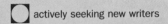
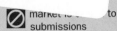
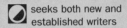
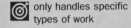
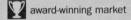
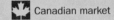
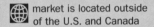
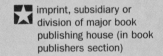
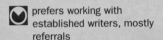

2008 NOVEL & SHORT STORY WRITER'S MARKET KEY TO SYMBOLS

 N market new to this edition

A publisher accepts agented submissions only

C publisher of graphic novels and comics

 market is closed to submissions

 actively seeking new writers

 seeks both new and established writers

 prefers working with established writers, mostly referrals

 only handles specific types of work

 award-winning market

 Canadian market

market is located outside of the U.S. and Canada

imprint, subsidiary or division of major book publishing house (in book publishers section)

$ market pays (in magazine sections)

● comment from the editor of *Novel & Short Story Writer's Market*

ms, mss manuscript(s)

SASE self-addressed, stamped envelope

SAE self-addressed envelope

IRC International Reply Coupon, for use in countries other than your own

(For definitions of words and expressions relating specifically to writing and publishing, see the Glossary in the back of this book.)

TEAR ALONG PERFORATION

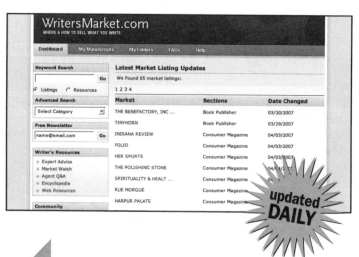
NSSM08

2008
Novel & Short Story Writer's Market

Lauren Mosko, Editor

Michael Schweer, Assistant Editor

WRITER'S DIGEST BOOKS
CINCINNATI, OH

Complaint Procedure

If you feel you have not been treated fairly by a listing in *Novel & Short Story Writer's Market*, we advise you to take the following steps:

- First try to contact the listing. Sometimes one phone call or a letter can quickly clear up the matter.

- Document all your correspondence with the listing. When you write to us with a complaint, provide the details of your submission, the date of your first contact with the listing and the nature of your subsequent correspondence.

We will enter your letter into our files and attempt to contact the listing. The number and severity of complaints will be considered in our decision whether or not to delete the listing from the next edition.

If you are a publisher of fiction and would like to be considered for a listing in the next edition of *Novel & Short Story Writer's Market*, send a SASE (or SAE and IRC) with your request for a questionnaire to *Novel & Short Story Writer's Market*—QR, 4700 East Galbraith Road, Cincinnati, Ohio 45236.

Editorial Director, Writer's Digest Books: Jane Friedman
Managing Editor, Writer's Digest Market Books: Alice Pope

Novel & Short Story Writer's Market Web page: www.nsswm.com
Writer's Market Web site: www.writersmarket.com
Writer's Digest Web site: www.writersdigest.com
F+W Publications Bookstore: http://fwbookstore.com

2008 Novel & Short Story Writer's Market. Copyright © 2007 by Writer's Digest Books. Published by F+W Publications, 4700 East Galbraith Rd., Cincinnati, Ohio 45236. Printed and bound in the United States of America. All rights reserved. No part of this book may be reproduced in any form or by any electronic or mechanical means including information storage and retrieval systems without written permission from the publisher. Reviewers may quote brief passages to be printed in a magazine or newspaper.

Distributed in Canada by Fraser Direct
100 Armstrong Ave.
Georgetown, ON, Canada L7G 5S4
Tel: (905) 877-4411

Distributed in the U.K. and Europe by David & Charles
Brunel House, Newton Abbot, Devon, TQ12 4PU, England
Tel: (+44) 1626 323200, Fax: (+44) 1626 323319
E-mail: postmaster@davidandcharles.co.uk

Distributed in Australia by Capricorn Link
P.O. Box 704, Windsor, NSW 2756, Australia
Tel: (02) 4577-3555

Distributed in New Zealand by David Bateman Ltd.
P.O. Box 100-242, N.S.M.C., Auckland 1330, New Zealand
Tel: (09) 415-7664, Fax: (09) 415-8892

Distributed in South Africa by Real Books
P.O. Box 1040, Auckland Park 2006, Johannesburg, South Africa
Tel: (011) 837-0643, Fax: (011) 837-0645
E-mail: realbook@global.co.za

ISSN: 0897-9790
ISBN-13: 978-1-58297-498-9
ISBN-10: 1-58297-498-5

Cover design and illustration by Josh Roflow
Interior design by Clare Finney
Production coordinated by Kristen Heller and Greg Nock
Photographs on selected pages © Frédéric Cirou/PhotoAlto

Attention Booksellers: This is an annual directory of F+W Publications. Return deadline for this edition is December 31, 2008.

fw
F+W PUBLICATIONS, INC.

Contents

From the Editor 1

You've Got a Story
So What Now? 2

THE WRITING LIFE

Percival Everett
Characteristically Uncharacteristic, by Joseph Bates 5

Sigrid Nunez
A Fiction Ever Closer to the Truth, by Lauren Mosko 11

Lisa See
Blending Culture, Myth and Research Into Fiction, by Janice Gable Bashman 18

James Alexander Thom
Bringing Historical Figures to Life, by Paula Deimling 23

Kelly Link
Nighttime Logic, Useful Obsessions and Following Your Inner Perv
by Alex DeBonis 28

Premier Voices
Three Debut Authors on the Importance of Teamwork, by Lauren Mosko 33
    Will Allison, *What You Have Left* (Free Press) 33
    Darren DeFrain, *The Salt Palace* (New Issues Press) 35
    Diana Holquist, *Make Me a Match* (Warner Forever) 37

CRAFT & TECHNIQUE

Does My Novel Have What It Takes?
by I.J. Schecter 40

Stay or Go?
Knowing When to Stick With Your Novel . . . or Toss It to the Curb
by W.E. Reinka 43

The Sweep of the Story
Broadening the Scope of Your Short Story, by Noelle Sterne 47

GETTING PUBLISHED

Testing the E-credential
Do Online Publications 'Count'?, by Jack Smith 54

Should You Hire a Publicist?
by Dena Harris 60

Writer Wanted
Partner Beware: Five Famous Teams Talk About Co-Authoring, by Jude Tulli 65

Blockbusters & Breakouts
The Elusive Art of Writing a BIG Book, by Roxanne St. Claire 73

Boost Your Mood
Bouncing Back From Rejection, Rewrite Requests and Other Disappointments
by Eve Menezes Cunningham 77

Success Story
The Importance of Persistence, Friendship and Strawberry-rhubarb Pie
by David Mohan 81

The Business of Fiction Writing 83

FOR MYSTERY WRITERS

John Connolly
'It's About Moving On', by T.E. Lyons 92

Brian Freeman
Living in the Gray, by Lauren Mosko 98

Rochelle Krich
Making the Unknown Familiar, by Rachel A. McDonald 106

Resources for Mystery Writers 110

FOR ROMANCE WRITERS

Cheryl Holt
Proving Success Can Happen at Any Age, by Deborah Bouziden 112

Beverly Bartlett
Turning a Passion Into a Plot, by Ellen Birkett Morris 116

Resources for Romance Writers 119

FOR SCIENCE FICTION, FANTASY & HORROR WRITERS

Worlds and Wonders
Speculative Fiction Roundtable, by I.J. Schecter 120

Speculative Fiction
The Next Generation, by John Joseph Adams 125

More Than Little Green Men
Tips for Making Your Aliens Alien, by Carol D. Pinchefsky 129

Resources for Science Fiction, Fantasy & Horror Writers 133

FOR GRAPHIC NOVEL & COMICS WRITERS

Greg Rucka
Balancing Comics and Prose, It's a Gentleman's Game, by Greg Nock 134

Wonder Women
How Women Writers Are Changing the Perception of Comics
by Greg Hatfield 141

The Business of Comics
Finding a Job in Hollywood's Idea Factory, by John Jackson Miller 149

Resources for Graphic Novel & Comics Writers 153

MARKETS

Literary Agents 155

Literary Magazines 222

Small Circulation Magazines 306

Online Markets 325

Consumer Magazines 345

Book Publishers 365

Contests & Awards 448

Conferences & Workshops 486

RESOURCES

Publishers and Their Imprints 525

Canadian Writers Take Note 531

Printing & Production Terms Defined 533

Glossary 536

Genre Glossary 544
  Definitions of Fiction Subcategories

Professional Organizations 552

Literary Agents Category Index 557

Conference Index by Date 575

Category Index 581

General Index 621

From the Editor

Being a fiction writer is, largely, about taking risks. Every time you sit down at your computer, you face the mirror, your demons, your inner critic, the blank page, the anxiety of influence, and waves of guilt for not spending more time with your kids/ your significant other/your "real" job/your aging parents/your dog/whatever. Then, once you've written something, you've actually got to *put it out there* and face those outer critics, demons and influences.

The good news is the more you write and submit, just like practicing any new skill, the less scary it becomes. And, after a while, you actually want to up the ante for yourself. Of course, you can always take the comfortable, familiar route—writing the same stories with the same styles and themes, sending to the same publishers. But it's actually *good* to remain a little bit uncomfortable at your desk—to continue to reach farther and explore unfamiliar forms, characters or points of view; to seek new and different outlets for your work—because this is how you continue to grow as a writer.

Over the last three years, you've been with me as I've edited *Novel & Short Story Writer's Market*. You were with me when I made a pledge to revise and submit a story, and you were with me when I got my first rejection out of the way. (It wasn't that bad. I didn't even cry. Okay, maybe I got a little choked up.) I've learned so much about the market for fiction, and I've had the privilege to talk with dozens of fascinating writers whose insights I've shared with you in these pages. I've grown so much, as both a writer and an editor. And now it's time for me to challenge myself to grow again, to take new risks and add new skills to my writing and editing toolbox, and so this will be my last edition at the helm.

Thank you, readers, for inspiring me and for asking all the right questions—always challenging me and *NSSWM* to be better. Keep it up. Thank you, faithful contributors, for making this book vital and personal—so much more than just a collection of market stats. I couldn't have done it without you. And thank you, generous interviewees, for giving of your time and of yourselves.

My parting challenge is to push yourself; make yourself uncomfortable. (*You* know what that means for you.) Your fiction is important—it's vital, it's personal, it's your lifeblood on the page—so prove it. Onward!

Lauren Mosko

Lauren Mosko
Lauren.Mosko@fwpubs.com

You've Got a Story

So What Now?

To make the most of *Novel & Short Story Writer's Market*, you need to know how to use it. And with more than 600 pages of fiction publishing markets and resources, a writer could easily get lost amid the information. This quick-start guide will help you wind your way through the pages of *Novel & Short Story Writer's Market*, as well as the fiction publishing process, and emerge with your dream accomplished—to see your fiction in print.

1. Read, read, read. Read numerous magazines, fiction collections and novels to determine if your fiction compares favorably with work currently being published. If your fiction is at least the same caliber as that you're reading, then move on to step two. If not, postpone submitting your work and spend your time polishing your fiction. Writing and reading the work of others are the best ways to improve craft.

For help with craft and critique of your work:

- You'll find advice and inspiration from best-selling authors and top fiction editors in the Writing Life section, beginning on page 5.
- You'll find articles on the craft and business aspects of writing fiction in the Craft & Technique section, beginning on page 40, and in the Getting Published section, beginning on page 54.
- If you're a genre writer, you will find information in For Mystery Writers, beginning on page 92, For Romance Writers, beginning on page 112; For Science Fiction, Fantasy & Horror Writers, beginning on page 120; and For Graphic Novel & Comics Writers, beginning on page 134.
- You'll find Contest listings beginning on page 448.
- You'll find Conference & Workshop listings beginning on page 486.

2. Analyze your fiction. Determine the type of fiction you write to best target markets most suitable for your work. Do you write literary, genre, mainstream or one of many other categories of fiction? For definitions and explanations of genres and subgenres, see the Glossary beginning on page 536 and the Genre Glossary beginning on page 544. There are magazines and presses seeking specialized work in each of these areas as well as numerous others.

For editors and publishers with specialized interests, see the Category Index beginning on page 581.

3. Learn about the market. Read *Writer's Digest* magazine (F + W Publications, Inc.); *Publishers Weekly*, the trade magazine of the publishing industry; and *Independent Publisher*, which contains information about small- to medium-sized independent presses. And don't forget the Internet. The number of sites for writers seems to grow daily, and among them you'll find www.writersmarket.com and www.writersdigest.com.

4. Find markets for your work. There are a variety of ways to locate markets for fiction. The periodicals sections of bookstores and libraries are great places to discover new journals and magazines that might be open to your type of short stories. Read writing-related magazines and newsletters for information about new markets and publications seeking fiction submissions. Also, frequently browse bookstore shelves to see what novels and short story collections are being published and by whom. Check acknowledgment pages for names of editors and agents, too. Online journals often have links to the Web sites of other journals that may publish fiction. And last but certainly not least, read the listings found here in *Novel & Short Story Writer's Market*.

Also, don't forget to utilize the Category Indexes at the back of this book to help you target your market for your fiction.

5. Send for guidelines. In the listings in this book, we try to include as much submission information as we can get from editors and publishers. Over the course of the year, however, editors' expectations and needs may change. Therefore, it is best to request submission guidelines by sending a self-addressed stamped envelope (SASE). You can also check each magazine's and press' Web site, which usually contains a page with guideline information. And for an even more comprehensive and continually updated online markets list, you can obtain a subscription to www.writersmarket.com.

6. Begin your publishing efforts with journals and contests open to beginners. If this is your first attempt at publishing your work, your best bet is to begin with local publications or those you know are open to beginning writers. Then, after you have built a publication history, you can try the more prestigious and nationally distributed magazines. For markets most open to beginners, look for the ◻ symbol preceding listing titles. Also, look for the ◪ symbol that identifies markets open to exceptional work from beginners as well as work from experienced, previously published writers.

7. Submit your fiction in a professional manner. Take the time to show editors that you care about your work and are serious about publishing. By following a publication's or book publisher's submission guidelines and practicing standard submission etiquette, you

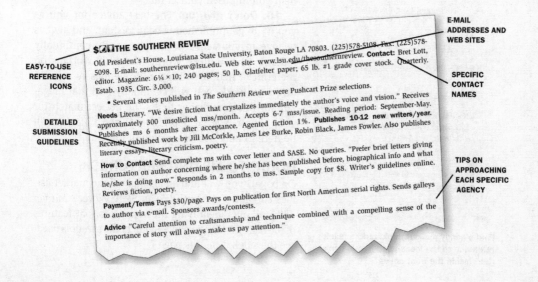

EASY-TO-USE REFERENCE ICONS

DETAILED SUBMISSION GUIDELINES

E-MAIL ADDRESSES AND WEB SITES

SPECIFIC CONTACT NAMES

TIPS ON APPROACHING EACH SPECIFIC AGENCY

$ 🔲📧 THE SOUTHERN REVIEW

Old President's House, Louisiana State University, Baton Rouge LA 70803. (225)578-5108. Fax: (225)578-5098. E-mail: southernreview@lsu.edu. Web site: www.lsu.edu/thesouthernreview. **Contact:** Bret Lott, editor. Magazine: 6¼ × 10; 240 pages; 50 lb. Glatfelter paper; 65 lb. #1 grade cover stock. Quarterly. Estab. 1935. Circ. 3,000.

• Several stories published in *The Southern Review* were Pushcart Prize selections.

Needs Literary. "We desire fiction that crystalizes immediately the author's voice and vision." Receives approximately 300 unsolicited mss/month. Accepts 6-7 mss/issue. Reading period: September-May. Publishes ms 6 months after acceptance. Agented fiction 1%. **Publishes 10-12 new writers/year.** Recently published work by Jill McCorkle, James Lee Burke, Robin Black, James Fowler. Also publishes literary essays, literary criticism, poetry.

How to Contact Send complete ms with cover letter and SASE. No queries. "Prefer brief letters giving information on author concerning where he/she has been published before, biographical info and what he/she is doing now." Responds in 2 months to mss. Sample copy for $8. Writer's guidelines online. Reviews fiction, poetry.

Payment/Terms Pays $30/page. Pays on publication for first North American serial rights. Sends galleys to author via e-mail. Sponsors awards/contests.

Advice "Careful attention to craftsmanship and technique combined with a compelling sense of the importance of story will always make us pay attention."

2008 NOVEL & SHORT STORY WRITER'S MARKET KEY TO SYMBOLS

[N] market new to this edition

[A] publisher accepts agented submissions only

[Ø] market is closed to submissions

[○] actively seeking new writers

[◐] seeks both new and established writers

[◑] prefers working with established writers, mostly referrals

[◎] only handles specific types of work

[♕] award-winning market

[❖] Canadian market

[🌐] market located outside of U.S. and Canada

[★] imprint, subsidiary or division of larger book publishing house (in book publishers section)

[C] publisher of graphic novels or comics

$ market pays (in magazine sections)

● comment from the editor of *Novel & Short Story Writer's Market*

ms, mss manuscript(s)

SASE self-addressed, stamped envelope

SAE self-addressed envelope

IRC International Reply Coupon, for use in countries other than your own

(For definitions of words and expressions relating specifically to writing and publishing, see the Glossary in the back of this book.)

Find a handy pull-out bookmark, a quick reference to the icons used in this book, right inside the front cover.

can increase your chances that an editor will want to take the time to read your work and consider it for publication. Remember, first impressions last, and a carelessly assembled submission packet can jeopardize your chances before your story or novel manuscript has had a chance to speak for itself. For help with preparing submissions read "The Business of Fiction Writing," beginning on page 83.

8. Keep track of your submissions. Know when and where you have sent fiction and how long you need to wait before expecting a reply. If an editor does not respond by the time indicated in his market listing or guidelines, wait a few more months and then follow up with a letter (and SASE) asking when the editor anticipates making a decision. If you still do not receive a reply from the editor within a month or two, send a letter withdrawing your work from consideration and move on to the next market on your list.

9. Learn from rejection. Rejection is the hardest part of the publication process. Unfortunately, rejection happens to every writer, and every writer needs to learn to deal with the negativity involved. On the other hand, rejection can be valuable when used as a teaching tool rather than a reason to doubt yourself and your work. If an editor offers suggestions with his or her rejection slip, take those comments into consideration. You don't have to automatically agree with an editor's opinion of your work. It may be that the editor has a different perspective on the piece than you do. Or, you may find that the editor's suggestions give you new insight into your work and help you improve your craft.

10. Don't give up. The best advice for you as you try to get published is be persistent, and always believe in yourself and your work. By continually reading other writers' work, constantly working on the craft of fiction writing, and relentlessly submitting your work, you will eventually find that magazine or book publisher that's the perfect match for your fiction. *Novel & Short Story Writer's Market* will be here to help you every step of the way.

GUIDE TO LISTING FEATURES

On page 3 you will find an example of the market listings contained in *Novel & Short Story Writer's Market* with call-outs identifying the various format features of the listings. (For an explanation of the symbols used, see the sidebar on this page.)

Percival Everett

Characteristically Uncharacteristic

© Danzy Senna

by Joseph Bates

I n an industry where writers are often expected to label or be labeled by their work, Percival Everett has remained unapologetically, and to our great benefit, unpredictable. His novels have ranged from muted realism to dystopian science fiction to scathing satire and open farce; have reexamined Native American land treaties, reimagined the mythos of the Old and New West, and retold Greek myth; have been narrated by a parodic Wild West cowpoke, a constantly metamorphosed servant of the god Dionysos, an infant with an uberintellect who composes thoughts on ontological inquiry and poststructuralist academic posturing while taking moments to lay a load in his "big-boy underwear." Reading the next Percival Everett novel, in other words, is never the same experience as reading the last. "[It's] as if he likes making 90 degree turns to see what's around the corner," Terry McMillan has noted, "and then over the edge."

This is not to say that Everett's work isn't recognizably his. On the contrary, over the course of 16 novels—from his debut *Suder* (Viking, 1983), the story of a slumping third baseman for the Seattle Mariners who sets off on a journey to reconcile his past traumas and present troubles, to his latest, *The Water Cure* (Graywolf, 2007)—Everett has crafted a literature known for its intelligence, lyricism and savage humor, for its abilities not only to reveal the tragic through the absurd and vice versa but to show the two as so often one and the same. In the process of creating this singular opus corpus—which includes also three well-received collections of stories, *The Weather and Women Treat Me Fair* (August House, 1987), *Big Picture* (Graywolf, 1996) and *Damned If I Do* (2004); a book of poems, *Re:f (gesture)* (Red Hen Press, 2004); even a children's book, *The One That Got Away*, with illustrator Dirk Zimmer (Clarion Books, 1992)—Everett has earned high praise from his critics and readers and such high honors as the New American Writing Award, the American Academy of Arts and Letters award, the Hurston/Wright Legacy Award and, most recently, the PEN USA Literary Award for his novel *Wounded* (Graywolf, 2005). In lauding both novel and novelist, the judges pointed out their pleasure in recognizing one "who has accomplished so much in so many interesting directions in his body of work."

Indeed, Everett's talent for tackling uncommon subjects has become a very common point of praise for reviewers, from the *The New York Times'* noting him as a writer of "unexpected directions" to *Playboy's* declaration of his work as "predictable only in its provocation" to

JOSEPH BATES holds a Ph.D. in Literature and Creative Writing from the University of Cincinnati. His short fiction has appeared or is forthcoming in *The South Carolina Review*, *Fresh Boiled Peanuts*, and *Lunch Hour Stories*. He is a visiting assistant professor of English at Miami University in Oxford, Ohio, and is eternally working on a novel.

Boston Globe reviewer James Sallis' contention that Everett's divergent subject matters and styles mark him as something of a "literary wild card." But if to another writer such praise might run the risk of limitation—if "uncategorizable" might threaten to become a categorization in itself—Everett seems to have no such concerns.

"I don't think about categories," he admits. "I make novels, and I make them about what interests me at a particular moment." But this seeming understatement belies an important fact: It is precisely the scope of those interests and his skill in exploring them that have made Percival Everett one of the most dynamic, catholic fiction writers working today.

Reprinted with permission from University Press of New England.

Perhaps part of the creative heterogeneity Everett enjoys might be traced to his itinerant background: Like Ralph Ellison and Mark Twain, both of whom are cited as influences, Everett is a novelist of Southern roots—born and raised in South Carolina, educated as an undergraduate at the University of Miami—who found himself pulling up stakes, following the pull West and, like those writers of the American Grain, becoming part of all he has seen. His resumé includes a range of occupations from ranch-hand to musician to high school math teacher to that most difficult of all, college professor of English at such universities as Notre Dame, Wyoming, the University of California at Riverside and, currently, the University of Southern California. (Everett lives outside Los Angeles with his wife, the novelist Danzy Senna, and their young son, Henry.) His free-time pursuits reflect this distinction, running from abstract painting to jazz and blues guitar to fly fishing, woodworking and the raising and training of horses, donkeys and mules. It's an unconventional CV, but of the kind one might expect for a writer whose work has appeared in imprints as varied as LSU's Voices of the South and Akashic's Urban Surreal.

Philosophy and the forms of fiction

Everett's entry into the world of fiction was equally atypical; his undergraduate study at the University of Miami was not in literature but philosophy, with Everett taking particular interest in Ludwig Wittgenstein and the ideas of ordinary language philosophy. While still an undergrad, Everett earned admittance into the MFA program at Brown University—with, reportedly, one of his first stories—and used his time there to write *Suder*, which was promptly snatched up by Viking, marking his novelistic debut at age 25. As to whether his unusually quick success played some role in his tendency to take risks and avoid the trends and constraints of the market, the author confesses, "I don't know. I'd like to think that it's in my nature to write what I want to write."

But Everett's philosophical framework has undoubtedly played an important role in his career, not only in terms of the intellectual curiosity which suggests his subject matters and the intense reading habits that feed his research—though he asserts that his research extends only to the point where he knows enough "that I don't need to show I know it"—but in terms of one of the central questions of his fiction: the degree to which language reflects both our readings and misreadings of reality.

For example, consider *Frenzy* (Graywolf, 1997), Everett's raucous take on the Dionysian myth which sees the god trying to circumvent his divinity in order to fully experience the human. He attempts this earnest cosmic slumming through reportage from his long-suffering servant, Vlepo, who is able to recount to the god—and to the reader—events both near and far by way of his master's continual transporting of him through time and space, transforming him into such eavesdropping, and thus narrating, objects as the blade of a saw, the hull of a ship, a stem of grapes, even the mythological labyrinth. Thus, rather than engaging a more traditional first-or third-person omniscient narrator, Everett burdens Vlepo as both at once, as an unwillingly omnipresent narrator quantum leaping—quantum thrown—into continuously shifting states of being and reality and yet remaining through it all hysterically, achingly, recognizably human. Still, despite the narrative's foray into the fantastic, for Everett the construction of the voice seemed a necessary choice to tell the story he wanted to tell. "I imagine that I thought the god, wanting to experience what it was to be human, would have to create a conduit to that experience," he says. "And so, Vlepo."

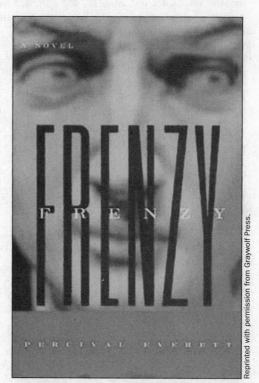

For another example of Everett's testing our preconceptions of and through narrative, there's *Glyph* (Graywolf, 1999), the story of Ralph, a toddler with a 475 IQ who refuses to speak but rather writes himself into existence through notes he keeps on his failed academic father, his struggling-artist mother, and his kidnapping and re-kidnapping by adults—including crazed psychiatrists and government agents—out to exploit his intellect. Ralph's narrative is a pastiche of footnoted, intellectually dense treatise, adventure story, and coming-of-age (the age is four), and while Ralph's inquiries into the realities of his existence mirror our own amazement—"i.e.," Ralph writes, "there is at least one baby who can write a paragraph"—the novel stretches the limits of our belief without once straining credulity. Added to this, *Glyph* highlights one of the great ironies of Everett's career: that those institutions or entities his work targets are often those who embrace his work most enthusiastically. The novel, besides a compelling adventure and laugh-out-loud comedy, is a wicked send-up of academia and deconstruction which has become, since its publication, a favorite text in the university classroom for academics to deconstruct.

Politics of race and voice

But there is, famously, another aspect of narrative and representation that Everett plays with in *Glyph*. Fifty pages into the book, young Ralph comments on the difficulty his kidnappers face due to the "discrepancy between my skin color and my abductors'." This leads Ralph to pose a question startling to the reader because it calls into question one's very habit of reading:

> Have you to this point assumed that I am white? In my reading I discovered that if a character was black, then he at some point was required to comb his Afro hairdo, speak on the street using an obvious, ethnically identifiable idiom, live in a certain part of town, or be called a nigger by someone. White characters, I assumed they were white (often, because of the ways they spoke of other kinds of people), did not seem to need that kind of introduction, or perhaps legitimization, to exist on the page. But you, dear reader, no doubt, whether you share my pigmentation or cultural origins, probably assumed that I was white. It is not important unless you want it to be and I will say no more about it . . .

Everett's work—as this passage typifies—consistently challenges our common conceptions and misconceptions of race and voice by pointing out readers' false, automatic assumptions or, as in the case of his brief, brutal novel of maternity and morality *Cutting Lisa* (Ticknor & Fields, 1986), by not pointing out race at all. Yet no less a discerning reader than Madison Smartt Bell, an Everett admirer, has admitted that upon finishing *Cutting Lisa* and seeing Everett's author photo on the last page, his automatic first thought was, "Oh, did it say somewhere those characters are *black*?"

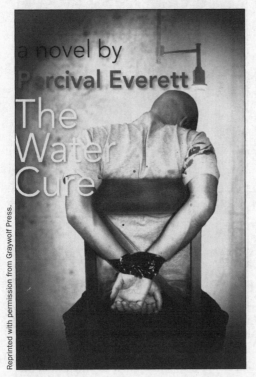

"Our culture teaches us to read with racist eyes," Everett says. "White characters need no codes to announce their whiteness, unless of course they are stuck in the middle of South Central LA. I don't think about readers. If they assume things, they assume things. If they discover their assumptions have been wrong, then fine, but I'm not on some cultural mission to correct the reading habits of the West. However, I do exploit and find the habits of great interest."

Which brings us to *Erasure* (UPNE, 2001), Everett's masterpiece of race, voice and the politics of publishing. The book's protagonist is Thelonius "Monk" Ellison, a writer who, finding that his novels face the same insistent, misguided criticism of not being "black" enough, fires off a blistering parody of expectedly ghettoized, "authentic" Black literature entitled *My Pafology* (and later retitled as a four-letter word unprintable here). But the parody, meant to skewer such misinformed habits of reading, is instead hailed as a model of the Black experience, the "kind of book that they will be reading in high schools thirty years from now," his agent tells him. The novel earns Monk's pseudonym, Stagg R. Lee, a six-hundred-thousand-dollar advance and a major literary award and forces Monk to come to terms with his creation, his aesthetic and himself.

A tour de force exploration into the industry's marketing of race, *Erasure* was nevertheless immediately recognized and embraced—rightly so—by the publishing world; it was eagerly introduced into numerous universities' African American literature curricula; and, most ironic of all, it very nearly, infamously, became the launch for Doubleday's African-American imprint, Harlem Moon.

Turning another corner

But true to form, Everett hasn't allowed *Erasure*'s success to dictate his directions since; his follow-up, *American Desert* (Hyperion, 2004), is the strange tale of Theodore Street, a failed academic who intends to commit suicide but is beaten to the punch when he is decapitated in a car accident . . . and who is further thwarted when he comes back from the dead three days later. *A History of the African-American People [proposed] By Strom Thurmond* (Akashic, 2004) is a novel-in-correspondence between Percival Everett; his co-author James Kincaid; Barton Wilkes, the devious, Kinbote-esque editor who has devised and orchestrated the proposed history without Thurmond's input; and even, intermittently, missives from the confused former Senator himself. And most recently there's *Wounded*, Everett's haunting look at racial and sexual prejudices as seen through the eyes of John Hunt, a reserved rancher who gets caught up in the murder investigation of a young gay man and its aftermath. As for the novel's evocation of the brutal 1998 murder of Matthew Shepard, Everett suggests both parallel and divergence. ''I certainly use the tragic case of Matthew Shepard to set up my novel,'' he says, ''but it was not the source of the work. The work was actually generated by sudden and inexplicable interest in caves, actual caves and then caves as metaphor.'' The metaphor works as a place of both safety and isolation for Hunt, a characteristic not limited to this particular narrator; even while being drawn into action, Everett's protagonists often remain, and retain an awareness of themselves as, outsiders.

The Writing Life

For Further Reading

- *American Desert* (Hyperion, 2004)

- *Big Picture: Stories* (Graywolf Press, 1996)

- *Cutting Lisa* (Ticknor & Fields, 1986; reiss. LSU Press, 1999)

- *Damned If I Do: Stories* (Graywolf, 2004)

- *Erasure* (University Press of New England, 2001)

- *Frenzy* (Graywolf, 1997)

- *God's Country* (Faber and Faber, 1994; reiss. Beacon Press, 2003)

- *Glyph* (Graywolf, 1999)

- *A History of the African-American People [proposed] by Strom Thurmond, as told to Percival Everett and James Kincaid* (Akashic Books, 2004)

- *Suder* (Viking, 1983; reiss. LSU Press, 1999)

- *Watershed* (Graywolf, 1996; reiss. Beacon Press, 2003)

- *Wounded* (Graywolf, 2005)

- *Zulus* (Permanent Press, 1990)

Readers can expect another unexpected turn from Percival Everett with his latest *The Water Cure*, once again published by St. Paul's Graywolf Press, with whom the author has enjoyed a celebrated, rewarding relationship.

"At Graywolf I get to talk about books," Everett says. "I'm no good talking about money and marketing. I might not be any good at talking about books, but I like to do it. Fiona McCrae [Everett's editor at Graywolf] is as smart as they come. I'm lucky; she gets me, understands what I'm about. She's no pushover. She speaks her mind and we've had some good fights. We're both interested in making the book its best. There is no ego there with her, no attempt to make the book hers in some way, no desire to satisfy her own aesthetic."

Of his work with Graywolf on *The Water Cure*, the author admits that it's "a tough book in a lot of ways. Combined words, non-sequitur sections. Fiona returned the manuscript with edits to me in what seemed a week. She helped the book. That's what an editor does."

Indeed, Everett's devotion to a particular artistic vision and to the unique needs of a given project is the characteristic which best and most completely defines his work, and it's this lesson above all he tries to impart to his students in USC's writing program: "I don't talk about publishing with my students until they have something they want to publish. My advice is always the same. Be true to yourself. Be true to your art.

"That might not get you rich," Everett says, "but it will keep you whole."

The Writing Life

Sigrid Nunez

A Fiction Ever Closer to the Truth

© Marion Ettlinger

by Lauren Mosko

ast spring at a small writers' conference in South Carolina, I was approached by a middle-aged woman with an apprehensive expression on her face. "I'm Violet," she said with a thick Eastern European accent. "I'm not a writer, but I have a story to tell . . ." She went on to explain that her parents were Hungarian refugees and that she wanted to write about their escape to America, their immigrant experience, and their struggles with language. "And maybe there will be room for my own story, too. I'm very passionate about gardening," she laughed. "Is all this possible in one book?" A smile crept across my face. "Have you ever read Sigrid Nunez' *A Feather on the Breath of God?*"

This novel—Nunez' first (HarperCollins, 1995)—draws upon the immigrant experiences of her own mother and father to create the opposing characters of Chang (the narrator's Chinese-Panamanian father who does not speak) and Christa (her German mother who is constantly lamenting), while deftly weaving the narrator's passion for the practice of ballet and her reckless affair with Vadim, a Russian ESL student. Though all of the relationships—between Chang and Christa, Christa and her daughters, the narrator and Chang, and the narrator and Vadim—are complicated and tenderly rendered, Nunez (rightfully and thankfully) offers us no saccharine resolutions, and each relationship brings us closer to understanding the novel's larger questions concerning the bonds and barriers of language and their relationship to identity. In this story and in each of Nunez' four successive novels, the author tackles themes, events, figures and eras that are seemingly mythic in proportion, but she treats them in such a thoughtful way that both the mythic and narrative complexities are reduced—and therefore elevated—to the realm of human complexity.

In *Naked Sleeper* (1996), a woman struggles to define herself and rewrite her own story when her background and context suddenly shift. In *Mitz: The Marmoset of Bloomsbury* (1998), Nunez presents us with an uncommon and endearing look at the lives of Leonard and Virginia Woolf, through the biography of their pet monkey. *For Rouenna* (FSG, 2001) tells the story of two childhood acquaintances from the projects of Staten Island—one who becomes a combat nurse in Vietnam and the other, the writer who will record her memories. Nunez' latest, *The Last of Her Kind* (FSG, 2005), follows another pair of female friends, this time Barnard College roommates in 1968, one of them (Ann Drayton) a child of privilege turned radical activist, the other (our narrator, Georgette George) pleased just to rise above her impoverished roots to live the life of a conventional adult. Though the women's lives diverge for a time, their time together proves a lasting, irrevocable bond.

LAUREN MOSKO is the editor of *Novel & Short Story Writer's Market*.

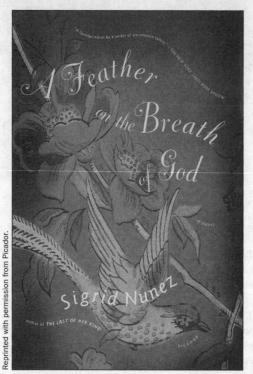

Reprinted with permission from Picador.

As a reader, you soon become so intimate with Nunez' characters that Leonard and Virginia begin to feel more like your quirky aunt and uncle than literary icons. You know you wouldn't have lasted a week in that combat hospital. Or maybe you would have marched with SDS at Barnard, too. And yes, each of these feats of the expansive and the personal is possible in one book.

Though some have labeled Nunez a writer of "hybrid" works, she is a fiction writer in the truest sense in that she perfectly balances history, imagination, others' stories, and her own—giving us just enough of herself in each novel to see ourselves more clearly. In this interview, she discusses her writing vocation and aspects of each of her novels.

What is it about writing fiction that has compelled you to devote your life to it? At what point did you decide to pursue writing as a vocation?

I've been interested in storytelling for about as long as I can remember. I wrote stories, mostly about animals, when I was very young, and early on I had the idea I would grow up to write children's books. I'd still love to write a children's book someday. At all the public schools I attended, creative writing was very much encouraged, so it's always been part of my life. For a time when I was a teenager, my dream was to become a dancer rather than a writer. But even before I graduated from college, I was quite sure that writing fiction would be my profession.

One of my favorite moments in *A Feather on the Breath of God* is the story the narrator tells about a man who is about to marry an Italian woman but has no intention of learning Italian. "What kind of love is that?" the narrator remarks. I was moved by the idea that to share language—to make the effort to share language—is to love more deeply. How did you arrive at this sentiment? Can you elaborate on the power of language for you? How does this translate to your craft and your relationship with the reader?

Really, it was just a thought that came to me while writing that book. I was thinking that if I were to marry someone whose native language was different from mine, I would surely try to learn that language, as a way of getting closer to him. I was brought up believing that a person's language and literature are a deep part of his or her identity. That's something Christa, the narrator's mother, says: "Your language is who you are." I believe that when someone reads my work, he or she is discovering, among other things, who I am. I was very struck once when I heard someone say, "I don't like that woman. I don't like her vocabulary." I wouldn't ever say that about anyone myself, but I do understand it.

In *Naked Sleeper*, Nona keeps insisting that background is important. I understood this both literally and figuratively: setting, context, history. What compelled you to focus on these elements of story?

I was taken with the idea that a person's behavior can change, in unexpected ways, simply because of a change of scenery. A woman in a strange place can fall in love with a man she would never fall in love with back home. Place this same woman and the man she's fallen in love with in yet another setting, and the whole relationship could change again. I'm not saying all of life is this unstable or arbitrary, of course. But I do think we are different, depending on our external circumstances. And I do think that many of our most important experiences have everything to do with sheer randomness, and that this is part of what makes human life difficult and complicated.

I've read that it was Virginia Woolf's own *Flush* that inspired you to write *Mitz*. When did you first encounter a record of the existence of Mitz? What was it about *Flush* that impressed you enough to try your own hand at a pet's "unauthorized biography"?

I first learned about Mitz from reading Woolf's diaries. I'm not sure when I read *Flush*, but it was definitely before I read the diaries. I thought it was such a charming idea Woolf had, to write a mock biography of Elizabeth Barrett Browning's cocker spaniel, and then I thought what fun it would be to write a biography of the Woolf's pet marmoset. Of course, what I really wanted was to write about the Woolfs and about Bloomsbury, and in fact *Mitz*, like *Flush*, is as much nonfiction as fiction.

There's a part in *Mitz* where you talk about Virginia's experience writing *Flush* and her fear of the backlash of negative reviews. You noted that one reviewer wrote, "as a serious writer Mrs. Woolf was now dead." Did you have those sorts of anxieties about *Mitz*, as well? It's certainly a departure from the intense family dramas of *A Feather . . .* and *Naked Sleeper*.

I wasn't concerned about anything I'd call "backlash," specifically, but like most writers I'm always anxious about the possibility of bad reviews.

Your interview with Renee Shea in *Poets & Writers* focused on your blending of fact and fiction; Shea wrote, "With each succeeding book, Nunez discloses more of herself . . ." And in *Glimmer Train*'s *Writers Ask* newsletter, you were quoted as saying: "There's something about writing passionately or intensely that enables you to expose yourself, in a way, and show your mind at work and your imagination at play and what kind of sensibility you truly have." How does it feel for you to create fiction from the personal elements of your life— do you feel free or raw when you write this way? Has such disclosure become easier with each novel?

First, I have to disagree: It isn't true that I've disclosed more of myself with each book. In fact, my most personal and most autobiographical book is my first book. As for my most recent novel, *The Last of Her Kind*, although part of it is set at Barnard during the same years I was a student there, none of the characters is based on myself or on people I actually knew. Unlike the narrator, Georgette, I didn't drop out of school, I've never worked for a fashion magazine, I've never been an editor of a literary journal, I've never been married, I've never had children, I don't have a troubled runaway kid sister, et cetera, et cetera. That novel, like *For Rouenna*, is a first-person narrative that is autobiographical in form but not in content.

What makes me feel "free" is precisely the fact that, even though there are personal elements in all my work (true of most novelists, surely), I'm writing fiction. Writing a memoir I'm sure I'd feel a lot more exposed and "raw" than I've felt writing my novels.

On a related note, George remarks in *The Last of Her Kind* that "I have no curiosity, not the least interest in what they [her journals] might tell me about the past today. Whatever happened, I prefer to re-create it. Even at the inevitable risk of getting some things wrong, I want this to be a work of pure memory and imagination. Instinct tells me that, in the end, what I'll have made will be closer to the truth." Your own fiction is a blend of memory and invention that creates a history. Where does research fit in? At what point, if any, do you feel like "getting some things wrong" matters? (I also call to mind Chuck in *For Rouenna*: "What difference does it make? It's a great story.")

It makes all the difference in the world, Chuck! For me, with a book like *For Rouenna*, nothing could have been more important to me than getting things right. Never having been a nurse, never having been in the Army, never having been to Vietnam—needless to say, I had to do a lot of research to tell Rouenna's story so that it sounded authentic. I never knew a woman like Rouenna; she is a totally invented character. But it was absolutely critical to me that I do everything possible to construct an accurate story of what it was like to be an Army nurse serving in Vietnam. Otherwise, I wouldn't have had any interest in writing that novel, nor would I have had any business writing it.

Similarly, in *The Last of Her Kind*, historical accuracy mattered a great deal to me. I wanted to be sure to get things right: how people talked, dressed, thought, and so on. I didn't have to do the same kind of research, of course, because much of what I wrote about was drawn from memory. Again, it's a question of authenticity. As a writer you want to cast a spell. You want the reader to be thinking, *All this really happened*, just as if it *were* a memoir. And for that to work, you have to get things right.

How does the relationship between memory, fact, and invention change for you as you work on autobiographical essays?

When I write nonfiction, I don't invent anything. There isn't any confusion for me in this regard, as there seems to be for some other writers. For me, as soon as you begin to make things up, saying "this happened" when in fact it did not happen, you've crossed the border into fiction. And if it's going to be published, it has to be published as fiction.

I was struck several times throughout *The Last . . .* by how vivid and complex a character Ann Drayton is; she and her counterculture experience are so clear, in fact, that she felt like a historical figure (more real to me than Patty Hearst). Rouenna and her Vietnam experience became like history to me, as well. What was your inspiration for Ann's life and voice? For Rouenna's? How much did you know about them before you started their novels?

Ann is an extreme version of a type that was fairly common on college campuses in the late sixties and early seventies. She wasn't modeled on any particular historical person, but I'd say she's a lot closer to someone like Kathy Boudin than to Patty Hearst. As for her voice— a character's voice comes to me while I'm actually writing about him or her; it's not something I can plan beforehand.

About Rouenna, I'd always known there were women who served as nurses in Vietnam, but I'd never given them much thought until I read some interviews and personal histories that came out in the eighties. Then I thought how one day I'd love to write about a woman who'd been through such an intense and unusual experience. It took a long time, but I finally got around to it. As I said before, I had to do a lot of research to write *For Rouenna*. For *The Last of Her Kind*, the most extensive research I had to do was about the criminal justice system and prison life.

It's hard to say how much I knew about either Rouenna or Ann before I started writing about them. Not much, since I tend to invent everything as I go along. Though it's fair to say I knew both of them would be complicated.

When and how did you learn that Barnard wanted to give a copy of *The Last . . .* to every incoming student? How did that feel? After your reading there, what sort of questions did the class of 2010 ask you?

I found out in June 2006, about five months after the book was published. I was thrilled, of course. The students asked so many different kinds of questions . . . . The one that struck me most was "Do you have a message for us?" I said no, without hesitation. The student— and the audience in general—seemed surprised at this response. I explained that I hadn't written the novel because I had a message for anyone, but rather because I had a story.

In your "Backstory" on MJ Rose's blog, you wrote (about *The Last . . .*) that you "wanted to write about specific individuals who happened to come of age in that revolutionary time and whose lives were shaped and marked by it forever, as mine was." Please talk a little more about this. How did this time affect you as a woman and also as a writer? Is the "writing as healing" motif that recurs throughout *The Last . . .* something you embraced at that time or as a result of that time in your life?

How that time affected me—I think the answer to that question has to be the novel itself. As I said before, the choices a writer makes—choices not only about subject but also about language and style—will tell you who that person is. Or as V.S. Naipaul said: "Fiction reveals the writer totally." My thoughts and feelings about that era and its aftermath are revealed in the novel, through the characters and their experiences, and through the way I write about them.

"Writing as healing" is something that comes up more than once in the book, and it's something certain characters might embrace, but it's not an idea I myself embrace. Of course I know that practicing any art can have beneficial effects, but I think there's something naïve and even false about the idea that you can exorcise your demons or achieve catharsis through writing. If life really worked that way, writers would be far happier, better-adjusted people than we all know them to be, wouldn't they?

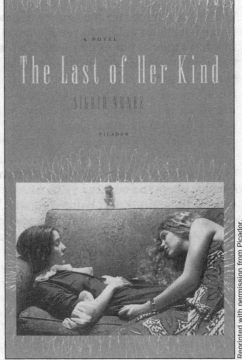

Reprinted with permission from Picador.

The narrator in *For Rouenna* recalls a comment Primo Levi made about Holocaust literature and applies it to the Vietnam war: "I believe that at times Rouenna was troubled by . . . the fear that the more stories that got told, the more novels and memoirs and movies and TV shows about the Big Event that got put out into the world, the greater the gap between those imagined or reconstructed versions and the Big Event itself." Did you share a similar fear as you were writing this novel? What do you think is fiction's role or responsibility when it draws from a historical event—especially something as tragic as the Holocaust or Vietnam (or 9-11)?

Writing about historical events of any kind, I feel a responsibility to be as accurate as possible. Any fears I had writing about the Vietnam War had to do with not getting things right. Primo Levi's fear is well founded, of course, and its realization is surely inevitable. But needless to say, he didn't mean that people should stop writing about "Big Events." In fact, we have a duty to write about them. But we also always have to bear in mind that what comes to us through memory is often more imagination than history.

You've been awarded fellowships to both Rome and Berlin and have taught at a handful of different colleges. How has the fairly regular change in scenery—especially your time abroad—affected your writing life? How do you balance teaching and writing?

I don't have a permanent teaching position, so it isn't that hard for me to balance teaching and writing. Of course I get more writing done when I'm not teaching. As for living for periods away from home, that's given me enormous pleasure, of course, but I don't really know that it's had that much of an effect on the writing itself. So far, at least, it certainly hasn't affected me in terms of subject matter for fiction.

You've also served on the faculty at several writing workshops, including Bread Loaf. How useful do you feel such conferences are for writers and why? At what stage in her career would you encourage a writer to attend?

How useful these conferences are depends entirely on the individual participant. For some people they can be extremely useful, though not always for the same reason. It might be because the writer had a really great workshop, or because he or she connected with other writers, or managed to catch the interest of a visiting agent or editor. I've seen all these things happen to people at conferences. In general I think conferences are probably most useful—and fun—for those who are just beginning their careers, whatever age they might be.

In your interview with Linda B. Swanson-Davies, you said that sensitivity to language was the quality in your students' creative writing that most excited you, and that one can't write without it. How do you teach such a thing to students who arrive in your classroom without already having cultivated that understanding of and respect for the English language?

What you do is show them examples of good writing, and you talk about the choice of words and the shape of the sentences and the narrative structure, and you try to explain what makes the writing beautiful. And you hope the students will learn to recognize good writing for themselves and will want to imitate it. Because that's really how you learn to write. In the beginning, it's mostly about trying to do what those writers whose work you admire do. Joan Didion once sat down at the typewriter with a work of Hemingway's and began copying it word for word, hoping to learn, as she typed, how he did it. I've heard of another writer who claimed to have typed *Moby-Dick* several times with the same purpose in mind.

Looking back on your experiences writing and publishing five successful novels, what is the lesson you've learned with respect to craft that you most wish you could travel back in time and tell your pre-*Feather* self in order to save her anxiety and/or grief? What bit of publishing knowledge would you share with her?

To begin with publishing knowledge, I think many writers believe that if they could just get that first book sold, all their problems would be solved. The truth is, only one problem would be solved, and a great many others would arise. If you're going to survive as a writer, you need a lot of patience in order to deal with the inevitable frustrations and disappointments of being published. Few writers I know have not been dismayed to learn they have almost no say in how their book will be produced, presented to the world, and marketed.

With regard to craft, I wish I'd learned earlier to be braver and more ruthless about cutting or abandoning drafts. Just because you spent hours or weeks, or perhaps even longer, revising and polishing something doesn't mean in the end it will be any good. It may still have to be discarded, and you have to learn to see this not as failure, or as wasted time, but rather as part of the process. Writing well is something you have to learn, and as with most human endeavors, much of what is essential can be learned best by doing it wrong first.

For more information on Sigrid Nunez and her work, visit www.sigridnunez.com.

Lisa See

Blending Culture, Myth and Research Into Fiction

© Patricia Williams

by Janice Gable Bashman

Writers often state that they've always wanted to write, that they need to write, and that writing has been part of their lives since they were young. Lisa See only wanted to travel. "I didn't know myself very well back in the day," she says. "I knew I didn't want to get married or have kids. I only wanted to live out of a suitcase. I thought the only way to have the life I wanted was to be a writer."

Although she eventually married and had two sons, she didn't change her mind about her love for and fascination with other places. "Travel is one of the most important things you can do as a human being. It truly broadens your horizons and makes you think about yourself, other people, other cultures, and the world in different ways. Writers have to get out of their rooms and live," she says. In addition to her travels, her love for her Chinese heritage has thoroughly informed her writing.

See's nonfiction book, *On Gold Mountain: The One Hundred Year Odyssey of My Chinese-American Family* (Vintage, 1996), and her page-turning novels, including *Flower Net* (Harper-Collins, 1997), *The Interior* (1999), *Dragon Bones* (Random House, 2003), and *Snow Flower and the Secret Fan* (2005), are acclaimed for depicting Chinese culture—helping to transport readers from their rooms—and continually land on the best-seller lists. Her work has been praised by *Publishers Weekly*, *The Los Angeles Times*, *The New York Times*, *The Washington Post*, National Public Radio, and Booksense.

See's newest work, *Peony in Love: A Novel* (Random House, 2007), is set in the 17th century in the Yangzi Delta. It is based on the true story of three maidens who were married to the same man. See describes it as a "ghost story within a ghost story."

Draw me into the world of this ghost story and tell me why I would want to visit.

I'm drawn to history that's been lost, deliberately covered up, or forgotten. This is one of the reasons I wrote *On Gold Mountain* about the Chinese side of my family. It's why I wrote the mysteries, which dealt with stories that I didn't feel were getting enough attention—the smuggling of endangered animal parts used for Chinese herbal medicine, how American

---

JANICE GABLE BASHMAN has published extensively in the field of psychology and has written and directed videos on psychodrama. More recently, she has been a book reviewer for *Elle* magazine and the *Borzoi Reader*, completed an author profile for *Bucks* magazine (July/August 2006) and is an ongoing contributor to *Wild River Review* literary magazine. She is working in collaboration with best-selling author Jonathan Maberry on a book for writers about the inner workings of the publishing business.

goods are made in China, and the building of the Three Gorges Dam. *Snow Flower and the Secret Fan* used as its backdrop *nu shu*, a writing system invented, used and kept secret by women in China for 1,000 years.

I look at the new book as a kind of reverse-mirror image of *Snow Flower*. It's based on the true story of three women who lived in 17th-century China. Peony, the beautiful, well-educated and cloistered daughter of a wealthy Hangzhou scholar, loves an opera called *The Peony Pavilion*. (In real life, this opera was known to cause lovesickness in many young women with resulting death by age 16.) One night while wandering in her garden, she meets by accident the man to whom she's been betrothed in an arranged marriage. Quite unexpectedly, they fall in love. But for Peony it's more serious than that. She's caught a case of lovesickness, writes obsessively about love in the margins of a copy of opera, wastes away, and dies. She isn't buried properly and returns to earth as a ghost to complete her project on love and to be recognized as the rightful wife of the man she loves. He, however, marries two more times. Peony gets her sister-wives to continue writing in the margins of the opera. The second wife also dies of lovesickness.

The third wife pawns her wedding jewelry and uses it to have the project published. (It became the first book of its kind to be published by women anywhere in the world and it remained in print for nearly 300 years). The novel uses the richness and magic of the Chinese afterlife to explore the different manifestations of love—mother love, romantic love, erotic love, deep-heart love—and how they can transcend death. Ultimately it's about female friendship, the cost of expressing creativity under oppressive circumstances, and the desire and need for women to be heard—all as timely and pertinent today as they were three centuries ago. And it's a story that remained hidden for a long time, but shows the great courage and ingenuity of women.

China plays an important role in your novels and the Chinese culture informs your work. Why?

I'm part Chinese. My great-great-grandfather came here to work on the building of the transcontinental railroad. My great-grandfather was the godfather/patriarch of Los Angeles Chinatown. I don't look at all Chinese, but I grew up in a very large Chinese-American family.

All writers are told to write what they know, and this is what I know. And when I don't know something—*nu shu*, for example—I love to find out whatever I can about it and then bring my sensibility to the subject. In many ways I straddle two cultures, and I try to bring that into my work. The American side of me tries to open a window into China and things Chinese for non-Chinese, while the Chinese side of me makes sure that what I'm writing is true to the Chinese culture without making it seem too "exotic" or "foreign."

You use Chinese culture to explore universal themes such as love, friendship, betrayal, passion and death. Explain the significance of this in your work.

Chinese culture is what I know best because of how I was raised. Frankly, I don't know what else I would write about. I try to use the Chinese experience to get people to think about their own lives and relationships. What I really want people to get from my books is that all people on the planet share common life experiences—falling in love, getting married, having children, dying—and share common emotions—love, hate, greed, jealousy. These are the universals; the differences are in the particulars of customs and culture.

You stated that when you read, you love to "open the pages, fly to a different world, time or culture and connect to the characters and by extension to the human condition." Explain the process you use to provide this experience for your readers.

Reprinted with permission from Random.

I try to create a place and the people who inhabit it using all five senses. Isn't smell supposed to be the strongest sense? If you look, you'll see that I use a lot of odors, fragrances and aromas in my work. I try to create descriptions that you can see as though you were there, humidity that you can really feel on your skin, unique sounds that really put you in a place, and sensations—like foot binding—that you can feel as though you're going through them yourself.

Creating characters that are believable and empathetic comes next. This is important whether a character is real or imagined. Characters must be real to the writer in order for them to be real to the reader. If their emotions are real and true, then readers—myself included—will connect to them. As a writer, I hope then that people will move from those characters to thinking about themselves, and yes, about the human condition.

Obviously all this hinges on two things: doing research (not just reading in a library or seeing what you can find on the Internet, but going out and seeing and experiencing for yourself), and finding the emotional truth for every single character.

Once you have a story in mind, do you discover your location, character or plot first? Explain how they evolve.

I don't think one comes before the other. They're all entwined. Let's use *Snow Flower* as an example. I knew I wanted to write something about the secret language. I went to a very remote part of China to see what I could see. As I was going there, I had an incredible meal where they brought in a live chicken, killed it, and then we cooked it in a hot pot. They made taro and caramelized sugar for dessert. This meal became the favorite special meal for Lily and Snow Flower.

I didn't know that Snow Flower was going to marry a butcher until I sat on the porch of a house in a tiny village and learned that this was the home of a butcher. There was a big wok embedded in the porch where the butcher slaughtered the pig and then boiled the body to remove the skin—right outside the front door!

I didn't know the overall form for the novel until I was leaving China. I had one night in a nice hotel room. I had my first hot shower in a long time and a meal that didn't involve pig penis or pig's blood. This voice came to me that was a bit of my grandmother, a bit of my great-aunt, and a bit of a 96-year-old woman I'd met in one of the villages. I got in bed and wrote the opening chapter. It involved an old woman filled with regrets looking back on her life. So the novel was written from her point of view as an old woman looking back on her life in a kind of autobiography. The point I'd like to make is that these things could have happened in any order. One thing just builds upon another. You have to be open and receptive to what the universe brings you.

Incorporating historical fact and myths into fiction seems like a daunting process. What methods do you use to make this process successful?

I think you have to get very straight in your mind what you want your story to be. I over-research, use it all, and then cut a tremendous amount of it. As a teenager, I used to read James Michener. He did all this research, but when I came to it as a reader, the story would stop dead. I would skip paragraphs and sometimes pages. So I really watch out for that in my own work. For a short time, I need to be the world's greatest expert on a subject. The art comes in cutting most of it out and letting the characters tell their story. What I hope happens is that the history and research are holding the story like a good foundation, not like a big brick wall separating the reader from the characters, the emotions and the action.

Myths are a little different. Why are you using a myth? If it pertains to the story, then use it. If it doesn't and you just happen to like the myth, then it shouldn't be there. It has to have some meaning in the story you're trying to tell.

How do you research your work?

I go to the library, look on the Internet, go to locations, search for out-of-print books, take photos, look at art (if I'm writing about a time before photography was invented). I love research and I do it all myself, because you never know what you'll come across that will be an *aha!* moment.

Do you find your characters' voices or do they find you?

A little of both. I already explained how Lily came to me. With Snow Flower, I thought about how I would have felt living my entire life in an upstairs room with just one window to look out of. I would have been desperate to get out, which would have been impossible, given the time and the circumstances. So, if I had been in that upstairs room, I would have looked inward and relied on my imagination. Snow Flower always talks about birds in flight, soaring, and flying.

With the new book I'm writing, Peony is a ghost—forever sixteen. She lived in the 17th century, so her language is different from what a sixteen-year-old might use today. I drew on poetry written by women in 17th century China to find her voice. But even though she's forever sixteen, ghosts aren't dumb and they don't remain the same, so 300 years later her language, her concerns, and the way she views the world are very different, so naturally her voice changes and evolves through the novel.

In his book, *On Writing*, Stephen King discusses the necessity for all writers to have a writer's toolbox. The toolbox, at its most basic level, must contain vocabulary, grammar, the elements of style and the commitment of the writer to the work. What tools have you added to your toolbox and what benefit do they serve?

I think my greatest tool is my work habits. I work every day, all day doing research, or writing 1,000 words, editing 20 pages of the first-draft, or polishing 50 pages of clean copy. The house can be falling down around me—and often it is—but I have to get my work done first. (This is especially important for women, because we have the added burdens—gifts!—of caring for our homes and families. I can't tell you how many times my husband and kids have had to eat cheese and crackers for dinner. But they've survived and I've been happy, so what's the harm?)

I have a good attitude about editing. I figure you have to divide criticism from others into three categories: a third of the time they're completely wrong, a third of the time they're completely right, and a third of the time you have to acknowledge that something wasn't quite working and then try to fix it.

You also have to take good care of yourself. Others like warm baths and candles, but I take walks, swallow lots of vitamins, and reward myself with a good stiff drink on occasion.

James Alexander Thom

Bringing Historical Figures to Life

Courtesy of the author

by Paula Deimling

James Alexander Thom's books have taken us into the landscape of historical figures—like Lewis and Clark and Tecumseh—but also into their struggles, joys and heartbreaks. And Thom constructs his stories with great passion, earnestness and wisdom. "If I was writing about someone I admired, or something that was inspiring in some way, or things that were admirable, the reader response is so much better," says Thom. This realization—which came with the publication of *Long Knife* (Avon, 1979) and *Follow the River* (Ballantine, 1981)—set the tone for his career.

While serving as a reporter and columnist for *The Indianapolis Star* in the 1960s, Thom was working on novels. "I *liked* the newspaper work, but the novels were more important," he admits. His first published novel in 1978, *Spectator Sport*, was about the 1973 Indianapolis 500 race. In 1974, the Indiana Historical Society suggested he bring out a dramatization of George Rogers Clark's victory at Vincennes in time for the 1979 bicentennial of the event. Thom began researching Clark, and the result was the novel *Long Knife*.

During this research, Thom learned about a woman from Virginia who was captured by Indians in 1755, but who escaped and trekked 450 miles through mountainous terrain and along riverbanks to return home. This story eventually became the bestseller, *Follow the River*, which, like all of Thom's nine historical novels, has remained in print. (*Follow the River* is now in its 40th printing.)

For Thom, the idea for a book must "assert itself *irresistibly*" in his mind before the writing can begin. "It is always part of my desire to find marvelous stories not that familiar. . . . I generally tend to go with a story that has inspired me or lifted me in such a way that I want to spread the story. It's the old story-telling urge: to share a story that amazed me in some good way."

Choosing the voice

The planning of a book starts on the emotional level, but then a crucial decision must be made. "I approach each book with the feeling that I have to get a voice for that book. I have to figure out how I am going to sound as I tell this story." The hardest part is figuring out this voice, he says. "How am I going to tell this? . . . I have very seldom started off right."

PAULA DEIMLING wrote 45 published interviews with authors and editors, including John F. Baker, Russell Banks and Jane Smiley. A contributor to *Agents, Editors, and You* (Writer's Digest Books, 2002) and former editor of *Writer's Market*, she was a full-time writer whose subjects ranged from genealogy and history to human-interest stories.

When writing *From Sea to Shining Sea* (Ballantine, 1984), Thom finished the entire 1,200-page manuscript before he realized something more was needed to bind it together and give it the right tone. While the manuscript ended as Lewis and Clark reached the Pacific Ocean, Thom realized the overriding story was at the hearthside—a story of family. His solution was to add soliloquies in the words of Ann Rogers Clark and an epilogue. Now at the novel's beginning and end, Mrs. Clark talks of her family and famous sons. "There is a roundness to every story," he says. This is true of everything, he notes—the universe, the seasons, the shape of a story.

His latest novel, *Saint Patrick's Battalion* (Ballantine, 2006), which covers the Mexican-American War of 1846-1848, started out in the point of view of Irish soldier John Riley, but three or four chapters into the book, Thom wanted a wider overview of Riley's life and created two characters who know him—young boys on opposite sides of the conflict—through which the story is told. The realization, which came just six or seven years ago (after nearly 25 years of novel writing), that a fictional observer can tell an accurate historical story was a pleasant discovery for Thom. "I'm still learning," he acknowledges.

Building a believable world, rooted in history

Once voice is chosen, Thom can begin to fill in a character's world. "I must understand the main character to the point where I become the character or that character's whole family," he says. The next aspect is "to see the surroundings, environment and action so vividly that I feel like the action is happening to me. Therefore it will feel like that to the reader."

To write authentically about historical characters *and* to create characters who are historically accurate, Thom seeks out first-person accounts, government records, letters and diaries. "The hardest part of writing true historical fiction is not having the liberty of making up a plot," he says. "My difficulty is I have to find out as much as I possibly can about the characters, events and environment."

Environment and opposition, he says, affect the point of view in a book. For instance, mountains and rivers were obstacles to characters like Mary Draper Ingles and William Clark. Not so for Tecumseh in *Panther in the Sky* (Random House Value, 1991) or Indian interpreter George Drouillard in *Sign-Talker* (Ballantine, 2000). And every novel has an opposition—the enemy—and the author must understand that enemy. "Your enemy makes the struggle what it is," explains Thom.

The writer-historian at work

Thom collects about five times as much information as he uses in a book, and the research takes about three times as long as the actual writing. His 14 × 16-foot office is filled with two dozen file cabinets. (The desks are actually tabletops laid over file cabinets.) Thom and his wife, author Dark Rain Thom, share this office; he uses a typewriter and she prefers a computer.

"The historian stands in the present and tells his reader 'here's what happened 200 years ago and here's how it affects us now,' " Thom observes. "But what I have to do as a historical fiction writer is to take the reader back there with me to that day and, not knowing what comes after. . . . I have to make everything vivid." And to write vividly, it helps to see and experience the places first hand.

Saint Patrick's Battalion includes illustrations by Thom, some of which were done in the 1950s, as he traveled by train through Mexico with a sketch pad and fell in love with the country. Padraic Quinn, a main character and young boy in the book, is a sketch artist and diarist, too, experiencing Mexico for the first time. Thom wrote *From Sea to Shining Sea* in a tent as he was reconstructing an 1840s log house. He used block and tackle and other primitive tools, as his characters would. "Everything I do has some research value," he explains. The log house became his home, and he has lived in it ever since. (Thom found out after the book was published that an actual historical character in that book, a Revolutionary War veteran, was the first white man to own this Indiana land where this log house sits.) Thom even traveled the entire route of the Lewis and Clark Expedition while writing *From Sea to Shining Sea*. He hiked the route that Mary Ingles took, including climbing over the palisade cliffs she traversed on the final day of her journey. He has fasted for a week to understand what hunger does to a body and mind. This sort of research helps him and the reader to *feel* just how desperate Ingles was to get home.

"If you're writing fictional narrative, write to the reader's senses," Thom says. The reader needs to smell and taste and feel the textures, and feel the fatigue. This sensory experience gives the reader the sense of being there as part of the scene. Thom even feels his experience as a U.S. Marine in the Korean War was useful for his writing life because it has given him insight into warriors' fear and discomfort. "Otherwise, I'd just be guessing," he quips.

Thom doesn't hire researchers to help with the details. A researcher will focus on what the author asks him or her to find, and that creates a sort of tunnel vision, he believes. When researching, Thom not only looks for specific information but is open to other aspects that might enhance the story or even become the focus of a later book. Studying the culture of a character and the character's worldview—what was known and not known in the time period of the book—is crucial. It takes research to know what details to leave out of a book, he says. In fact, one of the last and hardest skills for him to master was selectivity: deciding what to include and what to leave out of a book. It's a skill that brings momentum to a narrative because paragraphs aren't bogged down with details that don't advance the story. If you put everything in a book or try to preach a particular viewpoint, the book suffers. Readers want story telling, not philosophizing, he explains.

Thom holds on to a manuscript as long as he can because it can always be improved, particularly the connecting chapters or minor chapters. "We do have a tendency to hurry through things while we're carried away with the story. . . . When I go back to such a chapter, then I can take the leisure to apply my whole imagination to enhancing the details and vividness, and even making the language more powerful or more cogent. Very often, too, when you get to the end of the book, you have learned certain things that make you re-evaluate the importance of all the preceding chapters."

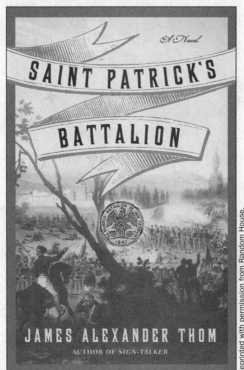

Reprinted with permission from Random House.

The Writing Life

Co-authoring a saga

Dark Rain, the Water Panther Clan Mother of the Shawnee Nation, East of the River Band of Ohio, received a contract to do a book on Nonhelema, the Women's Peace Chief of the Shawnee Nation, as far back as 1994, but she and Thom decided to combine their research and skills to create a novel. *Warrior Woman* (Ballantine, 2003) tells the story of 17 crucial years in the long life of Nonhelema.

As part of the research, Dark Rain consulted old traders' records to know how the Native Americans dressed—in what colors and using what materias—and what objects they had access to in the 1700s. "Then you're able to flesh out what they looked like and how they would have appeared when they walked in," she explains.

Like her husband, Dark Rain has a keen eye for detail. "Peripheral vision," she points out. "It makes the setting that makes the tree I'm focusing on pop out. The surroundings are as important as what you're focusing on. . . . If you want people to understand the breathtaking beauty of something, you have to put it in its proper setting. You can't just have this nugget of gold without showing some sort of support or some light that makes it shine."

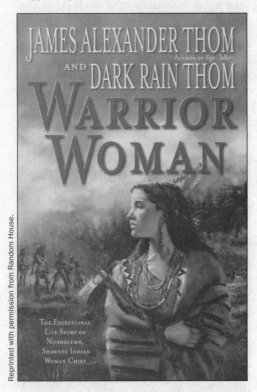

The author of the Shawnee history, *Koh-kumthena's Grandchildren/The Shawnee* (Guild Press of Indiana, Inc., 1994), she is fascinated by the way voice and character evolve with the writing of a novel. "Sometimes you think one of your characters will be the voice or their viewpoint, or it's just going to be a narrator, and as you write, a voice becomes apparent and. . . you realize that one of the characters has developed a bigger role than you anticipated him to, or his opinion, his attitude or his experiences put things into focus more than you realized in the beginning. Once we begin, the story begins to tell itself and identifies whose voice it wants to be told by. So you can have your plans and your plots and believe you've got it all nailed down and then all of a sudden, the story actually says, 'That's pretty good; however, I have a different view or I have a better view or I have a fuller view and here is the way *I'm* telling it,' and you look at it and you don't know where it came from, but *my goodness, that's good.*"

James and Dark Rain reiterate that mutual trust and respect are crucial to a successful co-authorship. They spent the first 10 months thinking about *Warrior Woman* and being polite to one another, says Dark Rain. One day, he said, "By the way, I started the book yesterday."

"You did? I did too. Where did you start?"

"The Battle of Point Pleasant."

But the men, Dark Rain pointed out, couldn't have gone to war without the approval of the Women's Council.

"You're right," she recalls him saying.

They began the book with Nonhelema preparing for the Women's Council.

James' editorial tweaking gave *Warrior Woman* its singular voice so it didn't sound like two people writing, Dark Rain says. He kept it from becoming full of sidebars of information. "We have to write tight," he'd say. Sometimes just deleting three or four sentences and adding five or six words to what was left gives more impact to the narrative.

"The story never ends. You never capture it all," says Dark Rain, currently writing a novel based on her grandfather, *The Odyssey of Henry P.* In the past few years, she has come to realize that every novel requires that two or three novels worth of material be deleted. "There is a specific story. What you find is the story is richer than you ever imagined it."

She'd heard her husband say over the years that characters will modify and change in their own ways almost independent of the writer, but seeing this and the effects of characters' lives continuing. . . it is like the spreading of fairy dust. "Listen to the wisdom of your characters," she advises.

This allows the wisdom of the author *and* many decades. . . and centuries. . . to shine through.

For a list of titles and other information, visit www.jamesalexanderthom.com.

Kelly Link

*Nighttime Logic, Useful Obsessions
and Following Your Inner Perv*

Courtesy of author

by Alex DeBonis

In Kelly Link's short story "Lull," a son gives his father the number of a phone sex line where an operator named Starlight will spin out stories for her callers. The teenager claims she's capable of much more than pornographic tales—that she will tell whatever kind of story the father wants, even a mish-mash of his favorite tropes. The son describes her storytelling as "Stephen King and sci-fi and the *Arabian Nights* and *Penthouse Letters* all at once."

A narrative with this DNA would be at home in either of Link's own short story collections. Her fictions are mongrels, exhibiting traits from a variety of genres, such as ruminations on suburban angst populated by ghosts and witches or a lonely man reaching out to a writer with mysterious sci-fi tales about blonde-haired female aliens redolent of dish-soap. Link transports us to worlds that operate by the arbitrary and surreal rules of dreams and, in doing so, defies both genre expectations and the conventions of literary realism. But these excursions are less about bucking categories than they are about experiencing the loopy pleasures and dark turns of her own quirky imagination. Link's stories make us wonder why more fiction doesn't dwell on haunted cellos or have zombies scraping through its corridors.

Link's work has been noticed both by the literary establishment and those pushing the envelope of genre fiction. Her 2001 collection *Stranger Things Happen* (Small Beer Press) was a Salon.com and *Village Voice* book of the year. Her most recent collection from Small Beer, *Magic for Beginners* (2005), was a Book Sense pick (and a Best of Book Sense 2005 pick) and selected for best of the year lists by *Salon, TIME, Village Voice, San Francisco Chronicle, Boldtype,* and *Capitol Times.* Stories from the collection have been published in *McSweeney's Mammoth Treasury of Thrilling Tales, Conjunctions* and *One Story,* among others. Her story "Stone Animals" was selected by Michael Chabon for the 2005 edition of *Best American Short Stories.* Link has edited the collection *Trampoline,* and (along with Ellen Datlow and Gavin J. Grant) she edits *The Year's Best Fantasy & Horror* (St. Martin's).

Here, Link takes some time out of teaching at the Clarion South workshop in Brisbane, Australia, to discuss the journal and press she started, her methods of composition, and her own burgeoning body of work.

ALEX DEBONIS grew up in Indiana, lived in Ohio, and recently moved to Chicago with his wife, Loraine, after earning his Ph.D. in American literature and fiction writing from the University of Cincinnati. He's served as an editorial assistant at *The Cincinnati Review*, and his work has appeared in Storyglossia, *Review of Contemporary Fiction* and *Cincinnati CityBeat*.

The Writing Life

What prompted you to start Small Beer Press (with your husband Gavin J. Grant) and the journal *Lady Churchill's Rosebud Wristlet*?

Gavin wanted to start a zine because he thought it would be fun. I wanted to help because I liked Gavin, and I knew I liked editing as well. I'd worked on a literary review, and I'd read slush for a magazine called *Crank*. We've been putting out *LCRW* twice a year for 10 years now, and besides having fun and wanting to break even while doing so, our goal was to publish interesting work by newer writers, as well as work that didn't quite fit into genre magazines like *Asimov's* or *The Magazine of Fantasy & Science Fiction*.

What have you learned from starting your own press?

That I'm a control freak. I liked being able to design my own books. I loved working with Shelley Jackson on cover art and illustrations. I like thinking about fonts. Making books is physically satisfying in a way that writing fiction isn't. (Perhaps best of all would be knitting my own books. Not that I can knit.)

Most of my own stories have been published at least once in a magazine or anthology before I self-published them in the two collections. So I'd had at least some feedback from an editor. When I begin to revise, I am attempting to think about my work in the way I would, as an editor, approach someone else's work. I try to notice words, sentences, paragraphs, and scenes that feel like place-holders, that are make-do rather than what they need to be.

Keep your editor cap on. What does a submission to *LCRW* have to do to excite you?

This may sound horrible, but what makes me happiest, besides finding a good story is when the submissions are properly formatted. Which means Courier, 12-point, double-spaced, as short a cover letter as possible, and all the paragraphs properly indented rather than with space breaks between them. Especially that last one! I also want to get the sense that the writer submitting the story has had a look at *LCRW*, and thought about whether or not her work is a good fit for us. As far as content goes, I want stories that feel as if they mattered to the writer. I want ambitious short stories and poetry, and I want to find work with a strong sense of voice.

When you first began writing for publication, how did you recognize your strengths and weaknesses? How did you overcome your weaknesses?

I'm a big fan of workshops. I went through an MFA program at the University of North Carolina at Greensboro, and then, afterwards, I attended Clarion, which is an intensive six-week genre workshop. I think I needed both of these kinds of workshops in order to figure out certain things not only about how I write, but also about how I read. I like feedback, and I also like conversation about writing. I like the company of other writers.

When I wrote my first stories, I liked metaphors and similes a great deal. Plot not so much. Now I'm much more fond of thinking about plot and narrative structure, and I spend a lot less time coming up with interesting similes. Of course, now I have a whole new set of weaknesses. A lack of similes is probably one of them. The problem with overcoming weaknesses is that strengths can be just as much of a problem for a writer. If you only write toward your strengths, you'll end up using the same set of techniques, strategies, narratives, etc., which rapidly turns your strengths into weaknesses.

In a previous interview, you said, "I don't abandon stories once I've started working on them. . . But I do reject most of the ideas for stories that I come up with." Can you describe the litmus test you run on a story idea to decide if it's viable?

The first litmus test, although that sounds far too scientific, is whether I immediately think, "That is a really stupid idea." The second litmus test is whether or not I forget about a particular idea after deciding that it isn't too stupid. If I still have that idea in my head when I sit down to work, the second test is whether I'm interested enough in the first paragraph to go on writing.

Is the notion of telling an unconventional story (or telling a story in a way that hasn't been done before) important to you?

When I start a new story, what I usually think about is a particular character, or a situation that seems as if it would go somewhere interesting. Like a woman in a yard yelling, "Tree! Tree!" Or two women with the same first name who have been friends for years (one of whom has had a string of lovers, all cellists). Or a series of towers, all built close together, with wizards at the top of each and child servants running up and down the stairs on mysterious errands. Or a boy who puts on a cat suit. Usually the starting place for the story determines how I go on to write the story. Every once in a while, it will seem to me that I'm writing the same kind of characters over and over, or using the same narrative rhythms, and I'll attempt to put things together differently. I might try writing a first draft with dialogue only, or I might see what breaking up the story into three distinct parts does to it. Figuring out how to break certain kinds of rules is one kind of motivation. Figuring out how not to sound like myself is another. But the basic motivation is always: How can I make this funny? How can I make it scary? How much can I leave out?

When I sit down to write, I hope that I'm producing original work. But I'm also responding to the work of other writers, whether I'm aware of it as I write or whether I notice it later on or whether I don't notice it until someone points it out. I'm engaged in a conversation.

Many of your stories deal with loneliness and abandonment (in particular "Carnation, Lily, Lily, Rose," "Stone Animals," and "Lull"). Could you describe why you choose to approach those themes through speculative fiction?

Two of those are ghost stories, one is an epistolary story, and in "Lull," the devil shows up and makes out in a closet with a time-traveling cheerleader. I love ghost stories. I like stories where the devil causes trouble. I don't think about themes until after I have a finished draft. What I do think about is what I can do with a devil, or with the epistolary format. Loss and consolation are the business of most kinds of fiction, art, pop music, etc., or at least that's how it seems to me when I read or listen to music or, for that matter, when I watch television shows. *Buffy the Vampire Slayer*, for example.

My father read all the Tolkien novels to me before I knew how to read for myself, and the most recent novel that I've finished is Rose Macaulay's *The Towers of Trebizond*. Both of these writers are working in the same territory, really, in terms of theme. I don't know whether science fiction or fantasy or horror or romance or mystery has a built-in advantage over more mainstream fiction. Do musicians have an advantage over novelists? Do novelists have an advantage over short-story writers?

Does your genre-straddling approach make those issues more relevant to you in some way?

I write stories with zombies and witches in them because zombies and witches throw me—and, hopefully, readers—off balance in useful ways. I need to be knocked sideways a bit in order to find an interesting way into a story. But I'm not sure that what I'm writing about is so much a decision as a kind of stubbornness. I don't see "why" I can't write about zombies if I want to.

If all writers are, more or less, working in the same territory as far as thematic material goes, why don't more writers put zombies in their work? Why don't more writers tackle a ghost story now and then? Every good writer has at least one good ghost story in them, or at least I'm hopeful that that's the case.

Some stories seem infatuated with people having dreams (like "Most of My Friends Are Two-Thirds Water" in *Stranger Things Happen*) or with the logic of dreams ("The Hortlak" in *Magic for Beginners* springs to mind). What appeals to you about dreams?

The writer Howard Waldrop says that there are two kinds of logic in fiction. One is daytime logic and the other is nighttime logic. Dreams and fairytales operate on nighttime logic: Being polite will make witches like you. The third son is luckier than his brothers. Daytime logic is complicated, but less fun to talk about. Most stories need a bit of both kinds of logic. But what I love about dreams is that mixture of the ridiculous and the uncanny and the profound.

You've said that you like "mysteries better than solutions" in fiction. Which of your stories do you think best reflects this inclination and why?

I've been thinking, recently, about how the beginnings of mystery novels and horror novels are almost always better than the endings, explanations, and resolutions. Once a motivation or a mystery or a monster has been explained too thoroughly, it's somehow a bit like a birthday party where all the presents have been unwrapped, opened and then wrapped up again and put away. I love the ending of Ann Patchett's *Bel Canto* and the ending of Dodie Smith's *I Capture The Castle*, where we're pulled back away from understanding, or where the narrative simply breaks off before resolution. Of my stories, I like the ending of "The Wrong Grave," which is actually three endings in one, or "The Great Divorce," where the story changes shape in the very last sentence. But I have to admit that I like all my endings—what I usually hope is that the story has built up enough momentum that the reader keeps on moving forward even after I've stopped. (Imagine a slide in an amusement park, where the slide stops but the rider doesn't.)

Though you've professed a desire to write a novel, you've mainly stuck to the form of short fiction. What draws you to the short story?

I like to leave things out. I love short stories. If I had to choose between short stories and novels, I could stick with short stories happily—I've been writing much longer short stories than usual in the last year or so, and I'm much more anxious to get back to the 5,000-7,000 word range than I am to get up to the 60,000.

Also, I'm not sure that I've professed anything as strong as a "desire" to write a novel, but I dearly love to read novels, and I will probably try to write one at some point. Probably a young adult novel. Let's call it a strong interest rather than a desire.

A side note: Hardly anyone asks me if I want to write poetry. Are poets, too, always being asked if they plan to write novels? What I'd really like to do is write a picture book.

[Editor's note: Since this interview, Kelly Link has contracted with Viking Children's Books to publish a young-adult story collection, scheduled for release in fall 2008.]

You've also said that "Every writer has particular, useful obsessions—which translate into characters or situations or kinds of narrative arcs—that they come back to again and again." What do you identify as your own useful obsessions?

There was a period when I wrote a lot of stories that seemed to be about shoes or feet in some way. Then I stopped. More recently, I've been obsessed with zombies, but it's ghost stories that I end up writing over and over again. I suppose the best way to keep your fiction fresh is to develop new, useful obsessions. The young-adult writer Cecil Castellucci has an excellent piece of advice, which I love to pass on to writers: "Follow your inner rage and your inner perv."

Premier Voices

Three Debut Authors on the Importance of Teamwork

by Lauren Mosko

Writing can be a lonesome endeavor. Whether we spend hours buried in stale, silent library stacks doing research or staring at our monitor trying to actually create, it's no surprise that our fictional characters start to seem like real people. After all, if the writing's going well, we spend more time with them than we do our friends and family.

But the three authors in this year's first-books roundup happen to echo the same bit of wisdom and encouragement: While writing is a solitary pursuit, publishing is certainly not. Each writer acknowledges the tremendous contributions of different individuals—academic mentors, editors, agents, critique partners, spouses, writers' organizations—all of which he or she feels made each book better, each career possible, each agonizing wait by the mailbox more tolerable.

It's easy to get discouraged and start interpreting the bored looks on our cats' faces as indictments of our latest story when the only voices we hear all day come through our iTunes. So maybe it's time to give your writing life a boost and rejoin the living—to take a workshop or commit to an MFA program (full-time or low-res, whatever fits your schedule), to join a writers organization or critique group. At the very least, send your story to a smart, well-read friend you can trust to give you thoughtful feedback.

But first, read on to discover the steps these three authors took to move from the shadows of their writing desk and into the light (of your local Barnes & Noble, and other fine retailers).

Will Allison
What You Have Left (Free Press)

Will Allison knew he wanted to be a writer after taking a workshop with Lee K. Abbott during his sophomore year at Case Western University. "I wasn't particularly good at fiction writing, but that didn't stop me," Allison says. "At the time, I had plans to be a literary prodigy. I remember sharing this good news with a friend over a pitcher of beer at the aptly named Club Illusion. Thinking about that conversation still makes me cringe."

Big dreams aside, it would be seven years before Allison

Will Allison

© Lizzie Himmel

LAUREN MOSKO is the editor of *Novel & Short Story Writer's Market*. If you'd like to be considered for next year's Premier Voices column, please e-mail her at Lauren.Mosko@fwpubs.com.

published his first story and another eleven years before he sold his first book. In between, he "took a year off to write stories and be underemployed" and then followed Abbott to the fledgling MFA program at Ohio State University. He also took a turn as executive editor of the well-respected (and now-defunct) literary journal *Story*.

"Working at *Story* was, hands down, my most valuable experience as a young writer," Allison says. "It gave me a chance to learn about publishing, to meet authors and editors and agents, to read a lot of fiction and call it work. Most of all, the job afforded me a chance to edit some amazing stories, which is a great way to learn what makes them tick."

While working at *Story*, he began a story of his own called "The Gray Man." "I distinctly remember sneaking down to what was then the smoking lounge—a picnic area behind the building, next to some train tracks—to work on the first page again and again," recalls Allison. "For some reason, I had an awful hard time with the first two paragraphs."

Reprinted with permission from Free Press.

That story would become the penultimate chapter of his debut novel *What You Have Left*, a story of love, loss, abandonment and forgiveness, set in motion by Wylie Greer, who deserts his five-year-old daughter Holly after the death of his wife, Maddy. As the novel opens, we find a teenaged Holly "sentenced to life on my grandfather's dairy farm" in Columbia, SC—frustrated, lonely and desperate for information about the father she barely remembers and the mother her grandfather refuses to discuss. What she *does* know is that her father was an expert racecar mechanic and that her mother, much to the chagrin of the local menfolk, was a pioneering NASCAR "lady driver." As Holly searches for—and eventually finds—the elusive Wylie, the two must decide if their tenuous relationship is worth salvaging.

Allison himself had a bit of a precarious relationship with the novel when it began: After penning the first story, he wasn't quite sure what it was. "I knew I wanted to keep writing about the characters in that story, but it wasn't clear to me if I was writing a collection, a novel, a novel in stories, linked stories or something else," he says. "I told people it was a 'collection of interrelated stories,' in part, I think, because I was afraid to call it a novel: Writing stories seemed (almost) doable; writing a novel seemed scary."

Because each of the chapters in the novel is told during a different year by one of three characters (Holly, Wylie, or Holly's husband, Lyle), Allison could treat them as stand-alone stories, publishing them in several prestigious literary journals, including *The Cincinnati Review, One Story, Zoetrope, Glimmer Train Stories, The Kenyon Review* and *Shenandoah*. In this way, he laid the foundation for his book project, but he did not aggressively seek representation.

"I decided early on that I wouldn't go looking for an agent; I'd wait (or rather, hope) for agents to come to me," Allison explains. "I figured that was the best way to guarantee that I didn't pester anyone before my work was up to snuff." He was, however, savvy enough to know that he couldn't just wait in his apartment for the phone to ring; Allison had been an active member of the Community of Writers at Squaw Valley since 1999. And that's where he ended up meeting his agent, Julie Barer (a fellow housemate at the annual writers' workshop), in 2001. Barer took Allison as a client in 2003.

Once Barer had the manuscript in hand, Allison had a two-book deal with Free Press in a matter of weeks. "What it boils down to is I was very lucky," says Allison, "lucky to have an agent who was enthusiastic about the book, and lucky to find a publisher, Martha Levin, and an editor, Wylie O'Sullivan, who were likewise enthusiastic.

"One thing I've learned about the business of publishing is the extent to which it's a team sport," he says. "It takes a lot of people working closely together—agent, editor, editorial director, managing editor, publisher, associate publisher, publicist, publicity director, book designer, production editor, production manager, marketing manager, salespeople—you get the picture. They are invariably smart, friendly, dedicated people who could spend more time with their families and make more money if they'd chosen a different line of work, but they're in publishing because they care deeply about books. This sets them apart from the vast majority of Americans. Possibly they are mad. Those of us who write literary fiction have a relatively minuscule voice in our culture. If it weren't for these folks—and the editors of literary magazines—we'd have no voice at all."

In addition to the vast support network Allison recognizes at Free Press, he also acknowledges another contributor, his wife, magazine editor Deborah Way. "My friend, the late Max Steele, used to say, 'I've never seen a story that couldn't be improved by editing.' I don't understand writers who don't like to be edited. I want all the good editing I can get. Happily, I'm married to a brilliant, exacting, generous editor. If *What You Have Left* is any good, a lot of the credit goes to Deborah."

Allison is now at work on his second novel, which he says is much different from *What You Have Left*. "It's not a Southern book; it's set in New Jersey. And the structure is more linear than *What You Have Left*," he says. "The process is pretty much the same. I suppose there's more pressure this time in the sense that there's a due date in my contract, but, on the other hand, I get to write fiction full-time, at least for a while. That's the most I could ask for."

For more information about Will Allison and his novels and stories, visit www.willallison.com.

Darren DeFrain
The Salt Palace (New Issues Press)

What do the game of basketball, the state of Utah, and footnotes have in common? According to author Darren DeFrain: simultaneous narrative. This concept was not only the impetus for his debut novel, *The Salt Palace*, it also serves as the unifying principle for what might otherwise seem a bizarre tale.

© New Issues Press.

Darren DeFrain

Perfect mismatched strangers Brian (inert, aloof, works at a bank) and Randy (moody, mysterious, has a checkered past and a prosthetic steel claw for an arm) have only three things in common: They are rabid Utah Jazz fans, fallen sons of the Church of Jesus Christ of Latter-day Saints, and companions on an ill-fated road trip from Michigan home to Utah.

"Utah is such a wonderfully peculiar place whose culture and history so heavily informs your experience that I wanted to try to capture that on the page," explains DeFrain. "When I started integrating basketball into the primary narrative, I started thinking about the physical act of watching a game on television. There are at least three simultaneous narratives (and more and more simultaneous narratives in our daily lives with the greater intrusion of technology and text). First, there's the action on the court. That would be Brian and Randy's story. Then there are all the stats and history of the game that splash across the bottom of the screen. That's the Mormon and state history. And then there's the announcers' banter. That's the self-aware authorial voice coming into the story.''

DeFrain achieves the effect of simultaneous narrative by moving much of what other writers might consider back story, such as historical and statistical information, into footnotes. Often, footnoted text is as substantial as the primary chapter, obviously playing with the fictional form.

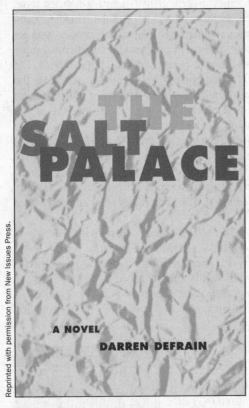

Reprinted with permission from New Issues Press.

"I knew there would be a lot of comparisons to the David Foster Wallaces of the world (to which I would pale), but I didn't want to simply utilize that implied academic sarcasm that I typically see employed with footnotes," DeFrain says. "These notes, I feel, are crucial to a more profound understanding of Brian's struggles. At the same time, I know they're skimmable. My late editor Herb Scott and I went round a bit on the footnotes. He wanted me to list them as endnotes primarily so they'd be easier to print. But I really thought that undermined the nature of the simultaneous narrative that was at the heart of this novel.''

Even though DeFrain admits that the great footnote debate slowed down his book's editorial process, his willingness to play with form was one element of the novel that helped him connect with New Issues Press. He had previously sent the press a collection of his stories (which they'd returned with a "Dear Writer" type of rejection) as he was finishing his doctoral degree at Western Michigan University. (WMU also houses New Issues Press.)

Press editor Herb Scott happened to run into Jaimy Gordon, DeFrain's writing mentor, on campus one day and mentioned that he didn't think DeFrain's collection was working. She suggested Scott take a look at *The Salt Palace* and then called DeFrain and told him to hurry and send the novel to Scott's attention. DeFrain was encouraged and decided to take the chance despite the earlier rejection.

"I'd heard that Herb Scott was looking for novels with a Michigan link that took some stylistic risks. He was also a big fan of basketball, so I can't imagine a better fit," he says.

DeFrain sent the manuscript (which took him two years to draft and another year to revise) to Scott in 2002. "He read the novel over a weekend and called me the next Monday and said he wanted to publish it. My wife asked if I shouldn't think about shopping it around a little to larger presses, but I knew I couldn't top Herb's enthusiasm, which was very important to me."

In addition to acknowledging the support of Gordon and Scott, DeFrain is quick to recognize the invaluable encouragement and opportunities he gained from his time in academic writing programs. "I saw—and now see, as director of the MFA program at Wichita State University—a lot of grad students with entitlement issues who don't necessarily realize what a terrific opportunity an MFA is and how, at the same time, it is also comes with no guarantees," he says. "There won't be a line of agents or hiring committees waiting for you to show them your diploma; you've got to take advantage of every single opportunity to work with your mentors, to get feedback on your writing, to sharpen your own critical aesthetic, and to hear visiting writers read and answer questions. Unless you're some kind of savant, which I'm not, all of those opportunities are expressly helpful to the beginning writer.

"The other important thing I learned from working with Steve [Heller], Debra [Monroe], Stu [Dybek], Jaimy and the late Andre Dubus was the amount of dedication and work it takes to be a writer. I think I entered writing believing too much in inspiration as the source of good writing. Dubus was particularly inspiring because he was so afflicted from a hit-and-run accident that he couldn't comfortably hold a pen to the page. He 'wrote' on a tape recorder and then had his work transcribed for him. He was my thesis reader and he sent me a cassette tape discussing my thesis stories. That struck me as a hell of an example of dedication to craft and work, not to mention just a wonderfully generous person with a beginning writer."

The experience of publishing his first novel taught DeFrain an important lesson, too. "Stick to your guns. When I tried to show people early, early drafts of the novel, even friends, they'd see the footnotes and the roughly hewn prose and be inclined to discourage me," he recalls. "If you've got a vision for your work, you need to pursue that and not turn it into a committee project (with workshops, peers, editors or anyone). You should listen to what they have to say, but you need to be your own advocate for what you want to do at all points in the process."

For more information on Darren DeFrain and his work, visit www.darrendefrain.com.

Diana Holquist
Make Me a Match (Warner Forever)

When her husband's job relocated Diana Holquist, an advertising copywriter, and her family from Manhattan to a tiny town in upstate New York, there were no jobs for her. She cried for a week. Then she decided it was the perfect time to start something new.

© Warner Forever.

Diana Holquist

"Because I was incredibly naïve, I opened a file on my computer and typed 'Chapter One,' sure I was going to write the Great American Novel," she says. "Three years and three unsold manuscripts later, I began to educate myself on the business of fiction writing. After a lot of research, I decided that the romance genre was the place to start."

Holquist may have felt like she was starting her new career at square one, but in truth, a lot of the skills she learned as a business writer translated to her fiction writing. "Business writing was crucial to making me a successful fiction writer because, ultimately, fiction writing *is* a business," she explains. "With my advertising work, I learned to write funny on a deadline. There's no writer's block when you have a client meeting at 9 a.m. Also, in advertising, there are no solo efforts, so I came to fiction with that spirit of collaboration. It wasn't about ownership (or authorship); it was about ending up with the best work possible. But the most important thing I learned from business writing was how to take criticism and learn from it. In a New York City ad agency, it's incredibly competitive. So you listen and you watch and you learn—or else."

It was a combination of such creativity and observation that led her to the inspiration for her novel *Make Me a Match*. Holquist started following the story of a woman searching for a husband through the woman's Web site and was astounded by the extensive list of criteria the woman expected her husband-to-be to meet. "I knew it was a good story, so I started writing it. But there was no spark, nothing distinctive—no hook," she says. "Then, I read a short story about a man who curses a town by telling every citizen the exact day they'll die. I loved the idea of knowledge as a curse. I couldn't get it out of my head. I realized that this Web-searching woman's greatest curse would be to learn that there actually is a man destined to be her One True Love on this earth—but he's her worst nightmare. Thus, Amy, the psychic gypsy who can tell you the name of your One True Love was born. It was a fun, magic hook that let me explore a theme that had been done to death in a way that had never been done before. Once I had the hook, I made the sale."

WARNER ☙ FOREVER

If True Love is a gift, what's the return policy?

Make Me a Match

Diana Holquist

Reprinted with permission from Warner Forever.

In *Make Me a Match*, the aforementioned Amy—a gypsy in every sense of the word—crashes the engagement party of her estranged older sister Cecelia, a successful cardiologist who has done everything she can to forget her wandering Romani roots. But Amy hasn't just come to eat caviar out of the serving bowl (or make off with the silver candlesticks); she's come to tell Cel that her wealthy, gorgeous fiancé, Jack, is not only *not* her One True Love, but Fate has destined her to be matched with a man named Finn Franklin Concord—who's dying. Now Cecelia has to decide if she's prepared to risk the tidy life she's built for herself to explore the possibility of true happiness. . . before it's too late.

Even with a great story, great characters and a great hook, it still took Holquist seven months and 18 rejections to find an agent. Another seven months (and more rejections) passed before her agent got two simultaneous offers from Warner and a smaller press. "The editor at the smaller press was very senior and loved it as is. The Warner editor was very junior and wanted huge changes. But the changes she wanted were so smart, I didn't have any question that I would go with Warner," says Holquist. "It was a great working relationship from day one."

Holquist's editors at Warner asked for a complete overhaul of one of the secondary characters, which required cutting over 150 pages from the original manuscript, but she was all for it. "It was an *enormous* change and it made the book 100% better," she says. "I love the revision process. I think it's where most of the magic happens. There's no page of a manuscript that can't be funnier; no character that can't be more interesting; no plot that can't have one more brilliant twist. A good editor can do all that. I was just along for the ride."

Holquist also attributes much of her success to her active participation in Romance Writers of America, which she joined after finishing her first "practice" novel in 2002. (That manuscript was a finalist for RWA's Golden Heart award for unpublished manuscripts in 2003, but Holquist doesn't intend to sell it.) "I'll never forget my first meeting in the Liverpool public library in upstate New York. Twenty women sitting around a table guffawing and telling bawdy jokes, and halfway through I realize, hey, that's Maggie Shayne, who's been on every best-seller's list in existence, giving a newbie query advice. And that's Deirdre Martin, *USA Today* best-selling author, critiquing an unpublished writer on a Saturday morning like it's no big deal. Romance writers are amazing that way,'' she says. ''Writers helping other writers. Let me restate that: Published, successful best-selling writers spending their Saturday in a dreary town in a dark library *helping unpublished wannabes* like it's no big deal. Can you imagine anything more remarkable? I wouldn't be published today without RWA.''

Now that Holquist has joined the ranks of the published—the sequel *Sexiest Man Alive* was released in October 2007 and the third book in the series is in the works—she has a few pieces of advice and encouragement of her own to pass on: ''You can't get better if you work alone. You need to show people your work, the sooner the better, and then you have to listen to what they say. I know it's scary, but it's a necessary part of the process. I work with a critique group that saves my butt every time. They make my work so much better than it would have been if I had written it my way. If you find the courage to put your work out there and then you listen to feedback, you'll get published. It's just a matter of time.''

(And for those of you grumbling bitterly right now about overnight success, just in case you were wondering, *Make Me a Match*—from page one to bookstore shelf—took four years.

For more information on Diana Holquist and her books, visit www.dianaholquist.com.

The Writing Life

Does My Novel Have What It Takes?

by I.J. Schecter

U ndertaking a novel is a bit like succumbing to a teenage infatuation. That first power-ful spark, though it's probably been laying in wait, seems swift and unexpected. Without warning the spark becomes an obsession, transforming you into a loon who swings daily between elation and anguish. At the first hint of self-doubt, you press on, mildly panicked but hoping contradictory evidence will emerge. Further indications that it might not meet your ideal vision lead to agonized moments of soul-searching and silent questions about whether what you're doing is really worthwhile.

In a relationship, sometimes your gut is the best guide. With a novel, the same can't be said. To succeed in a competitive marketplace, you need to rely upon something more con-crete than instinct. Though no one has invented an infallible Novel Success Predictor, there are certain questions you can ask yourself to help decide whether your manuscript is ready to be sent into the hands of agents or publishers. Here are half a dozen.

Do I know who, and what, this story is about?

A great novel, though it may seem like a mystical confluence of uncontrollable forces, is really a product of two things: a good idea, and the firm resolve of a writer to know what he's trying to say and through whom he's trying to say it. Successful novels change over time—Dickens doesn't sound much like, say, Jonathan Franzen—but they all share something crucial: Readers know who and what they're about. Ask a handful of people to describe *Wuthering Heights* in one sentence. Easy, most will say—it's a story about how love can eat you up. How about *To Kill a Mockingbird?* Sure—lawyer takes on bigoted system. *Christine*? No problem—teenage loser falls in love with his car, which is, unfortunately for him, possessed.

Ask the same people *who* these books are about, and the answers should come just as quickly. Heathcliff and Catherine. Atticus Finch. A '58 Plymouth Fury. They're novels written at different times by different people, but all are memorable because they're clear on who's at the center of the story and just what that story is about.

Subject your manuscript to the same test. Who's the protagonist, and what's his or her story? If you can answer right away—"It's about Dexter Knight, a glass blower who inadver-tently gets caught up with the Mafia"—good for you. If you can't—"It's about this guy who's

I.J. SCHECTER (www.ijschecter.com) writes for leading magazines, newspapers and Web sites throughout the world, including *Condé Nast Brides*, *Golf Monthly*, *Men's Exercise*, *The Globe & Mail* and iParenting.com. He is also the author of two collections, *The Bottom of the Mug* (Aegina Press Inc) and *Slices: Observations from the Wrong Side of the Fairway* (John Wiley & Sons).

a glass blower . . . oh, but he also has a girlfriend who's having an affair with a CIA guy, then the guy, not the CIA guy but the glass blower, gets caught up with drug smugglers, who are actually the Mafia, so it's about the drug trade, and the Mafia, but also about, you know, relationships, especially how hard it is to have one with someone in the CIA''—it's time to get more focused.

Is the synopsis clear?
One of the best ways to identify narrative gaps or weak points in your story is to have a go at writing the synopsis, a condensed—*extremely* condensed—version of the entire beast. The synopsis is similar to those one-paragraph movie descriptions you read to help decide what you should see on Saturday night. Readers often conduct the same exercise with books. If your synopsis doesn't stand up to scrutiny, those readers might never even get to page one of the actual book. If the story is clear in your head, you won't have any trouble condensing it into a few paragraphs. If it's still fuzzy, your attempt at a synopsis will give you fits, telling you where you need to take action.

Could I recognize my leads walking down the street?
You know Dexter Knight the glass blower is the story's protagonist. Good. You also know that his girlfriend, Trish Walters, is going to be along for the ride as Dex accidentally becomes a pawn in the operations of an organized drug ring, and that he's going to have to eventually face off against the boss of that ring, Paul Puccini. You deserve kudos for establishing a solid framework for the story. Now pretend you're talking a stroll to replenish the Diet Coke supply you always keep on hand when writing. If Dexter were to walk out of the store as you were walking in, would you know it was him? How about Trish, or Paul?

Before you submit that manuscript, the answer to this question—not just for these three main characters, but for every other character as well—must be an unequivocal yes. When they talk, the reader should know instantly it's them talking and not someone else. When they appear, there should be no hesitation in the recognition that it is them on stage. When they perform any act, small or large, it should be known without question that it's them acting because you've described them so clearly that the reader feels they can predict what they'll do before they do it. And when finally they show behavior demonstrating change or growth—when habitually mild Dexter confronts Paul Puccini because Trish's life is at stake, say—it should be a believable change consistent with how you've set them up to that point. The reader shouldn't be saying to herself, ''Hmm, that seems weird.'' She should be saying, ''Way to go, Dex. I knew you had it in you.''

How strong is a randomly chosen chapter?
While we all battle the perception that our writing is superb one day and dismal the next, the truth is you write to a certain skill range anytime you take pen to paper or fingers to keyboard. Some days you may be closer to the bottom of that range and some days closer to the top, but for the most part you aren't spontaneously rising to Shakespeare's level or reverting to your three-year-old nephew's, despite how it may feel.

Therefore, any chapter in your novel should serve as a pretty good gauge of the manuscript's overall quality. Pick any chapter and read it, trusting that it isn't much worse than the best or much better than the worst. If after one chapter you're finding it difficult to make this judgment, read another. If you still aren't sure, read a third. If after three chapters you still can't decide, then the overall story isn't good enough—at least not yet.

What do three of my friends think?
Should you give the manuscript to your spouse for feedback? No harm. How about your mom? Sure, why not—good for the ego. But if you really want to know whether your story

has the goods, give the manuscript to three friends you trust and ask them for their objective reactions. Tell them not to hold back. Tell them you need comments on everything: whether certain parts crackle and others fall flat, whether the antagonist strikes the right chord but the villain feels stock, whether the whole thing starts with a bang but ends with a fizzle.

When you get parallel responses regarding one aspect or another—for example, all three readers say Trish's personality is inconsistent—trust them, and go to work on improving those aspects. If you get conflicting answers—one person says Trish is note-perfect, one says she's somewhat vague and another says she's nothing but a big distraction—give the manuscript to three more friends. Keep doing this until you get significant majority responses. Fix the things that are wrong, keep the things that are right, and then send that sucker off.

How does this compare with the book I'm reading now?

Pitting your novel against other stuff you've written isn't very useful, because, let's face it, you just aren't a very objective judge of your own work. One moment you're probably too high on that great sentence you wrote in Chapter 1, the next you're probably in the throes of despair because of that inconsistency in Chapter 2 you somehow didn't catch until the fourth draft.

Forget the other stuff *you've* written, and instead perform the ultimate anxiety-inducing test: Weigh your manuscript against the books *others* have written. I'm not talking about people in your writing group, the blogger next door, or casual correspondents of yours whose e-mails would make grammarians everywhere cringe. I'm talking about those men and women whose names are on the spines in your local Barnes & Noble.

When I'm writing a humor manuscript and can't tell whether it's good enough yet to send to my publisher, I go to my local bookstore and start to flip through Dave Barry's latest. Usually I laugh to tears for twenty minutes and then leave depressed because I'll never measure up. But when I get home and dare to peek at my manuscript again, I might come across a sentence that makes me chuckle, and my faith begins to restore itself. The manuscript still has a long way to go, I'll realize, but it has potential. I've reminded myself where the bar is set, and that's key. In any competition, after all, you need to know what you're aiming for.

Stay or Go?

*Knowing When to Stick With Your Novel. . .
or Toss It to the Curb*

by W.E. Reinka

Writing a novel is a lot like a love affair.

Even on those days when we're not writing, we're thinking about the book. Some days go along beautifully. Words flow like the waves that kiss the shore on the beach walks in personal ads. On the other hand, some days the novel gets stubborn. We wonder why we ever thought we could make it work.

Writing or loving, we ask ourselves the same question: When to stay, when to go?

Hit the road, Jack

Like legions of college theater majors before her, Sheri Holman headed to the Big Apple to trod the boards. While waiting for stardom, she had to eat regularly so she took a job as an assistant to Molly Friedrich, who happens to be one of the hottest literary agents in New York. It was like an aerospace engineer heading to L.A. and taking work with some guy named Spielberg until something opened up at Lockheed.

Holman was soon swept into the literary world. After spending her days reading other people's manuscripts, she went home at night to work on her own. One day she presented her first novel to Friedrich who took it home over the weekend. On Monday, Friedrich returned it to her with a shake of the head.

So did Holman stick with the novel, adding a twist or two and deepening the characters to try to make it work?

No, she dropped it. The affair was over. Good thing, too, because if she'd stayed with it she might never have published her second effort, *A Stolen Tongue* (Atlantic Monthly Press, 1997), or hit the big time with *The Dress Lodger* (2000) which, at least so it seems, every book club in the country has tackled at one time or another.

Robert Ward got lucky after bar hopping.

"One night I went out in Greenwich Village and came home all bummed out over the book I'd been working on, thinking it's never going to work. I went to bed all sweaty after drinking too much and in my twilight asleep I heard a voice in my head say, 'My name is Red Baker and the story I'm about to tell you . . .' It was really the first line of a new book. So I went in the other room and, pre-computers, started typing away. I typed from one in the morning till seven. The voice had come. The characters were all there and the plot was there."

The result was *Red Baker* (Dial Press), a novel that went on to win the 1985 PEN West prize for Best Novel. His latest title is *Four Kinds of Rain* (St. Martin's Minotaur, 2006) and he

W. E. REINKA, who frequently writes about books and authors, contributes to magazines and newspapers nationwide.

might still be out in the rain himself if he hadn't left his first book to run off with *Red Baker*.

What happened to the novel he was working on? Ward never wrote another word of it. He thinks he might have the original 600 pages stashed in his garage.

Hold on tight

On the other hand, literary novelist Margot Livesey decided to hang in there with *Eva Moves the Furniture* (Henry Holt & Co, 2001), though it felt like a dysfunctional relationship at times. She started that novel in 1987 and finished it 14 years later. During that span, she played around—publishing three other novels—but always went back to Eva.

One reason the novel took so long (and one reason she couldn't let it go) was that its primary character, Eva, was based on Livesey's mother, who died when she was still a toddler. It was intensely personal. "I'd give up on it and I'd write another novel that would be published. Then I'd say to myself, 'Now I know what to do with *Eva Moves the Furniture*.' I'd get back to it for maybe six months and think, 'No, no this is just disappearing into a black hole again' and I'd stop and write another publishable book."

But it's important to note that Livesey didn't continually revise *Eva Moves the Furniture* after countless rejections. The book's long evolution derived from bringing the novel into focus for herself. "When I finally came back to it after I'd written and published *The Missing World*, it wasn't with the expectation of publishing the book. It was with the expectation of finishing it to my own satisfaction."

Sometimes things are too hot not to cool down.

Back in the 1980s, Richard A. Lupoff wrote a sweeping thriller about Super Bowl betting and drug usage in the National Football League, a bit of a departure from his established career as a novelist in the horror, science fiction, and mystery genres. Maybe Lupoff himself even sensed this book might too hot—he submitted it under a pseudonym. Every editor who read it loved it. Every editor also turned it down. However prescient, the novel was too far ahead of its time—the NFL remained something of a sacred cow in American culture, and drug abuse in sports hadn't yet made the front page.

So did Lupoff mope like a star-crossed lover?

"I could've been bummed out and I certainly wasn't happy. But I wasn't going to spend the rest of my career sulking because of this incident. I said 'Okay, too bad. Throw it in the drawer and write another book.' And that's what I did. I'm not like the God Janus who could look in two directions at once. You gotta choose. Look to the future or look to the past. I'm not going to the past. I can't control that. I can only control the future."

Sometimes it's okay to chase after someone.

S.J. Rozan was enjoying a career as an architect in New York City when a voice inside her head began nagging her, "Weren't we going to write a book?" Soon she joined the legions of other writers with day jobs. She completed her first novel, *Stone Quarry* (Minotaur Books, 1999). "Then mostly," she recalls, "as a matter of not wanting to give up the joy of writing, as opposed to confidence, drive, or any sensible reason," she plunged ahead before she had an agent, let alone a book contract, into what she envisioned as the second in her detective series.

Even after she completed the second book, *Concourse* (Minotaur, 1995), without a sale, she remained undeterred. It wasn't until Rozan had written her third novel that she finally struck pay dirt. Those first two books wound up being the second and sixth installments in the two-time Edgar winner's Lydia Chin/Bill Smith series.

So how do you know?

A former bartender, mystery novelist J.A. Konrath sees a common parallel between certain wannabe novelists and some of the bar-scene regulars. "They flit from one project to another without ever letting things develop." At least for the literary lounge lizards, Konrath suggests following the same four steps over and over. "Write when you can. Finish what you write. Revise what you finish. Submit your revision and start all over again if it doesn't go."

Lupoff sounds a lot like Konrath when he talks about three friends who seem blind to déjà vu rejections on novels they won't divorce.

All three of Lupoff's writer-friends have nursed first novels for going on 10 years, submitting them, watching them get rejected, revising them again and submitting them again (and again). "I have given each of them identical advice which goes as follows: Write another book. Spend a year on it. Then write another book and spend a year on that. Write another book and spend a year on that. In the meantime, these are all out in the marketplace. Any reasonably literate intelligent person can write a novel in a year and if you do this for 10 years, I guarantee by the end of the ten years you will be selling your books." Lupoff pauses for emphasis. "I have not gotten one of the three to heed this advice. They all nod their heads and say 'yeah, yeah, yeah' and go back and revise chapter six again thinking somehow that this is going to have a magical effect and turn an unsaleable book into saleable book."

Seeing how Konrath wrote 10 novels over 12 years before his first sale, it's no wonder that he echoes Lupoff's advice. How did he let go of the first nine novels, especially when he thinks that his best work remains unpublished? "If a project has accumulated between 30 and 100 rejections from editors and agents, then it's time to move on. Writing a publishable novel doesn't mean that it's going to get published. I wrote over a million words and had 450 rejections from editors and agents before I sold my first book."

While acknowledging that "once you start pouring work into something, it's hard to give up," Margot Livesey advises her students at Emerson College that often writing a novel, especially a first novel, is a learning experience. "There may come that awful moment when you actually have to accept that the novel into which you've put so much time and hope and effort was a way for you to learn to be a better writer. It's a tricky moment for everyone involved. Usually the news comes to the young writer from agents and editors rather than from their teachers."

Sheri Holman observes that novels, like relationships, are often easier to throw away than to fix. "The best gift you can give yourself as a writer is to hear and accept criticism from people who know more than you. It's hard. It's something that's deeply painful and mortifying to hear. But if you can hear and accept it, you can grow as a writer."

Konrath likes to compare editing to marriage counseling. "You don't necessarily think you need it. You don't necessarily want it. But it's going to be good for the marriage."

And sometimes it just clicks.

Robert Ward who came home from the bar and started a new novel says that he's had his

Craft & Technique

When to Stay

- If you're passionate about your book and make it a priority in your busy schedule to write about characters who increasingly are taking on minds of their own.

- If it's an exclusive relationship where you're not tempted to start three other novels while you "search for direction" with this one.

- If rejection letters offer specific and lengthy encouragement which you can use as revision guidelines.

share of tough relationships where everything seemed hard, along with book projects where everything seemed hard. "But when I saw Red Baker and those characters popping out of my typewriter it was like falling in love. The other book I'd been working on was all forced. It was all will, in a way—I'm going to make this work, by God. Red Baker was just the opposite. Its characters existed previously and all I had to do was write about them. If you're in a tough romantic relationship, everything is really hard—we've got to act right, let's try to be good to each other—then all of a sudden you meet someone with whom you just hit it off. You don't have to will it to work, it works! That's where creativity and love meet."

When to Go

- If you're hundreds of pages into the manuscript and its shape is still evolving, you likely have a patch of quicksand, not a concrete plot with sharply defined characters.

- If you've received over 30 agent and publisher rejections that do not offer any specific encouragement other than standard phrases meant to soften the blow ("while we found much that we liked . . .")

- If friends clamor for a copy of the manuscript, whip through the first chapters and then take ages to complete it, if ever. When even clamoring friends don't think it's a compelling read, you're dead.

Craft & Technique

The Sweep of the Story

Broadening the Scope of Your Short Story

by Noelle Sterne

Most short stories illumine a single dark corner, narrowly circumscribed. They follow the time-revered rule: Limit your story to a specific time, place, event, interaction or character's evolution. But the story can be a more versatile genre than your high school English teacher sermonized. If we stick to tradition only, we may restrict or dilute our subjects or abandon potentially powerful ideas.

Many wonderful stories remain small in conception and scale, yet others maintain the short story character but introduce an outlook that's much broader than we've been taught to expect. This is the sweep of the story.

Where's the sweep?

You may never have heard of the sweep; it's not discussed in texts or fiction seminars and may sound a lot like background, setting, exposition, or backstory. The sweep certainly incorporates elements of these and, like them, can be used for effective foreshadowing. But it's more. With a sweep, the story opens like a movie camera panning a wide-ranging view, from the swirling galaxy and down through the heavens to the earth to a countryside to a neighborhood to a single home, and finally to the protagonist in the kitchen in his underwear.

The sweep encompasses grand events—physical, historical, generational, psychological, emotional—and involves a sense of time and distance, stretching the reader's mind beyond the expected confines of the short story. For example, in that camera's panoramic lens, a sweep may synopsize a cataclysmic climate change, the long years of a religious war, a king's rule, a civilization's demise and regeneration, a terrible pattern resounding through family generations.

To illustrate, look at these two passages. The first is conventional:

> Jason's father was always hard on him. From earliest childhood, Jason knew
> this was what to expect. It was almost a family tradition.

The second is a sweep:

> Patriarchal discipline was ingrained into the very fabric of the family. It had
> gone on for generations and didn't break for holidays, births, funerals, or world

NOELLE STERNE publishes in writers' and other magazines and has contributed monthly columns to lifestyle and writers' publications. She specializes in motivational, psychological, philosophical, inspirational and spiritual approaches. Long a reader and writer of fiction, she won an award and publication of a short story in the *CrossTIME Science Fiction Anthology, Vol. V*. She is currently completing a book of candid counsel and relentless support for writers.

wars. It always got transmitted in torturous exactness from father to son to son—and even to sons-in-law (by some bonded osmotic process) as men married into the family. None of the children could escape, and this oppressive mantle was now being passed to Jason.

You can see from these examples how the sweep differs from typical exposition. They both establish necessary grounding, but the sweep's dimension is wider (in Jason's family, no child can escape) and its design larger (the discipline is passed down through the generations).

The range of the sweep is also more courageous than the normal background. It asks you to push beyond the accepted rules of the short story and lands you at the precipice of a novel—in the second example, following the sweep, an entire chapter could easily be devoted to Jason's great-grandfather's mode of discipline and its influence on each family member, another chapter to Jason's grandfather as father, and a third to Jason's father, finally introducing Jason. But in a short story, you don't have the luxury of chapters for each scenario.

On the other hand, the sweep isn't mere rambling or lazy writing. Let's say that in the above sweep, instead of continuing with Jason, you talked about his two sisters and how they were (or weren't) disciplined. This would be straying from the promised focus—Jason. Just because your train of thought started running away with the daughters' experiences doesn't mean you don't apply the brakes of conscious writing and thinking.

When to sweep

Not many short stories make use of the sweep, and this, in addition to the usual strictures, may be why you haven't entertained the idea. A sweep is appropriate when you want to give your story—or your main character's struggles or conflicts—a larger context, more than generally expected in a short story. In our Jason example above, I wanted to show that he was up against not only his father's habitual actions but the strength of successive generations of disciplinarians. As the story unfolds and Jason begins to question his father's authority and power, the sweep makes us realize Jason's victory is that much more profound.

Many sweep-less short stories grip us from the first word, but with a sweep, some supreme stories captivate our interest and draw us into their mesmerizing, expansive environment without losing the essence of the form. They show us a compelling picture, present many clues about the story and protagonist, pull us in, and entice us. Here we'll consider five elements that help you discover, create, manage and integrate the sweep of your story.

1. Establish your sweep

The sweep can take place at the opening of your story or several paragraphs into it. In ''The Rocking Horse Winner,'' D.H. Lawrence opens with the sweep, covering at least 30 years as he recounts the wife's psychological history, from her adult beginnings to the present and her marriage and children, whom she somehow cannot love. Lawrence compounds this void by portraying the family's chronic lack of money, their expensive tastes and the necessity of keeping up their London social position. This is how he begins:

> There was a woman who was beautiful, who started with all the advantages, yet she had no luck. She married for love, and the love turned to dust. She had bonny children, yet she felt they had been thrust upon her, and she could not love them. . . . This troubled her, and in her manner she was all the more gentle and anxious for her children, as if she loved them very much. Only she herself knew that at the centre of her heart was a hard little place that could not feel love, no, not for anybody. . . . Although they lived in style, they felt always an anxiety in the house. . . . There must be more money, there must be more money.

This sweep is successful because it narrates not simply one or two events in the mother's life but sums up her entire past, including motivation (married for love) and results (love turned to dust, children thrust on her). Added to this past is the family's chronic anxiety about lack of money, an ironic outcome since she "started with all the advantages," and this lack, as we shall see, governs many of her responses to her son.

The passage also brings us to the verge of the present action, telling how she now always attempts to compensate for the hardness of her heart (acting all the more gentle toward her children). In this passage, we're given both a history of physical events that cover many years and their accumulated psychological and emotional effects on the mother. The sweep thus fills in a larger, more complex and multidimensional picture than the customary backstory.

In another illustration, Steve Lazarowitz in "A Creative Edge" opens with a sweep every writer can relate to:

> Sandros Lefrak was a writer. At least, he claimed to be. He certainly spent enough time on it, as he sat before his antiquated typewriter, hour after hour, day after day. One page after another of tripe. The worst kind of tripe. And everyone knew it, except for him.
>
> His agent, if you could call him an agent, would barely accept his calls anymore. What was left of his friends avoided him for fear he might ask them to read something he'd written. Even his own mother, rest her soul, had lied to him, claiming her eyes had become too bad to read. It wasn't his style that was bad, but rather his imagination that couldn't conjure a new idea, even on a good day.

This outline gives us a sweeping insight, probably more than we're comfortable with, into Sandros' chronically failing writing life. And the sweep explains why he takes the extreme measure he does to acquire new ideas and reach the writing gratification he craves.

2. Make your sweep relate

As you can see from these two examples, the successful sweep must relate precisely to the heart of your story. It's easy to get carried away with, say, a lush description of war-torn years, à la *Gone With the Wind*. But readers will recognize the self-indulgence of a sweep that doesn't specifically connect to your protagonist and the main conflict. They'll sense you're overly enamored with those brilliant descriptions and will likely turn to the TV.

Lawrence's initial psychological and social history frames the motivation for the son's compulsive and desperate actions and his inevitable destruction. And Lawrence's use of the thematic word "luck" in the first sentence foreshadows the son's tragic obsession with it. Lazarowitz's unflinching introduction encapsulating Sandros' sorry writing saga makes us understand what pushes him to take a drastic, irrevocable step.

In another example with a conventional opening, Shirley Jackson starts her classic and bone-chilling story "The Lottery" with immediate action. On a balmy summer day, the citizens of a typically pleasant small town gather as if at a county fair. We're introduced to the townsfolk by name as the men exchange sage words about the crops and weather, the women gossip and the boys collect smooth stones, as boys will, and play boisterously.

But then, in the fourth paragraph, we're given the first real indication of the day's sinister nature. The townsfolk aren't preparing for a county fair but for a macabre ritual—involving those apparently innocent stones—as old as the village. Now Jackson turns to her sweep with the history of the lottery's focal point, the "black box":

> The original paraphernalia for the lottery had been lost long ago, and the black box now resting on the stool had been put into use even before Old Man

Warner, the oldest man in town, was born. Mr. Summers spoke frequently to the villagers about making a new box, but no one liked to upset even as much tradition as was represented by the black box. There was a story that the present box had been made with some pieces of the box that had preceded it, the one that had been constructed when the first people settled down to make a village here. Every year, after the lottery, Mr. Summers began talking again about a new box, but every year the subject was allowed to fade off without anything's being done. The black box grew shabbier each year: by now it was no longer completely black but splintered badly along one side to show the original wood color, and in some places faded or stained.

This precise and detailed account emphasizes the centrality of the black box to the ancient, outdated rite that is still mandatory and very much alive. With this background, Jackson quickly refocuses on the present as the citizens take their turns drawing slips of paper from the box, to the story's final horrific end.

Ruth Prawer Jhabvala uses a different kind of sweep in "The Interview," a tale of the crucial job interview faced by one of the two men in an extended family. Like Jackson, Jhabvala introduces the sweep after several opening paragraphs. Dreading his impending interview, and certain his inherent nature is not to work, the man ruminates how his mother, grandmother and aunt have brought him up:

> I have found that women are usually kind to me. I think they realize that I am a rather sensitive person and that therefore I must be treated very gently. My mother has always treated me very gently. I am her youngest child. . . . Right from the time when I was a tiny baby, she understood that I needed greater care and tenderness than other children. . . .

At great length, he then describes this care—how his mother and female relatives have always protected him from work and hardship, giving him the best food, shielding him from other men in the neighborhood, and always making excuses for him to his brother, the sole, steady family breadwinner.

At the interview, he sits in the dank room, loathing the idea of a dead-end job calculating figures. During the interminable wait, he becomes more and more anxious, finds it increasingly hard to breathe, and finally runs out before his name is called. Taking refuge in a café, he treats himself, as the family women have always done for him, to a delectable sweet. With the early sweep, Jhabvala shows us his "sensitive" nature and place as the family darling, preparing us for his responses at the interview and these final actions.

3. Sweep smoothly in and out

The sweep requires a smooth introduction and graceful exit. When your story starts with a sweep, obviously a transition to introduce it isn't needed. Lawrence's opening sweep recounts the wife's sad history and at the same time plants the story's themes—lack of luck, lack of love, lack of money. With this groundwork, he immediately illustrates the lack of money and glides into the story proper with the son's pointed question: "Mother . . . why don't we keep a car of our own?" The mother replies with an explanation that at once reannounces the theme and propels the action: "Because we're the poor members of the family . . . it's because your father has no luck." With this answer, which the sweep foreshadowed, the story quickly focuses on how the son attempts to reverse the curse of "no luck" by incessantly riding his rocking horse in a frenzied attempt to "win" a real race and thus win his mother's love and the needed money for the family.

But when the sweep takes place a few paragraphs into the story, we must watch its entry and departure. If the transition is too abrupt, the sweep will seem artificial, superfluous, an intrusion. Jackson positions the sweep artfully, setting the scene with the day's action and slowly, with carefully planted descriptions (about the smooth stones and Mr. Summers, keeper of the box) segues into the sweep. Here's the sentence immediately before the sweep and its first sentence, quoted earlier:

> Mr. Martin and his oldest son, Baxter, came forward to hold the box steady on the stool while Mr. Summers stirred up the papers inside it.
>
> The original paraphernalia for the lottery had been lost long ago, and the black box now resting on the stool had been put into use even before Old Man Warner, the oldest man in town, was born.

Just as skillfully, in a kind of sandwich with the same characters, after the box's history Jackson picks up the story's action. Notice her almost exact repetition of the words introducing the sweep. Here's the last line of the sweep and the next of the story:

> The black box grew shabbier each year: by now it was no longer completely black but splintered badly along one side to show the original wood color, and in some places faded or stained.
>
> Mr. Martin and his oldest son, Baxter, held the black box securely on the stool until Mr. Summers had stirred the papers thoroughly with his hand.

Jackson uses the sweep here and the minute, repetitive detail before and after it to elongate the action, heighten the tension and rivet our attention.

So, we can think of the transition into and out of the sweep as a contraction-expansion-contraction. From the narrower action or narrative, the movie screen-scene expands, embedding aspects of the action, allowing the sweep in naturally and then narrowing again back to the main focus, resuming the story's forward motion.

4. Decide the length of your sweep

Once you've established your sweep and worked out your transitions, decide how long to stay. "Test" it, expanding or reigning it in. My story "Casey" is about a middle-school adolescent boy who's sure he's a "loser." In an early draft, at the start I described how the teachers ignored Casey and lavished attention on his nemesis Clive, the perfect student. In the process, I got fired up about the why the teachers responded so strongly to Clive. This is only some of the original lengthy passage:

> Clive was the student they were sure would be the norm as they had proudly accepted their degrees at graduation from teacher ed college. Clive was the student they were sure would still appear, even after years of slogging through gradebooks and writing parents never-delivered notes. Clive was the student who made worthwhile their initial desire to become a teacher, even when they were all but drowning in mountains of paperwork and endless staff meetings and seriously considering quitting two years before retirement, not caring any more about sacrificing their pension.

After several drafts, in which I kept going on about the teachers, I saw that this story could easily veer off into their plight and a diatribe of the educational system. So, bracing for the surgery, I cut out a thousand words (of course saving them) and reduced the passage to two paragraphs that centered on Clive. As in the examples above, the sweep should always focus on character, so cut away exposition that digresses—like my paragraph above—in favor of character development. Here's my revised version:

Like his mother, Casey's teachers seemed to look on Clive as almost a religious figure. Through the dark years of blank-faced children, their faces blurred with stupid sameness, Clive appeared, a comet in the black. Casey saw how the teachers' faces lit up when Clive raised his hand, how they called on him too quickly, knowing they'd be saved from the class's incipient noisy rebellion and embarrassing visit from the principal.

The English teacher loved Clive. He could conjugate verb tenses without a hiccup and interpret a poem correctly. The science teacher loved Clive. He could recite the planets in their correct order from the sun and even tell how many moons each had. The coach loved Clive. He scored the most points in every basketball game and, as captain of the swim team, kept his men motivated. The music teacher loved Clive. He played lead trumpet in the band, learned all the music faster than anyone else, and always showed up on time for practice.

Measuring your sweep will also help you gain perspective, assuring you haven't roamed too far afield or cut the reader off at the pass. Count the words that treat the larger sphere, compare them to the story's total length and calculate the percentage. In Lawrence's 5,423-word story, the sweep is 663 words, 12%. This rather high percentage is key to the impetus of the story. But Lazarowitz's sweep, a short 125 of the 3,155-word story, is 4%. It's enough, though, to plant the motivational seed for the extreme remedy Sandros chooses, to his (literal) everlasting regret.

Jackson's sweep of the black box is 166 words, 5% of the total 3,378. If she had continued the ominous history for two or three more paragraphs, reporting details about previous "winners," it would have been too much (and rambling writing), and she would have given away the climax. But in Jhabvala's 5,940-word story of the interviewee, the 690-word sweep that recaps his coddled upbringing is 12%. Somehow, just right.

Deciding how long to make your sweep is largely a matter of aesthetic judgment and distance. Often only trial and error will reveal the right length. First write your heart out in the sweep, as I did in "Casey." Then obey an essential rule of good writing: Let it sit. Walk away, forget it, bury it under your novel in progress, go clean out the garage.

Later, inch up on your story again and reread it. If the sweep is too short, you may not have given enough context for the main character's later actions. If Lazarowitz had stopped at his first sentence (presumably thinking he'd explained enough or being just too lazy to expand), we'd never know about Sandros' central conflict. If the sweep is too long and tangential, readers lose patience or become confused about your point, as in my pre-excised "Casey" draft. Listen to your writerly intuition, and you'll probably spot immediately where the sweep is too scant or drawn out.

You can also test the sweep by showing your story to someone you trust and watching for responses. If you see a suddenly furrowed brow (too short) or hear suppressed sighs or outright yawns (too long), there's your answer.

5. Try a succinct sweep

A brief sweep, done well, can also evoke just the scope and range of the story you envision. Science fiction and fantasy writers are known for their opening sweeps—time continuums, light years, far galaxies, alien species. Here are a few variations:

A fearsome civilization from David Zindell's "Shanidar":

> For me, the end of civilization came on the seventieth night of my fiftieth— or was it fifty-first?—deep winter in this City of Pain. Icefall, some called it, or Unreal City, city of lights and mists, the topological and, some say, spiritual center of a thousand decaying worlds. . . . ice and snow and cold so deep that

your breath shatters into ice crystals on the hard air, and flesh—should any man be foolish enough to let the air of this forsaken city touch his naked flesh—flesh turns to stone as you watch. What matters is men who deny the importance of flesh, men who seek new beginnings.

Another species and plane from Ursula LeGuin's "The Seasons of the Ansaracs":

> I talked for a long time once with an old Ansar. I met him at his Interplanary Hostel, which is on a large island far out in the Great Western Ocean, well away from the migratory routes of the Ansarac. It is the only place visitors from other planes are allowed, these days.

Another planet and astonishing environmental chronicle, slightly longer, from Ray Bradbury's "All Summer in a Day":

> It had been raining for seven years; thousands upon thousands of days compounded and filled from one end to the other with rain, with the drum and gush of water, with the sweet crystal fall of showers and the concussion of storms so heavy they were tidal waves come over the islands. A thousand forests had been crushed under the rain and grown up a thousand times to be crushed again. And this was the way life was forever on the planet Venus, and this was the schoolroom of the children of the rocket men and women who had come to a raining world to set up civilization and live out their lives.

Such sweeps instantly involve us, intrigue us and convey the flavor of the story. More concise sweeps can be as effective as longer ones, but of course they must be twined like tendons into the body of the story.

Summary: How to sweep

Study these steps. They will help reduce any lingering fears and guide you into sweeping adventures.

1. Tell yourself you don't have to be bound by the standard limitations or confines imposed on the short story.
2. Tell yourself you're free to think and visualize on a broad scale.
3. Think about the "history" of your characters, their family, their living situation, the events that surround them, their country, era, planet, their growth (or lack of it).
4. Ask yourself, Why do I want to place my characters in this larger context? (If the answer is that you don't, you really have no need for a sweep in this story.)
5. How will the sweeping context make more dramatic, poignant, meaningful the theme, conflict, resolution?
6. See your mind as the movie camera panning toward that main action. Where will you first focus your lens?
7. Now, write what comes to you, censoring nothing, whatever the length.
8. Let it sit, go back to it, and get editing!

Understanding the sweep frees you from limiting your stories to single circumscribed subjects and extends your repertoire of narrative techniques. Observe how other writers use the sweep and experiment with your own. With better acquaintance, you won't rule out any subject, scene or setting as too big or broad. Your work will gain breadth and richness when you use the sweep in your stories.

Craft & Technique

Testing the E-credential

Do Online Publications 'Count'?

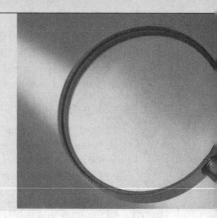

by Jack Smith

Getting a story published in a reputable magazine or journal in today's highly competitive market is no easy matter, as writers who have been at it for a while can tell you. Getting a book contract is considerably harder, and the word is: Get a lot of stories published first, and get them published in good places. What exactly, though, is a *good place*? How about those innumerable online markets? Will your online publications count when you approach a book publisher? Or, assuming you want to teach creative writing at the college-level, will hiring committees look favorably upon them?

For writers, publication has usually been viewed as a validation of one's talent and ability, or as a gauge of the artistic merit of one's work. And for a number of editors at book presses—though not all—a strong bio serves an indispensable gate-keeping purpose as they wade through the huge slush pile. After all, who is likely to attract the attention of a busy editor, the writer with a strong publication record, or one with only a few publications—or even none?

Ed Wilson of Absey Press states, "If the author has no bio, I still look at the work, but the writing has to be great to be seriously considered." Mark Cull of Red Hen Press emphasizes getting published in the right places: "I would suggest to writers that they really think about where they get published and what their ultimate intention is. If we were given a new book submission and 75 percent of the publication history for it was with mid-list journals, online or in print, we are unlikely to give it the consideration the author would like." For Katie Dublinski, editorial manager of Graywolf, the bio is a gauge of the writer's success in marketing his or her work: "In general, what an author's list of journal/magazine publications signals to me is to what extent (and with what success) the author has been trying to get their work read by a broader audience before approaching a book publisher. This is especially important when considering a short-story manuscript."

For these publishers, and others like them, a strong bio is step one in the editorial process. But where do online publications fit in? Which ones are likely to be viewed as quality publications—and which ones not? Adam Brooke Davis, managing editor of *The Green Hills Literary Lantern*, an online journal published at Truman State University, offers a useful checklist for

JACK SMITH has published short fiction in a number of literary magazines, including *The Southern Review, Happy, In Posse Review, Savoy, Southern Ocean Review, Roswell Literary Review, B&A: New Fiction* and *X-Connect.* He has stories forthcoming in *North American Review* and *Texas Review.* His reviews have been published in *Missouri Review, Texas Review, Georgia Review, Pleaides, X-Connect, RE:AL* and *Environment* magazine. He has contributed seven stories to *Novel & Short Story Writer's Market* and has co-authored the nonfiction work *Killing Me Softly* (Monthly Review Press, 2002). He co-edits *The Green Hills Literary Lantern*, an online journal, published by Truman State University.

evaluating any journal—either online or print. (Consider that the same criteria you use to choose a publisher for your story could also be applied by book editors judging your publishing credentials.)

- Does it have an editorial board consisting of well-published authors and/or academics?
- Has it been in publication for at least 10 years?
- If it's an online journal, did it begin as a print journal or does it have a print counterpart?
- Is it listed in the standard directories?
- Does its author list include important names, those who regularly appear in first-tier journals?
- Is it linked to a college, university or other reputable organization?

Of course, not every item on this list need apply. For instance, if the publication is linked to a college or university, with a notable editorial staff, it will not matter how new the publication is. Still, a fairly lengthy history of publication, where this exists, can serve as a record of the quality of the work being published. Even the editorial board, as Davis points out, is not an absolute must: an "estimable" journal might be edited entirely by one individual, as is the case with *The Chariton Review*, a magazine with a long history of excellence, edited entirely by Jim Barnes.

Book publishers weigh in

What do book publishers themselves have to say?

The bottom line: Online publishers must "publish," not "post," authors' work. They must exercise solid editorial standards. Jordan Jones, editor of Leaping Dog Press, states it well: "If an online venue accepts and posts all submissions, or most, or does so based on criteria that are lax, then it doesn't help to mention them." Jim Gilbert, editor of River City Publishing, emphasizes that the legitimate online publications are those that judge the author's work "critically" and with "competent editing." A good example of solid editorial standards at work occurred recently, he points out, in the flash fiction contest held by Square Books, with the winners published on the Square Books' MySpace page.

As with regular print magazines, name recognition and reputation certainly do matter. Publications such as *Salon*, *Mississippi Review online*, *The Barcelona Review*, and *McSweeney's* are high-profile magazines, and editors are likely to take notice. Yet the inner circle is gradually widening: Ben Furnish of BkMk Press mentions other, lesser-known ones that he is "taking serious notice of" these days—such publications as *Drunken Boat*, *Pedestal*, and *Del Sol Review* at Web del Sol. "I think that online publications have to earn their reputations just as traditionally printed journals do, based on the impressions that they make over time," Furnish says. Some online magazines earn their reputations much more quickly, of course, such as *Narrative Magazine* (launched in 2003), which features the work of such literary heavy-weights as Rick Bass, Ann Beattie, T.C. Boyle, E.L. Doctorow, Andre Dubus, Joyce Carol Oates, Jayne Anne Phillips, Jane Smiley, Jean Stafford and Tobias Wolff.

Third, writers would do well to demonstrate a good mix of both regular print and online publications. "A mix," says Katie Dublinski, "of reputable, high quality print and online publications would tell me that they are exploring all avenues, and that a variety of editors had responded positively to their work. If I were considering a submission by an author who had published a number of stories, but all in the same online journal that I'd never heard of, I'd be skeptical." Mark Cull seconds this idea: "If an author is published *only* in online journals, as an editor, I might not take them too seriously. The fact is, and I'm sure you can appreciate this, I don't have the time to invest in researching the details of a new author's publication history. If every journal they have been published in is "http://www. . . ." I just might skip ahead to the next person in the stack."

A note of warning

And now for an interesting paradox: For book editors judging your bio, some of your online publication credits may not "count"—that is, the e-journals may seem too obscure, the editors are unknown, the authors being published are unknown, the publication isn't connected to a reputable institution, or the publication itself my not seem viable or worthy of an editor's attention—but make no mistake, these *are*, in fact, real publications, and you won't be able to re-market your published stories unless you seek a magazine or journal that takes reprints. As a writer, you should always be discriminating, because an online publication, no matter how shaky, is still a publication. Michael Czyzniejewski, editor-in-chief of *Mid-American Review* says, "We certainly acknowledge them as pubs in the publishing industry, and something that's appeared online is not eligible for publication in *MAR*; I would say 98 percent of my fellow editors agree. Hey, if a billion people can read it online, it's no longer exclusive to us. So it certainly 'counts' to us." The lesson here: Be selective where you publish.

Academia weighs in

Some writers—particularly those who are academically trained—may wish to use their graduate degrees (and support their writing habits) by teaching creative writing at the college level. In this case, building a strong and reputable publishing history is even more important than it is when seeking a book publisher and so the question of the credibility of online publication again comes into play.

Judith Claire Mitchell, director of the MFA program in creative writing at the University of Wisconsin-Madison, sums up the general resistance in academe to online publications: "What we tell our students when advising them about applying for teaching jobs is that our general sense, at this point in time, is that most online publications are deemed less prestigious than established print publications by most academic institutions and hiring committees (which almost always include literature professors and other scholars who know little about creative writing or online journals and tend to be slow to embrace less traditional standards). At the same time, we never disparage online journals; in fact, we express our hope that they will thrive and acquire the same importance as print publications. The more venues making good writing available, the better. We do, however, point out the realities of the current marketplace to our students who are just beginning to publish their work and who almost always are hoping to secure teaching jobs upon graduation."

Gary Fincke, who directs the creative writing program at Susquehanna University, states that at his institution online publications are, for the most part, of secondary status. "Online publication isn't ignored by us, but given that nearly every candidate has a number of print publication credits, they don't carry much weight in our decisions unless the online journal is one of the few that are genuinely respected," he says. "We'd rather see fewer publications in better journals than a long list of publications in obscure ones."

It's the general obscurity as well as the lack of longevity of online pubs that concerns Claire Davis, Creative Writing chair at Lewis and Clark State College. "Okay, I have to admit, we tend to take the printed work much more seriously," Davis says. "There's just so much online out there, that it's hard to genuinely assess the quality of the zine. Additionally, because of the transitory nature of online work, it's hard to judge the merit of a particular zine, or its long-term effects in terms of literature. On the other hand, if we see someone published in *The Georgia Review* or *Shenandoah*, we're going to pay attention."

Is this response to online pubs endemic to academic culture? No, this depends, according to Michael Czyzniejewski, on "who's on that committee. If they themselves have a lot of online pubs, or if they are aware of online pubs, even familiar with them specifically, then that's going to help. But for now, I'm thinking that print pubs will help you more. Will this change as time goes by? More and more every day, probably.'' Claudia Keelan, who directs the creative writing program at University of Nevada, Las Vegas, sees this change coming and urges students to prepare for it. ''My advice to students is publish as much and in as many places as possible,'' she says. ''Time is real, and the times are changing *vis à vis* publishing. The universities will eventually catch up. How they 'count' re: jobs is entirely up to the individual search committee, and I tend to think any person who has come into academe since the early 1980s is and must be conversant with the electronic medium.''

Writers weigh in

Overall, there's a general reluctance and guardedness out there, at present, with respect to online publications. But where do writers themselves stand? Author Ian MacMillan, who teaches at the University of Hawaii, states, ''Most writers I know balk at the idea until they see good ones, and also until they find out that some of them pay (I assume because they can, having reduced the cost by going online). But my guess is that it'll take a decade or so before writers start to feel comfortable with it, because they all tend to see the object you pull out of an envelope and hold in your hand as the conclusion of the process. Something you can hand to someone else, and put on your shelf.''

Judith Claire Mitchell, speaking of the MFA students at the University of Wisconsin-Madison, makes essentially the same point: ''There is a certain thrill to having a piece appear in a magazine with a long and impressive history, of feeling somehow affiliated with the writers who have previously appeared in, say, *Ploughshares* or *The Paris Review*. And a lot of writers still like the idea of paper, of bookstores, of something to hold in your hand. Obviously, this is changing, but as far as I can tell, it is changing slowly.''

For Some, the Writing Is Paramount

For some book publishers, a writer's publication background itself—whether online or print—is much less important than the present work being submitted.

Chris Hebert, acquisitions editor at the **University of Michigan Press**: ''In my own experience, I've taken on books by writers who have never published anywhere, online or otherwise, as well as some with very long track records. For me, and I think for a lot of editors, there's a certain thrill in discovering unknown writers. My only considerations are how much I like the book, and how well I think I can sell it.''

Scott Schmidt of **Salvo Press**: ''I don't worry about the writing history of my authors. I've had authors come to me with 30 books under their belt by major New York publishers, and the book they're asking me to review does not meet my standards. On the contrary, I've had authors with no publishing history whatsoever, with a book better than I've read in years and better than most published by those same New York publishers. Bottom line, I let the writing speak for itself. Send me a damn good book and I'll publish it.''

Martin Shepard, co-publisher of **Permanent Press**: ''An author's credentials mean absolutely nothing to us. We receive about 6,000 submissions a year and only select twelve books—a one-release-a-month schedule. Most of what we do is quality fiction. The writer's background and contacts might prove useful after we make a selection if it helps us promotion-wise. But it has no relevance at all when it comes to choosing what we want to publish.''

Getting Published

One development that pleases writers who balk at online pubs is the online journal that has a print annual. Examples include *X-Connect*, *Painted Bride Quarterly* and *Night Train*, which is currently moving in that direction. "This hybrid approach makes good sense to me," says MacMillan, "because those who like the annual will go to the online mag, and those familiar with the online mag might order the print annual. As for what it's going to be like in 30 years? It might be that online mags will outnumber print ones by 10 to one, and be the first choice for writers."

If this is truly the case, writing and publishing will undergo a radical shift, ushering in a new age—but one which is, in fact, already emerging. It's this radical shift, this Copernican kind of revolution involving author, text, publisher, critic, the whole academic enterprise and the reading public that Tom Jenks, co-editor of *Narrative Magazine*, traces to a new revolution in print media—namely, digital. This revolution has had a number of implications, and like any paradigm shift, the dust hasn't settled yet:

> The question about the place or validity of literature online is a non-question. As early as 1995, the rising popularity—the sheer call on imagination and inspiration—of the Internet made it plain that writers would have to move online or be marginalized.

> Today, major university libraries have moved more and more toward digital media, and, as you know, Google is working to make major university library collections available for online indexing. The conventional publishing industry is depressed by competition from other media; literary reading is declining dramatically, especially among readers aged 18 to 30. We're in the midst of a revolution in the written word, surpassing Gutenberg. The revolution has been going on for more than a decade and will likely proceed for another 20 years or so before we know exactly what the future of reading looks like.

> The future of the written word is digital. Traditional, familiar forms will continue to exist popularly, but the means of their delivery to readers will evolve remarkably, with great opportunities for economies of scale in production and distribution. This is good news amid the general confusion about the direction of contemporary literary publishing.

> The issue of prestige, or quality, of literature online is part of a larger issue involving the fall of the canon of western literature, the sometimes mistaken invocation of political correctness and diversity as defining of literary value, the decades-long increasingly abstract and theoretical approach to literature within the academy, the defection from fiction and literature by hard-pressed publishers pursuing more seemingly saleable material, the general loss of reliable literary commentary from developed reviewers and critics in all but a few major periodicals, the marketing-driven public fascination with the cult of personality and celebrity, the Internet-based sense of authorship by plurality in hypertext, and, finally, the resulting popular notion that whatever anyone says is good is as valid as what anyone else says is good.

Whatever status is enjoyed ultimately by online pubs—and however the many questions surrounding the medium are answered—for now, a central question persists: Should the medium *itself*—print or online—be connected to the question of quality? Says Ian MacMillan: "As for me, I see two editors, one of a print journal, and another of an online journal. Both are likely going to be picky, are going to use their space wisely, and are not going to jeopardize their own standards. The same goes for editors of online publishing houses." Ben Furnish adds, "Online publications are here to stay, and their medium in no way renders them inferior (or superior) per se."

While the question of quality is being debated, decided on, or simply bracketed in the turmoil created by so many online journals coming onto the literary scene, a number of literary bellwethers do point the way toward excellence in electronic publishing. One such leader in the field is *Narrative Magazine*. As Tom Jenks points out, "*Narrative Magazine* exists to demonstrate what literature can look like in the digital age, to offer continuity and excellence in a narrative tradition, and to encourage readers and writers in a non-commercial community created around good writing. We are very optimistic and excited about the years ahead and the opportunities and challenges offered by the vast changes taking place. The human spirit and imagination—and new stories—are, as ever, re-creating and reinterpreting the world."

Should You Hire a Publicist?

by Dena Harris

You've written a book. After signing with a flourish the copies begged for by friends, relatives and hometown neighbors, you're shocked when sales skid to a standstill after a mere two months on the open market. The book's cover art is eye-popping. Your writing is brilliant. So where are the throngs of book buyers? Why isn't Oprah calling? Where is the *love*?

The love is being held hostage in publishers' lists overflowing with fiction titles. Media reps are so bombarded with pitches for the next Great American Novel that they run for cover every time the fax machine whirs to life. And yet, novels by unknown writers do manage to find footholds in literary sales and claim varying degrees of success. Is it because the writing found in their pages is so much more compelling than that of the average Joe? Perhaps. But it's also likely the authors of novels that vault to new heights have well-executed media plans to thank for their rising book sales.

Who needs a publicist?

Whether you need (or want) a publicist to promote your book is a personal—and often a financial—decision. Although many houses offer the services of an in-house publicist, this person is an employee of the publisher and is responsible for promoting many titles simultaneously. They will spend the majority of their promotional efforts on the titles expected to pull in the most revenue—the 80/20 rule. The involvement of an in-house publicist may range from as little as preparing a press kit to as much as overseeing a four-month media campaign. But regardless of how much coverage an in-house publicist provides, the reality is your novel will receive declining attention as new titles shoot down the pipeline.

A lack of ongoing (or sometimes even initial) PR support is one of the biggest disillusionments of new authors. Finding time to write a book is enough of a challenge—finding the additional time to market, promote and sell a book is an even greater struggle.

Kim Byerly, director of publicity for Blair Publishing notes, "Once the initial tour is over, our authors are responsible for setting up their own events and doing their own publicity."

Many authors prefer to go it alone. Margaret H. Bonham is the author of 22 books, three of which are novels published by small presses with no in-house publicity.

DENA HARRIS writes from her home in North Carolina. Her credits include *Writer's Digest*, *The Toastmaster*, *Art Jewelry*, *Motorhome Magazine* and *Chicken Soup for the Cat Lover's Soul*, among others. She is the author of two books on cats, including the humor book *Lessons in Stalking*. Her mother is still her best PR agent. Learn more about Dena at www.denaharris.com.

"I decided to handle my own promotion because I'm good at it," says Bonham, who counts blogs, plogs, podcasts and seven Web sites among her marketing endeavors. "New writers making it versus new writers not making it is based on what they're willing to do. I'm not afraid to get out there and hawk my books."

But Quinn Dalton, author of the short-story collection *Bulletproof Girl* (Washington Square Press, 2005) and the novel *High Strung* (Atria, 2003), found there were limits to self-promotion. A former director of public relations for an advertising agency, Dalton assumed she had the know-how to market herself. "But I learned the painful lesson that when you promote yourself to the media, you're sometimes seen as arrogant or grabby," she recalls. Dalton consulted with her in-house publicist before deciding to hire an independent publicist—called an indy—for marketing *Bulletproof Girl*.

Finding the right publicist

If you decide to hire an indy publicist, take the time to ensure you hire the right one. Anywhere from eight months to a year before your book release is the time frame for interviewing. Why so early? Magazines average three- to six-month lag times. Radio and TV shows schedule guests months prior. Most publicists will want to start working with you at least two to four months before your book ever sees print.

Once you have a timeline for your book's release, look at several publicists and firms. You might correspond initially by e-mail, moving to phone interviews after you've narrowed the field. Ask about media timelines, target markets, pricing and what expectations the publicist holds for your book. Beware anyone who "guarantees" you a slot on Oprah or promises to "make you a star." When it comes to what will grab the media's attention, there *are* no guarantees. In fact, good publicists will be upfront in sharing any concerns they have about marketing your book.

Ask for referrals and review examples of work conducted on prior book campaigns. Call authors the firm has worked with and ask if they would work with that firm again. Be zealous (but not obnoxious) in your search to find the firm right for you.

And then, says Marika Flatt, founder and owner of the literary publicity firm PR by the Book, "Go with your gut. Your publicist should understand what you're about and that's not going to be everyone."

Be forewarned that while you weed out firms, firms may also shun you. Novelist Lynn York had difficulty finding an indy publicist for her first book, *The Piano Teacher* (Plume, 2004). "Some firms are reluctant to work with first-time authors, especially if it's a small budget," says York.

Note the differences between literary publicists and general publicity firms. Publicists tend to specialize, and a firm that gets great coverage for non-profits or restaurants won't have the same contacts of an established book publicist. Book publicists generate media awareness through review houses, trade magazines, radio and TV. They have inside contacts and know who to pitch and how to approach them. Even within the literary industry, promotion tactics differ for fiction versus nonfiction. If you've written a cookbook, you can conduct workshops and a mini-cooking segment on early-morning TV. Finding speaking outlets for your novel on 18th-century vampires run amok may present more of a challenge.

Still, novels have their hooks. Look no further than the rounds of discussion sparked by *The Da Vinci Code* or reading groups and workshops centered on Mitch Albom's *The Five People You Meet in Heaven*. The right publicist can find the hook that turns your fiction into a hot topic of discussion.

What's this going to cost me?

It's no surprise the cost of hiring a publicist drives many an author to self-promotion. And yet, a structured, well-thought-out media campaign will often pay for itself in terms of book sales and author exposure.

After York hired a publicist to do the ancillary media her in-house publicist didn't cover, her book sold better then initial projections. This garnered in-house attention from her publisher, and additional dates were added to her tour, "probably doubling the original in-house PR budget for my book," says York.

Decide how much of your advance you can afford to spend (after agent's cut and taxes) and squirrel that money away in an account labeled "marketing."

Prices for publicists range anywhere from $2,000 to $20,000, depending on length of hire and tasks assigned. Some firms charge on retainer, some quote hourly rates and still others charge by "hit" (i.e., per booking). York, for example, paid a flat fee for her publicist to pull together her press kit, with fees for radio/TV exposure calculated by city.

Many authors prefer hiring on retainer as they feel it makes the publicist feel like a part of the team. If you're paying by retainer, ask upfront what you're getting for that amount. It would be a rude awakening to think your publicist is booking speaking engagements only to discover they spent their time, and your money, on ad placement.

In all cases, ask your publicist to provide you with his or her media goals and targets for your book. York worked with her indy publicist to compile a list of the most effective media coverage but says, "We ended up tossing some national stuff out due to cost."

And what *are* you getting for all your hard-earned money? Different firms offer varying degrees of promotion. Some won't touch speaking engagements or book tours while others handle anything. A publicist's services may include but are not limited to:

- Press kit preparation and dispersal to targeted media
- Soliciting reviews
- Review copies sent to TV, radio and newspapers in tour or targeted cities
- Soliciting interviews and speaking engagements on radio, TV, Internet chat forums
- Arranging book signings at trade shows, book stores, etc.
- Strategic ad placement
- Tying your book to hot or breaking news stories
- Media training
- Finding book contests
- Mailings
- Copy writing for Web sites, mailers, newsletters, etc.
- Coordinating book tours

Above all, remember you're paying for your publicist's contacts within the media. You might be capable of writing your own press release (and chose to do so), but many journalists are more receptive to a third-party contact versus dealing with the author. Your publicist also knows the best way to gain the attention of a much-coveted contact.

Finally, your publicist can—at your instruction—promote not just your book but you as well. Author branding is often worth the cost of hiring a publicist.

The publicist's perspective

Believe it or not, some publicists have the gall to hold opinions on what makes a good client (as if the fact that you've written the next Great American Novel isn't enough).

Let's look first to the in-house publicist. Byerly notes the authors easiest to work with—and often the most successful—are those who listen to the advice she has to offer and then do their best to implement it. "Authors who believe they know better than anyone what they need to do to market and sell their book often end up hurting their sales more than helping them," she observes.

Byerly also stresses the importance of authors being prepared and notes her reputation—as well as that of Blair Publishing—is at stake every time an author does an interview. "If an author is unprepared, forgets about an interview, or is just plain rude, a producer or reporter may choose not to work with me again." Byerly concludes by stating if she sees an author appreciates the work she's doing, she's motivated to work that much harder for him or her.

Almost any in-house publicist will be grateful for the added resource of an indy publicist paid for by the author. York's publisher was delighted when she hired a publicist, noting it showed an additional commitment on her part. Just make sure your publicist doesn't become a drag on the in-house staff with constant phone calls or duplicate marketing efforts.

York found her publicist through her agent's recommendation. Although agents will have little to no contact with an author's publicist, many are able to offer referrals to publicists based on prior author experience. Also try online searches, author referrals, and even the yellow pages for publicist listings. The annual *Guide to Literary Agents* (Writer's Digest Books) also lists publicists.

Agent Emily Russo at Sobel Weber notes they expect their authors "to do as much as they want in terms of self-promotion, but they can't go about it half-heartedly." Publicists can be godsends for authors too shy or time-constrained for serious self-promotion. Reinvesting your advance money toward promoting your book also sends a message to your agent that you're serious about growing your career as a writer.

Flatt at PR by the Book notes some clients have chosen to be heavily involved in their media campaigns while others have full-time jobs and families, which is why they hired her firm in the first place. Either scenario is fine with her, as long as clients are quick to respond (24-hour turnaround at the most) to her calls and e-mails.

"Authors need to understand media has the upper hand in scheduling and we're on their timeline," says Flatt. "I need authors to be as flexible as possible and available to do media interviews on short notice—otherwise we're losing opportunities."

If you're not confident in your speaking skills, enlisting media training on your own time is appreciated. Your publicist may land you numerous interviews, but if you're off-topic or not engaging, sales may still lag.

Is it ever too late to hire a publicist?

Suppose your book has been on the market for close to a year with no targeted media campaign. Is hiring a publicist at this late start date still worth your time and money?

Maybe. "A publicist could help you . . . if your book relates to something that is in the news at the moment," says Byerly.

Flatt agrees, noting, "Never say never." She points out even in a traditionally run campaign, there comes a point when the book publicist knows to switch the pitch from, "This is a new release," to "Here's an expert with good advice." Authors with great track records or something interesting in their experience where the author (more so then the novel) is the story for the media can also be reasons to ignite a late-season PR campaign.

What your publicist won't be able to get you with a late start is book reviews in trade journals such as *Publishers Weekly* or *The New York Times*, which review only new releases. Still, small or regional newspapers may be willing to promote your work.

If you do approach a publicist about promoting a novel or short-story collection that's been on the market for some time, ask them to outline hurdles you'll face. "A publicist should share if they feel your hook isn't strong enough to support a campaign," says Flatt.

Getting Published

Final considerations

Part of evaluating the value of a publicist is evaluating the relationship—is your publicist receptive to your ideas and feedback? Are you happy with the direction the campaign is going? Is she available to take your calls? Be fair in your evaluation. Remember—one month of promotion won't shoot you to the top of the best-seller charts.

Even if you hire a publicist, don't forget to do your part. Stay on top of leads your publicist may not have time to follow up on. Update your Web site. Accept any speaking engagements—paid or not—that come your way.

York reminds authors there's a "switchover" that needs to be made once the book is written. "Your book is a product you're selling. Don't be modest," she advises.

If you find it difficult to brag on yourself, hire a publicist to do it for you. Just remember that doesn't leave you free to while away your time.

"I'd do a lot of PR even if I had a publicist," states Bonham, who estimates she spends 20-30% of her time on promotion. Why?

"No one cares about the success of my book as much as I do," she says.

Can you say the same?

What You Can Do

Even if you hire a publicist, do all you can to assist them in their effort to get the word out. Remember, the only thing worse than people talking about you is people *not* talking about you . . .

Ideas for self-promotion:

- Create an engaging Web site with a professional author photo, recent book reviews, press updates, FAQs, list of upcoming appearances, etc.
- Start a blog about your book. Have blog readers sign up for book giveaway contests to gain e-mail addresses for your mailing list.
- Host your own "ask the author" chat session online and write PR announcing it.
- Keep a box of books in your car—you never know who you might run into that it would be advantageous to hand a copy to.
- Become a pro at cross-promotion. Flaunt your book on your Web site and your Web site in your book.
- Send letters or e-mails announcing your book to family, friends, alumni groups, former colleagues, pen pals, high school sweethearts and that kid with the runny nose you sat next to in second grade.
- Move past the shyness factor and talk yourself up to everyone you meet.
- Pay attention to the media. Read local, regional and national newspapers and watch for stories or trends you can tie your book to.
- Volunteer to give readings at bookstores, trade shows, writers conferences, AM radio stations, restaurants, Junior Leagues, coffee shops, Rotary clubs and anyone else who'll have you.
- If you've written fantasy or sci-fi, attend conventions.
- Serialize your book on a podcast (listeners who don't want to wait 14 weeks to find out how your book ends will purchase the book).
- Be willing to cross promote. Look for authors or artists you might partner with for readings, book signings, etc.

Writer Wanted

Partner Beware: Five Famous Teams
Talk About Co-Authoring

by Jude Tulli

Loneliness can cloud a writer's judgment. Or perception. For many it can become difficult even to discern between the two. Authors coop themselves up for hours, days, weeks, months, years, often degrading their spinal integrity in sub-standard home office chairs as they whisk or trudge through page after page, draft after draft. They cast off their hopes and dreams along with finished manuscripts only to wait more days, weeks, months, years; sometimes with nary a shred of feedback from agents, editors, or even a friend's sister's uncle who "loves books just like that!"

At some point, bobbing up and down in the midst of this fathomless ocean of waiting, water-logged and synonym-depleted, it is not uncommon for writers of both the published and unpublished variety to consider teaming up for anything from a single project to a long-term partnership of Lennon-McCartney magnitude (phantasmagorical success not included). After all, it's possible that two or more heads are truly better than one, right? And at the very least, feedback, while still not instantaneous, is likely to be more reliably forthcoming. A friendly rap on the old noggin at this juncture may help intuit whether the aforementioned judgment/perception is still capable of discriminating a dolphin from a shark. Even so, proceed with caution.

Dysfunctional pairings

Some pairings are not meant to be. Others, while perhaps fated, clearly fall beneath some star-crossed genus. Here are some archetypal examples of potentially toxic collaborations, some of which you, dear reader, may have already fled screaming.

Dictator/Secretary: One year in elementary school, my class was forced to write in teams. I don't quite remember how the pairings were established, but I suspect it had something to do with counting off. My "partner" used to talk. I would write. For well-matched teams this works. In this case, the problem was that he deliberately talked faster than I wrote. This left me feeling like George Harrison, had he been stripped of even his token two tracks per album.

Writer/Nay-sayer: When I did get an idea out, it was immediately shot down and my partner continued the story his way. Granted, I was writing; I had ultimate veto power. But I hadn't hit my rebellious stage yet.

JUDE TULLI is a part-time writer who, in his scant free time, somehow manages to churn out projects of all shapes and sizes much faster than he can find markets for them. When not calculating his astounding rejection: acceptance ratio, he revels in a generous handful of modest print credits and short film scripts that, in a manner he likes to imagine as being not entirely dissimilar to migrating hummingbirds, found their merry way to becoming short films. He resides in the Grand Canyon state with his beloved wife Trish and their indoor-to-add-at-least-10-years-to-the-old-life-expectancy cats Tasha, Max, Cassandra, Little Cat, Tesha and Sebastian.

Writer/Credit-Hog: He also used to claim intellectual ownership of "his" stories. Fortunately there were never any royalties to fight over (of which I'm aware).

Writer/Pencil-Tapper: Guess who does all the work here.

Writer/Plagiarist: Be sure your partner isn't especially enamored with the copy/paste function. This can be a predictable escalation of the Writer/Pencil-Tapper combination when the latter is cornered into doing actual work other than practicing to be the next Ringo Starr.

Writer/Ghostwriter: The latter of this combination rewrites when the former least expects it. If such action is provoked, it may be a Dictator/Ghostwriter dynamic. Like what I should have done in grade school. . .

Existing Team/New Player: Though honored as the only non-member artist to receive a label performance credit, Billy Preston might well have been dubbed the sole indisputable Fifth Beatle had he arrived before the group was nearly ready to disband. New additions seldom get their fair share of respect up front.

Writer/Insert-Whatever-Most-Gets-On-Your-Nerves: Believe it or not, your worst nightmares *can* come true in the collaborative arena. You can attempt to avoid long-term detrimental partnerships by building in a trial period. Hammer out a few pages together or apart (however you plan to work on the project as a whole) and come together to compare notes and determine whether your styles and sympathies jibe.

Realities of teaming up

There are many different motivators for initiating and sustaining a writing team. Some scribes prefer company as they venture into the uncertain territory of a new genre. Others may seek to find someone who is strong in areas where they feel weak, or vice versa. There are many positive aspects to writing in cahoots with another, although there are drawbacks to consider as well.

Successful writing teams navigate the give-and-take and see their projects through to publication and beyond. Some prominent teams with first-hand experience on the subject were kind enough to share their insights with us. Each collaborator cited granted a separate interview by e-mail or phone. Through their responses we can see both similarities and differences in partner selection criteria (some prefer dual relationships, for example, while others eschew them), working styles, preferences and arrangements.

Nearly universally they endorse agreeing to terms up front and in writing, yet not all of them have done so. Their biggest quibbles, it seems, tend to arise not over money, rights or attributions, but over the direction of the creative work itself. Perhaps second only to that ranks the mundane if not harrowing travel they must endure together to promote their finished products. Indeed some may prefer not to tour at all, a valid stance especially well supported by the precedent the Beatles set in the late 1960s. Surely if music can be sold *en masse* without touring, so too can books.

Many openly embrace the freedom of writing alone; they savor the facility to paint every last verbal brushstroke by their own sovereign hand. Yet in co-writing they certainly find some testament to the old adage "the whole is greater than the sum of its parts," as their mutual creations occupy no less sacred a space in their hearts than their lone accomplishments both within and beyond the writing arena.

And so without further hullabaloo, I invite you to drink deep from the fountain of their wisdom. Or at least enjoy a quick sip or two.

Julianna Baggott and Steve Almond

These co-authors of *Which Brings Me to You: A Novel in Confessions* (Algonquin Books, 2006) didn't know each other personally when they agreed to conspire to bring Baggott's novel idea to fruition. "We knew one another's work and had seen each other read," says Almond.

Despite having rubbed elbows, they remained but literary acquaintances. Baggott deems it for the best. "We didn't have a friendship to burn," she explains.

The book is about a love affair that begins with a rendezvous in the coatroom of a wedding and continues through an old-fashioned medium: letters. You know, the kind you write by hand. "We each wrote from the point of view of one character, alternating chapters," Almond explains. "We did offer comments on one another's sections, but steered away from interfering with each other any more than that."

But as with any partnership, there are sacrifices. When asked about the benefits of writing alone, both writers remain on the same page in perpetuity. "I like being God. The one all-powerful God, as opposed to the Greek god who has to share power," Baggott admits without a shred of apology. Likewise, Almond confesses, "As a control freak, I get to call all the shots."

Indeed there were times when the pair considered packing up their characters' baggage and going their separate ways. Almond explains, "We did a lot of yelling at each other, mostly around revising the initial draft. We basically just battled things out. We considered quitting the project, but the book seemed too good to allow our bickering to bring it down."

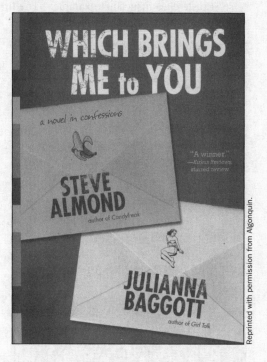

Reprinted with permission from Algonquin.

Baggott asserts that ultimately the conflict made the book better. Furthermore, she believes the characters are better off together than they would have been apart. Still, she found it "difficult. . . to let go of my character for the ending," as Almond wrote the end of the book. His greatest frustrations? "The second draft. And the third."

For wanna-be co-writers Baggott cautions, "You have to be willing to fight, and pretty loudly," while Almond admonishes, "Check your ego at the door." They both recognize the work as a life-long bond, and suggest taking that likelihood into account from the beginning. "It's not just writing the book, but revising it, selling it, marketing it, including potentially trying to adapt it for the screen," says Almond. Baggott concurs, "These books, they don't go away."

Jennifer Crusie and Bob Mayer

Crusie and Mayer met in Maui when they taught in adjacent classrooms at a writer's conference. Serendipity and timing may have each played a role in Mayer's decision to initiate a collaboration: "We were both at points in our careers where we were looking at doing something different," he reflects.

Since then, the two have co-written *Don't Look Down* (St. Martin's Press, 2006) and *Agnes and the Hitman* (2007) with a third collaboration in the works. "I'm continuing to collaborate with Bob because I love collaborating with Bob," says Crusie.

To the untrained ear, their process sounds simple: "We write in third person limited," Mayer explains, "Jennifer writes the female POV character and I write the male POV characters." That's how they get through the first draft, anyway.

According to Mayer, the two count on each other to provide "a unique perspective. . . we wouldn't have on our own" that includes "real reactions from the opposite sex characters." Crusie cites a succinct example: "The first thing Bob does with his character in my scenes is cut the dialogue. Too much chatting."

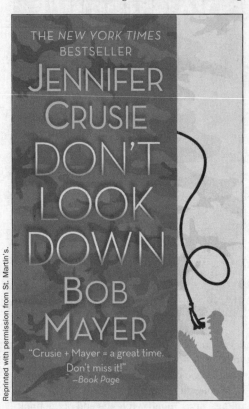

THE *NEW YORK TIMES* BESTSELLER

JENNIFER CRUSIE

DON'T LOOK DOWN

BOB MAYER

"Crusie + Mayer = a great time. Don't miss it!" *—Book Page*

Reprinted with permission from St. Martin's.

Mayer asserts that his partner "loves rewriting." Crusie says, "Once the book is done, we both go in and write over each other. If the original writer can't tell the change has been made, it's a good change. And if he or she can tell, there is much yelling." Still, Mayer maintains that the conflict inherent to any collaboration is tempered by the fact that, "We keep 600 miles between us and work mostly in e-mail." Crusie mentions that they do meet in person though, "fairly regularly, probably every month or two."

What guidance can they offer to up-and-coming collaborators? "Choose your partner very carefully," Crusie says. "It's amazingly hard to find the right [one]." Mayer suggests, "Have good contracts drawn up. Be prepared for a lot of emotional turmoil in the writing, as you are bleeding on the page and it spills over." But don't just collaborate for collaboration's sake; "have a good reason for doing it," he adds. "Find someone who is already a *New York Times* best-selling author," he jests with a touch of seriousness, having learned from less successful partnerships that for him it's best to avoid "dealing with people who aren't experienced." Ultimately, he emphasizes, "it's always about the writing."

Jennifer Crusie, Anne Stuart and Eileen Dreyer

Despite the implications of playing on more than one writing team, Crusie doesn't see herself as having any particular penchant for collaboration. "The collaboration with [Anne] and Eileen began as a novella anthology and as we talked about it, it turned into a collaborative novel," she says. "I didn't choose to do two collaborations, one of them became a collaboration."

Dreyer explains, "I had an idea for an anthology and tried to think of the two strongest voices and best authors I could find to join me. Serendipity led me to Jen and [Anne] on the same evening at a conference, and they were crazy enough to say yes."

She took them up on the promise, despite the influence of "too much champagne." According to Stuart, "A couple of months later, when the champagne had worn off, she e-mailed Jenny and me and said 'let's do it' and we said 'cool'." As soon as they realized they could weave the three characters' stories together into one narrative, *The Unfortunate Miss Fortunes* (St. Martin's Press, 2007) was conceived.

The novel was completed in three face-to-face meetings, with the synapses between devoted to e-mail collaboration. Of the first meeting, Dreyer says, "The brainstorming. . . should have sent sparks flying up the chimney like Ghostbusters."

Once the synergy faded, naturally conflict arose. For this they had prepared by setting ground rules. Dreyer explains, "only the writer of her character had final say over what her character was. The others were only allowed suggestions." Stuart adds, "We decided ahead of time that if two of the three of us felt one way, the other would agree. That didn't always happen, but often enough that it worked." Dreyer found the virtual work to be more frustrating than face-to-face conspiring, "It's very easy to miscommunicate in an e-mail. And I loathe emoticons."

Their writing dynamics were further punctuated by their interpersonal interactions. "To this day, I don't know whether we became the sisters or the sisters became us, but it was spooky. At one point, we started calling each other by the character names," says Crusie. Stuart agrees, "we became our characters. . . I took the role my character had, that of peacemaker."

Stuart describes their final meeting: "We got together with our finished (mine) and almost finished (theirs) versions and played 52 pick-up." Then what? She readily admits that the trio "argued, ignored each other, argued some more." Dreyer concurs that they had to "slug it out." Still, Crusie believes the book is better for the brouhaha. "Being polite does not make for a good book," she says. "Be polite at the party, fight it out for the sake of the book."

Their caveats to others who may seek to venture down a similar path? "Make sure you can adapt," Dreyer cautions. "Make sure you can. . . communicate with each other. And make sure at least one of you can organize things." Though she's proud of the book they bore together, Crusie suggests "avoiding a triad. It's hard collaborating with one person; getting three people lined up in the same book is really difficult."

JENNIFER CRUSIE
EILEEN DREYER
ANNE STUART

THE ONLY THING
WILDER THAN THEIR MAGIC
IS THEIR MEN...

The UNFORTUNATE
MISS FORTUNES
A NOVEL

Reprinted with permission from St. Martin's.

On selecting a cohort Stuart says, "A writing partner needs to be someone you can both love and respect, or you're headed for disaster." Such feelings are generally reserved for friends, yet Stuart warns that it can be a balancing act to make sure the book is as good as it can be without infuriating a confidante. "Somewhat along the lines of never, ever lend money to a friend," she explains, "friends don't tend to mix well with money, sex or the book of your heart."

Still, these three writers managed to forge a communal book they all adore. They happily report that their friendships emerged from the process unscathed.

Hallie Ephron and Donald Davidoff

Hallie Ephron and Donald Davidoff had known each other as friends for more than 30 years before a burst of synchronicity struck them. Don, a neuropsychologist who evaluates criminal defendants and testifies as an expert witness, described a case one night at a dinner party involving the memory of an eyewitness. "Don explained his role, how memory is fallible, and how he'd be testing the person and testifying in court. I was fascinated," Ephron says. "We agreed to get together that Sunday and see if we could work together. . . that was nine years and five books ago." Together they co-write the Dr. Peter Zak mystery series (St. Martin's Minotaur), which so far includes the titles *Amnesia*, *Addiction*, *Delusion*, *Obsessed* and *Guilt*.

The two approached the undertaking with common fears. Davidoff says, "When we started the collaboration, her biggest fear was that I was going to want to put pen to paper. *My* biggest fear was that she was going to *make* me put pen to paper." Ephron mirrors his musings exactly, "Don was afraid I was going to make him write; I was afraid he was going to want to write."

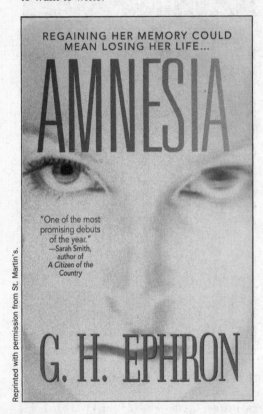

REGAINING HER MEMORY COULD MEAN LOSING HER LIFE...

AMNESIA

"One of the most promising debuts of the year."
—Sarah Smith, author of *A Citizen of the Country*

G. H. EPHRON

Reprinted with permission from St. Martin's.

What makes this team unique among those profiled here is that Davidoff, who is well versed in academic and nonfiction writing, is not a self-described fiction writer. Ephron says, "I think our partnership has worked because we have virtually no overlapping talents." Davidoff too states that they have "basically no overlapping skills. . . I would talk, developing the characters, developing the action. She would take notes. . . and make that into literature." In his line of work, Davidoff is "confronted with these mini-mysteries all the time" and his experience has "created a way for me to think about people, in terms of understanding motivations and where those motivations take us." Add to that his knowledge of the "wrong turns psychopathology pushes people into" and his contribution to the series is clearly no less than essential.

Though each consistently critiques the other's area of expertise, "all of the disagreements are solved fairly easily," Davidoff says. "Hallie is the final arbiter about writing. Character, personality and such, she deferred to me." Ephron explains one such conflict: "Our protagonist Peter Zak is very much based on [Don]. Occasionally I've written Peter doing something and Don objects, like in *Obsessed* Peter gets a red Miata. . . Turns out Don would never get a red car, so I had to change it." Yet like their novels, life too has many unforeseen twists and turns: "The final irony. . . I now own a red Nissan 350Z!" Davidoff says.

Davidoff explains his unique relationship to their protagonist succinctly, "He's the person I wish I could be, because in fact we can control not only the situation but the reactions, and in life you can't do that. He's a little better looking and a little smarter. . . He is me, but he's not me." As a result, Davidoff admits that he may be "overly invested in making [Peter] look like an idiot."

Though they genuinely enjoy collaborating and have few complaints, co-authoring has its drawbacks for every team. According to Ephron, "The major downside, of course, is having to split the money—so neither of us has quit our day jobs." Yet for Davidoff that's not necessarily a downside; for him writing is a side trip rather than a major throughway in his professional life and identity. He explains it well, "Neither Hallie nor I come to this as 20-year-olds. We come to this both with established careers, both with a sense of who we are, and so the stakes are very different. It does allow us to invest in the product rather than ourselves."

As for advice, Ephron warns, "There are a million ways to get burned—your ego, your finances, your trust. So enter a partnership with caution." Davidoff recommends finding "someone who is your complement, whose skills and abilities and knowledge do not directly overlap yours." Half-kidding, he also proffers the following sage wisdom: "Don't collaborate with your spouse. Because then it raises the ante considerably."

Lori and Tony Karayianni

Lori and Tony Karayianni met "at a Greek diner, of course." Lori recalls that it was "over coffee and baklava no less. It was a clearly defining moment—until then I believed 'love' and 'first sight' were words reserved solely for romance novels. Not anymore."

Together they comprise the only husband-and-wife team among our interviewees; under the pen name Tori Carrington they have co-authored more than 35 novels, including *Sofie Metropolis*, *Dirty Laundry* and *Foul Play* (for their entire bibliography, visit www.toricarrington.net), and they're still going strong. Neither has ever tried writing a novel alone, a tidbit that testifies to their joy and success in working together. "We get each other," Lori says. "I suspect there are few who can say this about their working relationships."

As for the mechanics of their arrangement, "We write from about eight in the morning until one in the afternoon, break for lunch and a siesta, then are back in our shared office again by seven or eight at night until about eleven or so most every day," Lori explains. "Half our evenings are devoted to keeping our extensive Web sites. . . updated and chatting online with fellow readers." Indeed they have met many people from all around the world as a result of their books. They consider the accessibility the Internet lends to writers and their readerships to be a constant blessing.

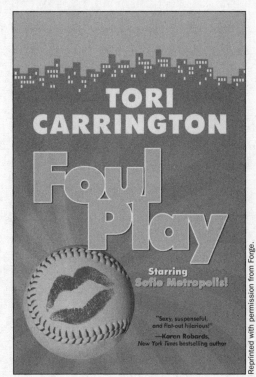

Reprinted with permission from Forge.

Having tried many and varied work styles, Lori says that, "It wasn't until we tried my being the chief writer and Tony the master plotter. . . that everything slid into place for us." When disagreements arise, she says they've learned to "compromise, compromise, compromise. Since we're so prolific, opportunities to pull out the compromise wild card in subsequent disagreements are many. . . the trump card the miffed one gets as a result is pure gold."

The secret to their long-lived success is no secret at all. Lori says, "A successful marriage is built on a foundation of love, mutual respect, the ability to compromise, a joint vision of the future together, and a putting aside of ego for the greater good of the union.'' What does that have to do with writing together? Everything, according to Lori. ''Coincidence that the elements that go into creating a successful marriage are the same ones needed to forge a successful collaboration? We don't think so.''

Her advice to the would-be collaborator could just as easily apply to selecting a life partner: ''Choose someone you respect, cherish and love.''

Blockbusters & Breakouts

The Elusive Art of Writing a BIG Book

© Dick Stanley

by Roxanne St. Claire

Why does one story of star-crossed lovers in a small town languish on the remainder pile, while the other one is *The Bridges of Madison County*? Why do one woman's musings about sex and the single life sit spine-out until stripped, and another become *Bridget Jones's Diary*? Why does one introspective, heartbreaking tale of tragedy and triumph suffer a print run of 5,000, while a little story written from the point of view of a young, dead girl becomes *The Lovely Bones*? Why does *You on a Diet* become a publisher's number one hardcover seller of all time . . . when that publisher has Dan Brown's backlist?

The difference is what some call "high concept." A breakout title. A blockbuster. A cross-over. A bestseller. A mega-hit. Whatever handle you hang on this beast, it's the kind of book that appeals to a vast and diverse audience, that delves into subject matter that is relevant to millions, and that tells a story so compelling that nothing could stop the wildfire word-of-mouth campaign it launches.

This is a big book, and authors want to write them, editors want to publish them, bookstores want to sell them, and readers will devour every one they can.

What makes a book BIG?

What makes one book "bigger" than another? It is the voice, the premise, the characters, the marketing, the cover, the conflict, the title, the timing, the table in the store where it is placed? Is it the pacing, the drama, the details, the sex, the stakes? Is it the author, the publisher, the day of release? Is it kismet? Is it fate? Is it possible?

Yes. To all of the above.

A big book is born of so many factors that it is virtually impossible to pinpoint one element every time. Or, more important, it is impossible for a writer, publisher or bookseller to *control* any or all of the factors. A big book is not necessarily a long book, or a lofty literary tome. It doesn't always hit the top of the *New York Times*, and it can be written in any genre, by a seasoned household name or a debut author. It doesn't have to put the world in jeopardy; it doesn't have to have a complicated plot; it doesn't have

ROXANNE ST. CLAIRE is a national best-selling author of 20 novels, of varying levels of bigness. She writes romantic suspense for Pocket Books, recently launching a popular bodyguard series known as The Bullet Catchers. She is the recipient of numerous prestigious writing awards, including the Bookseller's Best and The Maggie Award, and is a frequent speaker to writers and readers groups.

to be licensed for film rights pre-publication. Big books happen. When, why, and how often constitute the great mystery of the publishing universe.

Supersizing your novel

As a writer, you can take two approaches to the big book. You can consciously attempt to write one, controlling aspects of the craft by making specific big-book choices along the way. *New York Times* best-selling author of women's fiction Debbie Macomber made just that type of decision years ago when she decided to transition from writing category romances to what the industry calls "single title" novels. She wrote a longer, more involved romance and added a subplot. Although they did well, Macomber still didn't feel like she was writing the type of books that resonate with millions of people.

"Because I'm basically a storyteller, I had to devise a system to gauge which stories were worthy of development because the ideas had universal appeal," Macomber says. "My stories had to be provocative, relevant, creative and honest." The system worked, and the mix of all four elements has translated into phenomenal international publishing success for this prolific and popular author, including a coveted Quill Award.

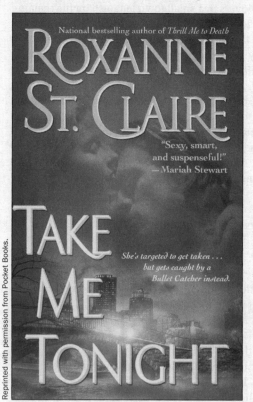

National bestselling author of *Thrill Me to Death*

ROXANNE ST. CLAIRE

"Sexy, smart, and suspenseful!"
— Mariah Stewart

TAKE ME TONIGHT

She's targeted to get taken... but gets caught by a Bullet Catcher instead.

Reprinted with permission from Pocket Books.

Writers and publishers will generally agree that blockbuster fiction is likely to have larger-than-life characters, believable, yet "fantastic" conflicts, and the capacity to draw on universal and well-founded emotions and truths. Usually, the stakes are high enough that the lives of many people, or even just a few important characters, are at risk if the protagonist doesn't succeed in his journey. Of course, there are other ways to raise the stakes—hearts can be permanently broken, money can be lost, homes can be destroyed, life-shattering secrets can be revealed, careers ruined, dreams dashed. Whatever hangs in the balance, it has to *matter* to the reader.

At the root of many big books, there is a struggle between good and evil, whether it is on a grand, international scale pitting country against country or planet against planet, or simply one good guy trying to take down one bad guy. However, many thriller writers will tell you: the bigger the evil, the bigger the book.

There are other factors at play, too. The depth of research and realism will add to the scope of the book, as will the wow factor of the pacing and structure of the story. Even the genre can impact the perception of a book—thrillers and suspense novels generally have a better shot at being labeled as "big" than most romances or mysteries, however there are numerous exceptions to that rule.

In general, an author can simply "think big" while writing, and the best way to do this is not to limit the work. Editors repeatedly say they are looking for the "really" factor: the books that push the envelope, regardless of the genre. Really sexy, really scary, really dark, really funny, really thrilling. A big book doesn't hold back.

This is true in nonfiction as well, whether it is a memoir, a biography, a cookbook, self-help or essays of a bemused dog owner. Even in nonfiction, the "really" factor will help a book to be perceived as one that tackles a subject matter more thoroughly than the competition, one that entertains as it educates, and inspires as it informs.

New York Times best-selling author Jo-Ann Ross agrees that the writer can control, to some extent, the "bigness" of the book. "I use a larger canvas for a long and involved suspense novel," Ross says. "And I layer the paint on thicker than I would for smaller, genre romances. The layering always includes more secondary characters who are helpful in showing the protagonist's various dimensions. I also focus on continually rising conflict, and high stakes that force the character to grow. The more readers care about the character, the more they care about the outcome, which keeps them turning pages."

Few argue that no matter the size or scope of the book, the depth and dimension of the characters will heavily influence whether or not readers connect with the book in a "big" way.

Leaving it up to fate (and the market)

There are certainly writers and industry professionals who don't believe the author has any ability to control whether or not a book is destined to be big, beyond telling the story they have in their heart and head. Renowned best-selling author Linda Howard says she doesn't think about the finished product when she starts a manuscript, but writes the story, whatever it is. "If it has a 'big' feel, that's simply the way things worked out."

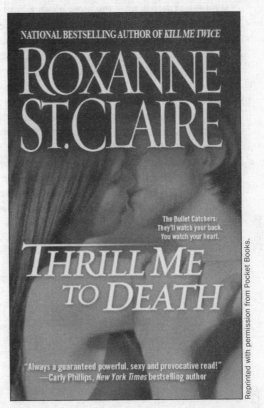

NATIONAL BESTSELLING AUTHOR OF *KILL ME TWICE*

ROXANNE ST. CLAIRE

The Bullet Catchers:
They'll watch your back.
You watch your heart.

THRILL ME TO DEATH

"Always a guaranteed powerful, sexy and provocative read!"
—Carly Phillips, *New York Times* bestselling author

Reprinted with permission from Pocket Books.

Kim Whalen, vice president of the Trident Media Group, a leading literary agency, thinks much of the magic happens in rooms where the writer isn't even present. From the moment a book is sold, the intangible element of editorial enthusiasm comes into play. And even if that enthusiasm is off the charts and spreads throughout the publishing house, there are no guarantees. Although she believes that nonfiction success is easier to predict, based on the author's platform, credentials and contacts, fiction can be "a gamble." The betting, Whalen says, starts even before a contract is negotiated.

Few argue that publisher support will influence the perception of a book. The quality of the cover art, the acquisition of key author cover quotes, even the 'tone' the sales force takes during the sell-in process will impact how a book is positioned and received in the marketplace. When the book reaches the bookstore, co-op placement that sends a title to the front of the larger stores makes a huge difference in sales, and the physical size (hard cover or trade versus mass market paperback) helps dictate a book's perceived value. Add to that national advertising, important reviews, high-profile promotions and an aggressive book tour, and there's no doubt the publisher plays a key part in the game.

Another player has a critical role in this process: the bookseller. Whether it is a major chain, a privately operated indie, or a national retailer like Target and Wal-Mart, once the books are in the hands of booksellers, the art of hand-selling, the magic of word of mouth, and the reality of sell-through and reorders all influence how a book is perceived, and ultimately, sold.

And then there is fate, the most elusive, and sometimes most influential, of all aspects of publishing. A movie deal. The Oprah nod. An extraordinary review, an unexpected related news story, a single snapshot of a celebrity holding that book. Something no one ever predicted can catapult a title from the mid-list purgatory to best-seller paradise, or transform a little story into a major publishing event.

It starts at the desk

The birth of a big book might not end with the writer, but it certainly starts with one. Everyone agrees there are certain ''must haves'' for a book to have a chance at being perceived as ''big''—and every one of these fundamental, essential elements is in the writer's control. A big book always features distinct and memorable characters. A big book has relevant, universal themes layered into escalating conflict. A big book is always told in a powerful voice that resonates on an emotional and entertaining level.

That means that every time a writer sits down to make magic at the keyboard, the next ''big'' book could be right under his fingertips.

Boost Your Mood

Bouncing Back From Rejection, Rewrite Requests and Other Disappointments

by Eve Menezes Cunningham

All writers face rejection and other setbacks at some point. Creative writers can feel even more exposed in their work. But whatever you're facing, you're not alone. Here, published novelists share their strategies for dealing with disappointments.

Negative self-talk

All writers know that sinking feeling of being so close to their work they can't tell if it has any redeeming features. Even award-winning, best-selling authors struggle with fears that the story they're currently writing won't be good enough.

Sara Paretsky, most famous for her delightful V.I. Warshawski novels, still gets "terrified. I'm starting work on a new book now and I think, 'I don't know what I'm doing and I don't know how to do it and maybe it would just be better if I jumped off the bridge.'

"I just have to fight through it. I have this sense that if I don't look after myself, there's no one to pick up the pieces. So in the back of my mind is, 'Sara, you've got to pull yourself together and do it.' And then, when I'm actually writing I'm fine. It's only when I'm thinking about it . . . ."

If you find yourself struggling through similar unhelpful self-doubt, write. Many of my clients share Sara's experience and feel completely in the zone while writing, only to beat themselves up by putting on their Editor hat too soon.

When doubts flood your mind, ask yourself, "Whose voice am I hearing?" It may be that you've internalized a critical parent or early English teacher's insults. Recognizing that the critical thought is a thought (and not the reality) is the first step to freeing yourself from it.

Once you've identified the voice, speak out loud to really get a sense of it. Then play around with it. You've been giving the critical voice in your head authority and free reign for too long. Dilute its authority by saying the same words but in a silly voice (Bart Simpson, your neighbor's cat, or any other voice that will have no power over you). Try it out. It really works. This releases the power you've given it and allows you to approach your writing more objectively.

Sometimes, you'll hear a little voice telling you what needs to be changed to make your writing better. So how can you tell the difference?

The best way to distinguish is the way you feel when the "voice" is talking. The one you should ignore makes you feel terrible about your writing and yourself. It's completely

EVE MENEZES CUNNINGHAM is a writer and life coach specializing in confidence coaching and NLP for writers. For more information and to sign up for a free monthly newsletter, please visit www.CoachingWriters.co.uk.

unhelpful. The helpful voice will inspire you to make your writing even better. You'll suddenly see areas for improvement and feel really good about making the changes.

If you still can't tell, ask the voice for specific feedback. If your gut tells you that some of the dialogue could be more believable and this rings true for you, get your manuscript out again and make those changes. But if that voice is telling you, "You're a worthless idiot and literary fraud," use the technique above to disarm it.

The one that got away

Sue Moorcroft, author of *Uphill All the Way* (Transita, 2005) says, "The thing I try to remember about rejection and rewrites is that there's nothing personal behind either. Editors and agents have more to do with their time and energy than come up with ways to give me a disappointment. So my first coping strategy is always that the rejection has come because my work wasn't right for them. If their comments strike a chord with me then I use their insight to make my work better. I get back to work, because where there's work on editor's desks, there's hope that it'll sell.

"But when I almost got a novel to contract with a publisher and the publisher then ceased to trade, that was a particular kind of disappointment. It was outside of my control and probably outside of the publisher's control, too. The temptation was to sulk. I probably did sulk! I was entitled. But sulking is a singularly unproductive activity and it doesn't get work on editors' desks! So, again, I worked."

If, like Moorcroft, something completely out of your control has knocked the wind out of your sails, give yourself a moment to catch your breath. Take several deep breaths. Nothing (legal) works faster to change your state completely. And as more oxygen reaches your blood and organs, you'll also notice your mood changing for the better.

Once you're feeling better, make a list of every single thing you can do to bring yourself closer to the outcome you're after. And if you're not clear about the outcome you want, give it some serious thought. List all the steps you can take. Tiny things you can do immediately include researching other publishers and getting back to work on your book to see if there's anything more you can do to improve it. A larger step might be asking a trusted reader to read and tell you what they liked. Once you've identified everything you can do, schedule each step into your calendar or planner. Don't lose momentum. Keep moving towards your goal, and you'll find the right publisher for you and your book.

Back to the drawing board

Bernardine Kennedy (www.bernardinekennedy.com) has published several successful novels including *Old Scores* (Headline Publishing Group, 2006), *Taken* (2004), *Chain of Deception* (2003), *My Sister's Keeper* (2002) and *Everything is Not Enough* (2001). Even so, when her editor showed her the rewrites wanted for her current novel, Kennedy was "horrified! But after stomping around and threatening to throw my PC through the window, I thought about it sensibly and realized that the suggestions were good. Unfortunately, it's all part of an author's life and although I would love to never have to edit/rewrite, it happens! I probably felt sorry for myself for about a day."

Kennedy got back on track by "writing up the new suggestions and re-plotting. The hardest part is when it's an additional storyline throughout the whole book and then it has to be threaded through nearly every chapter. I went into a phase of work displacement for a couple of weeks. Shopping, lunching, e-mailing, blogging—even housework! Anything rather than write. Then I knuckled down and got on with it. It's my job."

If you're in a similar situation, again, remind yourself that you're not alone. This is part of the editing process. Everyone involved is working together to make this novel or story the best it can be. Now take a break. Seeing all those amendments can feel overwhelming, so your first task is to get yourself into the most resourceful state possible. If you find it unnatural to be kind and compassionate towards yourself, imagine your writer-self is your child. Do something really indulgent (a day trip, pampering treat, or a "cheer up" present within your budget) to boost the way you feel. If you try to tackle the rewrites from the disappointed, frazzled state you were in when you found out about them, you'll feel awful and your writing will be flat.

When you're feeling good again, revisit it. If it's an enormous task, break it down into smaller chunks and list them. Assign yourself a celebration for each thing you'll be ticking off. This will keep you motivated and stop you from burning out. Kennedy adds, "Accept that most of the time editors know best and their experienced eyes will be an asset to the manuscript in the long run. But it's still a pain nonetheless!"

Family matters

Before publishing her debut novel, *Zade* (Saqi Books, 2004), Heather Reyes taught and wrote short stories for more than 20 years. Reyes says, "My immediate family is fine, but my parents don't really understand how much time it takes. There's a certain amount of sympathy, but people don't understand what you feel is at stake.

"Although I'm female, I'm not terribly interested in shopping and the house. But in my family, as a woman, mother and grandmother, there is the expectation that I'm happy to spend three months planning Christmas. Five months into the year, my mother was already asking about what I was going to do," she says. "Taking part in the life of the tribe takes time. If a distant relative is having a barbeque, you have to give up a precious Sunday and you have to talk to them about what interests them. As a woman trained very much to be nice to other people, this feels like a life of continual emotional admin. If you love somebody, like I do my family, it's very difficult to say, 'I don't think like you. I don't want my life to be like yours.' And as a writer, you're more sensitive to other people's needs. But that can be a trap because you feel that your life is being sucked away from you.

"It's important to have an ally," she adds. "If I were on my own trying to deal with it, I would have gone under. For me, having a partner like Malcolm [Burgess, also a writer] makes all the difference in the world. It doesn't have to be a partner—even mixing with other creative people stops you from thinking you're quite mad. At the Society of Authors you meet people who are just as mad as you are! I want to be writing and meeting people who are stimulating and interesting. There's something that drives you as a creative person and, if you're not like that, it's really hard to imagine."

If this feels familiar, there's no reason for you to stop loving your friends and family who aren't creative. But if you feel marginalized at all, surround yourself with as many writers and other creative people as possible. Join a local group or find a friendly forum for writers on the Internet. When you have your need for support and empathy met by people who truly understand what it's like, you won't need it from your family.

Many writers dismiss their writing. Until they're published or have awards or some other kind of external validation, there can be a sense that they're not entitled to call themselves "writers." Your loved ones may be picking up on this insecurity, so reclaim your writing for yourself and make it a priority in your life. You'll find that when you start taking your writing seriously yourself, other people will also recognize that it's an important part of your life.

Believe to achieve

Whatever situation you're in, keep your focus on what you want to happen. Wallowing won't make you feel better and it certainly won't help you succeed. There is always something you can do to improve your chances. If you've had a rejection, send your manuscript off to another suitable publisher. Don't let it get buried under a pile of papers. Keep things flowing and don't stop writing. You can't control what an editor or agent is going to think about your work, but you can control your attitude to give yourself the best possible chance. If you're waiting to hear from an agent or publisher, what do you think they'll find more appealing when they do get in touch? Someone who's been waiting by the phone with their life and writing on hold or someone with loads of exciting projects on the go and a happy, positive attitude about making them all a success?

Keep following up your great ideas and enjoy your writing.

For More Information

Many of the techniques described in this article are part of a practice known as Neuro-linguistic Programming (NLP). The "Neuro" aspect is about how we think and the link between our bodies and minds. "Linguistic" refers to our understanding of the world through language (what we say, what we think and how we interpret what we hear). "Programming" is how we put it all together. NLP can help with everything from changing unhelpful internal beliefs to improving communication and goal setting. At it's simplest, NLP is about deciding on an outcome (what exactly do you want to happen?), paying attention to the feedback from the world (is what you've been doing working for you?) and changing your behavior until you get the outcome you're after. To find out more about NLP, visit www.bbnlp.com, www.nlp-world.com/directory/NLP_Information/index.html and www.applecoaching.com or read *Introducing Neuro-linguistic Programming: The New Psychology of Personal Excellence* by Joseph O'Connor et al, and *Introducing NLP* by Sue Knight.

Success Story

The Importance of Persistence, Friendship, and Strawberry-rhubarb Pie

by David Mohan

In fourth grade, my sister gave me Ellen Conford's *Dreams of Victory*. When I finished it, I knew I wanted to be a writer. It wasn't long before I'd be at the library with my mom, who'd say, "David, you're not going to find *The Hobbit* in reference—oh, you're looking at the *Novel & Short Story Writer's Market* again."

A few years later I submitted a story to a magazine for the first time. My story involved a boy who talked to a houseplant possessed by the devil. If I'd been a bit wiser, I would have realized that *Cricket*, a magazine for middle-schoolers, is not a market open to stories of demons and exorcisms.

By the early '90s I was buying my own copies of *NSSWM* annually. However, I did not write that much. I hadn't counted on being afflicted with depression or the resulting heartbreak from creating and submitting. In the next 10 years, I only wrote seven stories.

In 2002, I attended a writing group where a man I'll call McGrudge was bellowing, "I don't need my characters to have any emotions because Hemingway's never did!" I knew there was something (or many somethings) that Hemingway had done to make his writing compelling that McGrudge hadn't, but I didn't know what. I decided to try emulating Hemingway. Perhaps I could figure out what he had done and also learn spare, powerful writing.

I wrote a variation on the Hemingway story "Hills Like White Elephants" in which a couple discusses abortion without mentioning the term. In my version, it is a gay couple, and the topic they are dancing around is HIV. I incorporated similar dialogue and used Spain as a setting. I originally titled the story "Hills Like Pink Elephants" but decided that was too obvious, not to mention too silly. It was a long way from Hemingway, but my friend, Kimberly, told me the experiment was a success.

David Mohan

Depression kept me from working on it often, but I'd change it based on commentary I received, cutting adverbs and adjectives. I occasionally submitted other stories, but mostly I'd lament that I wasn't good enough for publication, so Kimberly would take me to get strawberry-rhubarb pie, or I'd terrorize the residents of my Sim City with aliens and earthquakes.

In 2004, I sent the story, now called "Like All The Things You've Waited For" to *Confronta-*

IF YOU HAVE A SUCCESS STORY in which *Novel & Short Story Writer's Market* helped you find a publisher for your work and you would like to be featured, please e-mail a brief synopsis to Lauren Mosko at lauren.mosko@fwpubs.com.

tion. NSSWM listed it as entry level, but many of its authors were famous. They said no. More pie and Sim City. Then I submitted it to a *Glimmer Train* contest for unpublished writers. While they also said no, they said it was "a good read." Considering how many submissions they have, positive feedback from them was very heartening.

I'd read years ago in *NSSWM* that one should submit a story at least 12 times before moving on. Thus, for dietary purposes, I told myself I had to wait for 10 additional rejections before I could have more pie. Meanwhile, I kept writing. My Sim City exploits generated a series of stories about a terrible town where the fire department is always on strike, the mayor gleefully allows factories to commit environmental atrocities, and occasionally the houseplants are possessed.

Driving makes me nervous, so reaching the post office is difficult, and the level of wealth I have to buy sample copies of magazines conjures the words "church mouse." Therefore, I searched the *NSSWM* for new markets that I could read and submit to online. I tried e-magazines with fiction I loved, such as *Failbetter* and *Slow Trains,* without luck. Meanwhile, I submitted another story to another great e-magazine, *SNReview.* They said no, but they also said they would enjoy reading more of my work. Wow! I'd never been told that before. Kimberly said, "Send 'Like All The Things' to them tomorrow! That's my favorite!" On May 18, 2006, almost 18 years and 100,000 words after I first submitted a story, *SNReview*'s editor Joe Conlin wrote to tell me he would be "honored to publish it." That was exhilarating.

I don't feel able to dispense wisdom to other writers. However, I will say again that in the fight against discouragement, I cannot emphasize enough the importance of good pie. Also, writing is often solitary, and rejection is depressing. So much more important than the pie is a good friend with similar writing dreams, a supportive writing group, and the recognition that every year there are emerging markets that may be just perfect.

[Editor's note: Since writing this article, David was published again in Nuvein Magazine. *David can be reached at DavidMohan@sbcglobal.net.]*

The Business of Fiction Writing

I t's true there are no substitutes for talent and hard work. A writer's first concern must always be attention to craft. No matter how well presented, a poorly written story or novel has little chance of being published. On the other hand, a well-written piece may be equally hard to sell in today's competitive publishing market. Talent alone is just not enough.

To be successful, writers need to study the field and pay careful attention to finding the right market. While the hours spent perfecting your writing are usually hours spent alone, you're not alone when it comes to developing your marketing plan. *Novel & Short Story Writer's Market* provides you with detailed listings containing the essential information you'll need to locate and contact the markets most suitable for your work.

Once you've determined where to send your work, you must turn your attention to presentation. We can help here, too. We've included the basics of manuscript preparation, along with information on submission procedures and how to approach markets. We also include tips on promoting your work. No matter where you're from or what level of experience you have, you'll find useful information here on everything from presentation to mailing to selling rights to promoting your work—the "business" of fiction.

APPROACHING MAGAZINE MARKETS

While it is essential for nonfiction markets, a query letter by itself is usually not needed by most magazine fiction editors. If you are approaching a magazine to find out if fiction is accepted, a query is fine, but editors looking for short fiction want to see *how* you write. A cover letter can be useful as a letter of introduction, but it must be accompanied by the actual piece. The key here is brevity. A successful cover letter is no more than one page (20 lb. bond paper). It should be single spaced with a double space between paragraphs, proofread carefully and neatly typed in a standard typeface (not script or italic). The writer's name, address and phone number appear at the top, and the letter is addressed, ideally, to a specific editor. (If the editor's name is unavailable, address to "Fiction Editor.")

The body of a successful cover letter contains the name and word count of the story, a brief list of previous publications if you have any, and the reason you are submitting to this particular publication. Mention that you have enclosed a self-addressed, stamped envelope or postcard for reply. Also let the editor know if you are sending a disposable manuscript that doesn't need to be returned. (More and more editors prefer disposable manuscripts that save them time and save you postage.) When sending a computer disk (only do so if the submission guidelines request one), identify the program you are using. Remember, however, that even editors who appreciate receiving your story on a disk usually also want a printed copy. Finally, don't forget to thank the editor for considering your story. See the sample short story cover letter on page 85.

APPROACHING BOOK PUBLISHERS

Some book publishers do ask for queries first, but most want a query plus sample chapters or an outline or, occasionally, the complete manuscript. Again, make your letter brief. Include the essentials about yourself—name, address, phone number and publishing experience. Include a 3 or 4 sentence ''pitch'' and only the personal information related to your story. Show that you have researched the market with a few sentences about why you chose this publisher. See the sample book query on page 86.

BOOK PROPOSALS

A book proposal is a package sent to a publisher that includes a cover letter and one or more of the following: sample chapters, outline, synopsis, author bio, publications list. When asked to send sample chapters, send up to three *consecutive* chapters. **An outline** covers the highlights of your book chapter by chapter. Be sure to include details on main characters, the plot and subplots. Outlines can run up to 30 pages, depending on the length of your novel. The object is to tell what happens in a concise, but clear, manner. **A synopsis** is a shorter summary of your novel, written in a way that expresses the emotion of the story in addition to just explaining the essential points. Evan Marshall, literary agent and author of *The Marshall Plan for Getting Your Novel Published* (Writer's Digest Books), suggests you aim for a page of synopsis for every 25 pages of manuscript. Marshall also advises you write the synopsis as one unified narrative, without section, subheads or chapters to break up the text. The terms synopsis and outline are sometimes used interchangeably, so be sure to find out exactly what each publisher wants.

A FEW WORDS ABOUT AGENTS

Agents are not usually needed for short fiction and most do not handle it unless they already have a working relationship with you. For novels, you may want to consider working with an agent, especially if you intend to market your book to publishers who do not look at unsolicited submissions. For more on approaching agents and to read listings of agents willing to work with beginning and established writers, see our Literary Agents section beginning on page 155 or refer to this year's edition of *Guide to Literary Agents*, edited by Chuck Sambuchino.

MANUSCRIPT MECHANICS

A professionally presented manuscript will not guarantee publication. But a sloppy, hard-to-read manuscript will not be read—publishers simply do not have the time. Here's a list of suggested submission techniques for polished manuscript presentation:

• **Use white, 8½×11 bond paper,** preferably 16 or 20 lb. weight. The paper should be heavy enough so it will not show pages underneath it and strong enough to take handling by several people.

• **Type your manuscript** on a computer and print it out using a laser or ink jet printer, or use a typewriter with a new ribbon.

• **Proofread carefully.** An occasional white-out is okay, but don't send a marked-up manuscript with many typos. Keep a dictionary, thesaurus and stylebook handy and use the spellcheck function on your computer.

• **Always double space and leave a 1 inch margin** on all sides of the page.

• **For a short story manuscript,** your first page should include your name, address, phone number and e-mail address (single-spaced) in the upper left corner. In the upper right, indicate an approximate word count. Center the name of your story about one-third of the way down, skip a line and center your byline (byline is optional). Skip four lines and begin your story. On subsequent pages, put last name and page number in the upper right hand corner.

Short Story Cover Letter

Lauren Mosko
4700 East Galbraith Rd.
Cincinnati, OH 45236
Phone (513) 531-2690
Fax (513) 531-2687
lauren.mosko@fwpubs.com

March 2, 2006

Toni Graham
Cimarron Review
Oklahoma State University
205 Morrill Hall
Stillwater, OK 74078-0135

Dear Toni Graham:

I am submitting my short story, "Things From Which You Can Never Recover" (6,475 words), for your consideration in *Cimarron Review.*

I am the editor of *Novel & Short Story Writer's Market* (F + W Publications) and my essays, interviews and reviews have been published in several other books in the Writer's Market series, as well as *The Writer's Digest Handbook of Magazine Article Writing* (2nd ed.), *I.D. Magazine*, and the alt weeklies *Louisville Eccentric Observer* and (Cincinnati's now-defunct) *Everybody's News.*

Enclosed you will also find an SASE for your response; you may recycle the manuscript. This is a simultaneous submission.

Your listing in *Novel & Short Story Writer's Market* said you are seeking work with "unusual perspective, language, imagery and character," and I think my story fits this description. I hope you enjoy it. Thank you in advance for your time and consideration.

Sincerely,

Lauren Mosko

Encl: Short story, "Things From Which You Can Never Recover"
      SASE

This sample cover letter is professional, brief and succinct so I don't waste a second of the editor's time and I allow my writing to speak for itself. The power is in the precise details: the name of the editor, the title of my story, the word count, my publishing history, and attention to their submission guidelines (noting that I've enclosed a SASE and that this is a simultaneous submission).

Query to Publisher: Novel

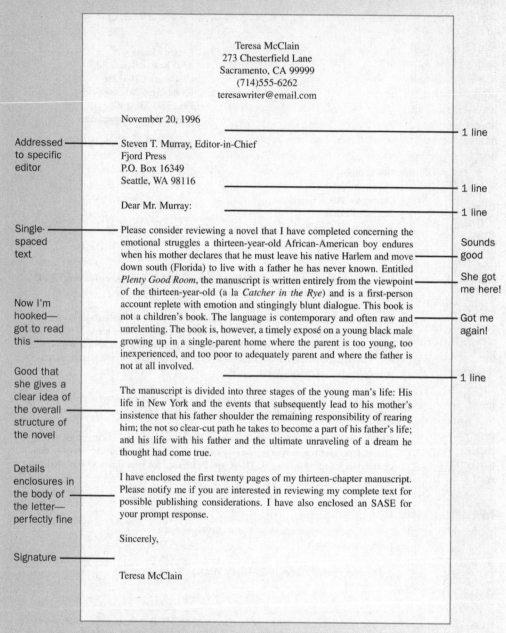

Teresa McClain
273 Chesterfield Lane
Sacramento, CA 99999
(714)555-6262
teresawriter@email.com

November 20, 1996
_____ 1 line

Addressed to specific editor

Steven T. Murray, Editor-in-Chief
Fjord Press
P.O. Box 16349
Seattle, WA 98116
_____ 1 line

Dear Mr. Murray:
_____ 1 line

Single-spaced text

Please consider reviewing a novel that I have completed concerning the emotional struggles a thirteen-year-old African-American boy endures when his mother declares that he must leave his native Harlem and move down south (Florida) to live with a father he has never known. Entitled *Plenty Good Room*, the manuscript is written entirely from the viewpoint of the thirteen-year-old (a la *Catcher in the Rye*) and is a first-person account replete with emotion and stingingly blunt dialogue. This book is not a children's book. The language is contemporary and often raw and unrelenting. The book is, however, a timely exposé on a young black male growing up in a single-parent home where the parent is too young, too inexperienced, and too poor to adequately parent and where the father is not at all involved.

Sounds good

She got me here!

Got me again!

Now I'm hooked— got to read this

_____ 1 line

Good that she gives a clear idea of the overall structure of the novel

The manuscript is divided into three stages of the young man's life: His life in New York and the events that subsequently lead to his mother's insistence that his father shoulder the remaining responsibility of rearing him; the not so clear-cut path he takes to become a part of his father's life; and his life with his father and the ultimate unraveling of a dream he thought had come true.

Details enclosures in the body of the letter— perfectly fine

I have enclosed the first twenty pages of my thirteen-chapter manuscript. Please notify me if you are interested in reviewing my complete text for possible publishing considerations. I have also enclosed an SASE for your prompt response.

Sincerely,

Signature

Teresa McClain

Comments provided by Steven Murray of Fjord Press.

• **For book manuscripts,** use a separate title page. Put your name, address, phone number and e-mail address in the lower right corner and word count in the upper right. If you have representation, list your agent's name and address in the lower right. (This bumps your name and contact information to the upper left corner.) Center your title and byline about halfway down the page. Start your first chapter on the next page. Center the chapter number and title (if there is one) one-third of the way down the page. Include your last name and the novel's title in all caps in the upper left and put the page number in the upper right of this page and each page to follow. Start each chapter with a new page.

• **Include a word count.** If you work on a computer, chances are your word processing program can give you a word count. If you are using a typewriter, there are a number of ways to count the number of words in your piece. One way is to count the words in five lines and divide that number by five to find an average. Then count the number of lines and multiply to find the total words. For long pieces, you may want to count the words in the first three pages, divide by three and multiply by the number of pages you have.

• **Always keep a copy.** Manuscripts do get lost. To avoid expensive mailing costs, send only what is required. If you are including artwork or photos but you are not positive they will be used, send photocopies. Artwork is hard to replace.

• **Suggest art where applicable.** Most publishers do not expect you to provide artwork and some insist on selecting their own illustrators, but if you have suggestions, please let them know. Magazine publishers work in a very visual field and are usually open to ideas.

• **Enclose a self-addressed, stamped envelope (SASE)** if you want a reply or if you want your manuscript returned. For most letters, a business-size (#10) envelope will do. Avoid using any envelope too small for an 8½×11 sheet of paper. For manuscripts, be sure to include enough postage and an envelope large enough to contain it. If you are requesting a sample copy of a magazine or a book publisher's catalog, send an envelope big enough to fit.

• **Consider sending a disposable manuscript** that saves editors time and saves you money.

• **When sending electronic (disk or e-mail) submissions,** check the publisher's Web site or contact them first for specific information and follow the directions carefully. Always include a printed copy with any disk submission.

• **Keep accurate records.** This can be done in a number of ways, but be sure to keep track of where your stories are and how long they have been "out." Write down submission dates. If you do not hear about your submission for a long time—about one to two months longer than the reporting time stated in the listing—you may want to contact the publisher. When you do, you will need an accurate record for reference.

MAILING TIPS
When mailing short correspondence or short manuscripts:

• Fold manuscripts under five pages into thirds and send in a business-size (#10) envelope.

• Mail manuscripts five pages or more unfolded in a 9×12 or 10×13 envelope.

• Mark envelopes in all caps, FIRST CLASS MAIL or SPECIAL FOURTH CLASS MANU-SCRIPT RATE.

• For return envelope, fold it in half, address it to yourself and add a stamp or, if going to a foreign country, International Reply Coupons (available at the main branch of your local post office).

• Don't send by certified mail. This is a sign of an amateur and publishers do not appreciate receiving unsolicited manuscripts this way.

• For the most current postage rates, visit the United States Postal Service online at www.usps.com.

When mailing book-length manuscripts:

First Class Mail over 11 ounces (about 65 8½×11 20 lb.-weight pages) automatically becomes **PRIORITY MAIL.**

Metered Mail may be dropped in any post office box, but meter strips on SASEs should not be dated.

The Postal Service provides, free of charge, tape, boxes and envelopes to hold up to two pounds for those using PRIORITY and EXPRESS MAIL. Requirements for mailing FOURTH CLASS and PARCEL POST have not changed.

Main branches of local banks will cash foreign checks, but keep in mind payment quoted in our listings by publishers in other countries is usually payment in their currency. Also note reporting time is longer in most overseas markets. To save time and money, you may want to include a return postcard (and IRC) with your submission and forgo asking for a manuscript to be returned. If you live in Canada, see "Canadian Writers Take Note" on page 531.

Important note about IRCs: Foreign editors sometimes find IRCs have been stamped incorrectly by the U.S. post office when purchased. This voids the IRCs and makes it impossible for foreign editors to exchange the coupons for return postage for your manuscript. When buying IRCs, make sure yours have been stamped correctly before you leave the counter. (Each IRC should be stamped on the bottom *left* side of the coupon, not the right.) More information about International Reply Coupons, including an image of a correctly stamped IRC, is available on the USPS Web site (www.usps.com).

RIGHTS

The Copyright Law states that writers are selling one-time rights (in almost all cases) unless they and the publisher have agreed otherwise. A list of various rights follows. Be sure you know exactly what rights you are selling before you agree to the sale.

• **Copyright** is the legal right to exclusive publication, sale or distribution of a literary work. As the writer or creator of a written work, you need simply to include your name, date and the copyright symbol © on your piece in order to copyright it. Be aware, however, that most editors today consider placing the copyright symbol on your work the sign of an amateur and many are even offended by it.

To get specific answers to questions about copyright (but not legal advice), you can call the Copyright Public Information Office at (202)707-3000 weekdays between 8:30 a.m. and 5 p.m. EST. Publications listed in *Novel & Short Story Writer's Market* are copyrighted *unless* otherwise stated. In the case of magazines that are not copyrighted, be sure to keep a copy of your manuscript with your notice printed on it. For more information on copyrighting your work see *The Copyright Handbook: How to Protect & Use Written Works*, 8th edition, by Stephen Fishman (Nolo Press, 2005).

Some people are under the mistaken impression that copyright is something they have to send away for, and that their writing is not properly protected until they have "received" their copyright from the government. The fact is, you don't have to register your work with the Copyright Office in order for your work to be copyrighted; any piece of writing is copyrighted the moment it is put to paper.

Although it is generally unnecessary, registration is a matter of filling out an application form (for writers, that's Form TX) and sending the completed form, a nonreturnable copy of the work in question and a check for $45 to the Library of Congress, Copyright Office, Register of Copyrights, 101 Independence Ave. SE, Washington DC 20559-6000. If the thought of paying $45 each to register every piece you write does not appeal to you, you can cut costs by registering a group of your works with one form, under one title for one $45 fee.

Most magazines are registered with the Copyright Office as single collective entities themselves; that is, the individual works that make up the magazine are *not* copyrighted individually in the names of the authors. You'll need to register your article yourself if you wish to have the additional protection of copyright registration.

For more information, visit the United States Copyright Office online at www.copyright.gov.

• **First Serial Rights**—This means the writer offers a newspaper or magazine the right to publish the article, story or poem for the first time in a particular periodical. All other rights to the material remain with the writer. The qualifier "North American" is often added to this phrase to specify a geographical limit to the license.

When material is excerpted from a book scheduled to be published and it appears in a magazine or newspaper prior to book publication, this is also called first serial rights.

• **One-time Rights**—A periodical that licenses one-time rights to a work (also known as simultaneous rights) buys the *nonexclusive* right to publish the work once. That is, there is nothing to stop the author from selling the work to other publications at the same time. Simultaneous sales would typically be to periodicals without overlapping audiences.

• **Second Serial (Reprint) Rights**—This gives a newspaper or magazine the opportunity to print an article, poem or story after it has already appeared in another newspaper or magazine. Second serial rights are nonexclusive; that is, they can be licensed to more than one market.

• **All Rights**—This is just what it sounds like. All rights means a publisher may use the manuscript anywhere and in any form, including movie and book club sales, without further payment to the writer (although such a transfer, or *assignment*, of rights will terminate after 35 years). If you think you'll want to use the material later, you must avoid submitting to such markets or refuse payment and withdraw your material. Ask the editor whether he is willing to buy first rights instead of all rights before you agree to an assignment or sale. Some editors will reassign rights to a writer after a given period, such as one year. It's worth an inquiry in writing.

• **Subsidiary Rights**—These are the rights, other than book publication rights, that should be covered in a book contract. These may include various serial rights; movie, television, audiotape and other electronic rights; translation rights, etc. The book contract should specify who controls these rights (author or publisher) and what percentage of sales from the licensing of these sub rights goes to the author.

• **Dramatic, Television and Motion Picture Rights**—This means the writer is selling his material for use on the stage, in television or in the movies. Often a one-year option to buy such rights is offered (generally for 10% of the total price). The interested party then tries to sell the idea to other people—actors, directors, studios or television networks, etc. Some properties are optioned over and over again, but most fail to become dramatic productions. In such cases, the writer can sell his rights again and again—as long as there is interest in the material. Though dramatic, TV and motion picture rights are more important to the fiction writer than the nonfiction writer, producers today are increasingly interested in nonfiction material; many biographies, topical books and true stories are being dramatized.

• **Electronic Rights**—These rights cover usage in a broad range of electronic media, from online magazines and databases to CD-ROM magazine anthologies and interactive games. The editor should specify in writing if—and which—electronic rights are being requested. The presumption is that unspecified rights are kept by the writer.

Compensation for electronic rights is a major source of conflict between writers and publishers, as many book publishers seek control of them and many magazines routinely include electronic rights in the purchase of print rights, often with no additional payment. Alternative ways of handling this issue include an additional 15 percent added to the amount to purchase first rights and a royalty system based on the number of times an article is accessed from an electronic database.

MARKETING AND PROMOTION

Everyone agrees writing is hard work whether you are published or not. Yet, once you achieve publication the work changes. Now, not only do you continue writing and revising your next project, you must also concern yourself with getting your book into the hands of readers. It becomes time to switch hats from artist to salesperson.

While even best-selling authors whose publishers have committed big bucks to marketing are asked to help promote their books, new authors may have to take it upon themselves to plan and initiate some of their own promotion, sometimes dipping into their own pockets. While this does not mean that every author is expected to go on tour, sometimes at their own expense, it does mean authors should be prepared to offer suggestions for promoting their books.

About Our Policies

Important

We occasionally receive letters asking why a certain magazine, publisher or contest is not in the book. Sometimes when we contact listings, the editors do not want to be listed because they:

- do not use very much fiction.
- are overwhelmed with submissions.
- are having financial difficulty or have been recently sold.
- use only solicited material.
- accept work from a select group of writers only.
- do not have the staff or time for the many unsolicited submissions a listing may bring.

Some of the listings do not appear because we have chosen not to list them. We investigate complaints of unprofessional conduct in editors' dealings with writers and misrepresentation of information provided to us by editors and publishers. If we find these reports to be true, after a thorough investigation, we will delete the listing from future editions.

There is no charge to the companies that list in this book. Listings appearing in *Novel & Short Story Writer's Market* are compiled from detailed questionnaires, phone interviews and information provided by editors, publishers, and awards and conference directors. The publishing industry is volatile and changes of address, editor, policies and needs happen frequently. To keep up with the changes between editors of the book, we suggest you check the market information on the *Writer's Market* Web site at www.writersmarket.com, or on the *Writer's Digest* Web site at www.writersdigest.com. Many magazine and book publishers offer updated information for writers on their Web sites. Check individual listings for those Web site addresses.

Club newsletters and small magazines devoted to helping writers also list market information. For those writers with access to online services, several offer writers' bulletin boards, message centers and chat lines with up-to-the-minute changes and happenings in the writing community.

We rely on our readers, as well, for new markets and information about market conditions. Write us if you have any new information or if you have suggestions on how to improve our listings to better suit your writing needs.

Depending on the time, money and personal preferences of the author and publisher, a promotional campaign could mean anything from mailing out press releases to setting up book signings to hitting the talk-show circuit. Most writers can contribute to their own promotion by providing contact names—reviewers, hometown newspapers, civic groups, organizations—that might have a special interest in the book or the writer.

Above all, when it comes to promotion, be creative. What is your book about? Try to capitalize on it. Focus on your potential audiences and how you can help them to connect with your book.

Important Listing Information

- Listings are not advertisements. Although the information here is as accurate as possible, the listings are not endorsed or guaranteed by the editor of *Novel & Short Story Writer's Market*.

- *Novel & Short Story Writer's Market* reserves the right to exclude any listing that does not meet its requirements.

John Connolly

'It's About Moving On'

© Brian L. Velenchenko

by T.E. Lyons

Private-eye mystery, crime thriller, weird tale—John Connolly wouldn't observe the distinctions even if he believed that storytelling had such boundaries.

At a signing, he's an energetic figure in a white poet's shirt or tight black pullover. Engaging the audience with a fast and slightly sharp Irish lilt, he quickly shows he has much more to offer than an appealing delivery of predictable genre conventions. Connolly is glad to divert a reading, for example, with an update on the preservation of the Sedlec Ossuary— a unique church property near Prague (written into the 2005 novel *The Black Angel* [Atria]) that has startling features, including a chandelier containing every bone of the human body.

History, religion, violence: These can all shade or jolt the life course of John Connolly's characters. His fiction—eight novels and a short-story collection to date—is redolent with atonement, regret and retribution.

The protagonist of most of Connolly's books, a private investigator named Charlie Parker, is a self-effacing ex-NYPD detective who has gradually reassembled his life after losing both wife and daughter to a serial killer. Parker lives in Maine and takes on cases that involve unusual crimes, unique characters, and, occasionally, a touch of the supernatural. (For those who wonder at the PI sharing the name of the great bebop saxophonist, Connolly isn't much of a jazz fan—but musical references [often indie rock] show up often in his novels. The author gratefully acknowledges his debt to music, going so far as to compile CDs of songs and artists that have inspired him, and including the discs in special editions [at great cost for licensing the recordings].)

Parker was introduced in *Every Dead Thing* (Simon & Schuster, 1999), which won the 1999 Shamus Award for Best First Novel. This mystery begins with a prologue that Connolly recalls rewriting dozens of times. In conversation with the author, it's clear he has plumbed his own capabilities and found a *modus operandi* that works for him (but, as he admits, won't work for everyone): a veritable campaign of focused rewriting that will yield a novel over a not-too-varying period.

Connolly's protagonist can't be considered a doppelganger for the author himself—though

T. E. LYONS has been writing actively since his daughter's birth in 1990. This included a residency at the Mary Anderson Center for the Arts in Mt. St. Francis, Indiana. He's written more than 800 music reviews and 50 book reviews in markets in the Ohio Valley and Midatlantic regions. He has also sold several dozen works of both speculative and erotic fiction to print and online publications. He's served as both the Music and Associate Arts Editor for the *Louisville Eccentric Observer* alt-weekly paper and, during his tenure there, earned five Metro Louisville (Ky.) Awards from the Society of Professional Journalists.

many of Connolly's carefully constructed sentences bring readers close to Parker's inner thoughts. "[Parker] constantly picks at things, turning them this way and that in his mind, trying to understand them or to reveal some previously unsuspected facet of the case," Connolly explains. "Maybe, for those who like the books, that's why Parker comes alive. We're privy to almost everything that goes on in his head." Through six Parker novels (as well as other works in which the character has made an appearance), Connolly has maintained an ambiguity to the PI's physical description. Parker is, however, an American, although the author has spent limited time on the western side of the Atlantic. The only real similarity: The investigator shares the author's tastes in music.

In recent years, Connolly has explored both new styles and subjects. In 2004, there was *Nocturnes*, a short-story collection begun through a radio collaboration with the BBC. 2006 saw publication of *The Book of Lost Things*, a stand-alone work in which archetypes and variants of folk tales and fairy tales challenge a troubled boy on the cusp of adolescence. "I think of it as a book about childhood for adults," the author says, and the American Library Association agreed by conferring one of its Alex Awards, which recognizes adult books with special appeal to teen readers.

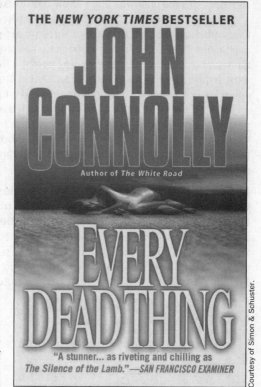

THE *NEW YORK TIMES* BESTSELLER

JOHN CONNOLLY

Author of *The White Road*

EVERY DEAD THING

"A stunner... as riveting and chilling as *The Silence of the Lamb*."—SAN FRANCISCO EXAMINER

Courtesy of Simon & Schuster.

Connolly, once a full-time journalist, continues to make freelance contributions to *The Irish Times*. Though some of his articles are related to his fiction (e.g., interviews with other authors), Connolly sees journalism as "a very different discipline, and fulfilling in a way that writing fiction isn't. It's more immediate."

In this interview, Connolly speaks about what it takes to write through an entire draft without getting stuck, the fascination commanded by killers without empathy, the value of serendipitous research into local history, continuing the work of M.R. James, and what it's like to dive into short-story writing after becoming a well-established novelist.

When I'm reading a page in a John Connolly novel, how many times will it have been rewritten?

The first one was different because it took five years to write—and like most people, I had another job at the time. It was about 40 start-to-finish drafts. Now they're on about a dozen before it goes to proof stage. And they always start the same way: I spend a long time going through the first draft . . . where there'll be sections that are left out, bits of dialogue I haven't done properly, and there'll be characters that are half-developed. But nobody's standing over my shoulder, criticizing me. My main priority is to know that there's a book there. If I can get it from start to finish—once I know that it more or less follows a logical sequence—I can begin fixing it.

That first draft is like a preliminary sketch. Then I go over it, start to finish, again and again and again. It's the only way that I know how to do it. I'll begin to get into the rhythm of it.

Each book will have its own rhythm—because I don't go in jerkily, dipping into chapters. Even if I know that the first two or three [chapters] are probably okay, and the problem is in chapters 40 to 50, I'd rather go back to the start, find my way into the book again . . . and then, you sense when things are going wrong. I'll occasionally read bits aloud, and the same thing happens—you can tell when the rhythm isn't right. If you're reading something aloud and it sounds wrong in your mouth, then it'll sound wrong to the reader, as well.

I want the books to flow. I want the readers to get into the flow of it. And I'm not any person who shies away from poetic language or from using metaphor. I think it has its place in mystery fiction, as in any other fiction. So, if you want to get around to [writing for publication], part is in the background of being taught the basics of English. That every sentence has a rhythm.

In *Book of Lost Things* you write, "Stories compel themselves to be told." One story that keeps being told is that of the serial killer. Why do you think this one maintains its interest with readers?

I get criticized sometimes for using supernatural elements in my stories. There are people who would like to see the mystery novel set in aspic somewhere between Sherlock Holmes going over the Reichenbach Falls and the death of Poirot, and this would be "the Golden Period." They're very much proponents of a rationalist approach to crime fiction.

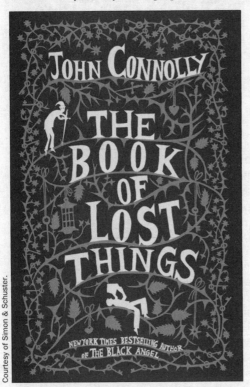

Courtesy of Simon & Schuster.

Yet it seems to me that crime fiction and supernatural fiction have the same basis: a fear of disorder, of chaos. Of what happens if you stray from the path, or what happens if something strays from the forest into *your* path. The idea that you could be confronted by a type of evil—whether that's criminal evil or supernatural evil—that will just completely distort the path of your life.

I think, at some elemental level, that's the appeal of the serial killer. It is the equivalent of the boogieman—this thing that comes out of the forest, this implacable evil that can't be reasoned with. In the supernatural novel, the entity has no empathy because it is from outside human experience. In the serial-killer novel, it is a human being without empathy.

Professionals in psychiatry and psychology [have frequently told me] that evil is the absence of empathy. The inability or the reluctance to accept that people suffer as you do. And we are curious about the monstrous—about that thing that seems beyond our camp.

Unusual historical locations, artifacts and incidents have been important to your novels (e.g., the Sedlec Ossuary, the Maine religious cult in *The Killing Kind*). Do you keep a file of anomalies and enigmas?

Usually, I trip over them by accident. While I do have files in my office, once I put something in the file I tend to forget about it.

With *The Killing Kind*, I wanted to write about religious obsession. Since I wrote about Maine, I thought I'd look and see if there was a little bit of religious history in Maine. I found this wonderful paper written in the 1920s. It turned out that Maine was a hotbed of religious lunacy for pretty much its entire history! So it was a coincidence and nothing more: I had this idea about religious history, and it turned out that the history of Maine suited it.

I don't think Maine is unique in that way—if you begin delving into the history of a state or a place . . . it's not just that people are curious: People are odd! So I've gotten used to having an idea and then trying to tinker around in history and see if there's something there.

Regarding writing logistics—do you have a standard office space?

I have an office. No music—no distractions of any kind. A place where I write from 9 to 2 pretty much every working day. I might do a little bit more in the late afternoon or early evening.

Sometimes, after a glass of wine, I think I'm being really witty and I go upstairs and write some dialogue. Sometimes it works . . . mostly, it doesn't: I wake up the next morning and look at what I wrote and say, "God, you must be an ass when you're drunk."

That next morning, do you dive into something you thought about at the very end of your previous session, or do you have to review and see where you were leading up to . . .?

No, I never read back over anything I've done. When I wrote my first book, I spent about six months trying to get the prologue perfect—and it was never going to be. It took me all that time to realize that this wasn't the way to write for me. Because I'm quite obsessive about it—I go over things again and again. It was like getting trapped in a cul de sac.

So now I don't look back—I can't do it. Because I know it's not right. If I were to read it again, I wouldn't make any progress. I'd feel that I had to get that part *just right*. I don't mind going back over stuff again and again—as long as I do it in progression and don't get caught up in any one thing.

I set myself a very easily attainable target: a thousand words a day. Sometimes I can get my thousand words done in an hour. Other times, I'll slog through two, three, four hours of sweating it out—and I'll think it's rubbish. But I still won't go back over it again. It goes to one side and I move on.

Does Charlie Parker ever show up when you're writing about other characters?

I suppose, like most writers, I have a default narrative voice. Which is one of the reasons why, when I was doing *The Book of Lost Things*, it was set in England—almost to force myself not to fall into that American rhythm that I have. It was important for that book to be entirely different. And the *Nocturnes* stories were part of an experiment with that: A lot of those stories are set in a kind of English never-never land of the 1930s, because I wanted to see if I could carry that off.

The world of those stories seems to have picked up a lot from M.R. James.

James had a huge influence on me. None of the *Nocturnes* stories are very original—they are part of a tradition that I think is in danger of being lost. That classic ghost story tradition is largely English, and so the tone has to be English and the setting is going to have to be English, as well.

My fans may not agree—and neither would my editor or my agent—but there's always been a progression in my books. What usually happened in a novel was developed in the novel that came after. So, you know, *Nocturnes* was quite clearly a dry run for *The Book of Lost Things*.

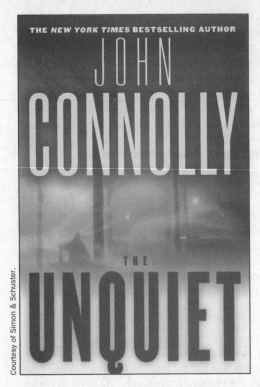

Courtesy of Simon & Schuster.

You build—and you learn by trying new things. The short stories are a way of doing it. My agent said, "Your books are doing pretty well, you've earned a certain amount of freedom now . . . but you have to be careful not to do *little* things." What he meant, I think, was the short stories—it's the commercial kiss of death. But if I hadn't done *Nocturnes*, I probably wouldn't have been able to do *Book of Lost Things*. I wouldn't have been able to do *The Unquiet*, the Parker novel that develops from one of the stories in *Nocturnes*. Everything is done for a purpose—even if it seems like a side-wise step, and commercially you're sacrificing sales and it looks bad on your record with the chain stores.

But you can't look at your sales. Walt Disney once said, "I make movies so I can make more movies." Yes, you want to write books that sell . . . so you can continue writing books. I *like* being published. I *like* that people read what I do. But I don't want to hear what I should write—that's not going to be helpful to me. And, to be fair, by the time that a book has hit the shelves, I've written the next book anyway. If it tanks, it's too late. I've already written the next thing that I'm going to do—and it's good to work that way.

Your short-story collection was different from those of many authors in that a lot of it was written all at one time, and written with intent for radio readings.
The BBC came to me and said, "What would you like to do?" I think they were thinking of TV scripts or short movies. My immediate reaction was that I wanted to write for the radio—I wanted to write a series of short stories. Because I love that tradition of James sitting his students down and telling them a story. They weren't written down, originally—they were *told*. It was this tradition that James had established, where he would tell a new ghost story every Christmas.

My stories went on the radio and people seemed to like them. The producer said, "Would you consider doing more?" and I said, "I want to do ghost stories that are interlinked. I want stories that echo each other," and I took a year out from writing novels. It was desperately hard work—and I'll never do it again! It was like writing a mini-novel every time. It's very difficult to keep 15 or 16 separate entities in your mind at once. But the discipline of it was good.

How many things do you have going in your mind right now?
One. And when it's in my head, I don't get very far with it. There are writers who can plan out almost entire novels in their minds. I tend to keep going over the same two or three images until I know what—probably—the first chapter is about. And vaguely, the second chapter.

Not a planner . . . so you don't use software, charts . . .?

If I planned out a book, I wouldn't write it. I'd be bored. When I write a novel, it's like reading it for the first time. It's one of the nice things about it—that you're surprised about what's sitting in your subconscious.

I know, now, that's how I write. And the book will come out, it'll develop. I was accused once of 'pinball plotting,' but it never seemed like that to me. It was actually that each thousand words seemed to lay possibilities for the next thousand words—rather than knowing you've got five incidents and you've got to try to link them all.

For Further Reading

In addition to the books mentioned in this article, John Connolly also has written*:

- *Dark Hollow* (2002)
- *The White Road* (2004)
- *Bad Men* (2005)

Mentioned in interview:

- *The Unquiet* (2007)
- *The Killing Kind* (2003)
- *Nocturnes* (2006)
- *The Book of Lost Things* (2006)
- *The Black Angel* (2005)
- *Every Dead Thing* (1999)

*All dates for Simon & Schuster/Atria printings.

Brian Freeman

Living in the Gray

© Marcia Freeman

by Lauren Mosko

While some writers make military weaponry or crime scene investigation the focal point of their mystery novels, Brian Freeman chooses to plumb the darker recesses of the human heart and the murky corners of morality for the questions that drive his fiction. His first two novels have been acclaimed for their breathtaking, harrowing twists and turns, but Freeman has consistently taken care to make his characters every bit as intricate as his plots.

"My books always have solutions, but I hope they don't necessarily have easy answers. I think that if everything about the conflict is black and white, then the plot and characters become pretty two-dimensional," Freeman says. "I try to write books where the villains aren't all evil and the heroes aren't all good and strong. They all sort of live in that gray area, and I think that makes it more dramatic."

In his debut novel, *IMMORAL* (St. Martin's Minotaur, 2005), intense but good-natured lieutenant Jonathan Stride is tasked with hunting down a serial killer when two local teenage girls—all-American Kerry McGrath and dark, seductive Rachel Deese—vanish from the streets of Duluth, Minnesota. But the more Stride uncovers about the latter girl, the more complicated the case becomes, both professionally and personally. In the sequel, *STRIPPED* (2006), Stride has relocated to Las Vegas, where a string of murders—including the shooting of a celebrity millionaire's son and the hit-and-run death of a 10-year-old boy—seem to be puppeted by a hand from the past. As Stride becomes more involved in the investigation and the city's perilous web of cut-throat ambition, revenge, and divided loyalties, he is forced to question his own loyalties—to Sin City and to his new love interest, detective Serena Dial.

"I want readers to realize that all these characters face difficult choices and to ask themselves how they would react if they were in the same circumstance and what they would do if they were tempted to cross some terrible lines," Freeman adds.

In this interview, Freeman discusses his own writerly choices; his novels, past and future; as well as his international publishing experiences.

In your video interview with the Literary Guild, you said the point of the architecture of *IMMORAL* was to keep the reader guessing and to keep you one step ahead. Do you know who committed the murders when you start your books, or are you along for the ride as you write, as well?

When I begin the actual drafting process for the book, I have a pretty detailed outline of the plot at that point. The different threads of the back story in my novels are usually so complex

---

LAUREN MOSKO is the editor of *Novel & Short Story Writer's Market*.

that I have to map it out like a puzzle before I start. But even so, the reality is that the books and the characters often take on a life of their own as I write. Even with very complex plots, they have a way of evolving and going in new directions during the writing process. There are some major characters in both books I think people would be surprised weren't actually in the original plan until I started writing.

Can you share one with us?

One of the popular characters from *IMMORAL* is Stride's partner Maggie, and in the very first outline of the book I pulled together, Maggie wasn't in there. As I was working on Stride, however, I knew he needed a foil for his seriousness and his passion and I wrote Maggie in. In the process of writing, she demanded a larger role in the book and so became a much more significant character than I originally envisioned.

Courtesy of St. Martin's.

How long does it take you to write such a detailed outline?

The process of mapping out the book usually takes three to four months. I spend a lot of time thinking and playing out different ideas in my head and jotting a lot of notes that don't seem to go anywhere. Eventually I reach a point where I feel like I've got enough of the big picture in my head that I can start thinking about how it might go chapter by chapter. Once I've done the first round, I go back and start tweaking it from there.

You said, "the past has its hands around the throat of the present" in both your novels. Why is this a compelling idea for you?

I love the idea that the past is never quite dead, that sin and mysteries from years ago can come back to life. I think it's so compelling because writers and readers hate to let go of the past. They like to think it's still within our grasp. Of course, the trouble is, be careful what you wish for. Whenever the past rears its head in mysteries, it means bad things happening. Oh, and the past is just as much a part of my third and fourth books as it was books one and two.

IMMORAL's victim/villain, Rachel, seems so purely evil (especially after reading the bonus scenes on your Web site)—and several other characters think of her that way. Does she have a redeeming quality for you?

I'll start by saying that my male readers have no trouble seeing Rachel's redeeming qualities. [Laughs] She's one of those women who can seduce a man even when he knows perfectly well that it is bound to end in disaster. I've even found that quite a few women readers like Rachel. For as evil as she is, she has such a life force about her. She may be immoral, but she gets to do things people might long to do in the darker parts of their soul. And she is bent on revenge and she gets her revenge, even if it's at a terrible price.

She is a very sympathetic character, as rotten as she is. Were you crafting her very consciously?

Yes. I wanted a character who would be in many ways thoroughly despicable but also someone who had had her own significant challenges growing up and had never given up on herself. For as evil as many of her choices turned out to be, she didn't simply break down or accept her suffering. She turned around and insisted that she was going to get what she wanted out of life. So there's something twisted and admirable in that. I find it interesting that I've actually had some comments from teenage girls who've read the book and who find Rachel to be an empowering figure. Again, for as immoral as she is, she wraps all the adults in the book around her finger.

Can you offer some advice for writers who are trying to learn to craft in this gray area of morality—learning not to make their characters so stereotypical?

I think the most important thing is to try to understand why people do the things they do. When you're looking at people who actually commit crimes, try to put yourself inside their head and understand what is driving them and what is going on in their backgrounds and in their minds that would lead them across that line. And do the same for the people on the other side of that line, who are trying to track down these people. Try to think through the source of mental stresses that go along with that process—what it does to your family life and your mind when you're exposed to some of the darkest sides of the human soul on a daily basis. The more you think about it, the more you realize that there is good and evil, but rarely does one person embody only one side or the other—that's life. You want your books to carry the same feeling.

Speaking of dark motivators, desire is hands-down the greatest motivator of action in your books, and you don't shy away from explicit love scenes. What do you think this sexual dimension adds to your work?

Well, you know what they say, write what you know. [Laughs] Seriously, I do think desire is one of the strongest motivators, and desire often tempts ordinary people across some very dark lines. So the crimes in my books have a sexual dimension to them, and even the heroes in the books often struggle with their sexuality and with sexual issues. I hope that's part of what makes them real and what makes people relate to them. I don't write about military technology or forensic minutiae; there are plenty of writers who tell wonderful stories about that sort of thing, but I prefer to deal with raw human emotion—stories and plots that really arise out of who the characters are and what drives them.

Your novels are full of wonderful, fresh description like, "At 5 in the morning, the parking lot was a vast, empty stretch of pavement, just a handful of lonely cars spread out like pins on a map." Does imagery like this just come to you? Do you have any advice for writers on conceiving original metaphor?

Sometimes the images come easily. But a lot times you really have to spend time visualizing places and people and thinking through how you can make the two-dimensional become three-dimensional. Writers like James Lee Burke and John Connolly do that so well—their writing is just so astoundingly visual—but that's one of the hardest challenges writers face during the editing process: to wring out the tired phrases and the stale images. For me there's nothing to do but go paragraph by paragraph, word by word. Always ask yourself if you've truly captured what it is you're trying to describe. Until you see high-definition television, you don't realize how fuzzy your current television screen is. And every writer should always be striving to make sure their words are in HDTV.

At one point in _STRIPPED_, you wrote, "Violence was part of the city . . . . Part of the immoral world." Both Duluth and Vegas have "immoral" qualities but for different reasons—Duluth because its forests and lakes seem wild and amoral like the natural world, and Vegas because it's known as the town where anything goes. Is that why you chose these locations?

I should say that it's interesting that you can get almost nowhere on a nonstop flight from Duluth, but you _can_ get to Las Vegas from there. [Laughs] So even without me, there's some strange symbiotic relationship between the cities.

I think they're kind of mirror images of each other in their extremes. One is very frigid and forbidding, the other is arid and burning hot. One sexually liberated, one sexually closed off. I think they reflect each other. In _STRIPPED_, even though it's set in Las Vegas, I think Duluth casts a pretty long shadow over the book through the character Stride. You wind up seeing Vegas through Duluth eyes. And then when Serena goes to Duluth, it's the reverse. You wind up seeing Duluth through someone who's lived in a very different area. In book three, Serena talks about Vegas being like a snake and Duluth being like a bear. I think that's the kind of contrast you have set up between the cities.

Setting can easily be considered a character in your novels. Since you live in Minnesota, I imagine most of the detail of scene and tone for _IMMORAL_ came from experience. How much (and what kind of) research on Las Vegas did you have to do to make _STRIPPED_ so vivid?

Research in Vegas—that's really hard work. [Laughs] I was mostly there in July when it was 118 degrees. I spent a lot of time in the library pouring over old newspapers and magazines from the Rat Pack days. Even though the book is set in the present, I wanted the recollections of the characters to carry authenticity. Other than the prologue, the only place that you see old Las Vegas is when other people are talking about it, and so I really needed to have those memories carry both the glamour and the seediness of that era, as well as the yearning and nostalgia of the older characters for what they had lost back in that era. I really needed to understand what it was like living back then, and you can pick up so much just by reading those old newspapers and seeing what was going on in the world and what people were seeing on a day to day basis through that. I also scouted out setting for scenes in the novel, just like you would for a movie. Even when I invent places, I want them to feel as real as the settings you'd find if you actually drove down the Strip.

I read that the idea for _IMMORAL_ came from an unsolved case in Minnesota and a trial without a body. Where did the idea for _STRIPPED_ come from?

In some instances, the plot will be triggered by a crime I read about and I'll start playing with it in my head, but not in the case of _STRIPPED_. That really just popped into my

STRIPPED

R.I.P!

BRIAN FREEMAN

A NOVEL BY THE BESTSELLING AUTHOR OF _IMMORAL_

Courtesy of St. Martin's.

head. I think it was the ambiance of Las Vegas that did that for me. I think when you're there it has the flavor of everything that's gone on in the past. And even though the past is long gone and torn down and imploded in Las Vegas, I think it still resonates throughout the present there. The more time I spent there, the more I really felt this place was ripe for a novel where you see that the past is still alive and ripples through in some terrible crimes going on today.

The theme of the whole city is in line with the theme of your first book, so it's almost a natural fit.

Exactly. People sort of wonder—well Duluth and Las Vegas, how does that fit, but once they see that and read *STRIPPED*, it seems to flow so naturally.

Was any of the crime in *STRIPPED* taken from the kernel of a true crime like *IMMORAL* was?

No, it really was not. I pulled all those ideas out of my imagination, whereas in *IMMORAL*, the kernel really was based on a true crime that happened in Minnesota about 10 years ago. That was a situation where the concept of the crime intrigued me and then I started changing the factors around and playing with them and putting in new twists and turns and letting the plot emerge from there.

Book four is based in part on a murder that took place a number of years ago on the East Coast. Again, I started playing with the details and applying them to the settings and characters in Minnesota. Book three, however, is like *STRIPPED* and simply came out of the dark recesses of my mind.

Since it's come up twice now, can you give us a little scoop on third book?

STALKED is due out early in 2008. Stride and Serena are back in Duluth, and Maggie—who a lot of readers missed from *IMMORAL*—is back, too. As for the plot, I'll only say that Maggie's marriage does not last long or end well.

Are Stride and Dial sticking around for book four?

Yes, book four will be part of the same series.

I moderated a panel at a literary festival last fall during which two acclaimed mystery/thriller writers got into a huge argument over whether plot or character is the most essential element of fiction. Where do you weigh in on the conversation?

That's like debating whether your arms are more important than your legs. It just seems utterly pointless. You need to pay attention to both. I've read very lyrical writers who have beautifully drawn characters but whose pacing is glacial. And I've read writers who write page-turners but they have cardboard characters. So the ideal, and what I aspire to, is to write page-turners that will also linger in your mind because of who the characters are. If you can do that, then I think you have something really special.

You've been practicing the craft of the novel since sixth grade, with five attempts before *IMMORAL*. At what point did you begin actively pursuing publication? Seventh grade?

That's probably true. [Laughs] I'm pretty sure I was sending stories to *The New Yorker* when I was 12. [Laughs] I pursued publication off and on for a very long time. Like a lot of writers, I knew nothing about the business side of the industry. I was really laboring under the foolish belief that if you write a book that's good enough, it will sell itself. Nothing could be further from the truth. You have to market yourself—to agents, publishers, booksellers, readers—and if you're serious about writing for a living then you have to make it your career and treat it like what it is, which is a business.

Fortunately, I spent a lot of time in the business world doing marketing and public relations and so I learned a lot of lessons that helped me break through and helped me build the right relationships. But it was a lot of work. If you think your career means spending your days writing and letting other people worry about the details, then I think you're going to be unhappy with the results.

And I had a lot to learn about storytelling. I remember James Michener, who actually published his first book at the same age I did, saying that you shouldn't try to publish seriously until you've written about a million words, and I must have been pretty close to that when I broke through. I could put the words together; I just needed a lot more life experience to make the plots and the characters work.

Can you give me some examples of lessons you learned from your marketing and public relations experience that applied to the business side of your writing life?

I think a lot of aspiring writers don't understand just how relationship-driven the industry is. That may be somewhat counterintuitive because you think it's a consumer business and writers are selling books to individuals all over the country and all over the world. And yet the reality is that the publishing industry is pretty small and most people know each other and it's intensely competitive. The way to break through is to build relationships and find people that can help you get your foot in the door.

I began to look at first novels and I would read the acknowledgements page. I'd read the book and say, "I think my work is every bit as good as this; what is this person doing that I'm not that this book got published?" Almost every time when you read the acknowledgements, you see there was some key relationship that helped the person get in the door and helped introduce them to an agent or publisher who would read their work and take them seriously. You have to very thoughtfully go about building those kinds of relationships and looking for people that can help you make the right connections in the industry. That doesn't always come easily. It often means putting yourself out on the line and putting your ego out on the line in a way that may not be very comfortable, but there's no other way to get it done.

I took a job in 1997 as director of marketing at an international law firm and when I was taking that job, I remember specifically commenting to my wife that one of the advantages was that it would give me the opportunity to meet a lot of people who would have connections in the publishing industry and may be able to help me when I was ready to put a new book out there. In fact, that's very much the way it worked out. A lawyer I worked with extensively in the firm's London office turned out to have a relationship with an agent at one of London's largest literary agencies and he made an introduction for me and got me around the Praetorian guard of people who read the queries that come in. The agent herself read the book, and a week later, she wrote to me and said she couldn't put it down, stayed up until one in the morning reading it, and had already pitched it in the UK as the next Harlan Coben—"Call me immediately." [Laughs] And after I peeled myself off the ceiling, we were off to the races. It can happen quickly even after 20 years of dismal failure, but it does take a thoughtful process of getting to know people who can be helpful to you.

What was it like having an agent in London? How much did it help you? Was it ever frustrating?

I think it has been a tremendous advantage. I love the people in New York, but I do think the New York wing of the publishing industry can sometimes get a little U.S.-centric. Sometimes they don't really look outside the borders. From the beginning, my agent in London saw this as an international project; the U.S. was an important deal, but it was not the only deal. She marched right into the process of making European and Asian sales right after she got the U.K. and U.S. deals done, and we've now sold IMMORAL in 16 languages. I don't think that would have happened—and certainly not nearly as quickly—if I didn't have a primary agent in London. I think they just approach the business from a more international perspective, being outside the US.

Has it ever caused any problems? No. These days international communication is so seamless that I don't notice distance at all. But I must say that no matter how seamless electronic communication is, there's still no substitute for face to face. I make it a point to meet and build personal relationships with all my editors. I have managed to meet nearly all of my overseas editors at this point. You don't "need" to do it, but I think it adds tremendous value to a relationship when you've actually had a chance to shake their hand and talk to them face to face about the book.

How does it feel to see your book in translation? With the different covers . . .

All my life I was waiting for that moment when I would hold my published book in my hands for the first time. I certainly never gave any thought to the idea that it might be in a different language. And that's exactly what happened. The very first time I got my book in my hands, it was actually in Dutch. The Dutch and the Spanish came out with IMMORAL before the U.S. and U.K. did, so I now tell people they can read the book in the original Dutch. [Laughs]

Are you conscious of having readers all over the world as you write now? Will it influence future books?

Sure. I'm very conscious of the international side of things at this point. I receive e-mails from readers all over the world and often in foreign languages. It's amazing what a broadening experience it is. I got an e-mail not long ago from a British soldier serving in Afghanistan, and that kind of e-mail is a very humbling experience because you get a sense of the work that people have to do in this world. It was also astonishingly gratifying because it really brought home to me the difference writers can make in lifting people out of their daily surroundings and for a while transporting them to another world.

Those kinds of connections with people around the world mean a lot to me, and I think what it does in terms of my writing is that I become more conscious of the fact that I'm not just selling to an American audience. I'm conscious of the language and images that I'm using, and for me, my approach works well for that audience because I'm not just trying to focus on political thrillers or things that are unique to the U.S. I try to come up with plots and characters that are universal, where the drivers and motivators are emotionally based, and those are things anyone can relate to anywhere in the world. They don't have to be American.

You said that being nominated for the Edgar for Best First Novel was really the beginning of your journey to continually challenge and raise the bar for your own work. What challenges do you have in store for yourself?

In the end, the biggest challenge is to write a book every time where readers will say, "That's his best one yet." So I do all this for the readers. I want to give them the same thoughtful entertainment that so many other writers have given me over the years. That's my challenge—to keep raising the bar each time so that a reader says, "How can he top that last one?" Then they read it and say, "Well, he did."

Is this a source of more anxiety or excitement for you?
A little of both, but the reality is I've worked my whole life to get to the point where I have this amazing opportunity to pursue this as a career, so I can't let the anxiety stop me. I'm so excited about having the chance to sit down and craft books. Even when I'm starting the outline process for number four, I'm sitting up at night thinking about what I'm going to do in book five and book six and book seven.

For more information about Brian Freeman and his novels, visit *www.bfreemanbooks.com*.

Rochelle Krich

Making the Unknown Familiar

Courtesy of the author.

by Rachel A. McDonald

Rochelle Krich takes something few people know much about—Orthodox Judaism—and combines it with the familiar—mystery novels—to create new and rich experiences for her readers. Giving her characters various connections to the Orthodox Jewish community and culture allows Krich to look at larger themes and issues in a different context, all while giving the reader a thrilling mystery.

An Orthodox Jew herself, Krich isn't what you think of when people mention mystery writers. Krich describes herself as "much like a stereotypical Jewish mother because I worry all the time. I suppose that comes in handy when you're detecting." A mother of six and daughter of Holocaust survivors, Krich has put her worries and life experiences to good use in her writing.

And that writing has been good indeed. Krich's novel *Grave Endings* (Ballantine, 2004)—starring true-crime writer Molly Blume—won the Mary Higgins Clark Award and the Left Coast Crime Calavera Award, and her latest book, *Now You See Me* (2005), was nominated for the Barry Award.

In addition to writing, Krich keeps herself highly active in the mystery writing community. She is the National President of Sisters in Crime and a member of Mystery Writers of America the American Crime Writers League.

While not all of her novels have the Jewish connection, all of them are engaging mysteries that thrill readers. Here, Krich discusses her world of mystery writing and gives some tips for fellow writers.

How did you get interested in writing mysteries?

I can't recall a time when mysteries weren't my passion. As a child and adolescent, I always went straight to the mystery section in the library. I loved the puzzle, the game. I loved trying to play along with the detective and figure out whodunit.

As an adult reader, I still love the puzzle in mysteries, and I appreciate the gratification that comes with finding a world restored to order, with seeing justice served. As the writer, I get to put the bad guys away. More and more, as a reader and writer, I find myself interested not only in the whodunit, but also in the *why*dunit. I fantasize that if we could solve the mystery of the whydunit, we could, in some measure, prevent the whodunit.

RACHEL A. McDONALD is a recent graduate of the University of Cincinnati where she received a MA in Comparative Literature, Professional Writing and Editing. She has served as the prose editor for *Ellipsis . . . Literature and Art* and interned with Writer's Digest Books.

You are an active member of Sisters in Crime and several other organizations. How has that helped you as a writer? Would you recommend new writers get involved in similar organizations?

I'll answer the last part of your question first: Absolutely!

I'm the national Sisters in Crime president, but 20 years ago, when a parent of one of my students suggested that I attend a Sisters in Crime meeting, I'd never heard of the organization. I attended a meeting, became a member, and found myself part of a group that offered me advice, networking opportunities, and most importantly, long-lasting friendships. Through Sisters in Crime I learned how to set up book signings and do PR, and I joined a critique group that provided me with valuable feedback and taught me to relax my defenses and learn how to accept constructive criticism. I'm also a member of Mystery Writers of America (I served on the national board) and the American Crime Writers League. Writing is a solitary occupation. Belonging to these organizations, all of which have newsletters and online listservs where members can exchange ideas and concerns, makes me feel that I'm part of a close knit, supportive community.

In a few interviews, you have spoken about the theme or message that your novels portray. Which comes first, the theme or the plot? Or are they concurrent?

I find myself drawn to social issues, and my mind invariably comes up with the "what if." I've written about domestic violence, elder abuse, Holocaust denial, date rape, infertility. In my current Molly Blume mystery, *Now You See Me . . .*, I write about teens at risk, and focus on a high-school senior who runs off with a man she meets in an Internet chat room. (I wrote the book before MySpace and other similar online sites began to make almost daily headlines.) I'm interested in exploring these issues and others and taking the reader along on the journey. I don't promise answers to these often complex issues—often, there aren't any.

A Novel of Suspense

NOW YOU SEE ME...

Nationally bestselling author of *Grave Endings*
ROCHELLE KRICH
Winner of the Mary Higgins Clark Award

Courtesy of Ballantine.

One of the marvelous things about your novels is how you integrate the Jewish culture into the mystery. What advice can you give to new writers who want to do the same thing with their own culture?

Readers, I have found, enjoy being allowed to peek into a world that is exotic and unfamiliar to them. I certainly do. As the writer, you have to be careful not to overwhelm your story with details of your culture. You also have to make sure that, while the characters you have created are unique *because* of their culture, they possess universal qualities and face challenges with which readers can identify. I get mail from many readers unfamiliar with Judaism who enjoy learning about Jewish life and culture through my protagonists. They

Courtesy of Ballantine.

tell me they can relate to Molly Blume, and to Jessie Drake. (Jessie is an LAPD homicide detective who is exploring her newly discovered Judaism.)

What kind of guidelines do you have for yourself regarding how much detail to go into when you are explaining things like Sabbath day observances and the prohibition against married women having their hair uncovered? How do you know when you're giving too much background, or not enough?

You *don't* know, really—not when you're writing your first draft, and sometimes not until your agent or editor gives you an objective response to the book. Or until a reviewer tells you! My guidelines are simple: I use the cultural details to enhance character, setting, and plot, and I'm gratified by readers who tell me they appreciate the seamless way I blend Judaism into my mysteries.

You write both series and stand-alone novels. What are some of the joys and difficulties in writing these differing types of books? Are any specific to the mystery genre?

Writing the series provides a comfort level that the stand-alone doesn't provide: Although the plot is unique (I hope!) and the characters are specific to that novel (the victim, victim's family, the suspects), the protagonist and the other people I introduced in the first book in the series—family, friends, people with whom the protagonist connects professionally and romantically—are all continuing. Writing the subsequent books is like revisiting family. I know the characters and can slip easily into their "voices." The challenge is to maintain the freshness of the characters, to allow the characters— particularly the protagonist—to grow in ways that aren't contrived, and to sustain your interest in your characters. If I'm not interested in them, the reader definitely won't be.

Writing a stand-alone allows me to create a new world with a brand new set of characters. I'm not limited by the choices I've made for my series character—age, physical description, profession, family and romantic relationships, psychological makeup, worldview. I'm beginning with a blank page. On the other hand, that blank page can be daunting, and it takes a while to understand my protagonist and the other characters, to get their "voices."

In *Now You See Me . . .*, Jessie Drake and Molly Blume, the main characters in two of your series, met. Are you going to keep developing that friendship? Will we get to see a book where the two of them work closely together on a case?

I'd like to develop the friendship, and down the road I'd like to write a mystery where they collaborate. They seem like a natural pair: Jessie is a homicide detective. Molly is a true-crime writer who collects data from the police for a weekly crime sheet column. It's surprising they didn't meet before!

Have you ever considered, or tried, writing in a different genre?

Aside from a number of articles I've written for magazines and newspapers, I haven't tried writing in a different genre. My daughters are pushing me to write a screenplay—a romantic comedy. That's my second love.

What's in the works right now?

I'm working on a stand-alone, *Mind Games*. It's a thriller about a widow who places herself and her young daughter in grave danger when she tries to prove that her psychiatrist husband's apparent suicide was really murder.

Books by Rochelle Krich

Molly Blume mysteries

- *Now You See Me . . .* (Ballantine, 2005)
- *Blues in the Night* (Ballantine, 2002)
- *Dream House* (Ballantine, 2003)
- *Grave Endings* (Ballantine, 2004)

Jessie Drake mysteries

- *Fair Game* (Mysterious Press, 1993)
- *Angel of Death* (Mysterious Press, 1994)
- *Blood Money* (Avon, 1999)
- *Dead Air* (William Morrow & Co., 2000)
- *Shadows of Sin* (William Morrow & Co., 2001)

Stand-alone mysteries

- *Where's Mommy Now?* (1990)
- *Till Death Do Us Part*, (Avon Books, 1992)
- *Nowhere to Run*, (Avon Books, 1994)
- *Speak No Evil*, (Mysterious Books, 1996)
- *Fertile Ground*, (William Morrow & Co., 1998)

FOR MYSTERY WRITERS

Resources

Where to Look for More Information

Below is a list of invaluable resources specifically for mystery writers. To order any of the Writer's Digest Books titles or to get a consumer book catalog, call (800)448-0915. You may also order Writer's Digest Books selections through www.fwbookstore .com, Amazon.com, or www.barnesandnoble.com.

MAGAZINES:

- *Mystery Readers Journal*, Mystery Readers International, P.O. Box 8116, Berkeley CA 94707. Web site: www.mysteryreaders.org.
- *Mystery News*, Black Raven Press, PMB 152, 105 E. Townline Rd., Vernon Hills IL 60061-1424. Web site: www.blackravenpress.com.
- *Mystery Scene*, 331 W. 57th St., Suite 148, New York NY 10019. Web site: www.mysteryscenemag.com.

BOOKS:
Howdunit series (Writer's Digest Books):
- *Modus Operandi: A Writer's Guide to How Criminals Work*, by Mauro V. Corvasce and Joseph R. Paglino
- *Missing Persons: A Writer's Guide to Finding the Lost, the Abducted and the Escaped*, by Fay Faron
- *Book of Poisons*, by Serita Stevens and Anne Bannon
- *Scene of the Crime: A Writer's Guide to Crime Scene Investigation*, by Anne Wingate, Ph.D.
- *Book of Police Procedure and Investigation*, by Lee Lofland

Other Writer's Digest Books for mystery writers:
- *The Criminal Mind, A Writer's Guide to Forensic Psychology*, by Katherine Ramsland
- *Writing Mysteries: A Handbook by the Mystery Writers of America*, edited by Sue Grafton
- *Writing and Selling Your Mystery Novel: How to Knock 'em Dead With Style*, by Hallie Ephron
- *You Can Write a Mystery*, by Gillian Roberts

ORGANIZATIONS & ONLINE:
- Crime Writers of Canada. Web site: www.crimewriterscanada.com.
- Crime Writers' Association. Web site: www.thecwa.co.uk.
- Mystery Writers of America, 17 E. 47th St., 6th Floor, New York NY 10017. Web site: www.mysterywriters.org

- The Private Eye Writers of America, 4342 Forest DeVille Dr., Apt. H, St. Louis MO 63129. Web site: http://hometown.aol.com/rrandisi/myhomepage/writing.html
- Sisters in Crime, P.O. Box 442124, Lawrence KS 66044-8933. Web site: www.sistersincrime.org
- Writer's Market Online. Web site: www.writersmarket.com.
- Writer's Digest Online. Web site: www.writersdigest.com.

Cheryl Holt

*Proving Success Can Happen
at Any Age*

© Kristin Zabawa Photography

by Deborah Bouziden

Cheryl Holt is an author who has proven anyone can become a success in publishing, at any time, at any age. All one needs is a will and desire. Holt, an attorney and one-time city prosecutor, had both of her children late in life. She began her writing career when she turned 40 after the birth of her second child.

"I thought, since I'm going to be home and have all this 'free time'," Holt says, "this is the perfect opportunity to write that book I've always talked about. I was so clueless about what it took to write a novel, but more importantly, about how one sold it and established oneself in the industry."

Her first try, in her own words, was awful. However, she was undaunted and, with her usual enthusiasm, called a New York agent.

"I had written a pitiful attempt at a suspense novel and figured I had to find an agent because 'that's what writers do.' I *did* find an agent and phoned her," Holt recalls. "After I was in to my pitch about 30 seconds, she could tell I was an idiot and cut me off. I've never forgotten what she said though. *'You sound like a fairly intelligent person and you have the sort of work background editors look for in a novelist, but you don't have any idea what you're doing. Go read 50 novels that were published in the past year, rewrite your manuscript, and call me back.'* "

Holt was offended at first, but after she "stewed" for a few days, she calmed down enough to think that perhaps the agent was right. She hadn't read as much as she had in the past.

"I started reading novels and realized I *didn't* have a clue—my career theme—as to what was selling or how good my writing technique would have to be before I could sell to a New York publisher," she says.

Holt set to work. She started reading and, while she always thought she would write suspense, realized she enjoyed historical romances. So she decided to write one. At age 44, her first historical romance, *The Way of the Heart*, sold to Zebra. The editor who acquired it told her it was the best manuscript she'd found in her slush pile in years.

Holt's story could very well end there with 'and the rest is history', but her career didn't go as planned. After five books with Zebra, they let her go saying "she wouldn't make it in the business." But someone else thought differently.

"My agent at the time convinced me the new trend would be erotic romances and he suggested I try one," Holt said. "I wrote a synopsis, chapters, and we put it out on the market."

DEBORAH BOUZIDEN has been writing and publishing fiction and nonfiction, books and articles, since 1985. To discover more about her work visit her Web site at www.deborahbouziden.com.

Love Lessons was Holt's sixth novel and her first erotic story for St. Martin's. After writing 12 novels for the house, St. Martin's can't seem to get enough of Holt's books, and in 2006, the author signed contracts for at least three more.

Holt continues to find her books on the *USA Today* Bestseller's List and Waldenbooks Romance bestseller list. She won the *Romantic Times* Career Achievement Award for Best Historical Storyteller in 2005, and in February 2006 in a *Romantic Times* article titled, "Top 25 Erotic Writers of All Time," Holt was called a "modern erotic phenom" and named a "Master of Erotica."

Now that Holt is a mega-star in romance publishing, what does she say about her late start?

"I don't think I could have written a novel at age 20 or 25 or even into my 30s. It simply takes a lot of focus, attention, and work. I don't think I was ready until I was older. It wasn't that I felt I had more to say at age 40; it was simply that I could finally sit down at the keyboard and put words together.

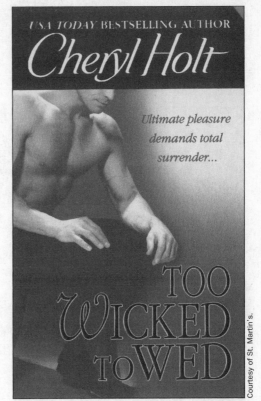

Courtesy of St. Martin's.

Over the years you've had many professional careers like schoolteacher, lobbyist, bartender, and attorney. How does that experience figure into your novels?

I've never felt they had any effect on my writing career. The process of writing commercial fiction is so different from anything I'd ever done before that there was very little crossover from any employment I'd had.

One real benefit out of my past was I was quite a gifted pianist as a child. I received a bachelor's degree in piano and organ performance as a young adult. So I spent many, many years sitting at a keyboard.

Writing novels is exactly the same cognitive process as playing the piano. Art starts in your head and flows out through your fingers onto a keyboard.

You have been called the "queen of erotica" and your stories are very explicit. How do you decide what to write so your plot moves along?

The pressure to create interesting stories with intriguing characters is enormous, so as I went along, I adopted a few tactics that seem to work and help me drive the story.

Because they're marketed as erotic books, I have to keep the sexual tenor very high. My editor expects something sexual to happen on the first page, and to continue happening till the very last. During our initial years of working together, we set a few standards for ourselves that make the stories hot and titillate readers in great ways. My heroines are always virgins, and we start the books that way because when she falls off her virginal pedestal, it's a long, slow and delicious plunge.

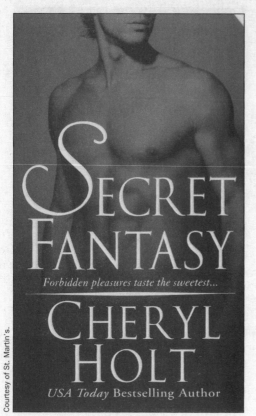

Courtesy of St. Martin's.

As time went along and I wrote more and more of these, I also changed my villains. My villains were always awful, but now, they're "sexual" villains, such as rapists or pedophiles who have evil designs on the heroine or one of her family members.

Every character is chosen for how they can drive the sexual flavor of the story. Their various sexual machinations, either for good or evil, keep the pace flying.

Because of the nature of your books, how do you keep from repeating the same things over and over again?

I try very hard to make each book very different, to make them interesting and compelling for the reader. I don't picture myself as a writer. I consider myself to be working in "sales." I'm creating a product that will entice the maximum number of people to read it, and I have to put it together so they like it and are willing to buy the next one.

I think the sex scenes end up being so different because all of my stories are very different. I try to have a hero and heroine who are extremely diverse from one that's appeared in an earlier book. The factors and stakes driving them are always very different, too, so the reasons they get together, and the "ways" they get together are always changing. I'm constantly looking for ways to keep the sexual scenes very fresh, very alive and real.

How has your writing changed over the years? What is one area of writing you have mastered?

My writing has changed in that I'm better at editing out what doesn't need to be there, which gives a better "flow" to the story. I credit my editor for cleaning me up, until it now seems I simply write "noun-verb-noun-verb" and that's it. Once, she read a finished manuscript of mine and in her editorial letter, she told me to "take out 1,000 adverbs"—which I did—and it made the flow stronger. Now, I try to write with the fewest descriptive words I can, so the text can fly along.

I leave out nearly all "backstory" and hardly ever waste paragraphs on characters' thoughts or motivations. If I do, I try not to use more than a paragraph or two. I move the story through dialogue, because it makes the story simple, fast, and exciting.

I don't feel I've mastered any area. It's a very labor-intensive process, very difficult, and it takes many years of practice before you start to get it right.

What changes do you see for the romance industry? Do you think these changes are a positive for authors?

The main trend I've seen lately is companies reprinting old (early) books from writers who are starting to get famous—rather than buying books from new writers. It is a disappointing trend. Every time a publisher reprints a novel, it takes up shelf space that a new writer will never be able to have. There are only so many spaces in the stores, and the more books that are reprinted, the less chances there are for new writers to break in. I often wonder—if I were starting out now instead of 12 years ago—how I would ever break in.

What is the most rewarding part of your job?

The coolest part of my job is that I sit in my home, write these great love stories and then a year or two later, I'll get a letter from someone who read it in Singapore, Pakistan, or South Africa. That makes all the hard work worth it.

The letter I like the most came from a male U.S. soldier serving in Iraq in '04. He was an avid reader, so he'd blazed through all the novels in the Baghdad base commissary and with no other choice left to him, he picked up one of my romances and read it. He liked it so much, he had to write and tell me. That was very cool because I'd brought him some fun and entertainment when he was so far from home, but also because he's a guy and my books are very gender specific. From the looks of the cover alone, a man would rarely be caught dead reading one, so I considered his letter to be an enormous compliment.

What advice would you give beginning or struggling writers?

I have two pieces of advice: Write all the time, and read everything you can get your hands on, especially books that have sold in the last two years.

New writers tend to think, "I'll just write a novel. How hard can that be?" The reality is writing a novel is extremely difficult. If you want to get published, you have to practice and practice, so your craft rises to the level of those who are already published.

Start reading books in the genre you want to be published in. If you're hoping to do cop dramas, then you should read every single cop drama that's published. The more you read, the better your own writing will become.

I'm sure for some new writers this sounds cold and calculated, but this is a *business*, and it's BIG business. This is commercial fiction, and if a publisher buys from you, they will expect you to make them money. You do this by writing hot, fast, great stories. If you can't give publishers fast pacing and exciting plot lines, they will look to the next person in the slush pile who can.

Beverly Bartlett

Turning a Passion Into a Plot

© Mary Ann Gerth

by Ellen Birkett Morris

Novelist Beverly Bartlett was always intimidated by the adage "Write what you know." "I feel like I've had a sort of boring life," she says. "I had a nice childhood. I've taken some nice trips. But I didn't have any fodder for dramatic material."

What Bartlett did have was an enduring obsession with Princess Diana, fueled by the royal wedding she got up at 4 a.m. to watch on television as a 14-year-old girl. Her interest grew to include other royals like the mischievous Sarah Ferguson, Duchess of York and Princess Kiko of Japan. She enjoyed reading royal biographies for an insider's look at the lives and loves of royal families and the barely hidden agendas of the authors, often former butlers or family confidants. She parlayed that interest into her first novel *Princess Izzy and The E Street Shuffle* (5 Spot/Warner), the "biography" of a princess who gleans advice about love from the lyrics of Bruce Springsteen songs. In the novel, Bartlett plays with the conventions of royal biographies, including the unreliable narrator (often armed with a hidden agenda) and the media's obsessive attention to all aspects of royal life.

"I came up with the concept way before I came up with the plot. I knew I had things to say about royal-watching and thought there would be a market for it. There were fits and starts as I actually tried to come up with a story to go with it. I didn't want it to be just Diana's story. I drew on the story of other royals and how our obsession with them reflects on us," says Bartlett.

She wrote the prologue in 1997, and continued to craft the novel on and off for a number of years between job changes, moves, and having a baby. In spring of 2003, she quit her job as a journalist with the goal of publishing the book and began writing in earnest. Working as a freelance writer by day and stealing a few hours to write at night while her husband watched the baby, Bartlett completed her first book.

A royal opportunity

During a private coaching session from romance novelist Elizabeth Beverly at the Green River Writers' Novels in Progress Workshop in 2003, Bartlett got a much-needed boost. "The most important thing I got from her was encouragement, a sense that my goal was not unrealistic and that I should keep going," she says.

ELLEN BIRKETT MORRIS has been a freelance journalist and writer for 11 years. She worked as a stringer for *The New York Times* and has contributed to dozens of publications including *Cooking Light* and *www.drkoop.com*. Her essays have appeared in six anthologies including *The Writing Group Book* (Chicago Review Press). Her fiction has been published in *Alimentum*, *Mindprints*, and www.thepedestalmagazine.com.

The following year she returned to the conference armed and ready. She expected to pitch Scott Hoffman of Folio Literary Management later that day but ended up being one of several people who took the agent to lunch. They were waiting for the car to pull up when he asked what her book was about.

"I came up with a short paragraph to describe what my book is about before I went to the conference—an elevator pitch of sorts. I'm so glad I did," she says.

Later that afternoon, Bartlett and Hoffman sat down for a formal pitch session and Bartlett presented the agent with 20 pages of manuscript and a synopsis. He liked what he read and asked to see the entire manuscript. After deciding to represent the book, Hoffman sent the book to 25 publishers, and the 5 Spot imprint at Warner Books (now Grand Central Publishing) offered Bartlett a two-book deal.

Courtesy of Hachette Book Group.

From black & white to pink all over

Making the transition from journalist to novelist was challenging for Bartlett. For one, the writing style was much different. She was used to tackling complex issues in less than 30 inches and had to learn how to draw the story out. However, she did appreciate the advantage of already knowing how to do deal with red ink. "I was used to having things rewritten entirely and torn apart. It made it much easier for me to not take my editor's feedback personally and to pick my battles," she says.

The tougher problem was one of identity. How did a self-described "serious journalist" from the world of newsprint feel about her entry into the chick-lit land of pink covers, sassy tag lines, and high-heeled cover models?

"I was worried what my former editors, bosses and colleagues would think. I wondered what some of the community leaders that I'd interviewed in the past would think. But, for the most part, people have been thrilled for me," says Bartlett.

"What [chick lit] has actually turned out to be is something that I don't see how anyone could object to. Most of the time it isn't the most serious literature out there or Pulitzer Prize-winning or anything—few novels are. I think that it is what it is: fun reading about modern women. There is some pleasure in reading about other women, their struggles and triumphs," she says.

Sassy *and* smart

In addition to just being fun, Bartlett believes that chick lit can take on larger issues and explore society's biases. "Society's expectations for royal women are the expectations for all women, magnified a lot," she explains, citing issues like weight gain and marital problems.

Her second book, *Cover Girl Confidential*, is the "tell all" autobiography of the fictional Addison McGhee, a former refugee and currently America's sweetheart. Bartlett describes the book as partly fun and partly a commentary on the absurdity of immigration policy. She plans to continue taking on social issues in her work.

"The proposal for a third book explores some of the identity issues I had going from being a driven, ambitious career women to being more focused on family. I am still the capable feminist I was before, but people make assumptions about me. I am looking for a somewhat wacky way to tackle that issue," says Bartlett.

She aims to write a particular brand of chick lit that appeals to women much like herself: educated, curious and not afraid to have fun.

Courtesy of Hachette Book Group.

"There is a certain level of wackiness to a Beverly Bartlett book. I hope there is also a certain amount of social commentary, so that it is the kind of book you can read on the beach and chuckle, but you also don't feel like it was just completely froth. I hope that there are strong women characters—not necessarily strong as what we think of in serious feminist literature, but strong in that they are carving out the life that they want for themselves," she says.

The tagline for Bartlett's books is "smart books for smart women," something she came up with on the spot when the graphic designer was looking to complete the cover's design.

"It came pretty quickly to me. What I liked about it is that "smart" means a couple of different things. When you are talking about a smart-looking princess there is a certain element of being put together. Because I knew that chick lit is not taken very seriously, I wanted to try to convey that even though these characters are wacky and the book has pink stripes on the cover that the story still has some substance to it," she says.

A little dreaming and a lot of hard work

Following her interests, parodying the format of the "tell all" biography, and finding time in her busy day to write helped Bartlett reach her goal of becoming a novelist. She hopes that her success encourages other writers.

"It is so easy to be intimidated by the idea of how rare it is to get a book published. It's good to be realistic about how hard it is, but you shouldn't be intimidated to the point that you don't follow your dream. Agents don't make a living by rejecting people. They make a living by the people they accept," says Bartlett. "It is easy to talk your way out of finishing your book and sending it out, but you'll never know unless you pursue it. Pursuing your dream can be a lot less traumatic than you think."

Resources

Where to Look for More Information

Below is a list of invaluable resources specifically for romance writers. To order any of the Writer's Digest Books titles or to get a consumer book catalog, call (800)448-0915. You may also order Writer's Digest Books selections through www.fwbookstore .com, Amazon.com or www.barnesandnoble.com.

MAGAZINES:
- *Romance Writers Report*, Romance Writers of America, 16000 Stuebner Airline Rd., Suite 140, Spring TX 77379. (832)717-5200. Fax: (832)717-5201. E-mail: info@rwanational.or g.
- *Romantic Times Bookclub Magazine*, 55 Bergen St., Brooklyn NY 11201. (718)237-1097. Web site: www.romantictimes.com.

BOOKS:
- *On Writing Romance: How to Craft a Novel That Sells*, by Leigh Michaels.
- *Writing Romances: A Handbook by the Romance Writers of America*, edited by Rita Clay Estrada and Rita Gallagher.
- *You Can Write a Romance*, by Rita Clay Estrada and Rita Gallagher (Writer's Digest Books)
- *Writing the Christian Romance*, by Gail Gaymer Martin

ORGANIZATIONS & ONLINE:
- Canadian Romance Authors' Network. Web site: www.canadianromanceauthors.com.
- Romance Writers of America, Inc. (RWA), 16000 Stuebner Airline Rd., Suite 140, Spring TX 77379. (832)717-5200. Fax: (832)717-5201. E-mail: info@rwanational.org. Web site: www.rwanational.org.
- Romance Writers of America regional chapters. Contact National Office (address above) for information on the chapter nearest you.
- The Romance Club. Web site: http://theromanceclub.com.
- Romance Central. Web site: www.romance-central.com. Offers workshops and forum where romance writers share ideas and exchange advice about romance writing.
- Writer's Market Online. Web site: www.writersmarket.com.
- Writer's Digest Online. Web site: www.writersdigest.com.

Worlds and Wonders

Speculative Fiction Roundtable

by I.J. Schecter

The speculative fiction genre has come a long way since its first passing mention in an 1889 issue of *Lippincott's Monthly Magazine*. Today, this realm encompasses a number of sub-genres, including science fiction, fantasy, horror, supernatural, alternate history and magic realism, and continues to draw new readers every day. Here, four speculative writers discuss the history of this enchanting genre and its growing place in the literary landscape.

Victoria Strauss (victoriastrauss.com) is the author of seven fantasy novels, including the Stone duology (*The Arm of the Stone* and *The Garden of the Stone*) and the Way of Arata duology (*The Burning Land* and *The Awakened City*). In 2006, she served as a judge for the World Fantasy Awards. An active member of the Science Fiction and Fantasy Writers of America, she is vice chair of the SFWA Writing Scams Committee and maintains the Writer Beware Web site (writerbeware.org).

Born in Derbyshire, England, **Simon Rose** (simon-rose.com) has lived in Canada since 1990. He is also a graduate of the Institute of Children's Literature of West Redding, Connecticut. Rose's first novel for young readers, *The Alchemist's Portrait*, was published in 2003 and *The Sorcerer's Letterbox* followed in 2004. A third novel, *The Clone Conspiracy*, was published in June 2005 and *The Emerald Curse* in July 2006.

Kathleen Ann Goonan (www.goonan.com) burst into prominence with *Queen City Jazz*, a finalist for the 1998 British Science Fiction Award. *The Bones of Time*, her acclaimed second novel, was a finalist for the Arthur C. Clarke Award in 2000. Her third novel, *Mississippi Blues*, made her, according to *Publishers Weekly*, ". . . a major voice in the field." She has since continued to publish unique novels blending social change, biotechnology and jazz, like *Crescent City Rhapsody*, *Light Music* and, most recently, *In War Times*.

Novelist, poet, editor, critic and reviewer—there is little in speculative fiction **John Clute** (johnclute.co.uk) hasn't done. The winner of multiple awards and co-editor of *The Encyclopedia of Science Fiction*, CluteJohn writes the monthly column Excessive Candour for the online *Science Fiction Weekly* and is a trustee of both the Telluride Institute in Colorado and The Science Fiction Foundation in England. His novel *Appleseed* was a *New York Times* Notable Book for 2002.

I. J. SCHECTER (www.ijschecter.com) writes for leading magazines, newspapers and Web sites throughout the world, including *Condé Nast Brides*, *Golf Monthly*, *Men's Exercise*, *The Globe & Mail* and iParenting.com. He is also the author of two collections, *The Bottom of the Mug* (Aegina Press Inc) and *Slices: Observations from the Wrong Side of the Fairway* (John Wiley & Sons).

How has the speculative genre evolved since its origins?

Victoria Strauss: While maintaining genre identity, I think speculative fiction has become steadily less distinguishable, in terms of literary quality, from mainstream fiction. There's still room for straight-ahead space adventure and classic sword-and-sorcery, but there's also a lot of very serious literary and experimental stuff happening now, especially in fantasy.

Simon Rose: I agree that it is now taken more seriously as a genre—not to mention enjoyed by more young readers.

Kathleen Ann Goonan: Of interest to me is also the fact that women are writing it, and women and girls appear as viable characters in the genre.

Victoria Strauss

John Clute: There has always been speculation, of course. But science fiction as the primary speculative genre has evolved enormously over the past century, in significant large part because it is precisely a *genre*, an evolving set of codes and shortcuts, of questions and answers. It is like a great long conversation, growing daily.

Can you remember the first moment you decided, "THIS is the kind of stuff I want to write?"

Clute: Reading *The Man Who Japed* by Philip K. Dick. It was minor Dick, but maybe because it was fairly simple, and at the same time mysterious, I thought, *Hey, maybe I can follow this guy. Maybe I can do some of this travelling, too.*

Rose: When my own children were very young, I began to write and quickly realized that I wanted to create stories like the ones I enjoyed growing up—science fiction, time travel, other dimensions, parallel universes and so on.

Strauss: I don't ever remember making a conscious decision to write speculative stories. Given the amount of fantasy, science fiction, folklore and myth I read growing up, it seemed natural.

Goonan: I don't think I decided; it chose me. I wanted to write books and stories that embodied the strangeness of the world I felt.

Say I'm about to tackle my first speculative story. What advice do you have?

Clute: Read, read, read. Speculative stories are stories about the world, and you need to know some of the workings of the world to pull one off. And they are part of a long "conversation of genre," which means that it may be the case that your first Brilliant Idea may have been told and retold, rebuked and praised and revised, a dozen times already.

Strauss: Make sure you've read widely in your chosen area—both the classics and what is currently being published. Other than actually writing, reading is the best way to learn your craft and increase your skill—seeing what other writers do that works, and, when it doesn't work, analyzing why not. It's also a good idea to know what has already been

John Clute

done so you won't unwittingly repeat it. If you're going to break rules, you need to know what they are first.

Goonan: Never think of yourself as any particular kind of writer, following any artificial literary rules. Write your first story, and any story, as if the world is burning down around you and only the process of writing can save it—and you.

Rose: Don't worry too much about being completely original, as it's tough to do something that some way or other has never been done before. Also, although the premise may be fantastic, the story should be grounded in reality.

What is it about this particular genre that compels you?

Goonan: Speculative fiction is the only fiction that truly uses all the information we've discovered since Darwin showed us we're part of the natural world, not separate from it. It is an attempt to humanize what is mostly abstract, to explore the present and the future, and to understand science through intermediaries. Speculative writing has the power to illuminate and to engender new thought.

Clute: What compels me is that, despite its ample faults, speculative fiction opens windows to the world. There is an old adage about the stage: that the audience is the fourth wall, and that one shouldn't break through that fourth wall. The world is the fourth wall of speculative fiction, and every great speculative story breaks through that wall in different ways.

Kathleen Ann Goonan

Rose: For me, the answer is simple: It never fails to stir the imagination.

Strauss: As a reader, the opportunity to explore unfamiliar worlds and experience wonders created by someone else's imagination. As a writer, trying to create those worlds and wonders.

Where do you write? What's your typical process?

Rose: At home on the computer, mostly at night, until the wee hours.

Goonan: I travel a lot, so I write wherever I find myself. I usually fool around way too much when I start writing. The first 45 minutes or so are crap, or seem like it. Sometimes that feeling can last for the entire writing session, which in the best of circumstances lasts five or six hours. But sometimes the magic happens.

Clute: No particular place. First and second draft are always on an old DOS word processor because it is not as idiotically unfriendly to writers' needs as Windows.

Simon Rose

Strauss: Mostly, I write in my office. I do e-mail and business stuff in the morning, then go for a run or a walk and have lunch, then sit down to write mid-afternoon. I usually write from around 3 p.m. until 9 or 10, with a break for dinner. I'm a slow writer compared to others in my genre; I don't usually manage more than 1,000 to 1,500 words a day, and often much less. The advantage of my method is that I end up with a polished manuscript, and don't need to do too much more to get it into submittable shape.

What are the most important attributes in speculative fiction?

Goonan: Evoking a sense of wonder; creating something entirely new. Language is not new, but it can be constantly used in new ways.

Strauss: Science fiction is about what could be; fantasy is about what never was. Science fiction is about scientific and technological possibilities; fantasy is about myths and archetypes. Ultimately, I think the most important attribute of speculative fiction is the same as for any kind of fiction: good writing.

Clute: I would say it's the wonderful marriage of passion and knowledge.

Rose: There are many important attributes, but I would say the most important is, as I said, that the characters and premise have some grounding in reality no matter how fantastic the idea. Also, time machines must at least seem feasible in the way that they work, as do any scientific procedures, equipment or weapons that appear in the story.

If you could be transported to the distant past or distant future, which would you choose? Any particular place, period or moment?

Clute: Eighteenth-century Italy, with a fortune and good health and a Secret Garden on a canal in the heart of Venice.

Strauss: I'd love to go back to ancient Rome. I've always been fascinated by that society.

Rose: First-century Palestine. The French Revolution. The Napoleonic era. Ancient Rome. The Barbarian Invasions. The entire Medieval Period. And on and on.

Goonan: Wind me back to Victorian-age London, and then let me live through all of the astonishing intellectual changes that have taken place since then.

Given the nature of speculative fiction, is most of your work research-free, or are there things you end up having to investigate in the course of writing?

Clute: As I referred to before, I think speculative fiction needs to know something about what it is speculating about, that is, the world itself.

Goonan: Doing research is one of my great joys—and expenses. While writing *In War Times*, I read over a hundred books about World War II. Almost every sentence of the book is informed by several books. Another vector of the book involves, of course, jazz, and in particular modern jazz, or bebop. Again, I digested many bios, lots of music theory and a lifetime of fascinating listening. I'm no scientist, but my research on scientific issues is exhaustive.

Rose: Most of my work is research-free, even with historical fiction or time-travel stories. I have a history degree, so I end up checking only occasional facts to make sure I'm accurate.

Strauss: A lot of people think if you write fantasy you can just make it up. But in order to convincingly make things up, you need a foundation of knowledge. If there are battle scenes in your book, it's a good idea to read up on weaponry and military strategy. If one of your characters is a metalsmith, you'll need to know something about metalworking techniques if you want him to be credible.

Name a piece of speculative fiction you wish you could have written.

Rose: *The Door Into Summer* by Robert Heinlein, or *Elleander Morning* by Jerry Yulsman.

Goonan: *Gravity's Rainbow* by Thomas Pynchon.

Strauss: *Little, Big* by John Crowley.

Clute: *The Book of the New Sun* by Gene Wolfe.

As a reader, do you gravitate toward speculative fiction or deliberately stay away from it?

Goonan: Actually, I stay away from it—although I also try to keep up with it, and make time for what seems the best or most important work out there. I'm a review junkie, so I'm constantly tempted to read all kinds of things.

Rose: I gravitate towards speculative fiction, but also read a lot of reference and non-fiction material, and read literature in a wide variety of genres in my work as a reviewer.

Clute: The ghetto structure of the publishing industry ensures that ''non-genre'' writers, when they write science fiction, are not identified as doing so. This intellectual bankruptcy on the part of the gnomes who do publicity for publishers means most of us are reading speculative fiction much of the time but calling it something else. The last two books I reviewed—Cormac McCarthy's *The Road* and *Against the Day* by Thomas Pynchon—are both pure science fiction, but neither is called that.

Strauss: I do gravitate toward speculative fiction, both fantasy and science fiction, because I love it, of course, but also because I feel the need to keep current with what's going on in the field. I also read a good deal of mystery, and pick mainstream novels off the shelf as they pique my interest.

Why is speculative fiction important?

Clute: We have no world to waste, and so we had better understand it—and what we're doing to it—as fast as we can.

Strauss: It's one of the oldest forms of storytelling. It springs from something that I think is hardwired into the human brain, the need to imagine a reality beyond our own. And there is a lot of really wonderful writing in the genre—more every year.

Rose: And for that reason, speculative writing is more accepted as a genre now and taken more seriously in the literary community.

Goonan: I think most literary people would say speculative fiction is not at all important. One stereotype is that, in science fiction, ideas are foregrounded at the expense of character and writing quality, but I don't believe this is the case. In fact, I think a speculative viewpoint is becoming more prevalent, and is being used more and more by mainstream writers as they discover the scope and freedom it allows.

Strauss: I agree. Of course I think speculative writing is important, but the majority of the population does not agree. In terms of sales, speculative fiction is the smallest of the genres, and people who don't read it or write it are often inclined to dismiss it on the basis of pulp stereotypes that reflect just a fraction of what's actually being produced in the genre. That's a shame. For every mainstream reader who steers clear of the speculative aisles in the bookstore, there's a science fiction or fantasy author I guarantee they would love.

Do your friends and family consider you someone often in his or her own world?

Strauss: Absolutely.

Clute: Just enough. They're used to it by now.

Rose: It's the nature of the writing life—otherwise where would ideas come from?

Goonan: Like most artists, I tend to see everything through the lens of whatever I'm working on at the time—or I simply tune out and work on a story in my head. This can be annoying to others, or dangerous when attention is required. I'm not fantasizing, though; I'm working.

Speculative Fiction

The Next Generation

by John Joseph Adams

Thirteen is said to be the magical age at which readers discover and fall in love with the science fiction genre. But while some of those 13-year-olds become life-long readers, others don't just want to read it—they want to write it, too.

So what drives people to create rather than just consume? And why is it that so many young people choose science fiction, fantasy and horror instead of other genres?

Tor Books editor Liz Gorinsky says that one factor is that aside from a few major exceptions like Harry Potter, there's still that unfortunate correlation between liking SF/F/H and being socially removed from one's peers. "Maybe because young people who feel like weirdos are likelier to respond to the keening call of the literature of the weird, or maybe because SF&F really can claim some of the great escapist literature, which is bound to be attractive to adolescents who are bored and frustrated with trying to fit in in middle school," Gorinsky says. "So it seems pretty natural that a certain percentage of those kids would parlay that satisfaction with the literature into a drive to create escapist fantasies of their own. In recent years that phenomenon has been augmented by the droves of teenagers and twentysomethings . . . who have found resilient, fulfilling communities within fanfiction circles and have consequently taken up writing genre tropes as a form of social commerce, but it's too soon to tell how many of them will ever try their hands at original fiction."

The most prominent example of a youngster who *has* tried his hand at original fiction is probably author Christopher Paolini. Though he wrote *Eragon* (Knopf, 2004) during his teenage years, and he is only now in his early 20s, his books have sold millions of copies worldwide—and *Eragon* has been made into a successful film (and a dozen spin-off products).

A more recent success story is Drew C. Bowling, whose novel *The Tower of Shadows* was published by Del Rey in December 2006. Bowling began writing his novel during his senior year of high school and had sold it (as part of a three-book deal) during his freshman year of college.

Even younger than these two is Amelia Atwater-Rhodes; her first novel, *In the Forests of the Night*, was published in 1999 when she was just 15, and she has gone on to publish a new novel every year since then.

These three are among the more high-profile young authors, but many others have and

JOHN JOSEPH ADAMS is the assistant editor of *The Magazine of Fantasy & Science Fiction.* His nonfiction has appeared in *Amazing Stories, Intergalactic Medicine Show, The Internet Review of Science Fiction, Kirkus, Locus Magazine, Publishers Weekly, Science Fiction Weekly, Strange Horizons, Subterranean Magazine* and *Writer's Digest.* You can visit his blog, The Slush God Speaketh, at www.tuginternet.com/jja/journal.

currently are achieving success at a young age in the field of science fiction, fantasy, and horror. There's John W. Campbell Award nominee Brandon Sanderson, Stoker Award nominees Brian Freeman (aka James Kidman) and Kealan Patrick Burke, Stephen Chambers, Anselm Audley, Catherynne M. Valente, and Scott Lynch, to name but a few.

So what is the reason for this? Is tere something about these genres in particular that makes them more receptive to younger writers? To get a better understanding of this phenomenon, I spoke with four young authors like those mentioned above to find out how they managed their success and what's responsible for it.

First steps in fiction

© Courtesy of the author

Cherie Priest, author of the critically acclaimed *Four and Twenty Blackbirds* (Tor, 2005) and *Wings to the Kingdom* (2006), says that getting an early start helped her achieve writing success while still in her twenties. "I completed my first draft of my first novel when I was 15, and oh God help me it was terrible, but I finished it," she says. "I was sure it would make a million dollars, and I was convinced that people would be beating down my door to buy it and turn me into an overnight sensation. I made all the standard etiquette mistakes, I committed every possible query error, and I shattered rules of writing that Strunk & White never even imagined."

Cherie Priest

Crystal Rain (Tor, 2006) author **Tobias S. Buckell** says that his success came as a result of focus and goal setting, with lots of hard work and passion for writing. "I've seriously wanted to be a writer since I was 15, and certainly thought writing was interesting since even younger," he says. "I have a quote on my desk by H. Jackson Brown that says, 'Don't say you don't have enough time. You have exactly the same number of hours per day that were given to Helen Keller, Pasteur, Michelangelo, Mother Teresa, Leonardo da Vinci, Thomas Jefferson, and Albert Einstein.' I try to remember that when I complain about not having enough time to work on the things I want to achieve in life."

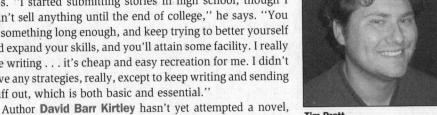

© Heather Shaw

Tim Pratt, the Nebula Award-winning author of *The Strange Adventures of Rangergirl* (Spectra, 2005), says that starting young and perseverance is what led to his early success. "I started submitting stories in high school, though I didn't sell anything until the end of college," he says. "You do something long enough, and keep trying to better yourself and expand your skills, and you'll attain some facility. I really like writing . . . it's cheap and easy recreation for me. I didn't have any strategies, really, except to keep writing and sending stuff out, which is both basic and essential."

Tim Pratt

Author **David Barr Kirtley** hasn't yet attempted a novel, but he achieved great success in the short story market in his teens, which has continued in his twenties. "I've been writing fiction regularly since my earliest childhood, so the success I've had is the result of two decades of hard work," he says. "First I submitted to contests for young writers. Success there was a strong hint that I possessed an unusual talent, and that made me more confident about taking risks and making sacrifices to nurture that talent. I also investigated the markets for short fiction. I read the magazines and studied their guidelines. I read dozens of books on writing. I took writing classes in college. I attended writers' workshops, such as Clarion. I wrote and submitted regularly, and collected dozens of rejections, and didn't give up. I got to know other young writers, and swapped info on writing techniques and the literary marketplace. I studied the writers I most admired, going so far as to copy out whole novels longhand to examine every detail. I attended author readings, [and] I devoted as much time as I could to reading and writing."

Choosing the writing life

But their successes did not come without sacrifices. Every writer, no matter what age, must give up much of his or her free time in order to write, but for many young people the things they give up are the things they're most drawn to: television, parties, videogames. "I read and I wrote with most of my free time," Buckell says. "I'm a pretty social person; it was hard at times to pass up on all that fun to keep my eyes on the prize, but I don't regret those sacrifices for a moment. It was hard at times to sit down and tell myself I had to work for several hours on a story when people were heading out to party. . . . But I believed in myself, and believed that it would be cool to have my novel sitting on a shelf in a bookstore. And it was every bit as cool as I'd hoped."

Priest struggled with the lack of leisure time as well. "For the last few years, it seems like I've had nothing of the sort—because I'm constantly operating under deadlines," she says. "It's like being a permanent senior in college, with infinite term papers hanging over your head. Every time I sit around and watch a movie, take a nap, lounge in front of the TV, or surf the Internet, in the back of my head there's a little voice saying, 'You *really* ought to be working on the edits for that next book.' . . . But there's no such thing as a day off."

Writing in the digital age

Priest and Buckell both used online writing to help with their fiction writing. "One of the things I did was create a blog to chronicle my attempt to become a writer back in 1998," Buckell says. "I felt that declaring something and trying to achieve it in front of an audience would light a fire under me, as well as keep me on task regarding my goals. And it did just that. And more. The blog spun out of control into becoming a way in which my readers found out about me, and a way for me to interact with them, as well as other authors around me."

Tobias S. Buckell

"Writing online has done a lot to help hone my sense of audience," says Priest. "It's one thing to sit at home and type on a laptop, hoarding your words and telling yourself that they're beautiful; it's another thing altogether to know with absolute certainty that people are reading and evaluating them. It's hard to do, at first. It's tough to put yourself out there and take whatever blows may come. But it's something you have to get accustomed to—and writing for an Internet audience is something of a crash course in finding out what works and what doesn't."

Required reading

One reason younger writers may be finding success in the genre is because over the years it has gained more credibility as a viable form of literature. As a result, academic institutions have become more open to including SF in their curriculum. Many colleges offer classes that focus on genre writing or literature. The University of Kansas even has a Center for the Study of Science Fiction, which was founded and is directed by SFWA Grand Master James Gunn—whose efforts are largely responsible for this newfound academic acceptance. Previously many would-be authors were discouraged from writing SF in college, and so gravitated toward other kinds of writing, such as mainstream lit, only to later return to their first love: SF.

But high schools are now more receptive to genre literature as well, with many works being used as assigned reading. Most of us probably had to read *Brave New World, 1984* and *Flowers for Algernon* in high school—three brilliant science fiction novels that are classified as Literature (with a capital L) rather than science fiction—but it was not until the last 10 years or so that high schools have commonly taught modern, core genre works such as *Ender's Game* by Orson Scott Card, *Neuromancer* by William Gibson, and *Doomsday Book* by Connie Willis.

The influence of pop culture

In addition to the advantages the Internet has brought to writing and publishing and the introduction of increasing amounts of contemporary speculative fiction in the classroom, some think the sheer amount of sophisticated SF available to eager readers has contributed to the recent influx of new, young talent in the genre.

David Barr Kirtley

"When Mary Shelley wrote *Frankenstein*, the very concept was considered so shocking and grotesque that she was widely denounced," Kirtley says. "Obviously that society isn't going to produce a tidal wave of young SF writers. Even my parents' generation grew up with a relative scarcity of fantasy and science fiction. You could read or watch most of what there was, and it was still something of a fringe interest. By contrast, our generation has come of age in a pop culture landscape in which conceptual audacity is a given. The entire iconography of my childhood, from television (*Transformers* and *Dungeons & Dragons*) to movies (*Back to the Future* and *Ghostbusters*) to video games (*King's Quest* and *Metroid*) to books (*Narnia* and *Prydain*) is that of fantasy and science fiction. Obviously young writers today are going to want to write fiction that reflects the world we grew up in."

Pratt agrees. "I think SF is just part of the background noise of the culture now," he says. "The most popular multiplayer gaming sites are fantasy-related (a lot more kids play *World of Warcraft* than will *ever* read a book of fiction voluntarily!). Many of the most popular movies of all time are SF and Fantasy (and some of those movies are even based on books, which, as a writer, I find a bit heartening). There's tons of SF and fantasy stuff on TV. . . . It's even becoming more acceptable in college classes, among the intelligentsia; they just gave a MacArthur Genius Grant to a guy [Jonathan Lethem] who published stories in *Asimov's*! It's over, dude. Science fiction won."

Buckell says that a lot of writers in their 20s and 30s seem to have been heavily influenced—or at least tempted into the field—by *Star Wars* and *Star Trek*. "I think most of them then go on to find out the amazing breadth beyond those properties that the field has to offer," he says. "I meet a lot of younger writers who started out writing 'fanfic' [fanfiction] in those worlds, who then moved on to doing their own original work."

Not your brother's books

Priest, meanwhile, sees another revolution of sorts: the influx of female readers and writers of SF. "My genre writer buddies [and I have] been talking amongst ourselves about how many young women (in particular) have found their way into genre fiction— even into areas like hard science fiction that have been largely dominated by men, historically speaking," she says. "Our general conclusion is that this is due to the fact that we are the first generation of girls who were raised with strong, sophisticated female role models in genre fiction. We grew up with Princess Leia, Sarah Connor, and Ellen Ripley—and we won't settle for writing about brass-bra babes in need of rescue. But . . . it's more far-reaching than feminism. Better genre fiction means more genre fiction. More people want to read it, so more people want to publish it, and therefore publishers are looking for more people who write it."

More Than Little Green Men

Tips for Making Your Aliens Alien

by Carol D. Pinchefsky

Little Green Men. Bug-eyed monsters. The thing from another planet. Clichés of science fiction aliens are, well, a dime a dozen: tentacled, utterly unscrutable menaces from beyond who have designs on Earth women. But as good science fiction writers know, alien characters can be as lifelike and sympathetic as their human counterparts.

Science fiction writers have to imagine highly advanced technology, star-voyaging ships, and the future of civilization. But for some, creating an alien character is the most challenging aspect of writing science fiction. (Fantasy novels also have their versions of "aliens"—races of elves or dragons have to be carefully imagined to avoid clichés.) Even though writers must infuse their characters with at least some identifiable traits, aliens have to be just that: alien. It's easy to create characters with blue skin and antennae and call them "alien," but author Larry Niven, whose acclaimed Known Space universe set a standard for creative alien races, cautions writers against the easy way out. "Beware of creating actors in rubber suits," he says. "Don't put a mask on a human being and think you've made an alien."

In other words, when it comes to aliens, anything that can be imagined *should* be imagined. Do this well and you'll find yourself with unique, memorable characters—who happen to come from another planet.

Here are 10 tips to help you imagine your own alien species:

1) Start with the opposite of normal.

Niven says, "What I do: take an assumption contrary to human fact, and follow the implications."

These assumptions include something as basic as using your mouth to speak or needing two people to procreate. Niven's Pierson's Puppeteers (*Ringworld*) contradict those very human abilities. His Puppeteers use their mouths as hands, and reproduction works when two males inseminate a female. His other aliens, Moties (*The Mote in God's Eye*), lack bilateral symmetry; one side of the Motie's body does not mirror the other.

2) Remember: home is where the third heart is.

"Believable aliens must both look and act in ways that grow logically out of the place where they evolved," says Stanley Schmidt, author of *Aliens and Alien Societies: A Writer's*

CAROL D. PINCHEFSKY is a New York City-based freelance writer who specializes in science fiction journalism. Her articles have appeared in SciFi.com, *SciFi Weekly*, *The New York Review of Science Fiction*, *SFX*, IGN.com and *Battlestar Galactica Magazine*.

Guide to Creating Extraterrestrial Life-forms (Writer's Digest Books, 1996) and the editor of *Analog* magazine.

When creating aliens, think about their homeworld, even if the reader never sees it. Starfaring aliens who evolved from an ocean planet may have advantages that land-dwellers do not, such as an ability to withstand extremes in pressure. They would also be at a disadvantage on a land with a limited water supply. Creating aliens with Achilles' heels (or Achilles' lungs) adds tension, as well as introduces a wonderful opportunity for a writer to find—and then solve—problems.

3) Do not create all beings alike.

Elizabeth Bear, the Campbell and Locus Award-winning author of *Carnival, Blood & Iron*, and *The Chains That You Refuse*, refers to "the Klingon problem, where all of the members of the alien race all have similar thoughts, they're all stereotyped." Think of all the different cultures on earth—not one person can really represent an entire planet's inhabitants. The same is true for aliens: A planet of a reasonable size would not have a monoculture (unless, of course, they have a hive mind or other programmed reason for sameness).

Be prepared to introduce more than one alien race if your protagonists visit a planet. After you've considered your home world (step two), also consider what other types of aliens may be on your planet, such as the oft-forgotten alien animals or alien insects. Do your aliens keep pets? Hunt for sport? How your aliens interact with their own environment may give clues as to how they interact with your protagonists.

4) Study insects, predators, and other cultures on Earth.

Look around. Alien behavior can be gleaned right here on this planet. Best-selling author David Brin (*Earth, Kiln People*) suggests, "Look to animal behavior on Earth—carnivores, insects, arthropods—and extrapolate intelligence into some plausible mix of traits."

Humans with worldviews other than your own can also offer insight. Bear says, "I read Temple Grandin, who's a slaughterhouse designer and a high-functioning autistic. Her perspective is very different from that of most people. She has interesting thoughts on animal psychology and how it differs from human psychology."

Studying cultural anthropology can teach us how alien other people can be. See how other cultures treat kinship ties, art, religion and politics, and incorporate some of the differences that fascinate you. They should fascinate your readers, too.

5) Let stereotypes work for you.

You can use stereotypes as a kind of shorthand when differentiating individuals from races, as well as two other races from each other. Brin does, and with a minimum of effort. "I say [the character] was chosen as an ambassador because he is what passes for an extremely stodgy and responsible person, for a Tymbrimi. This implies that tymbrimi are in general very rascally types."

6) Keep it simple, sort of.

How far does a writer go? Create a language from scratch, complete with dictionary? Chart a new civilization from its multicelled origins?

Lest the answers to these questions seem like too much information, Schmidt suggests restraint when describing the unknown: "I advise writers to know as much as they can about their backgrounds, and tell no more than they have to. Knowing a lot ensures that the story will feel solidly coherent and consistent with a larger whole, even if much it is not explicitly mentioned in the story. Telling too much risks boring readers and having them catch you in mistakes.''

7) Fix their level of technology.

Alien antagonists frequently have a higher level of technology than your human or alien protagonists. There are reasons for this.

Brin says, ''On a galactic scale of things, we are obviously a very young technological species.'' And Bear says, ''If aliens have a higher level of tech, they can come to us rather than us go to them.'' This simplifies the task of creating faster-than-light travel and a space-faring civilization for our protagonist.

But Bear warns that creating aliens with a lower level of technology often comes across as ''thinly disguised allegories for colonialism.'' Brin adds, ''Recall the purpose of a story is to produce . . . adventure! Hence your heroes . . . have to get into trouble so they can have harrowing escapes and daring deeds! Well, doesn't it help such a plot for them to be tech-backward, at least at the start?''

However, superior technology does not always equate to superior beings. Bear says, ''I can think of a lot of good stories where the aliens don't have that much more tech than we do, or the tech they have may be more advanced—but it's not advanced enough to help them.''

8) Remember the humans of the past.

Are humans alien? We can be, according to Bear, who says writing about people in the past ''involves getting into something of an alien mindset, somebody who's from a different culture and different time and whose base assumptions are nothing like yours and mine.''

A 15-year-old girl in 21st century America would have a different outlook on life than a 15-year-old girl from 1st century Rome. The American may look forward to driving, but the Roman might worry for her husband and children.

Before she wrote a book set in the Elizabethan era, Bear submerged herself in the written works of the time. ''I read a lot of period material to alienate myself,'' she says. Many good history books can introduce you to a slice of life that no longer exists, a valuable resource in creating alien worlds and characters.

9) Read more science fiction.

It's no secret. Learning how other authors shape their aliens is a great way to spur the imagination. When you read, do so actively. Ask yourself, ''How did she do that?'' and ''What makes his aliens so compelling?'' Go back through this list and use it to sketch out and study the author's alien characters, taking note of things like how much description is given and what kind, how the characters relate to each other and their homeworld, how their technology is used.

Even professional science fiction writers have their favorites that they return to often for inspiration. Schmidt admires, among others, ''Marc Stiegler's Rosans, who live their entire adult lives in 36 intensely frenzied hours and have to cooperate with humans.''

10) Engage the reader.

All of the work you've put into your characters will go to waste if your aliens aren't compelling. Pull your readers in with sensory detail and emotional appeal.

Readers won't soon forget their alien encounter if it's engaging to all five senses. To bring your aliens to life, ask yourself what they might smell like. Are they physically repulsive, so much so that contact is difficult? When they speak, do they sound like a choir? Is their skin wet or dry? Do they even have skin?

Pathos is also a powerful tool. Brin says, "Trace the inevitable poignant ironies. Take one example: friends of two races, one who lives a much longer life and the other who can fly, each of them deeply envying the other. Or find strange ways to engender mutual respect, as Barry Longyear did in *Enemy Mine*."

Even though alien desires, motivations and values may be vastly different than ours, it's up to you to find common ground between your alien and your audience.

Resources

Where to Look for More Information

B elow is a list of invaluable resources specifically for science fiction, fantasy and horror writers. To order any of the Writer's Digest Books titles or to get a consumer book catalog, call (800)448-0915. You may also order Writer's Digest Books selections through www.fwbookstore.com, Amazon.com, or www.barnesandnoble.com.

MAGAZINES:
- *Locus*, P.O. Box 13305, Oakland CA 94661. E-mail: locus@locusmag.com. Web site: www.locusmag.com.
- *The Horror Writer*, P.O. Box 1188, Long Beach NY 11561. Web site: www.bloodmoonrising magazine.com/horrorwritermag.html.
- SPECFICME! (bimonthly PDF newsletter). Web site: www.specficworld.com.

BOOKS (by Writer's Digest Books):
- *How to Write Science Fiction & Fantasy*, by Orson Scott Card
- *The Writer's Complete Fantasy Reference*, from the editors of Writer's Digest Books
- *On Writing Horror*, edited by Mort Castle

ORGANIZATIONS & ONLINE:
- Fantasy-Writers.org. Web site: www.fantasy-writers.org.
- Horror Writers Association, P.O. Box 50577, Palo Alto CA 94303. Web site: www.horror.org.
- Science Fiction & Fantasy Writers of America, Inc., P.O. Box 877, Chestertown MD 21620. E-mail: execdir@sfwa.org. Website: www.sfwa.org/.
- SF Canada, 303-2333 Scarth St., Regina SK S4P 2J8. Web site: www.sfcanada.ca.
- SpecFicWorld. Web site: www.specficworld.com. Covers all 3 speculative genres (science fiction, fantasy and horror).
- Books and Writing Online. Web site: www.interzone.com/Books/books.html.
- Writer's Market Online. Web site: www.writersmarket.com.

Greg Rucka

Balancing Comics and Prose,
It's a Gentleman's Game

© Jason E. Kaplan

by Greg Nock

As both a prose novelist and a graphic novelist, Greg Rucka has crafted stories around characters as diverse as Carrie Stetko, a United States Marshal banished to the South Pole, and DC Comics icon Superman. Rucka's debut novel, *Keeper* (Bantam, 1996), was the first in a series starring personal security agent Atticus Kodiak (with one novel in the series, *Shooting at Midnight* [1999], centered around Kodiak's sometimes-girlfriend, private investigator Bridgett Logan). Rucka's early work captured the attention of Oni Press, an independent comic book publisher in Portland, Oregon, leading to an offer to adapt Kodiak in comic-book form. Rucka decided against that idea, instead choosing to write a mystery-thriller set on the ice of Antarctica. Illustrated by Steve Lieber, *Whiteout* put Rucka on the comics map, especially when its sequel, *Whiteout: Melt*, won the 2000 Eisner Award for Best Limited Series.

Rucka's career in comics continued to flourish, with assignments from DC to write their Big Three: Batman, Wonder Woman and Superman. He also created *Gotham Central* with Ed Brubaker and Michael Lark, a street-level police drama set in Batman's crime-plagued home city. The series won Rucka his third Eisner Award in 2004 for Best Serialized Story. Rucka's success at DC also garnered the attention of Marvel Comics, where he was assigned characters like Elektra, Spider-Man and the Black Widow, along with a high-profile run on Wolverine.

But Rucka never strayed too far from creator-owned, independent comics. Inspired by the 1970s British television series *The Sandbaggers*, he launched *Queen & Country* at Oni. Blending well-researched espionage intrigue with the very real emotional effects such work would have on those involved, *Queen & Country* stars Tara Chace, one of three special operatives (code-named "Minders") for Britain's Special Intelligence Service.

All the while, Rucka worked in prose, continuing the Kodiak series as well as branching out with the stand-alone novel *A Fistful of Rain* (Bantam, 2003) and two books based on the videogame "Perfect Dark." DC Comics also commissioned Rucka to novelize *Batman: No Man's Land*, a series that ran in comics over a large number of issues.

In 2004, Rucka again bridged the gap between his two careers by publishing *A Gentleman's Game*, a novel featuring Tara Chace and other characters from *Queen & Country*. Dramatically affecting the continuity of the series, Rucka followed this a year later with *Private Wars*,

---

GREG NOCK first appeared in *Nifty Comics* #74, and is currently a member of the F+W Production Super-team. He's also illustrating the forthcoming title *For Boys Only/For Girls Only* for HOW Books.

crafting the novels carefully to allow both incarnations of the series to fit together seamlessly, or exist independently for non-comics-readers.

More recently, Rucka has helped shape the DC Comics Universe by writing *O.M.A.C. Project* and (with co-writers Geoff Johns, Grant Morrison, Mark Waid and Keith Giffen) by working on *52*, a year-long, weekly series spun out of the events of the company's crossover event *Infinite Crisis*. His current DC assignment is the super-hero-espionage series *Checkmate*.

For fans of his novels, late 2007 saw the publication of *Patriot Acts*, the sixth Kodiak novel.

'Does she get cramps?': Developing character

No matter what he's working on, however, Rucka's approach remains the same.

"I write all characters the same way," he says. "I try to find the universality of the character, and I've always felt that the heart of good literature is literature that makes the reader empathize. I can be writing somebody that I've created or I can be writing Superman—but if I can get into that personality to find those things that are universal to us all—that's how it works for me."

"When writers say 'write what you know,' they're not saying you have to have traveled to outer space to write science fiction. What they mean is that we all know universal concepts; we know what it's like to be cold, or to love somebody who isn't loving us back. We know what it's like to eat something that gets us excited, and we know what it's like to eat something we can't stand the taste of. Writing is about finding little truths that reveal big truths. It's very hard to write a story about coming to terms with death—that's enormous. But, in its own way, it's just as hard to convey the meaning of a good piece of chocolate."

For Rucka, those little truths add up to create a full character, even though a reader will only see one-tenth of what's there, which he likens to seeing only the tip of an iceberg.

"I had an interesting experience when I sat down to write my fourth novel [*Shooting at Midnight*]. I knew that I wanted Bridgett to be the primary character, but I was very nervous about it. I hadn't really tried a first-person, female point of view, and I knew I damn well better do it right. I've always been interested in gender issues—not just equality but the differences in sexuality—and it was critical for me that I write a character that was a *woman*, not just a guy with breasts. So I sat down one day with my wife and a female friend of ours, and had them asking me questions about Bridgett that I'd never even conceived of. I remember this friend asking 'does she get cramps?' I said I had no idea, and she said 'I get cramps. When I have my period I get cramps so badly I curl up and I lose a day just because it hurts so bad.' And it was a question I should have been able to answer, even though it may never, ever enter the writing."

At the same time, Rucka is aware that crafting character is an act of fiction—an act of creation on the author's part. "If I'm asked what Atticus Kodiak's favorite color is, I can say

A GENTLEMAN'S GAME

A QUEEN & COUNTRY NOVEL

GREG RUCKA

'blue,' and that can just as easily be a lie.'' Nevertheless, Rucka considers this method ''a willingness to embrace the creation, to look at the character as a totality.''

While this general approach is consistent in all of Rucka's writing, the time spent inside each character's head in preparation for a project is more difficult to anticipate. Before sitting down to begin his assignment writing *Wonder Woman*, Rucka says he spent two years passively thinking about the character, followed by 12 months where he and the book's editor exchanged frequent e-mails and talked about the character very actively. In this case, however, Wonder Woman was an existing character with over 60 years of stories establishing her personality, giving Rucka plenty of material to base his work on.

Atticus Kodiak, by contrast, sprung entirely from Rucka's mind and only came to life after six months of very directed thought. Inspired by the works of Dashiell Hammett and Raymond Chandler, ''Atticus was the result of a concerted effort and went through many iterations. I first wrote Atticus when I was in graduate school at USC, and I approached him from the principle that he had to be 'the best man in his world, and a good enough man in any world.' ''

The cemetery on Staten Island? He's been there, too

But the believability of Rucka's stories does not hinge entirely upon the depth of his characters; he's earned a reputation as a master researcher, an element of writing he takes very seriously. His comics and novels are rich with real-world detail and are not afraid to embrace delicate issues like abortion or the Taliban's mistreatment of women (in a story Rucka wrote *before* the events of September 11, 2001). In an interview for silverbulletcomicbooks.com, he stated that his greatest fear is that someone reading one of his novels would be able to say ''that's totally wrong,'' so he takes great care to ensure that he gets the details right— even on something as simple as a wild goose chase.

When one of Atticus Kodiak's clients is kidnapped by an international assassin-for-hire in *Critical Space* (2001), Kodiak is forced to bounce all over New York City in an effort to get the client back safely. The assassin, code-named ''Drama,'' leads Kodiak from location to location through pre-arranged notes, a pager and a walkie-talkie. Starting at a Starbucks on Third Avenue in the Murray Hill neighborhood of Manhattan, Atticus is instructed to cross town on foot, run to a subway station, board a train headed South for the Staten Island Ferry Terminal, take the Ferry, drive from Staten Island to Brooklyn, and finally end up in Brighton Beach (where he's then knocked unconscious and taken to Hoboken).

Rucka actually took that trip himself, and says it was the most fun he's ever had doing research.

''I had a stopwatch and three friends—one of whom was a native New Yorker, one of whom was a high-school buddy, and a guy I met doing research for another novel and has since become one of my dearest friends. We ran around the city with a video camera, and I'm proud of this: You can pick up the novel and follow it step by step; you can follow that map.''

In a particularly serendipitous example of research supporting writing, one of Kodiak's stops on the route puts him in a cemetery on Staten Island. At this point, Bridgett Logan is still tailing him, trying to provide some backup. Via pager, Drama directs Atticus to sit on a bench and look at a headstone to his right. The headstone is marked ''Logan''—Drama has just warned Atticus to tell Bridgett to back off. ''That headstone is actually there,'' Rucka says, laughing. ''I had to put that in.''

This tendency to experience situations firsthand has led Rucka into some unusual situations. His novel *Finder* (1997) opens with Atticus Kodiak working as a bouncer in a bondage club. Visiting such establishments to understand that setting was ''the oddest research I've ever done,'' he says.

And by establishing contacts in both government and law-enforcement organizations,

Rucka ensures that his procedural depictions are as close to reality as possible.

The theory behind the amount of research he does is similar to the process behind thinking through his characters: "Do a lot of it so you can show just enough."

"If you know something very well, then you don't have to prove to anybody that you know it," he says. "It just comes through naturally, in the same way that if you know a character very well, you don't have to sit there and design things to show that character. If you're researching life in Antarctica and you've learned everything you reasonably can about how the mess-hall works, then all you need to show is what you need for the story. Everything else is what supports it." So scenes in *Whiteout* showing the sparseness of life in base-camp are meant to underscore the harshness of the surroundings, enhancing the mood of the story and the ever-present threat of the environment.

Rucka is careful not to let the details get in the way of the story, however. "I say this as a guy who is fairly specific about equipment, but I've never enjoyed reading 'this is what they use'—that sort of Clancy-ish 'tech-fetishism.'"

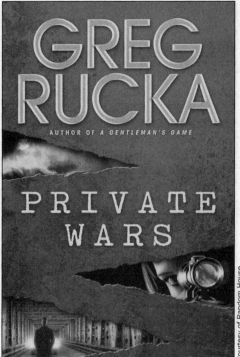

Courtesy of Random House.

"That said, there's a bit in *Private Wars* where Chace gets a specific pistol at an arms bazaar. That pistol was very crucial for what she needed to do, so it was important for me to explain how this pistol would come to be there; how it could have survived Vietnam, made its way to Central Asia to be sold at this arms bazaar at the border between Uzbekistan and Kazakhstan for her to use." For Rucka, this level of detail served the story.

The passage of 30 years in two panels

While Rucka's general approach to creating stories remains the same regardless of the project, writing for comics and writing prose present different opportunities and different challenges.

"The different mediums have different strengths," he states. "If I write a play, it's going to be very hard for me, for instance, to show you, in the course of one scene, the passing of 30 years. But in a comic book, I can do that in one page. I can do it in two panels! One of the things we can do in comics beautifully is deal with time. You can also change point of view and voice effortlessly."

Novels, on the other hand, allow much more space for intimate richness and texture. This is what led Rucka to take the characters from *Queen & Country* from graphic novels to prose. "There were stories that I would've loved to be able to show, but just couldn't do in a comic. The novels provided a way to tell stories about Chace that I felt were too big—not necessarily in scope, but in emotional importance. They were written so that fans of the comics would get a deeper, richer experience, while people who read only the novels (and not the comics) would be able to enjoy them as well."

Rucka's work has also attracted attention from Hollywood (*Whiteout* is in production, due for a summer 2008 release) and he's aware that adapting a story from one medium to

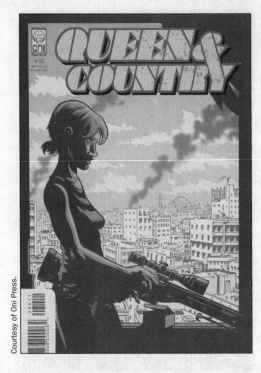

Courtesy of Oni Press.

the other is not always advisable—or possible—without taking into account the different requirements of each. "I think it's a little disingenuous when a creator sells the rights to do something as a movie and then complains that the final product isn't what they wrote. Of course it isn't! With very rare exceptions, these people are writing novels that *then* get sold, rather than screenplay treatments."

"It's a truism, but a comic is not a novel . . . is not a short story . . . is not a movie. I get infuriated when people say 'well, y'know, Peter Jackon's *Lord of the Rings* is totally different from the novel.' I wanna say 'DUH!' You cannot mistake one for the other."

Rucka is quick to point to *Whiteout* as an example of the differences between comics and prose. "That story works because it's a graphic novel," he says. "I could spend 500 words trying to convey a specific expanse in Antarctica. Or I could have Steve Lieber draw it, and wow, it's cold and empty and awful and beautiful in a way I'm not sure I could get words to convey."

This dependence on a collaborator is another key difference between the two fields.

"When you write a novel, you own it. You're on your own. But for those of us who can't draw, comics must be collaborative. The artist is easily half, if not more, of the final creation. I have great, great respect for people who can draw anything. I can't draw somebody that looks the same way twice!"

This collaboration is not without its challenges, however. For one thing, the fast-paced production schedules inherent in comics publishing don't always allow for ideal partnerships. "They have to come out monthly," he says. "So in many cases it becomes less a question of 'who do I want to work with,' than 'who is available at a given time?' "

In addition, Rucka admits that he's not as good at tailoring a story to his artistic partners as he'd like to be. With a storytelling approach he classifies as "fairly compressed," Rucka is reluctant to turn over any of the finite amount of storytelling space present in a standard 22-page comic book to a double-page spread, for example—despite an artist's desire for big, eye-grabbing visuals. "Very rarely do I think a moment deserves a double-page splash . . . but I realize there are whole swaths of readers out there looking for them. I'm not the writer for those fans."

Rucka is steadfast in this belief that writing should not be dictated by the whims of the audience. "You can't write to order," he states. "Decisions have been made for the worst reasons; if you're trying to make people happy, you can't. Nobody is going to write anything that everybody likes. You're going to become preoccupied with what the audience will think, how they'll react, when ultimately your job is to serve the character." Rucka keeps this in mind particularly when working on long-standing properties like Superman or Batman. "They'll be around longer than me; those characters will endure."

As for his own characters, Rucka risked angering his fans with *Critical Space*. Due to his involvement with the assassin Drama, Atticus Kodiak leaves the events of that novel in a very different, much darker place than he occupies in the previous books. Rucka has left this story dangling since 2001, *Patriot Acts* finally picked up where *Critical Space* left off. "Going back to the quote about Atticus being the best man in his world, *Critical Space* was about changing that world," he says.

This gives Rucka a chance to explore the question of "Nature vs. Nurture." "And while Atticus was changed by Alena [Drama's real name], Alena is changed by him." Rucka teases that there's a point in the novel where Alena is given the opportunity to kill someone—a situation in which killing that person would make tactical sense—and where she would have done so without hesitation before her association with Atticus, she's no longer quite the ruthless assassin she once was.

From chains on the doors to a two-book deal

In addition to working with artists, Rucka also appreciates the valuable input he gets from his editors and his agent. "I like working with editors. I put a lot of trust in them, and for the most part, that has served me well. I've yet to write anything that couldn't be made better by a good editor," he laughs. In fact, Rucka attributes some very valuable advice to an editor-turned-agent.

"I came out of graduate school with the first—unpublished—Kodiak novel, called *Minder*. I took it to my advisor who signed off on it as my thesis and then said he wanted to send it to an editor he knew who had just become an agent [Peter Rubie]. I asked him why, and he told me Peter would explain why I would never be able to sell it.

"Well, he sent it to Peter, and Peter called me and said he'd very much like to represent the book. He tried for about a year to sell that first one, and just couldn't do it. We got huge rejections, instead of just the usual 'we do not require this novel at this time'—double-page, single-spaced letters with 'I hated this book and here's why!' So we figured we were onto something then, that we'd hit a nerve."

One piece of criticism Rucka received at this stage still makes him laugh; one editor reacted unfavorably to the fact that Atticus shares an apartment with his friend Rubin. "He said, 'two men in their mid-twenties would not be sharing an apartment in New York unless they're gay!' Uh, ever see 'Friends'? "

While Peter Rubie was busy trying to build interest in Rucka's work, Rucka was continuing to hammer out problems. "We'd moved so my wife [writer Jennifer Van Meter] could start graduate school, and I had been unable to find regular work for months. I went eight months basically doing odd jobs. I finally found semi-regular work at a business college teaching, of all things, job-finding skills. I was teaching four nights a week, and I was doing some technical writing for a software game company. By the end of August, I'd re-written *Keeper* three or four times. I'd keep handing it into Peter, and he'd keep saying, 'This is what you need to do.' I was getting really frustrated."

"So this business college was going to close down for two weeks for, quote, Summer, unquote. And I arrived at the school the last day before vacation to find all the students milling around outside; the doors had been chained closed and everything was being repossessed. We were so poor at that point," Rucka remembers, "we were getting fat because we couldn't eat well. So I called Peter and said, 'I don't care what you have to do now, you're going out with the book. I'm not going to re-write it again. You go out and sell the damn novel.' "

While the teaching job had vanished, Rucka still had the technical-writing job, and it was while working there that he received some good news. "I got a call from Jen telling me I needed to come home; Peter needed to talk to me. I guess what he had done was gone ahead and sent it out to four or five publishers, told them there was a window of availability on it, and so we were getting offers from these publishers."

One of these offers came from Bantam Books. With money tight, Rucka suddenly found himself with the choice between a two-book deal, or a minimum bid from Bantam if the book should go to auction.

"I loved the idea of going to auction," Rucka remembers. "I'm practically yelling, 'Oh my God! We're not gonna be poor!' and Peter gave me one of the best bits of advice he ever gave me. He said: 'An auction can get you a lot of money. It can also kill your career. Because if it sells at auction for two million dollars, and your book doesn't make it back, you're dead. You'll have a one-book career. Bantam is guaranteeing two books; my advice is to take the deal.' "

Going against his initial instincts, Rucka listened to Rubie's suggestion and has since published eight novels through Bantam, with a ninth on the way.

With his workload, balancing both sides of his career has been a constant challenge, particularly over the last year while working on *52*. When asked how he manages to juggle all his projects, he answers "badly," laughing. "My goal for the coming year is to do less, better. Lately my job has become writing to deadline—writing to put out fires, rather than to complete the story. That said, it's still possible to get in there and lose myself in the story and enjoy it. I have nothing to complain about."

For Further Reading

Prose novels

- *Patriot Acts* (Bantam)
- *Critical Space* (Bantam)
- *Shooting at Midnight* (Bantam)
- *Smoker* (Bantam)
- *Finder* (Bantam)
- *Keeper* (Bantam)
- *Private Wars* (Bantam)
- *A Gentleman's Game* (Bantam)
- *A Fistful of Rain* (Bantam)
- *Batman: No Man's Land* (Pocket)
- *Perfect Dark: Second Front* (Tor)
- *Perfect Dark: Initial Vector* (Tor)

Graphic novels

- *Whiteout* (Oni Press)
- *Whiteout: Melt* (Oni Press)
- *Queen & Country* (Oni Press)
- *Gotham Central* (DC)
- *52* (DC)
- *Checkmate* (DC)

Wonder Women

*How Women Writers Are Changing
the Perception of Comics*

by Greg Hatfield

C an women write comic books? Can women write comics that males will actually want to read? The answer to both questions is a resounding *Yes!* Not only are more and more women writing comics that have a strong readership, but women writers outside the field are also being recruited to write for the big comics companies.

With the advent of original graphic novels and the ever-growing fuzziness between genres, women writers are writing comics and comics-related material that have become best-selling works. It's been a long and rocky trip, but women writers have definitely come into their own in comics.

Comic books have always been considered a male medium. In the beginning of the Golden Age, in the mid-1930s, comics were written by men mostly for boys who glorified superheroes like Superman, Batman and Captain America and who imagined themselves the juvenile sidekick—Jimmy Olsen, Robin or Bucky.

Though there were women characters in comics, most were offshoots of their male counterparts. Mary Marvel had all the powers of Captain Marvel, and Wonder Woman really was a Superman equivalent, a position she still holds to this day.

Where women writers excelled in those early days was in comic strips. Marjorie Henderson Buell wrote and drew *Little Lulu*, Dale Messick wrote and drew *Brenda Starr,* and Tarpe Mills wrote and drew the Sunday superhero strip *Miss Fury*. Women writers for comic books were scarce, however, with notables being Toni Blum and Marilyn Mercer, both of whom worked for the Eisner-Iger Studios on *The Spirit*, among other projects.

It wasn't until the 1970s that women writers and illustrators struck out on their own and began getting attention for their work. Independent presses began publishing zines containing the works of Trina Robbins, Carla Speed MacNeil, Roberta Gregory and others. These women used the medium of comics to express the views and opinions they shared but could not find elsewhere in print, such as feminism and political idealism. Their works were frequently autobiographical, with topics ranging from sex to female empowerment.

As comics continued to expand their range, creator Wendy Pini began her work on the groundbreaking title *ElfQuest*. The book was a hit, opening the door for more independent

GREG HATFIELD coordinates publicity for Writer's Digest Books and Impact Books. He has coordinated the Impact University: How to Write and Draw Comics and Graphic Novels panel for Comic-Con International in San Diego for the past four years and helped develop a companion comic book for Free Comic Book Day. He is also co-coordinator of the BookExpo America/Writer's Digest Books Writers Conference, a national writing conference held each year prior to the annual publishing trade show. In addition, he has contributed to *Novel & Short Story Writer's Market* and *The Writer's Encyclopedia*.

comics. That's when writer/artist Colleen Doran began work on her series *A Distant Soil*, one of the most popular and longest running independent comics in the industry. "I never expected [*A Distant Soil*] to be successful," says Doran. "I never expected it to be published. It was something I was doing for my own entertainment. My work and story caught the eye of several publishers. I never approached a publisher with *A Distant Soil*, myself. It all came as a surprise to me. So, when it ended up selling over 40,000 of the first issue, I was quite shocked. It just never seemed that this could happen.

Though Doran enjoyed the success of her series, the overall climate for women in comics was not quite as favorable. "It was very difficult early on because there just wasn't much opportunity for women creators, and there wasn't much room in the mainstream for non-superhero work. I love superheroes, but if you wanted to make a living in comics, you really had to work for Marvel or DC. There were few options elsewhere," she explains. "There are always a handful of exceptions we can name of people who made it big in the independent press, but on the whole, most creators worked for very low pay or for free. Even though I had a successful comic in the independents, I didn't make money from it and was making less than $10,000 a year. Lots of small press companies had bad money management, or simply folded up shop when it came time to pay their bills, and creators expecting big paydays never saw their money."

In order to better understand the legacy of women in comics and to find out where today's wonder women are headed, we checked in with independent comics pioneer **Colleen Doran**; comics industry journalist **Heidi MacDonald**; **Gail Simone**, quite possibly the most popular woman comics writer today; and best-selling novelist and relative comics newcomer **Jodi Picoult** for their views on women writing comics.

What is the perception of women writing comics?

MacDonald: I think the perception, at least in the superhero comics world, is that women writers are an anomaly, although it is much different in the indie and manga fields. There are still only a handful of women written comics for the big two publishers, Marvel and DC, although back in the '50s and '60s, when comics credits weren't routinely printed, there were more, mostly working in genres like romance and children's comics.

What perspective can women bring to the table when writing comics male writers can't?

Doran: Well, we certainly have a different series of life experiences than most men do, but a good writer ought to be able to observe, listen and translate the life experiences of others into their work, regardless. Perhaps women do not devalue the life experiences of women and girls as often as some men do.

Simone: Oh, I don't know. I certainly wouldn't phrase it that way. There's no question that there are male writers writing female characters brilliantly, and vice versa. The thing is that historically, or at least for the last few decades, there hasn't been much emphasis put on the female perspective in comics, so regardless of who was writing, the stories were about and aimed at males nearly exclusively.

It wasn't always that way—girls were huge purchasers of comics long ago, and with manga, once again they're becoming a driving force in the audience, and "mainstream" comics are beginning to reflect that as well.

MacDonald: I think that's one of those questions with a no-win answer. The short version is that men and woman can and should write about all different genres and themes. Every individual writer has their own quirks and viewpoint and shouldn't be shoehorned into any parameters. That said, as comics for kids and teens—YA comics—are gaining ground at major book publishers, I think there are probably more opportunities for woman there, since these are traditionally considered fields where many of the top writers are women. YA authors like Cecil Castellucci, Laurell K. Hamilton and Tamora Pierce have written comics; obviously it's harder to break in if you're not a best-selling author like Laurell K. Hamilton, but they've kind of broken the ground for new writers as well.

Novelist Jodi Picoult is writing a *Wonder Woman* story. As an outsider, can she bring a new perspective to the character, or is it better to let someone who writes comics regularly handle the book?

MacDonald: I think she can definitely bring a new—and welcome!—perspective. However, as I mentioned above, I think being a good *comics* writer has different skills than just being a good writer. Storytelling and characterization are universals, of course, but there is a particular way of plotting and pacing and writing for artists that is really important in writing good comics, and I think even Jodi has admitted she had to learn all this, as it doesn't come naturally to writers in other fields.

As in any field, knowing the rules, understanding the intangibles, and having a real vision and voice are what will make any writer, whatever their gender, succeed.

Jodi, you're doing a story arc for *Wonder Woman*. What drew you to the character? What do you hope you can bring to the character that others may not have?

Picoult: What I think I can bring to Wonder Woman is something she's been sorely lacking—a way for readers to relate to her. Unlike most DC superheroes, she's not human with a superhero identity—she's larger than life, and slumming it as a human (kind of like Superman). However, Superman had the whole Clark Kent story for readers to identify with— Wonder Woman is just strong, powerful, and pretty much perfect.

It's my belief though that even when we're really good in one area of our lives, we have doubts about another area. Think of how the term "wonder woman" is used to describe women who juggle it all—it also hints that those very women worry they are not giving 100% to any one area; or in other words, that there's some self-doubt amidst the vision of strength and ease. Without sacrificing Wonder Woman's strength, smarts and power, I want to give her a bit of emotional vulnerability—enough that the reader picking up the issue can say, "Hey, I've felt like that before."

When you were working on *The Tenth Circle*, how did graphic novel elements come into play in your story?

Picoult: I wanted to show all the stories we tell to ourselves, and the way we tell a story— which led me to the graphic novel format. The only way you get to learn about the main character's thoughts and feelings in the wake of his daughter's rape is through the graphic novel he presents to the reader.

Were you always a comics fan?

Picoult: Every Sunday when I was a kid my dad and I would go to the newsstand and while he bought *The New York Times*, I was allowed to buy a Charms lollipop and a comic book. I was a big X-Men fan back then.

Gail, you've been working with DC now for a long time and you've had a chance to work on many of their major characters. When you're writing for Batman or Superman, is there a shorthand that you use since you don't have to keep re-inventing them? What qualities can you give them when you're working on such established characters?

Simone: It's the mark of greatness in some of these characters that after thousands of stories over multiple decades in many different media that a good writer can still find something new to say about them, and it happens all the time, thank goodness. There's no real shorthand—the shared universe is a blessing, because you get to stand on the shoulders of some amazingly innovative stuff, but you still have to tell a proper story with all the elements in place.

What stereotypes have you all encountered when working on comics?

Doran: There used to be the oddest prejudices against women working in comics. There are still some glass ceilings waiting to be shattered, but in the 1980s when I first got into comics, the prejudice against women creators was absolutely ridiculous and sometimes bizarre. I was frequently told flat out that women simply could not draw. They certainly could not draw comics. I was told over and over that women artists were historically inferior to men, and that women didn't understand the storytelling process. The work was too hard. And even when work was available, jobs often went to male creators because, as a young girl, I didn't need jobs as much as men with families needed jobs. There was no excuse I did not hear that every woman did not hear that was directed at keeping women out of comics.

The only good thing about any of this is that when I speak to a 19-year-old girl getting into comics and I tell her these stories, I might as well be describing the life cycle of a bug from Alpha Centauri. While girls today have no frame of reference for the sexism women encountered 20 years ago, at the same time, they don't have to fight as hard for success, or carry so much baggage, and that is a good thing.

MacDonald: I think mainly, as I said earlier, there is the idea that there are certain books that men and women can or cannot write. Chris Claremont wrote some of the best-loved female characters of all when he was writing the X-Men. Likewise, there's a rap against women not being able to write action, but writers like Louise Simonson, Devin Grayson, and Gail Simone have proven that's wrong.

Simone: Well, again, and this isn't the case with all writers, but there are a fair number of writers in comics who still can only write a female character if she's primarily defined by her sexuality. They are more comfortable with swimsuit models and softcore porn imagery than anything approaching a real human character. It's the same kind of fear, I think, that prevents some writers in all media from writing, say, a black man or a Latino. It's a reliance on comfortable, but ultimately empty, stereotypes.

As for how the industry has treated me, I know everyone wants to hear horror stories, but I can't give any—not a one. I've been treated phenomenally well by every company I've worked for, and the readership has been more than welcoming. I think everyone knows it's time to open up the sandbox.

Jodi, obviously you're coming into comics from a different place in the world, that is, from the perspective of a successful author. What challenges do you face when approaching comics? Are you aware of the struggles that women writers have had to face over the years in a male-dominated industry?

Picoult: I didn't know much about what other women comics writers faced; I just dove into the challenge. However, in a comic book format, you're confined to 22 pages; you have to think about pacing between emotional scenes and action; you have to worry about how long your dialogue is—all constraints I've never had before. The hardest part was working with the historical reality of Wonder Woman. I couldn't just re-create her in a vacuum—I had to think about who she's been and where she's headed; what she does for the Justice League and all the other elements of the DC Universe. It was a bit like being given a puzzle with one piece missing and being told to create a storyline that fits that little shaped hole.

We know that many look at comics as sexist and misogynistic, i.e., Superman always saving Lois from trouble, a total absence of unattractive women. How do you combat those issues?

Doran: Well, we know that many comics don't offer only sexist viewpoints today. I prefer to read those comics. There are so many new readers who are enjoying comics written and drawn by women and for women, as well as comics for general readerships. One of the fastest growing markets in comics is for shoujo manga, girls comics from Japan.

Now, I would not say that all superhero comics are sexist and misogynistic, and I certainly grew up reading them. Wonder Woman was a role model for me. And of course, Superman is the hero of his book. He gets to do the saving. I liked Lois and thought it would be cool to be a reporter. But I could do without a lot of what I see in comics, especially those directed at kids. That includes some of what I see in some manga.

Simone: Well, first, I disagree with this to some degree, regarding Lois. Lois, as originally conceived, is an absolute hell-raising ass-kicker. She was braver and smarter than all the other reporters, including Clark Kent. In the '50s, I think she was actually *too* strong and they felt they had to tone her down. But when I write her—and most other Superman writers do the same—she's still that incredibly smart and intimidating woman. She's a fantastic role model, and a huge believer in freedom of press. I find her just as heroic as Superman.

As for ugly women, it's an idealized artform. But the best thing is to have characters with some sense of real humanity, good and bad. That's what I shoot for more than some perceived injustice in physical appearance.

MacDonald: It's more a question of who the comics are aimed at. *Buffy the Vampire Slayer* was tremendously influential in showing that having a female fanbase and male fanbase weren't mutually exclusive for a genre show. (And it was written by a man.) I think getting more women in as writers anywhere will open up themes and bring in a wider audience. Any time you broaden your appeal, you broaden your audience. I do think there are some themes that come more naturally to women writers—romance and interpersonal relationships—and having more of this in superhero comics couldn't help but broaden the audience. It's a question of just opening the window and letting in some fresh ideas. And I do think that will combat some of the more obviously "comic book" stereotypes.

In manga, half the audience and creators are female to begin, so this isn't really an issue. They have no problem saying a book like *Dramacon* or *Bizenghast* is for girls, and these books have no trouble reaching a female audience. The risk is less.

Indie and literary comics have a more eclectic base in many ways. These aren't really a place for comics writers, per se, since most literary comics tend to be created by writer/artists. But it isn't impossible. Marguerite Abouet is an example of a woman writer for a literary comic.

Picoult: I'll be letting Wonder Woman resolve some issues with her mom. (Tricky, because mom's dead!) Who hasn't struggled with whether we grow up to be the people our parents want and expect us to be . . . or who we want to become? I don't think this will conflict with the male's version of a female superhero. For one thing, she's still fighting crime in her bustier. (Something any *woman* knows is ludicrous!) One of the questions for me in writing Wonder Woman was to figure out who she was being pitched to—men? boys? girls? I wanted to create a story arc that would draw in all those readers, the same way my novels have readers who range from 13 to 103, and are nearly evenly split between male and female fans.

The opportunities for women writers in comics seem to be in the independent and alternative markets, including manga. Have these markets equalized the playing field for women writers?

Picoult: Again, I don't feel like I can really speak to this, as I was asked specifically by DC to "guest write." However, it stunned me that a major female superhero like Wonder Woman has only had one former female writer. I'd think that was a no-brainer!

Doran: Oh absolutely. There are more women and girls reading and making manga than other kinds of comics. Girls like the storylines and the style of art in manga better.

There are more opportunities for women throughout comics nowadays. Publishers used to claim that girls don't read comics, therefore they didn't make comics for girls and they didn't hire women. Now they can't say that. The readers are voting with their dollars. And the publishers are paying attention. Publishers want to make money, and if they see a market available, they will want to make money off that market.

I've had editors go purple in the face raging about how much they hate manga. Who cares about them? Some other publisher will make manga, some other publisher will hire women to draw it, some other girls will buy it, and some other people will make money off of it. And eventually, these dinosaur-industry editors will be winnowed out of the business. No publisher can afford to hire editors who don't know the market and treat their publishing offices like a personal fan press. Publishers want editors who can stay on top of market trends.

Colleen, as someone who regularly moves from independent to mainstream comics, what are the advantages and disadvantages of working with both?

Doran: The most obvious negative is that the independent press is not well funded, as a rule. Creating a graphic novel is a huge labor investment. It is one thing to write a scene that calls for a cast of thousands. It is another thing to draw a cast of thousands. And most independent publishers don't pay page rates like the mainstream publishers do. So, if you are only working for a small advance against royalties, the labor you have put into your graphic novel may never pay off. Drawing a graphic novel is full-time work for a year for an artist. That's a lot of work for no guaranteed pay. In the mainstream, you are getting a guaranteed page rate. No matter what, you will be paid for the time and effort you put into your project.

While most independent companies allow creators to maintain copyright and trademark ownership as well as a lot of creative control, some companies don't. A publisher like Image Comics gives creators huge benefits in their work. The drawback is there is not much upfront money, if any. The payoff—if you have a hit—you get a huge return. It's much harder to get creative control of your work in the mainstream, though I have actually had a lot of leeway on some of my mainstream projects. My editors are very flexible and they trust me. But it can take years to build up that kind of rapport. A beginner shouldn't expect that.

Heidi, still for all the success women have had writing independent comics, there just aren't that many successful mainstream women writers. Is the outlook any brighter?

MacDonald: Not really. While there are many more women cartoonists than there used to be, there are still only a handful of women who are comics writers alone. As I mentioned, women novelists coming in has swelled the ranks a bit. I think what it will take is just women who are very focused and don't let the past get in their way.

To be brutally honest, there is a sort of "There can be only one" attitude here. You will almost never see two women successfully writing superhero comics at the same time. Right now it's Gail Simone; a few years ago, it was Devin Grayson. I think in order to succeed, you have to have talent and really like superheroes and know a lot about continuity. And, of course, it doesn't hurt to really understand the workings of action/genre pop culture. The most successful comics are much like the most successful action movies and TV shows, and have a lot of the same beats and conventions. It makes a lot of sense to study these, and also to understand comics artists and how they work.

About Our Panelists

Colleen Doran is an award-winning illustrator and writer, known for her lush and detailed artwork, who seems to be more in demand each year. She began her work on *A Distant Soil* when she was 12 years old and now has produced four graphic novel collections and 40 comics. The fifth graphic novel is now in production, which will wrap up the main storyline. Doran was one of the early supporters of manga, working as a consultant to Japanese publishers trying to break into the American market. She was Artist in Residence at the Smithsonian Institute in May 2006, where she lectured on manga. Doran recently completed *Girl to Grrrl Manga* (Impact Books, 2006), an instruction book on how to draw shoujo-manga-style art. Her latest work includes *The Book of Lost Souls* for Marvel Comics and *Stealth Tribes* for DC's Vertigo imprint.

Heidi MacDonald has been a force in comics for over a decade as a critic, an editor and most recently, a blogger. From her early days as a critic for *The Comics Journal*, she was comics editor at *Disney Adventures Magazine* where she developed the comics adventures of such world-renowned characters as Donald Duck, Mickey Mouse, *Toy Story*, and *The Lion King*. At DC Comics, she oversaw such properties as Scooby-Doo and The Powerpuff Girls before moving to Vertigo where she developed best-sellers such as Brian K. Vaughn's *Y: The Last Man* and *Orbiter*. She has also been senior producer at *The Pulse*, one of the top news sites for the comics industry, and she most recently developed *The Beat*, a must-read blog of comics pop culture, currently housed at *Publishers Weekly*, where she is also contributing editor.

Gail Simone has become possibly the most prolific female comics writer in history, working on such titles as *Deadpool*, *Teen Titans*, *Gus Beezer*, *Agent X*, *X-Men Unlimited*, *Action Comics*, *JLA: Classified*, *Rose and Thorn*, *Legion*, the *All-New Atom*, *Gen13*, her creator-owned Wildstorm book, *Welcome to Tranquility*, and a long and respected run of *Birds of Prey*. She also wrote the acclaimed "Double Date" episode of *Justice League Unlimited*, and is currently writing a screenplay and several animation projects.

Best-selling author **Jodi Picoult** released the novel *Nineteen Minutes* (Atria) in March 2007, which topped the fiction lists of the *New York Times*, *Publishers Weekly*, the *Wall Street Journal*, and the Associated Press. Her previous novel, also a bestseller, was *The Tenth Circle* (Atria, 2006). In it, the main character is also a comic book artist, and there are illustrated pages to show his work. That led to a call from a DC editor asking if Picoult would be interested in writing *Wonder Woman*. She began a five-issue storyline for *Wonder Woman* in the March 2007 issue.

Gail, throughout the years, you've been outspoken about the treatment of women in comics. You've said if comics keep killing off characters female readers relate to, then there won't be any female readers. Has your opinion changed since your original comment?

Simone: Yes, and no. When I first posited that theory, comics were already making a change for the better. It's a self-fulfilling prophecy, that if no effort is made to appeal to the female readers, you can't turn around and whine that, hey, where are all the female readers?

But the quality of writing in comics, the sophistication involved, has gone up considerably in recent years, and you can't write about human characters for any period of time without bringing in female characters and points of view. And we've seen that now, female characters can lead teams and hold their own books.

I think the next generation of comics writers is going to skew much more towards more females, I see the signs everywhere. Women already occupy a lot of the editorial positions and make up a huge amount of the most interesting voices on the comics Internet. Change is coming; those slow to see it are just going to be run over.

The Business of Comics

Finding a Job in Hollywood's Idea Factory

by John Jackson Miller

Creating comics, it has been said, has something in common with golf. You can't watch either being done without being inspired, at some point, to try your own hand at it—advisedly or not. Indeed, there are more aspiring comic-book creators in the aisles of comic-book conventions than there are behind the signing tables.

That kind of power to inspire consumers to action is certainly a strength of comics, but it can also be a problem. Few markets have such fierce creative competition. One of comics' best-known scribes once famously said he had no fans—just people who wanted his job. Indeed, there have been times when the greatest fear in comics was that we were one big craft circle, selling only to ourselves.

Fortunately, comics in the 21st century are in a much better place. Bouncing back from a historic speculation-driven collapse in the early 1990s, comics have claimed a position as a factory of creative ideas for other media. With more than 170,000 comic-book issues having been published in North America alone, Hollywood has found a seemingly inexhaustible supply of reader-tested material—and mass-market booksellers have taken notice.

Now, squarebound comics are no longer relegated to the "Humor" shelves of bookstores but are racked on their own in most venues. Some farsighted retailers are even beginning to rack comics alongside related prose works in their individual genres—putting comics mysteries, comics SF, and comics romances where their customers are, regardless of the format. For creators of what used to be considered a second-class or children's medium, that's a dream come true.

But comics are deceptive. Looking at the growing presence of bound editions of comics in mass-market bookstores, a novice writer might assume they're just another kind of book, as far as publishers are concerned. But, however they're eventually packaged, almost all American comics begin as *magazines*, and the production model is, at heart, a magazine production model.

Understanding the product

The term "graphic novel," coined in comics in the 1970s, has become popular in the mainstream press, allowing coverage of comics to appear in places where it might not have before. But a graphic novel—correctly defined as complete comics work (usually of more than 64

JOHN JACKSON MILLER (www.johnjacksonmiller.com) writes comics, in titles including Star Wars, Simpsons and Iron Man, and writes about them in books and magazines, including *The Standard Catalog of Comic Books* and *Comics Buyer's Guide*. He also runs the comic-book resourse site the Comics Chronicles (www.comichron.com).

pages) appearing for the first time in a single squarebound volume—is actually a rarity in comics publishing.

In fact, 98% or more of the comics seen on the bookshelves of Borders and Barnes & Noble are collections reprinting material that's already appeared in monthly comics in the United States or in Japanese manga. They're the DVD release of the TV series, if you will. Within the comics field, they're called "trade paperbacks" (despite that term meaning something else for the book-publishing world), and they helped revitalize the industry in the early 2000s by allowing periodical publishers both a second stream of income and a vital inroad into mass-market stores, many of which had surrendered their business in the 32-page monthlies to the 2,500 or so comics shops in North America.

Without the pre-existing series, few bound editions would be published. Many of the original graphic novels green-lit by major publishers are by people who've already made their names, either in comics, the outside world, or both. Before there was a place for comics in bookstores in addition to the spinner rack, Harvey Pekar's award-winning *American Splendor* (Ballantine, 2003) was serialized in periodical form. His later *Quitter* (Vertigo, 2005) was not, there being, by then, both a wider market for his work and a place for bookstores to actually stock that work. Apart from art houses and specialty imprints of major prose publishers, most comics publishers look on the original graphic novel as a prestige—and, thus, a luxury—item.

As much as sales of bound editions of comics (reprint and otherwise) have grown, prior serialization remains a must for most comics publishers. The reasons are many. Without the revenue from the periodical, the publisher loses both revenue and exposure. It's the word-of-mouth from the periodical version that helps sell the trade-paperback collection—often to the very same people who bought the individual issues.

Furthermore, the work simply won't get done. A 132-page comics story (the equivalent of a six-issue arc of a comic-book series) might take a writer a few weeks to complete. But it requires *months* of time for one or more artists, not to mention colorists and letterers involved. Experience has shown that the monthly tempo, enforcing deadlines of a chapter a month, brings more stories to market than you'd see if a graphic novel had to be completed before its initial publication.

And comics is a cash-on-delivery business. Just as with magazine writing, creators rarely, if ever, are paid in advance. Publishers usually pay on delivery of the work, which means one thing if you're turning in 22 pages at a time—and starvation at 132 pages at a time.

Creators hope that as bookstore sales of comics in bound form grow, comics publishers will increasingly adopt such prose-market devices as advances, which will then allow for longer-form original works.

But for now, aspiring comics creators with ideas for their own graphic novels have a decision to make: If they eschew serialization in comic books, the odds against publication by an existing publisher escalate. A first-time creator can find an opportunity with a longer-form work at a smaller art house (of which there are several in comics), but with the larger firms, serialized periodicals are often a necessary part of the equation.

Breaking in—and in and in again . . .

More than 300 new comic books are released every month in North America, which would seem to suggest a lot of opportunities for new entries. Unfortunately, the publishing market is not as broad as it is deep. The two longtime market leaders, Marvel and DC, combine for nearly two-thirds of the offerings each month and nearly four-fifths of the sales. And, while getting an assignment with one or the other is an invaluable stamp of approval, the competition for positions with either reflects that.

The news is good here for artists who make it onto the larger publishers' radar screens:

So *much* material is moving through the system that the partnership with a competent and punctual artist can be an editor's most valuable commodity. Artists also have an advantage in a more streamlined path to discovery. Major publishers hold portfolio review sessions at the hobby's major conventions—and many artists have earned assignments just by setting up in "Artists Alley" and being seen when an editor in need walks by.

Here, the importance of taking any assignment at all, for however small the publisher, becomes obvious for most artists. Published work in one's portfolio isn't just the best visual cue to one's talent; it also suggests the artist both made a deadline and has had exposure. Comics fans are obsessive when it comes to indexing creators' careers—online sites and the *Standard Catalog of Comic Books* are to comics what The Internet Movie Database (IMDb) is to film—so every credit is magnified many times. The career paths of most artists working regularly in monthly comics today can be traced through the "rookie leagues" to the larger publishers, as editors see their ability (and, what's more important, reliability).

Opportunities for artists multiplied with the arrival of next-day shipping and multiplied again with the introduction of the Internet. Where most chances for work used to go to artists in New York City, now artists can live virtually anywhere, communicating with their writers and delivering their image files electronically. That's changed how comics are produced. The "Marvel method" (in which a writer dialogues pages that an artist has drawn based on an agreed-upon plot) still exists but has largely been replaced by full scripts (in which the writer has provided panel-by-panel direction). In-person collaboration has thus vanished, for most. (I wrote an entire year of a series without ever meeting my artist, who lived in Argentina.)

Finding work tends to be harder for new writers. Consider the numbers: An artist may have time to draw a little more than one 22-page comic book a month—two, if he's working full-time and has the speed of Mercury. Meanwhile, it's not unusual to see full-time comics writers hammering out several titles a month. In the early 1990s, Fabian Nicieza was both editing at Marvel and writing nine monthlies and, in the 1960s, Stan Lee wrote every Marvel series! A monthly title might provide work to as many as a dozen cover artists, interior artists, and colorists in a year, yet might be only *one* of the titles a writer is scripting. Since writers are generally paid less per page than artists, they often have to take more assignments—thus, assignments tend to coalesce around a small number of contributors.

So it is that the power of being an insider—or a familiar face—is greatly magnified when it comes to writers. In periods of business contraction, many assignments understandably go to insiders-turned-freelancers. Some majors have been known to stop accepting writing submissions for years at a time. Complicating the process for comics writers, too, is that the characters being written about are usually owned by the publisher, so idea submission agreements are usually required beforehand. Which puts many writers in a Catch-22 with the majors: A pitch about Copyrighted Character X can only go to one publisher, yet publishers are not often in the market for work from beginning writers about brand new characters.

Another challenge comics creators face is remaining in the public's eye, year after year. Even the creative superstars of comics say that "paying your dues" is a process that never really stops. While longevity can translate to royalties where it couldn't before, the market is so volatile and dynamic that assignments on the corporate-owned titles must be won, and won, and won again. Even with creator-owned characters and concepts, a continuing supply of new material in periodical form makes it far easier to help retailers sell the older collections. It's a lot easier to maintain an ongoing franchise than to revive it.

However, in recent years many comics fans have gone from being brand-loyal to author-loyal—an easier thing now that the creators' names appear on the covers and elsewhere inside. (For years, they weren't listed in comic books at all!) It's increasingly possible for a creator to bring his or her fans with him to the next project, wherever it is—though this involves a great deal of personal marketing at conventions and online. With hundreds of comics released each month, it's vital for a creator to communicate where he is and what he's doing at all times—not just for the fans' information, but for the editors as well. Editors are accustomed to creators drifting into and out of the business, and without stoking the fires it's easy for a writer or artist to be counted in the latter group.

Guerilla marketing

Even without the visual advantages artists have in marketing their services, aspiring writers do have ways of being seen. The comics blogosphere and fan press is active and has generated name recognition for many who later became comics writers (myself included). Self-publishing, a mark of vanity elsewhere, is regarded as a declaration of independence in comics and has produced many writers who went on to long careers. Many, many comics series started at small presses have gone to the larger ones without much loss in the way of the creators' rights. Webcomics also can serve as a method of guerilla-marketing exposure; although comics remain—make no mistake—exclusively a print medium for most financial and artistic purposes. Finally, as with artists, traveling to major conventions where editors are is vital. Writers and artists may no longer work face-to-face, but face time with editors is necessary for both.

The major publishers do occasionally stage talent searches, whenever they're looking for fresh faces and a publicity boost. These are worth watching for, although the challenge is that the pent-up demand for consideration can be vast, resulting in a flood of proposals. These searches can work for a creator (one did for this writer), but they're always a reminder of just how many comics readers want to work behind the scenes.

As with artists, proof of reliability is everything. The writer, at the beginning of the chain, can start a cascade of delays that can upset everything.

Got what it takes?

Most everyone who reads comics wants to create them themselves. If you're an aspiring creator who's not an avid comics consumer already, the best advice is not to bother: Comics require a visual vocabulary that is learned only by reading comics. Trying to create comics without that background knowledge is like aspiring to write a prose story in a language you don't know. But, if you know the lingo, have interesting ideas, can hit a deadline, and don't mind a little competition, there may be a place among the *next* 170,000 comics published.

Resources

Where to Look for More Information

Below is a list of invaluable resources specifically for writers of graphic novels and comics. To order any of the Impact Books titles or to get a consumer book catalog, call (800)448-0915 or visit fwbookstore.com, amazon.com or barnesandnoble.com.

MAGAZINES

- *Comic Buyer's Guide*, published by Krause Publications (a division of F+W Publications, Inc.). Subscribe online at www.cbgxtra.com. Six issues for $19.95.
- *The Comics Journal*, published by Fantagraphics Books. Subscribe by writing *The Comics Journal*, 7563 Lake City Way NE, Seattle, WA 98115, by calling (800)657-1100, or online at www.tcj.com. Five issues for $36.

BOOKS

- *Alan Moore's Writing for Comics*, by Alan Moore. Avatar Press: 2003.
- *Best American Comics* anthology. Houghton Mifflin: annual.
- *Comics and Sequential Art*, by Will Eisner. Impact Books: 2004
- *The DC Comics Guide to Writing Comics*, by Dennis O'Neil. Watson-Guptill: 2001.
- *Graphic Storytelling and Visual Narrative*, by Will Eisner. Impact Books: 2004.
- *How to Draw and Sell Comics*, by Alan McKenzie. Impact Books: 2005.
- *The Writer's Guide to the Business of Comics*, by Lurene Haines. Watson-Guptill: 1998.
- *Writing for Comics with Peter David*, by Peter David. Impact Books: 2006.

ORGANIZATIONS

- Comic Book Legal Defense Fund. "Non-profit organization dedicated to the preservation of First Amendment rights for members of the comics community." Web site: www.cbldf.org.
- Friends of Lulu. Nonprofit organization dedicated to promoting and encouraging female readership and participation in the comic book industry. Web site: www.friends-lulu.org.
- International Comic Arts Association. Non-profit organization that strives to "support, promote, and strengthen the comic industry, its products, and professionals." Web site: www.comicarts.org.
- National Association of Comics Art Educators. International association that promotes the teaching and study of visual storytelling. Web site: www.teachingcomics.org.

ONLINE

- Artbomb. Reviews. Web site: www.artbomb.net.
- The Big Comic Book Database. Research guide. Web site: www.comics-db.com.
- Comic Book Resources. Daily news, columns and interviews. Web site: www.comicbookresources.com.
- Egon. Coverage of independent comics, including news, events and exhibits. Web site: www.egonlabs.com.
- ICV2. Industry business news. Web site: www.icv2.com.
- Newsarama. Breaking news, columns, previews, interviews. Web site: www.newsarama.com.
- The Pulse. News and interviews, updated daily. Web site: www.comicon.com/pulse/.
- Silver Bullet Comics. News, previews and industry gossip. Web site: www.silverbulletcomicbooks.com.
- SmallPressComics.com. Focuses on the creation, distribution, and promotion of small-press comics. Web site: www.smallpresscomics.com.
- The Beat. The News Blog of the Comics Culture, by Heidi MacDonald. Web site: pwbeat.publishersweekly.com/blog/.

Literary Agents

Many publishers are willing to look at unsolicited submissions but most feel having an agent is in the writer's best interest. In this section, we include agents who specialize in or represent fiction. These agents were also selected because of their openness to submissions from writers.

The commercial fiction field is intensely competitive. Many publishers have small staffs and little time. For that reason, many book publishers rely on agents for new talent. Some publishers are even relying on agents as "first readers" who must wade through the deluge of submissions from writers to find the very best. For writers, a good agent can be a foot in the door—someone willing to do the necessary work to put your manuscript in the right editor's hands.

It would seem today that finding a good agent is as hard as finding a good publisher. Yet those writers who have agents say they are invaluable. Not only can a good agent help you make your work more marketable, an agent also acts as your business manager and adviser, protecting your interests during and after contract negotiations.

Still, finding an agent can be very difficult for a new writer. If you are already published in magazines, you have a better chance than someone with no publishing credits. (Many agents routinely read periodicals searching for new writers.) Although many agents do read queries and manuscripts from unpublished authors without introduction, referrals from their writer clients can be a big help. If you don't know any published authors with agents, attending a conference is a good way to meet agents. Some agents even set aside time at conferences to meet new writers.

Almost all the agents listed here have said they are open to working with new, previously unpublished writers as well as published writers. They do not charge a fee to cover the time and effort involved in reviewing a manuscript or a synopsis and chapters, but their time is still extremely valuable. Only send an agent your work when you feel it is as complete and polished as possible.

USING THE LISTINGS

It is especially important that you read individual listings carefully before contacting these busy agents. The first information after the company name includes the address and phone, fax, e-mail address (when available) and Web site. **Member Agents** gives the names of individual agents working at that company. (Specific types of fiction an agent handles are indicated in parenthesis after that agent's name). The **Represents** section lists the types of fiction the agency works with. Reading the **Recent Sales** gives you the names of writers an agent is currently working with and, very importantly, publishers the agent has placed manuscripts with. **Writers' Conferences** identifies conferences an agent attends (and where you might possibly meet that agent). **Tips** presents advice directly from the agent to authors.

Also, look closely at the openness to submissions icons that precede most listings. They will indicate how willing an agency is to take on new writers.

☑ DOMINICK ABEL LITERARY AGENCY, INC.

146 W. 82nd St., #1B, New York NY 10024. (212)877-0710. Fax: (212)595-3133. E-mail: agency@dalainc.com. Estab. 1975. Member of AAR. Represents 100 clients. Currently handles: adult nonfiction books; adult novels.
How to Contact Query with SASE.
Terms Agent receives 15% commission on domestic sales; 20% commission on foreign sales.

☒ ☑ ACACIA HOUSE PUBLISHING SERVICES, LTD.

62 Chestnut Ave., Brantford ON N3T 4C2 Canada. Phone/Fax: (416)484-8356. **Contact:** (Ms.) Frances Hanna. Estab. 1985. Represents 100 clients. Currently handles: 30% nonfiction books; 70% novels.

- Ms. Hanna has been in the publishing business for 30 years, first in London as a fiction editor with Barrie & Jenkins and Pan Books, and as a senior editor with a packager of mainly illustrated books. She was condensed books editor for 6 years for *Reader's Digest* in Montreal and senior editor and foreign rights manager for William Collins & Sons (now HarperCollins) in Toronto. Mr. Hanna has more than 40 years of experience in the publishing business.

Member Agents Frances Hanna; Bill Hanna, vice president (self-help, modern history, military history).
Represents Nonfiction books, novels. **Considers these nonfiction areas:** Animals; biography/autobiography; language/literature/criticism; memoirs; military/war; music/dance; nature/environment; theater/film; travel. **Considers these fiction areas:** Action/adventure; detective/police/crime; literary; mainstream/contemporary; mystery/suspense; thriller.

- ⚬━ This agency specializes in contemporary fiction—literary or commercial. Actively seeking outstanding first novels with literary merit. Does not want to receive horror, occult or science fiction.

How to Contact Query with outline, SASE. *No unsolicited mss.* No e-mail or fax queries. Responds in 6 weeks to queries. Returns materials only with SASE.
Recent Sales This agency prefers not to share information on specific sales.
Terms Agent receives 15% commission on English language sales; 20% commission on dramatic sales; 25% commission on foreign sales. Charges clients for photocopying, postage, courier.
Tips "We prefer that writers be previously published, with at least a few short stories or articles to their credit. Strongest consideration will be given to those with three or more published books. However, we would take on an unpublished writer of outstanding talent."

☑ AGENTS INK!

P.O. Box 4956, Fresno CA 93744. (559)438-8289. **Contact:** Sydney H. Harriet, director. Estab. 1987. Member of APA. Represents 20 clients. 70% of clients are new/unpublished writers. Currently handles: 80% nonfiction books; 20% novels.

- Prior to opening his agency, Dr. Harriet was a psychologist, radio and television reporter, and professor of English. Ms. McNichols has a BA in classical Greek and an MA in classics. She has more than 20 years of experience as an editor for daily and alternative newspapers, major syndicates, and independent authors.

Member Agents Sydney Harriet; Dinah McNichols.
Represents Nonfiction books, novels. **Considers these nonfiction areas:** Animals; cooking/foods/nutrition; government/politics/law; health/medicine (mind/body healing); history; language/literature/criticism; psychology; science/technology; self-help/personal improvement; sociology; sports (medicine, psychology); foreign affairs; international topics.

- ⚬━ This agency specializes in writers who have education experience in the business, legal and health professions. It is helpful if the writer is licensed, but not necessary. Prior nonfiction book publication is not necessary. For fiction, previously published fiction is a prerequisite for representation. Does not want to receive memoirs, autobiographies, stories about overcoming an illness, science fiction, fantasy, religious materials or children's books.

How to Contact Query with SASE. Considers simultaneous submissions. Responds in 1 month.
Terms Agent receives 15% commission on domestic sales; 20% commission on foreign sales. Offers written contract, binding for 6-12 months (negotiable).

THE AHEARN AGENCY, INC.

2021 Pine St., New Orleans LA 70118. E-mail: pahearn@aol.com. **Contact:** Pamela G. Ahearn. Estab. 1992. Member of MWA, RWA, ITW. Represents 35 clients. 20% of clients are new/unpublished writers. Currently handles: 10% nonfiction books; 90% novels.

- Prior to opening her agency, Ms. Ahearn was an agent for 8 years and an editor with Bantam Books. **Considers these nonfiction areas:** Animals; child guidance/parenting; current affairs; ethnic/cultural interests; gay/lesbian issues; health/medicine; history; popular culture; self-help/personal improvement; theater/film; true crime/investigative; women's issues/studies. **Considers these fiction areas:** Action/adventure; contemporary issues; detective/police/crime; ethnic; family saga; feminist; glitz; historical; humor/satire; literary; mainstream/contemporary; mystery/suspense; psychic/supernatural; regional; romance; thriller.

- This agency specializes in historical romance and is also very interested in mysteries and suspense fiction. Does not want to receive category romance, science fiction or fantasy.

How to Contact Query with SASE. Accepts e-mail queries (no attachments). Considers simultaneous queries. Responds in 8 weeks to queries; 10 weeks to mss. Obtains most new clients through recommendations from others, solicitations, conferences.

Recent Sales *Red Chrysanthemum*, by Laura Joh Rowland; *Only a Duke Will Do*, by Sabrina Jeffries; *The Alexandria Link*, by Steve Berry.

Terms Agent receives 15% commission on domestic sales; 20% commission on foreign sales. Offers written contract, binding for 1 year; renewable by mutual consent.

Writers' Conferences Moonlight & Magnolias; RWA National Conference; Thriller Fest; Florida Romance Writers; Bouchercon; Malice Domestic.

Tips "Be professional! Always send in exactly what an agent/editor asks for—no more, no less. Keep query letters brief and to the point, giving your writing credentials and a very brief summary of your book. If one agent rejects you, keep trying—there are a lot of us out there!"

ALIVE COMMUNICATIONS, INC.

7680 Goddard St., Suite 200, Colorado Springs CO 80920. (719)260-7080. Fax: (719)260-8223. Web site: www.alivecom.com. Estab. 1989. Member of AAR, Authors Guild. Represents 100+ clients. 5% of clients are new/unpublished writers. Currently handles: 50% nonfiction books; 35% novels; 5% novellas; 10% juvenile books.

Member Agents Rick Christian, president (blockbusters, bestsellers); Lee Hough (popular/commercial nonfiction and fiction, thoughtful spirituality, children's); Beth Jusino (thoughtful/inspirational nonfiction, women's fiction/nonfiction, Christian living).

Represents Nonfiction books, novels, short story collections, novellas. **Considers these nonfiction areas:** Biography/autobiography; business/economics; child guidance/parenting; how-to; memoirs; religious/inspirational; self-help/personal improvement; women's issues/studies. **Considers these fiction areas:** Action/adventure; contemporary issues; detective/police/crime; family saga; historical; humor/satire; literary; mainstream/contemporary; mystery/suspense; religious/inspirational; thriller.

- This agency specializes in fiction, Christian living, how-to and commercial nonfiction. Actively seeking inspirational, literary and mainstream fiction, and work from authors with established track records and platforms. Does not want to receive poetry, young adult paperbacks, scripts or dark themes.

How to Contact Query with SASE. Be advised that this agency works primarily with well-established, best-selling, and career authors. Returns materials only with SASE. Obtains most new clients through recommendations from others.

Recent Sales Sold 300+ titles in the last year. A spiritual memoir, by Eugene Peterson (Viking); A biography of Rwandan president Paul Kagame, by Stephen Kinzer; *Ever After*, by Karen Klingsbury (Zondervan).

Terms Agent receives 15% commission on domestic sales; 15% commission on foreign sales. Offers written contract; 2-month notice must be given to terminate contract.

Tips "Rewrite and polish until the words on the page shine. Endorsements and great connections may help, provided you can write with power and passion. Network with publishing professionals by making contacts, joining critique groups, and attending writers' conferences in order to make personal connections and to get feedback. Alive Communications, Inc., has established itself as a premiere literary agency. We serve an elite group of authors who are critically acclaimed and commercially successful in both Christian and general markets."

MIRIAM ALTSHULER LITERARY AGENCY

53 Old Post Road N., Red Hook NY 12571. (845)758-9408. **Contact:** Miriam Altshuler. Estab. 1994. Member of AAR. Represents 40 clients. Currently handles: 45% nonfiction books; 45% novels; 5% story collections; 5% juvenile books.

• Ms. Altshuler has been an agent since 1982.

Represents Nonfiction books, novels, short story collections, juvenile books. **Considers these nonfiction areas:** Biography/autobiography; ethnic/cultural interests; history; language/literature/criticism; memoirs; multicultural; music/dance; nature/environment; popular culture; psychology; sociology; theater/film; women's issues/studies. **Considers these fiction areas:** Literary; mainstream/contemporary; multicultural.

○➤ Does not want self-help, mystery, how-to, romance, horror, spiritual, fantasy, poetry, screenplays, science fiction or techno-thriller.

How to Contact Query with SASE. Prefers to read materials exclusively. If no SASE is included, no response will be sent. No unsolicited mss. No e-mail or fax queries. Considers simultaneous queries. Responds in 3 weeks to mss. Returns materials only with SASE. Obtains most new clients through recommendations from others.

Terms Agent receives 15% commission on domestic sales; 20% commission on foreign sales. Charges clients for overseas mailing, photocopies, overnight mail when requested by author.

Writers' Conferences Bread Loaf Writers' Conference; Washington Independent Writers Conference; North Carolina Writers' Network Conference.

⊞ ◑ THE AMPERSAND AGENCY

Ryman's Cottages, Little Tew, Oxfordshire OX7 4JJ United Kingdom. (44)(16)868-3677. Fax: (44)(16)868-3449. E-mail: peter@theampersandagency.co.uk. Web site: www.theampersandagency.co.uk. **Contact:** Peter Buckman. Estab. 2003. Member of AAR. Represents 35 clients. 75% of clients are new/unpublished writers.

• Prior to opening his agency, Mr. Buckman was a writer and publisher in England and America.

Member Agents Peter Buckman (literary fiction and nonfiction); Peter Janson-Smith (crime, thrillers, biography); Anne-Marie Doulton (historical and women's fiction).

Represents Nonfiction books, novels, juvenile books, scholarly books. **Considers these nonfiction areas:** Animals; biography/autobiography; cooking/foods/nutrition; current affairs; education; ethnic/cultural interests; government/politics/law; health/medicine; history; humor/satire; language/literature/criticism; memoirs; military/war; music/dance; popular culture; psychology; theater/film; translation; true crime/investigative. **Considers these fiction areas:** Action/adventure; comic books/cartoon; confession; detective/police/crime; ethnic; family saga; fantasy; historical; juvenile; literary; mainstream/contemporary; mystery/suspense; romance; thriller; young adult; glitz.

○➤ "Being a new agency, we specialize in new writers, although we also represent well-established names. We are small, experienced, and professional. We know what we like, respond quickly, and enjoy working with the writers we take on to present their work in the best possible way. We also offer a foreign rights service and have well-established contacts on both sides of the Atlantic in film, TV, broadcasting, and publishing." Actively seeking commercial and literary fiction and nonfiction. Does not want science fiction or works with only regional appeal.

How to Contact Submit outline, 1-2 sample chapters. Accepts queries via e-mail. Considers simultaneous queries. Responds in 1 week to queries; 1 month to mss. Returns materials only with SASE. Obtains most new clients through recommendations, writers' handbooks, word of mouth.

Recent Sales Sold 14 titles in the last year. *Q&A*, by Vikas Swarup (Scribner/Doubleday); *My Side of the Story*, by Will Davis (Bloomsbury); *Digging Up the Dead*, by Dr. Druin Burch (Chatoo & Windus); *Neptune's Daughter*, by Beryl Kingston (Transita). Other clients include Geoff Baker, Max Barron, Rob Buckman, Anna Crosbie, Andrew Cullen, Tom Darke, Francis Ellen, Justin Elliott, Cora Harrison, Georgette Heyer, Michael Hutchinson, Jim McKenna, Euan Macpherson, Bolaji Odofin, Rosie Orr, Philip Purser, Penny Rumble, Nick van Bloss, Mike Walters, Norman Welch, Kirby Wright.

Terms Agent receives 10-15% commission on domestic sales; 20% commission on foreign sales. Offers written contract. "By agreement with the author, we charge for extra photocopying in the case of multiple submissions and for any lawyers or other profesional fees required by a negotiation."

◑ BETSY AMSTER LITERARY ENTERPRISES

P.O. Box 27788, Los Angeles CA 90027-0788. **Contact:** Betsy Amster. Estab. 1992. Member of AAR. Represents more than 65 clients. 35% of clients are new/unpublished writers. Currently handles: 65% nonfiction books; 35% novels.

• Prior to opening her agency, Ms. Amster was an editor at Pantheon and Vintage for 10 years, and served as editorial director for the Globe Pequot Press for 2 years.

Represents Nonfiction books, novels. **Considers these nonfiction areas:** Biography/autobiography; child guidance/parenting; ethnic/cultural interests; gardening; health/medicine; history; money/finance; psychology; sociology; women's issues/studies. **Considers these fiction areas:** Ethnic; literary; mystery/suspense (quirky); thriller (quirky); women's (high quality).

○⇥ Actively seeking strong narrative nonfiction, particularly by journalists; outstanding literary fiction (the next Richard Ford or Jhumpa Lahiri); witty, intelligent commerical women's fiction (the next Elinor Lipman or Jennifer Weiner); mysteries that open new worlds to us; and high-profile self-help and psychology, preferably research based. Does not want to receive poetry, children's books, romances, western, science fiction or action/adventure.

How to Contact For fiction, send query, first 3 pages, SASE. For nonfiction, send query or proposal with SASE. No e-mail or fax queries. Considers simultaneous queries. Responds in 1 month to queries; 2 months to mss. Obtains most new clients through recommendations from others, solicitations, conferences.

Recent Sales *The Blessing of a B Minus*, by Dr. Wendy Mogel (Scribner); *Winners and Lovers: Balancing Love and Power in All Your Relationships*, by Dr. Elaine N. Aron (Little, Brown); *Wild Indigo and Wild Inferno*, by Sandi Ault (Berkley Prime Crime); *Mona Lisa in Camelot: Jacqueline Kennedy and the True Story of the Painting's High-Stakes Journey to America*, by Margaret Leslie Davis (DaCapo); *The Girl I Left Behind: A Narrative History of the Sixties*, by Judith Nies (HarperCollins); *The Battle for Wine and Love (Or How I Saved the World from Parkerization)*, by Alice Feiring (Harcourt); *Mutts*, by Sharon Montrose (Stewart, Tabori & Chang); *A Vicky Hill Exclusive!*, by Hannah Dennison (Berkley Prime Crime); *100 Trees and How They Got Their Names*, by Diana Wells (Algonquin). Other clients include Dr. Linda Acredolo and Dr. Susan Goodwyn, Dwight Allen, Barbara DeMarco-Barrett, Robin Chotzinoff, Rob Cohen & David Wollock, Phil Doran, Ruth Andrew Ellenson, Maria Amparo Escandon, Paul Mandelbaum, Joy Nicholson, Christopher Noxon, Edward Schneider and R.J. Smith.

Terms Agent receives 15% commission on domestic sales; 20% commission on foreign sales. Offers written contract, binding for 1 year; 3-month notice must be given to terminate contract. Charges for photocopying, postage, long distance phone calls, messengers, galleys/books used in submissions to foreign and film agents and to magazines for first serial rights.

Writers' Conferences Squaw Valley Writers' Workshop; San Diego State University Writers' Conference; UCLA Extension Writers' Program; The Loft Literary Center.

⊞ ◎ ANUBIS LITERARY AGENCY

7 Birdhaven Close Lighthorne Heath, Banbury Road, Warwick Warwickshire CV35 0BE, United Kingdom. Phone/Fax: (44)(192)664-2588. E-mail: anubis.agency2@btopenworld.com. **Contact:** Steve Calcutt. Estab. 1994. Represents 15 clients. 50% of clients are new/unpublished writers. Currently handles: 100% novels.

• In addition to being an agent, Mr. Calcutt teaches creative writing and American history (U.S. Civil War) at Warwick University.

Represents Novels. **Considers these fiction areas:** Horror; science fiction; dark fantasy.

○⇥ Actively seeking horror fiction. Does not want to receive children's books, nonfiction, journalism or TV/film scripts.

How to Contact Query with proposal package, outline, SASE/IRCs. Returns materials only with SASE/IRCs. No e-mail or fax queries. Responds in 6 weeks to queries; 3 months to mss. Obtains most new clients through personal recommendation.

Recent Sales *Berserk* and *Dusk*, by Tim Lebbon (Dorchester); *The Beloved*, by J.F. Gonzalez; *Breeding Ground*, by Sarah Pinborough (Dorchester); *Gradisil*, by Adam Roberts (Orion). Other clients include Steve Savile, Lesley Asquith, Anthea Ingham, Brett A. Savory.

Terms Agent receives 15% commission on domestic sales; 20% commission on foreign sales.

◎ APPLESEEDS MANAGEMENT

200 E. 30th St., Suite 302, San Bernardino CA 92404. (909)882-1667. **Contact:** S. James Foiles. Estab. 1988. 40% of clients are new/unpublished writers. Currently handles: 15% nonfiction books; 85% novels.

Represents Nonfiction books, novels. **Considers these nonfiction areas:** True crime/investigative. **Considers these fiction areas:** Detective/police/crime; mystery/suspense.

How to Contact Query with SASE. Responds in 2 weeks to queries; 2 months to mss.

Recent Sales This agency prefers not to share information on specific sales.

Terms Agent receives 10-15% commission on domestic sales; 20% commission on foreign sales. Offers written contract, binding for 1-7 years.

Tips "Because readership of mysteries is expanding, Appleseeds specializes in mysteries with a detective who could be in a continuing series."

◎ ARCADIA

31 Lake Place N., Danbury CT 06810. E-mail: pryor@arcadialit.com. **Contact:** Victoria Gould Pryor. Member of AAR.

Represents Nonfiction books, literary and commercial fiction. **Considers these nonfiction areas:** Biography/autobiography; business/economics; current affairs; health/medicine; history; memoirs; psychology; science/

technology; true crime/investigative; women's issues/studies; investigative journalism; culture; classical music; life transforming self-help.

O— "I'm a very hands-on agent, which is necessary in this competitive marketplace. I work with authors on revisions until whatever we present to publishers is as perfect as it can be. I represent talented, dedicated, intelligent and ambitious writers who are looking for a long-term relationship based on professional success and mutual respect." Does not want to receive science fiction/fantasy, horror, humor or children's/YA. "We are only able to read fiction submissions from previously published authors."

How to Contact Query with SASE. This agency accepts e-queries (no attachments).

Recent Sales This agency prefers not to share information on specific sales.

◨ ARTISTS AND ARTISANS INC.

104 W. 29th St., 11th Floor, New York NY 10001. Fax: (212)931-8377. E-mail: adam@artistsandartisans.com. Web site: www.artistsandartisans.com. **Contact:** Adam Chromy. Estab. 2002. Represents 40 clients. 80% of clients are new/unpublished writers. Currently handles: 63% nonfiction books; 35% novels; 2% scholarly books.

• Prior to becoming an agent, Mr. Chromy was an entrepreneur in the technology field for nearly a decade.

Represents Nonfiction books, novels. **Considers these nonfiction areas:** Biography/autobiography; business/ economics; child guidance/parenting; cooking/foods/nutrition; current affairs; ethnic/cultural interests; health/ medicine; how-to; humor/satire; language/literature/criticism; memoirs; money/finance; music/dance; popular culture; religious/inspirational; science/technology; self-help/personal improvement; sports; theater/film; true crime/investigative; women's issues/studies; fashion/style. **Considers these fiction areas:** Confession; family saga; humor/satire; literary; mainstream/contemporary.

O— "My education and experience in the business world ensure that my clients' enterprise as authors gets as much attention and care as their writing." Working journalists for nonfiction books. No scripts.

How to Contact Query with SASE. Considers simultaneous queries. Responds in 2 weeks to queries; 2 weeks to mss. Returns materials only with SASE. Obtains most new clients through recommendations from others, solicitations, conferences.

Recent Sales Sold 12 titles in the last year. *Dr. Z on Scoring*, by Victoria Zdrok (Touchstone Fireside); *Winning Points with Your Woman*, by Jaci Rae (Touchstone); *From Binge to Blackout*, by Chris Volkmann and Toren Volkmann (NAL Penguin Group); *Modest Mouse*, by Alan Goldsher (Thomas Dunne Books); *Jewtopia*, by Brian Fogel and Sam Wolfson (Warner Books).

Terms Agent receives 15% commission on domestic sales; 25% commission on foreign sales. Offers written contract; 1-month notice must be given to terminate contract. "We only charge for extraordinary expenses (e.g., client requests check via FedEx instead of regular mail)."

Writers' Conferences ASJA Writers Conference.

Tips "Please make sure you are ready before approaching us or any other agent. If you write fiction, make sure it is the best work you can do and get objective criticism from a writing group. If you write nonfiction, make sure the proposal exhibits your best work and a comprehensive understanding of the market."

◨ THE AUGUST AGENCY, LLC

E-mail: submissions@augustagency.com. Web site: www.augustagency.com. **Contact:** Cricket Pechstein, Jeffery McGraw. Estab. 2004. Represents 25-40 clients. 50% of clients are new/unpublished writers. Currently handles: 75% nonfiction books; 20% novels; 5% other.

• Before opening The August Agency, Ms. Pechstein was a freelance writer, magazine editor and independent literary agent; Mr. McGraw worked as an editor for HarperCollins and publicity manager for Abrams.

Member Agents Jeffery McGraw (politics/current affairs, entertainment, business, psychology, self-help, narrative nonfiction, contemporary women's fiction, literary fiction); Cricket Pechstein (mystery/crime fiction, chick lit, thrillers).

Represents Nonfiction books, novels. **Considers these nonfiction areas:** Biography/autobiography; business/ economics; child guidance/parenting; cooking/foods/nutrition; current affairs; ethnic/cultural interests; gay/ lesbian issues; government/politics/law; health/medicine; history; how-to; humor/satire; interior design/decorating; memoirs; military/war; money/finance; music/dance; popular culture; psychology; self-help/personal improvement; sociology; sports; theater/film; true crime/investigative; women's issues/studies; inspirational. **Considers these fiction areas:** Action/adventure; detective/police/crime; ethnic; family saga; gay/lesbian; historical; humor/satire; literary; mainstream/contemporary; mystery/suspense; psychic/supernatural; thriller; smart chick lit (non-genre romance).

O— "We actively pursue an array of fiction and nonfiction writers to represent, with an emphasis in media (seasoned journalists receive special favor here), popular culture/entertainment, political science, diet/ fitness, health, cookbooks, psychology, business, memoir, highly creative nonfiction, accessible literary fiction, women's fiction, and high-concept mysteries and thrillers. When it comes to nonfiction, we favor persuasive and prescriptive works with a full-bodied narrative command and an undeniable contemporary relevance. Our favorite novelists are as eclectic as our minds are broad, yet they all share one common denominator that might explain a peculiar predisposition for what we prefer to call 'emotional fiction'—a brand of storytelling defined not so much by a novel's category as by its extraordinary power to resonate universally on a deeply emotional level." Does not want to receive academic textbooks, children's books, cozy mysteries, horror, poetry, science fiction/fantasy, short story collections, westerns, screenplays, genre romance or previously self-published works.

How to Contact Submit book summary (1-2 paragraphs), chapter outline (nonfiction only), first 1,000 words or first chapter, total page/word count, brief paragraph on why you have chosen to write the book. Send via e-mail only (no attachments). Responds in 2-3 weeks to queries; 3 months to mss. Obtains most new clients through recommendations from others, solicitations, conferences.

Terms Agent receives 15% commission on domestic sales; 20% commission on foreign sales. Offers written contract; 1-month notice must be given to terminate contract.

Writers' Conferences Surrey International Writers' Conference; Southern California Writers' Conference; Naples Writers' Conference, et al.

AUTHENTIC CREATIONS LITERARY AGENCY

911 Duluth Hwy., Suite D3-144, Lawrenceville GA 30043. (770)339-3774. Fax: (770)339-7126. E-mail: ron@authenticcreations.com. Web site: www.authenticcreations.com. **Contact:** Mary Lee Laitsch. Estab. 1993. Member of AAR, Authors Guild. Represents 70 clients. 30% of clients are new/unpublished writers. Currently handles: 60% nonfiction books; 40% novels.

Member Agents Mary Lee Laitsch; Ronald Laitsch; Jason Laitsch.

Represents Nonfiction books, novels, scholarly books. **Considers these nonfiction areas:** Anthropology/archaeology; biography/autobiography; child guidance/parenting; crafts/hobbies; current affairs; history; how-to; science/technology; self-help/personal improvement; sports; true crime/investigative; women's issues/studies. **Considers these fiction areas:** Action/adventure; detective/police/crime; family saga; literary; mainstream/contemporary; mystery/suspense; romance; sports; thriller.

How to Contact Query with SASE. No e-mail or fax queries. Considers simultaneous queries. Responds in 2 weeks to queries; 2 months to mss.

Recent Sales Sold 20 titles in the last year. *Secret Agent*, by Robyn Spizman and Mark Johnston (Simon & Schuster); *Beauchamp Beseiged*, by Elaine Knighton (Harlequin); *Visible Differences*, by Dominic Pulera (Continuum).

Terms Agent receives 15% commission on domestic sales; 15% commission on foreign sales. This agency charges clients for photocopying.

THE AXELROD AGENCY

55 Main St., P.O. Box 357, Chatham NY 12037. (518)392-2100. Fax: (518)392-2944. E-mail: steve@axelrodagency.com. **Contact:** Steven Axelrod. Estab. 1983. Member of AAR. Represents 20-30 clients. 1% of clients are new/unpublished writers. Currently handles: 5% nonfiction books; 95% novels.

• Prior to becoming an agent, Mr. Axelrod was a book club editor.

Represents Nonfiction books, novels. **Considers these fiction areas:** Mystery/suspense; romance; women's.

How to Contact Query with SASE. Considers simultaneous queries. Responds in 3 weeks to queries; 6 weeks to mss. Returns materials only with SASE. Obtains most new clients through recommendations from others.

Recent Sales This agency prefers not to share information on specific sales.

Terms Agent receives 15% commission on domestic sales; 20% commission on foreign sales. No written contract.

Writers' Conferences RWA National Conference.

BARER LITERARY, LLC

156 Fifth Ave., Suite 1134, New York NY 10010. Web site: www.barerliterary.com. **Contact:** Julie Barer. Member of AAR.

Represents Nonfiction books, novels, short story collections. **Considers these nonfiction areas:** Biography/autobiography; ethnic/cultural interests; history; memoirs; popular culture; women's issues/studies. **Considers these fiction areas:** Ethnic; family saga; historical; literary; mainstream/contemporary; young adult.

How to Contact Query with SASE.

Recent Sales *A Ticket to Ride*, by Paula McLain (Ecco); *What You Have Left*, by Will Allison (Free Press); *Still Life With Husband*, by Lauren Fox (Knopf); *Then We Came to the End*, by Joshua Ferris (Little, Brown); *Frenemies*, by Megan Crane (Warner Books); *The Time It Takes to Fall*, by Margaret Lazarus Dean (Simon & Schuster).

Terms Agent receives 15% commission on domestic sales; 20% commission on foreign sales. Offers written contract. Charges for photocopying and books ordered.

🗹 LORETTA BARRETT BOOKS, INC.

101 Fifth Ave., New York NY 10003. (212)242-3420. Fax: (212)807-9579. E-mail: query@lorettabarrettbooks.com. Web site: www.lorettabarrettbooks.com. **Contact:** Loretta A. Barrett, Nick Mullendore. Estab. 1990. Member of AAR. Currently handles: 50% nonfiction books; 50% novels.

- Prior to opening her agency, Ms. Barrett was vice president and executive editor at Doubleday and editor-in-chief of Anchor Books.

Represents Nonfiction books, novels. **Considers these nonfiction areas:** Biography/autobiography; child guidance/parenting; current affairs; ethnic/cultural interests; government/politics/law; health/medicine; history; memoirs; money/finance; multicultural; nature/environment; popular culture; psychology; religious/inspirational; science/technology; self-help/personal improvement; sociology; spirituality; sports; women's issues/studies; nutrition; creative nonfiction. **Considers these fiction areas:** Action/adventure; contemporary issues; detective/police/crime; ethnic; family saga; historical; literary; mainstream/contemporary; mystery/suspense; psychic/supernatural; thriller.

- ☛ This agency specializes in general interest books. No children's, juvenile, science fiction, or fantasy.

How to Contact Query with SASE. Accepts e-mail queries. No fax queries. Considers simultaneous queries. Responds in 2-3 weeks to queries. Returns materials only with SASE.

Recent Sales *Spiritual Progress*, by Thomas D. Williams (Hachette); *The Hazards of Space Travel*, by Neil Comins (Ballantine); *Mother Angelica's Little Book of Life Lessons*, by Raymond Arroyo (Doubleday) and more.

Terms Agent receives 15% commission on domestic sales; 20% commission on foreign sales. Offers written contract. Charges clients for shipping and photocopying.

🗹 FAYE BENDER LITERARY AGENCY

337 W. 76th St., #E1, New York NY 10023. E-mail: info@fbliterary.com. Web site: www.fbliterary.com. **Contact:** Faye Bender. Estab. 2004. Member of AAR.

Represents Nonfiction books, novels, juvenile books. **Considers these nonfiction areas:** Memoirs; popular culture; women's issues/studies; young adult; narrative; health; biography; popular science. **Considers these fiction areas:** Literary; young adult (middle-grade); women's; commercial.

- ☛ "I choose books based on the narrative voice and strength of writing. I work with previously published and first-time authors." Does not want genre fiction (western, romance, horror, fantasy, science fiction).

How to Contact Query with SASE and 10 sample pages via mail or e-mail. No fax queries.

Recent Sales *Science Experiments*, by Karen Romano Young (National Geographic Society); *The Last Beach Bungalow*, by Jennie Nash (Berkley).

Tips "Please keep your letters to the point, include all relevant information, and have a bit of patience."

🗹 MEREDITH BERNSTEIN LITERARY AGENCY

2095 Broadway, Suite 505, New York NY 10023. (212)799-1007. Fax: (212)799-1145. Estab. 1981. Member of AAR. Represents 85 clients. 20% of clients are new/unpublished writers. Currently handles: 50% nonfiction books; 50% fiction.

- Prior to opening her agency, Ms. Bernstein served at another agency for 5 years.

Represents Nonfiction books, novels. **Considers these nonfiction areas:** Any area of nonfiction in which the author has an established platform. **Considers these fiction areas:** Literary; mystery/suspense; romance; thriller; women's.

- ☛ This agency does not specialize. It is very eclectic.

How to Contact Query with SASE. No e-mail or fax queries. Considers simultaneous queries. Obtains most new clients through recommendations from others, conferences, developing/packaging ideas.

Recent Sales Three untitled novels of suspense, by Nancy Pickard (Ballantine); *Why Women Lie*, by Susan Baresh; *Bride's Diplomacy Guide*, by Sharon Naylor (Adams); *Mortgage Brokering*, by Darrin Seppinni (McGraw, Hill).

Terms Agent receives 15% commission on domestic sales; 20% commission on foreign sales. Charges clients $75 disbursement fee/year.

Writers' Conferences Southwest Writers' Conference; Rocky Mountain Fiction Writers' Colorado Gold; Pacific Northwest Writers' Conference; Willamette Writers' Conference; Surrey International Writers' Conference; San Diego State University Writers' Conference.

🗹 BIGSCORE PRODUCTIONS, INC.

(717)293-0247. E-mail: bigscore@bigscoreproductions.com. Web site: www.bigscoreproductions.com. **Contact:** David A. Robie. Estab. 1995. Represents 50-75 clients. 25% of clients are new/unpublished writers.

Represents Nonfiction and fiction (see Web site for categories of interest).

O⟶ Mr. Robie specializes in inspirational and self-help nonfiction and fiction, and has been in the publishing and agenting business for over 20 years.

How to Contact See Web site for submission guidelines. Query by e-mail only. Do not fax or mail queries. Considers simultaneous queries. Only responds if interested.

Terms Agent receives 15% commission on domestic sales. Offers written contract, binding for 6 months.

Tips "We are very open to taking on new nonfiction clients. We only consider established fiction writers. Submit a well-prepared proposal that will take minimal fine-tuning for presentation to publishers. Nonfiction writers must be highly marketable and media savvy—the more established in speaking or in your profession, the better. Bigscore Productions works with all major general and Christian publishers."

◢ BLEECKER STREET ASSOCIATES, INC.

532 LaGuardia Place, #617, New York NY 10012. (212)677-4492. Fax: (212)388-0001. **Contact:** Agnes Birnbaum. Estab. 1984. Member of AAR, RWA, MWA. Represents 60 clients. 20% of clients are new/unpublished writers. Currently handles: 75% nonfiction books; 25% novels.

• Prior to becoming an agent, Ms. Birnbaum was a senior editor at Simon & Schuster, Dutton/Signet, and other publishing houses.

Represents Nonfiction books, novels. **Considers these nonfiction areas:** Animals; biography/autobiography; business/economics; child guidance/parenting; computers/electronic; cooking/foods/nutrition; current affairs; ethnic/cultural interests; government/politics/law; health/medicine; history; how-to; memoirs; military/war; money/finance; nature/environment; New Age/metaphysics; popular culture; psychology; religious/inspirational; science/technology; self-help/personal improvement; sociology; sports; true crime/investigative; women's issues/studies. **Considers these fiction areas:** Ethnic; historical; literary; mystery/suspense; romance; thriller; women's.

O⟶ "We're very hands-on and accessible. We try to be truly creative in our submission approaches. We've had especially good luck with first-time authors." Does not want to receive science fiction, westerns, poetry, children's books, academic/scholarly/professional books, plays, scripts, or short stories.

How to Contact Query with SASE. No e-mail, phone, or fax queries. Considers simultaneous queries. Responds in 2 weeks to queries; 1 month to mss. Returns materials only with SASE. Obtains most new clients through recommendations from others, solicitations, conferences, "plus, I will approach someone with a letter if his/her work impresses me."

Recent Sales Sold 20 titles in the last year. *Following Sarah*, by Daniel Brown (Morrow); *Biology of the Brain*, by Paul Swingle (Rutgers University Press); *Tripoli*, by David Smethurst (Ballantine); *Phantom Warrior*, by Bryant Johnson (Berkley).

Terms Agent receives 15% commission on domestic sales; 25% commission on foreign sales. Offers written contract; 1-month notice must be given to terminate contract. Charges for postage, long distance, fax, messengers, photocopies (not to exceed $200).

Tips "Keep query letters short and to the point; include only information pertaining to the book or background as a writer. Try to avoid superlatives in description. Work needs to stand on its own, so how much editing it may have received has no place in a query letter."

◢ THE BLUMER LITERARY AGENCY, INC.

350 Seventh Ave., Suite 2003, New York NY 10001-5013. (212)947-3040. **Contact:** Olivia B. Blumer. Estab. 2002. Member of AAR. Represents 34 clients. 60% of clients are new/unpublished writers. Currently handles: 67% nonfiction books; 33% novels.

• Prior to becoming an agent, Ms. Blumer spent 25 years in publishing (subsidiary rights, publicity, editorial).

Represents Nonfiction books, novels. **Considers these nonfiction areas:** Agriculture/horticulture; animals; anthropology/archaeology; art/architecture/design; biography/autobiography; business/economics; cooking/foods/nutrition; ethnic/cultural interests; health/medicine; how-to; humor/satire; language/literature/criticism; memoirs; money/finance; nature/environment; photography; popular culture; psychology; religious/inspirational; self-help/personal improvement; true crime/investigative; women's issues/studies; New Age/metaphysics; crafts/hobbies; interior design/decorating. **Considers these fiction areas:** Detective/police/crime; ethnic; family saga; feminist; historical; humor/satire; literary; mainstream/contemporary; mystery/suspense; regional; thriller.

O⟶ Actively seeking quality fiction, practical nonfiction, and memoir with a larger purpose.

How to Contact Query with SASE. No e-mail or fax queries. Responds in 3 weeks to queries; 4-6 weeks to mss. Returns materials only with SASE. Obtains most new clients through recommendations from others, but significant exceptions have come from the slush pile.

Recent Sales *The Color of Law*, by Mark Gimenez; *Still Life with Chickens*, by Catherine Goldhammer; *Demoli-*

tion Desserts, by Elizabeth Falkner; *Fat* by Jennifer McLagan; *Carpool Diem*, by Nancy Star. Other clients include Joan Anderson, Marialisa Calta, Ellen Rolfes, Laura Karr, Liz McGregor, Lauri Ward, Susann Cokal, Dennis L. Smith, Sharon Pywell, Sarah Turnbull, Naomi Duguid, Jeffrey Alford.

Terms Agent receives 15% commission on domestic sales; 20% commission on foreign sales. Charges for photocopying, overseas shipping, FedEx/UPS.

BOOKENDS, LLC

Web site: www.bookends-inc.com; bookendslitagency.blogspot.com. **Contact:** Jessica Faust, Jacky Sach, Kim Lionetti. Estab. 1999. Member of AAR. Represents 50+ clients. 10% of clients are new/unpublished writers. Currently handles: 50% nonfiction books; 50% novels.

Member Agents Jessica Faust (Fiction: romance, erotica, chick lit, women's fiction, mysterious and suspense. Nonfiction: business, finance, career, parenting, psychology, women's issues, self-help, health, sex); Jacky Sach (mysteries, women's fiction, suspense, self-help, spirituality, alternative and mainstream health, business and career, addiction, chick-lit nonfiction).

Represents Nonfiction books, novels. **Considers these nonfiction areas:** Business/economics; child guidance/parenting; ethnic/cultural interests; gay/lesbian issues; health/medicine; how-to; money/finance; New Age/metaphysics; psychology; religious/inspirational; self-help/personal improvement; sex; spirituality; true crime/investigative; women's issues/studies. **Considers these fiction areas:** Detective/police/crime (cozies); mainstream/contemporary; mystery/suspense; romance; thriller; women's; chick lit.

⊶ BookEnds does not want to receive children's books, screenplays, science fiction, poetry, or technical/military thrillers.

How to Contact Review Web site for guidelines.

Recent Sales *1,000 Wine Secrets*, by Carolyn Hammond (Sourcebooks); *Wolf Tales III*, by Kate Douglas (Kensington Aphrodisia); *Women at Ground Zero*, by Mary Carouba and Susan Hagen (Alpha Books).

BOOKS & SUCH LITERARY AGENCY

52 Mission Circle, Suite 122, PMB 170, Santa Rosa CA 95409. E-mail: representative@booksandsuch.biz. Web site: www.booksandsuch.biz. **Contact:** Janet Kobobel Grant, Wendy Lawton. Estab. 1996. Member of CBA (associate), American Christian Fiction Writers. Represents 80 clients. 5% of clients are new/unpublished writers. Currently handles: 50% nonfiction books; 50% novels.

● Prior to becoming an agent, Ms. Grant was an editor for Zondervan and managing editor for *Focus on the Family*; Ms. Lawton was an author, sculptor and designer of porcelein dolls.

Represents Nonfiction books, novels. **Considers these nonfiction areas:** Child guidance/parenting; humor/satire; religious/inspirational; self-help/personal improvement; women's issues/studies. **Considers these fiction areas:** Contemporary issues; family saga; historical; mainstream/contemporary; religious/inspirational; romance; African American adult.

⊶ This agency specializes in general and inspirational fiction, romance, and in the Christian booksellers market. Actively seeking well-crafted material that presents Judeo-Christian values, if only subtly.

How to Contact Query with SASE. Considers simultaneous queries. Responds in 1 month to queries; 2 months to mss. Returns materials only with SASE. Obtains most new clients through recommendations from others, conferences.

Recent Sales Sold 112 titles in the last year. *Awaken My Heart*, by Diann Mills (Avon Inspire); *My Life As a Doormat (In Three Acts)*, by Rene Gutteridge; *Having a Mary Spirit*, by Joanna Weaver; *Finding Father Christmas*, by Robin Jones Gunn; *No More Mr. Christian Nice Guy*, by Paul Coughlin. Other clients include Janet McHenry, Jane Orcutt, Gayle Roper, Stephanie Grace Whitson, Dale Cramer, Patti Hill, Gayle Roper, Sara Horn.

Terms Agent receives 15% commission on domestic sales; 15% commission on foreign sales. Offers written contract; 2-month notice must be given to terminate contract. Charges clients for postage, photocopying, telephone calls, fax, express mail.

Writers' Conferences Mount Hermon Christian Writers' Conference; Wrangling With Writing; Glorieta Christian Writers' Conference; Writing for the Soul; Blue Ridge Mountains Christian Writers' Conference; American Christian Fiction Writers' Conference; Sandy Cove Christian Writers' Conference; San Francisco Writers' Conference.

Tips "The heart of our agency's motivation is to develop relationships with the authors we serve, to do what we can to shine the light of success on them, and to help be a caretaker of their gifts and time."

BRANDT & HOCHMAN LITERARY AGENTS, INC.

1501 Broadway, Suite 2310, New York NY 10036. (212)840-5760. Fax: (212)840-5776. **Contact:** Gail Hochman. Estab. 1913. Member of AAR. Represents 200 clients.

Member Agents Carl Brandt; Gail Hochman; Marianne Merola; Charles Schlessiger; Bill Contardi.

Represents Nonfiction books, novels, short story collections, juvenile books, journalism. **Considers these**

nonfiction areas: Biography/autobiography; current affairs; ethnic/cultural interests; government/politics/law; history; women's issues/studies. **Considers these fiction areas:** Contemporary issues; ethnic; historical; literary; mainstream/contemporary; mystery/suspense; romance; thriller; young adult.

How to Contact Query with SASE. No e-mail or fax queries. Considers simultaneous queries. Responds in 1 month to queries. Returns materials only with SASE. Obtains most new clients through recommendations from others.

Recent Sales *Season of Betrayal*, by Margaret Lowrie Robertson (Harcourt); *The Misremembered Man*, by Christina McKenna (Toby Press). Other clients include Scott Turow, Carlos Fuentes, Ursula Hegi, Michael Cunningham, Mary Pope Osborne, Julia Glass.

Terms Agent receives 15% commission on domestic sales; 20% commission on foreign sales. Charges clients for ms duplication or other special expenses agreed to in advance.

Tips "Write a letter which will give the agent a sense of you as a professional writer—your long-term interests as well as a short description of the work at hand."

⊙ BARBARA BRAUN ASSOCIATES, INC.

104 Fifth Ave., 7th Floor, New York NY 10011. Fax: (212)604-9041. E-mail: bba230@earthlink.net. Web site: www.barbarabraunagency.com. **Contact:** Barbara Braun. Member of AAR.

Member Agents Barbara Braun; John F. Baker.

Represents Nonfiction books, novels.

    ○ "Our fiction is strong on women's stories, historical and multicultural stories, as well as mysteries and thrillers. We're interested in narrative nonfiction and books by journalists. We do not represent poetry, science fiction, fantasy, horror, or screenplays." Look online for more details.

How to Contact Query with SASE. Accepts e-mail queries (no full mss).

Recent Sales *Luncheon of the Boating Party*, by Susan Vreeland (Viking/Penguin); *Looking for Salvation at the Dairy Queen* and a second novel, by Susan Gregg Gilmore (Shaye Areheart/Crown); *Vivaldi's Girls*, by Laurel Corona (Hyperion); *Heartbreak Town* and a sequel, by Marsha Moyer (Three Rivers/Crown); *The Lost Van Gogh*, by A.J. Zerries (Tor/Forge); *Terror in Michigan*, by Arnie Bernstein (Univ. of Michigan Press); *A Strand of Corpses* and *A Friend of Need*, by J.R. Benn (Soho Press).

Terms Agent receives 15% commission on domestic sales; 20% commission on foreign sales.

ℕ ⊞ ⊘ CURTIS BROWN (AUST) PTY LTD

P.O. Box 19, Paddington NSW 2021, Australia. (61)(2)9361-6161. Fax: (61)(2)9360-3935. E-mail: info@curtisbrown.com.au. Web site: www.curtisbrown.com.au. **Contact:** Submissions Department. Estab. 1967. Represents 350 clients. 10% of clients are new/unpublished writers. Currently handles: 30% nonfiction books; 30% novels; 25% juvenile books; 5% scholarly books; 5% textbooks; 5% other.

    ● "Prior to joining Curtis Brown, most of our agents worked in publishing or the film/theatre industries in Australia and the United Kingdom."

Member Agents Fiona Inglis, managing director; Fran Moore, agent/deputy managing director; Tara Wynne, agent; Pippa Masson, agent.

Represents Nonfiction books, novels, novellas, juvenile books.

    ○ "We are the oldest and largest literary agency in Australia and we look after a wide variety of clients." No poetry, short stories, film scripts, picture books or translations.

How to Contact Submit 3 sample chapters, cover letter with biographical information, synopsis (2-3 pages), SASE. No fax queries.

Recent Sales *The Messenger*, by Marcus Zusak (Pan Macmillan); *Holly, Jess and C*, by Jane Burke (Random House); *Dark Space*, by Marianne De Pierres (Orbit UK).

⊘ BROWN LITERARY AGENCY

410 7th St. NW, Naples FL 34120. Web site: www.brownliteraryagency.com. **Contact:** Roberta Brown. Estab. 1996. Member of AAR, RWA, Author's Guild. Represents 35 clients. 5% of clients are new/unpublished writers.

    ● This agency is not seeking new clients at this time.

Member Agents Roberta Brown (women's fiction, romance, erotica).

Represents Novels. **Considers these fiction areas:** Erotica; romance (single title and category); women's.

    ○ (This agency is not seeking new clients.)

How to Contact No e-mail or fax queries. Obtains most new clients through visitors to Web site.

Recent Sales Other clients include Clients include Emma Holly, Angela Knight, Karen Kay, Jenna Mills, Dianne Castell, Lora Leigh, Shiloh Walker, Kate Angell, Sue-Ellen Welfonder.

Terms Agent receives 15% commission on domestic sales; 15% commission on foreign sales. Offers written contract; 30-day notice must be given to terminate contract.

Writers' Conferences RWA National Conference; Romantic Times Convention.

Tips "Polish your manuscript. Be professional."

◙ CURTIS BROWN, LTD.

10 Astor Place, New York NY 10003-6935. (212)473-5400. Web site: www.curtisbrown.com. Alternate address: Peter Ginsberg, president at CBSF, 1750 Montgomery St., San Francisco CA 94111. (415)954-8566. Member of AAR; signatory of WGA.

Member Agents Laura Blake Peterson; Emilie Jacobson, senior vice president; Maureen Walters, senior vice president; Ginger Knowlton, vice president; Mitchell Waters; Elizabeth Harding; Holly Frederick; Timothy Knowlton, CEO; Ginger Clark; Katherine Fausset.

Represents Nonfiction books, novels, short story collections, juvenile books. **Considers these nonfiction areas:** Agriculture/horticulture; Americana; animals; anthropology/archaeology; art/architecture/design; biography/autobiography; business/economics; child guidance/parenting; computers/electronic; cooking/foods/nutrition; crafts/hobbies; current affairs; education; ethnic/cultural interests; gardening; gay/lesbian issues; government/politics/law; health/medicine; history; how-to; humor/satire; interior design/decorating; juvenile nonfiction; language/literature/criticism; memoirs; military/war; money/finance; multicultural; music/dance; nature/environment; New Age/metaphysics; philosophy; photography; popular culture; psychology; recreation; regional; religious/inspirational; science/technology; self-help/personal improvement; sex; sociology; software; spirituality; sports; theater/film; translation; travel; true crime/investigative; women's issues/studies; young adult; creative nonfiction. **Considers these fiction areas:** Action/adventure; comic books/cartoon; confession; contemporary issues; detective/police/crime; erotica; ethnic; experimental; family saga; fantasy; feminist; gay/lesbian; glitz; gothic; hi-lo; historical; horror; humor/satire; juvenile; literary; mainstream/contemporary; military/war; multicultural; multimedia; mystery/suspense; New Age; occult; picture books; plays; poetry; psychic/supernatural; regional; religious/inspirational; romance; science fiction; short story collections; spiritual; sports; thriller; translation; westerns/frontier; young adult; women's.

How to Contact Query individual agent with SASE. Prefers to read materials exclusively. *No unsolicited mss.* No e-mail or fax queries. Responds in 3 weeks to queries; 5 weeks to mss. Obtains most new clients through recommendations from others, solicitations, conferences.

Recent Sales This agency prefers not to share information on specific sales.

Terms Offers written contract. Charges for photocopying and some postage.

◙ BROWNE & MILLER LITERARY ASSOCIATES

410 S. Michigan Ave., Suite 460, Chicago IL 60605-1465. (312)922-3063. E-mail: mail@browneandmiller.com. **Contact:** Danielle Egan-Miller. Estab. 1971. Member of AAR, RWA, MWA, Author's Guild. Represents 150 clients. 2% of clients are new/unpublished writers. Currently handles: 40% nonfiction books; 60% novels.

Represents Nonfiction books, novels. **Considers these nonfiction areas:** Agriculture/horticulture; animals; anthropology/archaeology; biography/autobiography; business/economics; child guidance/parenting; cooking/foods/nutrition; crafts/hobbies; current affairs; ethnic/cultural interests; health/medicine; how-to; humor/satire; memoirs; money/finance; nature/environment; popular culture; psychology; religious/inspirational; science/technology; self-help/personal improvement; sociology; sports; true crime/investigative; women's issues/studies. **Considers these fiction areas:** Detective/police/crime; ethnic; family saga; glitz; historical; literary; mainstream/contemporary; mystery/suspense; religious/inspirational; romance (contemporary, gothic, historical, regency); sports; thriller.

    ○┓ "We are generalists looking for professional writers with finely honed skills in writing. We are partial to authors with promotion savvy. We work closely with our authors through the whole publishing process, from proposal to after publication." Actively seeking highly commercial mainstream fiction and nonfiction. Does not represent poetry, short stories, plays, screenplays, articles, or children's books.

How to Contact Query with SASE. *No unsolicited mss.* Prefers to read material exclusively. Responds in 6 weeks to queries. Returns materials only with SASE. Obtains most new clients through referrals, queries by professional/marketable authors.

Terms Agent receives 15% commission on domestic sales; 20% commission on foreign sales. Offers written contract, binding for 2 years. Charges clients for photocopying, overseas postage, faxes, phone calls.

Writers' Conferences BookExpo America; Frankfurt Book Fair; RWA National Conference; CBA National Conference; London Book Fair; Bouchercon.

Tips "If interested in agency representation, be well informed."

◙ PEMA BROWNE, LTD.

11 Tena Place, Valley Cottage NY 10989. Web site: www.pemabrowneltd.com. **Contact:** Pema Browne. Estab. 1966. Member of SCBWI, RWA; signatory of WGA. Represents 30 clients. Currently handles: 25% nonfiction books; 50% novels/romance novels; 25% juvenile books.

• Prior to opening her agency, Ms. Browne was an artist and art buyer.

Represents Nonfiction books, novels, juvenile books, reference books. **Considers these nonfiction areas:** Business/economics; child guidance/parenting; cooking/foods/nutrition; ethnic/cultural interests; gay/lesbian issues; health/medicine; how-to; juvenile nonfiction; money/finance; New Age/metaphysics; popular culture; psychology; religious/inspirational; self-help/personal improvement; spirituality; women's issues/studies; reference. **Considers these fiction areas:** Action/adventure; contemporary issues; feminist; gay/lesbian; glitz; historical; juvenile; literary; mainstream/contemporary (commercial); mystery/suspense; picture books; religious/inspirational; romance (contemporary, gothic, historical, regency); young adult.

Oₙ "We are not accepting any new projects or authors until further notice."

How to Contact Query with SASE.

Recent Sales *The Champion*, by Heather Grothaus (Kensington/Zebra); *The Highlander's Bride*, by Michele Peach (Kensington/Zebra); *Whispers*, by Samatha Garver (Kensington/Zebra); *Yellowstone Park*, by Linda Cargill (Cora Verlag); *The Daring Harriet Quimby*, by Suzane Whitaker (Holiday House); *One Night to Be Sinful*, by Samantha Garver (Kensington); *Point Eyes of the Dragon*, by Linda Cargill (Cora Verlag).

Terms Agent receives 20% commission on domestic sales; 20% commission on foreign sales.

Tips "We do not review manuscripts that have been sent out to publishers. If writing romance, be sure to receive guidelines from various romance publishers. In nonfiction, one must have credentials to lend credence to a proposal. Make sure of margins, double-space, and use clean, dark type."

⬤ SHEREE BYKOFSKY ASSOCIATES, INC.

16 W. 36th St., 13th Floor, New York NY 10018. E-mail: submitbee@aol.com. Web site: www.shereebee.com. **Contact:** Sheree Bykofsky. Estab. 1984, incorporated 1991. Member of AAR, ASJA, WNBA. Currently handles: 80% nonfiction books; 20% novels.

• Prior to opening her agency, Ms. Bykofsky served as executive editor of The Stonesong Press and managing editor of Chiron Press. She is also the author or co-author of more than 20 books, including *The Complete Idiot's Guide to Getting Published*. Ms. Bykofsky teaches publishing at NYU and SEAK, Inc.

Member Agents Janet Rosen, associate; Caroline Woods, associate.

Represents Nonfiction books, novels. **Considers these nonfiction areas:** Americana; animals; art/architecture/design; biography/autobiography; business/economics; child guidance/parenting; cooking/foods/nutrition; crafts/hobbies; current affairs; education; ethnic/cultural interests; gardening; gay/lesbian issues; government/politics/law; health/medicine; history; how-to; humor/satire; interior design/decorating; language/literature/criticism; memoirs; military/war; money/finance (personal finance); multicultural; music/dance; nature/environment; New Age/metaphysics; philosophy; photography; popular culture; psychology; recreation; regional; religious/inspirational; science/technology; self-help/personal improvement; sex; sociology; spirituality; sports; theater/film; translation; travel; true crime/investigative; women's issues/studies; anthropolgy; creative nonfiction. **Considers these fiction areas:** Literary; mainstream/contemporary; mystery/suspense.

Oₙ This agency specializes in popular reference nonfiction, commercial fiction with a literary quality, and mysteries. "I have wide-ranging interests, but it really depends on quality of writing, originality, and how a particular project appeals to me (or not). I take on fiction when I completely love it—it doesn't matter what area or genre." Does not want to receive poetry, material for children, screenplays, westerns, horror, science fiction, or fantasy.

How to Contact Query with SASE. No unsolicited mss, e-mail queries, or phone calls. Considers simultaneous queries. Responds in 3 weeks to queries with SASE. Responds in 1 month to requested mss. Returns materials only with SASE. Obtains most new clients through recommendations from others.

Recent Sales Sold 100 titles in the last year. *Self-Esteem Sickness*, by Albert Ellis (Prometheus); *When the Ghost Screams*, by Leslie Rule (Andrews McMeel); *225 Squares*, by Matt Gaffney (Avalon).

Terms Agent receives 15% commission on domestic sales; 20% commission on foreign sales. Offers written contract, binding for 1 year. Charges for postage, photocopying, fax.

Writers' Conferences ASJA Writers Conference; Asilomar; Florida Suncoast Writers' Conference; Whidbey Island Writers' Conference; Florida First Coast Writers' Festibal; Agents and Editors Conference; Columbus Writers Conference; Southwest Writers Conference; Willamette Writers Conferece; Dorothy Canfield Fisher Conference; Maui Writers Conference; Pacific Northwest Writers Conference; IWWG.

Tips "Read the agent listing carefully and comply with guidelines."

⬤ CANTON SMITH AGENCY

E-mail: bookhold2@yahoo.com; bookhold1@yahoo.com. Web site: www.cantonsmithagency.com. **Contact:** Eric Smith, senior partner (esmith@cantonsmithagency.com); Chamein Canton, partner (chamein@cantonsmithagency.com); Netta Beckford, associate (nettab@cantonsmithagency.com). Estab. 2001. Represents 28 clients. 100% of clients are new/unpublished writers.

• Prior to becoming agents, Mr. Smith was in advertising and bookstore retail; Ms. Canton was a writer and a paralegal; Ms. Beckford attended Johnson and Wales University.

Member Agents Eric Smith (science fiction, sports, literature); Chamein Canton (how-to, reference, literary, women's, multicultural, ethnic, crafts, cooking, health); Melissa Falcone (childrens, juvenile, young adult, teen, fantasy); Netta Beckford (cookbooks, health, new age, metaphysical, holistic healing, astrology, numerology, Eastern medicine).

Represents Nonfiction books, novels, juvenile books, scholarly books, textbooks, movie scripts. **Considers these nonfiction areas:** Art/architecture/design; business/economics; child guidance/parenting; cooking/foods/nutrition; education; ethnic/cultural interests; health/medicine; history; how-to; humor/satire; language/literature/criticism; memoirs; military/war; music/dance; photography; psychology; sports; translation; women's issues/studies. **Considers these fiction areas:** Fantasy; humor/satire; juvenile; multicultural; romance; young adult; Latina fiction; chick lit; African-American fiction; entertainment. **Considers these script subject areas:** Action/adventure; comedy; romantic comedy; romantic drama; science fiction.

O→ "We specialize in helping new and established writers expand their marketing potential for prospective publishers. We are currently focusing on women's fiction (chick lit), Latina fiction, African American fiction, multicultural, romance, memoirs, humor and entertainment, in addition to more nonfiction titles (cooking, how-to, fashion, home improvement, etc)."

How to Contact Only accepts e-queries. Send a query, not sample chapters and/or proposals, unless specifically requested. Considers simultaneous queries. Responds in 5 months to queries; 5 months to mss. Obtains most new clients through recommendations from others.

Recent Sales Sold 7 titles in the last year. Clients include Robert Koger, Olivia, Jennifer DeWit, Sheila Smestad, James Weil, Jaime Nava, JC Miller, Diana Smith, Robert Beers, Marcy Gannon, Keith Maxwell, Dawn Jackson, Jeannine Carney, Mark Barlow, Robert Marsocci, Anita Ballard Jones, Deb Mohr, Seth Ahonen, Melissa Graf, Robert Zavala, Cliff Webb, John and Carolyn Osborne.

Terms Agent receives 15% commission on domestic sales; 20% commission on foreign sales. Offers written contract; 2-month notice must be given to terminate contract.

Tips "Know your market. Agents, as well as publishers, are keenly interested in writers with their finger on the pulse of their market."

CASTIGLIA LITERARY AGENCY

1155 Camino Del Mar, Suite 510, Del Mar CA 92014. (858)755-8761. Fax: (858)755-7063. Estab. 1993. Member of AAR, PEN. Represents 50 clients. Currently handles: 55% nonfiction books; 45% novels.

Member Agents Julie Castiglia; Winifred Golden; Sally Van Haitsma.

Represents Nonfiction books, novels. **Considers these nonfiction areas:** Animals; anthropology/archaeology; biography/autobiography; business/economics; child guidance/parenting; cooking/foods/nutrition; current affairs; ethnic/cultural interests; health/medicine; history; language/literature/criticism; money/finance; nature/environment; psychology; religious/inspirational; science/technology; self-help/personal improvement; women's issues/studies. **Considers these fiction areas:** Ethnic; literary; mainstream/contemporary; mystery/suspense; women's.

O→ Does not want to receive horror, screenplays, poetry or academic nonfiction.

How to Contact Query with SASE. No fax queries. Returns materials only with SASE. Obtains most new clients through recommendations from others, solicitations, conferences.

Recent Sales Sold 26 titles in the last year. *Big Brown*, by Greg Neimann (Wiley); *From Baghdad With Love*, by Jay Kopelman with Melinda Roth (Lyons Press); *Illuminations*, by Mark Tompkins (Ten Speed/Celestial Arts); *Midnight Brunch*, by Marta Acosta (S&S); *Teardrops*, by Doug Keister (Gibbs Smith); *Orphan's Journey*, by Robert Buettner (Little, Brown/Orbit).

Terms Agent receives 15% commission on domestic sales; 25% commission on foreign sales. Offers written contract; 6-week notice must be given to terminate contract.

Writers' Conferences Santa Barbara Writers' Conference; Southern California Writers' Conference; Surrey International Writers' Conference; San Diego State University Writers' Conference; Willamette Writers' Conference.

Tips "Be professional with submissions. Attend workshops and conferences before you approach an agent."

JANE CHELIUS LITERARY AGENCY

548 Second St., Brooklyn NY 11215. (718)499-0236. Fax: (718)832-7335. E-mail: queries@janechelius.com. Web site: www.janechelius.com. Member of AAR.

Represents Nonfiction books, novels. **Considers these nonfiction areas:** Humor/satire; women's issues/studies; popular science; parenting; medicine; biography; natural history; narrative. **Considers these fiction areas:** Literary; mystery/suspense; women's; men's adventure.

O→ Does not want to receive children's books, stage plays, screenplays, or poetry.

How to Contact Query with synopsis, cover letter, SASE. Accepts e-mail queries. *No unsolicited chapters or mss.* Responds in 3-4 weeks to queries.

◖ WM CLARK ASSOCIATES

154 Christopher St., Suite 3C, New York NY 10014. (212)675-2784. Fax: (646)349-1658. E-mail: query@wmclark .com. Web site: www.wmclark.com. Estab. 1997. Member of AAR. 50% of clients are new/unpublished writers. Currently handles: 50% nonfiction books; 50% novels.

• Prior to opening WCA, Mr. Clark was an agent at the William Morris Agency.

Represents Nonfiction books, novels. **Considers these nonfiction areas:** Art/architecture/design; biography/ autobiography; current affairs; ethnic/cultural interests; history; memoirs; music/dance; popular culture; religious/inspirational (Eastern philosophy only); science/technology; sociology; theater/film; translation. **Considers these fiction areas:** Contemporary issues; ethnic; historical; literary; mainstream/contemporary; Southern fiction.

O—¬ "Building on a reputation for moving quickly and strategically on behalf of his clients, and offering individual focus and a global presence, William Clark practices an aggressive, innovative, and broad-ranged approach to the representation of content and the talent that creates it. His clients range from authors of first fiction and award-winning best-selling narrative nonfiction, to international authors in translation, musicians, and artists."

How to Contact E-mail queries only. Prefers to read requested materials exclusively. Responds in 1-2 months to queries.

Recent Sales Sold 25 titles in the last year. *Fallingwater Rising: E.J. Kaufman and Frank Lloyd Wright Create the Most Exciting House in the World*, by Franklin Toker (Alfred A. Knopf); *The Balthazar Cookbook*, by Riad Nasr, Lee Hanson, and Keith McNally (Clarkson Potter); *The Book of 'Exodus': The Making and Meaning of Bob Marley's Album of the Century*, by Vivien Goldman (Crown/Three Rivers Press); *Hungry Ghost*, by Keith Kachtick (HarperCollins). Other clients include Russell Martin, Daye Haddon, Bjork, Mian Mian, Jonathan Stone, Jocko Weyland, Peter Hessler, Rev. Billy (a.k.a. Billy Talen).

Terms Agent receives 15% commission on domestic sales; 20% commission on foreign sales. Offers written contract.

Tips "WCA works on a reciprocal basis with Ed Victor Ltd. (UK) in representing select properties to the US market and vice versa. Translation rights are sold directly in the German, Italian, Spanish, Portuguese, Latin American, French, Dutch, and Scandinavian territories in association with Andrew Nurnberg Associates Ltd. (UK); through offices in China, Bulgaria, Czech Republic, Latvia, Poland, Hungary, and Russia; and through corresponding agents in Japan, Greece, Israel, Turkey, Korea, Taiwan, and Thailand."

◖ FRANCES COLLIN, LITERARY AGENT

P.O. Box 33, Wayne PA 19087-0033. Web site: www.francescollin.com. **Contact:** Frances Collin. Estab. 1948. Member of AAR. Represents 90 clients. 1% of clients are new/unpublished writers. Currently handles: 50% nonfiction books; 48% novels; 1% textbooks; 1% poetry.

Represents Nonfiction books, fiction.

O—¬ "We are accepting almost no new clients unless recommended by publishing professionals or current clients." Does not want cookbooks, crafts, children's books, software, or original screenplays.

How to Contact Query with SASE, brief proposal. No phone, fax, or e-mail inquiries. Enclose sufficient IRCs if outside the US. Considers simultaneous queries.

Terms Agent receives 15% commission on domestic sales; 20% commission on foreign sales. Offers written contract. Charges clients for overseas postage for books mailed to foreign agents; photocopying of mss, books, proposals; copyright registration fees; registered mail fees; passes along cost of any books purchased.

◖ COLLINS LITERARY AGENCY

30 Bond St., New York NY 10012. (212)529-4909. Fax: (212)358-1055. Web site: www.collinsliterary.com. **Contact:** Nina Collins. Estab. 2005. Represents 30 clients. 40% of clients are new/unpublished writers.

• Prior to opening her agency, Ms. Collins was a literary scout for foreign publishers and American film companies.

Member Agents Nina Collins (memoir, literary fiction, lifestyle, young adult, travel, psychology, and women and/or mother/daughter issues); Matthew Elblonk (literary fiction, narrative nonfiction, pop culture, music, young adult and anything that is slightly quirky or absurd).

Represents Nonfiction books, novels.

O—¬ No genre fiction.

How to Contact Query with SASE. Send queries via snail mail. No e-mail or fax queries. Considers simultaneous queries. Responds in 2 weeks to queries; 1 month to mss. Returns materials only with SASE. Obtains most new clients through recommendations from others.

Recent Sales *Why the Devil Chose New England to Do His Work*, by Jason Brown (Open City Books); *The Mother Daughter Project*, by Hamkins & Schulz (Hudson St. Press); *Over the Hill and Between the Sheets*, by

Gail Belsky (Warner); *Evo-lution*, by Stephanie Staal (Bloomsbury); *Gonzo Gardening*, by Katherine Whiteside (Clarkson Potter).

Terms Agent receives 15% commission on domestic sales; 20% commission on foreign sales. Offers written contract; 1-month notice must be given to terminate contract.

◖ DON CONGDON ASSOCIATES INC.

156 Fifth Ave., Suite 625, New York NY 10010-7002. (212)645-1229. Fax: (212)727-2688. E-mail: dca@doncongdon.com. **Contact:** Don Congdon, Michael Congdon, Susan Ramer, Cristina Concepcion. Estab. 1983. Member of AAR. Represents 100 clients. Currently handles: 60% nonfiction books; 40% fiction.

Represents Nonfiction books, fiction. **Considers these nonfiction areas:** Anthropology/archaeology; biography/autobiography; child guidance/parenting; cooking/foods/nutrition; current affairs; government/politics/law; health/medicine; history; humor/satire; language/literature/criticism; memoirs; military/war; music/dance; nature/environment; popular culture; psychology; science/technology; theater/film; travel; true crime/investigative; women's issues/studies; creative nonfiction. **Considers these fiction areas:** Action/adventure; detective/police/crime; literary; mainstream/contemporary; mystery/suspense; short story collections; thriller; women's.

   Oⁿ Especially interested in narrative nonfiction and literary fiction.

How to Contact Query with SASE or via e-mail (no attachments). Responds in 3 weeks to queries; 1 month to mss. Obtains most new clients through recommendations from other authors.

Terms Agent receives 15% commission on domestic sales; 19% commission on foreign sales. Charges client for extra shipping costs, photocopying, copyright fees, book purchases.

Tips "Writing a query letter with a self-addressed stamped envelope is a must. We cannot guarantee replies to foreign queries via e-mail. No phone calls. We never download attachments to e-mail queries for security reasons, so please copy and paste material into your e-mail."

◖ CONNOR LITERARY AGENCY

2911 W. 71st St., Minneapolis MN 55423. (612)866-1486. E-mail: connoragency@aol.com. **Contact:** Marlene Connor Lynch. Estab. 1985. Represents 50 clients. 30% of clients are new/unpublished writers. Currently handles: 50% nonfiction books; 50% novels.

   • Prior to opening her agency, Ms. Connor served at the Literary Guild of America, Simon & Schuster and Random House. She is author of *Welcome to the Family: Memories of the Past for a Bright Future* (Broadway Books) and *What is Cool: Understanding Black Manhood in America* (Crown).

Member Agents Marlene Connor Lynch (all categories with an emphasis on these nonfiction areas: Child guidance/parenting; cooking/foods/nutrition; crafts/hobbies; current affairs; ethnic/cultural interests; government/politics/law; health/medicine; how-to; humor/satire; interior design/decorating; language/literature/criticism; money/finance; photography; popular culture; self-help/personal improvement; women's issues/studies; relationships. Considers these fiction areas: historical; horror; literary; mainstream/contemporary; multicultural; thriller; women's; suspense); Deborah Coker (mainstream and literary fiction, multicultural fiction, children's books, humor, politics, memoirs, narrative nonfiction, true crime/investigative); Nichole L. Shields/Chicago (multicultural fiction and nonfiction with an emphasis on African-American literature, poetry and children's content); Brenda Lee Mann (mainstream, historical, and women's fiction, general nonfiction including cooking, self improvement, spiritual/religious popular psychology, child guidance, etc.).

Represents Nonfiction books, novels.

   Oⁿ Actively seeking mysteries.

How to Contact Query with SASE. All unsolicited mss returned unopened. Obtains most new clients through recommendations from others, conferences, grapevine.

Recent Sales *Beautiful Hair at Any Age*, by Lisa Akbari; *12 Months of Knitting*, by Joanne Yordanou; *The Warrior Path: Confessions of a Young Lord*, by Felipe Luciano.

Terms Agent receives 15% commission on domestic sales; 25% commission on foreign sales. Offers written contract, binding for 1 year.

Writers' Conferences National Writers Union, Midwest Chapter; Agents, Agents, Agents; Texas Writers' Conference; Detroit Writers' Conference; Annual Gwendolyn Brooks Writers' Conference for Literature and Creative Writing.

Tips "Previously published writers are preferred; new writers with national exposure or potential to have national exposure from their own efforts preferred."

◖ THE DOE COOVER AGENCY

P.O. Box 668, Winchester MA 01890. (781)721-6000. Fax: (781)721-6727. Web site: doecooveragency.com. Estab. 1985. Represents more than 100 clients. Currently handles: 80% nonfiction books; 20% novels.

Member Agents Doe Coover (general nonfiction, cooking); Colleen Mohyde (literary and commercial fiction, general and narrative nonfiction); Amanda Lewis (children's books); Frances Kennedy, associate. **Considers**

these nonfiction areas: Biography/autobiography; business/economics; cooking/foods/nutrition; gardening; history; science/technology; social issues, narrative nonfiction. **Considers these fiction areas:** Literary; commercial.

○➤ This agency specializes in nonfiction, particularly books on history, popular science, biography, social issues, and narrative nonfiction, as well as cooking, gardening, and literary and commercial fiction. Does not want romance, fantasy, science fiction, poetry or screenplays.

How to Contact Query with SASE, outline. No e-mail or fax queries. Considers simultaneous queries. Returns materials only with SASE. Obtains most new clients through recommendations from others, solicitations.

Recent Sales Sold 25-30 titles in the last year. *More Fast Food My Way*, by Jacques Pepin (Houghton Mifflin); *Entertaining Simple*, by Matthew Mead (John Wiley & Sons); *International Grilling*, by Chris Schlesinger and John Willoughby (Dorling Kindersley); *The Setpoint Solution*, by George Blackburn (HarperCollins Publishers); *You're Never Too Old To Start Something New*, by Martha Manglesdorf (Ten Speed Press); *Openwork*, by Adria Bernardi (SMU Press); *See What You Can Be*, by Liz Suneby and Diane Heiman (American Girl). *Movie/TV MOW script(s) optioned/sold: A Crime in the Neighborhood*, by Suzanne Berne; *Mr. White's Confession*, by Robert Clark. Other clients include WGBH, New England Aquarium, Blue Balliett, Deborah Madison, Rick Bayless, Molly Stevens, David Allen, Adria Bernardi, Paula Poundstone.

Terms Agent receives 15% commission on domestic sales; 10% of original advance commission on foreign sales.

◉ RICHARD CURTIS ASSOCIATES, INC.

171 E. 74th St., New York NY 10021. (212)772-7363. Fax: (212)772-7393. Web site: www.curtisagency.com. Estab. 1979. Member of RWA, MWA, SFWA; signatory of WGA. Represents 100 clients. 1% of clients are new/unpublished writers. Currently handles: 70% nonfiction books; 20% genre fiction, 10% fiction.

● Prior to opening his agency, Mr. Curtis was an agent with the Scott Meredith Literary Agency for seven years. He has also authored more than 50 published books.

Represents Commercial nonfiction and fiction. **Considers these nonfiction areas:** Health/medicine; history; science/technology.

How to Contact Send 1-page query letter and no more than a 5-page synopsis. Don't send ms unless specifically requested. If requested, submission must be accompanied by a SASE. No e-mail or fax queries. Returns materials only with SASE.

Recent Sales Sold 150 titles in the last year. *The Terror*, by Dan Simmons; *The Side-Effects Solution*, by Dr. Frederic Vagnini and Barry Fox; *Quantico*, by Greg Bear. Other clients include Janet Dailey, Jennifer Blake, Leonard Maltin, D.J. MacHale, John Altman, Beverly Barton, Earl Mindell, Barbara Parker.

Terms Agent receives 15% commission on domestic sales; 25% commission on foreign sales. Offers written contract. Charges for photocopying, express mail, international freight, book orders.

Writers' Conferences SFWA Conference; HWA Conference; RWA National Conference; World Fantasy Convention; Backspace Writers Conference.

◉ D4EO LITERARY AGENCY

7 Indian Valley Road, Weston CT 06883. (203)544-7180. Fax: (203)544-7160. E-mail: d4eo@optonline.net. **Contact:** Bob Diforio. Estab. 1991. Represents more than 100 clients. 50% of clients are new/unpublished writers. Currently handles: 70% nonfiction books; 25% novels; 5% juvenile books.

● Prior to opening his agency, Mr. Diforio was a publisher.

Represents Nonfiction books, novels. **Considers these nonfiction areas:** Art/architecture/design; biography/autobiography; business/economics; child guidance/parenting; current affairs; gay/lesbian issues; health/medicine; history; how-to; humor/satire; juvenile nonfiction; memoirs; military/war; money/finance; psychology; religious/inspirational; science/technology; self-help/personal improvement; sports; true crime/investigative; women's issues/studies. **Considers these fiction areas:** Action/adventure; detective/police/crime; erotica; historical; horror; humor/satire; juvenile; literary; mainstream/contemporary; mystery/suspense; picture books; romance; science fiction; sports; thriller; westerns/frontier; young adult.

How to Contact Query with SASE. Accepts and prefers e-mail queries. Prefers to read material exclusively. Responds in 1 week to queries. Returns materials only with SASE. Obtains most new clients through recommendations from others.

Recent Sales Sold 125 titles in the last year. *Jaywalker* plus 2 novels, by Joseph Teller; *Skeleton Coast*, by Jack Du Brul; *Revenge* (Butch Karp #20), by Robert K. Tanenbaum; *Secrets of the Alchemist Dar*, by Michael Stadther; The Pleasure Series, by Cathryn Fox; *The Valorian Journals*, by Tawny Stokes. Other clients include Andrea DaRif, Tawny Stokes, Cathy Verge, Lynn Kerston, Bob Bly, Michael Levine, Mark Wiskup, George Parker, Michael Stodther, Evie Rhoder, Charlie Stella, Kathy Tracy.

Terms Agent receives 15% commission on domestic sales; 25% commission on foreign sales. Offers written contract, binding for 2 years; 60-day notice must be given to terminate contract. Charges for photocopying and submission postage.

◐ LAURA DAIL LITERARY AGENCY, INC.

350 Seventh Ave., Suite 2003, New York NY 10010. (212)239-7477. Fax: (212)947-0460. E-mail: queries@ldlainc.com. Web site: www.ldlainc.com. Member of AAR.

Member Agents Talia Cohen; Laura Dail; Tamar Ellman.

Represents Nonfiction books, novels.

> ⊶ "Due to the volume of queries and manuscripts received, we apologize for not answering every e-mail and letter." Specializes in historical, literary and some young adult fiction, as well as both practical and idea-driven nonfiction.

How to Contact Query with SASE. This agency prefers e-queries.

Recent Sales *This Year's Model*, by Carol Alt and Nina Malkin (Regan); *Skinny Bitch in the Kitch and Skinny Mama*, by Rory Freedman and Kim Barnoin (Running Press); *The Lost Memoirs of Jane Austin: A Novel*, by Syrie James (Avon).

◐ DARHANSOFF, VERRILL, FELDMAN LITERARY AGENTS

236 W. 26th St., Suite 802, New York NY 10001. (917)305-1300. Fax: (917)305-1400. Web site: www.dvagency.com. Estab. 1975. Member of AAR. Represents 120 clients. 10% of clients are new/unpublished writers. Currently handles: 25% nonfiction books; 60% novels; 15% story collections.

Member Agents Liz Darhansoff; Charles Verrill; Leigh Feldman.

Represents Nonfiction books, novels, short story collections.

How to Contact Obtains most new clients through recommendations from others.

◐ LIZA DAWSON ASSOCIATES

350 Seventh Ave., Ste. 2003, New York NY 10001. (212)465-9071. Member of AAR, MWA, Women's Media Group. Represents 50+ clients. 15% of clients are new/unpublished writers. Currently handles: 60% nonfiction books; 40% novels.

> • Prior to becoming an agent, Ms. Dawson was an editor for 20 years, spending 11 years at William Morrow as vice president and 2 years at Putnam as executive editor. Ms. Bladell was a senior editor at HarperCollins and Avon. Ms. Miller is an *Essence*-best-selling author and niche publisher. Ms. Olswanger is an author.

Member Agents Liza Dawson; Anna Olswanger; Havis Dawson; Caitlin Blasdell; Karen Quinones-Miller.

Represents Nonfiction books, novels and gift books (Olswanger only). **Considers these nonfiction areas:** Biography/autobiography; health/medicine; history; memoirs; psychology; sociology; women's issues/studies; politics; business; parenting. **Considers these fiction areas:** Fantasy (Blasdell only); historical; literary; mystery/suspense; regional; science fiction (Blasdell only); thriller; African-American (Miller only).

> ⊶ This agency specializes in readable literary fiction, thrillers, mainstream historicals, women's fiction, academics, historians, business, journalists and psychology. Does not want to receive western, sports, computers or juvenile.

How to Contact Query with SASE. Responds in 3 weeks to queries; 6 weeks to mss. Obtains most new clients through recommendations from others, conferences.

Recent Sales Sold 40 titles in the last year. *Going for It*, by Karen E. Quinones Miller (Warner); *Mayada: Daughter of Iraq*, by Jean Sasson (Dutton); *It's So Much Work to Be Your Friend: Social Skill Problems at Home and at School*, by Richard Lavoie (Touchstone); *WORDCRAFT: How to Write Like a Professional*, by Jack Hart (Pantheon); *...And a Time to Die: How Hospitals Shape the End of Life Experience*, by Dr. Sharon Kaufman (Scribner); *Zeus: A Biography*, by Tom Stone (Bloomsbury).

Terms Agent receives 15% commission on domestic sales; 20% commission on foreign sales. Offers written contract. Charges clients for photocopying and overseas postage.

◐ THE JENNIFER DECHIARA LITERARY AGENCY

31 East 32nd St., Suite 300, New York NY 10016. (212)481-8484. E-mail: jenndec@aol.com. Web site: www.jdlit.com. **Contact:** Jennifer DeChiara. Estab. 2001. Represents 100 clients. 50% of clients are new/unpublished writers. Currently handles: 50% nonfiction books; 25% novels; 25% juvenile books.

> • Prior to becoming an agent, Ms. DeChiara was a writing consultant, freelance editor at Simon & Schuster and Random House, and a ballerina and an actress.

Represents Nonfiction books, novels, juvenile books. **Considers these nonfiction areas:** Biography/autobiography; child guidance/parenting; cooking/foods/nutrition; crafts/hobbies; current affairs; education; ethnic/cultural interests; gay/lesbian issues; government/politics/law; health/medicine; history; how-to; humor/satire; interior design/decorating; juvenile nonfiction; language/literature/criticism; memoirs; military/war; money/finance; music/dance; nature/environment; photography; popular culture; psychology; science/technology; self-help/personal improvement; sociology; sports; theater/film; true crime/investigative; women's issues/studies. **Considers these fiction areas:** Confession; detective/police/crime; ethnic; family saga; fantasy; feminist; gay/lesbian; historical; horror; humor/satire; juvenile; literary; mainstream/contemporary; mystery/

suspense; picture books; regional; sports; thriller; young adult; chick lit; psychic/supernatural; glitz.

O→ "We represent both children's and adult books in a wide range of ages and genres. We are a full-service agency and fulfill the potential of every book in every possible medium—stage, film, television, etc. We help writers every step of the way, from creating book ideas to editing and promotion. We are passionate about helping writers further their careers, but are just as eager to discover new talent, regardless of age or lack of prior publishing experience. This agency is committed to managing a writer's entire career. For us, it's not just about selling books, but about making dreams come true. We are especially attracted to the downtrodden, the discouraged, and the downright disgusted." Actively seeking literary fiction, chick lit, young adult fiction, self-help, pop culture, and celebrity biographies. Does not want westerns, poetry, or short stories.

How to Contact Query with SASE. Considers simultaneous queries. Responds in 3-6 months to queries; 3-6 months to mss. Returns materials only with SASE. Obtains most new clients through recommendations from others, conferences, query letters.

Recent Sales Sold 30 titles in the last year. *I Was a Teenage Popsicle*, by Bev Katz Rosenbaum (Berkley/JAM); *Hazing Meri Sugarman*, by M. Apostolina (Simon Pulse); *The 10-Minute Sexual Solution* and *Virgin Sex: A Guy's Guide to Sex*, by Dr. Darcy Luadzers (Hatherleigh Press). *Movie/TV MOW script(s) optioned/sold:* Geography Club, by Brent Hartinger (East of Doheny). Other clients include Adam Meyer, Herbie J. Pilato, Chris Demarest, Jeff Lenburg, Joe Cadora, Tiffani Amber Thiessen, Bonnie Neubauer.

Terms Agent receives 15% commission on domestic sales; 20% commission on foreign sales. Offers written contract.

JOELLE DELBOURGO ASSOCIATES, INC.

516 Bloomfield Ave., Suite 5, Montclair NJ 07042. (973)783-6800. Fax: (973)783-6802. E-mail: info@delbourgo.com. Web site: www.delbourgo.com. **Contact:** Joelle Delbourgo, Molly Lyons. Estab. 2000. Represents 80 clients. 40% of clients are new/unpublished writers. Currently handles: 75% nonfiction books; 25% novels.

● Prior to becoming an agent, Ms. Delbourgo was an editor and senior publishing executive at HarperCollins and Random House.

Member Agents Joelle Delbourgo (parenting, self-help, psychology, business, serious nonfiction, narrative nonfiction, quality fiction); Molly Lyons (practical and narrative nonfiction, memoir, quality fiction).

Represents Nonfiction books, novels, short story collections. **Considers these nonfiction areas:** Biography/autobiography; business/economics; child guidance/parenting; cooking/foods/nutrition; current affairs; education; ethnic/cultural interests; gay/lesbian issues; government/politics/law; health/medicine; history; how-to; money/finance; music/dance; nature/environment; popular culture; psychology; religious/inspirational; science/technology; self-help/personal improvement; sociology; theater/film; true crime/investigative; women's issues/studies; New Age/metaphysics, interior design/decorating. **Considers these fiction areas:** Historical; literary; mainstream/contemporary; mystery/suspense; regional.

O→ "We are former publishers and editors, with deep knowledge and an insider perspective. We have a reputation for individualized attention to clients, strategic management of authors' careers, and creating strong partnerships with publishers for our clients." Actively seeking history, narrative nonfiction, science/medicine, memoir, literary fiction, psychology, parenting and biographies. Does not want to receive genre fiction or screenplays.

How to Contact Query with SASE. No e-mail or fax queries. Considers simultaneous queries. Responds in 3 weeks to queries; 2 months to mss. Returns materials only with SASE.

Recent Sales Sold 26 titles in the last year. *Washashores*, by Lynn Bonasia (Touchstone/Fireside); *Leftovers: The New Food Underclass and the Fight Against Obesity*, by Hank J. Cardello with Doug Garr (Regan/HarperCollins); *Mad Fish*, by Charlie Moore (St. Martin's Press); *Three Little Words*, by Ashley Rhodes Courer (Simon & Schuster); *Kissing Snowflakes*, by Abby Sher (Scholastic). Other clients include Pamela Duncan, Geeta Anand, Philip Mitchell Freeman, Roy Hoffman, Chris Farrell, David Cole, Marc Siegel, Joan Wester Anderson, Julie Fenster.

Terms Agent receives 15% commission on domestic sales; 20% commission on foreign sales. Offers written contract. Charges clients for postage and photocopying.

Tips "Do your homework. Do not cold call. Read and follow submission guidelines before contacting us. Do not call to find out if we received your material. No e-mail queries. Treat agents with respect, as you would any other professional, such as a doctor, lawyer or financial advisor."

DHS LITERARY, INC.

10711 Preston Road, Suite 100, Dallas TX 75230. (214)363-4422. Fax: (214)363-4423. E-mail: submissions@dhsliterary.com. Web site: www.dhsliterary.com. **Contact:** David Hale Smith, president. Estab. 1994. Represents 35 clients. 15% of clients are new/unpublished writers. Currently handles: 60% nonfiction books; 40% novels.

- Prior to opening his agency, Mr. Smith was an agent at Dupree/Miller & Associates.

Represents Nonfiction books, novels. **Considers these nonfiction areas:** Biography/autobiography; business/economics; child guidance/parenting; cooking/foods/nutrition; current affairs; ethnic/cultural interests; popular culture; sports; true crime/investigative. **Considers these fiction areas:** Detective/police/crime; ethnic; literary; mainstream/contemporary; mystery/suspense; thriller; westerns/frontier.

O→ This agency specializes in commercial fiction and nonfiction for the adult trade market. Actively seeking thrillers, mysteries, suspense, etc., and narrative nonfiction. Does not want to receive poetry, short fiction or children's books.

How to Contact Accepts new material by referral only and only responds if interested. *No unsolicited mss.* No fax queries.

Recent Sales *Officer Down*, by Theresa Schwegel; *Private Wars*, by Greg Rucka; *The Lean Body Promise*, by Lee Labrada.

Terms Agent receives 15% commission on domestic sales; 25% commission on foreign sales. Offers written contract; 10-day notice must be given to terminate contract. This agency charges for postage and photocopying.

Tips "Remember to be courteous and professional, and to treat marketing your work and approaching an agent as you would any formal business matter. If you have a referral, always query first via e-mail. Sorry, but we cannot respond to queries sent via mail, even with a SASE. Visit our Web site for more information."

DUNHAM LITERARY, INC.

156 Fifth Ave., Suite 625, New York NY 10010-7002. (212)929-0994. Web site: www.dunhamlit.com. **Contact:** Jennie Dunham. Estab. 2000. Member of AAR. Represents 50 clients. 15% of clients are new/unpublished writers. Currently handles: 25% nonfiction books; 25% novels; 50% juvenile books.

- Prior to opening her agency, Ms. Dunham worked as a literary agent for Russell & Volkening. The Rhoda Weyr Agency is now a division of Dunham Literary, Inc.

Represents Nonfiction books, novels, short story collections, juvenile books. **Considers these nonfiction areas:** Anthropology/archaeology; biography/autobiography; ethnic/cultural interests; government/politics/law; health/medicine; history; language/literature/criticism; nature/environment; popular culture; psychology; science/technology; women's issues/studies. **Considers these fiction areas:** Ethnic; juvenile; literary; mainstream/contemporary; picture books; young adult.

How to Contact Query with SASE. No e-mail or fax queries. Responds in 1 week to queries; 2 months to mss. Obtains most new clients through recommendations from others, solicitations.

Recent Sales *America the Beautiful*, by Robert Sabuda; *Dahlia*, by Barbara McClintock; *Living Dead Girl*, by Tod Goldberg; *In My Mother's House*, by Margaret McMulla; *Black Hawk Down*, by Mark Bowden; *Look Back All the Green Valley*, by Fred Chappell; *Under a Wing*, by Reeve Lindbergh; *I Am Madame X*, by Gioia Diliberto.

Terms Agent receives 15% commission on domestic sales; 20% commission on foreign sales.

DYSTEL & GODERICH LITERARY MANAGEMENT

1 Union Square W., Suite 904, New York NY 10003. (212)627-9100. Fax: (212)627-9313. E-mail: miriam@dystel.com. Web site: www.dystel.com. **Contact:** Miriam Goderich. Estab. 1994. Member of AAR. Represents 300 clients. 50% of clients are new/unpublished writers. Currently handles: 65% nonfiction books; 25% novels; 10% cookbooks.

- Dystel & Goderich Literary Management recently acquired the client list of Bedford Book Works.

Member Agents Stacey Glick; Jane Dystel; Miriam Goderich; Michael Bourret; Jim McCarthy; Lauren Abramo; Adina Kahn.

Represents Nonfiction books, novels, cookbooks. **Considers these nonfiction areas:** Animals; anthropology/archaeology; biography/autobiography; business/economics; child guidance/parenting; cooking/foods/nutrition; current affairs; education; ethnic/cultural interests; gay/lesbian issues; government/politics/law; health/medicine; history; humor/satire; military/war; money/finance; New Age/metaphysics; popular culture; psychology; religious/inspirational; science/technology; true crime/investigative; women's issues/studies. **Considers these fiction areas:** Action/adventure; detective/police/crime; ethnic; family saga; gay/lesbian; literary; mainstream/contemporary; mystery/suspense; thriller.

O→ This agency specializes in cookbooks and commercial and literary fiction and nonfiction.

How to Contact Query with SASE. Considers simultaneous queries. Responds in 1 month to queries; 6 weeks to mss. Obtains most new clients through recommendations from others, solicitations, conferences.

Terms Agent receives 15% commission on domestic sales; 19% commission on foreign sales. Offers written contract. Charges for photocopying. Galley charges and book charges from the publisher are passed on to the author.

Writers' Conferences Whidbey Island Writers' Conference; Backspace Writers' Conference; Iowa Summer Writing Festival; Pacific Northwest Writers' Association; Pike's Peak Writers' Conference; Santa Barbara Writers'

Conference; Harriette Austin Writers' Conference; Sandhills Writers' Conference; Denver Publishing Institute; Love Is Murder.

Tips "Work on sending professional, well-written queries that are concise and addressed to the specific agent the author is contacting. No dear Sir/Madam."

◢ ETHAN ELLENBERG LITERARY AGENCY

548 Broadway, #5-E, New York NY 10012. (212)431-4554. Fax: (212)941-4652. E-mail: agent@ethanellenberg.com. Web site: www.ethanellenberg.com. **Contact:** Ethan Ellenberg. Estab. 1983. Represents 80 clients. 10% of clients are new/unpublished writers. Currently handles: 25% nonfiction books; 75% novels.

- Prior to opening his agency, Mr. Ellenberg was contracts manager of Berkley/Jove and associate contracts manager for Bantam.

Represents Nonfiction books, novels, children's books. **Considers these nonfiction areas:** Biography/autobiography; current affairs; health/medicine; history; military/war; science/technology; narrative. **Considers these fiction areas:** Commerical fiction—specializing in romance/fiction for women, science fiction and fantasy, thrillers, suspense and mysteries, children's books (all types: picture books, middle grade and YA).

- ✱ This agency specializes in commercial fiction—especially thrillers, romance/women's, and specialized nonfiction. "We also do a lot of children's books, commercial fiction as noted above—romance/fiction for women, science fiction and fantasy, thrillers, suspense and mysteries. Our other two main areas of interest are children's books and narrative nonfiction. We are actively seeking clients, follow the directions on our Web site." Does not want to receive poetry, short stories, westerns, autobiographies or screenplays.

How to Contact For fiction, send introductory letter, outline, first 3 chapters, SASE. For nonfiction, send query letter, proposal, 1 sample chapter, SASE. For children's books, send introductory letter, up to 3 picture book mss, outline, first 3 chapters, SASE. No fax queries. Accepts e-mail queries (no attachments). Will only respond to e-mail queries if interested. Considers simultaneous queries. Responds in 4-6 weeks to mss. Returns materials only with SASE.

Recent Sales *Sleeping With the Fishes* and *Dead and Loving It*, by Maryjanice Davidson (Berkley); *The Summoner*, by Gail Martin (Solaris); *Empress of Mijak*, by Karen Miller (Harper Australia); *Hellgate: London*, by Mel Odom (Pocket Books); *The Last Colony* and *Android's Dream*, by John Scalzi (Tor Books); *General Winston's Daughter*, by Sharon Shinn (Ace Books); *Dead Sexy*, by Amanda Ashley (Kensington). Other clients include Rebecca York, Bertrice Small, Eric Rohmann.

Terms Agent receives 15% commission on domestic sales; 10% commission on foreign sales. Offers written contract. Charges clients (with their consent) for direct expenses limited to photocopying and postage.

Writers' Conferences RWA National Conference; Novelists, Inc; and other regional conferences.

Tips "We do consider new material from unsolicited authors. Write a good, clear letter with a succinct description of your book. We prefer the first 3 chapters when we consider fiction. For all submissions, you must include a SASE or the material will be discarded. It's always hard to break in, but talent will find a home. Check our Web site for complete submission guidelines. We continue to see natural storytellers and nonfiction writers with important books."

◢ THE NICHOLAS ELLISON AGENCY

Affiliated with Sanford J. Greenburger Associates, 55 Fifth Ave., 15th Floor, New York NY 10003. (212)206-6050. Fax: (212)463-8718. Web site: www.greenburger.com. **Contact:** Nicholas Ellison. Estab. 1983. Represents 70 clients. Currently handles: 50% nonfiction books; 50% novels.

- Prior to becoming an agent, Mr. Ellison was an editor at Minerva Editions and Harper & Row, and editor-in-chief at Delacorte.

Member Agents Nicholas Ellison; Sarah Dickman.

Represents Nonfiction books, novels. **Considers these nonfiction areas:** Considers most nonfiction areas. **Considers these fiction areas:** Literary; mainstream/contemporary.

How to Contact Query with SASE. Responds in 6 weeks to queries.

Recent Sales *School of Fortune*, by Amanda Brown and Janice Weber (St. Martin's); *You Suck*, by Christopher Moore (HarperCollins); *I'm Not Myself*, by Sarah Dunn (Little, Brown); next 3 Nelson DeMille Books (Warner). Other clients include Olivia Goldsmith, P.T. Deutermann, Nancy Geary, Jeff Lindsay, Thomas Christopher Greene, Bill Mason, Geoff Emerick, Howard Massey, Emily Benedek, Alan Weisman, Matthew Scott Hansen.

Terms Agent receives 15% commission on domestic sales; 20% commission on foreign sales.

◢ ANN ELMO AGENCY, INC.

60 E. 42nd St., New York NY 10165. (212)661-2880. Fax: (212)661-2883. **Contact:** Lettie Lee. Estab. 1959. Member of AAR, Authors Guild.

Member Agents Lettie Lee; Mari Cronin (plays); A.L. Abecassis (nonfiction).

Represents Nonfiction books, novels. **Considers these nonfiction areas:** Biography/autobiography; current affairs; health/medicine; history; how-to; popular culture; science/technology. **Considers these fiction areas:** Ethnic; family saga; mainstream/contemporary; romance (contemporary, gothic, historical, regency); thriller; women's.

How to Contact Only accepts mailed queries with SASE. Do not send full ms unless requested. No fax queries. Responds in 3 months to queries. Obtains most new clients through recommendations from others.

Recent Sales This agency prefers not to share information on specific sales.

Terms Agent receives 15% commission on domestic sales; 20% commission on foreign sales. Offers written contract. This agency charges clients for special mailings, shipping, multiple international calls. There is no charge for usual cost of doing business.

Tips "Query first, and only when asked send properly prepared manuscript. A double-spaced, readable manuscript is the best recommendation. Include a SASE, of course."

THE ELAINE P. ENGLISH LITERARY AGENCY

4701 41st St. NW, Suite D, Washington DC 20016. (202)362-5190. Fax: (202)362-5192. E-mail: elaine@elaineeng lish.com. Web site: www.elaineenglish.com. **Contact:** Elaine English. Member of AAR. Represents 16 clients. 25% of clients are new/unpublished writers. Currently handles: 100% novels.

• Ms. English has been working in publishing for more than 20 years. She is also an attorney specializing in media and publishing law.

Represents Novels. **Considers these fiction areas:** Historical; multicultural; mystery/suspense; romance (single title, historical, contemporary, romantic, suspense, chick lit, erotic); thriller; general women's fiction. The agency is slowly but steadily acquiring in all mentioned areas.

• Actively seeking women's fiction, including single-title romances. Does not want to receive any science fiction, time travel, children's, or young adult.

How to Contact Prefers e-queries sent to queries@elaineenglish.com. If requested, submit synopsis, first 3 chapters, SASE. Accepts e-mail queries. No fax queries. Responds in 6-12 weeks to queries; 6 months to requested ms. Returns materials only with SASE. Obtains most new clients through recommendations from others, conferences, submissions.

Recent Sales *The Blue-Eyed Devil*, by Diane Whiteside (Kensington).

Terms Agent receives 15% commission on domestic sales; 20% commission on foreign sales. Offers written contract; 30-day notice must be given to terminate contract. Charges only for copying and postage; generally taken from proceeds.

Writers' Conferences RWA National Conference; SEAK Medical & Legal Fiction Writing Conference; Novelists, Inc; Malice Domestic; Washington Romance Writers Retreat, among others.

FARBER LITERARY AGENCY, INC.

14 E. 75th St., #2E, New York NY 10021. (212)861-7075. Fax: (212)861-7076. E-mail: farberlit@aol.com. Web site: www.donaldfarber.com. **Contact:** Ann Farber, Dr. Seth Farber. Estab. 1989. Represents 40 clients. 50% of clients are new/unpublished writers. Currently handles: 25% nonfiction books; 35% novels; 15% scholarly books; 25% stage plays.

Member Agents Ann Farber (novels); Seth Farber (plays, scholarly books, novels); Donald C. Farber (attorney, all entertainment media).

Represents Nonfiction books, novels, juvenile books, textbooks, stage plays. **Considers these nonfiction areas:** Child guidance/parenting; cooking/foods/nutrition; music/dance; psychology; theater/film. **Considers these fiction areas:** Action/adventure; humor/satire; juvenile; literary; mainstream/contemporary; mystery/suspense; thriller; young adult.

How to Contact Submit outline, 3 sample chapters, SASE. Prefers to read materials exclusively. Responds in 1 month to queries; 2 months to mss. Obtains most new clients through recommendations from others.

Terms Agent receives 15% commission on domestic sales; 20% commission on foreign sales. Offers written contract, binding for 1 year. Client must furnish copies of ms, treatments, and any other items for submission.

Tips "Our attorney, Donald C. Farber, is the author of many books. His services are available to the agency's clients as part of the agency service at no additional charge."

FARRIS LITERARY AGENCY, INC.

P.O. Box 570069, Dallas TX 75357. (972)203-8804. E-mail: farris1@airmail.net. Web site: www.farrisliterary.c om. **Contact:** Mike Farris, Susan Morgan Farris. Estab. 2002. Represents 30 clients. 60% of clients are new/ unpublished writers.

• Both Mr. Farris and Ms. Farris are attorneys.

Represents Nonfiction books, novels. **Considers these nonfiction areas:** Biography/autobiography; business/ economics; child guidance/parenting; cooking/foods/nutrition; current affairs; government/politics/law;

health/medicine; history; how-to; humor/satire; memoirs; military/war; music/dance; popular culture; religious/inspirational; self-help/personal improvement; sports; women's issues/studies. **Considers these fiction areas:** Action/adventure; detective/police/crime; historical; humor/satire; mainstream/contemporary; mystery/suspense; religious/inspirational; romance; sports; thriller; westerns/frontier.

> O— "We specialize in both fiction and nonfiction books. We are particularly interested in discovering unpublished authors. We adhere to AAR guidelines." Does not consider science fiction, fantasy, gay and lesbian, erotica, young adult, or children's.

How to Contact Query with SASE. Considers simultaneous queries. Responds in 2-3 weeks to queries; 4-8 weeks to mss. Returns materials only with SASE. Obtains most new clients through recommendations from others, solicitations, conferences.

Recent Sales Sold 4 titles in the last year. *The Show Must Go On*, by Doug Snauffer (McFarland).

Terms Agent receives 15% commission on domestic sales; 20% commission on foreign sales. Offers written contract; 30-day notice must be given to terminate contract. Charges clients for postage and photocopying.

Writers' Conferences Oklahoma Writers Federation Conference; The Screenwriting Conference in Santa Fe; Pikes Peak Writers Conference; Women Writing the West Annual Conference.

◑ DIANA FINCH LITERARY AGENCY

116 W. 23rd St., Suite 500, New York NY 10011. (646)375-2081. E-mail: diana.finch@verizon.net. **Contact:** Diana Finch. Estab. 2003. Member of AAR. Represents 45 clients. 20% of clients are new/unpublished writers. Currently handles: 65% nonfiction books; 25% novels; 5% juvenile books; 5% multimedia.

- Prior to opening her agency, Ms. Finch worked at Ellen Levine Literary Agency for 18 years.

Represents Nonfiction books, novels, scholarly books. **Considers these nonfiction areas:** Biography/autobiography; business/economics; child guidance/parenting; computers/electronic; current affairs; ethnic/cultural interests; government/politics/law; health/medicine; history; how-to; humor/satire; juvenile nonfiction; memoirs; military/war; money/finance; music/dance; nature/environment; photography; popular culture; psychology; science/technology; self-help/personal improvement; sports; theater/film; translation; true crime/investigative; women's issues/studies. **Considers these fiction areas:** Action/adventure; detective/police/crime; ethnic; historical; literary; mainstream/contemporary; thriller; young adult.

> O— Actively seeking narrative nonfiction, popular science, and health topics. Does not want romance, mysteries, or children's picture books.

How to Contact Query with SASE or via e-mail (no attachments). No phone or fax queries. Considers simultaneous queries. Returns materials only with SASE. Obtains most new clients through recommendations from others.

Recent Sales *Armed Madhouse*, by Greg Palast (Penguin US/UK); *The Bush Agenda*, by Antonia Juhasz; *Journey of the Magi*, by Tudor Parfitt (Farrar, Straus & Giroux); *Radiant Days*, by Michael FitzGerald (Shoemaker & Hoard); *The Queen's Soprano*, by Carol Dines (Harcourt Young Adult); *Was the 2004 Election Stolen?*, by Steven Freeman and Joel Bleifuss (Seven Stories); *Lipstick Jihad*, by Azadeh Moaveni (Public Affairs); *Great Customer Connections*, by Rich Gallagher (Amacom). Other clients include Daniel Duane, Thomas Goltz, Hugh Pope, Owen Matthews, Dr. Robert Marion.

Terms Agent receives 15% commission on domestic sales; 20% commission on foreign sales. Offers written contract. "I charge for photocopying, overseas postage, galleys, and books purchased, and try to recap these costs from earnings received for a client, rather than charging outright."

Tips "Do as much research as you can on agents before you query. Have someone critique your query letter before you send it. It should be only 1 page and describe your book clearly—and why you are writing it—but also demonstrate creativity and a sense of your writing style."

◑ FLETCHER & PARRY

78 Fifth Ave., 3rd Floor, New York NY 10011. (212)614-0778. Fax: (212)614-0728. **Contact:** Christy Fletcher, Emma Parry. Estab. 2003. Member of AAR.

Represents Nonfiction books, novels. **Considers these nonfiction areas:** Current affairs; history; memoirs; sports; travel; African American; narrative; science; biography; business; health; lifestyle. **Considers these fiction areas:** Literary; young adult; commercial.

> O— Does not want genre fiction.

How to Contact Query with SASE. Responds in 4-6 weeks to queries.

Recent Sales *Let Them In: The Case for Open Borders*, by Jason Riley (Gotham); *The Vanishing Act of Esme Lennox*, by Maggie O'Farrell (Harcourt).

◑ THE FOLEY LITERARY AGENCY

34 E. 38th St., New York NY 10016-2508. (212)686-6930. **Contact:** Joan Foley, Joseph Foley. Estab. 1961. Represents 10 clients. Currently handles: 75% nonfiction books; 25% novels.

Represents Nonfiction books, novels.

How to Contact Query with letter, brief outline, SASE. Responds promptly to queries. Obtains most new clients through recommendations from others (rarely taking on new clients).

Recent Sales This agency prefers not to share information on specific sales.

Terms Agent receives 10% commission on domestic sales; 15% commission on foreign sales. 100% of business is derived from commissions on ms sales.

● SARAH JANE FREYMANN LITERARY AGENCY

59 W. 71st St., Suite 9B, New York NY 10023. (212)362-9277. E-mail: sarah@sarahjanefreymann.com. Web site: www.sarahjanefreymann.com. **Contact:** Sarah Jane Freymann, Steve Schwartz. Represents 100 clients. 20% of clients are new/unpublished writers. Currently handles: 75% nonfiction books; 23% novels; 2% juvenile books.

Member Agents Sarah Jane Freymann; Steve Schwartz, steve@sarahjanefreymann.com (historical novels, thrillers, crime, sports, humor, food, travel).

Represents Nonfiction books, novels, illustrated books. **Considers these nonfiction areas:** Animals; anthropology/archaeology; art/architecture/design; biography/autobiography; business/economics; child guidance/parenting; cooking/foods/nutrition; current affairs; ethnic/cultural interests; health/medicine; history; interior design/decorating; memoirs (narrative); nature/environment; psychology; religious/inspirational; self-help/personal improvement; women's issues/studies; lifestyle. **Considers these fiction areas:** Ethnic; literary; mainstream/contemporary.

How to Contact Query with SASE. Responds in 2 weeks to queries; 6 weeks to mss. Obtains most new clients through recommendations from others.

Recent Sales *Girl Stories*, by Lauren Weinstein (Henry Holt); *The Good, Good Pig*, by Sy Montgomery (Ballantine/Random House); *The Man Who Killed the Whale*, by Linda Hogan (W.W. Norton); *Writing the Fire! Yoga and the Art of Making Your Words Come Alive*, by Gail Sher (Harmoney/Bell Tower); *Mexicocina*, by Melba Levick and Betsy McNair (Chronicle); *Holy Play*, by Kirk Byron Jones (Jossey Bass).

Terms Agent receives 15% commission on domestic sales; 20% commission on foreign sales. Offers written contract. Charges clients for long distance, overseas postage, photocopying. 100% of business is derived from commissions on ms sales.

Tips "I love fresh, new, passionate works by authors who love what they are doing and have both natural talent and carefully honed skill."

● GELFMAN SCHNEIDER LITERARY AGENTS, INC.

250 W. 57th St., Suite 2515, New York NY 10107. (212)245-1993. Fax: (212)245-8678. E-mail: mail@gelfmanschneider.com. **Contact:** Jane Gelfman, Deborah Schneider. Estab. 1981. Member of AAR. Represents 300+ clients. 10% of clients are new/unpublished writers.

Represents Nonfiction books, novels. **Considers these nonfiction areas:** Biography; health; lifestyle; politics; science. **Considers these fiction areas:** Literary; mainstream/contemporary; mystery/suspense; women's.

　　O－ Does not want to receive romance, science fiction, westerns, or children's books.

How to Contact Query with SASE. Send queries via snail mail only. No e-mail or fax queries. Responds in 1 month to queries; 2 months to mss.

Terms Agent receives 15% commission on domestic sales; 20% commission on foreign sales; 15% commission on dramatic rights sales. Offers written contract. Charges clients for photocopying and messengers/couriers.

● THE GISLASON AGENCY

219 Main St. SE, Suite 506, Minneapolis MN 55414-2160. (612)331-8033. Fax: (612)331-8115. E-mail: gislasonbj @aol.com. Web site: www.thegislasonagency.com. **Contact:** Barbara J. Gislason. Estab. 1992. Member of Minnesota State Bar Association, American Bar Association, Art & Entertainment Law Section, Animal Law, Minnesota Intellectual Property Law Association Copyright Committee; Icelandic Association of Minnesota, American Academy of Acupuncture and Oriental Medicine. 80% of clients are new/unpublished writers. Currently handles: 10% nonfiction books; 90% novels.

　　● Ms. Gislason became an attorney in 1980, and continues to practice art and entertainment law. She has been nationally recognized as a Leading American Attorney and a Super Lawyer.

Represents Nonfiction books, novels. **Considers these nonfiction areas:** Animals (companion animals/pets, feral animals, working and service animals, domestic and farm animals, laboratory animals, caged animals and wild animals). **Considers these fiction areas:** Animals (companion animals/pets, feral animals, working and service animals, domestic and farm animals, laboratory animals, caged animals and wild animals).

　　O－ Do not send personal memoirs, poetry, short stories, screenplays, or children's books.

How to Contact For fiction, query with synopsis, first 3 chapters, SASE. For nonfiction, query with proposal, sample chapters. No e-mail or fax queries. Responds in 1 months to queries; 6 months to mss. Obtains most new clients through recommendations from others, conferences, *Guide to Literary Agents, Literary Market Place*, other reference books.

Terms Agent receives 15% commission on domestic sales; 20% commission on foreign sales. Offers written contract, binding for 1 year with option to renew. Charges clients for photocopying and postage.

Writers' Conferences Southwest Writers Conference; Willamette Writers Conference; Wrangling with Writing; other state and regional conferences.

Tips "We are looking for manuscripts for adults that express ideas and tell stories powerful enough to change people's views about animals, without overt sentimentality. Your cover letter should be well written and include a detailed synopsis (fiction) or proposal (nonfiction), the first 3 chapters, and author bio. Appropriate SASE required. If submitting nonfiction work, explain how the submission differs from and adds to previously published works in the field. Remember to proofread. If the work was written with a specific publisher in mind, this should be communicated."

🌐 ⊘ GOLVAN ARTS MANAGEMENT

P.O. Box 766, Kew VIC 3101 Australia. E-mail: golvan@ozemail.com.au. Web site: www.golvanarts.com.au. **Contact:** Colin Golvan.

Represents Nonfiction books, novels, juvenile books, poetry books, movie scripts, TV scripts, stage plays. **How to Contact** Query with author bio, SASE.

Recent Sales *The Runaway Circus*, by Gordon Reece (Lothian Books); *Two for the Road*, by Shirly Hardy-Rix and Brian Rix (Macmillan); *The Catch*, by Marg Vandeleur (Penguin).

Terms Agent receives 11% commission on domestic sales.

⊘ GOODMAN ASSOCIATES

500 West End Ave., New York NY 10024-4317. (212)873-4806. **Contact:** Elise Simon Goodman. Estab. 1976. Member of AAR. Represents 50 clients.

• Mr. Goodman is the former chair of the AAR Ethics Committee.

Member Agents Elise Simon Goodman; Arnold P. Goodman.

Represents Nonfiction books, novels.

➤ Accepting new clients by recommendation only. Does not want to receive poetry, articles, individual stories, children's or young adult material.

How to Contact Query with SASE. Responds in 10 days to queries; 1 month to mss.

Recent Sales *Urban Preservation*, by Eugenia Bone (Clarkson Potter).

Terms Agent receives 15% commission on domestic sales; 20% commission on foreign sales. Charges clients for certain expenses: faxes, toll calls, overseas postage, photocopying, book purchases.

⊘ JILL GROSJEAN LITERARY AGENCY

1390 Millstone Road, Sag Harbor NY 11963-2214. (631)725-7419. Fax: (631)725-8632. E-mail: jill6981@aol.com. **Contact:** Jill Grosjean. Estab. 1999. Represents 33 clients. 100% of clients are new/unpublished writers.

• Prior to becoming an agent, Ms. Grosjean was manager of an independent bookstore. She has also worked in publishing and advertising.

Represents Novels. **Considers these fiction areas:** Historical; literary; mainstream/contemporary; mystery/suspense; regional; romance.

➤ This agency offers some editorial assistance (i.e., line-by-line edits). Actively seeking literary novels and mysteries.

How to Contact Query with SASE. No cold calls, please. Considers simultaneous queries. Responds in 1 week to queries; 1 month to mss. Returns materials only with SASE. Obtains most new clients through recommendations from others, solicitations.

Recent Sales *Beating the Babushka*, by Tim Maleeny (Midnight Ink); *Whispers Within*, by Don Locke (Nav Press); *Rivers Edge*, by Marie Bostwick (Kensington Publishing); *Stealing the Dragon*, by Tim Maleeny (Midnight Ink); *I Love You Like a Tomato*, by Marie Giordano (Forge Books); *Nectar*, by David C. Fickett (Forge Books); *Cycling* and *Sanctuary*, by Greg Garrett (Kensington); *The Smoke*, by Tony Broadbent (St. Martin's Press/Minotaur); *Fields of Gold*, by Marie Bostwick (Kensington); *Spectres in the Smoke*, by Tony Broadbent (St. Martin's Press/Minotaur).

Terms Agent receives 15% commission on domestic sales; 20% commission on foreign sales. No written contract. Charges clients for photocopying and mailing expenses.

Writers' Conferences Book Passage's Mystery Writers' Conference; Agents and Editors Conference; Texas Writers' and Agents' Conference.

⊘ REECE HALSEY NORTH

98 Main St., #704, Tiburon CA 94920. Fax: (415)789-9177. E-mail: info@reecehalseynorth.com. Web site: www.reecehalseynorth.com. **Contact:** Kimberley Cameron. Estab. 1957 (Reece Halsey Agency); 1993 (Reece

Halsey North). Member of AAR. Represents 40 clients. 30% of clients are new/unpublished writers. Currently handles: 75% fiction, 25% nonfiction.

● The Reece Halsey Agency has had an illustrious client list of established writers, including the estate of Aldous Huxley, and has represented Upton Sinclair, William Faulkner, and Henry Miller.

Member Agents Kimberley Cameron, Elizabeth Evans.

Represents Nonfiction books, novels. **Considers these nonfiction areas:** Biography/autobiography; current affairs; history; language/literature/criticism; popular culture; science/technology; true crime/investigative; women's issues/studies. **Considers these fiction areas:** Action/adventure; contemporary issues; detective/police/crime; ethnic; family saga; historical; horror; literary; mainstream/contemporary; mystery/suspense; science fiction; thriller; women's.

0̶₁ "We are looking for a unique and heartfelt voice that conveys a universal truth."

How to Contact Query with SASE, first 50 pages of novel. Please do not fax queries. Responds in 3-6 weeks to queries; 1 month to mss. Obtains most new clients through recommendations from others, solicitations.

Terms Agent receives 15% commission on domestic sales; 10% commission on dramatic rights sales. Offers written contract, binding for 1 year. Requests 6 copies of ms if representing an author.

Writers' Conferences Maui Writers Conference; Aspen Summer Words Literary Festival; Willamette Writers Conference, numerous others.

Tips "Always send a polite, well-written query and please include a SASE with it."

THE JOY HARRIS LITERARY AGENCY, INC.

156 Fifth Ave., Suite 617, New York NY 10010. (212)924-6269. Fax: (212)924-6609. **Contact:** Joy Harris. Member of AAR. Represents more than 100 clients. Currently handles: 50% nonfiction books; 50% novels.

Represents Nonfiction books, novels. **Considers these fiction areas:** Ethnic; experimental; family saga; feminist; gay/lesbian; glitz; hi-lo; historical; humor/satire; literary; mainstream/contemporary; multicultural; multimedia; mystery/suspense; regional; short story collections; spiritual; translation; young adult; women's.

0̶₁ No screenplays.

How to Contact Query with sample chapter, outline/proposal, SASE. Accepts fax queries. No e-mail queries. Considers simultaneous queries. Responds in 2 months to queries. Returns materials only with SASE. Obtains most new clients through recommendations from clients and editors.

Recent Sales This agency prefers not to share information on specific sales.

Terms Agent receives 15% commission on domestic sales; 20% commission on foreign sales. Charges clients for some office expenses.

HARTLINE LITERARY AGENCY

123 Queenston Dr., Pittsburgh PA 15235-5429. (412)829-2495. Fax: (412)829-2432. E-mail: joyce@hartlineliterary.com. Web site: www.hartlineliterary.com. **Contact:** Joyce A. Hart. Estab. 1990. Represents 40 clients. 20% of clients are new/unpublished writers. Currently handles: 40% nonfiction books; 60% novels.

Member Agents Joyce A. Hart, principal agent; Andrea Boeshaar; Terry Burns; Tamela Hancock Murray.

Represents Nonfiction books, novels. **Considers these nonfiction areas:** Business/economics; child guidance/parenting; cooking/foods/nutrition; money/finance; religious/inspirational; self-help/personal improvement; women's issues/studies. **Considers these fiction areas:** Action/adventure; contemporary issues; family saga; historical; literary; mystery/suspense (amateur sleuth, cozy); regional; religious/inspirational; romance (contemporary, gothic, historical, regency); thriller.

0̶₁ This agency specializes in the Christian bookseller market. Actively seeking adult fiction, self-help, nutritional books, devotional, and business. Does not want to receive erotica, gay/lesbian, fantasy, horror, etc.

How to Contact Submit summary/outline, author bio, 3 sample chapters. Accepts e-mail and fax queries. Considers simultaneous queries. Responds in 2 months to queries; 3 months to mss. Returns materials only with SASE. Obtains most new clients through recommendations from others.

Recent Sales *I'm Not OK and Neither Are You*, by David E. Clarke, PhD (Barbour Publishers); *Along Came Love*, by Carrie Turansky (Steeple Hill); *Glory Be*, by Ron and Janet Benrey (Steeple Hill); *Overcoing the Top Ten Reasons Singles Stay Single*, by Tom and Beverly Rodgers (NavPress); *A Clearing in the Wild*, by Jane Kirkpatrick (Waterbrook); *The Mothers-in-Law*, by Andrea Boeshaar and Jeri Odel (Focus on the Family); *Ties to Home*, by Kim Sawyer (Bethany House); The Reluctant 3-book series, by Jill Nelson (Harvest House).

Terms Agent receives 15% commission on domestic sales. Offers written contract.

ANTONY HARWOOD LIMITED

103 Walton St., Oxford OX2 6EB, England. (44)(186)555-9615. Fax: (44)(186)531-0660. E-mail: mail@antonyharwood.com. Web site: www.antonyharwood.com. **Contact:** Antony Harwood, James Macdonald Lockhart. Estab. 2000. Represents 52 clients.

• Prior to starting this agency, Mr. Harwood and Mr. Lockhart worked at publishing houses and other literary agencies.

Represents Nonfiction books, novels. **Considers these nonfiction areas:** Agriculture/horticulture; Americana; animals; anthropology/archaeology; art/architecture/design; biography/autobiography; business/economics; child guidance/parenting; computers/electronic; cooking/foods/nutrition; creative nonfiction (1); current affairs; education; ethnic/cultural interests; gardening; gay/lesbian issues; government/politics/law; health/medicine; history; how-to; humor/satire; language/literature/criticism; memoirs; military/war; money/finance; multicultural; music/dance; nature/environment; philosophy; photography; popular culture; psychology; recreation; regional; religious/inspirational; science/technology; self-help/personal improvement; sex; sociology; software; spirituality; sports; theater/film; translation; travel; true crime/investigative; women's issues/studies. **Considers these fiction areas:** Action/adventure; comic books/cartoon; confession; detective/police/crime; erotica; ethnic; experimental; family saga; fantasy; feminist; gay/lesbian; gothic; hi-lo; historical; horror; humor/satire; literary; mainstream/contemporary; military/war; multicultural; multimedia; mystery/suspense; occult; picture books; plays; regional; religious/inspirational; romance; science fiction; spiritual; sports; thriller; translation; westerns/frontier; young adult.

O➡ "We accept every genre of fiction and nonfiction except for children's fiction for readers ages 10 and younger." No poetry or screenplays.

How to Contact Submit outline, 2-3 sample chapters via e-mail or postal mail (include SASE or IRC). No fax queries. Responds in 2 months to queries.

Terms Agent receives 15% commission on domestic sales; 20% commission on foreign sales.

🌙 JOHN HAWKINS & ASSOCIATES, INC.

71 W. 23rd St., Suite 1600, New York NY 10010. (212)807-7040. Fax: (212)807-9555. E-mail: jha@jhalit.com. Web site: www.jhalit.com. **Contact:** Moses Cardona (moses@jhalit.com). Estab. 1893. Member of AAR. Represents over 100 clients. 5-10% of clients are new/unpublished writers. Currently handles: 40% nonfiction books; 40% novels; 20% juvenile books.

Member Agents Moses Cardona; Warren Frazier; Anne Hawkins; John Hawkins; William Reiss.

Represents Nonfiction books, novels, young adult. **Considers these nonfiction areas:** Agriculture/horticulture; Americana; anthropology/archaeology; art/architecture/design; biography/autobiography; business/economics; current affairs; education; ethnic/cultural interests; gardening; gay/lesbian issues; government/politics/law; health/medicine; history; how-to; interior design/decorating; language/literature/criticism; memoirs; money/finance; multicultural; nature/environment; philosophy; popular culture; psychology; recreation; science/technology; self-help/personal improvement; sex; sociology; software; theater/film; travel; true crime/investigative; young adult; music; creative nonfiction. **Considers these fiction areas:** Action/adventure; detective/police/crime; ethnic; experimental; family saga; feminist; gay/lesbian; glitz; gothic; hi-lo; historical; literary; mainstream/contemporary; military/war; multicultural; multimedia; mystery/suspense; psychic/supernatural; religious/inspirational; short story collections; sports; thriller; translation; westerns/frontier; young adult; women's.

How to Contact Submit query, proposal package, outline, SASE. Considers simultaneous queries. Responds in 1 month to queries. Returns materials only with SASE. Obtains most new clients through recommendations from others.

Recent Sales *Catching Genius*, by Kristy Kiernan; *Raven Black*, by Ann Cleeves; *The Museum of Dr. Moses*, by Joyce Carol Oates; *Waltzing With Alligators*, by Lorelle Marinello (Avon).

Terms Agent receives 15% commission on domestic sales; 20% commission on foreign sales. Charges clients for photocopying.

🌙 RICHARD HENSHAW GROUP

22 West 23rd St., Fifth Floor, New York NY 10010. (212)414-1172. Fax: (212)414-1182. E-mail: submissions@he nshaw.com. Web site: www.rich.henshaw.com. **Contact:** Rich Henshaw. Estab. 1995. Member of AAR, SinC, MWA, HWA, SFWA, RWA. Represents 35 clients. 20% of clients are new/unpublished writers. Currently handles: 35% nonfiction books; 65% novels.

• Prior to opening his agency, Mr. Henshaw served as an agent with Richard Curtis Associates, Inc.

Represents Nonfiction books, novels. **Considers these nonfiction areas:** Animals; biography/autobiography; business/economics; child guidance/parenting; computers/electronic; cooking/foods/nutrition; current affairs; gay/lesbian issues; government/politics/law; health/medicine; how-to; humor/satire; military/war; money/finance; music/dance; nature/environment; New Age/metaphysics; popular culture; psychology; science/technology; self-help/personal improvement; sociology; sports; true crime/investigative; women's issues/studies. **Considers these fiction areas:** Action/adventure; detective/police/crime; ethnic; family saga; fantasy; glitz; historical; horror; humor/satire; literary; mainstream/contemporary; mystery/suspense; psychic/supernatural; romance; science fiction; sports; thriller.

O➜ This agency specializes in thrillers, mysteries, science fiction, fantasy and horror.

How to Contact Query with SASE. Responds in 3 weeks to queries; 6 weeks to mss. Obtains most new clients through recommendations from others, solicitations, conferences.

Recent Sales *Blindfold Game*, by Dana Stabenow (St. Martin's Press); *A Deeper Sleep*, by Dana Stabenow (St. Martin's Press); *The Drowning Man*, by Margaret Coel (Berkley); *The History of the Ancient World*, by Susan Wise Bauer (Norton); *Stone Butterfly*, by James D. Doss (St. Martin's Press); *Box Like the Pros*, by Joe Frazier and William Dettloff (HarperCollins); *The Raven Prince*, by Elizabeth Hoyt (Warner). Other clients include Jessie Wise, Peter van Dijk, Jay Caselberg, Judith Laik.

Terms Agent receives 15% commission on domestic sales; 20% commission on foreign sales. No written contract. 100% of business is derived from commissions on ms sales. Charges clients for photocopying and book orders.

Tips "While we do not have any reason to believe that our submission guidelines will change in the near future, writers can find up-to-date submission policy information on our Web site. Always include a SASE with correct return postage."

☑ FREDERICK HILL BONNIE NADELL, INC.

1842 Union St., San Francisco CA 94123. (415)921-2910. Fax: (415)921-2802. **Contact:** Elise Proulx. Estab. 1979. Represents 100 clients.

Member Agents Fred Hill, president; Bonnie Nadell, vice president; Elise Proulx, associate.

Represents Nonfiction books, novels. **Considers these nonfiction areas:** Current affairs; health/medicine; history; language/literature/criticism; nature/environment; popular culture; science/technology; biography; government/politics, narrative. **Considers these fiction areas:** Literary; mainstream/contemporary.

How to Contact Query with SASE. No e-mail or fax queries. Considers simultaneous queries. Returns materials only with SASE.

Recent Sales *It Might Have Been What He Said*, by Eden Collinsworth; *Consider the Lobster and Other Essays*, by David Foster Wallace; *The Underdog*, by Joshua Davis.

Terms Agent receives 15% commission on domestic sales; 20% commission on foreign sales; 15% commission on dramatic rights sales. Charges clients for photocopying and foreign mailings.

☑ HOPKINS LITERARY ASSOCIATES

2117 Buffalo Rd., Suite 327, Rochester NY 14624-1507. (585)352-6268. **Contact:** Pam Hopkins. Estab. 1996. Member of AAR, RWA. Represents 30 clients. 5% of clients are new/unpublished writers. Currently handles: 100% novels.

Represents Novels. **Considers these fiction areas:** Romance (historical, contemporary, category); women's.

O➜ This agency specializes in women's fiction, particularly historical, contemporary, and category romance, as well as mainstream work.

How to Contact Submit outline, 3 sample chapters. No e-mail or fax queries. Considers simultaneous queries. Responds in 2 weeks to queries; 1 month to mss. Returns materials only with SASE. Obtains most new clients through recommendations from others, solicitations, conferences.

Recent Sales Sold 50 titles in the last year. *Lady of Sin*, by Madeline Hunter (Bantam); *Silent in the Grave*, by Deanna Raybourn (Mira); *Passion*, by Lisa Valdez (Berkley).

Terms Agent receives 15% commission on domestic sales; 20% commission on foreign sales. No written contract.

Writers' Conferences RWA National Conference.

☑ IMPRINT AGENCY, INC.

240 West 35th St., Suite 500, New York NY 10001. Web site: www.imprintagency.com. **Contact:** Stephany Evans, president. Member of AAR.

● Prior to her current position, Ms. Evans began agenting in 1990 with Sandra Martin/Paraview; Ms. Reid formerly ran her own agency, JetReid.

Member Agents Stephany Evans, sevans@imprintagency.com (health and wellness, spirituality, psychology/ self-help, mind/body, pregnancy and parenting, lifestyle, popular reference, narrative nonfiction, women's fiction, both literary and commercial—including chick lit, mystery and light suspense); Gary Heidt, gheidt@imprintagency.com (mystery, thriller, romance, literary fiction, multicultural, speculative, humorous, satirical); Meredith Hays, mhays@imprintagency.com (sophisticated women's fiction—think urban chick lit, pop culture, lifestyle, animals, and absorbing nonfiction accounts); Janet Reid, jreid@imprintagency.com.

Represents Nonfiction books, novels. **Considers these nonfiction areas:** Government/politics/law; health/ medicine; history; music/dance; psychology; self-help/personal improvement; spirituality; relationship; parapsychology; parenting; pregancy; narrative nonfiction; lifestyle. **Considers these fiction areas:** Literary; multicultural; mystery/suspense; thriller; young adult; women's (chick-lit); commercial.

O— "Special areas of interest include alternative health and healing, spirituality, popular psychology, transpersonal psychology, parapsychology, pets, women's issues, history, popular science, parenting, multicultural issues, home decor and narrative nonfiction. We are not looking for historicals, westerns, fantasies, science fiction, plays, poetry or children's books."

How to Contact Query with SASE, proposal package, outline, outline/proposal, publishing history, author bio. No attachments on e-mails. If interested, the agency will contact you. Accepts e-mail queries. No fax queries.

Recent Sales Sold more than 25 titles in the last year. *Baby Proof*, by Emily Giffin (St. Martin's Press); *Crossing Into Medicine Country*, by David Carson (Arcade); *Rollergirl: Totally True Tales From the Track*, by Melissa Joulwan (Simon & Schuster); *The Pirate Primer*, by George Choundras (Writer's Digest Books).

Terms Agent receives 15% commission on domestic sales; 20% commission on foreign sales.

J DE S ASSOCIATES, INC.

9 Shagbark Road, Wilson Point, South Norwalk CT 06854. (203)838-7571. **Contact:** Jacques de Spoelberch. Estab. 1975. Represents 50 clients. Currently handles: 50% nonfiction books; 50% novels.

• Prior to opening his agency, Mr. de Spoelberch was an editor with Houghton Mifflin.

Represents Nonfiction books, novels. **Considers these nonfiction areas:** Biography/autobiography; business/economics; current affairs; ethnic/cultural interests; government/politics/law; health/medicine; history; military/war; New Age/metaphysics; self-help/personal improvement; sociology; sports; translation. **Considers these fiction areas:** Detective/police/crime; historical; juvenile; literary; mainstream/contemporary; mystery/suspense; New Age; westerns/frontier; young adult.

How to Contact Query with SASE. Responds in 2 months to queries. Obtains most new clients through recommendations from authors and other clients.

Terms Agent receives 15% commission on domestic sales; 20% commission on foreign sales. Charges clients for foreign postage and photocopying.

JABBERWOCKY LITERARY AGENCY

P.O. Box 4558, Sunnyside NY 11104-0558. (718)392-5985. Web site: www.awfulagent.com. **Contact:** Joshua Bilmes. Estab. 1994. Member of SFWA. Represents 40 clients. 15% of clients are new/unpublished writers. Currently handles: 15% nonfiction books; 75% novels; 5% scholarly books; 5% other.

Represents Nonfiction books, novels, scholarly books. **Considers these nonfiction areas:** Biography/autobiography; business/economics; cooking/foods/nutrition; current affairs; gay/lesbian issues; government/politics/law; health/medicine; history; humor/satire; language/literature/criticism; military/war; money/finance; nature/environment; popular culture; science/technology; sociology; sports; theater/film; true crime/investigative; women's issues/studies. **Considers these fiction areas:** Action/adventure; contemporary issues; detective/police/crime; ethnic; family saga; fantasy; gay/lesbian; glitz; historical; horror; humor/satire; literary; mainstream/contemporary; psychic/supernatural; regional; science fiction; sports; thriller.

O— This agency represents quite a lot of genre fiction and is actively seeking to increase the amount of nonfiction projects. It does not handle juvenile or young adult. Book-length material only—no poetry, articles, or short fiction.

How to Contact Query with SASE. Do not send mss unless requested. No e-mail or fax queries. Considers simultaneous queries. Responds in 2 weeks to queries. Returns materials only with SASE. Obtains most new clients through solicitations, recommendation by current clients.

Recent Sales Sold 30 US and 100 foreign titles in the last year. *All Together Dead*, by Charlaine Harris (Ace); *Command Decision*, by Elizabeth Moon (Del Rey); *Poltergeist*, by Kat Richardson (Ace); *Mistborn* series and *Alcatraz* series, by Brandon Sanderson (Scholastic). Other clients include Simon Green, Tanya Huff, Tobias Buckell.

Terms Agent receives 15% commission on domestic sales; 20% commission on foreign sales. Offers written contract, binding for 1 year. Charges clients for book purchases, photocopying, international book/ms mailing.

Writers' Conferences Malice Domestic; World Fantasy Convention.

Tips "In approaching with a query, the most important things to me are your credits and your biographical background to the extent it's relevant to your work. I (and most agents) will ignore the adjectives you may choose to describe your own work."

JCA LITERARY AGENCY

174 Sullivan St., New York NY 10012. (212)807-0888. E-mail: mel@jcalit.com. Web site: www.jcalit.com. **Contact:** Melanie Meyers Cushman. Estab. 1978. Member of AAR. Represents 100 clients.

Member Agents Tom Cushman; Melanie Meyers Cushman; Tony Outhwaite.

Represents Nonfiction books, novels. **Considers these nonfiction areas:** Biography/autobiography; current affairs; government/politics/law; history; language/literature/criticism; memoirs; popular culture; sociology; sports; theater/film; translation; true crime/investigative. **Considers these fiction areas:** Action/adventure;

contemporary issues; detective/police/crime; family saga; historical; literary; mainstream/contemporary; mystery/suspense; sports; thriller.

O⟶ Does not want to receive screenplays, poetry, children's books, science fiction/fantasy or genre romance.

Terms Agent receives 15% commission on domestic sales; 20% commission on foreign sales. No written contract.

◖ NATASHA KERN LITERARY AGENCY

P.O. Box 1069, White Salmon WA 98672. (509)493-3803. Web site: www.natashakern.com. **Contact:** Natasha Kern. Estab. 1986. Member of RWA, MWA, SinC.

● Prior to opening her agency, Ms. Kern worked as an editor and publicist for Simon & Schuster, Bantam, and Ballantine. "This agency has sold more than 700 books."

Represents Adult commercial nonfiction and fiction. **Considers these nonfiction areas:** Animals; child guidance/parenting; current affairs; ethnic/cultural interests; gardening; health/medicine; nature/environment; New Age/metaphysics; popular culture; psychology; religious/inspirational; self-help/personal improvement; spirituality; women's issues/studies; investigative journalism. **Considers these fiction areas:** Women's; chick lit; lady lit; romance (contemporary, historical); historical; mainstream/contemporary; multicultural; mystery/suspense; religious/inspirational; thriller.

O⟶ This agency specializes in commercial fiction and nonfiction for adults. "We are a full-service agency." Does not represent sports, true crime, scholarly works, coffee table books, war memoirs, software, scripts, literary fiction, photography, poetry, short stories, children's, horror, fantasy, genre science fiction, stage plays, or traditional westerns.

How to Contact See submission instructions online. Query with submission history, writing credits and length of ms. Don't include SASE. Considers simultaneous queries. Responds in 3 weeks to queries.

Recent Sales Sold 56 titles in the last year. *China Dolls*, by Michelle Yu and Blossom Kan (St. Martin's); *Bastard Tongues*, by Derek Bickerton (Farrar Strauss); *Bone Rattler*, by Eliot Pattison; *Wicked Pleasure*, by Nina Bangs (Berkley); *Inviting God In*, by David Aaron (Shambhala); *Perfect Killer*, by Lewis Perdue (Tor); *Unlawful Contact*, by Pamela Clare (Berkley); *Dead End Dating*, by Kimberly Raye (Ballantine); *A Scent of Roses*, by Nikki Arana (Baker Book House); *The Sexiest Man Alive*, by Diana Holquist (Warner Books).

Terms Agent receives 15% commission on domestic sales; 20% commission on foreign sales; 15% commission on dramatic rights sales.

Writers' Conferences RWA National Conference; MWA National Conference; ACFW Conference; and many regional conferences.

Tips "Your chances of being accepted for representation will be greatly enhanced by going to our Web site first. If we know what you need and want, we can help you achieve it. A dream client has a storytelling gift, a commitment to a writing career, a desire to learn and grow, and a passion for excellence. This client understands that many people have to work together for a book to succeed and that everything in publishing takes far longer than one imagines. Trust and communication are truly essential."

◎ KIRCHOFF/WOHLBERG, INC., AUTHORS' REPRESENTATION DIVISION

866 United Nations Plaza, #525, New York NY 10017. (212)644-2020. Fax: (212)223-4387. **Contact:** Liza Pulitzer Voges. Estab. 1930s. Member of AAR, AAP, Society of Illustrators, SPAR, Bookbuilders of Boston, New York Bookbinders' Guild, AIGA. Represents 50 clients. 10% of clients are new/unpublished writers. Currently handles: 5% nonfiction books; 25% novels; 5% young adult; 65% picture books.

● Kirchoff/Wohlberg has been in business for more than 60 years.

O⟶ This agency specializes in juvenile through young adult trade books.

How to Contact For novels, query with SASE, outline, a few sample chapters. For picture books, send entire ms, SASE. No e-mail or fax queries. Considers simultaneous queries. Responds in 1 month to queries; 2 months to mss. Returns materials only with SASE. Obtains most new clients through recommendations from authors, illustrators, and editors.

Recent Sales Sold more than 50 titles in the last year. *Dizzy*, by Jonah Winter (Scholastic); *Homework Machine*, by Dan Gutman (Simon and Schuster); Princess Power series, by Suzanne Williams (HarperCollins); My Weird School series, by Dan Gutman (HarperCollins); *Biscuit*, by Alyssa Capucilli (HarperCollins).

Terms Offers written contract, binding for at least 1 year. Agent receives standard commission, depending upon whether it is an author only, illustrator only, or an author/illustrator book.

◖ HARVEY KLINGER, INC.

300 W. 55th St., New York NY 10019. (212)581-7068. E-mail: queries@harveyklinger.com. Web site: www.harveyklinger.com. **Contact:** Harvey Klinger. Estab. 1977. Member of AAR. Represents 100 clients. 25% of clients are new/unpublished writers. Currently handles: 50% nonfiction books; 50% novels.

Member Agents David Dunton (popular culture, music-related books, literary fiction, crime novels, thrillers);

Sara Crowe (children's and young adult authors, adult fiction and nonfiction, foreign rights sales); Andrea Somberg (literary fiction, commercial fiction, romance, sci-fi/fantasy, mysteries/thrillers, young adult, middle grade, quality narrative nonfiction, popular culture, how-to, self-help, humor, interior design, cookbooks, health/fitness); Nikki Van De Car (science fiction/fantasy, horror, romance, literary fiction, popular culture, how-to, memoir).

Represents Nonfiction books, novels. **Considers these nonfiction areas:** Biography/autobiography; cooking/foods/nutrition; health/medicine; psychology; science/technology; self-help/personal improvement; spirituality; sports; true crime/investigative; women's issues/studies. **Considers these fiction areas:** Action/adventure; detective/police/crime; family saga; glitz; literary; mainstream/contemporary; mystery/suspense; thriller.

○━ This agency specializes in big, mainstream, contemporary fiction and nonfiction.

How to Contact Query with SASE. No phone or fax queries. Accepts e-mail queries. No fax queries. Responds in 2 months to queries and mss. Obtains most new clients through recommendations from others.

Recent Sales *Breakable You*, By Brian Morton; *The Money In You!*, by Julie Stav; *The Mercy Seller*, by Brenda Vantrease; *A Country Music Christmas*, by Edie Hand and Buddy Killen; *Keep Climbing*, by Sean Swarner; *The Cubicle Survival Guide*, by James F. Thompson; *Cookie Sensations*, by Meaghan Mountford; *Stranger*, by Justine Musk; *Laird Of The Mist*, by Paula Quinn. Other clients include Barbara Wood, Terry Kay, Barbara De Angelis, Jeremy Jackson.

Terms Agent receives 15% commission on domestic sales; 25% commission on foreign sales. Offers written contract. Charges for photocopying mss and overseas postage for mss.

◑ KNEERIM & WILLIAMS

225 Franklin St., Boston MA 02110. (617)542-5070. Fax: (617)542-8906. Web site: www.fr.com/kwfr. **Contact:** Melissa Grella. Estab. 1990. Represents 200 clients. 5% of clients are new/unpublished writers. Currently handles: 80% nonfiction books; 15% novels; 5% movie scripts.

● Prior to becoming an agent, Mr. Williams was a lawyer; Ms. Kneerim was a publisher and editor; Mr. Wasserman was an editor and journalist.

Member Agents John Taylor Williams; Jill Kneerim; Steve Wasserman; Bretthe Bloom.

Represents Nonfiction books, novels. **Considers these nonfiction areas:** Anthropology/archaeology; biography/autobiography; business/economics; child guidance/parenting; current affairs; government/politics/law; health/medicine; history; language/literature/criticism; memoirs; nature/environment; popular culture; psychology; religious/inspirational; science/technology; sociology; sports; women's issues/studies. **Considers these fiction areas:** Historical; literary; mainstream/contemporary.

○━ This agency specializes in narrative nonfiction, history, science, business, women's issues, commercial and literary fiction, film, and television. "We have 7 agents and 2 scouts in Boston, New York, and Santa Fe." Actively seeking distinguished authors, experts, professionals, intellectuals, and serious writers. Does not want to receive blanket multiple submissions, genre fiction, children's literature, or original screenplays.

How to Contact Query with SASE. Responds in 2 weeks to queries; 2 months to mss. Returns materials only with SASE. Obtains most new clients through recommendations from others.

Recent Sales *Frank Gehry and the Bilbao Museum*, by Nicolai Ouroussoff (Basic); *Nuclear Terrorism*, by Graham Allison (Times Books); *Beggar at the Gate*, by Thalassa Ali (Bantam); *The Future of Life*, by E.O. Wilson (Knopf); *Savage Mountain: The Women of K2*, by Jennifer Jordan (Morrow).

◑ ELAINE KOSTER LITERARY AGENCY, LLC

55 Central Park W., Suite 6, New York NY 10023. (212)362-9488. Fax: (212)712-0164. **Contact:** Elaine Koster, Stephanie Lehmann. Member of AAR, MWA; Author's Guild, Women's Media Group. Represents 40 clients. 10% of clients are new/unpublished writers. Currently handles: 30% nonfiction books; 70% novels.

● Prior to opening her agency in 1998, Ms. Koster was president and publisher of Dutton NAL, part of the Penguin Group.

Represents Nonfiction books, novels. **Considers these nonfiction areas:** Biography/autobiography; business/economics; child guidance/parenting; cooking/foods/nutrition; current affairs; ethnic/cultural interests; health/medicine; history; how-to; money/finance; nature/environment; popular culture; psychology; self-help/personal improvement; spirituality; women's issues/studies. **Considers these fiction areas:** Contemporary issues; detective/police/crime; ethnic; family saga; feminist; historical; literary; mainstream/contemporary; mystery/suspense (amateur sleuth, cozy, culinary, malice domestic); regional; thriller; young adult; chick lit.

○━ This agency specializes in quality fiction and nonfiction. Does not want to receive juvenile, screenplays, or science fiction.

How to Contact Query with SASE, outline, 3 sample chapters. Prefers to read materials exclusively. No e-mail or fax queries. Responds in 3 weeks to queries; 1 month to mss. Returns materials only with SASE. Obtains most new clients through recommendations from others.

Recent Sales Sold 50 titles in the last year. *The Opposite of Love*, by Julie Buxbaum (Dial Press); *Secret Sins*, by Francis Ray (St. Martin's); *No One Needs a Husband Seven Days a Week*, by Nina Foxx (Avon).

Terms Agent receives 15% commission on domestic sales. Bills back specific expenses incurred doing business for a client.

Tips "We prefer exclusive submissions. Don't e-mail or fax submissions. Please include biographical information and publishing history."

KRAAS LITERARY AGENCY

E-mail: irene@kraasliteraryagency.com. Web site: www.kraasliteraryagency.com. **Contact:** Irene Kraas. Estab. 1990. Represents 40 clients. 75% of clients are new/unpublished writers. Currently handles: 5% nonfiction books; 95% novels.

Member Agents Irene Kraas, principal (psychological thrillers, medical thrillers, literary fiction, young adult).

O→ Actively seeking books that are well written with commercial potential. No short stories, plays or poetry.

How to Contact Please refer to this agency's Web site, as its submission guidelines are in flux. No e-mail or fax queries. Considers simultaneous queries. Returns materials only with SASE.

Recent Sales See Web site for a list of recent sales. Offers written contract.

Writers' Conferences Southwest Writers Conference, Wrangling with Writing.

Tips "Material by unpublished authors will be accepted in the above areas only. Pay attention to the submission guidelines as they apply to all submissions."

KT PUBLIC RELATIONS & LITERARY SERVICES

1905 Cricklewood Cove, Fogelsville PA 18051. (610)395-6298. Fax: (610)395-6299. E-mail: kae@ktpublicrelatio ns.com or jon@ktpublicrelations.com. Web site: www.ktpublicrelations.com. **Contact:** Kae Tienstra, Jon Tienstra. Estab. 2005. Represents 12 clients. 75% of clients are new/unpublished writers. Currently handles: 50% nonfiction books; 50% novels.

● Prior to becoming an agent, Ms. Tienstra was publicity director for Rodale, Inc. for 13 years and then founded her own publicity agency; Mr. Tienstra joined the firm in 1995 with varied corporate experience and a master's degree in library science.

Member Agents Kae Tienstra (health, parenting, psychology, how-to, crafts, foods/nutrition, beauty, women's fiction, general fiction); Jon Tienstra (nature/environment, history, cooking/foods/nutrition, war/military, automotive, health/medicine, gardening, general fiction, science fiction/fantasy, popular fiction).

Represents Nonfiction books, novels, novellas. **Considers these nonfiction areas:** Agriculture/horticulture; animals; child guidance/parenting; cooking/foods/nutrition; crafts/hobbies; health/medicine; history; how-to; military/war; nature/environment; popular culture; psychology; science/technology; self-help/personal improvement; interior design/decorating. **Considers these fiction areas:** Action/adventure; detective/police/crime; family saga; fantasy; historical; literary; mainstream/contemporary; mystery/suspense; romance; science fiction; thriller.

O→ Specializes in parenting, history, cooking/foods/nutrition, crafts, beauty, war, health/medicine, psychology, how-to, gardening, science fiction, fantasy, women's fiction, and popular fiction. Does not want to see unprofessional material.

How to Contact Query with SASE. Accepts e-mail and fax queries. Considers simultaneous queries. Responds in 2 weeks to queries; 3 months to mss. Returns materials only with SASE. Obtains most new clients through recommendations from others.

Terms Agent receives 15% commission on domestic sales; 20% commission on foreign sales. Offers written contract. Charges clients for long-distance phone calls, fax, postage, photocopying (only when incurred). No advance payment for these out-of-pocket expenses.

THE LA LITERARY AGENCY

P.O. Box 46370, Los Angeles CA 90046. (323)654-5288. E-mail: laliteraryag@aol.com. **Contact:** Ann Cashman, Eric Lasher. Estab. 1980.

● Prior to becoming an agent, Mr. Lasher worked in publishing in New York and Los Angeles.

Represents Nonfiction books, novels. **Considers these nonfiction areas:** Animals; anthropology/archaeology; art/architecture/design; biography/autobiography; business/economics; child guidance/parenting; cooking/foods/nutrition; current affairs; ethnic/cultural interests; government/politics/law; health/medicine; history; how-to; nature/environment; popular culture; psychology; science/technology; self-help/personal improvement; sociology; sports; true crime/investigative; women's issues/studies; narrative nonfiction. **Considers these fiction areas:** Action/adventure; detective/police/crime; family saga; feminist; historical; literary; mainstream/contemporary; sports; thriller.

How to Contact Query with SASE, outline, 1 sample chapter. No e-mail or fax queries.

Recent Sales *Full Bloom: The Art and Life of Georgia O'Keeffe*, by Hunter Drohojowska-Philp (Norton); *And the*

Walls Came Tumbling Down, by H. Caldwell (Scribner); *Italian Slow & Savory*, by Joyce Goldstein (Chronicle); *A Field Guide to Chocolate Chip Cookies*, by Dede Wilson (Harvard Common Press); *Teen Knitting Club* (Artisan); *The Framingham Heart Study*, by Dr. Daniel Levy (Knopf).

☉ PETER LAMPACK AGENCY, INC.

551 Fifth Ave., Suite 1613, New York NY 10176-0187. (212)687-9106. Fax: (212)687-9109. E-mail: alampack@ve rizon.net. **Contact:** Andrew Lampack. Estab. 1977. Represents 50 clients. 10% of clients are new/unpublished writers. Currently handles: 20% nonfiction books; 80% novels.

Member Agents Peter Lampack (president); Rema Delanyan (foreign rights); Andrew Lampack (new writers).

Represents Nonfiction books, novels. **Considers these fiction areas:** Action/adventure; detective/police/ crime; family saga; historical; literary; mainstream/contemporary; mystery/suspense; thriller; contemporary relationships.

    0→ This agency specializes in commercial fiction and nonfiction by recognized experts. Actively seeking literary and commercial fiction, thrillers, mysteries, suspense, and psychological thrillers. Does not want to receive horror, romance, science fiction, westerns, historical literary fiction or academic material.

How to Contact Query with SASE. *No unsolicited mss.* Accepts e-mail queries. No fax queries. Considers simultaneous queries. Responds in 2 months to queries and mss. Obtains most new clients through referrals made by clients.

Recent Sales *Inner Workings*, by J.M. Coetzee; *Treasure of Kahn*, by Clive Cussler and Dick Cussler; *Skeleton Coast*, by Clive Cussler and Jack Du Brul; *The Navigator*, by Clive Cussler with Paul Kemprecos; *Dust*, by Martha Grimes; *Bloodthirsty Bitches and Pious Pimps of Power*, by Gerry Spence.

Terms Agent receives 15% commission on domestic sales; 20% commission on foreign sales.

Writers' Conferences BookExpo America.

Tips "Submit only your best work for consideration. Have a very specific agenda of goals you wish your prospective agent to accomplish for you. Provide the agent with a comprehensive statement of your credentials—educational and professional."

☉ LAURA LANGLIE, LITERARY AGENT

239 Carroll St., Garden Apartment, Brooklyn NY 11231. (718)855-8102. Fax: (718)855-4450. E-mail: laura@laur alanglie.com. **Contact:** Laura Langlie. Estab. 2001. Represents 25 clients. 50% of clients are new/unpublished writers. Currently handles: 25% nonfiction books; 48% novels; 2% story collections; 25% juvenile books.

    • Prior to opening her agency, Ms. Langlie worked in publishing for 7 years and as an agent at Kidde, Hoyt & Picard for 6 years.

Represents Nonfiction books, novels, short story collections, novellas, juvenile books. **Considers these nonfiction areas:** Animals (not how-to); anthropology/archaeology; biography/autobiography; current affairs; ethnic/ cultural interests; gay/lesbian issues; government/politics/law; history; humor/satire; memoirs; nature/environment; popular culture; psychology; theater/film; women's issues/studies; history of medicine and science; language/literature. **Considers these fiction areas:** Detective/police/crime; ethnic; feminist; gay/lesbian; historical; humor/satire; juvenile; literary; mystery/suspense; romance; thriller; young adult; mainstream.

    0→ "I love working with first-time authors. I'm very involved with and committed to my clients. I also employ a publicist to work with all my clients to make the most of each book's publication. Most of my clients come to me via recommendations from other agents, clients and editors. I've met very few at conferences. I've often sought out writers for projects, and I still find new clients via the traditional query letter." Does not want to receive children's picture books, science fiction, poetry, men's adventure or erotica.

How to Contact Query with SASE. Accepts queries via fax. Considers simultaneous queries. Responds in 1 week to queries; 1 month to mss. Returns materials only with SASE. Obtains most new clients through recommendations, submissions.

Recent Sales Sold 30 titles in the last year. *Pants on Fire* by Meg Cabot (HarperCollins Children's); *It's About Your Husband*, by Lauren Lipton (Warner Books); *Price of Admission*, by Leslie Margolis (Simon Pulse); *Island of the Lost*, by Joan Druett (Algonquin Books of Chapel Hill). Other clients include Renee Ashley, Mignon F. Ballard, Jessica Benson, Jack El-Hai, Sarah Elliott, Fiona Gibson, Robin Hathaway, Melanie Lynne Hauser, Mary Hogan, Jonathan Neale, Eric Pinder, Delia Ray, Cheryl L. Reed, Jennifer Sturman.

Terms Agent receives 15% commission on domestic sales; 20% commission on foreign sales. No written contract.

Tips "Be complete, forthright and clear in your communications. Do your research as to what a particular agent represents."

☉ MICHAEL LARSEN/ELIZABETH POMADA, LITERARY AGENTS

1029 Jones St., San Francisco CA 94109-5023. (415)673-0939. E-mail: larsenpoma@aol.com. Web site: www.lar sen-pomada.com. **Contact:** Mike Larsen, Elizabeth Pomada. Estab. 1972. Member of AAR, Authors Guild, ASJA,

PEN, WNBA, California Writers Club, National Speakers Association. Represents 100 clients. 40-45% of clients are new/unpublished writers. Currently handles: 70% nonfiction books; 30% novels.

- ● Prior to opening their agency, Mr. Larsen and Ms. Pomada were promotion executives for major publishing houses. Mr. Larsen worked for Morrow, Bantam and Pyramid (now part of Berkley); Ms. Pomada worked at Holt, David McKay and The Dial Press. Mr. Larsen is the author of the third editions of *How to Write a Book Proposal* and *How to Get a Literary Agent*.

Member Agents Michael Larsen (nonfiction); Elizabeth Pomada (fiction, narrative nonfiction, nonfiction for women); Laurie McLean, laurie@agentsavant.com (fantasy, science, romance, middle-grade and YA fiction).

Represents Adult book-length fiction and nonfiction that will interest New York publishers or are irresistibly written or conceived. **Considers these nonfiction areas:** Anthropology/archaeology; art/architecture/design; biography/autobiography; business/economics; cooking/foods/nutrition; current affairs; ethnic/cultural interests; gay/lesbian issues; government/politics/law; health/medicine; history; how-to; humor/satire; memoirs; money/finance; music/dance; nature/environment; New Age/metaphysics; popular culture; psychology; religious/inspirational; science/technology; self-help/personal improvement; sociology; sports; theater/film; travel; true crime/investigative; women's issues/studies; futurism. **Considers these fiction areas:** Action/adventure; contemporary issues; detective/police/crime; ethnic; experimental; family saga; fantasy; feminist; gay/lesbian; glitz; historical; humor/satire; literary; mainstream/contemporary; mystery/suspense; religious/inspirational; romance (contemporary, gothic, historical); chick lit.

- ⊶ "We have diverse tastes. We look for fresh voices and new ideas. We handle literary, commercial and genre fiction, and the full range of nonfiction books." Actively seeking commercial, genre and literary fiction. Does not want to receive children's books, plays, short stories, screenplays, pornography, poetry or stories of abuse.

How to Contact Query with SASE, submit first 10 pages of completed novel, 2-page synopsis, SASE. Make sure the query is 1 page. For nonfiction, send a promotion plan done according to the advice on the Web site. Accepts e-mail queries. No fax queries. Responds in 2 weeks to queries; 2 months to mss.

Recent Sales Sold at least 15 titles in the last year. *Banana Hear Summer*, by Merlinda Bobis (Bantam); *Guerilla Marketing: Secrets for Making Big Profits from Your Small Business, 4th edition*, by Jay Levinson (Houghton Mifflin); *The Tender Carnivore: How to Be a Thoughtful Meat-Eater*, by Catherine Friend (Marlowe).

Terms Agent receives 15% commission on domestic sales; 20% (30% for Asia) commission on foreign sales. May charge for printing, postage for multiple submissions, foreign mail, foreign phone calls, galleys, books, legal fees.

Writers' Conferences BookExpo America; Santa Barbara Writers' Conference; San Francisco Writers' Conference.

Tips "We love helping writers get the rewards and recognition they deserve. If you can write books that meet the needs of the marketplace and you can promote your books, now is the best time ever to be a writer. We must find new writers to make a living, so we are very eager to hear from new writers whose work will interest large houses, and nonfiction writers who can promote their books. For a list of recent sales, helpful info, and three ways to make yourself irresistible to any publisher, please visit our Web site."

◎ THE STEVE LAUBE AGENCY

5501 N. Seventh Ave., #502, Phoenix AZ 85013. (602)336-8910. Fax: (602)532-7123. E-mail: krichards@stevelaube.com. Web site: www.stevelaube.com. **Contact:** Steve Laube. Estab. 2004. Member of CBA. Represents 60+ clients. 5% of clients are new/unpublished writers. Currently handles: 48% nonfiction books; 48% novels; 2% novellas; 2% scholarly books.

- ● Prior to becoming an agent, Mr. Laube worked 11 years as a Christian bookseller and 11 years as editorial director of nonfiction with Bethany House Publishers.

Represents Nonfiction books, novels. **Considers these nonfiction areas:** Religious/inspirational. **Considers these fiction areas:** Religious/inspirational.

- ⊶ "We primarily serve the Christian market (CBA)." Actively seeking Christian fiction and religious nonfiction. Does not want to receive children's picture books, poetry or cookbooks.

How to Contact Submit proposal package, outline, 3 sample chapters, SASE. No e-mail submissions. Consult Web site for guidelines. Considers simultaneous queries. Responds in 6-8 weeks to queries. Returns materials only with SASE. Obtains most new clients through recommendations from others, solicitations, conferences.

Recent Sales Sold 80 titles in the last year. *Day With a Perfect Stranger*, by David Gregory (Kelly's Filmworks). Other clients include Deborah Raney, Bright Media, Allison Bottke, H. Norman Wright, Ellie Kay, Jack Cavanaugh, Karen Ball, Tracey Bateman, Clint Kelly, Susan May Warren, Lisa Bergren, John Rosemond, David Gregory, Cindy Woodsmall.

Terms Agent receives 15% commission on domestic sales; 20% commission on foreign sales. Offers written contract; 30-day notice must be given to terminate contract.

Writers' Conferences Mount Hermon Christian Writers' Conference; American Christian Fiction Writers' Conference; Glorieta Christian Writers' Conference.

◪ LAZEAR AGENCY, INC.

431 Second St., Suite 300, Hudson WI 54016. (715)531-0012. Fax: (715)531-0016. E-mail: admin@lazear.com. Web site: www.lazear.com. **Contact:** Editorial Board. Estab. 1984. 20% of clients are new/unpublished writers. Currently handles: 55% nonfiction books; 40% novels; 5% juvenile books.

• The Lazear Agency opened a New York office in September 1997.

Member Agents Jonathon Lazear; Christi Cardenas; Julie Mayo; Anne Blackstone.

Represents Nonfiction books, novels, short story collections, novellas, juvenile books, graphic novels. **Considers these nonfiction areas:** Agriculture/horticulture; Americana; animals; anthropology/archaeology; art/architecture/design; biography/autobiography; business/economics; child guidance/parenting; computers/electronic; cooking/foods/nutrition; current affairs; education; ethnic/cultural interests; gardening; gay/lesbian issues; government/politics/law; health/medicine; history; how-to; humor/satire; interior design/decorating; juvenile nonfiction; language/literature/criticism; memoirs; military/war; money/finance; multicultural; music/dance; nature/environment; New Age/metaphysics; philosophy; photography; popular culture; psychology; recreation; regional; religious/inspirational; science/technology; self-help/personal improvement; sex; sociology; software; spirituality; sports; theater/film; travel; true crime/investigative; women's issues/studies; young adult; creative nonfiction. **Considers these fiction areas:** Action/adventure; confession; detective/police/crime; ethnic; family saga; fantasy; feminist; gay/lesbian; gothic; hi-lo; historical; humor/satire; juvenile; literary; mainstream/contemporary; military/war; multicultural; multimedia; mystery/suspense; New Age; occult; picture books; plays; psychic/supernatural; religious/inspirational; romance; science fiction; short story collections; spiritual; sports; thriller; translation; westerns/frontier; young adult; women's.

○┐ Actively seeking new voices in commercial fiction and nonfiction. "It's all in the writing, no matter the subject matter." Does not want to receive horror, poetry, scripts and/or screenplays.

How to Contact Query with SASE, submit outline/proposal, synopsis, author bio, SASE. No phone calls or faxes. We prefer snail mail queries. Responds in 2 weeks to queries; 3 weeks to mss. Returns materials only with SASE. Obtains most new clients through recommendations from others, solicitations.

Recent Sales Sold more than 50 titles in the last year. Untitled book, by Jane Goodall (Warner); Untitled book, by Tony Hendra (Holt); Untitled YA series, by Will Weaver (FSG); *The Truth (with Jokes)*, by Al Franken (Dutton); *Harvest for Hope*, by Jane Goodall with Gary McAvoy and Gail Hudson (Warner); *Mommy Knows Worst*, by James Lileks (Crown); *The Prop*, by Pete Hautman (Simon & Schuster). Other clients include Margaret Weis, Gerry Gross, Noah Adams, and many more.

Terms Agent receives 15% commission on domestic sales; 20% commission on foreign sales. Offers written contract. Charges clients for photocopying, international express mail, bound galleys, books used for subsidiary rights sales. No fees charged if book is not sold.

Tips "The writer should first view himself as a salesperson in order to obtain an agent. Sell yourself, your idea, your concept. Do your homework. Notice what is in the marketplace. Be sophisticated about the arena in which you are writing. Please note that we also have a New York office, but the primary office remains in Hudson, Wis., for the receipt of any material."

◎ THE NED LEAVITT AGENCY

70 Wooster St., Suite 4F, New York NY 10012. (212)334-0999. Web site: www.nedleavittagency.com. **Contact:** Ned Leavitt. Member of AAR. Represents 40+ clients.

Member Agents Ned Leavitt, founder and agent; Britta Alexander, agent; Jill Beckman, editorial assistant.

Represents Nonfiction books, novels.

○┐ "We are small in size, but intensely dedicated to our authors and to supporting excellent and unique writing."

How to Contact This agency now only takes queries/submissions through referred clients. Do *not* cold query. No fax queries.

Recent Sales *In Time of War*, by Allen Appel (Carroll & Graf); *From Father to Son*, by Allen Appel (St. Martin's); *The Way of Song*, by Shawna Carol (St. Martin's); *Alchemy of Illness*, by Kat Duff (Pantheon); *Are You Getting Enlightened or Losing Your Mind?*, by Dennis Gersten (Harmony).

Tips Look online for this agency's recently changed submission guidelines.

▣ LESCHER & LESCHER, LTD.

47 E. 19th St., New York NY 10003. (212)529-1790. Fax: (212)529-2716. **Contact:** Robert Lescher, Susan Lescher. Estab. 1966. Member of AAR. Represents 150 clients. Currently handles: 80% nonfiction books; 20% novels.

Represents Nonfiction books, novels. **Considers these nonfiction areas:** Current affairs; history; memoirs;

popular culture; biography; cookbooks/wines; law; contemporary issues; narrative nonfiction. **Considers these fiction areas:** Literary; mystery/suspense; commercial.

    O➤ Does not want to receive screenplays, science fiction or romance.

How to Contact Query with SASE. Obtains most new clients through recommendations from others.

Recent Sales Sold 35 titles in the last year. This agency prefers not to share information on specific sales. Clients include Neil Sheehan, Madeleine L'Engle, Calvin Trillin, Judith Viorst, Thomas Perry, Anne Fadiman, Frances FitzGerald, Paula Fox, Robert M. Parker Jr.

Terms Agent receives 15% commission on domestic sales; 20% commission on foreign sales.

◙ LEVINE GREENBERG LITERARY AGENCY, INC.

307 Seventh Ave., Suite 2407, New York NY 10001. (212)337-0934. Fax: (212)337-0948. Web site: www.levinegr eenberg.com. Estab. 1989. Member of AAR. Represents 250 clients. 33% of clients are new/unpublished writers. Currently handles: 70% nonfiction books; 30% novels.

    ● Prior to opening his agency, Mr. Levine served as vice president of the Bank Street College of Education.

Member Agents James Levine; Arielle Eckstut; Daniel Greenberg; Stephanie Kip Rostan; Jenoyne Adams.

Represents Nonfiction books, novels. **Considers these nonfiction areas:** Animals; art/architecture/design; biography/autobiography; business/economics; child guidance/parenting; computers/electronic; cooking/ foods/nutrition; gardening; gay/lesbian issues; health/medicine; money/finance; nature/environment; New Age/metaphysics; religious/inspirational; science/technology; self-help/personal improvement; sociology; spirituality; sports; women's issues/studies. **Considers these fiction areas:** Literary; mainstream/contemporary; mystery/suspense; thriller (psychological); women's.

    O➤ This agency specializes in business, psychology, parenting, health/medicine, narrative nonfiction, spiri-
       tuality, religion, women's issues, and commercial fiction.

How to Contact See Web site for full submission procedure. Prefers e-mail queries. Obtains most new clients through recommendations from others.

Recent Sales *Sharp Objects*, by Gillian Flynn; *Love is a Mix Tape*, by Rob Sheffield; *Growing Great Employees*, Erika Anderson.

Terms Agent receives 15% commission on domestic sales; 20% commission on foreign sales. Offers written contract. Charges clients for out-of-pocket expenses—telephone, fax, postage, photocopying—directly connected to the project.

Writers' Conferences ASJA Writers' Conference.

Tips "We focus on editorial development, business representation, and publicity and marketing strategy."

◙ PAUL S. LEVINE LITERARY AGENCY

1054 Superba Ave., Venice CA 90291-3940. (310)450-6711. Fax: (310)450-0181. E-mail: pslevine@ix.netcom.c om. Web site: www.paulslevine.com. **Contact:** Paul S. Levine. Estab. 1996. Member of the State Bar of California. Represents over 100 clients. 75% of clients are new/unpublished writers. Currently handles: 30% nonfiction books; 30% novels; 10% movie scripts; 30% TV scripts.

Represents Nonfiction books, novels, movie scripts, feature film, TV scripts, TV movie of the week, episodic drama, sitcom, animation, documentary, miniseries, syndicated material. **Considers these nonfiction areas:** Art/architecture/design; biography/autobiography; business/economics; child guidance/parenting; computers/electronic; cooking/foods/nutrition; crafts/hobbies; current affairs; education; ethnic/cultural interests; gay/lesbian issues; government/politics/law; health/medicine; history; how-to; humor/satire; interior design/ decorating; language/literature/criticism; memoirs; military/war; money/finance; music/dance; nature/environment; New Age/metaphysics; photography; popular culture; psychology; religious/inspirational; science/ technology; self-help/personal improvement; sociology; sports; theater/film; true crime/investigative; women's issues/studies; creative nonfiction. **Considers these fiction areas:** Action/adventure; comic books/cartoon; confession; detective/police/crime; erotica; ethnic; experimental; family saga; feminist; gay/lesbian; glitz; historical; humor/satire; literary; mainstream/contemporary; mystery/suspense; regional; religious/inspirational; romance; sports; thriller; westerns/frontier. **Considers these script subject areas:** Action/adventure; biography/autobiography; cartoon/animation; comedy; contemporary issues; detective/police/crime; erotica; ethnic; experimental; family saga; feminist; gay/lesbian; glitz; historical; horror; juvenile; mainstream; multimedia; mystery/suspense; religious/inspirational; romantic comedy; romantic drama; sports; teen; thriller; western/ frontier.

    O➤ Actively seeking commercial fiction and nonfiction. Also handles children's and young adult fiction
       and nonfiction. Does not want to receive science fiction, fantasy, or horror.

How to Contact Query with SASE. Accepts e-mail and fax queries. Considers simultaneous queries. Responds in 1 day to queries; 2 months to mss. Returns materials only with SASE. Obtains most new clients through conferences, referrals, listings on various Web sites and in directories.

Recent Sales Sold 25 titles in the last year. This agency prefers not to share information on specific sales.

Terms Agent receives 15% commission on domestic sales; 20% commission on foreign sales. Offers written contract. Charges clients for messengers, long distance calls, postage (only when incurred). No advance payment necessary.

Writers' Conferences California Lawyers for the Arts Workshops; Selling to Hollywood Conference; Willamette Writers Conference; and many others.

⬛ LIPPINCOTT MASSIE MCQUILKIN

80 Fifth Ave., Suite 1101, New York NY 10011. (212)337-2044. Fax: (212)352-2059. E-mail: info@lmqlit.com. Web site: www.lmqlit.com. **Contact:** Molly Lindley, assistant. Estab. 2003. Represents 90 clients. 30% of clients are new/unpublished writers. Currently handles: 40% nonfiction books; 40% novels; 10% story collections; 5% scholarly books; 5% poetry.

Member Agents Maria Massie (fiction, memoir, cultural criticism); Will Lippincott (politics, current affairs, history); Rob McQuilkin (fiction, history, psychology, sociology, graphic material).

Represents Nonfiction books, novels, short story collections, scholarly books, graphic novels. **Considers these nonfiction areas:** Animals; anthropology/archaeology; art/architecture/design; biography/autobiography; business/economics; child guidance/parenting; current affairs; ethnic/cultural interests; gay/lesbian issues; government/politics/law; health/medicine; history; language/literature/criticism; memoirs; military/war; money/finance; music/dance; nature/environment; popular culture; psychology; religious/inspirational; science/technology; self-help/personal improvement; sociology; theater/film; true crime/investigative; women's issues/studies. **Considers these fiction areas:** Action/adventure; comic books/cartoon; confession; family saga; feminist; gay/lesbian; historical; humor/satire; literary; mainstream/contemporary; regional.

> ○━ LMQ focuses on bringing new voices in literary and commercial fiction to the market, as well as popularizing the ideas and arguments of scholars in the fields of history, psychology, sociology, political science, and current affairs. Actively seeking fiction writers who already have credits in magazines and quarterlies, as well as nonfiction writers who already have a media platform or some kind of a university affiliation. Does not want to receive romance, genre fiction, or children's material.

How to Contact Send query via e-mail. Only send additional materials if requested. Considers simultaneous queries. Responds in 1 week to queries; 1 month to mss. Obtains most new clients through recommendations from others, solicitations, conferences.

Recent Sales Sold 27 titles in the last year. *The Abstinence Teacher*, by Tom Perrotta (St. Martins); *Queen of Fashion*, by Caroline Weber (Henry Holt); *Whistling Past Dixie*, by Tom Schaller (Simon & Schuster); *Pretty Little Dirty*, by Amanda Boyden (Vintage). Other clients include Peter Ho Davies, Kim Addonizio, Don Lee, Natasha Trethewey, Anatol Lieven, Sir Michael Marmot, Anne Carson, Liza Ward, David Sirota, Anne Marie Slaughter, Marina Belozerskaya, Kate Walbert.

Terms Agent receives 15% commission on domestic sales; 20% commission on foreign sales. Offers written contract; 30-day notice must be given to terminate contract. Only charges for reasonable business expenses upon successful sale.

⬛ THE LITERARY GROUP

51 E. 25th St., Suite 401, New York NY 10010. (212)274-1616. Fax: (212)274-9876. E-mail: fweimann@theliterarygroup.com. Web site: www.theliterarygroup.com. **Contact:** Frank Weimann. Estab. 1985. 65% of clients are new/unpublished writers. Currently handles: 50% nonfiction books; 50% fiction.

Member Agents Frank Weimann; Ian Kleinert.

Represents Nonfiction books, novels. **Considers these nonfiction areas:** Animals; anthropology/archaeology; biography/autobiography; business/economics; child guidance/parenting; crafts/hobbies; current affairs; education; ethnic/cultural interests; government/politics/law; health/medicine; history; how-to; humor/satire; juvenile nonfiction; language/literature/criticism; memoirs; military/war; money/finance; multicultural; music/dance; nature/environment; popular culture; psychology; religious/inspirational; science/technology; self-help/personal improvement; sociology; sports; theater/film; true crime/investigative; women's issues/studies; creative nonfiction. **Considers these fiction areas:** Action/adventure; contemporary issues; detective/police/crime; ethnic; family saga; fantasy; feminist; horror; humor/satire; mystery/suspense; psychic/supernatural; romance (contemporary, gothic, historical, regency); sports; thriller; westerns/frontier.

> ○━ This agency specializes in nonfiction (memoir, military, history, biography, sports, how-to).

How to Contact Query with SASE, outline, 3 sample chapters. Prefers to read materials exclusively. Only responds if interested. Returns materials only with SASE. Obtains most new clients through referrals, writers' conferences, query letters.

Recent Sales Sold 150 titles in the last year. *The Alchemyst*, by Michael Scott; *Dog and Bear*, by Laura Vaccaro Seeger; *How To Be Sexy*, by Carmen Electra; *Ship of Ghosts*, by James Hornfischer; *Push*, by Relentless Aaron; *Falling Out of Fashion*, by Karen Yampolsky. Other clients include Robert Anderson, Michael Reagan, J.L. King.

Terms Agent receives 15% commission on domestic sales; 20% commission on foreign sales. Offers written contract; 30-day notice must be given to terminate contract.

Writers' Conferences San Diego State University Writers' Conference; Maui Writers' Conference; Agents and Editors Conference.

JULIA LORD LITERARY MANAGEMENT

38 W. Ninth St., #4, New York NY 10011. (212)995-2333. Fax: (212)995-2332. E-mail: julialordliterary@nyc.rr.com. Estab. 1999. Member of AAR.

Member Agents Julia Lord, owner; Riley Kellogg, subagent.

Represents Nonfiction books, novels. **Considers these nonfiction areas:** Biography/autobiography; history; sports; travel; African-American; lifestyle; narrative nonfiction. **Considers these fiction areas:** Action/adventure; historical; literary; mainstream/contemporary; mystery/suspense.

How to Contact Query with SASE or via e-mail. Obtains most new clients through recommendations from others, solicitations.

STERLING LORD LITERISTIC, INC.

65 Bleecker St., 12th Floor, New York NY 10012. (212)780-6050. Fax: (212)780-6095. E-mail: info@sll.com. Web site: www.sll.com. Estab. 1952. Member of AAR; signatory of WGA. Represents 600 clients. Currently handles: 50% nonfiction books; 50% novels.

Member Agents Marcy Posner; Philippa Brophy; Laurie Liss; Chris Calhoun; Peter Matson; Sterling Lord; Claudia Cross; Neeti Madan; George Nicholson; Jim Rutman; Charlotte Sheedy (affiliate); Douglas Stewart; Robert Guinsler.

Represents Nonfiction books, novels.

How to Contact Query with SASE. Query by snail mail. No e-mail or fax queries. Responds in 1 month to mss. Obtains most new clients through recommendations from others.

Recent Sales This agency prefers not to share information on specific sales. Clients include Kent Haruf, Dick Francis, Mary Gordon, Sen. John McCain, Simon Winchester, James McBride, Billy Collins, Richard Paul Evans, Dave Pelzer.

Terms Agent receives 15% commission on domestic sales; 20% commission on foreign sales. Offers written contract. Charges clients for photocopying.

LOWENSTEIN-YOST ASSOCIATES

121 W. 27th St., Suite 601, New York NY 10001. (212)206-1630. Fax: (212)727-0280. Web site: www.lowenstein yost.com. **Contact:** Barbara Lowenstein or Nancy Yost. Estab. 1976. Member of AAR. Represents 150 clients. 20% of clients are new/unpublished writers. Currently handles: 60% nonfiction books; 40% novels.

Member Agents Barbara Lowenstein, president (nonfiction interests include narrative nonfiction, health, money, finance, travel, multicultural, popular culture and memoir; fiction interests include literary fiction and women's fiction); Nancy Yost, vice president (mainstream/contemporary fiction, mystery, suspense, contemporary/historical romance, thriller, women's fiction); Norman Kurz, business affairs; Zoe Fishman, foreign rights (young adult, literary fiction, narrative nonfiction); Rachel Vater (fantasy, young adult, women's fiction); Natanya Wheeler (narrative nonfiction, literary fiction, historical, women's fiction, birds).

Represents Nonfiction books, novels. **Considers these nonfiction areas:** Animals; anthropology/archaeology; biography/autobiography; business/economics; child guidance/parenting; current affairs; education; ethnic/cultural interests; government/politics/law; health/medicine; history; how-to; language/literature/criticism; memoirs; money/finance; multicultural; nature/environment; popular culture; psychology; self-help/personal improvement; sociology; travel; women's issues/studies; music; narrative nonfiction; science; film. **Considers these fiction areas:** Detective/police/crime; erotica; ethnic; feminist; historical; literary; mainstream/contemporary; mystery/suspense; romance (contemporary, historical, regency); thriller; women's; fantasy; young adult.

> ○→ This agency specializes in health, business, creative nonfiction, literary fiction and commercial fiction—especially suspense, crime and women's issues. "We are a full-service agency, handling domestic and foreign rights, film rights and audio rights to all of our books."

How to Contact Query with SASE. Prefers to read materials exclusively. For fiction, send outline and first chapter. *No unsolicited mss.* Responds in 4 weeks to queries. Returns materials only with SASE. Obtains most new clients through recommendations from others, solicitations, conferences.

Recent Sales *Body After Baby*, by Jackie Keller (Avery); *Creating Competitive Advantage*, by Jaynie Smith & Bill Flanagan (Doubleday); *To Keep a Husband*, by Lindsay Graves (Ballantine); *The Notorious Mrs. Winston*, by Mary Mackey (Berkley); *Gleason's Gym Total Body Boxing Workout for Women*, by Hector Roca & Bruce Silverglade (Fireside); *More Than A Champion: A Biography of Mohammed Ali*, by Ishmael Reed (Shaye Areheart); *Dreams of A Caspian Rain*, by Gina Nahai; *House of Dark Delights*, by Louisa Burton (Bantam); a new thriller by Perri O'Shaughnessy (Pocket); the debut thriller by N.P.R. writer Susan Arnout Smith (St. Martin's);

Sworn to Silence, by Linda Castillo; *Thinner or Pretty on the Outside*, by Valerie Frankel; *In the Stars*, by Eileen Cook; *The Dark Lantern*, by Gerri Brightwell. Other clients include Stephanie Laurens, Dr. Ro, Penny McFall, Deborah Crombie, Liz Carlyle, Suzanne Enoch, Gaelen Foley, Tamar Myers, Sandi K. Shelton, Kathryn Smith, Cheyenne McCray, Barbara Keesling.

Terms Agent receives 15% commission on domestic sales; 20% commission on foreign sales. Offers written contract. Charges for large photocopy batches, messenger service, international postage.

Writers' Conferences Malice Domestic; Bouchercon; RWA National Conference.

Tips "Know the genre you are working in and read! Also, please see our Web site for details on which agent to query for your project."

🖤 DONALD MAASS LITERARY AGENCY

121 W. 27th St., Suite 801, New York NY 10001. (212)727-8383. Web site: www.maassagency.com. Estab. 1980. Member of AAR, SFWA, MWA, RWA. Represents more than 100 clients. 5% of clients are new/unpublished writers. Currently handles: 100% novels.

- Prior to opening his agency, Mr. Maass served as an editor at Dell Publishing (New York) and as a reader at Gollancz (London). He also served as the president of AAR.

Member Agents Donald Maass (mainstream, literary, mystery/suspense, science fiction); Jennifer Jackson (commercial fiction, romance, science fiction, fantasy, mystery/suspense); Cameron McClure (literary, mystery/suspense, urban, fantasy, narrative nonfiction and projects with multicultural, international, and environmental themes, gay/lesbian); Stephen Barbara (literary fiction, young adult novels, middle grade, narrative nonfiction, historical nonfiction, mainstream, genre).

Represents Novels. **Considers these nonfiction areas:** Young adult. **Considers these fiction areas:** Detective/police/crime; fantasy; historical; horror; literary; mainstream/contemporary; mystery/suspense; psychic/supernatural; romance (historical, paranormal, time travel); science fiction; thriller; women's.

- ⊶ This agency specializes in commercial fiction, especially science fiction, fantasy, mystery and suspense. Actively seeking to expand in literary fiction and women's fiction. Does not want to receive nonfiction, picture books, prescriptive nonfiction, or poetry.

How to Contact Query with SASE, synopsis, first 5 pages. Returns material only with SASE. Considers simultaneous queries. Responds in 2 weeks to queries; 3 months to mss.

Recent Sales *Afternoons With Emily*, by Rose MacMurray (Little, Brown); *Denial: A Lew Fonesca Mystery*, by Stuart Kaminsky (Forge); *The Shifting Tide*, by Anne Perry (Ballantine); *Midnight Plague*, by Gregg Keizer (G.P. Putnam's Sons); *White Night: A Novel of The Dresden Files*, by Jim Butcher (Roc).

Terms Agent receives 15% commission on domestic sales; 20% commission on foreign sales.

Writers' Conferences Donald Maass: World Science Fiction Convention; Frankfurt Book Fair; Pacific Northwest Writers Conference; Bouchercon. Jennifer Jackson: World Science Fiction Convention; RWA National Conference.

Tips "We are fiction specialists, also noted for our innovative approach to career planning. Few new clients are accepted, but interested authors should query with a SASE. Works with subagents in all principle foreign countries and Hollywood. No prescriptive nonfiction, picture books or poetry will be considered."

🖤 GINA MACCOBY LITERARY AGENCY

P.O. Box 60, Chappaqua NY 10514. (914)238-5630. **Contact:** Gina Maccoby. Estab. 1986. Represents 25 clients. Currently handles: 33% nonfiction books; 33% novels; 33% juvenile books; illustrators of children's books.

Represents Nonfiction books, novels, juvenile books. **Considers these nonfiction areas:** Biography/autobiography; current affairs; ethnic/cultural interests; history; juvenile nonfiction; popular culture; women's issues/studies. **Considers these fiction areas:** Juvenile; literary; mainstream/contemporary; mystery/suspense; thriller; young adult.

How to Contact Query with SASE. Considers simultaneous queries. Responds in 3 months to queries. Returns materials only with SASE. Obtains most new clients through recommendations from clients and publishers.

Recent Sales Sold 21 titles in the last year.

Terms Agent receives 15% commission on domestic sales; 25% commission on foreign sales. Charges clients for photocopying. May recover certain costs, such as legal fees or the cost of shipping books by air to Europe or Japan.

🖤 CAROL MANN AGENCY

55 Fifth Ave., New York NY 10003. (212)206-5635. Fax: (212)675-4809. E-mail: will@carolmannagency.com. **Contact:** Will Sherlin. Estab. 1977. Member of AAR. Represents roughly 200 clients. 15% of clients are new/unpublished writers. Currently handles: 90% nonfiction books; 10% novels.

Member Agents Carol Mann; Will Sherlin; Laura Yorke.

Represents Nonfiction books, novels. **Considers these nonfiction areas:** Anthropology/archaeology; art/architecture/design; biography/autobiography; business/economics; child guidance/parenting; current affairs; ethnic/cultural interests; government/politics/law; health/medicine; history; money/finance; popular culture; psychology; self-help/personal improvement; sociology; sports; women's issues/studies; music. **Considers these fiction areas:** Literary; commercial.

> O—┓ This agency specializes in current affairs, self-help, popular culture, psychology, parenting, and history. Does not want to receive genre fiction (romance, mystery, etc.).

How to Contact Query with outline/proposal, SASE. Responds in 3 weeks to queries.

Recent Sales Clients include novelists Paul Auster and Marita Golden; National Book Award Winners Tim Egan, Hannah Storm, and Willow Bay; Pulitzer Prize-winner Fox Butterfield; bestselling essayist Shelby Steele; sociologist Dr. William Julius Wilson; economist Thomas Sowell; bestselling diet doctors Mary Dan and Michael Eades; ACLU president Nadine Strossen; pundit Mona Charen; memoirist Lauren Winner; photography project editors Rick Smolan and David Cohen (*America 24/7*); Kevin Liles, executive vice president of Warner Music Group and former president of Def Jam Records; and Jermaine Dupri.

Terms Agent receives 15% commission on domestic sales; 20% commission on foreign sales. Offers written contract.

MANUS & ASSOCIATES LITERARY AGENCY, INC.

425 Sherman Ave., Suite 200, Palo Alto CA 94306. (650)470-5151. Fax: (650)470-5159. E-mail: manuslit@manus lit.com. Web site: www.manuslit.com. 445 Park Ave., New York NY 10022. (212)644-8020. Fax (212)644-3374. **Contact**: Janet Manus. **Contact:** Jillian Manus, Jandy Nelson, Stephanie Lee, Donna Levin, Penny Nelson. Estab. 1985. Member of AAR. Represents 75 clients. 30% of clients are new/unpublished writers. Currently handles: 70% nonfiction books; 30% novels.

> ● Prior to becoming an agent, Ms. Manus was associate publisher of two national magazines and director of development at Warner Bros. and Universal Studios; she has been a literary agent for 20 years.

Member Agents Jandy Nelson, jandy@manuslit.com (self-help, health, memoirs, narrative nonfiction, women's fiction, literary fiction, multicultural fiction, thrillers); Stephanie Lee, slee@manuslit.com (self-help, narrative nonfiction, commercial literary fiction, quirky/edgy fiction, pop culture, pop science); Jillian Manus, jillian-@manuslit.com (political, memoirs, self-help, history, sports, women's issues, Latin fiction and nonfiction, thrillers); Penny Nelson, penny@manuslit.com (memoirs, self-help, sports, nonfiction); Dena Fischer (literary fiction, mainstream/commercial fiction, chick lit, women's fiction, historical fiction, ethnic/cultural fiction, narrative nonfiction, parenting, relationships, pop culture, health, sociology, psychology).

Represents Nonfiction books, novels. **Considers these nonfiction areas:** Biography/autobiography; business/economics; child guidance/parenting; current affairs; ethnic/cultural interests; health/medicine; how-to; memoirs; money/finance; nature/environment; popular culture; psychology; science/technology; self-help/personal improvement; women's issues/studies; Gen X and Gen Y issues; creative nonfiction. **Considers these fiction areas:** Literary; mainstream/contemporary; multicultural; mystery/suspense; thriller; women's; quirky/edgy fiction.

> O—┓ "Our agency is unique in the way that we not only sell the material, but we edit, develop concepts, and participate in the marketing effort. We specialize in large, conceptual fiction and nonfiction, and always value a project that can be sold in the TV/feature film market." Actively seeking high-concept thrillers, commercial literary fiction, women's fiction, celebrity biographies, memoirs, multicultural fiction, popular health, women's empowerment and mysteries. No horror, romance, science fiction, fantasy, western, young adult, children's, poetry, cookbooks or magazine articles.

How to Contact Query with SASE. If requested, submit outline, 2-3 sample chapters. All queries should be sent to the California office. Accepts e-mail queries. No fax queries. Considers simultaneous queries. Responds in 3 months to queries; 3 months to mss. Returns materials only with SASE. Obtains most new clients through recommendations from others, solicitations, conferences.

Recent Sales *Nothing Down for the 2000s* and *Multiple Streams of Income for the 2000s*, by Robert Allen; *Missed Fortune* and *Missed Fortune 101*, by Doug Andrew; *Cracking the Millionaire Code*, by Mark Victor Hansen and Robert Allen; *Stress Free for Good*, by Dr. Fred Luskin and Dr. Ken Pelletier; *The Mercy of Thin Air*, by Ronlyn Domangue; *The Fine Art of Small Talk*, by Debra Fine; *Bone Man of Bonares*, by Terry Tarnoff.

Terms Agent receives 15% commission on domestic sales; 20-25% commission on foreign sales. Offers written contract, binding for 2 years; 60-day notice must be given to terminate contract. Charges for photocopying and postage/UPS.

Writers' Conferences Maui Writers' Conference; San Diego State University Writers' Conference; Willamette Writers' Conference; BookExpo America; MEGA Book Marketing University.

Tips "Research agents using a variety of sources."

☑ MARCH TENTH, INC.

4 Myrtle St., Haworth NJ 07641-1740. (201)387-6551. Fax: (201)387-6552. E-mail: hchoron@aol.com. Web site: www.marchtenthinc.com. **Contact:** Harry Choron, vice president. Estab. 1982. Represents 40 clients. 30% of clients are new/unpublished writers. Currently handles: 75% nonfiction books; 25% novels.

Represents Nonfiction books, novels. **Considers these nonfiction areas:** Biography/autobiography; current affairs; health/medicine; history; humor/satire; language/literature/criticism; music/dance; popular culture; theater/film. **Considers these fiction areas:** Confession; ethnic; family saga; historical; humor/satire; literary; mainstream/contemporary.

    O┐ "We prefer to work with published/established writers."

How to Contact Query with SASE. Considers simultaneous queries. Responds in 1 month to queries. Returns materials only with SASE.

Recent Sales Sold 24 titles in the last year. *Art of the Chopper*, by Tom Zimberoff; *Bruce Springstein Live*, by Dave Marsh; *Complete Annotated Grateful Dead Lyrics*, by David Dodd.

Terms Agent receives 15% commission on domestic sales; 20% commission on foreign sales; 20% commission on dramatic rights sales. Charges clients for postage, photocopying, overseas phone expenses. Does not require expense money upfront.

☑ THE DENISE MARCIL LITERARY AGENCY, INC.

156 Fifth Ave., Suite 625, New York NY 10010. (212)337-3402. Fax: (212)727-2688. Web site: www.DeniseMarci lAgency.com. **Contact:** Denise Marcil, Maura Kye-Casella. Estab. 1977. Member of AAR. Represents 50 clients. 10% of clients are new/unpublished writers.

    ● Prior to opening her agency, Ms. Marcil served as an editorial assistant with Avon Books and as an assistant editor with Simon & Schuster.

Member Agents Denise Marcil (women's commercial fiction, thrillers, suspense, popular reference, how-to, self-help, health, business, and parenting. "I am looking for fresh, new voices in commercial women's fiction—stories that capture women's experiences today. I'd love to find a well-written historical novel about a real-life woman from another century"); Maura Kye-Casella (narrative nonfiction, adventure, pop culture, parenting, cookbooks, humor, memoir; and for fiction: multicultural, paranormal, suspense, well-written novels with an edgy voice, quirky characters, and/or unique plots and settings); Anne Marie O'Farrell (manuscripts in the following areas: quantum physics, New Age, business, human potential, personal growth/self-help, healing, children's books and books about drama and acting); Chris Morehouse (manuscripts in the following areas: sports, memoirs, biography, historical fiction and young adult fiction and nonfiction).

How to Contact Query with SASE.

Recent Sales Sold 43 titles in the last year. *My Next Phase*, by Eric Sundstrom, Michael Burnham and J. Randolph Burnham; *How Women are Getting Ahead by Working Abroad*, by Stacie Nevadomski Berdan and C. Perry Yeatman; *Diet for a Pain Free Life*, by Dr. Harris McIlwain and Debra Fulghum Bruce; *Feels Like Family* and *Mending Fences* by Sherryl Woods; *Devour* by Melina Morel; and *Red Cat* by Peter Spiegelman.

Terms Agent receives 15% commission on domestic sales; 20% commission on foreign sales. Offers written contract, binding for 2 years; 100% of business is derived from commissions on ms sales. Charges $100/year for postage, photocopying, long-distance calls, etc.

Writers' Conferences Pacific Northwest Writers' Conference; RWA National Conference; Oregon Writers' Colony.

☑ THE EVAN MARSHALL AGENCY

Six Tristam Place, Pine Brook NJ 07058-9445. (973)882-1122. Fax: (973)882-3099. E-mail: evanmarshall@theno velist.com. **Contact:** Evan Marshall. Estab. 1987. Member of AAR, MWA, RWA, Sisters in Crime. Currently handles: 100% novels.

    ● Prior to opening his agency, Mr. Marshall served as an editor with Houghton Mifflin, New American Library, Everest House, and Dodd, Mead & Co., and then worked as a literary agent at The Sterling Lord Agency.

Represents Novels. **Considers these fiction areas:** Action/adventure; erotica; ethnic; historical; horror; humor/satire; literary; mainstream/contemporary; mystery/suspense; religious/inspirational; romance (contemporary, gothic, historical, regency); science fiction; westerns/frontier.

How to Contact Query first with SASE; do not enclose material. No e-mail queries. Responds in 1 week to queries; 3 months to mss. Obtains most new clients through recommendations from others.

Recent Sales *Last Known Victim*, by Erica Spindler (Mira); *Julia's Chocolates*, by Cathy Lamb (Kensington); *Maverick*, by Joan Hohl (Silhouette).

Terms Agent receives 15% commission on domestic sales; 20% commission on foreign sales. Offers written contract.

☑ HELEN MCGRATH

1406 Idaho Court, Concord CA 94521. (925)672-6211. Fax: (925)672-6383. E-mail: hmcgrath_lit@yahoo.com. **Contact:** Helen McGrath. Estab. 1977. Currently handles: 50% nonfiction books; 50% novels.
Represents Nonfiction books, novels. **Considers these nonfiction areas:** Biography/autobiography; business/economics; current affairs; health/medicine; history; how-to; military/war; psychology; self-help/personal improvement; sports; women's issues/studies. **Considers these fiction areas:** Detective/police/crime; literary; mainstream/contemporary; mystery/suspense; psychic/supernatural; romance; science fiction; thriller.
How to Contact Submit proposal with SASE. *No unsolicited mss.* Responds in 2 months to queries. Obtains most new clients through recommendations from others.
Terms Agent receives 15% commission on domestic sales. Offers written contract. Charges clients for photocopying.

☑ MENDEL MEDIA GROUP, LLC

115 West 30th St., Suite 800, New York NY 10001. (646)239-9896. Fax: (212)685-4717. E-mail: scott@mendelme dia.com. Web site: www.mendelmedia.com. Estab. 2002. Member of AAR. Represents 40-60 clients.

- Prior to becoming an agent, Mr. Mendel was an academic. "I taught American literature, Yiddish, Jewish studies, and literary theory at the University of Chicago and the University of Illinois at Chicago while working on my PhD in English. I also worked as a freelance technical writer and as the managing editor of a healthcare magazine. In 1998, I began working for the late Jane Jordan Browne, a long-time agent in the book publishing world."

Represents Nonfiction books, novels, scholarly books (with potential for broad/popular appeal). **Considers these nonfiction areas:** Americana; animals; anthropology/archaeology; art/architecture/design; biography/autobiography; business/economics; child guidance/parenting; cooking/foods/nutrition; current affairs; education; ethnic/cultural interests; gardening; gay/lesbian issues; government/politics/law; health/medicine; history; how-to; humor/satire; language/literature/criticism; memoirs; military/war; money/finance; multicultural; music/dance; nature/environment; philosophy; popular culture; psychology; recreation; regional; religious/inspirational; science/technology; self-help/personal improvement; sex; sociology; software; spirituality; sports; true crime/investigative; women's issues/studies; Jewish topics; creative nonfiction. **Considers these fiction areas:** Action/adventure; contemporary issues; detective/police/crime; erotica; ethnic; feminist; gay/lesbian; glitz; historical; humor/satire; juvenile; literary; mainstream/contemporary; mystery/suspense; picture books; religious/inspirational; romance; sports; thriller; young adult; Jewish fiction.

- ☐ "I am interested in major works of history, current affairs, biography, business, politics, economics, science, major memoirs, narrative nonfiction, and other sorts of general nonfiction." Actively seeking new, major or definitive work on a subject of broad interest, or a controversial, but authoritative, new book on a subject that affects many people's lives.

How to Contact Query with SASE. Do not e-mail or fax queries. For nonfiction, include a complete, fully-edited book proposal with sample chapters. For fiction, include a complete synopsis and no more than 20 pages of sample text. Responds in 2 weeks to queries; 4-6 weeks to mss. Returns materials only with SASE. Obtains most new clients through recommendations from others.
Terms Agent receives 15% commission on domestic sales; 20% commission on foreign sales. Offers written contract, binding for 2 years; 1-month notice must be given to terminate contract. Charges clients for ms duplication, expedited delivery services (when necessary), any overseas shipping, telephone calls/faxes necessary for marketing the author's foreign rights.
Writers' Conferences BookExpo America; Frankfurt Book Fair; London Book Fair; RWA National Conference; Modern Language Association Convention; Jerusalem Book Fair.
Tips "While I am not interested in being flattered by a prospective client, it does matter to me that she knows why she is writing to me in the first place. Is one of my clients a colleague of hers? Has she read a book by one of my clients that led her to believe I might be interested in her work?"

☑ HENRY MORRISON, INC.

105 S. Bedford Road, Suite 306A, Mt. Kisco NY 10549. (914)666-3500. Fax: (914)241-7846. **Contact:** Henry Morrison. Estab. 1965. Signatory of WGA. Represents 53 clients. 5% of clients are new/unpublished writers. Currently handles: 5% nonfiction books; 95% novels.
Represents Nonfiction books, novels. **Considers these nonfiction areas:** Anthropology/archaeology; biography/autobiography; government/politics/law; history. **Considers these fiction areas:** Action/adventure; detective/police/crime; family saga; historical.
How to Contact Query with SASE. Responds in 2 weeks to queries; 3 months to mss. Obtains most new clients through recommendations from others.
Recent Sales Sold 15 titles in the last year. *The Bourne Betrayal,* by Eric Lustbader (Warner Books/Hachette); *The Vampire of New York,* by R.L. Stevens (Signet); *Glass Tiger,* by Joe Gores (Penzler Harcourt); *Prion,* by

Daniel Kalla (Forge); *Dark Reflections*, by Samuel R. Delany (Carroll & Graf); *City of Glory*, by Beverly Swerling (Simon & Schuster). Other clients include Daniel Cohen, Joel Ross, Dan Kalla, Christopher Hyde, Charles W. Henderson.

Terms Agent receives 15% commission on domestic sales; 25% commission on foreign sales. Charges clients for ms copies, bound galleys, finished books for submissions to publishers, movie producers and foreign publishers.

MUSE LITERARY MANAGEMENT

189 Waverly Place, #4, New York NY 10014. (212)925-3721. E-mail: museliterarymgmt@aol.com. **Contact:** Deborah Carter. Estab. 1998. Member of MediaBistro, Author's Guild, SCBWI, International Thriller Writers. Represents 10 clients. 80% of clients are new/unpublished writers.

- Prior to starting her agency, Ms. Carter trained with an AAR literary agent and worked in the music business and as a talent scout for record companies in artist management. She has a BA in English and music from Washington Square University College at NYU.

Represents Novels, short story collections, novellas, juvenile books. **Considers these nonfiction areas:** Narrative-only nonfiction (memoir, outdoors, music, writing). Please query other narrative nonfiction subjects. **Considers these fiction areas:** Action/adventure; detective/police/crime; picture books; young adult; espionage; middle-grade novels; literary short story collections; literary fiction with popular appeal; mystery/suspense/thriller (no cozies).

- Specializes in manuscript development, the sale and administration of print, performance, and foreign rights to literary works, and post-publication publicity and appearances. Actively seeking progressive, African-American, and multicultural fiction for adults and children in the U.S. market. Does not want to receive category fiction (romance, chick lit, fantasy, science fiction, horror), or fiction/nonfiction with religious/spiritual matter, illness or victimhood.

How to Contact Query with SASE. Query via e-mail (no attachments). Discards unwanted queries. Responds in 2 weeks to queries; 2-3 weeks to mss. Obtains most new clients through recommendations from others, conferences.

Recent Sales Sold 2 titles in the last year. Untitled children's folktale collection, by Anne Shelby (UNC Press); foreign rights sales: *The Fund*, by Wes DeMott in Russian. Other clients include various new writers.

Terms Agent receives 15% commission on domestic sales; 20% commission on foreign sales. Offers written contract, binding for 1 year; 1-day notice must be given to terminate contract. Sometimes charges for postage and photocopying. All expenses are subject to client approval.

Writers' Conferences BookExpo America.

JEAN V. NAGGAR LITERARY AGENCY, INC.

216 E. 75th St., Suite 1E, New York NY 10021. (212)794-1082. E-mail: jvnla@jvnla.com. Web site: www.jvnla.com. **Contact:** Jean Naggar. Estab. 1978. Member of AAR, PEN, Women's Media Group, Women's Forum. Represents 80 clients. 20% of clients are new/unpublished writers. Currently handles: 35% nonfiction books; 45% novels; 15% juvenile books; 5% scholarly books.

- Ms. Naggar has served as president of AAR.

Member Agents Jean Naggar (mainstream fiction, nonfiction); Jennifer Weltz, director (subsidiary rights, children's books); Alice Tasman, senior agent (commercial and literary fiction, thrillers, narrative nonfiction); Mollie Glick, agent (specializes in literary and practical nonfiction); Jessica Regel, agent (young adult fiction and nonfiction).

Represents Nonfiction books, novels. **Considers these nonfiction areas:** Biography/autobiography; child guidance/parenting; current affairs; government/politics/law; health/medicine; history; juvenile nonfiction; memoirs; New Age/metaphysics; psychology; religious/inspirational; self-help/personal improvement; sociology; travel; women's issues/studies. **Considers these fiction areas:** Action/adventure; detective/police/crime; ethnic; family saga; feminist; historical; literary; mainstream/contemporary; mystery/suspense; psychic/supernatural; thriller.

- This agency specializes in mainstream fiction and nonfiction and literary fiction with commercial potential.

How to Contact Query with SASE. Prefers to read materials exclusively. No e-mail or fax queries. Responds in 1 day to queries; 2 months to mss. Returns materials only with SASE. Obtains most new clients through recommendations from others.

Recent Sales *Dark Angels*, by Karleen Koen; *Poison*, by Susan Fromberg Schaeffer; *Unauthorized*, by Kristin McCloy; *Voyage of the Sea Turtle: The Search for the Last Dinosaurs*, by Carl Safina; *Enola Holmes*, by Nancy Springer; *The Liar's Diary*, by Patry Francis; *Closing Costs*, by Seth Margolis; *Blind Faith*, by Richard Sloan.

Terms Agent receives 15% commission on domestic sales; 20% commission on foreign sales. Offers written contract. Charges for overseas mailing, messenger services, book purchases, long-distance telephone, photocopying—all deductible from royalties received.

Literary Agents

Writers' Conferences Willamette Writers Conference; Pacific Northwest Writers Conference; Bread Loaf Writers Conference; Marymount Manhattan Writers Conference; SEAK Medical & Legal Fiction Writing Conference.
Tips "We will now only guarantee to read and respond to queries from writers who come recommended by someone we know. Our areas are general fiction and nonfiction—no children's books by unpublished writers, no multimedia, no screenplays, no formula fiction, and no mysteries by unpublished writers."

◙ NELSON LITERARY AGENCY
1020 15th St., Suite 26L, Denver CO 80202. (303)463-5301. E-mail: query@nelsonagency.com. Web site: www.nelsonagency.com. **Contact:** Kristin Nelson. Estab. 2002. Member of AAR.
• Prior to opening her own agency, Ms. Nelson worked as a literary scout and subrights agent for agent Jody Rein.
Represents Novels, select nonfiction. **Considers these nonfiction areas:** Memoirs; narrative nonfiction. **Considers these fiction areas:** Literary; romance (includes fantasy with romantic elements, science fiction, fantasy, young adult); women's; chick lit (includes mysteries); commercial/mainstream.
⚬➤ NLA specializes in representing commercial fiction and high caliber literary fiction. Actively seeking Latina writers who tackle contemporary issues in a modern voice (think *Dirty Girls Social Club*). Does not want short story collections, mysteries (except chick lit), thrillers, Christian, horror, or children's picture books.
How to Contact Query by e-mail only.
Recent Sales *Schemes of Love*, by Sherry Thomas (Bantam Dell); *The Camelot Code*, by Mari Mancusi (Dutton Children's); *Magic Lost, Trouble Found*, by Lisa Shearin (Ace); *Magellan's Witch*, by Carolyn Jewel (Hachette/Warner); *No Place Safe*, by Kim Reid (Kensington); *Plan B*, by Jennifer O'Connell (MTV/Pocket Books); *Code of Love*, by Cheryl Sawyer (NAL/Penguin Group); *Once Upon Stilettos*, by Shanna Swendson (Ballantine); *I'd Tell You I Love You But Then I'd Have to Kill You*, by Ally Carter (Hyperion Children's); *An Accidental Goddess*, by Linnea Sinclair (Bantam Spectra). Other clients include Paula Reed, Becky Motew, Jack McCallum, Jana Deleon.

◙ HAROLD OBER ASSOCIATES
425 Madison Ave., New York NY 10017. (212)759-8600. Fax: (212)759-9428. **Contact:** Craig Tenney. Estab. 1929. Member of AAR. Represents 250 clients. 10% of clients are new/unpublished writers. Currently handles: 35% nonfiction books; 50% novels; 15% juvenile books.
Member Agents Phyllis Westberg; Pamela Malpas; Craig Tenney (few new clients, mostly Ober backlist).
Represents Nonfiction books, novels, juvenile books.
⚬➤ "We consider all subjects/genres of fiction and nonfiction."
How to Contact Submit query letter only with SASE. No e-mail or fax queries. Responds as promptly as possible. Obtains most new clients through recommendations from others.
Terms Agent receives 15% commission on domestic sales; 20% commission on foreign sales. Charges clients for photocopying and express mail/package services.

◙ THE RICHARD PARKS AGENCY
Box 693, Salem NY 12865. Web site: www.richardparksagency.com. **Contact:** Richard Parks. Estab. 1988. Member of AAR. Currently handles: 55% nonfiction books; 40% novels; 5% story collections.
Represents Nonfiction books, novels. **Considers these nonfiction areas:** Animals; anthropology/archaeology; art/architecture/design; biography/autobiography; business/economics; child guidance/parenting; cooking/foods/nutrition; crafts/hobbies; current affairs; ethnic/cultural interests; gardening; gay/lesbian issues; government/politics/law; health/medicine; history; how-to; humor/satire; language/literature/criticism; memoirs; military/war; money/finance; music/dance; nature/environment; popular culture; psychology; science/technology; self-help/personal improvement; sociology; theater/film; travel; women's issues/studies.
⚬➤ Actively seeking nonfiction. Considers fiction by referral only. Does not want to receive unsolicited material.
How to Contact Query with SASE. No e-mail or fax queries. Considers simultaneous queries Responds in 2 weeks to queries. Returns materials only with SASE. Obtains most new clients through recommendations/referrals.
Terms Agent receives 15% commission on domestic sales; 20% commission on foreign sales. Charges clients for photocopying or any unusual expense incurred at the writer's request.

◙ L. PERKINS ASSOCIATES
5800 Arlington Ave., Riverdale NY 10471. (718)543-5344. Fax: (718)543-5354. E-mail: lperkinsagency@yahoo.com. **Contact:** Lori Perkins, Amy Stout (jrlperkinsagency@yahoo.com). Estab. 1990. Member of AAR. Represents 90 clients. 10% of clients are new/unpublished writers.

• Ms. Perkins has been an agent for 20 years. She is also the author of *The Insider's Guide to Getting an Agent* (Writer's Digest Books), as well as three other nonfiction books. She has also edited two anthologies.
Represents Nonfiction books, novels. **Considers these nonfiction areas:** Popular culture. **Considers these fiction areas:** Erotica; fantasy; horror; literary (dark); science fiction.

> 0→ Most of Ms. Perkins' clients write both fiction and nonfiction. "This combination keeps my clients publishing for years. I am also a published author, so I know what it takes to write a good book." Actively seeking a Latino *Gone With the Wind* and *Waiting to Exhale,* and urban ethnic horror. Does not want to receive anything outside of the above categories (westerns, romance, etc.).

How to Contact Query with SASE. Considers simultaneous queries. Responds in 12 weeks to queries; 3-6 months to mss. Returns materials only with SASE. Obtains most new clients through recommendations from others, solicitations, conferences.
Recent Sales Sold 100 titles in the last year. *How to Make Love Like a Porn Star: A Cautionary Tale*, by Jenna Jameson (Reagan Books); *Everything But ...?*, by Rachel Krammer Bussel (Bantam); *Dear Mom, I Always Wanted You to Know*, by Lisa Delman (Perigee Books); *The Illustrated Ray Bradbury*, by Jerry Weist (Avon); *The Poet in Exile*, by Ray Manzarek (Avalon); *Behind Sad Eyes: The Life of George Harrison*, by Marc Shapiro (St. Martin's Press).
Terms Agent receives 15% commission on domestic sales; 20% commission on foreign sales. No written contract. Charges clients for photocopying.
Writers' Conferences San Diego State University Writers' Conference; NECON; BookExpo America; World Fantasy Convention.
Tips "Research your field and contact professional writers' organizations to see who is looking for what. Finish your novel before querying agents. Read my book, *An Insider's Guide to Getting an Agent*, to get a sense of how agents operate. Read agent blogs—litsoup.blogspot.com and missnark.blogspot.com."

◪ STEPHEN PEVNER, INC.
382 Lafayette St., Eighth Floor, New York NY 10003. (212)674-8403. Fax: (212)529-3692. E-mail: spevner@aol.com. **Contact:** Stephen Pevner.
Represents Nonfiction books, novels, feature film, TV scripts, TV movie of the week, episodic drama, animation, documentary, miniseries. **Considers these nonfiction areas:** Biography/autobiography; ethnic/cultural interests; gay/lesbian issues; history; humor/satire; language/literature/criticism; memoirs; music/dance; New Age/metaphysics; photography; popular culture; religious/inspirational; sociology; travel. **Considers these fiction areas:** Comic books/cartoon; erotica; ethnic; experimental; gay/lesbian; glitz; horror; humor/satire; literary; mainstream/contemporary; psychic/supernatural; thriller; urban. **Considers these script subject areas:** Comedy; contemporary issues; detective/police/crime; gay/lesbian; glitz; horror; romantic comedy; romantic drama; thriller.

> 0→ This agency specializes in motion pictures, novels, humor, pop culture, urban fiction, and independent filmmakers.

How to Contact Query with SASE, outline/proposal. Prefers to read materials exclusively. No e-mail or fax queries. Responds in 2 weeks to queries; 1 month to mss. Obtains most new clients through recommendations from others.
Recent Sales *Matt and Ben*, by Mindy Kaling and Brenda Withers; *In the Company of Men* and *Bash: Latterday Plays*, by Neil Labote; *Guide to Life*, by The Five Lesbian Brothers; *Noise From Underground*, by Michael Levine. Other clients include Richard Linklater, Gregg Araki, Tom DiCillo, Genvieve Turner/Rose Troche, Todd Solondz, Neil LaBute.
Terms Agent receives 15% commission on domestic sales; 20% commission on foreign sales. Offers written contract, binding for 1 year; 6-week notice must be given to terminate contract. 100% of business is derived from commissions on ms sales.
Tips "Be persistent, but civilized."

⊘ ALISON J. PICARD, LITERARY AGENT
P.O. Box 2000, Cotuit MA 02635. Phone/Fax: (508)477-7192. E-mail: ajpicard@aol.com. **Contact:** Alison Picard. Estab. 1985. Represents 48 clients. 30% of clients are new/unpublished writers. Currently handles: 40% nonfiction books; 40% novels; 20% juvenile books.
• Prior to becoming an agent, Ms. Picard was an assistant at a literary agency in New York.
Represents Nonfiction books, novels, juvenile books. **Considers these nonfiction areas:** Animals; biography/autobiography; business/economics; child guidance/parenting; cooking/foods/nutrition; current affairs; education; ethnic/cultural interests; gay/lesbian issues; government/politics/law; health/medicine; history; how-to; humor/satire; juvenile nonfiction; memoirs; military/war; money/finance; multicultural; nature/environment; New Age/metaphysics; popular culture; psychology; religious/inspirational; science/technology; self-help/personal improvement; travel; true crime/investigative; women's issues/studies; young adult. **Considers these**

fiction areas: Action/adventure; contemporary issues; detective/police/crime; erotica; ethnic; family saga; feminist; gay/lesbian; glitz; historical; horror; humor/satire; juvenile; literary; mainstream/contemporary; multicultural; mystery/suspense; New Age; picture books; psychic/supernatural; romance; sports; thriller; young adult.

○→ "Many of my clients have come to me from big agencies, where they felt overlooked or ignored. I communicate freely with my clients and offer a lot of career advice, suggestions for revising manuscripts, etc. If I believe in a project, I will submit it to a dozen or more publishers, unlike some agents who give up after four or five rejections." No science fiction/fantasy, western, poetry, plays or articles.

How to Contact Query with SASE. Considers simultaneous queries. Responds in 2 weeks to queries; 4 months to mss. Returns materials only with SASE. Obtains most new clients through recommendations from others, solicitations.

Recent Sales Two untitled mysteries, by David Housewright (St. Martin's Press); *Simply Scandalous* and two untitled romances by Tamara Lejeune (Kensington Publishing Corp.); two untitled erotic novels by Fiona Zedde (Kensington Publishing Corp.); *The Right Kind of People,* by Daniel Kimmel (Ivan R. Dee); *The Merchants of Fear,* by Christopher Catherwood and Joe Divanna (Lyons Press); *Hoops of Steel* and *Running With the Wind,* by John Foley (Llewellyn/Flux); *A Habit of Death* and *Ice in His Veins,* by Charles Zito (Llewellyn/Midnight Ink); four mysteries by Richard Schwartz (Llewellyn/Midnight Ink); *Breathing Underwater,* by Lu Vickers (Alyson); *One Size Fits All,* by Ben Patrick Johnson (Alyson). Other clients include Theresa Alan, Tom Eslick, Nancy Means Wright, Dina Friedman and Margi Preus.

Terms Agent receives 15% commission on domestic sales; 20% commission on foreign sales. Offers written contract, binding for 1 year; 1-week notice must be given to terminate contract.

Tips "Please don't send material without sending a query first via mail or e-mail. I don't accept phone or fax queries. Always enclose an SASE with a query."

ALICKA PISTEK LITERARY AGENCY, LLC

302A W. 12th St., #124, New York NY 10014. E-mail: info@apliterary.com. Web site: www.apliterary.com. **Contact:** Alicka Pistek. Estab. 2003. Represents 15 clients. 50% of clients are new/unpublished writers. Currently handles: 60% nonfiction books; 40% novels.

● Prior to opening her agency, Ms. Pistek worked at ICM and as an agent at Nicholas Ellison, Inc.

Represents Nonfiction books, novels. **Considers these nonfiction areas:** Animals; anthropology/archaeology; biography/autobiography; child guidance/parenting; current affairs; government/politics/law; health/medicine; history; how-to; language/literature/criticism; memoirs; military/war; money/finance; nature/environment; psychology; science/technology; self-help/personal improvement; travel; creative nonfiction. **Considers these fiction areas:** Detective/police/crime; ethnic; family saga; historical; literary; mainstream/contemporary; mystery/suspense; romance; thriller.

○→ Does not want to receive fantasy, science fiction or western.

How to Contact Send e-query to info@apliterary.com. The agency will only respond if interested. Accepts e-mail queries. No fax queries. Considers simultaneous queries. Responds in 2 months to queries; 8 weeks to mss. Returns materials only with SASE.

Recent Sales *The Animal Girl,* by John Fulton; *Elephants on Acid,* by Alex Boese; *Living on the Fly,* by Amanda Switzer and Daniel A. Shaw. Other clients include Matthew Zapruder, Steven R. Kinsella, Julie Tilsner, Michael Christopher Carroll, Quinton Skinner, Erin Grady.

Terms Agent receives 15% commission on domestic sales; 20% commission on foreign sales. Offers written contract. This agency charges for photocopying more than 40 pages and international postage.

Tips "Be sure you are familiar with the genre you are writing in and learn standard procedures for submitting your work. A good query will go a long way."

AARON M. PRIEST LITERARY AGENCY

708 Third Ave., 23rd Floor, New York NY 10017-4103. (212)818-0344. Fax: (212)573-9417. Estab. 1974. Member of AAR. Currently handles: 25% nonfiction books; 75% novels.

Member Agents Aaron Priest, querypriest@aaronpriest.com (thrillers and fiction); Lisa Erbach Vance, queryvance@aaronpriest.com (general fiction, mystery, thrillers, historical fiction, up market women's fiction, narrative nonfiction, memoir); Lucy Childs, querychilds@aaronpriest.com (literary and commercial fiction, memoir, historical fiction, upscale commercial women's fiction); Nicole Kenealy, querykenealy@aaronpriest.com (chicklit/commercial women's fiction, literary fiction, young adult fiction and nonfiction).

Represents Commercial fiction, literary fiction, some nonfiction.

How to Contact Query with SASE, submit publishing history, author bio. Make sure your query is one page. Paste first chapter into body e-mail. Do not query more than one agent here. Accepts e-mail queries. No fax queries. Considers simultaneous queries. Responds in 3 weeks, only if interested.

Recent Sales *She is Me,* by Kathleen Schine; *Killer Smile,* by Lisa Scottoline.

Terms Agent receives 15% commission on domestic sales. This agency charges for photocopying and postage expenses.

◪ PROSPECT AGENCY LLC

285 Fifth Ave., PMB 445, Brooklyn NY 11215. (718)788-3217. E-mail: esk@prospectagency.com. Web site: www.prospectagency.com. **Contact:** Emily Sylvan Kim. Estab. 2005. Represents 15 clients. 50% of clients are new/unpublished writers. Currently handles: 66% novels; 33% juvenile books.

● Prior to starting her agency, Ms. Kim briefly attended law school and worked for another literary agency.

Represents Nonfiction books, novels, juvenile books. **Considers these nonfiction areas:** Memoirs; science/technology; juvenile. **Considers these fiction areas:** Action/adventure; detective/police/crime; erotica; ethnic; family saga; juvenile; literary; mainstream/contemporary; mystery/suspense; picture books; romance; science fiction; thriller; westerns/frontier; young adult.

O⊸ "We are currently looking for the next generation of writers to shape the literary landscape. Our clients receive professional and knowledgeable representation. We are committed to offering skilled editorial advice and advocating our clients in the marketplace." Actively seeking romance, literary fiction, and young adult submissions. Does not want to receive poetry, short stories, textbooks, or most nonfiction.

How to Contact Upload outline and 3 sample chapters to the Web site. Considers simultaneous queries. Responds in 3 weeks to queries; 1 month to mss. Obtains most new clients through recommendations from others, conferences, unsolicited mss.

Recent Sales *Love Potion #10*, by Janice Maynard (NAL); *God's Own Drunk*, by Tim Tharp (Knopf Children). Other clients include Diane Perkins, Regina Scott, Opal Carew, Marissa Doyle, Meagan Brothers, Elizabeth Scott, Bonnie Edwards.

Terms Agent receives 15% commission on domestic sales; 20% commission on foreign sales. Offers written contract.

Writers' Conferences SCBWI Annual Winter Conference; Pikes Peak Writers Conference; RWA National Conference.

◪ PSALTIS LITERARY

Post Office: Park West Finance, P.O. Box 20736, New York NY 10025. E-mail: psaltisliterary@mpsaltis.com. Web site: www.mpsaltis.com. **Contact:** Michael Psaltis. Member of AAR. Represents 30-40 clients.

Represents Nonfiction books, novels. **Considers these nonfiction areas:** Biography/autobiography; business/economics; cooking/foods/nutrition; health/medicine; history; memoirs; popular culture; psychology; science/technology. **Considers these fiction areas:** Mainstream/contemporary.

How to Contact Submit outline/proposal. Responds in 2-4 weeks to queries; 6-8 weeks to mss.

Recent Sales *Hometown Appetites*, by Kelly Alexander and Cindy Harris (Gotham Books); *A Life in Twilight*, by Mark Wolverton (Joseph Henry Press); *Cooked*, by Jeff Henderson (William Morrow).

Terms Agent receives 15% commission on domestic sales; 20% commission on foreign sales. Offers written contract.

◪ QUICKSILVER BOOKS: LITERARY AGENTS

508 Central Park Ave., #5101, Scarsdale NY 10583. Phone/Fax: (914)722-4664. Web site: www.quicksilverbooks .com. **Contact:** Bob Silverstein. Estab. 1973 as packager; 1987 as literary agency. Represents 50 clients. 50% of clients are new/unpublished writers. Currently handles: 75% nonfiction books; 25% novels.

● Prior to opening his agency, Mr. Silverstein served as senior editor at Bantam Books and Dell Books/Delacorte Press.

Represents Nonfiction books, novels. **Considers these nonfiction areas:** Anthropology/archaeology; biography/autobiography; business/economics; child guidance/parenting; cooking/foods/nutrition; current affairs; ethnic/cultural interests; health/medicine; history; how-to; language/literature/criticism; memoirs; nature/environment; New Age/metaphysics; popular culture; psychology; religious/inspirational; science/technology; self-help/personal improvement; sociology; sports; true crime/investigative; women's issues/studies. **Considers these fiction areas:** Action/adventure; glitz; mystery/suspense; thriller.

O⊸ This agency specializes in literary and commercial mainstream fiction and nonfiction, especially psychology, New Age, holistic healing, consciousness, ecology, environment, spirituality, reference, self-help, cookbooks and narrative nonfiction. Does not want to receive science fiction, pornography, poetry or single-spaced mss.

How to Contact Query with SASE. Authors are expected to supply SASE for return of ms and for query letter responses. No fax queries. Considers simultaneous queries. Responds in 2 weeks to queries; 1 month to mss. Returns materials only with SASE. Obtains most new clients through recommendations, listings in sourcebooks, solicitations, workshop participation.

Recent Sales Sold more than 20 titles in the last year. *See Jane Lead*, by Lois Frankel (Warner); *28-Day Shapeover*, by Brad Schoenfeld (Human Kinetics); *Don't Sabotage Your Career*, by Lois Frankel (Warner); *Beyond the Indigo Children*, by P.M.H. Atwater (Bear & Company); *Dinner at Mr. Jefferson's*, by Charles Cerami (Wiley); *Nice Girls Don't Get Rich*, by Lois P. Frankel (Warner Books); *The Young Patriots*, by Charles Cerami (Source-

books); *The Coming of the Beatles*, by Martin Goldsmith (Wiley); *The Real Food Daily Cookbook*, by Ann Gentry (Ten Speed Press); *The Complete Book of Vinyasa Yoga*, by Srivatsa Ramaswami (Marlowe & Co.).
Terms Agent receives 15% commission on domestic sales; 20% commission on foreign sales. Offers written contract.
Writers' Conferences National Writers Union.
Tips "Write what you know. Write from the heart. Publishers print, authors sell."

RAINES & RAINES

103 Kenyon Road, Medusa NY 12120. (518)239-8311. Fax: (518)239-6029. **Contact:** Theron Raines (member of AAR); Joan Raines; Keith Korman. Represents 100 clients.
Represents Nonfiction books, novels. **Considers these nonfiction areas:** All subjects. **Considers these fiction areas:** Action/adventure; detective/police/crime; fantasy; historical; mystery/suspense; picture books; science fiction; thriller; westerns/frontier.
How to Contact Query with SASE. Responds in 2 weeks to queries.
Terms Agent receives 15% commission on domestic sales; 20% commission on foreign sales. Charges for photocopying.

HELEN REES LITERARY AGENCY

376 North St., Boston MA 02113-2013. (617)227-9014. Fax: (617)227-8762. E-mail: reesagency@reesagency.com. **Contact:** Joan Mazmanian, Ann Collette, Helen Rees, Lorin Rees. Estab. 1983. Member of AAR, PEN. Represents more than 100 clients. 50% of clients are new/unpublished writers. Currently handles: 60% nonfiction books; 40% novels.
Member Agents Ann Collette (literary fiction, women's studies, health, biography, history); Helen Rees (business, money/finance/economics, government/politics/law, contemporary issues, literary fiction); Lorin Rees (business, money/finance, management, history, narrative nonfiction, science, literary fiction, memoir).
Represents Nonfiction books, novels. **Considers these nonfiction areas:** Biography/autobiography; business/economics; current affairs; government/politics/law; health/medicine; history; money/finance; women's issues/studies. **Considers these fiction areas:** Historical; literary; mainstream/contemporary; mystery/suspense; thriller.
How to Contact Query with SASE, outline, 2 sample chapters. No unsolicited e-mail submissions. No multiple submissions. No e-mail or fax queries. Responds in 3-4 weeks to queries. Obtains most new clients through recommendations from others, conferences, submissions.
Recent Sales Sold more than 35 titles in the last year. *Get Your Ship Together*, by Capt. D. Michael Abrashoff; *Overpromise and Overdeliver*, by Rick Berrara; *Opacity*, by Joel Kurtzman; *America the Broke*, by Gerald Swanson; *Murder at the B-School*, by Jeffrey Cruikshank; *Bone Factory*, by Steven Sidor; *Father Said*, by Hal Sirowitz; *Winning*, by Jack Welch; *The Case for Israel*, by Alan Dershowitz; *As the Future Catches You*, by Juan Enriquez; *Blood Makes the Grass Grow Green*, by Johnny Rico; *DVD Movie Guide*, by Mick Martin and Marsha Porter; *Words That Work*, by Frank Luntz; *Stirring It Up*, by Gary Hirshberg; *Hot Spots*, by Martin Fletcher; *Andy Grove: The Life and Times of an American*, by Richard Tedlow; *Girls Most Likely To*, by Poonam Sharma.
Terms Agent receives 15% commission on domestic sales; 20% commission on foreign sales.

REGAL LITERARY AGENCY

1140 Broadway, Penthouse, New York NY 10001. (212)684-7900. Fax: (212)684-7906. E-mail: Shannon@regal-literary.com. Web site: www.regal-literary.com. **Contact:** Shannon Firth, Marcus Hoffmann. Estab. 2002. Member of AAR. Represents 100 clients. 20% of clients are new/unpublished writers. Currently handles: 48% nonfiction books; 46% novels; 6% poetry.
  ● Prior to becoming agents, Mr. Regal was a musician; Mr. Steinberg was a filmmaker and screenwriter; Ms. Reid and Ms. Schott Pearson were magazine editors; Mr. Hoffman worked in the publishing industry in London.
Member Agents Joseph Regal (literary fiction, science, history, memoir); Peter Steinberg (literary and commercial fiction, history, humor, memoir, narrative nonfiction, young adult); Bess Reed (literary fiction, narrative nonfiction, self-help); Lauren Schott Pearson (literary fiction, commercial fiction, memoir, narrative nonfiction, thrillers, mysteries); Markus Hoffmann (foreign rights manager, literary fiction, mysteries, thrillers, international fiction, science, music). Michael Psaltis of Psaltis Literary also works with Regal Literary agents to form the Culinary Cooperative—a joint-venture agency dedicated to food writing, cookbooks, and all things related to cooking. Recent sales include *Cooked* (William Morrow); *Carmine's Family Style* (St. Martin's Press); *Fish On a First-Name Basis* (St. Martin's Press); *The Reverse Diet* (John Wiley & Sons); and *The Seasoning of a Chef* (Doubleday/Broadway).
Represents Nonfiction books, novels, short story collections, novellas. **Considers these nonfiction areas:** Anthropology/archaeology; art/architecture/design; biography/autobiography; business/economics; cooking/

foods/nutrition; current affairs; ethnic/cultural interests; gay/lesbian issues; history; humor/satire; language/ literature/criticism; memoirs; military/war; music/dance; nature/environment; photography; popular culture; psychology; religious/inspirational; science/technology; sports; translation; women's issues/studies. **Considers these fiction areas:** Comic books/cartoon; detective/police/crime; ethnic; historical; literary; mystery/suspense; thriller; contemporary.

> ⦿ "We have discovered more than a dozen successful literary novelists in the last 5 years. We are small, but are extraordinarily responsive to our writers. We are more like managers than agents, with an eye toward every aspect of our writers' careers, including publicity and other media." Actively seeking literary fiction and narrative nonfiction. Does not want romance, science fiction, horror, or screenplays.

How to Contact Query with SASE, 5-15 sample pages. No phone calls. No e-mail or fax queries. Considers simultaneous queries. Responds in 2-3 weeks to queries; 4-12 to mss. Returns materials only with SASE. Obtains most new clients through recommendations from others, unsolicited submissions.

Recent Sales Sold 20 titles in the last year. *The Stolen Child*, by Keith Donohue (Nan Talese/Doubleday); *What Elmo Taught Me*, by Kevin Clash (HarperCollins); *The Affected Provincial's Companion*, by Lord Breaulove Swells Whimsy (Bloomsbury); *The Three Incestuous Sisters*, by Audrey Niffenegger (Abrams); *The Traveler*, by John Twelve Hawks (Doubleday). Other clients include James Reston Jr., Tony Earley, Dennie Hughes, Mark Lee, Jake Page, Cheryl Bernard, Daniel Wallace, John Marks, Keith Scribner, Cathy Day, Alicia Erian, Gregory David Roberts, Dallas Hudgens, Tim Winton, Ian Spiegelman, Brad Barkley, Heather Hepler, Gavin Edwards, Sara Voorhees, Alex Abella.

Terms Agent receives 15% commission on domestic sales; 20% commission on foreign sales. No written contract. Charges clients for typical/major office expenses, such as photocopying and foreign postage.

⊘ JODY REIN BOOKS, INC.

7741 S. Ash Ct., Centennial CO 80122. (303)694-4430. Fax: (303)694-0687. Web site: www.jodyreinbooks.com. **Contact:** Winnefred Dollar. Estab. 1994. Member of AAR, Authors' Guild. Currently handles: 70% nonfiction books; 30% novels.

> ● Prior to opening her agency, Ms. Rein worked for 13 years as an acquisitions editor for Contemporary Books and as executive editor for Bantam/Doubleday/Dell and Morrow/Avon.

Represents Nonfiction books, novels. **Considers these nonfiction areas:** Business/economics; child guidance/ parenting; current affairs; ethnic/cultural interests; government/politics/law; history; humor/satire; music/ dance; nature/environment; popular culture; psychology; science/technology; sociology; theater/film; women's issues/studies. **Considers these fiction areas:** Literary; mainstream/contemporary.

> ⦿ This agency specializes in commercial and narrative nonfiction and literary/commercial fiction.

How to Contact "We're not accepting new clients at this time."

Recent Sales *How to Remodel a Man*, by Bruce Cameron (St. Martin's Press); *8 Simple Rules for Dating My Teenage Daughter*, by Bruce Cameron (ABC/Disney); *Skeletons on the Zahara*, by Dean King (Little, Brown); *The Big Year*, by Mark Obmascik (The Free Press).

Terms Agent receives 15% commission on domestic sales; 25% commission on foreign sales; 20% commission on dramatic rights sales. Offers written contract. Charges clients for express mail, overseas expenses, photocopying mss.

Tips "Do your homework before submitting. Make sure you have a marketable topic and the credentials to write about it. We want well-written books on fresh and original nonfiction topics that have broad appeal, as well as novels written by authors who have spent years developing their craft. Authors must be well established in their fields and have strong media experience."

⊙ JODIE RHODES LITERARY AGENCY

8840 Villa La Jolla Drive, Suite 315, La Jolla CA 92037-1957. **Contact:** Jodie Rhodes, president. Estab. 1998. Member of AAR. Represents 50 clients. 60% of clients are new/unpublished writers. Currently handles: 60% nonfiction books; 35% novels; 5% middle grade/young adult books.

> ● Prior to opening her agency, Ms. Rhodes was a university-level creative writing teacher, workshop director, published novelist, and vice president/media director at the N.W. Ayer Advertising Agency.

Member Agents Jodie Rhodes; Clark McCutcheon (fiction); Bob McCarter (nonfiction).

Represents Nonfiction books, novels. **Considers these nonfiction areas:** Biography/autobiography; child guidance/parenting; ethnic/cultural interests; government/politics/law; health/medicine; history; memoirs; military/war; science/technology; women's issues/studies. **Considers these fiction areas:** Ethnic; family saga; historical; literary; mainstream/contemporary; mystery/suspense; thriller; young adult; women's.

> ⦿ Actively seeking witty, sophisticated women's books about career ambitions and relationships; edgy/ trendy YA and teen books; narrative nonfiction on groundbreaking scientific discoveries, politics, economics, military and important current affairs by prominent scientists and academic professors. Does

not want to receive erotica, horror, fantasy, romance, science fiction, religious/inspirational, or children's books (does accept young adult/teen).

How to Contact Query with brief synopsis, first 30-50 pages, SASE. Do not call. Do not send complete ms unless requested. This agency does not return unrequested material weighing a pound or more that requires special postage. Include e-mail address with query. No e-mail or fax queries. Considers simultaneous queries. Responds in 3 weeks to queries. Returns materials only with SASE. Obtains most new clients through recommendations from others, agent sourcebooks.

Recent Sales Sold 40 titles in the last year. *A Matter of Gravity*, by John Moffat (HarperCollins); *A Girl Named Indie*, by Kavita Daswani (Simon and Schuster); *First Six Minutes of Life on Earth*, by Christina Reed (John Wiley & Sons); *Flak Jacket Rock*, by Dean Kohler (HarperCollins); *Roots and Wings*, by Many Ly (Random House); *The Art of Solving Crime*, by Max Houck (Praeger); *Murder at the Universe*, by Dan Craig (Midnight Ink); *Into Jerusalem*, by Craig Eisendrath (The Permanent Press); *Preventing Alzheimer's* by Marwan Sabbagh (John Wiley & Sons); *The Genie Machine*, by Robert Plotkin (Stanford University Press); *Take Charge of Your Diabetes*, by Sarfraz Zaidi (Da Capo Press).

Terms Agent receives 15% commission on domestic sales; 20% commission on foreign sales. Offers written contract; 1-month notice must be given to terminate contract. Charges clients for fax, photocopying, phone calls, postage. Charges are itemized and approved by writers upfront.

Tips "Think your book out before you write it. Do your research, know your subject matter intimately, and write vivid specifics, not bland generalities. Care deeply about your book. Don't imitate other writers. Find your own voice. We never take on a book we don't believe in, and we go the extra mile for our writers. We welcome talented, new writers."

☾ ANN RITTENBERG LITERARY AGENCY, INC.

30 Bond St., New York NY 10012. (212)684-6936. Fax: (212)684-6929. Web site: www.rittlit.com. **Contact:** Ann Rittenberg, president. Estab. 1992. Member of AAR. Currently handles: 50% nonfiction books; 50% novels.

Represents Nonfiction books, novels. **Considers these nonfiction areas:** Biography/autobiography; history (social/cultural); memoirs; women's issues/studies. **Considers these fiction areas:** Literary.

    ○▸ This agent specializes in literary fiction and literary nonfiction.

How to Contact Query with SASE, submit outline, 3 sample chapters, SASE. Query via snail mail *only*. No e-mail or fax queries. Considers simultaneous queries. Responds in 6 weeks to queries; 2 months to mss. Obtains most new clients through referrals from established writers and editors.

Recent Sales *Bad Cat*, by Jim Edgar (Workman); *A Certain Slant of Light*, by Laura Whitcomb (Houghton Mifflin); *New York Night*, by Mark Caldwell (Scribner); *In Plain Sight*, by C.J. Box (Putnam); *Improbable*, by Adam Fawer (HarperCollins); *Colleges That Change Lives*, by Loren Pope (Penguin Books).

Terms Agent receives 15% commission on domestic sales; 20% commission on foreign sales. Offers written contract. This agency charges clients for photocopying only.

☾ RIVERSIDE LITERARY AGENCY

41 Simon Keets Road, Leyden MA 01337. (413)772-0067. Fax: (413)772-0969. E-mail: rivlit@sover.net. **Contact:** Susan Lee Cohen. Estab. 1990. Represents 40 clients. 20% of clients are new/unpublished writers.

Represents Adult nonfiction, adult novels.

How to Contact Query with SASE, outline. Accepts e-mail queries. No fax queries. Considers simultaneous queries. Responds in 2 weeks to queries. Obtains most new clients through referrals.

Recent Sales *Writing to Change the World*, by Mary Pipher (Riverhead/Penguin Putnam); *The Sociopath Next Door: The Ruthless Versus the Rest of Us*, by Martha Stout (Broadway); *The Secret Magdalene*, by Ki Longfellow (Crown); *Buddha is as Buddha Does*, by Lama Surya Das (Broadway).

Terms Agent receives 15% commission on domestic sales. Offers written contract. Charges clients for foreign postage, photocopying large mss, express mail deliveries, etc.

☾ B.J. ROBBINS LITERARY AGENCY

5130 Bellaire Ave., North Hollywood CA 91607-2908. (818)760-6602. E-mail: robbinsliterary@aol.com. **Contact:** (Ms.) B.J. Robbins. Estab. 1992. Member of AAR. Represents 40 clients. 50% of clients are new/unpublished writers. Currently handles: 50% nonfiction books; 50% novels.

Represents Nonfiction books, novels. **Considers these nonfiction areas:** Biography/autobiography; current affairs; ethnic/cultural interests; health/medicine; how-to; humor/satire; memoirs; music/dance; popular culture; psychology; self-help/personal improvement; sociology; sports; theater/film; travel; true crime/investigative; women's issues/studies. **Considers these fiction areas:** Detective/police/crime; ethnic; literary; mainstream/contemporary; mystery/suspense; sports; thriller.

How to Contact Query with SASE, submit outline/proposal, 3 sample chapters, SASE. Accepts e-mail queries (no attachments). No fax queries. Considers simultaneous queries. Responds in 2-6 weeks to queries; 6-8 weeks to mss. Returns materials only with SASE. Obtains most new clients through conferences, referrals.

Recent Sales Sold 15 titles in the last year. *Getting Stoned with Savages*, by J. Maarten Troost (Broadway); *Hot Water*, by Kathryn Jordan (Berkley); *Between the Bridge and the River*, by Craig Ferguson (Chronicle); *I'm Proud of You*, by Tim Madigan (Gotham); *Man of the House*, by Chris Erskine (Rodale); *Bird of Another Heaven*, by James D. Houston (Knopf); *Tomorrow They Will Kiss*, by Eduardo Santiago (Little, Brown).

Terms Agent receives 15% commission on domestic sales; 20% commission on foreign sales. Offers written contract; 3-month notice must be given to terminate contract. 100% of business is derived from commissions on ms sales. This agency charges clients for postage and photocopying (only after sale of ms).

Writers' Conferences Squaw Valley Writers Workshop; San Diego State University Writers' Conference; Santa Barbara Writers' Conference.

☑ THE ROSENBERG GROUP

23 Lincoln Ave., Marblehead MA 01945. (781)990-1341. Fax: (781)990-1344. Web site: www.rosenberggroup.com. **Contact:** Barbara Collins Rosenberg. Estab. 1998. Member of AAR, recognized agent of the RWA. Represents 25 clients. 15% of clients are new/unpublished writers. Currently handles: 30% nonfiction books; 30% novels; 10% scholarly books; 30% college textbooks.

- Prior to becoming an agent, Ms. Rosenberg was a senior editor for Harcourt.

Represents Nonfiction books, novels, textbooks (college textbooks only). **Considers these nonfiction areas:** Current affairs; popular culture; psychology; sports; women's issues/studies; women's health; food/wine/beverages. **Considers these fiction areas:** Romance; women's.

    O→ Ms. Rosenberg is well-versed in the romance market (both category and single title). She is a frequent speaker at romance conferences. Actively seeking romance category or single title in contemporary chick lit, romantic suspense, and the historical subgenres. Does not want to receive inspirational or spiritual romances.

How to Contact Query with SASE. No e-mail or fax queries. Responds in 2 weeks to queries; 4-6 weeks to mss. Returns materials only with SASE. Obtains most new clients through recommendations from others, solicitations, conferences.

Recent Sales Sold 21 titles in the last year.

Terms Agent receives 15% commission on domestic sales; 15% commission on foreign sales. Offers written contract; 1-month notice must be given to terminate contract. Charges maximum of $350/year for postage and photocopying.

Writers' Conferences RWA National Conference; BookExpo America.

☑ ROSENSTONE/WENDER

38 E. 29th St., 10th Floor, New York NY 10016. (212)725-9445. Fax: (212)725-9447. **Contact:** Phyllis Wender. Member of AAR. Currently handles: 100% stage plays.

Member Agents Phyllis Wender; Sonia Pabley.

Represents Theatrical stage play.

    O→ Interested in literary, adult and dramatic material.

How to Contact Query with SASE. No e-mail or fax queries. Obtains most new clients through recommendations from others.

Recent Sales *River of Heaven*, by Lee Martin (Shaye Areheart Books).

☑ JANE ROTROSEN AGENCY LLC

318 E. 51st St., New York NY 10022. (212)593-4330. Fax: (212)935-6985. E-mail: firstinitiallastname@janerotrosen.com. Estab. 1974. Member of AAR, Authors Guild. Represents over 100 clients. Currently handles: 30% nonfiction books; 70% novels.

Member Agents Jane R. Berkey; Andrea Cirillo; Annelise Robey; Margaret Ruley; Kelly Harms; Christina Hogrebe; Peggy Gordijn, director of translation rights.

Represents Nonfiction books, novels. **Considers these nonfiction areas:** Biography/autobiography; business/economics; child guidance/parenting; cooking/foods/nutrition; current affairs; health/medicine; how-to; humor/satire; money/finance; nature/environment; popular culture; psychology; self-help/personal improvement; sports; true crime/investigative; women's issues/studies. **Considers these fiction areas:** Action/adventure; detective/police/crime; family saga; historical; horror; mainstream/contemporary; mystery/suspense; romance; thriller; women's.

How to Contact Query with SASE. No e-mail or fax queries. Responds in 2 months to mss. Responds in 2 weeks to writers who have been referred by a client or colleague. Returns materials only with SASE. Obtains most new clients through referrals.

Recent Sales This agency prefers not to share information on specific sales.

Terms Agent receives 15% commission on domestic sales; 20% commission on foreign sales. Offers written contract, binding for 3-5 years; 2-month notice must be given to terminate contract. Charges clients for photocopying, express mail, overseas postage, book purchase.

☑ THE PETER RUBIE LITERARY AGENCY

240 W. 35th St., Suite 500, New York NY 10001. (212)279-1776. Fax: (212)279-0927. E-mail: peterrubie@prlit.com. Web site: www.prlit.com. **Contact:** Peter Rubie (peterrubie@prlit.com); June Clark (pralit@aol.com); and Amy Tipton (assist@prlit.com). Estab. 2000. Member of AAR. Represents 130 clients. 20% of clients are new/unpublished writers.

• Prior to opening his agency, Mr. Rubie authored two novels and a number of nonfiction books. He was also the fiction editor at Walker and Co. Ms. Clark is the author of several books and plays, and previously worked in cable TV marketing and promotion. Ms. Tipton is also a writer and has worked as a literary assistant and office manager at several agencies.

Member Agents Peter Rubie (crime, science fiction, fantasy, literary fiction, thrillers, narrative/serious nonfiction, business, self-help, how-to, popular, food/wine, history, commercial science, music, education, parenting); June Clark (celebrity biographies, parenting, pets, women's issues, teen nonfiction, how-to, self-help, offbeat business, food/wine, commercial New Age, pop culture, entertainment, gay/lesbian); Amy Tipton (edgy/gritty fiction, urban, women's fiction, memoir and young adult).

Represents Nonfiction books, novels. **Considers these nonfiction areas:** Business/economics; current affairs; ethnic/cultural interests; gay/lesbian issues; how-to; popular culture; science/technology; self-help/personal improvement; TV; creative nonfiction (narrative); health/nutrition; cooking/food/wine; music; theater/film; prescriptive New Age; parenting/education; pets; commercial academic material. **Considers these fiction areas:** Fantasy; historical; literary; science fiction; thriller.

How to Contact For fiction, submit short synopsis, first 30-40 pages. For nonfiction, submit 1-page overview of the book, TOC, outline, 1-2 sample chapters. Accepts e-mail queries. No fax queries. Responds in 2 months to queries; 3 months to mss. Returns materials only with SASE. Obtains most new clients through recommendations from others.

Recent Sales Sold 50 titles in the last year. *Walking Money*, by James Born (Putnam); *Atherton*, by Patrick Carman (Little, Brown); *One Nation Under God*, by James P. Moore (Doubleday); *28 Days*, by Gabrielle Lichterman (Adams); *Shattered Dreams*, by Harlan Ullman (Carroll & Graf); *Chef on Fire*, by Joseph Carey (Taylor); *Laughing with Lucy*, by Madelyn Pugh Davis (Emis); *Read My Hips*, by Eve Marx (Adams); *Black Comedians on Black Comedy*, by Darryl Littleton (Applause).

Terms Agent receives 15% commission on domestic sales; 20% commission on foreign sales. Offers written contract. Charges clients for photocopying and some foreign mailings.

Tips "We look for writers who are experts, have a strong platform and reputation in their field, and have an outstanding prose style. Be professional and open-minded. Know your market and learn your craft. Go to our Web site for up-to-date information on clients and sales."

☑ RUSSELL & VOLKENING

50 W. 29th St., #7E, New York NY 10001. (212)684-6050. Fax: (212)889-3026. Web site: www.randvinc.com. **Contact:** Timothy Seldes, Jesseca Salky. Estab. 1940. Member of AAR. Represents 140 clients. 20% of clients are new/unpublished writers. Currently handles: 45% nonfiction books; 50% novels; 3% story collections; 2% novellas.

Represents Nonfiction books, novels, short story collections. **Considers these nonfiction areas:** Anthropology/archaeology; art/architecture/design; biography/autobiography; business/economics; cooking/foods/nutrition; current affairs; education; ethnic/cultural interests; gay/lesbian issues; government/politics/law; health/medicine; history; language/literature/criticism; military/war; money/finance; music/dance; nature/environment; photography; popular culture; psychology; science/technology; sociology; sports; theater/film; true crime/investigative; women's issues/studies; creative nonfiction. **Considers these fiction areas:** Action/adventure; detective/police/crime; ethnic; literary; mainstream/contemporary; mystery/suspense; picture books; sports; thriller.

O➔ This agency specializes in literary fiction and narrative nonfiction.

How to Contact Query with SASE, submit synopsis, several pages. No e-mail or fax queries. Responds in 4 weeks to queries.

Recent Sales *Digging to America*, by Anne Tyler (Knopf); *Get a Life*, by Nadine Gardiner (Penguin); *The Franklin Affair*, by Jim Lehrer (Random House).

Terms Agent receives 15% commission on domestic sales; 20% commission on foreign sales. Charges clients for standard office expenses relating to the submission of materials.

Tips "If the query is cogent, well written, well presented, and is the type of book we'd represent, we'll ask to see the manuscript. From there, it depends purely on the quality of the work."

VICTORIA SANDERS & ASSOCIATES

241 Avenue of the Americas, Suite 11 H, New York NY 10014. (212)633-8811. Fax: (212)633-0525. E-mail: queriesvsa@hotmail.com. Web site: www.victoriasanders.com. **Contact:** Victoria Sanders, Diane Dickensheid. Estab. 1993. Member of AAR; signatory of WGA. Represents 135 clients. 25% of clients are new/unpublished writers. Currently handles: 50% nonfiction books; 50% novels.

Represents Nonfiction books, novels. **Considers these nonfiction areas:** Biography/autobiography; current affairs; ethnic/cultural interests; gay/lesbian issues; government/politics/law; history; humor/satire; language/literature/criticism; music/dance; popular culture; psychology; theater/film; translation; women's issues/studies. **Considers these fiction areas:** Action/adventure; contemporary issues; ethnic; family saga; feminist; gay/lesbian; literary; thriller.

How to Contact Query by e-mail only.

Recent Sales Sold 20+ titles in the last year. *Faithless, Triptych & Skin Privilege,* by Karin Slaughter (Delacorte); *Jewels: 50 Phenomenal Black Women Over 50,* by Connie Briscoe and Michael Cunningham (Bulfinch); *B Mother,* by Maureen O'Brien (Harcourt); *Vagablonde,* by Kim Green (Warner); *Next Elements,* by Jeff Chang (Basic Civitas); *The Ties That Bind,* by Dr. Bertice Berry.

Terms Agent receives 15% commission on domestic sales; 20% commission on foreign sales. Offers written contract. Charges for photocopying, messenger, express mail. If in excess of $100, client approval is required.

Tips "Limit query to letter (no calls) and give it your best shot. A good query is going to get a good response."

SCHIAVONE LITERARY AGENCY, INC.

236 Trails End, West Palm Beach FL 33413-2135. (561)966-9294. Fax: (561)966-9294. E-mail: profschia@aol.com. New York office: 3671 Hudson Manor Terrace, No. 11H, Bronx, NY, 10463-1139, phone: (718)548-5332; fax: (718)548-5332; e-mail: jendu77@aol.com **Contact:** Dr. James Schiavone. CEO, corporate offices in Florida; Jennifer DuVall, president, New York office. Estab. 1996. Member of National Education Association. Represents 60+ clients. 2% of clients are new/unpublished writers. Currently handles: 50% nonfiction books; 49% novels; 1% textbooks.

- Prior to opening his agency, Dr. Schiavone was a full professor of developmental skills at the City University of New York and author of 5 trade books and 3 textbooks. Jennifer DuVall has many years of combined experience in office management and agenting.

Represents Nonfiction books, novels, juvenile books, scholarly books, textbooks. **Considers these nonfiction areas:** Animals; anthropology/archaeology; biography/autobiography; child guidance/parenting; current affairs; education; ethnic/cultural interests; gay/lesbian issues; government/politics/law; health/medicine; history; how-to; humor/satire; juvenile nonfiction; language/literature/criticism; military/war; nature/environment; popular culture; psychology; science/technology; self-help/personal improvement; sociology; spirituality (mind and body); true crime/investigative. **Considers these fiction areas:** Ethnic; family saga; historical; horror; humor/satire; juvenile; literary; mainstream/contemporary; science fiction; young adult.

- ⊶ This agency specializes in celebrity biography and autobiography and memoirs. Does not want to receive poetry.

How to Contact Query with SASE. Do not send unsolicited materials or parcels requiring a signature. Send no e-attachments. Accepts e-mail queries. No fax queries. Considers simultaneous queries. Responds in 2 weeks to queries; 6 weeks to mss. Returns materials only with SASE. Obtains most new clients through recommendations from others, solicitations, conferences.

Terms Agent receives 15% commission on domestic sales; 20% commission on foreign sales. Offers written contract. Charges clients for postage only.

Writers' Conferences Key West Literary Seminar; South Florida Writers' Conference; Tallahassee Writers' Conference, Million Dollar Writers' Conference.

Tips "We prefer to work with established authors published by major houses in New York. We will consider marketable proposals from new/previously unpublished writers."

SCRIBE AGENCY, LLC

5508 Joylynne Dr., Madison WI 53716. E-mail: queries@scribeagency.com. Web site: www.scribeagency.com. **Contact:** Kristopher O'Higgins. Estab. 2004. Represents 8 clients. 50% of clients are new/unpublished writers. Currently handles: 100% novels.

- "We have 15 years of experience in publishing and have worked on both agency and editorial sides in the past, with marketing expertise to boot. We love books as much or more than anyone you know. Check our Web site to see what we're about and to make sure you jive with the Scribe vibe."

Member Agents Kristopher O'Higgins; Jesse Vogel.

Represents Nonfiction books, novels, short story collections, novellas, juvenile books, poetry books. **Considers these nonfiction areas:** Cooking/foods/nutrition; ethnic/cultural interests; gay/lesbian issues; humor/satire; memoirs; music/dance; popular culture; true crime/investigative; women's issues/studies. **Considers these**

fiction areas: Action/adventure; comic books/cartoon; detective/police/crime; erotica; ethnic; experimental; fantasy; feminist; gay/lesbian; horror; humor/satire; literary; mainstream/contemporary; mystery/suspense; psychic/supernatural; science fiction; thriller; young adult.

    ⊶ Actively seeking excellent writers with ideas and stories to tell. Does not want cat mysteries or anything not listed above.

How to Contact Query with SASE. Responds in 3-4 weeks to queries; 3-4 months to mss. Returns materials only with SASE.

Recent Sales Sold 2 titles in the last year.

Terms Agent receives 15% commission on domestic sales; 20% commission on foreign sales. Offers written contract. Charges for postage and photocopying.

Writers' Conferences BookExpo America; The Writer's Institute; Spring Writer's Festival; WisCon; Wisconsin Book Festival; World Fantasy Convention.

🖉 LYNN SELIGMAN, LITERARY AGENT

400 Highland Ave., Upper Montclair NJ 07043. (973)783-3631. **Contact:** Lynn Seligman. Estab. 1985. Member of Women's Media Group. Represents 32 clients. 15% of clients are new/unpublished writers. Currently handles: 60% nonfiction books; 40% novels.

    • Prior to opening her agency, Ms. Seligman worked in the subsidiary rights department of Doubleday and Simon & Schuster, and served as an agent with Julian Bach Literary Agency (which became IMG Literary Agency). Foreign rights are represented by Books Crossing Borders, Inc.

Represents Nonfiction books, novels. **Considers these nonfiction areas:** Anthropology/archaeology; art/architecture/design; biography/autobiography; business/economics; child guidance/parenting; cooking/foods/nutrition; current affairs; education; ethnic/cultural interests; government/politics/law; health/medicine; history; how-to; humor/satire; interior design/decorating; language/literature/criticism; money/finance; music/dance; nature/environment; photography; popular culture; psychology; science/technology; self-help/personal improvement; sociology; theater/film; true crime/investigative; women's issues/studies. **Considers these fiction areas:** Detective/police/crime; ethnic; fantasy; feminist; gay/lesbian; historical; horror; humor/satire; literary; mainstream/contemporary; mystery/suspense; romance (contemporary, gothic, historical, regency); science fiction.

    ⊶ This agency specializes in general nonfiction and fiction. "I also do illustrated and photography books and have represented several photographers for books." This agency does not handle children's or young adult books.

How to Contact Query with SASE, sample chapters, outline/proposal. Prefers to read materials exclusively. No e-mail or fax queries. Considers simultaneous queries. Responds in 2 weeks to queries; 2 months to mss. Returns materials only with SASE. Obtains most new clients through referrals from other writers and editors.

Recent Sales Sold 15 titles in the last year. *Naughty in Deed* by Barbara Pierce; *Morbid Curiousity*, by Deborah Leblanc.

Terms Agent receives 15% commission on domestic sales; 25% commission on foreign sales. Charges clients for photocopying, unusual postage, express mail, telephone expenses (checks with author first).

🖉 SERENDIPITY LITERARY AGENCY, LLC

305 Gates Ave., Brooklyn NY 11216. (718)230-7689. Fax: (718)230-7829. E-mail: rbrooks@serendipitylit.com. Web site: www.serendipitylit.com. **Contact:** Regina Brooks. Estab. 2000. Represents 50 clients. 50% of clients are new/unpublished writers. Currently handles: 50% nonfiction books; 50% fiction.

    • Prior to becoming an agent, Ms. Brooks was an acquisitions editor for John Wiley & Sons, Inc. and McGraw-Hill Companies.

Represents Nonfiction books, novels, juvenile books, scholarly books, children's books. **Considers these nonfiction areas:** Business/economics; current affairs; education; ethnic/cultural interests; history; juvenile nonfiction; memoirs; money/finance; multicultural; New Age/metaphysics; popular culture; psychology; religious/inspirational; science/technology; self-help/personal improvement; sports; women's issues/studies; health/medical; narrative; popular science; biography; politics; crafts/design; food/cooking; contemporary culture. **Considers these fiction areas:** Action/adventure; confession; ethnic; historical; juvenile; literary; multicultural; picture books; thriller; suspense; mystery; romance.

    ⊶ African-American nonfiction, commercial fiction, young adult novels with an urban flair and juvenile books. No stage plays, screenplays or poetry.

How to Contact Prefers to read materials exclusively. For nonfiction, submit outline, 1 sample chapter, SASE. Responds in 2 months to queries; 3 months to mss. Obtains most new clients through conferences, referrals.

Recent Sales This agency prefers not to share information on specific sales. Recent sales available upon request.

Terms Agent receives 15% commission on domestic sales; 20% commission on foreign sales. Offers written contract; 2-month notice must be given to terminate contract. Charges clients for office fees, which are taken from any advance.

Tips "We are eagerly looking for young adult books and fiction and nonfiction targeted to 20- and 30-year-old's. We also represent illustrators."

◙ THE SEYMOUR AGENCY

475 Miner St., Canton NY 13617. (315)386-1831. E-mail: marysue@slic.com. Web site: www.theseymouragency .com. **Contact:** Mary Sue Seymour. Estab. 1992. Member of AAR, RWA, Authors Guild; signatory of WGA. Represents 50 clients. 5% of clients are new/unpublished writers. Currently handles: 50% nonfiction books; 50% fiction.

- Ms. Seymour is a retired New York State certified teacher.

Represents Nonfiction books, novels. **Considers these nonfiction areas:** Business/economics; health/medicine; how-to; self-help/personal improvement; Christian books; cookbooks; any well-written nonfiction that includes a proposal in standard format and 1 sample chapter. **Considers these fiction areas:** Religious/inspirational (Christian books); romance (any type).

How to Contact Query with SASE, synopsis, first 50 pages for romance. Accepts e-mail queries. No fax queries. Considers simultaneous queries. Responds in 1 month to queries; 3 months to mss. Returns materials only with SASE.

Recent Sales Two romance books, by Tracy Willouer; two romance books, by Kimberly Kaye Terry; Maryanne Raphael's authorized biograohy of Mother Teresa; *Interference*, by Shelley Wernlein; *The Doctor's Daughter*, by Donna MacQuigg.

Terms Agent receives 12-15% commission on domestic sales.

Writers' Conferences BookExpo America; Start Your Engines; Romantic Times Convention; ICE Escape Writers Conference; Spring Into Romance; Silicon Valley RWA Conference; Put Your Heart in a Book; RWA National.

◙ WENDY SHERMAN ASSOCIATES, INC.

450 Seventh Ave., Suite 2307, New York NY 10123. (212)279-9027. Fax: (212)279-8863. Web site: www.wsherm an.com. **Contact:** Wendy Sherman. Estab. 1999. Member of AAR. Represents 50 clients. 30% of clients are new/unpublished writers. Currently handles: 50% nonfiction books; 50% novels.

- Prior to opening the agency, Ms. Sherman worked for The Aaron Priest agency and served as vice president, executive director, associate publisher, subsidary rights director, and sales and marketing director in the publishing industry.

Member Agents Wendy Sherman; Michelle Brower.

Represents Nonfiction books, novels. **Considers these nonfiction areas:** Psychology; narrative; practical. **Considers these fiction areas:** Literary; women's (suspense).

- ⛏ "We specialize in developing new writers, as well as working with more established writers. My experience as a publisher has proven to be a great asset to my clients."

How to Contact Query with SASE or send outline/proposal, 1 sample chapter. No e-mail queries. Considers simultaneous queries. Responds in 1 month to queries. Returns materials only with SASE. Obtains most new clients through recommendations from others.

Recent Sales *America's Boy: A Memoir*, by Wade Rouse; *Marked Man*, by William Lashner; *The Vanishing Point*, by Mary Sharratt; *Spooning: The Cooking Club Divas Turn Up The Heat*, by Darri Stephens and Megan DeSales; *The Kindergarten Wars: The Battle To Get Into America's Best Private Schools*, by Alan Eisenstock; *The Judas Field: A Novel Of The Civil War*, by Howard Bahr. Other clients include Fiction clients include: William Lashner, Nani Power, DW Buffa, Howard Bahr, Suzanne Chazin, Sarah Stonich, Ad Hudler, Mary Sharratt, Libby Street, Heather Estay, Darri Stephens, Megan Desales. Nonfiction clients include: Rabbi Mark Borovitz, Alan Eisenstock, Esther Perel, Clifton Leaf, Maggie Estep, Greg Baer, Martin Friedman, Lundy Bancroft, Alvin Ailey Dance, Lise Friedman, Liz Landers, Vicky Mainzer.

Terms Agent receives 15% commission on domestic sales; 20% commission on foreign sales. Offers written contract.

Tips "The bottom line is: Do your homework. Be as well prepared as possible. Read the books that will help you present yourself and your work with polish. You want your submission to stand out."

◙ ROSALIE SIEGEL, INTERNATIONAL LITERARY AGENCY, INC.

1 Abey Dr., Pennington NJ 08543. (609)737-1007. Fax: (609)737-3708. **Contact:** Rosalie Siegel. Estab. 1977. Member of AAR. Represents 35 clients. 10% of clients are new/unpublished writers. Currently handles: 45% nonfiction books; 45% novels; 10% young adult books; short story collections for current clients.

How to Contact Obtains most new clients through referrals from writers and friends.

Terms Agent receives 15% commission on domestic sales; 20% commission on foreign sales. Offers written contract; 2-month notice must be given to terminate contract. Charges clients for photocopying.

Tips "I'm not looking for new authors in an active way."

⊞ ☑ JEFFREY SIMMONS LITERARY AGENCY

15 Penn House, Mallory St., London NW8 8SX England. (44)(207)224-8917. E-mail: jasimmons@btconnect.com. **Contact:** Jeffrey Simmons. Estab. 1978. Represents 43 clients. 40% of clients are new/unpublished writers. Currently handles: 65% nonfiction books; 35% novels.

• Prior to becoming an agent, Mr. Simmons was a publisher. He is also an author.

Represents Nonfiction books, novels. **Considers these nonfiction areas:** Biography/autobiography; current affairs; government/politics/law; history; language/literature/criticism; memoirs; music/dance; popular culture; sociology; sports; theater/film; translation; true crime/investigative. **Considers these fiction areas:** Action/adventure; confession; detective/police/crime; family saga; literary; mainstream/contemporary; mystery/suspense; thriller.

○➔ This agency seeks to handle good books and promising young writers. "My long experience in publishing and as an author and ghostwriter means I can offer an excellent service all around, especially in terms of editorial experience where appropriate." Actively seeking quality fiction, biography, autobiography, showbiz, personality books, law, crime, politics, and world affairs. Does not want to receive science fiction, horror, fantasy, juvenile, academic books, or specialist subjects (e.g., cooking, gardening, religious).

How to Contact Submit sample chapter, outline/proposal, SASE (IRCs if necessary). Prefers to read materials exclusively. Responds in 1 week to queries; 1 month to mss. Obtains most new clients through recommendations from others, solicitations.

Terms Agent receives 10-15% commission on domestic sales; 15% commission on foreign sales. Offers written contract, binding for lifetime of book in question or until it becomes out of print.

Tips "When contacting us with an outline/proposal, include a brief biographical note (listing any previous publications, with publishers and dates). Preferably tell us if the book has already been offered elsewhere."

⧗ ☺ BEVERLEY SLOPEN LITERARY AGENCY

131 Bloor St. W., Suite 711, Toronto ON M5S 1S3 Canada. (416)964-9598. Fax: (416)921-7726. E-mail: beverly@slopenagency.ca. Web site: www.slopenagency.ca. **Contact:** Beverley Slopen. Estab. 1974. Represents 70 clients. 20% of clients are new/unpublished writers. Currently handles: 60% nonfiction books; 40% novels.

• Prior to opening her agency, Ms. Slopen worked in publishing and as a journalist.

Represents Nonfiction books, novels, scholarly books, textbooks (college). **Considers these nonfiction areas:** Anthropology/archaeology; biography/autobiography; business/economics; current affairs; psychology; sociology; true crime/investigative; women's issues/studies. **Considers these fiction areas:** Literary; mystery/suspense.

○➔ This agency has a strong bent toward Canadian writers. Actively seeking serious nonfiction that is accessible and appealing to the general reader. Does not want to receive fantasy, science fiction, or children's books.

How to Contact Query with SAE and IRCs. Returns materials only with SASE (Canadian postage only). Accepts short e-mail queries. Considers simultaneous queries. Responds in 2 months to queries.

Recent Sales Sold over 40 titles in the last year. *Court Lady* and *Country Wife*, by Lita-Rose Betcherman (HarperCollins Canada/Morrow/Wiley UK); *Vermeer's Hat*, by Timothy Brook (HarperCollins Canada); *Midnight Cab*, by James W. Nichol (Canongate US/Droemer); *Lady Franklin's Revenge*, by Ken McGoogan (HarperCollins Canada/Bantam UK); *Understanding Uncertainty*, by Jeffrey Rosenthal (HarperCollins Canada); *Damaged Angels*, by Bonnie Buxton (Carroll & Graf US); *Sea of Dreams*, by Adam Mayers (McClelland & Stewart Canada); *Memory Book*, by Howard Engel (Carroll & Graf); *Written in the Flesh*, by Edward Shorter (University of Toronto Press); *Punch Line*, by Joey Slinger (Key Porter Books). Other clients include Modris Eksteins, Michael Marrus, Robert Fulford, Morley Torgov, Elliott Leyton, Don Gutteridge, Joanna Goodman, Roberta Rich, Jennifer Welsh, Margaret Wente, Frank Wydra.

Terms Agent receives 15% commission on domestic sales; 10% commission on foreign sales. Offers written contract, binding for 2 years; 3-month notice must be given to terminate contract.

Tips "Please, no unsolicited manuscripts."

☑ SPECTRUM LITERARY AGENCY

320 Central Park W., Suite 1-D, New York NY 10025. Fax: (212)362-4562. Web site: www.spectrumliteraryagency.com. **Contact:** Eleanor Wood, president. Represents 90 clients. Currently handles: 10% nonfiction books; 90% novels.

Member Agents Lucienne Diver.

Represents Nonfiction books, novels. **Considers these fiction areas:** Fantasy; historical; mainstream/contemporary; mystery/suspense; romance; science fiction.

How to Contact Query with SASE, submit author bio, publishing credits. No unsolicited mss will be read. Snail mail queries **only**. No e-mail or fax queries. Responds in 1-3 months to queries. Obtains most new clients through recommendations from authors.

Recent Sales Sold more than 100 titles in the last year. Sales available on this agency's Web site.

Terms Agent receives 15% commission on domestic sales. Deducts for photocopying and book orders.

⬛ SPENCERHILL ASSOCIATES

P.O. Box 374, Chatham NY 12037. (518)392-9293. Fax: (518)392-9554. E-mail: ksolem@klsbooks.com; jennifer @klsbooks.com. **Contact:** Karen Solem or Jennifer Schober. Estab. 2001. Member of AAR. Represents 40 clients. 5% of clients are new/unpublished writers. Currently handles: 5% nonfiction books; 90% novels; 5% novellas.

• Prior to becoming an agent, Ms. Solem was editor-in-chief at HarperCollins and an associate publisher.

Member Agents Karen Solem; Jennifer Schober (new agent actively seeking clients).

Represents Nonfiction books, novels. **Considers these nonfiction areas:** Animals; religious/inspirational. **Considers these fiction areas:** Detective/police/crime; historical; mainstream/contemporary; religious/inspirational; romance; thriller.

    ○┐ "We handle mostly commercial women's fiction, historical novels, romance (historical, contemporary, paranormal), thrillers, and mysteries. We also represent Christian fiction and nonfiction." No poetry, science fiction, juvenile, or scripts.

How to Contact Query with SASE, proposal package, outline. Responds in 1 month to queries. Returns materials only with SASE.

Recent Sales Sold 225 titles in the last year.

Terms Agent receives 15% commission on domestic sales; 20% commission on foreign sales. Offers written contract; 3-month notice must be given to terminate contract.

⬛ THE SPIELER AGENCY

154 W. 57th St., Suite 135, New York NY 10019. **Contact:** Katya Balter. Estab. 1981. Represents 160 clients. 2% of clients are new/unpublished writers.

• Prior to opening his agency, Mr. Spieler was a magazine editor.

Member Agents Joe Spieler; John Thornton (nonfiction); Lisa M. Ross (fiction, nonfiction); Deirdre Mullane (nonfiction); Eric Myers (nonfiction, fiction); Victoria Shoemaker (fiction, nonfiction).

Represents Nonfiction books, novels, children's books. **Considers these nonfiction areas:** Biography/autobiography; business/economics; child guidance/parenting; current affairs; gay/lesbian issues; government/politics/law; history; memoirs; money/finance; music/dance; nature/environment; religious/inspirational; sociology; spirituality; theater/film; travel; women's issues/studies. **Considers these fiction areas:** Detective/police/crime; feminist; gay/lesbian; literary; mystery/suspense.

How to Contact Query with SASE. Prefers to read materials exclusively. Returns materials only with SASE; otherwise materials are discarded when rejected. No fax queries. Considers simultaneous queries. Responds in 2 weeks to queries; 2 months to mss. Obtains most new clients through recommendations, listing in *Guide to Literary Agents*.

Recent Sales *Tilt-A-Whirl*, by Chris Grabenstein (Carroll and Graf); *What's the Matter with Kansas*, by Thomas Frank (Metropolitan/Holt); *Natural History of the Rich*, by Richard Conniff (W.W. Norton); *Juicing the Game*, by Howard Bryant (Viking).

Terms Agent receives 15% commission on domestic sales. Charges clients for messenger bills, photocopying, postage.

Writers' Conferences London Book Fair.

⬛ PHILIP G. SPITZER LITERARY AGENCY, INC

50 Talmage Farm Ln., East Hampton NY 11937. (631)329-3650. Fax: (631)329-3651. E-mail: spitzer516@aol.com. **Contact:** Philip Spitzer, Lukas Ortiz. Estab. 1969. Member of AAR. Represents 60 clients. 10% of clients are new/unpublished writers. Currently handles: 50% nonfiction books; 50% novels.

• Prior to opening his agency, Mr. Spitzer served at New York University Press, McGraw-Hill, and the John Cushman Associates literary agency.

Represents Nonfiction books, novels. **Considers these nonfiction areas:** Biography/autobiography; business/economics; current affairs; ethnic/cultural interests; government/politics/law; health/medicine; history; language/literature/criticism; military/war; music/dance; nature/environment; popular culture; psychology; sociology; sports; theater/film; true crime/investigative. **Considers these fiction areas:** Detective/police/crime; literary; mainstream/contemporary; mystery/suspense; sports; thriller.

    ○┐ This agency specializes in mystery/suspense, literary fiction, sports and general nonfiction (no how-to).

How to Contact Query with SASE, outline, 1 sample chapter. Responds in 1 week to queries; 6 weeks to mss. Obtains most new clients through recommendations from others.

Recent Sales *The Overlook*, by Michael Connelly; *Acts of Nature*, by Jonathon King; *Dead Connections*, by

Alafair Burke; *Pegasus Descending*, by James Lee Burke; *Four Kinds of Rain*, by Robert Ward; *Ty & Babe*, by Tom Stanton; *Con Ed*, by Matthew Klein; *Kidnapped*, by Jan Burke.

Terms Agent receives 15% commission on domestic sales; 20% commission on foreign sales. Charges clients for photocopying.

Writers' Conferences BookExpo America.

⦿ NANCY STAUFFER ASSOCIATES

P.O. Box 1203, Darien CT 06820. (203)655-3717. Fax: (203)655-3704. E-mail: nanstauf@optonline.net. Web site: www.publishersmarketplace.com/members/nstauffer. **Contact:** Nancy Stauffer Cahoon. Estab. 1989. Member of Authors Guild. 5% of clients are new/unpublished writers. Currently handles: 15% nonfiction books; 85% novels. **Considers these nonfiction areas:** Current affairs; ethnic/cultural interests; creative nonfiction (narrative). **Considers these fiction areas:** Contemporary issues; literary; regional.

How to Contact Obtains most new clients through referrals from existing clients.

Recent Sales New novels by Sherman Alexie, Mark Spragg, and William C. Harris.

Terms Agent receives 15% commission on domestic sales; 20% commission on foreign sales; 15% commission on dramatic rights sales.

⦿ STEELE-PERKINS LITERARY AGENCY

26 Island Ln., Canandaigua NY 14424. (585)396-9290. Fax: (585)396-3579. E-mail: pattiesp@aol.com. **Contact:** Pattie Steele-Perkins. Member of AAR, RWA. Currently handles: 100% novels.

Represents Novels. **Considers these fiction areas:** Romance and women's, including multicultural and inspirational.

How to Contact Submit outline, 3 sample chapters, SASE. Considers simultaneous queries. Responds in 6 weeks to queries. Returns materials only with SASE. Obtains most new clients through recommendations from others, queries/solicitations.

Recent Sales This agency prefers not to share information on specific sales.

Terms Agent receives 15% commission on domestic sales. Offers written contract, binding for 1 year; 1-month notice must be given to terminate contract.

Writers' Conferences RWA National Conference; BookExpo America; CBA Convention; Romance Slam Jam.

Tips "Be patient. E-mail rather than call. Make sure what you are sending is the best it can be."

⦿ STERNIG & BYRNE LITERARY AGENCY

2370 S. 107th St., Apt. #4, Milwaukee WI 53227-2036. (414)328-8034. Fax: (414)328-8034. E-mail: jackbyrne@hotmail.com. Web site: www.sff.net/people/jackbyrne. **Contact:** Jack Byrne. Estab. 1950s. Member of SFWA, MWA. Represents 30 clients. 10% of clients are new/unpublished writers. Currently handles: 5% nonfiction books; 85% novels; 10% juvenile books.

Represents Nonfiction books, novels, juvenile books. **Considers these fiction areas:** Fantasy; horror; mystery/suspense; science fiction.

　　○╼ "Our client list is comfortably full and our current needs are therefore quite limited." Actively seeking science fiction/fantasy and mystery by established writers. Does not want to receive romance, poetry, textbooks, or highly specialized nonfiction.

How to Contact Query with SASE. Prefers e-mail queries (no attachments); hard copy queries also acceptable. Accepts e-mail queries. No fax queries. Responds in 3 weeks to queries; 3 months to mss. Returns materials only with SASE.

Recent Sales Sold 16 titles in the last year. *Cybermancy*, by Kelly McCullough; *Ha'Penny*, by Jo Walton; *Mirador*, by Sarah Monette. Other clients include Lyn McConche, Betty Ren Wright, Jo Walton, Moira Moore, Sarah Monette, John C. Wright, Bill Gagliani.

Terms Agent receives 15% commission on domestic sales; 20% commission on foreign sales. Offers written contract; 2-month notice must be given to terminate contract.

Tips "Don't send first drafts, have a professional presentation (including cover letter), and know your field. Read what's been done—good and bad."

⦿ PAM STRICKLER AUTHOR MANAGEMENT

1 Water St., New Paltz NY 12561. (845)255-0061. Web site: www.pamstrickler.com. **Contact:** Pamela Dean Strickler. Member of AAR.

　　● Prior to opening her agency, Ms. Strickler was senior editor at Ballantine Books..

　　○╼ Specializes in romance and women's fiction. Does not want to receive nonfiction or children's books.

How to Contact Query via e-mail with 1-page letter including brief plot description and first 10 pages of ms (no attachments). *No unsolicited mss.*

Recent Sales *Lady Dearing's Masquerade*, by Elena Greene (New American Library); *Her Body of Work*, by Marie Donovan (Harlequin/Blaze); *Deceived*, by Nicola Cornick (Harlequin/HQN).

☕ REBECCA STRONG INTERNATIONAL LITERARY AGENCY

235 W. 108th St., #35, New York NY 10025. (212)865-1569. **Contact:** Rebecca Strong. Estab. 2003.
• Prior to opening her agency, Ms. Strong was an industry executive with experience editing and licensing in the US and UK. She has worked at Crown/Random House, Harmony/Random House, Bloomsbury, and Harvill.

Represents Nonfiction books, novels. **Considers these nonfiction areas:** Biography/autobiography; business/economics; health/medicine; history; memoirs; science/technology; travel. **Considers these fiction areas:** General fiction.

O→ "We are a consciously small agency dedicated to established and building writers' book publishing careers rather than representing one-time projects." Does not want to receive poetry, screenplays or any unsolicited mss.

How to Contact Query with SASE. No e-mail or fax queries. Considers simultaneous queries. Responds in 2 months to queries. Returns materials only with SASE. Obtains most new clients through recommendations from others, conferences.

Terms Agent receives 15% commission on domestic sales; 20% commission on foreign sales. Offers written contract, binding for 10 years; 30-day notice must be given to terminate contract.

Tips "I represent writers with prior publishing experience only: journalists, magazine writers or writers of fiction who have been published in anthologies or literary magazines. There are exceptions to this guideline, but not many."

☕ THE STROTHMAN AGENCY, LLC

One Faneuil Hall Marketplace, Third Floor, Boston MA 02109. (617)742-2011. Fax: (617)742-2014. Web site: www.strothmanagency.com. **Contact:** Wendy Strothman, Dan O'Connell. Estab. 2003. Represents 50 clients. Currently handles: 70% nonfiction books; 10% novels; 20% scholarly books.
• Prior to becoming an agent, Ms. Strothman was head of Beacon Press (1983-1995) and executive vice president of Houghton Mifflin's Trade & Reference Division (1996-2002).

Member Agents Wendy Strothman; Dan O'Connell.

Represents Nonfiction books, novels, scholarly books. **Considers these nonfiction areas:** Current affairs; government/politics/law; history; language/literature/criticism; nature/environment. **Considers these fiction areas:** Literary.

O→ "Because we are highly selective in the clients we represent, we increase the value publishers place on our properties. We seek out public figures, scholars, journalists and other acknowledged and emerging experts in their fields. We specialize in narrative nonfiction, memoir, history, science and nature, arts and culture, literary travel, current affairs and some business. We have a highly selective practice in literary fiction and children's literature." Does not want to receive commercial fiction, romance, science fiction or self-help.

How to Contact Query with SASE. Considers simultaneous queries. Responds in 3 weeks to queries; 1 month to mss. Returns materials only with SASE. Obtains most new clients through recommendations from others.

Recent Sales Sold 25 titles in the last year. *Flights Against the Sunset*, by Kenn Kaufman (Houghton Mifflin); *Guantanamo Bay: A History*, by Jonathan Hansen (Random House); *Backcast: A Memoir of Fly Fishing, Fatherhood, and Divorce*, by Lou Ureneck (St. Martin's); *Model-Wives: Madame Cezanne, Madame Monet, Madame Rodin*, by Ruth Butler (Yale University Press); *Smithsonian Ocean*, by Deborah Cramer (Smithsonian Books); *Free Fall: The Rising Economic Risk Facing America's Working Families*, by Peter Gosselin (Basic Books).

Terms Agent receives 15% commission on domestic sales; 20% commission on foreign sales. Offers written contract; 30-day notice must be given to terminate contract.

☕ THE SWETKY AGENCY

2150 Balboa Way, No. 29, St. George UT 84770. E-mail: fayeswetky@amsaw.org. Web site: www.amsaw.org/swetkyagency/index.html. **Contact:** Faye M. Swetky. Estab. 2000. Member of American Society of Authors and Writers. Represents 40+ clients. 80% of clients are new/unpublished writers. Currently handles: 30% nonfiction books; 30% novels; 20% movie scripts; 20% TV scripts.
• Prior to becoming an agent, Ms. Swetky was an editor and corporate manager. She has also raised and raced thoroughbred horses.

Represents Nonfiction books, novels, short story collections, juvenile books, movie scripts, feature film, TV scripts, TV movie of the week, sitcom, documentary. **Considers these nonfiction areas:** All major nonfiction genres. **Considers these fiction areas:** All major fiction genres. **Considers these script subject areas:** Action/adventure; biography/autobiography; cartoon/animation; comedy; contemporary issues; detective/police/

crime; erotica; ethnic; experimental; family saga; fantasy; feminist; gay/lesbian; glitz; historical; horror; juvenile; mainstream; multicultural; multimedia; mystery/suspense; psychic/supernatural; regional; religious/inspirational; romantic comedy; romantic drama; science fiction; sports; teen; thriller; western/frontier.

○→ "We handle only book-length fiction and nonfiction and feature-length movie and television scripts. Please visit our Web site before submitting. All agency-related information is there, including a sample contract, e-mail submission forms, policies, clients, etc." Actively seeking young adult material. Do not send unprofessionally prepared mss and/or scripts.

How to Contact See Web site for submission instructions. Accepts e-mail queries only. Considers simultaneous queries. Response time varies. Obtains most new clients through queries.

Recent Sales *Zen and the Art of Pond Building*, by J.D. Herda (Sterling); *Solid Stiehl*, by D.J. Herda (Archebooks); *24/7*, by Susan Diplacido (Zumaya Publications); *House on the Road to Salisbury*, by Lisa Adams (Archebooks). *Movie/TV MOW script(s) optioned/sold: Demons 5*, by Jim O'Rear (Katzir Productions); *Detention* and *Instinct Vs. Reason*, by Garrett Hargrove (Filmjack Productions).

Terms Agent receives 15% commission on domestic sales; 20% commission on foreign sales; 20% commission on dramatic rights sales. Offers written contract, binding for 1 year; 30-day notice must be given to terminate contract.

Tips "Be professional. Have a professionally prepared product."

◧ TALCOTT NOTCH LITERARY

276 Forest Road, Milford CT 06460. (203)877-1146. Fax: (203)876-9517. E-mail: gpanettieri@talcottnotch.net; rdowen@talcottnotch.net. Web site: www.talcottnotch.net. **Contact:** Gina Panettieri, president. Estab. 2003. Represents 25 clients. 30% of clients are new/unpublished writers.

• Prior to becoming an agent, Ms. Panettieri was a freelance writer and editor.

Member Agents Gina Panettieri (nonfiction, mystery); Rachel Dowen (children's fiction, mystery).

Represents Nonfiction books, novels, juvenile books, scholarly books, textbooks. **Considers these nonfiction areas:** Agriculture/horticulture; animals; anthropology/archaeology; art/architecture/design; biography/autobiography; business/economics; child guidance/parenting; computers/electronic; cooking/foods/nutrition; current affairs; education; ethnic/cultural interests; gay/lesbian issues; government/politics/law; health/medicine; history; how-to; memoirs; military/war; money/finance; music/dance; nature/environment; popular culture; psychology; science/technology; self-help/personal improvement; sociology; sports; true crime/investigative; women's issues/studies; New Age/metaphysics, interior design/decorating, juvenile nonfiction. **Considers these fiction areas:** Action/adventure; detective/police/crime; juvenile; mystery/suspense; thriller; young adult.

○→ Actively seeking prescriptive nonfiction, children's fiction and mysteries. Does not want to receive poetry or picture books.

How to Contact Query via e-mail (preferred) or with SASE. Considers simultaneous queries. Responds in 1 week to queries; 2 weeks to mss. Returns materials only with SASE.

Recent Sales Sold 24 titles in the last year. *The Connected Child*, by Dr. Karyn Purvis, Dr. David Cross and Wendy Sunshine (Mcgraw-Hill); *Parenting Your Defiant Child*, by Dr. Philip Hall And Dr. Nancy Hall (Amacom); *Fall: The Rape and Murder of Innocence in a Small Town*, by Ron Franscell (New Horizon Press); *The New Supervisor's Handbook*, by Brette Sember and Terry Sember (Career Press); *The Executive's Guide To E-mail Correspondance*, by Dr. Dawn-Michelle Baude (Career Press). Other clients include Dr. Leslie Young, Moira Mccarthy, Corrie Lynne Player, David Evans Katz, Erik Lawrence, Dagmara Scalise, Nancy Whitney Reiter, A.E. Rought/Savannah Jordan.

Terms Agent receives 15% commission on domestic sales; 20% commission on foreign sales. Offers written contract, binding for 1 year.

Tips "Present your book or project effectively in your query. Don't include links to a Web page rather than a traditional query, and take the time to prepare a thorough but brief synopsis of the material. Make the effort to prepare a thoughtful analysis of comparison titles. How is your work different, and will it appeal to those same readers?"

◖ PATRICIA TEAL LITERARY AGENCY

2036 Vista Del Rosa, Fullerton CA 92831-1336. Phone/Fax: (714)738-8333. **Contact:** Patricia Teal. Estab. 1978. Member of AAR. Represents 20 clients. Currently handles: 10% nonfiction books; 90% fiction.

Represents Nonfiction books, novels. **Considers these nonfiction areas:** Animals; biography/autobiography; child guidance/parenting; health/medicine; how-to; psychology; self-help/personal improvement; true crime/investigative; women's issues/studies. **Considers these fiction areas:** Glitz; mainstream/contemporary; mystery/suspense; romance (contemporary, historical).

○→ This agency specializes in women's fiction, commercial how-to, and self-help nonfiction. Does not want to receive poetry, short stories, articles, science fiction, fantasy, or regency romance.

How to Contact Published authors only may query with SASE. No e-mail or fax queries. Considers simultaneous queries. Responds in 10 days to queries; 6 weeks to mss. Returns materials only with SASE. Obtains most new clients through conferences, recommendations from authors and editors.

Recent Sales Sold 30 titles in the last year. *Texas Rose,* by Marie Ferrarella (Silhouette); *Watch Your Language,* by Sterling Johnson (St. Martin's Press); *The Black Sheep's Baby*, by Kathleen Creighton (Silhouette); *Man With a Message,* by Muriel Jensen (Harlequin).

Terms Agent receives 10-15% commission on domestic sales; 20% commission on foreign sales. Offers written contract, binding for 1 year. Charges clients for postage.

Writers' Conferences RWA Conferences; Asilomar; BookExpo America; Bouchercon; Maui Writers Conference.

Tips ''Include SASE with all correspondence. I am taking on published authors only.''

● TESSLER LITERARY AGENCY, LLC

27 W. 20th St., Suite 1003, New York NY 10011. (212)242-0466. Fax: (212)242-2366. Web site: www.tessleragen cy.com. **Contact:** Michelle Tessler. Member of AAR.

   ● Prior to forming her own agency, Ms. Tessler worked at Carlisle & Co. (now a part of Inkwell Management). She has also worked at the William Morris Agency and the Elaine Markson Literary Agency..

   O→ The Tessler Agency is a full-service boutique agency that represents writers of high-quality nonfiction and literary and commercial fiction.

How to Contact Submit query through Web site only.

● 3 SEAS LITERARY AGENCY

P.O. Box 8571, Madison WI 53708. (608)221-4306. E-mail: queries@threeseaslit.com. Web site: www.threeseasl it.com. **Contact:** Michelle Grajkowski, Cori Deyoe. Estab. 2000. Member of RWA, Chicago Women in Publishing. Represents 40 clients. 10% of clients are new/unpublished writers. Currently handles: 5% nonfiction books; 80% novels; 15% juvenile books.

   ● Prior to becoming an agent, Ms. Grajkowski worked in both sales and purchasing for a medical facility. She has a degree in journalism from the University of Wisconsin-Madison. Prior to joining the agency in 2006, Ms. Deyoe was a multi-published author. She is excited to be part of the agency and is actively building her client list.

Member Agents Michelle Grajkowski; Cori Deyoe.

Represents Nonfiction books, novels, juvenile books, scholarly books.

   O→ 3 Seas focuses on romance (including category, historical, regency, western, romantic suspense, para-normal), women's fiction, mysteries, nonfiction, young adult and children's stories. No poetry, screen-plays or short stories.

How to Contact For fiction and young adult, query with first 3 chapters, synopsis, bio, SASE. For nonfiction, query with complete proposal, first 3 chapters, word count, bio, SASE. For picture books, query with complete ms. Considers simultaneous queries. Responds in 1 month to queries. Responds in 3 months to partials. Returns materials only with SASE. Obtains most new clients through recommendations from others, conferences.

Recent Sales Sold 75 titles in the last year. *Even Vampires Get the Blues* and *Light My Fire*, by Katie MacAlister (NAL); *Vamps in the City,* by Kerrelyn Sparks (Avon); *Date Me Baby, One More Time* and *Must Love Dragons*, by Stephanie Rowe (Warner); *From the Dark,* by Michelle Hauf (Harlequin Nocturne); *The Runaway Daughter*, by Anna DeStefano; *Calamity Jayne Rides Again,* by Kathleen Bacus (Leisure); *Daddy Daycare*, by Laura Marie Altom (Harlequin American); *Dark Protector*, by Alexis Morgan (Pocket); *Seduced By the Night*, by Robin T. Popp (Warner); *What Happens In Paris*, by Nancy Robards Thompson (Harlequin NEXT). Other clients include Naomi Neale, Brenda Mott, Winnie Griggs, Barbara Jean Hicks, Cathy McDavid, Lisa Mondello, R. Barri Flowers, Dyanne Davis, Catherine Kean, Pat White, Mary Buckham.

Terms Agent receives 15% commission on domestic sales; 20% commission on foreign sales. Offers written contract.

Writers' Conferences RWA National Conference.

● TRIADA U.S. LITERARY AGENCY, INC.

P.O. Box 561, Sewickley PA 15143. (412)401-3376. E-mail: uwe@triadaus.com. Web site: www.triadaus.com. **Contact:** Dr. Uwe Stender. Estab. 2004. Represents 47 clients. 58% of clients are new/unpublished writers. Currently handles: 45 nonfiction books; 45 novels; 12 juvenile books; 3 scholarly books.

Member Agents Paul Hudson (science fiction, fantasy).

Represents Nonfiction books, novels, short story collections, juvenile books, scholarly books. **Considers these nonfiction areas:** Biography/autobiography; business/economics; child guidance/parenting; education; how-to; humor/satire; memoirs; popular culture; self-help/personal improvement; sports. **Considers these fiction areas:** Action/adventure; detective/police/crime; ethnic; fantasy; historical; horror; juvenile; literary; main-stream/contemporary; mystery/suspense; romance; science fiction; sports; thriller; young adult.

O— "We are now focusing on self-help and how-to. Additionally, we specialize in literary novels and suspense. Education, business, popular culture, and narrative nonfiction are other strong suits. Our response time is fairly unique. We recognize that neither we nor the authors have time to waste, so we guarantee a 5-day response time. We usually respond within 24 hours." Actively looking for nonfiction, especially self-help, how-to, and prescriptive nonfiction. De-emphasizing fiction, although great writing will always be considered.

How to Contact E-mail queries preferred; otherwise query with SASE. Considers simultaneous queries. Responds in 1-5 weeks to queries; 2-6 weeks to mss. Returns materials only with SASE. Obtains most new clients through recommendations from others, conferences.

Recent Sales *Unlocking the Secret of Lost*, by Poter/Robson/Lavery (Sourcebooks); *Confessions of Emergency Room Doctors*, by Rocky Lang (Andrew McMeel); *365 Ways to Save Gas*, by Ron Weiers (DK Publishing); *Parenting Beyond Belief*, by Dale McGowan (Amacom); *Yellowstone Drift*, by John Holt (Univ. of Nebraska Press); *Out of the Pocket*, by Tony Moss (Univ. of Nebraska Press); *Lost World*, by Lynnette Porter and David Lavery (Sourcebooks); *Cinderella*, by Michael Lito (Sourcebooks); *Joss Whedon: Wonder Boy*, by David Lavery (IB Tauris).

Terms Agent receives 15% commission on domestic sales; 20% commission on foreign sales. Offers written contract; 30-day notice must be given to terminate contract.

Tips "I comment on all requested manuscripts which I reject."

TRIDENT MEDIA GROUP

41 Madison Ave., 36th Floor, New York NY 10010. E-mail: levine.assistant@tridentmediagroup.com. Web site: www.tridentmediagroup.com. **Contact:** Ellen Levine. Member of AAR.

Member Agents Jenny Bent; Scott Miller; Paul Fedorko; Alex Glass; Melissa Flashman; Eileen Cope.

O— Actively seeking new or established authors in a variety of fiction and nonfiction genres.

How to Contact Query with SASE or via e-mail. Check Web site for more details.

BETH VESEL LITERARY AGENCY

80 Fifth Ave., Suite 1101, New York NY 10011. (212)924-4252. Fax: (212)675-1381. E-mail: mlindley@bvlit.com. **Contact:** Molly Lindley, assistant. Estab. 2003. Represents 65 clients. 10% of clients are new/unpublished writers. Currently handles: 75% nonfiction books; 10% novels; 5% story collections; 10% scholarly books.

• Prior to becoming an agent, Ms. Vesel was a poet and a journalist.

Represents Nonfiction books, novels. **Considers these nonfiction areas:** Biography/autobiography; business/economics; ethnic/cultural interests; health/medicine; how-to; memoirs; photography; psychology; self-help/personal improvement; true crime/investigative; women's issues/studies; cultural criticism. **Considers these fiction areas:** Detective/police/crime; literary.

O— "My specialties include serious nonfiction, psychology, cultural criticism, memoir, and women's issues." Actively seeking cultural criticism, literary psychological thrillers, and sophisticated memoirs. No uninspired psychology or run-of-the-mill first novels.

How to Contact Query with SASE. Considers simultaneous queries. Responds in 2 weeks to queries; 1 month to mss. Returns materials only with SASE. Obtains most new clients through referrals, reading good magazines, contacting professionals with ideas.

Recent Sales Sold 10 titles in the last year. *The Female Thing*, by Laura Kipnis (Pantheon); *The Little Book of Plagarism*, by Richard Posner (Pantheon); *Meet*, by Virginia Vitzthum (Little, Brown). Other clients include Martha Beck, Linda Carroll, Tracy Thompson, Vicki Robin, Paul Raeburn, John Head, Joe Graves.

Terms Agent receives 15% commission on domestic sales; 20% commission on foreign sales. Offers written contract.

Writers' Conferences Squaw Valley Writers Workshop, Iowa Summer Writing Festival.

Tips "Try to find out if you fit on a particular agent's list by looking at his/her books and comparing yours. You can almost always find who represents a book by looking at the acknowledgements."

WADE & DOHERTY LITERARY AGENCY

33 Cormorant Lodge, Thomas Moore St., London E1W 1AU England. (44)(20)7488-4171. Fax: (44)(20)7488-4172. E-mail: rw@rwla.com. Web site: www.rwla.com. **Contact:** Robin Wade. Estab. 2001.

• Prior to opening his agency, Mr. Wade was an author; Ms. Doherty worked as a production assistant, editor and editorial director.

Member Agents Robin Wade, agent; Broo Doherty, agent.

Represents Nonfiction books, novels, juvenile books.

O— "We are young and dynamic and actively seek new writers across the literary spectrum." No poetry, plays or short stories.

How to Contact Submit synopsis (1-6 pages), bio, first 10,000 words via e-mail (Word or PDF documents only). If sending by post, include SASE or IRC. Responds in 1 week to queries; 1 month to mss.

Recent Sales *The Solitude of Thomas Cave*, by Georgina Harding; *The Hunt for Atlantis*, by Andy McDermott; *The Opposite House*, by Helen Oyeyemi; *A Tangled Summer*, by Caroline Kington; *The Truth Will Out: Unmasking the Real Shakespeare*, by Brenda James.

Terms Agent receives 10% commission on domestic sales; 20% commission on foreign sales. Offers written contract; 1-month notice must be given to terminate contract.

Tips "We seek manuscripts that are well written, with strong characters and an original narrative voice. Our absolute priority is giving the best possible service to the authors we choose to represent, as well as maintaining routine friendly contact with them as we help develop their careers."

◧ WALES LITERARY AGENCY, INC.

P.O. Box 9428, Seattle WA 98109-0428. (206)284-7114. E-mail: waleslit@waleslit.com. Web site: www.waleslit. com. **Contact:** Elizabeth Wales, Josie di Bernardo. Estab. 1988. Member of AAR, Book Publishers' Northwest, Pacific Northwest Booksellers Association, PEN. Represents 65 clients. 10% of clients are new/unpublished writers. Currently handles: 60% nonfiction books; 40% novels.

- Prior to becoming an agent, Ms. Wales worked at Oxford University Press and Viking Penguin.

Member Agents Elizabeth Wales; Neal Swain.

➤ This agency specializes in narrative nonfiction and quality mainstream and literary fiction. Does not handle screenplays, children's literature, genre fiction, or most category nonfiction.

How to Contact Query with cover letter, writing sample (about 30 pages), SASE. No phone or fax queries. Prefers regular mail queries, but accepts 1-page e-mail queries with no attachments. Considers simultaneous queries. Responds in 3 weeks to queries; 6 weeks to mss. Returns materials only with SASE.

Recent Sales *Fashion Statements*, edited by Michelle Tea (Seal Press/Avalon); *The Mom and Pop Store: Minding the American Dream*, by Robert Specter (Walker Books); *The Million Dollar Chicken: How I Won the Grand Prize at the Pillsbury Bake-Off*, by Ellie Mathews (Berkley/Penguin).

Terms Agent receives 15% commission on domestic sales; 20% commission on foreign sales.

Writers' Conferences Pacific Northwest Writers Conference; Willamette Writers Conference.

Tips "We are especially interested in work that espouses a progressive cultural or political view, projects a new voice, or simply shares an important, compelling story. We also encourage writers living in the Pacific Northwest, West Coast, Alaska, and Pacific Rim countries, and writers from historically underrepresented groups, such as gay and lesbian writers and writers of color, to submit work (but does not discourage writers outside these areas). Most importantly, whether in fiction or nonfiction, the agency is looking for talented storytellers."

◧ JOHN A. WARE LITERARY AGENCY

392 Central Park W., New York NY 10025-5801. (212)866-4733. Fax: (212)866-4734. **Contact:** John Ware. Estab. 1978. Represents 60 clients. 40% of clients are new/unpublished writers. Currently handles: 75% nonfiction books; 25% novels.

- Prior to opening his agency, Mr. Ware served as a literary agent with James Brown Associates/Curtis Brown, Ltd., and as an editor for Doubleday & Co.

Represents Nonfiction books, novels. **Considers these nonfiction areas:** Anthropology/archaeology; biography/autobiography; current affairs; health/medicine (academic credentials required); history (oral history, Americana, folklore); language/literature/criticism; music/dance; nature/environment; popular culture; psychology (academic credentials required); science/technology; sports; true crime/investigative; women's issues/studies; social commentary; investigative journalism; bird's eye views of phenomena. **Considers these fiction areas:** Detective/police/crime; mystery/suspense; thriller; accessible literary noncategory fiction.

➤ Does not want personal memoirs.

How to Contact Query with SASE. Send a letter only. No e-mail or fax queries. Considers simultaneous queries. Responds in 2 weeks to queries.

Recent Sales Untitled on Afghanistan, by Jon Krakauer (Doubleday); *High School*, by Jennifer Niven (Simon Spotlight Entertainment); *The Man Who Made the Blues: A Biography of W.C. Handy*, by David Robertson (Knopf); *Abundance of Valor*, by Will Irwin (Presidio); *Ledyard*, by Bill Gifford (Harcourt); *The Star Garden*, by Nancy E. Turner (Thomas Dunne/St. Martin's); *Sunday*, by Craig Harline (Doubleday); *The Family Business: The Story of Tabasco*, by Jeff Rothfeder (HarperBusiness); *Hawking the Empire*, by Tim Shorrock (Simon & Schuster); *The Jedburghs*, by Will Irwin (PublicAffairs).

Terms Agent receives 15% commission on domestic sales; 20% commission on foreign sales; 15% commission on dramatic rights sales. Charges clients for messenger service and photocopying.

Tips "Writers must have appropriate credentials for authorship of proposal (nonfiction) or manuscript (fiction); no publishing track record required. I am open to good writing and interesting ideas by new or veteran writers."

◖ WATKINS LOOMIS AGENCY, INC.

133 E. 35th St., Suite 1, New York NY 10016. (212)532-0080. Fax: (212)889-0506. **Contact:** Jacqueline S. Hackett. Estab. 1908. Represents 150 clients.
Member Agents Gloria Loomis, president; Jacqueline S. Hackett, agent.
Represents Nonfiction books, novels, short story collections. **Considers these nonfiction areas:** Art/architecture/design; biography/autobiography; current affairs; ethnic/cultural interests; history; nature/environment; popular culture; science/technology; investigative journalism. **Considers these fiction areas:** Literary.
   O—₮ This agency specializes in literary fiction and nonfiction.
How to Contact *No unsolicited mss.*
Recent Sales This agency prefers not to share information on specific sales. Clients include Walter Mosley and Cornel West.
Terms Agent receives 15% commission on domestic sales; 20% commission on foreign sales.

◖ WAXMAN LITERARY AGENCY, INC.

80 Fifth Ave., Suite 1101, New York NY 10011. Web site: www.waxmanagency.com. **Contact:** Scott Waxman. Estab. 1997. Represents 60 clients. 50% of clients are new/unpublished writers. Currently handles: 80% nonfiction books; 20% novels.
   • Prior to opening his agency, Mr. Waxman was an editor at HarperCollins.
Member Agents Scott Waxman (all categories of nonfiction, commercial fiction); Byrd Leavell; Farley Chase.
Represents Nonfiction books, novels. **Considers these nonfiction areas:** Narrative nonfiction. **Considers these fiction areas:** Literary.
   O—₮ "We're looking for serious journalists and novelists with published works."
How to Contact All unsolicited mss returned unopened. Query through Web site. Considers simultaneous queries. Responds in 2 weeks to queries; 6 weeks to mss. Returns materials only with SASE. Obtains most new clients through recommendations from others, solicitations, conferences.
Recent Sales *Grip It and Sip It*, by John Daly (Harper); *That First Season*, by John Eisenberg (Houghton Mifflin); *The Fighting 69th: The Remarkable Journey of New York's Weekend Warriors From Ground Zero to Baghdad*, by Sean Michael Flynn (Viking Penguin).
Terms Agent receives 15% commission on domestic sales; 25% commission on foreign sales. Offers written contract; 2-month notice must be given to terminate contract.

◖ CHERRY WEINER LITERARY AGENCY

28 Kipling Way, Manalapan NJ 07726-3711. (732)446-2096. Fax: (732)792-0506. E-mail: cherry8486@aol.com. **Contact:** Cherry Weiner. Estab. 1977. Represents 40 clients. 10% of clients are new/unpublished writers. Currently handles: 10-20% nonfiction books; 80-90% novels.
Represents Nonfiction books, novels. **Considers these nonfiction areas:** Self-help/personal improvement. **Considers these fiction areas:** Action/adventure; contemporary issues; detective/police/crime; family saga; fantasy; historical; mainstream/contemporary; mystery/suspense; psychic/supernatural; romance; science fiction; thriller; westerns/frontier.
   O—₮ This agency is currently not accepting new clients except by referral or by personal contact at writers' conferences. Specializes in fantasy, science fiction, westerns, mysteries (both contemporary and historical), historical novels, Native-American works, mainstream and all genre romances.
How to Contact Query with SASE. Prefers to read materials exclusively. No fax queries. Responds in 1 week to queries; 2 months to mss. Returns materials only with SASE.
Recent Sales Sold 75 titles in the last year. This agency prefers not to share information on specific sales.
Terms Agent receives 15% commission on domestic sales; 15% commission on foreign sales. Offers written contract. Charges clients for extra copies of mss, first-class postage for author's copies of books, express mail for important documents/mss.
Tips "Meet agents and publishers at conferences. Establish a relationship, then get in touch with them and remind them of the meeting and conference."

◖ THE WEINGEL-FIDEL AGENCY

310 E. 46th St., 21E, New York NY 10017. (212)599-2959. **Contact:** Loretta Weingel-Fidel. Estab. 1989. Currently handles: 75% nonfiction books; 25% novels.
   • Prior to opening her agency, Ms. Weingel-Fidel was a psychoeducational diagnostician.
Represents Nonfiction books, novels. **Considers these nonfiction areas:** Art/architecture/design; biography/autobiography; memoirs; music/dance; psychology; science/technology; sociology; women's issues/studies; investigative journalism. **Considers these fiction areas:** Literary; mainstream/contemporary.
   O—₮ This agency specializes in commercial and literary fiction and nonfiction. Actively seeking investigative journalism. Does not want to receive genre fiction, self-help, science fiction, or fantasy.

How to Contact Accepts writers by referral only. *No unsolicited mss.*

Terms Agent receives 15% commission on domestic sales; 20% commission on foreign sales. Offers written contract, binding for 1 year with automatic renewal. Bills sent back to clients are all reasonable expenses, such as UPS, express mail, photocopying, etc.

Tips "A very small, selective list enables me to work very closely with my clients to develop and nurture talent. I only take on projects and writers about which I am extremely enthusiastic."

WINSUN LITERARY AGENCY

3706 NE Shady Lane Dr., Gladstone MO 64119. Phone/Fax: (816)459-8016. E-mail: mlittleton@earthlink.net. Estab. 2004. Represents 20 clients. 50% of clients are new/unpublished writers. Currently handles: 75% nonfiction books; 20% novels; 5% juvenile books.

- Prior to becoming an agent, Mr. Littleton was a writer and a speaker.

Represents Nonfiction books, novels, juvenile books. **Considers these nonfiction areas:** Biography/autobiography; child guidance/parenting; current affairs; how-to; humor/satire; memoirs; religious/inspirational; self-help/personal improvement. **Considers these fiction areas:** Action/adventure; detective/police/crime; family saga; humor/satire; juvenile; literary; mainstream/contemporary; mystery/suspense; picture books; psychic/supernatural; religious/inspirational; romance; thriller.

O┐ "We mainly serve Christian clients in the CBA."

How to Contact Query with SASE. E-queries accepted. Considers simultaneous queries. Responds in 6 weeks to queries; 3 months to mss. Returns materials only with SASE. Obtains most new clients through recommendations from others, conferences.

Recent Sales Sold 8 titles in the last year. Sold several titles in 2006 to Howard Publishing, Adams Media, Jordan House, Bethany House and others.

Terms Agent receives 15% commission on domestic sales; 20% commission on foreign sales. Offers written contract, binding for 1 year; 30-day notice must be given to terminate contract.

WORDSERVE LITERARY GROUP

10152 S. Knoll Circle, Highlands Ranch CO 80130. (303)471-6675. Web site: www.wordserveliterary.com. **Contact:** Greg Johnson. Estab. 2003. Represents 30 clients. 25% of clients are new/unpublished writers. Currently handles: 30% nonfiction books; 40% novels; 10% story collections; 5% novellas; 10% juvenile books; 5% multimedia.

- Prior to becoming an agent in 1994, Mr. Johnson was a magazine editor and freelance writer of more than 20 books and 200 articles.

Represents Primarily religious books in these categories: nonfiction, fiction, short story collections, novellas. **Considers these nonfiction areas:** Biography/autobiography; child guidance/parenting; memoirs; religious/inspirational.

O┐ Materials with a faith-based angle.

How to Contact Query with SASE, proposal package, outline, 2-3 sample chapters. Considers simultaneous queries. Responds in 1 week to queries; 2 months to mss. Returns materials only with SASE. Obtains most new clients through recommendations from others.

Recent Sales Sold 1,300 titles in the last 10 years. Redemption series, by Karen Kingsbury (Tyndale); *Loving God Up Close*, by Calvin Miller (Warner Faith); *Christmas in My Heart*, by Joe Wheeler (Tyndale). Other clients include Steve Arterburn, Wanda Dyson, Catherine Martin, David Murrow, Leslie Haskin, Gilbert Morris, Calvin Miller, Robert Wise, Jim Burns, Wayne Cordeiro, Denise George, Susie Shellenberger, Tim Smith, Joe Wheeler, Athol Dickson, Bob DeMoss, Patty Kirk, John Shore.

Terms Agent receives 15% commission on domestic sales; 10-15% commission on foreign sales. Offers written contract; up to 60-day notice must be given to terminate contract.

Tips "We are looking for good proposals, great writing, and authors willing to market their books as appropriate. Also, we're only looking for projects with a faith element bent. See the Web site before submitting."

WRITERS HOUSE

21 W. 26th St., New York NY 10010. (212)685-2400. Fax: (212)685-1781. Web site: www.writershouse.com. Estab. 1974. Member of AAR. Represents 440 clients. 50% of clients are new/unpublished writers. Currently handles: 25% nonfiction books; 40% novels; 35% juvenile books.

Member Agents Albert Zuckerman (major novels, thrillers, women's fiction, important nonfiction); Amy Berkower (major juvenile authors, women's fiction, art/decorating, psychology); Merrilee Heifetz (quality children's fiction, science fiction/fantasy, popular culture, literary fiction); Susan Cohen (juvenile/young adult fiction and nonfiction, Judaism, women's issues); Susan Ginsburg (serious and popular fiction, true crime, narrative nonfiction, personality books, cookbooks); Michele Rubin (serious nonfiction); Robin Rue (commercial fiction and nonfiction, young adult fiction); Jodi Reamer (juvenile/young adult fiction and nonfiction, adult commercial fiction, popular culture); Simon Lipskar (literary and commercial fiction, narrative nonfiction); Steven Malk (juvenile/young adult fiction and nonfiction); Dan Lazar (commercial and literary fiction, pop culture, narrative nonfiction, women's interest, memoirs, Judaica and humor); Rebecca Sherman (juvenile, young adult); Ken Wright (juvenile, young adult).

Represents Nonfiction books, novels, juvenile books. **Considers these nonfiction areas:** Animals; art/architecture/design; biography/autobiography; business/economics; child guidance/parenting; cooking/foods/nutrition; health/medicine; history; humor/satire; interior design/decorating; juvenile nonfiction; military/war; money/finance; music/dance; nature/environment; psychology; science/technology; self-help/personal improvement; theater/film; true crime/investigative; women's issues/studies. **Considers these fiction areas:** Action/adventure; contemporary issues; detective/police/crime; erotica; ethnic; family saga; fantasy; feminist; gay/lesbian; gothic; hi-lo; historical; horror; humor/satire; juvenile; literary; mainstream/contemporary; military/war; multicultural; mystery/suspense; New Age; occult; picture books; psychic/supernatural; regional; romance; science fiction; short story collections; spiritual; sports; thriller; translation; westerns/frontier; young adult; women's; cartoon.

> O→ This agency specializes in all types of popular fiction and nonfiction. Does not want to receive scholarly or professional text, poetry, plays, or screenplays.

How to Contact Query with SASE. No e-mail or fax queries. Responds in 1 month to queries. Obtains most new clients through recommendations from authors and editors.

Recent Sales Sold 200-300 titles in the last year. *Moneyball*, by Michael Lewis (Norton); *Cut and Run*, by Ridley Pearson (Hyperion); *Report from Ground Zero*, by Dennis Smith (Viking); *Northern Lights*, by Nora Roberts (Penguin/Putnam); Captain Underpants series, by Dav Pilkey (Scholastic); Junie B. Jones series, by Barbara Park (Random House). Other clients include Francine Pascal, Ken Follett, Stephen Hawking, Linda Howard, F. Paul Wilson, Neil Gaiman, Laurel Hamilton, V.C. Andrews, Lisa Jackson, Michael Gruber, Chris Paolini, Barbara Delinsky, Ann Martin, Bradley Trevor Greive, Erica Jong, Kyle Mills, Andrew Guess, Tim Willocks.

Terms Agent receives 15% commission on domestic sales; 20% commission on foreign sales. Offers written contract, binding for 1 year. Agency charges fees for copying mss/proposals and overseas airmail of books.

Tips "Do not send manuscripts. Write a compelling letter. If you do, we'll ask to see your work."

⬤ ZACHARY SHUSTER HARMSWORTH

1776 Broadway, Suite 1405, New York NY 10019. (212)765-6900. Fax: (212)765-6490. E-mail: kfleury@zshlitera ry.com; reception@zshliterary.com. Web site: www.zshliterary.com. Alternate address: 535 Boylston St., 11th Floor. (617)262-2400. Fax: (617)262-2468. **Contact:** Kathleen Fleury. Estab. 1996. Represents 125 clients. 20% of clients are new/unpublished writers. Currently handles: 45% nonfiction books; 45% novels; 5% story collections; 5% scholarly books.

> • "Our principals include two former publishing and entertainment lawyers, a journalist, and an editor/agent."

Member Agents Esmond Harmsworth (commercial mysteries, literary fiction, history, science, adventure, business); Todd Shuster (narrative and prescriptive nonfiction, biography, memoirs); Lane Zachary (biography, memoirs, literary fiction); Jennifer Gates (literary fiction, nonfiction).

Represents Nonfiction books, novels. **Considers these nonfiction areas:** Animals; biography/autobiography; business/economics; current affairs; gay/lesbian issues; government/politics/law; health/medicine; history; how-to; language/literature/criticism; memoirs; money/finance; music/dance; psychology; science/technology; self-help/personal improvement; sports; true crime/investigative; women's issues/studies. **Considers these fiction areas:** Detective/police/crime; ethnic; feminist; gay/lesbian; historical; literary; mainstream/contemporary; mystery/suspense; thriller.

> O→ This agency specializes in journalist-driven narrative nonfiction and literary and commercial fiction. No poetry.

How to Contact Query with SASE. *No unsolicited manuscripts.* No e-mail or fax queries. Obtains most new clients through recommendations from others.

Recent Sales *Can You Tell a Sunni from a Shiite?*, by Jeff Stein; *Christmas Hope*, by Donna Van Liere; *Female Chauvinist Pigs*, by Ariel Levy; *War Trash*, by Ha Jin; *Women Who Think Too Much*, by Susan Nolen-Hoeksema, PhD; *The Red Carpet*, by Lavanya Sankaran; *Grapevine*, by David Balter and John Butman.

Terms Agent receives 15% commission on domestic sales; 20% commission on foreign sales. Offers written contract, binding for 1 work only; 30-day notice must be given to terminate contract. Charges clients for postage, copying, courier, telephone. "We only charge expenses if the manuscript is sold."

Tips "We work closely with all our clients on all editorial and promotional aspects of their works."

🅐 SUSAN ZECKENDORF ASSOC., INC.

171 W. 57th St., New York NY 10019. (212)245-2928. **Contact:** Susan Zeckendorf. Estab. 1979. Member of AAR. Represents 15 clients. 25% of clients are new/unpublished writers. Currently handles: 50% nonfiction books; 50% novels.

● Prior to opening her agency, Ms. Zeckendorf was a counseling psychologist.

Represents Nonfiction books, novels. **Considers these nonfiction areas:** Biography/autobiography; child guidance/parenting; health/medicine; history; music/dance; psychology; science/technology; sociology; women's issues/studies. **Considers these fiction areas:** Detective/police/crime; ethnic; historical; literary; mainstream/contemporary; mystery/suspense; thriller.

○┓ Actively seeking mysteries, literary fiction, mainstream fiction, thrillers, social history, parenting, classical music, and biography. Does not want to receive science fiction, romance, or children's books.

How to Contact Query with SASE. No e-mail or fax queries. Considers simultaneous queries. Responds in 10 days to queries; 3 weeks to mss. Returns materials only with SASE.

Recent Sales *How to Write a Damn Good Mystery*, by James N. Frey (St. Martin's Press); *The Hardscrabble Chronicles*, by Laurie Bogart Morrow (Berkley); *Haunted Heart: A Biography of Susannah McCorkle*, by Linda Dahl (University of Michigan Press); *Garden of Aloes*, by Gayle Jandrey (Permanent Press).

Terms Agent receives 15% commission on domestic sales; 20% commission on foreign sales. Charges for photocopying and messenger services.

Writers' Conferences Frontiers in Writing Conference; Oklahoma Festival of Books.

Tips "We are a small agency giving lots of individual attention. We respond quickly to submissions."

Literary Magazines

This section contains markets for your literary short fiction. Although definitions of what constitutes "literary" writing vary, editors of literary journals agree they want to publish the best fiction they can acquire. Qualities they look for in fiction include fully developed characters, strong and unique narrative voice, flawless mechanics, and careful attention to detail in content and manuscript preparation. Most of the authors writing such fiction are well read and well educated, and many are students and graduates of university creative writing programs.

Please also review our Online Markets section, page 325, for electronic literary magazines. At a time when paper and publishing costs rise while funding to small and university presses continues to be cut or eliminated, electronic literary magazines are helping generate a publishing renaissance for experimental as well as more traditional literary fiction. These electronic outlets for literary fiction also benefit writers by eliminating copying and postage costs and providing the opportunity for much quicker responses to submissions. Also notice that some magazines with Web sites give specific information about what they offer online, including updated writer's guidelines and sample fiction from their publications.

STEPPING STONES TO RECOGNITION

Some well-established literary journals pay several hundred or even several thousand dollars for a short story. Most, though, can only pay with contributor's copies or a subscription to their publication. However, being published in literary journals offers the important benefits of experience, exposure and prestige. Agents and major book publishers regularly read literary magazines in search of new writers. Work from these journals is also selected for inclusion in annual prize anthologies. (See next page for a list of anthologies.)

You'll find most of the well-known prestigious literary journals listed here. Many, including *The Southern Review* and *Ploughshares*, are associated with universities, while others like *The Paris Review* are independently published.

SELECTING THE RIGHT LITERARY JOURNAL

Once you have browsed through this section and have a list of journals you might like to submit to, read those listings again carefully. Remember this is information editors provide to help you submit work that fits their needs. You've Got a Story, starting on page 2, will guide you through the process of finding markets for your fiction.

Note that you will find some magazines that do not read submissions all year long. Whether limited reading periods are tied to a university schedule or meant to accommodate the capabilities of a very small staff, those periods are noted within listings (when the editors notify us). The staffs of university journals are usually made up of student editors and a managing editor who is also a faculty member. These staffs often change every year. Whenever possible, we indicate this in listings and give the name of the current editor and the length of that editor's term. Also be aware that the schedule of a university journal usually coincides with that university's academic year, meaning that the editors of most university publications are difficult or impossible to reach during the summer.

FURTHERING YOUR SEARCH

It cannot be stressed enough that reading the listings for literary journals is only the first part of developing your marketing plan. The second part, equally important, is to obtain fiction guidelines and to read with great care the actual journal you'd like to submit to. Reading copies of these journals helps you determine the fine points of each magazine's publishing style and sensibility. There is no substitute for this type of hands-on research.

Unlike commercial periodicals available at most newsstands and bookstores, it requires a little more effort to obtain some of the magazines listed here. The super-chain bookstores are doing a better job these days of stocking literaries, and you can find some in independent and college bookstores, especially those published in your area. The Internet is an invaluable resource for submission guidelines, as more and more journals establish an online presence. You may, however, need to send for a sample copy. We include sample copy prices in the listings whenever possible. In addition to reading your sample copies, pay close attention to the **Advice** section of each listing. There you'll often find a very specific description of the style of fiction the editors at that publication prefer.

Another way to find out more about literary magazines is to check out the various prize anthologies and take note of journals whose fiction is being selected for publication in them. Studying prize anthologies not only lets you know which magazines are publishing award-winning work, but it also provides a valuable overview of what is considered to be the best fiction published today. Those anthologies include:

- *Best American Short Stories*, published by Houghton Mifflin.
- *New Stories from the South: The Year's Best*, published by Algonquin Books of Chapel Hill.
- *The O. Henry Prize Stories*, published by Doubleday/Anchor.
- *Pushcart Prize: Best of the Small Presses*, published by Pushcart Press.

At the beginnings of listings, we include symbols to help you narrow your search. Keys to those symbols can be found on the inside covers of this book.

$⊘ AFRICAN AMERICAN REVIEW

Saint Louis University, Humanities 317, 3800 Lindell Boulevard, St. Louis MO 63108-3414. (314)977-3688. Fax: (314)977-1514. E-mail: keenanam@slu.edu. Web site: aar.slu.edu. **Contact:** Joycelyn Moody, editor; Aileen Keenan, managing editor. Magazine: 7×10; 200 pages; 55 lb., acid-free paper; 100 lb. skid stock cover; illustrations; photos. "Essays on African-American literature, theater, film, art and culture generally; interviews; poetry and fiction by African-American authors; book reviews." Quarterly. Estab. 1967. Circ. 2,067.

- *African American Review* is the official publication of the Division of Black American Literature and Culture of the Modern Language Association. The magazine received American Literary Magazine Awards in 1994 and 1995.

Needs Ethnic/multicultural, experimental, feminist, literary, mainstream. "No children's/juvenile/young adult/teen." Receives 15 unsolicited mss/month. Accepts 16 mss/year. Publishes ms 1 year after acceptance. Agented fiction 10%. Recently published work by Solon Timothy Woodward, Eugenia Collier, Jeffery Renard Allen, Patrick Lohier, Raki Jones, Olympia Vernon. Length: 2,500-5,000 words; average length: 3,000 words. Also publishes literary essays, literary criticism, poetry. Sometimes comments on rejected mss.

How to Contact Responds in 1 week to queries; 3 months to mss. Sample copy for $12. Writer's guidelines online. Reviews fiction.

Payment/Terms Pays $25-100, 1 contributor's copy and 5 offprints. Pays on publication for first North American serial rights. Sends galleys to author.

$⊘ ▣ AGNI

Boston University, 236 Bay State Rd., Boston MA 02215. (617)353-7135. Fax: (617)353-7134. E-mail: agni@bu.edu. Web site: www.agnimagazine.org. **Contact:** Sven Birkerts, editor. Magazine: 5³/₈×8¹/₂; 240 pages; 55 lb. booktext paper; art portfolios. "Eclectic literary magazine publishing first-rate poems, essays, translations and stories." Biannual. Estab. 1972. Circ. 4,000.

- Founding editor Askold Melnyczuk won the 2001 Nora Magid Award for Magazine Editing. Work from *AGNI* has been included and cited regularly in the *Pushcart Prize* and *Best American* anthologies.

Needs Translations, stories, prose poems. "No science fiction or romance." Receives 500 unsolicited mss/month. Accepts 3-5 mss/issue; 6-10 mss/year. Reading period September 1 through May 31 only. Publishes ms 6 months after acceptance. **Publishes 30 new writers/year.** Recently published work by Rikki Ducornet, Phong Nguyen, Jack Pulaski, David Foster Wallace, Lise Haines, Gania Barlow and Nicholas Montemarano.

How to Contact Responds in 2 weeks to queries; 4 months to mss. Accepts simultaneous submissions. Sample copy for $10 or online. Writer's guidelines for #10 SASE or online.

Payment/Terms Pays $10/page up to $150, 2 contributor's copies, 1-year subscription, and 4 gift copies. Pays on publication for first North American serial rights, rights to reprint in *AGNI* anthology (with author's consent). Sends galleys to author.

Advice "Read *AGNI* and other literary magazines carefully to understand the kinds of stories we do and do not publish. It's also important for artists to support the arts."

⊘ THE AGUILAR EXPRESSION

1329 Gilmore Ave., Donora PA 15033-2228. (724)379-8019. E-mail: xyz0@access995.com. Web site: www.wordrunner.com/xfaguilar. **Contact:** Xavier F. Aguilar, editor. Magazine: 8¹/₂×11; 4-20 pages; 20 lb. bond paper; illustrations. "We are open to all writers of a general theme—something that may appeal to everyone." Publishes in October. Estab. 1986. Circ. 300.

Needs Adventure, ethnic/multicultural, experimental, horror, mainstream, mystery/suspense (romantic suspense), romance (contemporary). "No religious or erotic stories. Want more current social issues." Receives 15 unsolicited mss/month. Accepts 1-2 mss/year. Reading period: January, February, March. Publishes ms 1 month to 1 year after acceptance. **Publishes 2-4 new writers/year.** Recently published work by Ken Bennet. Length: 250-1,000 words; average length: 1,000 words. Also publishes poetry.

How to Contact Send a disposable copy of ms with SASE for reply. "We do not return any manuscripts and discard rejected works. If we decide to publish, we contact within 30 days." Responds in 1 month to mss. No simultaneous submissions. Sample copy for $8. Guidelines for first-class stamp.

Payment/Terms Pays 2 contributor's copies for lead story; additional copies at a reduced rate of $3. Acquires one-time rights. Not copyrighted.

Advice "We would like to see more social issues worked into fiction."

$⊘ ALASKA QUARTERLY REVIEW

ESB 208, University of Alaska-Anchorage, 3211 Providence Dr., Anchorage AK 99508. (907)786-6916. E-mail: ayaqr@uaa.alaska.edu. Web site: www.uaa.alaska.edu/aqr. **Contact:** Ronald Spatz, fiction editor. Magazine: 6×9; 232-300 pages; 60 lb. Glatfelter paper; 12 pt. C15 black ink or 4-color; varnish cover stock; photos on cover and photo essays. *AQR* "publishes fiction, poetry, literary nonfiction and short plays in traditional and experimental styles." Semiannual. Estab. 1982. Circ. 3,500.

• Two stories selected for inclusion in the 2004 edition of *The O'Henry Prize Stories*.

Needs Experimental, literary, translations, contemporary, prose poem. "If the works in *Alaska Quarterly Review* have certain characteristics, they are these: freshness, honesty and a compelling subject. What makes a piece stand out from the multitude of other submissions? The voice of the piece must be strong—idiosyncratic enough to create a unique persona. We look for the demonstration of craft, making the situation palpable and putting it in a form where it becomes emotionally and intellectually complex. One could look through our pages over time and see that many of the pieces published in the *Alaska Quarterly Review* concern everyday life. We're not asking our writers to go outside themselves and their experiences to the absolute exotic to catch our interest. We look for the experiential and revelatory qualities of the work. We will, without hesitation, champion a piece that may be less polished or stylistically sophisticated, if it engages me, surprises me, and resonates for me. The joy in reading such a work is in discovering something true. Moreover, in keeping with our mission to publish new writers, we are looking for voices our readers do not know, voices that may not always be reflected in the dominant culture and that, in all instances, have something important to convey." Receives 200 unsolicited mss/month. Accepts 7-18 mss/issue; 15-30 mss/year. Does not read mss May 10-August 25. Publishes ms 6 months after acceptance. **Publishes 6 new writers/year.** Recently published work by Howard Norman, Douglas Light, Courtney Angela Brkic, Alison Baker, Lindsay Fitz-Gerald, John Fulton, Ann Stapleton, Edith Pearlman. Publishes short shorts.

How to Contact Responds in 4 months to queries; 4 months to mss. Simultaneous submissions "undesirable, but will accept if indicated." Sample copy for $6. Writer's guidelines online.

Payment/Terms Pays $50-200 subject to funding; pays in contributor's copies and subscriptions when funding is limited. Honorariums on publication when funding permits. Acquires first North American serial rights. Upon request, rights will be transferred back to author after publication.

Advice "Professionalism, patience and persistence are essential. One needs to do one's homework and know the market. The competition is very intense, and funding for the front-line journals is generally inadequate, so staffing is low. It takes time to get a response, and rejections are a fact of life. It is important not to take the rejections personally, and also to know that editors make decisions for better or worse, and they make mistakes too. Fortunately there are many gatekeepers. *Alaska Quarterly Review* has published many pieces that had been turned down by other journals—including pieces that then went on to win national awards. We also know of instances in which pieces *Alaska Quarterly Review* rejected later appeared in other magazines. We haven't regretted that we didn't take those pieces. Rather, we're happy that the authors have made a good match. Disappointment should *never* stop anyone. Will counts as much as talent, and new writers need to have confidence in themselves and stick to it."

☑ ◎ ALIMENTUM, The Literature of Food

P.O. Box 776, New York NY 10163. E-mail: submissions@alimentumjournal.com. Web site: www.alimentumjournal.com. **Contact:** Submissions editor. Literary magazine/journal: 6×7½, 128 pages, matte cover. Contains illustrations. "All of our stories, poems and essays have food as a theme." Semiannual. Estab. 2005.

Needs Literary. Special interests: food related. Receives 100 mss/month. Accepts 20-24 mss/issue. Manuscript published one to two years after acceptance. **Publishes average of 2 new writers/year.** Published Mark Kurlansky, Oliver Sacks, Dick Allen, Ann Hood, Carly Sachs. Length: 4,500 words (max). Average length: 2,000-3,000 words. Publishes short shorts. Also publishes literary essays, poetry, spot illustrations. Rarely comments on/critiques rejected manuscripts.

How to Contact Send complete ms with cover letter. Snail mail only. No previously published work. 5-poem limit per submission. Simultaneous submissions okay." Responds to queries in 1-3 months. Responds to mss in 1-3 months. Send either SASE (or IRC) for return of ms or disposable copy of ms and #10 SASE for reply only. Sample copy available for $10. Guidelines available on Web site.

Payment and Terms Writers receive 1 contributor's copy. Additional contributor's copies $8. Pays on publication. Acquires first North American serial rights. Publication is copyrighted.

Advice "Write a good story, no clichés, attention to style, strong voice, memorable characters and scenes."

☑ ◎ THE ALLEGHENY REVIEW, A National Journal of Undergraduate Literature

Box 32 Allegheny College, Meadville PA 16335. E-mail: review@allegheny.edu. Web site: http://review.allegheny.edu. **Contact:** Senior editor. Magazine: 6×9; 100 pages; illustrations; photos. "*The Allegheny Review* is one of America's only nationwide literary magazines exclusively for undergraduate works of poetry, fiction and nonfiction. Our intended audience is persons interested in quality literature." Annual. Estab. 1983.

Needs Adventure, ethnic/multicultural, experimental, family saga, fantasy, feminist, gay, historical, horror, humor/satire, lesbian, literary, mainstream, military/war, mystery/suspense, New Age, psychic/supernatural/occult, religious/inspirational (general), romance, science fiction, western. "We accept nothing but fiction by currently enrolled undergraduate students. We consider anything catering to an intellectual audience." Receives 50 unsolicited mss/month. Accepts 3 mss/issue. Publishes ms 2 months after deadline. **Publishes roughly 90% new writers/year.** Recently published work by Dianne Page, Monica Stahl and DJ Kinney. Publishes short shorts. Also publishes literary essays, literary criticism, poetry. Sometimes comments on rejected mss.

How to Contact Send complete mss with a cover letter. Accepts submissions on disk. Responds in 2 weeks to queries; 4 months to mss. Send disposable copy of ms and #10 SASE for reply only. Sample copy for $4. Writer's guidelines for SASE, by e-mail or on Web site.

Payment/Terms Pays 1 contributor's copy; additional copies $3. Sponsors awards/contests.

Advice "We look for quality work that has been thoroughly revised. Unique voice, interesting topic and playfulness with the English language. Revise, revise, revise! And be careful how you send it—the cover letter says a lot. We definitely look for diversity in the pieces we publish."

☐ THE AMERICAN DRIVEL REVIEW, A Unified Field Theory of Wit

3561 SE Cora Drive, Portland OR 97202. (720)494-8719. E-mail: info@americandrivelreview.com. Web site: www.americandrivelreview.com. **Contact:** Tara Blaine and David Wester, editors. Magazine: 6×9; 90-100 pages; black and white illustrations and photos. *The American Drivel Review* is a journal of literary humor dedicated to formulating a Unified Field Theory of Wit. Estab. 2004. Circ. 200.

Needs "We are delighted to consider any categories, styles, forms or genres—real or imagined. We are interested in quality humorous writing in every conceivable form." Receives 75-100 unsolicited mss/month. Accepts 20-30 mss/issue; 60-80 mss/year. Publishes ms 2 months after acceptance. **Publishes 10-15 new writers/year.** Recently published work by Willie Smith, Laird Hunt, Matthew Summers-Sparks, Jack Collom, Richard Froude, Guy R. Beining, and Larry Fagin. Publishes short shorts. Also publishes literary essays, literary criticism, poetry.

How to Contact Send complete ms. Accepts submissions by e-mail, disk. Send SASE for return of ms. Responds in 2-3 months to queries. Accepts multiple submissions. No simultaneous submissions. Sample copy for $4.50. Writer's guidelines for #10 SASE, online or by e-mail.

Payment/Terms Pays 2 contributor's copies. Pays on publication for one-time rights.

Advice "We look primarily for sublime, funny, brilliant writing and a unique or experimental voice."

◪ AMERICAN LITERARY REVIEW

University of North Texas, P.O. Box 311307, Denton TX 76203-1307. (940)565-2755. Fax: (940)565-4355. E-mail: americanliteraryreview@gmail.com. Web site: www.engl.unt.edu/alr/. **Contact:** Ann McCutchan, prose editor. Magazine: 6×9; 128 pages; 70 lb. Mohawk paper; 67 lb. Wausau Vellum cover. "Publishes quality, contemporary poems and stories." Semiannual. Estab. 1990. Circ. 1,200.

Needs Literary, mainstream. "No genre works." Receives 150-200 unsolicited mss/month. Accepts 5-6 mss/issue; 12-16 mss/year. Reading period: October 1-May 1. Publishes ms within 2 years after acceptance. Recently published work by Dana Johnson, Bill Roorbach, Cynthia Shearer, Mark Jacobs and Sylvia Wantanabe. Also publishes literary essays, poetry. Critiques or comments on rejected mss.

How to Contact Send complete ms with cover letter. Responds in 2-4 months to mss. Accepts simultaneous submissions. Sample copy for $8. Writer's guidelines for #10 SASE.

Payment/Terms Pays in contributor's copies. Acquires one-time rights.

Advice "We would like to see more short shorts and stylisically innovative and risk-taking fiction. We like to see stories that illuminate the various layers of characters and their situations with great artistry. Give us distinctive character-driven stories that explore the complexities of human existence." Looks for "the small moments that contain more than at first possible, that surprise us with more truth than we thought we had a right to expect."

$◪ ◎ ANCIENT PATHS

P.O. Box 7505, Fairfax Station VA 22039. Web site: www.editorskylar.com. **Contact:** Skylar H. Burris, editor. Magazine: digest size; 80+ pages; 20 lb. plain white paper; cardstock cover; perfect bound; illustrations. "*Ancient Paths* publishes quality fiction and creative nonfiction for a literate Christian audience. Religious themes are usually subtle, and the magazine has non-Christian readers as well as some content by non-Christian authors. However, writers should be comfortable appearing in a Christian magazine." Annual. Estab. 1998. Circ. 175-200.

Needs Historical, humor/satire, literary, mainstream, novel excerpts, religious/inspirational (general religious/ literary), science fiction (Christian), slice-of-life vignettes. No retelling of Bible stories. Literary fiction favored over genre fiction. Receives 10+ unsolicited mss/month. Accepts 7-10 mss/issue. Publishes ms 2-4 months after acceptance. Recently published work by Larry Marshall Sams, Erin Tocknell, Maureen Stirsman and Chris Williams. Length: 250-2,500 words; average length: 1,500 words. Publishes short shorts. Often comments on rejected mss.

How to Contact Send complete ms. Accepts submissions by e-mail ssburris@msn.com. [only international submissions]. Include estimated word count. Send SASE for return of ms or send a disposable copy of ms and #10 SASE for reply only. Responds in 1 week to queries; 4-5 weeks to mss. Accepts simultaneous, multiple submissions and reprints. Sample copy for $5; make checks payable to Skylar Burris *not to Ancient Paths*. Writer's guidelines online. Reviews fiction.
Payment/Terms Pays $6, 1 copy, and discount on additional copies. Pays on publication for one-time rights. Not copyrighted.
Advice "We look for fluid prose, intriguing characters and substantial themes in fiction manuscripts."

$ 💷 🖊 THE ANTIGONISH REVIEW

St. Francis Xavier University, P.O. Box 5000, Antigonish NS B2G 2W5 Canada. (902)867-3962. Fax: (902)867-5563. Web site: www.antigonishreview.com. **Contact:** Bonnie McIsaac, office manager. Literary magazine for educated and creative readers. Quarterly. Estab. 1970. Circ. 1,000.
Needs Literary, translations, contemporary, prose poem. No erotica. Receives 50 unsolicited mss/month. Accepts 6 mss/issue. Publishes ms 4 months after acceptance. **Publishes some new writers/year.** Recently published work by Arnold Bloch, Richard Butts and Helen Barolini. Sometimes comments on rejected mss.
How to Contact Send complete ms. Accepts submissions by fax. Accepts electronic (disk compatible with WordPerfect/IBM and Windows) submissions. Prefers hard copy with disk submission. Responds in 1 month to queries; 6 months to mss. No simultaneous submissions. Sample copy for $7 or online. Writer's guidelines for #10 SASE or online.
Payment/Terms Pays $50 for stories. Pays on publication. Rights retained by author.
Advice "Learn the fundamentals and do not deluge an editor."

Ⓝ 🖊 APALACHEE REVIEW

Apalachee Press, P.O. Box 10469, Tallahassee FL 32302. (850)644-9114. Web site: http://apalacheereview.org/index.html. **Contact:** Michael Trammell, editor; Mary Jane Ryals, fiction editor. Literary magazine/journal: trade paperback size, 100-140 pages. Includes photographs. "At *Apalachee Review*, we are especially interested in poetry, fiction, and nonfiction that addresses intercultural issues in a domestic or international setting/context." Annual. Estab. 1976. Circ. 500. Member CLMP.
Needs Ethnic/multicultural, experimental, fantasy/sci-fi (with a literary bent), feminist, historical, humor/satire, literary, mainstream, mystery/suspense, new age, translations. Does not want cliché-filled genre-oriented fiction. Receives 60-100 mss/month. Accepts 5-10 mss/issue. Manuscript published 1 yr after acceptance. Agented fiction .5%. **Publishes 1-2 new writers/year.** Recently published Lu Vickers, Joe Clark, Justin Courter, Joe Taylor, Jane Arrowsmith Edwards, Vivian Lawry, Linda Frysh. Length: 600 words (min)-5,500 words (max). Average length: 3,500 words. Publishes short shorts. Average length of short shorts: 250 words. Also publishes literary essays, book reviews, poetry. Send review copies to Michael Trammell, editor. Sometimes comments on/critiques rejected mss.
How to Contact Send complete ms with cover letter. Include brief bio, list of publications. Responds to queries in 4-6 weeks. Responds to mss in 3-14 months. Send either SASE (or IRC) for return of ms or disposable copy of ms and #10 SASE for reply only. Considers simultaneous submissions. Sample copy available for $8 (current issue), $5 (back issue). Guidelines available for SASE, on Web site.
Payment and Terms Writers receive 2 contributor's copies. Additional copies $5/each. Pays on publication. Acquires one-time rights, electronic rights. Publication is copyrighted.

🖊 ◎ ARKANSAS REVIEW, A Journal of Delta Studies

Department of English and Philosophy, P.O. Box 1890, Arkansas State University, State University AR 72467-1890. (870)972-3043. Fax: (501)972-3045. E-mail: tswillia@astate.edu. Web site: www.clt.astate.edu/arkreview. **Contact:** Tom Williams, fiction editor. Magazine: $8\frac{1}{4} \times 11$; 64-100 pages; coated, matte paper; matte, 4-color cover stock; illustrations; photos. Publishes articles, fiction, poetry, essays, interviews, reviews, visual art evocative of or responsive to the Mississippi River Delta. Triannual. Estab. 1996. Circ. 700.
Needs Literary (essays and criticism), regional (short stories). "No genre fiction. Must have a Delta focus." Receives 30-50 unsolicited mss/month. Accepts 2-3 mss/issue; 5-7 mss/year. Publishes ms 6-12 months after acceptance. Agented fiction 1%. **Publishes 3-4 new writers/year.** Recently published work by Susan Henderson, George Singleton, Scott Ely and Pia Erhart. Also publishes literary essays, poetry. Sometimes comments on rejected mss.
How to Contact Accepts submissions by e-mail, fax. Send SASE for reply, return of ms or send a disposable copy of ms. Responds in 1 week to queries; 4 months to mss. Sample copy for $7.50. Writer's guidelines for #10 SASE.
Payment/Terms Pays 3 contributor's copies; additional copies for $5. Acquires first North American serial rights.

Advice "We see a lot of stories set in New Orleans but prefer fiction that takes place in other parts of the Delta. We'd love more innovative and experimental fiction too but primarily seek stories that involve and engage the reader and evoke or respond to the Delta natural and/or cultural experience."

THE ARMCHAIR AESTHETE

Pickle Gas Press, 31 Rolling Meadows Way, Penfield NY 14526. (585)388-6968. E-mail: bypaul@netacc.net. **Contact:** Paul Agosto, editor. Magazine: 5½ × 8½; 60-75 pages; 20 lb. paper; 110 lb. card stock color cover. "*The Armchair Aesthete* seeks quality writing that enlightens and entertains a thoughtful audience (ages 9-90) with a 'good read." Tri-annual. Estab. 1996. Circ. 100.

Needs Adventure, fantasy (science fantasy, sword and sorcery), historical (general), horror, humor/satire (satire), mainstream (contemporary), mystery/suspense (amateur sleuth, cozy, police procedural, private eye/ hard-boiled, romantic suspense), science fiction (soft/sociological), western (frontier, traditional). "No racist, pornographic, overt gore; no religious or material intended for or written by children. Receives 90 unsolicited mss/month. Accepts 13-18 mss/issue; 60-80 mss/year. Publishes ms 3-9 months after acceptance. Agented fiction 5%. **Publishes 15-25 new writers/year.** Recently published work by Alan Reynolds, Frank Andreotti, Joyce G. Bradshaw, Rachel Lapidow, D'Arcy Ann Pryciak. Average length: 3,500 words. Publishes short shorts. Also publishes poetry. Sometimes comments on rejected mss.

How to Contact Accepts submissions by e-mail. Send SASE for reply, return of ms or send a disposable copy of ms. Responds in 2-3 weeks to queries; 3-6 months to mss. Accepts simultaneous, multiple submissions and reprints. Sample copy for $4 (paid to P. Agosto, Ed.) and 3 first-class stamps. Writer's guidelines for #10 SASE. Reviews fiction.

Payment/Terms Pays 1 contributor's copy; additional copies for $3 (pay to P. Agosto, editor). Pays on publication for one-time rights.

Advice "Clever, compelling storytelling has a good chance here. We look for a clever plot, thought-out characters, something that surprises or catches us off guard. Write on innovative subjects and situations. Submissions should be professionally presented and technically sound."

BACKWARDS CITY REVIEW

Backwards City Publications, P.O. Box 41317, Greensboro NC 27404-1317. (336)275-9777. E-mail: editors@backwardscity.net. Web site: www.backwardscity.net. **Contact:** Gerry Canavan, editor. Literary magazine/journal: 6 × 9, 128 pages, white, 50 lb. paper, 10 pt CIS cover. Contains illustrations. Includes photographs. "At Backwards City Review, we seek to gather strong voices from different genres to create a journal that caters to the world above, beyond, below, around, near, within sight of, and slightly out of tune with conventional literary outlets." Semiannual. Estab. 2004. Circ. 400. Member CLMP.

Needs Comics/graphic novels, experimental, literary, mainstream, science fiction (soft/sociological), translations. Does not want religious, historical. List of upcoming themes available on Web site. Receives 100+ mss/ month. Accepts 5-6 mss/issue; 10-12 mss/year. Manuscript published 6 months after acceptance. Agented fiction 0%. **Publishes 3-5 new writers/year.** Published Jonathan Lethem, George Singleton, Chris Offutt, Chris Bachelder, Cory Doctorow, Alix Ohlin, Michael Parker, Kurt Vonnegut. Length: 10,000 words max. Average length: 3,000-5,000 words. Publishes short shorts. Average length of short shorts: 1,000 words. Also publishes literary essays, poetry. Sometimes comments on/critiques rejected manuscripts.

How to Contact Send complete ms with cover letter. Include estimated word count, brief bio, list of publications, SASE. Responds to queries in 4 weeks. Responds to mss in 4 months. Send disposable copy of ms and #10 SASE for reply only. Considers simultaneous submissions. Sample copy available for $5. Guidelines available on Web site.

Payment and Terms Writers receive 3 contributor's copies. Additional copies $3 each. Acquires first North American serial rights. Sends galleys to author. "Sponsors an Annual Fiction Contest. Deadline is April 15th. See Web site for additional contests." Cash prize for contest winners.

Advice "We're looking for something both well written and unconventional. We showcase the different. We love stories we've never seen before. Be original. Read a sample issue. Visit our blog. Send us only your best work."

BALLYHOO STORIES

Ballyhoo Stories, LLC, P.O. Box 170, Prince Street Station, New York NY 10012. E-mail: editors@ballyhoostories. com. Web site: www.ballyhoostories.com. **Contact:** Joshua Mandelbaum or Suzanne Pettypiece, editors. Literary magazine/journal. 88 pages, matte cover. "*Ballyhoo Stories* publishes the best in creative nonfiction and fiction. Each issue has a theme. We look for imaginative interpretation of each theme. We also have an online-only '50 States project.' The goal of this project is to collect one story with each state as either the subject or the setting." Bimonthly. Estab. 2005. Circ. 500. Member CLMP.

Needs Literary. List of upcoming themes available on Web site. Receives 100 mss/month. Accepts 10 mss/

issue; 20 mss/year. Manuscript published 2 months after acceptance. **Publishes 4 new writers/year.** Length: 7,000 words (max). Average length: 5,000. Also publishes literary essays. Sometimes comments on/critiques rejected manuscripts.

How to Contact Send complete ms with cover letter. Accepts e-mail submissions for 50 States project ONLY. Include brief bio. Responds to queries in 1 week. Responds to mss in 3 months. Include e-mail address for reply. Send disposable copy of ms and #10 SASE for reply only. Considers simultaneous submissions. Sample copy available for $8. Guidelines available via e-mail, on Web site.

Payment and Terms Writers receive 2 contributor's copies. Additional copies $8. Acquires first North American serial rights. Publication is copyrighted.

THE BALTIMORE REVIEW

P.O. Box 36418, Towson MD 21286. Web site: www.baltimorereview.org. **Contact:** Susan Muaddi Darraj, managing editor. Magazine: 6×9; 150 pages; 60 lb. paper; 10 pt. CS1 gloss film cover. Showcase for the best short stories, creative nonfiction and poetry by writers in the Baltimore area and beyond. Semiannual. Estab. 1996.

Needs Ethnic/multicultural, literary, mainstream. "No science fiction, westerns, children's, romance, etc." Accepts 20 mss/issue; approx. 40 mss/year. Publishes ms 1-9 months after acceptance. **Publishes "at least a few" new writers/year.** Average length: 3,000 words. Publishes short shorts. Also publishes poetry.

How to Contact Send SASE for reply, return of ms or send a disposable copy of ms. Responds in 4-6 months to mss. Accepts simultaneous submissions. No e-mail or fax submissions. Sample copy online.

Payment/Terms Pays 2 contributor's copies. Acquires first North American serial rights.

Advice "We look for compelling stories and a masterful use of the English language. We want to feel that we have never heard this story, or this voice, before. Read the kinds of publications you want your work to appear in. Make your reader believe and care."

BARBARIC YAWP

Bone World Publishing, 3700 County Rt. 24, Russell NY 13684-3198. (315)347-2609. **Contact:** Nancy Berbrich, fiction editor. Magazine: digest-size; 60 pages; 24 lb. paper; matte cover stock. "We publish what we like. Fiction should include some bounce and surprise. Our publication is intended for the intelligent, open-minded reader." Quarterly. Estab. 1997. Circ. 120.

Needs Adventure, experimental, fantasy (science, sword and sorcery), historical, horror, literary, mainstream, psychic/supernatural/occult, regional, religious/inspirational, science fiction (hard, soft/sociological). "We don't want any pornography, gratuitous violence or whining." Wants more suspense and philosophical work. Receives 30-40 unsolicited mss/month. Accepts 10-12 mss/issue; 40-48 mss/year. Publishes ms up to 6 months after acceptance. **Publishes 4-6 new writers/year.** Recently published work by Francine Witte, Jeff Grimshaw, Thaddeus Rutkowski and Holly Interlandi. Length: 1,500 words; average length: 600 words. Publishes short shorts. Also publishes literary essays, literary criticism, poetry. Often comments on rejected mss.

How to Contact Send SASE for reply, return of ms or send a disposable copy of ms. Responds in 2 weeks to queries; 4 months to mss. Accepts simultaneous, multiple submissions and reprints. Sample copy for $4. Writer's guidelines for #10 SASE.

Payment/Terms Pays 1 contributor's copy; additional copies $3. Acquires one-time rights.

Advice "Don't give up. Read much, write much, submit much. Observe closely the world around you. Don't borrow ideas from TV or films. Revision is often necessary—grit your teeth and do it. Never fear rejection."

BATHTUB GIN

Pathwise Press, P.O. Box 1164, Champaign IL 61824. (814)455-5498. E-mail: pathwisepress@hotmail.com. Web site: www.pathwisepress.com. **Contact:** Fiction Editor. Magazine: 8½×5½; 60 pages; recycled 20-lb. paper; 80-lb. card cover; illustrations; photos. "*Bathtub Gin* is looking for work that has some kick to it. We are very eclectic and publish a wide range of styles. Audience is anyone interested in new writing and art that is not being presented in larger magazines." Semiannual. Estab. 1997. Circ. 250.

Needs Condensed novels, experimental, humor/satire, literary. "No horror, science fiction, historical unless they go beyond the usual formula. We want more experimental fiction." Receives 20 unsolicited mss/month. Accepts 2-3 mss/issue. Reads mss for two issues June 1st-September 15th. "We publish in mid-October and mid-April." **Publishes 10 new writers/year.** Recently published work by J.T. Whitehead and G.D. McFetridge. Publishes short shorts. Also publishes literary essays, literary criticism, poetry. Often comments on rejected mss.

How to Contact Accepts submissions by e-mail. Send cover letter with a 3-5 line bio. Send SASE for reply, return of ms or send a disposable copy of ms. Responds in 1-2 months to queries. Accepts simultaneous, multiple submissions and reprints. Sample copy for $5. Writer's guidelines for #10 SASE. Reviews fiction.

Payment/Terms Pays 2 contributor's copies; discount on additional copies. Rights revert to author upon publication.

Advice "We are looking for writing that contains strong imagery, is complex, and is willing to take a chance with form and structure."

○ BEGINNINGS PUBLISHING INC., A Magazine for the Novice Writer

Beginnings Publishing, P.O. Box 214-W, Bayport NY 11705. (631)645-3846. E-mail: jenineb@optonline.net. Web site: www.scbeginnings.com. **Contact:** Jenine Killoran, fiction editor. Magazine: 8½×11; 54 pages; matte; glossy cover; illustrations; photographs. "*Beginnings* publishes only beginner/novice writers. We do accept articles by professionals pertaining to the craft of writing. We have had many new writers go on to be published elsewhere after being featured in our magazine." Triannual. Estab. 1999. Circ. 2,500.

Needs Adventure, family saga, literary, mainstream, mystery/suspense (amateur slueth), romance (contemporary), science fiction (soft/sociological), western. "No erotica, horror." Receives 425 unsolicited mss/month. Accepts 10 mss/issue; 20 mss/year. Does not read mss during January and April. Publishes ms 3-4 months after acceptance. **Publishes 100 percent new writers/year.** Recently published work by Harvey Stanbrough, Sue Guiney, Tom Cooper and Stephen Wallace. Average length: 2,500 words. Publishes short shorts. Also publishes poetry. Usually comments on rejected mss.

How to Contact Send complete ms. Send disposable copy of ms and #10 SASE for reply only; however, will accept SASE for return of ms. Responds in 3 weeks to queries; 10-13 weeks to mss. Accepts simultaneous submissions and reprints. Sample copy for $4. Writer's guidelines for SASE, e-mail or on Web site.

Payment/Terms Pays one contributor's copy; additional copies $4. Pays on publication for first North American serial, first rights.

Advice "Originality, presentation, proper grammar and spelling a must. Non-predictable endings. Many new writers confuse showing vs. telling. Writers who have that mastered stand out. Study the magazine. Check and double check your work. Original storylines, well thought out, keep up a good pace. Presentation is important, too! Rewrite, rewrite!"

○ BELLEVUE LITERARY REVIEW, A Journal of Humanity and Human Experience

Dept. of Medicine, NYU School of Medicine, 550 First Avenue, OBV-A612, New York NY 10016. (212)263-3973. Fax: (212)263-3206. E-mail: info@blreview.org. Web site: http://blreview.org. **Contact:** Ronna Wineberg, fiction editor. Magazine: 6×9; 160 pages. "The *BLR* is a literary journal that examines human existence through the prism of health and healing, illness and disease. We encourage creative interpretations of these themes." Semiannual. Estab. 2001. Member CLMP.

Needs Literary. No genre fiction. Receives 100 unsolicited mss/month. Accepts 9 mss/issue; 18 mss/year. Publishes ms 3-6 months after acceptance. Agented fiction 1%. **Publishes 3-6 new writers/year.** Recently published work by Amy Hempel, Sheila Kohler, Abraham Verghese, Stephen Dixon. Length: 5,000 words; average length: 2,500 words. Publishes short shorts. Also publishes literary essays, poetry. Sometimes comments on rejected mss.

How to Contact Submit online at www.blreview.org. (preferred). Also accepts mss via regular mail. Send complete ms. Send SASE (or IRC) for return of ms or disposable copy of the ms and #10 SASE for reply only. Responds in 3-6 months to mss. Accepts simultaneous submissions. Sample copy for $7. Writer's guidelines for SASE, e-mail or on Web site.

Payment/Terms Pays 2 contributor's copies, 1-year subscription and 1 year gift subscription; additional copies $5. Pays on publication for first North American serial rights. Sends galleys to author.

◑ BELLINGHAM REVIEW

Mail Stop 9053, Western Washington University, Bellingham WA 98225. (360)650-4863. E-mail: bhreview@cc. wwu.edu. Web site: www.wwu.edu/~bhreview. **Contact:** Fiction Editor. Magazine: 6×8¼; 150 pages; 60 lb. white paper; four-color cover." *Bellingham Review* seeks literature of palpable quality; stories, essays and poems that nudge the limits of form or execute traditional forms exquisitely. Semiannual. Estab. 1977. Circ. 1,600.

• The editors are actively seeking submissions of creative nonfiction, as well as stories that push the boundaries of the form. The Tobias Wolff Award in Fiction Contest runs December 1-March 15; see Web site for guidelines or send SASE.

Needs Experimental, humor/satire, literary, regional (Northwest). Does not want anything nonliterary. Accepts 3-4 mss/issue. Does not read ms February 2-September 14. Publishes ms 6 months after acceptance. Agented fiction 10%. **Publishes 10 new writers/year.** Recently published work by Patricia Vigderman, Joshua Rolnick, and A.G. Harmon. Publishes short shorts. Also publishes poetry.

How to Contact Send complete ms. Responds in 3 months to mss. Accepts simultaneous submissions. Sample copy for $7. Writer's guidelines online.

Payment/Terms Pays on publication when funding allows. Acquires first North American serial rights.
Advice "We look for work that is ambitious, vital and challenging both to the spirit and the intellect."

☑ ☒ BELLOWING ARK, A Literary Tabloid

P.O. Box 55564, Shoreline WA 98155. E-mail: bellowingark@bellowingark.org. **Contact:** Fiction Editor. Tabloid: $11\frac{1}{2} \times 17\frac{1}{2}$; 32 pages; electro-brite paper and cover stock; illustrations; photos. "We publish material we feel addresses the human situation in an affirmative way. We do not publish academic fiction." Bimonthly. Estab. 1984. Circ. 650.

● Work from *Bellowing Ark* appeared in the *Pushcart Prize* anthology.

Needs Literary, mainstream, serialized novels. "No science fiction or fantasy." Receives 30-70 unsolicited mss/month. Accepts 2-5 mss/issue; 700-1,000 mss/year. Publishes ms 6 months after acceptance. **Publishes 6-10 new writers/year.** Recently published work by Tom Cook, Diane Trzcinski, Myra Love, Shelley Uva, D.C. Taylor, and E.R. Romaine. Also publishes literary essays, literary criticism, poetry. Sometimes comments on rejected mss.
How to Contact Send complete ms and SASE. Responds in 6 weeks to mss. No simultaneous submissions. Sample copy for $4, $9\frac{1}{2} \times 12\frac{1}{2}$ SAE and $1.43 postage.
Payment/Terms Pays in contributor's copies. Acquires one-time rights.
Advice "*Bellowing Ark* began as (and remains) an alternative to the despair and negativity of the workshop/academic literary scene; we believe that life has meaning and is worth living—the work we publish reflects that belief. Learn how to tell a story before submitting. Avoid 'trick' endings; they have all been done before and better. *Bellowing Ark* is interested in publishing writers who will develop with the magazine, as in an extended community. We find *good* writers and stick with them. This is why the magazine has grown from 12 to 32 pages."

☑ ☒ BELOIT FICTION JOURNAL

Box 11, 700 College St., Beloit College WI 53511. (608)363-2577. E-mail: bfj@beloit.edu. Web site: www.beloit. edu/~english/bfjournal.htm. **Contact:** Chris Fink, editor-in-chief. Literary magazine: 6×9; 250 pages; 60 lb. paper; 10 pt. C1S cover stock; illustrations; photos on cover; ad-free. "We are interested in publishing the best contemporary fiction and are open to all themes except those involving pornographic, religiously dogmatic or politically propagandistic representations. Our magazine is for general readership, though most of our readers will probably have a specific interest in literary magazines." Annual. Estab. 1985.

● Work first appearing in *Beloit Fiction Journal* has been reprinted in award-winning collections, including the Flannery O'Connor and the Milkweed Fiction Prize collections, and has won the Iowa Short Fiction award.

Needs Literary, mainstream, contemporary. Wants more experimental and short shorts. Would like to see more "stories with a focus on both language and plot, unusual metaphors and vivid characters. No pornography, religious dogma, science fiction, horror, political propaganda or genre fiction." Receives 200 unsolicited mss/month. Accepts 20 mss/year. Publishes ms 9 months after acceptance. **Publishes 3 new writers/year.** Recently published work by Dennis Lehane, Silas House and David Harris Ebenbach. Length: 250-10,000 words; average length: 5,000 words. Sometimes comments on rejected mss.
How to Contact Our reading period is from August 1st to December 1st only. No fax, e-mail or disk submissions. Responds in 2 weeks to queries; 2 months to mss. Accepts simultaneous submissions if identified as such. Please send one story at a time. Always include SASE. Sample copy for $15 (new issue), $12 (back issue, double issue), $6 (back issue, single issue). Writer's guidelines for #10 SASE or on Web site.
Payment and Terms Buys first North American serial rights only. Payment in copies.
Advice "Many of our contributors are writers whose work we had previously rejected. Don't let one rejection slip turn you away from our—or any—magazine."

☑ ☒ BIG MUDDY: A JOURNAL OF THE MISSISSIPPI RIVER VALLEY

Southeast Missouri State University Press, MS2650 English Dept., Southeast MO State University, Cape Girardeau MO 63701. E-mail: sswartwout@semo.edu. Web site: www6.semo.edu/universitypress/. **Contact:** Susan Swartwout, editor. Magazine: $8\frac{1}{2} \times 5\frac{1}{2}$ perfect-bound; 150 pages; acid-free paper; color cover stock; layflat lamination; illustrations; photos. "*Big Muddy* explores multidisciplinary, multicultural issues, people, and events mainly concerning the 10-state area that borders the Mississippi River, by people who have lived here, who have an interest in the area, or who know the River Basin. We publish fiction, poetry, historical essays, creative nonfiction, environmental essays, biography, regional events, photography, art, etc." Semiannual. Estab. 2001. Circ. 500.
Needs Adventure, ethnic/multicultural, experimental, family saga, feminist, historical, humor/satire, literary, mainstream, military/war, mystery/suspense, regional (Mississippi River Valley; Midwest), translations. "No

romance, fantasy or children's." Receives 50 unsolicited mss/month. Accepts 7-10 mss/issue. Publishes ms 6 months after acceptance.

How to Contact Send SASE for return of ms or send a disposable copy of ms and #10 SASE for reply only. Responds in 10 weeks to mss. Accepts multiple submissions. Sample copy for $6. Writer's guidelines for SASE, e-mail, fax or on Web site. Reviews fiction.

Payment/Terms Pays 2 contributor's copies; additional copies $5. Acquires first North American serial rights.

Advice "In fiction manuscripts we look for clear language, avoidance of clichés except in necessary dialogue, a *fresh* vision of the theme or issue. Find some excellent and honest readers to comment on your work-in-progress and final draft. Consider their viewpoints carefully. Revise."

☑ ◎ BILINGUAL REVIEW

Hispanic Research Center, Arizona State University, Box 875303, Tempe AZ 85287-5303. (480)965-3867. E-mail: brp@asu.edu. Web site: www.asu.edu/brp. **Contact:** Gary D. Keller, editor-in-chief. Magazine: 7×10; 96 pages; 55 lb. acid-free paper; coated cover stock. Scholarly/literary journal of US Hispanic life: poetry, short stories, other prose and short theater. 3 times/year. Estab. 1974. Circ. 2,000.

Needs US Hispanic creative literature. "We accept material in English or Spanish. We publish orginal work only—no translations." US Hispanic themes only. Receives 50 unsolicited mss/month. Accepts 3 mss/issue; 9 mss/year. Publishes ms 1 year after acceptance. Recently published work by Daniel Olivas, Virgil Suárez, Ibis Gomez-Vega. Also publishes literary criticism, poetry. Often comments on rejected mss.

How to Contact Accepts submissions by mail only. Accepts simultaneous submissions and high-quality photo-copied submissions. Sample copy for $8. Reviews fiction.

Payment/Terms Pays 2 contributor's copies; 30% discount for extras. Acquires 50% of reprint permission fee given to author as matter of policy rights.

Advice "We do not publish literature about tourists in Latin America and their perceptions of the 'native culture.' We do not publish fiction about Latin America unless there is a clear tie to the United States (characters, theme, etc.)."

☑ THE BITTER OLEANDER

4983 Tall Oaks Dr., Fayettville NY 13066-9776. (315)637-3047. Fax: (315)637-5056. E-mail: info@bitteroleander. com. Web site: www.bitteroleander.com. **Contact:** Paul B. Roth. Zine specializing in poetry and fiction: 6×9; 128 pages; 55 lb. paper; 12 pt. CIS cover stock; photos. "We're interested in the surreal; deep image particulariza-tion of natural experiences." Semiannual. Estab. 1974. Circ. 2,000.

Needs Experimental, translations. "No pornography; no confessional; no romance." Receives 100 unsolicited mss/month. Accepts 1-2 mss/issue; 2-4 mss/year. Does not read in July. Publishes ms 4-6 months after accep-tance. Recently published work by Tom Stoner, John Michael Cummings, Sara Leslie. Average length: 2,500 words. Publishes short shorts. Also publishes literary essays, poetry. Always comments on rejected mss.

How to Contact Send SASE for reply, return of ms. Responds in 1 week to queries; 1 month to mss. Accepts multiple submissions. Sample copy for $8. Writer's guidelines for #10 SASE.

Payment/Terms Pays 1 contributor's copy; additional copies $8. Acquires first rights.

Advice "If within the first 100 words my mind drifts, the rest rarely makes it. Be yourself and listen to no one but yourself."

$☑ ⚓ BLACK WARRIOR REVIEW

P.O. Box 862936, Tuscaloosa AL 35486-0027. (205)348-4518. E-mail: bwr@ua.edu. Web site: www.webdelsol. com/bwr. **Contact:** Andy Farkas, fiction editor. Magazine: 6×9; 160 pages; color artwork. "We publish contem-porary fiction, poetry, reviews, essays and art for a literary audience. We publish the freshest work we can find." Semiannual. Estab. 1974. Circ. 2,000.

● Work that appeared in the *Black Warrior Review* has been included in the *Pushcart Prize* anthology, *Harper's Magazine*, *Best American Short Stories*, *Best American Poetry* and *New Stories from the South*.

Needs Literary, contemporary, short and short-short fiction. Wants "work that is conscious of form and well crafted. We are open to good experimental writing and short-short fiction. No genre fiction, please." Receives 300 unsolicited mss/month. Accepts 5 mss/issue; 10 mss/year. Unsolicited novel excerpts are not considered unless the novel is already contracted for publication. Publishes ms 6 months after acceptance. **Publishes 5 new writers/year.** Recently published work by Eric Maxon, Gary Parks, Gary Fincke, Anthony Varallo, Wayne Johnson, Jim Ruland, Elizabeth Wetmore, Bret Anthony Johnston, Rick Bass, Sherri Flick. Length: 7,500 words; average length: 2,000-5,000 words. Occasionally comments on rejected mss.

How to Contact Send complete ms with SASE (1 story per submission). Responds in 4 months to mss. Accepts simultaneous submissions if noted. Sample copy for $10. Writer's guidelines online.

Payment/Terms Pays up to $100, copies, and a 1-year subscription. Pays on publication for first rights.

Advice "We look for attention to language, freshness, honesty, a convincing and sharp voice. Send us a clean, well-printed, proofread manuscript. Become familiar with the magazine prior to submission."

☑ ◎ BLUELINE

125 Morey Hall, Department of English and Communication, SUNY Potsdam, Postdam NY 13676. (315)267-2043. E-mail: blueline@postdam.edu. Web site: www.potsdam.edu/ENGL/Blueline/blue.html. **Contact:** Fiction Editor. Magazine: 6×9; 200 pages; 70 lb. white stock paper; 65 lb. smooth cover stock; illustrations; photos. "*Blueline* is interested in quality writing about the Adirondacks or other places similar in geography and spirit. We publish fiction, poetry, personal essays, book reviews and oral history for those interested in Adirondacks, nature in general, and well-crafted writing." Annual. Estab. 1979. Circ. 400.

Needs Adventure, humor/satire, literary, regional, contemporary, prose poem, reminiscences, oral history, nature/outdoors. No urban stories or erotica. Receives 8-10 unsolicited mss/month. Accepts 6-8 mss/issue. Does not read January-August. Publishes ms 3-6 months after acceptance. **Publishes 2 new writers/year.** Recently published work by Joan Connor, Laura Rodley and Ann Mohin. Length: 500-3,000 words; average length: 2,500 words. Also publishes literary essays, poetry. Occasionally comments on rejected mss.

How to Contact Accepts simultaneous submissions. Sample copy for $6.

Payment/Terms Pays 1 contributor's copy; charges $7 each for 3 or more copies. Acquires first rights.

Advice "We look for concise, clear, concrete prose that tells a story and touches upon a universal theme or situation. We prefer realism to romanticism but will consider nostalgia if well done. Pay attention to grammar and syntax. Avoid murky language, sentimentality, cuteness or folkiness. We would like to see more good fiction related to the Adirondacks and more literary fiction and prose poems. If manuscript has potential, we work with author to improve and reconsider for publication. Our readers prefer fiction to poetry (in general) or reviews. Write from your own experience, be specific and factual (within the bounds of your story) and if you write about universal features such as love, death, change, etc., write about them in a fresh way. Triteness and mediocrity are the hallmarks of the majority of stories seen today."

☑ BOGG, Journal of Contemporary Writing

Bogg Publications, 422 N. Cleveland St., Arlington VA 22201-1424. E-mail: boggmag@aol.com. **Contact:** John Elsberg, US editor. Magazine: 6×9; 56 pages; 70 lb. white paper; 70 lb. cover stock; line illustrations. "Poetry (to include prose poems, haiku/tanka and experimental forms), experimental short fiction, reviews." Published 2 or 3 times a year. Estab. 1968. Circ. 750.

Needs Very short experimental fiction and prose poems. Receives 25 unsolicited mss/month. Accepts 4-6 mss/issue. Publishes ms 3-18 months after acceptance. **Publishes 40-80 new writers/year.** Recently published work by Linda Bosson, Brian Johnson, Pamela Gay, Art Stein and Hugh Fox. Also publishes essays on small press history and literary criticism. Occasionally comments on rejected mss.

How to Contact Responds in 1 week to queries; 2 weeks to mss. Sample copy for $4 or $6 (current issue). Reviews fiction. Does not consider e-mail or simultaneous submissions.

Payment/Terms Pays 2 contributor's copies; reduced charge for extras. Acquires one-time rights.

Advice "We look for voice and originality. Read magazine first. We are most interested in prose of experimental or wry nature to supplement poetry and are always looking for innovative/imaginative uses of British references."

⊕ ◻ BOOK WORLD MAGAZINE

Christ Church Publishers Ltd., 2 Caversham Street, London England SW3 4AH United Kingdom. 0207 351 4995. Fax: 0207 3514995. E-mail: leonard.holdsworth@btopenworld.com. **Contact:** James Hughes. Magazine: 64 pages; illustrations; photos. "Subscription magazine for serious book lovers, book collectors, librarians and academics." Monthly. Estab. 1971. Circ. 6,000.

Needs Also publishes literary essays, literary criticism.

How to Contact Query. Send IRC (International Reply Coupon) for return of ms. Responds in 3 months to queries; 3 months to mss. Accepts simultaneous submissions. Sample copy for $7.50. Writer's guidelines for IRC.

Payment/Terms Pays on publication for one-time rights.

Advice "Always write to us before sending any mss."

$☑ BOULEVARD

Opojaz, Inc., 6614 Clayton Rd., PMB 325, Richmond Heights MO 63117. (314)862-2643. Fax: (314)862-2982. E-mail: ballymon@hotmail.com. Web site: www.richardburgin.com. **Contact:** Richard Burgin, editor; Edmund de Chasca, senior editor. Magazine: 5½×8½; 150-250 pages; excellent paper; high-quality cover stock; illustrations; photos. "*Boulevard* is a diverse literary magazine presenting original creative work by well-known authors, as well as by writers of exciting promise." Triannual. Estab. 1985. Circ. 11,000.

Needs Confessions, experimental, literary, mainstream, novel excerpts. "We do not want erotica, science fiction, romance, western or children's stories." Receives over 600 unsolicited mss/month. Accepts about 10 mss/issue. Does not accept manuscripts between May 1 and October 1. Publishes ms 9 months after acceptance. **Publishes 10 new writers/year.** Recently published work by Joyce Carol Oates, Floyd Skloot, Alice Hoffman, Stephen Dixon and Frederick Busch. Length: 9,000 words maximum; average length: 5,000 words. Publishes short shorts. Also publishes literary essays, literary criticism, poetry. Sometimes comments on rejected mss.

How to Contact Send complete ms. Accepts submissions on disk. SASE for reply. Responds in 2 weeks to queries; 3-4 months to mss. Accepts multiple submissions. No simultaneous submissions. Sample copy for $9. Writer's guidelines online.

Payment/Terms Pays $50-700. Pays on publication for first North American serial rights.

Advice "We pick the stories that move us the most emotionally, stimulate us the most intellectually, are the best written and thought out. Don't write to get published—write to express your experience and vision of the world."

◖ THE BRIAR CLIFF REVIEW

Briar Cliff University, 3303 Rebecca St., Sioux City IA 51104-0100. (712)279-5477. E-mail: curranst@briarcliff.edu. Web site: www.briarcliff.edu/bcreview. **Contact:** Phil Hey or Tricia Currans-Sheehan, fiction editors. Magazine: 8½×11; 100 pages; 70 lb. 100# Altima Satin Text; illustrations; photos. "*The Briar Cliff Review* is an eclectic literary and cultural magazine focusing on (but not limited to) Siouxland writers and subjects. We are happy to proclaim ourselves a regional publication. It doesn't diminish us; it enhances us." Annual. Estab. 1989. Circ. 750.

Needs Ethnic/multicultural, feminist, historical, humor/satire, literary, mainstream, regional. "No romance, horror or alien stories." Accepts 5 mss/year. Reads mss only between August 1 and November 1. Publishes ms 3-4 months after acceptance. **Publishes 10-14 new writers/year.** Recently published work by Jenna Blum, Brian Bedard, Christian Michener, Rebecca Tuch, and Josip Novakovich. Length: 2,500-5,000 words; average length: 3,000 words. Also publishes literary essays, literary criticism, poetry. Sometimes comments on rejected mss.

How to Contact Send SASE for return of ms. Does not accept electronic submissions (unless from overseas). Responds in 4-5 months to mss. Accepts simultaneous submissions. Sample copy for $12 and 9×12 SAE. Writer's guidelines for #10 SASE. Reviews fiction.

Payment/Terms Pays 2 contributor's copies; additional copies available for $9. Acquires first rights.

Advice "So many stories are just telling. We want some action. It has to move. We prefer stories in which there is no gimmick, no mechanical turn of events, no moral except the one we would draw privately."

◖ ◎ BRILLANT CORNERS, A Journal of Jazz & Literature

Lycoming College, Williamsport PA 17701. (570)321-4279. Fax: (570)321-4090. E-mail: feinstein@lycoming.edu. **Contact:** Sascha Feinstein, editor. Journal: 6×9; 100 pages; 70 lb. Cougar opaque, vellum, natural paper; photographs. "We publish jazz-related literature—fiction, poetry and nonfiction." Semiannual. Estab. 1996. Circ. 1,200.

Needs Condensed novels, ethnic/multicultural, experimental, literary, mainstream, romance (contemporary). Receives 10-15 unsolicited mss/month. Accepts 1-2 mss/issue; 2-3 mss/year. Does not read mss May 15-September 1. Publishes ms 4-12 months after acceptance. Publishes short shorts. Also publishes literary essays, literary criticism, poetry. Rarely comments on rejected mss.

How to Contact SASE for return of ms or send a disposable copy of ms. Accepts unpublished work only. Responds in 2 weeks to queries; 1-2 months to mss. Sample copy for $7. Reviews fiction.

Payment/Terms Acquires first North American serial rights. Sends galleys to author when possible.

Advice "We look for clear, moving prose that demonstrates a love of both writing and jazz. We primarily publish established writers, but we read all submissions carefully and welcome work by outstanding young writers."

◖ BROKEN BRIDGE REVIEW, The Best New Work By Emerging Writers

Pomfret School, 398 Pomfret St., Pomfret CT 06258-0128. (860)963-5220. E-mail: eds@brokenbridge.us. Web site: www.brokenbridge.us. **Contact:** Brad Davis, editor. Literary magazine/journal: 6×9, 200 pages, matte color cover. "Neither for beginners nor A-list writers; think 'on the cusp'. A journal of interest for new writers, college and MFA writers, established writers—with an eye for the best new work by emerging writers." Annual. Estab. 2006.

Needs Experimental, literary, mainstream, regional. Does not read December-August. Manuscript published 10 months after acceptance. Length: 1,000 words (min)-4,000 words (max). Average length: 3,000 words. Publishes short shorts. Also publishes poetry. Never comments on/critiques rejected manuscripts.

How to Contact Send complete ms with cover letter. Include estimated word count, brief bio, list of publications, e-mail address and (if any) private school connection. Responds to mss in 1-3 months. Send disposable copy of ms. Replies by e-mail. Sample copy available for $10. Guidelines available via e-mail, on Web site.

Payment and Terms Writers receive 2 contributor's copies. Additional copies $10. Pays on publication. Acquires one-time rights. Sends galleys to author.

N ☑ BROKEN PENCIL

P.O. Box 203 STN P, Toronto ON M5S 2S7 Canada. (416)204-1700. E-mail: editor@brokenpencil.com. Web site: www.brokenpencil.com. **Contact:** Hal Niedzviecki, fiction editor. Magazine. "Founded in 1995 and based in Toronto, Canada, *Broken Pencil* is a Web site and print magazine published four times a year. It is one of the few magazines in the world devoted to underground culture and the independent arts. We are a great resource and a lively read. A cross between the *Utne Reader*, an underground *Reader's Digest*, and the now defunct *Factsheet15*, *Broken Pencil* reviews the best zines, books, Web sites, videos, and artworks from the underground and reprints the best articles from the alternative press. Also, ground-breaking interviews, original fiction, and commentary on all aspects of the independent arts. From the hilarious to the perverse, *Broken Pencil* challenges conformity and demands attention." Quarterly. Estab. 1995. Circ. 5,000.

Needs Adventure, erotica, ethnic/multicultural, experimental, fantasy, historical, horror, humor/satire, amateur sleuth, romance, science fiction. Accepts 8 mss/year. Manuscript published 2-3 months after acceptance. Length: 500 words (min)-3,000 words (max).

How to Contact Accepts submissions by e-mail.

Payment and Terms Acquires first rights.

Advice "Write to receive a list of upcoming themes and then pitch us stories based around these themes. If you keep your ear to the ground in alternative and underground arts communities, you will be able to find content appropriate for *Broken Pencil*."

☑ BRYANT LITERARY REVIEW

Bryant University, 1150 Douglas Pike, Faculty Suite F, Smithfield RI 02917. (401)232-6802. Fax: (401)232-6270. E-mail: blr@bryant.edu. Web site: http://web.bryant.edu/ ~ blr. **Contact:** M.J. Kim. Magazine: 6 × 9; 125 pages; photos. Annual. Estab. 2000. Circ. 2,400. Member CLMP.

Needs Adventure, ethnic/multicultural, experimental, family saga, fantasy, feminist, historical, humor/satire, literary, mainstream, military/war, mystery/suspense, New Age, psychic/supernatural/occult, regional, science fiction, thriller/espionage, translations, western. "No novellas or serialized novels; only short stories." Receives 100 unsolicited mss/month. Accepts approx. 7 mss/issue. Does not read January through August. Publishes ms 4-5 months after acceptance. **Publishes 1-2 new writers/year.** Recently published work by Lyzette Wanzer, K.S. Phillips, Richard N. Bentley. Publishes short shorts. Also publishes poetry.

How to Contact Send a disposable copy of ms and #10 SASE for reply only. Responds in 2 weeks to queries; 12 weeks to mss. No simultaneous submissions. Sample copy for $8. Writer's guidelines by e-mail or on Web site.

Payment/Terms Pays 2 contributor's copies; additional copies $8. Pays on publication.

N ☑ BUFFALO CARP

Quad City Arts, 1715 2nd Avenue, Rock Island IL 61201. (309)793-1213. Web site: www.quadcityarts.com. **Contact:** Tracy Alan White, managing editor. Literary magazine/journal: 6 × 9, 100 pages, 60 lb. paper, glossy, four-color with original artwork cover. "*Buffalo Carp* is a hybrid, an amalgam, unique, surprising and yet somehow inevitable. The works range from the factual to the fanciful, from fascinating to frightening, and everything in between." Annual. Estab. 2002. Circ. 500.

Needs Adventure, experimental, family saga, historical, horror (dark fantasy, futuristic, psychological), humor/satire, literary, mainstream, amateur sleuth, religious (inspirational), romance (contemporary), science fiction (hard science/technological), thriller/espionage, western (frontier saga). Receives 15 mss/month. Accepts 8-10 mss/issue. Does not read May-August. Manuscript published 6-12 months after acceptance. Agented fiction 5%. Publishes 1-2 new writers/year. Length: 3,000 words (max). Average length: 1,500-3,000 words. Publishes short shorts. Also publishes poetry. Rarely comments on/critiques rejected mss.

How to Contact Send complete ms with cover letter. Accepts submissions by e-mail. Include estimated word count, brief bio. Responds to queries in 2 weeks. Responds to mss in 6-12 weeks. Send disposable copy of ms and #10 SASE for reply only. Considers simultaneous submissions, multiple submissions. Sample copy available for. Guidelines available for SASE, via e-mail, on Web site.

Payment and Terms Writers receive 2 contributor's copies. Pays on publication. Publication is copyrighted.

Advice "Good writing contains the same qualities found in a breeze-blown Midwestern lake; the surface exudes a sparkle and liveliness which compels deeper examination. Soon many details, movements and meaning are discovered, and a clarity surprising for the depth."

◐ BUTTON, New England's Tiniest Magazine of Poetry, Fiction and Gracious Living

Box 77, Westminster, MA 014 73. Web site: www.moonsigns.net. **Contact:** W.M. Davies, fiction editor. Magazine: 4×5; 34 pages; bond paper; color cardstock cover; illustrations; photos. "*Button* is New England's tiniest magazine of poetry, fiction and gracious living, published once a year. As 'gracious living' is on the cover, we like wit, brevity, cleverly conceived essay/recipe, poetry that isn't sentimental or song lyrics. I started *Button* so that a century from now, when people read it in landfils or, preferably, libraries, they'll say, 'Gee, what a great time to have lived. I wish I lived back then.' " Annual. Estab. 1993. Circ. 1,500.

Needs Literary. "No genre fiction, science fiction, techno-thriller." Wants more of "anything Herman Melville, Henry James or Betty MacDonald would like to read." Receives 20-40 unsolicited mss/month. Accepts 1-2 mss/issue; 3-5 mss/year. Publishes ms 3-9 months after acceptance. Recently published work by Ralph Lombreglia, John Hanson Mitchell, They Might Be Giants and Lawrence Millman. Also publishes literary essays, poetry. Sometimes comments on rejected mss.

How to Contact Send complete ms with bio, list of publications and explain how you found magazine. Include SASE. Responds in 1 month to queries; 2 months to mss. Sample copy for $2.50 and 1 41¢ stamp. Writer's guidelines for #10 SASE. Reviews fiction.

Payment/Terms Honorium, subscription and copies. Pays on publication for first North American serial rights.

Advice "What makes a manuscript stand out? Flannery O'Connor once said, 'Don't get subtle till the fourth page,' and I agree. We look for interesting, sympathetic, believable characters and careful setting. I'm really tired of stories that start strong then devolve into dialogue uninterrupted by further exposition. Also, no stories from a mad person's POV unless it's really tricky and skillful. Advice to prospective writers: Continue to read at least 10 times as much as you write. Read the best, and read intelligent criticism if you can find it. *No beginners please*. Please don't submit more than once a year; it's more important that you work on your craft rather than machine-gunning publications with samples, and don't submit more than 3 poems in a batch (this advice goes for other places, you'll find)."

$◐ BYLINE

P.O. Box 111, Albion NY 14411. (585)355-3290. E-mail: robbi@bylinemag.com. Web site: www.bylinemag.com. **Contact:** Robbi Hess. Magazine "aimed at encouraging and motivating all writers toward success, with special information to help new writers. Articles center on how to write better, market smarter, sell your work." Monthly. Estab. 1981.

Needs Literary, genre, general fiction. "Does not want to see erotica or explicit graphic content. No science fiction or fantasy." Receives 100-200 unsolicited mss/month. Accepts 1 mss/issue; 11 mss/year. Publishes ms 3 months after acceptance. **Publishes many new writers/year.** Recently published work by Ami Elizabeth Reeves, David Dumitru, William Eisner. Also publishes poetry.

How to Contact No cover letter needed. Responds in 6-12 weeks to mss. Accepts simultaneous submissions "if notified." Writer's guidelines for #10 SASE or online.

Payment/Terms Pays $75 and 3 contributor's copies. Pays on publication for first North American serial rights.

Advice "We look for good writing that draws the reader in; conflict and character movement by story's end. We're very open to new writers. Submit a well-written, professionally prepared ms with SASE. No erotica or senseless violence; otherwise, we'll consider most any theme. We also sponsor short story and poetry contests. Read what's being published. Find a good story, not just a narrative reflection. Keep submitting."

◐ ◎ CALYX, A Journal of Art & Literature by Women

Calyx, Inc., P.O. Box B, Corvallis OR 97339. (541)753-9384. Fax: (541)753-0515. E-mail: calyx@proaxis.com. Web site: www. calyxpress.org. **Contact:** Editor. Magazine: 6×8; 128 pages per single issue; 60 lb. coated matte stock paper; 10 pt. chrome coat cover; original art. Publishes prose, poetry, art, essays, interviews and critical and review articles. "*Calyx* exists to publish fine literature and art by women and is committed to publishing the work of all women, including women of color, older women, working class women and other voices that need to be heard. We are committed to discovering and nurturing beginning writers." Biannual. Estab. 1976. Circ. 6,000.

Needs Receives approximately 1,000 unsolicited prose and poetry mss when open. Accepts 4-8 prose mss/issue; 9-15 mss/year. Reads mss October 1-December 31; submit only during this period. Mss received when not reading will be returned. Publishes ms 4-12 months after acceptance. **Publishes 10-20 new writers/year.** Recently published work by M. Evelina Galang, Chitrita Banerji, Diana Ma , Catherine Brady. Also publishes literary essays, literary criticism, poetry.

How to Contact Responds in 4-12 months to mss. Accepts simultaneous submissions. Sample copy for $9.50 plus $3 postage. Include SASE.

Payment/Terms "Combination of free issues and 1 volume subscription.

Advice Most mss are rejected because "The writers are not familiar with *Calyx*. Writers should read *Calyx* and be familar with the publication. We look for good writing, imagination and important/interesting subject matter."

◎ ⛎ THE CARIBBEAN WRITER

The University of the Virgin Islands, RR 1, Box 10,000-Kinghill, St. Croix 00850 Virgin Islands. (340)692-4152. Fax: (340)692-4026. E-mail: qmars@uvi.edu. Web site: www.TheCaribbeanWriter.com. **Contact:** Quilin B. Mars, managing editor. Magazine: 6×9; 304 pages; 60 lb. paper; glossy cover stock; illustrations; photos. "*The Caribbean Writer* is an international magazine with a Caribbean focus. The Caribbean should be central to the work, or the work should reflect a Caribbean heritage, experience or perspective." Annual. Estab. 1987. Circ. 1,500.

• Work published in *The Caribbean Writer* has received two Pushcart Prizes and Quenepon Award.

Needs Historical (general), humor/satire, literary, mainstream, translations, contemporary and prose poem. Receives 65 unsolicited mss/month. Accepts 60 mss/issue. **Publishes approximately 20% new writers/year.** Recently published work by Carolina Paiz, Calvin Mills, and Opal Palmer Adisa. Also publishes literary essays, fiction, translations, plays, nad book reviews.

How to Contact Accepts submissions by e-mail. "Blind submissions only. Send name, address and title of manuscript on separate sheet. Title only on manuscript. Accepts simultaneous, multiple submissions. Sample copy for $7 and $4 postage.

Payment/Terms Pays 2 contributor's copies. Annual prizes for best story ($400); for best poem ($300); $200 for first time publication; best work by Caribbean Author ($500); best work by Virgin Islands author ($200). Acquires one-time rights.

Advice Looks for "work which reflects a Caribbean heritage, experience or perspective."

Ⓝ ◯ CC&D, CHILDREN, CHURCHES & DADDIES MAGAZINE: THE UNRELIGIOUS, NONFAMILY-ORIENTED LITERARY AND ART MAGAZINE

Scars Publications and Design, 829 Brian Court, Gurnee IL 60031-3155. (847)281-9070. E-mail: ccandd96@scars. tv. Web site: scars.tv. **Contact:** Janet Kuypers, editor in chief. Literary magazine/journal: 5×7, 60 lb paper. Contains illustrations & photographs. Monthly. Estab. 1993.

Needs Adventure, ethnic/multicultural, experimental, feminist, gay, historical, lesbian, literary, mystery/suspense, new age, psychic/supernatural/occult, science fiction. Does not want religious or rhyming or family-oriented material. Manuscript published 1 yr after acceptance. Published Mel Waldman, Kenneth DiMaggio, Pat Dixon, Robert William Meyers, Troy Davis, G.A. Scheinoha, Ken Dean. Average length: 1,000 words. Publishes short shorts. Also publishes poetry. Always comments on/critiques rejected mss if asked.

How to Contact Send complete ms with cover letter or query with clips of published work. Prefers submissions by e-mail. Responds to queries in 2 weeks; mss in 2 weeks. "Responds much faster to e-mail submissions and queries." Send either SASE (or IRC) for return of ms or disposable copy of ms and #10 SASE for reply only, "but if you have e-mail PLEASE send us an electronic submission instead. (If we accept your writing, we'll only ask for you to e-mail it to us anyway.)" Considers simultaneous submissions, previously published submissions, multiple submissions. Sample copy available for $6. Guidelines available for SASE, via e-mail, on Web site. "Reviews fiction, essays, journals, editorials, short fiction."

◪ CENTER, A Journal of the Literary Arts

University of Missouri, 202 Tate Hall, Columbia MO 65211. (573)882-4971. E-mail: cla@missouri.edu. Web site: www.missouri.edu/~center. **Contact:** Fiction editor. Magazine: 6×9; 125-200 pages; perfect bound, with 4-color card cover. *Center*'s goal is to publish the best in literary fiction, poetry and creative nonfiction by previously unpublished and emerging writers, as well as more established writers. Annual. Estab. 2000. Circ. 500.

Needs Ethnic/multicultural, experimental, humor/satire, literary. Receives 30-50 unsolicited mss/month. Accepts 3-5 mss/year. Reads mss from July 1-December 1 only. Publishes ms 6 months after acceptance. **Publishes 25% new writers/year.** Recently published work by Lisa Glatt and Robert Root. Publishes short shorts. Also publishes literary essays, poetry. Sometimes comments on rejected mss.

How to Contact Send SASE (or IRC) for return of ms or send a disposable copy of ms and #10 SASE for reply only. Responds in 1 month to queries; 3-4 months to mss. Accepts simultaneous, multiple submissions. Sample copy for $3, current copy $6. Writer's guidelines for SASE.

Payment/Terms Pays 2 contributor's copies; additional copies $3. Pays on publication for one-time rights.

◪ CHAFFIN JOURNAL

English Department, Eastern Kentucky University, Case Annex 467, Richmond KY 40475-3102. (859)622-3080. E-mail: robert.witt@eku.edu. Web site: www.english.eku.edu/chaffin_journal. **Contact:** Robert Witt, editor. Magazine: 8×5½; 120-130 pages; 70 lb. paper; 80 lb. cover. "We publish fiction on any subject; our only consideration is the quality." Annual. Estab. 1998. Circ. 150.

Needs Ethnic/multicultural, historical, humor/satire, literary, mainstream, regional (Appalachia). "No erotica, fantasy." Receives 20 unsolicited mss/month. Accepts 6-8 mss/year. Does not read mss October 1 through May

31. Publishes ms 6 months after acceptance. **Publishes 2-3 new writers/year.** Recently published work by Meridith Sue Willis, Marie Manilla, Raymond Abbott, Marjorie Bixler, Chris Helvey. Length: 10,000 words; average length: 5,000 words.

How to Contact Send SASE for return of ms. Responds in 1 week to queries; 3 months to mss. Accepts simultaneous, multiple submissions. Sample copy for $6. Writer's guidelines for SASE or e-mail submission are online.

Payment/Terms Pays 1 contributor's copy; additional copies $6. Pays on publication for one-time rights.

Advice ''All manuscripts submitted are considered.''

🌐 CHAPMAN

Chapman Publishing, 4 Broughton Place, Edinburgh Scotland EH1 3RX United Kingdom. (+44)131 557 2207. E-mail: chapman-pub@blueyonder.co.uk. Web site: www.chapman-pub.co.uk. **Contact:** Joy Hendry, editor. ''*Chapman*, Scotland's quality literary magazine, is a dynamic force in Scotland—publishing poetry; fiction; criticism; reviews; articles on theatre, politics, language and the arts. Our philosophy is to publish new work, from known and unknown writers, mainly Scottish, but also worldwide.'' Published three times a year. Estab. 1970. Circ. 2,000.

Needs Experimental, historical, humor/satire, literary, Scottish/international. ''No horror, science fiction.'' Accepts 4-6 mss/issue. Publishes ms 3 months after acceptance. **Publishes 50 new writers/year.**

How to Contact No simultaneous submissions. Writer's guidelines by e-mail.

Payment/Terms Pays by negotiation. Pays on publication for first rights.

Advice ''Keep your stories for six months and edit carefully. We seek challenging work which attempts to explore difficult/new territory in content and form, but lighter work, if original enough, is welcome.''

$ 🖊 THE CHARITON REVIEW

821 Camino de Jemez, Santa Fe, NM 87501. (660)785-4499. Fax: (660)785-7486. **Contact:** Jim Barnes. Magazine: 6×9; approximately 100 pages; 60 lb. paper; 65 lb. cover stock; photographs on cover. ''We demand only excellence in fiction and fiction translation for a general and college readership.'' Estab. 1975. Circ. 600.

Needs Experimental, literary, mainstream, novel excerpts (if they can stand alone), translations, traditional. ''We are not interested in slick or sick material.'' Accepts 3-5 mss/issue; 6-10 mss/year. Publishes ms 6 months after acceptance. **Publishes some new writers/year.** Recently published work by Ann Townsend, Glenn Del-Grosso, Paul Ruffin, Kenneth Lincoln. Also publishes literary essays, poetry. Sometimes comments on rejected mss.

How to Contact Send complete ms. No book-length mss. Responds in 1 week to queries; 1 month to mss. No simultaneous submissions. Sample copy for $5 and 7×10 SAE with 4 first-class stamps. Reviews fiction.

Payment/Terms Pays $5/page (up to $50). Pays on publication for first North American serial rights.

Advice ''Do not ask us for guidelines; the only guidelines are excellence in all matters. Write well and study the publication you are submitting to. We are interested only in the very best fiction and fiction translation. We are not interested in slick material. We do not read photocopies, dot-matrix or carbon copies. Know the simple mechanics of submission—SASE, no paper clips, no odd-sized SASE, etc. Know the genre (short story, novella, etc.). Know the unwritten laws. There is too much manufactured fiction—assembly-lined, ego-centered personal essays offered as fiction.''

$ 🖊 🎦 THE CHATTAHOOCHEE REVIEW

Georgia Perimeter College, 2101 Womack Rd., Dunwoody GA 30338-4497. (770)274-5145. Web site: www.chattahoochee-review.org. **Contact:** Marc Fitten, editor. Magazine: 6×9; 150 pages; 70 lb. paper; 80 lb. cover stock; illustrations; photos. ''We publish a number of Southern writers, but *Chattahoochee Review* is not a regional magazine by design. All themes, forms and styles are considered as long as they impact the whole person: heart, mind, intuition and imagination.'' Quarterly. Estab. 1980. Circ. 1,350.

• Fiction from *The Chattahoochee Review* has been included in *New Stories from the South* and was a 2003 winner of a Governor's Award in Humanities.

Needs ''No juvenile, romance, science fiction.'' Accepts 5 mss/issue. Does not read mss June 1-August 31. Publishes ms 3 months after acceptance. **Publishes 5 new writers/year.** Recently published work by George Singleton, William Gay, Martha Witt, Ignacio Padilla. Length: 6,000 words maximum; average length: 2,500 words. Sometimes comments on rejected mss.

How to Contact Send complete ms with SASE. Responds in 2 weeks to queries; 4 months to mss. Accepts simultaneous submissions. Sample copy for $6. Writer's guidelines online. Reviews fiction.

Payment/Terms Pays $20/page ($250 max) and 2 contributor's copies. Pays on publication for first rights.

Advice ''Arrange to read magazine before you submit to it.''

CHICAGO QUARTERLY REVIEW

Monadnock Group Publishers, 517 Sherman Ave., Evanston IL 60202-2815. (719)633-9794. **Contact:** Syed Afzal Haider, Jane Lawrence and Lisa McKenzie, editors. Magazine: 6×9; 125 pages; illustrations; photos. Annual. Estab. 1994. Circ. 300.

Needs Literary. Receives 20-30 unsolicited mss/month. Accepts 6-8 mss/issue; 8-16 mss/year. Publishes ms 1 year after acceptance. Agented fiction 10%. **Publishes 8-10 new writers/year.** Length: 5,000 words; average length: 2,500 words. Publishes short shorts. Also publishes literary essays, poetry. Sometimes comments on rejected mss.

How to Contact Send a disposable copy of ms and #10 SASE for reply only. Responds in 2 months to queries; 6 months to mss. Accepts simultaneous submissions. Sample copy for $9.

Payment/Terms Pays 4 contributor's copies; additional copies $9. Pays on publication for one-time rights.

Advice "The writer's voice ought to be clear and unique and should explain something of what it means to be human. We want well-written stories that reflect an appreciation for the rhythm and music of language, work that shows passion and commitment to the art of writing."

CHICAGO REVIEW

5801 S. Kenwood Ave., Chicago IL 60637. (773)702-0887. E-mail: chicago-review@uchicago.edu. Web site: humanities.uchicago.edu/orgs/review. **Contact:** Joshua Kotin, editor. Magazine for a highly literate general audience: 6×9; 128 pages; offset white 60 lb. paper; illustrations; photos. Quarterly. Estab. 1946. Circ. 3,500.

Needs Experimental, literary, contemporary. Receives 200 unsolicited mss/month. Accepts 2 mss/issue; 8 mss/ year. Recently published work by Harry Mathews, Tom House, Viet Dinh and Doris Dörrie. Also publishes literary essays, literary criticism, poetry.

How to Contact SASE. Responds in 3-6 months to mss. No simultaneous submissions. Sample copy for $10. Guidelines via Web site or SASE.

Payment/Terms Pays 3 contributor's copies and subscription.

Advice "We look for innovative fiction that avoids cliché."

$ ◎ CHRYSALIS READER

1745 Gravel Hill Road, Dillwyn VA 23936. (434)983-3021. E-mail: chrysalis@hovac.com. Web site: www.swede nborg.com/chrysalis. **Contact:** Robert Tucker, fiction editor. Book series: 7½×10; 192 pages; coated cover stock; illustrations; photos. *"The Chrysalis Reader* audience includes people from numerous faiths and backgrounds. Many of them work in psychology, education, religion, the arts, sciences, or one of the helping professions. The style of writing may be humorous, serious, or some combination of these approaches. Essays, poetry, and fiction that are not evangelical in tone but that are unique in addressing the Chrysalis Reader theme are more likely to be accepted. Our readers are interested in expanding, enriching, or challenging their intellects, hearts, and philosophies, and many also just want to enjoy a good read. For these reasons the editors attempt to publish a mix of writings. Articles and poetry must be related to the theme; however, you may have your own approach to the theme not written in our description." Estab. 1985. Circ. 3,000.

• This journal explores contemporary questions of spirituality from the perspective of Swedenborg theology.

Needs Adventure, experimental, historical, literary, mainstream, mystery/suspense, science fiction, fiction (leading to insight), contemporary, spiritual, sports. No religious works. Upcoming theme: "Other Worlds" (Fall 2007). Receives 50 unsolicited mss/month. Accepts 15-20 mss/issue; 20-40 mss/year. Publishes ms 9 months after acceptance. **Publishes 10 new writers/year.** Recently published work by Robert Bly, Larry Dossey, Dr. Bernie Siegel, Virgil Suárez, Carol Lem, Alan Magee, John Hitchcock. Also publishes literary essays, literary criticism, poetry. Sometimes comments on rejected mss.

How to Contact Query with SASE. Accepts submissions by e-mail. Responds in 1 month to queries; 4 months to mss. No simultaneous submissions. Sample copy for $10 and 8½×11 SAE. Writer's guidelines online.

Payment/Terms Pays $50-150. Pays at page-proof stage. Acquires first rights, makes work-for-hire assignments. Sends galleys to author.

Advice Looking for "1: *Quality*; 2. appeal for our audience; 3. relevance to/illumination of an issue's theme."

CIMARRON REVIEW

Oklahoma State University, 205 Morrill Hall, Stillwater OK 74078-0135. (405)744-9476. Web site: cimarronrevie w.okstate.edu. **Contact:** Toni Graham, fiction editor. Magazine: 6×9; 110 pages. "Poetry and fiction on contemporary themes; personal essays on contemporary issues that cope with life in the 21st century. We are eager to receive manuscripts from both established and less experienced writers who intrigue us with their unusual perspective, language, imagery and character." Quarterly. Estab. 1967. Circ. 600.

Needs Literary-quality short stories and novel excerpts. No juvenile or genre fiction. Accepts 3-5 mss/issue; 12-15 mss/year. Publishes ms 2-6 months after acceptance. **Publishes 2-4 new writers/year.** Recently published work by Adam Braver, Gary Fincke, Catherine Brady, Nona Caspers, David Ryan. Also publishes literary essays, literary criticism, poetry.

How to Contact Send complete ms with SASE. Responds in 2-6 months to mss. Accepts simultaneous submissions. Sample copy for $7. Reviews fiction.

Payment/Terms Pays 2 contributor's copies. Acquires first North American serial rights.

Advice "In order to get a feel for the kind of work we publish, please read an issue or two before submitting."

$ ◖ THE CINCINNATI REVIEW

P.O. Box 210069, Cincinnati OH 45221-0069. (513)556-3954. E-mail: editors@cincinnatireview.com. Web site: www.cincinnatireview.com. **Contact:** Brock Clarke, fiction editor. Magazine: 6×9; 180-200 pages; 60 lb. white offset paper. "A journal devoted to publishing the best new literary fiction and poetry as well as book reviews, essays and interviews." Semiannual. Estab. 2003.

Needs Literary. Does not want genre fiction. Accepts 13 mss/year. Reads submissions September 1-May 31. Manuscripts arriving during June, July and August will be returned unread.

How to Contact Send complete ms with SASE. Does not consider e-mail submissions. Responds in 2 weeks to queries; 6 weeks to mss. Accepts simultaneous submissions with notice. Sample copy for $9, subscription $15. Writer's guidelines online or send SASE.

Payment/Terms Pays $25/page. Pays on publication for first North American serial, electronic rights. All rights revert to author upon publication.

◪ ◯ ◎ THE CLAREMONT REVIEW, The Contemporary Magazine of Young Adult Writers

The Claremont Review Publishers, 4980 Wesley Rd., Victoria BC V8Y 1Y9 Canada. (250)658-5221. Fax: (250)658-5387. E-mail: editor@theClaremontReview.ca. Web site: www.theClaremontReview.ca. **Contact:** Lacy Bashford (managing editor), Susan Stenson, editors. Magazine: 6×9; 110-120 pages; book paper; soft gloss cover; b&w illustrations. "We are dedicated to publishing young writers aged 13-19 from anywhere in the English-speaking world, but primarily Canada and the U.S." Biannual. Estab. 1992. Circ. 700.

Needs Young adult/teen ("their writing, not writing for them"). No science fiction, fantasy. Receives 20-30 unsolicited mss/month. Accepts 10-12 mss/issue; 20-24 mss/year. Publishes ms 3 months after acceptance. **Publishes 100 new writers/year.** Recently published work by Danielle Hubbard, Kristina Lucas, Taylor McKinnon. Length: 5,000 words; average length: 1,500-3,000 words. Publishes short shorts. Also publishes poetry. Always comments on rejected mss.

How to Contact Responds in 3 months to mss. Accepts multiple submissions. Sample copy for $10.

Payment/Terms Pays 1 contributor's copy. Additional copies for $6. Acquires first North American serial, one-time rights. Sponsors awards/contests.

Advice Looking for "good concrete narratives with credible dialogue and solid use of original detail. It must be unique, honest and have a glimpse of some truth. Send an error-free final draft with a short cover letter and bio. Read us first to see what we publish."

◯ COAL CITY REVIEW

Coal City Press, University of Kansas, Lawrence KS 66045. E-mail: coalcity@sunflower.com. **Contact:** Mary Wharff, fiction editor. Literary magazine/journal: 8½×5½, 124 pages, heavy cover. Includes photographs. Annual. Estab. 1990. Circ. 200.

Needs Experimental, literary. Does not want erotica, horror, romance, mystery. Receives 10-20 mss/month. Accepts 8-10 mss/issue. Does not read November-March. Manuscript published up to 1 year after acceptance. Agented fiction 0%. **Publishes 5-10 new writers/year.** Published Daniel A. Hoyt, Bill Church, Laurie Martin-Frydman (debut), Tasha Haas, Marc Dickinson (debut), Elspeth Wood. Length: 50 words (min)—4,000 words (max). Average length: 2,000 words. Publishes short shorts. Average length of short shorts: 250 words. Also publishes literary criticism, poetry. Sometimes comments on/critiques rejected manuscripts.

How to Contact Submit via e-mail to coalcity@sunflower.com. Attach Word file. Include estimated word count, brief bio, list of publications. Responds to mss in 4 months. Send disposable copy of ms and #10 SASE for reply only. Considers simultaneous submissions. Sample copy available for $7. Guidelines available via e-mail.

Payment and Terms Writers receive 2 contributor's copies. Additional copies $5. Pays on publication. Acquires one-time rights. Publication is copyrighted.

Advice "We are looking for artful stories—with great language and great heart. Please do not send work that has not been thoughtfully and carefully revised or edited."

$ ◖ COLORADO REVIEW

Center for Literary Publishing, Department of English, Colorado State University, Fort Collins CO 80523. (970)491-5449. E-mail: creview@colostate.edu. Web site: http://coloradoreview.colostate.edu. **Contact:** Stephanie G'Schwind, editor. Literary journal: 224 pages; 60 lb. book weight paper. Estab. 1956. Circ. 1,300.

Needs Ethnic/multicultural, experimental, literary, mainstream, contemporary. "No genre fiction." Receives 1,000 unsolicited mss/month. Accepts 4-5 mss/issue. Does not read mss May-August. Publishes ms within 1 year after acceptance. Recently published work by Paul Mandelbaum, Ann Hood, Kent Haruf, Kelly Magee, Bret Lott. Also publishes poetry.

How to Contact Send complete ms. Responds in 2 months to mss. Sample copy for $10. Writer's guidelines online. Reviews fiction.

Payment/Terms Pays $5/page plus two contributor's copies. Pays on publication for first North American serial rights. Rights revert to author upon publication. Sends galleys to author.

Advice "We are interested in manuscripts that show craft, imagination and a convincing voice. If a story has reached a level of technical competence, we are receptive to the fiction working on its own terms. The oldest advice is still the best: persistence. Approach every aspect of the writing process with pride, conscientiousness— from word choice to manuscript appearance. Be familiar with the *Colorado Review*; read a couple of issues before submitting your manuscript."

$◻ ◙ CONFRONTATION, A Literary Journal

Long Island University, Brookville NY 11548. (516)299-2720. Fax: (516)299-2735. **Contact:** Jonna Semeiks. Magazine: 6×9; 250-350 pages; 70 lb. paper; 80 lb. cover; illustrations; photos. "We are eclectic in our taste. Excellence of style is our dominant concern." Semiannual. Estab. 1968. Circ. 2,000.

● *Confrontation* has garnered a long list of awards and honors, including the Editor's Award for Distinguished Achievement from CCLP and NEA grants. Work from the magazine has appeared in numerous anthologies including the *Pushcart Prize*, *Best Short Stories* and *The O. Henry Prize Stories*.

Needs Experimental, literary, mainstream, novel excerpts (if they are self-contained stories), regional, slice-of-life vignettes, contemporary, prose poems. "No 'proselytizing' literature or genre fiction." Receives 400 unsolicited mss/month. Accepts 30 mss/issue; 60 mss/year. Does not read June-September. Publishes ms 6 months to 1 year after acceptance. Agented fiction approximately 10-15%. **Publishes 20-30 new writers/year.** Recently published work by Susan Vreeland, Lanford Wilson, Tom Stacey, Elizabeth Swados and Sallie Bingham. Publishes short shorts. Also publishes literary essays, poetry.

How to Contact Send complete ms. Accepts e-mail submissions only. "Cover letters acceptable, not necessary. We accept simultaneous submissions but do not prefer them." Responds in 3 weeks to queries; 2 months to mss. Sample copy for $3. Writer's guidelines not available. Reviews fiction.

Payment/Terms Pays $25-250. Pays on publication for first North American serial, first, one-time rights.

Advice "We look for literary merit. Keep trying."

◩ ◙ CONNECTICUT REVIEW

Connecticut State University System, 39 Woodland St., Hartford CT 06105-2337. (203)837-9043 for senior editor. Web site: www.connecticutreview.com. **Contact:** John Briggs, senior editor. Magazine: 6×9; 208 pages; white/heavy paper; glossy/heavy cover; color and b&w illustrations and photos; artwork. *Connecticut Review* presents a wide range of cultural interests that cross disciplinary lines. "We're looking for the best in literary writing in a variety of genres. Some issues contain sections devoted to announced themes. The editors invite the submission of academic articles of general interest, creative essays, translations, short stories, short-shorts, plays, poems and interviews." Semiannual. Estab. 1968. Circ. 2,500. Member CLMP.

● Work published in *Connecticut Review* has won the Pushcart Prize and inclusion in *Best American Poetry*, *Best American Short Stories* (2000). *CR* has also received the Phoenix Award for Significant Editorial Achievement and National Public Radio's Award for Literary Excellence (2001).

Needs Literary. "Content must be under 4,000 words and suitable for circulation to libraries and high schools." Receives 250 unsolicited mss/month. Accepts 40 mss/issue; 80 mss/year. Does not accept mss to read May 15-September 1. Publishes ms 1-2 years after acceptance. **Publishes 15-20 new writers/year.** Has published work by John Searles, Michael Schiavone, Norman German, Tom Williams, Paul Ruffin, Dick Allen.

How to Contact Send two disposable copies of ms and #10 SASE for reply only. Responds in 6 months to queries. Considers simultaneous submissions. Sample copy for $12. Writer's guidelines for SASE, but forms for submissions and guidelines available on Web site.

Payment/Terms Pays 2 contributor's copies; additional copies $10. Pays on publication for first rights. Rights revert to author on publication. Sends galleys to author.

◩ COTTONWOOD

Box J, 400 Kansas Union, University of Kansas, Lawrence KS 66045-2115. (785)864-2516. Fax: (785)864-4298. E-mail: tlorenz@ku.edu. **Contact:** Tom Lorenz, fiction editor. Magazine: 6×9; 100 pages; illustrations; photos. "*Cottonwood* publishes high quality prose, poetry and artwork and is aimed at an audience that appreciates the same. We have a national scope and reputation while maintaining a strong regional flavor." Semiannual. Estab. 1965. Circ. 500.

Needs "We publish literary prose and poetry." Receives 25-50 unsolicited mss/month. Accepts 5-6 mss/issue; 10-12 mss/year. Publishes ms 6-18 months after acceptance. Agented fiction 10%. **Publishes 1-3 new writers/ year.** Recently published work by Connie May Fowler, Oakley Hall, Cris Mazza. Length: 1,000-8,000 words; average length: 2,000-5,000 words. Publishes short shorts. Also publishes literary essays, literary criticism, poetry.

How to Contact SASE for return of ms. Responds in 6 months to mss. Accepts simultaneous submissions. Sample copy for $8.50, 9 × 12 SAE and $1.90. Reviews fiction.

Payment/Terms Acquires one-time rights.

Advice "We're looking for depth and/or originality of subject matter, engaging voice and style, emotional honesty, command of the material and the structure. *Cottonwood* publishes high quality literary fiction, but we are very open to the work of talented new writers. Write something honest and that you care about and write it as well as you can. Don't hesitate to keep trying us. We sometimes take a piece from a writer we've rejected a number of times. We generally don't like clever, gimmicky writing. The style should be engaging but not claim all the the attention itself."

$CRAZYHORSE

College of Charleston, Dept. of English, 66 George St., Charleston SC 29424. (843)953-7740. E-mail: crazyhorse@ cofc.edu. Web site: http://crazyhorse.cofc.edu. **Contact:** Anthony Varallo, fiction editor. Literary magazine: 8³/₄ × 8¹/₄; 150 pages; illustrations; photos. "*Crazyhorse* publishes writing of fine quality regardless of style, predilection, subject. Editors are especially interested in original writing that engages in the work of honest communication." Raymond Carver called *Crazyhorse* "an indispensable literary magazine of the first order." Semiannual. Estab. 1961. Circ. 2,000.

• Richard Jackson's "This" won a 2004 Pushcart Prize for *Crazyhorse*.

Needs All fiction of fine quality. Receives 200 unsolicited mss/month. Accepts 8-10 mss/issue; 16-20 mss/year. Publishes ms 6-12 months after acceptance. Recently published work by W.D. Wetherell, T.M. McNally, Lia Purpura, Elizabeth Weld, Steven Schwarz. Length: 25 pages; average length: 15 pages. Publishes short shorts. Also publishes literary essays, poetry.

How to Contact Send SASE for return of ms or disposable copy of ms and #10 SASE for reply only. Responds in 1 week to queries; 3 months to mss. Accepts simultaneous submissions. Sample copy for $5. Writer's guidelines for SASE or by e-mail.

Payment/Terms Pays $20 per page and 2 contributor's copies; additional copies $5. Acquires first North American serial rights. Sends galleys to author.

Advice "Write to explore subjects you care about. Clarity of language; subject is one in which something is at stake."

THE CREAM CITY REVIEW

University of Wisconsin-Milwaukee, Box 413, Milwaukee WI 53201. (414)229-4708. E-mail: tccr@uwm.edu. Web site: www.uwm.edu/dept/english/ccr. **Contact:** Bayard Godsave and Suzanne Heagy, fiction editors. Magazine: 5¹/₂ × 8¹/₂; 150-300 pages; 70 lb. offset/perfect bound paper; 80 lb. cover stock; illustrations; photos. "General literary publication—an eclectic and electric selection of the best fiction we can find." Semiannual. Estab. 1975. Circ. 2,000.

Needs Ethnic/multicultural, experimental, literary, regional, translations, flash fiction, literary humor, magical realism, prose poem. "Would like to see more quality fiction. No horror, formulaic, racist, sexist, pornographic, homophobic, science fiction, romance." Receives 300 unsolicited mss/month. Accepts 6-10 mss/issue. Does not read fiction or poetry April-September. **Publishes 10 new writers/year.** Recently published work by Stuart Dybek, Laurence Goldstein, Harold Jaffe, Bradford Morrow, Gordon Weaver, Gordon Henry, Louis Owens, Arthur Boozhoo, George Makana Clark, Kyoko Mori. Publishes short shorts. Also publishes literary essays, literary criticism, poetry, memoir.

How to Contact Responds in 6 months to mss. Accepts simultaneous, multiple submissions. Sample copy for $7 (back issue), $12 (current issue). Reviews fiction.

Payment/Terms Pays 1-year subscription. Acquires first rights. Rights revert to author after publication. Sponsors awards/contests.

Advice "The best stories are those in which the reader doesn't know what is going to happen or what the writer is trying to do. Avoid formulas. Surprise us with language and stunning characters."

CRUCIBLE

English Dept., Barton College, College Station, Wilson NC 27893. (252)399-6343. Editor: Terrence L. Grimes. **Contact:** Fiction Editor. Magazine of fiction and poetry for a general, literary audience. Annual. Estab. 1964. Circ. 500.

Needs Ethnic/multicultural, experimental, feminist, literary, regional. Would like to see more short shorts.

Receives 20 unsolicited mss/month. Accepts 5-6 mss/year. Does not normally read mss from April 30 to December 1. Publishes ms 4-5 months after acceptance. **Publishes 5 new writers/year.** Recently published work by Sally Buckner.

How to Contact Send 3 complete copies of ms unsigned with cover letter which should include a brief biography, "in case we publish." Responds in 6 weeks to queries; 4 months to mss. Sample copy for $7. Writer's guidelines free.

Payment/Terms Pays in contributor's copies. Acquires first rights.

Advice "Write about what you know. Experimentation is fine as long as the experiences portrayed come across as authentic, that is to say, plausible."

DESCANT, Ft. Worth's Journal of Fiction and Poetry

Texas Christian University, TCU Box 297270, Ft. Worth TX 76129. (817)257-6537. Fax: (817)257-6239. E-mail: descant@tcu.edu. Web site: www.descant.tcu.edu. **Contact**: Dave Kuhne, editor. Magazine: 6×9; 120-150 pages; acid free paper; paper cover. "*descant* seeks high quality poems and stories in both traditional and innovative form." Annual. Estab. 1956. Circ. 500-750. Member CLMP.

• Offers four cash awards: The $500 Frank O'Connor Award for the best story in an issue; the $250 Gary Wilson Award for an outstanding story in an issue; the $500 Betsy Colquitt Award for the best poem in an issue; the $250 Baskerville Publishers Award for outstanding poem in an issue. Several stories first published by *descant* have appeared in *Best American Short Stories*.

Needs Literary. "No horror, romance, fantasy, erotica." Receives 20-30 unsolicited mss/month. Accepts 25-35 mss/year. Publishes ms 1 year after acceptance. **Publishes 50% new writers/year.** Recently published work by William Harrison, Annette Sanford, Miller Williams, Patricia Chao, Vonesca Stroud, and Walt McDonald. Length: 1,000-5,000 words; average length: 2,500 words. Publishes short shorts. Also publishes poetry.

How to Contact Send complete ms with cover letter. Include estimated word count and brief bio. Responds in 6-8 weeks to mss. Accepts simultaneous submissions. Sample copy for $10. SASE, e-mail or fax.

Payment/Terms 2 Contributor's copies, additional copies $6. Pays on publication for one-time rights. Sponsors awards/contests.

Advice "We look for character and quality of prose. Send your best short work."

DISLOCATE

English Department, University of Minnesota, 222 Lind Hall, 207 Church St. SE, Minneapolis MN 55455. E-mail: dislocate.magazine@gmail.com. Web site: http://dislocate.org. **Contact:** Andrew Luckham. Magazine has revolving editor. Editorial term: 2006-2007. Literary magazine/journal: 5½× 8½, 128 pages. Annual. Estab. 2005. Circ. 2,000.

Needs Literary fiction. Receives 25-50 mss/month. Accepts 2-3 mss/year. Publishes short shorts. Also publishes literary essays, poetry.

How to Contact Send complete ms with cover letter. Send either SASE (or IRC) for return of ms or disposable copy of ms and #10 SASE for reply only. Considers simultaneous submissions, multiple submissions. Guidelines available on Web site.

Payment and Terms Pays on publication.

Advice "Looking for quality and originality."

$ DOWNSTATE STORY

1825 Maple Ridge, Peoria IL 61614. (309)688-1409. Web site: www.wiu.edu/users/mfgeh/dss. **Contact:** Elaine Hopkins, editor. Magazine: includes illustrations. "Short fiction—some connection with Illinois or the Midwest." Annual. Estab. 1992. Circ. 250.

• Fiction received the Best of Illinois Stories Award.

Needs Adventure, ethnic/multicultural, experimental, historical, horror, humor/satire, literary, mainstream, mystery/suspense, psychic/supernatural/occult, regional, romance, science fiction, suspense, western. No porn. Accepts 10 mss/issue. Publishes ms 1 year after acceptance. Publishes short shorts. Also publishes literary essays.

How to Contact Send complete ms with a cover letter. SASE for return of ms. Responds "ASAP" to mss. Accepts simultaneous submissions. Sample copy for $8. Writer's guidelines online.

Payment/Terms Pays $50. Pays on acceptance for first rights.

ECLIPSE, A Literary Journal

Glendale College, 1500 N. Verdugo Rd., Glendale CA 91208. (818)240-1000. Fax: (818)549-9436. E-mail: eclipse @glendale.edu. **Contact:** Michael Ritterbrown, fiction editor. Magazine: 8½× 5½; 150-200 pages; 60 lb. paper. "*Eclipse* is committed to publishing outstanding fiction and poetry. We look for compelling characters and stories executed in ways that provoke our readers and allow them to understand the world in new ways." Annual. Circ. 1,800. CLMP.

Needs Ethnic/multicultural, experimental, literary. "Does not want horror, religious, science fiction or thriller mss." Receives 50-100 unsolicited mss/month. Accepts 10 mss/year. Publishes ms 6-12 months after acceptance. **Publishes 5 new writers/year.** Recently published work by Amy Sage Webb, Ira Sukrungruang, Richard Schmitt, George Rabasa. Length: 6,000 words; average length: 4,000 words. Publishes short shorts. Also publishes poetry. Sometimes comments on rejected mss.

How to Contact Send complete ms. Responds in 2 weeks to queries; 4-6 weeks to mss. Accepts simultaneous submissions. Sample copy for $8. Writer's guidelines for #10 SASE or by e-mail.

Payment/Terms Pays 2 contributor's copies; additional copies $6. Pays on publication for first North American serial rights.

Advice "We look for well-crafted fiction, experimental or traditional, with a clear unity of elements. A good story is important, but the writing must transcend the simple act of conveying the story."

⬛ ECOTONE, REIMAGINING PLACE

UNCW Dept. of Creative Writing, 601 South College Road, Wilmington NC 28403-3297. E-mail: ecotone@uncw. edu. Web site: www.uncw.edu/ecotone. **Contact:** David Gessner, editor-in-chief. Literary magazine/journal: 6×9. "Our magazine is focused on the writing of place and borders, be them geographical, international, sexual, spiritual, etc." Semiannual. Estab. 2005. Circ. 1,500.

Needs Ethnic/multicultural, experimental, historical, literary, mainstream. Does not want genre (fantasy, horror, sci-fi, etc.) or young adult fiction. Receives 90-100 mss/month. Accepts 5-7 mss/issue; 10-12 mss/year. Does not read mss May 1-August 14. Manuscript published 6-8 months after acceptance. Publishes 5-10 new writers/year. Published Alicia Erian, Luis Alberto Urrea, Brad Land, Paul Lisicky, Clyde Edgerton, Jill McCorkle, Rebecca Barry, Sheila Kohler. Length: 2,000 words (min)-6,000 words (max). Average length: 4,500 words. Also publishes literary essays, poetry.

How to Contact Send complete ms with cover letter. Include brief bio, list of publications. Send either SASE (or IRC) for return of ms or disposable copy of ms and #10 SASE for reply only. Considers multiple submissions. Sample copy available for $5. Guidelines available for SASE, via e-mail, on Web site.

Payment and Terms Writers receive 2 contributor's copies. Additional copies $5. Pays on publication. Acquires first North American serial rights. Sends galleys to author. Publication is copyrighted.

⬛ EMRYS JOURNAL

The Emrys Foundation, P.O. Box 8813, Greenville SC 29604. E-mail: ldishman@charter.net. Web site: www.emrys.org. **Contact:** L.B. Dishman. Catalog: 9×9¾; 120 pages; 80 lb. paper. "We publish short fiction, poetry and creative nonfiction. We are particularly interested in hearing from women and other minorities." Annual. Estab. 1984. Circ. 400.

Needs Literary, contemporary. No religious, sexually explicit or science fiction mss. Accepts approx 18 mss/issue. Reading period: August 1-November 1, no ms will be read outside the reading period. Publishes mss in April. **Publishes several new writers/year.** Recently published work by Jessica Goodfellow and Ron Rash. Length: 5,000 words; average length: 3,500 words. Publishes short shorts.

How to Contact Send complete ms with SASE. Responds after end of reading period. Does not accept simultaneous submissions. Accepts multiple submissions. Sample copy for $15 and 7×10 SAE with 4 first-class stamps. Writer's guidelines for #10 SASE.

Payment/Terms Pays in contributor's copies. Acquires first rights.

Advice Looks for previously unpublished literary fiction.

$ ⬛ 🏆 EPOCH

Cornell University, 251 Goldwin Smith Hall, Cornell University, Ithaca NY 14853. (607)255-3385. Fax: (607)255-6661. **Contact:** Joseph Martin, senior editor. Magazine: 6×9; 128 pages; good quality paper; good cover stock. "Well-written literary fiction, poetry, personal essays. Newcomers always welcome. Open to mainstream and avant-garde writing." Estab. 1947. Circ. 1,000.

● Work originally appearing in this quality literary journal has appeared in numerous anthologies including *Best American Short Stories*, *Best American Poetry*, *Pushcart Prize*, *The O. Henry Prize Stories*, *Best of the West* and *New Stories from the South*.

Needs Ethnic/multicultural, experimental, literary, mainstream, novel excerpts, literary short stories. "No genre fiction. Would like to see more Southern fiction (Southern US)." Receives 500 unsolicited mss/month. Accepts 15-20 mss/issue. Does not read in summer (April 15-September 15). Publishes ms an average of 6 months after acceptance. **Publishes 3-4 new writers/year.** Recently published work by Antonya Nelson, Doris Betts, Heidi Jon Schmidt. Also publishes poetry. Sometimes comments on rejected mss.

How to Contact Send complete ms. Responds in 2 weeks to queries; 6 weeks to mss. No simultaneous submissions. Sample copy for $5. Writer's guidelines for #10 SASE.
Payment/Terms Pays $5 and up/printed page. Pays on publication for first North American serial rights.
Advice "Read the journals you're sending work to."

⊘ EUREKA LITERARY MAGAZINE

300 E. College Ave., Eureka College, Eureka IL 61530-1500. (309)467-6591. E-mail: elm@eureka.edu. **Contact:** Eric Freeze, editor. Magazine: 6×9; 120 pages; 70 lb. white offset paper; 80 lb. gloss cover; photographs (occasionally). "We seek to be open to the best stories that are submitted to us. Our audience is a combination of professors/writers, students of writing and literature, and general readers." Semiannual. Estab. 1992. Circ. 500.
Needs Adventure, ethnic/multicultural, experimental, fantasy (science), feminist, historical, humor/satire, literary, mainstream, mystery/suspense (private eye/hard-boiled, romantic), psychic/supernatural/occult, regional, romance (historical), science fiction (soft/sociological), translations. Would like to see more "good literary fiction stories, good magical realism, historical fiction. We try to achieve a balance between the traditional and the experimental. We look for the well-crafted story, but essentially any type of story that has depth and substance to it is welcome." Receives 100 unsolicited mss/month. Accepts 10-12 mss/issue; 20-30 mss/year. Does not read mss in summer (May-August). **Publishes 5-6 new writers/year.** Recently published work by Jane Guill, Sarah Strickley, Ray Bradbury, Patrick Madden, Virgil Suárez, Cynthia Gallaher, Wendell Mayo. Length: 4,000-6,000 words; average length: 5,000 words. Also publishes short shorts, flash fiction and poetry.
How to Contact Accepts submissions by e-mail. Send SASE for reply, return of ms or send disposable copy of ms. Responds in 2 weeks to electronic queries; 4 months to mss. Accepts simultaneous, multiple submissions. Sample copy for $7.50.
Advice "Do something that hasn't been done a thousand times already. Give us unusual characters in unusual conflicts—clear resolution isn't always necessary, but it's nice. We don't hold to hard and fast rules about length, but most stories could do with some cutting. Make sure your title is relevant and eye-catching. Please do not send personal gifts or hate mail. We're a college-operated magazine, so we do not actually exist in summer. If we don't take a submission, that doesn't automatically mean we don't like it—we try to encourage authors who show promise to revise and resubmit. Order a copy if you can."

⊘ EVANSVILLE REVIEW

University of Evansville, 1800 Lincoln Ave., Evansville IN 47722. (812)488-1042. **Contact:** Corinna McClanahan, editor. Magazine: 6×9; 180 pages; 70 lb. white paper; glossy full-color cover; perfect bound. Annual. Estab. 1989. Circ. 1,000.
Needs Does not want erotica, fantasy, experimental or children's fiction. "We're open to all creativity. No discrimination. All fiction, screenplays, nonfiction, poetry, interviews and anything in between." List of upcoming themes available for SASE. Receives 70 unsolicited mss/month. Does not read mss January-August. Agented fiction 2%. **Publishes 20 new writers/year.** Recently published work by John Updike, Arthur Miller, X.J. Kennedy, Jim Barnes, Rita Dove. Also publishes literary essays, poetry.
How to Contact Send SASE for reply, or send a disposable copy of ms. Responds in 1 month to queries; 3 months to mss. Accepts simultaneous, multiple submissions and reprints. Sample copy for $5. Writer's guidelines free.
Payment/Terms Pays 2 contributor's copies. Pays on publication for one-time rights. Not copyrighted.
Advice "Because editorial staff rolls over every 1-2 years, the journal always has a new flavor."

⊘ FAULTLINE, Journal of Art and Literature

Dept. of English and Comparative Literature, University of California, Irvine, Irvine CA 92697-2650. (949)824-1573. E-mail: faultline@uci.edu. Web site: www.humanities.uci.edu/faultline. **Contact:** Editors change in September each year. Literary magazine: 6×9; 200 pages; illustrations; photos. "We publish the very best of what we recieve. Our interest is quality and literary merit." Annual. Estab. 1992.
Needs Translations, literary fiction, nonfiction up to 20 pages. Receives 150 unsolicited mss/month. Accepts 6-9 mss/year. Does not read mss April-September. Publishes ms 9 months after acceptance. Agented fiction 10-20%. **Publishes 30-40% new writers/year.** Recently published work by Maile Meloy, Aimee Bender, David Benioff, Steve Almond, Helen Maria Viramontes, Thomas Keneally. Publishes short shorts. Also publishes literary essays, poetry.
How to Contact Send SASE for reply, return of ms or send a disposable copy of ms. Responds in 2 weeks to queries; 4 months to mss. Accepts simultaneous submissions. Sample copy for $5. Writer's guidelines for business-size envelope.
Payment/Terms Pays 2 contributor's copies. Pays on publication for one-time rights.
Advice "Our commitment is to publish the best work possible from well-known and emerging authors with vivid and varied voices."

▣ ◎ FEMINIST STUDIES

0103 Taliaferro, University of Maryland, College Park MD 20742-7726. (301)405-7415. Fax: (301)405-8395. E-mail: creative@feministstudies.org. Web site: www.feministstudies.org. **Contact:** Minnie Bruce Pratt, creative writing editor. Magazine: journal-sized; about 200 pages; photographs. "We are interested in work that addresses questions of interest to the feminist studies audience, particularly work that pushes past the boundaries of what has been done before. We look for creative work that is intellectually challenging and aesthetically adventurous, that is complicated in dialogue with feminist ideas and concepts, and that shifts our readers into new perspectives on women/gender." Triannual. Estab. 1974. Circ. 7,500.

Needs Ethnic/multicultural, feminist, LGBT, contemporary. Receives 20 unsolicited mss/month. Accepts 2-3 mss/issue. "We review fiction and poetry twice a year. Deadline dates are May 1 and December 1. Authors will recieve notice of the board's decision by July 15 and February 15, respectively." Recently published work by Grace M. Cho, Dawn McDuffie, Susanne Davis, Liz Robbins, Maria Mazziotti Gillan, Cathleen Calbert, and Mary Ann Wehler. Sometimes comments on rejected mss.

How to Contact No simultaneous submissions. Sample copy for $17. Writer's guidelines at Web site.

Payment/Terms Pays 2 contributor's copies and 10 tearsheets.

$▣ ▣ FICTION

Department of English, The City College of New York, 138th St. & Convent Ave., New York NY 10031. (212)650-6319. E-mail: fictionmagazine@yahoo.com. Web site: www.fictioninc.com. **Contact:** Mark J. Mirsky, editor. Magazine: 6×9; 150-250 pages; illustrations; occasionally photos. "As the name implies, we publish only fiction; we are looking for the best new writing available, leaning toward the unconventional. *Fiction* has traditionally attempted to make accessible the unaccessible, to bring the experimental to a broader audience." Semiannual. Estab. 1972. Circ. 4,000.

- Stories first published in *Fiction* have been selected for inclusion in the *Pushcart Prize* and *Best of the Small Presses* anthologies.

Needs Experimental, humor/satire (satire), literary, translations, contemporary. No romance, science fiction, etc. Receives 200 unsolicited mss/month. Accepts 12-20 mss/issue; 24-40 mss/year. Reads mss September 15-April 15. Publishes ms 1 year after acceptance. Agented fiction 10-20%. Recently published work by Joyce Carol Oates, Robert Musil, Romulus Linney. Publishes short shorts. Sometimes comments on rejected mss.

How to Contact Send complete ms with cover letter and SASE. No e-mail submissions. Responds in 3 months to mss. Accepts simultaneous submissions. Sample copy for $5. Writer's guidelines online.

Payment/Terms Pays $75 plus subscription. Acquires first rights.

Advice "The guiding principle of *Fiction* has always been to go to *terra incognita* in the writing of the imagination and to ask that modern fiction set itself serious questions, if often in absurd and comical voices, interrogating the nature of the real and the fantastic. It represents no particular school of fiction, except the innovative. Its pages have often been a harbor for writers at odds with each other. As a result of its willingness to publish the difficult, experimental, unusual, while not excluding the well known, *Fiction* has a unique reputation in the U.S. and abroad as a journal of future directions."

▣ FIRST CLASS

Four-Sep Publications, P.O. Box 86, Friendship IN 47021. E-mail: christopherm@four-sep.com. Web site: www.four-sep.com. **Contact:** Christopher M, editor. Magazine: 4¼×11; 60+ pages; 24 lb./60 lb. offset paper; craft cover; illustrations; photos. "*First Class* features short fiction and poetics from the cream of the small press and killer unknowns—mingling before your very hungry eyes. I publish plays, too." Biannual. Estab. 1995. Circ. 200-400.

Needs Erotica, literary, science fiction (soft/socialogical), satire, drama. "No religious or traditional poetry, or 'boomer angst'—therapy-driven self loathing." Receives 50-70 unsolicited mss/month. Accepts 4-6 mss/issue; 10-12 mss/year. Publishes ms 1 month after acceptance. **Publishes 10-15 new writers/year.** Recently published work by Gerald Locklin, John Bennnet, B.Z. Niditch. Length: 5,000-8,000; average length: 2,000-3,000 words. Publishes short shorts. Also publishes poetry. Sometimes comments on rejected mss.

How to Contact Send SASE or send a disposable copy of ms and #10 SASE for reply only. Responds in 1 week to queries. Accepts simultaneous submissions and reprints. Sample copy for $6. Writer's guidelines for #10 SASE. Reviews fiction.

Payment/Terms Pays 1 contributor's copy; additional copies $5. Acquires one-time rights.

Advice "Don't bore me with puppy dogs and the morose/sappy feeling you have about death. Belt out a good, short, thought-provoking, graphic, uncommon piece."

$▣ ▣ FIVE POINTS, A Journal of Literature and Art

P.O. Box 3999, Georgia State University, Atlanta GA 30302 . (404)463-9484. Fax: (404)651-3167. E-mail: msexton @gsu.edu. Web site: www.webdelsol.com/Five_Points. **Contact:** Megan Sexton, associate editor. Magazine:

6×9; 200 pages; cotton paper; glossy cover; photos. *Five Points* is "committed to publishing work that compels the imagination through the use of fresh and convincing language." Triannual. Estab. 1996. Circ. 2,000.

- Fiction first appearing in *Five Points* has been anthologized in *Best American Fiction*, Pushcart anthologies, and *New Stories from The South*.

Needs List of upcoming themes available for SASE. Receives 250 unsolicited mss/month. Accepts 4 mss/issue; 15-20 mss/year. Does not read mss April 30-September 1. Publishes ms 6 months after acceptance. **Publishes 1 new writer/year.** Recently published work by Frederick Busch, Ursula Hegi, Melanie Rae Thon. Average length: 7,500 words. Publishes short shorts. Also publishes literary essays, poetry. Sometimes comments on rejected mss.

How to Contact Send SASE for reply to query. No simultaneous submissions. Sample copy for $7.

Payment/Terms Pays $15/page minimum ($250 maximum) , free subscription to magazine and 2 contributor's copies; additional copies $4. Acquires first North American serial rights. Sends galleys to author. Sponsors awards/contests.

Advice "We place no limitations on style or content. Our only criteria is excellence. If your writing has an original voice, substance and significance, send it to us. We will publish distinctive, intelligent writing that has something to say and says it in a way that captures and maintains our attention."

FLINT HILLS REVIEW

Dept. of English, Box 4019, Emporia State University, Emporia KS 66801-5087. (620)341-6916. Fax: (620)341-5547. E-mail: webbamy@emporia.edu. Web site: www.emporia.edu/fhr/. **Contact:** Amy Sage Webb, co-editor. Magazine: 9×6; 115 pages; 60 lb. paper; glossy cover; illustrations; photos. "*FHR* seeks work informed by a strong sense of place or region, especially Kansas and the Great Plains region. We seek to provide a publishing venue for writers of the Great Plains and Kansas while also publishing authors whose work evidences a strong sense of place, writing of literary quality, and accomplished use of language and depth of character development." Annual. Estab. 1996. Circ. 500. CLMP.

Needs Ethnic/multicultural, gay, historical, regional (Plains), translations. "No religious, inspirational, children's." Want to see more "writing of literary quality with a strong sense of place." List of upcoming themes online. Receives 5-15 unsolicited mss/month. Accepts 2-5 mss/issue; 2-5 mss/year. Does not read mss April-December. Publishes ms 4 months after acceptance. **Publishes 4 new writers/year.** Recently published work by Kim Stafford, Elizabeth Dodd, Bart Edelman, and Jennifer Henderson. Length: 1 page-5,000; average length: 3,000 words. Publishes short shorts. Also publishes literary essays, literary criticism, poetry.

How to Contact Send a disposable copy of ms and #10 SASE for reply only. Responds in 5 weeks to queries; 6 months to mss. Accepts simultaneous, multiple submissions. Sample copy for $5.50. Writer's guidelines for SASE, by e-mail, fax or on Web site. Reviews fiction.

Payment/Terms Pays 2 contributor's copies; additional copies $5.50. Acquires one-time rights.

Advice "Strong imagery and voice, writing that is informed by place or region, writing of literary quality with depth of character development. Hone the language down to the most literary depiction that is possible in the shortest space that still provides depth of development without excess length."

FLORIDA REVIEW

Dept. of English, University of Central Florida, P.O. Box 161346, Orlando FL 32816-1346. (407)823-2038. E-mail: flreview@mail.ucf.edu. Web site: www.english.ucf.edu/~flreview. **Contact:** Jeanne Leiby, editor. Magazine: 6×9; 144 pages; semi-gloss full color cover, perfect bound. "We publish fiction of high 'literary' quality—stories that delight, instruct and take risks. Our audience consists of avid readers of fiction, poetry and creative nonfiction." Semiannual. Estab. 1972. Circ. 1,500.

Needs Experimental, literary. "We aren't particularly interested in genre fiction (sci-fi, romance, adventure, etc.) but a good story can transcend any genre." Receives 400 unsolicited mss/month. Accepts 5-7 mss/issue; 10-14 mss/year. Publishes ms 3 months after acceptance. **Publishes 2-4 new writers/year.** Recently published work by Billy Collins, David Huddle, Wendell Mayo, Virgil Suárez. Length: 2,000-7,000 words; average length: 5,000 words. Publishes short shorts. Also publishes creative nonfiction, poetry. Rarely comments on rejected mss.

How to Contact Send complete ms. Send SASE (or IRC) for return of the ms or send disposable copy of the ms and #10 SASE for reply only. Responds in 2 weeks to queries; 2 months to mss. Accepts simultaneous submissions. Sample copy for $6. Writer's guidelines for #10 SASE or online.

Payment/Terms Rights held by UCF, revert to author after publication.

Advice "We're looking for writers with fresh voices and original stories. We like risk."

FLYWAY, A Literary Review

Iowa State University, 206 Ross Hall, Ames IA 50011. (515)294-8273. Fax: (515)294-6814. E-mail: flyway@iastate.edu. Web site: www.flyway.org. **Contact:** Stephen Pett, editor. Literary magazine: 6×9; 64 pages; quality paper; cover stock; some illustrations; photos. "We publish quality fiction. Our stories are accompanied by brief commentaries by their authors, the sort of thing a writer might say introducing a piece at a reading." Biannual. Estab. 1995. Circ. 500.

Needs Literary. Receives 50 unsolicited mss/month. Accepts 2-5 mss/issue; 10-12 mss/year. Reads mss September 1-May. Publishes ms 5 months after acceptance. **Publishes 7-10 new writers/year.** Recently published work by Naomi Shihab Nye, Gina Ochsner, Ted Kooser. Length: 5,000; average length: 3,500 words. Publishes short shorts. Often comments on rejected mss.

How to Contact Send SASE. Sample copy for $8. Writer's guidelines for SASE.

Payment/Terms Pays 2 contributor's copies; additional copies $6. Acquires one-time rights.

Advice "Quality, originality, voice, drama, tension. Make it as strong as you can."

☐ FOLIATE OAK LITERARY MAGAZINE, Foliate Oak Online

University of Arkansas-Monticello, MCB 113, Monticello AR 71656. (870)460-1247. E-mail: foliate@uamont.edu. Web site: www. foliateoak.uamont.edu. **Contact**: Diane Payne, faculty advisor. Magazine: 6×9; 80 pages. Monthly. Estab. 1980. Circ. 500.

Needs Adventure, comics/graphic novels, ethnic/multicultural, experimental, family saga, feminist, gay, historical, humor/satire, lesbian, literary, mainstream, science fiction (soft/sociological). No religious, sexist or homophobic work. Receives 30 unsolicited mss/month. Accepts 7 mss/issue; 50 mss/year. Does not read mss May-August. Publishes ms 1 month after acceptance. **Publishes 60 new writers/year.** Recently published work by David Barringer, Thom Didato, Joe Taylor, Molly Giles, Patricia Shevlin, Tony Hoagland. Length: 50-3,500 words; average length: 1,500 words. Publishes short shorts. Also publishes literary essays, literary criticism, poetry. Rarely comments on rejected mss.

How to Contact Send complete ms as an e-mail attachment (Word or RTF). Postal submissions will not be read. Please include author's name and title of story/poem/essay in e-mail header. In the e-mail, please send contact information and a short bio. Responds in 8 weeks. Only accepts submissions August through April. Accepts simultaneous submissions and multiple submissions. Please contact ASAP if work is accepted elsewhere. Sample copy for SASE and 6×8 envelope. Writer's guidelines online. Reviews fiction.

Payment/Terms Pays contributor's copy. Acquires electronic rights. Sends galleys to author. Not copyrighted.

Advice "We're open to honest, experimental, offbeat, realistic and surprising writing, if it has been edited. Limit poems to five per submission, and one short story or creative nonfiction (less than 2,500 words). You may send up to three flash fictions. Please don't send more writing until you hear from us regarding your first submission. We are also looking for artwork sent as .jpg or .gif files."

⊕ $FRANK, An International Journal of Contemporary Writing & Art

Association Frank, 32 rue Edouard Vaillant, Montreuil France. (33)(1)48596658. Fax: (33)(1)48596668. E-mail: submissions@readfrank.com. Web site: www.readfrank.com. or www.frank.ly. **Contact:** David Applefield. "Writing that takes risks and isn't ethnocentric is looked upon favorably." Biannual. Estab. 1983. Circ. 4,000.

Needs Experimental, novel excerpts, international. "At *Frank*, we publish fiction, poetry, literary and art interviews, and translations. We like work that falls between existing genres and has social or political consciousness." Accepts 20 mss/issue. Publishes ms 1 year after acceptance.

How to Contact Send complete ms. Send IRC or $5 cash. Must be previously unpublished in English (world). E-mail submissions as Word attachments are welcome and should be saved in RTF. Responds in 1 month to queries; 2 months to mss. Sample copy for $10. Writer's guidelines online.

Payment/Terms Pays $10/printed page. Pays on publication for one-time rights.

Advice "Send your most daring and original work. At *Frank*, we like work that is not too parochial or insular, however, don't try to write for a 'French' market."

♻ ☑ FREEFALL MAGAZINE

The Alexandra Writers' Centre Society, 922 Ninth Ave. SE, Calgary AB T2G 0S4 Canada. (403)264-4730. E-mail: michelinem@shaw.ca. Web site: www.alexandrawriters.org. **Contact:** Micheline Maylor, editor-in-chief; Lynn Fraser, managing editor. Magazine: 8½×5¾; 100 pages; bond paper; bond stock; illustrations; photos. "*FreeFall* features the best of new, emerging writers and gives them the chance to get into print along with established writers. Now in its 16th year, *FreeFall* seeks to attract readers looking for well-crafted stories, poetry and artwork." Semiannual. Estab. 1990. Circ. Under 500. Alberta Magazine Publishers Association (AMPA).

Needs Literary fiction, poetry, non-fiction, artwork, photography, and reviews. Accepts 3-5 mss/issue; 6-10 mss/year. Reads July and January. Publishes ms 4-6 months after acceptance. **Publishes 40% new writers/year.** Length: 500-3,000 words.

How to Contact Send SASE (or IRC) for return of ms, or send a disposable copy of ms with e-mail address or #10 SASE for reply only. Responds in 3 months to mss. Accepts reprint submissions. Sample copy for $10 (US). Writer's guidelines for SASE, e-mail or on Web site.

Payment/Terms Pays 1 contributor's copy; additional copies $10 (US). Acquires first North American serial, one-time rights.

Advice "We look for thoughtful word usage that conveys clear images and encourages further exploration of the story's idea and neat, clean presentation of work. Carefully read *FreeFall* guidelines before submitting. Do not fold manuscript, and submit 9×11 envelope. Include SASE/IRC for reply and/or return of manuscript. You may contact us by e-mail after initial hardcopy submission. For accepted pieces a request is made for disk or e-mail copy. Web presence attracts submissions from writers all over the world."

○ FRESH BOILED PEANUTS

P.O. Box 43194, Cincinnati OH 45243-0194. E-mail: contact@freshboiledpeanuts.com. Web site: www.freshboil edpeanuts.com. "We embrace the fact that literary magazines are a dime a dozen. We have no grand illusions of money or fame. We publish for the sake of the work itself. So it better be good." Semiannual. Estab. 2004.

Needs "Open to all fiction categories." Also publishes literary essays, literary criticism, poetry. Sometimes comments on rejected mss.

How to Contact Send complete ms. Accepts submissions by e-mail (must be a .doc file or .txt file). Send SASE (or IRC) for return of ms. Responds in 2-3 months to mss. Accepts simultaneous, multiple submissions. Sample copy online. Writer's guidelines online.

Payment/Terms Pays 1 contributor's copy. Acquires one-time rights.

Advice "Please be sure to visit our Web site for up-to-date submission guidelines."

🍁 ○ FRONT & CENTRE

Black Bile Press, 573 Gainsborough Ave., Ottawa ON K2A 2Y6 Canada. (613)729-8973. E-mail: firth@istar.ca. Web site: www.ardentdreams.com/blackbilepress. **Contact:** Matthew Firth, editor. Magazine: half letter-size; 40-50 pages; illustrations; photos. "We look for new fiction from Canadian and international writers—bold, aggressive work that does not compromise quality." Three issues per year. Estab. 1998. Circ. 500.

Needs Literary ("contemporary realism/gritty urban"). "No science fiction, horror, mainstream, romance or religious." Receives 30-40 unsolicited mss/month. Accepts 6-7 mss/issue; 10-20 mss/year. Publishes ms 6 months after acceptance. Agented fiction 10%. **Publishes 4-5 new writers/year.** Recently published work by Kenneth J. Harvey, David Rose, Laura Hird, Jon Boillard, Nichole McGill, John Swan. Length: 50-4,000 words; average length: 2,500 words. Publishes short shorts. Always comments on rejected mss.

How to Contact Send SASE (from Canada) (or IRCs from USA) for return of ms or send a disposable copy of ms with #10 SASE for reply only. Responds in 2 weeks to queries; 4 months to mss. Accepts multiple submissions. Sample copy for $6. Writer's guidelines for SASE or by e-mail. Reviews fiction.

Payment/Terms Acquires first rights. Not copyrighted.

Advice "We look for attention to detail, unique voice, not overtly derivative, bold writing, not pretentious. We should like to see more realism. Read the magazine first—simple as that!"

○ GARGOYLE

3819 N. 13th St., Arlington VA 22201. (703)525-9296. E-mail: gargoyle@gargoylemagazine.com. Web site: www.gargoylemagazine.com. **Contact:** Richard Peabody and Lucinda Ebersole, editors. Literary magazine: 5½×8½; 200 pages; illustrations; photos. "*Gargoyle* began in 1976 with twin goals: to discover new voices and to rediscover overlooked talent. These days we publish a lot of fictional efforts written by poets. We have always been more interested in how a writer tells a story than in plot or story per se." Annual. Estab. 1976. Circ. 2,000.

Needs Erotica, ethnic/multicultural, experimental, gay, lesbian, literary, mainstream, translations. "No romance, horror, science fiction." Wants "edgy realism or experimental works. We run both." Wants to see more Canadian, British, Australian and Third World fiction. Receives 50-200 unsolicited mss/month. Accepts 10-15 mss/issue. Accepts submissions during June, July, and Aug. Publishes ms 6-12 months after acceptance. Agented fiction 5%. **Publishes 2-3 new writers/year.** Recently published work by Naomi Ayala, Toby Barlow, Laura Chester, Pat MacEnulty, Toby Olson, Kit Reed, Megan Elizabeth Swades and Paul West. Length: 30 pages maximum; average length: 5-10 pages. Publishes short shorts. Also publishes literary essays, literary criticism, poetry. Sometimes comments on rejected mss.

How to Contact We prefer electronic submissions. Please send in the body of a letter. For *snail mail*, send SASE for reply, return of ms or send a disposable copy of ms. Responds in 2 weeks to queries; 3 months to mss. Accepts simultaneous submissions. Sample copy for $12.95.

Payment/Terms Pays 1 contributor's copy; additional copies for ½ price. Acquires first North American serial, first British and first rights. Sends galleys to author.

Advice "We have to fall in love with a particular fiction."

◯ GEORGETOWN REVIEW

G and R Publishing, Box 227, 400 East College St., Georgetown KY 40324. (502)863-8308. Fax: (502)868-8888. E-mail: gtownreview@georgetowncollege.edu. Web site: http://georgetownreview.georgetowncollege.edu. **Contact:** Steven Carter, editor. Literary magazine/journal: 6×9, 192 pages, 20 lb. paper, four-color 60 lb. glossy cover. "We publish the best fiction we receive, regardless of theme or genre." Annual. Estab. 1993. Circ. 1,000. Member CLMP.

Needs Ethnic/multicultural (general), experimental, literary. Does not want adventure, children's, fantasy, romance. Receives 100-125 mss/month. Accepts 8-10 mss/issue; 15-20 mss/year. Does not read March 16-August 31. Manuscript published 1 month-2 years after acceptance. Agented fiction 0%. **Publishes 3-4 new writers/year.** Published Liz Funk (debut), Laura Selby, Sallie Bingham, David Romtvedt, Carla Panciera. Average length: 4,000 words. Publishes short shorts. Average length of short shorts: 500-1,500 words. Also publishes literary essays, poetry. Sometimes comments on/critiques rejected manuscripts.

How to Contact Send complete ms with cover letter. Include brief bio, list of publications. Responds to queries in 1 month. Responds to mss in 1-3 months. Send either SASE (or IRC) for return of ms or disposable copy of ms and #10 SASE for reply only. Considers simultaneous submissions. Sample copy available for $6.50. Guidelines available on Web site.

Payment and Terms Writers receive 2 contributor's copies, free subscription to the magazine. Additional copies $5. Pays on publication. Acquires first North American serial rights. Publication is copyrighted. "Sponsors annual contest with $1,000 prize. Check Web site for guidelines."

Advice "We look for fiction that is well written and that has a story line that keeps our interest. Don't send a first draft, and even if we don't take your first, second, or third submission, keep trying."

$◯ 🔲 THE GEORGIA REVIEW

The University of Georgia, 012 Gilbert Hall, University of Georgia, Athens GA 30602-9009. (706)542-3481. Fax: (706)542-0047. Web site: www.uga.edu/garev. **Contact:** Stephen Corey, editor. Journal: 7×10; 208 pages (average); 50 lb. woven old-style paper; 80 lb. cover stock; illustrations; photos. "Our readers are educated, inquisitive people who read a lot of work in the areas we feature, so they expect only the best in our pages. All work submitted should show evidence that the writer is at least as well educated and well-read as our readers. Essays should be authoritative but accessible to a range of readers." Quarterly. Estab. 1947. Circ. 4,000.

● Stories first published in *The Georgia Review* have been anthologized in *Best American Short Stories*, *Best American Mystery Stories*, *New Stories from The South* and the *Pushcart Prize Collection*. *The Georgia Review* was a finalist for the National Magazine Award in essays in 2007.

Needs "Ordinarily we do not publish novel excerpts or works translated into English, and we strongly discourage authors from submitting these." Receives 300 unsolicited mss/month. Accepts 3-4 mss/issue; 12-15 mss/year. Does not read unsolicited mss May 5-August 15. Publishes ms 6 months after acceptance. **Publishes some new writers/year.** Recently published work by Lee K. Abbot, Mary Hood, Joyce Carol Oates, George Singleton. Also publishes literary essays, literary criticism, poetry. Occasionally comments on rejected mss.

How to Contact Send complete ms. Responds in 2 weeks to queries; 2-4 months to mss. No simultaneous submissions. Sample copy for $7. Writer's guidelines online.

Payment/Terms Pays $40/published page. Pays on publication for first North American serial rights. Sends galleys to author.

◯ GERTRUDE, A Journal of Voice & Vision

PO Box 83948, Portland OR 97283. **Contact:** Eric Delehoy, editor. Magazine: 5×8½; 64-72 pages; perfect bound; 60 lb. paper; glossy card cover; illustrations; photos. *Gertrude* is a "annual publication featuring the voices and visions of the gay, lesbian, bisexual, transgender and supportive community." Estab. 1999. Circ. 400.

Needs Ethnic/multicultural, feminist, gay, humor/satire, lesbian, literary, mainstream. "No romance, pornography or mystery." Wants more multicultural fiction. "We'd like to publish more humor and positive portrayals of gays—steer away from victim roles, pity." Receives 15-20 unsolicited mss/month. Accepts 4-8 mss/issue; 4-8 mss/year. Publishes ms 1-2 months after acceptance. **Publishes 4-5 new writers/year.** Recently published work by Carol Guess, Demrie Alonzo, Henry Alley and Scott Pomfret. Length: 200-3,000 words; average length: 1,800 words. Publishes short shorts. Also publishes poetry.

How to Contact Send SASE for reply to query and a disposable copy of ms. Responds in 4 months to mss. Accepts multiple submissions No simultaneous submissions. Sample copy for $5, 6×9 SAE and 4 1st class stamps. Writer's guidelines for #10 SASE.

Payment/Terms Pays 1-2 contributor's copies; additional copies $4. Pays on publication. Author retains rights upon publication. Not copyrighted.

Advice "We look for strong characterization, imagery and new, unique ways of writing about universal experiences. Follow the construction of your work until the ending. Many stories start out with zest, then flipper and die. Show us, don't tell us."

◯ GINOSKO

P.O. Box 246, Fairfax CA 94978. (415)785-2802. E-mail: ginoskoeditor@aol.com. **Contact:** Robert Cesaretti, editor. Magazine: 5½×8½; 50-60 pages; standard paper; photo glossy cover. Ghin-*oce*-koe: to perceive, understand, come to know; knowledge that has an inception, an attainment; the recognition of truth by personal experience. "Writing that lifts up the grace and beauty of human frailty yet carries with it the strength and veracity of humility, compassion, belief." Published semiannually. Estab. 2003. Circ. 2,000+.

Needs Experimental, literary, stylized. Strong on theme; poetic and imagistic magical realism. Receives 80-100 unsolicited mss/month. **Publishes 4 new writers/year.** Recently published work by Stephanie Dickinson, Michael Hettich.

How to Contact Send complete ms. Accepts submissions by e-mail (ginoskoeditor@aol.com) and snail mail. Responds in 1-3 months to mss. Accepts simultaneous submissions and reprints.

Payment/Terms Pays one contributor's copy. Pays on publication for one-time rights. Not copyrighted.

Advice "I am looking for a style that conveys spiritual hunger and yearning, yet avoids religiosity and convention—*between literary vision and spiritual realities.*"

$◯ ◯ GLIMMER TRAIN STORIES

Glimmer Train Press, Inc., 1211 NW Glisan St. #207, Portland OR 97209. (503)221-0836. Fax: (503)221-0837. Web site: www.glimmertrain.org. **Contact:** Susan Burmeister-Brown and Linda B. Swanson-Davies. Magazine: 7¼×9¼; 260 pages; recycled; acid-free paper; 12 photographs. "We are interested in well-written, emotionally-moving short stories published by unknown, as well as known, writers." Quarterly. Estab. 1991. Circ. 16,000.

• The magazine also sponsors an annual short story contest for new writers and a very short fiction contest.

Needs Literary. Receives 4,000 unsolicited mss/month. Accepts 10 mss/issue; 40 mss/year. Publishes ms up to 2 years after acceptance. Agented fiction 5%. **Publishes 18 new writers/year.** Recently published work by Judy Budnitz, Nancy Reisman, Herman Carrillo, Andre Dubus III, William Trevor, Alberto Rios, Alice Mattison. Sometimes comments on rejected mss.

How to Contact Submit work online at www.glimmertrain.org. Reads in January, April, July, October. Accepted work published in *Glimmer Train Stories*. Responds in 3 months to mss. No simultaneous submissions. Sample copy for $12 on Web site. Writer's guidelines online.

Payment/Terms Pays $700 for standard submissions, up to $2,000 for contest winning stories. Pays on acceptance for first rights.

Advice "When a story stays with us after the first reading, it gets another reading. Those stories that simply don't let us set them aside get published. Read good fiction. It will often improve the quality of your own writing."

◯ ◯ GLOBAL CITY REVIEW

City College of New York, 138th St. and Convent Ave., New York NY 10031. (212)650-7382. E-mail: globalcityreview@ccny.cuny.edu. Web site: www.webdelsol.com/globalcityreview. **Contact:** Linsey Abrams. Magazine: 4.125×6.75; 140 pages; stock paper; cardstock cover. "The perspective of *GCR* is feminist—women are an important focus, as are writers who write from a gay and lesbian or minority position, culturally decentralized voices because of age or culture, international perspectives, the silenced, the poor, etc. The point is an opening of literary space." Semiannual. Estab. 1993. Circ. 500. CLMP.

Needs Ethnic/multicultural (general), experimental, feminist, gay, lesbian, literary, translations. "No genre fiction." Receives 25-30 unsolicited mss/month. Accepts 4-6 mss/issue; 8-12 mss/year. Publishes short shorts. Also publishes literary essays, literary criticism, poetry.

How to Contact Send a disposable copy of ms and #10 SASE for reply only. Responds in 2-6 months to mss. Accepts simultaneous submissions. Sample copy for $8.50. Writer's guidelines for SASE or on Web site. Reviews fiction.

Payment/Terms Pays 2 contributor's copies; additional copies $8.50. Acquires one-time rights.

$◯ ◯ GRAIN LITERARY MAGAZINE

Saskatchewan Writers Guild, P.O. Box 67, Saskatoon SK S7K 3K1 Canada. (306)244-2828. Fax: (306)244-0255. Web site: www.grainmagazine.ca. **Contact:** Kent Bruyneel, editor. Literary magazine: 6×9; 128 pages; Chinook offset printing; chrome-coated stock; some photos. "*Grain* publishes writing of the highest quality, both traditional and innovative in nature. *Grain* aim: To publish work that challenges readers; to encourage promising new writers; and to produce a well-designed, visually interesting magazine." Quarterly. Estab. 1973. Circ. 1,500.

Needs Experimental, literary, mainstream, contemporary, prose poem, poetry. "No romance, confession, science fiction, vignettes, mystery." Receives 80 unsolicited mss/month. Accepts 8-12 mss/issue; 32-48 mss/year. Publishes ms 11 months after acceptance. Recently published work by Yann Martel, Tom Wayman, Lorna Crozier. Also publishes poetry. Occasionally comments on rejected mss.

How to Contact Send complete ms with SASE (or IRC) and brief letter. Accepts queries by e-mail, mail, fax, phone. Responds in 1 month to queries; 4 months to mss. No simultaneous submissions. Sample copy for $13 or online. Writer's guidelines for #10 SASE or online.

Payment/Terms Pays $50-225. Pays on publication for first Canadian serial rights.

Advice "Submit a story to us that will deepen the imaginative experience of our readers. *Grain* has established itself as a first-class magazine of serious fiction. We receive submissions from around the world. Do not use U.S. postage stamps on your return envelope. Without sufficient Canadian postage or an International Reply Coupon, we *will not* read or reply to your submission. We look for attention to detail, credibility, lucid use of language and metaphor and a confident, convincing voice. Make sure you have researched your piece, that the literal and metaphorical support one another."

GRANTA, The Magazine of New Writing

Granta Publications, 2-3 Hanover Yard, Noel Rd., London England NI 8BE United Kingdom. (44)(0)20 7704 9776. E-mail: editorial@granta.com. Web site: www.granta.com. **Contact:** Ian Jack, editor. Magazine: paperback, 256 pages approx; photos. "*Granta* magazine publishes fiction, reportage, biography and autobiography, history, travel and documentary photography. It does not publish 'writing about writing.' The realistic narrative—the story—is its primary form." Quarterly. Estab. 1979. Circ. 80,000.

Needs Literary, novel excerpts. No genre fiction. Themes decided as deadline approaches. Receives 100 unsolicited mss/month. Accepts 0-1 mss/issue; 1-2 mss/year. **Publishes 1-2 new writers/year.**

How to Contact Send SAE and IRCs for reply, return of ms or send a disposable copy of ms. Responds in 3 months to mss. Accepts simultaneous submissions. Sample copy for $14.95. Writer's guidelines online.

Payment/Terms Payment varies. Pays on publication. Buys world English language rights, first serial rights (minimum). "We hold more rights in pieces we commission." Sends galleys to author.

Advice "We are looking for the best in realistic stories; originality of voice; without jargon, connivance or self-conscious 'performance'—writing that endures."

GREEN MOUNTAINS REVIEW

Johnson State College, Johnson VT 05656. (802)635-1350. E-mail: gmr@jsc.vsc.edu. Web site: http://greenmou ntainsreview.jsc.vsc.edu. **Contact:** Leslie Daniels, fiction editor. Magazine: digest-sized; 160-200 pages. Semiannual. Estab. 1975. Circ. 1,700.

- *Green Mountains Review* has received a Pushcart Prize and Editor's Choice Award.

Needs Adventure, experimental, humor/satire, literary, mainstream, serialized novels, translations. Receives 100 unsolicited mss/month. Accepts 6 mss/issue; 12 mss/year. "Manuscripts received between March 1 and September 1 will not be read and will be returned." Publishes ms 6-12 months after acceptance. **Publishes 0-4 new writers/year.** Recently published work by Howard Norman, Debra Spark, Valerie Miner, Peter LaSalle. Publishes short shorts. Also publishes literary criticism, poetry. Sometimes comments on rejected mss.

How to Contact Send complete ms and SASE. Responds in 1 month to queries; 6 months to mss. Accepts simultaneous submissions if advised. Sample copy for $7.

Payment/Terms Pays contributor's copies, 1-year subscription and small honorarium, depending on grants. Acquires first North American serial rights. Rights revert to author upon request.

THE GREENSBORO REVIEW

3302 Hall for Humanities and Research Administration, UNC Greensboro, P.O. Box 26170, Greensboro NC 27402-6170. (336)334-5459. E-mail: jlclark@uncg.edu. Web site: www.greensororeview.com. **Contact:** Jim Clark, editor. Magazine: 6×9; approximately 128 pages; 60 lb. paper; 80 lb. cover. Literary magazine featuring fiction and poetry for readers interested in contemporary literature. Semiannual. Circ. 800.

- Stories for *The Greensboro Review* have been included in *Best American Short Stories, The O. Henry Prize Stories, New Stories from The South,* and *Pushcart Prize.*

Needs Accepts 6-8 mss/issue; 12-16 mss/year. Unsolicited manuscripts must arrive by September 15 to be considered for the spring issue and by February 15 to be considered for the fall issue. Manuscripts arriving after those dates may be held for the next consideration. **Publishes 10% new writers/year.** Recently published work by Robert Morgan, George Singleton, Robert Olmstead, Brock Clarke, Dale Ray Phillips, Kelly Cherry.

How to Contact Responds in 4 months to mss. Accepts multiple submissions. No simultaneous submissions. Sample copy for $5.

Payment/Terms Pays in contributor's copies. Acquires first North American serial rights.

Advice "We want to see the best being written regardless of theme, subject or style."

THE GRIFFIN

Gwynedd-Mercy College, P.O. Box 901, 1325 Sumneytown Pike, Gwynedd Valley PA 19437-0901. (215)646-7300, ext. 256. Fax: (215)641-5517. E-mail: allego.d@gmc.edu. **Contact:** Donna Allego, editor. Literary magazine: $8^1/_2 \times 5^1/_2$; 112 pages. "*The Griffin* is a literary journal sponsored by Gwynedd-Mercy College. Its mission is to enrich society by nurturing and promoting creative writing that demonstrates a unique and intelligent voice. We seek writing which accurately reflects the human condition with all its intellectual, emotional and ethical challenges." Annual. Estab. 1999. Circ. 500.

Needs Short stories, essays and poetry. Open to genre work. "No slasher, graphic violence or sex." Accepts mss depending on the quality of work submitted. Receives 20-30 unsolicited mss/month. Publishes ms 6-9 months after acceptance. **Publishes 10-15 new writers/year.** Length: 2,500 words; average length: 2,000 words. Publishes short shorts. Also publishes literary essays, poetry.

How to Contact Send complete ms. Send SASE for return of ms or send disposable copy of ms and #10 SASE for reply only. Responds in 2-3 months to queries; 6 months to mss. Accepts simultaneous submissions "if notified." Sample copy for $6.

Payment/Terms Pays 2 contributor's copies; additional copies for $6.

Advice "Looking for well-constructed works that explore universal qualities, respect for the individual and community, justice and integrity. Check our description and criteria. Rewrite until you're sure every word counts. We publish the best work we find regardless of industry needs."

☑ GSU REVIEW

Georgia State University, Campus P.O. Box 1894, MSC 8R0322 Unit 8, Atlanta GA 30303-3083. (404)651-4804. Fax: (404)651-1710. Web site: www.review.gsu.edu. **Contact:** Jody Brooks, prose editor. Literary journal. "*GSU Review* is a biannual literary magazine publishing poetry, fiction, creative nonfiction, and visual art. We're looking for original voices and well-written manuscripts. No subject or form biases." Biannual.

Needs Literary fiction and creative nonfiction. Receives 200 unsolicited mss/month. Publishes short shorts.

How to Contact Include SASE for notification. Responds in 3-4 months. Sample copy for $5. Writer's guidelines for SASE or on Web site.

Payment/Terms Pays in contributor's copy. Acquires one-time rights.

☑ GUD MAGAZINE

Greatest Uncommon Denominator Publishing, P.O. Box 1537, Laconia NH 03247. (603)397-3843. E-mail: editor @gudmagazine.com. Web site: www.gudmagazine.com. **Contact:** Sal Coraccio, editor. Literary magazine/journal. "*GUD Magazine* transcends and encompasses the audiences of both genre and literary fiction. Published twice a year in an attractive 5×8 perfect bound, 200+ page format, *GUD* features fiction (from flash to 15,000 word stories), art, poetry, essays and reports and short drama. See www.gudmagazine.com. for more." Estab. 2006.

Needs Adventure, erotica, ethnic/multicultural, experimental, fantasy, horror, humor/satire, literary, science fiction. Accepts 40 mss/year. Manuscript published 6 months after acceptance. Length: 15,000 words (max).

How to Contact Send complete ms with cover letter. Responds to mss in 6 months. Considers simultaneous submissions, previously published submissions, multiple submissions. Guidelines available on Web site.

Advice "Be warned: We read a lot. We've seen it all before. We are not easy to impress. Is your work original? Does it have something to say? Read it again. If you genuinely believe it to be so, send it."

$ ☑ ☑ GULF COAST, A Journal of Literature & Fine Arts

Dept. of English, University of Houston, Houston TX 77204-3013. (713)743-3223. Fax: (713)743-3229. Web site: www.gulfcoast mag.org. **Contact:** Casey Fleming, David MacLean, Oindrila Murherdee, fiction editors. Magazine: 7×9; approx. 300 pages; stock paper, gloss cover; illustrations; photos. "Innovative fiction for the literary-minded." Estab. 1987. Circ. 2,300.

• Work published in *Gulf Coast* has been selected for inclusion in the *Pushcart Prize* anthology, *The O'Henry Prize Stories* anthology and *Best American Short Stories*.

Needs Ethnic/multicultural, experimental, literary, regional, translations, contemporary. "No children's, genre, religious/inspirational." Wants more "cutting-edge, experimental" fiction. Receives 300 unsolicited mss/ month. Accepts 4-8 mss/issue; 12-16 mss/year. Publishes ms 6 months-1 year after acceptance. Agented fiction 5%. **Publishes 2-8 new writers/year.** Recently published work by Justin Cronin, Cary Holladay, Holiday Reinhorn, Michael Martone, Joe Meno, Karen An-hwei Lee. Publishes short shorts. Sometimes comments on rejected mss.

How to Contact Responds in 6 months to mss. Accepts simultaneous submissions. Back issue for $7, 7×10 SASE with 4 first-class stamps. Writer's guidelines for #10 SASE or on Web site.

Payment/Terms Pays $50-100. Acquires one-time rights.

Advice "Rotating editorship, so please be patient with replies. As always, please send one story at a time."

☑ GULF STREAM MAGAZINE

Florida International University, English Dept., Biscayne Bay Campus, 3000 N.E. 151st St., N. Miami FL 33181-3000. (305)919-5599. E-mail: gulfstreamfiu@yahoo.com. **Contact:** Denise Sebesta Lanier, editor. Magazine:

$5\frac{1}{2} \times 8\frac{1}{2}$; 124 pages; recycled paper; 80 lb. glossy cover; cover illustrations. "We publish *good quality*—fiction, nonfiction and poetry for a predominately literary market." Semiannual. Estab. 1989. Circ. 1,000.

Needs Literary, mainstream, contemporary. Does not want romance, historical, juvenile or religious work. Receives 250 unsolicited mss/month. Accepts 5 mss/issue; 10 mss/year. Does not read mss during the summer. Publishes ms 3-6 months after acceptance. **Publishes 2-5 new writers/year.** Recently published work by Leonard Nash, Jesse Millner, Lyn Millner, Peter Meinke, Susan Neville. Length: 7,500 words; average length: 5,000 words. Publishes short shorts. Also publishes poetry.

How to Contact Responds in 3 months to mss. Accepts simultaneous submissions "if noted." Sample copy for $5. Writer's guidelines for #10 SASE.

Payment/Terms Pays in gift subscriptions and contributor's copies. Acquires first North American serial rights.

Advice "Looks for fresh, original writing—well plotted stories with unforgettable characters, fresh poetry and experimental writing. Usually longer stories do not get accepted. There are exceptions, however."

$ ◙ HAPPY

46 St. Paul's Avenue, Jersey City, NJ 07306. E-mail: bayardx@gmail.com. **Contact:** Bayard, fiction editor. Magazine: $5\frac{1}{2} \times 8$; 150-200 pages; 60 lb. text paper; 150 lb. cover; perfect-bound; illustrations; photos. Quarterly. Estab. 1995. Circ. 500.

Needs Erotica, ethnic/multicultural, experimental, fantasy, feminist, gay, horror, humor/satire, lesbian, literary, novel excerpts, psychic/supernatural/occult, science fiction, short stories. No "television rehash or religious nonsense." Wants more work that is "strong, angry, empowering, intelligent, God-like, expressive." Receives 300-500 unsolicited mss/month. Accepts 30-40 mss/issue; 100-150 mss/year. Publishes ms 6-12 months after acceptance. **Publishes 25-30 new writers/year.** Length: 6,000 words maximum; average length: 1,000-3,500 words. Publishes short shorts. Often comments on rejected mss.

How to Contact Send complete ms. Include estimated word count. Send SASE for reply, return of ms or send a disposable copy of ms. Responds in 1 month to queries. Accepts simultaneous submissions. Sample copy for $20. Writer's guidelines for #10 SASE.

Payment/Terms Pays 1-5¢/word. Pays on publication for one-time rights.

Advice "Excite me!"

◙ HARPUR PALATE, A Literary Journal at Binghamton University

English Department, P.O. Box 6000, Binghamton University, Binghamton NY 13902-6000. E-mail: harpur.palate @gmail.com. Web site: harpurpalate.binghamton.edu. **Contact:** Kathryn Henion, editor. Magazine: 6×9; 180-200 pages; coated or uncoated paper; 100 lb. coated cover; 4-color art portfolio insert. "We have no restrictions on subject matter or form. Quite simply, send us your highest-quality prose or poetry." Semiannual. Estab. 2000. Circ. 500.

Needs Adventure, ethnic/multicultural, experimental, historical, humor/satire, mainstream, mystery/suspense, novel excerpts, literary, fabulism, magical realism, metafiction, slipstream. Receives 400 unsolicited mss/ month. Accepts 5-10 mss/issue; 12-20 mss/year. Publishes ms 1-2 months after acceptance. **Publishes 5 new writers/year.** Recently published work by Lee K. Abbott, Jaimee Wriston Colbert, Joan Connor, Stephen Corey, Viet Dinh, Andrew Farkas, Mary Ann Mohanraj, Michael Steinberg, Martha Witt. Length: 250-8,000 words; average length: 2,000-4,000 words. Publishes short shorts. Also publishes poetry. Sometimes comments on rejected mss.

How to Contact Send complete ms with a cover letter. Include e-mail address on cover. Include estimated word count, brief bio, list of publications. Send a disposable copy of ms and #10 SASE for reply only. Responds in 1-3 week to queries; 4- 8 months to mss. Accepts simultaneous submissions if stated in the cover letter. Sample copy for $10. Writer's guidelines online.

Payment/Terms Pays 2 copies. Pays on publication for first North American serial, electronic rights. Sponsors awards/contests.

Advice "*Harpur Palate* accepts submissions all year; deadline for the Winter issue is October 15, for the Summer issue March 15. *Harpur Palate* sponsors a fiction contest for the Summer issue. We do not accept submissions via e-mail. Almost every literary magazine already says this, but it bears repeating: Look at a recent copy of our publication to get an idea of the kind of writing published."

◙ HARVARD REVIEW

Harvard University, Lamont Library, Level 5, Cambridge MA 02138. (617)495-9775. E-mail: harvrev@fas.harvar d.edu. Web site: http://hcl.harvard.edu/harvardreview. **Contact:** Christina Thompson, editor. Magazine: 6×9; 192-240 pages; illustrations; photographs. Semiannual. Estab. 1992. Circ. 2,000.

Needs Literary. Receives 130 unsolicited mss/month. Accepts 4 mss/issue; 8 mss/year. Publishes ms 3-6 months after acceptance. **Publishes 3-4 new writers/year.** Recently published work by Joyce Carol Oates, Alice Hoffman, Alan Heathcock, Jim Crace, and Karen Bender. Length: 1,000-7,000 words; average length: 3,000-5,000 words. Publishes short shorts. Also publishes literary essays, literary criticism, poetry, and plays. Sometimes comments on rejected mss.

How to Contact Send SASE for return of ms or disposable copy of ms and SASE for reply only. Responds within 6 months to queries. Accepts simultaneous submissions. Writer's guidelines online.

Payment/Terms Pays 2 contributor's copies; additional copies $7. Pays on publication for first North American serial rights. Sends galleys to author.

🖉 HAWAI'I PACIFIC REVIEW

Hawai'i Pacific University, 1060 Bishop St., Honolulu HI 96813. (808)544-1108. Fax: (808)544-0862. E-mail: pwilson@hpu.edu. Web site: www.hpu.edu. **Contact:** Patrice M. Wilson, editor. Magazine: 6×9; 100 pages; glossy coated cover. *"Hawai'i Pacific Review* is looking for poetry, short fiction and personal essays that speak with a powerful and unique voice. We encourage experimental narrative techniques and poetic styles, and we welcome works in translation." Annual.

Needs Ethnic/multicultural (general), experimental, fantasy, feminist, historical (general), humor/satire, literary, mainstream, regional (Pacific), translations. "Open to all types as long as they're well done. Our audience is adults, so nothing for children/teens." Receives 30-50 unsolicited mss/month. Accepts 5-10 mss/year. Does not read mss January-August each year. Publishes ms 10 months after acceptance. **Publishes 1-2 new writers/ year.** Recently published work by Wendell Mayo, Elizabeth Crowell, Janet Flora. Publishes short shorts. Also publishes literary essays, poetry. Sometimes comments on rejected mss.

How to Contact Send SASE for return of ms or send a disposable copy of ms and SASE for reply only. Responds in 2 weeks to queries; 15 weeks to mss. Accepts simultaneous submissions but must be cited in the cover letter. Sample copy for $5.

Payment/Terms Pays 2 contributor's copies; additional copies $7. Pays on publication for first North American serial rights.

Advice "We look for the unusual or original plot; prose with the texture and nuance of poetry. Character development or portrayal must be unusual/original; humanity shown in an original insightful way (or characters); sense of humor where applicable. Be sure it's a draft that has gone through substantial changes, with supervision from a more experienced writer, if you're a beginner. Write about intense emotion and feeling, not just about someone's divorce or shaky relationship. No soap-opera-like fiction."

🖉 🖾 HAYDEN'S FERRY REVIEW

The Virginia G. Piper Center for Creative Writing at Arizona State University, Box 875002, Arizona State University, Tempe AZ 85287-5002. (480)965-1243. E-mail: hfr@asu.edu. Web site: www.haydensferryreview.org. **Contact:** Fiction editor. Editors change every 1-2 years. Magazine: 7×9¾; 128 pages; fine paper; illustrations; photos. *"Hayden's Ferry Review* publishes best quality fiction, poetry, and creative nonfiction from new, emerging and established writers." Semiannual. Estab. 1986. Circ. 1,300.

● Work from *Hayden's Ferry Review* has been selected for inclusion in *Pushcart Prize* anthologies.

Needs Ethnic/multicultural, experimental, humor/satire, literary, regional, slice-of-life vignettes, contemporary, prose poem. Possible special fiction issue. Receives 250 unsolicited mss/month. Accepts 5 mss/issue; 10 mss/ year. Publishes ms 6 months after acceptance. Recently published work by T.C. Boyle, Raymond Carver, Ken Kesey, Rita Dove, Chuck Rosenthal and Rick Bass. Publishes short shorts. Also publishes literary criticism.

How to Contact Send complete ms. SASE. Responds in 2 weeks to queries; 3 months to mss. Accepts simultaneous submissions. Sample copy for $7.50. Writer's guidelines online.

Payment/Terms Pays $25-100. Pays on publication for first North American serial rights. Sends galleys to author.

$🖉 ◎ HEARTLANDS, A Magazine of Midwest Life and Art

(formerly *The Heartlands Today*), The Firelands Writing Center, Firelands College of BGSU, Huron OH 44839. (419)433-5560. E-mail: lsmithdog@aol.com. Web site: www.theheartlandstoday.org. **Contact:** Fiction editor. Magazine: 8½×11; perfect bound; 96 pages; b&w illustrations; 15 photos. *Material must be set in the Midwest.* "We prefer material that reveals life in the Midwest today for a general, literate audience." Biannual. Estab. 1991.

Needs Ethnic/multicultural, humor/satire, literary, mainstream, regional (Midwest). Receives 15 unsolicited mss/month. Accepts 6 mss/issue. Does not read August-December. "We edit between January 1 and May 15." Publishes ms 6 months after acceptance. Recently published work by Wendell Mayo, Tony Tomassi, Gloria Bowman. Also publishes literary essays, poetry. Sometimes comments on rejected mss.

How to Contact Send SASE for ms, not needed for query. Responds in 2 months to mss. Accepts simultaneous submissions if noted. Sample copy for $5.

Payment/Terms Pays $10-20 and 2 contributor's copies. Pays on publication for first rights.

Advice "We look for writing that connects on a human level, that moves us with its truth and opens our vision of the world. If writing is a great escape for you, don't bother with us. We're in it for the joy, beauty or truth of the art. We look for a straight, honest voice dealing with human experiences. We do not define the Midwest, we hope to be a document of the Midwest. If you feel you are writing from the Midwest, send your work to us. We look first at the quality of the writing.''

⬛ ◎ HEAVEN BONE

Heaven Bone Press, 62 Woodrock Mtn. Dr. Washingtonville, NY 10992. (845)469-4109. E-mail: heavenbone@hv c.rr.com. **Contact:** Steven Hirsch and Kirpal Gordon, editors. Magazine: 8½×11; 96-116 pages; 60 lb. recycled offset paper; full color cover; computer clip art, graphics, line art, cartoons, halftones and photos scanned in .tif format. ''Expansive, fine surrealist and experimental literary, earth and nature, spiritual path. We use current reviews, essays on spiritual and esoteric topics, creative stories. Also: reviews of current poetry releases and expansive literature.'' Readers are ''scholars, surrealists, poets, artists, muscians, students.'' Annual. Estab. 1987. Circ. 2,500.

Needs Experimental, fantasy, regional, esoteric/scholarly, spiritual. ''No violent, thoughtless, exploitive or religious fiction.'' Receives 45-110 unsolicited mss/month. Accepts 5-15 mss/issue; 12-30 mss/year. Publishes ms 2 weeks-10 months after acceptance. **Publishes 3-4 new writers/year.** Recently published work by Keith Abbot and Stephen-Paul Martin. Length: 1,200-5,000 words; average length: 3,500 words. Publishes short shorts. Also publishes literary essays, literary criticism, poetry. Sometimes comments on rejected mss.

How to Contact Send SASE for reply or return of ms. Responds in 3 weeks to queries; 10 months to mss. Accepts reprints submissions. Sample copy for $10. Writer's guidelines for SASE. Reviews fiction.

Payment/Terms Pays in contributor's copies; charges for extras. Acquires first North American serial rights. Sends galleys to author.

Advice ''Read a sample issue first. Our fiction needs are temperamental, so please query first before submitting. We prefer shorter fiction. Do not send first drafts to test them on us. Please refine and polish your work before sending. Always include SASE. We are looking for the unique, unusual and excellent.''

⬛ ⬚ HOME PLANET NEWS

Home Planet Publications, P.O. Box 455, High Falls NY 12440. (845)687-4084. **Contact:** Donald Lev, editor. Tabloid: 11½×16; 24 pages; newsprint; illustrations; photos. ''*Home Planet News* publishes mainly poetry along with some fiction, as well as reviews (books, theater and art) and articles of literary interest. We see *HPN* as a quality literary journal in an eminently readable format and with content that is urban, urbane and politically aware.'' Triannual. Estab. 1979. Circ. 1,000.

● *HPN* has received a small grant from the Puffin Foundation for its focus on AIDS issues.

Needs Ethnic/multicultural, experimental, feminist, gay, historical, lesbian, literary, mainstream, science fiction (soft/sociological). No ''children's or genre stories (except rarely some science fiction).'' Publishes special fiction issue or anthology. Receives 12 unsolicited mss/month. Accepts 1 mss/issue; 3 mss/year. Publishes ms 1 year after acceptance. Recently published work by Hugh Fox, Walter Jackman, Jim Story. Length: 500-2,500 words; average length: 2,000 words. Publishes short shorts. Also publishes literary criticism.

How to Contact Send complete ms. Send SASE for reply, return of ms or send a disposable copy of the ms. Responds in 6 months to mss. Sample copy for $4. Writer's guidelines for SASE.

Payment/Terms Pays 3 contributor's copies; additional copies $1. Acquires one-time rights.

Advice ''We use very little fiction, and a story we accept just has to grab us. We need short pieces of some complexity, stories about complex people facing situations which resist simple resolutions.''

$⬚ ICONOCLAST

1675 Amazon Rd., Mohegan Lake NY 10547-1804. **Contact:** Phil Wagner, editor. Magazine: 8×10½; 80-96 pages; 20 lb. white paper; 50 lb. cover stock; illustrations. ''Aimed for a literate general audience with interests in fine (but accessible) fiction and poetry.'' Bimonthly. Estab. 1992. Circ. 700.

Needs Adventure, ethnic/multicultural, experimental, humor/satire, literary, mainstream, novel excerpts, science fiction, literary. No character studies, slice-of-life, pieces strong on attitude/weak on plot. Receives 150 unsolicited mss/month. Accepts 3-6 mss/issue; 25-30 mss/year. Publishes ms 9-12 months after acceptance. **Publishes 8-10 new writers/year.** Publishes short shorts. Also publishes literary essays, poetry. Sometimes comments on rejected mss.

How to Contact Send complete ms. Send SASE for reply, return of ms or send a disposable copy of the ms labeled as such. Responds in 2 weeks to queries; 5 weeks to mss. No simultaneous submissions. Sample copy for $5. Writer's guidelines for #10 SASE. Reviews fiction.

Payment/Terms Pays 1¢/word. Pays on publication for first North American serial rights.

Advice ''We like fiction that has something to say (and not about its author). We hope for work that is observant, intense and multi-leveled. Follow Pound's advice—'make it new.' Write what you want in whatever style you want without being gross, sensational or needlessly explicit—then pray there's someone who can appreciate your sensibility. Read good fiction. It's as fundamental as learning how to hit, throw and catch is to baseball. With the increasing American disinclination towards literature, stories must insist on being heard. Read what is being published—then write something better—and different. Do all rewrites before sending a story out. Few editors have time to work with writers on promising stories; only polished ones."

$⬚⬚⬚ THE IDAHO REVIEW

Boise State University, English Dept., 1910 University Dr., Boise ID 83725. (208)426-1002. Fax: (208)426-4373. E-mail: mwieland@boisestate.edu. **Contact:** Mitch Wieland, editor. Magazine: 6×9; 180-200 pages; acid-free accent opaque paper; coated cover stock; photos. "A literary journal for anyone who enjoys good fiction." Annual. Estab. 1998. Circ. 1,000. Member CLMP.
  • Recent stories reprinted in *The Best American Short Stories*, *The O. Henry Prize Stories*, *Pushcart Prize*, and *New Stories from The South*.
Needs Experimental, literary. "No genre fiction of any type." Receives 150 unsolicited mss/month. Accepts 5-7 mss/issue; 5-7 mss/year. "We do not read from May 1-August 31." Publishes ms 1 year after acceptance. Agented fiction 5%. **Publishes 1 new writers/year.** Recently published work by Rick Bass, Melanie Rae Thon, Ron Carlson, Joy Williams, Madison Smart Bell, Carolyn Cooke. Length: open; average length: 7,000 words. Publishes short shorts. Also publishes literary essays, poetry. Sometimes comments on rejected mss.
How to Contact Send SASE for return of ms or send a disposable copy of ms and #10 SASE for reply only. Responds in 3-5 months to mss. Accepts simultaneous, multiple submissions. Sample copy for $8.95. Writer's guidelines for SASE. Reviews fiction.
Payment/Terms Pays $100 when funds are available plus 2 contributor's copies; additional copies $5. Pays on publication for first North American serial rights. Sends galleys to author.
Advice "We look for strongly crafted work that tells a story that needs to be told. We demand vision and intlligence and mystery in the fiction we publish."

⬚ THE IDIOT

E-mail: idiotsubmission@yahoo.com. Web site: www.theidiotmagazine.com. **Contact:** Brian Campbell and Toni Plummer, lackeys. Magazine: 5½×8½; 48 pages; 20 lb. white paper; cardboard glossy cover; illustrations. "For people who enjoy Triumph The Insult Comic Dog, *The Daily Show*, *South Park*, *Ali G*, Louis Black, old Woody Allen, S.J. Perelman, James Thurber and Albert Camus. We're looking for black comedy. Death, disease, God, religion and micronauts are all potential subjects of comedy. Nothing is sacred, but it needs to be funny. I don't want whimsical, I don't want amusing, I don't want some fanciful anecdote about a trip you took with your uncle when you were eight. I want laugh-out-loud-fall-on-the-floor-funny. If it's cute, give it to your mom, your sweetheart, or your puppy dog. Length doesn't matter, but most comedy is like soup. It's an appetizer, not a meal. Short is often better. Bizarre, obscure, referential and literary are all appreciated. My audience is mostly comprised of bitter misanthropes who play Russian Roulette between airings of *The Simpsons* each day. I want dark." Annual. Estab. 1993. Circ. 1,000.
Needs Humor/satire. Wants more short, dark humor. Publishes ms 6-12 after acceptance. **Publishes 1-3 new writers/year.** Recently published work by Judd Trichter, Freud Pachenko, Brad Hufford and Johnny "John-John" Kearns. Length: 2,000 words; average length: 500 words. Publishes short shorts. Also publishes poetry. Sometimes comments on rejected mss.
How to Contact Accepts submissions by e-mail only. Responds in 1-12 months to mss. Accepts simultaneous submissions and reprints. Sample copy for $5, subscription $10.
Payment/Terms Pays 1 contributor's copy when applicable. Acquires one-time rights. Sends galleys to author.
Advice "We almost never use anything over 1,500 words, but if it's really funny I'll take a look at it."

⬚ ILLUMINATIONS, An International Magazine of Contemporary Writing

Dept. of English, College of Charleston, 66 George St., Charleston SC 29424-0001. (843)953-1920. Fax: (843)953-1924. E-mail: lewiss@cofc.edu. Web site: www.cofc.edu/illuminations. **Contact:** Simon Lewis, editor. Magazine: 5×8; 80 pages; illustrations. "*Illuminations* is one of the most challengingly eclectic little literary magazines around, having featured writers from the United States, Britain and Romania , as well as Southern Africa." Annual. Estab. 1982. Circ. 500.
Needs Literary. Receives 5 unsolicited mss/month. Accepts 1 mss/year. **Publishes 1 new writer/year.** Recently published work by John Michael Cummings. Also publishes poetry. Sometimes comments on rejected mss.
How to Contact Send SASE for reply, return of ms or send a disposable copy of ms. Responds in 2 weeks to queries; 2 months to mss. No simultaneous submissions. Sample copy for $10 and 6×9 envelope. Writer's guidelines free.
Payment/Terms Pays 2 contributor's copies of current issue; 1 of subsequent issue. Acquires one-time rights.

ILLYA'S HONEY

The Dallas Poets Community, a non-profit corportation, P.O. Box 700865, Dallas TX 75370. E-mail: info@dallasp oets.org. Web site: www.dallaspoets.org. **Contact:** Ann Howells, editor. Magazine: 5½×8½; 34 pages; 24 lb. paper; glossy cover; photos. "We publish poetry and flash fiction under 200 words. We try to present quality work by writers who take time to learn technique—aimed at anyone who appreciates good literature." Semi-annual. Estab. 1994. Circ. 125.

Needs Ethnic/multicultural, experimental, feminist, gay, historical, humor/satire, lesbian, literary, mainstream, regional, flash fiction. "We accept only flash (also known as micro) fiction." Receives 10 unsolicited mss/ month. Accepts 2-8 mss/issue. Publishes ms 3-5 months after acceptance. **Publishes 2-3 new writers/year.** Recently published work by Paul Sampson, Susanne Bowers, Denworthy. Also publishes poetry. Sometimes comments on rejected mss.

How to Contact Send complete ms. Send SASE for return of ms or send a disposable copy of ms and #10 SASE for reply only. Responds in 6 months to mss. Sample copy for $6. Writer's guidelines for SASE.

Payment/Terms Pays 1 contributor's copy; additional copies $8. Pays on publication for first North American serial rights.

Advice "We would like to see more character studies, humor."

$ ◻ ◎ IMAGE, Art, Faith, Mystery

3307 Third Ave. W, Seattle WA 98119. (206)281-2988. E-mail: image@imagejournal.org. Web site: www.imagej ournal.org. **Contact:** Gregory Wolfe. Magazine: 7×10; 136 pages; glossy cover stock; illustrations; photos. "*Image* is a showcase for the encounter between religious faith and world-class contemporary art. Each issue features fiction, poetry, essays, memoirs, an in-depth interview and articles about visual artists, film, music, etc. and glossy 4-color plates of contemporary visual art." Quarterly. Estab. 1989. Circ. 4,500. Member CLMP.

Needs Literary, translations. Receives 100 unsolicited mss/month. Accepts 2 mss/issue; 8 mss/year. Publishes ms 1 year after acceptance. Agented fiction 5%. Recently published work by Annie Dillard, David James Duncan, Robert Olen Butler, Bret Lott, Melanie Rae Thon. Length: 4,000-6,000 words; average length: 5,000 words. Also publishes literary essays, poetry.

How to Contact Send SASE for reply, return of ms or send disposable copy of ms. Responds in 1 month to queries; 3 months to mss. Sample copy for $16. Reviews fiction.

Payment/Terms Pays $10/page and 4 contributor's copies; additional copies for $6. Pays on acceptance . Sends galleys to author.

Advice "Fiction must grapple with religious faith, though the settings and subjects need not be overtly religious."

$ ◻ ◪ INDIANA REVIEW

Indiana University, Ballantine Hall 465, 1020 E. Kirkwood, Bloomington IN 47405-7103. (812)855-3439. Web site: www.indiana.edu/~inreview. **Contact:** Fiction editor. Magazine: 6×9; 160 pages; 50 lb. paper; Glatfelter cover stock. "*Indiana Review,* a nonprofit organization run by IU graduate students, is a journal of previously unpublished poetry and fiction. Literary interviews and essays also considered. We publish innovative fiction and poetry. We're interested in energy, originality and careful attention to craft. While we publish many well-known writers, we also welcome new and emerging poets and fiction writers." Semiannual. Estab. 1976. Circ. 2,000.

• Work published in *Indiana Review* received a Pushcart Prize (2001) and was included in *Best New American Voices* (2001). *IR* also received an Indiana Arts Council Grant and a NEA grant.

Needs Ethnic/multicultural, experimental, literary, mainstream, novel excerpts, regional, translations. No genre fiction. Receives 300 unsolicited mss/month. Accepts 7-9 mss/issue. Does not read mss from June 1 to October 31. Publishes ms an average of 3-6 months after acceptance. **Publishes 6-8 new writers/year.** Recently published work by Stuart Dybek, Marilyn Chin, Ray Gonzalez, Abby Frucht. Also publishes literary essays, poetry.

How to Contact Send complete ms. Accepts submissions by e-mail. Cover letters should be *brief* and demonstrate specific familiarity with the content of a recent issue of *Indiana Review.* Include SASE. Responds in 4 months to mss. Accepts simultaneous submissions if notified *immediately* of other publication. Sample copy for $9. Writer's guidelines online.

Payment/Terms Pays $5/page, plus 2 contributor's copies. Pays on publication for first North American serial rights. Sponsors awards/contests.

Advice "Because our editors change each year, so do our literary preferences. It's important that potential contributors are familiar with our most recent issue of *Indiana Review* via library, sample copy or subscription. Beyond that, we look for prose that is well crafted and socially relevant. Dig deep. Don't accept your first choice descriptions when you are revising. Cliché and easy images sink 90% of the stories we reject. Understand the magazines you send to—investigate!"

☑ INKWELL MAGAZINE

Manhattanville College, 2900 Purchase St., Purchase NY 10577. (914)323-7239. E-mail: inkwell@mville.edu. Web site: www.inkwelljournal.org. **Contact:** Fiction editor. Literary Journal: $5^{1}/_{2} \times 7^{1}/_{2}$; 120-170 pages; 60 lb. paper; 10 pt C1S, 4/c cover; illustrations; photos. "*Inkwell Magazine* is committed to presenting top quality poetry, prose and artwork in a high quality publication. *Inkwell* is dedicated to discovering new talent and to encouraging and bringing talents of working writers and artists to a wider audience. We encourage diverse voices and have an open submission policy for both art and literature." Annual. Estab. 1995. Circ. 1,000. Member CLMP.

Needs Experimental, humor/satire, literary. "No erotica, children's literature, romance, religious." Receives 120 unsolicited mss/month. Accepts 45 mss/issue. Does not read mss December-July. Publishes ms 2 months after acceptance. **Publishes 3-5 new writers/year.** Recently published work by Alice Quinn, Margaret Gibson, Benjamin Cheever. Length: 5,000 words; average length: 3,000 words. Publishes short shorts. Also publishes poetry.

How to Contact Send a disposable copy of ms and #10 SASE for reply only. Responds in 1 month to queries; 4-6 months to mss. Sample copy for $6. Writer's guidelines for SASE.

Payment/Terms Pays contributor's copies and sends complimentary copies; additional copies $8. Acquires first North American serial, first rights. Sponsors awards/contests.

Advice "We look for well-crafted original stories with a strong voice."

☑ ◎ IRIS, A Journal About Women

P.O. Box 800588, University of Virginia, Charlottesville VA 22908. (434)924-4500. E-mail: iris@virginia.edu. **Contact:** Fiction Editor. Magazine: $8^{1}/_{2} \times 11$; 80 pages; glossy paper; heavy cover; illustrations; artwork; photos. "Material of particular interests to women. For a feminist audience, college educated and above." Semiannual. Estab. 1980. Circ. 3,500.

Needs Experimental, feminist, lesbian, literary, mainstream. "We're just looking for well-written stories of interest to women (particularly feminist women)." Receives 25 unsolicited mss/month. Accepts 5 mss/year. Publishes ms 1 year after acceptance. **Publishes 1-2 new writers/year.** Recently published work by Sheila Thorne, Lizette Wanzer, Marsha Recknagel and Denise Laughlin. Average length: 2,500-4,000 words. Sometimes comments on rejected mss.

How to Contact Accepts submissions by e-mail. SASE. Responds in 3 months to mss. Accepts simultaneous submissions. Sample copy for $5. Writer's guidelines for SASE. Label: Fiction Editor.

Payment/Terms Pays in contributor's copies and 1 year subscription. Acquires one-time rights.

Advice "My major complaint is with stories that don't elevate the language above the bland sameness we hear on the television everyday. Read the work on the outstanding women writers, such as Alice Munro and Louise Erdrich."

$ ☑ ◎ ISOTOPE

A Journal of Literary Nature and Science Writing, 3200 Old Main Hill, Logan UT 84322-3200. (435)797-3697. Fax: (435)797-3797. E-mail: lbrown@cc.usu.edu. Web site: isotope.usu.edu. **Contact:** Charles Waugh, fiction editor. Literary magazine/journal: $8^{1}/_{2} \times 11$, 52 pages. Contains illustrations. Includes photographs. "Focus on nature and science writing that meditates on and engages in the varied and complex relations among the human and non-human worlds." Semiannual. Estab. 2003. Circ. 1,000. Member CLMP.

Needs Experimental, humor/satire, literary, translations. Special interests: nature and science. Receives 10 mss/month. Accepts 1-2 mss/issue; 2-4 mss/year. Does not read December 1 to August 31. Manuscript published 6-18 months after acceptance. **Publishes 2 new writers/year.** Published Jill Stegman, Emily Doak, Janette Fecteau. Length: 250-7,500. Average length: 5,000. Publishes short shorts. Average length of short shorts: 500. Also publishes literary essays, poetry. Rarely comments on/critiques rejected mss.

How to Contact Send complete ms with cover letter. Include brief bio, list of publications. Send either SASE (or IRC) for return of ms or disposable copy of ms and #10 SASE for reply only. Considers simultaneous submissions, multiple submissions. Sample copy available for $5. Guidelines available on Web site.

Payment and Terms Writers receive $100 per story, 4 contributor's copies, free subscription to the magazine. Additional copies $4. Pays on publication. Acquires first North American serial rights. Sends galleys to author. Publication is copyrighted.

☑ THE JABBERWOCK REVIEW

Mississippi State University, Drawer E, Dept. of English, Mississippi State MS 39762. (662)325-3644. E-mail: jabberwock@org.msstate.edu. Web site: www.msstate.edu/org/jabberwock. **Contact:** Fiction Editor (revolving editorship). Magazine: $8^{1}/_{2} \times 5^{1}/_{2}$; 120 pages; glossy cover; illustrations; photos. "We are located in the South—love the South—but we publish good writing from anywhere and everywhere. And from anyone. We respect writers of reputation—and print their work—but we take great delight in publishing new and emerging writers as well.'' Semiannual. Estab. 1979. Circ. 500.

Needs Ethnic/multicultural, experimental, feminist, gay, literary, mainstream, regional, translations. ''No science fiction, romance.'' Receives 150 unsolicited mss/month. Accepts 7-8 mss/issue; 15 mss/year. ''We do not read during the summer (May 1 to September 1). Publishes ms 4-6 months after acceptance. **Publishes 1-5 new writers/year.** Recently published work by Margo Rabb, Chris Mazza, Charles Harper Webb, Alyu Miller, Alison Baker. Length: 250-5,000 words; average length: 4,000 words. Publishes short shorts. Also publishes literary essays, poetry. Sometimes comments on rejected mss.

How to Contact Send SASE (or IRC) for return of ms. Responds in 5 months to mss. Accepts simultaneous submissions ''with notification of such.'' Sample copy for $6. Writer's guidelines for SASE.

Payment/Terms Pays 2 contributor's copies. Sponsors awards/contests.

Advice ''It might take a few months to get a response from us, but your manuscript will be read with care. Our editors enjoy reading submissions (really!) and will remember writers who are persistent and commited to getting a story 'right' through revision.''

$⬚ THE JOURNAL

The Ohio State University, 164 W. 17th Ave., Columbus OH 43210. (614)292-4076. Fax: (614)292-7816. E-mail: thejournal@osu.edu. Web site: http://english.osu.edu/journals/the_journal.cfm/. **Contact:** Kathy Fagan (poetry); Michelle Herman (fiction). Magazine: 6×9; 150 pages. ''We're open to all forms; we tend to favor work that gives evidence of a mature and sophisticated sense of the language.'' Semiannual. Estab. 1972. Circ. 1,500.

Needs Novel excerpts, literary short stories. No romance, science fiction or religious/devotional. Receives 100 unsolicited mss/month. Accepts 2 mss/issue. Publishes ms 1 year after acceptance. Agented fiction 10%. **Publishes some new writers/year.** Recently published work by Michael Martone, Gregory Spatz and Stephen Graham Jones. Sometimes comments on rejected mss.

How to Contact Send complete ms with cover letter and SASE. Responds in 2 weeks to queries; 2 months to mss. Accepts simultaneous submissions. No electronic submissions. Sample copy for $7 or online. Writer's guidelines online.

Payment/Terms Pays $20. Pays on publication for first North American serial rights. Sends galleys to author.

Advice ''Manuscripts are rejected because of lack of understanding of the short story form, shallow plots, undeveloped characters. Cure: Read as much well-written fiction as possible. Our readers prefer 'psychological' fiction rather than stories with intricate plots. Take care to present a clean, well-typed submission.''

⬚ ⬚ KARAMU

English Dept., Eastern Illinois University, 600 Lincoln Ave., Charleston IL 61920. (217)581-6297. E-mail: cfoxa@eiu.edu. **Contact:** Fiction Editor. Literary magazine: 5×8; 132-136 pages; illustrations; photos. ''*Karamu* is a literary magazine of ideas and artistic expression independently produced by the faculty members and associates of Eastern Illinois University. We publish writing that captures something essential about life, which goes beyond superficial, and which develops voice genuinely. Contributions of creative non-fiction, fiction, poetry and artwork of interest to a broadly educated audience are welcome.'' Annual. Estab. 1966. Circ. 500.

● *Karamu* has received three Illinois Arts Council Awards.

Needs Adventure, ethnic/multicultural, experimental, feminist, gay, historical, humor/satire, lesbian, literary, mainstream, regional. ''No pornographic, science fiction, religious, political or didactic stories—no dogma or proselytizing.'' List of upcoming editorial themes available for SASE. Receives 80-90 unsolicited mss/month. Accepts 10-15 mss/issue. Does not read February 16-September 1. Publishes ms 1 year after acceptance. **Publishes 3-6 new writers/year.** Recently published work by Pinky Feria, Aaron Sanders, Donna Steiner, Henry Miller, Martin McGowan, and Sybil Smith. Publishes short shorts. Also publishes poetry. Sometimes comments on rejected mss.

How to Contact Send SASE for reply. Responds in 1 week to queries. Does not accepts simultaneous submissions. Sample copy for $8 or $6 for back issues. Writer's guidelines for SASE.

Payment/Terms Pays 1 contributor's copy; additional copies at discount. Acquires one-time rights.

Advice Looks for ''convincing, well-developed characters and plots expressing aspects of human nature or relationships in a perceptive, believable and carefully considered and written way.''

$⬚ ⬚ THE KENYON REVIEW

Walton House, 104 College Dr., Gambier OH 43022. (740)427-5208. Fax: (740)427-5417. E-mail: kenyonreview @kenyon.edu. Web site: www.kenyonreview.org. **Contact:** Fiction Editor. An international journal of literature, culture and the arts dedicated to an inclusive representation of the best in new writing (fiction, poetry, essays, interviews, criticism) from established and emerging writers. Estab. 1939. Circ. 6,000.

Literary Magazines

• Work published in the *Kenyon Review* has been selected for inclusion in *The O Henry Prize Stories*, *Pushcart Prize* anthologies, *Best American Short Stories*, and *Best American Poetry*.

Needs Excerpts from novels, condensed novels, ethnic/multicultural, experimental, feminist, gay, historical, humor/satire, lesbian, literary, mainstream, translations, contemporary. Receives 900 unsolicited mss/month. Unsolicited mss typically read only from September 1-January 31. Publishes ms 1 year after acceptance. Recently published work by Alice Hoffman, Beth Ann Fennelly, Romulus Linney, John Koethe, Albert Goldbarth, Erin McGraw.

How to Contact Only accepting mss via online submissions program. Please visit Web site for instructions. Do not submit via e-mail or snail mail. No simultaneous submissions. Sample copy $12 single issue, includes postage and handling. Please call or e-mail to order. Writer's guidelines online.

Payment/Terms Pays $15-40/page. Pays on publication for first rights.

Advice "We look for strong voice, unusual perspective, and power in the writing."

☐ ◎ KEREM, Creative Explorations in Judaism

Jewish Study Center Press, Inc., 3035 Porter St. NW, Washington DC 20008. (202)364-3006. E-mail: langner@er ols.com. Web site: www.kerem.org. **Contact:** Sara R. Horowitz and Gilah Langner, editors. Magazine: 6×9; 128 pages; 60 lb. offset paper; glossy cover; illustrations; photos. "*Kerem* publishes Jewish religious, creative, literary material—short stories, poetry, personal reflections, text study, prayers, rituals, etc." Estab. 1992. Circ. 2,000.

Needs Jewish: feminist, humor/satire, literary, religious/inspirational. Receives 10-12 unsolicited mss/month. Accepts 1-2 mss/issue. Publishes ms 2-10 months after acceptance. **Publishes 2 new writers/year.** Also publishes literary essays, poetry.

How to Contact Prefers submissions by e-mail. Send SASE for reply, return of ms or send disposable copy of ms. Responds in 2 months to queries; 5 months to mss. Accepts simultaneous, multiple submissions. Sample copy for $8.50. Writer's guidelines online.

Payment/Terms Pays free subscription and 2-10 contributor's copies. Acquires one-time rights.

Advice "Should have a strong Jewish content. We want to be moved by reading the manuscript!"

$☐ THE KIT-CAT REVIEW

244 Halstead Ave., Harrison NY 10528. (914)835-4833. E-mail: kitcatreview@gmail.com. **Contact:** Claudia Fletcher, editor. Magazine: 8½×5½; 75 pages; laser paper; colored card cover stock; illustrations. "*The Kit-Cat Review* is named after the 18th Century Kit-Cat Club, whose members included Addison, Steele, Congreve, Vanbrugh and Garth. Its purpose is to promote/discover excellence and originality." *The Kit-Cat Review* is part of the collections of the University of Wisconsin (Madison) and State University of New York (Buffalo). Quarterly. Estab. 1998. Circ. 500.

Needs Ethnic/multicultural, experimental, literary, novel excerpts, slice-of-life vignettes. No stories with "O. Henry-type formula endings. Shorter pieces stand a better chance of publication." No science fiction, fantasy, romance, horror or new age. Receives 40 unsolicited mss/month. Accepts 6 mss/issue; 24 mss/year. Publishes ms 6-12 months after acceptance. **Publishes 14 new writers/year.** Recently published work by Chayym Zeldis, Michael Fedo, Louis Phillips, Elisha Porat. Length: 5,000 words maximum; average length: 2,000 words. Publishes short shorts. Also publishes literary essays, literary criticism, poetry.

How to Contact Send complete ms. Accepts submissions by disk. Send SASE (or IRC) for return of ms, or send disposable copy of ms and #10 SASE for reply only. Responds in 1 week to queries; 2 months to mss. Accepts simultaneous, multiple submissions. Sample copy for $7 (payable to Claudia Fletcher). Writer's guidelines not available.

Payment/Terms Pays $25-200 and 2 contributor's copies; additional copies $5. Pays on publication for first rights.

⊕ ◎ LA KANCERKLINIKO

% Laurent Septier, 162 rue Paradis, P.O. Box 174, 13444 Marseille Cantini Cedex France. (33)2-48-61-81-98. Fax: (33)2-48-61-81-98. E-mail: lseptier@hotmail.com. **Contact:** Laurent Septier. "An Esperanto magazine which appears 4 times annually. Each issue contains 32 pages. *La Kancerkliniko* is a political and cultural magazine." Quarterly. Circ. 300.

Needs Science fiction, short stories or very short novels. "The short story (or the very short novel) must be written only in Esperanto, either original or translation from any other language." Wants more science fiction. **Publishes 2-3 new writers/year.** Recently published work by Mao Zifu, Manuel de Sabrea, Peter Brown and Aldo de'Giorgi.

How to Contact Accepts submissions by e-mail, fax. Accepts disk submissions. Accepts multiple submissions. Sample copy for 3 IRCs from Universal Postal Union.

Payment/Terms Pays in contributor's copies.

⚫ LAKE EFFECT, A Journal of the Literary Arts

Penn State Erie, Humanities and Social Sciences, 5091 Station Rd., Erie PA 16563-1501. (814)898-6281. Fax: (814)898-6032. E-mail: goL1@psu.edu. **Contact:** George Looney, editor-in-chief. Magazine: $5^1/_2 \times 8^1/_2$; 136-150 pages; 55 lb. natural paper; 12 pt. C1S cover. "In addition to seeking strong, traditional stories, *Lake Effect* is open to more experimental, language-centered fiction as well." Annual. Estab. as *Lake Effect*, 2001; as *Tempest*, 1978. Circ. 500. Member CLMP.

Needs Experimental, literary, mainstream. "No children's/juvenile, fantasy, science fiction, romance or young adult/teen." Receives 120 unsolicited mss/month. Accepts 5-9 mss/issue. Publishes ms 1 year after acceptance. **Publishes 6 new writers/year.** Recently published work by Edith Pearlman, Francois Camoin, Cris Mazza, Joan Connor, Rick Henry, Joanna Howard. Length: 4,500 -5,000 words; average length: 2,600 -3,900 words. Publishes short shorts. Also publishes literary essays, poetry.

How to Contact Send SASE for return of ms or send a disposable copy of ms and #10 SASE for reply only. Responds in 3 weeks to queries; 4-6 months to mss. Accepts simultaneous submissions. Sample copy for $6. Writer's guidelines for SASE.

Payment/Terms Pays 2 contributor's copies; additional copies $2. Acquires first, one-time rights. Not copyrighted.

Advice "We're looking for strong, well-crafted stories that emerge from character and language more than plot. The language is what makes a story stand out (and a strong sense of voice). Be sure to let us know immediately should a submitted story be accepted elsewhere."

⚫ ◎ THE LAMP-POST, of the Southern California C.S. Lewis Society

1106 W. 16th St., Santa Ana CA 92706. (714)836-5257. E-mail: dgclark@adelphia. net. **Contact:** David G. Clark, editor. Magazine: $5^1/_2 \times 8^1/_2$; 34 pages; 7 lb. paper; 8 lb. cover; illustrations. "We are a literary review focused on C.S. Lewis and like writers." Quarterly. Estab. 1977. Circ. 200.

Needs "Literary fantasy and science fiction for children to adults." Publishes ms 3-12 months after acceptance. **Publishes 3-5 new writers/year.** Length: 1,000-5,000 words; average length: 2,500 words. Also publishes literary essays, literary criticism, poetry. Sometimes comments on rejected mss.

How to Contact Send via e-mail as Word file or rich text format. Send SASE for reply, return of ms or send a disposable copy of ms. Responds in 2 weeks to mss. Accepts reprint submissions . No simultaneous submissions. Sample copy for $3. Writer's guidelines for #10 SASE. Reviews fiction.

Payment/Terms Pays 2 contributor's copies; additional copies $3. Acquires first North American serial, one-time rights.

Advice "We look for fiction with the supernatural, mythic feel o f the fiction of C.S. Lewis and Charles Williams. Our slant is Christian but we want work of literary quality. No inspirational. Is it the sort of thing Lewis, Tolkien and Williams would like—subtle, crafted fiction? If so, send it. Don't be too obvious or facile. Our readers aren't stupid."

⊕ LANDFALL/UNIVERSITY OF OTAGO PRESS

University of Otago Press, P.O. Box 56, Dunedin New Zealand. Fax: (643)479-8385. E-mail: landfall@otago.ac. nz. **Contact:** Fiction Editor.

Needs Publishes fiction, poetry, commentary and reviews of New Zealand books.

How to Contact Send copy of ms with SASE. Sample copy not available.

Advice "We concentrate on publishing work by New Zealand writers, but occasionally accept work from elsewhere."

⚫ THE LAUREL REVIEW

Northwest Missouri State University, Dept. of English, Maryville MO 64468. (660)562-1739. E-mail: tlr@nwmiss ouri.edu. Web site: http://catpages.nwmissouri.edu/m/tlr. **Contact:** Rebecca Aronson, John Gallaher. Magazine: 6×9; 124-128 pages; good quality paper. "We publish poetry and fiction of high quality, from the traditional to the avant-garde. We are eclectic, open and flexible. Good writing is all we seek." Biannual. Estab. 1960. Circ. 900.

Needs Literary, contemporary. "No genre or politically polemical fiction." Receives 120 unsolicited mss/month. Accepts 3-5 mss/issue; 6-10 mss/year. Reading period: September 1-May 1. Publishes ms 1-12 months after acceptance. **Publishes 1-2 new writers/year.** Recently published work by Bruce Tallerman, Judith Kitchen, and John Vanderslice. Also publishes literary essays, poetry.

How to Contact Responds in 4 months to mss. No simultaneous submissions. Sample copy for $5.

Payment/Terms Pays 2 contributor's copies and 1 year subscription. Acquires first rights. Copyright reverts to author upon request.

Advice "Nothing really matters to us except our perception that the story presents something powerfully felt by the writer and communicated intensely to a serious reader. (We believe, incidentally, that comedy is just as serious a matter as tragedy, and we don't mind a bit if something makes us laugh out loud; we get too little that makes us laugh, in fact.) We try to reply promptly, though we don't always manage that. In short, we want good poems and good stories. We hope to be able to recognize them, and we print what we believe to the best work submitted."

LE FORUM, Supplement Littéraire

Franco-American Research Opportunity Group, University of Maine, Franco American Center, Orono ME 04469-5719. (207)581-3764. Fax: (207)581-1455. E-mail: lisa_michaud@umit.maine.edu. Web site: www.francomaine .org. **Contact:** Lisa Michaud, managing editor. Magazine: 56 pages; illustrations; photos. Publication was founded to stimulate and recognize creative expression among Franco-Americans, all types of readers, including literary and working class. This publication is used in classrooms. Circulated internationally. Quarterly. Estab. 1986. Circ. 5,000.

Needs "We will consider any type of short fiction, poetry and critical essays having to with Franco-American experience. They must be of good quality in French or English. We are also looking for Canadian writers with French-North American experiences." Receives 10 unsolicited mss/month. Accepts 2-4 mss/issue. **Publishes some new writers/year.** Length: 750-2,500 words; average length: 1,000 words. Occasionally comments on rejected mss.

How to Contact Include SASE. Responds in 3 weeks to queries; 1 month to mss. Accepts simultaneous submissions and reprints. Sample copy not available.

Payment/Terms Pays 3 copies. Acquires one-time rights.

Advice "Write honestly. Start with a strongly felt personal Franco-American experience. If you make us feel what you have felt, we will publish it. We stress that this publication deals specifically with the Franco-American experience."

THE LEDGE MAGAZINE

40 Maple Ave., Bellport NY 11713-2011. (631)286-5252. E-mail: tkmonaghan@aol.com. Web site: www.theledg emagazine.com. **Contact:** Tim Monaghan, publisher. Literary magazine/journal: 6×9, 192 pages, offset paper, glossy stock cover. "*The Ledge Magazine* publishes cutting-edge contemporary fiction by emerging and established wirters." Annual. Estab. 1988. Circ. 1,500.

Needs Erotica, ethnic/multicultural (general), literary. Receives 30 mss/month. Accepts 3-4 mss/issue. Manuscript published 6 months after acceptance. Published Franny French, Clifford Garstang, Elissa Minor Rust, Al Sims. Length: 2,500 words (min)-7,500 words (max). Average length: 6,000 words. Also publishes poetry. Rarely comments on/critiques rejected mss.

How to Contact Send complete ms with cover letter. Include estimated word count, brief bio. Responds to queries in 4 weeks. Responds to mss in 3 months. Send SASE (or IRC) for return of ms. Considers simultaneous submissions. Sample copy available for $10. Guidelines available for SASE.

Payment and Terms Writers receive 1 contributor's copy. Additional copies $6. Pays on publication. Acquires first North American serial rights. Sends galleys to author. Publication is copyrighted.

Advice "We seek stories that utilize language in a fresh, original way. Truly compelling stories are especially appreciated. We dislike sloppy or hackneyed writing."

THE LISTENING EYE

Kent State University Geauga Campus, 14111 Claridon-Troy Rd., Burton OH 44021. (440)286-3840. E-mail: grace_butcher@msn.com. **Contact:** Grace Butcher, editor. Magazine: $5\frac{1}{2} \times 8\frac{1}{2}$; 60 pages; photographs. "We publish the occasional very short stories (750 words/3 pages double spaced) in any subject and any style, but the language must be strong, unusual, free from cliché and vagueness. We are a shoestring operation from a small campus but we publish high-quality work." Annual. Estab. 1970. Circ. 250.

Needs Literary. "Pretty much anything will be considered except porn." Reads mss January 1-April 15 only. Publishes ms 3-4 months after acceptance. Recently published work by Elizabeth Scott, Sam Ruddick, H.E. Wright. Publishes short shorts. Also publishes poetry. Sometimes comments on rejected mss.

How to Contact Send SASE for return of ms or disposable copy of ms with SASE for reply only. Responds in 4 weeks to queries; 4 months to mss. Accepts reprint submissions. Sample copy for $3 and $1 postage. Writer's guidelines for SASE.

Payment/Terms Pays 2 contributor's copies; additional copies $3 with $1 postage. Pays on publication for one-time rights.

Advice "We look for powerful, unusual imagery, content and plot. Short, short."

LITERAL LATTÉ, Mind Stimulating Stories, Poems & Essays

Word Sci, Inc., 200 East 10th Street Suite 240, New York NY 10003. (212)260-5532. E-mail: litlatte@aol.com. Web site: www.literal-latte.com. **Contact:** Jeff Bockman, editor. Magazine: illustrations; photos. "Publishes great writing in many flavors and styles. *Literal Latté* expands the readership for literary magazines by offering free copies in New York coffeehouses and bookstores." Bimonthly. Estab. 1994. CLMP.

Needs Experimental, fantasy, literary, science fiction. Receives 4,000 unsolicited mss/month. Accepts 5-8 mss/issue; 40 mss/year. Agented fiction 5%. **Publishes 6 new writers/year.** Length: 500-6,000 words; average length: 4,000 words. Publishes short shorts. Often comments on rejected mss.

How to Contact Send SASE for return of mss or send a disposable copy of ms and #10 SASE for reply only or e-mail for reply only. Responds in 6 months to mss. Accepts simultaneous, multiple submissions. Sample copy for $3. Writer's guidelines for SASE, e-mail or check Web site. Reviews fiction.

Payment/Terms Pays 10 contributor's copies, a free subscription to the magazine and 2 gift certificates; additional copies $1. Pays on publication for first, one-time rights. Sponsors awards/contests.

Advice "Keeping free thought free and challenging entertainment are not mutually exclusive. Words make a manuscript stand out, words beautifully woven together in striking and memorable patterns."

THE LITERARY REVIEW, An International Journal of Contemporary Writing

Fairleigh Dickinson University, 285 Madison Ave., Madison NJ 07940. (973)443-8564. Fax: (973)443-8364. E-mail: tlr@fdu.edu. Web site: www.theliteraryreview.org. **Contact:** Walter Cummins, editor-in-chief. Magazine: 6×9; 160 pages; professionally printed on textpaper; semigloss card cover; perfect-bound. "Literary magazine specializing in fiction, poetry and essays with an international focus. Our audience is general with a leaning toward scholars, libraries and schools." Quarterly. Estab. 1957. Circ. 2,000.

- Work published in *The Literary Review* has been included in *Editor's Choice, Best American Short Stories* and *Pushcart Prize* anthologies.

Needs Works of high literary quality only. Does not want to see "overused subject matter or pat resolutions to conflicts." Receives 90-100 unsolicited mss/month. Accepts 20-25 mss/year. Does not read submissions during June, July and August. Publishes ms 1½-2 years after acceptance. Agented fiction 1-2%. **Publishes 80% new writers/year.** Recently published work by Irvin Faust, Todd James Pierce, Joshua Shapiro , Susan Schwartz Senstadt. Also publishes literary essays, literary criticism, poetry. Occasionally comments on rejected mss.

How to Contact Responds in 3-4 months to mss. Accepts multiple submissions. Sample copy for $7. Writer's guidelines for SASE. Reviews fiction.

Payment/Terms Pays 2 contributor's copies; $3 discount for extras. Acquires first rights.

Advice "We want original dramatic situations with complex moral and intellectual resonance and vivid prose. We don't want versions of familiar plots and relationships. Too much of what we are seeing today is openly derivative in subject, plot and prose style. We pride ourselves on spotting new writers with fresh insight and approach."

THE LONG STORY

18 Eaton St., Lawrence MA 01843. (978)686-7638. E-mail: rpburnham@mac.com. Web site: http://homepage.mac.com/rpburnham/longstory.html. **Contact:** R.P. Burnham. Magazine: 5½×8½; 150-200 pages; 60 lb. cover stock; illustrations (b&w graphics). For serious, educated, literary people. Annual. Estab. 1983. Circ. 1,200.

Needs Ethnic/multicultural, feminist, literary, contemporary. "No science fiction, adventure, romance, etc. We publish high literary quality of any kind but especially look for stories that have difficulty getting published elsewhere—committed fiction, working class settings, left-wing themes, etc." Receives 30-40 unsolicited mss/month. Accepts 6-7 mss/issue. Publishes ms 3 months to 1 year after acceptance. **Publishes 90% new writers/year.** Length: 8,000-20,000 words; average length: 8,000-12,000 words.

How to Contact Include SASE. Responds in 2 months to mss. Accepts simultaneous submissions "but not wild about it." Sample copy for $7.

Payment/Terms Pays 2 contributor's copies; $5 charge for extras. Acquires first rights.

Advice "Read us first and make sure submitted material is the kind we're interested in. Send clear, legible manuscripts. We're not interested in commercial success; rather we want to provide a place for long stories, the most difficult literary form to publish in our country."

LOUISIANA LITERATURE, A Review of Literature and Humanities

Southeastern Louisiana University, SLU 792, Hammond LA 70402. (985)549-5022. Fax: (504)549-5021. E-mail: ngerman@selu.edu. Web site: www. louisianaliterature.org. **Contact:** Norman German, fiction editor. Magazine: 6×9; 150 pages; 70 lb. paper; card cover; illustrations. "Essays should be about Louisiana material; preference is given to fiction and poetry with Louisiana and Southern themes, but creative work can be set anywhere." Semiannual. Estab. 1984. Circ. 400 paid; 500-700 printed.

Needs Literary, mainstream, regional. "No sloppy, ungrammatical manuscripts." Receives 100 unsolicited mss/month. May not read mss June-July. Publishes ms 6-12 after acceptance. **Publishes 4 new writers/year.** Recently published work by Anthony Bukowski, Tim Parrish, Robert Phillips, Andrew Otis Haschemeyer.

Length: 1,000-6,000 words; average length: 3,500 words. Also publishes literary essays, literary criticism, poetry. Sometimes comments on rejected mss.

How to Contact Include SASE. Responds in 3 months to mss. Sample copy for $8. Reviews fiction.

Payment/Terms Pays usually in contributor's copies. Acquires one-time rights.

Advice "Cut out everything that is not a functioning part of the story. Make sure your manuscript is professionally presented. Use relevant specific detail in every scene. We love detail, local color, voice and craft. Any professional manuscript stands out."

THE LOUISIANA REVIEW

Division of Liberal Arts, Louisiana State University at Eunice, P.O. Box 1129, Eunice LA 70535. (337)550-1315. E-mail: bfonteno@lsue.edu. **Contact:** Dr. Billy Fontenot, editors. Magazine: $5^{1}/_{2} \times 11^{1}/_{2}$; 100-200 pages; illustrations. "While we will accept some of the better works submitted by our own students, we prefer excellent work by Louisiana writers as well as those outside the state who tell us their connection to it." Annual. Estab. 1999. Circ. 300-600.

Needs Ethnic/multicultural (Cajun or Louisiana culture), historical (Louisiana-related or setting), regional (Louisiana). Receives 25 unsolicited mss/month. Accepts 5-7 mss/issue. Reads year-round. Publishes ms 6-12 months after acceptance. Recently published work by Tom Bonner, Laura Cario, Sheryl St. Germaine. Length: up to 9,000 words; average length: 2,000 words. Publishes short shorts. Also publishes poetry. Sometimes comments on rejected mss.

How to Contact Send SASE (or IRC) for return of ms. Responds in 5 weeks to queries; 10 weeks to mss. Accepts multiple submissions. Sample copy for $5.

Payment/Terms Pays 1 contributor's copy; additional copies $3. Pays on publication for one-time rights. Not copyrighted but has an ISSN number.

Advice "We do like to have fiction play out visually as a film would rather than static and undramatized. Louisiana or Gulf Coast settings and themes preferred."

THE LOUISVILLE REVIEW

Spalding University, 851 S. Fourth St., Louisville KY 40203. (502)585-9911, ext. 2777. E-mail: louisvillereview@spalding.edu. Web site: www.louisvillereview.org. **Contact:** Sena Jeter Naslund, editor. Literary magazine. "We are a literary journal seeking original stories with fresh imagery and vivid language." Semiannual. Estab. 1976.

Needs Literary. Receives 200 + unsolicited mss/month. Accepts 4-6 fiction mss/issue; 8-12 fiction mss/year. Publishes ms 6 months after acceptance. **Publishes 8-10 new writers/year.** Recently published work by Peter Macuck, Aleda Shirley and Murzban F. Schroff. Publishes essays, fiction, nonfiction and poetry.

How to Contact Send a disposable copy of ms and #10 SASE for reply only. Responds in 6 months to queries; 6 months to mss. Accepts multiple submissions.

Payment/Terms Pays 2 contributor's copies.

$ LUNCH HOUR STORIES

Lunch Hour Publications, 22833 Bothell-Everett Hwy, STE 110-PMB 1117, Bothell WA 98021-9366. (425)246-3726. Fax: (425)424-8859. E-mail: editor@lunchhourbooks.com. Web site: www.lunchhourstories.com. **Contact:** Nina Bayer, editor. Literary magazine/journal: $5^{1}/_{2} \times 8^{1}/_{2}$, 20 pages, natural linen paper, natural linen cover. "*Lunch Hour Stories* publishes only short stories and distributes them only to paid subscribers. *Lunch Hour Stories* are thin, easy-to-carry booklets that contain one short story each. They are designed to fit easily into a purse or briefcase and be read in less than 60 minutes. They are distributed by mail 16 times per year (minimum of one issue per month). Estab. Jan 2007.

Needs Literary, mainstream. Special interests: "Literary only." Does not want genre (romance, sci-fi, fantasy, etc.); experimental; religious; children's/young adult; feminist/gay; erotica. Accepts 1 mss/issue; 16 mss/year. Manuscript published 6-18 months after acceptance. Length: 4,000 words (min)-8,000 words (max). Average length: 6,000 words. Also publishes annual anthology of very short stories (less than 500 words). See Web site for full submissions guidelines. Often comments on/critiques rejected mss.

How to Contact Send one printed copy with a cover letter. Include word count, brief bio, contact information, SASE, synopsis of 100 words. Responds to mss in 3-6 months. Send disposable copy of ms and #10 SASE for reply only. Considers multiple and simultaneous submissions. Sample copy $2.50 in US, $4 worldwide with SASE ($6 \times 9$). Guidelines and annual contest information available on Web site.

Payment and Terms Writers receive $50 flat-rate payment, 10 contributor's copies, and free one-year subscription to the magazine. Additional copies $2.50 in US, $4 worldwide. Pays on publication. Acquires first worldwide English language serial rights. All stories must be previously unpublished. Rights revert back to author following publication, with some limitations for the first year. Sends galleys to author. Publication is copyrighted.

Advice "Stories should be well written and carefully edited. They should be engrossing, humorous, warm or moving. They should make us want to read them more than once and then share them with a friend. We encourage new writers to step out and take a chance! Do your best work, share it with a critique group, and then share it with us.''

THE MACGUFFIN

Schoolcraft College, Department of English, 18600 Haggerty Rd., Livonia MI 48152-2696. (734)462-4400, ext. 5327. Fax: (734)462-4679. E-mail: macguffin@schoolcraft.edu. Web site: www.schoolcraft.edu/macguffin/. **Contact:** Steven A. Dolgin, editor; Nausheen S. Khan, managing editor; Elizabeth Kircos, fiction editor; Carol Was, poetry editor. Magazine: 6×9; 164+ pages; 60 lb. paper; 110 lb. cover; b&w illustrations; photos. ''The *MacGuffin* is a literary magazine which publishes a range of material including poetry, creative nonfiction and fiction. Material ranges from traditional to experimental. We hope our periodical attracts a variety of people with many different interests.'' Triannual. Estab. 1984. Circ. 600.

Needs Adventure, ethnic/multicultural, experimental, historical (general), humor/satire, literary, mainstream, translations, contemporary, prose poem. ''No religious, inspirational, juvenile, romance, horror, pornography.'' Receives 35-55 unsolicited mss/month. Accepts 10-15 mss/issue; 30-50 mss/year. Does not read mss between July 1-August 15. Publishes ms 6 months to 2 years after acceptance. Agented fiction 10-15%. **Publishes 30 new writers/year.** Recently published work by Gerry LaFemina, Gail Waldstein, Margaret Karmazin, Linda Nemec Foster, Laurence Lieberman, Conrad Hilberry, and Thomas Lux. Length: 100-5,000 words; average length: 2,000-2,500 words. Publishes short shorts. Also publishes literary essays. Occasionally comments on rejected mss.

How to Contact Send SASE or e-mail. Responds in 4-6 months to mss. Sample copy for $6; current issue for $9. Writer's guidelines free.

Payment/Terms Pays 2 contributor's copies. Acquires one-time rights.

Advice ''We want to give promising new fiction writers the opportunity to publish alongside recognized writers. Be persistent. If a story is rejected, try to send it somewhere else. When we reject a story, we may accept the next one you send us. When we make suggestions for a rewrite, we may accept the revision. There seems to be a great number of good authors of fiction, but there are far too few places for publication. However, this is changing. Make your characters come to life. Even the most ordinary people become fascinating if they live for your readers.''

THE MADISON REVIEW

Department of English, Helen C. White Hall, 600 N. Park St., University of Wisconsin, Madison WI 53706. (608)263-0566. E-mail: madisonreview@yahoo.com. **Contact:** Laura Weingarten and Drew Salisbury, fiction editors. Magazine: 6×9; 180 pages. ''Magazine for fiction and poetry with special emphasis on literary stories and some emphasis on Midwestern writers.'' Semiannual. Estab. 1978. Circ. 1,000.

Needs Experimental, literary, novel excerpts, translations, prose poems. ''We would like to see more contemporary fiction; however, we accept fiction of any creative form and content. No historical fiction.'' Receives 10-50 unsolicited mss/month. Accepts 6 mss/issue. Does not read May-September. Publishes ms 4 months after acceptance. **Publishes 4 new writers/year.** Recently published work by Maurice Glenn Taylor and John McNally. Average length: 4,000 words. Also publishes poetry.

How to Contact Responds in 4 months to mss. Accepts multiple submissions. Sample copy for $3 via postal service or e-mail.

Payment/Terms Pays 2 contributor's copies; $5 charge for extras. Acquires first North American serial rights.

$ 🔲 ✅ 🔲 THE MALAHAT REVIEW

The University of Victoria P.O. Box 1700, STN CSC, Victoria BC V8W 2Y2 Canada. (250)721-8524. E-mail: malahat@uvic.ca. Web site: www.malahatreview.ca. **Contact:** John Barton, editor. ''We try to achieve a balance of views and styles in each issue. We strive for a mix of the best writing by both established and new writers.'' Quarterly. Estab. 1967. Circ. 1,000.

• *The Malahat Review* has received the National Magazine Award for poetry and fiction.

Needs ''General ficton and poetry.'' Accepts 3-4 mss/issue. Publishes ms within 6 months after acceptance. **Publishes 4-5 new writers/year.** Recently published work by Steven Hayward, Pauline Holdstock, Pasha Malla, Anne Sanow, J.M. Villaverde, Terrence Young.

How to Contact Send complete ms. ''Enclose proper postage on the SASE (or send IRC).'' Responds in 2 weeks to queries; 3 months to mss. No simultaneous submissions. Sample copy for $16.45 (US). Writer's guidelines online.

Payment/Terms Pays $35/magazine page. Pays on acceptance for second serial (reprint), first world rights.

Advice ''We do encourage new writers to submit. Read the magazines you want to be published in, ask for their guidelines and follow them. Check Web site for information on *Malahat*'s novella competition and *Far Horizons* award contest.''

$ ⬚ ⬚ MANOA, A Pacific Journal of International Writing

English Dept., University of Hawaii, Honolulu HI 96822. (808)956-3070. Fax: (808)956-3083. E-mail: mjournal-l@hawaii.edu. Web site: http://manoajournal.hawaii.edu. **Contact:** Frank Stewart, editor. Magazine: 7×10; 240 pages. "High quality literary fiction, poetry, essays, personal narrative, reviews. Most of each issue devoted to new work from Pacific and Asian nations. Our audience is primarily in the U.S., although expanding in Pacific countries. U.S. writing need not be confined to Pacific settings or subjects." Semiannual. Estab. 1989. Circ. 2,500.

- *Manoa* has received numerous awards, and work published in the magazine has been selected for prize anthologies.

Needs Literary, mainstream, translations (from U.S. and nations in or bordering on the Pacific), contemporary, excerpted novel. No Pacific exotica. Accepts 1-2 mss/issue. Agented fiction 10%. **Publishes 1-2 new writers/ year.** Recently published work by Ha Jin, Catherine Ryan Hyde, Samrat Upadhyay, Josip Novakovich. Also publishes poetry.

How to Contact Please query first before sending in mss. Include SASE. Does not accept submissions by e-mail. Responds in 3 weeks to queries; 1 month to poetry mss; 6 months to fiction to mss. Accepts simultaneous submissions. Sample copy for $10 (U.S.). Writer's guidelines online. Reviews fiction.

Payment/Terms Pays $100-500 normally ($25/printed page). Pays on publication for first North American serial, non-exclusive, one-time print rights. Sends galleys to author.

⬚ METAL SCRATCHES

P.O. Box 685, Forest Lake MN 55025. E-mail: metalscratches@aol.com. **Contact:** Kim Mark, editor. Magazine: $5\frac{1}{2} \times 8\frac{1}{2}$; 35 pages; heavy cover-stock. "*Metal Scratches* focuses on literary fiction that examines the dark side of humanity. We are not looking for anything that is 'cute' or 'sweet'." Semiannual. Estab. 2000.

Needs Erotica, experimental, horror (psychological), literary. "No poetry, science fiction, rape, murder or horror as in gore." Receives 20 unsolicited mss/month. Accepts 5-6 mss/issue; 20 mss/year. Publishes ms 6 months after acceptance. **Publishes 3 new writers/year.** Length: 3,500 words; average length: 3,000 words. Publishes short shorts. Sometimes comments on rejected mss.

How to Contact Send complete ms. Accepts submissions by e-mail. (No attachments.) Send disposable copy of ms and #10 SASE for reply only. Responds in 1 month to mss. Accepts simultaneous, multiple submissions. Sample copy for $3. Writer's guidelines for SASE or by e-mail.

Payment/Terms Pays 2 contributor's copies; additional copies for $2.50. Pays on publication for one-time rights. Not copyrighted.

Advice "Clean manuscripts prepared according to guidelines are a must. Send us something new and inventive. Don't let rejections from any editor scare you. Keep writing and keep submitting."

$ ⬚ MICHIGAN QUARTERLY REVIEW

3574 Rackham Bldg., 915 E. Washington, University of Michigan, Ann Arbor MI 48109-1070. (734)764-9265. E-mail: mqr@umich.edu. Web site: www.umich.edu/~mqr. **Contact:** Fiction Editor. "An interdisciplinary journal which publishes mainly essays and reviews, with some high-quality fiction and poetry, for an intellectual, widely read audience." Quarterly. Estab. 1962. Circ. 1,500.

- Stories from *Michigan Quarterly Review* have been selected for inclusion in *The Best American Short Stories, The O. Henry Prize Stories* and *Pushcart Prize* volumes.

Needs Literary. "No genre fiction written for a market. Would like to see more fiction about social, political, cultural matters, not just centered on a love relationship or dysfunctional family." Receives 200 unsolicited mss/month. Accepts 2 mss/issue; 8 mss/year. Publishes ms 1 year after acceptance. **Publishes 1-2 new writers/ year.** Recently published work by Robert Boyers, Herbert Gold, Alice Mattison, Joyce Carol Oates, Vu Tran. Length: 1,500-7,000 words; average length: 5,000 words. Also publishes literary essays, poetry.

How to Contact Send complete ms. "I like to know if a writer is at the beginning, or further along, in his or her career. Don't offer plot summaries of the story, though a background comment is welcome." Include SASE. Responds in 2 months to queries; 6 weeks to mss. No simultaneous submissions. Sample copy for $4. Writer's guidelines online.

Payment/Terms Pays $10/published page. Pays on publication. Buys first serial rights. Sponsors awards/ contests.

Advice "There's no beating a good plot, interesting characters and a fresh use of the English language. (Most stories fail because they're written in such a bland manner, or in TV-speak.) Be ambitious, try to involve the social world in the personal one, be aware of what the best writing of today is doing, don't be satisfied with a small slice-of-life narrative but think how to go beyond the ordinary."

⬚ ⬚ MID-AMERICAN REVIEW

Department of English Box W, Bowling Green State University, Bowling Green OH 43403. (419)372-2725. Fax: (419)372-6805. Web site: www.bgsu.edu/midamericanreview. **Contact:** Ashley Kaine, fiction editor. Magazine:

6×9; 232 pages; 60 lb. bond paper; coated cover stock. "We try to put the best possible work in front of the biggest possible audience. We publish serious fiction and poetry, as well as critical studies in contemporary literature, translations and book reviews." Semiannual. Estab. 1981.

Needs Experimental, literary, translations, memoir, prose poem, traditional. "No genre fiction. Would like to see more short shorts." Receives 700 unsolicited mss/month. Accepts 4-8 mss/issue. Publishes ms 6 months after acceptance. Agented fiction 5%. **Publishes 4-8 new writers/year.** Recently published work by Colleen Curran, Steve Almond, and Edith Pearlman. Also publishes literary essays, poetry. Occasionally comments on rejected mss.

How to Contact Send complete ms with SASE. Responds in 4 months to mss. Sample copy for $9 (current issue), $5 (back issue); rare back issues $10. Writer's guidelines online. Reviews fiction.

Payment/Terms Pays $10/page up to $50, pending funding. Pays on publication when funding is available. Acquires first North American serial, one-time rights. Sponsors awards/contests.

Advice "We look for well-written stories that make the reader want to read on past the first line and page. Cliché themes and sloppy writing turn us off immediately. Read literary journals to see what's being published in today's market. We tend to publish work that is more non-traditional in style and subject, but are open to all literary non-genre submissions."

☐ ◎ ☑ MINDPRINTS, A Literary Journal

Learning Assistance Program, Allan Hancock College, 800 S. College Dr., Santa Maria CA 93454-6399. (805)922-6966, ext. 3274. Fax: (805)922-3556. E-mail: pafahey@hancockcollege.edu. Web site: www.imindprints.com. **Contact:** Paul Fahey, editor. Magazine : 6×9; 125-150 pages; 70 lb. matte coated paper; glossy cover; illustrations; photos. "*Mindprints, A Literary Journal* is one of a very few college publications created as a forum for writers and artists with disabilities or for those with an interest in the field. The emphasis on flash fiction , as well as the fact that we are a national journal, puts us on the cutting edge of today's market." Annual. Estab. 2000. Circ. 600.

Needs Flash fiction: literary, mainstream. Receives 20-30 unsolicited mss/month. Accepts 50 mss/year. Does not read mss June-August. Publishes ms 6 months after acceptance. **Publishes 25-30 new writers/year.** Recently published work by Barbara Jacksha. Length: 250-750 words; average length: 500 words. Also publishes poetry. Often comments on rejected mss.

How to Contact Accepts submissions by e-mail (only from outside of the United States). Send a disposable copy of ms and cover letter and #10 SASE for reply only. Responds in 1 week to queries; 4 months to mss. Accepts simultaneous , multiple submissions and reprints. Sample copy for $6 and $2 postage or IRCs. Writer's guidelines for SASE, by e-mail or fax.

Payment/Terms Pays 1 contributor's copy; additional copies $5. Pays on publication for one-time rights. Not copyrighted.

Advice "We look for a great hook; a story that grabs us from the beginning; fiction and memoir with a strong voice and unusual themes; stories with a narrowness of focus yet broad in their appeal. Read and study the flash fiction genre. Revise, revise, revise. Do not send manuscripts that have not been proofed. Our mission is to showcase as many voices and worldviews as possible. We want our readers to sample creative talent from a national and international group of published and unpublished writers and artists."

◢ THE MINNESOTA REVIEW, A Journal of Committed Writing

Dept. of English, Carnegie Mellon University, Pittsburgh PA 15213. (412)268- 9825. E-mail: editors@theminnesotareview.org. Web site: http://theminnesotareview.org. **Contact:** Jeffrey Williams, editor. Magazine: 5¼×7½; approximately 200 pages; some illustrations; occasional photos. "We emphasize socially and politically engaged work." Semiannual. Estab. 1960. Circ. 1,500.

Needs Experimental, feminist, gay, historical, lesbian, literary. Receives 50-75 unsolicited mss/month. Accepts 3-4 mss/issue; 6-8 mss/year. Publishes ms 6-12 months after acceptance. **Publishes 3-5 new writers/year.** Recently published work by E. Shaskan Bumas, Carlos Fuentes, Maggie Jaffe , James Hughes. Publishes short shorts. Also publishes literary essays, literary criticism, poetry. Occasionally comments on rejected mss.

How to Contact Include SASE. Responds in 3 weeks to queries; 3 months to mss. Accepts simultaneous, multiple submissions. Sample copy for $15. Reviews fiction.

Payment/Terms Pays in contributor's copies. Charge for additional copies. Acquires first rights.

Advice "We look for socially and politically engaged work, particularly short, striking work that stretches boundaries."

◔ MISSISSIPPI REVIEW

University of Southern Mississippi, 118 College Dr. #5144, Hattiesburg MS 39406-0001. (601)266-4321. Fax: (601)266-5757. E-mail: rief@mississippireview.com. Web site: www.mississippireview.com. **Contact:** Rie Fortenberry, managing editor. Semiannual. Estab. 1972. Circ. 1,500.

Needs Annual fiction and poetry competition. $1,000 awarded in each category plus publication of all winners and finalists. Fiction entries 5,000 words or less. Poetry entry equals 1-3 poems, page limit is 10. $15 entry fee includes copy of prize issue. No limit on number of entries. Deadline October 1. No manuscripts returned. Does not read mss in summer. **Publishes 10-20 new writers/year.**
How to Contact Sample copy for $8. Writer's guidelines online.
Payment/Terms Acquires first North American serial rights.

$ 🖉 📺 THE MISSOURI REVIEW

1507 Hillcrest Hall, University of Missouri, Columbia MO 65211. (573)882-4474. Fax: (573)884-4671. E-mail: question@missourireview.com. Web site: www.missourireview.com. **Contact:** Speer Morgan, editor; Evelyn Somers, associate editor. Magazine: 6³/₄×10; 200 pages. "We publish contemporary fiction, poetry, interviews, personal essays, cartoons, special features for the literary and the general reader interested in a wide range of subjects." Estab. 1978. Circ. 5,500.

● This magazine had stories anthologized in the *Pushcart Prize, Best American Short Stories, The O. Henry Prize Stories, Best American Essays, Best American Mystery Stories, Best American Nature and Science Writing, Best American Erotica,* and *New Stories from The South.*

Needs Literary fiction on all subjects, novel excerpts. No genre fiction. Receives 500 unsolicited mss/month. Accepts 5-7 mss/issue; 16-20 mss/year. **Publishes 6-10 new writers/year.** Recently published work by Ed Falco, Lauren Slater, Jacob M. Appel, Fan Wu. Also publishes literary essays, poetry. Often comments on rejected mss.
How to Contact Send complete ms. May include brief bio and list of publications. Send SASE for reply, return of ms or send disposable copy of ms. International submissions via Web site. Responds in 2 weeks to queries; 12 weeks to mss. Sample copy for $8 or online. Writer's guidelines online.
Payment/Terms Pays $30/printed page up to $750. Offers signed contract. Sponsors awards/contests.

🖉 MOBIUS, The Journal of Social Change

505 Christianson, Madison WI 53714. (608)242-1009. E-mail: fmschep@charter.net. Web site: www.mobiusmagazine.com. **Contact:** Fred Schepartz, editor. Magazine: 8¹/₂×11; 16-24 pages; 60 lb. paper; 60 lb. cover. "Looking for fiction which uses social change as either a primary or secondary theme. This is broader than most people think. Need social relevance in one way or another. For an artistically and politically aware and curious audience." Quarterly. Estab. 1989. Circ. 1,500.
Needs Ethnic/multicultural, experimental, fantasy, feminist, gay, historical, horror, humor/satire, lesbian, literary, mainstream, science fiction, contemporary, prose poem. "No porn, no racist, sexist or any other kind of -ist. No Christian or spirituality proselytizing fiction." Wants to see more science fiction, erotica "assuming it relates to social change." Receives 15 unsolicited mss/month. Accepts 3-5 mss/issue , "however we are now doubling as a webzine, which means a dramatic change in how we operate. Any work considered suitable will first be published in the web version and will be held for further consideration for the print version." Publishes ms 3-9 months after acceptance. **Publishes 10 new writers/year.** Recently published work by Margaret Karmazin, Benjamin Reed, John Tuschen , Ken Byrnes. Length: 500-5,000 words; average length: 3,500 words. Publishes short shorts. Always comments on rejected mss.
How to Contact Include SASE. Responds in 4 months to mss. Accepts simultaneous, multiple submissions and reprints. Sample copy for $2, 9×12 SAE and 3 first class stamps. Writer's guidelines for SASE.
Payment/Terms Pays contributor's copies. Acquires one-time rights, electronic rights for www version.
Advice "Note that fiction and poetry may be simultaneously published in e-version of *Mobius.* Due to space constraints of print version, some works may be accepted in e-version, but not print version. We like high impact, we like plot and character-driven stories that function like theater of the mind. Looks for first and foremost, good writing. Prose must be crisp and polished; the story must pique my interest and make me care due to a certain intellectual, emotional aspect. Second, *Mobius* is about social change. We want stories that make some statement about the society we live in, either on a macro or micro level. Not that your story neeeds to preach from a soapbox (actually, we prefer that it doesn't), but your story needs to have *something* to say."

🖉 NASSAU REVIEW

Nassau Community College, State University of New York, 1 Education Dr., Garden City NY 11530-6793. (516)572-7792. **Contact:** Editorial Board. Magazine: 6¹/₂×9¹/₂; 200 pages; heavy stock paper and cover; illustrations; photos. "Looking for high-level, professionally talented fiction on any subject matter except science fiction. Intended for a college and university faculty-level audience. Not geared to college students or others of that age who have not yet reached professional competency." Annual. Estab. 1964. Circ. 1,200. Member Council of Literary Magazines & Presses.
Needs Historical (general), humor/satire, literary, mainstream, mystery/suspense (amateur sleuth, cozy). "No science fiction." Receives 200-400 unsolicited mss/month. Accepts 5-6 mss/year. Does not read mss April-

October. Publishes ms 6 months after acceptance. **Publishes 3-4 new writers/year.** Recently published work by Louis Phillips, Dick Wimmer, Norbert Petsch, Mike Lipstock. Length: 2,000-6,000 words; average length: 3,000-4,000 words. Publishes short shorts. Also publishes literary essays, literary criticism, poetry.

How to Contact Send 3 disposable copies of ms and #10 SASE for reply only. Responds in 2 weeks to queries; 6 months to mss. No simultaneous submissions. Sample copy free.

Payment/Terms Pays contributor's copies. Acquires one-time rights. Sponsors awards/contests.

Advice "We look for narrative drive, perceptive characterization and professional competence. Write concretely. Does not want over-elaborate details, and avoid digressions."

NERVE COWBOY

Liquid Paper Press, P.O. Box 4973, Austin TX 78765. Web site: www.onr.com/user/jwhagins/nervecowboy.html. **Contact:** Joseph Shields or Jerry Hagins, editors. Magazine: $7 \times 8\frac{1}{2}$; 64 pages; 20 lb. paper; card stock cover; illustrations. "*Nerve Cowboy* publishes adventurous, comical, disturbing, thought-provoking, accessible poetry and fiction. We like to see work sensitive enough to make the hardest hard-ass cry, funny enough to make the most helpless brooder laugh and disturbing enough to make us all glad we're not the author of the piece." Semiannual. Estab. 1996. Circ. 350.

Needs Literary. No "racist, sexist or overly offensive work. Wants more unusual stories with rich description and enough twists and turns that leave the reader thinking." Receives 40 unsolicited mss/month. Accepts 2-3 mss/issue; 4-6 mss/year. Publishes ms 6-12 months after acceptance. **Publishes 5-10 new writers/year.** Recently published work by Lori Jakiela, Tina Vincenti, Dave Newman, Brad Kohler, d.n. simmers, Paul Rogalus. Length: 1,500 words; average length: 750-1,000 words. Publishes short shorts. Also publishes poetry.

How to Contact Send SASE for reply, return of ms or send a disposable copy of ms. Responds in 4 weeks to queries; 3 months to mss. Accepts reprint submissions. No simultaneous submissions. Sample copy for $6. Writer's guidelines for #10 SASE or online.

Payment/Terms Pays 1 contributor's copy. Acquires one-time rights.

Advice "We look for writing which is very direct and elicits a visceral reaction in the reader. Read magazines you submit to in order to get a feel for what the editors are looking for. Write simply and from the gut."

NEW DELTA REVIEW

Louisiana State University, Dept. of English, 214 Allen Hall, Baton Rouge LA 70803-5001. (225)578-4079. E-mail: new-delta@lsu.edu. Web site: www.english.lsu.edu/journals/ndr. **Contact:** Editors change every year. Check Web site. Magazine: 6×9; 75-125 pages; high quality paper; glossy card cover; color artwork. "We seek vivid and exciting work from new and established writers. We have published fiction from writers such as Stacy Richter, Mark Poirier and George Singleton." Semiannual. Estab. 1984. Circ. 500.

- *New Delta Review* also sponsors the Matt Clark Prizes for fiction and poetry. Work from the magazine has been included in the *Pushcart Prize* anthology.

Needs Humor/satire, literary, mainstream, translations, contemporary, prose poem. "No Elvis stories, overwrought 'Southern' fiction, or cancer stories." Receives 150 unsolicited mss/month. Accepts 3-4 mss/issue; 6-8 mss/year. Reads from August 15-April 15. **Publishes 1-3 new writers/year.** Average length: 15 ms pages. Publishes short shorts. Also publishes poetry. Rarely comments on rejected mss.

How to Contact SASE (or IRC). Responds in 3 weeks to queries; 3 months to mss. Accepts simultaneous submissions only when stated in the cover letter. Sample copy for $7.

Payment/Terms Pays in contributor's copies. Charge for extras. Acquires first North American serial, electronic rights. Sponsors awards/contests.

Advice "Our staff is open-minded and youthful. We base decisions on merit, not reputation. The manuscript that's most enjoyable to read gets the nod. Be bold, take risks, surprise us."

$ NEW LETTERS

University of Missouri-Kansas City, University House, 5101 Rockhill Road., Kansas City MO 64110-2499. (816)235-1168. Fax: (816)235-2611. E-mail: newletters@umkc.edu. Web site: www.newletters.org. **Contact:** Robert Stewart, editor. Magazine: 6×9, 14 lb. cream paper; illustrations. "*New Letters* is intended for the general literary reader. We publish literary fiction, nonfiction, essays, poetry. We also publish art." Quarterly. Estab. 1934. Circ. 2,500.

Needs Ethnic/multicultural, experimental, humor/satire, literary, mainstream, translations, contemporary. No genre fiction. Does not read mss May 1-October 1. Publishes ms 5 months after acceptance. Recently published work by Thomas E. Kennedy, Sheila Kohler, Charlotte Holmes, Rosellen Brown, Janet Burroway. Publishes short shorts.

How to Contact Send complete ms. Do not submit by e-mail. Responds in 1 month to queries; 3 months to mss. No simultaneous submissions. Sample copy for $10 or sample articles on Web site. Writer's guidelines online.

Payment/Terms Pays $30-75 for fiction and $15 for single poem. Pays on publication for first North American serial rights. Sends galleys to author. $4,500 awarded annually in writing contest for short fiction, essay, and poetry. Visitwww.newletters.org for contest guidelines.

Advice "Seek publication of representative chapters in high-quality magazines as a way to the book contract. Try literary magazines first."

Ⓝ ☑ NEW MADRID

Murray State University, 7C Faculty Hall, Murray KY 42071. (270)809-4713, (270)809-2401. Fax: (270)809-4545. E-mail: newmadrid@murraystate.edu. Web site: http://murraystate.edu/newmadrid. **Contact:** Ann Neelon, fiction editor. Literary magazine/journal: 166 pages; contains illustrations & photographs. *"New Madrid* takes its name from the fault in the earth's crust in the middle of the United States. We are especially interested in work by writers in what some call 'the flyover zone.' " Semiannual. Estab. 1980. Circ. 1,500.

Needs Literary. List of upcoming themes available on Web site. "We have two reading periods, one during August and September, and one during February and March." Also publishes literary essays, literary criticism, poetry. Rarely comments on/critiques rejected mss.

How to Contact Send complete ms with cover letter. Accepts submissions by e-mail only. Include brief bio, list of publications. Considers multiple submissions. Guidelines available via e-mail, on Web site.

Payment and Terms Pays 1 contributor copy on publication. Acquires first North American serial rights. Publication is copyrighted.

Advice "Quality is the determining factor for breaking into *New Madrid*. We are looking for excellent work in a range of genres, forms and styles."

🔁 ☑ 🔍 THE NEW ORPHIC REVIEW

New Orphic Publishers, 706 Mill St., Nelson BC V1L 4S5 Canada. (250)354-0494. Fax: (250)352-0743. Web site: www3.telus.net/neworphicpublishers-hekkanen. **Contact:** Ernest Hekkanen, editor-in-chief. Magazine; $5^1/_2 \times 8^1/_2$; 120 pages; common paper; 100 lb. color cover. "In the traditional *Orphic* fashion, our magazine accepts a wide range of styles and approaches—from naturalism to the surreal, but, please, get to the essence of the narrative, emotion, conflict, state of being, whatever." Semiannual. Estab. 1998. Circ. 300.

● Margrith Schraner's story, "Dream Dig" was included in *The Journey Prize Anthology*, 2001.

Needs Ethnic/multicultural, experimental, fantasy, historical (general), literary, mainstream. "No detective or sword and sorcery stories." List of upcoming themes available for SASE. Receives 20 unsolicited mss/month. Accepts 10 mss/issue; 22 mss/year. Publishes ms 1 year after acceptance. **Publishes 6-8 new writers/year.** Recently published work by Eveline Hasler (Swiss), Leena Krohn (Finnish), Pekka Salmi. Length: 2,000-10,000 words; average length: 3,500 words. Publishes short shorts. Also publishes literary essays, literary criticism, poetry. Sometimes comments on rejected mss.

How to Contact Send SASE (or IRC) for return of ms or send a disposable copy of ms and #10 SASE for reply only. Responds in 1 month to queries; 4 months to mss. Accepts simultaneous, multiple submissions. Sample copy for $17.50. Writer's guidelines for SASE. Reviews fiction.

Payment/Terms Pays 1 contributor's copy; additional copies $14. Pays on publication for first North American serial rights.

Advice "I like fiction that deals with issues, accounts for every motive, has conflict, is well written and tackles something that is substantive. Don't be mundane; try for more, not less."

🌐 ☑ THE NEW WRITER

P.O. Box 60, Cranbrook TN17 2ZR United Kingdom. 01580 212626. Fax: 01580 212041. E-mail: editor@the newwriter.com. Web site: www.thenewwriter.com. **Contact:** Suzanne Ruthven, editor. Magazine: A4; 56 pages; illustrations; photos. Contemporary writing magazine which publishes "the best in fact, fiction and poetry." Publishes 6 issues per annum. Estab. 1996. Circ. 1,500.

Needs "We will consider most categories apart from stories written for children. No horror, erotic or cosy fiction." Accepts 4 mss/issue; 24 mss/year. Publishes ms 1 year after acceptance. Agented fiction 5%. **Publishes 12 new writers/year.** Recently published work by Alan Dunn, Alice Jolly, Kate Long, Annabel Lamb, Laureen Vonnegut and Stephen Finucan. Length: 2,000-5,000 words; average length: 3,500 words. Publishes short shorts. Also publishes literary essays, literary criticism, poetry. Often comments on rejected mss.

How to Contact Query with published clips. Accepts submissions by e-mail, fax. Send SASE (or IRC) for return of ms or send a disposable copy of ms and #10 SASE for reply only. "We consider short stories from subscribers only but we may also commission guest writers." Responds in 2 months to queries; 4 months to mss. Accepts simultaneous submissions. Sample copy for SASE and A4 SAE with IRCs only. Writer's guidelines for SASE. Reviews fiction.

Payment/Terms Pays £10 per story by credit voucher; additional copies for £1.50. Pays on publication for one-time rights. Sponsors awards/contests.

Advice "Hone it—always be prepared to improve the story. It's a competitive market."

◩ NIMROD, International Journal of Prose and Poetry

University of Tulsa, 600 S. College Ave., Tulsa OK 74104-3189. (918)631-3080. Fax: (918)631-3033. E-mail: nimrod@utulsa.edu. Web site: www.utulsa.edu/nimrod/. **Contact:** Gerry McLoud, fiction editor. Magazine: 6×9; 192 pages; 60 lb. white paper; illustrations; photos. "We publish one thematic issue and one awards issue each year. A recent theme was 'The Celtic Fringe,' a compilation of poetry and prose from all over the world. We seek vigorous, imaginative, quality writing. Our mission is to discover new writers and publish experimental writers who have not yet found a 'home' for their work." Semiannual. Estab. 1956. Circ. 3,000.

Needs "We accept contemporary poetry and/or prose. May submit adventure, ethnic, experimental, prose poem or translations. No science fiction or romance." Receives 120 unsolicited mss/month. **Publishes 5-10 new writers/year.** Recently published work by Felicia Ward, Ellen Bass, Jeanette Turner Hospital, Kate Small. Also publishes poetry.

How to Contact SASE for return of ms. Accepts queries by e-mail. Does not accept submissions by e-mail unless the writer is living outside the U.S. Responds in 5 months to mss. Accepts simultaneous, multiple submissions.

Payment/Terms Pays 2 contributor's copies.

Advice "We have not changed our fiction needs: quality, vigor, distinctive voice. We have, however, increased the number of stories we print. See current issues. We look for fiction that is fresh, vigorous, distinctive, serious and humorous, unflinchingly serious, ironic—whatever. Just so it is quality. Strongly encourage writers to send #10 SASE for brochure for annual literary contest with prizes of $1,000 and $2,000."

◩ ⬛ NOON

1324 Lexington Avenue PMB 298, New York NY 10128. **Contact:** Diane Williams, editor. Magazine: 5³/₁₆×8; 140 pages; illustrations; photographs. Annual. Estab. 2000. Circ. 5,000. Member: CLMP; AWP.

• Stories appearing in *Noon* have received Pushcart Prizes.

Needs Accepts 13-15 mss/year. **Publishes new writers each year.** Recently published work by Gary Lutz, Lydia Davis, Christine Schutt, Deb Olin Unferth and Tao Lin. Publishes short shorts. Also publishes literary essays, literary criticism. Sometimes comments on rejected mss.

How to Contact Send SASE (or IRC) for return of the ms. Responds in 4 weeks to queries; 3 months to mss. Accepts simultaneous, multiple submissions. Sample copy for $9.

Payment/Terms Acquires first rights. Sends galleys to author.

◎ NORTH CAROLINA LITERARY REVIEW, A Magazine of North Carolina Literature, Literary History and Culture

English Dept., East Carolina University, Greenville NC 27858-4353. (252)328-1537. Fax: (252)328-4889. E-mail: bauerm@ecu.edu. Web site: www.ecu.edu/nclr. "Articles should have a North Carolina literature slant. First consideration is always for quality of work. Although we treat academic and scholarly subjects, we do not wish to see jargon-laden prose; our readers, we hope, are found as often in bookstores and libraries as in academia. We seek to combine the best elements of a magazine for serious readers with the best of a scholarly journal." Annual. Estab. 1992. Circ. 750.

Needs Regional (North Carolina). Must be North Carolina related—either a North Carolina-connected writer or set in North Carolina. Publishes ms 1 year after acceptance.

How to Contact Query. Accepts queries by e-mail. Responds in 1 month to queries; within 6 months to mss. Sample copy for $10-25. Writer's guidelines online.

Payment/Terms Pays on publication for first North American serial rights. Rights returned to writer on request.

▢ ◎ NORTH CENTRAL REVIEW, YOUR UNDERGRADUATE LITERARY JOURNAL

North Central College, 30 N. Brainard St., CM #235, Naperville IL 60540. (630)637-5130. Fax: (630)637-5221. E-mail: nccreview@noctrl.edu. **Contact:** Dr. Anna Leahy, advisor. Magazine has revolving editor. Editorial term: Editor changes each year in the Fall. Literary magazine/journal: 5¹/₂×8¹/₂, 120 pages, perfect binding, color card-stock cover. Includes photographs. "The *North Central Review* is an undergraduate literary journal soliciting fiction, poetry, nonfiction and drama from around the country and the globe—but only from college students. This offers undergraduates a venue for sharing their work with their peers." Semiannual. Estab. 1936, undergraduate focus as of 2005. Circ. 500-750, depending on funding.

Needs Considers all categories. While we consider all fiction, longer works (more than 20 pages) are rarely published. Deadlines: February 15 and October 15. Does not read February 15-August 15. Accepts 4-8 mss/ issue; 8-16 mss/year. Manuscript published 2-3 months after acceptance. Agented fiction 0%. **Publishes "at least half, probably more" new writers/year.** Length: 6,000 words (max). Average length: 2,000 words. Publishes short shorts. Average length of short shorts: 100-700 words. Also publishes literary essays, poetry. Rarely comments on/critiques rejected manuscripts.

How to Contact Send complete ms with cover letter. Accepts submissions by e-mail. Include student (.edu) e-mail address or copy of student ID with ID number marked. Responds to queries in 1 week. Responds to mss in 4 months. Send disposable copy of ms and #10 SASE for reply only. Considers simultaneous submissions, multiple submissions. Sample copy free upon request (older issue) or available for $5 (most recent issue). Guidelines available for SASE, via e-mail.

Payment and Terms Writers receive 2 contributor's copies. Additional copies $5. Pays on publication. Acquires one-time rights.

Advice "The reading staff changes year to year (and sometimes from one academic term to the next) so tastes change. That said, at least three readers evaluate each submission, and there's usually a widespread agreement on the best ones. While all elements need to work together, readers take notice when one element—maybe setting or character—captivates and even teaches the reader something new. Don't send something you just drafted and printed. Give your work some time, revise it, and polish what you plan to send us. That said, don't hesitate to submit and submit again to the *North Central Review*. Undergraduates are beginners, and we welcome new voices."

⬛ ⬛ NORTH DAKOTA QUARTERLY

University of North Dakota, Merrifield Hall Room 110, 276 Centennial Drive Stop 7209 Grand Forks ND 58202-7209. (701)777-3322. Fax: (701)777-2373. E-mail: ndq@und.edu. Web site: www.und.nodak.edu/org/ndq. **Contact:** Robert W. Lewis, editor. Magazine: 6×9; 200 pages; bond paper; illustrations; photos. "*North Dakota Quarterly* is a literary journal publishing essays in the humanities; some short stories, some poetry. Occasional special topic issues." General audience. Quarterly. Estab. 1911. Circ. 700.

• Work published in *North Dakota Quarterly* was selected for inclusion in *The O. Henry Prize Stories*, *The Pushcart Prize*, and *Best American Essays*.

Needs Ethnic/multicultural, experimental, feminist, historical, literary, Native American. Receives 125-150 unsolicited mss/month. Accepts 4 mss/issue; 16 mss/year. Publishes ms 2 years after acceptance. **Publishes 4-5 new writers/year.** Recently published work by Louise Erdrich, Robert Day, Sandra Hunter. Average length: 3,000-4,000 words. Also publishes literary essays, literary criticism, poetry. Sometimes comments on rejected mss.

How to Contact SASE. Responds in 3 months to mss. Sample copy for $8. Reviews fiction.

Payment/Terms Pays 2-4 contributor's copies; 30% discount for extras. Acquires one-time rights. Sends galleys to author.

⬛ NORTHWEST REVIEW

369 PLC, University of Oregon, Eugene OR 97403. (541)346-3957. Web site: darkwing.uoregon.edu/~nwreview. **Contact:** Janice MacCrae, fiction editor. Magazine: 6×9; 140-160 pages; high quality cover stock; illustrations; photos. "A general literary review featuring poems, stories, essays and reviews, circulated nationally and internationally. For a literate audience in avant-garde as well as traditional literary forms; interested in the important writers who have not yet achieved their readership." Triannual. Estab. 1957. Circ. 1,200.

Needs Experimental, feminist, literary, translations, contemporary. Receives 150 unsolicited mss/month. Accepts 4-5 mss/issue; 12-15 mss/year. **Publishes some new writers/year.** Recently published work by Diana Abu-Jaber, Madison Smartt Bell, Maria Flook, Charles Marvin. Also publishes literary essays, literary criticism, poetry. Comments on rejected mss "when there is time."

How to Contact Responds in 4 months to mss. No simultaneous submissions. Sample copy for $4. Reviews fiction.

Payment/Terms Pays 3 contributor's copies and 1-year subscription; 40% discount on extras. Acquires first rights.

$⬛ NORTHWOODS JOURNAL, A Magazine for Writers

Conservatory of American Letters, P.O. Box 298, Thomaston ME 04861. (207)354-0998. Fax: (207)354-8953. E-mail: cal@americanletters.org. Web site: www.americanletters.org. **Contact:** S.M. Hall, fiction editor (submit fiction to S.M. Hall, III, 1A True St. Freeport ME 04032). Magazine: 5½×8½; 32-64 pages; white paper; 8 pt. glossy, full color cover; digital printing; some illustrations; photos. "No theme, no philosophy—for writers and for people who read for entertainment." Quarterly. Estab. 1993. Circ. 200.

Needs Adventure, experimental, fantasy (science fantasy, sword and sorcery), literary, mainstream, mystery/suspense (amateur sleuth, police procedural, private eye/hard-boiled, romantic suspense), psychic/supernatural/occult, regional, romance (gothic, historical), science fiction (hard science, soft/sociological), western (frontier, traditional), sports. "Would like to see more first-person adventure. No porn or evangelical." Publishes annual *Northwoods Anthology*. Receives 20 unsolicited mss/month. Accepts 12-15 mss/year. **Publishes 15 new writers/year.** Recently published work by J.F. Pytko, Richard Vaughn, Kelley Jean White. Also publishes literary criticism, poetry.

How to Contact Send SASE for reply, return of ms or send a disposable copy of ms. Responds in 2 days to queries; by next deadline plus 5 days to mss. No simultaneous submissions or electronic submissions. Sample copy for $6.50 next issue, $10 current issue, $14.50 back issue, all postage paid. Or send 7×10 SASE with $1.35 postage affixed and $6.50. Writer's guidelines for #10 SASE. Reviews fiction.

Payment/Terms Varies "but is generally 1 cent per word or more, based on experience with us. Pays an advance (non refundable) based on sales we can attribute to your influence." Pays on acceptance for first North American serial rights. 50/50 split of additional sales.

Advice "Read guidelines, read the things we've published. Know your market. Anyone submitting to a publication he/she has never seen deserves whatever happens to them."

$⬦ ⬛ NOTRE DAME REVIEW

University of Notre Dame, 840 Flanner Hall, Notre Dame IN 46556. (574)631-6952. Fax: (574)631-8209. Web site: www.nd.edu/~ndr/review.htm. **Contact:** William O'Rourke, fiction editor. Literary magazine: 6×9; 200 pages; 50 lb. smooth paper; illustrations; photos. "The *Notre Dame Review* is an indepenent, noncommercial magazine of contemporary American and international fiction, poetry, criticism and art. We are especially interested in work that takes on big issues by making the invisible seen, that gives voice to the voiceless. In addition to showcasing celebrated authors like Seamus Heaney and Czelaw Milosz, the *Notre Dame Review* introduces readers to authors they may have never encountered before, but who are doing innovative and important work. In conjunction with the *Notre Dame Review*, the online companion to the printed magazine engages readers as a community centered in literary rather than commercial concerns, a community we reach out to through critique and commentary as well as aesthetic experience." Semiannual. Estab. 1995. Circ. 1,500.

● Pushcart prizes in fiction and poetry.

Needs No genre fiction. Upcoming theme issues planned. Receives 75 unsolicited mss/month. Accepts 4-5 mss/issue; 10 mss/year. Does not read mss November-January or April-August. Publishes ms 6 months after acceptance. **Publishes 1 new writer/year.** Recently published work by Ed Falco, Jarda Cerverka, David Green. Publishes short shorts. Also publishes literary criticism, poetry.

How to Contact Send complete ms with cover letter. Include 4-sentence bio. Send SASE for response, return of ms, or send a disposable copy of ms. Responds in 6 months to mss. Accepts simultaneous submissions. Sample copy for $6. Writer's guidelines online. Mss sent during summer months will be returned unread.

Payment/Terms Pays $5-25. Pays on publication for first North American serial rights.

Advice "We're looking for high quality work that takes on big issues in a literary way. Please read our back issues before submitting."

◎ OBSIDIAN III, Literature in the African Diaspora

Dept. of English, North Carolina State University, Raleigh NC 27695-8105. (919)515-4153. Fax: (919)515-1836. E-mail: obsidian@social.chass.ncsu.edu. Web site: www.ncsu.edu/chass/obsidian/. **Contact:** Sheila Smith McKoy, editor. Magazine: 130 pages. "Creative works in English by black writers, scholarly critical studies by all writers on black literature in English." Published 2 times/year (spring/summer, fall/winter). Estab. 1975. Circ. 500.

Needs Ethnic/multicultural (Pan-African), feminist, literary. All writers on black topics. Accepts 7-9 mss/year. Publishes ms 4-6 months after acceptance. **Publishes 20 new writers/year.** Recently published work by Sean Henry, R. Flowers Rivera, Terrance Hayes, Eugene Kraft, Arlene McKanic, Pearl Bothe Williams, Kwane Dawes.

How to Contact Accepts submissions by e-mail. Responds in 4 months to mss. Sample copy for $10.

Payment/Terms Pays in contributor's copies. Acquires one-time rights. Sponsors awards/contests.

Advice "Following proper format is essential. Your title must be intriguing and text clean. Never give up. Some of the writers we publish were rejected many times before we published them."

⬦ ◎ OHIO TEACHERS WRITE

Ohio Council of Teachers of English Language Arts, 644 Overlook Dr., Columbus OH 43214. E-mail: rmcclain@b right.net. **Contact:** Scott Parsons, editor. Editors change every 3 years. Magazine: 8½×11; 50 pages; 60 lb. white offset paper; 65 lb. blue cover stock; illustrations; photos. "The purpose of the magazine is three fold: (1) to provide a collection of fine literature for the reading pleasure of teachers and other adult readers; (2) to encourage teachers to compose literary works along with their students; (3) to provide the literate citizens of Ohio a window into the world of educators not often seen by those outside the teaching profession." Annual. Estab. 1995. Circ. 1,000. Submissions are limited to Ohio Educators.

Needs Adventure, ethnic/multicultural, experimental, fantasy (science fantasy), feminist, gay, historical, humor/satire, lesbian, literary, mainstream, regional, religious/inspirational, romance (contemporary), science fiction (hard science, soft/sociological), western (frontier, traditional), senior citizen/retirement, sports, teaching. Receives 2 unsolicited mss/month. Accepts 7 mss/issue. "We read only in May when editorial board meets." Recently published work by Lois Spencer, Harry R. Noden, Linda J. Rice, June Langford Berkley. Publishes short shorts. Also publishes poetry. Often comments on rejected mss.

How to Contact Send SASE with postage clipped for return of ms or send a disposable copy of ms. Accepts multiple submissions. Sample copy for $6.

Payment/Terms Pays 2 contributor's copies; additional copies $6. Acquires first rights.

$☑ ONE-STORY

One-Story, LLC, P.O. Box 150618, Brooklyn NY 11215. Web site: www.one-story.com. **Contact:** Maribeth Batcha and Hannah Tinti, editors. "*One-Story* is a literary magazine that contains, simply, **one story**. It is a subscription-only magazine. Every 3 weeks subscribers are sent *One Story* in the mail. *One Story* is artfully designed, lightweight, easy to carry, and ready to entertain on buses, in bed, in subways, in cars, in the park, in the bath, in the waiting rooms of doctor's, on the couch, or in line at the supermarket. Subscribers also have access to a Web site, www.one-story.com, where they can learn more about *One-Story* authors, and hear about *One-Story* readings and events. There is always time to read *One Story*." Estab. 2002. Circ. 3,500.

Needs Literary short stories. *One-Story* only accepts short stories. Do not send excerpts. Do not send more than 1 story at a time. Publishes ms 3-6 months after acceptance. Recently published work by John Hodgman, Melanie Rae Thon, Daniel Wallace and Judy Budnitz.

How to Contact Send complete ms. Accepts online submissions only. Responds in 2-6 months to mss. Sample copy for $5. Writer's guidelines online.

Payment/Terms Pays $100. Pays on publication for first North American serial rights. Buys the rights to publish excerpts on Web site and in promotional materials.

☑ OPEN SPACES

Open Spaces Publications, Inc., PMB 134, 6327-C SW Capitol Hwy., Portland OR 97239-1937. (503)227-5764. Fax: (503)227-3401. Web site: www.open-spaces.com. **Contact:** Ellen Teicher, fiction editor. Magazine: 64 pages; illustrations; photos. "*Open Spaces* is a forum for informed writing and intelligent thought. Articles are written by experts in various fields. Audience is varied (CEOs and rock climbers, politicos and university presidents, etc.) but is highly educated and loves to read good writing." Quarterly. Estab. 1997.

Needs "Excellence is the issue—not subject matter." Accepts 2 mss/issue; 8 mss/year. Publishes ms 6 months after acceptance. **Publishes 12 new writers/year.** Recently published work by William Kittredge, Rick Bass, Pattiann Rogers,

David James Duncan. Publishes short shorts. Also publishes literary essays, poetry. Sometimes comments on rejected mss.

How to Contact Accepts submissions by fax. Send complete ms with a cover letter. Include short bio, social security number and list of publications. SASE for return of ms or send a disposable copy of ms. Accepts simultaneous submissions. Sample copy for $10. Writer's guidelines online.

Payment/Terms Payment varies. Pays on publication. Rights purchased vary with author and material.

Advice "The surest way for a writer to determine whether his or her material is right for us is to read the magazine."

⊕ ☑ OPEN WIDE MAGAZINE

The Flat, Yew Tree Farm, Sealand Rd., Chester Chesire CH1-6BS United Kingdom. E-mail: contact@openwidemagazine.co.uk. Web site: www.openwidemagazine.co.uk. **Contact:** Liz Roberts. Literary magazine/journal: A5, 50 pages. Quarterly. Estab. 2001. Circ. 700.

Needs Adventure, ethnic/multicultural, experimental, feminist, gay, horror, humor/satire, lesbian, mainstream, mystery/suspense, romance. Receives 100 mss/month. Accepts 25 mss/issue. Manuscript published 3 months after acceptance. **Publishes 30 new writers/year.** Length: 500-4,000. Average length: 2,500. Publishes short shorts. Also publishes poetry. Rarely comments on/critiques rejected mss.

How to Contact Accepts submissions by e-mail. Include estimated word count, brief bio. Send either SASE (or IRC) for return of ms or disposable copy of ms and #10 SASE for reply only. Sample copy available for $4.

Payment and Terms Additional copies $6. Acquires one-time rights. Publication is copyrighted.

$☑ OTHER VOICES

University of Illinois at Chicago, 601 S. Morgan St., Chicago IL 60607. (312)413-2209. Web site: www.othervoicesmagazine.org. **Contact:** Gina Frangello. Magazine: $5^{7}/_{8} \times 9$; 168-205 pages; 60 lb. paper; coated cover stock; occasional photos. "Original, fresh, diverse stories and novel excerpts" for literate adults. Semiannual. Estab. 1985. Circ. 1,800.

Needs Literary, contemporary, excerpted novel and one act-plays. Fiction only. "No taboos, except ineptitude and murkiness. No science fiction, romance, horror, fantasy." Receives 300 unsolicited mss/month. Accepts 17-20 mss/issue. **Publishes 6 new writers/year.** Recently published work by Mary Gaitskill, Joe Meno, Steve Almond, Dan Chaon. Length: 6,000 words; average length: 5,000 words.

How to Contact Send ms with SASE October 1-April 1 only. Mss received during non-reading period are returned unread. Cover letters "should be brief and list previous publications. Also, list title of submission. Most beginners' letters try to 'explain' the story—a big mistake." Responds in 10-12 weeks to mss. Accepts simultaneous submissions. Sample copy for $7 (includes postage). Writer's guidelines for #10 SASE.

Payment/Terms Pays $100 plus contributor's copies. Acquires one-time rights.

Advice "There are so *few* markets for *quality* fiction! By publishing up to 40 stories a year, we provide new and established writers a forum for their work. Send us your best voice, your best work, your best best."

N ☐ OYEZ REVIEW

Roosevelt University, Dept. of Literature, 430 S. Michigan Ave., Chicago IL . (312)341-2225. E-mail: oyezreview @roosevelt.edu. Web site: www.roosevelt.edu/oyezreview.edu. **Contact:** Dr. Janet Wondra, editor. Literary magazine/journal. "*Oyez Review* publishes fiction, creative nonfiction, poetry and art. There are no restrictions on style, theme, or subject matter." Annual. Estab. 1965. Circ. 600.

Needs Publish short stories and flash fiction on their merit as contemporary literature rather than the category within the genre.

How to Contact Accepts submissions by e-mail. Sample copy available for $5. Guidelines available on Web site.

Payment and Terms Writers receive 2 contributor's copies. Acquires first North American serial rights.

Advice "Writers should familiarize themselves with a variety of literary magazines in addition to ours in order to understand this niche and find out the scope of what contemporary literary magazines do and do not publish. Note that e-mail submissions, simultaneous submissions, work received without an SASE, and mss received before or after our August 1-October 1 reading period will not be read. We read complete manuscripts rather than queries."

OYSTER BOY REVIEW

P.O. Box 299, Pacifica CA 94044. E-mail: fiction@oysterboyreview.com. Web site: www.oysterboyreview.com. **Contact:** Craig Nelson, fiction editor. Damon Suave, editor/publisher. Electronic and print magazine. "We publish kick-ass, teeth-cracking stories." Published 4 times a year.

Needs No genre fiction. "Fiction that revolves around characters in conflict with themselves or each other; a plot that has a beginning, a middle, and an end; a narrative with a strong moral center (not necessarily 'moralistic'); a story with a satisfying resolution to the conflict; and an ethereal something that contributes to the mystery of a question, but does not necessarily seek or contrive to answer it." Submissions accepted January-September. **Publishes 4 new writers/year.** Recently published work by Todd Goldberg, Ken Wainio, Elisha Porat, Kevin McGowan.

How to Contact Accepts multiple submissions. Sample copy not available.

Advice "Keep writing, keep submitting, keep revising."

☑ PACIFIC COAST JOURNAL

French Bread Publications, P.O. Box 56, Carlsbad CA 92018. E-mail: paccoastj@frenchbreadpublications.com. Web site: www.frenchbreadpublications.com/pcj. **Contact:** Stephanie Kylkis, fiction editor. Magazine: $5\frac{1}{2}\times8\frac{1}{2}$; 40 pages; 20 lb. paper; 67 lb. cover; illustrations; b&w photos. "Slight focus toward Western North America/Pacific Rim." Quarterly. Estab. 1992. Circ. 200.

Needs Ethnic/multicultural, experimental, feminist, historical, humor/satire, literary, science fiction (soft/sociological, magical realism). "No children's, religious, or hard sci-fi." Receives 60-70 unsolicited mss/month. Accepts 3-4 mss/issue; 10-12 mss/year. Publishes ms 6-18 months after acceptance. Recently published work by Alan S. Bray and Abby Stewart. Length: 4,000 words; average length: 2,500 words. Publishes short shorts. Also publishes literary essays, poetry. Sometimes comments on rejected mss.

How to Contact Send SASE for reply, return of ms or send a disposable copy of ms. Also accepts e-mail address for response instead of SASE. Responds in 6-9 months to mss. Accepts simultaneous submissions and reprints. Sample copy for $2.50, 6×9 SASE and 3oz. postage. Reviews fiction.

Payment/Terms Pays 1 contributor's copy. Acquires one-time rights.

Advice "*PCJ* is an independent magazine and we have a limited amount of space and funding. We are looking for experiments in what can be done with the short fiction form. The best stories will entertain as well as confuse."

☑ PACIFIC REVIEW

Dept. of English and Comparative Lit., San Diego State University, 5500 Campanile Dr. MC8140, San Diego CA 92182-8140. E-mail: pacificREVIEW_sdsu@yahoo.com. Web site: http://pacificREVIEW.sdsu.edu. **Contact:** Leon Lanzbom, editor-in-chief. Magazine: 6×9; 200 pages; book stock paper; paper back, extra heavy cover stock; b&w illustrations, b&w photos. "*pacific REVIEW* publishes the work of emergent literati, pairing their efforts with those of established artists. It is available at West Coast independent booksellers and university and college libraries and is taught as text in numerous university literature and creative writing classes.'' Circ. 2,000.

Needs ''We seek high-quality fiction and give preference to pieces that explore the themes of omnivore as a compass to a wider field of implication and reinvention.'' For information on theme issues see Web site. **Publishes 15 new writers/year.** Recently published work by Ai, Alurista, Susan Daitch, Lawrence Ferlinghetti, William T. Vollmann.

How to Contact Responds in 3 months to mss. Sample copy for $10.

Payment/Terms Pays 2 contributor's copies. Aquires first serial rights. All other rights revert to author.

Advice ''We welcome all submissions, especially those created in or in the context of the West Coast/California and the space of our borders.''

✍ PAINTED BRIDE QUARTERLY

Drexel University, Dept. of English, 3141 Chestnut Street, Philadelphia PA 19104. E-mail: pbq@drexel.edu. Web site: http://pbq.drexel.edu. **Contact:** Kathleen Volk-Miller, managing editor. ''*PBQ* seeks literary fiction, experimental and traditional.'' Publishes online each quarter and a print annual each spring. Estab. 1973.

Needs Ethnic/multicultural, experimental, feminist, gay, lesbian, literary, translations. ''No genre fiction.''''- Publishes theme-related work, check Web site; holds annual fiction contests. **Publishes 24 new writers/year.** Length: 5,000 words; average length: 3,000 words. Publishes short shorts. Also publishes literary essays, literary criticism, poetry. Occasionally comments on rejected mss.

How to Contact Send complete ms. No electronic submissions. Responds in 6 months to mss. Sample copy online. Writer's guidelines online. Reviews fiction.

Payment/Terms Acquires first North American serial rights.

Advice We look for ''freshness of idea incorporated with high-quality writing. We receive an awful lot of nicely written work with worn-out plots. We want quality in whatever—we hold experimental work to as strict standards as anything else. Many of our readers write fiction; most of them enjoy a good reading. We hope to be an outlet for quality. A good story gives, first, enjoyment to the reader. We've seen a good many of them lately, and we've published the best of them.''

✍ ☒ PALO ALTO REVIEW, A Journal of Ideas

Palo Alto College, 1400 W. Villaret, San Antonio TX 78224. (210)921-5021. Fax: (210)921-5008. E-mail: eshull@accd.edu. **Contact:** Ellen Shull, editor. Magazine: $8^1/_2 \times 11$; 64 pages; 60 lb. gloss white paper; illustrations; photos. More than half of each issue is devoted to articles and essays. ''We select stories that we would want to read again. Not too experimental nor excessively avant-garde, just good fiction.'' Semiannual. Estab. 1992. Circ. 500.

• *Palo Alto Review* was awarded the Pushcart Prize for 2001.

Needs Adventure, ethnic/multicultural, experimental, fantasy, feminist, historical, humor/satire, literary, mainstream, mystery/suspense, regional, romance, science fiction, translations, western. Upcoming themes available for SASE. Receives 100-150 unsolicited mss/month. Accepts 2-3 mss/issue; 4-6 mss/year. Does not read mss April 1-May and October-December when putting out each issue. Publishes ms 2-15 months after acceptance. **Publishes 20 new writers/year.** Recently published work by Char Miller, Naveed Noori, E.M. Schorb, Louis Phillips, Tom Filer, Jo Lecoeur, H. Palmer Hall. Publishes short shorts. Also publishes poetry, essays, articles, memoirs, book reviews. Always comments on rejected mss.

How to Contact Send SASE for reply, return of ms or send a disposable copy of ms. ''Request sample copy and guidelines.'' Accepts submissions by e-mail only if outside the US. Responds in 4 months to mss. Accepts simultaneous submissions. Sample copy for $5. Writer's guidelines for #10 SASE or e-mail to eshull@accd.edu.

Payment/Terms Pays 2 contributor's copies; additional copies for $5. Acquires first North American serial rights.

Advice ''Good short stories have interesting characters confronted by a dilemma working toward a solution. So often what we get is 'a moment in time,' not a story. Generally, characters are interesting because readers can identify with them. Edit judiciously. Cut out extraneous verbiage. Set up a choice that has to be made. Then create tension—who wants what and why they can't have it.''

$☐ ◎ ☒ PARADOX, THE MAGAZINE OF HISTORICAL AND SPECULATIVE FICTION

Paradox Publications, P.O. Box 22897, Brooklyn NY 11202-2897. E-mail: editor@paradoxmag.com. Web site: www.paradoxmag.com. **Contact:** Christopher M. Cevasco, editor/publisher. Literary magazine/journal: $8^1/_2 \times 11$, 57 pages, standard white paper with b&w interior art, glossy color cover. Contains illustrations. Includes photographs. ''Paradox is the only English-language print magazine exclusively devoted to historical fiction in either its mainstream or genre forms.'' Semiannual. Estab. 2003. Circ. 600. Member Speculative Literature Foundation Small Press Co-operative. Awards: 6 honorable mentions (2003) and 3 honorable mentions (2004) in *Year's Best Fantasy & Horror*, edited by Ellen Datlow, Kelly Link and Gavin Grant; 2 honorable mentions (2004) in *Year's Best Science Fiction*, edited by Gardner Dozois.

Needs Fantasy (historical), horror (historical), military/war, historical mystery/suspense, science fiction (historical, e.g. time travel and alternate history), western (historical). Does not want children's stories, gratuitous erotica, vampires, werewolves. Receives 75 mss/month. Accepts 6-8 mss/issue; 12-16 mss/year. Manuscript published 6 months after acceptance. Agented fiction 5%. **Publishes 1-2 new writers/year.** Published Jack Whyte, Sarah Monette, Adam Stemple, Paul Finch, Eugie Foster, Darron T. Moore (debut). Length: 2,000 words (min)-15,000 words (max). Average length: 6,000 words. Publishes short shorts. Average length of short shorts: 1,200 words. Also publishes literary essays, book reviews, poetry. Send review copies to Christopher M. Cevasco. Always comments on/critiques rejected manuscripts.

How to Contact Send complete ms with cover letter. Include estimated word count. Responds to mss in 4 months. Send either SASE (or IRC) for return of ms or disposable copy of ms and #10 SASE for reply only. Sample copy available for $7.50 (includes postage), or for $8 to Canada, or for $11 elsewhere. Guidelines available on Web site.

Payment and Terms Writers receive 3¢-5¢/word, 4 contributor's copies. Additional copies ⅓ off cover price. Pays on publication. Acquires first world English-language rights. Sends galleys to author. Publication is copyrighted. "Offers periodic fiction writing contests; details posted in magazine and on Web site."

THE PARIS REVIEW

62 White St., New York NY 10013. Web site: www.theparisreview.com. **Contact:** Fiction Editor. Philip Gourevitch, editor. Magazine: 6⅝×9⅜; about 190 pages; illustrations; photography portfolios (unsolicited artwork not accepted). "Fiction, nonfiction and poetry of superlative quality. Our contributors include prominent, as well as less well-known and previously unpublished writers. The Writers at Work interview series features important contemporary writers discussing their own work and the craft of writing." Published quarterly.

Needs Fiction, nonfiction, poetry. Receives 1,000 unsolicited mss/month. Recently published work by Lisa Halliday, Haruki Murakami, Vladimir Nabokov, A.S. Byatt, Etgar Keret, Annie Proulx, Karl Taro Greenfeld.

How to Contact Send complete ms and SASE. Responds in 2 months to mss. Accepts simultaneous, multiple submissions. Sample copy for $12 (includes postage). Writer's guidelines online.

Payment/Terms Payment varies depending on length. Pays on publication for first English-language rights. Sends galleys to author. Sponsors awards/contests.

PARTING GIFTS

3413 Wilshire, Greensboro NC 27408-2923. E-mail: rbixby@earthlink.net. Web site: www.marchstreetpress.com. **Contact:** Robert Bixby, editor. Magazine: 5×7; 100 pages. "*Parting Gifts* seeks good, powerful, and short fiction that stands on its own and takes no prisoners." Semiannual. Estab. 1988.

Needs "Brevity is the second most important criterion behind literary quality." Publishes ms within one year after acceptance. Recently published work by Ray Miller, Katherine Taylor, Curtis Smith, William Snyder, Jr. Also publishes poetry. Sometimes comments on rejected mss.

How to Contact Include SASE. Responds in 1 day to queries; 1 week to mss. Accepts simultaneous, multiple submissions. Sample copy for $9. For a year subscription, $18.

Payment/Terms Pays in contributor's copies. Acquires one-time rights.

Advice "Read the works of Amy Hempel, Jim Harrison, Kelly Cherry, C.K. Williams and Janet Kaufman, all excellent writers who epitomize the writing *Parting Gifts* strives to promote. I look for original voice, original ideas, original setting and characters, language that makes one weep without knowing why, a deep understanding or keen observation of real people in real situations. The magazine is online, along with guidelines and feedback to authors; reading any one or all three will save a lot of postage."

PASSAGES NORTH

Northern Michigan University, Department of English, Gries Hall, Rm 229, Marquette MI 49855. (906)227-2711. Fax: (906)227-1203. E-mail: passages@nmu.edu. Web site: http://myweb.nmu.edu/~passages. Editor-in-Chief: Kate Myers Hanson. **Contact:** John Smolens, fiction editor; Austin Hummell, poetry editor; Paul Lehmberg, nonfiction editor. Magazine: 8×5½; 80 lb. paper. "*Passages North* publishes quality fiction, poetry and creative nonfiction by emerging and established writers." Readership: General and literary. Annual. Estab. 1979. Circ. 1,500.

Needs Ethnic/multicultural, literary, short-short fiction. No genre fiction, science fiction, "typical commercial press work." "Seeking more multicultural work." Receives 100-200 unsolicited mss/month. Accepts 20 mss/year. Reads mss September 1-April 15. **Publishes 25% new writers/year.** Recently published work by Bret Anthony Johnston, Michael Martone, Brett Garcia Myhren, Lee Martin, Anne Panning, David Dodd Lee, Bob Hicok, Jesse Lee Kercheval, Esther Lee and Dianna Joseph. Comments on rejected mss when there is time.

How to Contact Responds in 2 months to mss. Accepts simultaneous submissions.

Payment/Terms Pays 2 contributor's copies. Rights revert to author upon publication.

Advice "We look for voice, energetic prose, writers who take risks. Revise, revise. Read what we publish."

THE PATERSON LITERARY REVIEW

Passaic County Community College, One College Blvd., Paterson NJ 07505. (973)684-6555. Fax: (973)523-6085. E-mail: mgillan@pccc.edu. Web site: www.pccc.edu/poetry. **Contact:** Maria Mazziotti Gillan, editor. Magazine: 6×9; 400 pages; 60 lb. paper; 70 lb. cover; illustrations; photos. Annual.

* Work for *PLR* has been included in the *Pushcart Prize* anthology and *Best American Poetry*.

Needs Ethnic/multicultural, literary, contemporary. "We are interested in quality short stories, with no taboos on subject matter." Receives 60 unsolicited mss/month. Publishes ms 6-12 months after acceptance. **Publishes 5% new writers/year.** Recently published work by Robert Mooney and Abigail Stone. Also publishes literary essays, literary criticism, poetry.

How to Contact Send SASE for reply or return of ms. "Indicate whether you want story returned." Accepts simultaneous submissions. Sample copy for $13 plus $1.50 postage. Reviews fiction.

Payment/Terms Pays in contributor's copies. Acquires first North American serial rights.

Advice Looks for "clear, moving and specific work."

PEARL, A Literary Magazine

3030 E. Second St., Long Beach CA 90803-5163. (562)434-4523. E-mail: pearlmag@aol.com. Web site: www.pearlmag.com. **Contact:** Marilyn Johnson, editor. Magazine: 5½×8½; 96 pages; 60 lb. recycled, acid-free paper; perfect bound; coated cover; b &w drawings and graphics. "We are primarily a poetry magazine, but we do publish some *very short* fiction. We are interested in lively, readable prose that speaks to *real* people in direct, living language; for a general literary audience." Biannual. Estab. 1974. Circ. 600.

Needs Humor/satire, literary, mainstream, contemporary, prose poem. "We will consider short-short stories up to 1,200 words. Longer stories (up to 4,000 words) may only be submitted to our short story contest. All contest entries are considered for publication. Although we have no taboos stylistically or subject-wise, obscure, predictable, sentimental, or cliché-ridden stories are a turn-off." Publishes an all-fiction issue each year. Receives 30- 40 unsolicited mss/month. Accepts 15-20 mss/issue; 12-15 mss/year. Submissions accepted September-May *only*. Publishes ms 6-12 months after acceptance. **Publishes 1-5 new writers/year.** Recently published work by James D. McCallister, Heidi Rosenberg, W. Joshua Heffernan, Suzanne Greenberg, Fred McGavran, Gerald Locklin, Robert Perchan, Lisa Glatt. Length: 500-1,200 words; average length: 1,000 words. Also publishes poetry.

How to Contact Include SASE. Responds in 2 months to mss. Accepts simultaneous, multiple submissions. Sample copy for $8 (postpaid). Writer's guidelines for #10 SASE.

Payment/Terms Pays 1 contributor's copy. Acquires first North American serial rights. Sends galleys to author. Sponsors awards/contests.

Advice "We look for vivid, *dramatized* situations and characters, stories written in an original 'voice,' that make sense and follow a clear narrative line. What makes a manuscript stand out is more elusive, though— more to do with feeling and imagination than anything else."

PENNSYLVANIA ENGLISH

Penn State DuBois, College Place, DuBois PA 15801. (814)375-4814. Fax: (814)375-4784. E-mail: ajv2@psu.edu. "Mention *Pennsylvania English* in the subject line." **Contact:** Antonio Vallone, editor. Magazine: 5¼×8¼; up to 200 pages; perfect bound; full color cover featuring the artwork of a Pennsylvania artist. "Our philosophy is quality. We publish literary fiction (and poetry and nonfiction). Our intended audience is literate, college-educated people." Annual. Estab. 1985. Circ. 500.

Needs Literary, mainstream, contemporary. "No genre fiction or romance." Reads mss during the summer. Publishes ms up to 12 months after acceptance. **Publishes 4-6 new writers/year.** Recently published work by Dave Kress, Dan Leone and Paul West. Publishes short shorts. Also publishes literary essays, literary criticism, poetry. Sometimes comments on rejected mss.

How to Contact SASE. Does not normally accept electronic submissions. "We are creating Pennsylvania English Online—www.pennsylvaniaenglish.com—for electronic submissions and expanded publishing oppurtunities." Responds in up to 12 months to mss. Accepts simultaneous submissions. Does not accept previously published work. Sample copy for $10.

Payment/Terms Pays in 2 contributor's copies. Acquires first North American serial rights.

Advice "Quality of the writing is our only measure. We're not impressed by long-winded cover letters detailing awards and publications we've never heard of. Beginners and professionals have the same chance with us. We receive stacks of competently written but boring fiction. For a story to rise out of the rejection pile, it takes more than the basic competence."

◙ PEREGRINE

Amherst Writers & Artists Press, 190 University Drive, Amherst MA 01002. (413)253-3307. E-mail: peregrine@amherstwriters.com. Web site: www.amherstwriters.com. **Contact:** Nancy Rose, editor. Magazine: 6×9; 100 pages; 60 lb. white offset paper; glossy cover. "*Peregrine* has provided a forum for national and international writers since 1983, and is committed to finding excellent work by new writers as well as established authors. We publish what we love, knowing that all editorial decisions are subjective, and that all work has a home somewhere." Annual.

Needs Poetry and prose—short stories, short shorts. "No previously published work. No children's stories. We welcome work reflecting diversity of voice. We like to be surprised. We look for writing that is honest, unpretentious, and memorable." Short pieces have a better chance of publication. No electronic submissions. Accepts 6-12 mss/issue. Read February-June. Publishes ms 4 months after acceptance. **Publishes 8-10 new writers/ year.** Recently published work by Janet Aalfs, James Doyle, Sarah Durham, Willie James King, Jennifer Phillips, Ted Stein, William Yellow Robe, Jr., and Jane Yolen. Publishes short shorts.

How to Contact Enclose sufficiently stamped SASE for return of ms; if disposable copy, enclose #10 SASE for response. Deadline for submission: June 1. Accepts simultaneous, multiple submissions. Sample copy for $12. Writer's guidelines for #10 SASE or Web site.

Payment/Terms Pays contributor's copies. All rights return to writer upon publication.

Advice "We look for heart and soul as well as technical expertise. Trust your own voice. Familiarize yourself with *Peregrine*." Every ms is read by several readers; all decisions are made by editors.

◙ PHANTASMAGORIA

Century College English Dept., 3300 Century Ave. N, White Bear Lake MN 55110. (651)779-3410. E-mail: allenabigail@hotmail.com. **Contact:** Abigail Allen, editor. Magazine: 5½×8½; 140-200 pages. "We publish literary fiction, poetry and essays (no scholarly essays)." Semiannual. Estab. 2001. Circ. 1,000. Member CLMP.

Needs Experimental, literary, mainstream. "No children's stories or young adult/teen material." Receives 120 unsolicited mss/month. Accepts 20-40 mss/issue; 40-80 mss/year. Publishes ms 6 months after acceptance. **Publishes 5-10 new writers/year.** Recently published work by Greg Mulcahy, Hiram Goza, Simon Perchik, William Greenway. Length: 4,000 words; average length: 2,500 words. Publishes short shorts. Also publishes literary essays, poetry.

How to Contact Send SASE (or IRC) for return of ms or send a disposable copy of ms and #10 SASE for reply only. Responds in 2 weeks to queries. Sample copy for $9. Writer's guidelines for SASE. Reviews fiction.

Payment/Terms Pays 2 contributor's copies. Acquires first North American serial rights.

◌ PIKEVILLE REVIEW

Pikeville College, Sycamore St., Pikeville KY 41501. (606)218-5602. Fax: (606)218-5225. E-mail: sengland@pc.edu. Web site: www.pc.edu. **Contact:** Sydney England. Magazine: 8½×6; 120 pages; illustrations; photos. "Literate audience interested in well-crafted poetry, fiction, essays and reviews." Annual. Estab. 1987. Circ. 500.

Needs Ethnic/multicultural, experimental, feminist, humor/satire, literary, mainstream, regional, translations. Receives 60-80 unsolicited mss/month. Accepts 3-4 mss/issue. Does not read mss in the summer. Publishes ms 6-8 after acceptance. **Publishes 20 new writers/year.** Recently published work by Jim Wayne Miller, James Baker Hall, Robert Elkins, Robert Morgan. Length: 15,000 words; average length: 5,000 words. Publishes short shorts. Also publishes literary essays, poetry. Often comments on rejected mss.

How to Contact Accepts submissions by e-mail. Send SASE for reply, return of ms or send a disposable copy of ms. Sample copy for $4. Reviews fiction.

Payment/Terms Pays 5 contributor's copies; additional copies for $4. Acquires first rights. Sponsors awards/contests.

Advice "Send a clean manuscript with well-developed characters."

Ⓝ ◙ THE PINCH

(formerly *River City*) Dept. of English, The University of Memphis, Memphis TN 38152. (901)678-4591. E-mail: thepinch@memphis.edu. Web site: www.thepinchjournal.com or ww.mfainmemphis.com. **Contact:** Court Ogilvie, managing editor. Magazine: 7×10; 150 pages. Semiannual. Estab. 1980. Circ. 1,500.

Needs Short stories, poetry, creative nonfiction, essays, memoir, travel, or nature writing, art. **Publishes some new writers every year.** Recently published work by Bill Roorbach, Stephen Dunn, Denise Duhamel, Robert Morgan, and Beth Ann Fennelly.

How to Contact Send complete ms. Responds in 2 months to mss. Sample copy for $10.

Payment/Terms Pays 2 contributor's copies. Acquires first North American serial rights.

Advice "We have a new look and a new edge. We're soliciting work from writers with a national reputation as well as strong, interesting work from emerging writers. The River City Writing Awards in Fiction offers a $1,500 prize and publication. Check our Web site for details."

PINDELDYBOZ

Pindeldyboz, 23-55 38th St., Astoria NY 11105. E-mail: print@pindeldyboz.com. Web site: www.pindeldyboz.com. **Contact:** Whitney Pastorek, executive editor. Literary magazine: $5^{1}/_{2} \times 8^{1}/_{2}$; 272 pages; illustrations. *"Pindeldyboz* is dedicated to publishing work that challenges what a short story can be. We don't ask for anything specific—we only ask that people take chances. We like heightened language, events, relationships—stories that paint the world a little differently, while still showing us the places we already know." Semiannual. Estab. 2000.

Needs Comics/graphic novels, experimental, literary. Reads mss September 1-February 1 only. Publishes ms 3 months after acceptance. Recently published work by Jamie Attenberg, Carrie Hoffman, Matthew Derby, Amanda Eyre Ward, Dan Kennedy, Corey Mesler. Length: 250+; average length: 2,000 words. Publishes short shorts. Also publishes literary essays, poetry. Always comments on rejected mss.

How to Contact Send complete copy of ms with cover letter. Accepts mss by e-mail and disk. Include brief bio and phone number with submission. Send SASE (or IRC) for return of the ms and disposable copy of ms and #10 SASE for reply only. Responds in 2 weeks to queries; 3 months to mss. Accepts simultaneous, multiple submissions. Sample copy for $12. Writer's guidelines online.

Payment/Terms Pays 2 contributor's copies; additional copies $10. Pays on publication for one-time rights.

Advice "Good grammar, spelling, and sentence structure help, but what's more important is a willingness to take risks. Surprise us. And we will love it."

☑ PINYON

Mesa State College, Dept. of Languages, Lit and Comm, 1100 North Avenue, Grand Junction CO 81501-3122. E-mail: pinyonpoetry@hotmail.com. **Contact:** Fiction editor. Literary magazine/journal: $8^{1}/_{2} \times 5^{1}/_{2}$, 120 pages, heavy paper. Contains illustrations and photographs. Annual. Estab. 1996. Circ. 200.

Needs Literary. Receives 16-20 mss/month. Accepts 3-4 mss/issue; 3-4 mss/year. Does not read mss January-August. Manuscript published 6 months after acceptance. Length: 1,500 words (min)-5,000 words (max). Average length: 2,500 words. Publishes short shorts. Average length of short shorts: 500 words. Also publishes poetry.

How to Contact Send complete ms with cover letter. Include brief bio. Responds to queries in 1 month. Responds to mss in 6 months. Send either SASE (or IRC) for return of ms or disposable copy of ms and #10 SASE for reply only. Considers simultaneous submissions, multiple submissions. Sample copy available for $4.50. Send SASE for guidelines.

Payment and Terms Writers receive 2 contributor's copies. Acquires one-time rights. Publication is copyrighted.

Advice "Ask yourself if the work is something you would like to read in a publication."

Ⓝ ☐ PISGAH REVIEW

Department of Humanities, Brevard College, Brevard NC 28712. (828)586-1969. E-mail: jubaltara@yahoo.com. **Contact:** Jubal Tiner or Charles White, co-editors. Literary magazine/journal: $5^{1}/_{2}$ x $8^{1}/_{2}$, 120 pages. Includes cover photograph. *"Pisgah Review* publishes primarily literary short fiction, creative nonfiction and poetry. Our only criteria is quality of work; we look for the best. The magazine does give a small preference to work that is based evocatively on place, but we will look at any work of quality." Semiannual. Estab. 2005. Circ. 150.

Needs Ethnic/multicultural, experimental, literary, mainstream. Special interests: stories rooted in the theme of place—physical, psychological, or spiritual. Does not want genre fiction or inspirational stories. Receives 30 mss/month. Accepts 6-8 mss/issue; 12-15 mss/year. Manuscript published 6 months after acceptance. **Publishes 5 new writers/year.** Published Ron Rash, Lonnie Busch, Barbara Haas. Length: 2,000 words (min)-7,500 words (max). Average length: 4,000 words. Publishes short shorts. Average length of short shorts: 1,000 words. Also publishes poetry. Sometimes comments on/critiques rejected mss.

How to Contact Send complete ms with cover letter. Accepts submissions by e-mail. Responds to mss in 4-6 months. Send either SASE (or IRC) for return of ms or disposable copy of ms and #10 SASE for reply only. Considers simultaneous submissions. Sample copy available for $5. Guidelines available for SASE, via e-mail.

Payment and Terms Writers receive 2 contributor's copies. Additional copies $5. Pays on publication. Acquires first North American serial rights. Sends galleys to author if requested. Publication is copyrighted.

Advice "We select work only of the highest quality. Grab us from the beginning and follow through. Engage us with your language and characters. A clean manuscript goes a long way toward acceptance. Stay true to the vision of your work, revise tirelessly, and submit persistently."

$☑ ☑ PLEIADES

Pleiades Press, Department of English & Philosophy, Central Missouri State University, Martin 336, Warrensburg MO 64093. (660)543-4425. Fax: (660)543-8544. E-mail: ssteinberg@usfca.edu. Web site: www.cmsu.edu/englp

hil/pleiades. **Contact:** G.B. Crump, fiction editor. Magazine: 5½×8½; 150 pages; 60 lb. paper; perfect-bound; 8 pt. color cover. "We publish contemporary fiction, poetry, interviews, literary essays, special-interest personal essays, reviews for a general and literary audience." Semiannual. Estab. 1991. Circ. 3,000.

- Work from *Pleiades* appears in recent volumes of *The Best American Poetry*, *Pushcart Prize* and *Best American Fantasy and Horror*.

Needs Ethnic/multicultural, experimental, feminist, gay, humor/satire, literary, mainstream, novel excerpts, regional, translations, magical realism. No science fiction, fantasy, confession, erotica. Receives 100 unsolicited mss/month. Accepts 8 mss/issue; 16 mss/year. "We're slower at reading manuscripts in the summer." Publishes ms 9 months after acceptance. **Publishes 4-5 new writers/year.** Recently published work by Sherman Alexie, Edith Pearlman, Joyce Carol Oates, James Tate. Length: 2,000-6,000 words; average length: 3,000-6,000 words. Also publishes literary essays, literary criticism, poetry. Sometimes comments on rejected mss.

How to Contact Send complete ms. Include 75-100 word bio and list of publications. Send SASE for reply, return of ms or send a disposable copy of ms. Responds in 2 months to queries; 2 months to mss. Accepts simultaneous submissions. Sample copy for $5 (back issue), $6 (current issue). Writer's guidelines for #10 SASE.

Payment/Terms Pays $10. Pays on publication for first North American serial, second serial (reprint) rights. Occasionally requests rights for TV, radio reading, Web site.

Advice Looks for "a blend of language and subject matter that entices from beginning to end. Send us your best work. Don't send us formula stories. While we appreciate and publish well-crafted traditional pieces, we constantly seek the story that risks, that breaks form and expectations and wins us over anyhow."

POINTED CIRCLE

Portland Community College-Cascade, 705 N. Killingsworth St., Portland OR 97217. (503)978-5251. E-mail: kimball@pcc.edu. **Contact:** Cynthia Kimball, English instructor, faculty advisor. Magazine: 80 pages; b&w illustrations; photos. "Anything of interest to educationally/culturally mixed audience." Annual. Estab. 1980.

Needs Ethnic/multicultural, literary, regional, contemporary, prose poem. "We will read whatever is sent, but encourage writers to remember we are a quality literary/arts magazine intended to promote the arts in the community. No pornography. Be mindful of deadlines and length limits." Accepts submissions only October 1-March 1, for July 1 issue.

How to Contact Accepts submissions by e-mail, fax. Submitted materials will not be returned; SASE for notification only. Accepts multiple submissions. Writer's guidelines for #10 SASE.

Payment/Terms Pays 2 copies. Acquires one-time rights.

Advice "Looks for quality—topicality—nothing trite. The author cares about language and acts responsibly toward the reader, honors the reader's investment of time and piques the reader's interest."

POLYPHONY H.S., A STUDENT-RUN NATIONAL LITERARY MAGAZINE FOR HIGH SCHOOL WRITERS

The Latin School of Chicago, 59 W. North Blvd., Chicago IL 60610. (312)582-6405. Fax: (312)582-6401. E-mail: blombardo@latinschool.org. Web site: www.polyphonyhs.com. **Contact:** Billy Lombardo, editor-in-chief. Literary magazine/journal: 9×6, 70-120 pages, silk finish 80 lb. white paper, silk finish 100 lb. cover. "Our goal is to seek out the finest high school writers in the country, to work with them to grow as writers, and to exhibit their fiction before a national audience. Their work is edited by an actual staff of high school editors." Annual. Estab. 2005. Circ. 1,050.

Needs Literary works. Does not want erotica. Receives 20 mss/month. Accepts 20-40 mss/issue. **Publishes 20-40 new writers/year.** Length: 250 words (min)-4,000 words (max). Average length: 2,000 words. Publishes fiction and poetry. Always comments on/critiques rejected mss.

How to Contact See Web site. Accepts submissions by e-mail. Send complete mss as Word attachment and also paste within the e-mail text. Type title of piece, author's name in Subject line of e-mail. Include brief bio, name of school.Deadline: third Saturday in February. Responds to mss in 6 weeks. Send disposable copy of ms and #10 SASE for reply only. Considers simultaneous submissions. Sample copy available for $5. Guidelines available via e-mail.

Payment and Terms Writers receive 2 contributor's copies. Additional copies $3.50. Pays on publication. Acquires first rights. Publication is not copyrighted.

Advice "Revise, revise, revise. All first drafts are crappy, but absolutely essential to the final product. Care about the story."

PORCUPINE LITERARY ARTS MAGAZINE

P.O. Box 259, Cedarburg WI 53012-0259. (262)375-3128. E-mail: ppine259@aol.com. Web site: www.porcupine literaryarts.com. **Contact:** Chris Skoczynski, fiction editor. Magazine: 5×8½; 150 pages; glossy color cover stock; art work and photos. Publishes "primarily poetry and short fiction. Novel excerpts are acceptable if self-contained. No restrictions as to theme or style." Semiannual. Estab. 1996. Circ. 1,500.

Needs Condensed novels, ethnic/multicultural, literary, mainstream. "No pornographic or religious." Receives 40 unsolicited mss/month. Accepts 3 mss/issue; 6 mss/year. Publishes ms 6-12 months after acceptance. **Publishes 4-6 new writers/year.** Recently published work by Richard Thieme, Halina Duraj, Lauro Palomba, Jane Summer, Carol Lee Lorenzo. Length: 2,000-7,500 words; average length: 3,500 words. Also publishes literary essays, poetry. Sometimes comments on rejected mss.

How to Contact Accepts submissions by e-mail. Send SASE for reply, return of ms or send a disposable copy of ms. Responds in 2 weeks to queries; 2 months to mss. Sample copy for $5. Writer's guidelines for #10 SASE.

Payment/Terms Pays 1 contributor's copy; additional copies for $8.95. Pays on publication for one-time rights.

Advice Looks for "believable dialogue and a narrator I can see and hear and smell. Form or join a writers' group. Read aloud. Rewrite extensively."

☑ PORTLAND REVIEW

Portland State University, Box 347, Portland OR 97207-0347. (503)7254533. E-mail: jbrewer@pdx.edu. Web site: www.portlandreview.org. **Contact:** Jeff Brewer, editor. Magazine: 9×6; 100 pages; b&w art and photos. Triannual. Estab. 1956. Circ. 500.

Needs Experimental, historical, humor/satire, novel excerpts, regional, slice-of-life vignettes. Wants more humor. No fantasy, detective, western, or science fiction. Receives 100 unsolicited mss/month. Accepts 10-12 mss/issue; 30-40 mss/year. Publishes ms 3-6 months after acceptance. Recently published work by Katy Williams, Tina Boscha, Kathryn Ma, and Brian Turner.

How to Contact Send complete ms. Send SASE for return of ms. Responds in 6 weeks to queries; 2-4 months to mss. Accepts simultaneous submissions. Sample copy for $8. Writer's guidelines online.

Payment/Terms Pays contributor's copies. Acquires first North American serial rights.

Ⓝ ☑ POST ROAD

P.O. Box 400951, Cambridge MA 02140. E-mail: mary@postroadmag.com. Web site: www.postroadmag.com. **Contact:** Mary Cotton. Literary magazine/journal. 8½×11½, 240 pages, 60 lb. opaque paper, gloss cover. "*Post Road* is a nationally distributed literary magazine based out of New York and Boston that publishes work in the following genres: art, criticism, fiction, nonfiction, and poetry. *Post Road* also features two innovations: the Recommendations section, where established writers write 500-1,000 words on a favorite book(s) or author(s); and the Etcetera section where we publish interviews, profiles, translations, letters, classic reprints, documents, topical essays, travelogues, etc." Estab. 2000. Circ. 2,000.

● Work from *Post Road* has received the following honors: honorable mention in the 2001 O. Henry Prize Issue guest-edited by Michael Chabon, Mary Gordon, and Mona Simpson; the Pushcart Prize; honorable mention in *The Best American Nonfiction* series; and inclusion in the *Best American Short Stories* 2005.

Needs Literary. Receives 100 mss/month. Accepts 4-6 mss/issue; 8-12 mss/year. Does not read mss March 16-May 31 and September 2-January 14. Manuscript published 6 months after acceptance. Published Brian Booker, Louis E. Bourgeois, Becky Bradway, Adam Braver, Ashley Capps, Susan Choi, Lisa Selin Davis, Rebecca Dickson, Rick Moody. Average length: 5,000 words. Average length of short shorts: 1,500 words. Also publishes literary essays, literary criticism, poetry. Sometimes comments on/critiques rejected manuscripts.

How to Contact Accepts submissions by e-mail. Electronic submissions only. Include brief bio. Responds to mss in 1 months. Send SASE (or IRC) for return of ms. Considers simultaneous submissions. Guidelines available on Web site.

Payment and Terms Writers receive 2 contributor's copies. Pays on publication. Acquires first North American serial rights. Sends galleys to author. Publication is not copyrighted.

Advice "Looking for interesting narrative, sharp dialogue, deft use of imagery and metaphor. Be persistent and be open to criticism."

Ⓝ $ 🌐 ☑ POSTSCRIPTS: THE A TO Z OF FANTASTIC FICTION

PS Publishing LTD., Grosvenor House, 1 New Road, Hornsea, E. Yorks, HU18-1PG United Kingdom. 0-11-44-1964 537575. Fax: 0-11-44-1964 537535. E-mail: editor@pspublishing.co.uk. Web site: www.pspublishing.co.uk. **Contact:** Peter Crowther, editor/publisher. Literary magazine/journal: digest, 144 pages. Contains illustrations & photographs. "Science fiction, fantasy, horror and crime/suspense. We focus on the cerebral rather than the visceral, with an emphasis on quality literary fiction within the specified areas." Quarterly. Estab. 2004. Circ. around 1,000.

● PS Publishing has received five British Fantasy Awards, one World Fantasy Award, one International Horror Guild Award, and one Horror Writers Association Award.

Needs Fantasy (space fantasy, sword and sorcery), horror (dark fantasy, futuristic, psychological, supernatural), mystery (amateur sleuth, cozy, police procedural, private eye/hard-boiled), science fiction (hard science/technological, soft/sociological), List of upcoming themes available on Web site. Receives 20-50 mss/month. Accepts 10 mss/issue; 50 mss/year. Manuscript published up to 2 years after acceptance. Agented fiction less than 10%. **Publishes 4-8 new writers/year.** Length: 3,000 words (min)–8,000 words (max). Average length: 5,000 words. Publishes short shorts. Average length of short shorts: 1,000 words. Rarely comments on/critiques rejected mss.

How to Contact Send complete ms with cover letter. Accepts submissions by mail, e-mail. Include estimated word count, brief bio, list of publications. Responds to queries in 2 weeks; mss in 4 weeks. Send either SASE (or IRC) for return of ms or disposable copy of ms and #10 SASE for reply only. Sample copy available for $10 (and $5 IRCs). Guidelines available on Web site.

Payment and Terms Writers receive 4-7¢/word, 2 contributor's copies. Additional copies $10 (inc. postage). **Pays on acceptance.** Acquires first worldwide English rights. Publication is copyrighted.

Advice ''Read the magazine.''

✒ POTOMAC REVIEW, The Journal for Arts & Humanities

Montgomery College, Paul Peck Humanities Institute, 51 Mannakee St., Rockville MD 20850. (301)251-7417. Fax: (301)738-1745. E-mail: potomacrevieweditor@montgomerycollege.edu. Web site: www.montgomerycolle ge.edu/potomacreview. **Contact:** Julie Wakeman-Linn, editor. Magazine: 5½×8½; 175 pages; 50 lb. paper; 65 lb. color cover. *Potomac Review* '' reflects a view of our region looking out to the world, and in turn, seeks how the world views the region.'' Annual. Estab. 1994. Circ. 750.

Needs ''Stories and poems with a vivid, individual quality that get at 'the concealed side' of life.'' Essays and creative non-fiction pieces welcome. No themes. Recieves 300+ unsolicited mss/montyh. Accepts 40- 50 mss/issue. Publishes ms within 1 year after acceptance. Recently published work by Jim Tomilson, Tim Wendel, Rose Solari, Moira Egan, Martin Galvin, Elizabeth Murawski, Richard Peabody, Jeff Hardin, and Nancy Naomi Carlson. Length: 5,000 words; average length: 2,000 words.

How to Contact Send SASE with adequate postage for reply and/or return of ms. Responds in 3 -6 months to mss. Accepts simultaneous submissions. Sample copy for $10. Writer's guidelines on Web site.

Payment/Terms Pays 2 or more contributor's copies; additional copies for a 40% discount.

Advice ''Send us interesting, well crafted stories. Have something to say in an original, provacative voice. Read recent issue to get a sense of the journal's new direction.''

$ ☒ ✒ THE PRAIRIE JOURNAL, Journal of Canadian Literature

Prairie Journal Trust, P.O. Box 61203, Brentwood P.O., Calgary AB T2L 2K6 Canada. Web site: www.geocities. com/prairiejournal. **Contact:** A.E. Burke, editor. Journal: 7×8½; 50-60 pages; white bond paper; Cadillac cover stock; cover illustrations. ''The audience is literary, university, library, scholarly and creative readers/writers.'' Semiannual. Estab. 1983. Circ. 600.

Needs Literary, regional. No genre (romance, horror, western—sagebrush or cowboys—erotic, science fiction, or mystery). Receives 100 unsolicited mss/month. Accepts 10-15 mss/issue; 20-30 mss/year. Suggested deadlines: April 1 for spring/summer issue; October 1 for fall/winter. Publishes ms 4-6 months after acceptance. **Publishes 60 new writers/year.** Recently published work by Robert Clark, Sandy Campbell, Darcie Hasack, Christopher Blais. Length: 100-3,000 words; average length: 2,500 words. Also publishes literary essays, literary criticism, poetry. Sometimes comments on rejected mss.

How to Contact Send complete ms with SASE (IRC). Include cover letter of past credits, if any. Reply to queries for SAE with 55¢ for postage or IRC. No American stamps. Responds in 2 weeks to queries; 6 months to mss. No simultaneous submissions. No e-mail submissions. Sample copy for $6. Writer's guidelines online. Reviews fiction.

Payment/Terms Pays $10-75. Pays on publication for first North American serial rights. In Canada, author retains copyright with acknowledgement appreciated.

Advice ''We like character-driven rather than plot-centered fiction.'' Interested in ''innovational work of quality. Beginning writers welcome! There is no point in simply republishing known authors or conventional, predictable plots. Of the genres we receive, fiction is most often of the highest calibre. It is a very competitive field. Be proud of what you send. You're worth it.''

$ ☒ ✒ ☒ PRISM INTERNATIONAL

Department of Creative Writing, Buch E462-1866 Main Mall, University of British Columbia, Vancouver BC V6T 1Z1 Canada. (604)822-2514. Fax: (604)822-3616. E-mail: prism@interchange.ubc.ca. Web site: prism.arts. ubc.ca. **Contact:** Editor. Magazine: 6×9; 80 pages; Zephyr book paper; Cornwall, coated one-side cover; artwork on cover. ''An international journal of contemporary writing—fiction, poetry, drama, creative nonfiction and translation.'' Readership: ''public and university libraries, individual subscriptions, bookstores—a worldwide audience concerned with the contemporary in literature.'' Quarterly. Estab. 1959. Circ. 1,200.

• *Prism International* has won numerous magazine awards, and stories first published in *Prism International* have been included in the *Journey Prize Anthology* every year since 1991.

Needs Experimental, traditional. New writing that is contemporary and literary. Short stories and self-contained novel excerpts (up to 25 double-spaced pages). Works of translation are eagerly sought and should be accompanied by a copy of the original. Would like to see more translations. "No gothic, confession, religious, romance, pornography, or sci-fi." Also looking for creative nonfiction that is literary, not journalistic, in scope and tone. Receives over 100 unsolicited mss/month. Accepts 70 mss/year. "*PRISM* publishes both new and established writers; our contributors have included Franz Kafka, Gabriel García Márquez, Michael Ondaatje, Margaret Laurence, Mark Anthony Jarman, Gail Anderson-Dargatz and Eden Robinson." Publishes ms 4 months after acceptance. **Publishes 7 new writers/year.** Recently published work by Ibi Kaslik, Melanie Little, Mark Anthony Jarman. Publishes short shorts. Also publishes poetry.

How to Contact Send complete ms. Accepts submissions by fax, disk. "Keep it simple. U.S. contributors take note: Do not send SASEs with U.S. stamps, they are not valid in Canada. Send International Reply Coupons instead." Responds in 4 months to queries; 3-6 months to mss. Sample copy for $10 or on Web site. Writer's guidelines online.

Payment/Terms Pays $20/printed page and 1-year subscription. Pays on publication for first North American serial rights. Selected authors are paid an additional $10/page for digital rights. Sponsors awards/contests.

Advice "Read several issues of our magazine before submitting. We are committed to publishing outstanding literary work. We look for strong, believeable characters; real voices; attention to language; interesting ideas and plots. Send us fresh, innovative work which also shows a mastery of the basics of good prose writing."

◻ PUERTO DEL SOL

New Mexico State University, Box 3E, Las Cruces NM 88003-0001. (505)646-2345. Fax: (505)646-7755. E-mail: PUERTO@nmsu.edu. Web site: www.nmsu.edu/~puerto/welcome.html. **Contact:** Kevin McIlvoy, editor-in-chief and fiction editor; Kathleene West, poetry editor. Magazine: 6×9; 200 pages; 60 lb. paper; 70 lb. cover stock. "We publish quality material from anyone. Poetry, fiction, interviews, reviews, parts-of-novels, long poems." Semiannual. Estab. 1964. Circ. 2,000.

Needs Ethnic/multicultural, experimental, literary, mainstream, novel excerpts, translations, contemporary, prose poem. Accepts 8-10 mss/issue; 12-15 mss/year. Does not accept mss January-September. **Publishes 8-10 new writers/year.** Recently published work by Dagoberto Gilb, Wendell Mayo, William H. Cobb. Also publishes literary essays, poetry. Always comments on rejected mss.

How to Contact Responds in 3-6 months to mss. Accepts simultaneous submissions. Sample copy for $8.

Payment/Terms Pays 2 contributor's copies. Acquires one-time rights. Rights revert to author after publication.

Advice "We are open to all forms of fiction, from the conventional to the wildly experimental and we are pleased to work with emerging writers."

◧ ◎ QUARTER AFTER EIGHT, A Journal of Prose and Community

QAE, Ellis Hall, Ohio University, Athens OH 45701. (740)593-2827. E-mail: editor@quartereight.org. Web site: www.quartereight.org. **Contact:** Kelly Evans, co-editor-in-chief. Magazine: 6×9; 200 pages; 20 lb. glossy cover stock; photos. "We look to publish work which challenges boundaries of genre, style, idea, and voice." Annual.

Needs Condensed novels, ethnic/multicultural, experimental, gay, humor/satire, lesbian, literary, mainstream, translations. "No traditional, conventional fiction." Receives 150-200 unsolicited mss/month. Accepts 40-50 mss/issue. Does not read mss mid-March-mid-September. Publishes ms 6-12 months after acceptance. **Publishes 20-30 new writers/year.** Recently published work by Virgil Suárez, Maureen Sexton, John Gallagher and Amy England. Length: 10,000 words; average length: 3,000 words. Publishes short shorts. Also publishes literary essays, literary criticism, prose poetry. Occasionally comments on rejected mss.

How to Contact Send SASE for return of ms or send a disposable copy of ms. Responds in 3-5 months to mss. Accepts simultaneous, multiple submissions. Sample copy for $10, 8×11 SAE and $1.60 postage. Writer's guidelines for #10 SASE. Reviews fiction.

Payment/Terms Pays 2 contributor's copies; additional back copies $7. Acquires first North American serial rights. Rights revert to author upon publication. Sponsors awards/contests.

Advice "We look for fiction that is experimental, exploratory, devoted to and driven by language—that which succeeds in achieving the *QAE* aesthetic. Please subscribe to our journal and read what is published. We do not publish traditional lined poetry or straightforward conventional stories. We encourage writers to submit after they have gotten acquainted with the *QAE* aesthetic."

$ ◧ ◩ QUARTERLY WEST

University of Utah, 255 S. Central Campus Dr., Dept. of English, LNCO 3500, Salt Lake City UT 84112-9109. (801)581-3938. E-mail: quarterlywest@yahoo.com. Web site: www.utah.edu/quarterlywest. **Contact:** Halina

Duraj and Pam Balluck. Magazine: 7×10; 50 lb. paper; 4-color cover stock. "We publish fiction, poetry, and nonfiction in long and short formats, and will consider experimental as well as traditional works." Semiannual. Estab. 1976. Circ. 1,900.

● *Quarterly West* was awarded First Place for Editorial Content from the American Literary Magazine Awards. Work published in the magazine has been selected for inclusion in the *Pushcart Prize* anthology and *The Best American Short Stories* anthology.

Needs Ethnic/multicultural, experimental, humor/satire, literary, mainstream, novel excerpts, slice-of-life vignettes, translations, short shorts, translations. No detective, science fiction or romance. Receives 300 unsolicited mss/month. Accepts 6-10 mss/issue; 12-20 mss/year. Reads mss between September 1 and May 1 only. "Submissions received between May 2 and August 31 will be returned unread." Publishes ms 6 months after acceptance. **Publishes 3 new writers/year.** Recently published work by Steve Almond, Linh Dinh.

How to Contact Send complete ms. Brief cover letters welcome. Send SASE for reply or return of ms. Responds in 6 months to mss. Accepts simultaneous submissions if notified. Sample copy for $7.50. Writer's guidelines online.

Payment/Terms Pays $15-50, and 2 contributor's copies. Pays on publication for first North American serial rights.

Advice "We publish a special section of short shorts every issue, and we also sponsor a biennial novella contest. We are open to experimental work—potential contributors should read the magazine! We solicit occasionally, but tend more toward the surprises—unsolicited. Don't send more than one story per submission, and wait until you've heard about the first before submitting another."

◐ RAINBOW CURVE

P.O. Box 93206, Las Vegas NV 89193-3206. E-mail: rainbowcurve@sbcglobal.net. Web site: www.rainbowcurve.com. **Contact:** Daphne Young and Julianne Bonnet, editors. Magazine: 5½×8½; 100 pages; 60 lb. paper; coated cover. "*Rainbow Curve* publishes fiction and poetry that dabble at the edge; contemporary work that evokes emotion. Our audience is interested in exploring new worlds of experience and emotion; raw, visceral work is what we look for." Semiannual. Estab. 2002. Circ. 500.

Needs Ethnic/multicultural, experimental, feminist, gay, lesbian, literary. "No genre fiction (romance, western, fantasy, sci-fi)." Receives 60 unsolicited mss/month. Accepts 10-15 mss/issue; 20-30 mss/year. Publishes ms 6 months after acceptance. Agented fiction 1%. **Publishes 80% new writers/year.** Recently published work by Jonathan Barrett, Trent Busch, Rob Carney, Peter Fontaine, Bridget Hoida, and Karen Toloui. Length: 500-10,000 words; average length: 7,500 words. Publishes short shorts. Sometimes comments on rejected mss.

How to Contact Send SASE for return of ms or send a disposable copy of ms and #10 SASE for reply only. Responds in 3 months to mss. Accepts simultaneous submissions. Sample copy for $6. Writer's guidelines for SASE or on Web site.

Payment/Terms Pays 1 contributor's copy; additional copies $5. Acquires one-time rights. Sends galleys to author.

Advice "Unusual rendering of usual subjects and strong narrative voice make a story stand out. Unique glimpses into the lives of others—make it new."

$◐ THE RAMBLER

Rambler Publications, LLC, P.O. Box 5070, Chapel Hill NC 27514-5001. (919)545-9789. Fax: (919)545-0921. E-mail: editor@ramblermagazine.com. Web site: www.ramblermagazine.com. **Contact:** Elizabeth Oliver, editor. Magazine. 8⅛×10⅞, 64 pages, full color. Contains illustrations. Includes photographs. "*The Rambler, Your World, Your Stories*, features in-depth, personal interviews with artists, writers and performers as well as selections of fiction, poetry and essays." Bimonthly. Estab. Jan/Feb 2004. Circ. 4,000. Member IPA.

Needs Literary. Does not want any kind of genre fiction. Receives 150 mss/month. Accepts 1-2 mss/issue; 6-12 mss/year. Manuscript published 6-18 months after acceptance. Agented fiction 5%. **Publishes 15 new writers/year.** Published Marjorie Kemper, Lawrence Naumoff, Christopher Locke, Judith Cox, Laura Cruser, Marianne Gingher. Length: 8,000 words max. Average length: 4,000 words. Publishes short shorts. Average length of short shorts: 300-1,000 words. Also publishes nonfiction, poetry. Sometimes comments on/critiques rejected manuscripts.

How to Contact Send complete ms with cover letter. Include estimated word count, brief bio, list of publications. Prose submissions may also be sent by e-mail to fiction@ramblermagazine.com or nonfiction@ramblermagazine.com. Responds to queries in 2 months. Responds to mss in 4-6 months. Send either SASE (or IRC) for return of ms or disposable copy of ms and #10 SASE for reply only. Considers multiple submissions. Sample copy available for $7. Guidelines available for SASE, on Web site.

Payment and Terms Writers receive $25-$50 flat-rate payment, 1 contributors copy, complimentary one-year subscription to the magazine. Additional copies $6. Pays on publication. Acquires first North American serial rights. Sends galleys to author. Publication is copyrighted.

Advice "We're looking for stories that are well written with well-developed characters, believable dialogue and satisfying plots. A story that moves us in some way, connects us to something larger. Something that stays with us long after the story is finished."

◪ RATTAPALLAX

Rattapallax Press, 532 La Guardia Place, Suite 353, New York NJ 10012. E-mail: info@rattapallax.com. Web site: www.rattapallax.com. **Contact:** Alan Cheuse, fiction editor. Literary magazine: 9×12; 128 pages; bound; some illustrations; photos. "General readership. Our stories must be character driven with strong conflict. All accepted stories are edited by our staff and the writer before publication to ensure a well-crafted and written work." Semiannual. Estab. 1999. Circ. 2,000.

Needs Literary. Receives 15 unsolicited mss/month. Accepts 3 mss/issue; 6 mss/year. Publishes ms 3-6 months after acceptance. Agented fiction 15%. **Publishes 3 new writers/year.** Recently published work by Stuart Dybek, Howard Norman, Molly Giles, Rick Moody. Length: 1,000-10,000 words; average length: 5,000 words. Publishes short shorts. Also publishes poetry. Often comments on rejected mss.

How to Contact Send SASE for return of ms. Responds in 3 months to queries; 3 months to mss. Sample copy for $7.95. Writer's guidelines for SASE or on Web site.

Payment/Terms Pays 2 contributor's copies; additional copies for $7.95. Pays on publication for first North American serial rights. Sends galleys to author.

Advice "Character driven, well crafted, strong conflict."

$◪ THE RAVEN CHRONICLES, A Magazine of Transcultural Art, Literature and the Spoken Word

The Richard Hugo House, The Raven Chronicles, 1634 11th Ave., Seattle WA 98122-2419. (206)364-2045. E-mail: editors@ravenchronicles.org. Web site: www.ravenchronicles.org. **Contact:** Fiction editor. Magazine: 8½×11; 96 pages; 50 lb. book; glossy cover ; b&w illustrations; photos. "*The Raven Chronicles* is designed to promote transcultural art, literature and the spoken word." Triannual. Estab. 1991. Circ. 2,500-5,000.

Needs Ethnic/multicultural, literary, regional, political, cultural essays. "No romance, fantasy, mystery or detective." Receives 300-400 unsolicited mss/month. Accepts 35-60 mss/issue; 105-150 mss/year. Publishes ms 12 months after acceptance. **Publishes 50-100 new writers/year.** Recently published work by David Romtvedt, Sherman Alexie, D.L. Birchfield, Nancy Redwine, Diane Glancy, Greg Hischak , Sharon Hashimoto. Length: 2,500 words (but negotiable); average length: 2,000 words. Publishes short shorts. Also publishes literary essays, literary criticism, poetry. Sometimes comments on rejected mss.

How to Contact Send SASE for return of ms. Does not accept unsolicited submissions by e-mail (except foreign submissions). Responds in 3 months to mss. Does not accept simultaneous submissions. Sample copy for $6.50. Writer's guidelines for #10 SASE.

Payment/Terms Pays $10-40 and 2 contributor's copies; additional copies at half cover cost. Pays on publication for first North American serial rights. Sends galleys to author.

Advice Looks for "clean, direct language, written from the heart , and experimental writing. Read sample copy, or look at *Before Columbus* anthologies and *Greywolf Annual* anthologies."

◪ RED ROCK REVIEW

Community College of Southern Nevada, 3200 E. Cheyenne Ave. N., Las Vegas NV 89030. (702)651-4094. Fax: (702)651-4639. E-mail: richard_logsdon@ccsn.nevada.edu. Web site: www.ccsn.edu/english/redrockreview/index/html. **Contact:** Dr. Richard Logsdon, senior editor. Magazine: 5×8; 125 pages. "We're looking for the very best literature. Stories need to be tightly crafted, strong in character development, built around conflict. Poems need to be tightly crafted, characterised by expert use of language." Semiannual. Estab. 1995. Circ. 250.

Needs Experimental, literary, mainstream. Receives 350 unsolicited mss/month. Accepts 40-60 mss/issue; 80-120 mss/year. Does not read mss during summer. Publishes ms 3-5 after acceptance. **Publishes 5-10 new writers/year.** Recently published work by Charles Harper Webb, Mary Sojourner, Mark Irwin. Length: 1,500-5,000 words; average length: 3,500 words. Publishes short shorts. Also publishes literary essays, literary criticism, poetry. Sometimes comments on rejected mss.

How to Contact Send SASE (or IRC) for return of ms. Responds in 2 weeks to queries; 3 months to mss. Accepts simultaneous, multiple submissions. Sample copy for $5.50. Writer's guidelines for SASE, by e-mail or on Web site.

Payment/Terms Pays 2 contributor's copies. Pays on acceptance for first rights.

◪ RED WHEELBARROW

De Anza College, 21250 Stevens Creek Blvd., Cupertino CA 95014-5702. (408)864-8600. E-mail: splitterrandolph @fhda.edu. Web site: www.deanza.edu/redwheelbarrow. **Contact:** Randolph Splitter, editor-in-chief, or fiction editor. Magazine: 175-225 pages; photos. "Contemporary poetry, fiction, creative nonfiction, b&w graphics, comics and photos." Annual. Estab. 1976 as *Bottomfish*; 2000 as *Red Wheelbarrow*. Circ. 250-500.

Needs "Thoughtful, personal writing. We welcome submissions of all kinds, and we seek to publish a diverse range of styles and voices from around the country and the world." Receives 75 unsolicited mss/month. Accepts 30-50 mss/issue. Reads mss September through February. Submission deadline: January 31; publication date: Spring or Summer. Publishes mss 2-4 months after acceptance. Agented fiction 1%. **Publishes 0-2 new writers/ year.** Recently published work by Sandra Hunter, Susan Lennon, Gary Craig Powell, Mark Terrill, Mika Yamamoto. Length: 4,000 words; average length: 2,500 words. Publishes short shorts. Also publishes poetry.
How to Contact Accepts submissions by e-mail. Responds in 2-4 months to mss. Accepts simultaneous submissions. Sample copy for $8; back issues $2.50. Writer's guidelines online.
Payment/Terms Pays 2 contributor's copies. Acquires first North American serial rights.
Advice "Write freely, rewrite carefully. Resist clichés and stereotypes. We are not affiliated with Red Wheelbarrow Press or any similarly named publication."

☑ REDIVIDER

120 Boylston St., Emerson College, Boston MA 02116. E-mail: redivider@emerson.edu. Web site: www.redividerjournal.org. **Contact:** Prose Editor. Editors change each year. Magazine: $5^1/_2 \times 8^1/_2$; 160 pages; 60 lb. paper. *Redivider*, a journal of literature and art, is published twice a year by students in the graduate writing, literature and publishing department of Emerson College. Biannual. Estab. 1986. Circ. 1000.
Needs Literary. Receives 100 unsolicited mss/month. Accepts 6-8 mss/issue; 10-12 mss/year. Publishes ms 3-6 months after acceptance. Publishes short shorts. Also publishes poetry. Sometimes comments on rejected mss.
How to Contact Send disposable copy of ms. Accepts simultaneous submissions with notification. Sample copy for $6 with a #10 SASE. Writer's guidelines for SASE.
Payment/Terms Pays 2 contributor's copies; additional copies $6. Pays on publication for one-time rights. Sponsors awards/contests.

☑ REFLECTIONS LITERARY JOURNAL

Piedmont Community College, P.O. Box 1197, Roxboro NC 27573. (336)599-1181. E-mail: reflect@piedmontcc.edu. **Contact:** Ernest Avery, editor. Magazine: 100-150 pages. Annual. Estab. 1999. Circ. 250.
Needs Literary. "Accepts mss from NC authors only (residents or natives) and from authors we've previously published. If time and space permit, we'll consider submissions from Southeastern U.S. authors. "Receives 30 unsolicited mss/month. Accepts 25-30 mss/issue. Publishes mss 6-10 months after acceptance. **Publishes 3-5 new writers/year.** Recently published work by Maureen Sherbondy, Dainiel Green, Betty Moffett, Lian Gouw, Sejal Badani Ravani, Donna Conrad. Max Length: 4,000 words; average length: 2,500 words. Publishes short shorts. Also publishes poetry and essays.
How to Contact Send SASE for return of ms or #10 SASE for reply only. Sample copy for $3. Writer's guidelines for SASE or by e-mail.
Payment/Terms Pays 1 contributor's copy; additional copies $6 pre-publication; $7 post-publication. Acquires first North American serial rights. Sponsors awards/contests.
Advice "We look for good writing with a flair, which captivates an educated lay audience. Don't take rejection letters personally. We turn away many submissions simply because we don't have room for everything we like. For that reason, we're more likely to accept shorter well-written stories than longer stories of the same quality. Also, stories containing profanity that doesn't contribute to the plot, structure or intended tone are rejected immediately."

$ ☑ THE REJECTED QUARTERLY, A Journal of Quality Literature Rejected at Least Five Times

P.O. Box 1351, Cobb CA 95426. E-mail: bplankton@juno.com. **Contact:** Daniel Weiss, Jeff Ludecke, fiction editors. Magazine: $8^1/_2 \times 11$; 36-44 pages; 60 lb. paper; 10 pt. coated cover stock; illustrations. "We want the best literature possible, regardless of genre. We do, however, have a bias toward the unusual and toward speculative fiction. We aim for a literate, educated audience. *The Rejected Quarterly* believes in publishing the highest quality rejected fiction and other writing that doesn't fit anywhere else. We strive to be different, but will go for quality every time, whether conventional or not." Semiannual. Estab. 1998.
Needs Experimental, fantasy, historical, humor/satire, literary, mainstream, mystery/suspense, romance (futuristic/time travel only), science fiction (soft/sociological), sports. Accepts poetry about being rejected. Receives 30 unsolicited mss/month. Accepts 3-6 mss/issue; 8-12 mss/year. Publishes ms 1-12 months after acceptance. **Publishes 2- 4 new writers/year.** Recently published work by Matthew Babcock, RC Cooper , Stephen Jones. Length: 8,000 words. Publishes short shorts (literature related), literary criticism, rejection-related poetry. Often comments on rejected mss.
How to Contact Send SASE for reply, return of ms or send a disposable copy of ms. Responds in 2 -4 weeks to queries; 1-9 months to mss. Accepts reprint submissions. Sample copy for $6 (IRCs for foreign requests). Reviews fiction.

Payment/Terms Pays $10 and 1 contributor's copy; additional copies $5. Pays on acceptance for first rights.
Advice "We are looking for high-quality writing that tells a story or expresses a coherent idea. We want unique stories, original viewpoints and unusual slants. We are getting far too many inappropriate submissions. Please be familiar with the magazine. Be sure to include your rejection slips! Send out quality rather than quantity."

⚫ ☑ RIVER STYX

Big River Association, 634 N. Grand Blvd., 12th Floor, St. Louis MO 63103. (314)533-4541. Fax: (314)533-3345. Web site: www.riverstyx.org. **Contact:** Richard Newman, editor. Magazine: 6×9; 100 pages; color card cover; perfect-bound; b&w visual art. "*River Styx* publishes the highest quality fiction, poetry, interviews, essays, and visual art. We are an internationally distributed multicultural literary magazine." Mss read May-November. Estab. 1975.

• *River Styx* has had stories appear in *New Stories from the South* and has been included in *Pushcart* anthologies.

Needs Ethnic/multicultural, experimental, feminist, gay, lesbian, literary, mainstream, novel excerpts, translations, short stories, literary. "No genre fiction, less thinly veiled autobiography." Receives 350 unsolicited mss/month. Accepts 2-6 mss/issue; 6-12 mss/year. Reads only May through November. Publishes ms 1 year after acceptance. **Publishes 20 new writers/year.** Recently published work by Julianna Baggott, Philip Graham, Katherine Min, Richard Burgin, Nancy Zafris, and Eric Shade. Publishes short shorts. Also publishes poetry. Sometimes comments on rejected mss.
How to Contact Send complete ms. SASE required. Responds in 4 months to mss. Accepts simultaneous submissions "if a note is enclosed with your work and if we are notified immediately upon acceptance elsewhere." Sample copy for $8. Writer's guidelines online.
Payment/Terms Pays 2 contributor copies, plus 1-year subscription; $8/page if funds are available. Pays on publication for first North American serial, one-time rights.
Advice "We want high-powered stories with well-developed characters. We like strong plots, usually with at least three memorable scenes, and a subplot often helps. No thin, flimsy fiction with merely serviceable language. Short stories shouldn't be any different than poetry—every single word should count. One could argue every word counts more since we're being asked to read 10 to 30 pages."

⚫ RIVERWIND

Hocking College, 3301 Hocking Parkway, Nelsonville OH 45764. (740)753-3591. E-mail: williams_k@hocking.edu. **Contact:** Kristine Williams, co-editor. Magazine: 7×7; 125-150 pages; 60 lb. offset paper; illustrations; photos. *Riverwind* is an established magazine that prints fiction, poetry, black and white photos and prints, drawings, creative nonfiction, book reviews and plays. Special consideration is given to writers from the Appalachian region. Annual. Estab. 1976. Circ. 200-400.
Needs Adventure, ethnic/multicultural (Appalachian), humor/satire, literary, mainstream, regional. DOES NOT WANT erotica, fantasy, horror, experimental, religious, children's/juvenile. Receives 25 unsolicited mss/month. Does not read mss June-September. Publishes ms 6-9 months after acceptance. **Publishes many new writers/year.** Recently published work by Gerald Wheeler, Wendy McVicker, Roy Bentley, Perry A. White, Tom Montag, Beau Beadreaux. Length: 500-2,500 words; average length: 1,750 words. Publishes short shorts. Also publishes literary essays, literary criticism, poetry. Rarely comments on rejected mss.
How to Contact Send complete ms. Accepts submissions by e-mail, disk. Send disposable copy of ms and #10 SASE for reply only. Responds in 4 weeks to queries; 8-16 weeks to mss. Accepts simultaneous, multiple submissions. Sample copy for $5. Writer's guidelines for #10 SASE or by e-mail.
Payment/Terms Pays 2 contributor's copies. Pays on publication for first North American serial rights.
Advice "Avoid stereotypical plots and characters. We tend to favor realism but not sentimentality."

$⚫ ROANOKE REVIEW

Roanoke College, 221 College Lane, Salem VA 24153-3794. (540)375-2380. E-mail: review@roanoke.edu. **Contact:** Paul Hanstedt, editor. Magazine: 6×9; 200 pages; 60 lb. paper; 70 lb. cover. "We're looking for fresh, thoughtful material that will appeal to a broader as well as literary audience. Humor encouraged." Annual. Estab. 1967. Circ. 500.
Needs Feminist, gay, humor/satire, lesbian, literary, mainstream, regional. No pornography, science fiction or horror. Receives 150 unsolicited mss/month. Accepts 5-10 mss/year. Does not read mss February 1-September 1. Publishes ms 6 months after acceptance. **Publishes 1-5 new writers/year.** Recently published work by Robert Morgan, Lucy Ferriss, Francine Witte. Length: 1,000-6,000 words; average length: 1,500 words. Publishes short shorts. Also publishes poetry. Sometimes comments on rejected mss.
How to Contact Send SASE for return of ms or send a disposable copy of ms and #10 SASE for reply only. Responds in 1 month to queries; 6 months to mss. Sample copy for 8×11 SAE with $2 postage. Writer's guidelines for SASE.

Payment/Terms Pays $10-50/story (when budget allows) and 2 contributor's copies; additional copies $5. Pays on publication for one-time rights.

Advice "Pay attention to sentence-level writing—verbs, metaphors, concrete images. Don't forget, though, that plot and character keep us reading. We're looking for stuff that breaks the MFA story style."

Ⓝ Ⓓ Ⓒ ROCK & SLING: A JOURNAL OF LITERATURE, ART AND FAITH

7920 S. Parway Ln., Cheney WA 99004. (509)624-2678. E-mail: editors@rock@sling.org. Web site: http://rockandsling.org. **Contact:** Kris Christensen, editor. Literary magazine/journal: 6×9, 152 pages, 70# Anthem Matte 488 paper, 10 PT. C1S cover. Contains illustrations & photographs. "As writers who experience life as a spiritual journey, the editors of *Rock & Sling* have found themselves caught between the narrow religious market, which is driven more by theology than literary quality, and the literary world which is often dismissive of faith. Very few publications of fine literary quality welcome writing concerned with the travel of the spirit. Our vision is to create a hallmark of quality writing while being unafraid of broad differences in experience, to create a forum for writers and artists to search both the depths and the near misses of spirituality. In order to bring focus within the vast plains of spirituality, *Rock & Sling* will be limited to writing that nudges up against Christian faith. *Rock & Sling* is not interested in evangelizing. We don't want preachy tales, retelling of Bible stories, or the usual didacticism and platitudes. While advocating a critical mind, *Rock & Sling* wants writing that brushes against Christianity, both celebratory and questioning, historical and personal, as well as reportage. *Rock & Sling* is looking for accomplished writers; pieces will be selected based on literary quality and complexity of thought and emotion. An accepted *Rock & Sling* submission may not even make explicit references to Christianity, but it will maintain a universal spiritual curiosity." Semiannual. Estab. 2004. Circ. 200. Member CLMP.

Needs Experimental, literary. Does not want children's/juvenile, New Age, supernatural/occult, glitz, comics/graphic novels, erotica. Receives 15 mss/month. Accepts 1-5 mss/issue; 2-10 mss/year. Manuscript published 5 months after acceptance. Published Susanna Childress, Christopher Howell, Sydney Lea, Robert Cording, and Luci Shaw. Length: 5,000 words (max). Average length: 2,500-4,000 words. Publishes short shorts. Average length of short shorts: 150 words. Also publishes literary essays, literary criticism, poetry. Sometimes comments on/critiques rejected mss.

How to Contact Send complete ms with cover letter. Accepts submissions on disk. Include estimated word count, brief bio, list of publications. Responds to queries in 3 weeks. Responds to mss in 5 months. Send disposable copy of ms and #10 SASE for reply only. Considers simultaneous submissions. Sample copy available for $10. Guidelines available for SASE, via e-mail, on Web site.

Payment and Terms Writers receive 2 contributor's copies. Additional copies $7. Pays on publication. Acquires first North American serial rights. Sends galleys to author. Publication is copyrighted.

Advice "Not predictable, scene and dialogue excellence. Read the guidelines. No typos."

Ⓓ THE ROCKFORD REVIEW

The Rockford Writers Guild, P.O. Box 858, Rockford IL 61105. E-mail: daveconnieross@aol.com. Web site: http://writersguild1.tripod.com. **Contact:** David Ross, editor. Magazine: 100 pages; perfect bound; color illustrations; b&w photos. "We look for prose and poetry with a fresh approach to old themes or new insights into the human condition." Semiannual. Estab. 1971. Circ. 600.

Needs Ethnic/multicultural, experimental, fantasy, humor/satire, literary, regional, science fiction (hard science, soft/sociological). "No graphic sex, translations or overly academic work." Recently published work by James Bellarosa, Sean Michael Rice, John P. Kristofco, L.S. Sedishiro. Also publishes literary essays.

How to Contact Include SASE. Responds in 2 months to mss. Accepts simultaneous, multiple submissions. Sample copy for $9. Writer's guidelines for SASE or online.

Payment/Terms Pays contributor's copies. "Two $25 editor's choice cash prizes per issue." Acquires first North American serial rights.

Advice "We're wide open to new and established writers alike—particularly short satire."

Ⓓ Ⓥ SANSKRIT, Literary Arts Magazine of UNC Charlotte

University of North Carolina at Charlotte, 168 Conf. University Center, 9201 University City Blvd., Charlotte NC 28223-0001. (704)687-2326. Fax: (704)687-3394. E-mail: sanskrit@email.uncc.edu. Web site: www.sanskritlam.com. **Contact:** Sanskrit editor. "*Sanskrit* is an award-winning magazine produced with two goals in mind: service to the student body, and promotion of unpublished and beginning artists. Our intended audience is the literary/arts community of UNCC, Charlotte, other schools and contributors, and specifically individuals who might never have read a literary magazine before." Annual. Estab. 1968.

• *Sanskrit* has received the Pacemaker, Associated College Press, Gold Crown and Columbia Scholastic Press Award.

Needs "We are looking for short fiction or poetry that meets our guidelines." Receives 50 unsolicited mss/month. Accepts 2-3 mss/issue.

How to Contact Send complete ms. Accepts submissions by e-mail (sanskrit@email.uncc.edu) or postal mail. Include complete manuscript with cover letter. Accepts simultaneous, multiple submissions. Sample copy for $10. Writer's guidelines for #10 SASE or online.

Payment/Terms Pays contributor's copy. Acquires one-time rights.

☑ SANTA MONICA REVIEW

Santa Monica College, 1900 Pico Blvd., Santa Monica CA 90405. (310)434-4242. **Contact:** Andrew Tonkovich, editor. Magazine: 250 pages. ''The editors are committed to fostering new talent as well as presenting new work by established writers. There is also a special emphasis on presenting and promoting writers who make their home in Southern California.'' Estab. 1989. Circ. 4,000.

Needs Experimental, literary, memoirs. ''No crime and detective, mysogyny, footnotes, TV, dog stories. We want more self-conscious, smart, political, humorous, digressive, meta-fiction.'' Receives 250 unsolicited mss/ month. Accepts 10 mss/issue; 20 mss/year. Agented fiction 10%. **Publishes 5 new writers/year.** Recently published work by Ed Skoog, Trini Dalton, Judith Grossman, John Peterson. Also publishes literary essays.

How to Contact Send complete ms. Send disposable copy of ms. Responds in 3 months to mss. Accepts simultaneous, multiple submissions. Sample copy for $7.

Payment/Terms Pays 5 contributor's copies. Acquires first North American serial rights. Sends galleys to author.

☑ THE SARANAC REVIEW

Suny Plattsburgh, Dept. of English, Champlain Valley Hall, Plattsburgh NY 12901. (518)564-5151. Fax: (518)564-2140. E-mail: saranacreview@plattsburgh.edu. Web site: http://research.plattsburgh.edu/saranacreview/. **Contact:** Fiction editor. Magazine: $5^1/_2 \times 8^1/_2$; 180-200 pages; 80 lb. cover/70 lb. paper; glossy cover stock; illustrations; photos. ''*The Saranac Review* is committed to dissolving boundaries of all kinds, seeking to publish a diverse array of emerging and established writers from Canada and the U.S. *The Saranac Review* aims to be a textual clearing in which a space is opened for cross-pollination between American and Canadian writers. In this way the magazine reflects the expansive bright spirit of the etymology of it's name, Saranac, meaning 'cluster of stars.'' Annual. Estab. 2004.

Needs Ethnic/multicultural, historical, literary. Publishes ms 8 months after acceptance. Publishes flash fiction. Also publishes poetry and literary/creative nonfiction. Sometimes comments on rejected mss.

How to Contact Send complete ms. Send SASE (or IRC) for return of ms or send disposable copy of the ms and #10 SASE for reply only. Responds in 4 months to mss. Accepts simultaneous submissions. Sample copy for $6. Writer's guidelines online, or by e-mail. ''Please send one story at a time.'' Maximum length: 7,000 words.

Payment/Terms Pays 2 contributor's copies; discount on extras and free subscription for following issue. Pays on publication for first North American serial, first rights.

Advice ''We publish serious, generous fiction.''

☑ THE SEATTLE REVIEW

Box 354330, University of Washington, Seattle WA 98195. (206)543-2302. E-mail: seaview@u.washington.edu. Web site: www.seattlereview.org. **Contact:** Andrew Feld, editor-in-chief. Magazine: 6×9; 150 pages; illustrations; photos. ''Includes fiction, nonfiction, poetry and one interview per issue with an established writer.'' Semiannual. Estab. 1978. Circ. 1,000.

Needs Literary. Nothing in ''bad taste (porn, racist, etc.).'' Receives 200 unsolicited mss/month. Accepts 2-4 mss/issue; 4-8 mss/year. Does not read mss May 31-October 1. Publishes ms $1-2^1/_2$ years after acceptance. **Publishes 3-4 new writers/year.** Recently published work by Rick Bass, Lauren Whitehurst, Martha Hurwitz. Length: 5,500 words; average length: 3,000 words.

How to Contact Send complete ms. Send SASE (or IRC) for return of ms or send disposable copy of ms and #10 SASE for reply only. Responds in 4-6 months to mss. No simultaneous submissions, accepts multiple submissions. Sample copy for $8. Writer's guidelines for #10 SASE, online or by e-mail.

Payment/Terms Pays 2 contributor's copies. Acquires first North American serial rights.

Advice ''Know what we publish: no genre fiction; look at our magazine and decide if your work might be appreciated.''

$ THE SEWANEE REVIEW

University of the South, 735 University Ave., Sewanee TN 37383-1000. (931)598-1246. Web site: www.sewanee. edu/sewanee-review. **Contact:** George Core. ''A literary quarterly, publishing original fiction, poetry, essays on literary and related subjects, and book reviews for well-educated readers who appreciate good American and English literature.'' Quarterly. Estab. 1892. Circ. 2,000.

Needs Literary, contemporary. No erotica, science fiction, fantasy or excessively violent or profane material.

How to Contact Responds in 6 weeks to mss. Sample copy for $8.50. Writer's guidelines online.

Payment/Terms Pays $10-12/printed page; 2 contributor copies. Pays on publication for first North American serial, second serial (reprint) rights.

$ SHENANDOAH, The Washington and Lee University Review

Washington and Lee University, Mattingly House, 2 Lee Avenue, Washington and Lee University, Lexington VA 24450-2116. (540)458-8765. E-mail: shenandoah@wlu.edu. Web site: http://shenandoah.wlu.edu. Triannual. Estab. 1950. Circ. 2,000.

Needs Mainstream, novel excerpts. No sloppy, hasty, slight fiction. Publishes ms 10 months after acceptance.

How to Contact Send complete ms. Responds in 2 months to mss. Sample copy for $10. Writer's guidelines online.

Payment/Terms Pays $25/page. Pays on publication for first North American serial, one-time rights.

SHORT STUFF, For Grown-ups

Bowman Publications, 712 W. 10th St., Loveland CO 80537. (970)669-9139. "We are perhaps an enigma in that we publish only clean stories in any genre. We'll tackle any subject, but don't allow obscene language or pornographic description. Our magazine is for grown-ups, *not* X-rated 'adult' fare." Bimonthly. Estab. 1989. Circ. 10,400.

Needs Adventure, historical, humor/satire, mainstream, mystery/suspense, romance, science fiction (seldom), western. "We want to see more humor—not essay format—real stories with humor; 1,000-word mysteries, historical pieces. The 1,000-word pieces have the best chance of publication. We are no longer accepting essays for publication in the magazine. In particular, we are absolutely, positively not accepting any Erma Bombeck-like essays, e.g. essays proclaiming how wonderful hubby is or bemoaning how your children are sticking pencils up their noses." No erotica; nothing morbid or pornographic. Issues are Valentines (February/March); Easter (April/May); Mom's and Dad's (June/July); Americana (August/September); Halloween (October/November); and Holiday (December/January). Receives 500 unsolicited mss/month. Accepts 9-12 mss/issue; 76 mss/year. **Publishes 90% new writers/year.** Recently published work by Bill Hallstead, Dede Hammond, Skye Gibbons.

How to Contact Send complete ms. Responds in 6 months to mss. Sample copy for $1.50 and 9×12 SAE with 5 first-class stamps. Writer's guidelines for #10 SASE.

Payment/Terms Payment varies. Payment and contract upon publication. Acquires first North American serial rights.

Advice "We seek a potpourri of subjects each issue. A new slant, a different approach, fresh viewpoints—all of these excite us. We don't like gore, salacious humor or perverted tales. Prefer third person, past tense. Be sure it is a story with a beginning, middle and end. It must have dialogue. Many beginners do not know an essay from a short story. We'd like to see more young (25 and over) humor; 'clean' humor is hard to come by. Length is a big factor. Writers who can tell a good story in a thousand words are true artists and their work is highly prized by our readers. Stick to the guidelines. We get manuscripts of up to 10,000 words because the story is 'unique and deserving.' We don't even read these. Too many writers fail to include SASE. These submissions are not considered."

SLEEPINGFISH

Calamari Press. E-mail: white@sleepingfish.net. Web site: www.sleepingfish.net. **Contact:** Derek White, editor. Literary magazine/journal: 6×8, 160 pages, 60 lb. vellum paper, card stock cover. Contains illustrations. Includes photographs. "*Sleepingfish* publishes an eclectic mix of flash fiction, prose and visual poetry, experimental texts, text/image and art." Published every 9 months. Estab. 2003. Circ. 500.

Needs Adventure, comics/graphic novels, ethnic/multicultural, experimental, literary. Does not want to see any fiction or writing that fits into a genre or that is written for any other reason except for the sake of art. Receives 250 mss/month. Accepts 25 mss/issue; 25 mss/year. Manuscript published less than 3 months after acceptance. **Publishes 2-3 new writers/year.** Published Norman Lock, Peter Markus, Kevin Sampsell, Christian Peet, Brian Evenson, Thurston Moore, Kim Chinquee, and Danielle Dutton. Length: 1 word (min)-2,500 words (max). Average length: 500 words. Publishes short shorts. Average length of short shorts: 500 words. Rarely comments on/critiques rejected mss.

How to Contact Send complete ms with cover letter. Only accepts submissions by e-mail. Include brief bio. Responds to queries in 2 weeks. Responds to mss in 2 months. Send SASE (or IRC) for return of ms. Considers simultaneous submissions, multiple submissions. Guidelines available on Web site.

Payment and Terms Writers receive 1 contributor copy. Additional copies half price. Pays on publication. Acquires first rights. Sends galleys to author. Publication is copyrighted.

Advice "Write or create what's true to yourself and find a publication where you think your work honestly fits in."

$✉ SNOWY EGRET

The Fair Press, P.O. Box 29, Terre Haute IN 47808. **Contact:** Editors. Magazine: 8½×11; 60 pages; text paper; heavier cover; illustrations. "We publish works which celebrate the abundance and beauty of nature and examine the variety of ways in which human beings interact with landscapes and living things. Nature writing from literary, artistic, psychological, philosophical and historical perspectives." Semiannual. Estab. 1922. Circ. 400.

Needs "No genre fiction, e.g., horror, western, romance, etc." Receives 25 unsolicited mss/month. Accepts up to 6 mss/issue; up to 12 mss/year. Publishes ms 6 months after acceptance. **Publishes 20 new writers/year.** Recently published work by James Hinton, Ron Gielgun, Tom Noyes, Alice Cross, Maeve Mullin Ellis. Length: 500-10,000 words; average length: 1,000-3,000 words. Publishes short shorts. Sometimes comments on rejected mss.

How to Contact Send complete ms with SASE. Cover letter optional: do not query. Responds in 2 months to mss. Accepts simultaneous submissions if noted. Sample copy for 9×12 SASE and $8. Writer's guidelines for #10 SASE.

Payment/Terms Pays $2/page plus 2 contributor's copies. Pays on publication for first North American serial, one-time anthology rights, or reprint rights. Sends galleys to author.

Advice Looks for "honest, freshly detailed pieces with plenty of description and/or dialogue which will allow the reader to identify with the characters and step into the setting; fiction in which nature affects character development and the outcome of the story."

✉ ◎ SO TO SPEAK, A Feminist Journal of Language and Art

George Mason University, 4400 University Dr., MS 2D6, Fairfax VA 22030. (703)993-3625. E-mail: sts@gmu.edu. Web site: www.gmu.edu/org/sts. **Contact:** Courtney Campbell; Amy Amoroso, fiction editor. Magazine: 5½×8½; approximately 100 pages. "We are a feminist journal of language and art." Semiannual. Estab. 1993. Circ. 1,000.

Needs Ethnic/multicultural, experimental, feminist, lesbian, literary, mainstream, regional, translations. "No science fiction, mystery, genre romance." Receives 100 unsolicited mss/month. Accepts 3-5 mss/issue; 6-10 mss/year. Publishes ms 6 months after acceptance. **Publishes 5 new writers/year.** Length: For fiction, up to 5,000 words; for poetry, 3-5 pages per submission; average length: 4,000 words. Publishes short shorts. Also publishes literary essays, literary criticism, poetry.

How to Contact Send complete ms. Include bio (50 words maximum) and SASE for return of ms or send a disposable copy of ms. Responds in 6 months to mss. Accepts simultaneous submissions. Sample copy for $7. Reviews fiction.

Payment/Terms Pays contributor copies. Acquires first North American serial rights. Sponsors awards/contests.

Advice "We do not read between March 15 and August 15. Every writer has something they do exceptionally well; do that and it will shine through in the work. We look for quality prose with a definite appeal to a feminist audience. We are trying to move away from strict genre lines. We want high quality fiction, nonfiction, poetry, art, innovative and risk-taking work."

✉ SONORA REVIEW

University of Arizona's Creative Writing MFA Program, University of Arizona, Dept. of English, Tucson AZ 85721. E-mail: sonora@email.arizona.edu. Web site: www.coh.arizona.edu/sonora. **Contact:** Patrick Griffis, Amy Knight, editors. Magazine: 6×9; approx. 100 pages; photos. "We look for the highest quality poetry, fiction, and nonfiction, with an emphasis on emerging writers. Our magazine has a long-standing tradition of publishing the best new literature and writers. Check out our Web site for a sample of what we publish and our submission guidelines, or write us for a sample back issue." Semiannual. Estab. 1980. Circ. 500.

Needs Ethnic/multicultural, experimental, literary, mainstream, novel excerpts. Receives 200 unsolicited mss/month. Accepts 2-3 mss/issue; 6-8 mss/year. Does not read in the summer (June-August). Publishes ms 3-4 months after acceptance. **Publishes 1-3 new writers/year.** Recently published work by Antonya Nelson, Steve Almond. Also publishes literary essays, literary criticism, poetry. Sometimes comments on rejected mss.

How to Contact Send complete ms. Send disposable copy of the ms and #10 SASE for reply only. Responds in 2-5 weeks to queries; 3 months to mss. Accepts simultaneous, multiple submissions. Sample copy for $6. Writer's guidelines online. Reviews fiction.

Payment/Terms Pays 2 contributor's copies; additional copies for $4. Pays on publication for first North American serial, one-time, electronic rights.

Advice "Send us your best stuff."

✉ SOUTH CAROLINA REVIEW

611 Strode Tower Box 340522, Clemson University, Clemson SC 29634-0522. (864)656-5399. Fax: (864)656-1345. E-mail: cwayne@clemson.edu. Web site: www.clemson.edu/caah/cedp. **Contact:** Wayne Chapman, edi-

tor. Magazine: 6×9; 200 pages; 60 lb. cream white vellum paper; 65 lb. cream white vellum cover stock. Semiannual. Estab. 1967. Circ. 500.

Needs Literary, mainstream, poetry, essays, reviews. Does not read mss June-August or December. Receives 50-60 unsolicited mss/month. Recently published work by Ronald Frame, Dennis McFadden, Dulane Upshaw Ponder, and Stephen Jones. Rarely comments on rejected mss.

How to Contact Send complete ms. Requires text on disk upon acceptance in WordPerfect or Microsoft Word in PC format. Responds in 2 months to mss. Sample copy for $15 includes postage. Reviews fiction.

Payment/Terms Pays in contributor's copies.

◨ ◎ SOUTHERN HUMANITIES REVIEW

Auburn University, 9088 Haley Center, Auburn University AL 36849. Web site: www.auburn.edu/english/shr/home.htm. **Contact:** Fiction Editor. Magazine: 6×9; 100 pages; 60 lb neutral pH, natural paper; 65 lb. neutral pH medium coated cover stock; occasional illustration; photos. "We publish essays, poetry, fiction and reviews. Our fiction has ranged from very traditional in form and content to very experimental. Literate, college-educated audience. We hope they read our journal for both enlightenment and pleasure." Quarterly. Estab. 1967. Circ. 800.

Needs Feminist, humor/satire, regional. Slower reading time in summer. Receives 25 unsolicited mss/month. Accepts 1-2 mss/issue; 4-6 mss/year. Recently published work by Chris Arthur, Andrea Deagon, Sheryl St. Germain, Patricia Foster, Janette Turner Hospital, Paula Köhlmeier, David Wagner. Also publishes literary essays, literary criticism, poetry. Sometimes comments on rejected mss.

How to Contact Send complete ms, cover letter with an explanation of the topic chosen—"special, certain book, etc., a little about the author if he/she has never submitted." No e-mail submissions. No simultaneous submissions. Responds in 3 months to mss.

Payment/Terms Pays in contributor copies. Rights revert to author on publication.

Advice "Send us the ms with SASE. If we like it, we'll take it or we'll recommend changes. If we don't like it, we'll send it back as promptly as possible. Read the journal. Send typewritten, clean copy, carefully proofread. We also award the annual Hoepfner Prize of $100 for the best published essay or short story of the year. Let someone whose opinion you respect read your story and give you an honest appraisal. Rewrite, if necessary, to get the most from your story."

$ ◨ ◩ THE SOUTHERN REVIEW

Old President's House, Louisiana State University, Baton Rouge LA 70803. (225)578-5108. Fax: (225)578-5098. E-mail: southernreview@lsu.edu. Web site: www.lsu.edu/thesouthernreview. **Contact:** Bret Lott, editor. Magazine: 6¼×10; 240 pages; 50 lb. Glatfelter paper; 65 lb. #1 grade cover stock. Quarterly. Estab. 1935. Circ. 3,000.

● Several stories published in *The Southern Review* were *Pushcart Prize* selections.

Needs Literary. "We desire fiction that crystalizes immediately the author's voice and vision." Receives approximately 300 unsolicited mss/month. Accepts 6-7 mss/issue. Reading period: September-May. Publishes ms 6 months after acceptance. Agented fiction 1%. **Publishes 10-12 new writers/year.** Recently published work by Jill McCorkle, James Lee Burke, Robin Black, James Fowler. Also publishes literary essays, literary criticism, poetry.

How to Contact Send complete ms with cover letter and SASE. No queries. "Prefer brief letters giving information on author concerning where he/she has been published before, biographical info and what he/she is doing now." Responds in 2 months to mss. Sample copy for $8. Writer's guidelines online. Reviews fiction, poetry.

Payment/Terms Pays $30/page. Pays on publication for first North American serial rights. Sends galleys to author via e-mail. Sponsors awards/contests.

Advice "Careful attention to craftsmanship and technique combined with a compelling sense of the importance of story will always make us pay attention."

◨ SOUTHWEST REVIEW

P.O. Box 750374, Dallas TX 75275-0374. (214)768-1037. Fax: (214)768-1408. E-mail: swr@mail.smu.edu. Web site: www.southwestreview.org. **Contact:** Jennifer Cranfill, managing editor. Magazine: 6×9; 144 pages. "The majority of our readers are college-educated adults who wish to stay abreast of the latest and best in contemporary fiction, poetry, and essays in all but the most specialized disciplines." Quarterly. Estab. 1915. Circ. 1,600.

Needs "High literary quality; no specific requirements as to subject matter, but cannot use sentimental, religious, western, poor science fiction, pornographic, true confession, mystery, juvenile or serialized or condensed novels." Receives 200 unsolicited mss/month. Publishes ms 6-12 months after acceptance. Recently published work by Tracy Daugherty, Millicent Dillon, Mark Jacobs. Also publishes literary essays, poetry. Occasionally comments on rejected mss.

How to Contact Mail complete ms. Responds in 6 months to mss. Accepts multiple submissions. Sample copy for $6. Writer's guidelines for #10 SASE or on Web site.

Payment/Terms Pays negotiable rate and 3 contributor copies. Acquires first North American serial rights. Sends galleys to author.

Advice "We have become less regional. A lot of time would be saved for us and for the writer if he or she looked at a copy of review before submitting. We like to receive a cover letter because it is some reassurance that the author has taken the time to check a current directory for the editor's name. When there isn't a cover letter, we wonder whether the same story is on 20 other desks around the country."

SOUTHWESTERN AMERICAN LITERATURE

Center for the Study of the Southwest, Texas State University-San Marcos, 601 University Drive, San Marcos TX 78666. (512)245-2224. Fax: (512)245-7462. E-mail: mb13@txstate.edu. Web site: http://swrhc.txstate.edu/cssw/. **Contact:** Twister Marquiss, assistant editor; Mark Busby, co-editor; Dick Maurice Heaberlin, co-editor. Magazine: 6×9; 125 pages; 80 lb. cover stock. "We publish fiction, nonfiction, poetry, literary criticism and book reviews. Generally speaking, we want material covering the Greater Southwest, or material written by Southwest writers." Biannual. Estab. 1971. Circ. 300.

Needs Ethnic/multicultural, literary, mainstream, regional. "No science fiction or romance." Receives 10-15 unsolicited mss/month. Accepts 1-2 mss/issue; 4-5 mss/year. Publishes ms 6 months after acceptance. **Publishes 1-2 new writers/year.** Recently published work by Greg Garrett, Andrew Geyer, Robert Flynn, Walt McDonald, Carol Hamilton, Larry D. Thomas. Length: 6,250 words; average length: 4,000 words. Also publishes literary essays, literary criticism, poetry. Sometimes comments on rejected mss.

How to Contact Send complete ms. Include cover letter, estimated word count, 2-5 line bio and list of publications. Does not accept e-mail submissions. Responds in 3-6 months to mss. Sample copy for $8. Writer's guidelines free.

Payment/Terms Pays 2 contributor copies. Acquires first rights.

Advice "We look for crisp language, an interesting approach to material; a regional approach is desired but not required. Read widely, write often, revise carefully. We are looking for stories that probe the relationship between the tradition of Southwestern American literature and the writer's own imagination in creative ways. We seek stories that move beyond stereotype and approach the larger defining elements and also ones that, as William Faulkner noted in his Nobel Prize acceptance speech, treat subjects central to good literature—the old verities of the human heart, such as honor and courage and pity and suffering, fear and humor, love and sorrow."

SPEAK UP

Speak Up Press, P.O. Box 100506, Denver CO 80250. (303)715-0837. Fax: (303)715-0793. Web site: www.speakuppresss.org. **Contact:** Senior editor. Magazine: 5½×8½; 128 pages; 55 lb. Glat. Supple Opaque Recycled Natural paper; 12 CIS cover; illustrations; photos. "*Speak Up* features the original fiction, nonfiction, poetry, plays, photography and artwork of young people 13-19 years old. *Speak Up* provides a place for teens to be creative, honest and expressive in an uncensored environment." Annual. Estab. 1999. Circ. 2,900.

Needs Teen writers. Receives 30 unsolicited mss/month. Accepts 30 mss/issue; 30 mss/year. Publishes ms 3-12 months after acceptance. **Publishes 20 new writers/year.** Length: 5,000 words; average length: 500 words. Publishes short shorts. Also publishes literary essays, poetry.

How to Contact Send complete ms. Accepts submissions by e-mail, fax. Responds in 3 months to queries; 3 months to mss. Accepts simultaneous, multiple submissions and reprints. Sample copy free. Please include required submission forms. See Web site for details.

Payment/Terms Pays 2 contributor copies. Acquires first North American serial, one-time rights.

STAND MAGAZINE

North American Office: Department of English, VCU, Richmond VA 23284-2005. (804)828-1331. E-mail: dlatane @vcu.edu. Web site: www.standmagazine.org. "*Stand Magazine* is concerned with what happens when cultures and literatures meet, with translation in its many guises, with the mechanics of language, with the processes by which the policy receives or disables its cultural makers. *Stand* promotes debate of issues that are of radical concern to the intellectual community worldwide." Quarterly. Estab. 1952 in Leeds UK. Circ. 3,000 worldwide.

Needs "No genre fiction." Publishes ms 10 months after acceptance.

How to Contact Send complete ms. Responds in 6 weeks to queries; 3 months to mss. Sample copy for $12. Writer's guidelines for #10 SASE with sufficient number of IRCs or online.

Payment/Terms Payment varies. Pays on publication. Aquires first world rights.

STAPLE MAGAZINE

114-116 St. Stephen's Road, Nottingham NG2 4JS United Kingdom. E-mail: e.barrett@shu.ac.uk. **Contact:** Wayne Burrows, editor. Magazine: A5; 100 pages; illustrations; photos. Quarterly. Estab. 1982. Circ. 500.

Needs Receives 1,000 unsolicited mss/month. Recently published work by David Swann, Penny Feeny. Length: 5,000 words; average length: 3,000 words. Publishes short shorts. Also publishes literary essays, literary criticism, poetry. Sometimes comments on rejected mss.

How to Contact Send complete ms. Send SASE (or IRC) for return of ms. Responds in 8 weeks to queries; 12 weeks to mss. Sample copy for $15. Writer's guidelines for SASE.

Payment/Terms Pays 2 contributor's copies; additional copies $12. Pays on publication for one-time rights.

$☐ ◎ ☒ STONE SOUP, The Magazine by Young Writers and Artists

Children's Art Foundation, P.O. Box 83, Santa Cruz CA 95063-0083. (831)426-5557. Fax: (831)426-1161. Web site: www.stonesoup.com. **Contact:** Ms. Gerry Mandel, editor. Magazine: 7×10; 48 pages; high quality paper; photos. Audience is children, teachers, parents, writers, artists. "We have a preference for writing and art based on real-life experiences; no formula stories or poems. We only publish writing by children ages 8 to 13. We do not publish writing by adults." Bimonthly. Estab. 1973. Circ. 20,000.

- This is known as "the literary journal for children." *Stone Soup* has previously won the Ed Press Golden Lamp Honor Award and the Parent's Choice Award.

Needs Adventure, ethnic/multicultural, experimental, fantasy, historical, humor/satire, mystery/suspense, science fiction, slice-of-life vignettes, suspense. "We do not like assignments or formula stories of any kind." Receives 1,000 unsolicited mss/month. Accepts 10 mss/issue. Publishes ms 4 months after acceptance. **Publishes some new writers/year.** Also publishes literary essays, poetry.

How to Contact Send complete ms. "We like to learn a little about our young writers, why they like to write, and how they came to write the story they are submitting." Please do not include SASE. Do not send originals. Responds only to those submissions being considered for possible publication. "If you do not hear from us in 4 to 6 weeks it means we were not able to use your work. Don't be discouraged! Try again!" No simultaneous submissions. Sample copy for $5 or online. Writer's guidelines online.

Payment/Terms Pays $40 for stories. Authors also receive 2 copies, a certificate, and discounts on additional copies and on subscriptions. Pays on publication.

Advice Mss are rejected because they are "derivatives of movies, TV, comic books, or classroom assignments or other formulas. Go to our Web site, where you can see many examples of the kind of work we publish."

$▣ ◲ STORIE, All Write

Leconte Press, Via Suor Celestina Donati 13/E, Rome 00167 Italy. (+39)06 614 8777. Fax: (+39)06 614 8777. E-mail: storie@tiscali.it. Web site: www.storie.it. **Contact:** Gianluca Bassi, editor; Barbara Pezzopane, assistant editor; George Lerner, foreign editor. Magazine: 186 pages; illustrations; photographs. "*Storie* is one of Italy's leading literary magazines. Committed to a truly crossover vision of writing, the bilingual (Italian/English) review publishes high quality fiction and poetry, interspersed with the work of alternative wordsmiths such as filmmakers and musicians. Through writings bordering on narratives and interviews with important contemporary writers, it explores the culture and craft of writing." Bimonthly. Estab. 1989. Circ. 20,000.

Needs Literary. Receives 150 unsolicited mss/month. Accepts 6-10 mss/issue; 30-50 mss/year. Does not read mss in August. Publishes ms 2 months after acceptance. **Publishes 20 new writers/year.** Recently published work by Joyce Carol Oates, Haruki Murakami, Paul Auster, Robert Coover, Raymond Carver, T.C. Boyle, Ariel Dorfman, Tess Gallagher. Length: 2,000-6,000 words; average length: 1,500 words. Publishes short shorts. Also publishes literary essays, literary criticism, poetry. Sometimes comments on rejected mss.

How to Contact Accepts submissions by e-mail or on disk. Include brief bio. Send complete ms with cover letter. "Manuscripts may be submitted directly by regular post without querying first; however, we do not accept unsolicited manuscripts via e-mail. Please query via e-mail first. We only contact writers if their work has been accepted. We also arrange for and oversee a high-quality, professional translation of the piece." Responds in 1 month to queries; 6 months to mss. Accepts multiple submissions. Sample copy for $ 10. Writer's guidelines online.

Payment/Terms Pays $30-600 and 2 contributor's copies. Pays on publication for first (in English and Italian) rights.

Advice "More than erudite references or a virtuoso performance, we're interested in the recording of human experience in a genuine, original voice. *Storie* reserves the right to include a brief review of interesting submissions not selected for publication in a special column of the magazine."

☐ STRAYLIGHT

UW-Parkside, English Dept., 900 Wood Rd., P.O. Box 2000, Kenosha WI 53141. (262)595-2139. Fax: (262)595-2271. E-mail: admin@straylightontheweb.net. Web site: www.litspot.net/straylight. **Contact:** Fiction editor. Magazine has revolving editor. Editorial term: 2 years. Literary magazine/journal: 6¼×9½, 75 pages, quality paper, uncoated index stock cover. Contains illustrations. Includes photographs. "*Straylight* is a new literary journal. We are interested in publishing high quality, character-based fiction of any style. We tend not to publish strict genre pieces, though we may query them for future special issues. We do not publish erotica.'' Biannual with special issues. Estab. 2005.

Needs Ethnic/multicultural (general), experimental, gay, lesbian, literary, mainstream, regional. Special interests: genre fiction in special theme issues. Accepts 5-7 mss/issue; 10-14 mss/year. Does not read June-August. Manuscript published 6 months after acceptance. Agented fiction 0%. Length: 1,000 words (min)-5,000 words (max). Average length: 2,500 words. Publishes short shorts. Also publishes poetry. Rarely comments on/ critiques rejected mss.

How to Contact Send complete ms with cover letter. Accepts submissions by e-mail. Include brief bio, list of publications. Responds to queries in 2 weeks. Responds to mss in 2 months. Send either SASE (or IRC) for return of ms or disposable copy of ms and #10 SASE for reply only. Sample copy available for $4. Guidelines available for SASE, on Web site.

Payment and Terms Writers receive 3 contributor's copies. Additional copies $2. Pays on publication. Acquires first North American serial rights. Publication is copyrighted.

Advice ''We tend to publish character-based and inventive fiction with cutting-edge prose. We are unimpressed with works based on strict plot twists or novelties. Read a sample copy to get a feel for what we publish.''

STRUGGLE, A Magazine of Proletarian Revolutionary Literature

Detroit MI 48213-0261. (213)273-9039. E-mail: timhall11@yahoo.com. **Contact:** Tim Hall, editor. Magazine: $5^1/_2 \times 8^1/_2$; 36-72 pages; 20 lb. white bond paper; colored cover; illustrations; occasional photos. Publishes material related to ''the struggle of the working class and all progressive people against the rule of the rich—including their war policies, repression, racism, exploitation of the workers, oppression of women and general culture, etc.'' Quarterly. Estab. 1985.

Needs Ethnic/multicultural, experimental, feminist, historical, humor/satire, literary, regional, science fiction, translations, young adult/teen (10-18), prose poem, senior citizen/retirement. ''The theme can be approached in many ways, including plenty of categories not listed here. Readers would like fiction about anti-globalization, the fight against racism, prison conditions, neo-conservatism and the Iraq War. Would also like to see more fiction that depicts life, work and struggle of the working class of every background; also the struggles of the 1930s and '60s illustrated and brought to life. No romance, psychic, mystery, western, erotica, religious.'' Receives 10-12 unsolicited mss/month. Recently published work by Gregory Alan Norton, Paris Smith, Keith Laufenberg. Length: 4,000 words; average length: 1,000-3,000 words. Publishes short shorts. Normally comments on rejected mss.

How to Contact Send complete ms. Accepts submissions by e-mail. ''Tries to'' report in 3-4 months to queries. Accepts simultaneous, multiple submissions and reprints. Sample copies for $3; $5 for double-size issues; subscriptions $10 for 4 issues; make checks payable to Tim Hall, Special Account, not to *Struggle*.

Payment/Terms Pays 1 contributor's copy. No rights acquired . Not copyrighted.

Advice ''Write about the oppression of the working people, the poor, the minorities, women and, if possible, their rebellion against it—we are not interested in anything which accepts the status quo. We are not too worried about plot and advanced technique (fine if we get them!)—we would probably accept things others would call sketches, provided they have life and struggle. For new writers: just describe for us a situation in which some real people confront some problem of oppression, however seemingly minor. Observe and put down the real facts. Experienced writers: try your 'committed'/experimental fiction on us. We get poetry all the time. We have increased our fiction portion of our content in the last few years. The quality of fiction that we have published has continued to improve. If your work raises an interesting issue of literature and politics, it may get discussed in letters and in my editorial. I suggest ordering a sample.''

$ SUBTERRAIN, Strong words for a polite nation

P.O. Box 3008, MPO, Vancouver BC V6B 3X5 Canada. (604)876-8710. Fax: (604)879-2667. E-mail: subter@portal.ca. Web site: www.subterrain.ca. **Contact:** Fiction editor. Magazine: $8^1/_4 \times 10^7/_8$; 46-52 pages; gloss stock paper; color gloss cover stock; illustrations; photos. ''Looking for unique work and perspectives from Canada and beyond.'' Triannual. Estab. 1987. Circ. 3,000.

Needs Literary. Does not want genre fiction or children's fiction. Receives 100 unsolicited mss/month. Accepts 4 mss/issue; 10-15 mss/year. Publishes ms 4 months after acceptance. Recently published work by John Moore. Also publishes literary essays, literary criticism. Rarely comments on rejected mss.

How to Contact Send complete ms. Include disposable copy of the ms and #10 SASE for reply only. Responds in 3-4 weeks to queries; 2-4 months to mss. Accepts multiple submissions. Sample copy for $5. Writer's guidelines for #10 SASE or online.

Payment/Terms Pays $25 per page for prose. Pays on publication for first North American serial rights.

Advice ''Read the magazine first. Get to know what kind of work we publish.''

◖ SULPHUR RIVER LITERARY REVIEW

P.O. Box 19228, Austin TX 78760-9228. (512)292-9456. **Contact:** James Michael Robbins, editor. Magazine: 5½×8½; 145 pages; illustrations; photos. "*SRLR* publishes literature of quality—poetry and short fiction with appeal that transcends time. Audience includes a broad spectrum of readers, mostly educated, many of whom are writers, artists and educators." Semiannual. Estab. 1978. Circ. 350.

Needs Ethnic/multicultural, experimental, feminist, humor/satire, literary, mainstream, translations. "No religious, juvenile, teen, sports, romance or mystery. Wants to see more experimental, surreal and imaginative fiction." Receives 20 unsolicited mss/month. Accepts 4-5 mss/issue; 8-10 mss/year. Publishes ms 1-2 years after acceptance. Recently published work by William Jablonsky, Richard Vaughn, Frederic Boutet. Publishes short shorts. Also publishes literary essays, literary criticism, poetry.

How to Contact Send complete ms. Include short bio and list of publications. Send SASE for reply, return of ms, or send disposable copy of ms. Responds in 1 week to queries; 1 month to mss. Sample copy for $7.

Payment/Terms Pays 2 contributor copies. Additional copies $7. Acquires first North American serial rights.

Advice Looks for "quality. Imagination served perfectly by masterful control of language."

$◖ THE SUN

The Sun Publishing Co., 107 N. Roberson St., Chapel Hill NC 27516. (919)942-5282. Fax: (919)932-3101. Web site: www.thesunmagazine.org. **Contact:** Sy Safransky, editor. Magazine: 8½×11; 48 pages; offset paper; glossy cover stock; photos. "We are open to all kinds of writing, though we favor work of a personal nature." Monthly. Estab. 1974. Circ. 70,000.

Needs Literary. Open to all fiction. Receives 500 unsolicited mss/month. Accepts 2 mss/issue. Publishes ms 6-12 months after acceptance. Recently published work by Ronald F. Currie Jr., Davy Rothbart, Lindsay Fitzgerald, Jenny Bitner. Also publishes poetry.

How to Contact Send complete ms. Accepts reprint submissions. Sample copy for $5. Writer's guidelines online.

Payment/Terms Pays $300-1,000. Pays on publication for first, one-time rights.

Advice "We favor honest, personal writing with an intimate point of view."

◖ SYCAMORE REVIEW

Purdue University, Department of English, 500 Oval Drive, West Lafayette IN 47907. (765)494-3783. Fax: (765)494-3780. E-mail: sycamore@purdue.edu. Web site: www.sla.purdue.edu/sycamore. **Contact:** Fiction Editor. Magazine: 8×8; 100-150 pages; heavy, textured, uncoated paper; heavy laminated cover. "Journal devoted to contemporary literature. We publish both traditional and experimental fiction, personal essay, poetry, interviews, drama and graphic art. Novel excerpts welcome if they stand alone as a story." Semiannual. Estab. 1989. Circ. 1,000.

Needs Experimental, humor/satire, literary, mainstream, regional, translations. "We generally avoid genre literature but maintain no formal restrictions on style or subject matter. No romance, children's." Would like to see more experimental fiction. Publishes ms 11 months after acceptance. Recently published work by Lucia Perillo, June Armstrong, W.P. Osborn, William Giraldi. Also publishes poetry. Sometimes comments on rejected mss.

How to Contact Send complete ms with SASE, cover letter with previous publications and address. Responds in 4 months to mss. Accepts simultaneous submissions. Sample copy for $5. Writer's guidelines for #10 SASE or online.

Payment/Terms Acquires one-time rights.

Advice "We publish both new and experienced authors but we're always looking for stories with strong emotional appeal, vivid characterization and a distinctive narrative voice; fiction that breaks new ground while still telling an interesting and significant story. Avoid gimmicks and trite, predictable outcomes. Write stories that have a ring of truth, the impact of felt emotion. Don't be afraid to submit, send your best."

◖ TALKING RIVER REVIEW

Lewis-Clark State College, Division of Literature and Languages, 500 8th Ave., Lewiston ID 83501. (208)792-2307. Fax: (208)792-2324. **Contact:** Mark Sanders, editorial advisor. Magazine: 6×9; 150-200 pages; 60 lb. paper; coated, color cover; illustrations; photos. "We look for new voices with something to say to a discerning general audience." Semiannual. Estab. 1994. Circ. 500.

Needs Condensed novels, ethnic/multicultural, feminist, humor/satire, literary, regional. "Wants more well-written, character-driven stories that surprise and delight the reader with fresh, arresting yet unself-conscious language, imagery, metaphor, revelation." No stories that are sexist, racist, homophobic, erotic for shock value ; no genre fiction. Receives 400 unsolicited mss/month. Accepts 5-8 mss/issue; 10-15 mss/year. Reads mss September 1-May 1 only. Publishes ms 1-2 year s after acceptance. **Publishes 10-15 new writers/year.** Recently published work by X.J. Kennedy and Gary Fincke. Length: 7,500 words; average length: 3,000 words. Also publishes literary essays, poetry. Sometimes comments on rejected mss.

How to Contact Send complete manuscript with cover letter. Include estimated word count, 2-sentence bio and list of publications. Send SASE for reply, return of ms or send disposable copy of ms. Responds in 3 months to mss. Does not accept simultaneous submissions. Sample copy for $6. Writer's guidelines for #10 SASE.

Payment/Terms Pays contributor's copies; additional copies $4. Acquires one-time rights.

Advice "We look for the strong, the unique; we reject clichéd images and predictable climaxes."

$⊘ TAMPA REVIEW

University of Tampa Press, 401 W. Kennedy Blvd., Tampa FL 33606. (813)253-6266. Fax: (813)258-7593. Web site: tampareview.ut.edu. **Contact:** Lisa Birnbaum and Kathleen Ochshorn, fiction editors. Magazine: 7½×10½; hardback; approximately 100 pages; acid-free paper; visual art; photos. An international literary journal publishing art and literature from Florida and Tampa Bay as well as new work and translations from throughout the world. Semiannual. Estab. 1988. Circ. 500.

Needs Ethnic/multicultural, experimental, fantasy, historical, literary, mainstream, translations. "We are far more interested in quality than in genre. Nothing sentimental as opposed to genuinely moving, nor self-conscious style at the expense of human truth." Accepts 4-5 mss/issue. Reads September-December; reports January-May. Publishes ms 10 months after acceptance. Agented fiction 20%. Recently published work by Elizabeth Spencer, Lee K. Abbott, Lorrie Moore, Gordon Weaver, Tim O'Brien. Publishes short shorts. Also publishes literary essays, poetry.

How to Contact Send complete ms. Include brief bio. Responds in 5 months to mss. Accepts multiple submissions. Sample copy for $7. Writer's guidelines online.

Payment/Terms Pays $10/printed page. Pays on publication for first North American serial rights. Sends galleys to author.

Advice "There are more good writers publishing in magazines today than there have been in many decades. Unfortunately, there are even more bad ones. In T. Gertler's *Elbowing the Seducer*, an editor advises a young writer that he wants to hear her voice completely, to tell (he means 'show') him in a story the truest thing she knows. We concur. Rather than a trendy workshop story or a minimalism that actually stems from not having much to say, we would like to see stories that make us believe they mattered to the writer and, more importantly, will matter to a reader. Trim until only the essential is left, and don't give up belief in yourself. And it might help to attend a good writers' conference, e.g. Wesleyan or Bennington."

⊘ TAPROOT LITERARY REVIEW

Taproot Writer's Workshop, Inc., Box 204, Ambridge PA 15003. (724)266-8476. E-mail: taproot10@aol.com. **Contact:** Tikvah Feinstein, editor. Magazine: 5½×8½; 93 pages; 20 lb. paper; hardcover; attractively printed; saddle-stitched. "We select on quality, not topic. Variety and quality are our appealing features." Annual. Estab. 1987. Circ. 500.

Needs Literary. "No pornography, religious, popular, romance fiction. Wants more stories with multicultural themes, showing intensity, reality and human emotions that readers can relate to, learn from, and most importantly—be interesting." The majority of ms published are received through annual contest. Receives 20 unsolicited mss/month. Accepts 6 mss/issue. **Publishes 2-4 new writers/year.** Recently published work by Jennifer Renee Roediger, Janet Slike, Alicia Stankay, Margaret Karmazin, Alena Horowitz. Publishes short shorts. Also publishes poetry. Sometimes comments on rejected mss.

How to Contact Accepts submissions by e-mail. Send for guidelines first. Send complete ms with a cover letter. Include estimated word count and bio. Responds in 6 months to mss. No simultaneous submissions. Sample copy for $5, 6×12 SAE with 5 first-class stamps. Writer's guidelines for #10 SASE.

Payment/Terms Awards $25 in prize money for first place fiction and poetry winners each issue; certificate for 2nd and 3rd place; 1 contributor's copy. Additionally, *Taproot* offers a coveted literary prize, promotion, and $15 for the winner. Acquires first rights. Sponsors awards/contests.

Advice "Taproot is getting more fiction submissions, and every one is read entirely. This takes time, so response can be delayed at busy times of year. Our contest is a good way to start publishing. Send for a sample copy and read it through. Ask for a critique and follow suggestions. Don't be offended by any suggestions—just take them or leave them and keep writing. Looks for a story that speaks in its unique voice, told in a well-crafted and complete, memorable style, a style of signature to the author. Follow writer's guidelines. Research markets. Send cover letter. Don't give up."

⊘ THE TEXAS REVIEW

Texas Review Press at Sam Houston State University, P.O. Box 2146, Huntsville TX 77341-2146. (936)294-1992. Fax: (936)294-3070 (inquiries only). E-mail: eng_pdr@shsu.edu. Web site: www.shsu.edu. **Contact:** Paul Ruffin, editor. Magazine: 6×9; 148-190 pages; best quality paper; 70 lb. cover stock; illustrations; photos. "We publish top quality poetry, fiction, articles, interviews and reviews for a general audience." Semiannual. Estab. 1976. Circ. 1,200. A member of the Texas A&M University Press consortium.

Needs Humor/satire, literary, mainstream, contemporary fiction. "We are eager enough to consider fiction of quality, no matter what its theme or subject matter. No juvenile fiction." Receives 40-60 unsolicited mss/month. Accepts 4 mss/issue; 6 mss/year. Does not read mss May-September. Publishes ms 6-12 months after acceptance. **Publishes some new writers/year.** Recently published work by George Garrett, Ellen Gilchrist, Fred Chappell. Also publishes literary essays, literary criticism, poetry. Sometimes comments on rejected mss.
How to Contact Send complete ms. No mss accepted via fax. Send disposable copy of ms and #10 SASE for reply only. Responds in 2 weeks to queries; 3-6 months to mss. Accepts multiple submissions. Sample copy for $5. Writer's guidelines for SASE and on Web site.
Payment/Terms Pays contributor's copies and one year subscription. Pays on publication for first North American serial, one-time rights. Sends galleys to author.
Advice "Submit often; be aware that we reject 90% of submissions due to overwhelming number of mss sent."

N ⊕ ⊘ THE READER

19 Abercromby Square, Liverpool, Merseyside LG9 7ZG.01517942830. E-mail: readers@liv.ac.uk. Web site: www.thereader.co.uk. **Contact:** Jane Davis. Literary magazine/journal: 216×138 mm, 130 pages, 80 gsm (Silver Offset) paper. Includes photographs. "*The Reader* is a quarterly literary magazine aimed at the intelligent 'common reader'—from those just beginning to explore serious literary reading to professional teachers, academics and writers. As well as publishing short fiction and poetry by new writers and established names, the magazine features articles on all aspects of literature, language, and reading; regular features, including a literary quiz and 'Our Spy in NY', a bird's-eye view of literary goings-on in New York; reviews; and readers'recommendations of books that have made a difference to them. *The Reader* is unique among literary magazines in its focus on reading as a creative, important and pleasurable activity, and in its combination of high-quality material and presentation with a genuine commitment to ordinary but dedicated readers." Quarterly. Estab. 1997. Circ. 700.
Needs Literary. Receives 10 mss/month. Accepts 1-2 mss/issue; 8 mss/year. Manuscript published 16 months after acceptance. Publishes 4 new writers/year. Published Karen King Arbisala, Ray Tallis, Sasha Dugdale, Vicki Seal, David Constantine, Jonathan Meades, Ramesh Avadhani. Length: 1,000 words (min)-3,000 words (max). Average length: 2,300 words. Publishes short shorts. Average length of short shorts: 1,500 words. Also publishes literary essays, literary criticism, poetry. Sometimes comments on/critiques rejected mss.
How to Contact Send complete ms with cover letter. Include estimated word count, brief bio, list of publications. Responds to queries in 2 months; mss in 2 months. Send SASE (or IRC) for return of ms. Considers simultaneous submissions, multiple submissions. Guidelines available for SASE.
Payment and Terms Additional copies $6. Pays on publication. Sends galleys to author.
Advice "The style or polish of the writing is less important than the deep structure of the story (though of course, it matters that it's well written). The main persuasive element is whether the story moves us—and that's quite hard to quantify—it's something to do with the force of the idea and the genuine nature of enquiry within the story. When fiction is the writer's natural means of thinking things through, that'll get us. "

$⊘ THEMA

Box 8747, Metairie LA 70011-8747. (504)887-1263. **Contact:** Virginia Howard, editor. Magazine: 5½×8½; 150 pages; Grandee Strathmore cover stock; b&w illustrations. "*Thema* is designed to stimulate creative thinking by challenging writers with unusual themes, such as 'safety in numbers' and 'the power of whim.' Appeals to writers, teachers of creative writing, and general reading audience." Estab. 1988. Circ. 350.
Needs Adventure, ethnic/multicultural, experimental, fantasy, historical, humor/satire, literary, mainstream, mystery/suspense, novel excerpts, psychic/supernatural/occult, regional, religious/inspirational, science fiction, slice-of-life vignettes, western, contemporary, sports, prose poem. "No erotica." 2006 themes were "*Rage Over a Lost Penny*" (March 1); "*The Perfect Cup of Coffee*" (July 1); "*Written in Stone*" (November 1). Write for 2007 themes. Publishes ms within 6 months after acceptance. **Publishes 9 new writers/year.** Recently published work by Kristine Guile, Jennifer Hubbard, Serena Alibhai, Carol V. Paul. Publishes short shorts. Also publishes poetry. Sometimes comments on rejected mss.
How to Contact Send complete ms with SASE, cover letter, include "name and address, brief introduction, specifying the intended target issue for the mss." SASE. Responds in 1 week to queries; 5 months to mss. Accepts simultaneous, multiple submissions and reprints. Sample copy for $10. Writer's guidelines for #10 SASE.
Payment/Terms Pays $10-25. Pays on acceptance for one-time rights.
Advice "Do not submit a manuscript unless you have written it for a specified theme. If you don't know the upcoming themes, send for guidelines first before sending a story. We need more stories told in the Mark Twain/O. Henry tradition in magazine fiction."

THIRD COAST

Dept. of English, Western Michigan University, Kalamazoo MI 49008-5331. (269)387-2675. Fax: (269)387-2562. Web site: www.wmich.edu/thirdcoast. Peter Geye, editor. **Contact:** Rachel Swearingen and Kelly Daniels, fiction editors. Magazine: 6×9; 176 pages. "We will consider many different types of fiction and favor those exhibiting a freshness of vision and approach." Twice-yearly. Estab. 1995. Circ. 2,875.

● *Third Coast* has received *Pushcart Prize* nominations. The section editors of this publication change with the university year.

Needs Literary. "While we don't want to see formulaic genre fiction, we will consider material that plays with or challenges generic forms." Receives 200 unsolicited mss/month. Accepts 6-8 mss/issue; 15 mss/year. Recently published work by Keith Banner, Peter Ho Davies, Moira Crone, Lee Martin, John McNally, and Peter Orner. Also publishes literary essays, poetry, one-act plays. Sometimes comments on rejected mss.

How to Contact Send complete ms. Send SASE for reply. Responds in 4 months to mss. Accepts simultaneous submissions. Sample copy for $8. Writer's guidelines online. Reads mss from August to May.

Payment/Terms Pays 2 contributor's copies as well as a 1 year subscription to the publication; additional copies for $4. Acquires first North American serial rights.

Advice "We seek superior fiction from short-shorts to 30-page stories."

TICKLED BY THUNDER, Helping Writers Get Published Since 1990

Tickled By Thunder Publishing Co., 14076 86A Ave., Surrey BC V3W 0V9 Canada. (604)591-6095. E-mail: info@tickledbythunder.com. Web site: www.tickledbythunder.com. **Contact:** Larry Lindner, publisher. Magazine: digest-sized; 24 pages; bond paper; bond cover stock; illustrations; photos. "*Tickled By Thunder* is designed to encourage beginning writers of fiction, poetry and nonfiction." Quarterly. Estab. 1990. Circ. 1,000.

Needs Fantasy, humor/satire, literary, mainstream, mystery/suspense, science fiction, western. "No overly indulgent horror, sex, profanity or religious material." Receives 25 unsolicited mss/month. Accepts 3 mss/issue; 12 mss/year. Publishes ms 3-9 months after acceptance. **Publishes 10 new writers/year.** Recently published work by Rick Cook and Jerry Shane. Length: 2,000 words; average length: 1,500 words. Also publishes literary essays, literary criticism, poetry.

How to Contact Send complete ms. Include estimated word count and brief bio. Send SASE or IRC for return of ms; or send disposable copy of ms and #10 SASE for reply only. No e-mail submissions. Responds in 3 months to queries; 6 months to mss. Accepts simultaneous, multiple submissions and reprints. Writer's guidelines online.

Payment/Terms Pays on publication for first, second serial (reprint) rights.

Advice "Make your characters breathe on their own. Use description with action."

TRANSITION, An International Review

104 Mount Auburn St., 3R, Cambridge MA 02138. (617)496-2845. Fax: (617)496-2877. E-mail: transition@fas.harvard.edu. Web site: www.transitionmagazine.com. **Contact:** Laurie Calhoun, director of publications. Magazine: 9½×6½; 150-175 pages; 70 lb. Finch Opaque paper; 100 lb. White Warren Lustro dull cover; illustrations; photos. "*Transition* magazine is a quarterly international review known for compelling and controversial writing on race, ethnicity, culture, and politics. This prestigious magazine is edited at Harvard University, and editorial board members include such heavy-hitters as Toni Morrison, Jamaica Kincaid and bell hooks. The magazine also attracts famous contributors such as Spike Lee, Philip Gourevitch and Carolos Fuentes." Quarterly. Estab. 1961. Circ. 3,0 00.

● Four-time winner fo the Alternative Press Award for international reporting, (2001, 2000, 1999, 1995); finalist in the 2001 National Magazine Award in General Excellence category.

Needs Ethnic/multicultural, historical, humor/satire, literary, regional (African diaspora, Third World, etc.). Receives 40 unsolicited mss/month. Accepts 2 -4 mss/year. Publishes ms 6 -8 months after acceptance. Agented fiction 30-40%. **Publishes 5 new writers/year.** Recently published work by Wole Soyinka, Henry French, George Makana Clark, Brent Edwards, and Emily Raboteau . Length: 4,000-8,000 words; average length: 7,000 words. Also publishes literary essays, literary criticism. Sometimes comments on rejected mss.

How to Contact Query with published clips or send complete ms. Include brief bio and list of publications. Send disposable copy of ms and #10 SASE for reply only. Responds in 2 months to queries; 6 months to mss. Accepts simultaneous submissions. Sample copy not available. Writer's guidelines for #10 SASE.

Payment/Terms 4 contributor's copies. Sends galleys to author.

Advice "We look for a non-white, alternative perspective, dealing with issues of race, ethnicity and identity in an upredictable, provocative way."

UNDERSTANDING

Dionysia Press, 127 Milton Rd. West, 7 Duddingston House Courtyard, Edinburgh Scotland EH15 1JG United Kingdom. Magazine: A5; 200 pages. Annual. Estab. 1989. Circ. 500. Member: Scottish Publishing Association.

Needs Translations. Publishes ms 10 months after acceptance. **Publishes 100 new writers/year.** Publishes short shorts. Also publishes literary essays, poetry. Sometimes comments on rejected mss.

How to Contact Responds in 1 year to queries. Sample copy for $4.50 + postage. Writer's guidelines for SASE.

Payment/Terms Pays in contributor's copies.

VERSAL

wordsinhere, Amsterdam, The Netherlands. E-mail: versal@wordsinhere.com. Web site: http://versal.wordsinhere.com. **Contact:** Robert Glick, fiction editor. Literary magazine/journal: 20 cm×20 cm, 100 pages, offset, perfect bound paper, acid free color cover. Contains illustrations. Includes photographs. *"Versal* is the only English-language literary magazine in the Netherlands and publishes new poetry, prose and art from around the world. We publish writers with an instinct for language and line break, content and form that is urgent, involved and unexpected." Annual. Estab. 2002. Circ. 500.

Needs Experimental, literary. Receives 20 mss/month. Accepts 8 mss/year. Does not read mss January 16-September 14. Manuscript published 3 months after acceptance. **Publishes 2 new writers/year.** Published Russell Edson, Kathe Gray, Sandy Florian, Marius Benta, Rhonda Waterfall. Length: 3,000 words (max). Publishes short shorts. Average length of short shorts: 500 words. Also publishes poetry. Sometimes comments on/critiques rejected mss.

How to Contact Send complete ms with cover letter. Accepts submissions by e-mail only. Include brief bio. Responds to queries in 1 week. Responds to mss in 4 months. Considers simultaneous submissions. Guidelines available on Web site.

Payment and Terms Writers receive 1 contributor copy. Additional copies $8. Pays on publication. Acquires one-time rights. Sends galleys to author. Publication is copyrighted.

Advice "We are drawn to good pacing, varied tone and something out of the ordinary. Above all, we look for surprise and richness of detail in representing this surprise. We especially love something written in an unusual voice that also contains depth in content. For more traditional voices, we look for surprise within the story, either by giving us an unusual situation or by having characters surprise us with their actions. Nasty sex and drug adventures don't really shock us, so unless there's a fantastic twist to the tale, they don't provide a jump out of the slush pile. In flash fiction, we are less inclined to the purely anecdotal than to work that somehow manages to convey depth and/or tension."

WHISKEY ISLAND MAGAZINE

Dept. of English, Cleveland State University, Cleveland OH 44115-2440. (216)687-2056. Fax: (216)687-6943. E-mail: whiskeyisland@csuohio.edu. Web site: www.csuohio.edu/whiskey_island. Editors change each year. Magazine of fiction, creative nonfiction, theater writing and poetry. "We provide a forum for new writers and new work, for themes and points of view that are both meaningful and experimental, accessible and extreme." Semiannual. Estab. 1978. Circ. 2,500.

Needs "Would like to see more short shorts, flash fiction." Receives 100 unsolicited mss/month. Accepts 46 mss/issue. **Publishes 5-10 new writers/year.** Recently published work by Nin Andrews, Reginald Gibbons, Jim Daniels, Allison Luterman. Also publishes poetry.

How to Contact Send complete ms. Accepts submissions by e-mail. Responds in 4 months to queries; 4 months to mss. Sample copy for $6.

Payment/Terms Pays 2 contributor copies and 1-year subscription. Acquires one-time rights. Yearly contest issue for poetry and fiction with cash prizes. $10 per entry. Sponsors awards/contests.

Advice "We read manuscripts year round. We seek engaging writing of any style."

THE WILLIAM AND MARY REVIEW

The College of William and Mary, Campus Center, P.O. Box 8795, Williamsburg VA 23187-8795. (757)221-3290. E-mail: review@wm.edu. Web site: www.wm.edu/so/wmreview. **Contact:** Address all prose submissions ATTN: Prose Editor. Magazine: 6×9; 96 pages; coated paper; 4-color card cover; photos. "Our journal is read by a sophisticated audience of subscribers, professors, and university students." Annual. Estab. 1962. Circ. 1,600.

Needs Experimental, family saga, historical, horror (psychological), humor/satire, literary, mainstream, science fiction, thriller/espionage, translations, short stories. "We do not want to see typical genre pieces. Do not bother sending fantasy or erotica." Receives 35 unsolicited mss/month. Accepts 4-5 mss/year. Does not read mss from February to August. Publishes ms 1-2 months after acceptance. **Publishes 1-2 new writers/year.** Length: 250-7,000 words; average length: 3,500 words. Publishes short shorts. Also publishes poetry. Rarely comments on rejected mss.

How to Contact Send complete ms. Send SASE (or IRC) for return of the mss or send disposable copy of the ms and #10 SASE for reply only. Include a cover letter. Responds in 5-6 months to queries. Accepts simultaneous, multiple submissions but requires identification of those that are simultaneous and notification if they are accepted elsewhere. Sample copy for $5.50.

Payment/Terms Pays 5 contributor's copies; additional copies $5.50. Pays on publication for first North American serial rights.

Advice "We do not give much weight to prior publications; each piece is judged on its own merit. New writers should be bold and unafraid to submit unorthodox works that depart from textbook literary tradition. We would like to see more quality short shorts and nonfiction works. We receive far too many mediocre genre stories."

WILLARD & MAPLE, The Literary Magazine of Champlain College

163 South Willard Street, Freeman 302, Box 34, Burlington VT 05401. (802)860-2700 ext.2462. E-mail: willardan dmaple@champlain.edu. **Contact:** Fiction editor. Magazine: perfect bound; 125 pages; illustrations; photos. "*Willard & Maple* is a student-run literary magazine from Champlain College that publishes a wide array of poems, short stories, creative essays, short plays, pen and ink drawings, black and white photos, and computer graphics. We now accept color." Annual. Estab. 1996.

Needs We accept all types of mss. Receives 20 unsolicited mss/month. Accepts 1 mss/year. Does not read mss March 31-September 1. Publishes ms within 1 year after acceptance. **Publishes 10 new writers/year.** Recently published work by Robert Cooperman, Jackie Bishop, Kenneth Dimaggio, Richard Moyer, and Vladimir Swiryn-sky. Length: 5,000 words; average length: 2,500 words. Publishes short shorts. Also publishes literary essays, poetry. Sometimes comments on rejected mss.

How to Contact Send complete mss. Send SASE for return of ms or send disposable copy of mss and #10 SASE for reply only. Responds in 6 months to queries; 6 months to mss. Accepts simultaneous, multiple submissions. Sample copy for $8 10. Writer's guidelines for SASE or send e-mail. Reviews fiction.

Payment/Terms Pays 2 contributor's copies; additional copies $12. Pays on publication for one-time rights.

Advice "The power of imagination makes us infinite."

WILLOW REVIEW

College of Lake County, 19351 W. Washington, Grayslake IL 60030. (847)543-2956. E-mail: com426@clcillinois. edu. Web site: www.clcillinois.edu/community/willowreview.asp. **Contact:** Michael Latza, editor. Literary magazine/journal. 6×9, 110 pages. Annual. Estab. 1969. Circ. 800.

Needs Literary. Receives 10 mss/month. Accepts 3-5 mss/issue. Does not read mss May 1-September 1. Publishes 2-3 new writers/year. Published Patricia Smith, Tim Joycek. Length: 7,500 words (max). Publishes short shorts. Average length of short shorts: 500 words. Also publishes literary criticism. Rarely comments on/ critiques rejected manuscripts.

How to Contact Send complete ms with cover letter. Include estimated word count, brief bio, list of publications. Responds to mss in 3-4 months. Send either SASE (or IRC) for return of ms or disposable copy of ms and #10 SASE for reply only. Considers simultaneous submissions, multiple submissions. Sample copy available for $5. Guidelines available for SASE, via e-mail.

Payment and Terms Writers receive 2 contributors copies. Additional copies $7. Pays on publication. All rights revert to author upon publication.

WILLOW SPRINGS

705 W. First Ave., Spokane WA 99201. (509)623-4349. Web site: http://willowsprings.ewu.edu. **Contact:** Fiction Editor. Magazine: 9×6; 144 pages; 80 lb. glossy cover. "We publish quality contemporary fiction, poetry, nonfiction, interviews with notable authors, and works in translation." Semiannual. Estab. 1977. Circ. 1,500. Member CLMP, AWP.

• *Willow Springs* has received grants from the NEA and a CLMP excellence award.

Needs Literary short shorts, nonfiction, translations, short stories, prose poems, poems. "No genre fiction, please." Receives 200 unsolicited mss/month. Accepts 2-4 mss/issue; 4-8 mss/year. Reads mss year round, but expect slower response between July and October. Publishes ms 4 months after acceptance. **Publishes some new writers/year.** Recently published work by Imad Rahman, Deb Olin Unferth, Jim Daniels, Kirsten Sundberg Lunstrum, Robert Lopez, Stacey Richter. Also publishes literary essays, literary criticism, poetry. Rarely comments on rejected mss.

How to Contact Send complete ms. Prose submissions now accepted online. Responds in 2 months to queries; 2 months to mss. Simultaneous submissions encouraged. Sample copy for $6. Writer's guidelines for #10 SASE.

Payment/Terms Pays 2 contributor's copies. Acquires first North American serial, first rights.

Advice "We hope to attract good fiction writers to our magazine, and we've made a commitment to publish 3-4 stories per issue. We like fiction that exhibits a fresh approach to language. Our most recent issues, we feel, indicate the quality and level of our conmmitment."

○ WINDHOVER, A Journal of Christian Literature

University of Mary Hardin-Baylor, P.O. Box 8008, 900 College St., Belton TX 76513. (254)295-4561. E-mail: windhover@umhb.edu. **Contact:** D. Audell Shelburne, editor. Magazine: 6×9; white bond paper. "We accept poetry, short fiction, nonfiction, creative nonfiction. *Windhover* is devoted to promoting writers and literature with a Christian perspective and with a broad definition of that perspective." Annual. Estab. 1997. Circ. 500.

Needs Ethnic/multicultural, experimental, fantasy, historical, humor/satire, literary. No erotica. Receives 30 unsolicited mss/month. Accepts 5 mss/issue; 5 mss/year. Publishes ms 1 year after acceptance. **Publishes 5 new writers/year.** Recently published work by Walt McDonald, Cleatus Rattan, Greg Garrett, Barbara Crooker. Length: 1,500-4,000 words; average length: 3,000 words. Publishes short shorts. Also publishes literary essays, poetry. Sometimes comments on rejected mss.

How to Contact Send complete ms. Estimated word count, brief bio and list of publications. Include SASE postcard for acknowledgement. No submissions by e-mail. Responds in 4-6 weeks to queries; 4-6 months to mss. Accepts simultaneous submissions. Sample copy for $10. Writer's guidelines by e-mail.

Payment/Terms Pays 2 contributor copies. Pays on publication for first rights.

Advice "Be patient. We have an editorial board and it sometimes takes longer than I like. We particularly look for convincing plot and character development."

Ⓝ $○ WORKERS WRITE!

Blue Cubicle Press, LLC, P.O. Box 250382, Plano TX 75005-0382. (972)824-0646. E-mail: info@workerswritejour nal.com. Web site: www.workerswritejournal.com. **Contact:** David LaBounty, editor. Literary magazine/journal: 100-164 pages, 20 lb. bond paper paper, 80 lb. cover stock cover. "We publish stories that center on a particular workplace." Annual.

Needs Ethnic/multicultural (general), humor/satire, literary, mainstream, regional. Receives 100 mss/month. Accepts 12-15 mss/year. Manuscript published 3-4 months after acceptance. **Publishes 1 new writer/year.** Length: 500 words (min)-5,000 words (max). Average length: 3,000 words. Publishes short shorts. Also publishes poetry. Often comments on rejected mss.

How to Contact Send complete ms with cover letter. Accepts submissions by e-mail. Responds to queries in 1 weeks. Responds to mss in 3-4 weeks. Send either SASE (or IRC) for return of ms or disposable copy of ms and #10 SASE for reply only. Considers simultaneous submissions, previously published submissions, multiple submissions. Sample copy available for. Guidelines available for SASE, via e-mail, on Web site.

Payment and Terms Pays $50 maximum and contributor's copies. Additional copies $3. Pays on publication.

Advice "We publish stories from the worker's point of view."

◔ XAVIER REVIEW

Xavier University, 1 Drexel Dr., New Orleans LA 70125-1098. (504)520-7549. Fax: (504)485-7197. E-mail: rcollin s@xula.edu (correspondence only—no mss). **Contact:** Richard Collins, editor. Mark Whitaker, associate editor. Magazine: 6×9; 75 pages; 50 lb. paper; 12 pt. CS1 cover; photographs. Magazine of "poetry/fiction/nonfiction/ reviews (contemporary literature) for professional writers, libraries, colleges and universities." Semiannual. Estab. 1980. Circ. 500.

Needs Ethnic/multicultural, experimental, historical, literary, mainstream, regional (Southern, Latin American), religious/inspirational, serialized novels, translations. Receives 40 unsolicited mss/month. Accepts 2 mss/issue; 4 mss/year. **Publishes 2-3 new writers/year.** Recently published work by Andrei Codrescu, Terrance Hayes, Naton Leslie, Alvin Aubert. Also publishes literary essays, literary criticism. Occasionally comments on rejected mss.

How to Contact Send complete ms. Include 2-3 sentence bio. Sample copy for $5.

Payment/Terms Pays 2 contributor copies.

◔ ✉ YEMASSEE, The literary journal of the University of South Carolina

Department of English, University of South Carolina, Columbia SC 29208. (803)777-2085. Fax: (803)777-9064. E-mail: yemassee@gwm.sc.edu. Web site: www.cla.sc.edu/ENGL/yemassee/index.htm. **Contact:** Editors. Magazine: 5½×8½; 70-90 pages; 60 lb. natural paper; 65 lb. cover; cover illustration. "We are open to a variety of subjects and writing styles. We publish primarily fiction and poetry, but we are also interested in one-act plays, brief excerpts of novels, and interviews with literary figures. Our essential consideration for acceptance is the quality of the work." Semiannual. Estab. 1993. Circ. 500.

● Stories from *Yemassee* have been selected for publication in *New Stories from The South*.

Needs Condensed novels, ethnic/multicultural, experimental, feminist, gay, historical, humor/satire, lesbian, literary, regional. "No romance, religious/inspirational, young adult/teen, children's/juvenile, erotica. Wants more experimental work." Receives 30 unsolicited mss/month. Accepts 1-3 mss/issue; 2-6 mss/year. "We read from August-May and hold ms over to the next year if they arrive in the summer." **Publishes 6 new writers/**

year. Recently published work by Robert Coover, Chris Railey, Virgil Suárez, Susan Ludvigson , Kwame Dawes. Publishes short shorts. Also publishes literary essays, poetry.

How to Contact Send complete ms. Include estimated word count, brief bio , list of publications. Send SASE for reply, return of ms, or send disposable copy of ms. Responds in 2 weeks to queries; 4 months to mss. Accepts simultaneous submissions. Sample copy for $5. Writer's guidelines for #10 SASE.

Payment/Terms Acquires first rights.

Advice "Our criteria are based on what we perceive as quality. Generally that is work that is literary. We are interested in subtlety and originality, interesting or beautiful language, craft and precision. Read our journal and any other journal before you submit to see if your work seems appropriate. Send for guidelines and make sure you follow them."

$ ◎ ZYZZYVA, The Last Word: West Coast Writers & Artists

P.O. Box 590069, San Francisco CA 94159-0069. (415)752-4393. Fax: (415)752-4391. E-mail: editor@zyzzyva.o rg. Web site: www.zyzzyva.org. **Contact:** Howard Junker, editor. "We feature work by writers currently living on the West Coast or in Alaska and Hawaii only. We are essentially a literary magazine, but of wide-ranging interests and a strong commitment to nonfiction." Estab. 1985. Circ. 3,500.

Needs Ethnic/multicultural, experimental, humor/satire, mainstream. Receives 300 unsolicited mss/month. Accepts 10 mss/issue; 30 mss/year. Publishes ms 3 months after acceptance. Agented fiction 1%. **Publishes 15 new writers/year.** Recently published work by Amanda Field, Katherine Karlin, Margaret Weatherford. Publishes short shorts. Also publishes literary essays, poetry.

How to Contact Send complete ms. Responds in 1 week to queries; 1 month to mss. Sample copy for $7 or online. Writer's guidelines online.

Payment/Terms Pays $50. Pays on acceptance for first North American serial and one-time anthology rights.

Small Circulation Magazines

This section of *Novel & Short Story Writer's Market* contains general interest, special interest, regional and genre magazines with circulations under 10,000. Although these magazines vary greatly in size, theme, format and management, the editors are all looking for short stories. Their specific fiction needs present writers of all degrees of expertise and interests with an abundance of publishing opportunities. Among the diverse publications in this section are magazines devoted to almost every topic, every level of writing, and every type of writer. Some of the markets listed here publish fiction about a particular geographic area or by authors who live in that locale.

Although not as high-paying as the large-circulation consumer magazines, you'll find some of the publications listed here do pay writers 1-5¢/word or more. Also, unlike the big consumer magazines, these markets are very open to new writers and relatively easy to break into. Their only criteria is that your story be well written, well presented and suitable for their particular readership.

In this section you will also find listings for zines. Zines vary greatly in appearance as well as content. Some paper zines are photocopies published whenever the editor has material and money, while others feature offset printing and regular distribution schedules. A few have evolved into very slick four-color, commercial-looking publications.

SELECTING THE RIGHT MARKET

First, zero in on those markets most likely to be interested in your work. Begin by looking at the Category Index starting on page 581. If your work is more general—or conversely, very specialized—you may wish to browse through the listings, perhaps looking up those magazines published in your state or region. Also check the Online Markets section for other specialized and genre publications.

In addition to browsing through the listings and using the Category Index, check the openness icons at the beginning of listings to find those most likely to be receptive to your work. This is especially true for beginning writers, who should look for magazines that say they are especially open to new writers (□) and for those giving equal weight to both new and established writers (◑). For more explanation about these icons, see the inside covers of this book.

Once you have a list of magazines you might like to try, read their listings carefully. Much of the material within each listing carries clues that tell you more about the magazine. You've Got a Story, starting on page 2, describes in detail the listing information common to all the markets in our book.

The physical description appearing near the beginning of the listings can give you clues about the size and financial commitment to the publication. This is not always an indication of quality, but chances are a publication with expensive paper and four-color artwork on the cover has more prestige than a photocopied publication featuring a clip-art cover. For more information on some of the paper, binding and printing terms used in these descriptions, see Printing and Production Terms Defined on page 533.

FURTHERING YOUR SEARCH

It cannot be stressed enough that reading the listing is only the first part of developing your marketing plan. The second part, equally important, is to obtain fiction guidelines and read the actual magazine. Reading copies of a magazine helps you determine the fine points of the magazine's publishing style and philosophy. There is no substitute for this type of hands-on research.

Unlike commercial magazines available at most newsstands and bookstores, it requires a little more effort to obtain some of the magazines listed here. You may need to send for a sample copy. We include sample copy prices in the listings whenever possible. See The Business of Fiction Writing on page 83 for the specific mechanics of manuscript submission. Above all, editors appreciate a professional presentation. Include a brief cover letter and send a self-addressed, stamped envelope for a reply. Be sure the envelope is large enough to accommodate your manuscript, if you would like it returned, and include enough stamps or International Reply Coupons (for replies from countries other than your own) to cover your manuscript's return. Many publishers today appreciate receiving a disposable manuscript, eliminating the cost to writers of return postage and saving editors the effort of repackaging manuscripts for return.

Most of the magazines listed here are published in the U.S. You will also find some English-speaking markets from around the world. These foreign publications are denoted with a 🌐 symbol at the beginning of listings. To make it easier to find Canadian markets, we include a 🍁 symbol at the start of those listings.

🌐 🌐 ◔ ◎ **THE ABIKO ANNUAL WITH JAMES JOYCE, Finnegans Wake Studies**
ALP Ltd., 8-1-7 Namiki, Abiko-shi, Chiba 270-1165 Japan. (011)81-471-69-8036. E-mail: hamada-tatsuo@jcom.home.ne.jp. Web site: http://members.jcom.home.ne.jp/hamada-tatsuo/. **Contact:** Tatsuo Hamada. Magazine: A5; 350 pages; illustrations; photos. "We primarily publish James Joyce *Finnegans Wake* essays from writers here in Japan and abroad." Annual. Estab. 1989. Circ. 300.
Needs Experimental (in the vein of James Joyce), literary, inspirational. Also essays on James Joyce's *Finnegans Wake* from around the world. Receives very few unsolicited mss/month. Also publishes literary essays, literary criticism, poetry. Always comments on rejected mss.
How to Contact Send a disposable copy of ms or e-mail attachment. Responds in 1 week to queries; 3 months to mss. Accepts multiple submissions. Sample copy for $20. Guidelines for SASE. Reviews fiction.
Payment/Terms Pays 1 contributor's copy; additional copies $25. Copyright reverts to author upon publication.
Advice "We require camera-ready copy. The writer is welcome to accompany it with appropriate artwork."

🌐 $◔ ◎ **ALBEDO ONE, The Irish Magazine of Science Fiction, Fantasy and Horror**
Albedo One, 2 Post Rd., Lusk, Co Dublin Ireland. (+353)1-8730177. E-mail: bobn@yellowbrickroad.ie. Web site: www.albedo.com. **Contact:** Editor, *Albedo One*. Magazine: A4; 44 pages. "We hope to publish interesting and unusual fiction by new and established writers. We will consider anything, as long as it is well written and entertaining, though our definitions of both may not be exactly mainstream. We like stories with plot and characters that live on the page. Most of our audience are probably committed genre fans, but we try to appeal to a broad spectrum of readers." Triannual. Estab. 1993. Circ. 900.
Needs Experimental, fantasy, horror, literary, science fiction. Receives more than 80 unsolicited mss/month. Accepts 15-18 mss/year. Publishes ms 1 year after acceptance. **Publishes 6-8 new writers/year.** Length: 2,000-9,000 words; average length: 4,000 words. Also publishes literary criticism. Sometimes comments on rejected mss.
How to Contact Responds in 3 months to mss. Sample copy not available. Guidelines available by e-mail or on Web site. Reviews fiction.

Payment/Terms Pays 3 Euros per 1,000 words, and 1 contributor's copy; additional copies $5 plus p&p. Pays on publication for first rights.

Advice "We look for good writing, good plot, good characters. Read the magazine, and don't give up."

🌀 ANY DREAM WILL DO REVIEW, Short Stories and Humor from the Secret Recesses of our Minds

Any Dream Will Do, Inc., 1830 Kirman Ave., C1, Reno NV 89502-3381. (775)786-0345. E-mail: cassjmb@iqemail.com. Web site: www.willigocrazy.org/Ch08.htm. **Contact**: Dr . Jean M. Bradt, editor and publisher. Magazine: $5\frac{1}{2} \times 8\frac{1}{2}$; 52 pages; 20 lb. bond paper; 12pt. Carolina cover stock. "The *Any Dream Will Do Review* showcases a new literary genre, Fiction In The Raw, which attempts to fight the prejudice against consumers of mental-health services by touching hearts, that is, by exposing the consumers' deepest thoughts and emotions. In the *Review*'s stories, accomplished authors honestly reveal their most intimate secrets. See www.willigocrazy.org/Ch09a.htm for detailed instructions on how to write Fiction In The Raw." Published every 1 or 2 years. Estab. 2001. Circ. 200.

Needs Ethnic/multicultural, mainstream, psychic/supernatural/occult, romance (contemporary), science fiction (soft/sociological). No pornography, true-life stories, black humor, political material, testimonials, experimental fiction, or depressing accounts of hopeless or perverted people. Accepts 10 mss/issue; 20 mss/year. Publishes ms 12 months after acceptance. **Publishes 10 new writers/year.** Publishes short shorts. Often comments on rejected mss.

How to Contact Send complete ms. Accepts submissions by e-mail (cassjmb@iqemail.com). Please submit by e-mail. If you must submit by hardcopy, please send disposable copies. No queries, please. Responds in 8 weeks to mss. Sample copy for $4 plus postage. Writer's guidelines online.

Payment/Terms Pays in contributor's copies; additional copies $4 plus postage. Acquires first North American serial rights.

Advice "Read several stories on www.willigocrazy.org before starting to write. Proof your story many times before submitting. Make the readers think. Above all, present people (preferably diagnosed with mental illness) realistically rather than with prejudice."

$🌀 APEX SCIENCE FICTION AND HORROR DIGEST

Apex Publications, P.O. Box 2223, Lexington KY 40588. (859)312-3974. E-mail: jason@apexdigest.com. Web site: www.apexdigest.com. **Contact:** Jason Sizemore, editor-in-chief. Magazine: $5\frac{1}{2} \times 8\frac{1}{2}$, 128 pages, 70 lb. white offset paper, glossy #120 cover. Contains illustrations. "We publish dark sci-fi with horror elements. Our readers are those that enjoy speculative fiction with dark themes." Quarterly. Estab. 2005. Circ. 3,000.

Needs Dark science fiction. "We're not fans of 'monster' fiction." Receives 150-250 mss/month. Accepts 8 mss/issue; 32 mss/year. Manuscript published 3 months after acceptance. Publishes 10 new writers/year. Published Ben Bova, William F. Nolan, Tom Piccirilli, M.M. Buckner, JA Rourath, and James P. Hogan. Length: 200 words (min)-10,000 words (max). Average length: 4,000 words. Publishes short shorts. Average length of short shorts: 500 words. Also publishes literary essays. Often comments on/critiques rejected manuscripts.

How to Contact Send complete ms with cover letter. Include estimated word count, brief bio. Responds to queries in 3-4 weeks. Responds to mss in 3-4 weeks. Prefers submissions by e-mail, or send disposable copy of ms and #10 SASE for reply only. Considers previously published submissions; "must query, however." Sample copy available for $5. Guidelines available via e-mail, on Web site.

Payment and Terms Writers receive 2¢/word and two comp copies of magazine. Additional copies $4. Pays on publication. Acquires first North American serial rights. Publication is copyrighted.

Advice "Be professional. Be confident. Remember that any criticisms offered are given for your benefit."

THE BINNACLE

University of Maine at Machias, 9 O'Brien Ave., Machias ME 04654. E-mail: ummbinnacle@maine.edu. Web site: www.umm.maine.edu/binnacle. "We publish an alternative format journal of literary and visual art. We are restless about the ossification of literature and what to do about it." Semiannual. Estab. 1957. Circ. 300.

Needs Ethnic/multicultural, experimental, humor/satire, mainstream, slice-of-life vignettes. No extreme erotica, fantasy, horror, or religious, but any genre attuned to a general audience can work. Publishes ms 3 months after acceptance.

How to Contact Submissions by e-mail preferred. Responds in 1 month to queries; 3 months to mss. Accepts simultaneous submissions. Sample copy for $5. Writer's guidelines online at Web site or by e-mail.

Payment/Terms Acquires one-time rights.

$⬜ ◎ BLACK LACE

BLK Publishing CO., P.O. Box 83912, Los Angeles CA 90083-0912. (310)410-0808. Fax: (310)410-9250. E-mail: newsroom@blk.com. Web site: www.blacklace.org. **Contact:** Fiction Editor. Magazine: $8\frac{1}{8} \times 10\frac{5}{8}$; 48 pages;

book stock; color glossy cover; illustrations; photos. "*Black Lace* is a lifestyle magazine for African-American lesbians. Its content ranges from erotic imagery to political commentary." Quarterly. Estab. 1991.

Needs Ethnic/multicultural, lesbian. "Avoid interracial stories of idealized pornography." Accepts 4 mss/year. Recently published work by Nicole King, Wanda Thompson, Lynn K. Pannell, Sheree Ann Slaughter, Lyn Lifshin, JoJo and Drew Alise Timmens. Publishes short shorts. Also publishes literary essays, literary criticism, poetry.

How to Contact Query with published clips or send complete ms. Send a disposable copy of ms. No simultaneous submissions. Accepts electronic submissions. Sample copy for $7. Writer's guidelines free.

Payment/Terms Pays $50 and 2 contributor's copies. Acquires first North American serial rights. Right to anthologize.

Advice "*Black Lace* seeks erotic material of the highest quality. The most important thing is that the work be erotic and that it feature black lesbians or themes. Study the magazine to see what we do and how we do it. Some fiction is very romantic, other is highly sexual. Most articles in *Black Lace* cater to black lesbians between two extremes."

$ BRUTARIAN, The Magazine of Brutiful Art

9405 Ulysses Ct., Burke VA 22015. E-mail: brutarian@msn.com. Web site: www.brutarian.com. "A healthy knowledge of the great works of antiquity and an equally healthy contempt for most of what passes today as culture." Quarterly. Estab. 1991. Circ. 5,000.

Needs Adventure, confessions, erotica, experimental, fantasy, horror, humor/satire, mystery/suspense, novel excerpts, suspense. Publishes ms 3 months after acceptance.

How to Contact Send complete ms. Responds in 1 week to queries; 2 months to mss. Accepts simultaneous submissions. Sample copy for $6. Writer's guidelines online.

Payment/Terms Pays up to 10¢/word. Pays on publication for first, electronic rights.

$ ◎ CHARACTERS, Kids Short Story & Poetry Outlet

Davis Publications, P.O. Box 708, Newport NH 03773. (603)86 3-5896. Fax: (603)863-8198. E-mail: hotdog@nhv t.net. **Contact:** Cindy Davis, editor. Magazine: 5½×8½; 45 pages; saddle bound cover stock; illustrations. "We want to give kids a place to showcase their talents." Quarterly. Estab. 2003.

Needs "We accept all subjects of interest to kids. Particularly would like to see humor, mystery and adventure." Receives 60 unsolicited mss/month. Accepts 8-12 mss/issue; 36-48 mss/year. Publishes ms 1-6 months after acceptance. Publishes short shorts. Sometimes comments on rejected mss.

How to Contact Send complete ms. Accepts submissions by e-mail, fax. Send disposable copy of the ms and #10 SASE or e-mail address for reply. Responds in 2-4 weeks to mss. Accepts simultaneous submissions and reprints. Sample copy for $5. Writer's guidelines for #10 SASE, or by e-mail.

Payment/Terms Pays $5 and contributor's copy; additional copies $4. Pays on publication for one-time rights. Not copyrighted.

Advice "We love to see a well-thought-out plot and interesting, varied characters."

$ CHURCH EDUCATOR

Educational Ministries, Inc., 165 Plaza Dr., Prescott AZ 86303. (928)771-8601. Fax: (928)771-8621. E-mail: edmin2@aol.com. "*Church Educator* has programming ideas for the Christian educator in the mainline Protestant church. We are *not* on the conservative, fundamental side theologically, so slant articles to the liberal side. Programs should offer lots of questions and not give pat answers." Monthly. Estab. 1978. Circ. 2,500.

Needs Religious/inspirational; seasonal programs. Publishes ms 2 months after acceptance.

How to Contact Send complete ms. Accepts submissions by e-mail, fax, disk. Responds in 2 weeks to queries; 4 months to mss. Accepts simultaneous submissions. Sample copy for 9×12 SAE and 4 first-class stamps. Writer's guidelines free.

Payment/Terms Pays 3¢/word. Pays 60 days after publication. Acquires first rights.

$ ◪ ◎ CITY SLAB, Urban Tales of the Grotesque

City Slab Publications, 1705 Summit Ave. #314, Seattle WA 98122. (206)568-4343. E-mail: dave@cityslab.com. Web site: www.cityslab.com. **Contact:** Dave Lindschmidt, editor. Magazine: 8½×11; 72 gloss pages—at least 24 in color; illustrations; photos. "*City Slab* presents the best in urban horror today. *City Slab* offers an intriguing mix of familiar voices with new discoveries. Each page is a cold, wet kiss to the genre." —Evan Wright, *Rolling Stone*. Quarterly. Estab. 2002.

Needs "We're looking for taut, multi-leveled urban horror. Start the story with action. Capture the feel of your city whether it's real or imagined and have a story to tell! We love crime fiction but there has to be a horror slant to it. Steer away from first-person point of view." Publishes ms 3-6 months after acceptance. **Publishes**

6 new writers/year. Recently published work by Gerard Houarner, Jack Ketchum, Patricia Russo, and Robert Dunbar.

How to Contact Accepts submissions by e-mail (submission@cityslab.com with a copy to Scott@cityslab.com). Include estimated word count, brief bio and list of publications. Send disposable copy of ms and #10 SASE for reply only.'' Responds in 6 weeks to queries; 2 months to mss. Sample copy for $6. Writer's guidelines online.

Payment/Terms Pays 1-5¢ per word within sixty days of publication for first serial rights.

$ THE COUNTRY CONNECTION

Pinecone Publishing, P.O. Box 100, Boulter ON K0L 1G0 Canada. (613)332-3651. E-mail: editor@pinecone.on. ca. Web site: www.pinecone.on.ca. ''*The Country Connection* is a magazine for true nature lovers and the rural adventurer. Building on our commitment to heritage, cultural, artistic, and environmental themes, we continually add new topics to illuminate the country experience of people living within nature. Our goal is to chronicle rural life in its many aspects, giving 'voice' to the countryside.'' Estab. 1989. Circ. 5,000.

Needs Ontario history and heritage, humor/satire, nature, environment, the arts, country living. ''Canadian material by Canadian authors only.'' Publishes ms 4 months after acceptance.

How to Contact Send complete ms. Accepts submissions by e-mail, disk. Sample copy for $5.70. Writer's guidelines online.

Payment/Terms Pays 10¢/word. Pays on publication for first rights.

CREATIVE WITH WORDS PUBLICATIONS

Creative With Words Publications, P.O. Box 223226, Carmel CA 93922. Fax: (831)655-8627. E-mail: geltrich@m bay.net.. Web site: members.tripod.com/CreativeWithWords. **Contact:** Brigitta Geltrich, general editor.

Needs Ethnic/multicultural, humor/satire, mystery/suspense (amateur sleuth, private eye), regional (folklore), young adult/teen (adventure, historical). ''Do not submit essays.'' No violence or erotica, overly religious fiction or sensationalism. ''Once a year we publish an anthology of the writings of young writers titled, ''We are Writers, Too!'' List of upcoming themes available for SASE. Limit poetry to 20 lines or less, 46 characters per line or less. Receives 250-500 unsolicited mss/month. Accepts 50-80 mss/year. Publishes ms 1-2 months after acceptance. Recently published work by Najwa Salam Brax, Sirock Brighton, William Bridge and Maria Dickerhof. Average length: 800 words. Publishes short shorts. Also publishes poetry. Sometimes comments on rejected mss.

How to Contact Send complete ms with a cover letter with SASE. Include estimated word count. Responds in 2 weeks to queries; 2 months to mss. Sample copy for $6. Writer's guidelines for #10 SASE.

Payment/Terms 20% reduction cost on 1-9 copies ordered, 30% reduction on each copy on order of 10 or more. Acquires one-time rights.

Advice ''We offer a great variety of themes. We look for clean family-type fiction. Also, we ask the writer to look at the world from a different perspective, research topic thoroughly, be creative, apply brevity, tell the story from a character's viewpoint, tighten dialogue, be less descriptive, proofread before submitting and be patient. We will not publish every manuscript we receive. It has to be in standard English, well written, proofread. We do not appreciate receiving manuscripts where we have to do the proofreading and the correcting of grammar.''

DAN RIVER ANTHOLOGY

Conservatory of American Letters, P.O. Box 298, Thomaston ME 04861. (207)226-7528. Web site: www.america nletters.org. **Contact**: R.S. Danbury III, editor. Book: 6×9; 192 pages; 60 lb. paper; gloss 10 pt. full-color cover. Deadline every year is March 31, with acceptance/rejection by May 15, proofs out by June 15, and book released December 7. Annual. Estab. 1984. Circ. 750.

Needs Adventure, ethnic/multicultural, experimental, fantasy, historical, horror, humor/satire, literary, mainstream, psychic/supernatural/occult, regional, romance (contemporary and historical), science fiction, suspense, western, contemporary, prose poem, senior citizen/retirement. ''Virtually anything but porn, evangelical, juvenile. Would like to see more first-person adventure.'' Reads ''mostly in April.'' Length: 800-3,500 words; average length: 2,000-2,400 words. Also publishes poetry.

How to Contact Send complete ms. No simultaneous submissions. Nothing previously published. Sample copy for $16.95 paperback, $39.95 cloth, plus $3.50 shipping. Writer's guidelines available for #10 SASE or online.

Payment/Terms Payment ''depends on your experience with us, as it is a nonrefundable advance against royalties on all sales that we can attribute to your influence. For first-timers, the advance is about 1¢/word.'' Pays on acceptance for first rights.

Advice ''Read an issue or two, know the market. Don't submit without reading guidelines on the Web or send #10 SASE.''

◯ DOWN IN THE DIRT, The Publication Revealing all your Dirty Little Secrets

Scars Publications and Design, 829 Brian Court, Gurnee IL 60031-3155. (847)281-9070. E-mail: alexrand@scars. tv. Web site: scars.tv. **Contact**: Alexandria Rand, editor. Magazine: $5^1/_2 \times 8^1/_2$; 60 lb. paper; illustrations; photos. Monthly. Estab. 2000.

Needs Adventure, ethnic/multicultural, experimental, fantasy, feminist, gay, historical, horror, lesbian, literary, mystery/suspense, New Age, psychic/supernatural/occult, science fiction. No religious or rhyming or family-oriented material. Publishes ms within 1 year after acceptance. Recently published work by Simon Perchik, Jim Dewitt, Jennifer Connelly, L.B. Sedlacek, Aeon Logan, Helena Wolfe. Average length: 1,000 words. Publishes short shorts. Also publishes poetry. Always, if asked, comments on rejected mss.

How to Contact Query with published clips or send complete ms. Prefers submissions only by e-mail. Send SASE (or IRC) for return of the ms or disposable copy of the ms and #10 SASE for reply only. "If you have e-mail, please send electronic submisssions instead." Responds in 1 month to queries; 1 month to mss. Accepts simultaneous, multiple submissions and reprints. Sample copy for $6. Writer's guidelines for SASE, e-mail or on the Web site. Reviews fiction.

◈ $◎ DREAMS & VISIONS, Spiritual Fiction

Skysong Press, 35 Peter St. S., Orillia ON L3V 5A8 Canada. (705)329-1770. Fax: (705)329-1770. E-mail: skysong @bconnex.net. Web site: www.bconnex.net/~skysong. **Contact**: Steve Stanton, editor. Magazine: $5^1/_2 \times 8^1/_2$; 56 pages; 20 lb. bond paper; glossy cover. "Innovative literary fiction for adult Christian readers." Semiannual. Estab. 1988. Circ. 200.

Needs Experimental, fantasy, humor/satire, literary, mainstream, mystery/suspense, novel excerpts, religious/ inspirational, science fiction, slice-of-life vignettes. "We do not publish stories that glorify violence or perversity. All stories should portray a Christian worldview or expand upon Biblical themes or ethics in an entertaining or enlightening manner." Receives 20 unsolicited mss/month. Accepts 7 mss/issue; 14 mss/year. Publishes ms 4-8 months after acceptance. **Publishes 3 new writers/year.** Recently published work by Fred McGavran, Steven Mills, Donna Farley, and Michael Vance. Length: 2,000-6,000 words; average length: 2,500 words.

How to Contact Send complete ms. Responds in 3 weeks to queries; 3 months to mss. Accepts simultaneous submissions. Sample copy for $4.95. Writer's guidelines online.

Payment/Terms Pays 1¢/word. Pays on publication for first North American serial, one-time, second serial (reprint) rights.

Advice "In general we look for work that has some literary value, that is in some way unique and relevant to Christian readers today. Our first priority is technical adequacy, though we will occasionally work with a beginning writer to polish a manuscript. Ultimately, we look for stories that glorify the Lord Jesus Christ, stories that build up rather than tear down, that exalt the sanctity of life, the holiness of God, and the value of the family."

$◢ THE FIRST LINE

Blue Cubicle Press, LLC, P.O. Box 250382, Plano TX 75025-0382. (972)824-0646. E-mail: submissions@thefirstli ne.com. Web site: www.thefirstline.com. **Contact**: Robin LaBounty, manuscript coordinator. Magzine: 8×5; 64-72 pages; 20 lb. bond paper; 80 lb. cover stock. "We only publish stories that start with the first line provided. We are a collection of tales—of different directions writers can take when they start from the same place." Quarterly. Estab. 1999. Circ. 800.

Needs Adventure, ethnic/multicultural, fantasy, gay, humor/satire, lesbian, literary, mainstream, mystery/ suspense, regional, romance, science fiction, western. Receives 200 unsolicited mss/month. Accepts 12 mss/ issue; 48 mss/year. Publishes ms 1 month after acceptance. **Publishes 6 new writers/year.** Length: 300-3,000 words; average length: 1,500 words. Publishes short shorts. Also publishes literary essays, literary criticism. Often comments on rejected mss.

How to Contact Send complete ms. Accepts submissions by e-mail. Send SASE for return of ms or disposable copy of the ms and #10 SASE for reply only. Responds in 1 week to queries; 3 months to mss. Accepts multiple submissions. No simultaneous submissions. Sample copy for $3.50. Writer's guidelines for SASE, e-mail or on Web site. Reviews fiction.

Payment/Terms Pays $20 maximum and contributor's copy; additional copy $2. Pays on publication.

Advice "Don't just write the first story that comes to mind after you read the sentence. If it is obvious, chances are other people are writing about the same thing. Don't try so hard. Be willing to accept criticism."

$◎ FUN FOR KIDZ

Bluffton News Publishing and Printing Company, P.O. Box 227, 103 N. Main Street, Bluffton OH 45817-0227. (419)358-4610. Fax: (419)358-5027. Web site: www.funforkidz.com. **Contact**: Marilyn Edwards, editor. Magazine: 7×8; 49 pages; illustrations; photographs. "*Fun for Kidz* focuses on activity. The children are encouraged to solve problems, explore and develop character. Target age: 6-13 years." Bimonthly. Estab. 2002. Circ. 8,000.

Needs Children's/juvenile (adventure, animal, easy-to-read, historical, mystery, preschool, series, sports). Previous themes: Bugs; Oceans; Animals; Camping; Fun with Stars; Healthy Fun; Summer Splash; In the Mountains; Fun with Words. List of upcoming themes for SASE. Accepts 10 mss/issue; 60 mss/year. Publishes short shorts. Also publishes poetry. Sometimes comments on rejected mss.

How to Contact Send complete ms with cover letter. Include estimated word count and brief bio. Responds in 6 weeks to queries; 6 months to mss. Accepts simultaneous, multiple submissions. Sample copy for $5. Writer's guidelines for #10 SASE.

Payment/Terms Pays 5¢/word and 1 contributor's copy. Pays on publication for first rights.

Advice "Work needs to be appropriate for a children's publication ages 6-13 years. Request a theme list so story submitted will work into an upcoming issue."

◻ ◎ THE FUNNY PAPER

F/J Writers Service, 615 NW Jacob Dr. #206, Lee's Summit, MO 64081. E-mail: felixkcmo@aol.com. Web site: www.funnypaper.info. **Contact:** F.H. Fellhauer, editor. Zine specializing in humor, contest and poetry: 8½ × 11; 8 pages. Published 4 times/year. No summer or Christmas. Estab. 1984.

Needs Children's/juvenile, humor/satire, literary. "No controversial fiction." Receives 10-20 unsolicited mss/month. Accepts 1 mss/issue; 4-5 mss/year. Length:1,000 words; average length: 295 words. Publishes short shorts. Also publishes poetry. Sometimes comments on rejected mss.

How to Contact Accepts submissions by e-mail. Send for guidelines. Include estimated word count with submission. Send disposable copy of ms and #10 SASE for reply only. Responds in 2 weeks to queries; 1-3 months to mss. Accepts simultaneous submissions and reprints. Sample copy for $3.

Payment/Terms Prizes for stories, jokes and poems for $5-100 (humor, inspirational, fillers). Additional copies $3. Pays on publication for first, one-time rights.

Advice "Do your best work, no trash. We try to keep abreast of online publishing and provide information."

$ ◻ ◎ HARDBOILED

Gryphon Publications, P.O. Box 209, Brooklyn NY 11228. Web site: www.gryphonbooks.com. **Contact:** Gary Lovisi, editor. Magazine: Digest-sized; 100 pages; offset paper; color cover; illustrations. "Hard-hitting crime fiction and private-eye stories—the newest and most cutting-edge work and classic reprints." Semiannual. Estab. 1988. Circ. 1,000.

Needs Mystery/suspense (private eye, police procedural, noir), hard-boiled crime, and private-eye stories, all on the cutting edge. No "pastiches, violence for the sake of violence." Wants to see more non-private-eye hard-boiled. Receives 40-60 unsolicited mss/month. Accepts 10-20 mss/issue. Publishes ms 18 months after acceptance. **Publishes 5-10 new writers/year.** Recently published work by Andrew Vachss, Stephen Solomita, Joe Hensley, Mike Black. Sometimes comments on rejected mss.

How to Contact Query with or without published clips or send complete ms. Accepts submissions by fax. Query with SASE only on anything over 3,000 words. All stories must be submitted in hard copy. If accepted, e-mail as an attachment in a Word document. Responds in 2 weeks to queries; 1 month to mss. Accepts simultaneous submissions and reprints. Sample copy for $10 or double issue for $20 (add $1.50 book postage). Writer's guidelines for #10 SASE.

Payment/Terms Pays $5-50. Pays on publication for first North American serial, one-time rights.

Advice By "hardboiled" the editor does not mean rehashing of pulp detective fiction from the 1940s and 1950s but rather realistic, gritty material. We look for good writing, memorable characters, intense situations. Lovisi could be called a pulp fiction "afficionado," however he also publishes *Paperback Parade* and holds an annual vintage paperback fiction convention each year. "It is advisable new writers try a subscription to the magazine to better see the type of stories and writing I am looking for. $35 gets you the next 4 hard-hitting issues."

N ◻ ◎ IRREANTUM, Exploring Mormon Literature

The Association for Mormon Letters, P.O. Box 13 15, Salt Lake City UT 84 110. (801)582-2090. Web site: www.aml-online.org. **Contact:** Fiction Editor. Magazine or Zine: 8½ × 7½; 100-120 pages; 20 lb. paper; 20 lb. color cover; illustrations; photos. "While focused on Mormonism, *Irreantum* is a cultural, humanities-oriented magazine, not a religious magazine. Our guiding principle is that Mormonism is grounded in a sufficiently unusual, cohesive, and extended historical and cultural experience that it has become like a nation, an ethnic culture. We can speak of Mormon literature at least as surely as we can of a Jewish or Southern literature. *Irreantum* publishes stories, one-act dramas, stand-alone novel and drama excerpts, and poetry by, for, or about Mormons (as well as author interviews, essays, and reviews). The magazine's audience includes readers of any or no religious faith who are interested in literary exploration of the Mormon culture, mindset, and world-view through Mormon themes and characters. *Irreantum* is currently the only magazine devoted to Mormon literature." Bi-annual. Estab. 1999. Circ. 500.

Needs Adventure, ethnic/multicultural (Mormon), experimental, family saga, fantasy, feminist, historical, horror, humor/satire, literary, mainstream, mystery/suspense, New Age, psychic/supernatural/occult, regional (Western USA/Mormon), religious/inspirational, romance, science fiction, thriller/espionage, translations, young adult/teen. Receives 5 unsolicited mss/month. Accepts 3 mss/issue; 12 mss/year. Publishes ms 3-12 months after acceptance. **Publishes 6 new writers/year.** Recently published work by Anne Perry, Brady Udall, Brian Evenson and Robert Kirby. Length: 1,000-5,000 words; average length: 5,000 words. Publishes short shorts. Also publishes literary essays, literary criticism, poetry. Sometimes comments on rejected mss.

How to Contact Accepts submissions by e-mail. Send complete ms with cover letter. Include brief bio and list of publications. Send a disposable copy of ms and #10 SASE for reply only. Responds in 2 weeks to queries; 2 months to mss. Accepts simultaneous, multiple submissions and reprints. Sample copy for $6. Writer's guidelines by e-mail. Reviews fiction.

Payment/Terms Pays $0-100. Pays on publication for one-time, electronic rights.

Advice *"Irreantum* is not interested in didactic or polemical fiction that primarily attempts to prove or disprove Mormon doctrine, history or corporate policy. We encourage beginning writers to focus on human elements first, with Mormon elements introduced only as natural and organic to the story. Readers can tell if you are honestly trying to explore the human experience or if you are writing with a propagandistic agenda either for or against Mormonism. For conservative, orthodox Mormon writers, beware of sentimentalism, simplistic resolutions, and foregone conclusions."

ITALIAN AMERICANA

URI/CCE, 80 Washington Street, Providence RI 02903-1803. (401)277-5306. Fax: (401)277-5100. E-mail: bonom oal@etal.uri.edu. Web site: www.uri.edu/prov/italian/italian.html. **Contact:** C.B. Albright, editor. Magazine: 6×9; 240 pages; varnished cover; perfect bound; photos. *"Italian Americana* contains historical articles, fiction, poetry and memoirs, all concerning the Italian experience in the Americas." Semiannual. Estab. 1974. Circ. 1,200.

Needs Literary, Italian American. No nostalgia. Wants to see more fiction featuring "individualized characters." Receives 10 unsolicited mss/month. Accepts 3 mss/issue; 6-7 mss/year. Publishes ms up to 1 year after acceptance. Agented fiction 5%. **Publishes 2-4 new writers/year.** Recently published work by Mary Caponegro and Sal LaPuma. Publishes short shorts. Also publishes literary essays, literary criticism, poetry. Sometimes comments on rejected mss.

How to Contact Send complete ms (in duplicate) with a cover letter. Include 3-5 line bio, list of publications. Responds in 1 month to queries; 2 months to mss. No simultaneous submissions. Sample copy for $7. Writer's guidelines for #10 SASE. Reviews fiction.

Payment/Terms 1 contributor's copy; additional copies $7. Acquires first North American serial rights.

Advice "Please individualize characters, instead of presenting types (i.e., lovable uncle, etc.). No nostalgia."

KELSEY REVIEW

Mercer County College, P.O. Box B, Trenton NJ 08690. (609)586-4800. Fax: (609)586-2318. E-mail: kelsey.revie w@mccc.edu. Web site: www.mccc.edu. **Contact:** Ed Carmien, Holly-Katherine Mathews, editors. Magazine: 7×14; 98 pages; glossy paper; soft cover. "Must live or work in Mercer County, NJ." Annual. Estab. 1988. Circ. 1,900.

Needs Regional (Mercer County, NJ only), open. Receives 10 unsolicited mss/month. Accepts 24 mss/issue. Reads mss only in May. **Publishes 10 new writers/year.** Recently published work by Thom Beachamps, Janet Kirk, Bruce Petronio. Publishes short shorts. Also publishes literary essays, poetry.

How to Contact SASE for return of ms. Responds in June to mss. Accepts multiple submissions. Sample copy free.

Payment/Terms 5 contributor's copies. Rights revert to author on publication.

Advice Look for "quality, intellect, grace and guts. Avoid sentimentality, overwriting and self-indulgence. Work on clarity, depth and originality."

KRAX MAGAZINE

63 Dixon Lane, Leeds Yorkshire LS12 4RR United Kingdom. **Contact:** A. Robson, co-editor. *"Krax* publishes lighthearted, humorous and whimsical writing. It is for anyone seeking light relief at a gentle pace. Our audience has grown middle-aged along with us, especially now that we're annual and not able to provide the instant fix demanded by teens and twenties."

Needs "No war stories, horror, space bandits, boy-girl soap opera. We publish mostly poetry of a lighthearted nature but use comic or spoof fiction, witty and humorous essays. Would like to see more whimsical items, trivia ramblings or anything daft." Accepts 1 mss/issue. **Publishes 1 new writer/year.** Recently published work by Charles Stevens, Neil Lombardi.

How to Contact No specific guidelines but cover letter appreciated. Sample copy for $2.

Advice "Don't spend too long on scene-setting or character construction, as this inevitably produces an anti-climax in a short piece. We look for original settings, distinctive pacing, description related to plot, i.e. only dress character in bow tie and gumboots if you're having a candlelight dinner in The Everglades. Look at what you enjoy in all forms of fiction—from strip cartoons to novels, movies to music lyrics—then try to put some of this into your own writing.''

$🖅🖮 LADY CHURCHILL'S ROSEBUD WRISTLET

Small Beer Press, 176 Prospect Ave., Northampton MA 01060. E-mail: info@lcrw.net. Web site: www.lcrw.net/lcrw. **Contact:** Gavin Grant, editor. Zine: half legal size; 40 pages; 60 lb. paper; glossy cover; illustrations; photos. Semiannual. Estab. 1996. Circ. 700.

Needs Comics/graphic novels, experimental, fantasy, feminist, literary, science fiction, translations, short story collections. Receives 25 unsolicited mss/month. Accepts 4-6 mss/issue; 8-12 mss/year. Publishes ms 6-12 months after acceptance. **Publishes 2-4 new writers/year.** Recently published work by Amy Beth Forbes, Jeffrey Ford, Carol Emshwiller and Theodora Goss. Length: 200-7,000 words; average length: 3,500 words. Also publishes literary essays, poetry. Sometimes comments on rejected mss.

How to Contact Send complete ms with a cover letter. Include estimated word count. Send SASE (or IRC) for return of ms, or send a disposable copy of ms and #10 SASE for reply only. Responds in 2 weeks to queries; 1-3 months to mss. Sample copy for $5. Writer's guidelines online. Reviews fiction.

Payment/Terms Pays $.01/word, $20 minimum and 2 contributor's copies; additional copies contributor's discount 40%. Pays on publication for first, one-time rights.

Advice "I like fiction that tends toward the speculative."

🌐 $THE LONDON MAGAZINE, Review of Literature and the Arts

The London Magazine, 32 Addison Grove, London England W4 1ER United Kingdom. (00)44 0208 400 5882. Fax: (00)44 0208 994 1713. E-mail: admin@thelondonmagazine.net. Web site: www.thelondonmagazine.ukf.net. Bimonthly. Estab. 1732. Circ. 1,000.

Needs Adventure, confessions, erotica, ethnic/multicultural, experimental, fantasy, historical, humor/satire, mainstream, mystery/suspense, novel excerpts, religious/inspirational, romance, slice-of-life vignettes, suspense. Publishes ms 4 months after acceptance.

How to Contact Send complete ms. Include SASE. Responds in 1 month to queries; 4 months to mss. Accepts simultaneous submissions. Sample copy for £8.75. Writer's guidelines free.

Payment/Terms Pays minimum £20; maximum rate is negotiable. Pays on publication for first rights.

◎ NEW METHODS, The Journal of Animal Health Technology

713 S. Main St. C1, Willits CA 95490. (707)456-1262. E-mail: norwal13@yahoo.com. Web site: www.geocities.com/norwal13photos.yahoo.com/norwal13. **Contact:** Ronald S. Lippert, publisher. Newsletter ("could become a magazine again"): 8½×11; 2-4 pages; 20 lb. paper; illustrations; "rarely photos." Network service for mostly professionals in the animal field; e.g., animal health technicians. Monthly. Estab. 1976. Circ. 5,608.

Needs Animals: contemporary, experimental, historical, mainstream, regional. No stories unrelated to animals. Receives 12 unsolicited mss/month. Accepts 1 mss/issue; 12 mss/year. Publishes short shorts. Occasionally comments on rejected mss.

How to Contact Query first with theme, length, expected time of completion, photos/illustrations, if any, biographical sketch of author, all necessary credits, or send complete ms. Responds in up to 4 months to queries. Accepts simultaneous, multiple submissions. Sample copy for $2. Writer's guidelines for SASE.

Payment/Terms Acquires one-time rights. Sponsors awards/contests.

Advice "Emotion, personal experiences—make the person feel it. We are growing."

📖 ◎ THE NOCTURNAL LYRIC, Journal of the Bizarre

The Nocturnal Lyric, P.O. Box 542, Astoria OR 97103. E-mail: nocturnallyric@melodymail.com. Web site: www.angelfire.com/ca/nocturnallyric. **Contact:** Susan Moon, editor. Magazine: 8½×11; 40 pages; illustrations. "Fiction and poetry submitted should have a bizarre horror theme. Our audience encompasses people who stand proudly outside of the mainstream society." Annual. Estab. 1987. Circ. 400.

Needs Horror (dark fantasy, futuristic, psychological, supernatural, satirical). "No sexually graphic material—it's too overdone in the horror genre lately." Receives 25-30 unsolicited mss/month. Accepts 10-11 mss/issue; 10-11 mss/year. Publishes ms 1 year after acceptance. **Publishes 20 new writers/year.** Recently published work by Mary Blais, Brian Biswas, John Sunseri, and J.A. Davidson. Length: 2,000 words maximum; average length: 1,500 words. Publishes short shorts. Also publishes literary essays, poetry. Rarely comments on rejected mss.

How to Contact Send complete ms with cover letter. Include estimated word count. Responds in 3 month to queries; 8 months to mss. Accepts simultaneous, multiple submissions and reprints. Sample copy for $2 (back issue); $3 (current issue). Writer's guidelines online.

Payment/Terms Pays with discounts on subscriptions and discounts on copies of issue. Pays on acceptance Not copyrighted.

Advice "A manuscript stands out when the story has a very original theme and the ending is not predictable. Don't be afraid to be adventurous with your story. Mainstream horror can be boring. Surreal, satirical horror is what true nightmares are all about."

$ ⊘ ◎ NOVA SCIENCE FICTION MAGAZINE

Nova Publishing Company, 17983 Paseo Del Sol, Chino Hills CA 91709-3947. (909)393-0806. **Contact:** Wesley Kawato, editor. Zine specializing in evangelical Christian science fiction: $8^1/_2 \times 5^1/_2$; 64 pages; cardstock cover. "We publish religious science fiction short stories, no fantasy or horror. One story slot per issue will be reserved for a story written from an evangelical Christian viewpoint." Quarterly. Estab. 1999. Circ. 25.

Needs Science fiction (hard science/technological, soft/sociological, religious). "No stories where the villain is a religious fanatic and stories that assume the truth of evolution." Accepts 3 mss/issue; 12 mss/year. Publishes ms 3 months after acceptance. **Publishes 7 new writers/year.** Recently published work by Lawrence Dagstine, Brandon Barr, Jerry Olson, Brad Toner, Michael Cooper, and Chris Mazzoli. Length: 250-7,000 words; average length: 4,000 words. Publishes short shorts. Sometimes comments on rejected mss.

How to Contact Query first. Include estimated word count and list of publications. Responds in 3 months to queries and mss. Send SASE (or IRC) for return of ms. Accepts reprints, multiple submissions. Sample copy for $6. Guidelines free for SASE.

Payment/Terms Pays $1.25-35. Pays on publication for first North American serial rights. Not copyrighted.

Advice "Make sure your plot is believable and describe your characters well enough so I can visualize them. If I like it, I buy it. I like happy endings and heroes with a strong sense of faith."

⊘ NUTHOUSE, Your Place for Humor Therapy

Twin Rivers Press, P.O. Box 119, Ellenton FL 34222. E-mail: nuthous449@aol.com. Web site: hometown.aol. com/nuthous499/index2.html. **Contact:** Dr. Ludwig "Needles" Von Quirk, chief of staff. Zine: digest-sized; 12-16 pages; bond paper; illustrations; photos. "Humor of all genres for an adult readership that is not easily offended." Published every 2-3 months. Estab. 1993. Circ. 100.

Needs Humor/satire (erotica, experimental, fantasy, feminist, historical [general], horror, literary, mainstream/contemporary, mystery/suspense, psychic/supernatural/occult, romance, science fiction and westerns). Receives 30-50 unsolicited mss/month. Accepts 5-10 mss/issue; 50-60 mss/year. Publishes ms 6-12 months after acceptance. **Publishes 10-15 new writers/year.** Recently published work by Michael Fowler, Dale Andrew White, and Jim Sullivan. Length: 100-1,000 words; average length: 500 words. Publishes short shorts. Also publishes literary essays, literary criticism, poetry. Often comments on rejected mss.

How to Contact Send complete ms with a cover letter. Include estimated word count, bio (paragraph) and list of publications. SASE for return of ms or send disposable copy of ms. Sample copy for $1.25 (payable to Twin Rivers Press). Writer's guidelines for #10 SASE.

Payment/Terms Pays 1 contributor's copy. Acquires one-time rights. Not copyrighted.

Advice Looks for "laugh-out-loud prose. Strive for original ideas; read the great humorists—Saki, Woody Allen, Robert Benchley, Garrison Keillor, John Irving—and learn from them. We are turned off by sophomoric attempts at humor built on a single, tired, overworked gag or pun; give us a story with a beginning, middle and end."

⊘ THE OAK

1530 Seventh Street, Rock Island IL 61201. (309)788-3980. **Contact:** Betty Mowery, editor. Magazine: $8^1/_2 \times 11$; 8-10 pages. "To provide a showcase for new authors while showing the work of established authors as well; to publish wholesome work, something with a message." Bimonthly. Estab. 1991. Circ. 300.

Needs Adventure, experimental, fantasy, humor/satire, mainstream, contemporary, poems. No erotica or love poetry. "No killing of humans or animals." "Gray Squirrel" appears as a section in *Oak*, accepts poetry and fiction from seniors age 50 and up. Length: 500 words. Receives 25 unsolicited mss/month. Accepts 12 mss/issue. Publishes ms 3 months after acceptance. **Publishes 25 new writers/year.**

How to Contact Send complete ms. Responds in 1 week to mss. Accepts simultaneous, multiple submissions and reprints. Sample copy for $3; subscription $10. Writer's guidelines for #10 SASE.

Payment/Terms None, but not necessary to buy a copy in order to be published. Acquires first rights.

Advice "I do not want erotica, extreme violence or killing of humans or animals for the sake of killing. Just be yourself when you write. Also, write *tight*. Please include SASE or manuscripts will be destroyed. Be sure name and address are on the manuscript. Study the markets for length of manuscript and what type of material is wanted. *The Shepherd* needs inspirational fiction up to 500 words, poetry, and Biblical character profiles. Same address as *The Oak*. Sample $3."

⚡ $⬚ ON SPEC

P.O. Box 4727, Station South, Edmonton AB T6E 5G6 Canada. (780)413-0215. Fax: (780)413-1538. E-mail: onspec@onspec.ca. Web site: www.onspec.ca/. **Contact:** Diane L. Walton, editor. Magazine: 5¼×8; 112-120 pages; illustrations. "We publish speculative fiction by new and established writers, with a strong preference for Canadian authored works." Quarterly. Estab. 1989. Circ. 2,000.

Needs Fantasy, horror, science fiction, magic realism. No media tie-in or shaggy-alien stories. No condensed or excerpted novels, religious/inspirational stories, fairy tales. "We would like to see more horror, fantasy, science fiction—well-developed stories with complex characters and strong plots." Receives 100 unsolicited mss/month. Accepts 10 mss/issue; 40 mss/year. "We read manuscripts during the month after each deadline: February 28/May 31/August 31/November 30." Publishes ms 6-18 months after acceptance. **Publishes 10-15 new writers/year.** Recently published work by Mark Shainblum, Hugh Spencer and Leah Bobet. Length: 1,000-6,000 words; average length: 4,000 words. Also publishes poetry. Often comments on rejected mss.

How to Contact Send complete ms. Accepts submissions by disk. SASE for return of ms or send a disposable copy of ms plus #10 SASE for response. Include Canadian postage or IRCs. No e-mail or fax submissions. Responds in 2 weeks to queries; 4 months after deadline to mss. Accepts simultaneous submissions. Sample copy for $8. Writer's guidelines for #10 SASE or on Web site.

Payment/Terms Pays $50-180 for fiction. Short stories (under 1,000 words): $50 plus 1 contributor's copy. Pays on acceptance for first North American serial rights.

Advice "We're looking for original ideas with a strong SF element, excellent dialogue, and characters who are so believable, our readers will really care about them."

⚡ ⬚ ◎ OPEN MINDS QUARTERLY, A Psychosocial Literary Journal

NISA/Northern Initiative for Social Action, 680 Kirkwood Dr., Bldg 1, Sudbury ON P3E 1X3 Canada. (705)675-9193, ext. 8286. Fax: (705)675-3501. E-mail: openminds@nisa.on.ca. Web site: www.nisa.on.ca. **Contact:** Dinah Laprairie, editor. Magazine: 8½×11; 28 pages; illustrations; photos. "*Open Minds Quarterly* publishes quality, insightful writing from consumer/survivors of mental illness who have experiences to share and voices to be heard. We inform mental health professionals, family and friends, fellow consumer/survivors, and society at large of the strength, intelligence and creativity of our writers. The purpose is to eliminate the stigma associated with mental illness." Quarterly. Estab. 1998. Circ. 750.

Needs Mental illness, mental health. Receives 5-10 unsolicited mss/month. Accepts 1-2 mss/issue; 4-8 mss/year. **Publishes many new writers/year.** Occasionally publishes short shorts. Also publishes literary essays, poetry. Sometimes comments on rejected mss.

How to Contact Send complete ms with cover letter. Writers must be individuals who have experienced mental illness. Accepts submissions by e-mail, mail, disk. Send disposable copy of the ms and #10 SASE for reply only. Responds in 1 week to queries; 20 weeks to mss. Accepts simultaneous, multiple submissions and reprints. Sample copy for $5. Writer's guidelines for #10 SASE, online, or by e-mail.

Payment/Terms Pays 2-3 contributor's copies. Acquires first, one-time rights.

⚡ ⬚ ORACLE STORY & LETTERS

Rising Star Publishers, 7510 Lake Glen Drive, Glen Dale MD 20769. (301)352-233. Fax: (301)352-2529. E-mail: hekwonna@aol.com. **Contact:** Obi H. Ekwonna, publisher. Magazine: 5½×8½; 60 lb. white bound paper. Quarterly. Estab. 1989. Circ. 1,000.

Needs Adventure, children's/juvenile (adventure, fantasy, historical, mystery, series), comics/graphic novels, ethnic/multicultural, family saga, fantasy (sword and sorcery), historical, literary, mainstream, military/war, romance (contemporary, historical, suspense), thriller/espionage, western (frontier saga), young adult/teen (adventure, historical). Does not want gay/lesbian or erotica works. Receives 10 unsolicited mss/month. Accepts 7 mss/issue. Publishes ms 4 months after acceptance. **Publishes 5 new writers/year.** Recently published work by Joseph Manco, I.B.S. Sesay. Publishes short shorts. Also publishes literary essays, literary criticism, poetry. Rarely comments on rejected mss.

How to Contact Send complete ms. Accepts submissions by disk. Send SASE (or IRC) for return of the ms, or send a disposable copy of the ms and #10 SASE for reply only. Responds in 1 month to mss. Accepts multiple submissions. Sample copy for $10. Writer's guidelines for #10 SASE, or by e-mail.

Payment/Terms Pays 1 contributor's copy. Pays on publication for first North American serial rights.

Advice "Read anything you can lay your hands on."

🌐 ⬚ ◎ THE ORPHAN LEAF REVIEW

Orphan Leaf Press, J. Wallis, 26 Grove Park Terrace, Bristol BS16 2BN United Kingdom. E-mail: orphanleaf@jpwallis.co.uk. Web site: www.orphanleaf.co.uk. **Contact:** James Paul Wallis, editor. Zine specializing in creative writing: A5, 40 pages, mixed paper, card cover. Contains illustrations. "Each issue is a collection of orphan leaves. An orphan leaf is a page, seemingly torn from some parent book. Each page is a different size and texture. Read to the end of the leaf, let your imagination do the rest." Triannual. Estab. 2004. Circ. 100.

Needs All categories considered, but submission must be an orphan leaf. Receives 15 mss/month. Accepts 15 mss/issue. Manuscript published 2 months after acceptance. Length: 500 words (min)-800 words (max). Average length: 700 words. Also publishes literary essays, literary criticism, poetry. Never comments on/critiques rejected manuscripts.

How to Contact Accepts submissions by e-mail. Responds to queries in 1 weeks. Responds to mss in 6 months. Considers simultaneous submissions, previously published submissions, multiple submissions. Sample copy available for $10.

Payment and Terms Writers receive 1 contributor copy. Additional copies $10. Pays on publication. Publication is copyrighted.

Advice "Buy a copy to view the general standard. I have a surplus of fiction and poetry. So nonfiction and pieces from other types of book stand more chance of selection."

📁 ◎ 🉐 OUTER DARKNESS, Where Nightmares Roam Unleashed

Outer Darkness Press, 1312 N. Delaware Place, Tulsa OK 74110. **Contact**: Dennis Kirk, editor. Zine: $8^{1}/_{2} \times 5^{1}/_{2}$; 60-80 pages; 20 lb. paper; 90 lb. glossy cover; illustrations. Specializes in imaginative literature. "Variety is something I strive for in *Outer Darkness*. In each issue we present readers with great tales of science fiction and horror along with poetry, cartoons and interviews/essays. I seek to provide readers with a magazine which, overall, is fun to read. My readers range in age from 16 to 70." Quarterly. Estab. 1994. Circ. 500.

- Fiction published in *Outer Darkness* has received honorable mention in *The Year's Best Fantasy and Horror*.

Needs Fantasy (science), horror, mystery/suspense (with horror slant), psychic/supernatural/occult, romance (gothic), science fiction (hard science, soft/sociological). No straight mystery, pure fantasy—works which do not incorporate elements of science fiction and/or horror. Also, no slasher horror with violence, gore, sex instead of plot. Wants more "character driven tales—especially in the genre of science fiction and well-developed psychological horror. I do not publish works with children in sexual situations, and graphic language should be kept to a minimum." Receives 75-100 unsolicited mss/month. Accepts 7-9 mss/issue; 25-40 mss/year. **Publishes 2-5 new writers/year.** Recently published work by John Sunseri, Christopher Fulbright, Melinda Arnett, and James M. Steimle. Length: 1,500-5,000 words; average length: 3,000 words. Also publishes poetry. Always comments on rejected mss.

How to Contact Send complete ms with a cover letter. Include estimated word count, 50- to 75-word bio, list of publications and "any awards, honors you have received." Send SASE for reply, return of ms, or send a disposable copy of ms. Responds in 2 weeks to queries; 4 months to mss. Accepts simultaneous, multiple submissions. Sample copy for $4.95. Writer's guidelines for #10 SASE.

Payment/Terms Pays 3 contributor's copies for fiction; 2 for poetry and 3 for art. Pays on publication for one-time rights.

Advice "I look for strong characters and well-developed plot. And I definitely look for suspense. I want stories which move—and carry the reader along with them. Be patient and persistent. Often it's simply a matter of linking the right story with the right editor. I've received many stories which were good, but not what I wanted at the time. However, these stories worked well in another horror-sci-fi zine."

◎ PARADOXISM

University of New Mexico, 200 College Rd., Gallup NM 87301. Fax: (503)863-7532. E-mail: smarand@unm.edu. Web site: www.gallup.unm.edu/~smarandache/a/paradoxism.htm. **Contact:** Dr. Florentin Smarandache. Magazine: $8^{1}/_{2} \times 11$; 100 pages; illustrations. "*Paradoxism* is an avant-garde movement based on excessive use of antinomies, antitheses, contradictions, paradoxes in the literary creations set up by the editor in the 1980s as an anti-totalitarian protest." Annual. Estab. 1993. Circ. 500.

Needs Experimental, literary. "Contradictory, uncommon, experimental, avant garde." Plans specific themes in the next year. Publishes annual special fiction issue or anthology. Receives 5 unsolicited mss/month. Accepts 10 mss/issue. Recently published work by Mirecea Monu, Doru Motoc and Patrick Pinard. Publishes short shorts. Also publishes literary essays, literary criticism, poetry. Sometimes comments on rejected mss.

How to Contact Send a disposable copy of ms. Responds in 2 months to mss. Accepts simultaneous submissions. Sample copy for $19.95 and $8^{1}/_{2} \times 11$ SASE. Writer's guidelines online.

Payment/Terms Pays subscription. Pays on publication. Not copyrighted.

Advice "We look for work that refers to the paradoxism or is written in the paradoxist style. The Basic Thesis of the paradoxism: everything has a meaning and a non-meaning in a harmony with each other. The Essence of the paradoxism: a) the sense has a non-sense, and reciprocally B) the non-sense has a sense. The Motto of the paradoxism: 'All is possible, the impossible too!' The Symbol of the paradoxism: a spiral—optic illusion, or vicious circle."

☐ ◎ THE PEGASUS REVIEW

P.O. Box 88, Henderson MD 21640-0088. (410)482-6736. **Contact:** Art Bounds, editor. Magazine: $5^{1}/_{2} \times 8^{1}/_{2}$; 6-8 pages; illustrations. *"The Pegasus Review* is now a quarterly, done in a calligraphic format and occasionally illustrated. Each issue is based on a specific theme." Estab. 1980. Circ. 120.

- Because *The Pegasus Review* is done is a calligraphic format, fiction submissions must be very short. Two pages, says the editor, are the ideal length.

Needs Humor/satire, literary, religious/inspirational, prose poem. Wants more short-shorts ($2^{1}/_{2}$ pages ideal length) and essays. For 2008 themes please send SASE.

How to Contact Send complete ms. Send brief cover letter with author's background, name and prior credits, if any. Responds in 2 months to mss. Accepts simultaneous submissions. Sample copy for $2.50. Writer's guidelines for #10 SASE.

Payment/Terms Pays 2 contributor's copies. Acquires one-time rights. Sponsors awards/contests.

Advice "Perseverance is the key word. As a writer, encourage reading among young peple. Continue to check out marketing information and keep your work circulating in the mail."

☐ ◎ PRAYERWORKS, Encouraging God's people to do real work of ministry—intercessory prayer

The Master's Work, P.O. Box 301363, Portland OR 97294-9363. (503)761-2072. E-mail: vannm1@aol.com. Web site: www.prayerworksnw.org. **Contact:** V. Ann Mandeville, editor. Newsletter: $5^{1}/_{2} \times 8$; 4 pages; bond paper. "Our intended audience is 70% retired Christians and 30% families. We publish 350-500 word devotional material—fiction, nonfiction, biographical, poetry, clean quips and quotes. Our philosophy is evangelical Christian serving the body of Chirst in the area of prayer." Estab. 1988. Circ. 1,100.

Needs Religious/inspirational. "No nonevangelical Christian. Subject matter may include anything which will build relationship with the Lord—prayer, ways to pray, stories of answered prayer, teaching on a Scripture portion, articles that will build faith, or poems will all work." We even use a series occasionally. Publishes ms 2-6 months after acceptance. **Publishes 30 new writers/year.** Recently published work by Allen Audrey and Petey Prater. Length: 350-500 words; average length: 350-500 words. Publishes short shorts. Also publishes poetry. Often comments on rejected mss.

How to Contact Send complete ms with cover letter. Include estimated word count and a very short bio. Responds in 1 month to mss. Accepts simultaneous, multiple submissions and reprints. Writer's guidelines for #10 SASE.

Payment/Terms Pays free subscription to the magazine and contributor's copies. Pays on publication. Not copyrighted.

Advice Stories "must have a great take-away—no preaching; teach through action. Be thrifty with words—make them count."

$ ☐ PSI

P.O. Box 6218, Charlottesville VA 22906-6218. E-mail: asam@publisherssyndication.com. Web site: www.publisherssyndication.com. **Contact:** A.P. Samuels, editor. Magazine: $8^{1}/_{2} \times 11$; 32 pages; bond paper; self cover. "Mystery and romance." Bimonthly. Estab. 1987.

Needs Adventure, mystery/suspense (private eye), romance (contemporary, historical, young adult), western (traditional). No ghoulish, sex, violence. Wants to see more believable stories. Accepts 1-2 mss/issue. **Publishes 1-3 new writers/year.** Average length: 30,000 (novelettes) words. Publishes short shorts. Rarely comments on rejected mss.

How to Contact Send complete ms with cover letter. Responds in 2 weeks to queries; 6 weeks to mss.

Payment/Terms 1-4¢/word, plus royalty. Pays on acceptance.

Advice "Manuscripts must be for a general audience. Just good plain story telling (make it compelling). No explicit sex or ghoulish violence."

$ ☐ PURPOSE

616 Walnut Ave., Scottdale PA 15683-1999. (724)887-8500. Fax: (724)887-3111. E-mail: horsch@mph.org. Web site: www.mph.org. **Contact:** James E. Horsch, editor. Magazine: $5^{3}/_{8} \times 8^{3}/_{8}$; 8 pages; illustrations; photos. Weekly. Estab. 1968. Circ. 9,000.

Needs Historical (related to discipleship theme), humor/satire, religious/inspirational. No militaristic, narrow patriotism, or racist themes. Receives 150 unsolicited mss/month. Accepts 3 mss/issue; 140 mss/year. Publishes ms 1 year after acceptance. **Publishes 15-25 new writers/year.** Length: 600 words; average length: 400 words. Occasionally comments on rejected mss.

How to Contact Send complete ms. Send all submissions by Word attachment via e-mail. Responds in 3 months to queries. Accepts simultaneous submissions, reprints, multiple submissions. Sample copy and writer's guidelines for $2, 6×9 SAE and 2 first-class stamps. Writer's guidelines online.

Payment/Terms Pays up to 6¢/word for stories, and 2 contributor's copies. Pays on acceptance for one-time rights.

Advice "Many stories are situational, how to respond to dilemmas. Looking for first-person storylines. Write crisp, action moving, personal style, focused upon an individual, a group of people, or an organization. The story form is an excellent literary device to help readers explore discipleship issues. The first two paragraphs are crucial in establishing the mood/issue to be resolved in the story. Work hard on the development of these."

$ ▢ ◎ QUEEN'S QUARTERLY, A Canadian Review

Queen's University, Kingston ON K7L 3N6 Canada. (613)533-2667. Fax: (613)533-6822. E-mail: qquarter@post. queensu.ca. Web site: info.queensu.ca/quarterly. **Contact**: Boris Castel, editor. Magazine: 6×9; 800 pages/ year; illustrations. "A general interest intellectual review, featuring articles on science, politics, humanities, arts and letters. Book reviews, poetry and fiction." Quarterly. Estab. 1893. Circ. 3,000.

Needs Historical, literary, mainstream, novel excerpts, short stories, women's. "Special emphasis on work by Canadian writers." Accepts 2 mss/issue; 8 mss/year. Publishes ms 6-12 months after acceptance. **Publishes 5 new writers/year.** Recently published work by Gail Anderson-Dargatz, Tim Bowling, Emma Donohue, Viktor Carr, Mark Jarman, Rick Bowers and Dennis Bock. Also publishes literary essays, literary criticism, poetry.

How to Contact "Send complete ms with SASE and/or IRC. No reply with insufficient postage." Responds in 2-3 months to queries. Sample copy online. Writer's guidelines online. Reviews fiction.

Payment/Terms Pays $100-300 for fiction, 2 contributor's copies and 1-year subscription; additional copies $5. Pays on publication for first North American serial rights. Sends galleys to author.

Ⓝ ▢ SILENT VOICES

Ex Machina Press, LLC, P.O. Box 11180, Glendale CA 91226. (818)244-7209. E-mail: exmachinapag@aol.com. Web site: www.exmachinapress.com. **Contact:** Peter Balaskas, editor. Literary magazine/journal. *"Silent Voices* is an annual literary journal whose purpose is to publish fiction of a variety of styles and genres. By taking stories of a diverse nature and placing them in a specific order, we produce a creative mosaic that tells a larger story." Annual. Estab. 2,400. Circ. 1,000.

Needs Adventure, erotica, ethnic/multicultural, experimental, fantasy, historical, horror, humor/satire, mainstream, mystery, religious, romance, science fiction, western. Manuscript published 4-5 months after acceptance. Length: 15,000 words (max).

How to Contact Send complete ms with cover letter. Considers simultaneous submissions. Sample copy available for. Guidelines available on Web site.

Payment and Terms Acquires first North American serial rights.

▢ ◎ SLATE & STYLE, Magazine of the National Federation of the Blind Writers Division

NFB Writer's Division, 2704 Beach Drive, Merrick NY 11566. (516)868-8718. E-mail: loristay@aol.com. **Contact:** Lori Stayer, editor. Quarterly magazine: 28-32 print/40 Braille pages; e-mail, cassette and large print. "Articles of interest to writers, and resources for blind writers." Quarterly. Estab. 1982. Circ. 200.

Needs Adventure, fantasy, humor/satire, contemporary, blindness. No erotica. "Avoid theme of death." Does not read mss in June or July. **Publishes 2 new writers/year.** Recently published work by Rudy Makoul, Rochelle Caviness, and Nancy Scott. Publishes short shorts. Also publishes literary criticism, poetry. Sometimes comments on rejected mss.

How to Contact Accepts submissions by e-mail. Responds in 3-6 weeks to queries; 3-6 weeks to mss. Sample copy for $3.

Payment/Terms Pays in contributor's copies. Acquires one-time rights. Sponsors awards/contests.

Advice "The best advice I can give is to send your work out; manuscripts left in a drawer have no chance at all."

Ⓝ $◎ SOCKET SHOCKER MAGAZINE

Sample Press, P.O. Box 471159, Fort Worth TX 76147. E-mail: info@socketshocker.com. Web site: www.sockets hocker.com. **Contact:** Jennifer Farley, editor. Magazine. *"Socket Shocker Magazine* is a progressive publication which considers writing in every genre, but the major underlying theme marbled throughout everything we print is steadfast (not radical) environmentalism, vegetarianism, animal and human (particularly women's) rights, organic living and natural health." Quarterly. Estab. 2006. Circ. 1,500.

Needs Humor/satire, mainstream. Does not want erotica. Accepts 4-8 mss/year. Length: 1,000 words (min)-2,500 words (max).

How to Contact Send complete ms with cover letter. Accepts submissions by e-mail. Responds to queries in 6 weeks. Sample copy free upon request. Guidelines available on Web site.

Payment and Terms Acquires first rights, first North American serial rights, one-time rights, electronic rights. Pays ½¢ per word.

N ◎ SOLEADO

IPFW, CM 267 2101 E. Coliseum Blvd., Fort Wayne IN 46805. (260)481-6630. Fax: (260)481-6985. E-mail: summersj@ipfw.edu. Web site: ipfw.edu/summersj/soleado-Web site/soleportada.htm. **Contact:** Jason Summers, editor. Magazine. "We are looking for good literary writing in Spanish, from Magical Realism á la García Márquez, to McOndo-esque writing similiar to that of Edmundo Paz-Soldá and Alberto Fuguet, to Spanish pulp realism like that of Arturo Pérez-Reverte. Testimonials, experimental works like those of Diamela Eltit, and women's voices like Marcela Serrano and Zoé Valdés are also encouraged. We are not against any particular genre writing, but such stories do have to maintain their hold on the literary, as well as the genre, which is often a difficult task." Annual. Estab. 2004.

Needs Children's/juvenile, ethnic/multicultural, experimental, fantasy, historical, humor/satire, mainstream, mystery, science fiction. Accepts 2-6 mss/year. Length: 8,000 words (max).

How to Contact Send complete ms with cover letter. Accepts submissions by e-mail. Responds to queries in 1 week. Responds to mss in 3 months. Guidelines available on Web site.

Payment and Terms Acquires first rights, first North American serial rights, one-time rights, electronic rights.

$☐ THE STORYTELLER, A Writer's Magazine

2441 Washington Road, Maynard AR 72444. (870)647-2137. Fax: (870)647-2454. E-mail: storyteller1@hightowerco.com. Web site: http://freewebz.com/fossilcreek. **Contact**: Regina Cook Williams, editor. Tabloid: $8^{1}/_{2} \times 11$; 72 pages; typing paper; glossy cover; illustrations. "This magazine is open to all new writers regardless of age. I will accept short stories in any genre and poetry in any type. Please keep in mind, this is a family publication." Quarterly. Estab. 1996.

● Offers *People's Choice Awards* and nominates for a *Pushcart Prize.*

Needs Adventure, historical, humor/satire, literary, mainstream, mystery/suspense, religious/inspirational, romance, western, young adult/teen, senior citizen/retirement, sports. "I will not accept pornography, erotica, science fiction, new age, foul language, graphic horror or graphic violence." Wants more well-plotted mysteries. Publishes ms 3-9 months after acceptance. **Publishes 30-50 new writers/year.** Recently published work by Jodi Thomas, Jory Sherman, David Marion Wilkinson, Dusty Richards and Tony Hillerman. Publishes short shorts. Also publishes literary essays, poetry. Sometimes comments on rejected mss. Word length 2,500.

How to Contact Send complete ms with cover letter. Include estimated word count and 5-line bio. Submission by mail only. Responds in 1-2 weeks to mss. No queries. Accepts simultaneous submissions and reprints. Sample copy for $6. Writer's guidelines for #10 SASE.

Payment/Terms Pays $^{1}/_{4}$ ¢ per word. Sponsors awards/contests.

Advice "Follow the guidelines. No matter how many times this has been said, writers still ignore this basic and most important rule." Looks for "professionalism, good plots and unique characters. Purchase a sample copy so you know the kind of material we look for." Would like more "well-plotted mysteries and suspense and a few traditional westerns. Avoid sending anything that children or young adults would not (or could not) read, such as really bad language."

⊕ ☑ STUDIO, A Journal of Christians Writing

727 Peel Street, Albury 2640. Australia. (+61)26021-1135. E-mail: studio00@bigpond.net.au. **Contact:** Paul Grover, managing editor. Quarterly. Circ. 300.

Needs "*Studio* publishes prose and poetry of literary merit, offers a venue for new and aspiring writers, and seeks to create a sense of community among Christians writing." Accepts 30-40 mss/year. **Publishes 40 new writers/year.** Recently published work by Andrew Lansdown and Benjamin Gilmour.

How to Contact Accepts submissions by e-mail. Send SASE. "Overseas contributors must use International postal coupons in place of stamped envelope." Responds in 1 month to mss. Sample copy for $10 (Aus).

Payment/Terms Pays in copies; additional copies are discounted. Subscription $60 (Australian) for 4 issues (1 year). International draft in Australian dollars and IRC required, or Visa and Mastercard facilities available. "Copyright of individual published pieces remains with the author, while each collection is copyright to *Studio*."

$☑ TABARD INN, Tales of Questionable Taste

468 E. Vallette St., Elmhurst IL 60126. E-mail: tabardinnedgewoodent@yahoo.com. Web site: www.talesofquestionabletaste.com. **Contact:** John Bruni, editor. Magazine: $8^{1}/_{2} \times 11$, 60 pages, 60 lb. opaque smooth cover. Includes photographs. "*Tabard Inn* is a place for edgy stories that don't usually find a home in other magazines due to 'questionable' content." Estab. 2005. Circ. 560.

Needs Adventure, erotica, ethnic/multicultural, experimental, feminist, gay, historical, horror (dark fantasy, futuristic, psychological, supernatural), humor/satire, lesbian, literary, mainstream, military/war, mystery (amateur sleuth, cozy, police procedural, private eye/hard-boiled), religious (general), science fiction (soft/sociological), western. Does not want children's or fantasy works. Accepts 12 mss/issue. Manuscript published 6 months after acceptance. Publishes 3 new writers/year. Published John Bruni, Anthony Haversham, Jesse Russell, Edgar

Wells and David Fuller. Length: 1 words (min)-5,000 words (max). Average length: 2,000 words. Publishes short shorts. Average length of short shorts: 1,000 words. Also publishes poetry. Always comments on/critiques rejected manuscripts.

How to Contact Send complete ms with cover letter. Accepts submissions by e-mail, on disk. Include estimated word count, brief bio, list of publications. Responds to queries in 2 weeks. Responds to mss in 1 month. Send either SASE (or IRC) for return of ms or disposable copy of ms and #10 SASE for reply only. Considers simultaneous submissions, multiple submissions. Sample copy available for $6. Guidelines available for SASE, via e-mail.

Payment and Terms Writers receive $1 flat-rate payment, 2 contributors copies. Additional copies $3.50. Pays on publication. Acquires first North American serial rights. Publication is copyrighted.

Advice "Follow your heart. Write what you want to, not what you think has a good shot at getting published."

☑ TALEBONES, Fiction on the Dark Edge

Fairwood Press, 5203 Quincy Avenue SE, Auburn WA 98092-8723. (253)735-6552. E-mail: info@talebones.com. **Contact:** Patrick and Honna Swenson, editors. Magazine: digest size; 100 pages; standard paper; glossy cover stock; illustrations; photos. "We like stories that have punch, but still entertain. We like science fiction and dark fantasy, humor, psychological and experimental works." Published 2-3 times a year. Estab. 1995. Circ. 700.

Needs Fantasy (dark), humor/satire, science fiction (hard science, soft/sociological, dark). "No straight slash and hack horror. No cat stories or stories told by young adults." "Would like to see more science fiction." Receives 200 unsolicited mss/month. Accepts 8-10 mss/issue; 16-30 mss/year. Publishes ms 3-4 months after acceptance. **Publishes 2-3 new writers/year.** Recently published work by Louise Marley, Kay Kenyon, Nina Kiriki Hoffman, Anne Harris, and James Van Pelt. Length: 1,000-6,000 words; average length: 3,000-4,000 words. Publishes short shorts. Also publishes poetry.

How to Contact Send complete ms with cover letter. Include estimated word count and 1-paragraph bio. Responds in 1 week to queries; 1-2 months to mss. Sample copy for $7. Writer's guidelines for #10 SASE. Reviews fiction.

$☑ ◎ ☑ TALES OF THE TALISMAN

Hadrosaur Productions, P.O. Box 2194, Mesilla Park NM 88047-2194. E-mail: hadrosaur@zianet.com. Web site: www.hadrosaur.com. **Contact:** David L. Summers, editor. Zine specializing in science fiction: 8½×10½; 90 pages; 60 lb. white stock; 80 lb. cover. "*Tales of the Talisman* is a literary science fiction and fantasy magazine published 4 times a year. We publish short stories, poetry, and articles with themes related to science fiction and fantasy. Above all, we are looking for thought-provoking ideas and good writing. Speculative fiction set in the past, present, and future is welcome. Likewise, contemporary or historical fiction is welcome as long as it has a mythic or science fictional element. Our target audience includes adult fans of the science fiction and fantasy genres along with anyone else who enjoys thought-provoking and entertaining writing." Quarterly. Estab. 1995. Circ. 150.

 • Received an honorable mention in *The Year's Best Science Fiction* 2004 edited by Gardner Dozois.

Needs Fantasy (space fantasy, sword and sorcery), horror, science fiction (hard science/technological, soft/ sociological). "We do not want to see stories with graphic violence. Do not send 'mainstream' fiction with no science fictional or fantastic elements. Do not send stories with copyrighted characters, unless you're the copyright holder." Receives 15 unsolicited mss/month. Accepts 7-10 mss/issue; 21-30 mss/year. Publishes ms 9 months after acceptance. **Publishes 8 new writers/year.** Recently published work by Sonya Taaffe, Janni Lee Simner, Richard Harland, Tyree Campbell, Christina Sng, and Bruce Boston. Length: 1,000-6,000 words; average length: 4,000 words. Also publishes poetry. Often comments on rejected mss.

How to Contact Send complete ms. Accepts submissions by e-mail (hadrosaur@zianet.com). Include estimated word count, brief bio and list of publications. Send SASE (or IRC) for return of ms or send a disposable copy of ms and #10 SASE for reply only. Responds in 1 week to queries; 1 month to mss. Accepts reprint submissions. No simultaneous submissions. Sample copy for $8. Writer's guidelines online.

Payment/Terms Pays $6-10. Pays on acceptance for one-time rights.

Advice "First and foremost, I look for engaging drama and believable characters. With those characters and situations, I want you to take me someplace I've never been before. The story I'll buy is the one set in a new world or where the unexpected happens, but yet I cannot help but believe in the situation because it feels real. Read absolutely everything you can get your hands on, especially stories and articles outside your genre of choice. This is a great source for original ideas."

ℕ ◻ ◎ TEA, A MAGAZINE

Olde English Tea Company, Inc., 3 Devotion Road P.O. Box 348, Scotland CT 06264. (860)456-1145. Fax: (860)456-1023. E-mail: teamag@teamag.com. Web site: www.teamag.com. **Contact:** Jobina Miller, assistant to the editor. Magazine. "An exciting quarterly magazine all about tea, both as a drink and for its cultural significance in art, music, literature, history and society." Quarterly. Estab. 1994. Circ. 9,500.

Needs Needs fiction that is tea related.

How to Contact Send complete ms with cover letter. Responds to mss in 6 months. Guidelines available for SASE.

Payment and Terms Pays on publication. Acquires all rights.

$ ☑ TIMBER CREEK REVIEW

P.O. Box 16542, Greensboro NC 27416. E-mail: timber_creek_review@hoopsmail.com. **Contact:** John M. Freiermuth, editor; Rosyln Willette, associate editor. Newsletter: $5^1/_2 \times 8^1/_2$; 80-88 pages; computer generated on copy paper; saddle-stapled with colored paper cover; some illustrations. "Fiction, humor/satire, poetry and travel for a general audience." Quarterly. Estab. 1992. Circ. 140-160.

Needs Adventure, ethnic/multicultural, feminist, historical, humor/satire, literary, mainstream, mystery/suspense, regional, western, literary nonfiction, and one-act plays. "No religious, children's, gay, modern romance, and no reprints please!" Receives 50 unsolicited mss/month. Accepts 30-40 stories and 80-90 poems a year. Publishes ms 2-6 months after acceptance. **Publishes 0-3 new writers/year.** Recently published work by Christopher Dungey, Chris Brown, Richard Thieme, Hunter Huckabay, Kathleen Wheaton, Joan Fox, Carol Firth, Sid Miller, and Susan V. Carlos.

How to Contact Cover letter required. Accepts simultaneous submissions. Sample copy for $4.75, subscription $17.

Payment/Terms Pays $10-35, plus subscription. Acquires first North American serial rights. Not copyrighted.

Advice "Stop watching TV and read that literary magazine where your last manuscript appeared. There are no automatons here, so don't treat us like machines. We may not recognize your name at the top of the manuscript. Include a statement that the mss have previously not been published on paper nor on the internet, nor have they been accepted by others. A few lines about yourself breaks the ice, the names of three or four magazines that have published you in the last year or two would show your reality, and a bio blurb of 27 words including the names of 2 or 3 of the magazines you send the occasional subscription check (where you aspire to be?) could help. If you are not sending a check to some little magazine that is supported by subscriptions and the blood, sweat and tears of the editors, why would you send your manuscript to any of them and expect to receive a warm welcome? No requirement to subscribe or buy a sample, but they're available and are encouraged. There are no phony contests and never a reading fee. We read all year long, but may take 1 to 6 months to respond."

☐ ◎ TRAIL OF INDISCRETION

Fortress Publishing, Inc., 3704 Hartzdale Dr., Camp Hill PA 17011. (717)350-8760. E-mail: fortresspublishinginc @yahoo.com. Web site: www.fortresspublishinginc.com. **Contact:** Brian Koscienski, editor in chief. Zine specializing in genre fiction: digest ($5^1/_2 \times 8^1/_2$), 48 pages, 24 lb. paper, glossy cover. "We publish genre fiction—sci-fi, fantasy, horror, etc. We'd rather have a solid story containing great characters than a weak story with a surprise 'trick' ending." Quarterly. Estab. 2006. Circ. < 100.

Needs Adventure, fantasy (space fantasy, sword and sorcery), horror (dark fantasy, futuristic, psychological, supernatural), humor/satire, psychic/supernatural/occult, science fiction (hard science/technological, soft/sociological). Does not want "touchy-feely 'coming of age' stories or stories where the protagonist mopes about contemplating his/her own mortality." Accepts 5-7 mss/issue. Manuscript published 3-9 months after acceptance. **Publishes 2-10 new writers/year.** Published Nellie Batz (debut), Jeff Young, Den Wilson, Eric Hardenbrook (debut), Danielle Ackley-McPhail. Length: 5,000 words (max). Average length: 3,000 words. Publishes short shorts. Sometimes comments on/critiques rejected mss.

How to Contact Send complete ms with cover letter. Accepts submissions by e-mail. Include estimated word count, brief bio, list of publications. Responds to queries in 1-2 weeks. Responds to mss in 1-10 weeks. Send either SASE (or IRC) for return of ms or disposable copy of ms and #10 SASE for reply only. Considers simultaneous submissions, previously published submissions. Sample copy available for $4 or on Web site. Guidelines available for SASE, via e-mail, on Web site.

Payment and Terms Writers receive 2 contributors copies. Additional copies $2. Pays on publication. Acquires one-time rights. Publication is copyrighted.

Advice "If your story is about a 13-year-old girl coping with the change to womanhood while poignantly reflecting the recent passing of her favorite aunt, then we *don't* want it. However, if your story is about the 13-year-old daughter of a vampire cowboy who stumbles upon a government conspiracy involving unicorns and aliens while investigating the grizzly murder of her favorite aunt, then we'll look at it. Please read the magazine to see what we want. Love your story, but listen to advice."

◐ ◎ TRANSCENDENT VISIONS

Toxic Evolution Press, 251 S. Olds Blvd., 84-E, Fairless Hills PA 19030-3426. (215)547-7159. **Contact:** David Kime, editor. Zine: letter size; 24 pages; xerox paper; illustrations. "*Transcendent Visions* is a literary zine by and for people who have been labeled mentally ill. Our purpose is to illustrate how creative and articulate mental patients are." Annual. Estab. 1992. Circ. 200.

• *Transcendent Visions* has received excellent reviews in many underground publications.

Needs Experimental, feminist, gay, humor/satire, lesbian. Especially interested in material dealing with mental illness. "I do not like stuff one would find in a mainstream publication. No porn." Would like to see more "quirky, non-mainstream fiction." Receives 5 unsolicited mss/month. Accepts 7 mss/year. Publishes ms 3-4 months after acceptance. Recently published work by Brian McCarvill, Michael Fowler, Thomas A. Long, Lisa Donnelly, Roger D. Coleman and Emil Vachas. Publishes short shorts. Also publishes poetry.

How to Contact Send complete ms with cover letter. Include half-page bio. Send disposable copy of ms. Responds in 3 month to mss. Accepts simultaneous submissions and reprints. Sample copy for $3.

Payment/Terms Pays 1 contributor's copy. Pays on publication for one-time rights.

Advice "We like unusual stories that are quirky. We like shorter pieces. Please do not go on and on about what zines you have been published in or awards you have won, etc. We just want to read your material, not know your life story. Please don't swamp me with tons of submissions. Send up to five stories. Please print or type your name and address."

$🖉 VIRGINIA QUARTERLY REVIEW

University of Virginia, One West Range, P.O. Box 400223, Charlottesville VA 22904-4223. (434)924-3124. Fax: (434)924-1397. Web site: www.vqronline.org. **Contact:** Ted Genoways, editor. "A national journal of literature and discussion, featuring nonfiction, fiction, and poetry for both educated general readers and the academic audience." Quarterly. Estab. 1925. Circ. 6,000.

• Offers Emily Clark Balch Award for best short story and poetry, and the Staige D. Blackford prize for the best essay, published in its pages in the past year.

Needs Adventure, ethnic/multicultural, feminist, historical, humor/satire, literary, mainstream, mystery/suspense, novel excerpts, serialized novels, translations. Accepts 3 mss/issue; 20 mss/year. Publishes ms 3-6 months after acceptance.

How to Contact Send complete ms. SASE. No queries. Responds in 3-4 months to mss. Sample copy for $6. Writer's guidelines online.

Payment/Terms Pays $100/page maximum. $5 per line for poetry. Pays on publication for first North American rights and nonexclusive online rights.

$🖉🖉🖉 WEBER STUDIES, Voices and Viewpoints of the Contemporary West

1214 University Circle, Ogden UT 84408-1214. (801)626-6473. E-mail: blroghaar@weber.edu. Web site: weberstudies.weber.edu. **Contact:** Brad L. Roghaar, editor. Magazine: 7½×10; 120-140 pages; coated paper; 4-color cover; illustrations; photos. "We seek the following themes: preservation of and access to wilderness, environmental cooperation, insight derived from living in the West, cultural diversity, changing federal involvement in the region, women and the West, implications of population growth, a sense of place, etc. We love good writing that reveals human nature as well as natural environment." Triannual. Estab. 1984. Circ. 1,000.

Needs Adventure, comics/graphic novels, ethnic/multicultural, experimental, feminist, historical, humor/satire, literary, mainstream, military/war, mystery/suspense, New Age, psychic/supernatural/occult, regional (contemporary western US), translations, western (frontier sage, tradtional, contemporary), short story collections. No children's/juvenile, erotica, religious or young adult/teen. Receives 50 unsolicited mss/month. Accepts 3-6 mss/issue; 9-18 mss/year. Publishes ms up to 18 months after acceptance. **Publishes "few" new writers/year.** Recently published work by Gary Gildner, Ron McFarland and David Duncan. Publishes short shorts. Also publishes literary essays, poetry, art. Sometimes comments on rejected mss.

How to Contact Send complete ms with a cover letter. Include estimated word count, bio (if necessary), and list of publications (not necessary). Responds in 3 months to mss. Accepts multiple submissions. Sample copy for $10.

Payment/Terms Pays $150-$300. Pays on publication for first, electronic rights. Requests electronic archive permission. Sends galleys to author.

Advice "Is it true? Is it new? Is it interesting? Will the story appeal to educated readers who are concerned with the contemporary western United States? Declining public interest in reading generally is of concern. We publish both print media and electronic media because we believe the future will expect both options. The Dr. Neila C. Seshachari Fiction Award, a $500 prize, is awarded annually to the best fiction appearing in *Weber Studies* each year."

$🖉 WEIRD TALES

9710 Traville Gateway Drive #234, Rockville MD 20850. E-mail: weirdtales@comcast.net. **Contact:** George H. Scithers and Darrell Schweitzer, editors. Magazine: 8½×11; 80 pages; white, newsprint paper; glossy 4-color cover; illustrations. "We publish fantastic fiction, supernatural horror for an adult audience." Published 6 times a year. Estab. 1923. Circ. 5,000.

Needs Fantasy (sword and sorcery), horror, psychic/supernatural/occult, translations. No hard science fiction or non-fantasy. "We want to see a wide range of fantasy, from sword and sorcery to supernatural horror. We can use some unclassifiables." Receives 400 unsolicited mss/month. Accepts 8 mss/issue; 48 mss/year. Publishes ms 6-18 months after acceptance. Agented fiction 10%. **Publishes 8 new writers/year.** Recently published work by Tanith Lee, Thomas Ligotti, Ian Watson, and Lord Dunsany. Length: 15,000 words, but very few longer than 7,00; average length: 4,000 words. Publishes short shorts. Also publishes poetry. Always comments on rejected mss.

How to Contact Send complete ms. You must include SASE for reply and return of ms or send a disposable copy of ms with SASE. Responds in 4-6 weeks to mss. Accepts multiple submissions. No simultaneous submissions. Sample copy for $6. Writer's guidelines for #10 SASE or by e-mail. Reviews books of fantasy fiction.

Payment/Terms Pays 3¢/word and 2 contributor's copies on acceptance. Acquires first North American serial, plus anthology option rights. Sends galleys to author.

Advice "We look for imagination and vivid writing. Read the magazine. Get a good grounding in the contemporary horror and fantasy field through the various 'best of the year' anthologies. Avoid the obvious clichés of technicalities of the hereafter, the mechanics of vampirism, generic Tolkien-clone fantasy. In general, it is much better to be honest and emotionally moving rather than merely clever. Avoid stories which have nothing of interest but the allegedly 'surprise' ending."

$ ◨ ZAHIR, Unforgettable Tales

Zahir Publishing, 315 South Coast Hwy. 101, Suite U8, Encinitas CA 92024. E-mail: stempchin@zahirtales.com. Web site: www.zahirtales.com. **Contact:** Sheryl Tempchin, editor. Magazine: Digest-size; 80 pages; heavy stock paper; glossy, full color cover stock. "We publish quality speculative fiction for intelligent adult readers. Our goal is to bridge the gap between literary and genre fiction." Triannual. Estab. 2003.

Needs Fantasy, literary, psychic/supernatural/occult, science fiction, surrealism, magical realism. No children's stories, excessive violence or pornography. Accepts 6-8 mss/issue; 18-24 mss/year. Publishes ms 2-12 months after acceptance. **Publishes 6 new writers/year.** Sometimes comments on rejected mss.

How to Contact Send complete ms. Send SASE (or IRC) for return of ms, or send disposable copy of the ms and #10 SASE for reply only. E-mail queries okay. No e-mail mss except from writers living outside the U.S. Responds in 1-2 weeks to queries; 1-3 months to mss. Accepts reprints submissions. No simultaneous submissions. Sample copy for $6.50 (US). Writer's guidelines for #10 SASE, by e-mail, or online.

Payment/Terms Pays $10 and 2 contributor's copies. Pays on publication for first, second serial (reprint) rights.

Advice "The stories we are most likely to buy are well written, have interesting, well-developed characters and/or ideas that fascinate, chill, thrill, or amuse us. They must have some element of the fantastic or surreal."

Online Markets

As production and distribution costs go up and the number of subscribers falls, more and more magazines are giving up print publication and moving online. Relatively inexpensive to maintain and quicker to accept and post submissions, online fiction sites are growing fast in numbers and legitimacy. Jason Sanford, editor of *storySouth*, explains, "Online journals reach far greater audiences than print journals with far less cost. I have a friend who edits a print literary journal and he is constantly struggling to cover the cost of printing 500 copies twice a year. At *storySouth*, we reach 1,000 individual readers every single day without having to worry that we're going to break the bank with our printing budget. The benefit for writers is that your stories tend to gain more attention online than in small literary journals. Because small journals have print runs of 500-1,000 copies, there is a limit on how many people will read your work. Online, there is no limit. I've been published in both print and online literary journals, and the stories I've published online have received the most attention and feedback."

Writers exploring online opportunities for publication will find a rich and diverse community of voices. Genre sites are strong, in particular those for science fiction/fantasy and horror. (See *Alienskin* and *DargonZine*.) Mainstream short fiction markets are also growing exponentially. (See *Toasted Cheese* and *Paperplates*, among many others.) Online literary journals range from the traditional (*The Barcelona Review*, *The Green Hills Literary Lantern*) to those with a decidedly more quirky bent (*Timothy McSweeney's Internet Tendency*, *The Absinthe Literary Review*). Writers will also find here more highly experimental and multimedia work. (See *Convergence* and *Diagram*.)

Online journals are gaining respect for the writers who appear on their sites. As Jill Adams, publisher and editor of *The Barcelona Review*, says: "We see our Internet review, like the small independent publishing houses, as a means of counterbalancing the big-business mentality of the multi-national publishing houses. At the same time, we want to see our writers 'make it big.' Last year we heard from more and more big houses asking about some of our new writers, wanting contact information, etc. So I see a healthy trend in that big houses are finally—after being skeptical and confused—looking at it seriously and scouting online."

While the medium of online publication is different, the traditional rules of publishing apply to submissions. Writers should research the site and archives carefully, looking for a match in sensibility for their work. They should then follow submission guidelines exactly and submit courteously. True, these sites aren't bound by traditional print schedules, so your work theoretically may be published more quickly. But that doesn't mean online journals have a larger staff, so exercise patience with editors considering your manuscript.

Also, while reviewing the listings in this market section, notice they are grouped differently from other market listings. In our literary magazines section, for example, you'll find primarily only publications searching for literary short fiction. But Online Markets are grouped by medium, so you'll find publishers of mystery short stories listed next to those looking for horror next to those specializing in flash fiction, so review with care. In addition, online markets with print counterparts, such as *North American Review*, can be found listed in the print markets sections.

A final note about online publication: Like literary journals, the majority of these markets are either nonpaying or very low paying. In addition, writers will not receive print copies of the publications because of the medium. So in most cases, do not expect to be paid for your exposure.

$THE ABSINTHE LITERARY REVIEW

P.O. Box 328, Spring Green WI 53588. E-mail: staff@absinthe-literary-review.com. Web site: www.absinthe-literary-review.com. **Contact:** Charles Allen Wyman, editor-in-chief. Electronic literary magazine; print issue coming 2008. "*ALR* publishes short stories, novel excerpts, poems, book reviews, and literary essays. Our target audience is the literate individual who enjoys creative language use, character-driven fiction and the clashing of worlds—real and surreal, poetic and prosaic, sacred and transgressive."

Needs "Transgressive works dealing with sex, death, disease, madness, and the like; the clash of archaic with modern-day; archetype, symbolism; surrealism, philosophy, physics; existential, and post-modern flavoring; experimental or flagrantly textured (but not sloppy or casual) fiction; intense crafting of language from the writer's writer. Anathemas: mainstream storytellers, "Oprah" fiction, high school or beginner fiction, poetry or fiction that contains no capital letters or punctuation, "hot" trends, genre, and utterly normal prose or poetry; first, second or third drafts, pieces that exceed our stated word count (5,000 max.) by thousands of words." **Publishes 3-6 new writers/year.** Recently published work by Bruce Holland Rogers, David Schneiderman, Virgil Suarez, John Tisdale, James Reidel and Dan Pope.

How to Contact Due to a substantial backlog, *ALR* will not be accepting submissions or books for review for most if not all of the 2007 calendar year. Please check online guidelines in late 2007 for updated submission information. Any submissions received prior to the update will be disposed of without response. Questions? E-mail the *ALR* staff at staff@absinthe-literary-review.com.

Payment/Terms Pays $2-10 for fiction and essays; $1-10 for poetry.

Advice "Be erudite and daring in your writing. Draw from the past to drag meaning from the present. Kill ego and cliché. Invest your work with layers of meaning that subtly reveal multiple realities. Do not submit pieces that are riddled with spelling errors and grammatical snafus. Above all, be professional. For those of you who don't understand what this means, please send your manuscripts elsewhere until you have experienced the necessary epiphany."

N ⊘ THE ADIRONDACK REVIEW

Black Lawrence Press, P.O. Box 205619 % Diane Goettel, Sunset Station, Brooklyn NY 11220-7619. E-mail: tar@blacklawrencepress.com. Web site: http://adirondackreview.homestead.com. **Contact:** Diane Goettel, editor. Online literary magazine/journal. Contains illustrations & photographs. Estab. 2000.

Needs Adventure, experimental, family saga, gay, historical (general), psychological, translations. Does not want SciFi, fantasy. Receives over 200 mss/month. Accepts 5-10 mss/issue; 20-30 mss/year. Manuscript published 1-5 months after acceptance. Agented fiction 5%. **Publishes 15% new writers/year.** Published Frank Haberie, Steve Gillis, Melinda Misrala, Kate Swoboda. Length: 700 words (min)–8,000 words (max). Average length: 3,000 words. Publishes short shorts. Average length of short shorts: 800 words. Also publishes literary essays, literary criticism, book reviews, poetry. Send review copies to Diane Goettel. Rarely comments on/critiques rejected mss.

How to Contact Send complete ms with cover letter. Accepts submissions by e-mail. Include estimated word count, brief bio, list of publications, and "how they learned about the magazine." Responds to queries in 1-2 months. Responds to mss in 2-4 months. Send either SASE (or IRC) for return of ms or disposable copy of ms and #10 SASE for reply only. Considers simultaneous submissions, multiple submissions.

Payment and Terms Acquires first rights. Sponsors contests. See Web site for details.

$⊘ ALIENSKIN MAGAZINE, An Online Science Fiction, Fantasy & Horror Magazine

Froggy Bottom Press, P.O. Box 495, Beaver PA 15009. E-mail: alienskin@alienskinmag.com. Web site: www.alienskinmag.com. **Contact:** Feature fiction: K.A. Patterson; Flash fiction: Phil Adams. Online magazine. "Our magazine was created for, and strives to help, aspiring writers of SFFH. We endeavor to promote genre writers." Bimonthly. Estab. 2002. Circ. 1,000+ internet.

Needs Fantasy (dark fantasy, sword and sorcery), horror (dark fantasy, futuristic, psychological, psychic/supernatural/occult), science fiction (hard science/technological, soft/sociological). "No excessive blood, gore, erotica or vulgarity. No experimental or speculative fiction that does not use basic story elements of character, conflict, action and resolution. No esoteric ruminations." Receives 150-250 unsolicited mss/month. Accepts 27-30 mss/issue; 162-180 mss/year. Publishes ms 30-60 days after acceptance. **Publishes 10-15 new writers/year.** Recently published work by Doug Goodman, Stefan Schear, Rick McQuiston, and Elwin Estle. Length: 1,000-3,500 words; average length: 2,200 words. Publishes short shorts. Always comments on rejected mss.

How to Contact Send complete ms. Accepts submissions by e-mail only. Include estimated word count, brief bio, name, address, and e-mail address. Responds in 1-2 weeks to queries; 2 months to mss. Accepts multiple submissions. Sample copy online. Writer's guidelines online.

Payment/Terms 1/2¢/word for 1,001-3,500 words; $5 flat pay for 500-1,000 words. Pays on publication for first, electronic rights. Sponsors contests.

Advice "We look for interesting stories that offer something unique; stories that use basic story elements of character, conflict, action and resolution. We like the dark, twisted side of SFFH genres. Read our guidelines and follow the rules, treating the submission process as a serious business transaction. Only send stories that have been spell-checked, and proofread at least twice. Try to remember that editors who offer a critique on manuscripts do so to help you as a writer, not to hamper or dissuade you as a writer."

$◻ ◎ ▯ ALLEGORY, Tri-Annual Online Magazine of SF, Fantasy & Horror

(formerly Peridot Books) 1225 Liberty Bell Dr., Cherry Hill NJ 08003. (856)354-0786. E-mail: submissions@allegoryezine.com. Web site: www.allegoryezine.com. **Contact:** Ty Drago, editor. Online magazine specializing in science fiction, fantasy and horror. "We are an e-zine by writers for writers. Our articles focus on the art, craft and business of writing. Our links and editorial policy all focus on the needs of fiction authors." Triannual. Estab. 1998.

● Peridot Books won the Page One Award for Literary Contribution.

Needs Fantasy (space fantasy, sword and sorcery, sociological), horror (dark fantasy, futuristic, supernatural), science fiction (hard science/technological, soft/sociological). "No media tie-ins (Star Trek, Star Wars, etc., or space opera, vampires)." Receives 150 unsolicited mss/month. Accepts 8 mss/issue; 24 mss/year. Publishes ms 1-2 months after acceptance. Agented fiction 5%. **Publishes 10 new writers/year.** Length: 1,500-7,500 words; average length: 4,500 words. Also publishes literary essays, literary criticism. Often comments on rejected mss.

How to Contact Send complete ms with a cover letter, electronic only. Include estimated word count, brief bio, list of publications and name and e-mail address in the body of the story. Responds in 8 weeks to mss. Accepts simultaneous, multiple submissions and reprints. Writer's guidelines online.

Payment/Terms $15/story-article. Pays on publication for one-time, electronic rights.

Advice "Give us something original, preferably with a twist. Avoid gratuitous sex or violence. Funny always scores points. Be clever, imaginative, but be able to tell a story with proper mood and characterization. Put your name and e-mail address in the body of the story. Read the site and get a feel for it before submitting."

◓ THE ALSOP REVIEW

1880 Lincoln Ave., Calistoga, CA 94515. E-mail: alsop@alsopreview.com. Web site: www.alsopreview.com. **Contact:** Jaimes Alsop, editor. Web zine. "*The Alsop Review* is primarily a literary resource and as such does not solicit manuscripts. However, the review operates an e-zine which accepts manuscripts. *Octavo* is a quarterly magazine that accepts short stories and poetry. Send submissions to Andrew Boobier at andrew@netstep.co.uk."

Needs Experimental, literary. "No genre work or humor for its own sake. No pornography. We would like to see more experimental and unconventional works. Surprise me." Recently published work by Kyle Jarrard, Dennis Must, Kristy Nielsen, Bob Riche and Linda Sue Park.

How to Contact Accepts submissions by e-mail (alsop@alsopreview.com). Accepts reprints submissions. Sample copy not available.

Payment/Terms "None. We offer a permanent 'home' on the Web for writers and will pull and add material to their pages upon request."

Advice "Read, read, read. Treat submissions to Web zines as carefully as you would a print magazine. Research the market first. For every great Web zine, there are a hundred mediocre ones. Remember that once your work is on the Web, chances are it will be there for a very long time. Put your best stuff out there and take advantage of the opportunities to re-publish work from print magazines."

◪ AMERICAN FEED MAGAZINE

American Feed Magazine, 35 Hinsdale Ave., Winsted CT 06098. (860)469-8060. E-mail: editor@americanfeedmagazine.com. Web site: www.americanfeedmagazine.com. **Contact:** Shaw Izikson, editor. Online magazine.

"We like to give a place for new voices to be heard, and for established voices to get a wider audience for their work." Estab. 1994.

Needs Adventure, ethnic/multicultural, experimental, family saga, fantasy, feminist, glitz, historical, horror, humor/satire, literary, mainstream, mystery/suspense, New Age, psychic/supernatural/occult, science fiction, thriller/espionage. Receives 100 unsolicited mss/month. Accepts 15 mss/issue. **Publishes 20 new writers/year.** Recently published work by Richard Lind, Bill Glose, Angela Conrad, Ryan Miller, Joshua Farber and Daniel LaFabvre. Average length: 1,500 words. Publishes short shorts. Also publishes literary essays, literary criticism, poetry.

How to Contact Send complete ms. Include estimated word count and brief bio. Responds in 2 months to queries; 2 months to mss. Accepts simultaneous, multiple submissions and reprints. Sample copy online. Writer's guidelines by e-mail. Reviews fiction.

Payment/Terms Acquires one-time rights.

Advice "Make sure the story flows naturally, not in a forced way. You don't need a vivid imagination to write fiction, poetry or anything. Just look around you, because life is usually the best inspiration."

$⃝ ANTI MUSE

502 S. Main St., Saint Joseph TN 38481. (931)845-4838. E-mail: antimuse@antimuse.org. Web site: http://antimuse.org. **Contact:** Michael Haislip, editor. *Anti Muse* appeals to readers with a somewhat jaded and cynical outlook on life. Monthly. Estab. 2004. Circ. 10,000.

Needs Adventure, comics/graphic novels, erotica, ethnic/multicultural, experimental, fantasy, feminist, gay, historical, horror, humor/satire, lesbian, literary, mainstream, military/war, New Age, psychic/supernatural/occult, regional, science fiction, thriller/espionage, western. Receives 300 unsolicited mss/month. Accepts 5-10 mss/issue; 50 mss/year. Publishes ms 1 month after acceptance. **Publishes 50 new writers/year.** Recently published work by Robert Levin, Corey Mesler, and Trevor Davis. Length: 200-10,000 words; average length: 1,000 words. Publishes short shorts. Also publishes literary essays, literary criticism, poetry. Sometimes comments on rejected mss.

How to Contact Send complete ms. Accepts submissions by e-mail. Send SASE (or IRC) for return of the ms, or send disposable copy of the ms and #10 SASE for reply only. Responds in 1 month to mss. Accepts simultaneous, multiple submissions and reprints. Sample copy free. Writer's guidelines online.

Payment/Terms Pays $5-20. Pays on publication for one-time rights.

Advice "I want to be entertained by your submission. I want to feel as if I'd be foolish to put down your manuscript."

☒ ⃝ APPLE VALLEY REVIEW, A Journal of Contemporary Literature

Queen's Postal Outlet, Box 12, Kingston ON K7L 3R9. E-mail: editor@leahbrowning.net. Web site: www.applevalleyreview.com. **Contact:** Leah Browning, editor. Online literary magazine. Includes photographs/artwork on cover. "Each issue features a selection of beautifully crafted poetry, short fiction and essays. We prefer work that has both mainstream and literary appeal. As such, we avoid erotica, work containing explicit language and anything violent or extremely depressing. Our audience includes teens and adults of all ages." Semiannual. Estab. 2005. Member CLMP.

Needs Ethnic/multicultural (general), experimental, humor/satire, literary, mainstream, regional (American South, Southwest), translations, literary women's fiction (e.g. Barbara Kingsolver, Anne Tyler, Lee Smith, Elinor Lipman, Perri Klass). Does not want genre fiction, erotica, work containing explicit language, or anything violent or extremely depressing. Receives 20+ mss/month. Accepts 1-4 mss/issue; 2-8 mss/year. Manuscript published 3-6 months after acceptance. Published Hal Sirowitz, Anna Evans, David Thornbrugh, Steve Klepetar, Louie Crew, Arlene L. Mandell, Jéanpaul Ferro, Janet Zupan. Length: 100 words (min)-3,000 words (max). Average length: 2,000 words. Publishes short shorts. Average length of short shorts: 1,200 words. Also publishes literary essays, poetry. Sometimes comments on/critiques rejected manuscripts.

How to Contact Send complete ms with cover letter. Accepts submissions only via e-mail. Include estimated word count, brief bio. Responds to mss in 1 week-3 months. Considers multiple submissions. Guidelines available via e-mail, on Web site. Sample copy on Web site.

Payment and Terms Acquires first rights, right to archive online. Publication is copyrighted.

Advice "Excellent writing always makes a manuscript stand out. Beyond that, I look for stories and poems that I want to read again, and that I want to give to someone else to read—work so interesting for one reason or another that I feel compelled to share it. Please read at least some of the previously published work to get a feel for our style, and follow the submission guidelines as closely as possible. We accept submissions only via e-mail."

☒ ⃝ ASCENT ASPIRATIONS

Ascent, 1560 Arbutus Dr., Nanoose Bay BC C9P 9C8 Canada. E-mail: ascent aspirations@shaw.com. Web site: www.ascentaspirations.ca. **Contact:** David Fraser, editor. E-zine specializing in short fiction (all genres) and poetry, essays, visual art: 40 electronic pages; illustrations; photos. *Ascent* publishes two additional issues in print each year. "*Ascent Aspirations* magazine publishes quarterly online and semi-annually in print. The print issues are operated as contests. Please refer to current guidelines before submitting. *Ascent* is a quality electronic publication dedicated to the promotion and encouragement of aspiring writers of any genre. The focus however is toward interesting experimental writing in dark mainstream, literary, science fiction, fantasy and horror. Poetry can be on any theme. Essays need to be unique, current and have social, philosophical commentary." Quarterly online. Estab. 1997.

Needs Erotica, experimental, fantasy (space fantasy), feminist, horror (dark fantasy, futuristic, psychological, supernatural), literary, mainstream, mystery/suspense, New Age, psychic/supernatural/occult, science fiction (hard science/technological, soft/sociological). Receives 100-200 unsolicited mss/month. Accepts 40 mss/issue; 240 mss/year. Publishes ms 3 months after acceptance. **Publishes 10-50 new writers/year.** Recently published work by Taylor Graham, Janet Buck, Jim Manton, Steve Cartwright, Don Stockard, Penn Kemp, Sam Vargo, Vernon Waring, Margaret Karmazin, Bill Hughes. Length: 1,000 words or less. Publishes short shorts. Also publishes literary essays, literary criticism, poetry. Sometimes comments on rejected mss.

How to Contact "Query by e-mail with Word attachment." Include estimated word count, brief bio and list of publications. If you have to submit by mail because it is your only avenue, provide a SASE with either International Coupons or Canadian stamps only. Responds in 1 week to queries; 3 months to mss. Accepts simultaneous, multiple submissions and reprints. Guidelines by e-mail or on Web site. Reviews fiction.

Payment/Terms "No payment at this time. Rights remain with author."

Advice "Short fiction should, first of all, tell a good story, take the reader to new and interesting imaginary or real places. Short fiction should use language lyrically and effectively, be experimental in either form or content and take the reader into realms where they can analyze and think about the human condition. Write with passion for your material, be concise and economical and let the reader work to unravel your story. In terms of editing, always proofread to the point where what you submit is the best it possibly can be. Never be discouraged if your work is not accepted; it may just not be the right fit for a current publication."

BABEL, the Multilingual, Multicultural Online Journal and Community of Arts and Ideas

E-mail: submissions@towerofbabel.com. Web site: towerofbabel.com. **Contact:** Jennifer Low, submissions editor. Electronic zine. "We are an online community involving an extensive group of artists, writers and translators representing all of the world's languages. We publish regional reports from all over the planet, fiction, columns, poetry, erotica, travelogues, reviews of all the arts and editorials, as well as feature roundtable discussions."

Needs "While we appreciate all categories of fiction, we are not particularly interested in stories that delve no deeper than the typical supernatural, interplanetary alien, or horror stories. Also, stories written with the purpose of discriminating against a race or culture will not be considered. We are interested in stories that have a point and inspire readers to think."

How to Contact Query. Accepts submissions by e-mail. Reviews fiction.

Advice "Know what you are writing about and write passionately about it. Don't be afraid to explore new ideas and styles of writing. Try writing from the point of view of someone other than yourself, especially from the perspective of the opposite sex. By expanding your horizons, you will expand your imigination and, in turn, your writing."

THE BARCELONA REVIEW

Correu Vell 12-2, Barcelona 08002 Spain. (00) 34 93 319 15 96. E-mail: editor@barcelonareview.com. Web site: www.barcelonareview.com. **Contact:** Jill Adams, editor. "*TBR* is an international review of contemporary, cutting-edge fiction published in English, Spanish and Catalan. Our aim is to bring both new and established writers to the attention of a larger audience. Well-known writers such as Alicia Erian in the U.S., Michel Faber in the U.K., Carlos Gardini in Argentina, and Nuria Amat in Spain, for example, were not known outside their countries until appearing in *TBR*. Our multilingual format increases the audience all the more. Internationally known writers, such as Irvine Welsh and Douglas Coupland, have contributed stories that ran in small press anthologies available only in one country. We try to keep abreast of what's happening internationally and to present the best finds every two months. Our intended audience is anyone interested in high-quality contemporary fiction that often (but not always) veers from the mainstream; we assume that our readers are well read and familiar with contemporary fiction in general."

Needs Short fiction. "Our bias is towards potent and powerful cutting-edge material; given that general criteria, we are open to all styles and techniques and all genres. No slice-of-life stories, vignettes or reworked fables, and nothing that does not measure up, in your opinion, to the quality of work in our review, which we expect submitters to be familiar with." **Publishes 20 new writers/year.** Recently published work by Niall Griffiths, Adam Haslett, G.K. Wuori, Adam Johnson, Mary Wornov, Emily Carter, Jesse Shepard, and Julie Orringer.

How to Contact Send submissions by e-mail as an attached file. Hard copies accepted but cannot be returned. No simultaneous submissions.

Payment/Terms "In lieu of pay we offer a highly professional Spanish translation to English language writers and vice versa to Spanish writers."

Advice "Send top drawer material that has been drafted two, three, four times—whatever it takes. Then sit on it for a while and look at it afresh. Keep the text tight. Grab the reader in the first paragraph and don't let go. Keep in mind that a perfectly crafted story that lacks a punch of some sort won't cut it. Make it new, make it different. Surprise the reader in some way. Read the best of the short fiction available in your area of writing to see how yours measures up. Don't send anything off until you feel it's ready and then familiarize yourself with the content of the review/magazine to which you are submitting."

�‍ ✿ BIG COUNTRY PEACOCK CHRONICLE, Online Magazine

RR1, Box 89K-112, Aspermont TX 79502. (806)254-2322. E-mail: publisher@peacockchronicle.com. Web site: www.peacockchronicle.com. **Contact:** Audrey Yoeckel, owner/publisher. Online magazine. "We publish articles, commentaries, reviews, interviews, short stories, serialized novels and novellas, poetry, essays, humor, and anecdotes. Due to the nature of Internet publication, guidelines for length of written works are flexible and acceptance is based more on content. Content must be family friendly. Writings that promote hatred or violence will not be accepted. *The Big Country Peacock Chronicle* is dedicated to the preservation of community values and traditional folk cultures. In today's society, we are too often deprived of a solid feeling of community which is so vital to our security and well-being. It is our attempt to keep the best parts of our culture intact. Our goal is to build a place for individuals, no matter the skill level, to test their talents and get feedback from others in a non-threatening, friendly environment. The original concept for the magazine was to open the door to talented writers by providing not only a publishing medium for their work but support and feedback as well. It was created along the lines of a smalltown publication in order to remove some of the anxiety about submitting works for first-time publication." Quarterly. Estab. 2000.

Needs Adventure, children's/juvenile (adventure, easy-to-read, fantasy, historical, mystery, preschool, series, sports), ethnic/multicultural (general), family saga, fantasy (space fantasy, sword and sorcery), gay, historical (general), horror (futuristic, supernatural, psychological), humor/satire, literary, military/war, mystery/suspense (amateur sleuth, police procedural, private eye/hard-boiled), psychic/supernatural/occult, regional, religious/inspirational (children's religious), romance (gothic, historical, romantic suspense), science fiction (soft/sociological), thriller/espionage, translations (frontier saga, traditional), western. "While the genre of the writing or the style does not matter, excessive or gratuitous violence, foul language and sexually explicit material is not acceptable." Accepts 2-3 (depending on length) mss/issue. Publishes ms 3 months after acceptance. Average length: 2,500 words. Publishes short shorts. Also publishes literary essays, literary criticism, poetry. Always comments on rejected mss.

How to Contact Include estimated word count, brief bio, list of publications and Internet contact information; i.e., e-mail, Web site address. Responds in 3 weeks to queries; 6 weeks to mss. Accepts simultaneous, multiple submissions and reprints. Writer's guidelines online. Reviews fiction.

Payment/Terms Acquires electronic rights. Sends galleys to author.

Advice "We look for continuity and coherence. The work must be clean with a minimum of typographical errors. The advantage to submitting works to us is the feedback and support. We work closely with our writers, offering promotion, resource information, moral support and general help to achieve success as writers. While we recommend doing businesss with us via the Internet, we have also published writers who do not have access. For those new to the Internet, we also provide assistance with the best ways to use it as a medium for achieving success in the field."

ℕ $BURST

Terra Media, LLC, P.O. Box 133, Kohler WI 53044.(920)331-4904. E-mail: burst@terra-media.us. Web site: www.terra-media.us/burst. **Contact:** Kevin Struck, editor. E-zine. "*Burst* is a literary e-zine specifically designed for mobile devices, such as cell phones. Content must be short, entertaining, and get to the point. Material that is ambiguous and meaningful only to the writer is not for us. Specialize in flash fiction." Estab. 2006.

Needs Adventure, erotica, experimental, fantasy, humor/satire, mainstream, mystery, romance, science fiction. Accepts 20 mss/year. Manuscript published 3 months after acceptance. Length: 50 words (min)-1,000 words (max).

How to Contact Send complete ms with cover letter. Accepts submissions by e-mail. Responds to queries in 3 weeks. Responds to mss in 3 months. Considers simultaneous submissions, previously published submissions. Guidelines available on Web site.

Payment and Terms Acquires one-time rights. Pays flat rate of $10.

$☐ ✿ THE CAFE IRREAL, International Imagination

E-mail: editors@cafeirreal.com. Web site: www.cafeirreal.com. **Contact:** Alice Whittenburg, G.S. Evans, editors. E-zine: illustrations. "*The Cafe Irreal* is a webzine focusing on short stories and short shorts of an irreal nature." Quarterly. Estab. 1998.

Needs Experimental, fantasy (literary), science fiction (literary), translations. "No horror or 'slice-of-life' stories; no genre or mainstream science fiction or fantasy." Accepts 8-10 mss/issue; 30-40 mss/year. Recently published work by Ginacio Padilla, Charles Simic, Margarita Engle, Jiri Kratochvil, and Steven Schutzman. Publishes short shorts. Also publishes literary essays, literary criticism. Sometimes comments on rejected mss.

How to Contact Accepts submissions by e-mail. "No attachments, include submission in body of e-mail. Include estimated word count." Responds in 2-4 months to mss. No simultaneous submissions. Sample copy online. Writer's guidelines online.

Payment/Terms Pays 1¢/word, $2 minimum. Pays on publication for first-time electronic rights. Sends galleys to author.

Advice "Forget formulas. Write about what you don't know, take me places I couldn't possibly go, don't try to make me care about the characters. Read short fiction by writers such as Franz Kafka, Kobo Abe, Donald Barthelme, Mangnus Mills, Ana Maria Shua and Stanislaw Lem. Also read our Web site and guidelines."

CEZANNE'S CARROT, A Literary Journal of Fresh Observations

Spiritual, Transformational & Visionary Art, Inc., P.O. Box 6037, Santa Fe NM 87502-6037. E-mail: query@cezan nescarrot.org. Web site: www.cezannescarrot.org. **Contact:** Barbara Jacksha and Joan Kremer, editors. Online magazine. "*Cezanne's Carrot* publishes fiction, creative nonfiction, and art that explores spiritual, transformational, visionary or contemplative themes. We publish work that explores the higher, more expansive aspects of human nature, the integration of inner and outer worlds, and the exciting thresholds where the familiar meets the unknown." Quarterly. Estab. 2005.

Needs Ethnic/multicultural (general), experimental, fantasy (speculative), gay, humor/satire, lesbian, literary, mainstream, new age, psychic/supernatural/occult, religious, science fiction (soft/sociological), magical realism, irrealism, visionary, surrealism, metaphysical, spiritual. "Does not want horror, gore, murder, serial-killers, abuse stories, drug stories, vampires or other monsters, political stories, war stories, stories written for children, stories that primarily promote an agenda or a particular religion. We're not interested in dogma in any form." Receives 100 mss/month. Accepts 10-15 mss/issue; 40-60 mss/year. Manuscript published 4-12 weeks after acceptance. **Publishes 1-5 new writers/year.** Published Bruce Holland Rogers, Tamara Kaye Sellman, C.S. Fuqua, Margaret Frey, David Gaffney, Allen McGill, Paul Allen Fahey. Length: 100 words (min)-3,000 words (max). Average length: 1,800 words. Publishes short shorts.

How to Contact Send complete ms with cover letter. Accepts submissions by e-mail only. Include estimated word count, brief bio, list of publications. Responds to mss in 1-4 months. Considers simultaneous submissions, previously published submissions. Guidelines available on Web site.

Payment and Terms Acquires one-time rights, reprint rights.

Advice "We only accept work with a strong tie to our journal's mission and theme. Read our guidelines and mission statement carefully. Read previous issues to understand the kind of work we're looking for. Only submissions sent to the correct e-mail address will be considered."

$ CHALLENGING DESTINY, New Fantasy & Science Fiction

Crystalline Sphere Publishing, RR #6, St. Marys ON N4X 1C8 Canada. (519)885-6012. E-mail: csp@golden.net. Web site: challengingdestiny.com. **Contact:** David M. Switzer, editor. "We publish all kinds of science fiction and fantasy short stories." Quarterly. Estab. 1997. Circ. 200.

Needs Fantasy, science fiction. No horror, short short stories. Receives 40 unsolicited mss/month. Accepts 6 mss/issue; 24 mss/year. Publishes ms 5 months after acceptance. **Publishes 6 new writers/year.** Recently published work by Uncle River, A.R. Morlan, Jay Lake and Ken Rand. Length: 2,000-10,000 words; average length: 6,000 words. Often comments on rejected mss.

How to Contact Send complete ms. Send SAE and IRC for reply, return of ms or send disposable copy of ms. Responds in 1 week to queries; 1 month to mss. Accepts simultaneous submissions. Writer's guidelines for #10 SASE, 1 IRC, or online. Reviews fiction.

Payment/Terms Pays 1¢/word (Canadian), plus 1 contributor's copy. Pays on publication for first North American serial, electronic rights. Sends galleys to author.

Advice "Manuscripts with a good story and interesting characters stand out. We look for fiction that entertains and makes you think. If you're going to write short fiction, you need to read lots of it. Don't reinvent the wheel. Use your own voice."

CONVERGENCE

E-mail: editor@convergence-journal.com. Web site: www.convergence-journal.com. **Contact:** Lara Gularte, editor. *Convergence* seeks to unify the literary and visual arts and draw new interpretations of the written word by pairing poems and flash fiction with complementary art. Quarterly. Estab. 2003. Circ. 400.

Needs Ethnic/multicultural, experimental, feminist, gay, lesbian, literary, regional, translations. Accepts 10 mss/issue. Publishes ms 3 weeks after acceptance. Recently published work by Andrena Zawinski, Grace

Cavalieri, Lola Haskins, Molly Fisk, Renato Rosaldo. Publishes short shorts. Also publishes poetry. Sometimes comments on rejected mss.

How to Contact Send complete ms. E-mail submissions only. No simultaneous submissions. Responds in 2 weeks to queries; 4 months to mss. Writer's guidelines online.

Payment/Terms Acquires electronic rights.

Advice "We look for freshness and originality and a mastery of the craft of flash fiction."

◑ ◎ THE COPPERFIELD REVIEW, A Journal for Readers and Writers of Historical Fiction

E-mail: info@copperfieldreview.com. Web site: www.copperfieldreview.com. **Contact:** Meredith Allard, executive editor. "We are an online literary journal that publishes historical fiction and articles, reviews and interviews related to historical fiction. We believe that by understanding the lessons of the past through historical fiction we can gain better insight into the nature of our society today, as well as a better understanding of ourselves." Quarterly. Estab. 2000.

Needs Historical (general), romance (historical), western (frontier saga, traditional). "We will consider submissions in most fiction categories, but the setting must be historical in nature. We don't want to see anything not related to historical fiction." Receives 30 unsolicited mss/month. Accepts 7-10 mss/issue; 28-40 mss/year. Responds to mss during the months of January, April, July and October. **Publishes "between 30 and 40 percent" new writers/year.** Publishes short shorts. Also publishes literary essays, literary criticism, poetry. Seldom comments on rejected mss.

How to Contact Send complete ms. Accepts submissions by e-mail. Responds in 6 weeks to queries. Accepts simultaneous, multiple submissions and reprints. Sample copy online. Writer's guidelines online. Reviews fiction.

Payment/Terms Acquires one-time rights.

Advice "We wish to showcase the very best in literary historical fiction. Stories that use historical periods and details to illuminate universal truths will immediately stand out. We are thrilled to receive thoughtful work that is polished, poised and written from the heart. Be professional, and only submit your very best work. Be certain to adhere to a publication's submission guidelines, and always treat your e-mail submissions with the same care you would use with a traditional publisher. Above all, be strong and true to your calling as a writer. It is a difficult, frustrating but wonderful journey. It is important for writers to review our online submission guidelines prior to submitting."

$ ◑ DANA LITERARY SOCIETY ONLINE JOURNAL

Dana Literary Society, P.O. Box 3362, Dana Point CA 92629-8362. E-mail: ward@danaliterary.org. Web site: www.danaliterary.org. **Contact:** Robert L. Ward, director. Online journal. "Fiction we publish must be thought-provoking and well crafted. We prefer works that have a message or moral." Monthly. Estab. 2000. Circ. 8,000.

Needs Humor/satire. "Most categories are acceptable if work is mindful of a thinking audience. No romance, children's/juvenile, religious/inspirational, pornographic, excessively violent or profane work. Would like to see more humor/satire." Receives 120 unsolicited mss/month. Accepts 6 mss/issue; 72 mss/year. Publishes ms 3 months after acceptance. **Publishes 8 new writers/year.** Recently published work by A.B. Jacobs, Barbara Anton, and Gerald Eisman. Length: 800-2,500 words; average length: 2,000 words. Also publishes literary essays, poetry. Often comments on rejected mss.

How to Contact Send complete ms. Responds in 2 weeks to mss. Accepts simultaneous submissions and reprints. Sample copy online. Writer's guidelines online.

Payment/Terms Pays $50. Pays on publication for one-time rights. Not copyrighted.

Advice "Success requires two qualities: ability and tenacity. Perfect your technique through educational resources, expansion of your scope of interests and regular re-evaluation and, as required, revision of your works. Profit by a wide exposure to the writings of others. Submit works systematically and persistently, keeping accurate records so you know what went where and when. Take to heart responses and suggestions and plan your follow-up accordingly."

◎ DARGONZINE

E-mail: dargon@dargonzine.org. Web site: dargonzine.org. **Contact:** Ornoth D.A. Liscomb, editor. Electronic zine specializing in fantasy. "*DargonZine* is an electronic magazine that prints original fantasy fiction by aspiring Internet writers. The Dargon Project is a collaborative anthology whose goal is to provide a way for aspiring fantasy writers on the Internet to meet and become better writers through mutual contact and collaboration as well as contact with a live readership via the Internet."

Needs Fantasy. "Our goal is to write fantasy fiction that is mature, emotionally compelling, and professional. Membership in the Dargon Project is a requirement for publication." **Publishes 4-12 new writers/year.**

How to Contact Guidlines available on Web site. Sample copy online. Writer's guidelines online.

Payment/Terms "As a strictly noncommercial magazine, our writers' only compensation is their growth and membership in a lively writing community. Authors retain all rights to their stories."

Advice "The Readers and Writers FAQs on our Web site provide much more detailed information about our mission, writing philosophy and the value of writing for *DargonZine*."

$ ✉ DEATHLINGS.COM, Dark Fiction for the Discerning Reader

130 E. Willamette Ave., Colorado Springs CO 80903-1112. E-mail: cvgelvin@aol.com. Web site: www.deathlings .com. **Contact:** CV Gelvin, editor. E-zine specializing in dark fiction. "Our wonderfully quirky themes for the short story contests have included "Frozen Smiles" (dolls), "Burbian Horrors," "Technology Run Amuck" and "Love Gone Bad." Quarterly. Estab. 2000.

Needs Horror (futuristic, psychological, supernatural). "No children's, fantasy, poetry or romance." List of upcoming themes available on Web site. Receives 20-30 unsolicited mss/month. Accepts 3-4 mss/issue. Publishes ms 1-2 months after acceptance. **Publishes 3-6 new writers/year.** Recently published work by David Ballard, Fiona Curnow, Denise Dumars, Jason Franks, dgk Golberg, Darren O. Godfrey and CV Gelvin. Length: 4,000 words; average length: 3,000 words. Publishes short shorts. Sometimes comments on rejected mss.

How to Contact E-mail story attached in RTF. Include estimated word count, brief bio and list of publications with submission. Responds in 1-3 months to mss. Accepts simultaneous, multiple submissions and reprints. Guidelines free by e-mail or on Web site.

Payment/Terms 3¢/word. Pays on publication for electronic rights. Sponsors awards/contests.

✆ DIAGRAM, A Magazine of Art, Text, and Schematic

New Michigan Press, 648 Crescent NE, Grand Rapids MI 49503. E-mail: prose@thediagram.com. Web site: http://thediagram.com. **Contact:** Ander Monson, editor. "We specialize in work that pushes the boundaries of traditional genre or work that is in some way schematic. We do publish traditional fiction and poetry, too, but hybrid forms (short stories, prose poems, indexes, tables of contents, etc.) are welcome! We also publish diagrams and schematics (original and found). Bimonthly. Estab. 2001. Circ. 150,000 hits/month. Member CLMP.

Needs Experimental, literary. "We don't publish genre fiction, unless it's exceptional and transcends the genre boundaries." Receives 100 unsolicited mss/month. Accepts 2-3 mss/issue; 15 mss/year. **Publishes 15 new writers/year.** Average length: 250-1,000 words. Publishes short shorts. Also publishes literary essays, poetry. Often comments on rejected mss.

How to Contact Send complete ms. Accepts submissions by e-mail. Send SASE (or IRC) for return of the ms, or send disposable copy of the ms and #10 SASE for reply only. Responds in 2 weeks to queries; 1 month to mss. Accepts simultaneous submissions. Sample copy for $12 for print version. Writer's guidelines online.

Payment/Terms Acquires first, electronic rights.

Advice "We value invention, energy, experimentation and voice. When done very well, we like traditional fiction, too. Nearly all the work we select is propulsive and exciting."

⊕ ✆ DOTLIT, The Online Journal of Creative Writing

Creating Writing & Cultural Studies, Queensland University of Technology, Victoria Park Rd., Kelvin Grove Q 4059 Australia. E-mail: dotlitsubmissions@qut.edu.au. Web site: www.dotlit.qut.edu.au. Semiannual. Estab. 2000. "*dotlit* publishes a selection of the best new and innovative fiction, creative nonfiction and hypertexts, including commissioned pieces by established authors and new works by emerging writers. The journal's emphasis is on quality stories well told. Although it is by no means a prescriptive requirement, stories that innovate in terms of voice, structure, or other literary convention will be highly regarded."

Needs Literary fiction, poetry, experimental, young adult/teen, creative nonfiction. Receives 400 unsolicited mss/month. Accepts 12-20 mss/issue; 24-40 mss/year. Publishes ms 6-12 months after acceptance. Recently published work by Bruce Dawe, Graeme Turner, Olga Pavlinova and Lee Gutkind. Publishes short shorts. Also publishes literary essays, and especially wants scholarly articles on creative writing.

How to Contact Send complete ms (double-spaced in MS Word), 50-100 word biography of the author, including a relevant e-mail address. Length: 4,000 words (max). Accepts submissions only by e-mail. Responds in 10 weeks to mss. Submissions must be unpublished. Writer's guidelines online.

Payment/Terms Acquires electronic rights.

$ ✆ DRAGONS, KNIGHTS & ANGELS, The Magazine of Christian Fantasy and Science Fiction

Double-Edged Publishing, 9618 Misty Brook Cove, Cordova TN 38016. Toll Free: (866)888-9671. Fax: (901)213-3878. E-mail: editor@dkamagazine.com. Web site: www.dkamagazine.com. **Contact:** Selena Thomason, managing editor. Online magazine. "Works submitted to *DKA* for publication will be examined first on their merit as works of sci-fi/fantasy/poetry but also on how well they entertain, uplift, and enlighten. We are particularly interested in stories that meld the speculative and the spiritual, and scifi/fantasy stories that have a moral core without being preachy." Estab. 1999. Circ. 28,000 visits per month.

Needs Fantasy (space fantasy, sword and sorcery), religious, science fiction (hard science/technological, soft/ sociological), young adult/teen (adventure, fantasy/science fiction, horror, mystery/suspense, romance). Does not want lesbian, gay, erotica. Promotion of values and principles not compatible with Christianity will not be published. Receives 20-30 mss/month. Accepts 4-8 mss/issue; 48-96 mss/year. Manuscript published 2-8 weeks after acceptance. Average length: 3,500 words. Publishes short shorts. Average length of short shorts: 1,100 words. Also publishes poetry. Always comments on/critiques rejected manuscripts.

How to Contact Submit via Web site through online submission system. Responds to queries in 1 week. Responds to mss in 4 weeks, often less. Considers previously published submissions, multiple submissions. Guidelines available on Web site.

Payment and Terms *DKA* pays $10 for short stories (1,500-7,000 words), $5 for flash fiction (under 1,500 words), and $5 for poems. **Pays on acceptance.**

Advice "Please read our submission guidelines before submitting. It is also helpful to visit our forums, as well as read some of what we have published. After getting a sense of the publication, you will have a better idea of what we are looking for and whether or not your work will 'fit' with our publication. We are very open to working with new writers."

🖉 🖺 FAILBETTER.COM

Failbetter, 3222 Hanover Avenue, Richmond, VA 23221. E-mail: submissions@failbetter.com. Web site: www.failbtetter.com. **Contact:** Thom Didato, publisher. "We are a quarterly online magazine published in the spirit of a traditional literary journal—dedicated to publishing quality fiction, poetry, and artwork. While the Web plays host to hundreds, if not thousands, of genre-related sites (many of which have merit), we are not one of them." Quarterly. Estab. 2000. Circ. 50,000. Member CLMP.

Needs Literary, short stories, novel excerpts. "No genre fiction—romance, fantasy or science fiction." Always would like to see more "character-driven literary fiction where something happens!" Receives 50-75 unsolicited mss/month. Accepts 3-5 mss/issue; 12-20 mss/year. Publishes ms 4-8 months after acceptance. **Publishes 4-6 new writers/year.** Recently published work by Lou Mathews, Kevin Sampsell, Colleen Monder, and Terese Svoboda. Publishes short shorts. Often comments on rejected mss.

How to Contact Accepts submissions by e-mail. Include the word "submission" in the subject line. Responds in 8-12 weeks to queries; 4-6 month to mss. Accepts simultaneous submissions. All issues are available online.

Payment/Terms Acquires one-time rights.

Advice "Read an issue. Read our guidelines! We place a high degree of importance on originality, believing that even in this age of trends it is still possible. We are not looking for what is current or momentary. We are not concerned with length: One good sentence may find a home here, as the bulk of mediocrity will not. Most importantly, know that what you are saying could only come from you. When you are sure of this, please feel free to submit."

🖉 THE FAIRFIELD REVIEW

544 Silver Spring Rd., Fairfield CT 06824. (203)256-1960. Fax: (203)256-1970. E-mail: fairfieldreview@hpmd.com. Web site: www.fairfieldreview.org. **Contact:** Edward and Janet Granger-Happ, Pamela Pollak, editors. Electronic magazine. "Our mission is to provide an outlet for poetry, short stories and essays, from both new and established writers and students. We are accessible to the general public."

Needs Literary. Would like to see more stories "rich in lyrical imagery and those that are more humorous." **Publishes 20 new writers/year.** Recently published work by Nan Leslie (Pushcart nominee) and Richard Boughton.

How to Contact Strongly prefers submissions by e-mail. Replies by e-mail only. Right to retain publication in online archive issues, and the right to use in "Best of The Fairfield Review" anthologies. Sample copy online.

Payment/Terms Acquires first rights.

Advice "We encourage students and first-time writers to submit their work. In addition to the submission guidelines found in each issue on our Web site, we recommend reading the essay 'Writing Qualities to Keep in Mind' from our Editors and Authors page on the Web site. Keep to small, directly experienced themes; write crisply using creative, poetic images, avoid the trite expression."

5-TROPE

E-mail: editor.5trope@gmail.com. Web site: www.webdelsol.com/5_trope. **Contact:** Gunnar Benediktsson, editor. Online literary journal. "We aim to publish the new and original in fiction, poetry and new media. We are seeking writers with a playful seriousness about language and form." Quarterly. Estab. 1999. Circ. 5,000.

Needs Avant-garde prose, experimental, literary. "No religious, horror, fantasy, espionage." Receives 50 unsolicited mss/month. Accepts 6 mss/issue; 18 mss/year. Publishes ms 1-6 months after acceptance. **Publishes 5**

new writers/year. Recently published work by Cole Swensen, Carol Novack, Christopher Kennedy, Mike Topp, Norman Lock, Jeff Johnson, Peter Markus, Mandee Wright, and Jane Unrue. Length: 25-5,000 words; average length: 1,000 words. Publishes short shorts. Also publishes poetry. Sometimes comments on rejected mss.

How to Contact Accepts submissions by e-mail. Send complete mss electronically. Sample copy online.

Payment/Terms Acquires first rights. Sends galleys to author.

Advice "Before submitting, please visit our site, read an issue, and consult our guidelines for submission. Include your story within the body of an e-mail, not as an attachment. Include a descriptive subject line to get around spam filters. Experimental work should have a clarity about it, and should never be sentimental—our stories are about the moment of rupture, not the moment of closure."

FLUENT ASCENSION

Fierce Concepts, P.O. Box 6407, Glendale AZ 85312. E-mail: submissions@fluentascension.com. Web site: www.fluentascension.com. **Contact:** Warren Norgaard, editor. Online magazine. Quarterly. Estab. 2003.

Needs Comics/graphic novels, erotica, ethnic/multicultural, experimental, gay, humor/satire, lesbian, literary, translations. Receives 6-10 unsolicited mss/month. Accepts 1-3 mss/issue. Publishes short shorts. Also publishes literary essays, literary criticism, poetry. Sometimes comments on rejected mss.

How to Contact Send complete ms. Accepts submissions by e-mail. Include estimated word count, brief bio and list of publications. Send SASE (or IRC) for return of ms or send disposable copy of ms and #10 SASE for reply only. Responds in 4-8 weeks to queries; 4-8 weeks to mss. Accepts simultaneous, multiple submissions. Sample copy online. Writer's guidelines online.

Payment/Terms Acquires electronic rights. Sponsors awards/contests.

THE FURNACE REVIEW

E-mail: editor@thefurnacereview.com. Web site: www.thefurnacereview.com. **Contact:** Ciara LaVelle, editor. "We reach out to a young, well-educated audience, bringing them new, unique, fresh work they won't find elsewhere." Quarterly. Estab. 2004.

Needs Erotica, experimental, feminist, gay, historical, humor/satire, lesbian, literary, mainstream, military/war. Does not want children's, science fiction, or religious submissions. Receives 50-60 unsolicited mss/month. Accepts 1-3 mss/issue; 5-8 mss/year. **Publishes 5-8 new writers/year.** Recently published work by Amy Greene, Dominic Preziosi, and Sandra Soson. Length: 7,000 words; average length: 4,000 words. Publishes short shorts. Also publishes poetry.

How to Contact Send complete ms. Accepts submissions by e-mail only. Responds in 4 month to queries. Accepts simultaneous submissions.

Payment/Terms Acquires first North American serial rights.

THE GREEN HILLS LITERARY LANTERN

Published by Truman State University, Division of Language & Literature, Kirksville MO 63501. (660)785-4487. E-mail: adavis@truman.edu. Web site: http://ll.truman.edu/ghllweb. **Contact:** Fiction editor. "The mission of *GHLL* is to provide a literary market for quality fiction writers, both established and beginners, and to provide quality literature for readers from diverse backgrounds. We also see ourselves as a cultural resource for North Missouri. Our publication works to publish the highest quality fiction—dense, layered, subtle—and, at the same time, fiction which grabs the ordinary reader. We tend to publish traditional short stories, but we are open to experimental forms." Annual. Estab. 1990. The *GHLL* is now an online, open-access journal.

Needs Ethnic/multicultural, experimental, feminist, humor/satire, literary, mainstream, regional. "Our main requirement is literary merit. Wants more quality fiction about rural culture. No adventure, crime, erotica, horror, inspirational, mystery/suspense, romance." Receives 40 unsolicited mss/month. Accepts 15-17 mss/issue. Publishes ms 6-12 months after acceptance. **Publishes 0-3 new writers/year.** Recently published work by Karl Harshbarger, Mark Jacobs, J. Morris, Gary Fincke, Dennis Vannatta. Length: 7,000 words; average length: 3,000 words. Publishes short shorts. Also publishes poetry. Sometimes comments on rejected mss.

How to Contact SASE for return of ms. Responds in 4 months to mss. Accepts simultaneous, multiple submissions. Electronic submissions in .doc or .txt format also acceptable, but our manuscript readers still prefer hardcopy. E-mail attachment to adavis@truman.edu.

Payment/Terms No payment. Acquires one-time rights.

Advice "We look for strong character development, substantive plot and theme, visual and forceful language within a multilayered story. Make sure your work has the flavor of life, a sense of reality. A good story, well crafted, will eventually get published. Find the right market for it, and above all, don't give up."

KENNESAW REVIEW

Kennesaw State University, Dept. of English, Building 27, 1000 Chastain Rd., Kennesaw GA 30144-5591. (770)423-6346. Web site: www.kennesawreview.org. **Contact:** Robert W. Hill, editor. Online literary journal. "Just good litrary fiction, all themes, for an eclectic audience." Biannual. Estab. 1987.

Needs Short stories and flash fiction. "No formulaic genre fiction." Receives 25 unsolicited mss/month. Accepts 2-4 mss/issue. Publishes ms 12-18 months after acceptance. Recently published work by Ellen Lundquist, Michael Cadnum, and Robert Philips.

How to Contact Send complete ms. Include previous publications. Responds in 2 months to mss. Accepts simultaneous, multiple submissions. Writer's guidelines online.

Payment/Terms Acquires first rights.

Advice "Use the language well and tell an interesting story."

$ ⊞ ☑ LONE STAR STORIES, Speculative Fiction and Poetry

E-mail: submissions@erictmarin.com. Web site: www.lonestarstories.com. **Contact:** Eric T. Marin, editor. Online magazine. Contains illustrations and photographs. "*Lone Star Stories* publishes quality speculative fiction and poetry." Bimonthly. Estab. 2004.

Needs Speculative fiction (fantasy, dark fantasy, science fiction, and interstitial). Receives 100+ mss/month. Accepts 3 mss/issue; 18 mss/year. Manuscript published 2 months after acceptance. Average length: 5,000 words. Publishes short shorts. Average length of short shorts: 500 words. Also publishes poetry.

How to Contact Send complete ms with cover letter. Accepts submissions by e-mail. Include estimated word count. Responds to queries in 1 week. Responds to mss in 1 week. Considers simultaneous submissions, previously published submissions. Guidelines available on Web site.

Payment and Terms Writers receive $20 per story; $10 per poem. **Pays on acceptance.** Publication is copyrighted.

Advice "The standard advice applies: Read the current issue of *Lone Star Stories* to get a feel for what is likely to be published."

TIMOTHY MCSWEENEY'S INTERNET TENDENCY

826 Valencia Street, San Francisco CA 94110. E-mail: websubmissions@mcsweeneys.net. Web site: www.mcsweeneys.net. **Contact:** Dave Eggers, John Warner, editors. Online literary journal. "*Timothy McSweeney's Internet Tendency* is an offshoot of *Timothy McSweeney's Quarterly Concern*, a journal created by nervous people in relative obscurity, and published four times a year." Daily.

Needs Literate humor, sestinas. Sometimes comments on rejected mss.

How to Contact Accepts submissions by e-mail. "For submissions to the Web site, paste the entire piece into the body of an e-mail. Absolute length limit of 1,500 words, with a preference for pieces significantly shorter (700-1,000 words)." Sample copy online. Writer's guidelines online.

Advice "Do not submit your work to both the print submissions address and the Web submissions address, as seemingly hundreds of writers have been doing lately. If you submit a piece of writing intended for the magazine to the Web submissions address, you will confuse us, and if you confuse us, we will accidentally delete your work without reading it, and then we will laugh and never give it another moment's thought, and sleep the carefree sleep of young children. This is very, very serious."

☐ MIDNIGHT TIMES

1731 Shadwell Dr., Barnhart MO 63012. E-mail: editor@midnighttimes.com. Web site: www.midnighttimes.com. **Contact:** Jay Manning, editor. *Midnight Times* is an online literary magazine dedicated to publishing quality poetry and fiction by both previously unpublished as well as published writers. The primary theme is darkness, but this doesn't necessarily mean evil. There can be a light at the end of the tunnel. Quarterly. Estab. 2003.

Needs Fantasy (sword and sorcery), horror (dark fantasy, futuristic, psychological, supernatural), literary, mainstream, psychic/supernatural/occult, science fiction, vampires. No pornography. Accepts 3-6 mss/issue; 12-24 mss/year. Publishes ms 3-9 months after acceptance. **Publishes many new writers/year.** Length: 500-10,000 words; average length: 4,000 words. Publishes short shorts. Also publishes poetry. Sometimes comments on rejected mss.

How to Contact Send complete ms. Accepts submissions by e-mail. Send SASE (or IRC) for return of the ms, or send disposable copy of the ms and #10 SASE for reply only. Responds in 2 weeks to queries; 1 month to mss. Accepts simultaneous submissions and reprints. Writer's guidelines for SASE or by e-mail or on Web site.

Payment/Terms No payment. Acquires one-time, electronic rights.

Advice "Please read the submission guidelines on the Web site before submitting your work!"

☑ NEW WORKS REVIEW

P.O. Box 54, Friendswood TX 77549-0054. (281)482-7300. Fax: (281)482-7300. E-mail: timhealy@hal-pc.org. Web site: www.new-works.org. **Contact:** Tim Healy, editor-in-chief. Online magazine. Contains illustrations and photographs. "Our philosophy is to publish outstanding work suitable for all readers. All genres are published." Quarterly. Estab. 1998.

Needs Adventure, family saga, humor/satire, literary, mainstream, military/war, mystery/suspense (amateur sleuth, cozy, police procedural, private eye/hard-boiled), thriller/espionage, translations, western. Does not want porn, anti-religious, erotica, or use of obscenities. Receives 30 mss/month. Accepts 10 mss/issue; 40 mss/year. Manuscript published 3 months after acceptance. **Publishes 5-10 new writers/year.** Published Irving Greenfield, Lynn Strongin, Tom Sheehan, Michael Corrigan, Brett Alan Sanders and Diane Sawyer. Average length: 3,000 words. Also publishes literary essays, literary criticism, poetry, and book reviews. Often comments on/critiques rejected manuscripts.

How to Contact Send complete ms with cover letter. Accepts submissions by e-mail, on disk. Include estimated word count. Responds to queries in 1 week. Does not consider simultaneous submissions, previously published submissions, multiple submissions. Guidelines available on Web site.

Payment and Terms All rights retained by author. Sends galleys to author. Publication is copyrighted.

Advice ''Read established writers, edit and re-edit your stories, follow the guidelines.''

$⬛ NOCTURNAL OOZE, an Online Horror Magazine

Froggy Bottom Press, P.O. Box 495, Beaver PA 15009-0495. E-mail: submit@nocturnalooze.com. Web site: www.nocturnalooze.com. **Contact:** Katherine Patterson, Marty Hiller; senior editors. ''*Nocturnal Ooze* blends sight and sound in a themed enviroment, to create an atmosphere of the macabre which enhances the reading experience of visitors to our site. We seek to promote dark fiction, tales that make our spines tingle.'' Monthly. Estab. 2003. Circ. 650+. Member HWA.

Needs Horror (dark fantasy, psychological, supernatural), psychic/supernatural/occult. ''No silly or humorous horror. No excessive blood and gore just for mere shock value. No child abuse or baby mutilation stories.'' Receives 40-80 unsolicited mss/month. Accepts 10-12 mss/issue; 72 mss/year. Publishes ms 1-2 months after acceptance. **Publishes 10% new writers/year.** Recently published work by James Hartley, Matthew Lee Bain, Rayne Hall, Eric Christi, and Angeline Hawkes-Craig. Length: 750-3,500 words; average length: 1,250 words. Always comments on rejected mss.

How to Contact Send complete ms. Accepts submissions by e-mail only. Responds in 2 months to mss. Accepts multiple submissions. Writer's guidelines online.

Payment/Terms Pays $5-17.50. Pays on publication for first, electronic rights.

Advice ''We look for a story that grabs us at the start and draws us into the darkness of the unknown. Stories that put us on the brink of peril then either save us in the end or shove us into the abyss.''

⬛ NUVEIN ONLINE

(626)401-3466. Fax: (626)401-3460. E-mail: editor@nuvein.com. Web site: www.nuvein.com. **Contact:** Ahn Lottman, editor or Enrique Diaz, publisher. Electronic Zine. ''We are open to short works that explore topics divergent from the mainstream. Our vision is to provide a forum for new and experienced voices rarely heard in our global community.''

• *Nuvein Online* has received the Visionary Media Award.

Needs Fiction, poetry, plays and art. Wants more ''experimental fiction, ethnic works, and pieces dealing with the exploration of sexuality.'' **Publishes 20 new writers/year.** Recently published work by J. Knight, Paul A. Toth, Rick Austin, Robert Levin and Scott Essman.

How to Contact Query. Accepts submissions by e-mail. Send work as attachment. Sample copy online.

Advice ''Read over each submission before sending it, and if you, as the writer, find the piece irresistable, e-mail it to us immediately!''

◻ OPIUM MAGAZINE

Literary Humor for the Deliriously Captivated, 40 E. 3rd St., Suite 8, New York NY 10003-9213. (347)229-2443. E-mail: todd@opiummagazine.com. Web site: www.opiummagazine.com. **Contact:** Todd Zuniga, editor-in-chief. Online magazine. Contains illustrations and photographs. ''OpiumMagazine.com displays an eclectic mix of stories, poetry, reviews, cartoons, interviews and much more. It features 'estimated reading times' that precede each piece. It is updated daily. While the focus is often humorous literature, we love to publish heart-breaking, serious work. Our rule is that all work must be well written and engaging. While we publish traditional pieces, we're primarily engaged by writers who take risks.'' Updated daily. Estab. 2001. Circ. 25,000 hits/month. Member CLMP.

Needs Comics/graphic novels, experimental, humor/satire, literary, mainstream. ''Vignettes and first-person 'look at what a whacky time I had going to Spain' stories aren't going to get past first base with us.'' Receives 400 mss/month. Accepts 275 mss/year. Manuscript published 4 months after acceptance. Agented fiction 10%. **Publishes 50-75 new writers/year.** Published Darby Larson, John Leary, Grant Bailie, Angela Lovell, Tao Lin. Length: 50-1,200 words. Average length: 700 words. Publishes short shorts. Average length of short shorts: 400 words. Also publishes literary essays, literary criticism, poetry. Sometimes comments on/critiques rejected mss.

How to Contact Send complete ms with cover letter. Accepts submissions by e-mail. Include estimated word count, brief bio, list of publications, and your favorite book. Responds to queries in 1 week. Responds to mss in 2 weeks. Considers simultaneous submissions. Guidelines available via e-mail or on Web site.

Payment and Terms Acquires first North American serial rights. Publication is copyrighted.

Advice "We love sparkling, surprising, well-penned, brilliant stories. If you don't strike out in that first paragraph to expose something definitive or new, then you better by the second. We get scores of stories, and like the readers we want to attract, we demand to be engaged immediately. Every publication will say the same thing: read the magazine, read the site. And we, too, encourage that (obviously). But if you're short on time, send us your absolute best story. Tell us it's your first time, we'll be gentle, and our editors usually give thoughts and encouragement if a piece has promise, even if we reject it."

THE ORACULAR TREE, A Transformational E-Zine

The Oracular Tree, 208-167 Morgan Ave., Kitchener ON N2A 2M4 Canada. E-mail: editor@oracultree.com. Web site: www.oraculartree.com. **Contact:** Teresa Hawkes, publisher. E-zine specializing in practical ideas for transforming our lives. "The stories we tell ourselves and each other predict the outcome of our lives. We can affect gradual social change by transforming our deeply rooted cultural stories. The genre is not as important as the message and the high quality of the writing. We accept stories, poems, articles and essays which will reach well-educated, open-minded readers around the world. We offer a forum for those who see a need for change, who want to add their voices to a growing search for positive alternatives." Monthly. Estab. 1997. Circ. 250,000 hits/month.

Needs Serial fiction, poetry, essays, novels and novel excerpts, visual art, short fiction, news. "We'll look at any genre that is well written and can examine a new cultural paradigm. No tired dogma, no greeting card poetry, please." Receives 20-30 unsolicited mss/month. Accepts 80-100 mss/year. Publishes ms 3 months after acceptance. **Publishes 20-30 new writers/year.** Recently published work by Elisha Porat, Lyn Lyfshin, Rattan Mann, and Dr. Elaine Hatfield. Publishes short shorts. Also publishes literary essays, poetry. Often comments on rejected mss.

How to Contact Send complete ms. Accepts submissions by e-mail. Responds in 2 weeks to queries; 2 months to mss. Accepts simultaneous, multiple submissions and reprints. Sample copy online. Writer's guidelines online.

Payment/Terms Author retains copyright; one-time archive posting.

Advice "The underlying idea must be clearly expressed. The language should be appropriate to the tale, using creative license and an awareness of rhythm. We look for a juxtaposition of ideas that creates resonance in the mind and heart of the reader. Write from your honest voice. Trust your writing to unfold."

OUTER ART, the worst possible art in the world

The University of New Mexico, 200 College Road, Gallup NM 87301. (505)863-7647. Fax: (505)863-7532. E-mail: smarand@unm.edu. Web site: www.gallup.unm.edu/~smarandache/a/outer-art.htm. **Contact:** Florentin Smarandache, editor. E-zine. Annual. Estab. 2000.

Needs Experimental, literary, outer-art. Publishes ms 1 month after acceptance. Publishes short shorts. Also publishes literary essays, literary criticism.

How to Contact Accepts submissions by e-mail. Send SASE (or IRC) for return of the ms. Responds in 1 month to mss. Accepts simultaneous submissions and reprints. Writer's guidelines online.

OXFORD MAGAZINE

Bachelor Hall, Miami University, Oxford OH 45056. (513)529-1279. E-mail: oxmagfictioneditor@muohio.edu. Web site: www.oxfordmagazine.org. **Contact:** Fiction editor. Annual. Estab. 1985. Circ. 1,000.

• *Oxford* has been awarded two Pushcart Prizes.

Needs Wants quality fiction and prose, genre is not an issue but nothing sentimental. Receives 150 unsolicited mss/month. **Publishes some new writers/year.** Recently published work by Stephen Dixon, Andre Dubus and Stuart Dybek. Publishes short shorts. Also publishes poetry.

How to Contact SASE. Responds in 2 months, depending upon time of submissions; mss received after December 31 will be returned. Accepts simultaneous submissions if notified. Sample copy for $5.

Payment/Terms Acquires one-time rights.

Advice "*Oxford Magazine* accepts fiction, poetry, and essays (this last genre is a catch-all, much like the space under your couch cushions, and includes creative nonfiction, critical work exploring writing, and the like). Appearing once a year, OxMag is a Web-based journal that acquires first North American serial rights, one-time anthology rights and online serial rights. Simultaneous submissions are okay if you would kindly let us know if and when someone beats us to the punch."

PAPERPLATES, a magazine for fifty readers

Perkolator Kommunikation, 19 Kenwood Ave., Toronto ON M6C 2R8 Canada. (416)651-2551. E-mail: magazine @paperplates.org. Web site: www.paperplates.org. **Contact:** Bethany Gibson, fiction editor. Electronic magazine. Quarterly. Estab. 1990.

Needs Condensed novels, ethnic/multicultural, feminist, gay, lesbian, literary, mainstream, translations. ''No science fiction, fantasy or horror.'' Receives 12 unsolicited mss/month. Accepts 2-3 mss/issue; 6-9 mss/year. Publishes ms 6-8 months after acceptance. Recently published work by Lyn Fox, David Bezmozgis, Fraser Sutherland and Tim Conley. Length: 1,500-3,500 words; average length: 3,000 words. Publishes short shorts. Also publishes literary essays, literary criticism, poetry.

How to Contact Accepts submissions by e-mail and land mail. Responds in 6 weeks to queries; 6 months to mss. Accepts simultaneous submissions. Sample copy online. Writer's guidelines online.

Payment/Terms No payment. Acquires first North American serial rights.

🖉 THE PAUMANOK REVIEW

E-mail: submissions@paumanokreview.com. Web site: www.paumanokreview.com. **Contact:** Katherine Arline, editor. Online literary magazine. ''*TPR* is dedicated to publishing and promoting the best in world art and literature.'' Quarterly. Estab. 2000.

• J.P. Maney's *Western Exposures* was selected for inclusion in the *E2INK Best of the Web Anthology*.

Needs Mainstream, narrative, experimental, historical, mystery, horror, western, science fiction, slice-of-life vignette, serial, novel excerpt. Receives 100 unsolicited mss/month. Accepts 6-8 mss/issue; 24-32 mss/year. Publishes ms 6 weeks after acceptance. **Publishes 4 new writers/year.** Recently published work by Patty Friedman, Elisha Porat, Barry Spacks and Walt McDonald. Length: 1,000-6,000 words; average length: 3,000 words. Publishes short shorts. Also publishes literary essays, poetry. Usually comments on rejected mss.

How to Contact Send complete ms as attatchment (Word, RTF, HTML, TXT) or pasted in body of e-mail. Include estimated word count, brief bio, two ways to contact you, list of publications, and how you discovered *TPR*. Responds in 1 week to queries; 1 month to mss. Accepts simultaneous submissions and reprints. No multiple submissions. Sample copy online. Writer's guidelines online.

Payment/Terms Acquires one-time, anthology rights. Galleys offered in HTML or PDF format.

Advice ''Though this is an English-language publication, it is not US-or UK-centric. Please submit accordingly. *TPR* is a publication of Wind River Press, which also publishes *Critique* magazine and select print and electronic books.''

🖉 PBW

513 N. Central Ave., Fairborn OH 45324. (937)878-5184. E-mail: rianca@aol.com. Electronic disk zine; 700 pages, specializing in avant-garde fiction and poetry. ''*PBW* is an experimental floppy disk (CD-Rom) that prints strange and 'unpublishable' in an above-ground-sense writing.'' Twice per year. Estab. 1988.

How to Contact ''Manuscripts are only taken if they are submitted on disk or by e-mail.'' Send SASE for reply, return of ms. Sample copy not available.

Payment/Terms All rights revert back to author. Not copyrighted.

THE PINK CHAMELEON

E-mail: dpfreda@juno.com. Web site: http://www.geocities.com/thepinkchameleon/index.html. **Contact:** Mrs. Dorothy Paula Freda, editor/publisher. Family-oriented electronic magazine. Annual. Estab. 2000. Reading period from January to April and September to October.

Needs Short stories, adventure, family saga, fantasy, humor/satire, literary, mainstream, mystery/suspense, religious/inspirational, romance, science fiction, thriller/espionage, western, young adult/teen, psychic/supernatural. ''No violence for the sake of violence.'' Receives 20 unsolicited mss/month. Publishes ms within 1 year after acceptance. **Publishes 50% new writers/year.** Recently published work by Deanne F. Purcell, Martin Green, Albert J. Manachino, James W. Collins, Ken Sieben, Doris and Bob Papenmeyer, Thomas J. Misuraca, and Denise Noe. Length: 500-2,500 words; average length: 2,000 words. Publishes short shorts. No novels or novel excerpts. Also publishes literary essays, poetry. Sometimes comments on rejected mss.

How to Contact Send complete ms in the body of the e-mail. No attachments. Responds in 1 month to mss. Accepts reprints. No simultaneous submissions. Sample copy online. Writer's guidelines online.

Payment/Terms ''Non-profit. Acquires one-time rights for one year but will return rights earlier on request.''

Advice ''Simple, honest, evocative emotion, upbeat submissions that give hope for the future; well-paced plots; stories, poetry, articles, essays that speak from the heart. Read guidelines carefully. Use a good, but not ostentatious, opening hook. Stories should have a beginning, middle and end that make the reader feel the story was worth his or her time. This also applies to articles and essays. In the latter two, wrap your comments and conclusions in a neatly packaged final paragraph. Turnoffs include violence, bad language. Simple, genuine and sensitive work does not need to shock with vulgarity to be interesting and enjoyable.''

🖉 R-KV-R-Y, A Quarterly Literary Journal

90 Meetings in 90 Days Press, 499 North Canon Dr., Suite 400, Beverly Hills CA 90210. (323)217-5162. Fax: (323)852-1535. E-mail: recovery@ninetymeetingsinninetydays.com. Web site: www.ninetymeetingsinninetyda

ys.com. **Contact:** Victoria Pynchon, editor-in-chief. Online magazine. 25 Web pages. Contains illustrations. Includes photographs. "R-KV-R-Y publishes half a dozen short stories of high literary quality every quarter. We publish fiction that varies widely in style. We prefer stories of character development, psychological penetration, and lyricism, without sentimentality or purple prose. We ask that all submissions address issues related to recovery from any type of physical, psychological, or cultural loss, dislocation or oppression. We include but do not limit ourselves to issues of substance abuse. We do not publish the standard 'what it was like, what happened and what it is like now' recovery narrative. Works published by R-KV-R-Y embrace almost every area of adult interest related to recovery: literary affairs, history, folklore, fiction, poetry, literary criticism, art, music, and the theatre. Material should be presented in a fashion suited to a quarterly that is neither journalistic nor academic. We welcome academic articles from varying fields. We encourage our academic contributors to free themselves from the contraints imposed by academic journals, letting their knowledge, wisdom, and experience rock and roll on these pages. Our intended audience is people of discriminating taste, original ideas, heart, and love of narrative and language." Quarterly. Estab. 2004. Circ. 14,000 readers.

Needs Literary. List of upcoming themes available on Web site. Receives 5 mss/month. Accepts 5 mss/issue; 20 mss/year. Manuscript published 2-3 months after acceptance. Agented fiction 0%. **Publishes 5-6 new writers/year.** Published Rita Coleman (debut fiction), Anne LaBorde (debut literary nonfiction), Richard Wirick, Joseph Mockus, Birute Serota, Zoe Kiethley, Lee Patton, Nathan Leslie, Kathleen Wakefield, Sherry Lynne Maze (debut). Length: 5,000 words (max). Average length: 2,000 words. Publishes short shorts. Average length of short shorts: 1,000 words. Also publishes literary essays, book reviews, poetry. Sometimes comments on/critiques rejected manuscripts.

How to Contact Send complete ms with cover letter. Accepts submissions by e-mail. Include brief bio, list of publications. Responds to queries in 2 weeks. Responds to mss in 1-3 months. Considers simultaneous submissions, previously published submissions. Guidelines available on Web site.

Payment and Terms Acquires electronic rights. Sends galleys to author. Publication is copyrighted.

Advice "Wants strong focus on character development and lively writing style with strong voice. Read our present and former issues (archived online) as well as fiction found in such journals and magazines as *Granta*, *The New Yorker*, *Tri-Quarterly*, *The Atlantic*, *Harper's*, *Story* and similar sources of the highest quality fiction."

REALPOETIK, A Little Magazine of the Internet

E-mail: salasin@scn.org. Web site: www.scn.org/realpoetik. **Contact:** Fiction Editor. "We publish the new, lively, exciting and unexpected in vernacular English. Any vernacular will do." Weekly. Estab. 1993.

Needs "We do not want to see anything that fits neatly into categories. We subvert categories." Publishes ms 2-4 months after acceptance. **Publishes 20-30 new writers/year.** Average length: 250-500 words. Publishes short shorts. Also publishes literary essays, literary criticism, poetry. Sometimes comments on rejected mss.

How to Contact Query with or without published clips or send complete ms. Accepts submissions by e-mail. Responds in 1 month to queries. Sample copy online.

Payment/Terms Acquires one-time rights. Sponsors awards/contests.

Advice "Be different but interesting. Humor and consciousness are always helpful. Write short. We're a postmodern e-zine."

THE ROSE & THORN LITERARY E-ZINE, Showcasing Emerging and Established Writers and A Writer's Resource

E-mail: BAQuinn@aol.com. Web site: www.theroseandthornezine.com. **Contact:** Barbara Quinn, fiction editor, publisher, managing editor. E-zine specializing in literary works of fiction, nonfiction, poetry and essays. "We created this publication for readers and writers alike. We provide a forum for emerging and established voices. We blend contemporary writing with traditional prose and poetry in an effort to promote the literary arts." Quarterly. Circ. 12,000.

Needs Adventure, ethnic/multicultural, experimental, fantasy, historical, horror (dark fantasy, futuristic, psychological, supernatural), humor/satire, literary, mainstream, mystery/suspense, New Age, regional, religious/inspirational, romance (contemporary, futuristic/time travel, gothic, historical, regency, romantic suspense), science fiction, thriller/espionage, western. Receives "several hundred" unsolicited mss/month. Accepts 8-10 mss/issue; 40-50 mss/year. **Publishes many new writers/year.** Publishes short shorts. Also publishes literary essays, poetry. Sometimes comments on rejected mss.

How to Contact Query with or without published clips or send complete ms. Accepts submissions by e-mail. Include estimated word count, 150-word bio, list of publications and author's byline. Responds in 1 week to queries; 1 month to mss. Accepts simultaneous submissions and reprints. Sample copy free. Writer's guidelines online. 2,000 word limit.

Payment/Terms Writer retains all rights. Sends galleys to author.

Advice "Clarity, control of the language, evocative stories that tug at the heart and make their mark on the reader long after it's been read. We look for uniqueness in voice, style and characterization. New twists on old themes are always welcome. Use all aspects of good writing in your stories, including dynamic characters, strong narrative voice and a riveting original plot. We have eclectic tastes, so go ahead and give us a shot. Read the publication and other quality literary journals so you'll see what we look for. Always check your spelling and grammar before submitting. Reread your submission with a critical eye and ask yourself, 'Does it evoke an emotional response? Have I completely captured my reader?' Check your submission for 'it' and 'was' and see if you can come up with a better way to express yourself. Be unique.''

🖾 RPPS/FULLOSIA PRESS

Rockaway Park Philosophical Society, P.O. Box 280, Ronkonkoma NY 11779. E-mail: deanofrpps@aol.com. Web site: rpps_fullosia_press.tripod.com. **Contact:** J.D. Collins, editor. E-zine. ''One-person, part-time. Publishes fiction and non-fiction. Our publication is right wing and conservative, leaning to views of Patrick Buchanan but amenable to the opposition's point of view. We promote an independent America. We are anti-global, anti-UN. Collects unusual news from former British or American provinces. Fiction interests include military, police, private detective, courthouse stories.'' Monthly. Estab. 1999. Circ. 150.

Needs Historical (American), military/war, mystery/suspense, thriller/espionage. Christmas, St. Patrick's Day, Fourth of July. Publishes ms 1 week after acceptance. **Publishes 10 new writers/year.** Recently published work by Geoff Jasckson, 'Awesome' Dave Lawrence, Laura Stamps, John Grey, Dr. Kelly White, James Davies, Andy Martin, Michael Levy, and Peter Vetrano's class. Length: 500-2,000 words; average length: 750 words. Publishes short shorts. Also publishes literary essays. Always comments on rejected mss.

How to Contact Query with or without published clips. Accepts submissions by e-mail. Include brief bio and list of publications. Mail submissions must be on $3^1/_4$ floppy disk. Responds in 1 month to mss. Accepts simultaneous submissions, reprints, multiple submissions. Please avoid mass mailings. Sample copy online. Reviews fiction.

Payment/Terms Acquires electronic rights.

Advice ''Make your point quickly. If you haven't done so, after five pages, everybody hates you and your characters.''

🖾 🖾 SLOW TRAINS LITERARY JOURNAL

P.O. 4741, Denver CO 80155. E-mail: editor@slowtrains.com. Web site: www.slowtrains.com. **Contact:** Susannah Indigo. Quarterly. Estab. 2000.

Needs Literary. No romance, sci-fi, or other specific genre-writing. Receives 100+ unsolicited mss/month. Accepts 10-15 mss/issue; 40-50 mss/year. Publishes ms 3 months after acceptance. **Publishes 20-40 new writers/year.** Length: 1,000-5,000 words; average length: 3,500 words. Publishes short shorts. Also publishes literary essays, poetry. Rarely comments on rejected mss.

How to Contact Accepts submissions by e-mail. Responds in 4-8 weeks to mss. Accepts simultaneous submissions and reprints. Sample copy online. Writer's guidelines online.

Payment/Terms Pays 2 contributor's copies. Acquires one-time, electronic rights.

Advice ''The first page must be able to pull the reader in immediately. Use your own fresh, poetic, compelling voice. Center your story around some emotional truth, and be sure of what you're trying to say.''

🖾 SNREVIEW, Starry Night Review—A Literary E-Zine

197 Fairchild Ave., Fairfield CT 06825-4856. (203)366-5991. E-mail: editor@snreview.org. Web site: www.snreview.org. **Contact:** Joseph Conlin, editor. E-zine specializing in literary short stories, essays and poetry. ''We search for material that not only has strong characters and plot but also a devotion to imagery.'' Quarterly. Estab. 1999.

Needs Literary, mainstream. Receives 100 unsolicited mss/month. Accepts 20+ mss/issue; 80-100 mss/year. Publishes ms 6 months after acceptance. **Publishes 25 new writers/year.** Recently published work by Frank X. Walker, Adrian Louis, Barbara Burkhardt, E. Lindsey Balkan, Marie Griffin and Jonathan Lerner. Length: 1,000-7,000 words; average length: 4,000 words. Also publishes literary essays, literary criticism, poetry.

How to Contact Accepts submissions by e-mail only. Include 100 word bio and list of publications. Responds in 3 months to mss. Accepts simultaneous submissions and reprints. Sample copy online. Writer's guidelines online.

Payment/Terms Acquires first rights.

🖾 🖾 STEEL CITY REVIEW: A PITTSBURGH-BASED MAGAZINE OF SHORT FICTION

E-mail: editor@steelcityreview.com. Web site: www.steelcityreview.com. **Contact:** Julia LaSalle & Stefani Nellen, co-editors. Online magazine. ''We seek short fiction dealing with technology, industry, work, and how these issues intersect with individuals' lives. We also seek stories set in Pittsburgh and illuminating the ''feel'' of living there. Finally, we seek science fiction stories. We are an international, open, online magazine (one of the editors is German) with a local flavor.'' Quarterly. Estab. Jan. 2007. Circ. 1,200 reads per month.

Needs Ethnic/multicultural (general), literary, mainstream, regional (Pittsburgh/Allegheny County area), science fiction (hard science/technological, soft/sociological). Does not want religious/inspirational, mystery, romance or children's stories. No erotica please. Receives about 20 mss/month. Accepts about 6 mss/issue; about 24 mss/year. Manuscript published 3 months after acceptance. Agented fiction 0%. **Publishes 4 new writers/year.** Published GK Wuon, Steve Fellner, Vanessa Gebbie, Claudia Smith. Length: 500 words (min)-6,000 words (max). Average length: 2,500 words. Publishes short shorts. Average length of short shorts: 1,000 words. Often comments on/critiques rejected mss.

How to Contact Send complete ms with cover letter. Accepts submissions by e-mail only. Include estimated word count, brief bio, list of publications. Responds to mss in 8 weeks. Considers simultaneous submissions. Guidelines available via e-mail, on Web site.

Payment and Terms Acquires one-time electronic rights. Sends mock-up of Web page to author pre-publication for their approval. Publication is copyrighted.

Advice ''We want polished, confident manuscripts related to our themes/aesthetic. Manuscripts telling a full story with a minimum of words will enchant us. We want readable, original fiction that makes us forget we're reading. Don't try too hard. Dare to be funny, but don't force it. Read past issues before submitting. Please make sure your submission is grammatically clean and typo-free.''

🖉 STORY BYTES, Very Short Stories

E-mail: editor@storybytes.com. Web site: www.storybytes.com. **Contact:** M. Stanley Bubien, editor. Electronic zine. ''We are strictly an electronic publication, appearing on the Internet in three forms. First, the stories are sent to an electronic mailing list of readers. They also get placed on our Web site, both in PDF and HTML format.''

Needs ''Stories must be very short—having a length that is the power of 2, specifically: 2, 4, 8, 16, 32, etc.'' No sexually explicit material. ''Would like to see more material dealing with religion—not necessarily 'inspirational' stories, but those that show the struggles of living a life of faith in a realistic manner.'' **Publishes 33 percent new writers/year.** Recently published work by Richard K. Weems, Joseph Lerner, Lisa Cote and Thomas Sennet.

How to Contact Please query first. Query with or without published clips or send complete ms. Accepts submissions by e-mail. ''I prefer plain text with story title, authorship and word count. Only accepts electronic submissions. See Web site for complete guidelines.'' Sample copy online. Writer's guidelines online.

Advice ''In *Story Bytes* the very short stories themselves range in topic. Many explore a brief event—a vignette of something unusual, unique and at times something even commonplace. Some stories can be bizarre, while others quite lucid. Some are based on actual events, while others are entirely fictional. Try to develop conflict early on (in the first sentence if possible!), and illustrate or resolve this conflict through action rather than description. I believe we'll find an audience for electronic published works primarily in the short story realm.''

🖉 STORYSOUTH, The best from New South writers

898 Chelsea Ave., Columbus OH 43209. (614)545-0754. E-mail: storysouth@yahoo.com. Web site: www.storysouth.com. **Contact:** Jason Sanford, editor. ''*storySouth* is interested in fiction, creative nonfiction, and poetry by writers from the New South. The exact definition *New South* varies from person to person and we leave it up to the writer to define their own connection to the southern United States.'' Quarterly. Estab. 2001.

Needs Experimental, literary, regional (south), translations. Receives 70 unsolicited mss/month. Accepts 5 mss/issue; 20 mss/year. Publishes ms 1 month after acceptance. **Publishes 5-10 new writers/year.** Average length: 4,000 words. Publishes short shorts. Also publishes literary essays, literary criticism, poetry. Often comments on rejected mss.

How to Contact Send complete ms. Accepts submissions by e-mail. Responds in 2 months to mss. Accepts simultaneous, multiple submissions. Writer's guidelines online.

Payment/Terms Acquires one-time rights.

Advice ''What really makes a story stand out is a strong voice and a sense of urgency—a need for the reader to keep reading the story and not put it down until it is finished.''

$🖉 THE SUMMERSET REVIEW

25 Summerset Dr., Smithtown NY 11787. E-mail: editor@summersetreview.org. Web site: www.summersetreview.org. **Contact:** Joseph Levens, editor. Magazine: illustrations and photographs. ''Our goal is simply to publish the highest quality literary fiction and essays intended for a general audience. We love lighter pieces. We love romance and fantasy, as long as it isn't pure genre writing but rather something that might indeed teach us a thing or two. This is a simple online literary journal of high quality material, so simple you can call it unique.'' Quarterly. Estab. 2002.

- Several editors-in-chief of very prominent literary publications have done interviews for *The Summerset Review*: M.M.M. Hayes of *StoryQuarterly*, Gina Frangello of *Other Voices*, Jennifer Spiegel of *Hayden's Ferry Review*.

Needs Literary. No sci-fi, horror, or graphic erotica. Receives 90 unsolicited mss/month. Accepts 4 mss/issue; 18 mss/year. Publishes ms 2-3 months after acceptance. **Publishes 5-10 new writers/year.** Length: 8,000 words; average length: 3,000 words. Publishes short shorts. Also publishes literary essays. Usually critiques on mss that were almost accepted.

How to Contact Send complete ms. Accepts submissions by e-mail. Responds in 1-2 weeks to queries; 4-12 weeks to mss. Accepts simultaneous submissions and reprints. Writer's guidelines online.

Payment/Terms $25 per story/essay. Acquires no rights other than one-time publishing, although we request credit if first published in *The Summerset Review*. Sends galleys to author.

Advice "Style counts. We prefer innovative or at least very smooth, convincing voices. Even the dullest of premises or the complete lack of conflict make for an interesting story if it is told in the right voice and style. We like to find little, interesting facts and/or connections subtly sprinkled throughout the piece. Harsh language should be used only if/when necessary. If we are choosing between light and dark subjects, the light will usually win."

$⬛ THE SWORD REVIEW

Double-Edged Publishing, 9618 Misty Brook Cove, Cordova TN 38016. (901)213-3768. Fax: (901)213-3878. E-mail: editor@theswordreview.com. Web site: www.theswordreview.com. **Contact:** Bill Snodgrass, editor. Online magazine. Contains illustrations and photographs. "The purpose of *The Sword Review* is to entertain, uplift, and enlighten. It is a publication targeted to adult readers, with consideration to readers aged 14 and up. Although not a teen publication, we acknowledge that the fantasy and science fiction genres attract many readers in that demographic. While not all stories and articles will appeal to all readers, it is our intention to provide content that appeals across a wide range of ages." Estab. 2005. Circ. 3,000 plus.

Needs Adventure, ethnic/multicultural, fantasy (space fantasy, sword and sorcery), historical, horror, literary, mainstream, mystery/suspense, religious (inspirational, fantasy, mystery/suspense, thriller, romance), science fiction (hard science/technological, soft/sociological), thriller/espionage, young adult/teen (fantasy/science fiction, horror, mystery/suspense, romance). Does not want lesbian, gay, erotica. Promotion of values and principles not compatible with Christianity will not be published. Receives 20-30 mss/month. Accepts 4-6 mss/issue; 48-60 mss/year. Manuscript published 2-6 months after acceptance. Publishes 6 new writers/year. Published Terry Weide, Michale Ouellette, Marsheila Rockwell, Sean T. M. Stiennon and Marcie Lynn Tentchoff. Average length: 5,500 words. Publishes short shorts. Average length of short shorts: 1,100 words. Also publishes literary essays, literary criticism, poetry. Always comments on/critiques rejected manuscripts.

How to Contact Submit via Web Site through online submissions system. Responds to queries in 1 weeks. Responds to mss in 6 weeks. Considers previously published submissions, multiple submissions. Guidelines available on Web Site.

Payment and Terms Writers receive $5-25 flat-rate payment. **Pays on acceptance.** Acquires one-time rights, electronic rights and/or nonexclusive print rights (English language). Publication is copyrighted.

Advice "Meticulous editing is a must. Many begininning writers leave out details that are important to conveying the plot, themes, and character development. Other beginning writers include details that are unneeded. Be sure you know what your story is trying to do, then edit away what is not needed, and add what is lacking."

⬛ THE 13TH WARRIOR REVIEW

Asterius Press, P.O. Box 5122, Seabrook NJ 08302-3511. E-mail: theeditor@asteriuspress.com. Web site: www.asteriuspress.com. **Contact:** John C. Erianne, publisher/editor. Online magazine. Estab. 2000.

Needs Erotica, experimental, humor/satire, literary, mainstream. Receives 200 unsolicited mss/month. Accepts 4-5 mss/issue; 10-15 mss/year. Publishes ms 6 months after acceptance. **Publishes 1-2 new writers/year.** Recently published work by Marjolyn Deurloo, Suzanne Nelson, Stoyan Valev, Paul A. Toth and D. Olsen. Length: 300-3,000 words; average length: 1,500 words. Publishes short shorts. Also publishes literary essays, literary criticism, poetry, and book reviews. Sometimes comments on rejected mss.

How to Contact Send complete ms. Include estimated word count, brief bio and address/e-mail. Send SASE or IRC for return of ms or send a disposable copy of ms and #10 SASE for reply only. Accepts submissions by e-mail (text in in message body only, no file attachements). Responds in 1 week to queries; 1-2 months to mss. Accepts simultaneous submissions. Sample copy online at www.13thwr.org. Reviews fiction.

Payment/Terms Acquires first, electronic rights.

⬜ TOASTED CHEESE

E-mail: editors@toasted-cheese.com. Web site: www.toasted-cheese.com. **Contact:** submit@toasted-cheese.com. E-zine specializing in fiction, creative nonfiction, poetry and flash fiction. "*Toasted Cheese* accepts submissions of previously unpublished fiction, flash fiction, creative nonfiction and poetry. Our focus is on quality of work, not quantity. Some issues will therefore contain fewer/more pieces than previous issues. We don't restrict publication based on subject matter. We encourage submissions from innovative writers in all genres.'' Quarterly. Estab. 2001.

Needs Adventure, children's/juvenile, ethnic/multicultural, fantasy, feminist, gay, historical, horror, humor/satire, lesbian, literary, mainstream, mystery/suspense, New Age, psychic/supernatural/occult, romance, science fiction, thriller/espionage, western. ''No fan fiction. No chapters or excerpts unless they read as a stand-alone story. No first drafts.'' Receives 70 unsolicited mss/month. Accepts 1-10 mss/issue; 5-30 mss/year. **Publishes 15 new writers/year.** Publishes short shorts. Also publishes poetry.

How to Contact Send complete ms. Accepts submissions by e-mail. Responds in 4 months to mss. No simultaneous submissions. Sample copy online. Writer's guidelines online.

Payment/Terms Acquires electronic rights. Sponsors awards/contests.

Advice ''We are looking for clean, professional writing from writers of any level. Accepted stories will be concise and compelling. We are looking for writers who are serious about the craft: tomorrow's literary stars before they're famous. Take your submission seriously, yet remember that levity is appreciated. You are submitting not to traditional 'editors' but to fellow writers who appreciate the efforts of those in the trenches.''

Ⓝ Ⓞ VERBSAP.COM, CONCISE PROSE. ENOUGH SAID.

E-mail: editor@verbsap.com. Web site: www.verbsap.com. **Contact:** Laurie Seider, editor. Online magazine. ''Verbsap.com showcases an eclectic selection of the first in concise prose by established and emerging writers.'' Updated daily. Estab. 2005.

Needs Literary, mainstream. Does not want violent, racist or pornographic content. Accepts 200 mss/year. Manuscript published 2-4 weeks after acceptance. Length: 3,000 words (max). Average length: 2,000 words. Publishes short shorts. Average length of short shorts: 900 words. Also publishes literary essays, poetry. Always comments on/critiques rejected manuscripts.

How to Contact Follow online guidelines. Accepts submissions by e-mail. Responds to mss in 1 week. Considers simultaneous submissions. Guidelines available on Web site.

Payment and Terms Sends galleys to author. Publication is copyrighted.

Advice ''Show, don't tell. And write a story, not a T.V. episode. You might find our 'Editor's Notebook' essays helpful.''

Ⓞ WILD VIOLET

Wild Violet, P.O. Box 39706, Philadelphia PA 19106-9706. E-mail: wildvioletmagazine@yahoo.com. Web site: www.wildviolet.net. **Contact:** Alyce Wilson, editor. Online magazine: illustrations, photos. ''Our goal is to make a place for the arts: to make the arts more accessible and to serve as a creative forum for writers and artists. Our audience includes English-speaking readers from all over the world, who are interested in both 'high art' and pop culture.'' Quarterly. Estab. 2001.

Needs Comics/graphic novels, ethnic/multicultural, experimental, fantasy (space fantasy, sword and sorcery), feminist, gay, horror (dark fantasy, futuristic, psychological, supernatural), humor/satire, lesbian, literary, New Age, psychic/supernatural/occult, science fiction. ''No stories where sexual or violent content is just used to shock the reader. No racist writings.'' Receives 30 unsolicited mss/month. Accepts 5 mss/issue; 20 mss/year. **Publishes 30 new writers/year.** Recently published work by Deen Borok, Wayne Scheer, Jane McDonald and Eric Brown. Length: 500-6,000 words; average length: 3,000 words. Also publishes literary essays, literary criticism, poetry. Sometimes comments on rejected mss.

How to Contact Send complete ms. Accepts submissions by e-mail. Include estimated word count and brief bio. Send SASE for return of ms or send a disposable copy of ms and #10 SASE for reply only. Responds in 1 week to queries; 3-6 months to mss. Accepts simultaneous, multiple submissions. Sample copy online. Writer's guidelines by e-mail.

Payment/Terms Writers receive bio and links on contributor's page. Request limited electronic rights, for online publication and archival only. Sponsors awards/contests.

Advice ''We look for stories that are well-paced and show character and plot development. Even short shorts should do more than simply paint a picture. Manuscripts stand out when the author's voice is fresh and engaging. Avoid muddying your story with too many characters and don't attempt to shock the reader with an ending you have not earned. Experiment with styles and structures, but don't resort to experimentation for its own sake.''

Consumer Magazines

In this section of *Novel & Short Story Writer's Market* are consumer magazines with circulations of more than 10,000. Many have circulations in the hundreds of thousands or millions. And among the oldest magazines listed here are ones not only familiar to us, but also to our parents, grandparents and even great-grandparents: *The Atlantic Monthly* (1857); *The New Yorker* (1925); *Esquire* (1933); and *Ellery Queen's Mystery Magazine* (1941).

Consumer periodicals make excellent markets for fiction in terms of exposure, prestige and payment. Because these magazines are well known, however, competition is great. Even the largest consumer publications buy only one or two stories an issue, yet thousands of writers submit to these popular magazines.

Despite the odds, it is possible for talented new writers to break into print in the magazines listed here. Your keys to breaking into these markets are careful research, professional presentation and, of course, top-quality fiction.

TYPES OF CONSUMER MAGAZINES

In this section you will find a number of popular publications, some for a broad-based, general-interest readership and others for large but select groups of readers—children, teenagers, women, men and seniors. There are also religious and church-affiliated magazines, publications devoted to the interests of particular cultures and outlooks, and top markets for genre fiction.

SELECTING THE RIGHT MARKET

Unlike smaller journals and publications, most of the magazines listed here are available at newsstands and bookstores. Many can also be found in the library, and guidelines and sample copies are almost always available by mail or online. Start your search by reviewing the listings, then familiarize yourself with the fiction included in the magazines that interest you.

Don't make the mistake of thinking that just because you are familiar with a magazine, their fiction is the same today as when you first saw it. Nothing could be further from the truth. Consumer magazines, no matter how well established, are constantly revising their fiction needs as they strive to expand their audience base.

In a magazine that uses only one or two stories an issue, take a look at the nonfiction articles and features as well. These can give you a better idea of the audience for the publication and clues to the type of fiction that might appeal to them.

If you write genre fiction, look in the Category Index beginning on page 581. There you will find a list of markets that say they are looking for a particular subject.

FURTHERING YOUR SEARCH

See You've Got a Story (page 2) for information about the material common to all listings in this book. In this section in particular, pay close attention to the number of submissions a magazine receives in a given period and how many they publish in the same period. This will give you a clear picture of how stiff your competition can be.

While many of the magazines listed here publish one or two pieces of fiction in each issue, some also publish special fiction issues once or twice a year. When possible, we have indicated this in the listing information. We also note if the magazine is open to novel excerpts as well as short fiction, and we advise novelists to query first before submitting long work.

The Business of Fiction Writing, beginning on page 83, covers the basics of submitting your work. Professional presentation is a must for all markets listed. Editors at consumer magazines are especially busy, and anything you can do to make your manuscript easy to read and accessible will help your chances of being published. Most magazines want to see complete manuscripts, but watch for publications in this section that require a query first.

As in the previous section, we've included our own comments in many of the listings, set off by a bullet (●). Whenever possible, we list the publication's recent awards and honors. We've also included any special information we feel will help you in determining whether a particular publication interests you.

The maple leaf symbol (⬙) identifies our Canadian listings. You will also find some English-speaking markets from around the world. These foreign magazines are denoted with ⊕ at the beginning of the listings. Remember to use International Reply Coupons rather than stamps when you want a reply from a country other than your own.

Periodicals of Interest

For More Info

For more on consumer magazines, see issues of *Writer's Digest* (F+W Publications) and other industry trade publications available in larger libraries.

For news about some of the genre publications listed here and information about a particular field, there are a number of magazines devoted to genre topics, including *The Drood Review of Mystery*; *Science Fiction Chronicle*; *Locus* (for science fiction); and *Romance Writers' Report* (available to members of Romance Writers of America).

ADVENTURES

WordAction Publications, 6401 The Paseo, Kansas City MO 64131-1213. (816)333-7000. **Contact:** Julie Smith, editor. Magazine: 8¼×11; 4 pages; self cover; color illustrations. "This weekly take-home paper connects Sunday school learning to life for first and second graders (ages 6-8)." Weekly. Circ. 45,000.

✓ ADVOCATE, PKA'S PUBLICATION

PKA Publications, 1881 Little Westkill Rd. CO2, Prattsville NY 12468. (518)299-3103. Tabloid: 9⅜×12¼; 32 pages; newsprint paper; line drawings; color and b&w photographs. "Eclectic for a general audience." Bimonthly. Estab. 1987. Circ. 10,000.

Needs Adventure, children's/juvenile (5-9 years), ethnic/multicultural, experimental, fantasy, feminist, historical, humor/satire, literary, mainstream, mystery/suspense, regional, romance, science fiction, western, young adult/teen (10-18 years), contemporary, prose poem, senior citizen/retirement, sports. "Nothing religious, pornographic, violent, erotic, pro-drug or anti-enviroment. Currently looking for equine (horses) stories, poetry, art, photos and cartoons. The *Gaited Horse Newsletter* is currently published within the pages of PKA's *Advocate.*" Receives 60 unsolicited mss/month. Accepts 6-8 mss/issue; 34-48 mss/year. Publishes ms 4 months to 1 year after acceptance. Also publishes poetry. Sometimes comments on rejected mss.

How to Contact Send a complete ms with cover letter. Responds in 2 months to mss. No simultaneous submissions. "No work that has appeared on the Internet." Sample copy for $4 (US currency for inside US; $5.25 US currency for Canada). Writer's Guidelines with purchase of sample copy.

Payment/Terms Pays contributor copies. Acquires first rights.

Advice "The highest criterion in selecting a work is its entertainment value. It must first be enjoyable reading. It must, of course, be orginal. To stand out, it must be thought provoking or strongly emotive, or very cleverly plotted. Will consider only previously unpublished works by writers who do not earn their living principally through writing. We are currently very backed up on short stories. We are mostly looking for art, photos and poetry."

$ ✓ AIM MAGAZINE

Aim Publishing Co., P.O. Box 1174, Maywood IL 60153. (708)344-4414. Fax: (206)543-2746. Web site: aimmagazine.org. **Contact:** Ruth Apilado, associate editor. Magazine: 8½×11; 48 pages; slick paper; photos and illustrations. Publishes material "to purge racism from the human bloodstream through the written word—that is the purpose of *Aim Magazine.*" Quarterly. Estab. 1975. Circ. 10,000.

Needs Ethnic/multicultural, historical, mainstream, suspense. Open. No "religious" mss. Published special fiction issue last year; plans another. Receives 25 unsolicited mss/month. Accepts 15 mss/issue; 60 mss/year. Publishes ms 3 months after acceptance. **Publishes 40 new writers/year.** Recently published work by Christina Touregny, Thomas Lee Harris, Michael Williams and Jake Halpern. Publishes short shorts. Sometimes comments on rejected mss.

How to Contact Send complete ms. Accepts submissions by e-mail. Include SASE with cover letter and author's photograph. Responds in 2 months to queries; 1 month to mss. Accepts simultaneous submissions. Sample copy and writer's guidelines for $4 and 9×12 SAE with $1.70 postage or online.

Payment/Terms Pays $25-35. Pays on publication for first, one-time rights.

Advice "Search for those who are making unselfish contributions to their community and write about them. Write about your own experiences. Be familar with the background of your characters. Known for stories with social significance, proving that people from different ethnic, racial backgrounds are more alike than they are different."

$ ✓ 🖥 ANALOG SCIENCE FICTION & FACT

Dell Magazine Fiction Group, 475 Park Ave. S., 11th Floor, New York NY 10016. (212)686-7188. Fax: (212)686-7414. E-mail: analog@dellmagazines.com. Web site: www.analogsf.com. **Contact:** Stanley Schmidt, editor. Magazine: 144 pages; illustrations; photos. Monthly. Estab. 1930. Circ. 50,000.

• Fiction published in *Analog* has won numerous Nebula and Hugo Awards.

Needs Science fiction (hard science/technological, soft/sociological). "No fantasy or stories in which the scientific background is implausible or plays no essential role." Receives 500 unsolicited mss/month. Accepts 6 mss/issue; 70 mss/year. Publishes ms 10 months after acceptance. Agented fiction 5%. **Publishes 3-4 new writers/year.** Recently published work by Ben Bova, Stephen Baxter, Larry Niven, Michael F. Flynn, Timothy Zahn, Robert J. Sawyer, and Joe Haldeman. Length: 2,000-80,000 words; average length: 10,000 words. Publishes short shorts. Sometimes comments on rejected mss.

How to Contact Send complete ms with a cover letter. Accepts queries for serials and fact articles only; query by mail. Include estimated word count. Send SASE for return of ms or send a disposable copy of ms and #10

SASE for reply only. Responds in 1 month to queries. Accepts multiple submissions. No simultaneous submissions. Sample copy for $5. Writer's guidelines online. Reviews fiction.

Payment/Terms Pays 4¢/word for novels; 5-6¢/word for novelettes; 6-8¢/word for shorts under 7,500 words; $450-600 for intermediate lengths. Pays on acceptance for first North American serial, nonexclusive foreign serial rights. Sends galleys to author. Not copyrighted.

Advice "I'm looking for irresistibly entertaining stories that make me think about things in ways I've never done before. Read several issues to get a broad feel for our tastes, but don't try to imitate what you read."

$ ☑ ◎ THE ANNALS OF SAINT ANNE DE BEAUPRÉ

Redemptorist Fathers, 9795 St. Anne Blvd., St. Anne de Beaupre QC G0A 3C0 Canada. (418)827-4538. Fax: (418)827-4530. **Contact:** Father R. Théberge, C.Ss.R., editor. Magazine: 8×11; 32 pages; glossy paper; photos. "Our mission statement includes dedication to Christian family values and devotion to St. Anne." Releases 6 issues/year. Estab. 1885. Circ. 32,000.

Needs Religious/inspirational. "No senseless mockery." Receives 50-60 unsolicited mss/month. Recently published work by Beverly Sheresh. Always comments on rejected mss.

How to Contact Send complete ms. Include estimated word count. Send SASE for reply or return of ms. Responds in 4-6 weeks to queries. No simultaneous submissions.

Payment/Terms Pays 3-4¢/word. Pays on acceptance for first North American serial rights. Please state "rights" for sale.

$ ☑ ART TIMES, Commentary and Resources for the Fine and Performing Arts

P.O. Box 730, Mount Marion NY 12456-0730. (914)246-6944. Fax: (914)246-6944. Web site: www.arttimesjournal.com. **Contact:** Raymond J. Steiner, fiction editor. Magazine: 12×15; 24 pages; Jet paper and cover; illustrations; photos. "*Art Times* covers the art fields and is distributed in locations most frequented by those enjoying the arts. Our copies are distributed throughout the Northeast region as well as in most of the galleries of Soho, 57th Street and Madison Avenue in the metropolitan area; locations include theaters, galleries, museums, cultural centers and the like. Our readers are mostly over 40, affluent, art-conscious and sophisticated. Subscribers are located across U.S. and abroad (Italy, France, Germany, Greece, Russia, etc.)." Monthly. Estab. 1984. Circ. 28,000.

Needs Adventure, ethnic/multicultural, fantasy, feminist, gay, historical, humor/satire, lesbian, literary, mainstream, science fiction, contemporary. "We seek quality literary pieces. Nothing violent, sexist, erotic, juvenile, racist, romantic, political, etc." Receives 30-50 unsolicited mss/month. Accepts 1 mss/issue; 10 mss/year. Publishes ms 3 years after acceptance. **Publishes 6 new writers/year.** Publishes short shorts.

How to Contact Send complete ms with SASE. Responds in 6 months to mss. Accepts simultaneous, multiple submissions. Sample copy for 9×12 SAE and 6 first-class stamps. Writer's guidelines for #10 SASE or on Web site.

Payment/Terms Pays $25 maximum (honorarium) and 1 year's free subscription. Pays on publication for first North American serial, first rights.

Advice "Competition is greater (more submissions received), but keep trying. We print new as well as published writers."

$ ☑ ◎ ▼ ASIMOV'S SCIENCE FICTION

Dell Magazine Fiction Group, 475 Park Ave. S., 11th Floor, New York NY 10016. (212)686-7188. Fax: (212)686-7414. E-mail: asimovs@dellmagazines.com. Web site: www.asimovs.com. **Contact:** Sheila Williams, editor. Magazine: 5¼×8¼ (trim size); 144 pages; 30 lb. newspaper; 70 lb. to 8 pt. C1S cover stock; illustrations; rarely photos. Magazine consists of science fiction and fantasy stories for adults and young adults. Publishes "the best short science fiction available." Estab. 1977. Circ. 50,000.

- Named for a science fiction "legend," *Asimov's* regularly receives Hugo and Nebula Awards. Editor Gardner Dozois has received several awards for editing including Hugos and those from *Locus* magazine.

Needs Fantasy, science fiction (hard science, soft sociological). No horror or psychic/supernatural. Would like to see more hard science fiction. Receives approximately 800 unsolicited mss/month. Accepts 10 mss/issue. Publishes ms 6-12 months after acceptance. Agented fiction 10%. **Publishes 6 new writers/year.** Recently published work by Ursula LeGuin and Larry Niven. Publishes short shorts. Sometimes comments on rejected mss.

How to Contact Send complete ms with SASE. Responds in 2 months to queries; 3 months to mss. Accepts reprints submissions. No simultaneous submissions. Sample copy for $5. Writer's guidelines for #10 SASE or online. Reviews fiction.

Payment/Terms Pays 5-8¢/word. Pays on acceptance. Buys first North American serial, nonexclusive foreign serial rights; reprint rights occasionally. Sends galleys to author.

Advice "We are looking for character stories rather than those emphasizing technology or science. New writers will do best with a story under 10,000 words. Every new science fiction or fantasy film seems to 'inspire' writers—and this is not a desirable trend. Be sure to be familiar with our magazine and the type of story we like; workshops and lots of practice help. Try to stay away from trite, clichéd themes. Start in the middle of the action, starting as close to the end of the story as you possibly can. We like stories that extrapolate from up-to-date scientific research, but don't forget that we've been publishing clone stories for decades. Ideas must be fresh.''

$THE ATLANTIC MONTHLY

The Watergate, 600 New Hampshire Ave. NW, Washington DC 20037. (202)266-7083. Fax: (202)266-6388. Web site: www.theatlantic.com. **Contact:** C. Michael Curtis, fiction editor. General magazine for an educated readership with broad cultural interests. Monthly. Estab. 1857. Circ. 500,000.

Needs Literary and contemporary fiction. ''Seeks fiction that is clear, tightly written with strong sense of 'story' and well-defined characters.'' Receives 1,000 unsolicited mss/month. Accepts 7-8 mss/year. **Publishes 3-4 new writers/year.** Recently published work by Mary Gordon, Tobias Wolff.

How to Contact Send complete ms. Responds in 2 months to mss. Accepts multiple submissions. Writer's guidelines online.

Payment/Terms Pays $3,000. Pays on acceptance for first North American serial rights.

Advice When making first contract, ''cover letters are sometimes helpful, particularly if they cite prior publications or involvement in writing programs. Common mistakes: melodrama, inconclusiveness, lack of development, unpersuasive characters and/or dialogue.''

$BABYBUG

Carus Publishing Co., 70 E. Lake, Suite 300, Chicago IL 60601. (312)701-1720. Web site: www.cricketmag.com. ''Babybug is 'the listening and looking magazine for infants and toddlers,' intended to be read aloud by a loving adult to foster a love of books and reading in young children ages 6 months-2 years.'' Estab. 1994. Circ. 45,000.

Needs Very simple stories for infants and toddlers.

How to Contact Send complete ms. Accepts simultaneous submissions. Sample copy for $5. Writer's guidelines online.

Payment/Terms Pays $25 and up. Pays on publication for variable rights.

Advice ''Babybug is a board-book magazine. Study back issues before submitting.''

$BACKROADS, Motorcycles, Travel & Adventure

Backroads, Inc., P.O. Box 317, Branchville NJ 07826. (973)948-4176. Fax: (973)948-0823. E-mail: editor@backroadsusa.com. Web site: www.backroadsusa.com. ''Backroads is a motorcycle tour magazine geared toward getting motorcyclists on the road and traveling. We provide interesting destinations, unique roadside attractions and eateries, plus Rip & Ride Route Sheets. We cater to all brands. If you really ride, you need Backroads.'' Monthly. Estab. 1995. Circ. 40,000.

Needs Travel, motorcycle-related stories. Publishes ms 3 months after acceptance.

How to Contact Query. Accepts submissions by e-mail. Responds in 3 weeks to queries. Accepts reprints submissions. Sample copy for $2. Writer's guidelines free.

Payment/Terms Pays 5¢/word. Pays on publication for one-time rights.

$◫ THE BEAR DELUXE MAGAZINE

Orlo, P.O. Box 10342, Portland OR 97296. (503)242-1047. E-mail: bear@orlo.org. Web site: www.orlo.org. **Contact:** Tom Webb, editor. Magazine: 9 × 12; 48 pages; newsprint paper; Kraft paper cover illustrations; photos. ''The Bear Deluxe Magazine provides a fresh voice amid often strident and polarized environmental discourse. Street level, solution-oriented, and nondogmatic, The Bear Deluxe presents lively creative discussion to a diverse readership.'' Semiannual. Estab. 1993. Circ. 20,000.

● The Bear Deluxe has received publishing grants from the Oregon Council for the Humanities, Literary Arts, Regional Arts and Culture Council, Tides Foundation.

Needs Adventure, condensed novels, historical, horror, humor/satire, mystery/suspense, novel excerpts, western. ''No detective, children's or horror.'' Enviromentally focused: humor/satire, literary, science fiction. ''We would like to see more nontraditional forms.'' List of upcoming themes available for SASE. Receives 20-30 unsolicited mss/month. Accepts 2-3 mss/issue; 8-12 mss/year. Publishes ms 3 months after acceptance. **Publishes 5-6 new writers/year.** Recently published work by Peter Houlahan, John Reed and Karen Hueler. Length: 750-4,500 words; average length: 2,500 words. Publishes short shorts. Also publishes literary essays, literary criticism, poetry. Sometimes comments on rejected mss.

How to Contact Query with or without published clips or send complete ms. Send disposable copy of mss. Responds in 3 months to queries; 6 months to mss. Accepts simultaneous submissions and reprints. Sample copy for $3. Writer's guidelines for #10 SASE or on Web site. Reviews fiction.

Payment/Terms Pays free subscription to the magazine, contributor's copies and 5¢/word; additional copies for postage. Pays on publication for first, one-time rights.

Advice "Keep sending work. Write actively and focus on the connections of man, nature, etc., not just flowery descriptions. Urban and suburban enviroments are grist for the mill as well. Have not seen enough quality humorous and ironic writing. Interview and artist profile ideas needed. Juxtaposition of place welcome. Action and hands-on great. Not all that interested in enviromental ranting and simple 'walks through the park.' Make it powerful, yet accessible to a wide audience."

$ BOMB MAGAZINE

80 Hanson Place, Suite 703, Brooklyn NY 11217. (718)636-9100. Fax: (718)636-9200. E-mail: info@bombsite.com. Web site: www.bombsite.com. Magazine: 11×14; 104 pages; 70 lb. glossy cover; illustrations; photos. Written, edited and produced by industry professionals and funded by those interested in the arts. Publishes writing which is unconventional and contains an edge, whether it be in style or subject matter. Quarterly. Estab. 1981. Circ. 36,000.

Needs Experimental, novel excerpts, contemporary. No genre: romance, science fiction, horror, western. Receives 200 unsolicited mss/month. Accepts 6 mss/issue; 24 mss/year. Publishes ms 3-6 months after acceptance. Agented fiction 70%. **Publishes 2-3 new writers/year.** Recently published work by Lynne Tillman, Dennis Cooper, Susan Wheeler, and Laurie Sheck.

How to Contact SASE. Responds in 3-5 months to mss. Accepts multiple submissions. Sample copy for $7, plus $1.42 postage and handling. Writer's guidelines by e-mail.

Payment/Terms Pays $100, and contributor's copies. Pays on publication for first, one-time rights. Sends galleys to author.

Advice "We are committed to publishing new work that commercial publishers often deem too dangerous or difficult. The problem is, a lot of young writers confuse difficult with dreadful. Read the magazine before you even think of submitting something."

$ BOSTON REVIEW

35 Medford St., Suite 302, Sommerville, MA 02143. E-mail: review@bostonreview.net. Web site: www.bostonreview.net. **Contact:** Junot Diaz, fiction editor. Magazine: 10¾×14¾; 60 pages; newsprint. "The editors are committed to a society and culture that foster human diversity and a democracy in which we seek common grounds of principle amidst our many differences. In the hope of advancing these ideals, the *Review* acts as a forum that seeks to enrich the language of public debate." Bimonthly. Estab. 1975. Circ. 20,000.

• *Boston Review* is the recipient of a Pushcart Prize in poetry.

Needs Ethnic/multicultural, experimental, literary, regional, translations, contemporary, prose poem. Receives 150 unsolicited mss/month. Accepts 4-6 mss/year. Publishes ms 4 months after acceptance. Recently published work by David Mamet, Rhonda Stamell, Jacob Appel, Elisha Porat and Diane Williams. Length: 1,200-5,000 words; average length: 2,000 words. Occasionally comments on rejected mss.

How to Contact Send complete ms. Responds in 4 months to queries. Accepts simultaneous submissions if noted. Sample copy for $5 or online. Writer's guidelines online. Reviews fiction.

Payment/Terms Pays $300, and 3 contributor's copies. Acquires first North American serial, first rights.

$ CADET QUEST MAGAZINE

P.O. Box 7259, Grand Rapids MI 49501-7259. (616)241-5616. Fax: (616)241-5558. E-mail: submissions@calvinistcadets.org. Web site: www.calvinistcadets.org. **Contact:** G. Richard Broene, editor. Magazine: 8½×11; 24 pages; illustrations; photos. "*Cadet Quest Magazine* shows boys 9-14 how God is at work in their lives and in the world around them." Estab. 1958. Circ. 10,000.

Needs Adventure, children's/juvenile, religious/inspirational (Christian), spiritual, sports, comics. "Need material based on Christian perspective and articles on Christian role models. Avoid long dialogue and little action." No fantasy, science fiction, fashion, horror or erotica. List of upcoming themes available for SASE or on Web site in February. Receives 60 unsolicited mss/month. Accepts 3 mss/issue; 18 mss/year. Publishes ms 4-11 months after acceptance. **Publishes 0-3 new writers/year.** Length: 900-1,500 words; average length: 1,200 words. Publishes short shorts.

How to Contact Send complete ms by mail or send submissions in the body of the e-mail. Not as an attachment. Responds in 2 months to queries. Accepts simultaneous, multiple submissions and reprints. Sample copy for 9×12 SASE. Writer's guidelines for #10 SASE.

Payment/Terms Pays 4-6¢/word, and 1 contributor's copy. Pays on acceptance for first North American serial, one-time, second serial (reprint), simultaneous rights. Rights purchased vary with author and material.

Advice "On a cover sheet, list the point your story is trying to make. Our magazine has a theme for each issue, and we try to fit the fiction to the theme. All fiction should be about a young boy's interests—sports, outdoor activities, problems—with an emphasis on a Christian perspective. No simple moralisms. Best time to submit material is February-April.''

$ ☑ CALLIOPE, Exploring World History

Cobblestone Publishing Co., 30 Grove St., Suite C, Peterborough NH 03458-1454. (603)924-7209. Fax: (603)924-7380. Web site: www.cobblestonepub.com. **Contact:** Rosalie Baker, editor. Magazine. ''*Calliope* covers world history (east/west) and lively, original approaches to the subject are the primary concerns of the editors in choosing material. For 8-14 year olds.'' Estab. 1990. Circ. 13,000.

    ● Cobblestone Publishing also publishes the children's magazines *Appleseeds, Dig, Footsteps, Odyssey, Cobblestone* and *Faces,* some listed in this section. *Calliope* has received the Ed Press Golden Lamp and One-Theme Issue awards.

Needs Material must fit upcoming theme; write for themes and deadlines. Childrens/juvenile (8-14 years). ''Authentic historical and biographical fiction, adventure, retold legends, folktales, etc. relating to the theme.'' Send SASE for guidelines and theme list. Published after theme deadline. **Publishes 5-10 new writers/year.** Recently published work by Diane Childress and Jackson Kuhl. Publishes short shorts.

How to Contact Query with or without published clips. Send SASE (or IRC) for reply. Responds in several months (if interested, responds 5 months before publication date) to mss. No simultaneous submissions. Sample copy for $5.95 and 7½×10½ SASE with 4 first-class stamps or online. Writer's guidelines for #10 SAE and 1 first-class stamp or on Web site.

Payment/Terms Pays 20-25¢/word. Pays on publication.

Advice ''We primarily publish historical nonfiction. Fiction should be retold legends or folktales related to appropriate themes.''

☑ CANADIAN WRITER'S JOURNAL

P.O. Box 1178, New Liskeard ON P0J 1P0 Canada. (705)647-5424. Fax: (705)647-8366. Web site: www.cwj.ca. Accepts well-written articles by all writers. Bimonthly. Estab. 1984. Circ. 350.

Needs Requirements being met by annual contest. Send SASE for rules, or see guidelines on Web site. ''Does not want gratuitous violence, sex subject matter.'' Publishes ms 9 months after acceptance. **Publishes 40 new writers/year.** Also publishes poetry. Rarely comments on rejected mss.

How to Contact Accepts submissions by e-mail. Responds in 2 months to queries. Writer's guidelines online.

Payment/Terms Pays on publication for one-time rights.

$ ☑ ◎ CLUBHOUSE JR.

Focus on the Family, 8605 Explorer Drive, Colorado Springs CO 80920. (719)531-3400. Web site: www.clubhous ejr.com. **Contact:** Joanna Lutz, editorial assistant. Magazine: 8½×11; 24 pages; illustrations; photos. *Clubhouse Jr.* is designed to inspire, entertain, and teach Christian values to children 4-8. Estab. 1988. Circ. 75,000.

Needs Children's/juvenile (adventure, animal, preschool, sports), ethnic/multicultural, religious/inspirational. Receives 160 unsolicited mss/month. Accepts 1 mss/issue; 12 mss/year. Publishes ms 1 year after acceptance. **Publishes 2-3 new writers/year.** Recently published work by Laura Sassi, Nancy Sanders, Manfred Koehler, and Mary Manz Simon. Length: 250-1,000 words; average length: 250-700 words. Publishes short shorts. Also publishes poetry. Sometimes comments on rejected mss.

How to Contact Send complete ms. Send SASE (or IRC) for return of the ms or send disposable copy of the ms and #10 SASE for reply only. Responds in 6-8 weeks to mss. Does not accept simultaneous submissions. Sample copy for $1.25. Writer's guidelines for #10 SASE.

Payment/Terms Pays $125-200. Pays on acceptance for all rights.

Advice ''Fresh, inviting, creative; stories that explore a worthy theme without an obvious *moral*. Characters are well developed, story line fast-moving and interesting; built on Christian beliefs and values.''

$ ☑ ◎ CLUBHOUSE MAGAZINE

Focus on the Family, 8605 Explorer Dr., Colorado Springs CO 80920. (719)531-3400. Web site: www.clubhouse magazine.com. **Contact:** Joanna Lutz, editorial assistant. Magazine: 8×11; 24 pages; illustrations; photos. ''*Clubhouse* readers are 8-12 year old boys and girls who desire to know more about God and the Bible. Their parents (who typically pay for the membership) want wholesome, educational material with Scriptural or moral insight. The kids want excitement, adventure, action, humor, or mystery. Your job as a writer is to please both the parent and child with each article.'' Monthly. Estab. 1987. Circ. 95,000.

Needs Adventure, children's/juvenile (8-12 years), humor/satire, mystery/suspense, religious/inspirational, holiday. Avoid contemporary, middle-class family settings (existing authors meet this need), stories dealing with boy-girl relationships. ''No science fiction.'' Receives 150 unsolicited mss/month. Accepts 1 mss/issue. Publishes ms 6-12 months after acceptance. Agented fiction 15%. **Publishes 8 new writers/year.** Recently published work by Sigmund Brower and Nancy Rue.

How to Contact Send complete ms. Send SASE for reply, return of ms or send a disposable copy of ms. Responds in 2 months to mss. Sample copy for $1.50 with 9×12 SASE. Writer's guidelines for #10 SASE.

Payment/Terms Pays $200 and up for first time contributor and 5 contributor's copies; additional copies available. Pays on acceptance for first North American serial, first, one-time, electronic rights.

Advice Looks for "humor with a point, historical fiction featuring great Christians or Christians who lived during great times; contemporary, exotic settings; holiday material (Christmas, Thanksgiving, Easter, President's Day); parables; avoid graphic descriptions of evil creatures and sorcery; mystery stories; choose-your-own adventure stories. No contemporary, middle-class family settings (we already have authors who can meet these needs) or stories dealing with boy-girl relationships."

$ 🌐 COSMOS, A Magazine of Ideas, Science, Society and the Future

Luna Media Pty Ltd, Level 3, 13-15 Levey St., Chippendale, NSW 2008 Australia. (61)(2)9310 8500. Fax: (61)(2)9281 2360. E-mail: fiction@cosmosmagazine.com. Web site: www.cosmosmagazine.com. **Contact:** Damien Broderick, fiction editor. Magazine: 230 mm×275 mm, 112 pages, 80 gsm paper, 150 gsm cover. Contains illustrations and photographs. "We look for stories that are well written, stylistically and imaginatively executed, and polished. They should involve some element of science: a new technology, a new idea, a different society or alternative reality, but based on scientific premises, principles and possibilities. It doesn't have to be set in the future, but it's kind of fun if it is." Bi-monthly. Estab. 2005. Circ. 25,000.

Needs Science fiction (hard science/technological, soft/sociological). Does not want thinly-disguised lectures, poetic effusions with no science or quasi-science content, media spinoffs or fantasy. Accepts 1 mss/issue. Manuscript published 6 months after acceptance. Published Gregory Benford, Charles Stross, Paul Di Filiippo, Joe Haldeman and others. Required length: "as close as possible to 2,000 words." Rarely comments on/critiques rejected manuscripts.

How to Contact E-mail complete ms with cover letter. Include brief bio, list of publications. Responds to queries in 2 weeks. Responds to mss in 2 weeks. No simultaneous submissions, multiple submissions. Guidelines available on Web site.

Payment and Terms Writers receive $500 flat-rate payment, 2 contributors copies. Additional copies $4. **Pays on acceptance.** Acquires first worldwide rights for 3 months following date of first publication. Publication is copyrighted.

Advice "Because both our standards and our pay rates are so high, we are only interested in seeing the best writing. Unless you are convinced that your work is of top-shelf, global standard—the sort of excellent fiction published by, for example, *Asimov's*—please don't bother."

$ 📄 📷 🏆 CRICKET

Carus Publishing Co., 70 E. Lake Suite 300, Chicago IL 60601. (312)701-1720. Web site: www.cricketmag.com. Marianne Carus, editor-in-chief. **Contact:** Submissions Editor. Magazine: 8×10; 64 pages; illustrations; photos. Magazine for children, ages 9-14. Monthly. Estab. 1973. Circ. 73,000.

● *Cricket* has received a Parents' Choice Award, and awards from EdPress. Carus Corporation also publishes *Spider, the Magazine for Children*; *Ladybug, the Magazine for Young Children*; *Babybug*; and *Cicada*.

Needs Adventure, children's/juvenile, ethnic/multicultural, fantasy, historical, humor/satire, mystery/suspense, novel excerpts, science fiction, suspense, thriller/espionage, western, folk and fairy tales. No didactic, sex, religious, or horror stories. All issues have different "mini-themes." Receives 1,100 unsolicited mss/month. Accepts 150 mss/year. Publishes ms 6-24 months after acceptance. Agented fiction 1-2%. **Publishes some new writers/year.** Recently published work by Aaron Shepard, Arnold Adoff, and Nancy Springer.

How to Contact Send complete ms. Responds in 3 months to mss. Accepts reprints submissions. Sample copy for $5 and 9×12 SAE. Writer's guidelines for SASE and on Web site.

Payment/Terms Pays 25¢/word maximum, and 6 contributor's copies; $2.50 charge for extras. Pays on publication. Rights vary. Sponsors awards/contests.

Advice "Do not write *down* to children. Write about well-researched subjects you are familiar with and interested in, or about something that concerns you deeply. Children *need* fiction and fantasy. Carefully study several issues of *Cricket* before you submit your manuscript."

$ 📷 DISCIPLESWORLD, A Journal of News, Opinion, and Mission for the Christian Church

DisciplesWorld, Inc., 6325 N. Guilford Ave., Dyr. 213, Indianapolis IN 46202. E-mail: editor@disciplesworld.com. Web site: www.disciplesworld.com. "We are the journal of the Christian Church (Disciples of Christ) in North America. Our denomination numbers roughly 800,000. Disciples are a mainline Protestant group. Our readers are mostly laity, active in their churches, and interested in issues of faithful living, political and church news, ethics, and contemporary social issues." Monthly. Estab. 2002. Circ. 14,000.

Needs Ethnic/multicultural, mainstream, religious/inspirational, slice-of-life vignettes. "We're a religious publication, so use common sense! Stories do not have to be overtly 'religious,' but they should be uplifting and positive." Publishes ms 6 months after acceptance.

How to Contact Send complete ms. Accepts submissions by e-mail (editor@disciplesworld.com). Responds in 2 weeks to queries; 2 months to mss. Accepts simultaneous submissions. Sample copy for #10 SASE. Writer's guidelines online.

Payment/Terms Pays 16¢/word. Pays on publication for first North American serial rights.

$ ☑ ⬚ ESQUIRE

Hearst, 1790 Broadway, 13th Floor, New York NY 10019. (212)649-4050. Web site: www.esquire.com. **Contact:** Adrienne Miller, literary editor. Magazine. Monthly magazine for smart, well-off men. General readership is college educated and sophisticated, between ages 30 and 45. Written mostly by contributing editors on contract. Rarely accepts unsolicited manuscripts. Monthly. Estab. 1933. Circ. 750,000.

• *Esquire* is well respected for its fiction and has received several National Magazine Awards. Work published in *Esquire* has been selected for inclusion in the *Best American Short Stories* and *O. Henry* anthologies.

Needs Novel excerpts, short stories, some poetry, memoirs, and plays. No "pornography, science fiction or 'true romance' stories." Publishes special fiction issue in July. Receives 800 unsolicited mss/month. Rarely accepts unsolicited fiction. Publishes ms 2-6 months after acceptance. Recently published work by Russell Banks, Tim O'Brien, Richard Russo and David Means.

How to Contact Send complete ms. Accepts simultaneous submissions. Writer's guidelines for SASE.

Payment/Terms Pays in cash on acceptance, amount undisclosed. Retains first worldwide periodical publication rights for 90 days from cover date.

Advice "Submit one story at a time. We receive over 10,000 stories a year, so worry a little less about publication, a little more about the work itself."

$ ☑ ◎ EVANGEL

Free Methodist Publishing House, P.O. Box 535002, Indianapolis IN 46253-5002. (317)244-3660. Magazine: 5½×8½; 8 pages; 2 and 4-color illustrations; color and b&w photos. Sunday school take-home paper for distribution to adults who attend church. Fiction involves people coping with everday crises, making decisions that show spiritual growth. Weekly distribution. Printed quarterly. Estab. 1897. Circ. 10,000.

Needs Religious/inspirational. "No fiction without any semblance of Christian message or where the message clobbers the reader. Looking for more short pieces of devotional nature of 500 words or less." Receives 300 unsolicited mss/month. Accepts 3-4 mss/issue; 156-200 mss/year. Publishes ms 18-36 months after acceptance. **Publishes 7 new writers/year.** Recently published work by Karen Leet and Dennis Hensley.

How to Contact Send complete ms. Responds in 4-6 weeks to queries. Accepts multiple submissions. Sample copy and writer's guidelines for #10 SASE.

Payment/Terms Pays 4¢/word and 2 contributor's copies. Pays on publication. Buys second serial (reprint) or one-time rights.

Advice "Desire concise, tight writing that supports a solid thesis and fits the mission expressed in the quidelines."

$ ◎ FIFTY SOMETHING MAGAZINE

Linde Graphics Co., 1168 S. Beachview Rd., Willoughby OH 44094. (440)951-2468. Fax: (440)951-1015. "We are focusing on the 50-and-better reader." Quarterly. Estab. 1990. Circ. 10,000.

Needs Adventure, confessions, ethnic/multicultural, experimental, fantasy, historical, humor/satire, mainstream, mystery/suspense, novel excerpts, romance, slice-of-life vignettes, suspense, western. No erotica or horror. Receives 150 unsolicited mss/month. Accepts 5 mss/issue. Publishes ms 6 months after acceptance. **Publishes 20 new writers/year.** Recently published work by Gail Morrisey, Sally Morrisey, Jenny Miller, J. Alan Witt, and Sharon McGreagor. Length: 500-1,000 words; average length: 1,000 words. Publishes short shorts.

How to Contact Send complete ms. Responds in 3 months to queries; 3 months to mss. Accepts simultaneous submissions and reprints. Sample copy for 9×12 SAE and 4 first-class stamps. Writer's guidelines for #10 SASE.

Payment/Terms Pays $10-100. Pays on publication for one-time, second serial (reprint), simultaneous rights.

🄽 $ FLAUNT MAGAZINE

1422 North Highland Avenue, Los Angeles CA 90028. (323)836-1000. E-mail: info@flauntmagazine.com. Web site: www.flaunt.com. **Contact:** Andrew Pogany, senior editor. Magazine. "Ten times a year *Flaunt* features the bold work of emerging photographers, writers, artists, and musicians. The quality of the content is mirrored in the sophisticated, interactive format of the magazine, using advanced printing techniques, fold-out articles, beautiful papers, and inserts to create a visually stimulating, surprisingly readable, and intelligent book that pushes the magazine format into the realm of art-object. *Flaunt* magazine has for the last eight years made it a point to break new ground, earning itself a reputation as an engine of the avant-garde and an outlet for the culture of the cutting edge. *Flaunt* takes pride in reinventing itself each month, while consistently representing a hybrid of all that is interesting in entertainment, fashion, music, design, film, art, and literature." Monthly. Estab. 1998. Circ. 100,000.

Needs Experimental. Accepts 4 mss/year. Manuscript published 3 months after acceptance. Length: 500 words (min)-5,000 words (max).

How to Contact Guidelines available via e-mail.

Payment and Terms Acquires one-time rights. Pays flat rate of $500.

$ ⬤ ◎ ▼ HIGHLIGHTS FOR CHILDREN

Manuscript Submissions, 803 Church St., Honesdale PA 18431-1824. (570)253-1080. Fax: (570)251-7847. Web site: www.highlights.com. **Contact:** Marileta Robinson, senior editor. Magazine: 8½×11; 42 pages; uncoated paper; coated cover stock; illustrations; photos. "This book of wholesome fun is dedicated to helping children grow in basic skills and knowledge, in creativeness, in ability to think and reason, in sensitivity to others, in high ideals, and worthy ways of living—for children are the world's most important people. We publish stories for beginning and advanced readers. Up to 500 words for beginners (ages 3-7), up to 800 words for advanced (ages 8-12)." Monthly. Estab. 1946. Circ. more than 2,000,000.

- *Highlights* has won the Parent's Guide to Children's Media Award, Parent's Choice Award, and Editorial Excellence Awards from the Association of Educational Publishers.

Needs Adventure, children's/juvenile (ages 2-12), fantasy, historical, humor/satire, animal, contemporary, folktales, multi-cultural, problem-solving, sports. "No war, crime or violence." Unusual stories appealing to both girls and boys; stories with good characterization, strong emotional appeal, vivid, full of action. "Needs stories that begin with action rather than description, have strong plot, believable setting, suspense from start to finish." Receives 600-800 unsolicited mss/month. **Publishes 30 new writers/year.** Recently published work by Eileen Spinelli, James M. Janik, Teresa Bateman, Maryilyn Kratz, Lissa Rouetch. Occasionally comments on rejected mss.

How to Contact Send complete ms. Responds in 2 months to queries. Accepts multiple submissions. Sample copy free. Writer's guidelines for SASE or on Web site.

Payment/Terms Pays $150 minimum, plus 2 contributor's copies. **Pays on acceptance.** Sends galleys to author.

Advice "We accept a story on its merit whether written by an unpublished or an experienced writer. Mss are rejected because of poor writing, lack of plot, trite or worn-out plot, or poor characterization. Children *like* stories and learn about life from stories. Children learn to become lifelong fiction readers by enjoying stories. Feel passion for your subject. Create vivid images. Write a child-centered story; leave adults in the background."

⬤ ◎ ▼ ALFRED HITCHCOCK'S MYSTERY MAGAZINE

Dell Magazines, 475 Park Ave. S., 11th Floor, New York NY 10016. Web site: www.themysteryplace.com. **Contact:** Linda Landrigan, editor. Mystery fiction magazine: 5½×8⅜; 144 pages; 28 lb. newsprint paper; 70 lb. machine-coated cover stock; illustrations; photos. Monthly. Estab. 1956. Circ. 125,000.

- Stories published in *Alfred Hitchcock's Mystery Magazine* have won Edgar Awards for "Best Mystery Story of the Year," Shamus Awards for "Best Private Eye Story of the Year" and Robert L. Fish Awards for "Best First Mystery Short Story of the Year."

Needs Mystery/suspense (amateur sleuth, private eye, police procedural, suspense, etc.). No sensationalism. Number of mss/issue varies with length of mss. Recently published work by Rhys Bowen, Doug Allyn, I.J. Parker, and Martin Limón.

How to Contact Send complete ms. Responds in 4 months to mss. Sample copy for $5. Writer's guidelines for SASE or on Web site.

Payment/Terms Payment varies. Pays on publication for first serial, foreign rights.

⬤ ◎ ▼ KALEIDOSCOPE, Exploring the Experience of Disability Through Literature and the Fine Arts

Kaleidoscope Press, 701 S. Main St., Akron OH 44311-1019. (330)762-9755. Fax: (330)762-0912. Web site: www.udsakron.org. **Contact:** Gail Willmott, editor-in-chief. Magazine: 8½×11; 64 pages; non-coated paper; coated cover stock; illustrations (all media); photos. Subscribers include individuals, agencies, and organizations that assist people with disabilities and many university and public libraries. Open to new writers but appreciates work by established writers as well. Especially interested in work by writers with a disability, but features writers both with and without disabilities. "Writers without a disability must limit themselves to our focus, while those with a disability may explore any topic (although we prefer original perspectives about experiences with disability)." Semiannual. Estab. 1979. Circ. 1,000.

- *Kaleidoscope* has received awards from the American Heart Association, the Great Lakes Awards Competition and Ohio Public Images.

Needs "We look for well-developed plots, engaging characters and realistic dialogue. We lean toward fiction that emphasizes character and emotions rather than action-oriented narratives. No fiction that is stereotypical, patronizing, sentimental, erotic, or maudlin. No romance, religious or dogmatic fiction; no children's literature.'' Receives 20-25 unsolicited mss/month. Accepts 10 mss/year. Agented fiction 1%. **Publishes 1 new writer/ year.** Recently published work by Susan Vreeland, Laurence A. Becker, Ph.D, and Sharon Wachsler. Also publishes poetry.

How to Contact Accepts submissions by fax. Query first or send complete ms and cover letter. Include author's education and writing background and, if author has a disability, how it influenced the writing. SASE. Responds in 3 weeks to queries; 6 months to mss. Accepts simultaneous, multiple submissions and reprints. Sample copy for $6 prepaid. Writer's guidelines online.

Payment/Terms Pays $10-125, and 2 contributor's copies; additional copies $6. Pays on publication for first rights, reprints permitted with credit given to original publication. Rights revert to author upon publication.

Advice ''Read the magazine and get submission guidelines. We prefer that writers with a disability offer original perspectives about their experiences; writers without disabilities should limit themselves to our focus in order to solidify a connection to our magazine's purpose. Do not use stereotypical, patronizing and sentimental attitudes about disability.''

$◎ KENTUCKY MONTHLY

Vested Interest Publications, 213 St. Clair St., Frankfort KY 40601. (502)227-0053. Fax: (502)227-5009. E-mail: jackie@kentuckymonthly.com. Web site: www.kentuckymonthly.com. **Contact:** Jackie Bentley, associate editor. ''We publish stories about Kentucky and by Kentuckians, including stories written by those who live elsewhere.'' Monthly. Estab. 1998. Circ. 40,000.

Needs Adventure, historical, mainstream, novel excerpts. Publishes ms 3 months after acceptance.

How to Contact Query with published clips. Accepts submissions by e-mail, fax. Responds in 3 weeks to queries; 1 month to mss. Accepts simultaneous submissions. Sample copy online. Writer's guidelines online.

Payment/Terms Pays $50-100. Pays within 3 months of publication. Acquires first North American serial rights.

Ⓝ $◲ ◎ 🌡 LADYBUG, The Magazine for Young Children

Carus Publishing Co., 70 E. Lake St., Suite 300, Chicago IL 60601. (312)701-1720. **Contact:** Alice Letvini, editor; Jenny Gillispie, assistant editor. Magazine: 8×10; 36 pages plus 4-page pullout section; illustrations. ''We look for quality writing—quality literature, no matter the subject. For young children, ages 2-6.'' Monthly. Estab. 1990. Circ. 134,000.

● *Ladybug* has received the Parents Choice Award; the Golden Lamp Honor Award and the Golden Lamp Award from Ed Press, and Magazine Merit awards from the Society of Children's Book Writers and Illustrators.

Needs ''Looking for age-appropriate read-aloud stories for preschoolers.''

How to Contact Send complete ms. SASE. Responds in 6-8 months to mss. Accepts reprints submissions. Sample copy for $5 and 9×12 SAE. Writer's guidelines online.

Payment/Terms Pays 25¢/word (less for reprints). Pays on publication. Rights purchased vary. For recurring features, pays flat fee and copyright becomes property of Cricket Magazine Group.

Advice Looks for ''well-written stories for preschoolers: age-appropriate, not condescending. We look for rich, evocative language and sense of joy or wonder.''

$◻ 🌡 LIGUORIAN

One Liguori Dr., Liguori MO 63057-9999. (636)464-2500. Fax: (636)464-8449. E-mail: liguorianeditor@liguori.o rg. Web site: www.liguorian.org. **Contact:** Fr. William Parker, C.Ss.R, editor-in-chief. Magazine: 10⅝×8; 40 pages; 4-color illustrations; photos. ''Our purpose is to lead our readers to a fuller Christian life by helping them better understand the teachings of the gospel and the church and by illustrating how these teachings apply to life and the problems confronting them as members of families, the church, and society.'' Estab. 1913. Circ. 175,000.

● *Liguorian* received Catholic Press Association awards for 2005 including second and third place for Best Short Story.

Needs Religious/inspirational, young adult/teen, senior citizen/retirement. ''Stories submitted to *Liguorian* must have as their goal the lifting up of the reader to a higher Christian view of values and goals. We are not interested in contemporary works that lack purpose or are of questionable moral value.'' Receives 25 unsolicited mss/month. Accepts 12 mss/year. **Publishes 8-10 new writers/year.**

How to Contact Send complete ms. Accepts submissions by e-mail, fax, disk. Responds in 3 months to mss. Sample copy for 9×12 SASE with 3 first-class stamps or online. Writer's guidelines for #10 SASE and on Web site.

Payment/Terms Pays 10-15¢/word and 5 contributor's copies. Pays on acceptance. Buys first rights.

Advice ''First read several issues containing short stories. We look for originality and creative input in each story we read. Since most editors must wade through mounds of manuscripts each month, consideration for the editor requires that the market be studied, the manuscript be carefully presented and polished before submitting. Our publication uses only one story a month. Compare this with the 25 or more we receive over the transom each month. Also, many fiction mss are written without a specific goal or thrust, i.e., an interesting incident that goes nowhere is *not a story*. We believe fiction is a highly effective mode for transmitting the Christian message and also provides a good balance in an unusually heavy issue.''

$ ☑ ◎ LISTEN MAGAZINE, Celebrating Positive Choices

The Health Connection, 55 W. Oak Ridge Dr., Hagerstown MD 21740. (301)393-4082. Fax: (301)393-4055. E-mail: editor@listenmagazine.org. Web site: www.listenmagazine.org. **Contact:** Celeste Perrino-Walker, editor. Magazine: 32 pages; glossy paper; illustrations; photos. ''*Listen* is used in many high school classes and by professionals: medical personnel, counselors, law enforcement officers, educators, youth workers, etc. *Listen* publishes true lifestories about giving teens choices about real-life situations and moral issues in a secular way.'' Monthly. Circ. 40,000.

Needs Young adult/teen (easy-to-read, sports), anti-drug, alcohol, tobacco, positive role models. Publishes ms 6 months after acceptance. Length: 800-1,000; average length: 800 words.

How to Contact Query with published clips or send complete ms. Accepts submissions by e-mail. Prefers submissions by e-mail. Responds in 2 months to queries. Accepts simultaneous and multiple submissions, and reprints. Sample copy for $2 and 9×12 SASE. Writer's guidelines for SASE, by e-mail, fax or on Web site.

Payment/Terms Pays $50-150, and 3 contributor's copies; additional copies $2. Pays on acceptance for first rights.

$ ☑ ◎ LIVE, A Weekly Journal of Practical Christian Living

Gospel Publishing House, 1445 N. Boonville Ave., Springfield MO 65802-1894. (417)862-2781. Fax: (417)862-6059. E-mail: rl-live@gph.org. Web site: www.radiantlife.org. **Contact:** Richard Bennett, editor. ''*LIVE* is a take-home paper distributed weekly in young adult and adult Sunday school classes. We seek to encourage Christians to live for God through fiction and true stories which apply Biblical principles to everyday problems.'' Weekly. Estab. 1928. Circ. 60,000.

Needs Religious/inspirational, inspirational, prose poem. No preachy fiction, fiction about Bible characters, or stories that refer to religious myths (e.g., Santa Claus, Easter Bunny, etc.). No science fiction or Biblical fiction. No controversial stories about such subjects as feminism, war or capital punishment. ''Inner city, ethnic, racial settings.'' Accepts 2 mss/issue. Publishes ms 18 months after acceptance. **Publishes 75-100 new writers/year.** Recently published work by Tiffany Stuart, David Faust, Joanne Schulte and Michael W. Reed.

How to Contact Send complete ms. Accepts submissions by e-mail, fax. Responds in 2 weeks to queries; 6 weeks to mss. Accepts simultaneous submissions. Sample copy for #10 SASE. Writer's guidelines for #10 SASE.

Payment/Terms Pays 7-10¢/word. Pays on acceptance for first, second serial (reprint) rights.

Advice ''Study our publication and write good, inspirational stories that will encourage people to become all they can be as Christians. Stories should go somewhere! Action, not just thought—life; interaction, not just insights. Heroes and heroines, suspense and conflict. Avoid simplistic, pietistic, preachy, or critical conclusions or moralizing. We don't accept science fiction or Biblical fiction. Stories should be encouraging, challenging, humorous. Even problem-centered stories should be upbeat.'' Reserves the right to change the titles, abbreviate length and clarify flashbacks for publication.

$ ◎ THE LUTHERAN JOURNAL

Apostolic Publishing Co., Inc., P.O. Box 28158, Oakdale MN 55128. (651)702-0086. Fax: (651)702-0074. E-mail: lutheran2@msn.com. **Contact:** Vance E. Lichty. ''A family magazine providing wholesome and inspirational reading material for the enjoyment and enrichment of Lutherans.'' Semiannual. Estab. 1938. Circ. 200,000.

Needs Literary, religious/inspirational, romance (historical), young adult/teen, senior citizen/retirement. Must be appropriate for distribution in the churches. Accepts 3-6 mss/issue.

How to Contact Send complete ms. Responds in 4 months to queries. Accepts simultaneous submissions. Sample copy for 9×12 SASE with 60¢ postage.

Payment/Terms Pays $50-300 and one contributor's copy. Pays on publication for first rights.

$ ☑ ◎ ⛛ THE MAGAZINE OF FANTASY & SCIENCE FICTION

Spilogale, Inc., P.O. Box 3447, Hoboken NJ 07030. E-mail: fsfmagf@fsmag.com. Web site: www.fsfmag.com. **Contact:** Gordon Van Gelder, editor. Magazine: 5×8; 160 pages; groundwood paper; card stock cover; illustrations on cover only. ''*The Magazine of Fantasy and Science Fiction* publishes various types of science fiction and fantasy short stories and novellas, making up about 80% of each issue. The balance of each issue is devoted to articles about science fiction, a science column, book and film reviews, cartoons, and competitions.'' Monthly. Estab. 1949. Circ. 5,000.

• The *Magazine of Fantasy and Science Fiction* won a Nebula Award for Best Novella for "Bronte's Egg" by Richard Chwedyk and a Nebula Award for Best Short Story for "Creature" by Carol Emshwiller. Also won the 2002 World Fantasy Award for Best Short Story for "Queen for a Day" by Albert E. Cowdrey.

Needs Adventure, fantasy (space fantasy, sword and sorcery), horror (dark fantasy, futuristic, psychological, supernatural), psychic/supernatural/occult, science fiction (hard science/technological, soft/sociological), young adult/teen (fantasy/science fiction, horror). "We're always looking for more science fiction." Receives 500-700 unsolicited mss/month. Accepts 5-8 mss/issue; 75-100 mss/year. Publishes ms 9-12 months after acceptance. **Publishes 1-5 new writers/year.** Recently published work by Peter S. Beuyle, Ursula K. LeGuin, Alex Irvine, Pat Murphy, Joyce Carol Oates and Robert Silverbery. Length: Up to 25,000 words; average length: 7,000 words. Publishes short shorts. Sometimes comments on rejected mss.

How to Contact Send complete ms with SASE (or IRC). No electronic submissions. Responds in 2 months to queries. Accepts reprint submissions. Sample copy for $5. Writer's guidelines for SASE, by e-mail or on Web site.

Payment/Terms Pays 6-9¢/word; additional copies $2.10. Pays on acceptance for first North American serial, foreign serial rights.

Advice "A well-prepared manuscript stands out better that one with fancy doo-dads. Fiction that stands out tends to have well-developed characters and thinks through the implications of its fantasy elements. It has been said 100 times before, but read an issue of the magazine before submitting. In the wake of the recent films, we are seeing more fantasy stories about sorcerers than we can possibly publish. Humorous stories about the future are in short supply nowadays."

$MAISONNEUVE

400 de Maisonneuve Blvd. West Suite 655, Montreal QC H3A 1L4 Canada. (514)482-5089. Fax: (514)482-6734. E-mail: submissions@maisonneuve.org. Web site: www.maisonneuve.org. **Contact:** Phillip Todd, managing editor. Magazine. "*Maisonneuve* has been described as a new *New Yorker* for a younger generation, or as *Harper's* meets *Vice*, or as *Vanity Fair* without the vanity—but *Maisonneuve* is its own creature. *Maisonneuve's* purpose is to keep its readers informed, alert, and entertained, and to dissolve artistic borders between regions, countries, languages and genres. It does this by providing a diverse range of commentary across the arts, sciences, daily and social life. The magazine has a balanced perspective, and 'brings the news' in a wide variety of ways. At its core, *Maisonneuve* asks questions about our lives and provides answers free of cant and cool." Quarterly. Estab. 2002. Circ. 10,000.

Needs Adventure, ethnic/multicultural, experimental, humor/satire, science fiction. Accepts 4 mss/year. Manuscript published 4-6 months after acceptance. Length: 1,000 words (min)-4,000 words (max).

How to Contact Send complete ms with cover letter. Responds to queries in 2 weeks. Responds to mss in 2 months. Considers simultaneous submissions. Sample copy free with SASE. Guidelines available on Web site.

Payment and Terms Pays on publication. Acquires first North American serial rights, electronic rights. Publication is copyrighted.

Advice "Please see submission guidelines at www.maisonneuve.org."

$ MATURE YEARS

The United Methodist Publishing House, 201 Eighth Ave. S., Nashville TN 37202-0801. (615)749-6292. Fax: (615)749-6512. E-mail: matureyears@umpublishing.org. **Contact:** Marvin Cropsey, editor. Magazine: $8\frac{1}{2} \times 11$; 112 pages; illustrations; photos. Magazine "helps persons in and nearing retirement to appropriate the resources of the Christian faith as they seek to face the problems and opportunities related to aging." Quarterly. Estab. 1954. Circ. 55,000.

Needs Humor/satire, religious/inspirational, slice-of-life vignettes, retirement years issues, intergenerational relationships. "We don't want anything poking fun at old age, saccharine stories or anything not for older adults. Must show older adults (age 55 plus) in a positive manner." Accepts 1 mss/issue; 4 mss/year. Publishes ms 1 year after acceptance. **Publishes some new writers/year.** Recently published work by Harriet May Savitz, Donita K. Paul and Ann Gray.

How to Contact Send complete ms. Responds in 2 weeks to queries; 2 months to mss. No simultaneous submissions. Sample copy for $5.75 and 9×12 SAE. Writer's guidelines for #10 SASE or by e-mail.

Payment/Terms Pays $60-125. Pays on acceptance for first North American serial rights.

Advice "Practice writing dialogue! Listen to people talk; take notes; master dialogue writing! Not easy, but well worth it! Most inquiry letters are far too long. If you can't sell me an idea in a brief paragraph, you're not going to sell the reader on reading your finished article or story."

$ THE MESSENGER OF THE SACRED HEART

Apostleship of Prayer, 661 Greenwood Ave., Toronto ON M4J 4B3 Canada. (416)466-1195. **Contact:** Rev. F.J. Power, S.J. and Alfred DeManche, editors. Magazine: 7×10; 32 pages; coated paper; self-cover; illustrations;

photos. Monthly magazine for "Canadian and U.S. Catholics interested in developing a life of prayer and spirituality; stresses the great value of our ordinary actions and lives." Estab. 1891. Circ. 11,000.

Needs Religious/inspirational, stories about people, adventure, heroism, humor, drama. No poetry. Accepts 1 mss/issue. Sometimes comments on rejected mss.

How to Contact Send complete ms. Responds in 1 month to queries. Sample copy for $1 and 7½×10½ SAE. Writer's guidelines for #10 SASE.

Payment/Terms Pays 8¢/word, and 3 contributor's copies. Pays on acceptance for first North American serial, first rights.

Advice "Develop a story that sustains interest to the end. Do not preach, but use plot and characters to convey the message or theme. Aim to move the heart as well as the mind. If you can, add a light touch or a sense of humor to the story. Your ending should have impact, leaving a moral or faith message for the reader."

$ MSLEXIA, For Women Who Write

Mslexia Publications Ltd., P.O. Box 656, Newcastle Upon Tyne NE99 1PZ United Kingdom. (00)44-191-2616656. Fax: (00)44-191-2616636. E-mail: postbag@mslexia.demon.co.uk. Web site: www.mslexia.co.uk. **Contact:** Daneet Steffens, editor. Magazine: A4; 60 pages; some illustrations; photos. "*Mslexia* is for women who write, who want to write, who have a specialist interest in women's writing or who teach creative writing. *Mslexia* is a blend of features, articles, advice, listings, and original prose and poetry. Many parts of the magazine are open to submission from any women. Please request contributor's guidelines prior to sending in work." Quarterly. Estab. 1999. Circ. 20,000.

Needs No work from men accepted, except on letters' page. Prose and poetry in each issue is to a specific theme (e.g. sins, travel, rain). Send SASE for themes. Publishes ms 1-2 months after acceptance. **Publishes 40-50 new writers/year.** Length: 3,000 words; average length: 2,000 words. Publishes short shorts to a specific theme and autobiography (800 words). Also publishes poetry.

How to Contact Accepts submissions by post, and by e-mail from overseas only (postbag@mslexia.demon.co.uk). Query first. Responds in 3 months to mss. Guidelines for SAE, e-mail, fax or on Web site.

Payment/Terms £25 per poem; £15 per 1,000 words prose; features by negotiation. Plus contributors' copies.

Advice "Well structured, short pieces preferred. We look for intelligence and a strong sense of voice and place. Consider the obvious interpretations of the theme—then try to think of a new slant. Dare to be different. Make sure the piece is strong on craft as well as content. Extracts from novels are unlikely to be suitable."

$ NA'AMAT WOMAN, Magazine of NA'AMAT USA

NA'AMAT USA, 350 Fifth Ave., Suite 4700, New York NY 10118. (212)563-5222. Fax: (212)563-5710. **Contact:** Judith A. Sokoloff, editor. "Magazine covering a wide variety of subjects of interest to the Jewish community—including political and social issues, arts, profiles; many articles about Israel and women's issues. Fiction must have a Jewish theme. Readers are the American Jewish community." Estab. 1926. Circ. 20,000.

Needs Ethnic/multicultural, historical, humor/satire, literary, novel excerpts, women-oriented. Receives 10 unsolicited mss/month. Accepts 3-5 mss/year.

How to Contact Query with published clips or send complete mss. Responds in 6 months to queries; 6 months to mss. Sample copy for 9×11½ SAE and $1.20 postage. Writer's guidelines for #10 SASE.

Payment/Terms Pays 10¢/word and 2 contributor's copies. Pays on publication for first North American serial, first, one-time, second serial (reprint) rights, makes work-for-hire assignments.

Advice "No maudlin nostalgia or romance; no hackneyed Jewish humor and no poetry."

$ THE NEW YORKER

The New Yorker, Inc., 4 Times Square, New York NY 10036. (212)286-5900. E-mail: fiction@newyorker.com. Web site: www.newyorker.com. **Contact:** Deborah Treisman, fiction editor. A quality magazine of interesting, well-written stories, articles, essays and poems for a literate audience. Weekly. Estab. 1925. Circ. 750,000.

Needs Accepts 1 mss/issue.

How to Contact Send complete ms. Accepts submissions by e-mail. No more than 1 story or 6 poems should be submitted. No attachments. Responds in 3 months to mss. No simultaneous submissions. Writer's guidelines online.

Payment/Terms Payment varies. Pays on acceptance.

Advice "Be lively, original, not overly literary. Write what you want to write, not what you think the editor would like. Send poetry to Poetry Department."

$ NEWWITCH

BBI, Inc., P.O. Box 641, Point Arena CA 95468. (707)882-2052. Fax: (707)882-2793. E-mail: meditor@newwitch.com. Web site: www.newwitch.com. **Contact:** Kenaz Filan, managing editor. Magazine. "*newWitch* is dedicated to Witches, Wiccans, Neo-Pagans, and various other earth-based, ethnic, pre-christian, shamanic and magical practitioners. We hope to reach not only those already involved in what we cover, but also the curious and completely new as well.'' Quarterly. Estab. 2002. Circ. 15,000.

Needs Adventure, erotica, ethnic/multicultural, fantasy, historical, horror, humor/satire, mainstream, mystery, religious, romance. Special interests: Pagan/Earth Religion material. Does not accept "faction"—fictionalized retellings of real events. Avoid gratuitous sex and violence: in movie rating terms think PG-13. Also avoid gratuitous sentimentality and Pagan moralizing: don't beat our readers with the Rede or the Threefold Law. Accepts 3-4 mss/year. Length: 1,000 words (min)-5,000 words (max).

How to Contact Send complete ms with cover letter. Accepts submissions by e-mail. Responds to queries in 1-2 weeks. Responds to mss in 1 months. Sample copy available for. Guidelines available on Web site.

Advice "Read the magazine, do your research, write the piece, send it in. That's really the only way to get started as a writer: Everything else is window dressing."

108, CELEBRATING BASEBALL

Sandlot Media, 517 N Mountain Ave. #237, Uplano CA 91786. (909)912-0134. Fax: (909)912-0197. E-mail: info@108mag.com. Web site: www.108mag.com. **Contact:** Phil Osterholt, managing editor. Magazine. "*108* celebrates baseball's contributions to and role in American history, culture, and community through in-depth feature articles, short fiction, photography and original artwork." Quarterly. Estab. 2006. Circ. 30,000.

Needs Historical, horror, humor/satire, mainstream, mystery. "As long as baseball is an integral part of the story, we'll take a look." Accepts 10-15 mss/year. Manuscript published 1-2 months after acceptance. Length: 2,000 words (min)-7,000 words (max).

How to Contact Send complete ms with cover letter. Accepts submissions by e-mail. Sample copy available for $7.95. Guidelines available via e-mail.

Payment and Terms Acquires first North American serial rights, one-time rights, electronic rights.

Advice "We tell the great stories that help make baseball the great game it is, and we're looking for just that—great stories, not statistical-laden entries from a baseball encyclopedia. We prefer complete manuscripts to queries."

OUTLOOKS

#1B, 1230A 17th Avenue SW, Calgary AB T2T 0B8 Canada. (403)228-1157. Fax: (403)228-7735. E-mail: main@outlooks.ca. Web site: www.outlooks.ca. **Contact:** Roy Heale, editor. Magazine. "National lifestyle publisher for Canada's Gay and Lesbian community." Monthly. Estab. 1997. Circ. 37,500.

Needs Adventure, erotica, humor/satire. Accepts 10 mss/year. Manuscript published 2 months after acceptance. Length: 1,200 words (min)-1,600 words (max).

How to Contact Query with clips of published work. Responds to queries in 2 weeks. Guidelines available on Web site.

Payment and Terms Acquires first rights. Pays between $120-$160 for fiction. Publication is copyrighted.

PAKN TREGER

National Yiddish Book Center, 1021 West Street, Amherst MA 01002. (413)256-4900. Fax: (413)256-4700. E-mail: aatherley@bikher.org. Web site: www.yiddishbookcenter.org. **Contact:** Anne Atherly, assistant editor. Literary magazine/journal. "*Pakn Treger* is looking for high-quality writing for a secular audience interested in Yiddish and Jewish history, literature, and culture." Triannual. Estab. 1980. Circ. 30,000.

Needs Historical, humor/satire, mystery. Accepts 2 mss/year. Manuscript published 4 months after acceptance. Length: 1,200 words (min)-5,000 words (max).

How to Contact Query first. Accepts submissions by e-mail. Responds to queries in 2 weeks; mss in 2 months. Sample copy available via e-mail. Guidelines available via e-mail.

Payment and Terms Acquires one-time rights.

Advice "Read the magazine and visit www.yiddishbookcenter.org."

PLAYBOY MAGAZINE

730 5th Avenue, New York NY 10019. (212)261-5000. Web site: www.playboy.com. **Contact:** Fiction Department. "As the world's largest general interest lifestyle magazine for men, *Playboy* spans the spectrum of contemporary men's passions. From hard-hitting investigative journalism to light-hearted humor, the latest in fashion and personal technology to the cutting edge of the popular culture, *Playboy* is and always has been guidebook and dream book for generations of American men . . . the definitive source of information and ideas for over 10 million readers each month. In addition, *Playboy*'s 'Interview' and '20 Questions' present profiles of politicians, athletes and today's hottest personalities." Monthly. Estab. 1953. Circ. 3,283,000.

Needs Humor/satire, mainstream/literary, mystery/suspense. Does not consider poetry, plays, story outlines or novel-length mss. Writers should remember that the magazine's appeal is chiefly to a well-informed, young male audience. Fairy tales, extremely experimental fiction and out-right pornography all have their place, but it is not in *Playboy*. Handwritten submissions will be returned unread. Writers who submit mss without including a SASE will receive neither the ms nor a printed rejection. ''We will not consider stories submitted electronically or by fax.''

How to Contact Query. Responds in 1 month to queries. No simultaneous submissions. Writer's guidelines for #10 SASE or online at Web site.

Payment/Terms Acquires first North American serial rights.

Advice ''*Playboy* does not consider poetry, plays, story outlines or novel-length manuscripts.''

$ ◎ POCKETS

The Upper Room, 1908 Grand Ave., P.O. Box 340004, Nashville TN 37203-0004. (615)340-7333. Fax: (615)340-7267. E-mail: pockets@upperroom.org. Web site: www.pockets.org. **Contact**: Lynn W. Gilliam, editor. Magazine: 7×11; 48 pages; some photos. ''We are a Christian, inter-denominational publication for children 6-11 years of age. Each issue reflects a specific theme.'' Estab. 1981. Circ. 96,000.

● *Pockets* has received honors from the Educational Press Association of America.

Needs Adventure, ethnic/multicultural, historical (general), religious/inspirational, slice-of-life vignettes. No fantasy, science fiction, talking animals. ''All submissions should address the broad theme of the magazine. Each issue is built around one theme with material which can be used by children in a variety of ways. Scripture stories, fiction, poetry, prayers, art, graphics, puzzles and activities are included. Submissions do not need to be overtly religious. They should help children experience a Christian lifestyle that is not always a neatly-wrapped moral package, but is open to the continuing revelation of God's will. Seasonal material, both secular and liturgical, is desired. No violence, horror, sexual, racial stereotyping or fiction containing heavy moralizing.'' Receives 200 unsolicited mss/month. Accepts 3-4 mss/issue; 33-44 mss/year. Publishes ms 1 year to 18 months after acceptance. **Publishes 15 new writers/year.** Length: 600-1,400 words; average length: 1,200 words.

How to Contact Send complete ms. Cover letter not required. Responds in 6 weeks to mss. Accepts one-time reprints, multiple submissions. For a sample copy, themes and/or guidelines send 9×12 SASE with 4 first-class stamps. Writer's guidelines, themes, and due dates available online.

Payment/Terms Pays 14¢/word, plus 2-5 contributor's copies. Pays on acceptance for first North American serial rights. Sponsors awards/contests.

Advice ''Listen to children as they talk with each other. Send for a sample copy. Study guidelines and themes before submitting. Many manuscripts we receive are simply inappropriate. Each issue is theme-related. Please send for list of themes. New themes published in December of each year. We strongly advise sending for themes or checking the Web site before submitting.'' Include SASE.

$ ◪ ◎ PORTLAND MONTHLY, Maine's City Magazine

722 Congress St., Portland ME 041012. (207)775-4339. Fax: (207)775-2334. E-mail: editor@portlandmonthly.com. Web site: www.portlandmagazine.com. **Contact**: Colin Sargent, editor. Magazine: 200 pages; 60 lb. paper; 100 lb. cover stock; illustrations; photos. ''City lifestyle magazine—fiction, style, business, real estate, controversy, fashion, cuisine, interviews and art relating to the Maine area.'' Monthly. Estab. 1986. Circ. 100,000.

Needs Historical, literary (Maine connection). Query first. Receives 20 unsolicited mss/month. Accepts 1 mss/issue; 10 mss/year. **Publishes 50 new writers/year.** Recently published work by Rick Mood, Ann Hood, C.D.B Bryan, Joan Connor, Mameve Medwed, Jason Brown and Sebastian Junger.

How to Contact Send complete ms. SASE.

Payment/Terms Pays on publication for first North American serial rights.

Advice ''We publish ambitious short fiction featuring everyone from Frederick Barthelme to newly discovered fiction by Edna St. Vincent Millay.''

$ ◎ ◪ ELLERY QUEEN'S MYSTERY MAGAZINE

Dell Magazines Fiction Group, 475 Park Ave. S., 11th Floor, New York NY 10016. (212)686-7188. Fax: (212)686-7414. E-mail: elleryqueen@dellmagazines.com. Web site: www.themysteryplace.com. **Contact**: Janet Hutchings, editor. Magazine: 5¼×8 1/3, 144 pages with special 240-page combined March/April and September/October issues. ''*Ellery Queen's Mystery Magazine* welcomes submissions from both new and established writers. We publish every kind of mystery short story: the psychological suspense tale, the deductive puzzle, the private eye case—the gamut of crime and detection from the realistic (including the policeman's lot and stories of police procedure) to the more imaginative (including ''locked rooms'' and ''impossible crimes''). *EQMM* has been in continuous publication since 1941. From the beginning, three general criteria have been employed in evaluating submissions: We look for strong writing, an original and exciting plot, and professional craftsmanship. We encourage writers whose work meets these general criteria to read an issue of *EQMM* before making a submission.'' Magazine for lovers of mystery fiction. Estab. 1941. Circ. 180,780 readers.

● *EQMM* has won numerous awards and sponsors its own award yearly for the best *EQMM* stories nominated by its readership.

Needs Mystery/suspense. No explicit sex or violence, no gore or horror. Seldom publishes parodies or pastiches.

"We accept only mystery, crime, suspense and detective fiction." 2,500-8,000 words is the preferred range. Also publishes minute mysteries of 250 words; novellas up to 20,000 words from established authors. Publishes ms 6-12 months after acceptance. Agented fiction 50%. **Publishes 10 new writers/year.** Recently published work by Jeffery Deaver, Joyce Carol Oates and Margaret Maron. Sometimes comments on rejected mss.

How to Contact Send complete ms. Responds in 3 months to mss. Accepts simultaneous, multiple submissions. Sample copy for $5. Writer's guidelines for SASE or online.

Payment/Terms Pays 5-8¢/word, occasionally higher for established authors. Pays on acceptance for first North American serial rights.

Advice "We have a Department of First Stories and usually publish at least one first story an issue, i.e., the author's first published fiction. We select stories that are fresh and of the kind our readers have expressed a liking for. In writing a detective story, you must play fair with the reader, providing clues and necessary information. Otherwise you have a better chance of publishing if you avoid writing to formula."

ℕ $⌀ **REDBOOK MAGAZINE**

224 W. 57th St., New York NY 10019. (212)649-2000. Web site: www.redbookmag.com. Magazine: 8×10¾; 150-250 pages; 34 lb. paper; 70 lb. cover; illustrations; photos. "*Redbook* addresses young married women between the ages of 28 and 44. Most of our readers are married with children 10 and under; over 60 percent work outside the home. The articles entertain, educate and inspire our readers to confront challenging issues. Each article must be timely and relevant to *Redbook* readers' lives." Monthly. Estab. 1903. Circ. 3,200,000.

Needs Publishes ms 6 months after acceptance.

How to Contact *Redbook* was not accepting unsolicited mss at the time of publication. Sample copy not available. Writer's guidelines online.

Payment/Terms Pays on acceptance. Rights purchased vary with author and material.

Advice "Read at least the last 6 issues of the magazine to get a better understanding of appropriate subject matter and treatment."

$⌀ ◎ **SEEK**

Standard Publishing, 8121 Hamilton Ave., Cincinnati OH 45231. (513)728-6822. Fax: (513)931-0950. E-mail: seek@standardpub.com. Web site: www.standardpub.com. Magazine: 5½×8½; 8 pages; newsprint paper; art and photo in each issue. "Inspirational stories of faith-in-action for Christian adults; a Sunday School take-home paper." Quarterly. Estab. 1970. Circ. 27,000.

Needs Religious/inspirational, Religious fiction and religiously slanted historical and humorous fiction. No poetry. List of upcoming themes available online. Accepts 150 mss/year. Publishes ms 1 year after acceptance.

How to Contact Send complete ms. Accepts submissions by e-mail. Prefers submissions by e-mail. Writer's guidelines online.

Payment/Terms Pays 7¢/word. Pays on acceptance for first North American serial, pays 5¢ for second serial (reprint) rights.

Advice "Write a credible story with a Christian slant—no preachments; avoid overworked themes such as joy in suffering, generation gaps, etc. Most manuscripts are rejected by us because of irrelevant topic or message, unrealistic story, or poor charater and/or plot development. We use fiction stories that are believable."

ℕ $⌀ ◎ **SPIDER, The Magazine for Children**

Cricket Magazine Group, 70 East Lake Street, Suite 300, Chicago IL 6 0601. (815)224-5803. Fax: (815)224-6615. Web site: www.cricketmag.com. **Contact:** Marianne Carus, editor-in-chief; May-May Sugihara, editor. Magazine: 8×10; 34 pages; illustrations; photos. "*Spider* introduces 6- to 9-year-old children to the highest quality stories, poems, illustrations, articles, and activities. It was created to foster in beginning readers a love of reading and discovery that will last a lifetime. We're looking for writers who respect children's intelligence." Monthly. Estab. 1994. Circ. 60,000.

• Carus Publishing also publishes *Cricket, Ladybug, Babybug* and *Cicada,* and more.

Needs Adventure, children's/juvenile (6-9 years), ethnic/multicultural, fantasy (children's fantasy), historical, humor/satire, mystery/suspense, science fiction, suspense, realistic fiction, folk tales, fairy tales. No romance, horror, religious. Publishes ms 2-3 years after acceptance. Agented fiction 2%. Recently published work by Polly Horvath, Andrea Cheng, and Beth Wagner Brust. Length: 300-1,000 words; average length: 775 words. Also publishes poetry. Often comments on rejected mss.

How to Contact Send complete ms. Send SASE for return of ms. Responds in 6 months to mss. Accepts simultaneous submissions and reprints. Sample copy for $5 and 9×12 SASE. Writer's guidelines on Web site.

Payment/Terms Pays 25¢/word and 6 contributor's copies; additional copies $2.50. Pays on publication. Rights vary.

Advice "Read back issues of *Spider.*" Look for "quality writing, good characterization, lively style, humor."

$ 🗋 ◎ 🗒 ST. ANTHONY MESSENGER

28 W. Liberty St., Cincinnati OH 45202-6498. (513)241-5615. Fax: (513)241-0399. E-mail: patm@americancathol ic.org. Web site: www.americancatholic.org. **Contact:** Father Pat McCloskey, O.F.M., editor. Magazine: 8×10¾; 60 pages; illustrations; photos. "*St. Anthony Messenger* is a Catholic family magazine which aims to help its readers lead more fully human and Christian lives. We publish articles which report on a changing church and world, opinion pieces written from the perspective of Christian faith and values, personality profiles, and fiction which entertains and informs." Estab. 1893. Circ. 308,884.

- This is a leading Catholic magazine, but has won awards for both religious and secular journalism and writing from the Catholic Press Association, the International Association of Business Communicators, and the Society of Professional Journalists.

Needs Mainstream, religious/inspirational, senior citizen/retirement. "We do not want mawkishly sentimental or preachy fiction. Stories are most often rejected for poor plotting and characterization; bad dialogue—listen to how people talk; inadequate motivation. Many stories say nothing, are 'happenings' rather than stories." No fetal journals, no rewritten Bible stories. Receives 60-70 unsolicited mss/month. Accepts 1 mss/issue; 12 mss/year. Publishes ms 1 year after acceptance. **Publishes 3 new writers/year.** Recently published work by Geraldine Marshall Gutfreund, John Salustri, Beth Dotson, Miriam Pollikatsikis and Joseph Pici. Sometimes requests revisions before acceptance.

How to Contact Send complete ms. Accepts submissions by e-mail, fax. "For quickest response send self-addressed stamped postcard with choices: "Yes, we're interested in publishing; Maybe, we'd like to hold for future consideration; No, we've decided to pass on the publication." Responds in 3 weeks to queries; 2 months to mss. No simultaneous submissions. Sample copy for 9×12 SASE with 4 first-class stamps. Writer's guidelines online. Reviews fiction.

Payment/Terms Pays 16¢/word maximum and 2 contributor's copies; $1 charge for extras. Pays on acceptance for first North American serial, electronic rights.

Advice "We publish one story a month and we get up to 1,000 a year. Too many offer simplistic 'solutions' or answers. Pay attention to endings. Easy, simplistic, deus ex machina endings don't work. People have to feel characters in the stories are real and have a reason to care about them and what happens to them. Fiction entertains but can also convey a point and sound values."

$ ST. JOSEPH'S MESSENGER & ADVOCATE OF THE BLIND

Sisters of St. Joseph of Peace, St. Joseph's Home, P.O. Box 288, Jersey City NJ 07303-0288. **Contact:** Sister Mary Kuiken, editor. Magazine: 8¼×11; 12-16 pages. Semiannual. Estab. 1898. Circ. 13,000.

Needs Mainstream, religious/inspirational, contemporary. Publishes ms 6 months after acceptance. Length: 700-900 words; average length: 800 words. Publishes short shorts. Also publishes poetry. Rarely comments on rejected mss.

How to Contact Send complete ms. Send SASE (or IRC) for return of the ms or send disposable copy of the ms and #10 SASE for reply only. Responds in 2 weeks to queries; 2 months to mss. Accepts simultaneous submissions and reprints. Sample copy and writer's guidelines for 9×12 SAE and 2 first-class stamps.

Payment/Terms Pays $10-20. Pays on acceptance. Buys first serial and second serial (reprint) rights; reassigns rights back to author after publication in return for credit line in next publication.

$ 🗋 ◎ STANDARD

Nazarene Publishing House, 2923 Troost, Kansas City MO 64109. (816)931-1900. Fax: (816)412-8306. E-mail: sdharris@wordaction.com. Web site: www.wordaction.com. **Contact:** Stephanie Harris, editor; Everett Leadingham, senior editor. Magazine: 8½×11; 8 pages; illustrations; photos. Inspirational reading for adults. "In *Standard* we want to show Christianity in action, and we prefer to do that through stories that hold the reader's attention." Weekly. Estab. 1936. Circ. 130,000.

Needs "Looking for stories that show Christianity in action." Accepts 200 mss/year. Publishes ms 14-18 months after acceptance. **Publishes some new writers/year.**

How to Contact Send complete ms. Accepts submissions by e-mail. SASE. Accepts simultaneous submissions But pays at reprint rates. Writer's guidelines and sample copy for SAE with 2 first-class stamps or available by e-mail request.

Payment/Terms Pays 3½¢/word for first rights; 2¢/word for reprint rights, and contributor's copies. Pays on acceptance for one-time rights, whether first or reprint rights.

Advice "Be conscientious in your use of Scripture; don't overload your story with quotations. When you quote the Bible, quote it exactly and cite chapter, verse, and version used. (We prefer NIV.) *Standard* will handle copyright matters for Scripture. Except for quotations from the Bible, written permission for the use of any other copyrighted material (especially song lyrics) is the responsibility of the writer. Keep in mind the international audience of *Standard* with regard to geographic references and holidays. We cannot use stories about cultural, national, or secular holidays. Do not mention specific church affiliations. *Standard* is read in a variety of denominations. Do not submit any manuscripts which has been submitted to or published in any of the following: *Vista, Wesleyan Advocate, Holiness Today, Preacher's Magazine, World Mission, Women Alive,* or various teen and children's publications produced by WordAction Publishing Company. These are overlapping markets.''

$⬚⬚⬚ THE STRAND MAGAZINE

P.O. Box 1418, Birmingham MI 48012-1418. (248)788-5948. Fax: (248)874-1046. E-mail: strandmag@strandmag .com. Web site: www.strandmag.com. **Contact:** A.F. Gulli, editor. ''After an absence of nearly half a century, the magazine known to millions for bringing Sir Arthur Conan Doyle's ingenious detective, Sherlock Holmes, to the world has once again appeared on the literary scene. First launched in 1891, *The Strand* included in its pages the works of some of the greatest writers of the 20th century: Agatha Christie, Dorothy Sayers, Margery Allingham, W. Somerset Maugham, Graham Greene, P.G. Wodehouse, H.G. Wells, Aldous Huxley and many others. In 1950, economic difficulties in England caused a drop in circulation which forced the magazine to cease publication.'' Quarterly. Estab. 1998. Circ. 50,000.
Needs Horror, humor/satire, mystery/suspense (detective stories), suspense, tales of the unexpected, tales of terror and the supernatural ''written in the classic tradition of this century's great authors. We are NOT interested in submissions with any sexual content.'' Stories can be set in any time or place, provided they are well written and the plots interesting and well thought out.'' Publishes ms 4 months after acceptance.
How to Contact SASE (IRCs if outside the US). Query first. Responds in 1 month to queries. Sample copy not available. Writer's guidelines for #10 SASE.
Payment/Terms Pays $50-175. Pays on acceptance for first North American serial rights.

🅽 $ WASHINGTON RUNNING REPORT

13710 Ashby Rd, Rockville MD 20853. (301)871-0006. Fax: (301)871-0005. E-mail: kathy@runwashington.com. Web site: www.runwashington.com. **Contact:** Kathy Freedman, editor. Magazine. ''Written by runners for runners, *Washington Running Report* covers the running and racing scene in metropolitan Washington DC. Features include runner rankings, training tips and advice, feature articles on races, race results, race calendar, humor, product reviews and other articles of interest to runners.'' Bimonthly. Estab. 1984. Circ. 35,000.
Needs Adventure, fantasy, historical, humor/satire, mainstream, mystery. Accepts 1-2 mss/year. Manuscript published 2-4 months after acceptance. Length: 750 words (min)-1,500 words (max).
How to Contact Send complete ms with cover letter. Accepts submissions by e-mail. Responds to queries in 2-3 weeks. Responds to mss in 1-2 months. Considers simultaneous submissions, previously published submissions. Sample copy free upon request.
Payment and Terms Acquires first rights, one-time rights, electronic rights.

🌐 $ WOMAN'S WEEKLY

IPC Magazines, The Blue Fin Building, 110 Southward Street, London SE1 0SU United Kingdom. **Contact:** Gaynor Davies. Publishes 1 serial and at least 2 short stories/week.
Needs ''Short stories can be on any theme, but must have warmth. No explicit sex or violence. Serials need not be written in installments. They are submitted as complete manuscripts and we split them up, or send first installment of serial (4,500 words) and synopsis of the rest.''
How to Contact Writer's guidelines free.
Payment/Terms Short story payment starts at £100 and rises as writer becomes a more regular contributor. Serial payments start at around £600/installment. Writer's also receive contributor's copies.
Advice ''Read the magazine and try to understand who the publication is aimed at.''

🌐 $⬚ WRITERS' FORUM, Britain's Best Magazine for Writers

Writers International Ltd., P.O. Box 3229, Bournemouth Dorset BH1 1ZS United Kingdom. (44)1202 589828. Fax: (44)1202 587758. E-mail: editorial@writers-forum.com. Web site: www.writers-forum.com. **Contact:** John Jenkins, editor. Monthly: A4; 76 pages; illustrations; photos. ''In each issue *Writers' Forum* covers the *who, why, what, where, when* and *how* of writing. You will find the latest on markets, *how-to* articles, courses/ holidays for writers and much more. There is also a short story competition in every issue—that means you have ten chances to get published and win some cash. Prizes range from £300 to £100. Monthly. Estab. 1995.
Needs Erotica, historical, horror (psychological), literary, mainstream, mystery/suspense (cozy, private eye/ hardboiled), romance (contemporary, futuristic/time travel, historical, romantic suspense), science fiction (soft/sociological), thriller/espionage, western (frontier saga, traditional), young adult/teen (adventure, easy-to-read, historical, problem novels, romance). Receives hundreds unsolicited mss/month. Accepts 3-4 mss/ issue; 20 mss/year. Publishes ms 2-3 months after acceptance. Length: 1,000-3,000 words; average length: 1,500 words. Also publishes literary essays, literary criticism, poetry. Always comments on rejected mss.
How to Contact Query. Accepts submissions by e-mail, fax. Send SASE (or IRC) for return of ms or send

disposable copy of the ms and #10 SASE for reply only. Responds in 2-3 weeks to queries; 2-3 weeks to mss. Accepts simultaneous submissions. Sample copy online. Writer's guidelines online. Reviews fiction.

Payment/Terms Pays $120 maximum and 1 contributor's copy; additional copies $5. Pays 1 month following publication. Acquires first rights. Sponsors awards/contests.

Advice "A good introduction and a original slant on a common theme. Always read the competition rules and our guidelines."

$ WRITERS' JOURNAL, The Complete Writer's Magazine

Val-Tech Media, P.O. Box 394, Perham MN 56573-0394. (218)346-7921. Fax: (218)346-7924. E-mail: editor@wri tersjournal.com. Web site: www.writersjournal.com. *"Writers' Journal* is read by thousands of aspiring writers whose love of writing has taken them to the next step: Writing for money. We are an instructional manual giving writers the tools and information necessary to get their work published. We also print works by authors who have won our writing contests." Bimonthly. Estab. 1980. Circ. 26,000.

Needs "We only publish winners of our fiction contests—16 contests/year." Receives 200 contest entries mss/month. Publishes 5-7 mss/issue; 30-40 mss/year. **Publishes 100 new writers/year.** Also publishes poetry.

How to Contact Accepts contest submissions by postal mail only. Responds in 6 weeks to queries; 6 months to mss. Accepts unpublished simultaneous submissions. Sample copy for $5.

Payment/Terms Pays prize money on publication for one-time rights.

Book Publishers

I n this section, you will find many of the "big name" book publishers. Many of these publishers remain tough markets for new writers or for those whose work might be considered literary or experimental. Indeed, some only accept work from established authors, and then often only through an author's agent. Although having your novel published by one of the big commercial publishers listed in this section is difficult, it is not impossible. The trade magazine *Publishers Weekly* regularly features interviews with writers whose first novels are being released by top publishers. Many editors at large publishing houses find great satisfaction in publishing a writer's first novel.

On page 525, you'll find the publishing industry's "family tree," which maps out each of the large book publishing conglomerates' divisions, subsidiaries and imprints. Remember, most manuscripts are acquired by imprints, not their parent company, so avoid submitting to the conglomerates themselves. (For example, submit to Dutton or Berkley Books, not their parent Penguin.)

Also listed here are "small presses" publishing four or more titles annually. Included among them are independent presses, university presses and other nonprofit publishers. Introducing new writers to the reading public has become an increasingly important role of these smaller presses at a time when the large conglomerates are taking fewer chances on unknown writers. Many of the successful small presses listed in this section have built their reputations and their businesses in this way and have become known for publishing prize-winning fiction.

These smaller presses also tend to keep books in print longer than larger houses. And, since small presses publish a smaller number of books, each title is equally important to the publisher, and each is promoted in much the same way and with the same commitment. Editors also stay at small presses longer because they have more of a stake in the business— often they own the business. Many smaller book publishers are writers themselves and know firsthand the importance of a close editor-author or publisher-author relationship.

TYPES OF BOOK PUBLISHERS

Large or small, the publishers in this section publish books "for the trade." That is, unlike textbook, technical or scholarly publishers, trade publishers publish books to be sold to the general consumer through bookstores, chain stores or other retail outlets. Within the trade book field, however, there are a number of different types of books.

The easiest way to categorize books is by their physical appearance and the way they are marketed. Hardcover books are the more expensive editions of a book, sold through bookstores and carrying a price tag of around $20 and up. Trade paperbacks are soft-bound books, also sold mostly in bookstores, but they carry a more modest price tag of usually around $10 to $20. Today a lot of fiction is published in this form because it means a lower financial risk than hardcover.

Mass market paperbacks are another animal altogether. These are the smaller ''pocket-size'' books available at bookstores, grocery stores, drug stores, chain retail outlets, etc. Much genre or category fiction is published in this format. This area of the publishing industry is very open to the work of talented new writers who write in specific genres such as science fiction, romance and mystery.

At one time publishers could be easily identified and grouped by the type of books they produce. Today, however, the lines between hardcover and paperback books are blurred. Many publishers known for publishing hardcover books also publish trade paperbacks and have paperback imprints. This enables them to offer established authors (and a very few lucky newcomers) hard-soft deals in which their book comes out in both versions. Thanks to the mergers of the past decade, too, the same company may own several hardcover and paperback subsidiaries and imprints, even though their editorial focuses may remain separate.

CHOOSING A BOOK PUBLISHER

In addition to checking the bookstores and libraries for books by publishers that interest you, you may want to refer to the Category Index at the back of this book to find publishers divided by specific subject categories. The subjects listed in the Index are general. Read individual listings to find which subcategories interest a publisher. For example, you will find several romance publishers listed, but read the listings to find which type of romance is considered—gothic, contemporary, regency or futuristic. See You've Got a Story on page 2 for more on how to refine your list of potential markets.

The icons appearing before the names of the publishers will also help you in selecting a publisher. These codes are especially important in this section, because many of the publishing houses listed here require writers to submit through an agent. The ⬛ symbol indicates that a publisher accepts agented submissions only. A ⬛ icon identifies those that mostly publish established and agented authors, while a ⬜ points to publishers most open to new writers. See the inside front cover of this book for a complete list and explanations of symbols used in this book.

IN THE LISTINGS

As with other sections in this book, we identify new listings with a ⬛ symbol. In this section, most with this symbol are not new publishers, but instead are established publishers who were unable or decided not to list last year and are therefore new to this edition.

In addition to the ⬛ symbol indicating new listings, we include other symbols to help you in narrowing your search. English-speaking foreign markets are denoted by a ⬛ . The maple leaf symbol ⬛ identifies Canadian presses. If you are not a Canadian writer but are interested in a Canadian press, check the listing carefully. Many small presses in Canada receive grants and other funds from their provincial or national government and are, therefore, restricted to publishing Canadian authors.

We also include editorial comments set off by a bullet (●) within listings. This is where we include information about any special requirements or circumstances that will help you know even more about the publisher's needs and policies. The star ⬛ signals that this market is an imprint or division of a larger publisher. The ⬛ symbol identifies publishers who have recently received honors or awards for their books. The ⬛ denotes publishers who produce comics and graphic novels.

Each listing includes a summary of the editorial mission of the house, an overarching principle that ties together what they publish. Under the heading **Contact** we list one or more editors, often with their specific area of expertise.

Book editors asked us again this year to emphasize the importance of paying close attention to the **Needs** and **How to Contact** subheads of listings for book publishers. Unlike magazine editors who want to see complete manuscripts of short stories, most of the book publishers listed here ask that writers send a query letter with an outline and/or synopsis and several chapters of their novel. The Business of Fiction Writing, beginning on page 83 of this book, outlines how to prepare work to submit directly to a publisher.

There are no subsidy book publishers listed in *Novel & Short Story Writer's Market*. By subsidy, we mean any arrangement in which the writer is expected to pay all or part of the cost of producing, distributing and marketing his book. We feel a writer should not be asked to share in any cost of turning his manuscript into a book. All the book publishers listed here told us that they *do not charge writers* for publishing their work. **If any of the publishers listed here ask you to pay any part of publishing or marketing your manuscript, please let us know**. See our Complaint Procedure on the copyright page of this book.

A NOTE ABOUT AGENTS

Some publishers are willing to look at unsolicited submissions, but most feel having an agent is in the writer's best interest. In this section more than any other, you'll find a number of publishers who prefer submissions from agents. That's why we've included a section of agents open to submissions from fiction writers (page 155).

If you use the Internet or another resource to find an agent not listed in this book, be wary of any agents who charge large sums of money for reading a manuscript. Reading fees do not guarantee representation. Think of an agent as a potential business partner and feel free to ask tough questions about his or her credentials, experience and business practices.

Periodicals of Interest

For More Info

Check out issues of *Publishers Weekly* for publishing industry trade news in the U.S. and around the world or *Quill & Quire* for book publishing news in the Canadian book industry.

For more small presses see the *International Directory of Little Magazines and Small Presses* published by Dustbooks. To keep up with changes in the industry throughout the year, check issues of two small press trade publications: *Small Press Review* (also published by Dustbooks) and *Independent Publisher* (Jenkins Group, Inc.).

◢ ABSEY & CO.

23011 Northcrest Drive, Spring TX 77389. (281)257-2340. E-mail: abseyandco@aol.com. Web site: www.absey. com. **Contact:** Edward E. Wilson, publisher. "We are interested in book-length fiction of literary merit with a firm intended audience." Publishes hardcover, trade paperback and mass market paperback originals. **Published 3-5 debut authors within the last year.** Averages 6-10 total titles, 6-10 fiction titles/year.

Needs Juvenile, mainstream/contemporary, short story collections. Published *Where I'm From*, by George Ella Lyon; *Blast Man Standing*, by Robert V. Spelleri.

How to Contact Accepts unsolicited mss. Query with SASE. Responds in 3 months to queries; 9 months to mss. No simultaneous submissions, electronic submissions.

Terms Royalty and advance vary. Publishes ms 1 year after acceptance. Ms guidelines online.

Advice "Since we are a small, new press looking for good manuscripts with a firm intended audience, we tend to work closely and attentively with our authors. Many established authors who have been with the large New York houses have come to us to publish their work because we work closely with them."

◢ ACADEMY CHICAGO PUBLISHERS

363 W. Erie St., Suite 7E., Chicago IL 60610-3125. (312)751-7300. Fax: (312)751-7306. E-mail: info@academychi cago.com. Web site: www.academychicago.com. **Contact:** Anita Miller, senior editor. Estab. 1975. Midsize independent publisher. Publishes hardcover originals and trade paperback reprints. Averages 15 total titles/year.

Needs Historical, mainstream/contemporary, military/war, mystery. "We look for quality work, but we do not publish experimental, avant-garde novels." Biography, history, academic and anthologies. Only the most unusual mysteries, no private-eyes or thrillers. No explicit sex or violence. Serious fiction, no romance/adventure. "We will consider historical fiction that is well researched. No science fiction/fantasy, no religious/inspirational, no how-to, no cookbooks. In general, we are very conscious of women's roles. We publish very few children's books." Published *Clean Start*, by Patricia Margaret Page (first fiction); *Cutter's Island: Caesar in Captivity*, by Vincent Panella (first fiction, historical); *Murder at the Paniomic Games*, by Michael B. Edward.

How to Contact Accepts unsolicited mss. Do not submit by e-mail. Submit 3 sample chapter(s), synopsis. Accepts queries by mail. Include cover letter briefly describing the content of your work. Send SASE or IRC. "Manuscripts without envelopes will be discarded. *Mailers* are a *must* even from agents." Responds in 3 months to queries. No electronic submissions.

Terms Pays 7-10% royalty on wholesale price. Average advance: modest. Publishes ms 18 months after acceptance. Ms guidelines online.

Advice "At the moment we are swamped with manuscripts and anything under consideration can be under consideration for months."

◎ ACME PRESS

P.O. Box 1702, Westminster MD 21158-1702. (410)848-7577. **Contact:** (Ms.) E.G. Johnston, managing editor. Estab. 1991. "We operate on a part-time basis." Publishes hardcover and trade paperback originals. **Published some debut authors within the last year.** Averages 1-2 total titles/year.

Needs Humor. "We accept submissions on any subject as long as the material is humorous; prefer full-length novels. No cartoons or art (text only). No pornography, poetry, short stories or children's material." Published *She-Crab Soup* by Dawn Langley Simmons (fictional memoir); *Biting the Wall*, by J.M. Johnston (mystery); *SuperFan*, by Lyn A. Sherwood (football); and *Hearts of Gold*, by James Magorian (caper).

How to Contact Accepts unsolicited mss. Agented fiction 25%. Responds in 2 weeks to queries; 2 months to mss. Accepts simultaneous submissions. Always comments on rejected mss.

Terms Pays 25 author's copies and 50% of profits. Average advance: small. Publishes ms 1 year after acceptance. Book catalog and ms guidelines for #10 SASE.

◢ ◎ AGELESS PRESS

3759 Collins St., Sarasota FL 34232. E-mail: irishope@comcast.net. Web site: http://irisforrest.com. **Contact:** Iris Forrest, editor. Estab. 1992. Independent publisher. Publishes paperback originals. Books: acid-free paper; notched perfect binding; no illustrations. Averages 1 total title/year.

Needs Experimental, fantasy, humor, literary, mainstream/contemporary, mystery, new age/mystic, science fiction, short story collections, thriller/espionage. Looking for material "based on personal computer experiences." Stories selected by editor. Published *Computer Legends, Lies & Lore*, by various (anthology); and *Computer Tales of Fact and Fantasy*, by various (anthology).

How to Contact Does not accept unsolicited mss. Query with SASE. Accepts queries by e-mail, fax, mail. Responds in 1 week to queries; 1 week to mss. Accepts simultaneous submissions, electronic submissions, submissions on disk. Sometimes comments on rejected mss.

Terms Average advance: negotiable. Publishes ms 6-12 months after acceptance.
Advice "Query! Don't send work without a query!"

ALGONQUIN BOOKS OF CHAPEL HILL
Workman Publishing, P.O. Box 2225, Chapel Hill NC 27515-2225. (919)967-0108. Web site: www.algonquin.c om. **Contact:** Editorial Department. Publishes hardcover originals. Averages 24 total titles/year.
Needs Literary fiction and nonfiction, cookbooks and lifestyle books (about family, animals, food, flowers, adventure, and other topics of interest). No poetry, genre fiction (romance, science fiction, etc.) or children's books. Recently published *Saving the World*, by Julia Alvarez; *Which Brings Me to You*, by Steve Almond and Julianna Baggott; *Hope and Other Dangerous Pursuits*, by Laila Lalami.
How to Contact Send a 20-page sample of your work, along with a cover letter, SASE, and a check for return postage (if you wish to have your mss returned). No phone, e-mail or fax queries or submissions.
Terms Ms guidelines online.

ANVIL PRESS
278 East First Avenue, Vancouver BC V5T 1A6 Canada. (604)876-8710. Fax: (604)879-2667. E-mail: info@anvilp ress.com. Web site: www.anvilpress.com. **Contact:** Brian Kaufman, publisher. Estab. 1988. "Three-person operation with volunteer editorial board." Publishes trade paperback originals. Canadian authors *only*. Books: offset or web printing; perfect bound. **Published some debut authors within the last year.** Averages 8-10 total titles/year.
Needs Experimental, literary, short story collections. Contemporary, modern literature—no formulaic or genre. Published *Stolen*, by Annette Lapointe (novel); *Suburban Pornography*, by Matthew Firth (stories); *A Small Dog Barking*, by Robert Strandquist (stories); *Cusp/Detritus*, by Catherine Owen and Karen Moe (poetry/photographs).
How to Contact Accepts unsolicited mss, or query with SASE. Include estimated word count, brief bio. Send SASE for return of ms or send a disposable ms and SASE for reply only. Responds in 2 months to queries; 6 months to mss. Accepts simultaneous submissions.
Terms Pays 15% royalty on net receipts. Average advance: $500. Publishes ms 8 months after acceptance. Book catalog for 9×12 SAE with 2 first-class stamps. Ms guidelines online.
Advice "We are only interested in writing that is progressive in some way—form, content. We want contemporary fiction from serious writers who intend to be around for a while and be a name people will know in years to come. Read back titles, look through our catalog before submitting."

ARCADE PUBLISHING
116 John St., Suite 2810, New York NY 10038. (212)475-2633. **Contact:** Richard Seaver, Jeannette Seaver, Cal Barksdale, Casey Ebro, and James Jayo. Estab. 1988. Independent publisher. Publishes hardcover originals, trade paperback reprints. Books: 50-55 lb. paper; notch, perfect bound; illustrations. **Published some debut authors within the last year.** Averages 35 total titles, 10 fiction titles/year. Distributes titles through Hachette Book Group USA.
Needs Ethnic, literary, mainstream/contemporary, short story collections. Published *Trying to Save Piggy Sneed*, by John Irving; *It Might Have Been What He Said*, by Eden Collinsworth; *Music of a Life*, by Andrei Makine; *The Last Song of Dusk*, by Siddharth Dhanvant Shanghvi; *Bibliophilia*, by Michael Griffith.
How to Contact Does not accept unsolicited mss. *Agented submissions only.* Agented fiction 100%. Responds in 1 month to queries; 4 months to mss.
Terms Pays royalty on retail price, 10 author's copies. Offers advance. Publishes ms within 18 months after acceptance. Ms guidelines for #10 SASE.

ARIEL STARR PRODUCTIONS, LTD.
P.O. Box 17, Demarest NJ 07627. E-mail: darkbird@aol.com. Cynthia Soroka, president. Estab. 1991. Publishes paperback originals. **Published 2 debut authors within the last year.**
How to Contact Submit outline, 1 sample chapter(s). Accepts queries by e-mail, mail. Include brief bio. Send SASE or IRC. Responds in 6 weeks to queries; 4 months to mss. Sometimes comments on rejected mss.
Terms Publishes ms one year after acceptance.

ARSENAL PULP PRESS
341 Water Street, Suite 200, Vancouver BC V6B 1B8 Canada. (604)687-4233. Fax: (604)687-4283. Web site: www.arsenalpulp.com. **Contact:** Linda Field, editor. Estab. 1980. Literary press. Publishes hardcover and trade paperback originals, and trade paperback reprints. **Published some debut authors within the last year.** Plans 1,500 first novels this year. Averages 20 total titles/year. Distributes titles through Whitecap Books (Canada) and Consortium (U.S.). Promotes titles through reviews, excerpts and print advertising.

Needs Gay/lesbian, literary, multicultural, regional (British Columbia), cultural studies, pop culture, political/sociological issues. No poetry.

How to Contact Accepts unsolicited mss. Submit outline, 2-3 sample chapter(s), synopsis. Include list of publishing credits. Send copy of ms and SASE. Agented fiction 10%. Responds in 2 months to queries; 4 months to mss. Accepts simultaneous submissions. Sometimes comments on rejected mss.

Terms Publishes ms 1 year after acceptance. Book catalog for 9 × 12 SAE with 2 first-class stamps or online. Ms guidelines for #10 SASE or online.

Advice "We are not currently considering mss by non-Canadian writers."

ARTE PUBLICO PRESS

University of Houston, 452 Cullen Performance Hall, Houston TX 77204-2004. Fax: (713)743-3080. Web site: www.artepublicopress.com. **Contact:** Dr. Nicolas Kanellos, editor. Estab. 1979. "Small press devoted to the publication of contemporary U.S.-Hispanic literature." Publishes hardcover originals, trade paperback originals and reprints. Averages 36 total titles/year.

- Arte Publico Press is the oldest and largest publisher of Hispanic literature for children and adults in the United States.

Imprint(s) Pinata Books featuring children's and young adult literature by U.S.-Hispanic writers.

Needs Ethnic, literary, mainstream/contemporary, written by U.S.-Hispanic authors. Published *Project Death*, by Richard Bertematti (novel, mystery); *A Perfect Silence*, by Alba Ambert; *Song of the Hummingbird*, by Graciela Limón; *Little Havana Blues: A Cuban-American Literature Anthology*.

How to Contact Accepts unsolicited mss. Query with SASE or submit 2 sample chapter(s), synopsis or submit complete ms. Agented fiction 1%. Responds in 2-4 months to queries; 3-6 months to mss. Accepts simultaneous submissions. Sometimes comments on rejected mss.

Terms Pays 10% royalty on wholesale price. Provides 20 author's copies; 40% discount on subsequent copies. Average advance: $1,000-3,000. Publishes ms 2 years after acceptance. Ms guidelines online.

Advice "Include cover letter in which you 'sell' your book—why should we publish the book, who will want to read it, why does it matter, etc."

AUNT LUTE BOOKS

P.O. Box 410687, San Francisco CA 94141. (415)826-1300. Fax: (415)826-8300. E-mail: books@auntlute.com. Web site: www.auntlute.com. **Contact:** Shahara Godfrey, first reader. Small feminist and women-of-color press. Publishes hardcover and paperback originals. Averages 4 total titles/year.

Needs Ethnic, feminist, lesbian.

How to Contact Accepts unsolicited mss. Query with SASE or submit outline, sample chapter(s), synopsis. Send SASE or IRC. Responds in 4 months to mss.

Terms Pays royalty.

Advice "We seek manuscripts, both fiction and nonfiction, by women from a variety of cultures, ethnic backgrounds and subcultures; women who are self-aware and who, in the face of all contradictory evidence, are still hopeful that the world can reserve a place of respect for each woman in it. We seek work that explores the specificities of the worlds from which we come, and which examines the intersections between the borders which we all inhabit."

AVALON BOOKS

Thomas Bouregy & Co., Inc., 160 Madison Ave., 5th Floor, New York NY 10016. (212)598-0222. Fax: (212)979-1862. E-mail: editorial@avalonbooks.com. Web site: www.avalonbooks.com. **Contact:** Erin Cartwright-Niumata, editorial director; Faith Black, associate editor. Estab. 1950. Publishes hardcover originals. **Published some debut authors within the last year.** Averages 60 total titles/year. Distributes titles through Baker & Taylor, libraries, Barnes&Noble.com and Amazon.com. Promotes titles through *Library Journal*, *Booklist*, *Publisher's Weekly* and local papers.

Needs Historical (romance), mystery, contemporary romance, western. "We publish wholesome contemporary romances, mysteries, historical romances and westerns. Our books are read by adults as well as teenagers, and the characters are all adults. All mysteries are contemporary. We publish contemporary romances (four every two months), historical romances (two every two months), mysteries (two every two months) and westerns (two every two months). Submit first 3 sample chapters, a 2-3 page synopsis and SASE. The manuscripts should be between 40,000 to 70,000 words. Manuscripts that are too long will not be considered. Time period and setting are the author's preference. The historical romances will maintain the high level of reading expected by our readers. The books shall be wholesome fiction, without graphic sex, violence or strong language." Published *Death Superior*, by Matthew Williams (mystery); *A Matter of Motive*, by Michael Williams (mystery); *Christmas in Carol*, by Sheila Robins (romantic comedy); *Night Calls*, by Holly Jacobs (romantic comedy).

How to Contact Does not accept unsolicited mss. Query with SASE or IRC. Responds in 1 month to queries; 6-10 months to mss.

Terms Average advance: $1,000. Publishes ms 8-12 months after acceptance. Ms guidelines online.

[N] [★] [✎] [◎] B & H PUBLISHING

LifeWay Christian Resources, 127 Ninth Ave. N., Nashville TN 37234. (615)251-2438. Fax: (615)251-3752. Web site: www.bhpublishinggroup.com/Fiction. **Contact:** David Webb, executive editor. Estab. 1934. Publishes hardcover and paperback originals. B & H is the book division of LifeWay, the world's largest publisher of Christian materials. Averages 90 total titles, 20 fiction titles/year. Member: ECPA.

Needs Religious/inspirational (contemporary women's fiction, suspense, romance, thriller, historical romance). Engaging stories told from a Christian worldview. Published *A Spring Frost*, by Jenifer O'Neill (contemporary); *A Man of Temperance*, by Gilbert Morris (historical); *The Assassins*, by Oliver North (adventure); and *Snow Angel*, by Jamie Carie.

How to Contact Does not accept unsolicited mss. Query with SASE. Accepts queries by e-mail. Include synopsis, estimated word count, brief bio, list of publishing credits. Agented fiction 75%. Responds in 3 months to queries. Accepts simultaneous submissions.

Terms Pays negotiable royalty. Publishes ms 10-12 months after acceptance. Ms guidelines for #10 SASE.

[✎] [◎] BAEN PUBLISHING ENTERPRISES

P.O. Box 1403, Riverdale NY 10471-0671. (718)548-3100. E-mail: slush@baen.com. Web site: www.baen.com. **Contact:** Toni Weisskopf, publisher. Estab. 1983. "We publish books at the heart of science fiction and fantasy." Publishes hardcover, trade paperback and mass market paperback originals and reprints. **Published some debut authors within the last year.** Plans 2-3 first novels this year. Averages 120 total titles, 120 fiction titles/year. Distributes titles through Simon & Schuster.

Imprint(s) Baen Science Fiction and Baen Fantasy.

Needs Fantasy, science fiction. Interested in science fiction novels (based on real science) and fantasy novels "that at least strive for originality." Length: 100,00-130,000 words. Published *In Fury Born*, by David Weber; *Music to My Sorrow*, by Mercedes Lackey and Rosemary Edghill; *Ghost*, by John Ringo.

How to Contact Submit synopsis and complete ms. "Electronic submissions are strongly preferred. Attach manuscript as a Rich Text Format (.rtf) file. Any other format will not be considered." Additional submission guidelines online. Include estimated word count, brief bio. Send SASE or IRC. Responds in 9-12 months. No simultaneous submissions. Sometimes comments on rejected mss.

Terms Pays royalty on retail price. Offers advance. Ms guidelines online.

Advice "Keep an eye and a firm hand on the overall story you are telling. Style is important but less important than plot. Good style, like good breeding, never calls attention to itself. Read *Writing to the Point*, by Algis Budrys. We like to maintain long-term relationships with authors."

[N] [✎] [◎] BAKER BOOKS

Baker Book House Company, P.O. Box 6287, Grand Rapids MI 49516-6287. (616)676-9185. Fax: (616)676-2315. Web site: www.bakerbooks.com. **Contact:** Jeanette Thomason, special projects editor (mystery, literary, women's fiction); Lonnie Hull DuPont, editoral director (all genres); Vicki Crumpton, aquisitions editor (all genres). Estab. 1939. "Midsize publisher of work that interests Christians." Publishes hardcover and trade paperback originals and trade paperback reprints. Books: web offset print. Plans 5 first novels this year. Averages 200 total titles/year. Distributes titles through Ingram and Spring Arbor into both CBA and ABA markets world-wide.

Needs Literary, mainstream/contemporary, mystery, picture books, religious. "We are mainly seeking fiction of two genres: contemporary women's fiction and mystery." Published *Praise Jerusalem!* and *Resting in the Bosom of the Lamb*, by Augusta Trobaugh (contemporary women's fiction); *Touches the Sky*, by James Schaap (western, literary); and *Face to Face*, by Linda Dorrell (mystery); *Flabbergasted*, by Ray Blackston; *The Fisherman*, by Larry Huntsberger.

How to Contact Does not accept unsolicited mss.

Terms Pays 14% royalty on net receipts. Offers advance. Publishes ms within 1 year after acceptance. Ms guidelines for #10 SASE.

Advice "We are not interested in historical fiction, romances, science fiction, biblical narratives or spiritual warfare novels. Do not call to 'pass by' your idea."

[A] [★] BALLANTINE BOOKS

Random House, Inc., 1745 Broadway, New York NY 10019. (212)782-9000. E-mail: bfi@randomhouse.com. Web site: www.randomhouse.com/BB. **Contact:** Julia Cheiffetz, editor. Estab. 1952. "Ballantine's list encompasses a large, diverse offering in a variety of formats." Publishes hardcover, trade paperback, mass market paperback originals

Imprint(s) Ballantine Books; Del Ray; Fawcett (mystery line); Ivy (romance); The Modern Library; One World; Strivers Row; Presidio Press; Random House Trade Paperbacks; Villard Books.

Needs Confession, ethnic, fantasy, feminist, gay/lesbian, historical, humor, literary, mainstream/contemporary (women's), military/war, multicultural, mystery, romance, short story collections, spiritual, suspense, general fiction.

How to Contact *Agented submissions only.*

Terms Pays 8-15% royalty. Average advance: variable. Ms guidelines online.

🅰 🕢 BANCROFT PRESS

P.O. Box 65360, Baltimore MD 21209-9945. (410)358-0658. Fax: (410)764-1967. Web site: www.bancroftpress.com. **Contact:** Bruce Bortz, publisher (health, investments, politics, history, humor); Fiction Editor (literary novels, mystery/thrillers, young adult). "Small independent press publishing literary and commercial fiction, often by journalists." Publishes hardcover and trade paperback originals. Also packages books for other publishers (no fee to authors). **Published 2 debut authors within the last year.** Plans several first novels this year. Averages 4 total titles, 2-4 fiction titles/year.

• *The Re-Appearance of Sam Webber*, by Scott Fugua is an ALEX Award winner.

Needs Ethnic (general), family saga, feminist, gay/lesbian, glitz, historical, humor, lesbian, literary, mainstream/contemporary, military/war, mystery (amateur sleuth, cozy, police procedural, private eye/hardboiled), new age/mystic, regional, science fiction (hard science/technological, soft/sociological), thriller/espionage, young adult (historical, problem novels, series. "Our No. 1 priority is publishing books appropriate for young adults, ages 10-18. All quality books on any subject that fit that category will be considered." Published *Those Who Trespass*, by Bill O'Reilly (thriller); *The Re-Appearance of Sam Webber*, by Scott Fugua (literary); and *Malicious Intent*, by Mike Walker (Hollywood).

How to Contact Accepts unsolicited mss. Query with SASE or submit outline, 2 sample chapter(s), synopsis, by mail or e-mail or submit complete ms. Accepts queries by e-mail, fax. Include brief bio, list of publishing credits. Send SASE for return of ms or send a disposable ms and SASE for reply only. Agented fiction 100%. Responds in 6-12 months to mss. Accepts simultaneous submissions. Sometimes comments on rejected mss.

Terms Pays various royalties on retail price. Average advance: $750. Publishes ms up to 3 years after acceptance. Ms guidelines online.

Advice "Be patient, send a sample, know your book's audience."

🅰 🕱 BANTAM DELL PUBLISHING GROUP

Random House, Inc., 1745 Broadway, New York NY 10019. (212)782-9000. Fax: (212)782-8890. Web site: www.bantamdell.com. Estab. 1945. "In addition to being the nation's largest mass market paperback publisher, Bantam publishes a select yet diverse hardcover list." Publishes hardcover, trade paperback and mass market paperback originals; mass market paperback reprints. Averages 350 total titles/year.

Imprint(s) Bantam Hardcover; Bantam Trade Paperback; Bantam Mass Market; Crimeline; Dell; Delta; Domain; DTP; Delacorte Press; The Dial Press; Fanfare; Island; Spectra.

Needs Adventure, fantasy, horror.

How to Contact Agented submissions only.

Terms Offers advance. Publishes ms 1 year after acceptance.

🅰 🕱 🕎 BANTAM DOUBLEDAY DELL BOOKS FOR YOUNG READERS

Random House Children's Publishing, Random House, Inc., 1745 Broadway, New York NY 10019. (212)782-9000. Fax: (212)782-8234. Web site: www.randomhouse.com/kids. **Contact:** Michelle Poplof, editorial director. Publishes hardcover, trade paperback and mass market paperback series originals, trade paperback reprints. Averages 300 total titles/year.

• *Bud, Not Buddy*, by Christopher Paul Curtis won the Newberry Medal and the Coretta Scott King Award.

Imprint(s) Delacorte Books for Young Readers; Doubleday Books for Young Readers; Laurel Leaf; Skylark; Starfire; Yearling Books.

Needs Adventure, fantasy, historical, humor, juvenile, mainstream/contemporary, mystery, picture books, suspense, chapter books, middle-grade. Published *Bud, Not Buddy*, by Christopher Paul Curtis; *The Sisterhood of the Traveling Pants*, by Ann Brashares.

How to Contact Does not accept unsolicited mss. *Agented submissions only.*

Terms Pays royalty. Average advance: varied. Publishes ms 2 years after acceptance. Book catalog for 9×12 SASE.

◎ BARBOUR PUBLISHING, INC.

P.O. Box 719, Uhrichsville OH 44683. (740)922-6045. Fax: (740)922-5948. E-mail: editors@barbourbooks.com. Web site: www.barbourpublishing.com. **Contact:** Rebecca Germany, senior editor (fiction). Estab. 1981. Publishes hardcover, trade paperback and mass market paperback originals and reprints. **Published 40% debut authors within the last year.** Averages 250 total titles/year.

Imprint(s) Heartsong Presents; Barbour Books and Heartsong Presents Mysteries.

Needs Historical, contemporary, religious, romance, western, mystery. All submissions must be Christian mss. "Heartsong romance is 'sweet'—no sex, no bad language. All stories must have Christian faith as an underlying basis. Common writer's mistakes are a sketchy proposal, an unbelieveable story, and a story that doesn't fit our guidelines for inspirational romances." Published *The Storekeeper's Daughter*, by Wanda E. Brunstetter (fiction).

How to Contact Submit 3 sample chapter(s), synopsis by e-mail. Responds in 3 months to mss. Accepts simultaneous submissions.

Terms Pays 8-16% royalty on net price or makes outright purchase of $1,000-5,000. Average advance: $1,000-8,000. Publishes ms 1-2 years after acceptance. Book catalog online or for 9×12 SAE with 2 first-class stamps; ms guidelines for #10 SASE or online.

Advice "Audience is evangelical/Christian conservative, non-denominational, young and old. We're looking for *great concepts*, not necessarily a big name author or agent. We want to publish books with mass appeal."

◎ BAREFOOT BOOKS

2067 Massachusetts Avenue, Cambridge MA 02140. Web site: www.barefootbooks.com. **Contact:** Submissions editor. Publishes hardcover and trade paperback originals. **Published 35% debut authors within the last year.** Averages 30 total titles/year.

Needs Juvenile. Barefoot Books only publishes children's picture books and anthologies of folktales. "We do not publish novels. We do accept query letters but prefer to receive full manuscripts." *The Prince's Bedtime*, by Joanne Oppenheim (picture book); *The Barefoot Book of Fairy Tales*, by Malachy Doyle (illustrated anthology).

How to Contact Full ms with SASE. Responds in 4 months to mss. Accepts simultaneous submissions. No phone calls, or e-mails, please.

Terms Pays 2½-5% royalty on retail price. Offers advance. Publishes ms 2 years after acceptance. Ms guidelines online.

Advice "Our audience is made up of children and parents, teachers and students of many different ages and cultures. Since we are a small publisher and we definitely publish for a 'niche' market, it is helpful to look at our books and our Web site before submitting, to see if your book would fit into our list."

◯ ◎ BARKING DOG BOOKS

758 Peralta Avenue, Berkeley CA 94708. (510)527-6274. E-mail: barkingdogbooks@yahoo.com. **Contact:** Michael Mercer, editor. Estab. 1996. "Focuses on expatriate life, especially in Mexico, and America viewed from exile." Publishes paperback originals. Books: quality paper; offset printing; perfect bound. Average print order: 1,000. Titles distributed through Sunbelt Publications.

Needs Ethnic (Mexican), experimental, historical, humor, literary, regional (Mexico/Southwest), short story collections, expatriate life. Published *Bandidos*, by Michael Mercer.

How to Contact Accepts unsolicited mss. Submit outline, 3 sample chapter(s). Accepts queries by mail. Include brief bio, list of publishing credits. Send copy of ms and SASE. Responds in 2 months to queries; 6 months to mss. Accepts simultaneous submissions. No submissions on disk. Sometimes comments on rejected mss.

Terms Publishes ms 1 year after acceptance.

Advice "Don't try to write for a market; write for yourself, be authentic, and trust readers to gravitate to an authentic voice."

◎ BARRON'S EDUCATIONAL SERIES, INC.

250 Wireless Blvd., Hauppauge NY 11788. (631)434-3311. Fax: (631)434-3394. E-mail: waynebarr@barronseduc.com. Web site: barronseduc.com. **Contact:** Wayne Barr, director of acquisitions. Estab. 1941. Publishes hardcover, paperback and mass market originals and software. **Published 20% debut authors within the last year.** Averages 400 total titles/year.

Needs Middle grade, YA.

How to Contact Submit sample chapter(s), synopsis. Responds in 3 months to queries; 8 months to mss. Accepts simultaneous submissions. E-mail queries only, no attachments.

Terms Pays 12-13% royalty on net receipts. Average advance: $3-4,000. Publishes ms 18 months after acceptance. Ms queries online.

Advice "The writer has the best chance of selling us a book that will fit into one of our series. Children's books have less chance for acceptance because of the glut of submissions. SASE must be included for the return of all materials. Please be patient for replies.''

● FREDERIC C. BEIL, PUBLISHER, INC.

609 Whitaker St., Savannah GA 31401. (912)233-2446. Fax: (912)233-6456. Web site: www.beil.com. **Contact:** Frederic C. Beil III, president; Mary Ann Bowman, editor. Estab. 1982. ''Our objectives are (1) to offer to the reading public carefully selected texts of lasting value; (2) to adhere to high standards in the choice of materials and bookmaking craftsmanship; (3) to produce books that exemplify good taste in format and design; and (4) to maintain the lowest cost consistent with quality.'' Publishes hardcover originals and reprints. Books: acid-free paper; letterpress and offset printing; Smyth-sewn, hardcover binding; illustrations. Plans 3 first novels this year. Averages 10 total titles, 4 fiction titles/year.

Imprint(s) The Sandstone Press, Hypermedia, Inc.

Needs Historical, literary, regional, short story collections, biography. Published *Dancing by The River*, by Marlin Barton; *Joseph Jefferson*, by Arthur Bloom (biography); *The Invisible Country*, by H.E. Francis (fiction).

How to Contact Does not accept unsolicited mss. Query with SASE. Responds in 2 weeks to queries. Accepts simultaneous submissions.

Terms Pays 7½% royalty on retail price. Publishes ms 20 months after acceptance.

Advice ''Write about what you love.''

● ● BEN BELLA BOOKS

6440 N. Central Expy Suite 508, Dallas TX 75206. (214)750-3600. Fax: (214)750-3645. E-mail: leah@benbellaboo ks.com. Web site: www.benbellabooks.com. **Contact:** Leah Wilson, editor. Estab. 2001. Small, growing independent publisher specializing in popular culture, smart nonfiction and science fiction; our fiction is largely reprints or by established authors. Publishes hardcover and paperback originals and paperback reprints. Averages 30 total titles.

Needs Currently not accepting fiction submissions.

● ● THE BERKLEY PUBLISHING GROUP

Penguin Putnam, Inc., 375 Hudson St., New York NY 10014. (212)366-2000. E-mail: online@penguinputnam.c om. Web site: www.penguinputnam.com. Estab. 1954. ''Berkley is proud to publish in paperback some of the country's most significant best-selling authors.'' Publishes paperback and mass market originals and reprints. Averages approximately 800 total titles/year.

Imprint(s) Ace Books, Berkley Books, HP Books, Perigee, Riverhead Books.

Needs Adventure, historical, literary, mystery, romance, spiritual, suspense, western, young adult.

How to Contact Does not accept unsolicited mss.

Terms Pays 4-15% royalty on retail price. Offers advance. Publishes ms 2 years after acceptance.

● ● BETHANY HOUSE PUBLISHERS

11400 Hampshire Ave. S., Minneapolis MN 55438. (952)829-2500. Fax: (952)996-1304. Web site: www.bethany house.com. Estab. 1956. ''The purpose of Bethany House Publisher's publishing program is to relate biblical truth to all areas of life—whether in the framework of a well-told story, of a challenging book for spiritual growth, or of a Bible reference work.'' Publishes hardcover and trade paperback originals, mass market paperback reprints. Averages 90-100 total titles/year.

Needs Adventure, children's/juvenile, historical, young adult. Published *The Still of Night*, by Kristen Heitzmann (fiction).

How to Contact Does not accept unsolicited mss. Accepts queries only by fax. Accepts simultaneous submissions. Query guidelines online.

Terms Pays negotiable royalty on net price. Average advance: negotiable. Publishes ms 1 year after acceptance.

● BIRCH BROOK PRESS

P.O. Box 81, Delhi NY 13753. Fax: (607)746-7453. Web site: www.birchbrookpress.info. **Contact:** Tom Tolnay, publisher. Estab. 1982. Small publisher of popular culture and literary titles in mostly handcrafted letterpress editions. Specializes in fiction anthologies with specific theme, and an occasional novella. ''Not a good market for full-length novels.'' Publishes hardcover and trade paperback originals. Books: 80 lb. vellum paper; letterpress printing; wood engraving illustrations. Averages 6 total titles, 2 fiction titles/year. Member, Small Press Center, Publishers Marketing Association, Academy of American Poets. Distributes titles through Baker and Taylor, Barnes&Noble.com, Amazon.com, Gazelle Book Services in Europe, Multicultural Books in Canada. Promotes titles through Web site, catalogs, direct mail and group ads.

Imprint(s) Birch Brook Press, Persephone Press and Birch Brook Impressions.

Needs Literary, regional (Adirondacks), popular culture, special interest (flyfishing, baseball, books about books, outdoors). "Mostly we do anthologies around a particular theme generated inhouse. We make specific calls for fiction when we are doing an anthology." Published *Magic and Madness in the Library* (fiction collection); *Life & Death of a Book*, by William MacAdams; *Kilimanjaro Burning*, by John B. Robinson; *A Punk in Gallows America*, by P.W. Fox; *White Buffalo*, by Peter Skinner; *The Suspense of Loneliness* (anthology); *Tales for the Trail* (anthology); *Sexy Sixties*, by Harry Smith; *Human/Nature*, by Lance Lee; *Jack's Beans*, by Tom Smith.

How to Contact Query with SASE or submit sample chapter(s), synopsis. Responds in 2 months to queries. Accepts simultaneous submissions. Sometimes comments on rejected mss.

Terms Modest flat fee on anthologies. Usually publishes ms 10-18 months after acceptance. Ms guidelines for #10 SASE.

Advice "Write well on subjects of interest to BBP, such as outdoors, flyfishing, baseball, music, literary novellas, books about books."

BKMK PRESS

University of Missouri-Kansas City, 5101 Rockhill Rd., Kansas City MO 64110-2499. (816)235-2558. Fax: (816)235-2611. E-mail: bkmk@umkc.edu. Web site: www.umkc.edu/bkmk. Estab. 1971. Publishes trade paperback originals. Averages 4 total titles/year.

Needs Literary, short story collections.

How to Contact Query with SASE or submit 2-3 sample stories. Responds in 8 months to mss. Accepts simultaneous submissions.

Terms Pays 10% royalty on wholesale price. Publishes ms 1 year after acceptance. Ms guidelines online.

🄰 🌐 🄲 BL PUBLISHING

Games Workshop Ltd., Willow Road, Lenton, Nottingham NG7 2WS. (+44)(115)900-4100. Fax: (+44)(115)900-4111. E-mail: publishing@games-workshop.co.uk. Web site: www.blacklibrary.com. **Contact:** Christian Dunn. Estab. 1997. Publishes paperback originals. Published 4 new writers last year. Averages 85 total titles/year; 85 fiction titles/year.

Imprint(s) Black Library, Solaris.

Needs Fantasy (space fantasy, sword and sorcery), horror (dark fantasy, futuristic), science fiction (hard science/technological, soft/sociological), short story collection, young adult/teen (fantasy/science fiction, horror). Published *Salvation*, by CS Goto (science fiction); *The Daemon's Curse*, by Dan Abnett (fantasy); *Fifteen Hours*, by Mitchel Scanlon (science fiction).

How to Contact Submit through agent only. Accepts queries by snail mail, e-mail. Include brief bio, list of publishing credits. Send SASE or IRC for return of ms or disposable copy of ms and SASE/IRC for reply only. Agented fiction: 5%. Responds to mss in 3 months. No unsolicited mss. Considers simultaneous submissions, e-mail submissions. Rarely critiques/comments on rejected mss.

Terms Sends pre-production galleys to author. Writer's guidelines on Web site.

Advice "Please check our Web site."

🄽 🄲 🅈 BLACK HERON PRESS

P.O. Box 95676, Seattle WA 98145. Web site: www.blackheronpress.com. **Contact:** Jerry Gold, publisher. Estab. 1984. Two-person operation; no immediate plans to expand. "We're known for literary fiction. We've done several Vietnam titles and several surrealistic fictions." Publishes hardcover and trade paperback originals. **Published 1-2 debut authors within the last year.** Averages 4 total titles, 4 fiction titles/year.

• Eight books published by Black Heron Press have won regional awards.

Needs Experimental, humor, literary, mainstream/contemporary, science fiction (surrealism), war novels (literary). Published *Infinite Kindness*, by Laurie Blauner (historical fiction); and *Moses in Sinai*, by Simone Zelitch (historical fiction).

How to Contact Query with SASE. Responds in 3 months to queries; 6 months to mss. Accepts simultaneous submissions.

Terms Pays 8% royalty on retail price.

Advice "A query letter should tell me: 1) number of words; 2) number of pages; 3) if ms is available on disk; 4) if parts of novel have been published; 5) if so, where? And at least scan some of our books in a bookstore or library. Most submissions we get have come to the wrong press."

🄲 🄾 JOHN F. BLAIR, PUBLISHER

1406 Plaza Dr., Winston-Salem NC 27103-1470. (336)768-1374. Fax: (336)768-9194. Web site: www.blairpub.com. **Contact:** Carolyn Sakowski, president. Estab. 1954. Small, independent publisher. Publishes hardcover originals and trade paperbacks. Books: Acid-free paper; offset printing; illustrations. Averages 20 total titles/year.

Needs Prefers regional material dealing with southeastern U.S. ''We publish one work of fiction per season relating to the Southeastern U.S. Our editorial focus concentrates mostly on nonfiction.'' Published *The Minotaur Takes a Cigarette Break*, by Steven Sherrill; *Rocks That Float*, by Kathy Steele.

How to Contact Accepts unsolicited mss. Query with SASE or submit complete ms with SASE or IRC. Responds in 3 months to queries. Accepts simultaneous submissions.

Terms Royalty negotiable. Offers advance. Publishes ms 18 months after acceptance. Book catalog for 9×12 SAE with 5 first-class stamps. Ms guidelines online.

Advice ''We are primarily interested in nonfiction titles. Most of our titles have a tie-in with North Carolina or the southeastern United States, we do not accept short-story collections. Please enclose a cover letter and outline with the manuscript. We prefer to review queries before we are sent complete manuscripts. Queries should include an approximate word count.''

BLEAK HOUSE BOOKS

923 Williamson St., Madison WI 53703. (608)259-8370. Web site: www.bleakhousebooks.com. Benjamin Le-Roy, publisher. Estab. 1995. Publisher hardcover and paperback originals. Averages 15-20 titles annually.

Needs Mysteries and literary fiction. ''Good psychological engagement. We aren't looking for big budget special effects and car chases. The best part of the story isn't in the distractions, it's in the heart. Characters need to be well drawn. We don't want formula fiction. We don't want rehashes of CSI. We don't want unqualified 'experts' writing books with plot holes. We don't want authors who are so married to their words that they can't see when something doesn't work.'' Published *The Blood Knot*, by John Galligan; *Chasing the Wolf*, by Nathan Singer; *Provincetown Follies: Bangkok Blues*, by Randall Peffer; *Hardboiled Brooklyn*, edited by Reed Farrel Coleman; *Hose Monkey*, by Tony Spinosa.

How to Contact Does not accept unsolicited mss. Any unsolicited mss we receive will be recycled without ever being read. Query with SASE. We accept queries during January, February, July and August. Materials received in any other month will be returned unopened and unread. Include estimated word count, brief bio, list of publishing credits. Agented fiction 75%. ''Responds as fast as we can to queries. Depending on when we receive them, it may take awhile. Same holds true for submitted manuscripts, but we'll keep you abreast of what's going on when we know it.'' Responds in 2 weeks to queries; 2 months to mss. Accepts simultaneous submissions. No electronic submissions. Check Web site for up-to-date guidelines.

Terms All contracts negotiable depending on author, market viability, etc. Our average royalty rate is somewhere between 7.5-15% depending on hardcover/paperback, print run, and many other factors. Advances range from $500-$10,000. Publishes ms 12-18 months after acceptance.

Advice ''We've grown from a two book a year publishing house to doing 20-25 books a year (combined with our sister company, Intrigue Press). We're still willing to take a chance on first-time authors with extraordinary books. We're still willing to take a chance on offbeat fiction. We are very busy in our office and sometimes our response time isn't as fast as we'd like it to be. But, between working with the books in house or looking at submissions, we feel it's very important to take care of our family of authors first. Please, if you value your work and you are serious about being published, do not send out first drafts. Edit your book. Then edit it again. Please also understand that for a book to be successful, the author and the publisher (and sometimes the agent) have to work together as a team. Good publishers need good writers as much as good writers need good publishers. It's a two-way street. Best of luck and keep writing.''

BOOKS FOR ALL TIMES, INC.

P.O. Box 202, Warrenton VA 20188. Web site: www.bfat.com. **Contact:** Joe David, publisher/editor. Estab. 1981. One-man operation. Publishes paperback originals.

Needs Literary, mainstream/contemporary, short story collections. ''No novels at the moment; hopeful, though, of publishing a collection of quality short stories. No popular fiction or material easily published by the major or minor houses specializing in mindless entertainment. Only interested in stories of the Victor Hugo or Sinclair Lewis quality.''

How to Contact Query with SASE. Responds in 1 month to queries. Sometimes comments on rejected mss.

Terms Pays negotiable advance. ''Publishing/payment arrangement will depend on plans for the book.''

Advice Interested in ''controversial, honest stories which satisfy the reader's curiosity to know. Read Victor Hugo, Fyodor Dostoyevsky and Sinclair Lewis for example.''

BOREALIS PRESS, LTD.

8 Mohawk Crescent and Tecumseh Press Ltd., Nepean ON K2H 7G6 Canada. (613)829-0150. Fax: (613)798-9747. E-mail: drt@borealispress.com. Web site: www.borealispress.com. **Contact:** David Tierney, editor; Glenn Clever, editor. Estab. 1972. ''Publishes Canadiana, especially early works that have gone out of print, but also novels of today and shorter fiction for young readers.'' Publishes hardcover and paperback originals and reprints. Books: standard book-quality paper; offset printing; perfect bound. **Published some debut authors**

within the last year. Averages 10-20 total titles/year. Promotes titles through web site, catalogue distribution, fliers for titles, ads in media.

• Borealis Press has a "New Canadian Drama," with 10 books in print.

Imprint(s) *Journal of Canadian Poetry*, Tecumseh Press Ltd., Canadian Critical Editions Series.

Needs Adventure, ethnic, historical, juvenile, literary, mainstream/contemporary, romance, short story collections, young adult. "Only material Canadian in content and dealing with significant aspects of the human situation." Published *Blue: Little Cat Come Home to Stay*, by Donna Richards (young adult); *Biography of a Beagle*, by Gail MacMillan (novel); *The Love of Women*, by Jennifer McVaugh (comic novel).

How to Contact Query with SASE or submit 1-2 sample chapter(s), synopsis. Accepts queries by email, fax. Responds in 2 months to queries; 4 months to mss. No simultaneous submissions.

Terms Pays 10% royalty on net receipts. 3 free author's copies. Ms guidelines online.

Advice "Have your work professionally edited. Our greatest challenge is finding good authors, i.e., those who submit innovative and original material."

BOSON BOOKS

C & M Online Media, Inc., 3905 Meadow Field Lane, Raleigh NC 27606. (919)233-8164. Fax: (919)233-8578. E-mail: cm@cmonline.com. Web site: www.cmonline.com. **Contact:** Aquisitions Editor. Estab. 1994. "We are an online book company with distribution through distributors such as CyberRead.com, powells.com, ebooks.com, mobipocket.com and Amazon.com." Publishes online originals and reprints. **Published 6 debut authors within the last year.** Member, Association of Online Publishers.

Needs "The quality of writing is our only consideration."

How to Contact Query with SASE. Accepts queries by e-mail.

Terms Pays 25% royalty.

Advice "We want to see only excellence in writing."

BRANDEN PUBLISHING CO., INC.

P.O. Box 812094, Wellesley MA 02482. (781)235-3634. Fax: (781)790-1056. Web site: www.brandenbooks.com. **Contact:** Adolph Caso, editor. Estab. 1909. Publishes hardcover and trade paperback originals, reprints and software. Books: 55-60 lb. acid-free paper; case—or perfect-bound; illustrations. Averages 15 total titles, 5 fiction titles/year.

Imprint(s) I.P.L; Dante University Press; Four Seas; Branden Publishing Co., Branden Books.

Needs Ethnic (histories, integration), historical, literary, military/war, religious (historical-reconstructive), short story collections. Looking for "contemporary, fast pace, modern society." Published *I, Morgain*, by Harry Robin; *The Bell Keeper*, by Marilyn Seguin; and *The Straw Obelisk*, by Adolph Caso.

How to Contact Does not accept unsolicited mss. Query with SASE. Responds in 1 month to queries.

Terms Pays 5-10% royalty on net receipts. 10 author's copies. Average advance: $1,000 maximum. Publishes ms 10 months after acceptance.

Advice "Publishing more fiction because of demand. *Do not make phone, fax or e-mail inquiries*. Do not oversubmit; single submissions only; do not procrastinate if contract is offered. Our audience is well-read general public, professionals, college students and some high school students. We like books by or about women."

BREAKAWAY BOOKS

P.O. Box 24, Halcottsville NY 12438. (212)898-0408. E-mail: information@breakawaybooks.com. Web site: www.breakawaybooks.com. **Contact:** Garth Battista, publisher. Estab. 1994. "Small press specializing in fine literary books on sports. We have a new line of children's illustrated books (ages 3-7)—dealing with sports, especially running, cycling, triathlon, swimming, and boating (canoes, kayaks, sailboats). Publishes hardcover and trade paperback originals. **Published 3 debut authors within the last year.** Averages 8-10 total titles, 5 fiction titles/year.

Needs Short story collections (sports stories).

How to Contact Accepts unsolicited mss. Query with SASE or submit complete ms. Accepts queries by e-mail. Include brief bio, list of publishling credits. Send SASE for return of ms or send a disposable ms and SASE for reply only. Agented fiction 50%. Responds in 1 month to queries; 2 months to mss. Accepts simultaneous submissions, electronic submissions. Rarely comments on rejected mss.

Terms Pays 6-15% royalty on retail price. Average advance: $2,000-3,000. Publishes ms 9 months after acceptance. Book catalog and ms guidelines free. Ms guidelines online.

BRIDGE WORKS PUBLISHING CO.

Box 1798, 221 Bridge Lane, Bridgehampton NY 11932. (631)537-3418. Fax: (631)537-5092. **Contact:** Barbara Phillips, editorial director. Estab. 1992. "We are very small, doing only 1-6 titles a year. We publish quality fiction. Our books are routinely reviewed in major publications.'' Publishes hardcover originals and reprints. **Published some debut authors within the last year.** Distributes titles through National Book Network.

Needs Humor, literary, mystery, short story collections. ''Query with SASE before submitting ms. First-time authors should have manuscripts vetted by freelance editors before submitting. We do not accept or read multiple submissions.'' Recent publications include *Blackbelly* and *Mineral Spirits*, by Heather Sharfeddin.

How to Contact Write to address above, including synopsis and estimated word count. Responds in one month to query and 50 pages, two months to entire ms. Sometimes comments on rejected mss.

Terms Pays 8% of net received from wholesalers and bookstores. Average advance: $1,000. Publishes ms 1 year after acceptance. Book catalog and ms guidelines for #10 SASE.

Advice ''We are interested in discovering new writers and we work closely with our authors in both the editorial and marketing processes.''

Ⓐ ✖ BROADWAY BOOKS

Doubleday Broadway Publishing Group, Random House, Inc., 1745 Broadway, New York NY 10019. (212)782-9000. Fax: (212)782-9411. Web site: www.broadwaybooks.com. **Contact:** William Thomas, editor-in-chief. Estab. 1995. Broadway publishes general interest nonfiction and fiction for adults. Publishes hardcover and trade paperback originals and reprints.

Needs Publishes a limited list of commercial literary fiction. Published *Freedomland*, by Richard Price.

How to Contact *Agented submissions only.*

🌐 ◎ BROWN SKIN BOOKS

Pentimento, Ltd., P.O. Box 46504, London England N1 3NT United Kingdom. E-mail: info@brownskinbooks.co.uk. Web site: www.brownskinbooks.co.uk. Estab. 2002. Publishes trade paperback originals. Averages 7 total titles/year.

Needs Erotica. ''We are looking for erotic short stories or novels written by women of color, or sensual crime thrillers.''

How to Contact Submit proposal package including 2 sample chapter(s), synopsis. Responds in 1 month to queries; 2 months to mss. Accepts simultaneous submissions.

Terms Pays 5-50% royalty or makes outright purchase. Publishes ms 12 months after acceptance. Ms guidelines online.

Ⓒ CALAMARI PRESS

202 E. 7th St. Apt. 1D, New York NY 10009. E-mail: derek@calamaripress.com. Web site: www.calamaripress.com. **Contact:** Derek White, editor. Estab. 2003. ''Calamari Press is a small, one-person operation on a part-time basis that devotes special attention to creating book objects of literary text and art. It has no preconceived notions of what exactly that means and tastes are admittedly whimsical.'' Publishes paperback originals. Format: 60 lb. natural finch opaque paper; digital printing; perfect or saddle-stitched bound. Average print order: 300. Debut novel print order: 200. Averages 5 total titles/year; 4 fiction titles/year.

Needs Adventure, comics/graphic novels, ethnic/multicultural, experimental, literary, short story collections. Published *Land of the Snow Men*, by George Belden (Norman Lock) (fictional literary canard with illustrations); *The Singing Fish*, by Peter Markus (prose poem/short fiction collection); *The Night I Dropped Shakespeare On The Cat*, by John Olson.

How to Contact Query with outline/synopsis and 3 sample chapters. Accepts queries by e-mail only. Include brief bio. Send SASE or IRC for return of ms. Responds to queries in 2 weeks. Accepts unsolicited mss. Considers e-mail submissions. Sometimes critiques/comments on rejected mss. Responds to mss in 2 weeks.

Terms Sends pre-production galleys to author. Manuscript published 2-6 months after acceptance. Writer's guidelines on Web site. Pays in author's copies. Book catalogs free upon request.

Advice ''Find your voice and write what's true to yourself. Find a press that fits what you're doing, and if you can't find one then publish it yourself.''

◎ ◎ CALYX BOOKS

P.O. Box B, Corvallis OR 97339-0539. (541)753-9384. Fax: (541)753-0515. **Contact:** M. Donnelly, director. Estab. 1986 for Calyx Books; 1976 for Calyx, Inc. ''Calyx exists to publish women's literary and artistic work and is committed to publishing the works of all women, including women of color, older women, lesbians, working-class women, and other voices that need to be heard.'' Publishes fine literature by women, fiction, nonfiction and poetry. Publishes hardcover and paperback originals. Books: offset printing; paper and cloth binding. **Published 1 debut author within the last year.** Averages 1-2 total titles/year. Distributes titles through Consortium Book Sale and Distribution. Promotes titles through author reading tours, print advertising (trade and individuals), galley and review copy mailings, presence at trade shows, etc.

Needs Ethnic, experimental, feminist, gay/lesbian, lesbian, literary, mainstream/contemporary, short story collections. Published *Forbidden Stitch: An Asian American Women's Anthology; Women and Aging: Present Tense; Writing and Art by Young Women*; and *A Line of Cutting Women*.

How to Contact Closed to submissions until further notice.

Terms Pays 10-15% royalty on net receipts. Average advance: depends on grant support. Publishes ms 2 years after acceptance. Ms guidelines for #10 SASE.

CANDLEWICK PRESS

2067 Massachusetts Ave., Cambridge MA 02140. (617)661-3330. Fax: (617)661-0565. E-mail: bigbear@candlewick.com. Web site: www.candlewick.com. **Contact:** Joan Powers, editor-at-large; Amy Ehrlich, editor-at-large; Deb Wayshak Noyes, senior editor; Liz Bicknell, editorial director/associate publisher (poetry, picture books, fiction); Mary Lee Donovan, executive editor (picture books, fiction); Sarah Ketchersid, editor (board, toddler); Hilary Breed Van Dusen, acquisitions editor. Estab. 1991. "We are a truly child-centered publisher." Publishes hardcover originals, trade paperback originals and reprints. Averages 200 total titles/year.

• *The Tale of Despereaux*, by Kate DiCamillo won the 2004 Newbery Medal.

Needs Juvenile, picture books, young adult. Published *The Tale of Despereaux*, by Kate DiCamillo; *Judy Moody*, by Megan McDonald, illustrated by Peter Reynolds; *Feed*, by M.T. Anderson; *Fairieality*, by David Ellwando.

How to Contact Does not accept unsolicited mss.

CARNIFEX PRESS

P.O. Box 1686, Ormond Beach FL 32175. E-mail: armand@carnifexpress.net. Web site: www.carnifexpress.net. **Contact:** Armand Rosamilia. Estab. 2005. "Small press publisher of fantasy and horror books from the fresh faces in the genres. We publish themed anthologies and single-author novellas. We try to be the midpoint between big publishers and the non-paying markets." Publishes paperback originals. Format: 24# paper with glossy cover; off-set printing; perfect bound (books). Average print order: 1,000. Debut novel print order: 2,000. **Published 4-5 new writers last year**. Plans 6 debut novels this year. Averages 12 total titles/year; 12 fiction titles/year. Distributes/promotes titles through our Web site and small-press distributors like Shocklines and Amazon.com.

Needs Fantasy (sword and sorcery), horror (dark fantasy, futuristic, psychological, supernatural). Writers may submit work during specific reading periods. See Web site for details. Published *Then Comes The Child*, by Christopher Fulbright and Angeline Hawkes (horror); *The King's World*, by Laura J. Underwood (fantasy); *Thoroughbred*, by Steven Shrewsbury (fantasy). Plans Freehold, a shared world fantasy book series.

How to Contact Accepts unsolicited mss. Query with outline/synopsis and 3 sample chapters. Accepts queries by e-mail. Include estimated word count, brief bio. Send disposable copy of ms and SASE for reply only. Responds to queries in 1-2 weeks. Responds to mss in 2-3 months. Considers e-mail submissions. Sometimes critiques/comments on rejected mss.

Terms Pays royalties of 10% and 5 author's copies. Sends pre-production galleys to author. Manuscript published 8 months after acceptance. Writer's guidelines on Web site. Book catalogs on Web site.

Advice "Small press is such a wide business but easy to get into, which is good and bad. So many new publishers are springing up but then closing only a few short months later without a business model and cash flow. Carnifex Press is new, but Armand Rosamilia has been in the small-press market for over 10 years and knows the challenges and rewards of the fantasy/horror niche. Send us the best possible copy of your work! Despite what some think, an editor isn't going to spend hours fixing grammar mistakes and rewriting paragraphs. We're looking for finished books ready to sell with a few minor changes to either plot or characterization that you make yourself. Small press doesn't rely on big advertising campaigns, we rely on word of mouth and the author to get behind their own work and hit book fairs, conventions, and do online promotion with us."

CAROLRHODA BOOKS, INC.

A Division of Lerner Publishing Group, 241 First Ave. N., Minneapolis MN 55401. Fax: (612)332-7615. Web site: www.lernerbooks.com. Estab. 1959. Publishes hardcover originals. Acquisitions: Zelda Wagner, submission editor.

Needs Historical, juvenile, multicultural, picture books, young reader, middle grade and young adult fiction. "We continue to add fiction for middle grades and 8-10 picture books per year. Not looking for folktales or anthropomorphic animal stories." Recently published *The Perfect Shot*, by Elaine Marie Alphin; *Noel*, by Tony Johnston.

How to Contact No unsolicited submissions. "We will continue to seek targeted solicitations at specific reading levels and in specific subject areas. The company will list these targeted solicitations on our Web site and in national newsletters, such as the SCBWI Bulletin. Unsoliciteds sent in November 2006 under our previous submissions policy will be read and replied to by November 2007."

Terms Pays royalty on wholesale price or makes outright purchase. Negotiates payments of advance against royalty. Average advance: varied. Book catalog for 9×12 SAE with $3.50 postage.

◎ CAVE BOOKS

277 Clamer Rd., Trenton NJ 08628-3204. (609)530-9743. E-mail: pddb@juno.com. Web site: www.cavebooks.c om. **Contact:** Paul Steward, managing editor. Estab. 1980. Small press devoted to books on caves, karst and speleology. Fiction: novels about cave exploration only. Publishes hardcover and trade paperback originals and reprints. Books: acid-free paper; offset printing. Averages 2 total titles, 1 fiction title/year.

Needs Adventure, historical, literary, caves, karst, speleology. Recently published *True Tales of Terror in The Caves of the World*, by Paul Jay Steward; *Prehistoric Cavers of Mammoth Cave*, by Colleen O'Connor Olson.

How to Contact Accepts unsolicited mss. Query with SASE or submit complete ms. Accepts queries by e-mail. Send SASE for return of ms or send a disposable ms and SASE for reply only. Responds in 2 weeks to queries; 3 months to mss. Accepts simultaneous submissions, electronic submissions. Sometimes comments on rejected mss.

Terms Pays 10% royalty on retail price. Publishes ms 18 months after acceptance.

Advice "In the last 3 years we have received only 3 novels about caves, and we have published one of them. We get dozens of inappropriate submissions. We only print books about caves."

CHARLESBRIDGE PUBLISHING

85 Main St., Watertown MA 02472. Web site: www.charlesbridge.com/school. Estab. 1980. Publishes hardcover and paperback nonfiction and fiction children's books and transitional books. Averages 36 total titles/year.

Needs Multicultural, nature, science, social studies, bedtime, math, etc. Recently published *A Mother's Journey*, by Sandra Markle; *Aggie and Ben*, by Lori Ries.

How to Contact Submit complete ms with SASE.

Terms Royalty and advance vary. Publishes ms 2 years after acceptance. Ms guidelines online.

⊕ CHRISTCHURCH PUBLISHERS LTD

2 Caversham St., London England SW3 4AH United Kingdom. Fax: (+00)44 171 351 4995. **Contact:** James Hughes, fiction editor.

Needs "Miscellaneous fiction, also poetry. More 'literary' style of fiction, but also thrillers, crime fiction, etc."

How to Contact Query with IRC.

Terms Pays royalty. Offers advance. "We have contacts and agents worldwide."

CHRONICLE BOOKS

Adult Trade Division, 680 Second St., San Francisco CA 94107. (415)537-4200. Fax: (415)537-4440. Web site: www.chroniclebooks.com. **Contact:** Editorial Dept., Adult Trade Division. Estab. 1966. Publishes hardcover and trade paperback originals. Averages 175 total titles/year.

Needs Novels and story collections. No genre fiction.

How to Contact Submit complete ms and SASE. Responds in 3 months to mss. Accepts simultaneous submissions.

Terms Publishes ms 18 months after acceptance. Ms guidelines online.

✪ ◎ CHRONICLE BOOKS FOR CHILDREN

680 Second St., San Francisco CA 94107. (415)537-4422. Fax: (415)537-4415. E-mail: kided@chroniclebooks.c om. Web site: www.chroniclekids.com. **Contact:** Victoria Rock, associate publisher. Publishes hardcover and trade paperback originals. **Published 5% debut authors within the last year.** Averages 50-60 total titles/year.

Needs Mainstream/contemporary, multicultural, young adult, picture books, middle grade fiction, young adult projects. Published *The Man Who Went to the Far Side of the Moon*; by Bea Uusma Shyffert; *Just a Minute: A Trickster Tale and Counting Book*; by Yuyi Morales; *Mama, Do You Love Me?*, by Barbara Joosse and Barbara Lavallee.

How to Contact Query with SASE. Responds in 2-4 weeks to queries; 3 months to mss. Accepts simultaneous submissions. No electronic submissions, submissions on disk.

Terms Royalty varies. Average advance: variable. Publishes ms 18-24 months after acceptance. Ms guidelines online.

Advice "We are interested in projects that have a unique bent to them—be it in subject matter, writing style or illustrative technique. As a small list, we are looking for books that will lend our list a distinctive flavor. Primarily, we are interested in fiction and nonfiction picture books for children ages up to 8 years, and nonfiction books for children ages up to 12 years. We publish board, pop-up and other novelty formats as well as picture books. We are also interested in early chapter books, middle grade fiction and young adult projects."

◎ ▼ CIRCLET PRESS, INC.

1770 Massachusetts Ave., #278, Cambridge MA 02140. (617)864-0492. E-mail: ctan@circlet.com. Web site: www.circlet.com. **Contact:** Cecilia Tan, publisher. Estab. 1992. Small, independent specialty book publisher.

"We are the only book publisher specializing in science fiction and fantasy of an erotic nature." Publishes hardcover and trade paperback originals. Books: perfect binding; illustrations sometimes. **Published 2 debut authors within the last year.** Averages 4 titles/year. Distributes titles through SCB Distribution in the US/Canada, Turnaround UK in the UK, and Bulldog Books in Australia. Promotes titles through reviews in book trade and general media, mentions in *Publishers Weekly*, *Bookselling This Week* and regional radio/TV.

- "Our titles were finalists in the Independent Publisher Awards in both science fiction and fantasy."

Imprint(s) The Ultra Violet Library (non-erotic lesbian/gay fantasy and science fiction).

Needs Short stories only. "Fiction must combine both the erotic and the fantastic. The erotic content needs to be an integral part of a science fiction story, and vice versa. Writers should not assume that any sex is the same as erotica." All books are anthologies of short stories. Published *Nymph*, by Francesca Lia Block; *The Darker Passions*, by Amarantha Knight.

How to Contact Accepts unsolicited mss only between April 15 and August 15. Check Web site for anthology topics which change annually. Query with SASE. Include estimated word count, brief bio, list of publishing credits. Send SASE for return of ms or send a disposable ms and SASE for reply only. Agented fiction 5%. Responds in 1 month to queries; 6-18 months to mss. Accepts simultaneous submissions, electronic submissions only from overseas authors. Always comments on rejected mss.

Terms Pays 4-12% royalty on retail price or makes outright purchase. Also pays in books, if author prefers. Publishes ms 18 months after acceptance. Ms guidelines online.

Advice "Read what we publish, learn to use lyrical but concise language to portray sex positively. No horror. Make sex and erotic interaction integral to your plot. Stay away from genre stereotypes. Use depth of character, internal monologue and psychological introspection to draw me in."

CITY LIGHTS BOOKS

261 Columbus Ave., San Francisco CA 94133. (415)362-8193. Fax: (415)362-4921. E-mail: staff@citylights.com. Web site: www.citylights.com. **Contact:** Robert Sharrard, editor. Estab. 1955. Publishes paperback originals. Plans 1-2 first novels this year. Averages 12 total titles, 4-5 fiction titles/year.

Needs Fiction, essays, memoirs, translations, poetry and books on social and political issues.

How to Contact Submit one-page description of the book and a sample chapter or two with SASE. Does not accept unsolicited mss. Does not accept queries by e-mail. See Web site for guidelines.

⚒ ◎ ▼ CLARION BOOKS

Houghton Mifflin Co., 215 Park Ave. S., New York NY 10003. Web site: www.houghtonmifflinbooks.com. **Contact:** Dinah Stevenson, vice-president and publisher (YA, middle-grade, chapter book); Jennifer B. Greene, senior editor (YA, middle-grade, chapter book); Jennifer Wingertzahn, editor (YA, middle-grade, chapter book); Lynne Polvino, associate editor (YA, middle-grade, chapter book). Estab. 1965. "Clarion is a strong presence in the fiction market for young readers. We are highly selective in the areas of historical and contemporary fiction. We publish chapter books for children ages 7-10 and middle-grade novels for ages 9-12, as well as picture books and nonfiction." Publishes hardcover originals for children. Averages 50 total titles/year.

- Clarion author Linda Sue Park received the 2002 Newbery Award for her book, *A Single Shard*. David Wiesner received the 2002 Caldecott Award for *The Three Pigs*.

Needs Adventure, historical, humor, mystery, suspense, strong character studies. Clarion is highly selective in the areas of historical fiction, fantasy and science fiction. A novel must be superlatively written in order to find a place on the list. Mss that arrive without an SASE of adequate size will *not* be responded to or returned. Accepts fiction translations. Published *The Great Blue Yonder*, by Alex Shearer (contemporary, middle-grade); *When My Name Was Keoko*, by Linda Sue Park (historical fiction); *Dunk*, by David Lubar (contemporary YA).

How to Contact Submit complete ms. Responds in 2 months to queries. Prefers no multiple submissions to mss.

Terms Pays 5-10% royalty on retail price. Average advance: minimum of $4,000. Publishes ms 2 years after acceptance. Ms guidelines for #10 SASE.

⚑ ▼ COFFEE HOUSE PRESS

27 N. Fourth St., Suite 400, Minneapolis MN 55401. Fax: (612)338-4004. **Contact:** Chris Fischbach, senior editor. Estab. 1984. "Nonprofit publisher with a small staff. We publish literary titles: fiction and poetry." Publishes trade paperback originals. Books: acid-free paper; cover illustrations. **Published some debut authors within the last year.** Averages 12 total titles, 6 fiction titles/year.

- This successful nonprofit small press has received numerous grants from various organizations including the NEA, the McKnight Foundation and Target.

Needs Ethnic, experimental, literary, mainstream/contemporary, short story collections, novels. Publishes anthologies, but they are closed to unsolicited submissions. Published *Miniatures*, by Norah Labiner (novel); *Circle K Cycles*, by Karen Yamashita (stories); *Little Casino*, by Gilbert Sorrentino (novel).

How to Contact Accepts unsolicited mss. Query with SASE. Agented fiction 10%. Responds in 1 month to queries; up to 4 months to mss. No electronic submissions.

Terms Pays 8% royalty on retail price. Provides 15 author's copies. Publishes ms 18 months after acceptance. Book catalog and ms guidelines for #10 SASE with 2 first-class stamps. Ms guidelines for #10 SAE with 55¢ first-class stamps.

[N] COPPER CANYON PRESS

P.O. Box 271, Building 313, Port Townsend WA 98368. (360)385-4925. Fax: (360)385-4985. E-mail: poetry@coppercanyonpress.org. Web site: www.coppercanyonpress.org. **Contact:** Michael Wiegers. Estab. 1972. Publishes trade paperback originals and occasional clothbound editions. Averages 18 total titles/year.

Needs Poetry.

How to Contact Responds in 4 months to queries.

Terms Pays royalty. Publishes ms 2 years after acceptance. Ms guidelines online.

Advice Please check Web site for updates and guidelines.

[icons] COTEAU BOOKS

AKA Thunder Creek Publishing Co-operative Ltd., 2517 Victoria Ave., Regina SK S4P 0T2 Canada. (306)777-0170. Fax: (306)522-5152. E-mail: coteau@coteaubooks.com. Web site: www.coteaubooks.com. **Contact:** Nik L. Burton, managing editor. Estab. 1975. "Coteau Books publishes the finest Canadian fiction, poetry, drama and children's literature, with an emphasis on western writers." Publishes trade paperback originals and reprints. Books: 2 lb. offset or 60 lb. hi-bulk paper; offset printing; perfect bound; 4-color illustrations. Averages 16 total titles, 4-6 fiction titles/year. Distributes titles through Fitzhenry & Whiteside.

- 2006 Giller Prize nominated title—*The Hour of Bad Decisions*, by Russel Wangersky.

Needs Ethnic, fantasy, feminist, gay/lesbian, historical, humor, juvenile, literary, mainstream/contemporary, multicultural, multimedia, mystery, regional, short story collections, spiritual, sports, young adult. Canadian authors *only*. Published *God of the Plains*, by Gail Robinson (fiction); *Morningstar: A Warrior's Spirit*, by Morningstar Mercedi (memoir); *Peacekeepers*, by Dianne Linden (young adult).

How to Contact Accepts unsolicited mss. Submit complete manuscript, or 3-4 sample chapter(s), author bio. Responds in 2-3 months to queries; 6 months to mss. No simultaneous submissions. Sometimes comments on rejected mss.

Terms Pays 10% royalty on retail price. "We're a co-operative and receive subsidies from the Canadian, provincial and local governments. We do not accept payments from authors to publish their works." Publishes ms 1-2 years after acceptance. Ms guidelines online.

Advice "We publish short-story collections, novels, drama, nonfiction and poetry collections. Canadian authors only! This is part of our mandate. The work speaks for itself! Be bold. Be creative. Be persistent!"

[icon] COVENANT COMMUNICATIONS, INC.

920 E. State Rd., American Fork UT 84003-0416. (801)756-9966. E-mail: info@covenant-lds.com. Web site: www.covenant-lds.com. Averages 50+ total titles/year.

Needs Adventure, historical, humor, juvenile, literary, mainstream/contemporary, mystery, picture books, regional, religious, romance, spiritual, suspense, young adult.

How to Contact Responds in 4 months to mss.

Terms Pays 6½-15% royalty on retail price. Publishes ms 6-12 months after acceptance. Ms guidelines online.

Advice Our audience is exclusively LDS (Latter-Day Saints, "Mormon").

[icons] CRICKET BOOKS

Carus Publishing, 70 E. Lake St. Suite 300, Chicago IL 60601. E-mail: cricketbooks@caruspub.net. Web site: www.cricketbooks.net. **Contact:** Submissions editor. Estab. 1999. "Small, independent publisher able to integrate publishing with related *Cricket* and *Cobblestone* magazine groups. We publish children's fiction and nonfiction, from picture books to high young adult." Publishes hardcover and paperback originals. Distributes titles through PGW. Promotes titles through in-house marketing.

- 2003 National Book Award finalist.

Imprint(s) Cricket Books, picture books to young adults.

Needs Children's/juvenile (adventure, animal, easy-to-read, fantasy, historical, mystery, preschool/picture book, sports), juvenile, young adult (adventure, easy-to-read, fantasy/science fiction, historical, horror, mystery/suspense, problem novels, romance, sports, western), Early chapter books and middle grade fiction. Plans anthologies for Christmas, dragons, poetry, and Cricket Magazine's anniversary edition. Editors select stories. Published *Seek* , by Paul Fleischman (YA fiction); *Robert and the Weird and Wacky Facts*, by Barbara Seuling (chapter book); and *Scorpio's Child*, by Kezi Matthews (fiction, ages 11-14).

How to Contact Currently only accepting submissions by authors previously published in *Cricket* magazine.

Does not accept unsolicited mss. Submit complete ms. Include estimated word count, list of publishing credits. Send SASE for return of ms or send a disposable ms and SASE for reply only. Agented fiction 20%. Responds in 4 months to queries; 6 months to mss. Accepts simultaneous submissions. No electronic submissions, submissions on disk. Sometimes comments on rejected mss.

Terms Pays 10% royalty on net receipts. Open to first-time and unagented authors. Pays up to 10% royalty on retail price. Average advance: $1,500 and up. Publishes ms 18 months after acceptance. Ms guidelines online.

CROSSQUARTER PUBLISHING GROUP

P.O. Box 23749, Santa Fe NM 87502. (505)438-9846. Web site: www.crossquarter.com. **Contact:** Anthony Ravenscroft. Publishes case and trade paperback originals and reprints. **Published 90% debut authors within the last year.** Averages 1-2 total titles/year.

Needs Science fiction, visionary fiction.

How to Contact Query with SASE. Responds in 3 months to queries. Accepts simultaneous submissions.

Terms Pays 8-10% royalty on wholesale or retail price. Publishes ms 1 year after acceptance. Book catalog for $1.75. Ms guidelines online.

Advice "Audience is earth-conscious people looking to grow into balance of body, mind, heart and spirit."

⚡ ⊘ CROSSTIME

Crossquarter Publishing Group, P.O. Box 86, Crookston MN 56716. (218)281-8065. Fax: (218)975-9715. E-mail: info@crossquarter.com. Web site: www.crossquarter.com. **Contact:** Anthony Ravenscroft. Estab. 1985. Small Publisher. Publishes paperback originals. Books: recycled paper; docutech or offset printing; perfect bound. **Published 2 debut authors within the last year.** Plans 2 first novels this year. Member SPAN, PMA.

Needs Mystery (occult), new age/mystic, psychic/supernatural, romance (occult), science fiction, young adult (fantasy/science fiction). Plans an anthology of Paul B. Duquette Memorial Short Science Fiction contest winners. Guidelines on Web site. Recently published *The Shamrock and the Feather*, by Dori Dalton (debut author); *Shyla's Initiative*, by Barbara Casey (occult romance); *Emperor of Portland*, by Anthony Ravenscroft (occult mystery); *CrossTIME SF Anthology Vol. II* (science fiction).

How to Contact Does not accept unsolicited mss. Query with SASE. No longer accepts queries by e-mail. Include estimated word count, brief bio, list of publishing credits. Send SASE for return of ms or send a disposable ms and SASE for reply only. Responds in 3 months to queries; 6 months to mss. Accepts simultaneous submissions, electronic submissions, submissions on disk.

Terms Pays 6-10% royalty. Publishes ms 6-9 months after acceptance. Ms guidelines online.

⚡ ⊘ ◎ CROSSWAY BOOKS

Division of Good News Publishers, 1300 Crescent St., Wheaton IL 60187-5800. (630)682-4300. Fax: (630)682-4785. Web site: www.crossway.com. **Contact:** Jill Carter. Estab. 1938. "Making a difference in people's lives for Christ as its maxim, Crossway Books lists titles written from an evangelical Christian perspective." Midsize evangelical Christian publisher. Publishes hardcover and trade paperback originals. Averages 85 total titles, 1 fiction titles/year. Member ECPA. Distributes titles through Christian bookstores and catalogs. Promotes titles through magazine ads, catalogs.

Needs *Currently not accepting fiction manuscripts.*

How to Contact Does not accept unsolicited mss. Agented fiction 5%.

Terms Pays negotiable royalty. Average advance: negotiable. Publishes ms 18 months after acceptance. Ms guidelines online.

Advice "With so much Christian fiction on the market, we are carefully looking at our program to see the direction we wish to proceed. Be sure your project fits into our guidelines and is written from an evangelical Christian worldview. 'Religious' or 'Spiritual' viewpoints will not fit."

◯ DAN RIVER PRESS

Conservatory of American Letters, P.O. Box 298, Thomaston ME 04861-0298. (207)226-7528. E-mail: cal@americanletters.org. Web site: www.americanletters.org. **Contact:** Richard S. Danbury, III, fiction editor. Estab. 1977. "Small press publisher of fiction and biographies owned by a non-profit foundation." Publishes hardcover and paperback originals. Books: paperback; offset printing; perfect and cloth binding; illustrations. Averages 3-4 fiction titles/year, plus the annual (since 1984) *Dan River Anthology*. Promotes titles through the author's sphere of influence. Distributes titles by mail order to libraries and bookstores, as well as by Amazon, Barnesandnoble.com, Baker & Taylor, Ingrams, 10 UK distributors, and author's influence.

Needs Adventure, family saga, fantasy (space fantasy, sword and sorcery), historical (general), horror (dark fantasy, futuristic, psychological, supernatural), humor, literary, mainstream/contemporary, military/war, mystery (amateur sleuth, police procedural, private eye/hard-boiled), new age/mystic, psychic/supernatural, religious (general religious, inspirational, religious mystery/suspense, religious thriller, religious romance),

romance (contemporary, futuristic/time travel, gothic, historical, romantic suspense), science fiction (hard science/technological, soft/sociological), short story collections, thriller/espionage, western (frontier saga, traditional), young adult, outdoors/fishing/hunting/camping/trapping. Accepts anything but porn, sedition, evangelical, and children's literature. Publishes poetry and fiction anthology (submission guidelines to *Dan River Anthology* on the Web).

How to Contact Accepts unsolicited mss. Accepts queries by mail. Include estimated word count, brief bio, list of publishing credits. Send SASE for return of ms or send a disposable ms and SASE for reply only. Responds in 2-3 days to queries; 1-2 weeks to mss. Accepts simultaneous submissions. No electronic submissions.

Terms Pays 10-15% royalty and 5 author's copies. Average advance: occasional. Publishes ms 3-4 months after acceptance. Book catalog for 6×9 SAE with 60¢ postage affixed. Ms guidelines online.

Advice "Spend some time developing a following."

JOHN DANIEL AND CO.

Daniel & Daniel, Publishers, Inc., P.O. Box 2790, McKinleyville CA 95519. (707)839-3495. Fax: (707)839-3242. E-mail: dand@danielpublishing.com. Web site: www.danielpublishing.com. **Contact:** John Daniel, publisher. Estab. 1980. "We publish small books, usually in small editions, but we do so with pride." Publishes hardcover originals and trade paperback originals. Publishes poetry, fiction and nonfiction. Averages 4 total titles/year. Distributes through SCB Distributors. Promotes through direct mail, reviews.

Needs Literary, short story collections. Publishes poetry, fiction and nonfiction; specializes in belles lettres, literary memoir. Published *Windstorm and Flood*, by Rosalind Brackenbury (novel); *Silence of Parents*, by Susan Geroe (novel); *Flight into Egypt*, by Julian Stamper (novel).

How to Contact Accepts unsolicited mss. Query with SASE or submit synopsis, 50 pages. Responds in 1 month to queries; 2 months to mss. Accepts simultaneous submissions.

Terms Pays 10% royalty on wholesale price. Average advance: $0-500. Publishes ms 1 year after acceptance. Ms guidelines online.

Advice "Having downsized from small to tiny, we can't publish as many books as before, and must be very selective. So it's a long shot. Never the less, we do consider all submissions."

DARK HORSE COMICS, INC.

10956 SE Main St., Milwaukie OR 97222. (503)652-8815. Web site: www.darkhorse.com. "In addition to publishing comics from top talent like Frank Miller, Mike Mignola, Stan Sakai and internationally-renowned humorist Sergio Aragonés, Dark Horse is recognized as the world's leading publisher of licensed comics."

Needs Comic books, graphic novels. Published *Astro Boy Volume 10 TPB*, by Osamu Tezuka and Reid Fleming; *Flaming Carrot Crossover #1* by Bob Burden and David Boswell.

How to Contact Submit synopsis.

Advice "If you're looking for constructive criticism, show your work to industry professionals at conventions."

MAY DAVENPORT, PUBLISHERS

26313 Purissima Rd., Los Altos Hills CA 94022. (650)947-1275. Fax: (650)947-1373. E-mail: mdbooks@earthlink .net. Web site: www.maydavenportpublishers.com. **Contact:** May Davenport, editor/publisher. Estab. 1976. "We prefer books which can be *used* in high schools as supplementary readings in English or creative writing courses. Reading skills have to be taught, and novels by humourous authors can be more pleasant to read than Hawthorne's or Melville's novels, war novels, or novels about past generations. Humor has a place in literature." Publishes hardcover and paperback originals. Averages 4 total titles/year. Distributes titles through direct mail order.

Imprint(s) md Books (nonfiction and fiction).

Needs Humor, literary. "We want to focus on novels junior and senior high school teachers can share with the reluctant readers in their classrooms." Published *Charlie and Champ*, by Allyson Wagoner; *Senioritis*, by Tate Thompson; *A Life on The Line*, by Michael Horton; *Matthew Livingston & The Prison of Souls*, by Marco Conelli.

How to Contact Query with SASE. Responds in 1 month to queries.

Terms Pays 15% royalty on retail price. Publishes ms 1 year after acceptance. Ms guidelines for #10 SASE.

Advice "Just write humorous novels about today's generation with youthful, admirable, believable characters to make young readers laugh. TV-oriented youth need role models in literature, and how a writer uses descriptive adjectives and similes enlightens youngsters who are so used to music, animation, special effects with stories."

DAW BOOKS, INC.

Penguin Group, Inc., 375 Hudson St., 3rd Floor, New York NY 10014-3658. (212)366-2096. Fax: (212)366-2090. E-mail: daw@us.penguingroup.com. Web site: www.dawbooks.com. **Contact:** Peter Stampfel, submissions editor. Estab. 1971. Publishes hardcover and paperback originals and reprints. Averages 60-80 total titles/year.

Needs Fantasy, science fiction. "We are interested in science fiction and fantasy novels. We need science fiction more than fantasy right now, but we're still looking for both. We like character-driven books. We accept both agented and unagented manuscripts. Long books are not a problem. We are not seeking collections of short stories or ideas for anthologies. We do not want any nonfiction manuscripts."

How to Contact Query with SASE or submit complete ms. "Please type your name, address and phone number in the upper right hand corner of the first page of your manuscript. Right under this, please put the length of your manuscript in number of words ." Responds in 6-9 weeks to queries.

Terms Pays in royalties with an advance negotiable on a book-by-book basis. Ms guidelines online.

Advice "We strongly encourage new writers. Research your publishers and submit only appropriate work."

A ⊠ ◎ DEL REY BOOKS

The Random House Publishing Group, Random House, Inc., 1745 Broadway, 18th Floor, New York NY 10019. (212)782-9000. Web site: www.delreybooks.com. **Contact:** Betsy Mitchell, editor-in-chief; Shelly Shapiro, editorial director; Steve Saffel, executive editor. Estab. 1977. "We are a long-established imprint with an eclectic frontlist. We're seeking interesting new voices to add to our best-selling backlist." Publishes hardcover, trade paperback, and mass market originals and mass market paperback reprints. Averages 120 total titles, 80 fiction titles/year.

Imprint(s) Imprints: Del Rey Manga, edited by Dallas Middaugh, publishes translations of Japanese comics.

Needs Fantasy (should have the practice of magic as an essential element of the plot), science fiction (well-plotted novels with good characterizations and interesting extrapolations), alternate history. Published *The Iron Council*, by China Mieville; *The Charnel Prince*, by Greg Keyes; *Marque and Reprisal*, by Elizabeth Moon; *Dragon's Kin*, by Ann McCaffrey and Todd McCaffrey; *Star Wars: Yoda: Dark Rendezvous*, by Sean Stewart.

How to Contact Does not accept unsolicited mss. *Agented submissions only.*

Terms Pays royalty on retail price. Average advance: competitive. Publishes ms 1 year after acceptance. Ms guidelines online.

Advice Has been publishing "more fiction and hardcovers, because the market is there for them. Read a lot of science fiction and fantasy, such as works by Anne McCaffrey, David Eddings, China Mieville, Arthur C. Clarke, Terry Brooks, Richard K. Morgan, Elizabeth Moon. When writing, pay particular attention to plotting (and a satisfactory conclusion) and characters (sympathetic and well rounded) because those are what readers look for."

⊠ ◎ DIAL BOOKS FOR YOUNG READERS

Penguin Group USA, 345 Hudson St., 14th Floor, New York NY 10014. (212)366-2000. Web site: www.us.penguingroup.com. **Contact:** Submissions Editor. Estab. 1961. Trade children's book publisher. Publishes hardcover originals. Averages 50 total titles/year.

Needs Adventure, fantasy, juvenile, picture books, young adult. Especially looking for "lively and well-written novels for middle grade and young adult children involving a convincing plot and believable characters. The subject matter or theme should not already be overworked in previously published books. The approach must not be demeaning to any minority group, nor should the roles of female characters (or others) be stereotyped, though we don't think books should be didactic, or in any way message-y. No topics inappropriate for the juvenile, young adult and middle grade audiences. No plays." Published *A Year Down Yonder*, by Richard Peck; *The Missing Mitten Mystery*, by Steven Kellog.

How to Contact Accepts unsolicited mss. "Submit entire picture book manuscript or the first three chapters of longer works. Please include a cover letter with brief bio and publication credits. Please note that, unless interested in publishing your book, Dial will not respond to unsolicited submissions. Please do NOT include a SASE. If Dial is interested, expect a reply from us within four months."

Terms Pays royalty. Average advance: varies.

A ⊠ DIAL PRESS

Bantam Dell Publishing Group, Random House, Inc., 1745 Broadway, New York NY 10019. (212)782-9000. Fax: (212)782-9523. Web site: www.randomhouse.com/bantamdell/. **Contact:** Susan Kamil, vice president, editorial director. Estab. 1924. Averages 6-12 total titles/year.

Needs Literary (general). Published *Mary and O'Neil* (short story collection); *Niagara Falls Over Again*, by Elizabeth Mccracken (fiction).

How to Contact *Agented submissions only.* Accepts simultaneous submissions.

Terms Pays royalty on retail price. Offers advance. Publishes ms 18 months after acceptance.

A ⊠ DOUBLEDAY

Doubleday Broadway Publishing Group, Random House, Inc., 1745 Broadway, New York NY 10019. (212)782-9000. Fax: (212)782-9700. Web site: www.randomhouse.com. Estab. 1897. Publishes hardcover originals. Averages 70 total titles/year.

Needs Adventure, confession, ethnic, experimental, feminist, gay/lesbian, historical, humor, literary, mainstream/contemporary, religious, short story collections.

How to Contact *Agented submissions only.* No simultaneous submissions.

Terms Pays royalty on retail price. Offers advance. Publishes ms 1 year after acceptance.

N ⚡ ◎ DOUBLEDAY BOOKS FOR YOUNG READERS

Random House Children's Books, 1540 Broadway, New York NY 10036. (212)782-9000. Web site: www.random house.com/kids.

A ⚡ ⚡ DOUBLEDAY CANADA

Random House of Canada, 1 Toronto Street, Suite 300, Toronto ON M5C 2V6 Canada. (416)364-4449. Web site: www.randomhouse.ca. Publishes hardcover and paperback originals. Averages 50 total titles/year.

Imprint(s) Doubleday Canada (hardcover and paperback publisher); Bond Street Books Canada (hardcover publisher of international titles); Seal Books (mass market publisher); Anchor Canada (trade paperback publisher).

How to Contact Does not accept unsolicited mss. *Agented submissions only.*

A ⚡ ◎ DOUBLEDAY RELIGIOUS PUBLISHING

Doubleday Broadway Publishing Group, Random House, Inc., 1745 Broadway, New York NY 10019. (212)782-9000. Web site: www.randomhouse.com. **Contact:** Eric Major, vice president, religious division; Trace Murphy, executive editor; Andrew Corbin, editor. Estab. 1897. Publishes hardcover and trade paperback originals and reprints. Averages 45-50 total titles/year.

Imprint(s) Image Books, Anchor Bible Commentary, Anchor Bible Reference, Galilee, New Jerusalem Bible.

Needs Religious.

How to Contact *Agented submissions only.* Accepts simultaneous submissions.

Terms Pays 7$\frac{1}{2}$-15% royalty. Offers advance. Publishes ms 1 year after acceptance. Book catalog for SAE with 3 first-class stamps.

⚡ ▢ ◎ DRAGON MOON PRESS

3521 43A Ave, Red Deer AB T4N 3W9 Canada. E-mail: publisher@dragonmoonpress.com. Web site: www.drag onmoonpress.com. **Contact:** Gwen Gades, publisher. Estab. 1994. "Dragon Moon Press is dedicated to new and exciting voices in science fiction and fantasy." Publishes trade paperback and electronic originals. Books: 60 lb. offset paper; short run printing and offset printing. Average print order: 250-3,000. **Published several debut authors within the last year.** Plans 5 first novels this year. Averages 4-6 total titles, 4-5 fiction titles/ year. Distributed through Baker & Taylor. Promoted locally through authors and online at leading retail bookstores like Amazon, Barnes & Noble, Chapters, etc.

Imprint(s) Dragon Moon Press, Gwen Gades publisher (fantasy and science fiction).

Needs Fantasy, science fiction (soft/sociological). No horror or children's fiction, short stories or poetry. "We seek out quality manuscripts and authors who are eager to participate in the marketing of their book.

How to Contact Please visit our Web site at www.dragonmoonpress.com for submission guidelines. Accepts simultaneous submissions. No submissions on disk. "All submissions are requested electronically—do not mail submissions, as we will not respond. All mailed submissions are shredded and recycled."

Terms Pays 8-15% royalty on retail price. Publishes ms 2 years after acceptance.

Advice "First, be patient. Read our guidelines. Not following our submission guidelines can be grounds for automatic rejection. Second, be patient, we are small and sometimes very slow as a result, especially during book launch season. Third, we view publishing as a family affair. Be ready to participate in the process and show some enthusiasm and understanding in what we do. Remember also, this is a business and not about egos, so keep yours on a leash! Show us a great story with well-developed characters and plot lines, show us that you are interested in participating in marketing and developing as an author, and show us your desire to create a great book and you may just find yourself published by Dragon Moon Press."

A ⚡ ♥ DUTTON (ADULT TRADE)

Penguin Putnam, Inc., 375 Hudson St., New York NY 10014. (212)366-2000. Web site: www.penguinputnam.c om. **Contact:** Editor-in-Chief: Brian Tart. Estab. 1852. Publishers hardcover originals. Averages 40 total titles/ year.

Needs Adventure, historical, literary, mainstream/contemporary, mystery, short story collections, suspense. Published *The Darwin Awards II*, by Wendy Northcutt (humor); *Falling Angels*, by Tracy Chevalier (fiction); *The Oath*, by John Lescroart (fiction).

How to Contact *Agented submissions only.* Responds in 6 months to queries. Accepts simultaneous submissions.

Terms Pays royalty. Average advance: negotiable. Publishes ms 12-18 months after acceptance.

Advice "Write the complete manuscript and submit it to an agent or agents. They will know exactly which editor will be interested in a project."

⬛ ⬜ ◎ DUTTON CHILDREN'S BOOKS

Penguin Group, Inc., 345 Hudson St., New York NY 10014. (212)414-3700. Fax: (212)414-3397. Web site: www.penguin.com. **Contact:** Stephanie Owens Lurie, president and publisher (picture books and fiction); Maureen Sullivan, executive editor (upper young adult, fiction and nonfiction); Lucia Monfried, senior editor (picture books, easy-to-read books, fiction); Mark McVeigh, senior editor (picture books and fiction); Julie Strauss-Gabel, senior editor (picture books and young adult fiction). Estab. 1852. Dutton Children's Books publishes fiction and nonfiction for readers ranging from preschoolers to young adults on a variety of subjects. Publishes hardcover originals as well as novelty formats. Averages 100 total titles/year.

Needs Dutton Children's Books has a diverse, general-interest list that includes picture books, easy-to-read books and fiction for all ages, from "first chapter" books to young adult readers. Published *My Teacher for President*, by Kay Winters, illustrated by Denise Brunkus (picture book); *The Best Pet of All*, by David LaRochelle, illustrated by Hanako Wakiyama (picture book); *The Schwa was Here*, by Neal Shusteman (novel); *Guitar Girl*, by Sarra Manning (novel).

How to Contact Does not accept unsolicited mss.

Terms Pays royalty on retail price. Offers advance.

⬛ ECW PRESS

2120 Queen St. E., Suite 200, Toronto ON M4E 1E2 Canada. (416)694-3348. Fax: (416)698-9906. E-mail: info@ecwpress.com. Web site: www.ecwpress.com. **Contact:** Jack David, publisher. Estab. 1979. Publishes hardcover and trade paperback originals. Averages 40 total titles/year.

Needs Canadian authored fiction, specializes in mystery.

How to Contact Accepts simultaneous submissions.

Terms Pays 8-12% royalty on net receipts. Average advance: $300-5,000. Publishes ms 18 months after acceptance. Book catalog and ms guidelines free. Ms guidelines online.

Advice "Make sure to include return postage (SASE, IRC if outside of Canada) it you wish your material to be returned."

⬛ ◎ EDGE SCIENCE FICTION AND FANTASY PUBLISHING

Box 1714, Calgary AB T2P 2L7 Canada. (403)254-0160. Fax: (403)254-0456. E-mail: publisher@hadespublications.com. Web site: www.edgeWeb site.com. **Contact:** Kimberly Gammon, editorial manager (science fiction/fantasy). Estab. 1996. "We are an independent publisher of science fiction and fantasy novels in hard cover or trade paperback format. We produce high-quality books with lots of attention to detail and lots of marketing effort. We want to encourage, produce and promote thought-provoking and fun-to-read science fiction and fantasy literature by 'bringing the magic alive: one world at a time' (as our motto says) with each new book released." Publishes hardcover and trade paperback originals. Books: natural offset paper; offset/web printing; HC/perfect binding; b&w illustration only. Average print order: 2,000-3,000. Plans 8 first novels this year. Averages 6-8 total titles/year. Member of Book Publishers Association of Alberta (BPAA), Independent Publishers Association of Canada (IPAC), Publisher's Marketing Association (PMA), Small Press Center.

Imprint(s) Edge, Alien Vistas, Riverbend.

Needs Fantasy (space fantasy, sword and sorcery), science fiction (hard science/technological, soft/sociological). "We are looking for all types of fantasy and science fiction, except juvenile/young adult, horror, erotica, religious fiction, short stories, dark/gruesome fantasy, or poetry." Published *Stealing Magic*, by Tanya Huff; *Forbidden Cargo*, by Rebecca K. Rowe.

How to Contact Accepts unsolicited mss. Submit first 3 chapters and synopsis, Check Web site for guidelines or send SAE & IRCs for same. Include estimated word count. Responds in 4-5 months to mss. No simultaneous submissions, electronic submissions. Rarely comments on rejected mss.

Terms Pays 10% royalty on wholesale price. Average advance: negotiable. Publishes ms 18 months after acceptance. Ms guidelines online.

Advice "Send us your best, polished, completed manuscript. Use proper manuscript format. Take the time before you submit to get a critique from people who can offer you useful advice. When in doubt, visit our Web site for helpful resources, FAQs and other tips."

⬛ EERDMANS BOOKS FOR YOUNG READERS

William B. Eerdmans Publishing Co., 2140 Oak Industrial Dr. NE, Grand Rapids MI 49505. (616)459-4591. Fax: (616)459-6540. **Contact:** Judy Zylstra, editor. Publishes picture books and middle reader and young adult fiction and nonfiction. Averages 12-15 total titles/year.

Needs Juvenile, picture books, young adult, middle reader. Published *Going for The Record*, by Julie Swanson; *Dancing With Elvis*, by Lynda Stephenson.

How to Contact Responds in 6 weeks to 3 months to queries. Accepts exclusive submissions.

Terms Pays 5-7½% royalty on retail price. Publishes middle reader and YA books in 1-2 years; publishes picture books 2-4 years after acceptance.

☑ ◎ ♥ WILLIAM B. EERDMANS PUBLISHING CO.

2140 Oak Industrial Dr. NE, Grand Rapids MI 49505. (616)459-4591. Fax: (616)459-6540. E-mail: info@eerdmans.com. Web site: www.eerdmans.com. **Contact:** Jon Pott, editor-in-chief, fiction editor (adult fiction); Judy Zylstra, fiction editor (children). Estab. 1911. "Although Eerdmans publishes some regional books and other nonreligious titles, it is essentially a religious publisher whose titles range from the academic to the semi-popular. We are a midsize independent publisher. We publish the occasional adult novel, and these tend to engage deep spiritual issues from a Christian perspective." Publishes hardcover and paperback originals and reprints. **Published some debut authors within the last year.** Averages 120-130 total titles, 6-8 (mostly for children) fiction titles/year.

- Wm. B. Eerdmans Publishing Co.'s titles have won awards from the American Library Association and The American Bookseller's Association.

Imprint(s) Eerdmans Books for Young Readers.

Needs Religious (children's, general, fantasy). Published *I Wonder as I Wander*, by Gwenyth Swain, illustrated by Ronald Himler; *Gilgamesh the Herd*, by Geraldine McCaughrean, illustrated by David Parkins; *The Enemy Has a Face*, by Gloria D. Miklowitz (young adult); *Down in the Piney Woods* and *Mariah's Pond*, by Ethel Footman Smothers.

How to Contact Accepts unsolicited mss. Submit outline, 2 sample chapter(s), synopsis. Include brief bio, list of publishing credits. Send SASE for return of ms or send a disposable ms and SASE for reply only. Agented fiction 5%. Responds in 6 weeks to queries. Accepts simultaneous submissions. Sometimes comments on rejected mss.

Terms Pays royalty. Average advance: occasional. Publishes ms usually within 1 year after acceptance.

Advice "Our readers are educated and fairly sophisticated, and we are looking for novels with literary merit."

◎ ELLORA'S CAVE PUBLISHING, INC.

1056 Home Avenue, Akron OH 44310-3205. E-mail: submissions@ellorascave.com. Web site: www.ellorascave.com and www.cerridwenpress.com. Estab. 2000. Publishes trade paperback and electronic originals and reprints. Averages 300 total titles/year.

Needs Erotica, fantasy, gay/lesbian, gothic, historical, horror, mainstream/contemporary, multicultural, mystery, romance, science fiction, suspense, western. All must be under genre romance. All must have erotic content. For Cerridwen Press, all mainstream fiction genres.

How to Contact Submit proposal package including detailed full synopsis, first three chapters, last chapter via e-mail. No paper submissions. Responds in 3-12 months to mss. Accepts simultaneous submissions.

Terms Pays royalty of 37.5% of cover price for digital, 7.5% of cover for print. Ms guidelines online.

☑ ◎ EMPIRE PUBLISHING SERVICE

P.O. Box 1344, Studio City CA 91614-0344. Estab. 1960. Midsize publisher with related imprints. Publishes hardcover reprints and trade paperback originals and reprints. Book: paper varies; offset printing; binding varies. Average print order: 5,000-10,000. First novel print order: 2,500-5,000. **Published 4 debut authors within the last year.** Averages 60 total titles, 5 fiction titles/year. Distributes and promotes titles by "Sales & Marketing Distribution offices in five countries."

Imprint(s) Paul Mould Publishing, Paul Mould, editor (historical); Gaslight Publications (Sherlock Holmes); Collectors Publications (erotica).

Needs Historical (pre-18th century), mystery (Sherlock Holmes). Plans anthology of Sherlock Holmes short stories. Published *God's Hammer*, by Eric Shumacher.

How to Contact Does not accept unsolicited mss. Query with SASE. Include estimated word count, brief bio, list of publishing credits, general background. Send SASE for return of ms or send a disposable ms and SASE for reply only. Agented fiction 2%. Responds in 1 month to queries; up to 1 year to mss. No simultaneous submissions, electronic submissions, submissions on disk.

Terms Pays 6-10% royalty on retail price. Average advance: variable. Publishes ms 6 months to 2 years after acceptance. Ms guidelines for $1 or #10 SASE.

Advice "Send query with SASE for only the type of material we publish, historical and Sherlock Holmes."

⬛ ◎ EMPYREAL PRESS

P.O. Box 1746, Place Du Parc, Montreal QC HZX 4A7 Canada. E-mail: empyrealpress@hotmail.com. Web site: www.skarwood.com. **Contact:** Colleen B. McCool. "Our mission is the publishing of literature which doesn't

fit into any standard 'mold'—writing which is experimental yet grounded in discipline, imagination." Publishes trade paperback originals. **Published 50% debut authors within the last year.** Averages 1-2 total titles/year.
Needs Experimental, feminist, gay/lesbian, literary, short story collections. "Empyreal Press is not currently accepting unsolicited manuscripts due to extremely limited resources."

✍ ◎ EROS BOOKS
463 Barlow Ave., Staten Island NY 10308. (718)317-7484. E-mail: marynicholaou@aol.com. Web site: www.eros.thecraze.com. **Contact:** Mary Nicholaou, fiction editor. Estab. 2000. "Small independent publisher of postmodern romance, short fiction and translations." Publishes paperback originals, e-books. Format: 20 lb. paper; offset printing. Average print order: 500. Debut novel print order: 500. **Published 5 new writers last year.** Plans 10 debut novels this year. Averages 5 total titles/year; 4 fiction titles/year.
Needs Postmodern, short, romance fiction, translations. Published *Cracks*, by Mary Nicholaou (postmodern romance); *Chimera*, by Clara Smith (postmodern romance).
How to Contact Query with outline/synopsis. Reads submissions June-September. Accepts queries by snail mail, e-mail. Include social security number. Send SASE or IRC for return of ms or disposable copy of ms and SASE/IRC for reply only. Agented fiction: 10%. Responds to queries in 2 weeks. Considers simultaneous submissions, submissions on CD or disk. Always critiques/comments on rejected mss. Responds to mss in 2 months.
Terms Pays in author's copies. Manuscript published 12 months after acceptance. Writer's guidelines available for SASE. Book catalogs available for SASE.

✍ ⛉ ⛏ FANTAGRAPHICS BOOKS
7563 Lake City Way NE, Seattle WA 98115. Fax: (206)524-2104. E-mail: fbicomix@fantagraphics.com. Web site: www.fantagraphics.com. **Contact:** Michael Dowers (all genres). Estab. 1976. "Fantagraphics Books has been a leading proponent of comics as a legitimate form of art and literature since it began publishing the critical trade magazine *The Comics Journal* in 1976. By the early 1980s, Fantagraphics found itself at the forefront of the burgeoning movement to establish comics as a medium as eloquent and expressive as the more established popular arts of film, literature, poetry, et al. Fantagraphics quickly established a reputation as an advocacy publisher that specialized in seeking out and publishing the kind of innovative work that traditional comics corporations who dealt almost exclusively in superheroes and fantasy either didn't know existed or wouldn't touch: serious, dramatic, historical, journalistic, political and satirical work by a new generation of alternative cartoonists, as well as many artists who gained prominence as part of the seminal underground comix movement of the '60s. Fantagraphics has since gained an international reputation for its literate and audacious editorial standards and its exacting production values." Publishes hardcover originals, paperback originals, hardcover reprints, paperpack reprints. Average print run: 3,000 (debut writer). **Publishes 3-4 debut writers/year.** Publishes 60 titles/year. Titles promoted/distributed by W.W. Norton & Co. Awards: Harvey Awards, Eisner Awards, Ignatz Awards, Quills nomination.
Needs All categories. Does not want superheros. Anthologies: MOME, Hotwire, Blab. Editors select stories.
How to Contact Prefers submissions from writer-artists. Detailed submission guidelines at www.fantagraphics.com/submissions.html. Agented submissions: less than 5%. Responds to queries and ms/art packages in 4 months. Often comments on rejected manuscripts.
Terms Creators paid royalty. Sends pre-publication galleys to author. Writer's and artist's guidelines on Web site. Book catalog free upon request.

▲ FARRAR, STRAUS & GIROUX
19 Union Square West, New York NY 10003. (212)741-6900. E-mail: fsg.editorial@fsgbooks.com. Web site: www.fsgbooks.com. Eric Chinski, editor-in-chief. Publishes hardcover and trade paperback books. Averages 180 total titles/year.
Needs Literary.
How to Contact Does not accept unsolicited mss.

✦ ◯ ◎ ⛉ FARRAR, STRAUS & GIROUX BOOKS FOR YOUNG READERS
Farrar Straus Giroux, Inc., 19 Union Square W., New York NY 10003. (212)741-6900. Fax: (212)633-2427. **Contact:** Margaret Ferguson, editorial director (children's); Wesley Adams, executive editor (children's); Beverly Reingold, executive editor (children's); Janine O'Malley, editor (children's). Estab. 1946. "We publish original and well-written materials for all ages." Publishes hardcover originals and trade paperback reprints. **Published some debut authors within the last year.** Averages 75 total titles/year.
Imprint(s) Frances Foster Books, edited by Frances Foster (children's); Melanie Kroupa Books, edited by Melanie Kroupa (children's).
Needs Children's/juvenile, picture books, young adult, nonfiction. "Do not query picture books; just send

manuscript. Do not fax queries or manuscripts." Published *So Sleepy Story*, by Uri Shulevity; *Alabama Moon*, by Walk Key.

How to Contact Query with SASE. Include brief bio, list of publishing credits. Agented fiction 25%. Responds in 2 months to queries; 4 months to mss. Accepts simultaneous submissions. No electronic submissions, submissions on disk.

Terms Pays 2-6% royalty on retail price for paperbacks, 3-10% for hardcovers. Average advance: $3,000-25,000. Publishes ms 18 months after acceptance. Book catalog for 9×12 SAE with $1.87 postage. Ms guidelines for #10 SASE.

Advice "Study our list to avoid sending something inappropriate. Send query letters for long manuscripts; don't ask for editorial advice (just not possible, unfortunately); and send SASEs!"

FARRAR, STRAUS & GIROUX PAPERBACKS

19 Union Square W., New York NY 10003. (212)741-6900. FSG Paperbacks emphasizes literary nonfiction and fiction, as well as poetry. Publishes hardcover and trade paperback originals and reprints. Averages 180 total titles/year.

Needs Literary. Published *The Corrections*, by Jonathan Franzen; *The Haunting of L.*, by Howard Norman.

How to Contact Does not accept unsolicited mss. Agented submissions only.

FC2

Dept. of English, FSU, Tallahassee FL 32306. E-mail: fc2@english.fsu.edu. Web site: http://fc2.org. **Contact:** Brenda L. Mills, executive editor. Estab. 1974. Publisher of innovative fiction. Publishes hardcover and paperback originals. Books: perfect/Smyth binding; illustrations. Average print order: 2,200. **Published some debut authors within the last year.** Plans 2 first novels this year. Averages 6 total titles, 6 fiction titles/year. Titles distributed through University of Alabama Press. No open submissions except through Ronald Sukenick Innovative Fiction Prize.

Needs Experimental, feminist, gay/lesbian, innovative; modernist/postmodern; avant-garde; anarchist; minority; cyberpunk. Published *Book of Lazarus*, by Richard Grossman; *Is It Sexual Harassment Yet?*, by Cris Mazza; *Liberty's Excess*, by Lidia Yuknavitch; *The Wavering Knife*, by Brian Evenson.

How to Contact Does not accept unsolicited mss. See Web site (http://fc2.org/Sukenick%20prize.htm) for contest info. Query with SASE or submit outline, publishing history, synopsis, author bio. Agented fiction 5%. Responds in 3 weeks to queries; 2-6 months to mss. Accepts simultaneous submissions.

Terms Pays 10% royalty. Publishes ms 1-3 years after acceptance. Ms guidelines online.

Advice "Be familiar with our list."

THE FEMINIST PRESS AT THE CITY UNIVERSITY OF NEW YORK

365 Fifth Ave., Suite 5406, New York NY 10016. (212)817-7917. Fax: (212)817-1593. E-mail: fhowe@gc.cuny.edu. Web site: www.feministpress.org. **Contact:** Gloria Jacobs. Estab. 1970. Small, nonprofit literary and educational publisher. "The Feminist Press publishes mainly fiction reprints by classic American women authors and translations of distinguished international women writers." Publishes hardcover and trade paperback originals and reprints. Publishes original fiction occasionally; exceptions are anthologies and international works. "We use an acid-free paper, perfect-bind our books, four color covers; and some cloth for library sales if the book has been out of print for some time; we shoot from the original text when possible. We always include a scholarly and literary afterword, since we are introducing a text to a new audience. Average print run: 2,500." Averages 15-20 total titles, 4-8 fiction titles/year. Member: CLMP, Small Press Association. Distributes titles through Consortium Book Sales and Distribution. Promotes titles through author tours, advertising, exhibits and conferences. Charges "permission fees (reimbursement)."

Needs Ethnic, feminist, gay/lesbian, literary, short story collections, women's. "The Feminist Press publishes mainly fiction reprints by classic American women authors and imports and translations of distinguished international women writers. Very little original fiction is considered." Needs fiction by "U.S. women of color writers from 1920-1970 who have fallen out of print." Published *Apples From the Desert*, by Savyon Liebrecht (short stories, translation); *The Parish and the Hill*, by Mary Doyle Curran (fiction reprint); *Allegra Maud Goldman*, by Edith Konecky (fiction, reprint); and *Still Alive*, by Ruth Kluger (memoir).

How to Contact Does not accept unsolicited mss. Include estimated word count, brief bio, list of publishing credits. Responds within 6 weeks to queries. Accepts simultaneous submissions, electronic submissions.

Terms Pays 10% royalty on net receipts. Pays 5-10 author's copies. Average advance: $1,000. Publishes ms 18-24 months after acceptance. Ms guidelines online.

FLORIDA ACADEMIC PRESS

P.O. Box 540, Gainesville FL 32602. (352)332-5104. Fax: (352)331-6003. E-mail: fapress@gmail.com. **Contact:** Florence Dusek, assistant editor (fiction). Publishes hardcover and trade paperback originals. **Published 85% debut authors within the last year.** Averages 10 total titles/year.

Needs Serious fiction and scholarly social science manuscripts.

How to Contact Submit complete ms. Responds in 4-12 weeks to mss.

Terms Pays 5-8% royalty on retail price, depending if paperback or hardcover. Publishes ms 3-5 months after acceptance.

Advice Considers complete mss only. "Manuscripts we decide to publish must be re-submitted in camera-ready form."

⭐ 🖉 🏆 FORGE AND TOR BOOKS

Tom Doherty Associates, LLC, 175 Fifth Ave. 14th Floor, New York NY 10010. (212)388-0100. Fax: (212)388-0191. Web site: www.tor.com. **Contact:** Melissa Ann Singer, senior editor (general fiction, mysteries, thriller); Patrick Nielsen Hayden, senior editor (science fiction, fantasy). Estab. 1980. "Tor Books are science fiction, fantasy and horror, and occasionally, related nonfiction. Forge books are everything else—general fiction, historical fiction, mysteries and suspense, women's fiction and nonfiction. Orb titles are trade paperback reprint editions of science fiction, fantasy and horror books." Publishes hardcover, trade paperback and mass market paperback originals, trade and mass market paperback reprints. **Published some debut authors within the last year.**

• Tor was named Best Publisher at the Locus Awards for the sixteenth consecutive year.

Imprint(s) Forge, Tor, Orb.

Needs Historical, horror, mainstream/contemporary, mystery (amateur sleuth, police procedural, private eye/hard-boiled), science fiction, suspense, thriller/espionage, western (frontier saga, traditional), thriller; general fiction and fantasy.

How to Contact Accepts unsolicited mss. Do not query; "submit only the first three chapters of your book and a synopsis of the entire book. Your cover letter should state the genre of the submission and previous sales or publications if relevant." Include estimated word count, brief bio, list of publishing credits. Agented fiction 95%. Sometimes comments on rejected mss. Responds in 4-6 months. No simultaneous submissions. Additional guidelines on Web site.

Terms Paperback: Pays 6-8% royalty for first-time authors, 8-10% royalty for established authors. Hardcover: Pays 10% first 5,000; 12½% second 5,000; 15% thereafter. Offers advance. Publishes ms 12-18 months after acceptance.

Advice "The writing must be outstanding for a new author to break into today's market."

◎ FORT ROSS INC. RUSSIAN-AMERICAN PUBLISHING PROJECTS

26 Arthur Place, Yonkers NY 10701. (914)375-6448. E-mail: fort.ross@optonline.net. Web site: www.fortrossinc.com. **Contact:** Dr. Vladimir P. Kartsev. Estab. 1992. "We welcome Russia-related manuscripts as well as books from well-established fantasy and romance novel writers who would like to have their novels translated in Russia and Eastern Europe by our publishing house in cooperation with the local publishers." Publishes paperback originals. **Published 3 debut authors within the last year.** Averages 40 total titles/year.

Needs Adventure, fantasy (space fantasy, sword and sorcery), horror, mainstream/contemporary, mystery (amateur sleuth, police procedural, private eye/hard-boiled), romance (contemporary, regency), science fiction (hard science/technological, soft/sociological), suspense, thriller/espionage.

How to Contact Does not accept unsolicited mss. Query with SASE. Include estimated word count, brief bio, list of publishing credits. Send SASE for return of ms or send a disposable ms and SASE for reply only. Responds in 1 month to queries; 3 months to mss. Accepts simultaneous submissions.

Terms Pays 5-10% royalty on wholesale price or makes outright purchase of $500-1,500. Average advance: $500-$1,000; negotiable.

🖉 ◎ 🏆 FRONT STREET

an imprint of Boyds Mills Press, Inc., 815 Church St., Honesdale PA 18431. Web site: www.frontstreetbooks.com. **Contact:** Manuscript Submissions. Estab. 1994. "High-quality fiction for children and young adults." Publishes hardcover originals and trade paperback reprints. Books: coated paper; offset printing; case binding; 4-color illustrations. Averages 15 fiction titles/year. Distributes titles through independed sales reps and via order line directly from Front Street. Promotes titles through sales and professional conferences, sales reps, reviews.

Needs Adventure, ethnic, historical, humor, juvenile, literary, picture books, young adult (adventure, fantasy/science fiction, historical, mystery/suspense, problem novels, sports). "We look for fresh voices for children and young adults. Titles on our list entertain, challenge, or enlighten, always employing novel characters whose considered voices resonate." Published *Keturah and Lord Death*, by Martine Leavitt; *The Big House*, by Carolyn Coman; *Long Gone Daddy*, by Helen Hemphill.

How to Contact Accepts unsolicited and international mss. Query with outline/synopsis, 3 sample chapters, and SASE and lable the package "Manuscript Submission." Agented fiction 30%. Responds in 3 months to mss. Accepts simultaneous submissions.

Terms Pays royalty on retail price. Offers advance.

Advice "Read through our recently published titles and review our Web site. Check to see what's on the market and in our catalog before submitting your story. Feel free to query us if you're not sure."

⚡ ◎ GASLIGHT PUBLICATIONS

Empire Publishing Services, P.O. Box 1344, Studio City CA 91614. (818)784-8918. **Contact:** Simon Waters, fiction editor (Sherlock Holmes only). Estab. 1960. Publishes hardcover and paperback originals and reprints. Books: paper varies; offset printing; binding varies; illustrations. Average print order: 5,000. **Published 1 debut author within the last year.** Averages 4-12 total titles, 2-4 fiction titles/year. Promotes titles through sales reps, trade, library, etc.

Needs Sherlock Holmes only. Recently published *Sherlock Holmes, The Complete Bagel Street Saga*, by Robert L. Fish; *Subcutaneously: My Dear Watson*, by Jack Tracy (all Sherlock Holmes).

How to Contact Accepts unsolicited mss. Query with SASE. Include estimated word count, brief bio, list of publishing credits. Send SASE for return of ms or send a disposable ms and SASE for reply only. Agented fiction 10%. Responds in 2 weeks to queries; 1 year to mss.

Terms Pays 8-10% royalty. Royalty and advance dependent on the material. Publishes ms 1-6 months after acceptance.

Advice "Please send only Sherlock Holmes material. Other stuff just wastes time and money."

Ⓐ ⚡ ◎ LAURA GERINGER BOOKS

HarperCollins Children's Books, 1350 Avenue of the Americas, New York NY 10019. (212)261-6500. Web site: www.harperchildrens.com. **Contact:** Laura Geringer, senior vice president/publisher. "We look for books that are out of the ordinary, authors who have their own definite take, and artists who add a sense of humor to the text." Publishes hardcover originals. **Published some debut authors within the last year.** Averages 15-20 total titles/year.

Needs Adventure, fantasy, historical, humor, juvenile, literary, picture books, young adult. Recently published *Regular Guy*, by Sarah Weeks; *Throwing Smoke*, by Bruce Brooks.

How to Contact Does not accept unsolicited mss. Agented fiction 90%.

Terms Pays 10-12½% royalty on retail price. Average advance: variable.

Advice "A mistake writers often make is failing to research the type of books an imprint publishes, therefore sending inappropriate material."

◙ GERTRUDE PRESS

P.O. Box 83948, Portland OR 97283. Web site: www.gertrudepress.org. **Contact:** Justus Ballard (all fiction). Estab. 2005. "Gertrude Press is a nonprofit organization developing and showcasing the creative talents of lesbian, gay, bisexual, trans, queer-identified and allied individuals. We publish limited-edition fiction and poetry chapbooks plus the biannual literary journal, *Gertrude*." Format: 60 lb. paper; high-quality digital printing; perfect (lit mag) or saddle-stitch (chapbook) bound. Average print order: 350. Published 5-10 new writers last year. Averages 4 total titles/year; 1 fiction title/year.

Needs Ethnic/multicultural, experimental, feminist, gay, humor/satire, lesbian, literary, mainstream, short story collections.

How to Contact Submit complete ms with cover letter. Submissions accepted year-round. Accepts queries by snail mail, e-mail. Include estimated word count, brief bio, list of publishing credits. Send disposable copy of ms and SASE for reply only. Responds to queries in 3-4 weeks; mss in 3-6 months. Accepts unsolicited mss. Considers simultaneous submissions, e-mail submissions. Sometimes critiques/comments on rejected mss.

Terms Manuscript published 3 months after acceptance. Writer's guidelines on Web site. Pays in author's copies (1 for lit mag, 50 for chapbook). Book catalogs not available.

Advice Sponsors poetry and fiction chapbook contest. Prize is $50 and 50 contributor's copies. Submission guidelines and fee information on Web site. "Read the journal and sample published work. We are not impressed by pages of publications; your work should speak for itself."

◘ GIVAL PRESS

P.O. Box 3812, Arlington VA 22203. (703)351-0079. E-mail: givalpress@yahoo.com. Web site: www.givalpress.com. **Contact:** Robert L. Giron, publisher. Estab. 1998. A small, award-winning independent publisher that publishes quality works by a variety of authors from an array of walks of life. Works are in English, Spanish and French and have a philosophical or social message. Publishes paperback originals and reprints and e-books. Books: perfect-bound. Average print order: 500. **Publishes established and debut authors.** Plans 2 first novels this year. Member AAP, PMA, Literary Council of Small Presses and Magazines. Distributes books through Ingram and BookMasters, Inc.

• Received a DIY Book Festival award for Compilations/Anthologies; Silver Award, 2003 *Foreword Magazine* for fiction—translation.

Needs Literary, ethnic, gay/lesbian. "Looking for French books with English translation." The Annual Gival Press Novel Award contest deadline is May 30th. The Annual Gival Press Short Story Award contest deadline is August 8th. Guidelines on Web site. Recently published *Fiction: The Last Day of Paradise*, by Kiki Denis and *Boys*; *Lost & Found*, by Charles Casillo.

How to Contact Does not accept unsolicited mss. Query by e-mail first. Include description of project, estimated word count, brief bio, list of publishing credits. Agented fiction 5%. Responds by e-mail within 2 weeks. Rarely comments on rejected mss.

Terms Pays 20 contributor's copies. Offers advance. Publishes ms 1 year after acceptance. For book catalog send SASE and on Web site. Ms guidelines by SASE or on Web site.

Advice "Study the types of books we have published—literary works with a message of high quality."

☐ ◉ THE GLENCANNON PRESS

P.O. Box 1428, El Cerrito CA 94530. (510)528-4216. Fax: (510)528-3194. E-mail: merships@yahoo.com. Web site: www.glencannon.com. **Contact:** Bill Harris (maritime, maritime children's). Estab. 1993. "We publish quality books about ships and the sea." Publishes hardcover and paperback originals and hardcover reprints. Books: Smyth: perfect binding; illustrations. Average print order: 1,000. First novel print order: 750. Averages 4-5 total titles, 1 fiction titles/year. Member PMA, BAIPA. Distributes titles through Quality Books, Baker & Taylor. Promotes titles through direct mail, magazine advertising and word of mouth.

Imprint(s) Palo Alto Books (any except maritime); Glencannon Press (merchant marine and Navy).

Needs Adventure, children's/juvenile (adventure, fantasy, historical, mystery, preschool/picture book), ethnic (general), historical (maritime), humor, mainstream/contemporary, military/war, mystery, thriller/espionage, western (frontier saga, traditional maritime), young adult (adventure, historical, mystery/suspense, western). Currently emphasizing children's maritime, any age. Recently published *Good Shipmates*, by Ernest F. Imhoff (anthology, merchant marine); *Fort Ross*, by Mark West (Palo Alto Books, western).

How to Contact Accepts unsolicited mss. Submit complete ms. Include brief bio, list of publishing credits. Send SASE for return of ms or send a disposable ms and SASE for reply only. Responds in 1 month to queries; 2 months to mss. Accepts simultaneous submissions. Often comments on rejected mss.

Terms Pays 10-20% royalty. Publishes ms 6-24 months after acceptance.

Advice "Write a good story in a compelling style."

🔀 ◪ ◉ 🔡 GOOSE LANE EDITIONS

500 Beaver Brook Court, Suite 330, Fredericton NB E3B 5X4 Canada. (506)450-4251. Fax: (506)459-4991. Web site: www.gooselane.com. **Contact:** Susanne Alexander, publisher. Estab. 1954. Publishes hardcover and paperback originals and occasional reprints. Books: some illustrations. Average print order: 3,000. First novel print order: 1,500. Averages 16-18 total titles, 6-8 fiction titles/year. Distributes titles through University of Toronto Press (UTP).

• *Elle*, by Douglas Glover, won the 2004 Governor General's Award for Fiction and was shortlisted for the International IMPAC Dublin Literary Award.

Needs Literary (novels), mainstream/contemporary, short story collections. "Our needs in fiction never change: substantial, character-centered literary fiction." Published *The Famished Lover*, by Alan Curnyn.

How to Contact Accepts unsolicited mss. Query with SASE. Responds in 6 months to mss. No simultaneous submissions.

Terms Pays 8-10% royalty on retail price. Average advance: $200-1,000, negotiable. Ms guidelines online.

Advice "We do not consider submissions from outside Canada."

◉ GOTHIC CHAPBOOK SERIES

Gothic Press, 1701 Lobdell Avenue, No. 32, Baton Rouge LA 70806-8242. E-mail: gothicpt12@aol.com. Web site: www.gothicpress.com. **Contact:** Gary W. Crawford, editor (horror, fiction, poetry and scholarship). Estab. 1979. "One person operation on a part-time basis." Publishes paperback originals. Books: printing or photocopying. Average print order: 150-200. Distributes titles through direct mail and book dealers.

Needs Horror (dark fantasy, psychological, supernatural). Need novellas and short stories.

How to Contact Accepts unsolicited mss. Query with SASE. Accepts queries by e-mail, phone. Include estimated word count, brief bio, list of publishing credits. Send SASE for return of ms or send a disposable ms and SASE for reply only. Responds in 2 weeks to queries; 2 months to mss. Sometimes comments on rejected mss.

Terms Pays 10% royalty. Ms guidelines for #10 SASE.

Advice "Know gothic and horror literature well."

⚅ GRAYWOLF PRESS

2402 University Ave., Suite 203, St. Paul MN 55114. E-mail: wolves@graywolfpress.org. Web site: www.graywo lfpress.org. **Contact:** Katie Dublinski, editorial manager. Estab. 1974. Growing independent literary press, nonprofit corporation. Publishes trade cloth and paperback originals. Books: acid-free quality paper; offset printing; hardcover and soft binding. Average print order: 3,000-10,000. First novel print order: 3,000-7,500. Averages 25 total titles, 5-7 fiction titles/year. Distributes titles nationally through Farrar, Straus & Giroux.

Needs Literary novels, short story collections. ''Familiarize yourself with our list before submitting your work.'' Published *Wounded*, by Percival Everett; *The Translation of Dr. Apelles,* by David Treuer; *When All is Said and Done*, by Robert Hill.

How to Contact Query or submit 1 sample chapter. Include SASE/IRC, estimated word count, brief bio, list of publishing credits. Agented fiction 90%. Responds in 3 months to queries.

Terms Pays royalty on retail price, author's copies. Average advance: $2,500-15,000. Publishes ms 18-24 months after acceptance. Ms guidelines online.

Advice ''Please review our catalog and submission guidelines before submitting your work. We rarely publish story collections or novels by authors who have not published work previously in literary journals or magazines.''

ⓃⓄⓄ GREENE BARK PRESS

P.O. Box 1108, Bridgeport CT 06601. (203)372-4861. Fax: (203)371-5856. Web site: www.greenebarkpress.com. **Contact:** Tara Maroney, associate publisher. Estab. 1991. ''We only publish children's fiction—all subjects, but usually picture book format appealing to ages 3-9 or all ages.'' Publishes hardcover originals. **Published some debut authors within the last year.** Averages 1-6 total titles/year. Distributes titles through Baker & Taylor and Quality Books. Promotes titles through ads, trade shows (national and regional), direct mail campaigns.

Needs Juvenile. Published *Edith Ellen Eddy*, by Julee Granger.

How to Contact Submit complete ms. Responds in 3 months to queries; 6 months to mss. Accepts simultaneous submissions. No electronic submissions.

Terms Pays 10-15% royalty on wholesale price. Publishes ms 1 year after acceptance. Ms guidelines for SASE or e-mail request.

Advice Audience is ''children who read to themselves and others. Mothers, fathers, grandparents, godparents who read to their respective children, grandchildren. Include SASE, be prepared to wait, do NOT inquire by telephone, fax or e-mail.''

ⓧⓄ GREENWILLOW BOOKS

HarperCollins Publishers, 1350 Avenue of the Americas, New York NY 10019. (212)261-6500. Web site: www.ha rperchildrens.com. **Contact:** Fiction Editor. Estab. 1974. Publishes hardcover originals and reprints. Averages 50-60 total titles/year.

Needs Fantasy, humor, literary, mystery, picture books. *The Queen of Attolia*, by Megan Whalen Turner; *Bo & Mzzz Mad*, by Sid Fleishman; *Whale Talk*, by Chris Crutcher; *Year of the Griffen*, by Diana Wynne Jones.

How to Contact Does not accept unsolicited mss. ''Unsolicited mail will not be opened and will not be returned.''

Terms Pays 10% royalty on wholesale price for first-time authors. Average advance: variable. Publishes ms 2 years after acceptance.

Ⓐ GROVE/ATLANTIC, INC.

841 Broadway 4th Floor, New York NY 10003. (212)614-7850. Fax: (212)614-7886. Web site: www.groveatlantic .com. Estab. 1952. Publishes hardcover originals, trade paperback originals and reprints. Averages 60-70 total titles/year.

Imprint(s) Grove Press (estab. 1952), Atlantic Monthly Press (estab. 1917), Black Cat (estab. 1961, revived 2004).

Needs Literary. Published *Halfway House*, by Katharine Noel; *A Killing in This Town*, by Olympia Vernon; *I Love You More Than You Know*, by Jonathan Ames.

How to Contact Does not accept unsolicited mss. *Agented submissions only.* Accepts simultaneous submissions.

Terms Pays 7½-15% royalty on retail price. Average advance: varies. Publishes ms 1 year after acceptance.

Ⓞ GRYPHON BOOKS

P.O. Box 209, Brooklyn NY 11228. (718)646-6126 (after 6 p.m. EST). Web site: www.gryphonbooks.com. **Contact:** Gary Lovisi, owner/editor. Estab. 1983. Publishes paperback originals and trade paperback reprints. Books: bond paper; offset printing; perfect binding. Average print order: 500-1,000. **Published some debut authors within the last year.** Averages 10-15 total titles, 12 fiction titles/year.

Imprint(s) Gryphon Books, Gryphon Doubles, Gryphon SF Rediscovery Series.

Needs Mystery (private eye/hard-boiled, crime), science fiction (hard science/technological, soft/sociological).

Published *The Dreaming Detective*, by Ralph Vaughn (mystery-fantasy-horror); *The Woman in the Dugout*, by Gary Lovisi and T. Arnone (baseball novel); *A Mate for Murder*, by Bruno Fischer (hard-boiled pulp).
How to Contact "Not looking for novels right now; will only see a 1-2 page synopsis with SASE." Include estimated word count, brief bio, list of publishing credits. Agented fiction 5-10%. Often comments on rejected mss.
Terms Publishes ms 1-3 years after acceptance. Ms guidelines for #10 SASE.
Advice "I am looking for better and better writing, more cutting-edge material with *impact*! Keep it lean and focused."

HARBOR HOUSE

111 Tenth St., Augusta GA 30901. (706)738-0354. Fax: (706)823-5999. E-mail: harborhouse@harborhousebooks .com. Web site: www.harborhousebooks.com. **Contact:** Peggy Cheney, editorial director and assistant publisher. Estab. 1997. Harbor House seeks to publish the best in original fiction (southern, thrillers, horror) and current events/social issue nonfiction. Publishes hardcover originals and paperback originals. Average print order: 5,000. **Published 8 debut authors within the last year.** Member: Publishers Association of the South. Distribution with Ingram; Baker & Taylor; Anderson; and American Wholesale.
● Received a Golden Eye Literary Award.
Imprint(s) Batwing Press, Southern Winds, Savannah River Press.
Needs Horror, thriller, Civil War, new age/mystic, unsolved mysteries.
How to Contact Accepts queries by mail. Does not accept phone queries or proposals by e-mail. Accepts unsolicited mss or send outline, 3 sample chapter(s). Include estimated word count, brief bio, list of publishing credits, marketing plans, SASE. Agented fiction 10%. Responds in 4 weeks to queries; 2 months to mss. Accepts simultaneous submissions. Does not accept previously published works. Sometimes comments on rejected mss.
Terms Royalty rates vary, depending on hardcover or paperback. Minimum advance: $500.
Advice "We strongly encourage authors to consult our Web site before submitting material. We are particularly interested in developing unpublished authors."

⃞ ⃞ HARCOURT, INC

Children's Books Division, 525 B St., Suite 1900, San Diego CA 92101. (619)281-6616. Fax: (619)699-6777. Web site: www.harcourtbooks.com/htm/childrens_index.asp. Estab. 1919. "Harcourt Inc. owns some of the world's most prestigious publishing imprints—which distinguish quality products for the juvenile, educational, scientific, technical, medical, professional and trade markets worldwide." Publishes hardcover originals and trade paperback reprints.
Imprint(s) Harcourt Children's Books, Red Wagon, Odyssey Paperbacks, Magic Carpet, Voyager Books/Libros Viajeros and Green Light Readers.
Needs Children's/juvenile, young adult.
How to Contact Does not accept unsolicited mss.

⃞ ⃞ ⃞ HARLEQUIN AMERICAN ROMANCE

a Harlequin book line, 233 Broadway, Suite 1001, New York NY 10279. (212)553-4200. Web site: www.eharlequi n.com. **Contact:** Melissa Jeglinski, associate senior editor. "Upbeat and lively, fast paced and well plotted, American Romance celebrates the pursuit of love in the backyards, big cities and wide-open spaces of America." Publishes paperback originals and reprints. Books: newspaper print paper; web printing; perfect bound.
Needs Romance (contemporary, American). Needs "all-American stories with a range of emotional and sensual content that are supported by a sense of community within the plot's framework. In the confident and caring heroine, the tough but tender hero, and their dynamic relationship that is at the center of this series, real-life love is showcased as the best fantasy of all!"
How to Contact Query with SASE. No simultaneous submissions, electronic submissions, or submissions on disk.
Terms Pays royalty. Offers advance. Ms guidelines online.

⃞ ⃞ ⃞ ⃞ HARLEQUIN BLAZE

a Harlequin book line, 225 Duncan Mill Road, Don Mills ON M3B 3K9 Canada. (416)445-5860. Web site: www.eharlequin.com. **Contact:** Brenda Chin, associate senior editor. "Harlequin Blaze is a red-hot series. It is a vehicle to build and promote new authors who have a strong sexual edge to their stories. It is also *the* place to be for seasoned authors who want to create a sexy, sizzling, longer contemporary story." Publishes paperback originals. Books: newspaper print; web printing; perfect bound. **Published some debut authors within the last year.**
Needs Romance (contemporary). "Sensuous, highly romantic, innovative plots that are sexy in premise and execution. The tone of the books can run from fun and flirtatious to dark and sensual. Submissions should

have a very contemporary feel—what it's like to be young and single today. We are looking for heroes and heroines in their early 20s and up. There should be a a strong emphasis on the physical relationship between the couples. Fully described love scenes along with a high level of fantasy and playfulness.''

How to Contact No simultaneous submissions, electronic submissions, submissions on disk.

Terms Pays royalty. Offers advance. Ms guidelines online.

Advice ''Are you a *Cosmo* girl at heart? A fan of *Sex and the City*? Or maybe you have a sexually adventurous spirit. If so, then Blaze is the series for you!''

HARLEQUIN EVERLASTING

Harlequin Enterprises, Ltd., 225 Duncan Mill Rd., Don Mills ON M3B 3K9. Web site: www.eharlequin.com. **Contact:** Paula Eykelhof, executive editor. Estab. February 2007. ''The novels in this series will follow the life and relationship/s of one couple. The books will therefore span considerably more time than the typical series romance—it could be years or even an entire lifetime. The focus of Harlequin Everlasting is on much more of the characters' lives, not just the weeks or months during which the romantic relationship develops and its initial resolution takes place.'' Publishes paperback originals. Format: newsprint paper; web printing; perfect bound. Averages 24 fiction titles/year.

Needs Romance. ''We are looking for emotionally intense stories with a strong emphasis on well-rendered and psychologically credible characters (who influence each other's lives over time). The series will be open to a wide range of plots and situations; each story will require a significant conflict that creates urgency, excitement and momentum. Structurally, there will be many more options—interesting and nonlinear ways of structuring the story—than the traditional series romance typically allows. The narrative can start at any point, can include diaries or letters, can move freely back and forth in time, etc. Points of view can vary—and first-person narrative can be used. We're looking for writers who can create a complex and believable world for the characters and their romance. We want to see an individual and engaging style that is appropriate to the scope of the story. Above all, we want you to write a romance that matters—a sweeping narrative, a memorable story that touches the reader emotionally.''

How to Contact Query with outline/synopsis and 1-3 sample chapters. Accepts submissions by snail mail.

Terms Pays royalties, advance. Writer's guidelines on Web site. Book catalogs on Web site.

HARLEQUIN HISTORICALS

a Harlequin book line, Eton House, 18-24 Paradise Road, Richmond Surrey TW9 1SR United Kingdom. (212)553-4200. Web site: www.eharlequin.com. **Contact:** Linda Fildew, senior editor. ''The primary element of a Harlequin Historical novel is romance. The story should focus on the heroine and how her love for one man changes her life forever. For this reason, it is very important that you have an appealing hero and heroine, and that their relationship is a compelling one. The conflicts they must overcome—and the situations they face—can be as varied as the setting you have chosen, but there must be romantic tension, some spark between your hero and heroine that keeps your reader interested.'' Publishes paperback originals and reprints. Books: newsprint paper; perfect bound. **Published some debut authors within the last year.**

Needs Romance (historical). ''We will not accept books set after 1900. We're looking primarily for books set in North America, England or France between 1100 and 1900 A.D. We do not buy many novels set during the American Civil War. We are, however, flexible and will consider most periods and settings. We are not looking for gothics or family sagas, nor are we interested in the kind of comedy of manners typified by straight Regencies. Historical romances set during the Regency period, however, will definitely be considered.''

How to Contact Submit the first three chapters along with a 1-2 page synopsis of your novel.

Terms Pays royalty. Offers advance. Ms guidelines online.

HARLEQUIN INTRIGUE

a Harlequin Book line, 233 Broadway, Suite 1001, New York NY 10279. (212)553-4200. Web site: www.eharlequin.com. **Contact:** Denise Zaza, senior editor; Sean Mackiewicz, editorial assistant. ''These novels are taut, edge-of-the-seat, contemporary romantic suspense tales of intrigue and desire. Kidnappings, stalkings and women in jeopardy coupled with best-selling romantic themes are the examples of story lines we love most.'' Publishes paperback originals and reprints. Books: newspaper print; perfect bound. **Published some debut authors within the last year.**

Needs Romance (romantic suspense). ''Murder mystery, psychological suspense or thriller, the love story must be inextricably bound to the resolution where all loose ends are tied up neatly—and shared dangers lead right to shared passions. As long as they're in jeopardy and falling in love, our heroes and heroines may traverse a landscape as wide as the world itself. Their lives are on the line—and so are their hearts!''

How to Contact Accepts unsolicited mss. Query with SASE. Send SASE for return of ms or send a disposable ms and SASE for reply only. No simultaneous submissions, electronic submissions, submissions on disk.

Terms Pays royalty. Offers advance. Ms guidelines online.

🌐 ⚔ HARLEQUIN MILLS & BOON, LTD.

Harlequin Enterprises, Ltd., Eton House, 18-24 Paradise Rd., Richmond Surrey TW9 1SR United Kingdom. (+44)0208-288-2800. Web site: www.millsandboon.co.uk. **Contact:** K. Stoecker, editorial director; Tessa Shapcott, senior editor (Mills & Boon Modern Romance); Bryony Green, senior editor (Mills & Boon Tender Romance); Linda Fildew, senior editor (Mills & Boon Historicals); Sheila Hodgson, senior editor (Mills & Boon Medicals). Estab. 1908-1909. Publishes mass market paperback originals. **Published some debut authors within the last year.** Plans 3-4 first novels this year.

Imprint(s) Mills & Boon Modern Romance (Harlequin Presents); Mills & Boon Tender Romance (Harlequin Romance); Mills & Boon Historicals; Mills & Boon Medicals.

Needs Romance (contemporary, historical, regency period, medical).

How to Contact Send query letter. No simultaneous submissions.

Terms Pays advance against royalty. Publishes ms 2 years after acceptance. Ms guidelines online.

🔄 ⚔ ⃝ HARLEQUIN SUPERROMANCE

a Harlequin book line, 225 Duncan Mill Road, Don Mills ON M3B 3K9 Canada. (416)445-5860. Web site: www.eharlequin.com. **Contact:** Laura Shin, senior editor. "The aim of Superromance novels is to produce a contemporary, involving read with a mainstream tone in its situations and characters, using romance as the major theme. To achieve this, emphasis should be placed on individual writing styles and unique and topical ideas." Publishes paperback originals. Books: newspaper print; perfect bound. **Published 5 debut authors in 2006.**

Needs Romance (contemporary). "The criteria for Superromance books are flexible. Aside from length, the determining factor for publication will always be quality. Authors should strive to break free of stereotypes, clichés and worn-out plot devices to create strong, believable stories with depth and emotional intensity. Superromance novels are intended to appeal to a wide range of romance readers."

How to Contact Accepts unsolicited submissions. Submit 3 sample chapter(s) and synopsis. Send SASE for return of ms or send a disposable ms and SASE for reply only. No simultaneous submissions, electronic submissions, submissions on disk.

Terms Pays royalty. Offers advance. Ms guidelines online.

Advice "A general familiarity with current Superromance books is advisable to keep abreast of ever-changing trends and overall scope, but we don't want imitations. We look for sincere, heartfelt writing based on true-to-life experiences the reader can identify with. We are interested in innovation."

🅰 ⚔ ⊘ ◎ HARPERCOLLINS CANADA LTD.

2 Bloor St. East, 20th Floor, Toronto ON M4W 1A8 Canada. (416)975-9334. Fax: (416)975-5223. Web site: www.harpercanada.com. Harpercollins is not accepting unsolicited material at this time.

🅰 ⚔ HARPERCOLLINS CHILDREN'S BOOKS

HarperCollins Publishers, 1350 Avenue of the Americas, New York NY 10019. (212)261-6500. Fax: (212)261-6689. Web site: www.harperchildrens.com. Publishes hardcover originals. Averages 350 total titles/year.

Imprint(s) Amistad, Avon, Joanna Cotler, EOS, Greenwillow Books, Laura Geringer Books, HarperFestival, HarperKids Entertainment, HarperTrophy, HarperTempest, Katherine Tegen Books, Rayo Books.

Needs Adventure, fantasy, historical, humor, juvenile, literary, picture books, young adult.

How to Contact *Agented submissions only.*

Terms Pays 10-12½% royalty on retail price. Average advance: variable. Publishes ms 1 year (novels) or 2 years (picture books) after acceptance.

⚔ HARPERCOLLINS GENERAL BOOKS GROUP

Division of HarperCollins Publishers, 10 East 53 Street, New York NY 10022. (212)207-7000. Fax: (212)207-7633. Web site: www.harpercollins.com. "HarperCollins, one of the largest English language publishers in the world, is a broad-based publisher with strengths in academic, business and professional, children's, educational, general interest, and religious and spiritual books, as well as multimedia titles." Publishes hardcover and paperback originals and paperback reprints.

Imprint(s) Amistad Press, Avon, Caedmon, Ecco, Eos, Haper Perennial, HarperAudio, HarperCollins, HarperEntertainment, HarperLargePrint, HarperSanFranciso, HarperTorch PerfectBound, Rayo, ReganBooks, William Morrow.

How to Contact: See imprint for specific guidelines.

Ⓝ ⚔ ⊘ HARPERTORCH

(formerly HarperPaperbacks), Imprint of HarperCollins Publishers, 10 E. 53rd St., New York NY 10022. (212)207-7000. Fax: (212)207-7901. **Contact:** Michael Morrison, publisher. Publishes paperback originals and reprints. **Published some debut authors within the last year.**

Needs Mainstream/contemporary, mystery, romance (contemporary, historical, romantic suspense), suspense, thriller/espionage.

How to Contact Does not accept unsolicited mss. Query with SASE.

Terms Pays royalty. Offers advance.

Ⓐ Ⓒ HARVEST HOUSE PUBLISHERS

990 Owen Loop N., Eugene OR 97402. (541)343-0123. Fax: (541)302-0731. E-mail: manuscriptcoordinator@harvesthousepublishers.com. Web site: www.harvesthousepublishers.com. **Contact:** Acquisitions. Estab. 1974. "Our mission is to glorify God by providing high-quality books and products that affirm biblical values, help people grow spiritually strong, and proclaim Jesus Christ as the answer to every human need." Publishes hardcover originals and reprints, trade paperback originals and reprints, and mass market paperback originals and reprints. Books: 40 lb. ground wood paper; offset printing; perfect binding. Average print order: 10,000. First novel print order: 10,000-15,000. **Published 20 debut authors within the last year.** Averages 175 total titles, 15-20 fiction titles/year.

Needs Harvest House no longer accepts unsolicited manuscripts, proposals, or artwork.

How to Contact Does not accept unsolicited mss.

Advice "Attend a writer's conference where you have an opportunity to pitch your book idea to an editor face to face. We also look at fiction represented by a reputable agent."

Ⓜ HAWK PUBLISHING GROUP

7107 S. Yale Ave., #345, Tulsa OK 74136. (918)492-3677. Fax: (918)492-3677. Web site: www.hawkpub.com. Estab. 1999. Independent publisher of general trade/commercial books, fiction and nonfiction. Publishes hardcover and trade paperback originals. **Published 4 debut authors within the last year.** Plans 2 first novels this year. Averages 6-8 total titles, 3 fiction titles/year. Member PMA. Titles are distributed by NBN/Biblio Distribution.

Needs Looking for good books of all kinds. Not interested in juvenile, poetry or short story collections. Published *I Survived Cancer*, by Jim Chastain; *Everlasting*, by Carol Johnson; *Ghost Band*, by John Wooley.

How to Contact Accepts unsolicited mss. Submit first 20 pages of your book, synopsis, author bio. Include list of publishing credits. Accepts simultaneous submissions.

Terms Pays royalty. Publishes ms 1-2 years after acceptance. Ms guidelines online.

Advice "Prepare a professional submission and follow the guidelines. The simple things really do count; use 12 pt. pitch with 1-inch margins and only send what is requested."

Ⓒ HELICON NINE EDITIONS

Subsidiary of Midwest Center for the Literary Arts, Inc., P.O. Box 22412, Kansas City MO 64113. (816)753-1016. E-mail: helicon9@aol.com. Web site: www.heliconnine.com. **Contact:** Gloria Vando Hickok. Estab. 1990. Small not-for-profit press publishing poetry, fiction, creative nonfiction and anthologies. Publishes paperback originals. Also publishes one-story chapbooks called *feuillets*, which come with envelope, 250 print run. Books: 60 lb. paper; offset printing; perfect bound; 4-color cover. Average print order: 1,000-5,000. **Published 1 debut author within the last year.** Distributes titles through Baker & Taylor, Brodart, Ingrams, Follet (library acquisitions), and booksellers. Promotes titles through reviews, readings, radio and television interviews.

How to Contact Does not accept unsolicited mss.

Terms Pays royalty. Author's copies. Offers advance. Publishes ms 12-18 months after acceptance.

Advice "We accept short story collections, welcome new writers and first books. Submit a clean, readable copy in a folder or box—paginated with title and name on each page. Also, do not pre-design book, i.e., no illustrations, unless they are an integral part of the book. We'd like to see books that will be read 50-100 years from now."

Ⓒ HENDRICK-LONG PUBLISHING CO., INC.

10635 Toweroaks D., Houston TX 77070. (832)912-7323. Fax: (832)912-7353. E-mail: hendrick-long@worldnet.att.net. Web site: hendricklongpublishing.com. **Contact:** Vilma Long. Estab. 1969. Only considers manuscripts with Texas theme. Publishes hardcover and trade paperback originals and hardcover reprints. Averages 4 total titles/year.

Needs Juvenile, young adult.

How to Contact Submit outline, 2 sample chapter(s), synopsis. Responds in 3 months to queries. No simultaneous submissions.

Terms Pays royalty on selling price. Offers advance. Publishes ms 18 months after acceptance. Book catalog for 8½×11 or 9×12 SASE with 4 first-class stamps. Ms guidelines online.

Book Publishers

◎ HOLIDAY HOUSE, INC.

425 Madison Ave., New York NY 10017. (212)688-0085. Fax: (212)421-6134. **Contact:** Aquisitions editor. Estab. 1935. "Holiday House has a commitment to publishing first-time authors and illustrators." Independent publisher of children's books, picture books, nonfiction and novels for young readers. Publishes hardcover originals and paperback reprints. **Published some debut authors within the last year.** Averages 60 total titles/year.

Needs Middle grade, YA, humor, literary, mainstream/contemporary, Judaica and holiday, animal stories for young readers. Children's books only. Published *There is a Frog in My Throat*, by Pat Street, illustrated by Loreen Leedy; *The Gorillas of Gill Park*, by Amy Gordon.

How to Contact Query with SASE. No simultaneous submissions.

Terms Pays royalty on list price, range varies. Average advance: flexible, depending on whether the book is illustrated. Publishes ms 18 months after acceptance. Ms guidelines for #10 SASE.

Advice "We're not in a position to be too encouraging, as our list is tight, but we're always open to good writing. Please submit only one project at a time."

◯ HOLLOWAY HOUSE PUBLISHING CO.

8060 Melrose Ave., Los Angeles CA 90046. (323)653-8060. Fax: (323)655-9452. **Contact:** Neal Colgrass, editor (multicultural). Estab. 1960. Publishes paperback originals. Book: Groundwood paper; offset printing; perfect binding; illustrations. Average print order: 10,000. Distributes through the National Distributer.

Imprint(s) Mankind Books (multicultural).

Needs Erotica, ethnic, multicultural.

How to Contact Accepts unsolicited mss. Query with SASE. Accepts queries by mail. Include estimated word count, list of publishing credits. Send SASE or IRC. Agented fiction 10%. No simultaneous submissions. Sometimes comments on rejected mss.

Terms Publishes ms 6-12 months after acceptance.

▨ ◎ HENRY HOLT & CO. BOOKS FOR YOUNG READERS

Henry Holt & Co., LLC, 175 Fifth Avenue, New York NY 10010. (646)307-5087. Web site: www.henryholtchildre nsbooks.com. **Contact:** Submissions editor, Books for Young Readers. Henry Holt Books for Young Readers publishes excellent books of all kinds (fiction, nonfiction, illustrated) for all ages, from the very young to the young adult. Publishes hardcover originals of picture books, chapter books, middle grade and young adult novels. Averages 70-80 total titles/year.

Needs Adventure, fantasy, historical, mainstream/contemporary, multicultural, picture books, young adult. Juvenile: adventure, animal, contemporary, fantasy, history, multicultural. Picture books: animal, concept, history, mulitcultural, sports. Young adult: contemporary, fantasy, history, multicultural, nature/environment, problem novels, sports. Published *When Zachary Beaver Came to Town*, by Kimberly Willis Holt (middle grade fiction); *The Gospel According to Larry*, by Janet Tashjian (YA fiction); *Visiting Langston*, by Willie Perdomo, illustrated by Bryan Collier (picture book); *Keeper of the Night*, by Kimberly Willis Holt; *Alphabet Under Construction*, by Denise Fleming (picture book).

How to Contact Accepts unsolicited mss. Include estimated word count, brief bio, list of publishing credits. Do not send SASE; publisher will not respond unless making an offer for publication.

Terms See Web site for complete guidelines, www.henryholtchildrensbooks.com/submissions.htm.

▣ ▨ HENRY HOLT

Henry Holt and Company, 175 Fifth Avenue, New York NY 10011. (212)886-9200. Web site: www.henryholt.c om. Publishes hardcover and paperback originals and reprints.

Imprint(s) Metropolitan Books; Times Books; Henry Holt; Owl Books ; Jack Macrae Books.

How to Contact: Closed to submissions. *Agented submissions only.*

▨ ◪ ◎ HOUGHTON MIFFLIN BOOKS FOR CHILDREN

Houghton Mifflin Company, 222 Berkeley St., Boston MA 02116. (617)351-5959. Fax: (617)351-1111. E-mail: children's_books@hmco.com. Web site: www.houghtonmifflinbooks.com. **Contact:** Submissions coordinator; Kate O'Sullivan senior editor; Ann Rider, senior editor; Margaret Raymo, editorial director. "Houghton Mifflin gives shape to ideas that educate, inform and, above all, delight." Publishes hardcover originals and trade paperback originals and reprints. **Published 12 debut authors within the last year.** Averages 100 total titles/year. Promotes titles through author visits, advertising, reviews.

Imprint(s) Clarion Books, New York City, Walter Lorraine Books, King Fisher Books.

Needs Adventure, ethnic, historical, humor, juvenile (early readers), literary, mystery, picture books, suspense, young adult, board books. Published *Snow Sounds*, by David A. Johnson; *Gossamer*, by Lois Lowry; *The Circuit*, by Francisco Jimenez.

How to Contact Accepts unsolicited mss. Responds only if interested. Do not send SASE. Accepts simultaneous submissions. No electronic submissions.

Terms Pays 5-10% royalty on retail price. Average advance: variable. Publishes ms 18-24 months after acceptance. Book catalog for 9×12 SASE with 3 first-class stamps. Ms guidelines online.

Ⓐ HOUGHTON MIFFLIN CO.

222 Berkeley St., Boston MA 02116. (617)351-5000. Web site: www.hmco.com. **Contact:** Submissions Editor. Estab. 1832. Publishes hardcover originals and trade paperback originals and reprints. **Published 5 debut authors within the last year.** Averages 250 total titles/year.

Needs Literary. "We are not a mass market publisher. Study the current list." Published *Extremely Loud and Incredibly Close*, by Jonathan Safran Foer; *The Plot Against America*, by Philip Roth; *Heir to the Glimmering World*, by Cynthia Ozick.

How to Contact Does not accept unsolicited mss. *Agented submissions only.* Accepts simultaneous submissions.

Terms Hardcover: pays 10-15% royalty on retail price, sliding scale or flat rate based on sales; paperback: 7½% flat rate, but negotiable. Average advance: variable. Publishes ms 3 years after acceptance.

Ⓝ HOWELLS HOUSE

P.O. Box 9546, Washington DC 20016-9546. (202)333-2182. **Contact:** W.D. Howells, publisher. Estab. 1988. "Our interests are institutions and institutional change." Publishes hardcover and trade paperback originals and reprints. Averages 4 total titles/year.

Imprint(s) The Compass Press, Whalesback Books.

Needs Historical, literary, mainstream/contemporary.

How to Contact No simultaneous submissions.

Terms Pays 15% net royalty or makes outright purchase. May offer advance. Publishes ms 8 months after acceptance.

Ⓐ ⭐ ⊘ HYPERION BOOKS FOR CHILDREN

Hyperion, 114 Fifth Ave., New York NY 10011. (212)633-440. Fax: (212)807-5880. Web site: www.hyperionbooksforchildren.com. **Contact:** Editorial director. "The aim of Hyperion Books for Children is to create a dynamic children's program informed by Disney's creative vision, direct connection to children, and unparalleled marketing and distribution." Publishes hardcover and trade paperback originals. Averages 210 total titles/year.

Needs Juvenile, picture books, young adult. Published *McDuff*, by Roesmary Wells and Susan Jeffers (picture book); *Split Just Right*, by Adele Griffin (middle grade).

How to Contact *Agented submissions only.* Accepts simultaneous submissions.

Terms Pays royalty. Average advance: varies. Publishes ms 1 year after acceptance.

Advice "Hyperion Books for Children are meant to appeal to an upscale children's audience. Study your audience. Look at and research current children's books. Who publishes what you like? Approach them."

Ⓝ 🌐 ◯ IGNOTUS PRESS

BCM-Writer, London England WC1N 3XX United Kingdom. E-mail: ignotuspress@aol.com. Web site: www.ignotuspress.com. **Contact:** Suzanne Ruthuen. Estab. 1996. The aim of ignotus press is to provide a wide base of genuine information for all esoteric traditions. Publishes paperback originals, hardcover reprints, paperback reprints and e-books. Books: litho and digital printing; perfect binding; illustrations. Average first novel print order: 300. **Published 12 debut authors within the last year.** Averages 20 total titles/year.

Imprint(s) Moonraker, Alphard, Past Tomes.

Needs Horror (psychological, supernatural), humor, new age/mystic, psychic/supernatural, religious (religious mystery/suspense, religious thriller). "ignotus press hopes to fill the gap left by main-stream publishers who are moving away from traditional sources. What we don't want is New Age idealism, sword & sorcery, fantasy, 'mind, body & spirit', the white-light brand of modern Wicca, pseudo-spirituality or any form of neo-Hammer House of Horror fiction." Recently published *The Google Tantra*, by Alan Richardson; *Starchild*, by Melusine Draco; *The Salamander Stone*, by Catherine Watling.

How to Contact Does not accept unsolicited mss. Submit 2 sample chapter(s). Accepts queries by mail. Include estimated word count, brief bio, list of publishing credits. Send SASE for return of ms or send a disposable ms and SASE for reply only. Responds in 1 month to mss. Sometimes comments on rejected mss.

Terms Pays royalty. Pays 6 contributor's copies. Publishes ms 6-12 months after acceptance. Ms guidelines for SASE.

Advice "Seriously study the guidelines and back list."

⚂ ⊘ IMAGES SI, INC

Imprint of Images Publishing, 109 Woods of Arden Rd., Staten Island NY 10312. (718)966-3964. Fax: (718)966-3695. Web site: www.imagesco.com/publishing/index.html. **Contact:** Acquisitions Editor. Estab. 1990. Publishes 2 audio books a year.

Needs Hard science fiction for audiocassettes and CDs. Published *Centauri III*, by George L. Griggs (science fiction print book); *Nova-Audio, Issues 1-3*, by Hoyt, Franklin, Schoen, Wild, Silverberg and Catelli (science fiction audio).

How to Contact Closed to submissions until 2008.

Terms Pays 10-20% royalty on wholesale price. Publishes stories 6 months-2 years after acceptance.

Ⓝ ⊘ IMAJINN BOOKS

P.O. Box 545, Canon City CO 81212-0545. (719)275-0060. Fax: (719)276-0746. E-mail: editors@imajinnbooks.com. Web site: www.imajinnbooks.com. **Contact:** Linda J. Kichline, editor. Estab. 1998. "ImaJinn Books is a small independent print-on-demand publishing house that specializes in Urban Fantasy and paranormal romances with story lines involving psychics or psychic phenomena, witches, vampires, werewolves, space travel, the future. Launching a Regency Romance line in late 2007." Publishes trade paperback originals. Books: print-on-demand; perfect binding; no illustrations. **Published 3-4 debut authors.** Member: SPAN. Distributes titles through Ingram Books and imajinnbooks.com. Promotes titles through advertising and review magazines.

Needs Fantasy (romance), horror (romance), psychic/supernatural (romance), and all Urban Fantasy story lines, Regency romance. "We look for specific story lines based on what the readers are asking for and what story lines in which we're short. We post our current needs on our Web site." Published *Dancing with The Devil*, by Keri Arthur (horror romance); and *My Lord Viking*, by J.A. Ferguson (Regency romance).

How to Contact Query with SASE. Prefers queries by email. Include estimated word count, brief bio, list of publishing credits. Unless otherwise requested prefers e-mail submissions. Agented fiction 20%. Responds in 3 months to queries; 9-12 months to mss. Often comments on rejected mss.

Terms Pays 6-10% royalty on retail price. Average advance: 100-200. Publishes ms 1-3 years after acceptance. Book catalog and ms guidelines for #10 SASE or online. Ms guidelines online.

Advice "Carefully read the author guidelines, and read books published by ImaJinn Books. Do not submit manuscript without querying first."

⊘ INGALLS PUBLISHING GROUP, INC

197 New Market Center, #135, Boone NC 28607. (828)964-0590. Fax: (828)262-1973. E-mail: editor@highcountrypublishers.com. Web site: www.highcountrypublishers.com. **Contact:** Wendy Dingwall, operations and sales manager. Estab. 2001. "We are a small regional house focusing on popular fiction and memoir. At present, we are most interested in regional fiction, historical fiction and mystery fiction." Publishes hardcover originals, paperback originals and paperback reprints. Books: 60# paper; offset printing; b&w illustrations. Average print order: 1,500-5,000. First novel print order: 1,500-3,000. **Published 1 debut author within the last year.** Plans 3 first novels this year. Member PMA, PAS, SEBA. Distributes titles through Biblio Distribution, sister company of NBN books.

Needs Ethnic, feminist, historical, mystery (amateur sleuth, cozy, police procedural, private eye/hard-boiled), regional (southern appalachian), romance (contemporary, historical, romantic suspense adventure), young adult (historical, mystery/suspense). Published *Dirty Deeds*, by Mark Terry (mystery); *Once Upon a Different Time*, by Marian Coe; *Gloria*, by Ann Chamberlin (historical fiction); *Mount Doomsday*, by Don Berman (thriller).

How to Contact Accepts unsolicited mss. Query with SASE or submit outline, 3 sample chapter(s). Reading period open from July to October. Accepts queries by e-mail, mail. Include estimated word count, brief bio, list of publishing credits. Send copy of ms and SASE. Agented fiction 10%. Responds in 6 months to queries; 6 months to mss. Accepts simultaneous submissions, electronic submissions. No submissions on disk. Often comments on rejected mss.

Terms Pays 10% royalty. Publishes ms 6 months-2 years after acceptance. Ms guidelines online.

Ⓝ ⚏ INSOMNIAC PRESS

192 Spadina Ave., Suite 403, Toronto ON M5T 2C2 Canada. (416)504-6270. Fax: (416)504-9313. E-mail: mike@insomniacpress.com. Web site: www.insomniacpress.com. Estab. 1992. "Midsize independent publisher with a mandate to produce edgy experimental fiction." Publishes trade paperback originals and reprints, mass market paperback originals, and electronic originals and reprints. First novel print order: 3,000. **Published 15 debut authors within the last year.** Plans 4 first novels this year. Averages 20 total titles, 5 fiction titles/year.

Needs Comic books, ethnic, experimental, gay/lesbian, humor, literary, mainstream/contemporary, multicultural, mystery, suspense. We publish a mix of commercial (mysteries) and literary fiction. Published *Pray For Us Sinners*, by Patrick Taylor (novel).

How to Contact Accepts unsolicited mss. Accepts queries by email. Include estimated word count, brief bio, list of publishing credits. Send SASE for return of ms or send a disposable ms and SASE for reply only. Agented fiction 5%. Responds in 1 week to queries; 2 months to mss. Accepts simultaneous submissions. Sometimes comments on rejected mss.

Terms Pays 10-15% royalty on retail price. Average advance: $500-1,000. Publishes ms 6 months after acceptance. Ms guidelines online.

Advice "Visit our Web site, read our writer's guidelines."

INTERLINK PUBLISHING GROUP, INC.

46 Crosby St., Northampton MA 01060. (413)582-7054. Fax: (413)582-7057. E-mail: editor@interlinkbooks.com. Web site: www.interlinkbooks.com. **Contact:** Michel Moushabeck, publisher; Pam Thompson, editor. Estab. 1987. "Midsize independent publisher specializing in world travel, world literature, world history and politics." Publishes hardcover and trade paperback originals. Books: 55 lb. Warren Sebago Cream white paper; web offset printing; perfect binding. Average print order: 5,000. **Published new writers within the last year.** Averages 50 total titles, 2-4 fiction titles/year. Distributes titles through Baker & Taylor. Promotes titles through book mailings to extensive, specialized lists of editors and reviews; authors read at bookstores and special events across the country.

Imprint(s) Interlink Books and Olive Branch Press.

Needs Ethnic, international. "Adult—We are looking for translated works relating to the Middle East, Africa or Latin America." Recently published *Everything Good Will Come*, by Sefi Atta (first novel); *The Gardens of Light*, by Amin Maalouf (novel translated from French); *War in the Land of Egypt*, by Yusef Al-Qaid (novel translated from Arabic).

How to Contact Does not accept unsolicited mss. Query with SASE and a brief sample. Responds in 3 months to queries. Accepts simultaneous submissions. No electronic submissions.

Terms Pays 6-8% royalty on retail price. Average advance: small. Publishes ms 18 months after acceptance. Ms guidelines online.

Advice "Our Interlink International Fiction Series is designed to bring writers who have achieved wide acclaim at home, to North America."

☑ INVERTED-A

P.O. Box 267, Licking MO 65542. E-mail: amnfn@well.com. **Contact:** Aya Katz, chief editor (poetry, novels, political); Nets Katz, science editor (scientific, academic). Estab. 1985. Publishes paperback originals. Books: offset printing. Average print order: 1,000. Average first novel print order: 500. Distributes through Baker & Taylor, Amazon, Bowker.

Needs Utopian, political. Needs poetry submission for our newsletter, *Inverted-A Horn*.

How to Contact Does not accept unsolicited mss. Query with SASE. Reading period open from January 2 to March 15. Accepts queries by e-mail. Include estimated word count. Responds in 1 month to queries; 3 months to mss. Accepts simultaneous submissions. Sometimes comments on rejected mss.

Terms Pays in 10 author's copies. Publishes ms 1 year after acceptance. Ms guidelines for SASE.

Advice "Read our books. Read the Inverted-A Horn. We are different. We do not follow industry trends."

◎ ION IMAGINATION PUBLISHING

Ion Imagination Entertainment, Inc., P.O. Box 210943, Nashville TN 37221-0943. Fax: (615)646-6276. E-mail: ionimagin@aol.com. Web site: www.flumpa.com. **Contact:** Keith Frickey, editor. Estab. 1994. Small independent publisher of science-related children's fiction, multimedia and audio products. Publishes hardcover and paperback originals. Average first novel print order: 10,000. Member SPAN and PMA.

• Received the Parents' Choice, National Parenting Centers Seal of Approval, Dr. Toy, Parent Council.

Needs Children's/juvenile (adventure, animal, preschool/picture book, science).

How to Contact Does not accept unsolicited mss. Query with SASE. Include brief bio, list of publishing credits. Responds in 1 month to queries. Accepts simultaneous submissions. Sometimes comments on rejected queries.

Terms Pays royalty.

☑ ◎ ITALICA PRESS

595 Main St., Suite 605, New York NY 10044-0047. (212)935-4230. Fax: (212)838-7812. E-mail: inquiries@italica press.com. Web site: www.italicapress.com. **Contact:** Ronald G. Musto and Eileen Gardiner, publishers. Estab. 1985. Small independent publisher of Italian fiction in translation. "First-time translators published. We would like to see translations of Italian writers who are well-known in Italy who are not yet translated for an American audience." Publishes trade paperback originals. Books: 50-60 lb. natural paper; offset printing; illustrations. Average print order: 1,500. Averages 6 total titles, 2 fiction titles/year. Distributes titles through Web site. Promotes titles through Web site.

Needs Translations of 20th century Italian fiction. Published *Eruptions*, by Monica Sarsini; *The Great Bear*, by Ginevra Bompianai; *Sparrow*, by Giovanni Verga.

How to Contact Accepts unsolicited mss. Query with SASE. Accepts queries by e-mail, fax. Responds in 1 month to queries; 2 months to mss. Accepts simultaneous submissions, electronic submissions, submissions on disk.

Terms Pays 7-15% royalty on wholesale price. Pays author's copies. Publishes ms 1 year after acceptance. Ms guidelines online.

Advice "Remember we publish *only* fiction that has been previously published in Italian. A *brief* call saves a lot of postage. 90% of proposals we receive are completely off base—but we are very interested in things that are right on target. Please send return postage if you want your manuscript back."

IVY PUBLICATIONS

72 Hyperion House, Somers Road, London England SW21HZ United Kingdom. Estab. 1989. Small book publisher. Publishes paperback originals.

Needs Adventure, children's/juvenile (adventure, historical), historical, humor, military/war, young adult (adventure, historical). "We are on the lookout for genius; a P.G. Wodehouse or Raymond Chandler would be most welcome."

How to Contact Accepts unsolicited mss. Query with SASE. Accepts queries by mail. Include list of publishing credits. Send SASE or IRC. Accepts simultaneous submissions. No electronic submissions, submissions on disk. Sometimes comments on rejected mss.

Terms "We pay all costs." Profit: 50% to author, 50% to publisher.

Advice "Write in top-class English that is used by top American, British, Indian, South African writers. Meaning of words, style and grammar are our yardsticks."

JAMESON BOOKS, INC.

722 Columbus St., P.O. Box 738, Ottawa IL 61350. (815)434-7905. Fax: (815)434-7907. **Contact:** Jameson G. Campaigne, publisher/editor. Estab. 1986. "Jameson Books publishes conservative/libertarian politics and economics, history, biography, Chicago-area themes and pre-cowboy frontier novels (1750-1840)." Publishes hardcover originals. Books: free sheet paper; offset printing. Average print order: 10,000. First novel print order: 5,000. Averages 6 total titles/year. Distributes titles through Midpoint Trade (New York).

Needs Very well researched western (frontier pre-1850). Interested in pre-cowboy "mountain men" in American west, before 1820 in east frontier fiction. Published *Yellowstone Kelly*, by Peter Bowen; *Wister Trace*, by Loren Estelman; and *One-Eyed Dream*, by Terry Johnston.

How to Contact Does not accept unsolicited mss. Query with SASE or submit outline, 1 sample chapter(s), synopsis. Agented fiction 70%. Responds in 6 months to queries. Accepts simultaneous submissions. Sometimes comments on rejected mss.

Terms Pays 6-15% royalty on retail price. Average advance: $1,000-25,000. Publishes ms 1 year after acceptance.

JIREH PUBLISHING COMPANY

P.O. Box 1911, Suisun City CA 94585-1911. E-mail: jireh_subms@yahoo.com. Web site: www.jirehpublishing.com. Estab. 1995. Small independent publisher. "We have just begun our fiction line." Publishes hardcover, trade paperback and electronic originals. Books: paper varies; digital and offset printed; binding varies. Average print order: varies. First novel print order: varies. Plans 2 first novels this year. Averages 2-5 total titles, 1-2 fiction titles/year. Distributes titles through online bookstores and booksellers (retailers).

Needs Mystery/suspense, religious (Christian e-books, general religious, mystery/suspense, thriller, romance). "We are looking for Christian values in the books that we publish."

How to Contact Accepts unsolicited mss. Query by e-mail only. Include brief bio, list of publishing credits. Go to Web site for guidelines. Responds in 2 months to queries; 8 months to mss. Accepts simultaneous submissions, electronic submissions. No submissions on disk. Sometimes comments on rejected mss.

Terms Pays 10-12% royalty on wholesale price. Publishes ms 9-12 months after acceptance. Ms guidelines online.

JOURNEYFORTH

BJU Press, 1700 Wade Hampton Blvd., Greenville SC 29614-0001. (864)242-5100, ext. 4350. E-mail: jb@bjup.com. Web site: www.bjupress.com. **Contact:** Nancy Lohr, acquisitions editor (juvenile fiction). Estab. 1974. "Small independent publisher of excellent, trustworthy novels for readers pre-school through high school. We desire to develop in our children a love for and understanding of the written word, ultimately helping them love and understand God's word." Publishes paperback originals and reprints. Books: 50 lb. white paper; Webb lithography printing; perfect binding. Average print order: 5,000. **Published some debut authors within the**

last year. Averages 10 total titles, 10 fiction titles/year. Distributes titles through Spring Arbor and Appalachian. Promotes titles through CBA Marketplace.

Needs Adventure (children's/juvenile, young adult), historical (children's/juvenile, young adult), juvenile (animal, easy-to-read, series), mystery (children's/juvenile, young adult), sports (children's/juvenile, young adult), suspense (young adult), western (young adult), young adult (series). "Our fiction is all based on a moral and Christian wordview." Published *Susannah and the Secret Coins*, by Elaine Schulte (historical children's fiction); *Arby Jenkins Meets His Match*, by Sharon Hambrick (contemporary children's fiction); *Over the Divide*, by Catherine Farnes (young adult fiction).

How to Contact Accepts unsolicited mss. Query with SASE or submit outline, 5 sample chapters or submit complete ms. Include estimated word count, brief bio, social security number, list of publishing credits. Send SASE for return of ms or send a disposable ms and SASE for reply only. Responds in 1 month to queries; 3 months to mss. Accepts simultaneous submissions.

Terms Pays royalty. Publishes ms 12-18 months after acceptance. Ms guidelines online.

Advice "Study the publisher's guidelines. Make sure your work is suitable or you waste time for you and the publisher."

N ◖ ◎ KAEDEN BOOKS

P.O. Box 16190, Rocky River OH 44116-0190. (440)617-1400. Fax: (440)617-1403. E-mail: curmston@kaeden.com. Web site: www.kaeden.com. **Contact:** Craig Urmston, editor. Estab. 1990. "We are an educational publisher of early readers for use in the pre-K to 2nd grade market. Our materials are used by teachers in reading instruction in the classroom. These are fully illustrated books with kid-catching, interesting themes that are age appropriate." Publishes paperback originals. Books: offset printing; saddle binding; illustrations. Average print order: 5,000. **Published 8 debut authors within the last year.** Averages 8-16 total titles/year. Distributes titles through school sales representatives. Promotes titles in professional teacher and reading journals.

Needs Wants realistic fiction using simple vocabulary and sentence structure. Rhythm, rhyme, patterned text, and predictable text are key features for developing early readers. Themes need to relate to young readers including sports, family, animal, and curriculum-related subjects. Published *The Balloon Ride*, by Mary Pearson; *Just One More Mom*, by Kit S. Grady; and *Paula's Pickle Picnic*, by Barbara J. Underwood.

How to Contact Accepts unsolicited mss. Query with SASE or submit outline, publishing history, synopsis, author bio. Include brief bio, list of publishing credits. Send copy of ms and SASE.

Terms Pays royalty. Negotiable, either royalties or flat fee by individual arrangement with author depending on book.

Advice "Our line is expanding with particular interest in fiction/nonfiction for grades K-2. Material must be suitable for use in the public school classroom, be multicultural and be high interest with appropriate word usage and a positive tone for the respective grade."

◎ KEARNEY STREET BOOKS

P.O. Box 2021, Bellingham WA 98227. (360)738-1355. E-mail: garyrmc@mac.com. Web site: http://kearneystreetbooks.com. **Contact:** Gary McKinney, managing editor. Estab. 2003. "Books that rock—written by or about musicians or music." Publishes paperback originals. Perfect bound. Average print order: 200-2,000. Debut novel print order: 200. Plans 1 debut novel this year. Averages 1-2 total titles/year; 1-2 fiction titles/year. Member PMA, BPNW, PNBA. Distributes/promotes titles "marginally."

Needs Only publishes books about music or musicians. Published *Such a Killing Crime*, Robert Lopresti (mystery).

How to Contact Send query letter. Accepts queries by e-mail. Send disposable copy of ms and SASE for reply only. Responds to queries in 1 week. Accepts unsolicited mss. Responds to mss in 6-10 months. Considers simultaneous submissions, submissions on CD or disk. Never critiques/comments on rejected mss. Does not return rejected mss.

Terms Sends pre-production galleys to author. Manuscript published 18 months after acceptance. Pays "after expenses, profits split 50/50."

Advice "We publish very few titles. Nobody makes any money. This is all about the love of good fiction shunned by the corporations."

N A KENSINGTON PUBLISHING CORP.

850 Third Ave., 16th Floor, New York NY 10022. (212)407-1500. Fax: (212)935-0699. Web site: www.kensingtonbooks.com. **Contact:** Michaela Hamilton, editor in chief; Kate Duffy, editorial director (romance); John Scognamiglio, editor-in-chief; Selena James, executive editor (African American fiction, Dafina Books); Audrey LaFehr, editorial director. Estab. 1975. Full service trade commercial publisher, all formats. Publishes hardcover and trade paperback originals, mass market paperback originals and reprints. Averages over 500 total titles/year.

Imprint(s) Dafina (Selena James, executive editor); Brava (Kate Duffy, editoral director); Kensington; Pinnacle; Zebra.

Needs Ethnic, gay/lesbian, historical, horror, mainstream/contemporary, multicultural, mystery, occult, romance (contemporary, historical, regency,), suspense, thriller/espionage, western (epic), thrillers; women's. Published *Sullivan's Law*, by Nancy Taylor Rosenberg.

How to Contact Does not accept unsolicited mss. *Agented submissions only.* Responds in 1 month to queries; 4 months to mss. Accepts simultaneous submissions.

Terms Pays 8-15% royalty on retail price or makes outright purchase. Average advance: $2,000 and up. Publishes ms 9-12 months after acceptance.

ALLEN A. KNOLL, PUBLISHERS

200 W. Victoria Street, Santa Barbara CA 93101. (805)564-3377. E-mail: bookinfo@knollpublishers.com. Web site: www.knollpublishers.com. **Contact:** Submissions. Estab. 1990. Small independent publisher, a few titles a year. Specializes in 'books for intelligent people who read for fun.' Publishes hardcover originals. Books: offset printing; sewn binding. Titles distributed through Ingram, Baker & Taylor.

Needs Published *They Fall Hard*, by Alistair Boyle (mystery); *To Die For*, by David Champion (mystery); *The Duchess to the Rescue*, by Alexandra Eden (children's fiction).

How to Contact Does not accept unsolicited mss.

Terms Varies.

ⒶⓍ ALFRED A. KNOPF

Knopf Publishing Group, Random House, Inc., 1745 Broadway, 21st Floor, New York NY 10019. Web site: www.randomhouse.com/knopf. **Contact:** Senior Editor. Estab. 1915. Publishes hardcover and paperback originals. **Published some debut authors within the last year.** Averages 200 total titles/year.

Needs Publishes book-length fiction of literary merit by known or unknown writers. Length: 40,000-150,000 words. Published *Gertrude and Claudius*, by John Updike; *The Emperor of Ocean Park*, by Stephen Carter; *Balzac and the Little Chinese Seamstress*, by Dai Sijie.

How to Contact *Agented submissions only.* Query with SASE or submit sample chapter(s). Responds in 2-6 months to queries. Accepts simultaneous submissions.

Terms Pays 10-15% royalty. Royalty and advance vary. Offers advance. Must return advance if book is not completed or is unacceptable. Publishes ms 1 year after acceptance. Book catalog for $7\frac{1}{2} \times 10\frac{1}{2}$ SAE with 5 first-class stamps.

Ⓝ KOMENAR PUBLISHING

1756 LaCassie Ave., Ste. #202, Walnut Creek CA 94596. (510)444-2261. E-mail: komenar@komenarpublishing.com. Web site: www.komenarpublishing.com. **Contact:** Charlotte Cook, president. Estab. 2005. "Komenar Publishing believes that a novel should be a compelling read. Readers are entitled to stories with strong forward momentum, engaging and dynamic characters, and evocative settings. The story must begin in the first chapter." Publishes hardcover originals. Averages 2-4 total titles/year.

Needs Adventure, ethnic, experimental, fantasy, historical, humor, literary, mainstream, multicultural, mystery/suspense, science fiction.

How to Contact Responds to queries in 1-3 months. Considers simultaneous submissions. Responds to mss in 1-3 months. Send first 10 pages of ms, bio, and a cover letter. Proposal package must not exceed 12 total pages.

Terms Manuscript published 12 months after acceptance. Pays royalties. Book catalogs on Web site.

Ⓐ◎ KREGEL PUBLICATIONS

Kregel, Inc., P.O. Box 2607, Grand Rapids MI 49501. (616)451-4775. Fax: (616)451-9330. Web site: www.kregelpublications.com. **Contact:** Steve Barclift, managing editor. Estab. 1949. Midsize independent Christian publisher. Publishes hardcover and trade paperback originals and reprints. Averages 70 total titles, 10-15 fiction titles/year. Member ECPA.

Imprint(s) Kregel Academic & Professional, Jim Weaver (academic/pastoral); Kregel Kid Zone, Steve Barclift (children).

Needs Adventure, children's/juvenile (adventure, historical, mystery, preschool/picture book, series, sports, Christian), historical, mystery, religious (children's, general, inspirational, fantasy/sci-fi, mystery/suspense, religious thriller, relationships), young adult (adventure). Fiction should be geared toward the evangelical Christian market. Wants "books with fast-paced, contemporary storylines—strong Christian message presented in engaging, entertaining style as well as books for juvenile and young adults, especially young women." Published *Divided Loyalties*, by L.K. Malone (action/thriller); *A Test of Love*, by Kathleen Scott (relationships); *Jungle Hideout*, by Jeanette Windle (juvenile/adventure).

How to Contact No longer accepting unsolicited material. *Agented submissions only.*

Terms Pays 8-16% royalty on wholesale price. Average advance: $200-2,000. Publishes ms 14 months after acceptance. Book catalog for 9×12 SASE. Submissions policy online.
Advice "Visit our Web site and review the titles listed under various subject categories. Does your proposed work duplicate existing titles? Does it address areas not covered by existing titles? Does it break new ground?"

WENDY LAMB BOOKS

Random House Children's Books Group, 1745 Broadway, New York NY 10019. Estab. 2001. Publishes hardcover originals. Averages 10-15 total titles/year.
Needs Juvenile (ages 8-18). "We are not currently accepting picture book submissions."
How to Contact Query with SASE. Responds in 1 month to queries. Accepts simultaneous submissions.
Terms Pays royalty on retail price. Ms guidelines for #10 SASE.

LAST KNIGHT PUBLISHING COMPANY

P.O. Box 270006, Fort Collins CO 80527. (970)391-6857. Fax: (720)596-6778. E-mail: ckaine@lastknightpublishi ng.com. Web site: www.LastKnightPublishing.com. **Contact:** Charles Kaine, publisher/owner. "Small independent publisher changing focus to narrow in on science fiction and fantasy. We are interested in making high quality books, both by the words written and how it is printed." Publishes paperback originals. Books: 70 lb. Vellum opaque paper; offset printed; perfect bound. Average print order: 1,500-4,000. Average first novel print order: 1,500. **Published 1 debut author within the last year.** Plans 2-3 first novels this year.
Needs Fantasy (space fantasy, sword and sorcery), magical realism, speculative fantasy, science fiction of all forms. Published *Ace on The River*, by Barry Greenstein, *The Breach*, by Brian Kaufman (historical fiction).
How to Contact Accepts unsolicited mss. Query with SASE or submit 3 sample chapter(s), synopsis. Accepts submissions by mail only. We do not respond to e-mail queries. Include estimated word count, brief bio, explanation of "why people will want to read the work." Send SASE for return of ms or send a disposable ms and SASE for reply only. Responds in 6 weeks to queries; 2-3 months to mss. Accepts simultaneous submissions. Often comments on rejected mss.
Terms Pays royalty. Average advance: negotiable. Publishes ms 9 months after acceptance. Ms guidelines online.

LEAPFROG PRESS

P.O. Box 1495, 95 Commercial Street, Wellfleet MA 02667-1495. (508)349-1925. Fax: (508)349-1180. E-mail: leapfrog@c4.net. Web site: www.leapfrogpress.com. **Contact:** Donna Szeker, acquisitions editor. Estab. 1996. "We search for beautifully written literary titles and market them aggressively to national trade and library accounts as well as to sell film, translation, foreign and book club rights." Publishes paperback originals and spoken word audio CDs. Books: acid-free paper; sewn binding. Average print order: 5,000. First novel print order: 3,000-5,000 (average). Member, Publishers Marketing Association, Bookbuilders of Boston and PEN. Distributes titles through Consortium Book Sales and Distribution, St. Paul, MN. Promotes titles through all national review media, bookstore readings, author tours, web site, radio shows, chain store promotions, advertisements, book fairs.
  • *The Devil and Daniel Silverman*, by Theodore Rosak, was nominated for the American Library Association Stonewall Award and it was a San Francisco Chronicle best seller. *The German Money*, by Lev Raphael was a Booksense 76 pick.
Needs "Genres often blur; we're interested in good writing. We are most interested in literary fiction." Published *The War at Home*, by Nora Eisenberg; *Junebug*, by Maureen McCoy; *Paradise Dance*, by Michael Lee; and *Waiting for Elvis*, by Toni Graham.
How to Contact Query with SASE. Accepts queries by e-mail. Send SASE for return of ms or send a disposable ms and SASE for reply only. No response to e-mail queries unless we are interested. Responds in 3-6 months to queries by letter; 6 months to mss. No simultaneous submissions. Sometimes comments on rejected mss.
Terms Pays 4-8% royalty on net receipts. Average advance: negotiable. Publishes ms 1-2 years after acceptance.
Advice "Because editors have so little time, you had best send them your very best work. Editors don't have a lot of time to line edit. They love to work with you but they do not want to rewrite your book for you. In fact, if you send good material that is poorly written, they may wonder if you actually can do the revisions necessary. So don't be impatient. Send your work only when you feel it is as good as you can make it.. and that means knowing what's out there in the market; knowing how to create characters and a dynamite beginning and a plot that doesn't meander all over the place because you don't know where the story is going. Learn your craft. Although we have been open to the work of novice writers, we have found that we have had much of our success recently from writers who were formerly published by large NYC presses and then came to us. For that reason, we're especially interested in knowing where you have published before and if the book has a history."

N LEAPING DOG PRESS

P.O. Box 90473, Raleigh NC 27675-0473. (877)570-6873. Fax: (877)570-6873. E-mail: editor@leapingdogpress.com. Web site: www.leapingdogpress.com. **Contact:** Jordan Jones, editor and publisher.

LEE & LOW BOOKS

95 Madison Ave., New York NY 10016. (212)779-4400. Fax: (212)532-6035. Web site: www.leeandlow.com. **Contact:** Louise May, editor-in-chief. Estab. 1991. "Our goals are to meet a growing need for books that address children of color, and to present literature that all children can identify with. We only consider multicultural children's fiction and nonfiction works. Of special interest are stories set in contemporary America." Publishes hardcover originals—picture books and middle grade works only. Averages 12-16 total titles/year.
Imprint(s) Bebop Books.
Needs Children's/juvenile (historical, multicultural, books for children ages 5-12), ethnic/multicultural, illustrated. Published *Shanghai Messenger*, by Andrea Cheng; *Brothers in Hope*, by Mary Williams.
How to Contact Accepts unsolicited mss. Send SASE for return of ms or send a disposable ms and SASE for reply only. Agented fiction 30%. Responds in 4 months to queries; 4 months to mss. Accepts simultaneous submissions. Sometimes comments on rejected mss.
Terms Pays royalty. Offers advance. Book catalog for SASE with $2.07 postage. Ms guidelines online.
Advice "Writers should familarize themselves with the styles and formats of recently published children's books. Lee & Low Books is a multicultural children's book publisher. Animal stories and folktales are not considered at this time."

LEISURE BOOKS

Dorchester Publishing Co., 200 Madison Ave., Suite 2000, New York NY 10016. (212)725-8811. Fax: (212)532-1054. Web site: www.dorchesterpub.com. **Contact:** Erin Galloway, editorial assistant. Estab. 1970. Publishes mass market paperback originals and reprints. Publishes romances, westerns, horrors, chick lit and thrillers only. Books: newsprint paper; offset printing; perfect bound. Average print order: variable. First novel print order: variable. Plans 25 first novels this year. Averages 255 total titles/year. Promotes titles through national reviews, ads, author readings, promotional items and on the Web site.
Imprint(s) Leisure Books (contact: Alicia Condon); Love Spell Books (contact: Christopher Keeslar); Making It (contact: Leah Hultenschmidt).
Needs Horror, romance, western, thrillers, chick lit. "We are strongly backing historical romance. All historical romance should be set pre-1900. Horrors and westerns are growing as well. No sweet romance, science fiction, cozy mysteries." Published *A Knight's Honor*, by Connie Mason (historical romance); *Shadow Touch*, by Marjorie M. Liu (paranormal romance); *The Lake*, by Richard Laymon (horror).
How to Contact Accepts unsolicited mss. Query with SASE or submit outline, first 3 sample chapters, synopsis. Agented fiction 70%. Responds in 6-8 months to queries. No simultaneous submissions, electronic submissions.
Terms Pays royalty on retail price. Average advance: negotiable. Publishes ms 18 months after acceptance. Book catalog for free (800)481-9191. Ms guidelines online.
Advice Encourage first novelists "if they are talented and willing to take direction *and* write the kind of genre fiction we publish. Please include a brief synopsis if sample chapters are requested."

N LERNER PUBLISHING GROUP

241 First Ave., Minneapolis MN 55401. (612)332-7615. Web site: www.lernerbooks.com. **Contact:** Jennifer Zimian, nonfiction submission editor. Estab. 1959. Publishes hardcover originals. "Our goal is to publish children's books that educate, stimulate, and stretch the imagination; foster global awareness; encourage critical thinking; and inform, inspire, and entertain."
Imprints Lerner Publications; Millbrook Press; Twenty-First Century Books; ediciones Lerner; Carolrhoda; Graphic Universe; First Avenue Editions; Kar-Ben Publishing; Lerner Classroom
Needs Biograhy, children's juvenile. Subjects include ethnic, history, nature/environment, science, sports.
How to Contact "As of 2007, due to significant increases in volume, Lerner Publishing Group no longer accepts unsolicited submissions in any of our imprints. We will continue to seek targeted solicitations at specific reading levels and in specific subject areas. The company will list these targeted solicitations on our Web site and in national newsletters, such as the SCBWI Bulletin. Unsoliciteds sent in November 2006 under our previous submissions policy will be read and replied to by November 2007."
Terms Provides author's copies. Average advance: varied. Publishes ms 12-18 months after acceptance. Book catalog for 9×12 SAE with $4.05 postage.

N LIFETIME BOOKS

Barclay Road Inc., 5005 Jean Talon #200, Montreal QC H3S 1G2 Canada. (514)807-5245. Fax: (206)350-5392. E-mail: pub@barclayroad.com. Web site: www.barclayroad.com. **Contact:** Barb Leonard, editor. Estab. 1998.

Publishes hardcover originals, paperback originals, hardcover reprints, paperback reprints, e-books. Averages 5 total titles/year.

Needs Adventure, historical, juvenile, military, short story collections, sports, western, young adult.

How to Contact Submit complete ms with cover letter. Responds to queries in 6 weeks. Considers simultaneous submissions. Responds to mss in 8 months.

Terms Manuscript published 18 months after acceptance. Writer's guidelines on Web site. Pays royalties, 3%-15%.

◐ LIONHEARTED PUBLISHING, INC.

P.O. Box 618, Zephyr Cove NV 89448-0618. (888)546-6478. E-mail: submissions@LionHearted.com. Web site: www.lionhearted.com. **Contact:** Historical or Contemporary Acquistions Editor. Estab. 1994. "Multiple award-winning, independent publisher of single title, mass market paperback, trade and e-book romance novels." Books: mass market paperback; perfect binding. **Published 10-12 debut authors within the last year.** Averages 12-72 total titles, 12 fiction titles/year. Distributes through Ingram, Barnes & Noble, Baker & Taylor, Amazon and Internet Web site. Promotes titles through trade romance reader magazines, Web site and Internet.

Needs Romance (contemporary, futuristic/time travel, historical, regency period, romantic suspense; over 65,000 words only), romantic comedies. Published *Before an Autumn Wind*, by Katherine Smith (historical romance); *The London Claimant*, by Sharon Sobel (Regency romance); *Starjumper's Bride,* by Joy Clarke (sci-fi romance); *Kiss Me Kat*, by Beverly Pironti (western romance); *Outside the Fire*, by Catherine Berlin (contemporary romance); *Beneath a Blazing Sun*, by J.A. Clarke (contemporary romance); *A Hallow Heart*, by John Strysik (contemporary paranormal romance).

How to Contact Accepts unsolicited mss. Submit outline, 3 sample chapter(s), publishing history, synopsis, estimated word count, cover letter and 1 paragraph story summary in cover letter. Accepts queries by e-mail. Agented fiction less than 10%. Responds in 1 month to queries; 3 months to mss. No simultaneous submissions. Always comments on rejected mss.

Terms Royalties of 10% maximum on paperbacks; 30% on electronic books. Average advance: $100. Publishes ms 18-24 months after acceptance. Ms guidelines online.

Advice "If you are not an avid reader and fan of romance novels, don't waste your time or an editor's by submitting to a publisher of romance. You have probably not written a romance, and likely do not understand the hidden code and language of romance. Read at least three of our novels; they are a bit different from the normal category romance. Reading our books is the smart way to discover what our editors like."

▲ ✖ LITTLE, BROWN AND CO. ADULT TRADE BOOKS

Hachette Book Group USA (formerly Time Warner Book Group), 237 Park Avenue, New York NY 10 169. (212)522-8700. Fax: (212)522-2067. Web site: www.twbookmark.com. **Contact:** Editorial dept. Estab. 1837. "The general editorial philosophy for all divisions continues to be broad and flexible, with high quality and the promise of commercial success as always the first considerations." Publishes hardcover originals and paperback originals and reprints. Averages 100 total titles/year.

Imprint(s) Little, Brown; Arcade Books; Back Bay Books; Bulfinch Press.

Needs Literary, mainstream/contemporary. Published *When the Wind Blows*, by James Patterson; *Angels Flight*, by Michael Connelly; *Sea Glass*, by Anita Shreve; *City of Bones*, by Michael Connelly.

How to Contact *Agented submissions only.*

Terms Pays royalty. Offers advance. Ms guidelines online.

▲ ✖ ◎ LITTLE, BROWN AND CO. BOOKS FOR YOUNG READERS

Division of Hachette Book Group USA (formerly AOL Time Warner Book Group), Time Life Building, 237 Park Avenue, New York NY 10169. (212)522-8700. Web site: www.twbookmark.com/children/index.html. Contact: Submissions editor. Estab. 1837. "We are looking for strong writing and presentation but no predetermined topics." Publishes hardcover originals, trade paperback reprints. Averages 100-150 total titles/year.

Imprint(s) Back Bay Books; Megan Tingley Books (Megan Tingley, VP publisher).

Needs Adventure, ethnic, fantasy, historical, humor, juvenile, mystery, picture books, science fiction, suspense, young adult. "We are looking for strong fiction for children of all ages in any area, including multicultural. We always prefer full manuscripts for fiction."

How to Contact *Agented submissions only.*

Terms Pays royalty on retail price. Average advance: negotiable. Publishes ms 2 years after acceptance. Ms guidelines online.

LIVINGSTON PRESS

University of West Alabama, Station 22, Livingston AL 35470. E-mail: jwt@uwa.edu. Web site: www.livingston press.uwa.edu. **Contact:** Joe Taylor, literary editor; Tina Jones, literary editor; Debbie Davis, literary editor.

Estab. 1984. ''Small university press specializing in offbeat and/or Southern literature.'' Publishes hardcover and trade paperback originals. Books: acid free; offset; some illustrations. Average print order: 2,500. First novel print order: 2,500. Plans 5 first novels this year. Averages 10 fiction titles/year.

Imprint(s) Swallow's Tale Press.

Needs Experimental, literary, short story collections, off-beat or southern. ''We are interested in form and, of course style.'' Published *The Gin Girl*, by River Jordan (novel); *Pulpwood*, by Scott Ely (stories); *Live Cargo*, by Paul Toutonghi (stories).

How to Contact Query with SASE. Include estimated word count, brief bio, list of publishing credits. Send SASE for return of ms or send a disposable ms and SASE for reply only. Responds in 1 month to queries; 1 year to mss. Accepts simultaneous submissions. Send only in June and July.

Terms Pays 10% of 1,500 print run, 150 copies; thereafter pays a mix of royalties and books. Publishes ms 18 months after acceptance. Book catalog for SASE. Ms guidelines online.

LLEWELLYN PUBLICATIONS

Llewellyn Worldwide, Ltd., 2143 Wooddale Drive, Woodbury MN 55125. (651)291-1970. Fax: (651)291-1908. E-mail: bill@llewellyn.com. Web site: www.llewellyn.com. **Contact:** Barbara Moore, acquisitions editor (mystery: Midnight Ink imprint); Eava Palma Zuniga (Spanish); Elysia Gallo (magic); Andrew Karre (YA); Lisa Finander (astrology). Estab. 1901. Publishes trade and mass market paperback originals. **Published 30% debut authors within the last year.** Averages 100 total titles/year.

Needs Occult, spiritual (metaphysical), mystery, teen/YA. ''Authentic and educational, yet entertaining.''

How to Contact Responds in 3 months to queries. Accepts simultaneous submissions.

Terms Pays 10% royalty on wholesale price or retail price. Book catalog for 9 × 12 SAE with 4 first-class stamps. Ms guidelines online.

LOST HORSE PRESS

105 Lost Horse Lane, Sandpoint ID 83864. (208)255-4410. Fax: (208)255-1560. E-mail: losthorsepress@mindspring.com. Web site: www.losthorsepress.org. **Contact:** Christine Holbert, publisher. Estab. 1998. Publishes hardcover and paperback originals. Books: 60-70 lb. natural paper; offset printing; b&w illustration. Average print order: 1,000-2,500. First novel print order: 500. **Published 2 debut authors within the last year.** Averages 4 total titles/year. Distributed by Small Press Distribution.

- *Woman on the Cross*, by Pierre Delattre, won the *ForeWord Magazine's* 2001 Book of the Year Award for literary fiction.

Needs Literary, regional (Pacific NW), short story collections, poetry. Published *Tales of a Dalai Lama*, by Pierre Delattre (literary fiction); *Love*, by Valerie Martin (short stories); *Hiding From Salesmen*, by Scott Poole; *Woman on the Cross*, by Pierre Delattre (literary).

Terms Publishes ms 1-2 years after acceptance. Please check submission guidelines on Web site before submitting ms.

LOVE SPELL

Dorchester Publishing Co., Inc., 200 Madison Ave., 20th Floor, New York NY 10016. (212)725-8811. Fax: (212)532-1054. Web site: www.dorchesterpub.com. **Contact:** Leah Hultenschmidt, editor (romance), and Chris Keeslar, editor (romance). Love Spell publishes the quirky sub-genres of romance: time-travel, paranormal, futuristic. ''Despite the exotic settings, we are still interested in character-driven plots.'' Publishes mass market paperback originals. Books: newsprint paper; offset printing; perfect bound. Average print order: varies. First novel print order: varies. Plans 15 first novels this year. Averages 48 total titles/year.

Needs Romance (futuristic, time travel, paranormal, historical), whimsical contemporaries. ''Books industry-wide are getting shorter; we're interested in 90,000 words.'' Published *A Knight's Honor*, by Connie Mason (historical romance); *Shadow Touch*, by Marjorie M. Liu (paranormal romance).

How to Contact Accepts unsolicited mss. Query with SASE or submit 3 sample chapter(s), synopsis. Send SASE or IRC. Agented fiction 70%. Responds in 6-8 months to mss. No simultaneous submissions.

Terms Pays royalty on retail price. Average advance: varies. Publishes ms 1 year after acceptance. Book catalog for free (800)481-9191. Ms guidelines online.

Advice ''The best way to learn to write a Love Spell Romance is by reading several of our recent releases. The best-written stories are usually ones writers feel passionate about—so write from your heart! Also, the market is very tight these days so more than ever we are looking for refreshing, standout original fiction.''

LOW FIDELITY PRESS

1912 16th Ave. South, Birmingham AL 35205. (205)930-0837. Fax: (205)918-0259. E-mail: info@lofipress.com. Web site: www.lofipress.com. **Contact:** Brad Armstrong, Jeff Parker, and Tobin O'Donnell. Estab. 2002. ''Low Fidelity Press is a small independent publisher committed to publishing new, exceptional work regardless of the marketability of the work. We're willing to lose money on a title if it is essential that the work be published.'' Publishes paperback originals. Average print order: 1,000. **Published 1 debut authors within the last year.** Averages 2-3 total titles, 1-2 fiction titles/year. Distributes books through Baker & Taylor.

Needs Experimental, literary, short story collections. Published *B*, by Jonathan Bambach.

How to Contact Does not accept or return unsolicited mss. Query with SASE. Accepts queries by e-mail, mail. Include list of publishing credits. Send copy of ms and SASE. Responds in 1 month to queries. Accepts simultaneous submissions. Rarely comments on rejected mss.

Terms Pays 10-20% royalty. Average advance: varies. Publishes ms 12-18 months after acceptance. Ms guidelines online.

Advice "We ignore trends. Trends are temporary, and we're interested in publishing books that transcend that."

🌐 🅙 LUATH PRESS LTD.

543/2 Castlehill, The Royal Mile, Edinburgh Scotland EH1 2ND United Kingdom. (+00)44 0131 225 4326. Fax: (+00)44 0131 225 4324. E-mail: gavin.macdougall@luath.co.uk. Web site: www.luath.co.uk. **Contact:** Gavin MacDougall, editor. Estab. 1981. Committed to publishing well-written books worth reading. Publishes paperback and hardcover originals. **Published 5-10 debut authors within the last year.** Plans 5-10 first novels this year. Member: Scottish Publishers Association.

Needs Literary, thriller, mystery/suspense, short story collections, humor/satire, speculative fiction, translations. "The best of fiction with a distinctly Scottish twist."

How to Contact Accepts unsolicited mss. Query with SASE or submit complete ms and SASE. Accepts queries by e-mail, fax, phone, mail. Include estimated word count, brief bio, list of publishing credits. No submissions on disk. Never comments on rejected mss.

Terms Pays royalty.

Advice "Check out our Web site and our books, and then get in touch with us."

🅙 MACADAM/CAGE PUBLISHING, INC.

155 Sansome St., Suite 550, San Francisco CA 94104. (415)986-7502. Fax: (415)986-7414. E-mail: info@macada mcage.com. Web site: www.macadamcage.com. **Contact:** Check Web site for guidelines. Estab. 1999. Mid-size independent publisher. Publishes hardcover and trade paperback originals. Books: web offset printing; case binding. Average first novel print order: 5,000-15,000. **Published 10 debut authors within the last year.** Averages 25-30 total titles/year. Member PMA, ABA, NCIBA. Distributes titles through Baker & Taylor, Ingram, Brodart, Koen and American Wholesale. Promotes titles via in-house marketing/publicity department.

Needs Historical, literary, mainstream/contemporary. Published *How To Be Lost*, by Amanda Eyre Ward (fiction); *The Time Traveler's Wife*, by Audrey Niffenegger (fiction); *Pinkerton's Sister*, by Peter Rushforth (fiction); *The God File*, by Frank Turner Hollon (fiction).

How to Contact Accepts unsolicited mss. Check Web site for ms submission guidelines. Submit proposal package including cover letter, brief synopsis, 30-page sample, SASE to ATTN: Manuscript Submissions. Agented fiction 50%. Responds in 4 months to queries; 4 months to mss. Accepts simultaneous submissions.

Terms Pays negotiable royalties. Average advance: negotiable. Publishes ms up to 1 year after acceptance. Ms guidelines on Web site.

🅝 🅥 🅙 JOHN MACRAE BOOKS

Henry Holt & Co., Inc., 115 W. 18th St., New York NY 10011. (212)886-9200. Estab. 1991. "We publish literary fiction and nonfiction. Our primary interest is in language; strong, compelling writing." Publishes hardcover originals. Averages 20-25 total titles/year.

Needs Literary, mainstream/contemporary. Recently published *Burning Their Boats*, by Angela Carter (novel).

How to Contact Does not accept unsolicited mss.

Terms Pays royalty. Average advance: varies. Publishes ms 9-12 months after acceptance.

◎ MARINE TECHNIQUES PUBLISHING, INC.

126 Western Ave., Suite 266, Augusta ME 04330-7249. (207)622-7984. Fax: (207)621-0821. E-mail: marinetechni ques@midmaine.com. **Contact:** James L. Pelletier, president/CEO (commercial marine or maritime international); Christopher S. Pelletier, vice president operations; Jenelle M. Pelletier, editor in chief (national and international maritime related properties). **Published 15% debut authors within the last year.** Averages 3-5 total titles/year.

Needs Must be commercial maritime/marine related.

How to Contact Submit complete ms. Responds in 2 months to queries; 6 months to mss. Accepts simultaneous submissions.

Terms Pays 25-43% royalty on wholesale or retail price. Publishes ms 6-12 months after acceptance.

Advice "Audience consists of commercial marine/maritime firms, persons employed in all aspects of the marine/maritime commercial and recreational fields, persons interested in seeking employment in the commercial marine industry, firms seeking to sell their products and services to vessel owners, operators and mangers in the commercial marine industry worldwide, etc."

▣ ▣ ▣ MARINER BOOKS

Houghton Mifflin, 222 Berkeley St., Boston MA 02116. (617)351-5000. Fax: (617)351-1202. Web site: www.hmc o.com. **Contact:** Paperback division. Estab. 1997. Publishes trade paperback originals and reprints.
  • Mariner Books' *Interpreter of Maladies*, by debut author Jhumpa Lahiri, won the 2000 Pulitzer Prize for fiction and *The Caprices*, by Sabina Murray, received the 2003 PEN/Faulkner Award.
Needs Literary, mainstream/contemporary. Recently published Timothy Egan, Donald Hall, Amitav Ghosh, and Edna O'Brien.
How to Contact *Agented submissions only.* Responds in 4 months to mss.
Terms Pays royalty on retail price or makes outright purchase. Average advance: variable.

▣ ▣ MCBOOKS PRESS

ID Booth Building, 520 N. Meadow St., Ithaca NY 14850. (607)272-2114. Fax: (607)273-6068. E-mail: jackie@mc books.com. Web site: www.mcbooks.com. **Contact:** Jackie Swift. Estab. 1979. Small independent publisher; specializes in historical fiction, American publisher of Alexander Kent's Richard Bolitho series, Dudley Pope's Ramage novels. Publishes trade paperback and hardcover originals and reprints. Averages 20 total titles, 14 fiction titles/year. Distributes titles through National Book Network.
Needs General historical, nautical (British and American naval), military historical.
How to Contact Does not accept unsolicited mss. Submission guidelines available on Web site. Query with SASE. Include list of publishing credits. Responds in 2 months to queries. Accepts simultaneous submissions.
Terms Pays 5-10% royalty on retail price. Average advance: $1,000-5,000.
Advice "We are small and do not take on many unpublished writers. Lookin for historical action-adventure stories that appeal to men, with a secondary appeal to women. Historical and military accuracy is a must. We are moving away from nautical fiction to some degree. Especially looking for stories with at least one strong female character."

▣ ▣ ▣ MARGARET K. MCELDERRY BOOKS

Simon & Schuster Children's Publishing Division, Simon & Schuster, 1230 Sixth Ave., New York NY 10020. (212)698-7605. Fax: (212)698-2797. Web site: www.simonsayskids.com. **Contact:** Emma D. Dryden, vice president/associate publisher. Estab. 1971. Publishes quality material for preschoolers to 18-year-olds. Publishes hardcover originals. Books: high quality paper; offset printing; three piece and POB bindings; illustrations. Average print order: 12,500. First novel print order: 7,500. **Published some debut authors within the last year.** Averages 35 total titles/year.
  • Books published by Margaret K. McElderry Books have received numerous awards, including the Newbery and Caldecott Awards.
Needs Adventure, fantasy, historical, mainstream/contemporary, mystery, picture books, young adult (or middle grade). All categories (fiction and nonfiction) for juvenile and young adult. "We will consider any category. Results depend on the quality of the imagination, the artwork and the writing." Published *Bear's New Friend*,by Karma Wilson and illustrated by Jane Chapman (picture books); *Victory*, by Susan Cooper (middle-grade fiction); *Freaks*, by Annette Curtis Klause (young adult fiction).
Terms Average print order is 5,000-10,000 for a first middle grade or young adult book; 7,500-20,000 for a first picture book. Pays royalty on hardcover retail price: 10% fiction; 5% author, 5% illustrator (picture book). Offers $5,000-8,000 advance for new authors. Publishes ms up to 3 years after acceptance. Ms guidelines for #10 SASE.
Advice "Imaginative writing of high quality is always in demand; also picture books that are original and unusual. Keep in mind that McElderry is a very small imprint, so we are very selective about the books we will undertake for publication. We try not to publish any 'trend' books. Be familiar with our list and with what is being published this year by all publishing houses."

▣ MEDALLION PRESS, INC.

26609 Castleview Way, Wesley Chapel, Fl 33543. Web site: www.medallionpress.com. **Contact:** Kerry Estevez, acquisitions editor. Estab. 2003. "We are an independent publisher looking for books that are outside of the box. Please do not submit to us if you are looking for a large advance. We reserve our funds for marketing the books." Publishes paperback originals. Average print order: 5,000. **Published 20 + debut authors within the last year.**
Imprint(s) Platinum/Hardcover; Gold/Mass Market; Silver/Trade Paper; Bronze/Young Adult; Jewel/Romance;

Amethyst/Fantasy, Sci-Fi, Paranormal; Emerald/Suspense; Ruby/Contemporary; Sapphire/Historical.

Needs Adventure, ethnic, fantasy (space fantasy, sword and sorcery), glitz, historical, horror (dark fantasy, futuristic, psychological, supernatural), humor, literary, mainstream/contemporary, military/war, mystery (amateur slueth, police procedural, private eye/hard-boiled), romance, science fiction (hard science/technological, soft/sociological), thriller/espionage, western (frontier saga), young adult. Published *Siren's Call*, by Mary Ann Mitchell (horror); *Grand Traverse*, by Michael Beres (mainstream fiction); *Memories of Empire*, by Django Wexler (epic fantasy).

How to Contact Does not accept unsolicited mss. "Minimum word count 80K for adult fiction, 55K for YA, no exceptions." No poetry, anthologies, erotica or inspirational. Submit first 3 consecutive chapters and a chapter-by-chapter synopsis. "Without the synopsis, the submission will be rejected." Accepts queries only by mail. No e-mail queries. Include estimated word count, brief bio, list of publishing credits. Send SASE or IRC. Responds in 4-8 months to mss. Accepts simultaneous submissions. Sometimes comments on rejected mss.

Terms Offers advance. Publishes ms 1-2 years after acceptance. Ms guidelines online.

Advice "We are not affected by trends. We are simply looking for well crafted, original, grammatically correct works of fiction. Please visit our Web site for the most current guidelines prior to submitting anything to us."

MERIWETHER PUBLISHING, LTD.

885 Elkton Dr., Colorado Springs CO 80907-3557. (719)594-4422. Fax: (719)594-9916. Web site: www.meriwetherpublishing.com; www.contemporarydrama.com. **Contact:** Rhonda Wray, associate editor (church plays); Ted Zapel, editor (school plays, comedies, books). Estab. 1969. "Mid-size, independent publisher of plays. We publish plays for teens, mostly one-act comedies, holiday plays for churches and musical comedies. Our books are on the theatrical arts." Publishes paperback originals and reprints. Books: quality paper; printing house specialist; paperback binding. Average print order: 5,000-10,000. **Published 25-35 debut authors within the last year.**

Needs Mainstream/contemporary, comedy, religious (children's plays and religious Christmas and Easter plays), suspense—all in playscript format. Published *Pirates and Petticoats*, by Pat Cook (a two-act pirate comedy); *Let Him Sleep Until it's Time for His Funeral*, by Peg Kehret (two-act play).

How to Contact Accepts unsolicited mss. Query with SASE. Accepts queries by e-mail. Include list of publishing credits. Send SASE for return of ms or send a disposable ms and SASE for reply only. Responds in 3 weeks to queries; 2 months to mss. Accepts simultaneous submissions. Sometimes comments on rejected mss.

Terms Pays 10% royalty on retail price or makes outright purchase. Publishes ms 6-12 months after acceptance. Book catalog and ms guidelines for $2 postage.

Advice "If you're interested in writing comedy/farce plays, we're your best publisher."

MID-LIST PRESS

4324 12th Ave S., Minneapolis MN 55407-3218. (612)432-8062. Fax: (612)823-8387. E-mail: guide@midlist.org. Web site: www.midlist.org. **Contact:** Marianne Nora, executive director. Estab. 1989. "We are a nonprofit literary press dedicated to the survival of the mid-list, those quality titles that are being neglected by the larger commercial houses. Our focus is on new and emerging writers." Publishes hardcover and trade paperback originals. Books: acid-free paper; offset printing; perfect or Smyth-sewn binding. Average print order: 2,000. Averages 5 total titles, 2 fiction titles/year. Distributes titles through Ingram, Baker & Taylor, Midwest Library Service, Brodart, Follett and Emery Pratt. Promotes titles through publicity, direct mail, catalogs, author's events and review and awards.

Needs General fiction. Published *The Woman Who Never Cooked*, by Mary L. Tabor; *The Echo of Sand*, by Gail Chehab (first novel).

How to Contact Accepts unsolicited mss. Agented fiction less than10%. Responds in 3 weeks to queries; 3 months to mss. Accepts simultaneous submissions. Ms guidelines online.

Terms Pays 40-50% royalty on net receipts. Average advance: $1,000. Publishes ms 12-18 months after acceptance.

Advice "Write first for guidelines or visit our Web site before submitting. And take the time to read some of the titles we've published."

MILKWEED EDITIONS

1011 Washington Ave. S., Suite 300, Minneapolis MN 55415. (612)332-3192. Fax: (612)215-2550. E-mail: editor @milkweed.org. Web site: www.milkweed.org. **Contact:** Daniel Slager, editor-in-chief; Elisabeth Fitz, first reader. Estab. 1984. Nonprofit publisher. Publishes hardcover originals and paperback originals and reprints. Books: book text quality—acid-free paper; offset printing; perfect or hardcover binding. Average print order: 4,000. First novel print order depends on book. **Published some debut authors within the last year.** Averages 15 total titles/year. Distributes through Publisher's Group West. Each book has its own marketing plan involving print ads, tours, conferences, etc.

- Seth Kantner's *Ordinary Wolves* received a Pacific Northwest Booksellers Award.

Needs Literary. Novels for adults and for readers 8-13. High literary quality. For adult readers: literary fiction, nonfiction, poetry, essays; for children (ages 8-13): literary novels. Translations welcome for both audiences. Published *The Blue Sky*, by Galsan Tschinag (translation); *Visigoth*, by Gary Amdahl (first fiction, short stories); *Sky Bridge*, by Laura Pritchett.

How to Contact Submit complete ms. Responds in 2 months to queries; 6 months to mss. Accepts simultaneous submissions.

Terms Pays 6% royalty on retail price. Average advance: varied. Publishes ms 1-2 years after acceptance. Book catalog for $1.50 postage. Ms guidelines online.

Advice "Read good contemporary literary fiction, find your own voice, and persist. Familiarize yourself with our list before submitting."

✴ ◎ ⚊ MILKWEED FOR YOUNG READERS

Milkweed Editions, 1011 Washington Ave. S., Suite 300, Minneapolis MN 55415. (612)332-3192. Fax: (612)215-2550. Web site: www.milkweed.org. **Contact:** Daniel Slager, editor in chief; Children's reader. Estab. 1984. "Milkweed for Young Readers are works that embody humane values and contribute to cultural understanding." Publishes hardcover and trade paperback originals. Averages 1-2 total titles/year. Distributes titles through Publishers Group West. Promotes titles individually through print advertising, Web site and author tours.

- *Perfect*, by Natasha Friend, was chosen as a Book Sense 76 Children's Book selection.

Needs Adventure, historical, humor, mainstream/contemporary, animal, environmental. For ages 8-13. Published *The Summer of the Pike*, by Jutta Richter; *Trudy*, by Jessica Lee Anderson.

How to Contact Query with SASE. Agented fiction 30%. Responds in 2 months to queries. Accepts simultaneous submissions.

Terms Pays 6% royalty on retail price. Average advance: variable. Publishes ms 1 year after acceptance. Book catalog for $1.50. Ms guidelines for #10 SASE or on the Web site.

Advice "Familiarize yourself with our books before submitting. You need not have a long list of credentials—excellent work speaks for itself."

⊕ ✴ ◯ ◎ MILLS & BOON MEDICAL ROMANCE

a Harlequin book line, Eton House, 18-24 Paradise Rd., Richmond Surrey TW9 1SR United Kingdom. (+44)0208 288 2800. Web site: www.millsandboon.co.uk. **Contact:** Sheila Hodgson, senior editor. "These are present-day romances in a medical setting." Publishes paperback originals and reprints. Books: newspaper print; web printing; perfect bound. **Published some debut authors within the last year.**

Needs Romance (medical). Looking for writing with "a good balance between the romance, the medicine, and the underlying story. At least one of the main characters should be a medical professional, and developing the romance is easier if the hero and heroine work together. Medical detail should be accurate but preferably without using technical language. An exploration of patients and their illnesses is permitted, but not in such numbers as to overwhelm the growing love story. Settings can be anywhere in the world." Manuscripts must be 50,000-55,000 words.

How to Contact No unsolicited mss. Query with SASE, synopsis. No simultaneous submissions, electronic submissions, submissions on disk.

Terms Pays royalty. Offers advance. Ms guidelines for SASE and on Web site.

Advice "More detailed guidelines are available on request with a stamped, addressed envelope."

⊕ ✴ ◯ ◎ MILLS & BOON MODERN ROMANCE (HARLEQUIN PRESENTS)

a Harlequin book line, Eton House, 18-24 Paradise Road, Richmond, Surrey, TW9 1SR, United Kingdom. (+44)20 8288 2800. Web site: www.millsandboon.co.uk. **Contact:** Tessa Shapcott, executive editor. Publishes paperback originals and reprints. Books: newspaper print; perfect-bound. **Published some debut authors within the last year.**

Needs Romance. Needs "novels written in the third person that feature spirited, independent heroines who aren't afraid to take the initiative and breathtakingly attractive, larger-than-life heroes. The conflict between these characters should be lively and evenly matched but always balanced by a developing romance that may include sensual lovemaking."

How to Contact Accepts unsolicited mss. Submit synopsis and first three chapters. Send SASE for return of ms or send a disposable ms and SASE for reply only. No simultaneous submissions, electronic submissions, submissions on disk.

Terms Pays royalty. Offers advance. Ms guidelines online.

Advice "Think fast-paced, emotionally intense, sexually passionate stories with compelling characters."

⊕ ✪ ◨ ◎ MILLS & BOON MODERN XTRA-SENSUAL

(formerly Harlequin Temptation) a Harlequin book line, Eton House 1 8-24 Paradise Road, Richmond Surrey TW9 1SR United Kingdom. Web site: www.eharlequin.com. **Contact:** Tessa Shapcott, editor. "Take an international city background that vividly conveys the sophistication and buzz of cosmopolitan life, an independent woman who knows what she wants from love and her career and a guy who's confident, easygoing and gorgeously sexy . . . and you have Modern Xtra-Sensual! These titles promise to deliver to the reader a feel-good experience, focusing on the kind of relationships that women between the ages of 18 and 35 aspire to. Young characters in affluent urban settings—either North American or international—meet, flirt, share experiences, have great, passionate sex and fall in love, finally making a commitment that will bind them together, forever. Though their stories are firmly based around emotional issues, other concerns—such as job and friendship—are also touched upon and resolved in an upbeat way." Publishes paperback originals and reprints. Books: newspaper print; perfect bound. **Published some debut authors within the last year.**
Needs Romance.
How to Contact Submit first 3 chapters along with a 1-2 page synopsis.
Terms Pays royalty. Offers advance. Ms guidelines online.

Ⓝ ⊕ ✪ ◯ ◎ MILLS & BOON ROMANCE (HARLEQUIN ROMANCE)

a Harlequin book line, Eton House, 18-24 Paradise Road, Richmond, Surrey TW9 1SR United Kingdom. (+44)208 288 2800. Web site: www.millsandboon.co.uk. **Contact:** Kimberley Young, senior editor. "You just can't beat the feeling—the excitement, the anticipation, the depth of emotion and *the sheer rush of falling in love!* This series captures this feeling—again and again!" Publishes paperback originals. Books: newspaper print; perfect bound. **Published some debut authors within the last year.**
Needs "The reader lives the romance through the heroine, so she must be likable and engaging. A strong, charismatic, aspirational hero is essential, and his point of view is welcomed. He can be an alpha male, but like the heroine, his character is highly developed, three-dimensional and convincing. Every story in this series must deliver on *emotional depth*, and be driven by strong, believable, character-driven emotional conflicts. There is scope for a wide range of storylines, themes and international settings. High sensual tension between the protagonists is vital, but our readers are primarily interested in the romance, not in explicit sexual detail. Above all, we're looking for original novels with a fresh unique voice: sparkling, feel-good stories brimming with emotion and that guaranteed rush of romantic excitement!"
How to Contact Accepts unsolicited submissions. Submit 3 sample chapters, synopsis. Send SASE for return of ms or send a disposable ms and SASE for reply only. No simultaneous submissions, electronic submissions, submissions on disk.
Terms Pays royalty. Offers advance. Ms guidelines online.

Ⓐ ✪ ✪ MIRA BOOKS

an imprint of Harlequin, 225 Duncan Mill Rd., Don Mills ON M3B 3K9 Canada. Web site: www.mirabooks.com. "MIRA Books is proud to publish outstanding mainstream women's fiction for readers around the world." Publishes original novels in hardcover, trade and paperback formats.
Needs Thrillers, contemporary literary fiction, historical fiction, paranormal, relationship novels. Published work by Debbie Macomber, Diana Palmer, Nan Ryan, Susan Wiggs.
How to Contact Does not accept unsolicited mss. *Agented submissions only.*
Terms Pays royalty. Offers advance.

⊕ ◨ MONSOON BOOKS

52 Telok Blangah Road, #03-05 Telok Blangah House, 098829 Singapore. (+65)63776272. Fax: (+65)62761743. E-mail: sales@monsoonbooks.com.sg. Web site: www.monsoonbooks.com.sg. **Contact:** Philip Tatham (all fiction). Estab. 2002. "Monsoon Books is a small independent publisher of fiction and memoirs, based in Asia with worldwide distribution." Publishes paperback originals, paperback reprints. Books: Mungken 80 gram paper; offset printing; threadsewn binding. Average print order: 3,000. First novel print order: 3,000. **Published 7 new writers last year**. Plans 10 first novels this year. Averages 20 total titles/year; 12 fiction titles/year. Distributes titles through Worldwide Distribution and promotes through Freelance Publicists for USA and Asia.
Needs Erotica, ethnic/multicultural, family saga, gay, historical, horror (supernatural), humor satire, literary, mainstream, military/war, mystery/suspense (police procedural, private eye/hard-boiled), regional (Asia), thriller/espionage, translations, young adult (romance). Special interests: Southeast Asia. Published *Rouge Raider*, by Nigel Barley (historical fiction); *In Lust We Trust*, by Gerrie Lim (new journalism); *Private Dancer*, by Stephen Leather (general fiction/international relationships).
How to Contact Query with outline/synopsis and submit complete ms with cover letter. Accepts queries by snail mail, fax and e-mail. Please include estimated word count, brief bio, list of publishing credits, and list of three comparative titles. Send SASE or IRC for return of ms. Agented fiction 20%. Responds in 1 week to queries;

12 weeks to manuscripts. Accepts simultaneous submissions, submissions on CD or disk. Rarely comments on rejected manuscripts.

Terms Pays 7-10% royalty. Advance is negotiable. Publishes ms 6-12 months after acceptance. Guidelines online.

Advice "Due to the difficulty of getting published in New York and London, Monsoon represents a more viable option and is attracting new writers from USA, UK and Australia."

MOODY PUBLISHERS

Moody Bible Institute, 820 N. LaSalle Blvd., Chicago IL 60610. (312)329-8047. Fax: (312)329-2019. E-mail: acquisitions@moody.edu. **Contact:** Acquistions Coordinator (all fiction). Estab. 1894. Small, evangelical Christian publisher. "We publish fiction that reflects and supports our evangelical worldview and mission." Publishes hardcover, trade and mass market paperback originals. Averages 60 total titles, 5-10 fiction titles/year. Member, CBA. Distributes and promotes titles through sales reps, print advertising, promotional events, Internet, etc.

Needs Children's/juvenile (series), fantasy, historical, mystery, religious (children's religious, inspirational, religious mystery/suspense), science fiction, young adult (adventure, fantasy/science fiction, historical, mystery/suspense, series). Recently published *Admission*, by Travis Thrasher (suspense novel); *The Rats of Hamlin*, by Adam & Keith McCune (fantasy novel); *Sweet Honesty*, by Stephanie Perry Moore (YA).

How to Contact Accepts unsolicited mss. Query with SASE. Accepts queries by e-mail, fax. Include estimated word count, brief bio, list of publishing credits. Send SASE for return of ms or send a disposable ms and SASE for reply only. Agented fiction 90%. Responds in 2-3 months to queries. Accepts electronic submissions. No simultaneous submissions, submissions on disk.

Terms Royalty varies. Average advance: $1,000-10,000. Publishes ms 9-12 months after acceptance. Ms guidelines for SASE and on Web site.

Advice "Get to know Moody Publishers and understand what kinds of books we publish. We will decline all submissions that do not support our evangelical Christian beliefs and mission."

MORTALIS

Random House Trade Paperbacks, The Random House Publishing Group, 1745 Broadway, 18th Floor, New York, NY 10019. **Contact:** Mark Tavani and Judy Sternlight, editors. Estab. 2007. Publishes paperback originals, paperback reprints.

Needs Mystery/thriller. Launch titles were Boris Akunin's *Sister Pelagia and the White Bulldog*, David Corbett's *Blood of Paradise*, and Alex Carr's *An Accidental American*.

How to Contact Agented submissions only.

PAUL MOULD PUBLISHING

Empire Publishing, P.O. Box 1344, Studio City CA 91614. (818)784-8918. **Contact:** Paul Mould. Estab. 1960. Small independent publisher. Publishes paperback and hardcover originals and reprints. Book: 50 lb. bond paper; offset printing. Average print order: 2,000-5,000. **Published 3 debut authors within the last year.**

Imprint(s) Gaslight Publications; Collectors Publications.

Needs Children's/juvenile (Sherlock Holmes), erotica, historical (medieval), mystery (Sherlock Holmes), western, young adult (Sherlock Holmes).

How to Contact Does not accept unsolicited mss. Query with SASE. Accepts queries by mail. Include estimated word count, brief bio, list of publishing credits. Send SASE or IRC. Responds in 2-3 weeks to queries; 3-4 months to mss. Rarely comments on rejected mss.

Terms Pays royalty. Publishes ms 6 months to 2 years after acceptance. Ms guidelines for #10 SASE.

MOUNTAIN STATE PRESS

2300 MacCorkle Ave. SE, Charleston WV 25304-1099. (304)357-4767. Fax: (304)357-4715. E-mail: msp1@mountainstatepress.org. Web site: www.mountainstatepress.org. **Contact:** Shareena Johnson. Estab. 1978. "A small nonprofit press run by a volunteer board. We specialize in books about West Virginia or by authors from West Virginia. We strive to give a voice to Appalachia." Publishes paperback originals and reprints. Plans 2 first novels this year. Distributes titles through bookstores, distributors, gift shops and individual sales (Amazon.com and Barnes & Noble online carry our titles). Promotes titles through newspapers, radio, mailings and book signings.

Needs Family saga, historical (West Virginia), military/war, new age/mystic, religious. Currently compiling an anthology of West Virginia authors. Published *The Bingo Cheaters*, by Belinda Anderson; *Trophies That I Can't Hang on My Wall*, by Jay Banks.

How to Contact Accepts unsolicited mss. Query with SASE or submit complete ms. Accepts queries by e-mail, fax. Include estimated word count, brief bio. Send SASE for return of ms or send a disposable ms and SASE for reply only. Responds in 6 months to mss. Often comments on rejected mss.

Terms Pays royalty.
Advice ''Topic of West Virginia is the best choice for our press. Send your manuscript in and it will be read and reviewed by the members of the Board of Mountain State Press. We give helpful suggestions and critique the writing.''

NBM PUBLISHING

40 Exchange Pl., Ste. 1308, New York NY 10005. Web site: www.nbmpub.com. **Contact:** Terry Nantier, editor/art director. Estab. 1976. ''One of the best regarded quality graphic novel publishers. Our catalog is determined by what will appeal to a wide audience of readers.'' Publishes hardcover originals, paperback originals. Format: offset printing; perfect binding. Average print order: 3,000-4,000; average debut writer's print order: 2,000. Publishes 1-2 debut writers/year. Publishes 30 titles/year. Member: PMA, CBC. Distributed/promoted ''ourselves.'' Imprints: ComicsLit (literary comics), Eurotica (erotic comics).
Publishes Children's/juvenile (especially fairy tales, classics), creative nonfiction (especially true crime), erotica, ethnic/multicultural, fantasy, gay, historical, horror (dark fantasy, psychological), humor (satire), literary, manga, mystery/suspense, romantic suspense, science fiction, thriller/espionage, translations, young adult/teen. Does not want superhero or overly violent comics. Published *North Country*, by Shane White (autobio/literary).
How to Contact Prefers submissions from writer-artists, creative teams. Send a one-page synopsis of story along with a few pages of comics (copies NOT originals) and a SASE. Attends San Diego Comicon. Agented submissions: 2%. Responds to queries in 1 week; to ms/art packages in 3-4 weeks. Sometimes comments on rejected manuscripts.
Terms Royalties and advance negotiable. Publishes ms 6 months to 1 year after acceptance. Writer's guidelines on Web site. Artist's guidelines on Web site. Book catalog free upon request.

THOMAS NELSON, INC.

Box 141000, Nashville TN 37214-1000. (615)889-9000. Web site: www.thomasnelson.com. **Contact:** Acquisitions Editor. ''Largest Christian book publishers.'' Publishes hardcover and paperback orginals. Averages 100-150 total titles/year.
Needs Publishes commercial fiction authors who write for adults from a Christian perspective. Published *Kingdom Come*, by Larry Burkett and T. Davis Bunn; Dakota Moon series, by Stephanie Grace Whitson (romance); *Empty Coffin*, by Robert Wise (mystery/suspense).
How to Contact Does not accept unsolicited mss or queries.
Terms Pays royalty on net receipts. Rates negotiated for each project. Offers advance. Publishes ms 1-2 years after acceptance. Ms guidelines online.
Advice ''We are a conservative publishing house and want material which is conservative in morals and in nature.''

NEW VICTORIA PUBLISHERS

P.O. Box 13173, Chicago IL 60613-0173. (773)793-2244. E-mail: newvicpub@aol.com. Web site: www.newvictoria.com. **Contact:** Patricia Feuerhaken, president. Estab. 1976. ''Publishes mostly lesbian fiction—strong female protagonists. Most well known for Stoner McTavish mystery series.'' Publishes trade paperback originals. Averages 2-3 total titles/year. Distributes titles through Bookworld (Sarasota, FL), Airlift (London) and Bulldog Books (Sydney, Australia). Promotes titles ''mostly through lesbian feminist media.''
● *Mommy Deadest*, by Jean Marcy, won the Lambda Literary Award for Mystery.
Needs Adventure, erotica, fantasy, feminist, historical, humor, lesbian, mystery (amateur sleuth), romance, science fiction, western. ''Looking for strong feminist, well drawn characters, with a strong plot and action. We will consider most any original, well written piece that appeals to lesbian/feminist audience.'' Publishes anthologies or special editions. Published *Killing at the Cat*, by Carlene Miller (mystery); *Queer Japan*, by Barbara Summerhawk (anthology); *Skin to Skin*, by Martha Miller (erotic short fiction); *Talk Show*, by Melissa Hartman (novel); *Flight From Chador*, by Sigrid Brunel (adventure); *Owl of the Desert*, by Ida Swearingen (novel).
How to Contact Accepts unsolicited mss. Submit outline, sample chapter(s), synopsis. Accepts queries by e-mail, fax. Send SASE or IRC. No simultaneous submissions.
Terms Pays 10% royalty. Publishes ms 1 year after acceptance. Ms guidelines for SASE.
Advice ''We are especially interested in lesbian or feminist mysteries, ideally with a character or characters who can evolve through a series of books. Mysteries should involve a complex plot, accurate legal and police procedural detail, and protagonists with full emotional lives. Pay attention to plot and character development. Read guidelines carefully.''

NEWEST PUBLISHERS LTD.

201, 8540-109 St., Edmonton AB T6G 1E6 Canada. (780)432-9427. Fax: (780)433-3179. E-mail: info@newestpres s.com. Web site: www.newestpress.com. **Contact:** Linda Huffman, general manager. Estab. 1977. Publishes trade paperback originals. **Published some debut authors within the last year.** Averages 13-16 total titles/ year. Promotes titles through book launches, media interviews, review copy mailings.

Imprint(s) Prairie Play Series (drama); Writer as Critic (literary criticisim); Nunatak New Fiction.

Needs Literary. "Our press is interested in Western Canadian writing." Published *Icefields*, by Thomas Wharton (novel); *Blood Relations and Other Plays*, by Sharon Pollock (drama); *A Thirst to Die For*, by Ian Waddell (mystery, debut author).

How to Contact Accepts unsolicited mss. Submit complete ms. Send SASE or IRC. Responds in 9-12 months to queries. Accepts simultaneous submissions.

Terms Pays 10% royalty. Publishes ms 24-30 months after acceptance. Book catalog for 9×12 SASE. Ms guidelines online.

Advice "We publish western Canadian writers only or books about western Canada. We are looking for excellent quality and originality."

W.W. NORTON CO., INC.

500 Fifth Ave., New York NY 10110. Fax: (212)869-0856. E-mail: manuscripts@wwnorton.com. Web site: www.wwnorton.com. **Contact:** Acquisitions editor. Midsize independent publisher of trade books and college textbooks. Publishes literary fiction. Estab. 1923. Publishes hardcover and paperback originals and reprints. Averages 300 total titles/year.

Needs Literary, poetry, poetry in translation, religious. High-qulity literary fiction. Published *Ship Fever*, by Andrea Barrett; *Oyster*, by Jannette Turner Hospital; *Power*, by Linda Hogan.

How to Contact Does not accept unsolicited mss by mail. If you would like to submit your proposal (6 pages or less) by e-mail, paste the text of your query letter and/or sample chapter into the body of the e-mail message. Do not send attachments. Responds in 2 months to queries. No simultaneous submissions.

Terms Pays royalty. Offers advance. Ms guidelines online.

OAK TREE PRESS

140 E. Palmer St., Taylorville IL 62568. (217)824-6500. Fax: (217)824-2040. E-mail: oaktreepub@aol.com. Web site: www.oaktreebooks.com. **Contact:** Billie Johnson, publisher (mysteries, romance, nonfiction); Sarah Wasson, acquisitions editor (all); Barbara Hoffman, senior editor (children's, young adult, educational). Estab. 1998. "Small independent publisher with a philosophy of author advocacy. Welcomes first-time authors, and sponsors annual contests in which the winning entries are published." Publishes hardcover, trade paperback and mass market paperback originals and reprints. Books: acid-free paper; perfect binding. First novel print order: 1,000. **Published 4 debut authors within the last year.** Plans 8 first novels this year. Averages 12 total titles, 8 fiction titles/year. Member: SPAN, SPAWN. Distributes through Ingram, Baker & Taylor and Amazon.com. Promotes through Web site, conferences, PR, author tours.

- *Affinity for Murder*, by Anne White, was an Agatha Award finalist. *Timeless Love*, by Mary Montague Sikes, received a Prism Award.

Imprint(s) Oak Tree Press, Dark Oak Mysteries, Timeless Love, Acorn Books for Children (children's, YA).

Needs Adventure, confession, ethnic, fantasy (romance), feminist, humor, mainstream/contemporary, mystery (amateur sleuth, cozy, police procedural, private eye/hard-boiled), new age/mystic, picture books, romance (contemporary, futuristic/time travel, romantic suspense), suspense, thriller/espionage, young adult (adventure, mystery/suspense, romance). Emphasis on mystery and romance novels. Recently published *Big Black Hole*, by Wilma Kahn (mystery); *Intent to Defraud*, by Mark Travis (mystery); *Veil of Illusion*, by Patricia Sheehy (romance); *Bottom of the Ninth*, by Peter Spring (mystery); *Beyond the Flames*, by Heather Smith Thomas (memoir).

How to Contact Does not accept or return unsolicited mss. Query with SASE. Accepts queries by e-mail, fax. Include estimated word count, brief bio, list of publishing credits, brief description of ms. Send SASE for return of ms or send a disposable ms and SASE for reply only. Agented fiction 5%. Responds in 4-6 weeks to queries; 2 months to proposals; 2-3 months to mss. Accepts simultaneous submissions, electronic submissions. No submissions on disk. Rarely comments on rejected mss.

Terms Pays 10-20% royalty on wholesale price. Average advance: negotiable. Publishes ms 9-18 months after acceptance. Book catalog for SASE or on Web site. Ms guidelines for SASE or on Web site.

Advice "Understand the business and be eager and enthusiastic about participating in the marketing and promotion of the title."

OMNIDAWN PUBLISHING

Omnidawn Corporation, P.O. Box 5224, Richmond CA 94805-5224. (510)237-5472. E-mail: submissions@omnid awn.com. Web site: www.omnidawn.com. **Contact:** Rusty Morrison and Ken Keegan, editors. Estab. 2001.

Omnidawn is a small independent publisher run by two part-time editors. "We specialize in new wave fabulist and fabulist fiction and innovative poetry. See Web site for complete description." Publishes primarily paperback originals. Books: archival quality paper; offset printing; trade paperback binding. Average print order: 3,000. Plans 1 first novel this year. Distributes titles through Small Press Distribution.

Needs New wave fabulist and fabulist.

How to Contact See Web site for details regarding submission policies and contact procedures, which are subject to change. No electronic or disk submissions.

Terms Publishes ms 6-12 months after acceptance. Ms guidelines online.

Advice "Check our Web site for latest information."

ORCA BOOK PUBLISHERS

P.O. Box 5626, Victoria BC V8R 6S4 Canada. (250)380-1229. Fax: (250)380-1892. E-mail: orca@orcabook.com. Web site: www.orcabook.com. **Contact:** Maggie deVries, children's book editor. Estab. 1984. Only publishes Canadian authors. Publishes hardcover and trade paperback originals, and mass market paperback originals and reprints. Books: quality 60 lb. book stock paper; illustrations. Average print order: 3,000-5,000. First novel print order: 3,000-5,000. Plans 3-4 first novels this year. Averages 50 total titles/year.

Needs Hi-lo, juvenile (5-9 years), literary, mainstream/contemporary, young adult (10-18 years). "Ask for guidelines, find out what we publish." Looking for "children's fiction."

How to Contact Query with SASE or submit proposal package including outline, 2-5 sample chapter(s), synopsis, SASE. Agented fiction 20%. Responds in 1 month to queries; 1-2 months to mss. No simultaneous submissions. Sometimes comments on rejected mss.

Terms Pays 10% royalty. Publishes ms 12-18 months after acceptance. Book catalog for 8½×11 SASE. Ms guidelines online.

Advice "We are looking to promote and publish Canadians."

ORIENT PAPERBACKS

A Division of Vision Books Pvt Ltd., 5-A/8 Ansari Road, 1st Floor, Daryaganj, New Delhi-110 002, India. (+91)11 2327 8877 / 8878. Fax: (+91)11 2327 8879. E-mail: mail@orientpaperbacks.com. Web site: www.orientpaperbacks.com. **Contact:** Sudhir Malhotra, editor. "We are one of the largest paperback publishers in S.E. Asia and publish both fiction and nonfiction by authors from this part of the world."

Needs Length: 40,000 words minimum.

Terms Pays royalties on copies sold.

OTHER PRESS

2 Park Avenue, 24th floor, New York NY 10016. (212)414-0054. Fax: (212)414-0939. E-mail: editor@otherpress.com. Web site: www.otherpress.com. **Contact:** Mindy Okura-Marszycki, editor; Katherine Obertance, editorial assistant. Estab. 1998. The Other Press is a small independent publisher. Publishes hardcover originals and paperback reprints. **Published 1 debut authors within the last year.** Plans 3 first novels this year.

Needs Literary. Published *San Remo Drive*, by Leslie Epstein (fiction); *Stories From the City of God*, by Pier Paolo Pasolini (fiction/translation); *Tigor*, by Peter Stephan Jungk (fiction).

How to Contact Only agented submissions.

Terms Pays 7½-10% royalty. Average advance: Negotiable.

OUR CHILD PRESS

P.O. Box 4379, Philadelphia PA 19118-8379. (610)308-8988. E-mail: ourchldpress@aol.com. Web site: www.ourchildpress.com. **Contact:** Carol Perrott, CEO. Estab. 1984. Publishes hardcover and paperback originals and reprints.

• Received the Ben Franklin Award for *Don't Call Me Marda*, by Sheila Welch.

Needs Especially interested in books on adoption or learning disabilities. Published *Things Little Kids Need to Know*, by Susan Uhlig.

How to Contact Does not accept unsolicited mss. Query with SASE. Responds in 2 weeks to queries; 2 months to mss. Accepts simultaneous submissions. Sometimes comments on rejected mss.

Terms Pays 5% royalty. Publishes ms 6 months after acceptance.

PALARI PUBLISHING

P.O. Box 9288, Richmond VA 23227-0288. (866)570-6724. Fax: (804)883-5234. E-mail: submissions@palaribooks.com. Web site: www.palaribooks.com. **Contact:** David Smitherman, fiction editor. Estab. 1998. Small publisher of fiction and nonfiction books. Publishes hardcover and trade paperback originals. **Published 2 debut authors within the last year.** Member Publishers Marketing Association. Distributes titles through Baker &

Taylor, Ingram, Amazon, mail order and Web site. Promotes titles through book signings, direct mail and the Internet.

Needs Adventure, ethnic, gay/lesbian, historical, literary, mainstream/contemporary, multicultural, mystery, suspense. "Tell why your idea is unique or interesting. Make sure we are interested in your genre before submitting." Published *We're Still Here* (cultural); *In and Out in Hollywood* (Hollywood, gay); *The Guessing Game* (mystery).

How to Contact Does not accept unsolicited mss. Query with SASE. Accepts queries by e-mail, fax. Include estimated word count, brief bio, list of publishing credits. Send SASE for return of ms or send a disposable ms and SASE for reply only. Responds in 1 month to queries; 2-3 months to mss. Accepts electronic submissions. No simultaneous submissions. Often comments on rejected mss.

Terms Pays royalty. Publishes ms 1 year after acceptance. Ms guidelines online.

Advice "Send a good bio. I'm interested in a writer's experience and unique outlook on life."

◙ PANTHER CREEK PRESS

P.O. Box 130233, Spring TX 77393-0233. E-mail: panthercreek3@hotmail.com. Web site: www.panthercreekpress.com. **Contact:** Ted Walthen, editor (literary); Jerry Cooke, assistant editor (mystery); Guida Jackson, editor (collections). Estab. 1999. "Mid-size publisher interested in Merchant-Ivory type fiction. Our production schedule is full for 2007 and we will be reading no new submissions until 2007." Publishes paperback originals. Books: 60 lb. white paper; docutech-printed; perfect bound. Average print order: 1,500. **Published 4 debut authors within the last year.** Distributes titles through Baker & Taylor, Amazon.

Imprint(s) Enigma Books, Jerry Cooke, editor (mystery); Claredon House, Guida Jackson (literary).

Needs Ethnic, experimental, humor, literary, mainstream/contemporary, multicultural, mystery (amateur sleuth), regional (Texana), short story collections. Published *The Caballeros of Ruby, Texas*, by Cynthia Leal Massey (literary); *Salvation and Other Stories*, by Terry Dalrymple (collection); *Sue Ellen Learns to Dance*, by Judy Alter (collection).

How to Contact Will not read unsolicited mss. Query with SASE. Accepts queries by e-mail. Include estimated word count, brief bio, list of publishing credits. Send SASE for return of ms or send a disposable ms and SASE for reply only. Responds in 3 weeks to queries; 2 months to mss. Accepts simultaneous submissions.

Terms Pays 10% royalty, 5 author's copies. Publishes ms 1 year after acceptance. Guidelines and catalog available on Web site.

Advice "We would enjoy seeing more experimental work, but 'schock' narrative does not interest us. We don't want to see thrillers, fantasies, horror. The small, thoughtful literary story that large publishers don't want to take a chance on is the kind that gets our attention."

◙ ◎ ◪ PAPERCUTZ

40 Exchange Pl., Ste. 1308, New York NY 10005. Fax: (212)643-1545. E-mail: salicrup@papercutz.com. Web site: www.papercutz.com. **Contact:** Jim Salicrup (material aimed at the tween and teen market). Estab. 2004. "Independent publisher of graphic novels based on popular existing properties aimed at the teen and tween market." Publishes hardcover originals, paperback originals. Format: glossy white 100 lb. paper; offset four-color printing; perfect bound; full-color comics illustrations. Publishes 10+ titles/year. Distributed by Holtzbrinck Publishers.

Publishes Licensed characters/properties aimed at a tween and teen market. Not looking for original properties at this point. "Looking for professional comics writers able to write material for tweens and teens without dumbing down their work. Also looking for comic book artists able to work in animated or manga styles." Published *Nancy Drew, Girl Detective # 1* "The Demon of River Heights," by Stefan Petrucha (tween/teen mystery); *The Hardy Boys # 1* "The Ocean of Osyria," by Scott Lobdell (tween/teen mystery/adventure); *Zorro #1* "Scars!," by Don McGregor (tween/teen action/adventure). Series projects: Nancy Drew, Girl Detective; The Hardy Boys; Zorro; and more.

How to Contact Prefers submissions from writers, artists. Accepts unsolicited submissions. Send low res files of comic art samples or a link to samples on artist's Web site. Attends New York comic book conventions, as well as the San Diego Comic-Con, and will review portfolios if time allows. Agented submissions: 0%. Responds to queries and ms/art packages in 1-2 weeks. Considers simultaneous submissions, e-mail submissions, submissions on disk. Never comments on rejected manuscripts.

Terms Pays an advance against royalties. Publishes ms 3-6 months after acceptance. Writer's and artist's guidelines not available. Book catalog free upon request.

Advice "Be familiar with our titles—that's the best way to know what we're interested in publishing. If you are somehow attached to a successful tween or teen property and would like to adapt it into a graphic novel, we may be interested."

⬚ ⊘ PAPYRUS PUBLISHERS & LETTERBOX SERVICE

10501 Broom Hill Drive, Las Vegas NV 89134-7339. (702)256-3838. Web site: www.booksbyletterbox.com. **Contact:** Geoffrey Hutchinson-Cleaves, editor-in-chief; Jessie Rosé, fiction editor. Estab. London 1946; USA 1982. Mid-size independent press. Publishes hardcover originals, audio books. Average print order 5,000. Promotes titles through mail, individual author fliers, author tours.

Imprint(s) Letterbox of London, USA: Difficult Subjects Made Easy.

Needs "Not accepting mss right now."

Advice "Don't send it, unless you have polished and polished and polished. Absolutely no established author sends a piece that has just been 'written' once. That is the first draft of many!"

⬚ ⊚ PARADISE CAY PUBLICATIONS, INC.

P.O. Box 29, Arcata CA 95518-0029. (707)822-9063. Fax: (707)822-9163. E-mail: mattm@humboldt1.com. Web site: www.paracay.com. **Contact:** Matt Morehouse, publisher. Publishes hardcover and trade paperback originals and reprints. Books: 50 lb. paper; offset printing; perfect bound and hardcover; illustrations. Average print order: 10,000. Average first novel print order: 3,000. **Published 3 debut authors within the last year.** Averages 5 total titles.

Needs Adventure (nautical, sailing). All fiction must have a nautical theme.

How to Contact Query with SASE or submit 2-3 sample chapters, synopsis. Responds in 1 month to queries; 2 months to mss.

Terms Pays 10-15% royalty on wholesale price or makes outright purchase of $1,000-$10,000. Average advance: $0-2,000. Publishes ms 6 months after acceptance. Book catalog and ms guidelines on Web site.

Advice "Must present in a professional manner. *Must* have a strong nautical theme."

⬚ PATHWISE PRESS

P.O. Box 1164, Champaign IL 61824. E-mail: pathwisepress@hotmail.com. Web site: www.pathwisepress.com. **Contact:** Christopher Harter. Estab. 1997. Small independent publisher interested in work that is neither academic or Bukowski. "We publish chapbooks only." Publishes paperback originals. Books: 20 lb. white linen paper; laser printing; saddle-stitch bound; illustrations. Average print order: 200-300.

Needs Experimental, literary, short story collections.

How to Contact "As of April 2007, Pathwise Press is going on hiatus and relocating to New Orleans. Interested parties should e-mail or check Web site for updates."

Terms Pays 10-20% royalty. Publishes ms 6 months after acceptance. Ms guidelines online.

Advice "Proofread your work. Finished book should be 48-60 pages, including front and back matter, so consider length before submitting."

⬚ PAYCOCK PRESS

3819 No. 13th St., Arlington VA 22201. (703)525-9296. E-mail: hedgehogz@erols.com. Web site: www.atticusbooks.com. **Contact:** Lucinda Ebersole and Ricard Peabody. Estab. 1976. "Too academic for underground, too outlaw for the academic world. We tend to be edgy and look for ultra-literary work." Publishes paperback originals. Books: off-set printing. Average print order: 500. Averages 1 total title/year. Member CLMP. Distributes through Amazon and Web site.

Needs Experimental, literary, short story collections.

How to Contact Accepts unsolicited mss. Accepts queries by e-mail. Include brief bio. Send SASE for return of ms or send a disposable ms and SASE for reply only. Agented fiction 5%. Responds in 1 month to queries; 4 months to mss. Accepts simultaneous submissions, electronic submissions. Rarely comments on rejected mss.

Terms Publishes ms 12 months after acceptance.

Advice "Check out our Web Site. Two of our favorite writers are Paul Bowles and Jeanette Winterson."

✦ ⬚ ⊚ PEACHTREE CHILDREN'S BOOKS

Peachtree Publishers, Ltd., 1700 Chattahoochee Avenue, Atlanta GA 30318-2112. (404)876-8761. Fax: (404)875-2578. E-mail: hello@peachtree-online.com. Web site: www.peachtree-online.com. **Contact:** Helen Harriss, acquisitions editor. "We publish a broad range of subjects and perspectives, with emphasis on innovative plots and strong writing." Publishes hardcover and trade paperback originals. Averages 30 total titles, 20-25 fiction titles/year.

Needs Juvenile, picture books, young adult. Looking for very well written middle grade and young adult novels. No adult fiction. No short stories. Published *Sister Spider Knows All*; *Shadow of A Doubt*; *My Life and Death*, by Alexandra Canarsie.

How to Contact Submit 3 sample chapter(s) or submit complete ms. Responds in 6 months to queries; 6 months to mss. Accepts simultaneous submissions.

Terms Pays royalty on retail price; advance varies. Publishes ms 1 year or more after acceptance. Book catalog for 6 first-class stamps. Ms guidelines online.

◎ PEACHTREE PUBLISHERS, LTD.

1700 Chattahoochee Ave., Atlanta GA 30318-2112. (404)876-8761. Fax: (404)875-2578. Web site: www.peachtree-online.com. **Contact:** Helen Harriss, submissions editor. Estab. 1978. Independent publisher specializing in children's literature, nonfiction and regional guides. Publishes hardcover and trade paperback originals. First novel print run 5,000. **Published 2 debut authors within the last year.** Averages 20-25 total titles, 1-2 fiction titles/year. Promotes titles through review copies to appropriate publications, press kits and book signings at local bookstores.

Imprint(s) Peachtree Jr. and FreeStone.

Needs Juvenile, young adult. "Absolutely no adult fiction! We are seeking YA and juvenile works including mystery and historical fiction of high literary merit."

How to Contact Accepts unsolicited mss. Query with SASE. Responds in 6 months to queries; 6 months to mss. Accepts simultaneous submissions. No electronic submissions.

Terms Pays royalty. Royalty varies. Offers advance. Publishes ms 1 year or more after acceptance. Ms guidelines online.

Advice "Check out our Web site or catalog for the kinds of things we are interested in."

⬛⊘ PEDLAR PRESS

P.O. Box 26, Station P, Toronto ON M5S 2S6 Canada. (416)534-2011. Fax: (416)535-9677. E-mail: feralgrl@interlog.com. **Contact:** Beth Follett, editor (fiction, poetry). Publishes hardcover and trade paperback originals. **Published 50% debut authors within the last year.** Averages 6 total titles/year. Distributes in Canada through LitDist Co.; in the US distributes directly through publisher.

Needs Experimental, feminist, gay/lesbian, literary, picture books, short story collections. Published *The Man in the Moon-Fixer's Mask*, by Jonarno Lawson.

How to Contact Query with SASE, sample chapter(s), synopsis. Not accepting mss in 2006 and 2007.

Terms Pays 10% royalty on retail price. Average advance: $200-400. Publishes ms 1 year after acceptance. Ms guidelines for #10 SASE.

Advice "We select manuscripts according to our taste. Be familiar with some if not most of our recent titles."

⬛⬛ PELICAN PUBLISHING CO.

1000 Burmaster St., Gretna LA 70053. (504)368-1175. Web site: www.pelicanpub.com. **Contact:** Nina Kooij, editor-in-chief. Estab. 1926. "We seek writers on the cutting edge of ideas. We believe ideas have consequences. One of the consequences is that they lead to a best-selling book." Publishes hardcover, trade paperback and mass market paperback originals and reprints. Books: hardcover and paperback binding; illustrations sometimes. Buys juvenile mss with illustrations. Averages 65 total titles/year. Distributes titles internationally through distributors, bookstores, libraries. Promotes titles at reading and book conventions, in trade magazines, in radio interviews, print reviews and TV interviews.

● *The Warlord's Puzzle*, by Virginia Walton Pilegard, was #2 on *Independent Bookseller's* Book Sense 76 list. *Dictionary of Literary Biography* lists; *Unforgotten*, by D.J. Meador, as "one of the best of 1999."

Needs Historical, juvenile (regional or historical focus). "We publish maybe one novel a year, usually by an author we already have. Almost all proposals are returned. We are most interested in historical Southern novels." Published *Jubal*, by Gary Penley (novel); *Toby Belfer Visits Ellis Island*, by Gloria Teles Pushker (young reader).

How to Contact Does not accept unsolicited mss. Query with SASE or submit outline, 2 sample chapter(s), synopsis. Responds in 1 month to queries; 3 months to mss. No simultaneous submissions. Rarely comments on rejected mss.

Terms Pays royalty on actual receipts. Average advance: considered. Publishes ms 9-18 months after acceptance. Book catalog for SASE. Writer's guidelines for SASE or on Web site.

Advice "Research the market carefully. Check our catalog to see if your work is consistent with our list. For ages 8 and up, story must be planned in chapters that will fill at least 90 double-spaced manuscript pages. Topic for ages 8-12 must be Louisiana related and historical. We look for stories that illuminate a particular place and time in history and that are clean entertainment. The only original adult work we might consider is historical fiction, preferably Civil War (not romance). Please don't send three or more chapters unless solicited. Follow our guidelines listed under 'How to Contact.'"

⬛⬛⊘◎ PEMMICAN PUBLICATIONS

150 Henry Ave., Main Floor RM 12, Winnipeg MB R3B 0J7 Canada. (204)589-6346. Fax: (204)589-2063. E-mail: rmcilroy@pemmican.mbc.ca. Web site: www.pemmican.mb.ca. **Contact:** Randal Milroy, managing editor. Es-

tab. 1980. Metis adult and children's books. Publishes paperback originals. Books: stapled-bound smaller books and perfect-bound larger ones; 4-color illustrations, where applicable. Average print order: 1,500. First novel print order: 1,000. **Published some debut authors within the last year.** Averages 6 total titles/year. Distributes titles through press releases, Web site, fax, catalogues, and book displays.

Needs Stories by and about the Canadian Metis experience, especially from a modern adult or young-adult perspective. Recently published *Me and My Canoe*, by Brad Bird (adult non-fiction); *Metis Spirits*, by Deborah L. Delaronde (children's fiction); and *Our Memories of Lenny Breau—The Love, the Music and the Man*, (adult biography).

How to Contact Accepts unsolicited mss by conventional mail only. Submit samples and synopsis. Send SASE for return of ms or send a disposable ms and SASE for reply only. Accepts simultaneous submissions.

Terms Pays 10% royalty. Provides 10 author's copies. Average advance: $350.

✅ PENGUIN GROUP USA

375 Hudson St., New York NY 10014. (212)366-2000. Web site: www.penguin.com. "The company possesses perhaps the world's most prestigious list of best-selling authors and a backlist of unparalleled breadth, depth and quality." General interest publisher of both fiction and nonfiction.

Imprint(s) Viking (hardcover); Dutton (hardcover); The Penguin Press (hardcover); Daw (hardcover and paperback); G P Putnam's Sons (hardcover and children's); Riverhead Books (hardcover and paperback); Tarcher (hardcover and paperback); Grosset/Putnam (hardcover); Putnam (hardcover); Avery; Viking Compass (hardcover); Penguin (paperback); Penguin Classics (paperback); Plume (paperback); Signet (paperback); Signet classics (paperback); Onyx (paperback); Roc (paperback); Topaz (paperback); Mentor (paperback); Meridian (paperback); Berkley Books (paperback); Jove (paperback); Ace (paperback); Prime Crime (paperback); HP-Books (paperback); Penguin Compass (paperback); Dial Books for Young Readers (children's); Dutton Children's Books (children's); Viking Children's Books (children's); Puffin (children's); Frederick Warne (children's); Philomel Books (children's); Grosset and Dunlap (children's); Wee Sing (children's); PaperStar (children's); Planet Dexter (children's); Berkely (hardcover); Gothom (hardcover and paperback); Portfolio (hard and paperback); NAL (hardcover).

How to Contact "Due to the high volume of manuscripts we receive, Penguin Group (USA) Inc. imprints do not normally accept unsolicited manuscripts. On rare occasion, however, a particular imprint may be open to reading such. The Penguin Group (USA) web site features a listing of which imprints (if any) are currently accepting unsolicited manuscripts." Continue to check Web site for updates to the list.

Terms Pays advance and royalties, depending on imprint.

✅ THE PERMANENT PRESS/SECOND CHANCE PRESS

4170 Noyac Rd., Sag Harbor NY 11963. (631)725-1101. Fax: (631)725-8215. Web site: www.thepermanentpress. com. **Contact:** Judith and Martin Shepard, publishers. Estab. 1978. Mid-size, independent publisher of literary fiction. "We keep titles in print and are active in selling subsidiary rights." Publishes hardcover originals. Average print order: 1,500. Averages 12 total titles, 12 fiction titles/year. Distributes titles through Ingram, Baker & Taylor and Brodart. Promotes titles through reviews.

Needs Literary, mainstream/contemporary, mystery. Especially looking for high-line literary fiction, "artful, original and arresting." Accepts any fiction category as long as it is a "well-written, original full-length novel." Published *The Last Refuge*, by Chris Knopf; *School for Hawaiian Girls*, by Georgia Ka'apuni McMillan; *Christmas in Paris*, by Ron Fried; *Brian in Three Seasons*, by Patricia Grossman.

How to Contact Accepts unsolicited mss. Send SASE for return of ms or send a disposable ms and SASE for reply only. Responds in 12 weeks to queries; 8 months to mss. Accepts simultaneous submissions.

Terms Pays 10-15% royalty on wholesale price. Offers $1,000 advance for Permanent Press books; royalty only on Second Chance Press titles. Publishes ms 18 months after acceptance. Ms guidelines for #10 SASE.

Advice "We are looking for good books; be they 10th novels or first ones, it makes little difference. The fiction is more important than the track record. Send us the first 25 pages, it's impossible to judge something that begins on page 302. Also, no outlines—let the writing present itself."

N ✅ ✅ DAVID PHILIP PUBLISHERS

P.O. Box 46962, Glosderry 7702 South Africa. Fax: (+21)6743358. Web site: www.newafricabooks.co.za.

Needs "Fiction with southern African concern or focus. Progressive, often suitable for school or university prescription, literary, serious."

How to Contact Submit 1 sample chapter(s), synopsis.

Terms Pays royalty. Write for guidelines.

Advice "Familiarize yourself with list of publishers to which you wish to submit work."

⊞ ◯ **PIATKUS BOOKS**

5 Windmill Street, London England W1T 2JA United Kingdom. (+02)07 631 0710. Fax: (+02)07 436 7137. E-mail: info@piatkus.co.uk. Web site: www.piatkus.co.uk. **Contact:** Gillian Green, editorial director (fiction); Emma Callagher, ficton editor. Estab. 1979. Piatkus is a medium-sized independent publisher of nonfiction and fiction. The fiction list is highly commercial and includes women's fiction, crime and thriller as well as literary fiction. Publishes hardcover originals, paperback originals and paperback reprints. **Published 14 debut authors within the last year.** Plans 10 first novels this year. Member: IPG.

Imprint(s) Portrait (general/nonfiction).

Needs Quality women's fiction, family saga, historical, literary, mainstream/contemporary, mystery (amateur sleuth, police procedural, private eye/hard-boiled), regional, romance (contemporary, historical, regency period, romantic suspense, paranormal romance), thriller/espionage. Published *Angeles Fall*, by Nora Roberts (romantic suspense); *Sex Wars*, by Margo Piercy (literary); *Seeing Stars*, by Christina Jones (commercial women's fiction).

How to Contact Accepts unsolicited mss. Query with SASE or submit first 3 sample chapter(s), synopsis. Accepts queries by mail. Include estimated word count, brief bio, list of publishing credits. Send SASE for return of ms or send a disposable ms and SASE for reply only. Agented fiction 80%. Responds in 12 weeks to mss. Accepts simultaneous submissions. No submissions on disk or via e-mail. Rarely comments on rejected mss.

Terms Pays royalty. Average advance: negotiable. Publishes ms 1 year after acceptance. Ms guidelines for SASE.

Advice "Study our list before submitting your work."

Ⓐ ★ ◯ ⓥ **PICADOR USA**

St. Martin's Press, 175 Fifth Ave., New York NY 10010. (212)674-5151. Web site: www.picadorusa.com. **Contact:** Frances Coady, publisher (literary fiction); Joshua Kendall, associate editor (literary fiction); Sam Douglas, associate editor; David Rogers, assistant editor. Estab. 1994. Picador publishes high-quality literary fiction and nonfiction. "We are open to a broad range of subjects, well written by authoritative authors." Publishes hardcover and trade paperback originals and reprints. Averages 70-80 total titles/year. Titles distributed through Von Holtzbrinck Publishers. Titles promoted through national print advertising and bookstore co-op.

- *The Amazing Adventures of Kavalier & Clay*, by Michael Chabon, won the Pulitzer Prize for fiction; *In America*, by Susan Sontag, won National Book Award; Jame Crace's *Being Dead* won the National Book Critics Circle Award.

Needs Literary. Published *No One Thinks of Greenland*, by John Griesmer (first novel, literary); *Summerland*, by Malcolm Knox (first novel, literary fiction); *Half a Heart*, by Rosellen Brown (literary fiction).

How to Contact Does not accept unsolicited mss. *Agented submissions only.* Accepts queries by e-mail, fax, mail. Responds in 2 months to queries. Accepts simultaneous submissions.

Terms Pays 7½-15% royalty on retail price. Average advance: varies. Publishes ms 18 months after acceptance. Book catalog for 9×12 SASE and $2.60 postage; ms guidelines for #10 SASE or online.

Ⓝ ◯ **PIÑATA BOOKS**

Arte Publico Press, University of Houston, 452 Cullen Performance Hall, Houston TX 77204-2004. (713)743-2841. Fax: (713)743-3080. Web site: www.artepublicopress.com. **Contact:** Nicolas Kanellos, director. Estab. 1994. Piñata Books is dedicated to the publication of children's and young adult literature focusing on US Hispanic culture by U.S. Hispanic authors. Publishes hardcover and trade paperback originals. **Published some debut authors within the last year.** Averages 10-15 total titles/year.

Needs Adventure, juvenile, picture books, young adult. Published *Trino's Choice*, by Diane Gonzales Bertrand (ages 11-up); *Delicious Hullabaloo/Pachanga Deliciosa*, by Pat Mora (picture book); and *The Year of Our Revolution*, by Judith Ortiz Cofer (young adult).

How to Contact Does not accept unsolicited mss. Query with SASE or submit 2 sample chapter(s), synopsis, SASE. Responds in 1 month to queries; 6 months to mss. Accepts simultaneous submissions.

Terms Pays 10% royalty on wholesale price. Average advance: $1,000-3,000. Publishes ms 2 years after acceptance. Book catalog and ms guidelines available via Web site or with #10 SASE.

Advice "Include cover letter with submission explaining why your manuscript is unique and important, why we should publish it, who will buy it, relevance to the U.S. Hispanic culture, etc."

◯ ◎ **PINEAPPLE PRESS, INC.**

P.O. Box 3889, Sarasota FL 34230. (941)739-2219. Fax: (941)739-2296. E-mail: info@pineapplepress.com. Web site: www.pineapplepress.com. **Contact:** June Cussen, editor. Estab. 1982. Small independent trade publisher. Publishes hardcover and trade paperback originals. Books: quality paper; offset printing; Smyth-sewn or perfect bound; illustrations occasionally. **Published some debut authors within the last year.** Averages 25 total titles/year. Distributes titles through Pineapple, Ingram and Baker & Taylor. Promotes titles through reviews, advertising in print media, direct mail, author signings and the World Wide Web.

Needs Historical, literary, mainstream/contemporary, regional (Florida). Published *The Bucket Flower*, by Donald Wilson (novel).

How to Contact Does not accept unsolicited mss. Query with sample, SASE. Responds in 2 months to queries. Accepts simultaneous submissions.

Terms Pays 6½-15% royalty on net receipts. Average advance: rare. Publishes ms 18 months after acceptance. Book catalog for 9×12 SAE with $1.29 postage.

Advice "Quality first novels will be published, though we usually only do one or two novels per year and they must be set in Florida. We regard the author/editor relationship as a trusting relationship with communication open both ways. Learn all you can about the publishing process and about how to promote your book once it is published. A query on a novel without a brief sample seems useless."

PIPERS' ASH, LTD.

Pipers' Ash, Church Rd., Christian Malford, Chippenham, Wiltshire SN15 4BW United Kingdom. (+44)1249 720-563. Fax: 0870 0568917. E-mail: pipersash@supamasu.com. Web site: www.supamasu.com. **Contact:** Manuscript Evaluation Desk. Estab. 1976. "Small press publisher. Considers all submitted manuscripts fairly—without bias or favor. This company is run by book lovers, not by accountants." Publishes hardcover and electronic originals. **Published 18 debut authors within the last year.** Averages 18 total titles, 18 fiction titles/year. Distributes and promotes titles through press releases, catalogues, Web site shopping basket, direct mail and the Internet.

Needs Adventure, children's/juvenile (adventure), confession, feminist, historical, literary, mainstream/contemporary, military/war, regional, religious, romance (contemporary, romantic suspense), science fiction (hard science/technological, soft/sociological), short story collections, sports, suspense, young adult (adventure,science fiction). "We publish 30,000-word novellas and short story collections. Visit our Web site for submission guidelines and tips. Authors are invited to submit collections of short stories and poetry for consideration for our ongoing programs." Published *Belly-Button Tales and Other Things*, by Sandra McTavish; *Cosmic Women*, by Margaret Karamazin; *A Sailor's Song*, by Leslie Wilkie.

How to Contact Accepts unsolicited mss. Query with SASE or IRC or submit sample chapter(s), 25-word synopsis (that sorts out the writers from the wafflers). Accepts queries by e-mail, fax, phone. Include estimated word count. Send SASE or IRC for return of ms or send a disposable ms and SASE or IRC for reply only. Responds in 1 month to queries; 3 months to mss. Accepts electronic submissions, submissions on disk. No simultaneous submissions. Always comments on rejected mss.

Terms Pays 10% royalty on wholesale price. Also gives 5 author's copies. Publishes ms 6 months after acceptance. Ms guidelines online, www.supumasu.com.

Advice "Study the market! Check your selected publisher's catalogue and Web site."

PIPPIN PRESS

229 E. 85th St., P.O. Box 1347, Gracie Station, New York NY 10028. (212)288-4920. Fax: (732)225-1562. **Contact:** Barbara Francis, publisher and editor-in-chief; Joyce Segal, senior editor. Estab. 1987. "Small, independent children's book company, formed by the former editor-in-chief of Prentice Hall's juvenile book division." Publishes hardcover originals. Books: 135-150 GSM offset-semi-matte paper (for picture books); offset, sheet-fed printing; Smythe-sewn binding; full color, black and white line illustrations and half tone, b&w and full color illustrations. Averages 2-4 total titles/year. Distributes titles through commission sales force. Promotes titles through reviews, trade convention exhibits, as well as book fairs.

Needs Children's/juvenile (ages 6-12), historical, humor, mystery. "We're especially looking for small chapter books for 7- to 11-year olds, especially by people of many cultures." Also interested in humorous fiction for ages 7-11. "At this time, we are especially interested in historical novels, 'autobiographical' novels, historical and literary biographies and humor." Recently published *A Visit from the Leopard: Memories of a Ugandan Childhood*, by Catherine Mudibo-Pinang (juvenile autobiography, middle readers; debut author); *Abigail's Drum*, by John A. Minahan (juvenile historical, middle readers; debut author); *The Spinner's Daughter*, by Amy Littlesugar (juvenile fiction, young readers; debut author).

How to Contact Does not accept unsolicited mss. Query with SASE. Responds in 3 weeks to queries. No simultaneous submissions. Sometimes comments on rejected mss.

Terms Pays royalty. Offers advance. Publishes ms 2 years after acceptance. Book catalog for 6×9 SASE. Ms guidelines for #10 SASE.

PLEXUS PUBLISHING, INC.

143 Old Marlton Pike, Medford NJ 08055-8750. (609)654-6500. Fax: (609)654-4309. E-mail: info@plexuspublishing.com. Web site: www.plexuspublishing.com. **Contact:** John B. Bryans, editor-in-chief. Estab. 1977. Small regional publisher focusing on titles for New Jersey residents and visitors. Publishes hardcover and paperback originals and reprints. **Published 70% debut authors within the last year.** Averages 4-5 total titles/year.

Needs Regional (New Jersey). Mysteries and literary novels with a strong regional (southern NJ) angle. Published *Boardwalk Empire,* by Nelson Johnson; *Wave,* by Wil Mara.

How to Contact Query with SASE. Accepts queries by mail. Include brief bio, list of publishing credits. Agented fiction 10%. Responds in 1 month to queries; 3 months to mss. Accepts simultaneous submissions. No submissions on disk.

Terms Pays 10-15% royalty on net receipts. Average advance: $500-1,000. Publishes ms 1 year after acceptance. Book catalog and ms guidelines for 10×13 SAE with 4 first-class stamps.

Advice "If it's not New Jersey focused, we are unlikely to publish it."

Ⓐ ✿ ◙ PLUME

Division of Penguin Putnam Inc., 375 Hudson St., New York NY 10014. (212)366-2000. Web site: www.penguin putnam.com. **Contact:** Trena Keating, editor-in-chief/associate publisher (literary fiction). Estab. 1948. Publishes paperback originals and reprints. **Published some debut authors within the last year.**

Needs "All kinds of commercial and literary fiction, including mainstream, historical, New Age, western, thriller, gay. Full length novels and collections." Published *Girl with a Pearl Earring*, by Tracy Chevalier; *Liar's Moon*, by Phillip Kimball; *The True History of Paradise*, by Margaret Cezain-Thompson.

How to Contact *Agented submissions only.* Accepts simultaneous submissions.

Terms Pays in royalties and author's copies. Offers advance. Publishes ms 12-18 months after acceptance. Book catalog for SASE.

Advice "Write the complete manuscript and submit it to an agent or agents."

Ⓝ ◯ POCOL PRESS

6023 Pocol Drive, Clifton VA 20124. (703)830-5862. E-mail: chrisandtom@erols.com. Web site: www.pocolpres s.com. **Contact:** J. Thomas Hetrick, editor (baseball history and fiction). Pocol Press publishes first-time, un-agented authors. Our fiction deals mainly with single author short story anthologies from outstanding niche writers. Publishes paperback originals. Books: 50 lb. paper; offset printing; perfect binding. Average print order: 500. **Published 2 debut authors within the last year.** Averages 4 total titles, 3 fiction titles/year. Member: Small Press Publishers Association. Distributes titles through Web site, authors, e-mail, word-of-mouth and readings.

Needs Horror (psychological, supernatural), literary, mainstream/contemporary, short story collections, baseball. Published *Believers*, by Nathan Leslie (short fiction); *A Collection of Friends*, by Thomas Sheehan (memoir); *Foul Ball in Beantown*, by G.S. Rowe (baseball, mystery).

How to Contact Does not accept or return unsolicited mss. Query with SASE or submit 1 sample chapter(s). Accepts queries by mail. Include estimated word count, brief bio, list of publishing credits. Responds in 2 weeks to queries; 2 months to mss. No simultaneous submissions, submissions on disk. Sometimes comments on rejected mss.

Terms Pays 10-12% royalty. Publishes ms 1 year or less after acceptance. Book catalog for SASE or on Web site. Ms guidelines for SASE or on Web site.

Advice "Pocol Press is unique; we publish good writing and great storytelling. Write the best stories you can. Read them to you friends/peers. Note their reaction. Publishes some of the finest fiction by a small press."

◯ ◎ ⓥ POISONED PEN PRESS

6962 E. 1st Ave. #103, Scottsdale AZ 85251. (480)945-3375. Fax: (480)949-1707. E-mail: info@poisonedpenpress .com. Web site: www.poisonedpenpress.com. **Contact:** editor@poisonedpenpress.com (mystery, fiction). Estab. 1997. Publishes hardcover originals and paperback reprints. Books: 60 lb. paper; offset printing; hardcover binding. Average print order: 3,500. First novel print order: 3,000. **Published 4 debut authors within the last year.** Plans 8 first novels this year. Member Publishers Marketing Associations, Arizona Book Publishers Associations, Publishers Association of West. Distributes through Ingram, Baker & Taylor, Brodart.

• Was nominated in 2002 for the *LA Times* Book Prize. Also the recipient of several Edgar and Agatha Awards.

Needs Mystery (amateur sleuth, cozy, police procedural, private eye/hard-boiled, historical). Published *The Heat of The Moon*, by Sandra Parshall (mystery/fiction); *Impulse*, by Frederick Ramsay (mystery/fiction); *The Do-Re-Mi*, by Ken Kuhlken (mystery/fiction); *Drive*, by James Sallis (mystery/fiction).

How to Contact Accepts unsolicited mss. Query with SASE. Accepts queries by e-mail. Responds in 1 week to queries; 6-9 months to mss. Only accepts electronic submissions. No simultaneous submissions. Often comments on rejected mss.

Terms Pays 9-15% royalty. Average advance: $1,000. Publishes ms 12-15 months after acceptance. Ms guidelines online.

◻ PORT TOWN PUBLISHING

5909 Tower Avenue, Superior WI 54880. (715)392-6843. E-mail: jhackensmith@porttownpublishing.com. Web site: www.porttownpublishing.com. **Contact:** Jean Hackensmith, senior fiction editor. Estab. 1999. Port Town Publishing is a medium-sized publisher of paperback fiction novels. Publishes 48 titles per year, including 36 adult fiction titles ranging in genre from romance, to sci-fi, to mystery, to horror. Publishes paperback originals. Books: 20 lb. stock paper; laser printing; perfect bound; color and pencil-sketch illustrations. Average print order: 400. **Published 6 debut authors within the last year.** Titles disributed by Ingram Book Group, Baker & Taylor Books.

Imprint(s) Little Ones; Growing Years; Teen Scene.

Needs Adventure, children's/juvenile (adventure, animal, easy-to-read, fantasy, historical, mystery, preschool/picture book, series), fantasy (space fantasy, sword and sorcery), historical, horror (dark fantasy, futuristic, psychological, supernatural), mainstream/contemporary, mystery (amateur sleuth, cozy, police procedural, private eye/hard-boiled), regional (Lake Superior area), romance (contemporary, futuristic/time travel, gothic, historical, regency period, romantic suspense), science fiction (hard science/technological, soft/sociological), thriller/espionage, young adult (adventure, easy-to-read, fantasy/science fiction, historical, horror, mystery/suspense, problem novels, romance, series, sports). Especially wants science fiction, thriller and mystery. Recently published *The Teacher*, by Robert Banfelder; *Best Intentions*, by Julie Compton; *For Jennie*, by Donna Gestri.

How to Contact Does not accept unsolicited mss. Query with SASE. Accepts queries by e-mail, mail. E-mail for faster reply. Include estimated word count, brief bio, list of publishing credits. Send SASE for return of ms or send a disposable ms and SASE for reply only. Agented fiction 5%. Responds in 1 week to queries; 4-6 months to mss. Accepts simultaneous submissions if notified. Check manuscript submissions page on Web site before sending a query or proposal to see if we are accepting submissions.

Terms Publishes ms 1-2 years after acceptance. Ms guidelines online.

Advice "We are looking for a sellable, well-plotted story above all else. We are not afraid to take on a manuscript that needs work, but we always hope the author will grow during the editorial process."

◻◻ ◻ THE POST-APOLLO PRESS

35 Marie St., Sausalito CA 94965. (415)332-1458. Fax: (415)332-8045. E-mail: postapollo@earthlink.net. Web site: www.postapollopress.com. **Contact:** Simone Fattal, publisher. Estab. 1982. Specializes in "woman writers published in Europe or the Middle East who have been translated into English for the first time." Publishes trade paperback originals and reprints. Books: acid-free paper; lithography printing; perfect-bound. Average print order: 1,000. **Published some debut authors within the last year.** Averages 4 total titles/year. Distributes titles through Small Press Distribution, Berkley, California. Promotes titles through advertising in selectted literary quarterlies, SPD catalog, ALA and ABA and SF Bay Area Book Festival participation.

Needs Experimental, literary (plays), spiritual. "Many of our books are first translations into English." Published *Some Life*, by Joanne Kyger; *In/Somnia*, by Etel Adnan; *9:45*, by Kit Robinson; and *Happily*, by Lyn Hejinian.

How to Contact Submit 1 sample chapter(s). Responds in 3 months to queries.

Terms Pays 5-7% royalty on wholesale price. Publishes ms 1½ years after acceptance. Book catalog and ms guidelines for #10 SASE.

Advice "We want to see serious, literary quality, informed by an experimental aesthetic."

◻◻ ◻ ◻ PRAIRIE JOURNAL PRESS

Prairie Journal Trust, P.O. Box 61203, Brentwood Postal Services, Calgary AB T2L 2K6 Canada. E-mail: prairiejournal@yahoo.com. Web site: www.geocities.com/prairiejournal/. **Contact:** Anne Burke, literary editor. Estab. 1983. Small-press, noncommercial literary publisher. Publishes paperback originals. Books: bond paper; offset printing; stapled binding; b&w line drawings. **Published some debut authors within the last year.** Distributes titles by mail and in bookstores and libraries (public and university). Promotes titles through direct mail, reviews and in journals.

● Prairie Journal Press authors have been nominees for The Journey Prize in fiction and finalists and honorable mention for the National Magazine awards.

Needs Literary, short story collections. Published *Prairie Journal Fiction, Prairie Journal Fiction II* (anthologies of short stories); *Solstice* (short fiction on the theme of aging); and *Prairie Journal Prose*.

How to Contact Accepts unsolicited mss. Sometimes comments on rejected mss.

Terms Pays 1 author's copy; honorarium depends on grant/award provided by the government or private/corporate donations. SAE with IRC for individuals. No U.S. stamps please.

Advice "We wish we had the means to promote more new writers. We look for something different each time and try not to repeat types of stories if possible. We receive fiction of very high quality. Short fiction is preferable although excerpts from novels are considered if they stand alone on their own merit."

★ ◐ ◎ PUFFIN BOOKS

Penguin Group (USA), Inc., 345 Hudson St., New York NY 10014. (212)366-2000. Web site: www.penguinputnam.com. **Contact:** Sharyn November, senior editor; Kristin Gilson, editorial director. Puffin Books publishes high-end trade paperbacks and paperback reprints for preschool children, beginning and middle readers, and young adults. Publishes trade paperback originals and reprints. Averages 175-200 total titles/year.

Needs Picture books, young adult, middle grade; easy-to-read grades 1-3. "We publish paperback reprints and original titles. We do not publish original picture books." Published *Looking for Alaska*, by John Green.

How to Contact Does not accept unsolicited mss. Send SASE or IRC. Responds in 3 months to mss. No simultaneous submissions.

Terms Royalty varies. Average advance: varies. Publishes ms 1 year after acceptance. Book catalog for 9×12 SAE with 7 first-class stamps; send request to Marketing Department.

Advice "Our audience ranges from little children 'first books' to young adult (ages 14-16). An original idea has the best luck."

Ⓝ ◯ ◎ ⓥ PUREPLAY PRESS

11353 Missouri Ave., Los Angeles CA 90025. (310)479-8773. Fax: (310)473-9384. E-mail: editor@pureplaypress. com. Web site: www.pureplaypress.com. **Contact:** David Landau. "We are a small, niche publisher devoted to Cuba's history and culture. We publish high-quality books that people will want to read for years to come." Books are in English, Spanish and bilingual formats. Publishes hardcover and paperback originals. **Published 3 debut authors within the last year.** Averages 6 total titles, 3-4 fiction titles/year.

  • Best Poetry Book 2004, Latino Book Awards.

Needs Children's/juvenile, historical, military/war.

How to Contact Accepts queries by e-mail. Include brief bio. Accepts electronic submissions of mss. Sometimes comments on rejected mss.

Terms Pays 10% royalty. Offers advance. Ms guidelines online.

Ⓐ G.P. PUTNAM'S SONS (Adult Trade)

Penguin Putnam, Inc., 375 Hudson, New York NY 10014. (212)366-2000. Fax: (212)366-2664. Web site: www.penguinputnam.com. **Contact:** Acquisition Editor. Publishes hardcover and trade paperback originals. **Published some debut authors within the last year.**

Imprint(s) Putnam, Riverhead, Jeremy P. Tarcher, Perigee.

Needs Adventure, literary, mainstream/contemporary, mystery, suspense, women's. Prefers agented submissions. Recently published *The Bear and the Dragon*, by Tom Clancy (adventure).

How to Contact *Agented submissions only.* Accepts simultaneous submissions.

Terms Pays variable royalties on retail price. Average advance: varies. Request book catalog through mail order department.

◯ ◎ QUIXOTE PRESS

3544 Blakslee St., Wever IA 52658. (800)571-2665. Fax: (319)372-7485. **Contact:** Bruce Carlson, president. Quixote Press specializes in humorous and/or regional folklore and special-interest cookbooks. Publishes trade paperback originals and reprints. **Published many debut authors within the last year.**

Needs Humor, short story collections. Published *Eating Ohio*, by Rus Pishnery (short stories about Ohio); *Lil' Red Book of Fishing Tips*, by Tom Whitecloud (fishing tales); *How to Talk Hoosier*, by Netha Bell (humor); *Cow Whisperer*, by Skip Holmes (humor); *Flour Sack Bloomers*, by Lucy Fetterhoff (history).

How to Contact Query with SASE. Accepts simultaneous submissions.

Terms Pays 10% royalty on wholesale price. Publishes ms 1 year after acceptance.

Advice "Carefully consider marketing considerations. Audience is women in gift shops, on farm sites, direct retail outlets, wineries, outdoor sport shops, etc. Contact us at *idea* stage, not complete ms stage. Be receptive to design input by us."

◉ RAGER MEDIA

Rager Media, Inc., 1016 West Abbey, Medina OH 44256. (330)622-2928. E-mail: editor@ragermedia.com. Web site: www.ragermedia.com. **Contact:** Christopher White, editor-in-chief. Estab. 2005. "We are a small, independent press with an international audience. We strive to publish emerging writers, but many of our authors are among the most highly esteemed in the world, including *New York Times*best sellers and major literary prize winners. We distinguish ourselves by our willingness to keep excellent books in print and by publishing work that is widely admired and critically acclaimed." Publishes hardcover originals, paperback originals, paperback reprints. Format: 50 lb. acid-free house natural paper; offset printing; smythe-sewn and perfect bound; some illustrations. Average print order: 1,000. Debut novel print order: 1,000. **Plans 3 debut novels this year.**

Averages 12+ total titles/year; 6+ fiction titles/year. Distributes/promotes titles in house and through SPD (spdbooks.org).

Needs Literary. Published *The Great Kisser, Stories*, by David Evanier. Plans The Ohio Distinguished Authors series, The Australian Poetry in America series, The Rager First Books series.

How to Contact E-mail query letter or e-mail query plus electronic version of ms. Accepts queries by snail mail, e-mail. Include estimated word count. Send disposable copy of ms and SASE for reply only or send e-copy. Agented fiction: 30%. Responds to queries in 1-6 months. Accepts unsolicited mss. Considers simultaneous submissions, submissions on CD or disk, e-mail submissions. Sometimes critiques/comments on rejected mss. Responds to mss in 1-9 months.

Terms Pays royalties of 20% minimum. Manuscript published 1-3 years after acceptance. Sends pre-production galleys to author. Writer's guidelines on Web site. Book catalogs free upon request, on Web site.

Advice "We intend to take books of high quality and market them as one would any other product. Often, presses which publish our sort of literature are nonprofit and do not take a commercial approach. We, on the other hand, are literary entrepreneurs. At the same time, we are taking on what was once the expectation of the university press; that is, keeping excellent books in print, even those books that might not sell as well as our more commercially viable titles. We have a relatively simple philosophy when it comes to acquiring titles. If we think it's good, we'll publish it. We are known for having high editorial standards, but we will encourage the careers of budding authors just as much as we will publish more established ones."

Ⓐ ✪ ◎ RANDOM HOUSE CHILDREN'S BOOKS

Division of Random House, Inc., 1745 Broadway, New York NY 10019. (212)782-9000. Fax: (212)782-9452. Web site: www.randomhouse.com/kids. **Contact:** Kate Klimo, editorial director of Random House Golden Books Young Readers Group; Beverly Horowitz, editorial director for Knopf Delacorte Dell Young Readers Group; Heidi Kilgras, editorial director for Step Into Reading; Jennifer Dussling, senior director for Stepping Stone; Jim Thomas, senior editor (fantasy). Estab. 1925. "Producing books for preschool children through young adult readers, in all formats from board to activity books to picture books and novels, Random House Children's Books brings together world-famous franchise characters, multimillion-copy series and top-flight, award-winning authors and illustrators."

Imprint(s) *For Knopf Delacorte Dell Young Readers Group*—Doubleday, Alfred A. Knopf, Crown, Delacorte Press, Wendy Lamb Books, David Fickling Books, Dragonfly Books, Yearling Books, Laurel-Leaf Books, Bantam, Swartz & Wade Books. *For Random House/Golden Books Young Readers Group*—Picturebacks, Beginner Books, Step Into Reading, Stepping Stone Books, Landmark Books, Disney Books for Young Readers, First Time Books, Sesame Workshop.

Needs "Random House publishes a select list of first chapter books and novels, with an emphasis on fantasy and historical fiction." Chapter books, middle-grade readers, young adult.

How to Contact Does not accept unsolicited mss. *Agented submissions only.* Accepts simultaneous submissions.

Advice "We look for original, unique stories. Do something that hasn't been done before."

Ⓐ ✪ RANDOM HOUSE TRADE PUBLISHING GROUP

Random House, Inc., 1745 Broadway, 17th Floor, New York NY 10019. (212)782-9000. Fax: (212)572-4960. Web site: www.randomhouse.com. Estab. 1925. "The flagship imprint of Random House, Inc." Publishes hardcover and trade paperback books. Averages 120 total titles/year.

Imprint(s) The Modern Library, Random House Trade Books, Random House Trade Paperbacks, Villard Books, Strivers Row, Ballantine Books.

Needs Adventure, confession, experimental, fantasy, historical, horror, humor, mainstream/contemporary, mystery, suspense.

How to Contact *Agented submissions only.* Accepts simultaneous submissions.

Terms Pays royalty on retail price. Offers advance. Ms guidelines online.

Ⓐ ◎ RANDOM HOUSE, INC.

Division of Bertelsmann Book Group, 1745 Broadway, New York NY 10013. (212)782-9000. Fax: (212)302-7985. E-mail: editor@randomhouse.com. Web site: www.randomhouse.com. Estab. 1925. "Random House has long been committed to publishing the best literature by writers both in the United States and abroad."

Imprint(s) Alfred A. Knopf; Anchor Books; Shaye Areheart Books; Ballantine Books; Bantam Hardcover; Bantam Mass Market; Bantam Trade Paperbacks; Bell Tower; Black Ink/Harlem Moon; Broadway; Clarkson Potter; Crown Books for Young Readers; Crown Publishers, Inc; Currency; Del Ray; Del Ray/Lucas; Delacorte; Dell; Dell Dragonfly; Dell Laurel-Leaf; Dell Yearling; Delta; The Dial Press; Domain; Doubleday; Doubleday Religion; Doubleday Graphic Novels; DTP; Everyman's Library; Fanfare; Fawcett; David Fickling Books; First Choice Chapter Books; Fodor's; Grammercy Book; Harmony Books; Island; Ivy; Knopf Books for Young Readers; Knopf Paperbacks; Library of Contemporary Thought; Main Street Books; The Modern Library; Nan A. Talese; One

World; Pantheon Books; Picture Yearling; Presidio Press; Random House Children's Publishing; Random House Large Print Publishing; Shocken Books; Spectra; Strivers Row; Three Rivers Press; Times Books; Villard Books; Vintage Books; Wings Books.

Terms Pays royalty. Offers advance. Ms guidelines online.

🌐 ◻ ◎ RANSOM PUBLISHING LTD.

Rose Cottage Howe Hill, Watlington Oxon OX49 5HB United Kingdom. (+44)01491 613711. Fax: (+44)01491 613733. E-mail: jenny@ransom.co.uk. Web site: www.ransom.co.uk. **Contact:** Jenny Ertie, editor. Estab. 1995. Independent UK publisher with distribution in English speaking markets throughout the world. Specializes in books for reluctant and struggling readers. One of the few English language publishers to publish books with very high interest age and very low reading age. Has a developing list of children's books for home and school use. Specializes in phonics and general reading programs. Publishes paperback originals. **Published 5 debut authors within the last year.** Member BESA (UK), IPG (UK).

Needs Easy reading for young adults. Books for reluctant and struggling readers.

How to Contact Accepts unsolicited mss. Query with SASE or submit outline/proposal. Prefers queries by e-mail. Include estimated word count, brief bio, list of publishing credits. Responds in 3-4 weeks to queries. Accepts simultaneous submissions, electronic submissions, submissions on disk. Never comments on rejected mss.

Terms Pays 10% royalty on net receipts. Ms guidelines by e-mail.

Ⓝ ◪ RAVENHAWK BOOKS

The 6DOF Group, 7739 Broadway Blvd., #95, Tucson AZ 85710. **Contact:** Carl Lasky, publisher (all fiction). Estab. 1998. ''Small, independent, literary press most interested in provocative and innovative works.'' Publishes hardcover and paperback originals. Books: 50 or 60 lb. paper; traditional, POD, e-book printing. First novel print order: 1,000. **Published 3 debut authors within the last year.** Plans 3 first novels this year. Distibutes titles through Ingram, Baker & Taylor, Amazon, Borders, Barnes & Noble.

Needs Children's/juvenile (adventure, animal, easy-to-read, fantasy, mystery, series), fantasy (space fantasy, sword and sorcery), horror (dark fantasy, futuristic, psychological, supernatural), humor, literary, mainstream/contemporary, mystery (amateur sleuth, cozy, police procedural, private eye/hard-boiled), psychic/supernatural, religious (religious mystery/suspense, religious thriller), romance (contemporary, romantic suspense), science fiction (hard science/technological, soft/sociological), short story collections, thriller/espionage, young adult (adventure, easy-to-read, fantasy/science fiction, horror, mystery/suspense, problem novels, series). Especially interested in young authors with an insightful and innovative perspective that influences their writing, and appeals to their peers.

How to Contact Does not accept unsolicited mss. Agented fiction 10%. No simultaneous submissions, electronic submissions, submissions on disk. Sometimes comments on rejected mss.

Terms Pays 45-60% royalty. Publishes ms 18 months after acceptance.

Advice ''Write dynamic prose utilizing a multi-dimensional edge (conflict). Although the majority of elitists that control the publishing industry won't admit it, it really is a crap shoot out there. Don't ever give up if you believe in yourself. Courage.''

Ⓝ ❖ ◻ ◎ ⅴ RED DEER PRESS

1512, 1800 4th St. SW, Calgary AB T2S 2S5 Canada. (403)220-4334. Fax: (403)210-8191. E-mail: rdp@ucalgary. ca. Web site: www.reddeerpress.com. **Contact:** Peter Carver, children's book editor. Estab. 1975. Publishes young adult and paperback originals ''focusing on books by, about, or of interest to Canadian youth.'' Books: offset paper; offset printing; hardcover/perfect-bound. Average print order: 5,000. First novel print order: 2,500. Distributes titles in Canada, the US, the UK, Australia and New Zealand.

● Red Deer Press has received numerous honors and awards from the Book Publishers Association of Alberta, Canadian Children's Book Centre, the Governor General of Canada and the Writers Guild of Alberta.

Imprint(s) Northern Lights Books for Children, Northern Lights Young Novels, Roundup Books, Sirrocco Books.

Needs Young adult (juvenile and early reader), contemporary. No romance or horror. Published *A Fine Daughter*, by Catherine Simmons Niven (novel); *The Kappa Child*, by Hiromi Goto (novel); *The Dollinage*, by Martine Leavitt; and *The Game*, by Teresa Toten (nominated for the Governor General's Award).

How to Contact Accepts unsolicited mss. Query with SASE. Responds in 6 months to mss. Accepts simultaneous submissions. No submissions on disk.

Terms Pays 8-10% royalty. Advance is negotiable. Publishes ms 1 year after acceptance. Book catalog for 9×12 SASE.

Advice ''We're very interested in young adult and children's fiction from Canadian writers with a proven track record (either published books or widely published in established magazines or journals) and for manuscripts with regional themes and/or a distinctive voice. We publish Canadian authors exclusively.''

ⓃⓄ◎ RED DRESS INK

Harlequin Enterprises, Ltd., 233 Broadway, New York NY 10279. Web site: www.eharlequin.com; www.reddres sink.com. **Contact:** Margaret O'Neill Marbury, executive editor; Farrin Jacobs, associate editor. "We launched *Red Dress Ink* to provide women with fresh and irreverent stories that reflect the lifestyles of today's modern women." Publishes trade paperback originals.

Needs Adventure, confession, humor, mainstream/contemporary, multicultural, regional, romance, short story collections, contemporary women's fiction. Red Dress Ink publishes "stories that reflect the lifestyles of today's urban, single women. They show life as it is, with a strong touch of humor, hipness and energy." Word length: 90,000-110,000 words. Point of view: first person/third person, as well as multiple viewpoints, if needed. Settings: urban locales in North America or well-known international settings, such as London or Paris. Tone: fun, up-to-the-minute, clever, appealing, realistic. Published *Fashionistas*, by Lynn Messina; *The Thin Pink Line*, by Lauren Baratz-Logsted; and *Engaging Men*, by Lynda Curnyn.

How to Contact Accepts unsolicited mss. Query with SASE. Accepts queries by mail. Send SASE or IRC. No electronic submissions, submissions on disk.

Terms Pays 7$\frac{1}{2}$% royalty. Offers advance. Ms guidelines online.

Ⓝ RED HEN PRESS

P.O. Box 3537, Granada Hills CA 91394. (818)831-0649. Fax: (818)831-6659. E-mail: editor@redhen.org. Web site: www.redhen.org. **Contact:** Mark E. Cull, publisher/editor (fiction); Katherine Gale, poetry editor (poetry, literary fiction). Estab. 1993. Publishes trade paperback originals. **Published 10% of books from debut authors within the last year.** Averages 10 total titles, 10 fiction titles/year.

Needs Ethnic, experimental, feminist, gay/lesbian, historical, literary, mainstream/contemporary, short story collections. "We prefer high-quality literary fiction." Published *The Misread City: New Literary Los Angeles*, edited by Dana Gioia and Scott Timberg; *Rebel*, by Tom Hayden.

How to Contact Query with SASE. Agented fiction 10%. Responds in 1 month to queries; 3 months to mss. Accepts simultaneous submissions.

Terms Publishes book 1 year after acceptance of ms. Publishes ms 1 year after acceptance. Book catalog and ms guidelines available via Web site or free.

Advice "Audience reads poetry, literary fiction, intelligent nonfiction. If you have an agent, we may be too small since we don't pay advances. Write well. Send queries first. Be willing to help promote your own book."

Ⓞ RISING TIDE PRESS, NEW MEXICO

American-Canadian Publishers, Inc., P.O. Box 6136, Santa Fe NM 87502-6136. (505)983-8484. Estab. 1981. Rising Tide Press, New Mexico is a midsize publisher. Books: 8$\frac{1}{2}$×11; vellum bound; 140-150 pages; white trove paper.

Needs Wants innovative fiction. Recently published *Empire Sweets*, by Stanley Berne (fiction). "We also publish innovative poetry—political in nature, mature in quality."

How to Contact Does not accept unsolicited mss.

Terms Pays royalty.

Ⓞ❧ RIVER CITY PUBLISHING

River City Publishing, LLC, 1719 Mulberry St., Montgomery AL 36106. (334)265-6753. Fax: (334)265-8880. E-mail: jgilbert@rivercitypublishing.com. Web site: www.rivercitypublishing.com. **Contact:** Jim Gilbert, editor. Estab. 1989. Midsize independent publisher (10-20 books per year). "We publish books of national appeal, with an emphasis on Southern writers and Southern stories." Publishes hardcover and trade paperback originals. **Published 2 debut authors within the last year.** Averages 12 total titles, 4 fiction titles/year.

● Had three nominees to *Foreword* fiction book of the year awards (2002); won Ippy for Short Fiction (2005).

Needs Ethnic, historical, literary, multicultural, regional (southern), short story collections. Published *The Assigned Visit*, by Shelley Fraser Mickel (novel); *King of Country*, by Wayne Greenhaw (novel); *The Bear Bryant Funeral Train*, by Brad Vice (short story collection).

How to Contact Accepts unsolicited submissions and submissions from unagented authors, as well as those from established and agented writers. Submit 5 consecutive sample chapters or entire manuscript for review. "Please include a short biography that highlights any previous writing and publishing experience, sales opportunities the author could provide, ideas for marketing the book, and why you think the work would be appropriate for River City." Send appropriate-sized SASE or IRC, "otherwise, the material will be recycled." Also accepts queries by e-mail. "Please include your electronic query letter as inline text and not an as attachment; we do not open unsolicited attachments of any kind. Please do not include sample chapters or your entire manuscript as inline text. We do not accept electronic submissions of manuscripts or portions of manuscripts as e-mail attachments. We do not field or accept queries by telephone." Agented fiction 25%. Responds in three to nine months; "please wait at least 3 months before contacting us about your submission." Accepts simultaneous submissions. No multiple submissions. Rarely comments on rejected mss.

Terms Pays 10-15% royalty on retail price. Average advance: $500-5,000. Publishes ms 1 year after acceptance.

Advice "Only send your best work after you have received outside opinions. From approximately 1,000 submissions each year, we publish no more than 20 books and few of those come from unsolicited material. Competition is fierce, so follow the guidelines exactly. All first-time novelists should submit their work to the Fred Bonnie Award contest."

RIVERHEAD BOOKS

Penguin Putnam, 375 Hudson Street, Office #4079, New York NY 10014.

Contact: Sean McDonald, executive editor. Estab. 1994. "Riverhead Books carries on expanding its role as a leading publisher of quality fiction and groundbreaking nonfiction." Publishes hardcover originals, paperback originals.

Needs Literary, mainstream, contemporary. Among the award-winning writers whose careers Riverhead has launched so far are Pearl Abraham (*The Romance Reader*; *Giving Up America*), Jennifer Belle (*Going Down*; *High Maintenance*), Adam Davies (*The Frog King*), Junot Díaz (*Drown*), Alex Garland (*The Beach*; *The Tesseract*), Nick Hornby (*High Fidelity*; *About a Boy*; *How to Be Good*), Khaled Hosseini (*The Kite Runner*), ZZ Packer (*Drinking Coffee Elsewhere*), Iain Pears (*The Dream of Scipio*; *Instance of the Fingerpost*), Danzy Senna (*Caucasia*), Gary Shteyngart (*The Russian Debutante's Handbook*), Aryeh Lev Stollman (*The Far Euphrates*; *The Illuminated Soul*; *The Dialogues of Time and Entropy*), Sarah Waters (*Tipping the Velvet*; *Affinity*; *Fingersmith*).

How to Contact Submit through agent only. No unsolicited mss.

RONSDALE PRESS

3350 W. 21st Ave., Vancouver BC V6S 1G7 Canada. (604)738-4688. Fax: (604)731-4548. E-mail: ronsdale@shaw.ca. Web site: www.ronsdalepress.com. **Contact:** Ronald B. Hatch, president/editor; Veronica Hatch, editor (YA historical). Estab. 1988. Ronsdale Press is "dedicated to publishing books that give Canadians new insights into themselves and their country." Publishes trade paperback originals. Books: 60 lb. paper; photo offset printing; perfect binding. Average print order: 1,500. **Published some debut authors within the last year.** Averages 10 total titles, 3 fiction titles/year. Sales representation: Literary Press Group. Distribution: LitDistco. Promotes titles through ads in *BC Bookworld* and *Globe & Mail* and interviews on radio.

Needs Literary, short story collections, novels. Canadian authors *only*. Published *The City in the Egg*, by Michel Tremblay (novel); *Jackrabbit Moon*, by Sheila McLeod Arnopoulos (novel); and *What Belongs*, by F.B. André (short story collections).

How to Contact Accepts unsolicited mss. Accepts queries by e-mail. Send SASE or IRC. Responds in 2 weeks to queries; 2 months to mss. Accepts simultaneous submissions. Sometimes comments on rejected mss.

Terms Pays 10% royalty on retail price. Publishes ms 1 year after acceptance. Ms guidelines online.

Advice "We publish both fiction and poetry. Authors *must* be Canadian. We look for writing that shows the author has read widely in contemporary and earlier literature. Ronsdale, like other literary presses, is not interested in mass-market or pulp materials."

SALVO PRESS

P.O. Box 9736, Beaverton, OR 97007. Web site: www.salvopress.com. **Contact:** Scott Schmidt, publisher (mystery, suspense, thriller & espionage). Estab. 1998. "We are a small press specializing in mystery, suspense, espionage and thriller fiction. Our press publishes in trade paperback and e-book format." Publishes hardcover, trade paperback originals and e-books in most formats. Books: $5\frac{1}{2}\times8\frac{1}{2}$; or 6×9 printing; perfect binding. **Published 3 debut authors within the last year.** Averages 3 total titles, 3 fiction titles/year.

Needs Adventure, literary, mystery (amateur sleuth, police procedural, private/hard-boiled), science fiction (hard science/technological), suspense, thriller/espionage. "Our needs change. Check our Web site." Published *Global Shot*, by Trevor Scott (mystery/thriller); *Mayan Equinox*, by Keith Jones (first fiction, mystery); and *The Devil's Racket*, by Tom Wallace (mystery).

How to Contact Query by e-mail only at query@salvopress.com. Please place the word "Query" as the subject. Include estimated word count, brief bio, list of publishing credits, "and something to intrigue me so I ask for more." Agented fiction 15%. Responds in 1 month to queries; 2 months to mss. No simultaneous submissions. Sometimes comments on rejected mss.

Terms Pays 10% royalty. Publishes ms 9 months after acceptance. Book catalog and ms guidelines online.

SARABANDE BOOKS, INC.

2234 Dundee Rd., Suite 200, Louisville KY 40205. (502)458-4028. Fax: (502)458-4065. E-mail: info@sarabandebooks.org. Web site: www.sarabandebooks.org. **Contact:** Sarah Gorham, editor-in-chief; Kirby Gann, managing editor. Estab. 1994. "Small literary press publishing poetry, short fiction and literary nonfiction." Publishes hardcover and trade paperback originals. **Published some debut authors within the last year.** Averages 12 total titles, 2-3 fiction titles/year. Distributes titles through Consortium Book Sales & Distribution. Promotes titles through advertising in national magazines, sales reps, brochures, newsletters, postcards, catalogs, press release mailings, sales conferences, book fairs, author tours and reviews.

  • Marjorie Sander's story collection *Portrait of My Mother Who Posed Nude in Wartime* won the 2004 National Jewish Book Award. *When It Burned to the Ground* by Yolanda Barnes won the 2006 Independent Publisher Award for Best Multicultural Fiction.

Needs Literary, novellas, short novels, 250 pages maximum, 150 pages minimum. Submissions to Mary McCarthy Prize in Short Fiction accepted January through February. Published *Other Electricities*, by Ander Monson; *More Like Not Running Away*, by Paul Shepherd.

How to Contact See Web site for McCarthy Contest entry form. Also open to query in September with sample, SASE or IRC. Responds in 3 months to queries. Accepts simultaneous submissions.

Terms Pays royalty of 10% on actual income received. Publishes ms 18 months after acceptance. Ms guidelines for #10 SASE.

Advice "Make sure you're not writing in a vacuum, that you've read and are conscious of contemporary literature. Have someone read your manuscript, checking it for ordering, coherence. Better a lean, consistently strong manuscript than one that is long and uneven. We like a story to have good narrative, and we like to be engaged by language."

ⒶⓇⓄⓄ SCHOLASTIC CANADA, LTD.

175 Hillmount Rd., Markham ON L6C 1Z7 Canada. (905)887-7323. Fax: (905)887-3643. Web site: www.scholasti c.ca. Publishes hardcover and trade paperback originals. Averages 40 total titles/year.

Imprint(s) Les Éditions Scholastic (contact Syvie Andrews, French editor).

Needs Children's/juvenile, juvenile (middle grade), young adult. Published *The Promise of the Unicorn*, by Vicki Blum (juvenile novel).

How to Contact No unsolicited mss. For up-to-date information on our current submissions policy, you can call our publishing status line at 905-887-7323, extension 4308 or visitwww.scholastic.ca/aboutscholastic/ manuscripts.htm.

Terms Pays 5-10% royalty on retail price. Average advance: $1,000-5,000 (Canadian). Publishes ms 1 year after acceptance. Book catalog for 8½×11 SAE with 2 first-class stamps (IRC or Canadian stamps only).

ⒶⓄⓋ SCHOLASTIC PRESS

Scholastic Inc., 557 Broadway, New York NY 10012. (212)343-6100. Fax: (212)343-4713. Web site: www.schola stic.com. **Contact:** Elizabeth Szabla, editorial director (picture books, middle grade, young adult); Dianne Hess, executive editor (picture books, middle grade, young adult); Tracy Mack, executive editor (picture books, middle grade, young adult); Kara LaReau, executive editor; Lauren Thompson, senior editor (picture books, middle grade) . Publishes hardcover originals. **Published some debut authors within the last year.** Averages 30 total titles/year. Promotes titles through trade and library channels.

Needs Juvenile, picture books, novels. Wants "fresh, exciting picture books and novels—inspiring, new talent." Published *Chasing Vermeer*, by Blue Balliet; *Here Today*, by Ann M. Martin; *Detective LaRue*, by Mark Teague.

How to Contact Does not accept unsolicited mss. *Agented submissions only.* No simultaneous submissions.

Terms Pays royalty on retail price. Average advance: variable. Publishes ms 18-24 months after acceptance.

Advice "Be a big reader of juvenile literature before you write and submit!"

Ⓝ SCIENCE & HUMANITIES PRESS

P.O. Box 7151, Chesterfield MO 63006-7151. (636)394-4950. E-mail: publisher@sciencehumanitiespress.com. Web site: www.sciencehumanitiespress.com. **Contact:** Dr. Bud Banis, publisher. Publishes trade paperback originals and reprints, and electronic originals and reprints. **Published 25% of books from debut authors within the last year.** Averages 20-30 total titles/year.

Imprint(s) Science & Humanities Press; BeachHouse Books; MacroPrintBooks (large print editions); Heuristic Books; Early Editions Books.

Needs Adventure, historical, humor, literary, mainstream/contemporary, military/war, mystery, regional, romance, science fiction, short story collections, spiritual, sports, suspense, western, young adult. "We prefer books with a theme that gives a market focus. Brief description by e-mail."

How to Contact Responds in 2 months to queries; 3 months to mss. Accepts simultaneous submissions.

Terms Pays 8% royalty on retail price. Publishes ms 6-12 after acceptance. Ms guidelines online.

Advice Sales are primarily through the Internet, special orders, reviews in specialized media, direct sales to libraries, special organizations and use as textbooks. "Our expertise is electronic publishing for continuous short-run-in-house production rather than mass distribution to retail outlets. This allows us to commit to books that might not be financially successful in conventional book store enviroments and to keep books in print and available for extended periods of time. Books should be types that would sell steadily over a long period of time, rather than those that require rapid rollout and bookstore shelf exposure for a short time. We consider the nurture of new talent part of our mission but enjoy experienced writers as well. We are proud that many or our books are second, third and fourth books from authors who were once first-time authors. A good book is not a one-time accident."

ℕ ◯ ◎ SEAL PRESS

Avalon Publishing Group, 1400 65th Street, Suite 250, Emeryville, CA 94608. E-mail: sealacquisitions@avalonpub.com. Web site: www.sealpress.com. **Contact:** Ingrid Emerick, editor/publisher; Leslie Miller, senior editor; Christina Henry, editor. Estab. 1976. "Midsize independent feminist book publisher interested in original, lively, radical, empowering and culturally diverse books by women." Publishes mainly trade paperback originals. Books: 55 lb. natural paper; Cameron Belt, Web or offset printing; perfect binding; illustrations occasionally. Averages 22 total titles/year. Titles distributed by Publishers Group West.

Imprint(s) Adventura (women's travel/outdoors), Live Girls (Third-Wave, pop culture, young feminist).

Needs Ethnic, feminist, gay/lesbian, literary, multicultural. "We are interested in alternative voices." Published *Valencia*, by Michelle Tea (fiction); *Navigating the Darwin Straits*, by Edith Forbes (fiction); and *Bruised Hibiscus*, by Elizabeth Nunez (fiction).

How to Contact Does not accept unsolicited mss. Query with SASE or submit outline, 2 sample chapter(s), synopsis. Responds in 2 months to queries. Accepts simultaneous submissions.

Terms Pays 7-10% royalty on retail price. Pays variable advance. Publishes ms 18 months after acceptance. Book catalog and ms guidelines for SASE or online. Ms guidelines online.

◎ SEVEN STORIES PRESS

140 Watts St., New York NY 10013. (212)226-8760. Fax: (212)226-1411. E-mail: info@sevenstories.com. Web site: www.sevenstories.com. **Contact:** Daniel Simon. Estab. 1995. "Publishers of a distinguished list of authors in fine literature, journalism and contemporary culture." Publishes hardcover and trade paperback originals. Average print order: 5,000. **Published some debut authors within the last year.** Averages 40-50 total titles, 10 fiction titles/year. Distributes through Consortium Book Sales and Distribution.

Needs Literary. Plans anthologies. Ongoing series of short story collections for other cultures (e.g., Contemporary Fiction from Central America; from Vietnam, etc.). *A Place to Live and Other Selected Essays of Natalia Ginzburg*, edited by Lynne Sharon Schwartz; *American Falls*, by Barry Gifford; *The Incantation of Frida K.*, by Kate Braverman.

How to Contact Currently not accepting submissions. Please check Web site for updates.

Terms Pays 7-15% royalty on retail price. Offers advance. Publishes ms 1-3 years after acceptance. Book catalog and ms guidelines free.

Advice "Writers should only send us their work after they have read some of the books we publish and find our editorial vision in sync with theirs."

✿ ◎ SILHOUETTE BOOKS

233 Broadway, Suite 101, New York NY 10279. (212)553-4200. Fax: (212)227-8969. Web site: www.eharlequin.com. Estab. 1979. Publishes mass market paperback originals. Averages over 350 total titles/year.

Needs Romance (contemporary romance for adults). "We are interested in seeing submissions for all our lines. No manuscripts other than the types outlined. Manuscript should follow our general format, yet have an individuality and life of its own that will make them stand out in the readers' minds." See our Web site for details.

How to Contact See guidelines for specific imprints. No simultaneous submissions.

Terms Pays royalty. Offers advance. Publishes ms 1-3 years after acceptance. Ms guidelines online.

✿ ◯ ◎ SILHOUETTE DESIRE

a Harlequin book line, 233 Broadway, Suite 1001, New York NY 10279. (212)553-4200. Web site: www.eharlequin.com. **Contact:** Melissa Jeglinski, senior editor. "Sensual, believable and compelling, these books are written for today's woman. Innocent or experienced, the heroine is someone we identify with; the hero is irresistible." Publishes paperback originals and reprints. Books: newspaper print; web printing; perfect bound. **Published some debut authors within the last year.**

Needs Romance. Looking for novels in which "the conflict is an emotional one, springing naturally from the unique characters you've chosen. The focus is on the developing relationship, set in a believable plot. Sensuality is key, but lovemaking is never taken lightly. Secondary characters and subplots need to blend with the core story. Innovative new directions in storytelling and fresh approaches to classic romantic plots are welcome." Manuscripts must be 57,000 words.

How to Contact Does not accept unsolicited mss. Query with word count, brief bio, publishing history, synopsis (no more than 2 single-spaced pages), SASE/IRC. No simultaneous submissions.

Terms Pays royalty. Offers advance. Detailed ms guidelines for SASE or on Web site.

⭐ ◐ ◎ SILHOUETTE INTIMATE MOMENTS

a Harlequin book line, 233 Broadway, Suite 1001, New York NY 10279. (212)553-4200. Web site: www.eharlequin.com. **Contact:** Patience Smith, associate senior editor. "Believable characters swept into a world of larger-than-life suspenseful romance are the hallmark of Silhouette Intimate Moment books. These books offer you the freedom to combine the universally appealing elements of a category romance with the flash and excitement of romantic suspense." Publishes paperback originals and reprints. Books: newspaper print; web printing; perfect bound. **Published some debut authors within the last year.**

Needs Romance (contemporary). Looking for "novels that explore new directions in romantic fiction or classic plots in contemporary ways, always with the goal of tempting today's demanding reader. Adventure, suspense, melodrama, glamour—let your imagination be your guide as you blend old and new to create a novel with emotional depth and tantalizing complexity." Manuscripts must be approximately 80,000 words.

How to Contact Accepts unsolicited mss. Query with SASE or submit complete ms. Send SASE for return of ms or send a disposable ms and SASE for reply only. No simultaneous submissions, submissions on disk.

Terms Pays royalty. Offers advance. Ms guidelines for SASE or on Web site.

⭐ ◐ ◎ SILHOUETTE NOCTURNE

Harlequin Enterprises, Ltd., 233 Broadway, Suite 1001, New York NY 10279. Web site: www.eharlequin.com. **Contact:** Tara Gavin, senior executive editor; Anne Leslie Tuttle, associate editor; Sean Mackiewicz, editorial assistant. Estab. October 2006. "Nocturne is looking for stories that deliver a dark, very sexy read that will entertain readers and take them from everyday life to an atmospheric, complex, paranormal world filled with characters struggling with life and death issues. These stories will be fast-paced, action-packed and mission-oriented, with a strong level of sensuality. The hero is a key figure—powerful, mysterious and totally attractive to the heroine. In fact, both main characters are very powerful, and their conflict is based on this element. The author must be able to set up a unique existence for the characters, with its own set of rules and mythologies. We are looking for stories of vampires, shape-shifters, werewolves, psychic powers, etc. set in contemporary times." Publishes paperback originals. Format: newsprint paper; web printing; perfect bound. Averages 24 fiction titles/year.

Needs Paranormal romance. "Stories with strong sexuality, fantasy and danger elements. Books that are good reference points for Nocturne include stories by Maggie Shayne, Christine Feehan and Sherrilyn Kenyon. Lindsay McKenna's *Heart of the Jaguar* and the subsequent books in her Jaguar series are also good reference points."

How to Contact Query with outline/synopsis and 3 sample chapters. Accepts submissions by snail mail. Send SASE or IRC for return of ms.

Terms Pays royalties, advance. Writer's guidelines on Web site. Book catalogs on Web site.

⭐ ◐ ◎ SILHOUETTE SPECIAL EDITION

a Harlequin book line, 233 Broadway, Suite 101, New York NY 10279. (212)553-4200. Web site: www.eharlequin.com. **Contact:** Gail Chasan, senior editor. "Whether the sensuality is sizzling or subtle, whether the plot is wildly innovative or satisfying and traditional, the novel's emotional vividness, its depth and dimension, clearly label it a very special contemporary romance." Publishes paperback originals. Books: newspaper print; web printing; perfect bound. **Published some debut authors within the last year.**

Needs Romance (contemporary). "Sophisticated, substantial and packed with emotions, Special Edition demands writers eager to probe characters deeply to explore issues that heighten the drama of living, loving and creating a family, to generate compelling romantic plots. Subplots are welcome, but must further or parallel the developing romantic relationship in a meaningful way." Manuscripts must be approximately 70,000-75,000 words.

How to Contact Does not accept unsolicited mss. Query with SASE. No simultaneous submissions, submissions on disk.

Terms Pays royalty. Offers advance. Ms guidelines for SASE or on Web site.

⭐ ◐ ◎ SILVER DAGGER MYSTERIES

325 West Walnut Street, Johnson City TN 37605. (423)926-2691. Fax: (423)232-1252. E-mail: beth@overmtn.com. Web site: www.silverdaggermysteries.com. **Contact:** Alex Foster, acquisitions editor (mystery). Estab. 1999. "Small imprint of a larger company. We publish Southern mysteries. Our house is unique in that we are a consortium of authors who communicate and work together to promote each other." Publishes hardcover and trade paperback originals and reprints. Books: 60 lb. offset paper; perfect/case binding. Average print

order: 2,000-5,000; first novel print order: 2,000. **Published 6 debut authors within the last year.** Averages 30 total titles, 15 fiction titles/year. Member PAS. Distributes titles through direct mail, Ingram, Baker & Taylor, Partners, trade shows.

• Julie Wray Herman was nominated for the Agatha Award for *Three Dirty Women & the Garden of Death*.
Needs Mystery (amateur sleuth, cozy, police procedural, private eye/hard-boiled), young adult (mystery). "We look for average-length books of 60-80,000 words." Publishes *Magnolias & Mayhem*, an anthology of Southern short mysteries. Published *Killer Looks*, by Laura Young; *Haunting Refrain*, by Ellis Vidler; *Justice Betrayed*, by Daniel Bailey.
How to Contact Closed to submissions. Check Web site for updates.
Terms Pays 15% royalty on realized price. Publishes ms 2 years after acceptance. Book catalog and ms guidelines online.
Advice "We are very author friendly from editing to promotion. Make sure your book is 'Southern' or set in the South before taking the time to submit."

SILVER LEAF BOOKS, LLC
P.O. Box 6460, Holliston MA 01746. (508)429-4240. E-mail: editor@silverleafbooks.com. Web site: www.silverl eafbooks.com. **Contact:** Brett Fried and Melissa Novak, editors. Estab. 2003. "Silver Leaf Books is a small press featuring primarily new and upcoming talent in the fantasy, science fiction and horror genres. Our editors work closely with our authors to establish a lasting and mutually beneficial relationship, helping both the authors and company continue to grow and thrive." Publishes hardcover originals, trade paperback originals, paperback originals, paperback reprints. Average print order: 3,000. Debut novel print order: 3,000. Published 1 new writer last year. Plans 2 debut novels this year. Averages 6 total titles/year; 6 fiction titles/year. Distributes/promotes titles through Baker & Taylor Books.
Needs Fantasy (space fantasy, sword and sorcery), horror (dark fantasy, futuristic, psychological, supernatural), mystery/suspense (amateur sleuth, cozy, police procedural, private eye/hard-boiled), science fiction (hard science/technological, soft/sociological), young adult (adventure, fantasy/science fiction, horror, mystery/suspense). Published *Trapped in Time*, by Clifford B. Bowyer (fantasy).
How to Contact Query with outline/synopsis and 3 sample chapters. Accepts queries by snail mail. Include estimated word count, brief bio and marketing plan. Send SASE or IRC for return of ms or disposable copy of ms and SASE/IRC for reply only. Agented fiction: 25%. Responds to queries in 6 months. Responds to mss in 4 months. Accepts unsolicited mss. Considers simultaneous submissions. Sometimes critiques/comments on rejected mss.
Terms Manuscript published 12-24 months after acceptance. Writer's guidelines on Web site. Pays royalties, and provides author's copies.
Advice "Follow the online guidelines, be thorough and professional."

SIMON & SCHUSTER
1230 Avenue of the Americas, New York NY 10020. (212)698-7000. Web site: www.simonsays.com.
Imprint(s) *Simon & Schuster Adult Publishing Group*: Simon & Schuster; Scribner (Scribner, Lisa Drew, Simple Abundance Press); The Free Press; Atria Books; Kaplan; Touchstone; Scribner Paperback Fiction; S&S Librow en Espanol; Simon & Schuster Source; Wall Street Journal Books; Pocket Books (Pocket Star; Washington Square Press; MTV Books; Sonnet Books; Star Trek; The New Fogler Shakespeare; VH-1 Books; WWF Books). *Simon & Schusters Children's Publishing*: Aladdin Paperbacks; Atheneum Books for Young Readers (Anne Schwartz Books; Richard Jackson Books); Little Simon (Simon Spotlight; Rabbit Ears Books & Audio); Margaret K. McElderry Books, (Archway Paperbacks; Minstreal Books); Simon & Schuster Books for Young Readers.
How to Contact *Agented submissions only.*
Terms Pays royalty. Offers advance. Ms guidelines online.

SIMON & SCHUSTER ADULT PUBLISHING GROUP
(formerly Simon & Schuster Trade Division, Division of Simon & Schuster), 1230 Avenue of the Americas, New York NY 10020. E-mail: ssonline@simonsays.com. Web site: www.simonsays.com. Estab. 1924.
Imprint(s) H&R Block; Lisa Drew Books; Fireside; The Free Press; Pocket Book Press; Rawson Associates; Scribner; Scribner Classics; Scribner Paperback Fiction; Scribner Poetry; S&S—Libros en Espanol; Simon & Schuster; Simon & Schuster Source; Simple Abundance Press; Touchstone; Wall Street Journal Books.
How to Contact *Agented submissions only.*

SMALL BEER PRESS
176 Prospect Ave., Northampton MA 01060. (413)584-0299. Fax: (413)584-2662. E-mail: info@lcrw.net. Web site: www.lcrw.net. **Contact:** Gavin J. Grant. Estab. 2000. Averages 3-6 fiction titles/year.

● Small Beer Press also publishes the zine *Lady Churchill's Rosebud Wristlet*. SBP's books have been Hugo and Locus Award winners, as well as BookSense Picks and finalists for The Story Prize.

Needs Literary, experimental, speculative, story collections. Recently published *Generation Loss: A Novel*, by Elizabeth Hand (post-punk lit thriller); *Interfictions: An Anthology of Interstitial Writing*, by Delia Sherman and Theodora Goss, editors; *Skinny Dipping in the Lake of the Dead*, by Alan DeNiro (story collection); *Mothers & Other Monsters*, by Maureen F. McHugh (story collection); *Magic for Beginners*, by Kelly Link.

How to Contact "We do not accept unsolicited novel or short story collection manuscripts. Queries are welcome. Please send queries with an SASE by mail."

Advice "Please be familiar with our books first to avoid wasting your time and ours, thank you."

SOHO PRESS, INC.

853 Broadway, New York NY 10003. (212)260-1900. Fax: (212)260-1902. E-mail: soho@sohopress.com. Web site: www.sohopress.com. **Contact:** Laura Hruska, editor-in-chief (literary fiction, literary mysteries); Katie Herman, editor (literary fiction, literary mysteries). Estab. 1986. "Independent publisher known for sophisticated fiction, mysteries set abroad, women's interest (no genre) novels and multicultural novels." Publishes hardcover and trade paperback originals and reprint editions. Books: perfect binding; halftone illustrations. First novel print order: 5,000. **Published 5 debut authors within the last year.** Averages 31 total titles, 28 fiction titles/year. Distributes titles through Consortium Book Sales & Distribution in the US and Canada, Turnaround in England.

Imprint(s) Soho Crime: procedural series set abroad.

Needs Adventure, ethnic, feminist, historical, literary, mainstream/contemporary, mystery (police procedural), suspense, multicultural. Published *Billy Boyle*, by James Benn; *The Texicans*, by Nina Vida; *Chinatown Beat*, by Henry Chang; *Living On Air*, by Anna Shapiro; *Disco For The Departed*, by Colin Cotterill; *Snapshot*, by Garry Disher.

How to Contact Include estimated word count, brief bio, list of publishing credits. Send SASE for return of ms or send a disposable ms and SASE for reply only. Agented fiction 82%. Responds in 3 months to queries; 3 months to mss. Accepts simultaneous submissions. No electronic submissions. Sometimes comments on rejected mss.

Terms Pays 10-15% royalty on retail price for harcovers, 7.5% on trade paperbacks. Offers advance. Publishes ms within 21 months after acceptance. Ms guidelines online.

SOUTHERN METHODIST UNIVERSITY PRESS

P.O. Box 750415, Dallas TX 75275-0415. (214)768-1433. Fax: (214)768-1428. Web site: www.tamu.edu/upress. **Contact:** Kathryn Lang, senior editor. Estab. 1937. "Small university press publishing in areas of film/theater, Southwest life and letters, medical ethics, sports, creative nonfiction and contemporary fiction." Publishes hardcover and trade paperback originals and reprints. Books: acid-free paper; perfect bound; some illustrations. Average print order: 2,000. **Published 2 debut authors within the last year.** Averages 10-12 total titles, 3-4 fiction titles/year. Distributes titles through Texas A&M University Press Consortium. Promotes titles through writers' publications.

Needs Literary, short story collections, novels. "We are willing to look at 'serious' or 'literary' fiction." No "mass market, science fiction, formula, thriller, romance." Published *Openwork*, by Adria Bernardi (a novel) and *Tris Speaker*, by Charles C. Alexander (a baseball biography).

How to Contact Accepts unsolicited mss. Query with SASE. Responds in 2 weeks to queries; up to 1 year to mss. No simultaneous submissions. Sometimes comments on rejected mss.

Terms Pays 10% royalty on wholesale price, 10 author's copies. Average advance: $500. Publishes ms 1 year after acceptance. Ms guidelines online.

Advice "We view encouraging first-time authors as part of the mission of a university press. Send query describing the project and your own background. Research the press before you submit—don't send us the kinds of things we don't publish." Looks for "quality fiction from new or established writers."

SPECTRA BOOKS

Subsidiary of Random House, Inc., 1745 Broadway, New York NY 10019. (212)782-8632. Fax: (212)782-9174. Web site: www.bantamdell.com. **Contact:** Anne Lesley Groell, senior editor. Estab. 1985. Large science fiction, fantasy and speculative line. Publishes hardcover originals, paperback originals and trade paperbacks.

● Many Bantam Spectra Books have recieved Hugos and Nebulas.

Needs Fantasy, literary, science fiction. Needs include novels that attempt to broaden the traditional range of science fiction and fantasy. Strong emphasis on characterization. Especially well-written traditional science fiction and fantasy will be considered. No fiction that doesn't have as least some element of speculation or the fantastic. Published *Storm of Swords*, by George R. Martin (medieval fantasy); *Fool's Fate*, by Robin Hobb (fantasy); *The Years of Rice and Salt*, by Stanley Robinson (science fiction, alternative history).

How to Contact Accepts agented submissions only. Accepts simultaneous submissions.
Terms Pays royalty. Average advance: negotiable.
Advice "Please follow our guidelines carefully and type neatly."

⬛ ⭐ ✅ ◎ SPICE

Harlequin Enterprises, Ltd., 225 Duncan Mill Rd., Toronto ON M3B 3K9 Canada. Web site: www.eharlequin.c om. **Contact:** Susan Pezzack, editor. Estab. May 2006. "Modern women have finally begun embracing and taking charge of their own sexuality. Everywhere you turn, the media is celebrating and promoting women and sex: on TV, in Hollywood, in every magazine on the rack. SPICE is Harlequin's new single-title imprint for really good, really smart erotic fiction for the modern woman who also wants a great read. We are looking to acquire bold, pushing-the-envelope, high-quality editorial from top authors and talented new voices that have the ability to deliver believable, high-wattage sexual content set within the context of contemporary mainstream fiction. We want novels that will take the genre above and beyond today's stereotypical erotica stories." Publishes paperback originals. Format: newsprint paper; web printing; perfect bound.
Needs Erotica. "Stories in this line will range from highly sensual love stories to more contemplative, humorous tales to gritty, slice-of-life experiences of sex and the modern woman. Our diverse editorial direction will include ethnic, literary (humorous, edgy, urban), mystery/suspense and paranormal genres in first or third person point-of-view (female only), or if it works for the story, multiple points of view. Prospective authors can familiarize themselves with some competitive titles, such as: *Wifey*, by Judy Blume; *100 Strokes of the Brush Before Bed*, by Melissa P.; *Story of O*, by Pauline Reage; *The Sexual Life of Catherine M.*, by Catherine Millet; *Addicted*, by Zane; *The Other Woman*, by Eric Jerome Dickey; *Sex and the City*, by Candace Bushnell; and authors such as Jaid Black, Emma Holly, Alison Tyler, Sherrilyn Kenyon and Toni Bentley."
How to Contact Please submit partial or full mss accompanied by synopsis. No e-mailed submissions. Agented submissions are preferred but not essential.
Terms Pays royalties, advance. Writer's guidelines on Web site. Book catalogs on Web site.

🅽 ◒ ◎ SPIRE PRESS

532 LaGuardia Pl. Ste. 298, New York NY 10012. E-mail: editor@spirepress.org. Web site: www.spirepress.org. **Contact:** Shelly Reed. Publishes 5-6 books/year. **Publishes 1-2 new writers/year.**
Needs Literary story collections. Also publishes memoir, poetry. No novels. No horror, romance, or religious work. Length: 30,000+ words. Recently published work by Richard Weems.
How to Contact Send first 15 pages and synopsis in August only. Send disposable copy and #10 SASE for reply only. Responds in 3 months. Accepts simultaneous submissions. Rarely comments on rejected queries. Writer's guidelines online.
Terms Pays in advance copies and 15% royalty.
Advice "You should have published short stories and/or essays in established literary journals before querying us."

✅ SPOUT PRESS

P.O. Box 581067, Minneapolis MN 55458. (612)782-9629. E-mail: spoutpress@hotmail.com. Web site: www.spo utpress.com. **Contact:** Chris Watercott, fiction editor. Estab. 1989. "Small independent publisher with a permanent staff of three—interested in experimental fiction for our magazine and books." Publishes paperback originals. Books: perfect bound; illustrations. Average print order: 1,000. **Published 1 debut author within the last year.** Distibutes and promotes books through the Web site, events and large Web-based stores such as Amazon.com.
Needs Ethnic, experimental, literary, short story collections. Published *I'm Right Here*, by Tony Rauch.
How to Contact Does not accept unsolicited mss. Query with SASE. Accepts queries by mail. Include estimated word count, brief bio, list of publishing credits. Send SASE for return of ms or send a disposable ms and SASE for reply only. Agented fiction 10%. Responds in 1 month to queries; 3-5 months to mss. Accepts simultaneous submissions. Rarely comments on rejected mss.
Terms Individual arrangement with author depending on the book. Publishes ms 12-15 months after acceptance. Ms guidelines for SASE or on Web site.
Advice "We tend to publish writers after we know their work via publication in our journal, *Spout Magazine*."

🅐 ST. MARTIN'S PRESS

175 Fifth Ave., New York NY 10010. (212)674-5151. Fax: (212)420-9314. Web site: www.stmartins.com. **Contact:** Hilary Rubin, associate editor. Estab. 1952. General interest publisher of both fiction and nonfiction. Publishes hardcover, trade paperback and mass market originals. Averages 1,500 total titles/year.
Imprint(s) Bedford Books; Buzz Books; Thomas Dunne Books; Forge; Minotaur; Picador USA; Stonewall Inn Editions; TOR Books; Griffin.

Needs Fantasy, historical, horror, literary, mainstream/contemporary, mystery, science fiction, suspense, western (contemporary), general fiction; thriller.
How to Contact *Agented submissions only.*
Terms Pays royalty. Offers advance. Ms guidelines online.

STARCHERONE BOOKS

P.O. Box 303, Buffalo NY 14201-0303. (716)885-2726. E-mail: publisher@starcherone.com. Web site: www.starcherone.com. **Contact:** Ted Pelton, publisher. Estab. 2000. Non-profit publisher of literary and experimental fiction. Publishes paperback originals and reprints. Books: acid-free paper; perfect bound; occasional illustrations. Average print order: 1,000. Average first novel print order: 1,000. **Published 2 debut authors within the last year.** Member CLMP. Titles distributed through Web site, Small Press Distribution, Amazon, independent bookstores.
Needs Experimental, literary. Published *Black Umbrella Stories*, by Nicolette de Csipkay (debut author, short stories); *Hangings*, by Nina Shope (debut author, short stories); *My Body in Nine Parts*, by Raymond Federman (experimental).
How to Contact Accepts queries by mail or e-mail during August and September of each year. Include brief bio, list of publishing credits. Send copy of ms and SASE. Responds in 2 months to queries; 6-10 months to mss. Accepts simultaneous submissions. "Almost all of our debut authors come to us through our contest, which has an annual deadline of Jan. 31. Please see Web site for details."
Terms Pays 15% royalty. Publishes ms 9-18 months after acceptance. Guidelines and catalog available on Web site.
Advice "Become familiar with our interests in fiction. We are interested in new strategies for creating stories and fictive texts. Do not send genre fiction unless it is unconventional in approach."

STEEPLE HILL

Harlequin Enterprises, 233 Broadway, New York NY 10279. Web site: www.eharlequin.com. **Contact:** Joan Marlow Golan, Krista Stroever, senior editors. Estab. 1997. Publishes mass market paperback originals.
Imprint(s) Love Inspired; Love Inspired Suspense; Steeple Hill Woman's Fiction; Steeple Hill Café.
Needs Romance (Christian, 80,000-125,000 words). Wants all genres of inspirational woman's fiction including contemporary and historical romance, chick/mom-lit, relationship novels, romantic suspense, mysteries, family sagas, and thrillers. Published *A Mother at Heart*, by Carolyne Aarsen.
How to Contact No unsolicited mss. Query with SASE, synopsis. No simultaneous submissions.
Terms Pays royalty. Offers advance. Detailed ms guidelines online.
Advice "Drama, humor and even a touch of mystery all have a place in this series. Subplots are welcome and should further the story's main focus or intertwine in a meaningful way. Secondary characters (children, family, friends, neighbors, fellow church members, etc.) may all contribute to a substantial and satisfying story. These wholesome tales of romance include strong family values and high moral standards. While there is no premarital sex between characters, a vivid, exciting romance that is presented with a mature perspective, is essential. Although the element of faith must clearly be present, it should be well integrated into the characterization and plot. The conflict between the main characters should be an emotional one, arising naturally from the well-developed personalities you've created. Suitable stories should also impart an important lesson about the powers of trust and faith."

STONE BRIDGE PRESS

P.O. Box 8208, Berkeley CA 94707. (510)524-8732. Fax: (510)524-8711. Web site: www.stonebridge.com. **Contact:** Peter Goodman, publisher. Estab. 1989. "Independent press focusing on books about Japan and Asia in English (business, language, culture, literature, animation)." Publishes hardcover and trade paperback originals. Books: 60-70 lb. offset paper; web and sheet paper; perfect bound; some illustrations. Averages 12 total titles/year. Distributes titles through Consortium. Promotes titles through Internet announcements, special-interest magazines and niche tie-ins to associations.
  • Stone Bridge Press received a Japan-U.S. Friendship Prize for *Life in the Cul-de-Sac*, by Senji Kuroi.
Imprint(s) Heian.
Needs Experimental, gay/lesbian, literary, Japan-themed. "Primarily looking at material relating to Japan. Translations only."
How to Contact Does not accept unsolicited mss. Query with SASE. Accepts queries by e-mail, fax. Agented fiction 25%. Responds in 4 months to queries; 8 months to mss. Accepts simultaneous submissions. Sometimes comments on rejected mss.
Terms Pays royalty on wholesale price. Average advance: variable. Publishes ms 2 years after acceptance. Book catalog for 2 first-class stamps and SASE. Ms guidelines online.
Advice "Fiction translations only for the time being. No poetry."

☑ ☒ SYNERGEBOOKS

32700 River Bend Rd. #5 P.O. Box 685, Chiloquin OR 97624. (541)783-7512. E-mail: synergebooks@aol.com. Web site: www.synergebooks.com. **Contact:** Debra Staples, editor. Estab. 1999. Small press publisher, specializing in quality e-books from talented new writers in a myriad of genres, including print-on-demand. SynergE-books "works together" with the author to edit and market each book. Publishes paperback originals and e-books. Books: 60 lb. paper; print-on-demand; perfect bound. Average first novel print order: 30. **Published 5-10 debut authors within the last year.** Averages 30 total titles, 15 fiction titles/year.
   • Authors have received EPPIES and other awards.

Needs Adventure, business, family saga, fantasy (space fantasy, sword and sorcery), historical, horror, humor, mainstream/contemporary, mystery, new age/mystic, religious (children's religious, inspirational, religious fantasy, religious mystery/suspense, religious thriller, religious romance), romance (contemporary, futuristic/time travel, historical, regency period, romantic suspense), science fiction, short story collections, western (frontier saga, traditional), young adult (adventure, fantasy/science fiction, historical, horror, mystery/suspense, romance), native american. Welcomes series books (1-9 in a series, with at least 1 title completed at time of submission.) Published *A Talent to Deceive: Who REALLY Killed the Lindberg Baby?*, by William Norris (nonfiction); *The Oberon Series*, by P.G Forte (romance); *The Caterpillar That Wouldn't Change*, by Nancy S. Mure (children).

How to Contact Accepts unsolicited mss. Query via e-mail ONLY, 3 sample chapter(s), synopsis via attached mail in .doc format. Include estimated word count, brief bio, list of publishing credits, and e-mail address. Agented fiction 1%. Responds in 3 weeks to queries; 3 months to mss. Accepts simultaneous submissions, submissions on disk. Sometimes comments on rejected mss.

Terms Pays 15-40% royalty. Publishes ms 3-6 months after acceptance. Ms guidelines online.

Advice "We do not care if you've ever been published. If your work is unique in some way, and you are willing to work together to market your book, there is a good chance you will be accepted. Keep in mind that we are first and foremost a digital publisher, so if you are not willing to market your work online, we suggest you submit to a different publisher."

☒ ☒ NAN A. TALESE

Random House, Inc., 1745 Broadway, New York NY 10019. (212)782-8918. Fax: (212)782-8448. Web site: www.nantalese.com. **Contact:** Nan A. Talese, editorial director. "Nan A. Talese publishes nonfiction with a powerful guiding narrative and relevance to larger cultural trends and interests, and literary fiction of the highest quality." Publishes hardcover originals. Averages 15 total titles/year.

Needs Literary. "We want well-written narratives with a compelling story line, good characterization and use of language. We like stories with an edge." *Agented submissions only.* Published *The Blind Assassin*, by Margaret Atwood; *Atonement*, by Ian McEwan; *Great Shame*, Thomas Keneally.

How to Contact Responds in 1 week to queries; 2 weeks to mss. Accepts simultaneous submissions.

Terms Pays variable royalty on retail price. Average advance: varying. Publishes ms 1 year after acceptance. Agented submissions only.

Advice "We're interested in literary narrative, fiction and nonfiction—we do not publish genre fiction. Our readers are highly literate people interested in good storytelling that's intellectual and psychologically significant. We want well-written material."

TCU PRESS

P.O. Box 298300, TCU, Fort Worth TX 76129. (817)257-7822. Fax: (817)257-5075. Estab. 1966. Publishes hardcover originals, some reprints. Averages 2-3 total titles/year.

Needs Regional (Texas and the Southwest)l, young adult.

How to Contact Responds in 3 months to queries. No simultaneous submissions.

Terms Pays 10% royalty on net receipts. Publishes ms 16 months after acceptance.

☒ THIRD WORLD PRESS

P.O. Box 19730, 7822 S. Dobson Ave., Chicago IL 60619. (773)651-0700. Fax: (773)651-7286. E-mail: TWPress3 @aol.com. Web site: www.thirdworldpressinc.com. **Contact:** Gwendolyn Mitchell, editor. Estab. 1967. Black-owned and operated independent publisher of fiction and nonfiction books about the black experience throughout the Diaspora. Publishes hardcover and trade paperback originals and reprints. Averages 20 total titles/year. Distibutes titles through Independent Publisher Group.

Needs Materials for literary, ethnic, contemporary, juvenile and children's books. "We publish nonfiction, primarily, but will consider fiction." Published *The Covenant with Black America*, with an introduction by Tavis Smiley; *1996*, by Gloria Naylor.

How to Contact Accepts unsolicited mss. Submit outline, 5 sample chapter(s), synopsis. Responds in 8 weeks to queries; 5 months to mss. Accepts simultaneous submissions.

Terms Pays royalty on net revenues. Individual arrangement with author depending on the book, etc. Publishes ms 18 months after acceptance. Ms guidelines for #10 SASE.

⊘ TIMBERWOLF PRESS, INC.

202 N. Allen Dr., Suite A, Allen TX 75013. E-mail: submissions@timberwolfpress.com. Web site: www.timberwolfpress.com. **Contact:** Carol Woods, senior editor. Publishes trade paperback originals. **Published 25% debut authors within the last year.** Averages 24-30 total titles/year.

Needs Fantasy, military/war, mystery, science fiction, suspense. "In addition to the e-book, we present each title in next generation fully-cast, dramatized, unabridged audio theatre, available in the usual formats; and downloadable in all formats from our Web site. So our stories must maintain tension and pace. Think exciting. Think breathless. Think terrific story, terrific characters, terrific writing." Published *Soldier of the Legion*, by Marshall Thomas; *Book Two Bronwyn Tetralogy: Silk & Steel*.

How to Contact Closed to submissions at this time. Submissions guidelines are available on Web site; all contact to come through submissions@timberwolfpress.com. "No paper submissions. No telephone calls. No faxes. Only electronic submissions will be considered." Responds in 3 months to queries; 6 months to mss. Accepts simultaneous submissions.

Terms "Various programs." Publishes ms 1 year after acceptance. Book catalog and ms guidelines on Web site.

Advice "Professionalism and proper etiquette yield results. Learn professionalism through the writing industry media, writing conferences, writing critique groups."

⊘ TIN HOUSE BOOKS

2601 NW Thurman St., Portland OR 97210. (503)219-0622. Fax: (503)222-1154. E-mail: meg@tinhouse.com. Web site: www.tinhouse.com. **Contact:** Lee Montgomery, editorial director; Michelle Wildgen, editor; Meg Storey, associate editor. Estab. 2005. "We are a small independent publisher dedicated to nurturing new, promising talent as well as showcasing the work of established writers. Our Tin House New Voice series features work by authors who have not previously published a book." Publishes hardcover originals, paperback originals, paperback reprints. **Plans 2 debut short story collections and 1 debut novel this year.** Averages 6-8 total titles/year; 4-6 fiction titles/year. Distributes/promotes titles through Publishers Group West.

Needs Literary, novels, short story collections, poetry, translations. Publishes a *Best of Tin House* anthology of stories. Stories selected from *Tin House* magazine. Publishes A New Voice series.

How to Contact Query with outline/synopsis and a 50-page excerpt. Accepts queries by snail mail, e-mail, phone. Include brief bio, list of publishing credits. Send SASE or IRC for return of ms or disposable copy of ms and SASE/IRC for reply only. Agented fiction 80%. Responds to queries in 2-3 weeks. Responds to mss in 2-3 months. Accepts unsolicited mss. Considers simultaneous submissions. Sometimes critiques/comments on rejected mss.

Terms Sends pre-production galleys to author. Manuscript published approximately one year after acceptance. Writer's guidelines on Web site. Advance is negotiable. Book catalogs not available.

Ⓝ ⊕ ◯ TINDAL STREET PRESS, LTD.

217 The Custard Factory, Gibb Street, Birmingham B9 4AA United Kingdom. (+01)21 773 8157. Fax: (+01)21 693 5525. E-mail: info@tindalstreet.co.uk. Web site: www.tindalstreet.co.uk. **Contact:** Emma Hargrave, managing editor. Estab. 1998. "Tindal Street is an independent, prize-winning publisher of strong contemporary fiction—novels and short stories—from the English regions. We are a small press—three members of staff—with a commitment to author development, diversity and excellence." Publishes paperback originals. Books: perfect bound. Average print order: 1,500-2,000. **Published 5 debut authors within the last year.** Averages 6 total titles, 6 fiction titles/year. Distributes in the UK through Turnaround and in the US through Dufour.

Needs Ethnic, feminist, literary, mainstream/contemporary, mystery (private eye/hardboiled), regional (England), short story collections. Published *Birmingham Noir*, edited by Joel Land and Steve Bishop (fiction/short stories); *Astonishing Splashes of Colour*, by Clare Morrall (contemporary fiction); *What Goes Round*, by Maeve Clarke (contemporary fiction).

How to Contact Accepts unsolicited mss. Query with SASE or submit 3 sample chapter(s). Accepts queries by e-mail. Include brief bio, list of publishing credits. Send SASE for return of ms or send a disposable ms and SASE for reply only. Agented fiction 10-30%. Responds in 1-2 weeks to queries; 3-6 months to mss. No submissions on disk. Always comments on rejected mss.

Terms Average advance: negotiable. Publishes ms 6-18 months after acceptance.

Advice "Please check out our list of titles and judge how well your work might fit with the aims/standards/ attitudes of Tindal Street Press."

☑ TITAN PRESS

PMB 17897, Encino CA 91416. (818)377-4006. E-mail: titan91416@yahoo.com. Web site: www.titanpress.com. **Contact:** Stephani Wilson, editor. Estab. 1981. Publishes hardcover originals and paperback originals. Books: recycled paper; offset printing; perfect bound. Average print order: 2,000. Average first novel print order: 1,000. **Published 3 debut authors within the last year.** Averages 12 total titles, 6 fiction titles/year. Distributed at book fairs and through the Internet and at Barnes & Noble.

Needs Literary, mainstream/contemporary, short story collections. Published *Orange Messiahs*, by Scott Alixander Sonders (fiction).

How to Contact Does not accept unsolicited mss. Query with SASE. Include brief bio, social security number, list of publishing credits. Agented fiction 50%. Responds in 3 months to mss. Accepts simultaneous submissions. Sometimes comments on rejected mss.

Terms Pays 20-40% royalty. Publishes ms 1 year after acceptance. Ms guidelines for #10 SASE.

Advice "Look, act, sound and *be* professional."

Ⓝ TORQUERE PRESS

P.O. Box 2545, Round Rock TX 78680. (512)586-6921. Fax: (866)287-4860. E-mail: torquere@torquerepress.com. Web site: www.torquerepress.com. **Contact:** Shawn Clement, submission editor (homoerotica, suspense) and Lorna Hinson, senior editor (gay and lesbian romance, historicals). Estab. 2003. "We are a gay and lesbian press focusing on romance. We particularly like paranormal and western romance." Publishes paperback originals. Averages 140 total titles/year.

Imprint(s) Top Shelf, Single Shots, Shawn Clements, editor. Screwdrivers, M. Rode, editor. High Balls, Alex Drauen, editor.

Needs All categories gay and lesbian themed. Adventure, erotica, historical, horror, mainstream, multicultural, mystery, occult, romance, science fiction, short story collections, suspense, western. Published *Broken Road*, by Sean Michael (romance); *Soul Mates: Bound by Blood*, by Jourdan Lane (para. romance).

How to Contact Query with outline/synopsis and 3 sample chapters. Responds to queries in 1 months; mss in 2 months.

Terms Manuscript published 6 months after acceptance. Pays royalties. Book catalogs on Web site.

Advice "Our audience is primarily persons looking for a familiar romance setting featuring gay or lesbian protagonists."

☑ Ⓞ TRADEWIND BOOKS

202-1807 Maritime Mews, Granville Island, Vancouver BC V6H 3W7 Canada. (604)662-4405. Fax: (604)730-0153. E-mail: tradewindbooks@eudoramail.com. Web site: www.tradewindbooks.com. **Contact:** Michael Katz, publisher (picturebooks, young adult); Carol Frank, art director (picturebooks); R. David Stephens (acquisitions editor). Publishes hardcover and trade paperback originals. **Published 10% debut authors within the last year.** Averages 5 total titles/year.

Needs Juvenile. Published *The Bone Collector's Son*, *The Alchemist's Portrait*, *The Clone Conspiracy*.

How to Contact Query with SASE or submit 1 sample chapter, synopsis. Agented fiction 15%. Responds in 2 months to mss. Accepts simultaneous submissions.

Terms Pays 8% royalty on retail price. Average advance: variable. Publishes ms 3 years after acceptance. Book catalog and ms guidelines online.

☑ Ⓥ TRICYCLE PRESS

P.O. Box 7123, Berkeley CA 94707. (510)559-1600. Web site: www.tricylepress.com. **Contact:** Nicole Geiger, publisher. Estab. 1993. "Tricycle Press is a children's book publisher that publishes picture books, board books, chapter books, and middle grade novels. As an independent publisher, Tricycle Press brings to life kid-friendly books that address the universal truths of childhood in an off-beat way." Publishes hardcover and trade paperback originals. **Published 3 debut authors within the last year.** Averages 20-24 total titles, 17-21 fiction titles/year.

- Received a SCBWI Golden Kite Award: Best Picturebook text for *George Hogglesberry, Grade School Alien*, by Sarah Wilson, illustrated by Chad Cameron.

Needs Children's/juvenile (adventure, historical, board book, preschool/picture book), preteen. "One-off middle grade novels—quality fiction, 'tween fiction." Published *Hugging The Rock*, by Susan Taylor Brown (middle grade); *Time Bomb*, by Nigel Hinton (middle grade); *Girl Wonders*, by Karen Salmansohn (middle grade).

How to Contact Accepts unsolicited mss. Include brief bio, list of publishing credits, e-mail address. Send SASE for return of ms or send a disposable ms and SASE for reply only. Agented fiction 60%. Responds in 4-6 months to mss. Accepts simultaneous submissions.

Terms Pays 15-20% royalty on net receipts. Average advance: $0-9,000. Publishes ms 1-2 years after acceptance. Book catalog and ms guidelines for 9×12 SASE with 3 first-class stamps, or visit the Web site.

☑ ◎ TRIUMVIRATE PUBLICATIONS

497 West Avenue 44, Los Angeles CA 90065-3917. (818)340-6770. Fax: (818)340-6770. E-mail: triumpub@aol.c om. Web site: www.triumpub.com. **Contact:** Vladimir Chernozemsky, publisher. Estab. 1985. Publishes hardcover and paperback originals. Books: Antique/natural paper; offset printing; case and perfect bound; illustrations. Average print order 5,000-10,000. Member PMA. Distributes books through wholesalers using direct mail, fax/e-mail/telephone, trade/consumer advertising, book exhibits, reviews, listings and Internet.

Needs Adventure, fantasy, historical, horror, military/war, mystery, psychic/supernatural, science fiction, thriller/espionage. Published *A Continent Adrift*, by Vladimir Chernozemsky (science fiction); *Dark Side of Time*, by Vladimir Chernozemsky (supernatural).

How to Contact Does not accept unsolicited mss. Submit outline, 2 sample chapter(s). Accepts queries by fax, mail. Include brief bio, list of publishing credits. Send SASE for return of ms or send a disposable ms and SASE for reply only. Responds in 6 weeks to queries; 3 months to mss. Sometimes comments on rejected mss.

Terms Pays royalty. Publishes ms 6-12 months after acceptance.

Advice "Please query first. If interested, we will request the manuscript. Query should include: cover letter, short synopsis/description, 2-3 sample chapters, author bio, and writing/publishing credits. Send by mail. Do not fax except for short, 1-2 page query letters only. Please do not submit by e-mail or phone. We will respond if interested."

☑ ⚑ TURTLE BOOKS

866 United Nations Plaza, Suite #525, New York NY 10017. (212)644-2020. Fax: (212)223-4387. Web site: www.turtlebooks.com. "We are an independent publishing house. Our goal is to publish a small, select list of quality children's picture books in both English and Spanish editions." Publishes hardcover and trade paperback originals. Averages 6-8 total titles/year. Member Association of American Publishers. Distributed by Publishers Group West.

• Received the Willa Cather Award for Best Children's Book of the Year.

Needs Children's/juvenile. Subjects suitable for children's picture books. "We are looking for good stories which can be illustrated as children's picture books." Published *The Crab Man*, by Patricia Van West; *Keeper of The Swamp*, by Ann Garret; *Prairie Dog Pioneers*, by Jo Harper.

How to Contact Accepts unsolicited mss. Submit complete ms and SASE. Include list of publishing credits. Accepts simultaneous submissions.

Terms Pays royalty on retail price. Offers advance. Publishes ms 12 months after acceptance.

Advice "We only publish children's books. Every book we've published has been under 2,000 words in length. Queries are a waste of time. Please send only complete manuscripts."

Ⓝ ☑ TWILIGHT TIMES BOOKS

P.O. Box 3340, Kingsport TN 37664. (423)323-0183. Fax: (423)323-2183. E-mail: publishes@twilighttimesbooks. .com. Web site: www.twilighttimesbooks.com. **Contact:** Ardy M. Scott, managing editor. Estab. 1999. "We publish compelling literary fiction by authors with a distinctive voice. Our cross-genre, intellectual and visionary works remain in print regardless of sales." Publishes hardcover and paperback originals and paperback reprints and e-books. Book: 60 lb. paper; offset and digital printing; perfect bound. Average print order: 1500. **Published 3 debut authors within the last year.** Averages 18 total titles, 12 fiction titles/year. Member: AAP, PAS, SPAN, SLF. Nationally distributed by Midpoint Trade Books.

Needs Historical, literary, mystery, nonfiction, science fiction, and young adult. Published *Angelos*, by Robina Williams; *Hudson Lake*, by Laurahia Ward.

How to Contact Accepts unsolicited mss. Query with SASE or submit 2 sample chapter(s). Do not send complete mss. Accepts queries by e-mail, mail. Include estimated word count, brief bio, list of publishing credits, marketing plan. Send copy of ms and SASE. Agented fiction 10%. Responds in 4 weeks to queries; 2 months to mss. Accepts electronic submissions, submissions on disk. Rarely comments on rejected mss.

Terms Pays 8-15% royalty. Ms guidelines online.

Advice "The only requirement for consideration at Twilight Times Books is that your novel must be entertaining and professionally written."

Ⓝ ☑ TYRANNOSAURUS PRESS

5486 Fairway Drive, Zachary LA 70791. (225)287-8885. Fax: (206)984-0448. E-mail: info@tyrannosauruspress.c om. Web site: www.tyrannosauruspress.com. **Contact:** Roxanne Reiken. Estab. 2002. We are an independent press specializing in speculative fiction (science fiction & fantasy). Publishes paperback originals. Member: PMA. Distributes books via Baker & Taylor and other wholesalers; promotes by numerous different means.

Needs Fantasy (space fantasy, sword and sorcery), science fiction (hard science/technological, soft/sociological).

How to Contact Query with SASE. Accepts queries by e-mail. Include estimated word count. Send copy of ms and SASE. Responds in 4-6 weeks to queries; 3-6 months to mss. Accepts simultaneous submissions. Sometimes comments on rejected mss.

Terms Pays 10-20% royalty on net receipts. Book catalog for SASE and on Web site. Ms guidelines online.

⬤ UNBRIDLED BOOKS

200 North 9th Street, Suite A, Columbia MO 65201. 573-256-4106. Fax: 573-256-5207. Web site: www.unbridled books.com. **Contact:** Greg Michalson and Fred Ramey, editors. Estab. 2004. "Unbridled Books aspires to become a premier publisher of works of rich literary quality that appeal to a broad audience." Publishes both fiction and creative nonfiction. Hardcover and trade paperback originals. **Published 1 debut author within the last year.** Averages 10-12 total titles, 8-10 fiction titles/year.

Needs Literary, nonfiction, memoir. *The Green Age of Asher Witherow*, by M. Allen Cunningham; *The Distance Between Us*, by Masha Hamilton; *Fear Itself*, by Candida Lawrence; *Lucky Strike*, by Nancy Zafris.

How to Contact Query with SASE. Accepts queries by mail. No electronic submissions.

⬤ ◎ UNITY HOUSE

1901 NW Blue Parkway, Unity Village MO 64065-0001. (816)524-3559 ext. 3190. Fax: (816)251-3559. Web site: www.unityonline.org. **Contact:** Sharon Sartin. Estab. 1903. "We are a bridge between traditional Christianity and New Age spirituality. Unity is based on metaphysical Christian principles, spiritual values and the healing power of prayer as a resource for daily living." Publishes hardcover and trade paperback originals and reprints.

Needs Spiritual, visionary fiction, inspirational, metaphysical.

How to Contact Send complete mss (3 copies). Responds in 6-8 months. No simultaneous submissions.

Terms Pays 10-15% royalty on net receipts. Offers advance. Publishes ms 13 months after acceptance. Ms guidelines online.

◎ UNIVERSITY OF MICHIGAN PRESS

839 Greene St., Ann Arbor MI 48106. (734)764-4388. Fax: (734)615-1540. E-mail: ump.fiction@umich.edu. Web site: www.press.umich.edu. **Contact:** Chris Hebert, editor (fiction). Midsize university press. Publishes hardcover originals. Member AAUP.

Imprint(s) Sweetwater Fiction Originals (literary/regional).

Needs Literary, short story collections, novels.

How to Contact Accepts unsolicited mss. Query with SASE or submit outline, 3 sample chapter(s). Accepts queries by mail. Include brief bio, list of publishing credits. Responds in 4-6 weeks to queries; 6-8 weeks to mss. Accepts simultaneous submissions. No electronic submissions, submissions on disk. Sometimes comments on rejected mss.

Terms Ms guidelines online.

Advice "Aside from work published through the Michigan Literary Fiction Awards, we seek only fiction set in the Great Lakes region."

⬤ UNIVERSITY PRESS OF NEW ENGLAND

1 Court St., Suite 250, Lebanon NH 03766. (603)448-1533. Fax: (603)448-7006. E-mail: university.press@dartmo uth.edu. Web site: www.upne.com. **Contact:** Phyllis Deutsch, acquisitions editor-in-chief. Estab. 1970. Publishes hardcover originals. Averages 85 total titles, 6 fiction titles/year.

Needs Literary. Only New England novels, literary fiction and reprints. Published *Rebecca Wentworh's Distraction*, by Robert J. Begiebing; *The Private Revolution of Geoffrey Frost*, by I.E. Fender; *The Romance of Eleanor Gray*; by Raymond Kennedy; and *the Nature Notebooks*, by Don Mitchell.

How to Contact "For publication in the Hardscrabble series, it is not essential that the author live in the New England area, but the work should evoke themes and characters, and at the very least be set, in the region. Since much of what constitutes 'regional' fiction is fairly subjective, it is best to send a query letter." Query with SASE or submit sample chapter(s). Responds in 2 months to queries.

Terms Pays standard royalty. Average advance: occasional. Book catalog and ms guidelines for 9×12 SASE and 5 first-class stamps. Detailed ms and query guidelines online.

◨ ◎ VÉHICULE PRESS

Box 125, Place du Parc Station, Montreal QC H2X 4A3 Canada. (514)844-6073. Fax: (514)844-7543. Web site: www.vehiculepress.com. **Contact:** Andrew Steinmetz, fiction editor. Estab. 1973. Small publisher of scholarly, literary and cultural books. Publishes trade paperback originals by Canadian authors *only*. Books: good quality paper; offset printing; perfect and cloth binding; illustrations. Average print order: 1,000-3,000. Averages 15 total titles/year.

Imprint(s) Signal Editions (poetry), Esplande Books (fiction).

Needs Literary, regional, short story collections. Published *Optique*, by Clayton Bailey; *Seventeen Tomatoes: Tales from Kashmir*, by Jaspreet Singh; *A Short Journey by Car*, by Liam Durcan.
How to Contact Query with SASE. Responds in 4 months to queries.
Terms Pays 10-15% royalty on retail price. Average advance: $200-500. "Depends on press run and sales. Translators of fiction can receive Canada Council funding, which publisher applies for." Publishes ms 1 year after acceptance. Book catalog for 9×12 SAE with IRCs.
Advice "Quality in almost any style is acceptable. We believe in the editing process."

Ⓐ ✖ VILLARD BOOKS

Random House Publishing Group, 1745 Broadway 18th Fl., New York NY 10019. (212)572-2600. Web site: www.atrandom.com. Estab. 1983. Publishes hardcover and trade paperback originals. Averages 40-50 total titles/year.
Needs Commercial fiction.
How to Contact *Agented submissions only.* Agented fiction 95%. Accepts simultaneous submissions.
Terms Pays negotiable royalty. Average advance: negotiable.

Ⓐ ✖ VINTAGE ANCHOR PUBLISHING

The Knopf Publishing Group, A Division of Random House, Inc., 1745 Broadway, New York NY 10019. Web site: www.randomhouse.com. **Contact:** Furaha Norton, editor. Publishes trade paperback originals and reprints.
Needs Literary, mainstream/contemporary, short story collections. Published *Snow Falling on Cedars*, by Guterson (contemporary); *Martin Dressler*, by Millhauser (literary).
How to Contact *Agented submissions only.* Accepts simultaneous submissions. No electronic submissions.
Terms Pays 4-8% royalty on retail price. Average advance: $2,500 and up. Publishes ms 1 year after acceptance.

Ⓝ 🌐 🄾 🄾 VIRGIN BOOKS

(formerly Black Lace Books), Thames Wharf Studios, Units 5-bh, Rainville Road, London England W6 9HA United Kingdom. (+44)0207 386 3300. Fax: (+44)0207 386 3360. E-mail: info@virgin-books.co.uk. Web site: www.nexus-books.com, www.cheek-books.com. **Contact:** Adam Nevill, erotica editor. Estab. 1993. Publishes paper originals.
Imprint(s) Nexus Fetish Erotic Fiction for Men; Black Lace Erotic Fiction for Women, Cheek Erotic Chick-lit fiction. "Nexus and Black Lace are the leading imprints of erotic fiction in the UK."
Needs Erotica. "Female writers only for the Black Lace Series." Especially needs erotic fiction in contemporary and paranormal erotica settings. Also considers exceptional historical and erotic memoir. Publishes 4 erotic short story anthologies by women per year, called *Wicked Words*. Also published 6 novels within the softer Erotica Cheek imprint, chick-lit with erotic content aimed at 20-30 somethings, written by American and Canadian authors.
How to Contact Accepts unsolicited mss. Query with SASE. Include estimated word count. Agented fiction 25%. Responds in 1 month to queries; 6-8 months to mss. No simultaneous submissions. Always comments on rejected mss.
Terms Pays 7½% royalty. Average advance: £1,000. Publishes ms 7 months after acceptance. Ms guidelines online. All novels to be 70,000-75,000 words long.
Advice "Black Lace is open to female authors only. Read the guidelines first."

Ⓝ 🌐 🄾 VISION BOOKS PVT LTD.

5A/Ansari Road, Daryaganj, New Delhi 110 002 India. (+91)11 23278877 or (+91)11 23278878. Fax: (+91)11 23278879. E-mail: orientpbk@vsnl.com. **Contact:** Sudhir Malhotra, fiction editor.
Imprint(s) Orient Paperbacks.
Needs "We are a large multilingual publishing house publishing fiction and other trade books."
Terms Pays royalty.

WALKER AND CO.

Walker Publishing Co., 104 Fifth Ave., New York NY 10011. Web site: www.walkeryoungreaders.com. **Contact:** Emily Easton, publisher (picture books, middle grade & young adult novels); Timothy Travaglini, editor; Beth Marhoffer, assistant editor. Estab. 1959. Midsize independent publisher. Publishes hardcover trade originals. Average first novel print order: 2,500-3,500. Averages 25 total titles/year.
Needs Juvenile (fiction, nonfiction), picture books (juvenile). Published *Things Change*, by Patrick Jones; *The (Short) Story of My Life*, by Jennifer Jones.
How to Contact Accepts unsolicited mss. Query with SASE. Include "a concise description of the story line, including its outcome, word length of story (we prefer 50,000 words maximum), writing experience, publishing credits, particular expertise on this subject and in this genre. Common mistake: not researching our publishing

program and forgetting SASE." Agented fiction 50%. Responds in 3 months to queries. Sometimes comments on rejected mss.

Terms Pays 6% on paperback, 10% on hardcover. Average advance: competitive. Publishes ms 1 year after acceptance.

Ⓐ ✖ WARNER BOOKS

Hachette Book Group USA, Time & Life Building, 1271 Avenue of the Americas, New York NY 10020. (212)522-7200. Fax: (212)522-7993. Web site: www.twbookmark.com. **Contact:** (Ms.) Jamie Raab, senior vice president/publisher (general nonfiction and fiction); Les Pockell, associate publisher (general nonfiction); Amy Einhorn, vice president, executive editor; Beth de Guzman, vice president, editor-in-chief, Warner Paperbacks; Rick Wolff, vice president/executive editor (business, humor, sports); Caryn Karmatz Rudy, senior editor (fiction, general nonfiction, popular culture); Diana Baroni, executive editor (health, fitness, general nonfiction and fiction); John Aherne, editor (popular culture, men's health, New Age, movie tie-ins, general fiction); Rolf Zettersten, vice president/Warner Faith (books for the CBA market); (Ms.) Jaime Levine, editor/Aspect (science fiction); Karen Koszto Inyik, senior editor (women's fiction) ; Colin Fox, senior editor. Estab. 1960. Warner publishes general interest fiction. Publishes hardcover, trade paperback and mass market paperback originals and reprints and e-books. Averages 250 total titles/year.

Imprint(s) Mysterious Press; Warner Business; Warner Forever; Warner Vision; Warner Wellness; 5 Spot; Warner Twelve; Solana.

Needs Fantasy, horror, mainstream/contemporary, mystery, romance, science fiction, suspense, thriller/espionage, thrillers. Published *Up Country*, by Nelson DeMille; *A Bend in the Road*, by Nicholas Sparks.

How to Contact *Agented submissions only.*

Terms Pays variable royalty. Average advance: variable. Publishes ms 2 years after acceptance.

Ⓞ ◎ WHITE MANE KIDS

White Mane Publishing, P.O. Box 708, Shippensburg PA 17257. (717)532-2237. Fax: (717)532-6110. E-mail: marketing@whitemane.com. Web site: www.whitemane.com. Publishes hardcover orginals and paperback originals.

Needs Children's/juvenile (historical), young adult (historical). Published *Anybody's Hero: Battle of Old Men & Young Boys*, by Phyllis Haslip; *Crossroads at Gettysburg*, by Alan Kay.

How to Contact Accepts unsolicited mss. Query with SASE. Accepts queries by fax, mail. Include estimated word count, brief bio, summary of work and marketing ideas. Send SASE for return of ms or send a disposable ms and SASE for reply only. Responds in 1 month to queries; 3-4 months to mss. Accepts simultaneous submissions. Rarely comments on rejected mss.

Terms Pays royalty. Publishes ms 12-18 months after acceptance. Ms guidelines for #10 SASE.

Advice "Make your work historically accurate."

Ⓞ WILLOWGATE PRESS

P.O. Box 6529, Holliston MA 01746. (508)429-8774. E-mail: willowgatepress@yahoo.com. Web site: www.willowgatepress.com. **Contact:** Robert Tolins, editor. Publishes trade paperback and mass market paperback originals. **Published 50% debut authors within the last year.** Averages 1-2 total titles/year.

Needs Fantasy, gothic, historical, horror, humor, literary, mainstream/contemporary, military/war, mystery, occult, regional, science fiction, short story collections, sports. "We are not interested in children's, erotica or experimental."

Advice "At the present time we are closed to new submissions, and will remain so until we can work through our backlog. Our Web site will have updates."

Ⓞ ◎ WILSHIRE BOOK CO.

9731 Variel Ave., Chatsworth, CA 92311-4315. (818)700-1522. Fax: (818)700-1527. E-mail: mpowers@mpowers .com. Web site: www.mpowers.com. **Contact:** Melvin Powers, publisher; editorial department (adult fables). Estab. 1947. "You are not only what you are today, but also what you choose to become tomorrow." Looking for adult fables that teach principles of psychological growth. Publishes trade paperback originals and reprints. **Published 7 debut authors within the last year.** Averages 25 total titles/year. Distributes titles through wholesalers, bookstores and mail order. Promotes titles through author interviews on radio and television.

Needs Adult allegories that teach principles of psychological growth or offer guidance in living. Minimum 25,000 words. Published *The Princess Who Believed in Fairy Tales*, by Marcia Grad; *The King in Rusty Armor*, by Robert Fisher; *The Dragon Slayer With a Heavy Heart*, by Marcia Powers.

How to Contact Accepts unsolicited mss. Query with SASE or submit 3 sample chapter(s), synopsis or submit complete ms. Accepts queries by e-mail. Responds in 2 months to queries. Accepts simultaneous submissions.

Terms Pays standard royalty. Offers advance. Publishes ms 6 months after acceptance. Ms guidelines online.

Advice "We are vitally interested in all new material we receive. Just as you hopefully submit your manuscript for publication, we hopefully read every one submitted, searching for those that we believe will be successful in the marketplace. Writing and publishing must be a team effort. We need you to write what we can sell. We suggest that you read the successful books mentioned above or others that are similar: *Greatest Salesman in the World, Illusions, Way of the Peaceful Warrior, Celestine Prophecy*. Analyze them to discover what elements make them winners. Duplicate those elements in your own style, using a creative new approach and fresh material, and you will have written a book we can successfully market."

WIND RIVER PRESS

E-mail: submissions@windriverpress.com. Web site: www.windriverpress.com. **Contact:** Katherine Arline, editor (mainstream, travel, literary, historical, short story collections, translations). Estab. 2002. Publishes full and chapbook length paperback originals and reprints and electronic books. "Wind River Press works closely with the author to develop a cost-effective production, promotion and distribution strategy."

Needs Historical, literary, mainstream/contemporary, short story collections. Plans anthology of works selected from Wind River Press's magazines (*Critique* and *The Paumanok Review*). Recently published books by Elisha Porat, Gaither Stewart and Rochelle Mass.

How to Contact Accepts unsolicited mss. Accepts queries by e-mail. Include estimated word count, brief bio, list of publishing credits. Agented fiction 5%. Responds in 3 weeks to queries; 2 months to mss. Accepts simultaneous submissions. Always comments on rejected mss.

Terms Individual arrangement depending on book formats and target audience. Publishes ms 6 months after acceptance. Guidelines and book catalog available on Web site.

WINDRIVER PUBLISHING, INC.

72 N. Windriver Road, Silverton ID 83867-0446. (208)752-1836. Fax: (208)752-1876. E-mail: info@windriverpublishing.com. Web site: www.windriverpublishing.com. Estab. 2003. Publishes hardcover originals and reprints, trade paperback originals, mass market originals. Averages 8 total titles/year.

Needs Adventure, fantasy, historical, humor, juvenile, literary, military/war, mystery, religious, science fiction, spiritual, suspense, young adult.

How to Contact Responds in 2 months to queries; 4-6 months to mss. Accepts simultaneous submissions.

Terms Pays 8-15% royalty on wholesale price. Publishes ms 12-18 months after acceptance. Ms guidelines online.

WIZARDS OF THE COAST

P.O. Box 707, Renton WA 98057-0707. (425)226-6500. Web site: www.wizards.com. **Contact:** Novel Submissions. "We publish shared-world fiction set in the worlds of Forgotten Realms, Dragonlance, Eberron, Ravenloft, and Magic: The Gathering. We also publish young reader ficiton, in such series as Knights of the Silver Dragon, and select original speculative fiction." Publishes hardcover, mass market and trade paperback originals and mass market and trade paperback reprints. Wizards of the Coast publishes games as well, including the Dungeons & Dragons role-playing game. Books: standard paperbacks; offset printing; perfect binding; b&w (usually) illustrations. Averages 70-90 total titles/year. Distributes titles through Random House.

Imprint(s) Mirrorstone Books.

Needs See wizards.com for current guidelines. Currently not accepting manuscripts or proposals for any of our shared world lines. Open to original speculative fiction novel proposals from September 1 to January 1 of each year. Recently published *Empire of Blood*, by Richard A. Knaak; *Promise of the Witch-King*, by R.A. Salvatore (fantasy); *Resurrection*, by Paul S. Kemp.

How to Contact Agented fiction 65%. Responds in 4-8 months to queries. Accepts simultaneous submissions.

Terms Pays royalty on retail price with advance. Publishes ms 1-3 years after acceptance. Ms guidelines for #10 SASE.

WOODLEY MEMORIAL PRESS

English Dept., Washburn University, Topeka KS 66621. (785)670-1445. E-mail: paul.fecteau@washburn.edu. Web site: www.washburn.edu/reference/woodley-press. **Contact:** Paul Fecteau, corresponding editor. Estab. 1980. "Woodley Memorial Press is a small, nonprofit press which publishes novels and fiction collections by Kansas writers only; by 'Kansas writers' we mean writers who reside in Kansas or have a Kansas connection." Publishes paperback originals.

Needs Literary, mainstream/contemporary, short story collections. Published *Great Blues*, by Steve Semken; *The Trouble With Campus Security*, by G.W. Clift; and *Loading The Stone*, by Harley Elliot.

How to Contact Accepts unsolicited mss. Accepts queries by e-mail. Responds in 2 weeks to queries; 3 months to mss. Often comments on rejected mss.

Terms Publishes ms 1 year after acceptance. Ms guidelines online.

Advice "We only publish one to three works of fiction a year, on average, and those will definitely have a Kansas connection. We seek authors who are dedicated to promoting their works."

⚡ ✪ ✐ ◎ WORLDWIDE LIBRARY

Division of Harlequin Enterprises Limited, 225 Duncan Mill Rd., Don Mills ON M3B 3K9 Canada. (416)445-5860. Fax: (416)445-8655/8736. **Contact:** Feroze Mohammed, executive editor. Estab. 1979. Large commercial category line. Publishes paperback originals and reprints. "Mystery program is reprint; no originals please."
Imprint(s) Worldwide Mystery; Gold Eagle.
Needs "Action-adventure series and future fiction."
How to Contact Send SASE or IRC. Responds in 10 weeks to queries. Accepts simultaneous submissions.
Terms Advance and sometimes royalties; copyright buyout. Publishes ms 1-2 years after acceptance.
Advice "Publishing fiction in very selective areas."

◖ YELLOW SHOE FICTION SERIES

Louisiana State University Press, P.O. Box 25053, Baton Rouge LA 70894-5053. Web site: www.lsu.edu/lsupress. **Contact:** Michael Griffith, editor. Estab. 2004. Literary fiction series. Averages 1 title/year.
Needs Literary. "Looking first and foremost for literary excellence, especially good manuscripts that have fallen through the cracks at the big commercial presses. I'll cast a wide net." Published *Uke Rivers Delivers*, by R.T. Smith.
How to Contact Does not accept unsolicited mss. Accepts queries by mail. No electronic submissions.
Terms Pays royalty. Offers advance. Ms guidelines online.

N̄ Ⓐ ZEBRA BOOKS

Kensington, 850 Third Ave., 16th Floor, New York NY 10022. (877)422-3665. Web site: www.kensingtonbooks.com. **Contact:** Michaela Hamilton, editor-in-chief; Ann La Farge, executive editor; Kate Duffy, editorial director (romance); John Scognamiglio, editorial director; Karen Thomas, editorial director (Dafina); Bruce Bender, managing director (Citadel); Margaret Wolf, editor; Richard Ember, editor; Bob Shuman, senior editor; Jeremie Ruby-Strauss, senior editor; Miles Lott, editor. Publishes hardcover originals, trade paperback and mass market paperback originals and reprints. Averages 600 total titles/year.
Needs Zebra books is dedicated to women's fiction, which includes, but is not limited to romance.
How to Contact *Agented submissions only.* Accepts simultaneous submissions.
Terms Publishes ms 12-18 months after acceptance. Please no queries. Send synopsis and sample chapters with SASE.

Contests & Awards

In addition to honors and, quite often, cash prizes, contests and awards programs offer writers the opportunity to be judged on the basis of quality alone without the outside factors that sometimes influence publishing decisions. New writers who win contests may be published for the first time, while more experienced writers may gain public recognition of an entire body of work.

Listed here are contests for almost every type of fiction writing. Some focus on form, such as short stories, novels or novellas, while others feature writing on particular themes or topics. Still others are prestigious prizes or awards for work that must be nominated, such as the Pulitzer Prize in Fiction. Chances are, no matter what type of fiction you write, there is a contest or award program that may interest you.

SELECTING AND SUBMITTING TO A CONTEST

Use the same care in submitting to contests as you would sending your manuscript to a publication or book publisher. Deadlines are very important, and where possible, we've included this information. At times contest deadlines were only approximate at our press deadline, so be sure to write, call or look online for complete information.

Follow the rules to the letter. If, for instance, contest rules require your name on a cover sheet only, you will be disqualified if you ignore this and put your name on every page. Find out how many copies to send. If you don't send the correct amount, by the time you are contacted to send more, it may be past the submission deadline. An increasing number of contests invite writers to query by e-mail, and many post contest information on their Web sites. Check listings for e-mail and Web site addresses.

One note of caution: Beware of contests that charge entry fees that are disproportionate to the amount of the prize. Contests offering a $10 prize, but charging $7 in entry fees, are a waste of your time and money.

If you are interested in a contest or award that requires your publisher to nominate your work, it's acceptable to make your interest known. Be sure to leave the publisher plenty of time, however, to make the nomination deadline.

☐ AIM MAGAZINE SHORT STORY CONTEST

P.O. Box 1174, Maywood IL 60153-8174. (708)344-4414. E-mail: apiladoone@aol.com. Web site: www.aimmag azine.org. **Contact:** Ruth Apilado, associate editor. $100 prize offered to contest winner for best unpublished short story (4,000 words maximum) "promoting brotherhood among people and cultures." Judged by staff members. No entry fee. Deadline: August 15. Competition receives 20 submissions per category. Guidelines available anytime. Accepts inquiries by e-mail and phone. Winners are announced in the autumn issue and notified by mail on September 1. List of winners available for SASE. Open to any writer.

◎ ALABAMA STATE COUNCIL ON THE ARTS INDIVIDUAL ARTIST FELLOWSHIP

201 Monroe St., Montgomery AL 36130-1800. (334)242-4076, ext. 224. Fax: (334)240-3269. E-mail: randy.shoult s@arts.alabama.gov. Web site: www.arts.state.al.us. **Contact:** Randy Shoults, literature program manager. "To recognize the achievements and potential of Alabama writers." Judged by independent peer panel. Guidelines available in January. For guidelines, fax, e-mail, visit Web site. Accepts inquiries by fax, e-mail and phone. "Two copies of the following should be submitted: a résumé and a list of published works with reviews, if available. A minimum of 10 pages of poetry or prose, but no more than 20 pages. Please label each page with title, artist's name and date. If published, indicate where and the date of publication." Winners announced in June and notified by mail. List of winners available for SASE, fax, e-mail or visit Web site. No entry fee. Deadline: March. Competition receives 25 submissions annually. Two-year residency required.

☐ NELSON ALGREN SHORT FICTION CONTEST

Chicago Tribune, Nelson Algren Awards, 435 N. Michigan Ave., Chicago IL 60611. E-mail: efigula@tribune.com. Web site: chicagotribune.com/news/specials/broadband/chi-litawards-sub,0,4141930.htmlstory. **Contact:** Erin Figula, senior marketing specialist. "Honors excellence in short story writing by previously unpublished authors." Prize: $5,000 grand prize, $1,500 runners-up prizes (3). Judged by a group of *Chicago Tribune* editors and contributors. No entry fee. Cover letter should include name, address, phone, e-mail, word count, title. "No info on manuscript besides title and page numbers." Results announced October. Winners notified by mail or phone in September. For contest results, visit Web site. Deadline: February 15. Entries must be unpublished and written by a U.S. citizen. Competition for short stories. Open to any writer. Guidelines also available by e-mail and on Web site. Accepts inquiries by e-mail.

◎ AMERICAN ASSOCIATION OF UNIVERSITY WOMEN AWARD IN JUVENILE LITERATURE

North Carolina Literary and Historical Association, 4610 Mail Service Center, Raleigh NC 27699-4610. (919)807-7290. Fax: (919)733-8807. E-mail: michael.hill@ncmail.net. **Contact:** Michael Hill, awards coordinator. Award's purpose is to "select the year's best work of literature for young people by a North Carolina writer." Annual award for published books. Award: cup. Competition receives 10-15 submissions per category. Judged by three-judge panel. No entry fee. Deadline: July 15. Entries must be previously published. Contest open to "residents of North Carolina (three-year minimum)." Guidelines available July 15. For guidelines, send SASE, fax, e-mail or call. Accepts inquiries by fax, e-mail, phone. Winners announced October 15. Winners notified by mail. List of winners available for SASE, fax, e-mail.

AMERICAN LITERARY REVIEW SHORT FICTION AWARD

American Literary Review, P.O. Box 311307, University of North Texas, Denton TX 76203-1307. (940)565-2755. Web site: www.engl.unt.edu/alr. "To award excellence in short fiction." Prize: $1,000 and publication. Judged by rotating outside writer. Past judges have included Marly Swick, Antonya Nelson and Jonis Agee. Entry fee: $15. For guidelines, send SASE or visit Web site. Accepts inquiries by fax and phone. Deadline: September 1. Entries must be unpublished. Contest open to anyone not affiliated with the University of North Texas. "Only solidly crafted, character-driven stories will have the best chance for success." Winners announced and notified by mail and phone in February. List of winners available for SASE.

☐ AMERICAN MARKETS NEWSLETTER SHORT STORY COMPETITION

American Markets Newsletter, 1974 46th Ave., San Francisco CA 94116. E-mail: sheila.oconnor@juno.com. Award is "to give short story writers more exposure." Accepts fiction and nonfiction up to 2,000 words. Entries are eligible for cash prizes and all entries are eligible for worldwide syndication whether they win or not. Send double-spaced manuscripts with your story/article title, byline, word count and address on the first page above your article/story's first paragraph (no need for separate cover page). There is no limit to the number of entries you may send. Prize: 1st Place: $300; 2nd Place: $100; 3rd Place: $50. Judged by a panel of independent judges. Entry fee: $10 per entry; $15 for 2; $20 for 3; $23 for 4; $4 each entry thereafter. For guidelines, send SASE, fax or e-mail. Deadline: June 30 and December 31. Contest offered biannually. Published and unpublished stories are actively encouraged. Add a note of where and when previously published. Open to any writer. "All kinds of fiction are considered. We especially want women's pieces—romance, with a twist in the tale—but all will be considered.'' Results announced within 3 months of deadlines. Winners notified by mail if they include SASE.

◎ AMERICAN SCANDINAVIAN FOUNDATION TRANSLATION PRIZE

American Scandinavian Foundation, 58 Park Ave., New York NY 10016. (212)879-9779. Fax: (212)686-2115. E-mail: info@amscan.org. Web site: www.amscan.org. **Contact:** Laura Broomhall. Award to recognize excellence in fiction, poetry and drama translations of Scandinavian writers born after 1800. Prize: $2,000 grand prize; $1,000 prize. No entry fee. Cover letter should include name, address, phone, e-mail and title. Deadline: June 1. Entries must be unpublished. Length: no more than 50 pages for drama, fiction; no more than 35 pages for poetry. Open to any writer. Guidelines available in January for SASE, by fax, phone, e-mail or on Web site. Accepts inquiries by fax, e-mail, phone. Results announced in November. Winners notified by mail. Results available for SASE or by fax, e-mail, Web site.

◑ THE SHERWOOD ANDERSON FOUNDATION FICTION AWARD

The Sherwood Anderson Foundation, 216 College Rd., Richmond VA 23229. (804)289-8324. Fax: (804)287-6052. E-mail: mspear@richmond.edu. Web site: www.sherwoodandersonfoundation.org. **Contact:** Michael M. Spear, foundation co-president. Contest is ''to honor, preserve and celebrate the memory and literary work of Sherwood Anderson, American realist for the first half of the 20th century.'' Annual award for short stories and chapters of novels to ''encourage and support developing writers.'' Entrants must have published at least 1 book of fiction or have had several short stories published in major literary and/or commercial publications. Do not send your work by e-mail. Only mss in English will be accepted. Prize: $15,000 grant. Judged by a committee established by the foundation. Entry fee: $20 application fee (payable to The Sherwood Anderson Foundation). Deadline: April 1. Send a detailed résumé that provides a bibliography of your publications. Self-published stories do not qualify. Include a cover letter that provides a history of your writing experience and your future plans for writing projects. Also, submit 2 or 3 examples of what you consider to be your best work. Open to any writer. Accepts inquiries by e-mail. Mail your application to the above address. No mss or publications will be returned.

▧ ◎ ANNUAL ATLANTIC WRITING COMPETITION

Writer's Federation of Nova Scotia, 1113 Marginal Road, Halifax NS B3H 4P7 Canada. (902)423-8116. Fax: (902)422-0881. E-mail: talk@writers.ns.ca. Web site: www.writers.ns.ca. **Contact:** Susan Mersereau, executive assistant. Award's purpose is ''to provide feedback to emerging writers and create a venue for their work to be considered against that of other beginning authors. Annual award to residents of Atlantic Canada for short stories, poetry, and novels as well as children's literature, YA novels, poetry and essay.'' Prize: In Canadian money: $200, $150, $100 for adult novel; $150, $75, $50 for children's literature and YA novel; $100, $75, $50 for short stories and essay/magazine article. Judged by a jury of professionals from the writing/literature field—authors, librarians, publishers, teachers. Entry fee: $25 per novel entry ($20 for WFNS members); $15 per entry in other categories ($10 members). Deadline: first Friday in December of each year. Entries must be unpublished. Length: story 3,000 words maximum; novel 100,000 words maximum; children's writing 20,000 words maximum, YA novel 75,000 words maximum. Writers must use pseudonym; use 8½×11 white paper (one side only); and format entry typed and double-spaced. To be eligible, writers must be residents of Atlantic Canada, older than 16 and not extensively published in the category they are entering. Guidelines available by SASE or on Web site. Accepts inquiries by e-mail, phone. Winners announced in August. List of winners available on Web site.

◎ ANNUAL BOOK COMPETITION

Washington Writers' Publishing House, Elisavietta Ritchie, P.O Box 298, Broomes Island MD 20615. E-mail: megan@bcps.org. Web site: www.wwph.org. **Contact:** Moira Egan, president. ''To award literary excellence in the greater Washington DC-Baltimore area.'' Annual. Competition/award for novels, story collections. Prize: $500, publication, and 50 copies of book. Categories: fiction (novel or collection of short stories). Receives about 50 entries per category. Judged by members of the press. Entry fee: $25. Make checks payable to WWPH. Guidelines available all year with SASE, on Web site. Accepts inquiries by e-mail. Deadline: Nov. 1. Entries should be unpublished. ''Individual stories or excerpts may have been published in journals and anthologies.'' Open to fiction writers living within 60 miles of the Capitol (Baltimore area included). Length: no more than 350 pages, double or 1½ spaced. Cover letter should include name, address, phone, e-mail, novel/collection title, place(s) where stories/excerpts were previously published. None of this information should appear on the actual manuscript. Writers may submit own work. Results announced January of each year. Winners notified by phone, by e-mail. Results made available to entrants on Web site.

◖ ANNUAL FICTION CONTEST

Women in the Arts, P.O. Box 2907, Decatur IL 62524. (217)872-0811. **Contact:** Vice President. Annual competition for essays, fiction, fiction for children, plays, rhymed poetry, unrhymed poetry. Prize: $50, $35, $15 in all categories. Categories: Essay (up to 1,500 words); fiction (up to 1,500 words); fiction for children (up to 1,500 words); play (one act, 10-page limit); rhymed and unrhymed poetry (up to 32 lines). Judged by published, professional writers who live outside the state of Illinois. All entries will be subject to blind judging. Entry fee: $2 per entry, unlimited entries. Deadline: November 1. Do not submit drawings for any category. Double-space prose. Entries must be typed on $8\frac{1}{2} \times 11$ paper and must be titled. Do not put your name on any page of the ms. Do put your name, address, telephone number, e-mail and titles of your entries on a cover sheet. Submit one cover sheet and one check, with all entries mailed flat in one envelope. Do not staple. No entries published by WITA, author retains rights. Open to any writer. Results announced March 15 annually. Winners notified by mail. "Send a perfect manuscript—no typos, Liquid Paper, or holes from 3-ring binders."

ANNUAL JUVENILE FICTION CONTEST

Women in the Arts, P.O. Box 2907, Decatur IL 62524. (217)872-0811. **Contact:** Vice President. Annual competition for essays, fiction, fiction for children, plays, rhymed poetry, unrhymed poetry. Prize: $15-$50. Judged by anonymous judges who are published, professional writers who live outside Illinois. Entry fee: $2 per entry. Word length: 1,500 maximum for fiction, essay, fiction for children; one act for plays; up to 32 lines for poetry. Deadline: November 1. Entries must be original work of the author. Entries must be typed on $8\frac{1}{2} \times 11$ white paper and must be titled. Do not put your name on any page of the entry. Instead, put your name, address, telephone number, e-mail and titles of your entries on a cover sheet. Submit one cover sheet and one check. Mail all entries flat in a single envelope. Do not staple. Open to any writer. "Entrants must send for contest rules and follow the specific format requirements."

ARROWHEAD REGIONAL ARTS COUNCIL INDIVIDUAL ARTIST CAREER DEVELOPMENT GRANT

Arrowhead Regional Arts Council, 1301 Rice Lake Rd., Suite 111, Duluth MN 55811. (218)722-0952 or (800)569-8134. Fax: (218)722-4459. E-mail: aracouncil@aol.com. Web site: www.aracouncil.org. Award to "provide financial support to regional artists wishing to take advantage of impending, concrete opportunities that will advance their work or careers." Prize: up to $1,000. Categories: novels, short stories, story collections and translations. Judged by ARAC Board. No entry fee. Guidelines available by phone, e-mail or on Web site. See Web site for 2008 deadlines. Entries must be unpublished. Award is offered 3 times per year. Applicants must live in the seven-county region of Northeastern Minnesota. Results announced approximately 6 weeks after deadline. Winners notified by mail. List of winners available by phone.

THE ART OF MUSIC ANNUAL WRITING CONTEST

Piano Press, P.O. Box 85, Del Mar CA 92014-0085. (619)884-1401. Fax: (858)755-1104. E-mail: pianopress@pianopress.com. Web site: www.pianopress.com. **Contact:** Elizabeth C. Axford. Offered annually. Categories are: essay, short story, poetry and song lyrics. All writings must be on music-related topics. The purpose of the contest is to promote the art of music through writing. Acquires one-time rights. All entries must be accompanied by an entry form indicating category and age; parent signature is required of all writers under age 18. Poems may be of any length and in any style; essays and short stories should not exceed five double-spaced, typewritten pages. All entries shall be previously unpublished (except poems and song lyrics) and the original work of the author. Guidelines and entry form for SASE, on Web site or by e-mail. Prize: Cash, medal, certificate, publication in the biannual anthology/chapbook titled *The Art of Music: A Collection of Writings*, and copies of the book. Judged by a panel of published poets, authors and songwriters. Entry fee: $20 fee. Inquiries accepted by fax, e-mail, phone. Deadline: June 30. Short stories should be no longer than five pages typed and double spaced. Open to any writer. "Make sure all work is fresh and original. Music-related topics only." Results announced October 31. Winners notified by mail. For contest results, send SASE or visit Web site.

ASTED/GRAND PRIX DE LITTERATURE JEUNESSE DU QUEBEC-ALVINE-BELISLE

Association pour l'avancement des sciences et des techniques de la documentation, 3414 Avenue du Parc, Bureau 202, Montreal QC H2X 2H5 Canada. (514)281-5012. Fax: (514)281-8219. E-mail: info@asted.org. Web site: www.asted.org. **Contact:** Brigitte Moreau and Olivia Marleau, co-presidents. "Prize granted for the best work in youth literature edited in French in the Quebec Province. Authors and editors can participate in the contest." Offered annually for books published during the preceding year. Prize: $1,000. No entry fee. Deadline: June 1. Entries must be previously published. Open to editors and authors with books published during the preceding year.

THE ATHENAEUM LITERARY AWARD

The Athenaeum of Philadelphia, 219 S. Sixth St., Philadelphia PA 19106-3794. (215)925-2688. Fax: (215)925-3755. E-mail: erose@PhilaAthenaeum.org. Web site: www.PhilaAthenaeum.org. **Contact:** Ellen L. Rose. Annual award to recognize and encourage outstanding literary achievement in Philadelphia and its vicinity. Prize: a certificate bearing the name of the award, the seal of the Athenaeum, the title of the book, the name of the author and the year. Categories: The Athenaeum Literary Award is granted for a work of general literature, not exclusively for fiction. Judged by a committee appointed by the Board of Directors. No entry fee. Deadline: December. Entries must be previously published. Nominations shall be made in writing to the Literary Award Committee by the author, the publisher, or a member of the Athenaeum, accompanied by a copy of the book. Open to work by residents of Philadelphia and its vicinity. Guidelines available for SASE, by fax, by e-mail and on Web site. Accepts inquiries by fax, e-mail and phone. Juvenile fiction is not included. Results announced in Spring. Winners notified by mail. For contest results, see Web site.

AWP AWARD SERIES IN THE NOVEL, CREATIVE NONFICTION AND SHORT FICTION

The Association of Writers & Writing Programs, Mail Stop 1E3, George Mason University, Fairfax VA 22030. (703)993-4301. Fax: (703)993-4302. E-mail: awp@awpwriter.org. Web site: www.awpwriter.org. **Contact:** Supriya Bhatnagar, director of publications. The AWP Award Series was established in cooperation with several university presses in order to publish and make fine fiction and nonfiction available to a wide audience. Offered annually to foster new literary talent. Guidelines for SASE and on Web site. Categories: novel ($2,000), Donald Hall Prize in Poetry ($4,000), Grace Paley Prize in Short Fiction ($4,000), and creative nonfiction ($2,000). Entry fee: $25 for nonmembers, $10 for members. Entries must be unpublished. Mss must be postmarked between January 1-February 28. Cover letter should include name, address, phone number, e-mail and title. "This information should appear in cover letter only." Open to any writer. Guidelines available on Web site in November. No phone calls, please. Manuscripts published previously in their entirety, including self-publishing, are not eligible. No mss returned. Results announced in August. Winners notified by mail or phone. For contest results send SASE, or visit Web site. No phone calls, please.

AWP INTRO JOURNALS PROJECT

Dept. of English, Bluffton University, 1 University Drive, Bluffton OH 45817-2104. E-mail: awp@gmu.edu. Web site: www.awpwriter.org. **Contact:** Jeff Gundy. "This is a prize for students in AWP member university creative writing programs only. Authors are nominated by the head of the creative writing department. Each school may nominate no more than one work of nonfiction, one work of short fiction and three poems." Prize: $100 plus publication in participating journal. 2006 journals included *Puerto del Sol, Quarterly West, Mid-American Review, Willow Springs, Tampa Review, Controlled Burn, Artful Dodge, Colorado Review,* and *Hayden's Ferry Review.* Categories: Short stories, nonfiction and poetry. Judged by AWP. No entry fee. Deadline: December 1. Entries must be unpublished. Open to students in AWP Member University Creative Writing Programs only. Accepts inquiries by e-mail, fax and phone. Guidelines available for SASE or on Web site. Results announced in Spring. Winners notified by mail in Spring. For contest results, send SASE or visit Web site.

BARD FICTION PRIZE

Bard College, P.O. Box 5000, Annandale-on-Hudson NY 12504-5000. (845)758-7087. Fax: (845)758-7043. E-mail: bfp@bard.edu. Web site: www.bard.edu/bfp. **Contact:** Irene Zedlacher. The Bard Fiction Prize is intended to encourage and support young writers of fiction to pursue their creative goals and to provide an opportunity to work in a fertile and intellectual environment. Prize: $30,000 cash award and appointment as writer-in-residence at Bard College for 1 semester. Judged by committee of 5 judges (authors associated with Bard College). No entry fee. Cover letter should include name, address, phone, e-mail and name of publisher where book was previously published. Guidelines available by SASE, fax, phone, e-mail or on Web site. Deadline: July 15. Entries must be previously published. Open to US citizens aged 39 and below. Accepts inquiries by fax, e-mail and phone. Results announced by October 15. Winners notified by phone. For contest results, e-mail or visit Web site.

GEORGE BENNETT FELLOWSHIP

Phillips Exeter Academy, 20 Main St., Exeter NH 03833-2460. Web site: www.exeter.edu. Annual award for fellow and family "to provide time and freedom from material considerations to a person seriously contemplating or pursuing a career as a writer. Applicants should have a manuscript in progress which they intend to complete during the fellowship period." Duties: To be in residency for the academic year; to make oneself available informally to students interested in writing. Guidelines for SASE or on Web site. The committee favors writers who have not yet published a book with a major publisher. Residence at the Academy during the fellowship period required. Prize: $10,000 stipend, room and board. Judged by committee of the English department. $10 application fee. Application form and guidelines for SASE and on Web site. Deadline: December 1. Results announced in March. Winners notified by letter or phone. List of winners available in March. All entrants will receive an announcement of the winner. "Stay within a few pages of the limit. (We won't read more anyway.) Trust us to recognize that what you are sending is a work in progress. (You have the chance to talk about that in your statement.) Hope, but don't expect anything. If you don't win, some well-known writers have been in your shoes—at least as many as have won the fellowship."

◎ BEST LESBIAN EROTICA

Cleis Press, P.O. Box 395, Greenville, NY 12083. E-mail: tristan@puckerup.com. **Contact:** Tristan Taormino, series editor. Categories: Novel excerpts, short stories, other prose; poetry will be considered but is not encouraged. No entry fee. Include cover page with author's name, title of submission(s), address, phone, fax, e-mail. All submissions must be typed and double-spaced. Also number the pages. Length: 5,000 words. You may submit a maximum of 3 different pieces of work. Submit 2 hard copies of each submission. No e-mail submissions will be accepted; accepts inquiries by e-mail. Accepts both previously published and unpublished material. Open to any writer. All submissions must include SASE or an e-mail address for response. No mss will be returned.

◎ "BEST OF OHIO WRITER" CONTEST

Ohio Writer Magazine, 12200 Fairhill Rd., Townhouse #3A, Cleveland OH 44120. (216)421-0403. Fax: (216)421-8874. E-mail: pwlgc@yahoo.com. Web site: www.pwlgc.com. **Contact:** Darlene Montonaro, executive director. Award "to promote and encourage the work of writers in Ohio." Prize: $150, $50. Judged by "a selected panel of prominent Ohio writers." Entry fee: $15, which includes 1-yr. subscription to the magazine. Deadline: July 31. Entries must be unpublished. Ohio residents only. Guidelines available after January 1 for SASE or e-mail. Accepts inquiries by e-mail and phone. Length: 2,500 words, "No cliché plots; we're looking for fresh unpublished voices." Results announced November 1. Winners notified by mail. For contest results, send SASE or e-mail after November 1.

◐ BINGHAMTON UNIVERSITY JOHN GARDNER FICTION BOOK AWARD

Binghamton Center for Writers, State University of New York, P.O. Box 6000, Binghamton NY 13902. (607)777-2713. Fax: (607)777-2408. E-mail: cwpro@binghamton.edu. Web site: english.binghamton.edu/cwpro. **Contact:** Maria Mazziotti Gillan, director. Award's purpose is "to serve the literary community by calling attention to outstanding books of fiction." Prize: $1,000. Categories: novels and short story collections. Judged by "rotating outside judges." No entry fee. Entry must have been published in book form with a minimum press run of 500. Each book submitted must be accompanied by an application form, available online or send SASE to above address. Submit three copies of the book; copies will not be returned. Publishers may submit more than one book for prize consideration. Deadline: March 1. Entries must have appeared in print between January 1 and December 31 of the year preceding the award. Open to any writer. Results announced in Summer. Winners notified by e-mail or phone. For contest results, send SASE or visit Web site.

◐ ◎ IRMA S. AND JAMES H. BLACK AWARD

Bank Street College of Education, 610 W. 112th St., New York NY 10025. (212)875-4450. Fax: (212)875-4558. E-mail: lindag@bnkst.edu. Web site: streetcat.bnkst.edu/html/isb.html. **Contact:** Linda Greengrass, award director. Offered annually for a book for young children, for excellence of both text and illustrations. Entries must have been published during the previous calendar year. Prize: press function and scroll and seals by Maurice Sendak for attaching to award winner's book run. Judged by adult children's literature experts and children 6-10 years old. No entry fee. Guidelines for SASE, fax, e-mail or on Web site. Accepts inquiries by phone, fax, e-mail. Deadline: December 15. Entries must be previously published. "Write to address above. Usually publishers submit books they want considered, but individuals can too. No entries are returned." Winners notified by phone in April and announced in May. A list of winners will be available on Web site.

⊕ ◐ JAMES TAIT BLACK MEMORIAL PRIZES

Department of English Literature, University of Edinburgh, David Hume Tower, George Square, Edinburgh Scotland EH8 9JX United Kingdom. (44-13)1650-3619. Fax: (44-13)1650-6898. E-mail: s.strathdee@ed.ac.uk. Web site: www.englit.ed.ac.uk/jtbinf.htm. **Contact:** Sheila Strathdee, Department of English Literature. "Two prizes each of £10,000 are awarded: one for the best work of fiction, one for the best biography or work of that nature, published during the calendar year January 1 to December 31." Judged by the professor of English Literature. No entry fee. Accepts inquiries by fax, e-mail, phone. Deadline: January 31. Entries must be previously published. "Eligible works are those written in English and first published or co-published in Britain in the year of the award. Works should be submitted by publishers." Open to any writer. Winners notified by phone, via publisher. Contact department of English Literature for list of winners or check Web site.

⊕ ◐ ◎ THE BOARDMAN TASKER AWARD FOR MOUNTAIN LITERATURE

The Boardman Tasker Charitable Trust, Pound House, Llangennith, Swansea Wales SA3 1JQ United Kingdom. Phone/fax: (44-17)9238-6215. E-mail: margaretbody@lineone.net. Web site: www.boardmantasker.com. **Contact:** Margaret Body. "The award is to honor Peter Boardman and Joe Tasker, who disappeared on Everest in 1982." Offered annually to reward a work of nonfiction or fiction, in English or in translation, which has made an outstanding contribution to mountain literature. Books must be published in the UK between November 1 of previous year and October 31 of year of the prize. Writers may obtain information, but entry is by publishers only. "No restriction of nationality, but work must be published or distributed in the UK." Prize: £2,000. Judged by a panel of 3 judges elected by trustees. No entry fee. "May be fiction, nonfiction, poetry or drama. Not an anthology. Subject must be concerned with a mountain environment. Previous winners have been books on expeditions, climbing experiences, a biography of a mountaineer, novels." Guidelines available in January for SASE, by fax, e-mail or on Web site. Deadline: August 1. Entries must be previously published. Publisher's entry only. Open to any writer. Results announced in November. Winners notified by phone or e-mail. For contest results, send SASE, fax, e-mail or visit Web site. "The winning book needs to be well written to reflect a knowledge of and a respect and appreciation for the mountain environment."

BOULEVARD SHORT FICTION CONTEST FOR EMERGING WRITERS

Boulevard Magazine, 6614 Clayton Rd., PMB #325, Richmond Heights MO 63117. (314)862-2643. Fax: (314)781-7250. E-mail: ballymon@hotmail.com. Web site: www.richardburgin.com. **Contact:** Richard Burgin, editor. Offered annually for unpublished short fiction to award a writer who has not yet published a book of fiction, poetry or creative nonfiction with a nationally distributed press. "We hold first North American rights on anything not previously published." Open to any writer with no previous publication by a nationally known press. Guidelines for SASE or on Web site. Prize: $1,500, and publication in 1 of the next year's issues. Judged by editors of *Boulevard*. Entry fee: $15 fee/story; includes 1-year subscription to *Boulevard*. Guidelines available in April for SASE, e-mail, on Web site and in publication. Accepts inquiries by e-mail, phone. Deadline: December 15. Entries must be unpublished. Length: 9,000 words. Open to any writer. Author's name, address, phone, e-mail, story title, word count and "Boulevard Emerging Writers Contest" should appear on page 1; last name on each page is helpful. Include a 3×5 index card with your name, address and title of your submission(s). Results announced in Spring issue. Winners notified by mail or phone usually during February/March.

☐ THE BRIAR CLIFF POETRY, FICTION & CREATIVE NONFICTION COMPETITION

The Briar Cliff Review, Briar Cliff University, 3303 Rebecca St., Sioux City IA 51104-0100. (712)279-5321. Fax: (712)279-5410. E-mail: curranst@briarcliff.edu. Web site: www.briarcliff.edu/bcreview. **Contact:** Tricia Currans-Sheehan, editor. Award "to reward good writers and showcase quality writing." Offered annually for unpublished poem, story and essay. Prize: $ 1,000, and publication in Spring issue. All entrants receive a copy of the magazine with winning entries. Judged by editors. "We guarantee a considerate reading." Entry fee: $15. Guidelines available in August for SASE. Inquiries accepted by e-mail. Deadline: Submissions between August 1 and November 1. No mss returned. Entries must be unpublished. Length: 6,000 words maximum. Open to any writer. Results announced in December or January. Winners notified by phone or letter around December 20. For contest results, send SASE with submission. "Send us your best. We want stories with a plot."

⊕ ☐ THE BRIDPORT PRIZE

Bridport Arts Centre, South Street, Bridport, Dorset DT6 3NR United Kingdom. (01308)485064. Fax: (01308)485120. E-mail: frances@poorton.demon.co.uk. Web site: www.bridportprize.org.uk. **Contact:** Frances Everitt, administrator. Award to "promote literary excellence, discover new talent." Prize: £5,000 sterling; £1,000 sterling; £500 sterling, plus various runners-up prizes and publication of approximately 13 best stories and 13 best poems in anthology. Categories: short stories and poetry. Judged by 1 judge for fiction (in 2007, Tracy Chevalier) and 1 judge for poetry (in 2007, Don Paterson). Entry fee: £6 sterling for each entry. Deadline: June 30. Entries must be unpublished. Length: 5,000 maximum for short stories; 42 lines for poetry. Open to any writer. Guidelines available in January for SASE or visit Web site. Accepts inquiries by fax, e-mail, phone. Results announced in November of year of contest. Winners notified by phone or mail in September. For contest results, send SASE.

⊠ ◎ BURNABY WRITERS' SOCIETY CONTEST

Burnaby Writers' Society, 6584 Deer Lake Ave., Burnaby BC V5G 3T7 Canada. E-mail: info@bws.bc.ca. Web site: www.bws.bc.ca. Offered annually for unpublished work. Open to all residents of British Columbia. Categories vary from year to year. Send SASE for current rules. Purpose is to encourage talented writers in all genres. Prize: 1st Place: $200; 2nd Place: $100; 3rd Place: $50; and public reading. Entry fee: $5. Guidelines available by e-mail, for SASE or on Web site. Accepts inquiries by e-mail. Deadline: May 31. Results announced in September. Winners notified by mail, phone, e-mail. Results available for SASE or on Web site.

◎ BUSH ARTIST FELLOWS PROGRAM

Bush Foundation, 332 Minnesota St., Suite E-900, St. Paul MN 55101. Fax: (651)297-6485. E-mail: BAFinfo@bushfoundation.org. Web site: www.bushfoundation.org. **Contact:** Julie Dalgliesh, program director. Award to "provide artists with significant financial support that enables them to further their work and their contributions to their communities. Fellows may decide to take time for solitary work or reflection, engage in collaborative or community projects, or embark on travel or research." Prize: $48,000 for 12-24 months. Categories: fiction, creative nonfiction, poetry. Judged by a panel of artists and arts professionals who reside outside of Minnesota, South Dakota, North Dakota or Wisconsin. No entry fee. Applications available in August. Accepts inquiries by fax and e-mail. Applicants must be at least 25 years old, U.S. citizens or Permanent Residents, and residents of Minnesota, South Dakota, North Dakota or Western Wisconsin. Students not eligible. Must meet certain publication requirements. Results announced in Spring. Winners notified by letter. List of winners available in May and sent to all applicants.

☐ ◎ BYLINE MAGAZINE AWARDS

P.O. Box 111, Albion NY 14411. (585)355-8172. E-mail: robbi@bylinemag.com. Web site: www.bylinemag.com. **Contact:** Robbi Hess, award director. Several monthly contests, open to anyone, in various categories that include fiction, nonfiction, poetry and children's literature; a semi-annual poetry chapbook award which is open to any poet; and an annual *ByLine* Short Fiction and Poetry Award open only to our subscribers. For chapbook award and subscriber awards, publication constitutes part of the prize; winners grant first North American rights to *ByLine*. Prize: for monthly contests, cash and listing in magazine; for chapbook award, publication of chapbook, 50 copies and $200; for *ByLine* Short Fiction and Poetry Award, $250 in each category, plus publication in the magazine. Entry fee: $3-5 for monthly contests and $15 for chapbook contest. Deadline: varies. Entries must be unpublished.

▦ ◒ ◎ THE CAINE PRIZE FOR AFRICAN WRITING

51a Southwark St., London England SE1 1RU United Kingdom. E-mail: info@caineprize.com. Web site: www.caineprize.com. **Contact:** Nick Elam, administrator. Annual award for a short story (3,000-15,000 words) by an African writer. "An 'African writer' is normally taken to mean someone who was born in Africa, who is a national of an African country, or whose parents are African, and whose work has reflected African sensibilities." Entries must have appeared for the first time in the 5 years prior to the closing date for submissions, which is January 31 each year. Publishers should submit 6 copies of the published original with a brief cover note (no pro forma application). Prize: $15,000 (£10,000). Judged by a panel of judges appointed each year. No entry fee. Cover letter should include name, address, phone, e-mail, title and publication where story was previously published. Deadline: January 31. Entries must be previously published. Word length: 3,000-15,000 words. "Manuscripts not accepted. Entries must be submitted in published form." Writer's work is submitted by publisher. Writing must reflect its "African-ness." Results announced in mid-July. Winners notified at event/banquet. For contest results, send fax, e-mail or visit our Web site.

◒ JOHN W. CAMPBELL MEMORIAL AWARD FOR BEST SCIENCE FICTION NOVEL OF THE YEAR

Center for the Study of Science Fiction, English Department, University of Kansas, Lawrence KS 66045. (785)864-3380. Fax: (785)864-1159. E-mail: jgunn@ku.edu. Web site: www.ku.edu/~sfcenter. **Contact:** James Gunn, professor and director. Award to "honor the best science fiction novel of the year." Prize: Trophy. Winners receive an expense-paid trip to the university (in 2007 Kansas City, MO) to receive their award. Their names are also engraved on a permanent trophy. Categories: novels. Judged by a jury. No entry fee. Deadline: see Web site. Entries must be previously published. Open to any writer. Accepts inquiries by e-mail and fax. "Ordinarily publishers should submit work, but authors have done so when publishers would not. Send for list of jurors." Results announced in July. For contest results, send SASE.

☐ THE ALEXANDER PATTERSON CAPPON FICTION AWARD

New Letters, 5101 Rockhill Rd., Kansas City MO 64110. (816)235-1168. Fax: (816)235-2611. Web site: www.newletters.org. Offered annually for unpublished work to discover and to reward new and upcoming writers. Buys first North American serial rights. Prize: 1st place: $1,500 and publication in a volume of *New Letters*; 1 runner-up will receive a copy of a recent book of poetry or fiction from affiliate BkMk Press. All entries will be given consideration for publication in future issues of *New Letters*. Judged by renowned writers. Previous judges have included Philip Levine, Charles Simic, Joyce Carol Oates, Rosellen Brown, Phillip Lopate, Maxine Kumin. Entry fee: $15 (includes a 1-year subscription to *New Letters*); $10 for each entry after first. Entries in fiction are not to exceed 8,000 words. Send two cover sheets—the first with complete name, address, e-mail/phone, category and title(s); the second with category and title(s) only. Personal information should not appear anywhere else on the entry. Also enclose a stamped, self-addressed postcard if you would like notification of receipt and entry number and an SASE for list of winners. Note that manuscripts will not be returned. Deadline: May 18. Entries must be unpublished. Simultaneous and multiple submissions welcome. Winners announced mid-September. Open to any writer.

▧ ◔ ◎ THE CHRISTOPER AWARDS

The Christophers, 12 E. 48th St., New York NY 10017-1091. (212)759-4050. Fax: (646)843-1547. E-mail: awardsinfo@christophers.org. Web site: www.christophers.org. **Contact:** Judith Trojan, program director. Award "to encourage authors and illustrators to continue to produce works which affirm the highest values of the human spirit in adult and children's books." Prize: bronze medallion. Categories: Adult nonfiction and young adult novels and nonfiction. Judged by a panel of juvenile reading and subject experts. Juvenile titles are "children tested." No entry fee. Submission period: June 1 through November 1 every year. Entries must be previously published. Potential winners are nominated and reviewed throughout the year by juvenile book professionals, members of the Christopher staff, and by specially supervised children's reading groups. Open to any writer. For guidelines send 6×9 SASE, e-mail or visit Web site. Inquiries accepted by letter, fax, e-mail and phone. Winners chosen in early January and notified by mail in late January. Awards are presented annually in March at a black-tie gala in New York City. For contest results, send SASE, fax or visit Web site. Example of book award: *The Miraculous Journey of Edward Tulane*, by Kate DiCamillo; illustrated by Bagram Ibatoulline (children's book category 2006). "Publishers generally submit fiction/nonfiction books for young people. Authors and illustrators should familiarize themselves with our awards criteria and encourage their publishers to submit applicable titles."

CITY OF TORONTO BOOK AWARDS

City of Toronto, 100 Queem St. West, City Hall, 10th Floor, West Tower, Toronto ON M9W 3X3 Canada. (416)392-8191. Fax: (416)392-1247. Web site: www.toronto.ca/book_awards. **Contact:** Bev Kurmey, protocol officer. "The Toronto Book Awards honour authors of books of literary or artistic merit that are evocative of Toronto." Categories: short stories, novels, story collections, translations. Judged by committee. No entry fee. Guidelines available by e-mail, on Web site. Accepts inquiries by phone, fax, e-mail. Writers may submit their own fiction. Cover letter should include name, address, phone, e-mail, title. Deadline: Feb. 28. Entries must be previously published. Books must have been published during the year prior to the award (i.e. in 2007 for the 2008 deadline). Open to any writer. Results announced in Sept., short list in June. Winners notified by mail, e-mail. Results available on Web site.

CNW/FFWA ANNUAL FLORIDA STATE WRITING COMPETITION

% CNW Publishing, Florida Freelance Writers Association, P.O. Box A, North Stratford NH 03590-0167. E-mail: contest@writers-editors.com. Web site: www.writers-editors.com. **Contact:** Dana K. Cassell, executive director. Annual award "to recognize publishable talent." Divisions & Categories: Nonfiction (previously published article/essay/column/nonfiction book chapter; unpublished or self-published article/essay/column/nonfiction book chapter); Fiction (unpublished or self-published short story or novel chapter); Children's Literature (unpublished or self-published short story/nonfiction article/book chapter/poem); Poetry (unpublished or self-published free verse/traditional). Prize: 1st Place: $100, plus certificate; 2nd Place: $75, plus certificate; 3rd Place: $50, plus certificate. Honorable Mention certificates will be awarded in each category as warranted. Judged by editors, librarians and writers. Entry fee: $5 (active or new CNW/FFWA members) or $10 (nonmembers) for each fiction/nonfiction entry under 3,000 words; $10 (members) or $20 (nonmembers) for each entry of 3,000 words or longer; and $3 (members) or $5 (nonmembers) for each poem. Guidelines for SASE or on Web site. Accepts inquiries by e-mail, phone and mail. Deadline: March 15. Open to any writer. Results announced May 31. Winners notified by mail and posted on Web site. Results available for SASE or visit Web site.

CONSEIL DE LA VIE FRANCAISE EN AMERIQUE/PRIX CHAMPLAIN

Conseil de la Vie Francaise en Amerique, Faculté des lettres, DKN-3219, Univesité Laval, Quebec City QC G1K 7P4 Canada. (418)806-23021. Fax: (418)644-7670. E-mail: cvfa@cvfa.ca. Web site: www.cvfa.ca. **Contact:** Director General. Award to encourage literary work in novel or short story in French by Francophiles living outside Quebec, in the US or Canada. Prize: $1,500 Canadian. Judged by 3 different judges each year. No entry fee. Deadline: December 31. Entries must be previously published. "There is no restriction as to the subject matter. If the author lives in Quebec, the subject matter must be related to French-speaking people living outside of Quebec." Submissions must have been published no more than 3 years before award. Open to any writer. Guidelines for SASE or IRC or on Web site. Author must furnish 4 examples of work, curriculum vitae, address and phone number.

CRAZYHORSE FICTION PRIZE

College of Charleston, Dept. of English, 66 George St., Charleston SC 29424. (843)953-7740. E-mail: crazyhorse@cofc.edu. Web site: http://crazyhorse.cofc.edu. **Contact:** Editors. Prize: $2,000 and publication in *Crazyhorse*. Judged by anonymous writer whose identity is disclosed when the winners are announced in April. Past judges: Charles Baxter (2002), Michael Martone (2003), Diana Abu-Jaber (2004), T.M. McNally (2005), Dan Chaon (2006). Entry fee: $15 (covers 1-yr subscription to *Crazyhorse*; make checks payable to *Crazyhorse*). To enter, please send up to 25 pages of prose. Include a detachable cover sheet with your name, address and telephone number; please do not include this information on the ms itself. Send SASE or see Web site for additional details. Deadline: December 16th of each year; see Web site. Open to any writer.

◻ THE CRUCIBLE POETRY AND FICTION COMPETITION

Crucible, Barton College, College Station, Wilson NC 27893. (252)399-6456. E-mail: tgrimes@barton.edu. **Contact:** Terrence L. Grimes, editor. Offered annually for unpublished short stories. Prize: $150 (1st Prize); $100 (2nd Prize) and publication in *Crucible*. Competition receives 300 entries. Categories: Fiction should be 8,000 words or less. Judged by in-house editorial board. No entry fee. Guidelines available in January for SASE, e-mail or in publication. Deadline: April. Open to any writer. "The best time to submit is December through April." Results announced in July. Winners notified by mail. For contest rules, send e-mail.

◻ DEAD OF WINTER

E-mail: editors@toasted-cheese.com. Web site: www.toasted-cheese.com. **Contact:** Stephanie Lenz, editor. The contest is a winter-themed short fiction contest with a new topic each year. Topic and word limit announced Nov. 1. The topic is usually geared toward a supernatural theme. Prize: Amazon gift certificates in the amount of $20, $15 and $10; publication in *Toasted Cheese*. Also offers honorable mention. Categories: short stories. Judged by two *Toasted Cheese* editors who blind judge each contest. Each judge uses her own criteria to rate entries. No entry fee. Cover letter should include name, address, e-mail, word count and title. Deadline: December 21. Entries must be unpublished. Word limit varies each year. Open to any writer. Guidelines available in November on Web site. Accepts inquiries by e-mail. "Follow guidelines. Write a smart, original story. We have further guidelines on the Web site." Results announced January 31. Winners notified by e-mail. List of winners on Web site.

◉ DOBIE/PAISANO FELLOWSHIPS

Dobie House, 702 E. Dean Keeton St., Austin TX 78705. (512)471-8542. Fax: (512)471-9997. E-mail: aslate@mail.utexas.edu. Web site: www.utexas.edu/ogs/Paisano. **Contact:** Audrey N. Slate, director. Award to honor the achievement and promise of two writers. Prize: $2,000/month for six months and rent-free stay at Paisano ranch southwest of Austin, TX. Judged by committee from Texas Institute of Letters and the University of Texas. Entry fee: $10. Deadline: January 26. Entries must be unpublished. "Open to writers with a Texas connection—native Texans, people who have lived in Texas at least three years, or writers with published work on Texas." Winners announced early May. List of winners available at Web site.

◻ EATON LITERARY AGENCY'S ANNUAL AWARDS PROGRAM

Eaton Literary Agency, P.O. Box 49795, Sarasota FL 34230. (941)366-6589. Fax: (941)365-4679. E-mail: eatonlit@aol.com. Web site: www.eatonliterary.com. **Contact:** Richard Lawrence, vice president. Offered biannually for unpublished mss. Prize: $2,500 (over 10,000 words); $500 (under 10,000 words). Judged by an independent agency in conjunction with some members of Eaton's staff. No entry fee. Guidelines available for SASE, by fax, e-mail, or on Web site. Accepts inquiries by fax, phone and e-mail. Deadline: March 31 (mss under 10,000 words); August 31 (mss over 10,000 words). Entries must be unpublished. Open to any writer. Results announced in April and September. Winners notified by mail. For contest results, send SASE, fax, e-mail or visit Web site.

◑ EMERGING VOICES ROSENTHAL FELLOWSHIP

PEN USA, % Antioch University, 400 Corporate Pointe, Culver City CA 90230. (310)862-1555. Fax: (310)862-1556. E-mail: ev@penusa.org. Web site: www.penusa.org. **Contact:** Christine Lanoie-Newman, program director. "To serve up-and-coming writers from traditionally underserved communities. To help these not-yet-published authors gain the creative and professional skills needed to flourish in the literary world." Annual. Competition/award for short stories, novels, story collections. Prize: $1,000 and 1-yr mentorship with established author, plus classes and workshops and the opportunity to meet authors, agents, editors and publishers. Categories: fiction, poetry, creative nonfiction. Receives about 60 entries per category. Entries judged by EV selection committee composed of PEN USA board members, former EV fellows and prominent local authors. Entry fee: $10. Make checks payable to PEN USA. Guidelines available in February by phone, on Web site, in publication. Accepts inquiries by e-mail, phone. Deadline: September 2008. "Candidates should be minimally published, with no full-length books." Fellowship is geared towards writers from traditionally underserved communities (immigrants, ethnic minorities, women) though anyone may apply. Length: 20 pages max. Entrants must complete EV application, which is available on PEN's Web site. Writers may submit own work. "Utilize EV application. Follow all instructions. Don't wait until the last minute to assemble letters of recommendation." Results announced November. Winners notified by mail, phone, e-mail. Results made available to entrants on Web site.

EMERGING WRITERS NETWORK SHORT FICTION CONTEST

Emerging Writers Network, 1334 Woodbourne Street, Westland MI 48186. E-mail: wickettd@yahoo.com. Web site: www.emergingwriters.typepad.com. **Contact:** Dan Wickett, president. Purpose to "find an excellent short story, get it published in *Storyglossia*, and award the author." Annual. Competition/award for short stories. Prize: $1,000, publication on EWN Blog, publication in spring issue of *Storyglossia*. Judging: All stories initially read by Dan Wickett. Top 20 go without author names to guest judge who chooses winner. 2007 guest judge was Alyson Hagy. Entry fee: $15. Make checks payable to Dan Wickett. Guidelines available in April on Web site. Accepts inquiries by e-mail. Submission period: January 1 through July 1, 2008. Entries should be unpublished. Open only to authors who have had, or will have had, less than 3 books published by December prior to contest. Length: 3,000-8,000 words. Cover letter should include name, address, e-mail, word count, story title. Writers may submit own work. "Have an idea of the type of fiction the Emerging Writers Network supports and is generally excited about by reading the Web site." Results announced during the month of December. Winners notified by mail, e-mail. Results made available to entrants on Web site.

THE EMILY CONTEST

West Houston Chapter Romance Writers of America, 5603 Chantilly Lane, Houston TX 77092. E-mail: ellen_watk ins@juno.com. Web site: www.whrwa.com. **Contact:** Ellen Watkins, Emily Contest chair. Award "to help people writing romance novels learn to write better books and to help them make contacts in the publishing world." Prize: first place entry in each category receives the Emily brooch; all finalists receive certificates. Judged by authors and experienced critiquers in the first round; final round judges are editors at a major romance publishing house. Entry fee: $20 for WHRWA members; $30 for non-members. Deadline: October 1. Entries must be unpublished. Length: first 35 pages of a novel. Open to all unpublished romance writers. Guidelines available in July for SASE, by e-mail or on Web site. Accepts inquiries by e-mail. "We look for dynamic, interesting romance stories with a hero and heroine readers can relate to and love. Hook us from the beginning and keep the level of excitement high." Results announced in February. Winners notified by mail or phone. For contest results, send SASE or visit Web site.

THE VIRGINIA FAULKNER AWARD FOR EXCELLENCE IN WRITING

Prairie Schooner, 201 Andrews Hall, P.O. Box 880334, Lincoln NE 68588-0334. (402)472-0911. Fax: (402)472-9771. E-mail: kgrey2@unl.edu. Web site: www.unl.edu/schooner/psmain.htm. **Contact:** Hilda Raz, editor. Offered annually for work published in *Prairie Schooner* in the previous year. Prize: $1,000. Categories: short stories, essays, novel excerpts and translations. Judged by Editorial Board. No entry fee. Guidelines for SASE or on Web site. Accepts inquiries by fax and e-mail. "We only read mss from September 1 through May 1." Winning entry must have been published in *Prairie Schooner* in the year preceeding the award. Results announced in the Spring issue. Winners notified by mail in February or March.

FISH ONE PAGE PRIZE

Fish Publishing, Durrus, Bantry, County Cork Ireland. E-mail: info@fishpublishing.com. Web site: www.fishpu blishing.com. **Contact:** Clem Cairns, editor. Prize: 1st prize: 1,000 Euro (approx. $1,300). Nine runners up get 100 Euro (approx. $130). The authors of the 10 best works of short short fiction will be published in the Fish Short Story Prize Anthology. Entry fee: $15 per story. Enter online. Deadline: March 4. Entries must be unpublished. Stories must fit on one A4 page. Entries can be in any style or format and can be on any subject. The competition is open to writers from all countries, but entries must be written in English. Guidelines on Web site or by e-mail.

FISH SHORT STORY PRIZE

Fish Publishing, E-mail: info@fishpublishing.com. Web site: www.fishpublishing.com. **Contact:** Clem Cairns, editor. Purpose is to "find and publish new and exciting short fiction from all over the world; to support the short story and those who practice it." Offered annually for unpublished fiction mss. Prize: 1st Prize: 10,000 Euros (approx. $13,000); 2nd Prize: 1 week at Anam Cara Writers' Retreat in the west of Ireland plus 250 Euros; third prize is 250 Euros. The top 15 stories will be published in Fish's anthology, which is launched at the West Cork Literary Festival in June. Judged by a panel of international judges which changes every year. Entry fee: $30 per story. Guidelines available in July by e-mail, on Web site or in publication. Enter online at www.fishpubli shing.com. Deadline: November 30. Length: 5,000 words maximum. Open to any writer except those who have won before or who have been a runner-up twice. "Don't be afraid to write with your own voice. We value originality. Do make sure that your story is as good as you can get it. Don't try to please a judge or judges. Make sure it is neat and easy to read." Results announced March 17 every year. Winners notified by mail, phone or e-mail and at prize ceremony book launch in Bantry, County Cork, last Saturday in June. For contest results, e-mail, or visit Web site. See Web site for additional contests, including "One Page Story Prize," "Short Fiction Prize," "Short Histories Prize," and "Fish-Knife Award."

FLORIDA FIRST COAST WRITERS' FESTIVAL NOVEL, SHORT FICTION, PLAYWRITING & POETRY AWARDS

Writers' Festival & Florida Community College at Jacksonville, FCCJ North Campus, 4501 Capper Road, Jacksonville FL 32218-4499. (904)766-6559. Fax: (904)766-6654. E-mail: dathomas@fccj.edu or sturner@fccj.edu. Web site: www.fccj.edu/wf. **Contact:** Dr. Dana Thomas, festival contest director. Conference and contest "to create a healthy writing environment, honor writers of merit and find a novel manuscript to recommend to New York publishers for 'serious consideration." Judged by university faculty and freelance and professional writers. Entry fee: $39 (novels); $30 (plays); $15 (short fiction); $7 (poetry). Deadline: November 1 for novels, plays and short fiction; December 1 for poetry. Entries must be unpublished. Word length: no limit for novel; 6,000 words for short fiction; 30 lines for poetry. Open to any writer. Guidelines available on the Web site or in the fall for SASE. Accepts inquiries by fax and e-mail. "For stories and novels, make the opening pages sparkle. For plays, make them at least two acts and captivating. For poems, blow us over with imagery and insight and avoid clichés and wordiness." Results announced on the Web site and at FCCJ's Florida First Coast Writers' Festival held in the spring.

FLORIDA STATE WRITING COMPETITION

Florida Freelance Writers Association, P.O. Box A, North Stratford NH 03590-0167. (603)922-8338. E-mail: contest@writers-editors.com. Web site: www.writers-editors.com. **Contact:** Dana K. Cassell, executive director. Award "to offer additional opportunities for writers to earn income and recognition from their writing efforts." Prize: varies from $50-100. Categories: novels and short stories; also children's lit and nonfiction. Judged by authors, editors and librarians. Entry fee: $5-20. Deadline: March 15. Entries must be unpublished or self-published; except for one previously published nonfiction category. Open to any writer. Guidelines are revised each year and are subject to change. New guidelines are available in summer of each year. Accepts inquiries by e-mail. Results announced May 31. Winners notified by mail and posted on the Web site. For contest results, send SASE marked "winners" or visit Web site.

H.E. FRANCIS SHORT STORY AWARD

The Ruth Hindman Foundation, University of Alabama English Dept., Department of English, Huntsville AL 35899. E-mail: MaryH71997@aol.com. Web site: www.uah.edu/colleges/liberal/english/whatnewcontest.html. **Contact:** Patricia Sammon. Offered annually for unpublished work not to exceed 5,000 words. Acquires first-time publication rights. Prize: $1,000. Judged by a panel of nationally recognized, award-winning authors, directors of creative writing programs, and editors of literary journals. Entry fee: $15 reading fee (make check payable to the Ruth Hindman Foundation). Deadline: December 31.

GIVAL PRESS NOVEL AWARD

Gival Press LLC, P.O. Box 3812, Arlington VA 22203. (703)351-0079. E-mail: givalpress@yahoo.com. Web site: www.givalpress.com. **Contact:** Robert L. Giron, publisher. "To award the best literary novel." Annual. Prize: $3,000 (USD), publication and author's copies. Categories: literary novel. Receives about 60-80 entries per category. Final judge for 2006 was Don Berger. Entries read anonymously. Entry fee: $50 (USD). Make checks payable to Gival Press, LLC. Guidelines with SASE, by phone, by e-mail, on Web site, in journals. Accepts inquiries by e-mail. Deadline: May 30, 2008. Entries should be unpublished. Open to any author who writes original work in English. Length: 30,000-100,000 words. Cover letter should include name, address, phone, e-mail, word count, novel title. Only the title and word count should appear on the actual ms. Writers may submit own work. "Review the types of mss Gival Press has published. We stress literary works." Results announced late fall of same year. Winners notified by phone. Results made available to entrants with SASE, by e-mail, on Web site.

GIVAL PRESS SHORT STORY AWARD

Gival Press, P.O. Box 3812, Arlington VA 22203. (703)351-0079. E-mail: givalpress@yahoo.com. Web site: www.givalpress.com. **Contact:** Robert L. Giron, publisher. "To award the best literary short story." Annual. Prize: $1,000 and publication on Web site. Category: literary short story. Receives about 60-80 entries per category. Entries are judged anonymously. Entry fee: $25. Make checks payable to Gival Press, LLC. Guidelines available online, via e-mail, or by mail. Deadline: Aug. 8th of every year. Entries must be unpublished. Open to anyone who writes original short stories in English. Length: 5,000-10,000 words. Include name, address, phone, e-mail, word count, title on cover letter. Only the title and word count should be found on ms. Writers may submit their own ficiton. "We publish literary works." Results announced in the fall of the same year. Winners notified by phone. Results available with SASE, by e-mail, on Web site.

THE GLASGOW PRIZE FOR EMERGING WRITERS

Washington and Lee University/*Shenandoah*, Mattingly House, 2 Lee Ave., Lexington VA 24450-2116. (540)458-8765. Fax: (540)458-8461. E-mail: lleech@wlu.edu. Web site: shenandoah.wlu.edu **Contact:** Lynn Leech, managing editor. Award for writer with only one published book in genre being considered. (Genre rotates: 2007, poetry; 2008, creative nonfiction, 2009, short story.) Prize: $2,500, publication of new work in *Shenandoah*, and a reading at Washington and Lee University. Judged by anonymous writer/editor, announced after prize winner is selected. Entry fee: $22 (includes 1-yr subscription to *Shenandoah*; send credit card information or make checks payable to *Shenandoah*). To apply, send first book, one unpublished piece of work, SASE, and vita, along with check for $22 (from either author or publisher). Cover letter should include name, address, phone and e-mail. Books submitted for consideration will not be returned and will be donated to the University library after the contest. Guidelines available on Web site. Accepts inquiries by e-mail. Results announced on Web site and winners notified by mail or e-mail in May. Deadline: post-marked between March 15-31. Open to any writer.

◻ GLIMMER TRAIN'S FALL SHORT-STORY AWARD FOR NEW WRITERS

Glimmer Train Press, Inc., 1211 NW Glisan St., Suite 207, Portland OR 97209. (503)221-0836. Fax: (503)221-0837. Web site: www.glimmertrain.org. Offered for any writer whose fiction hasn't appeared in a nationally distributed publication with a circulation over 5,000. Word limit: 1,200-12,000 words. Contest open the month of November. Follow online submission procedure at www.glimmertrain.org. Notification on March 1. Prize: Winner receives $1,200, publication in *Glimmer Train Stories*, and 20 copies of that issue. First/second runners-up receive $500/$300, respectively. Entry fee: $15/story. Entries must be unpublished.

ℕ GLIMMER TRAIN'S FAMILY MATTERS (APRIL)

Glimmer Train Stories, 1211 NW Glisan St. Suite 207, Portland OR 97209. (503)221-0836. Fax: (503)221-0837. Web site: www.glimmertrain.org. Offered annually for unpublished stories about family. Prize: 1st place: $1,200, publication in *Glimmer Train Stories*, and 20 copies of that issue; 1st/2nd runners up receive $500/$300, respectively. Entry fee: $15. Submission period: April 1-April 30. Entries should be unpublished. Length: 12,000 words. Make your submissions online at www.glimmertrain.org. Winners will be notified and results will be posted on August 1.

ℕ GLIMMER TRAIN'S FAMILY MATTERS (OCTOBER)

Glimmer Train Stories, 1211 NW Glisan St. Suite 207, Portland OR 97209. (503)221-0836. Fax: (503)221-0837. Web site: www.glimmertrain.org. Offered annually for unpublished stories about family. Prize: 1st place: $1,200, publication in *Glimmer Train Stories*, and 20 copies of that issue; 1st/2nd runners up receive $500/$300, respectively. Max length: 12,000 words. Entry fee: $15. Submission period: October 1-31. Make your submissions online at www.glimmertrain.org. Winners will be notified and results will be posted on February 1.

◻ GLIMMER TRAIN'S SPRING SHORT-STORY AWARD FOR NEW WRITERS

Glimmer Train Press, Inc., 1211 NW Glisan St., Suite 207, Portland OR 97209. (503)221-0836. Fax: (503)221-0837. Web site: www.glimmertrain.org. Offered for any writer whose fiction hasn't appeared in a nationally distributed publication with a circulation over 5,000. Word limit: 1,200-12,000 words. Contest open the month of May. Follow online submission procedure at www.glimmertrain.org. Notification on September 1. Prize: Winner receives $1,200, publication in *Glimmer Train Stories*, and 20 copies of that issue. First/second runners-up receive $500/$300, respectively. Entry fee: $15/story. Entries must be unpublished.

◻ GLIMMER TRAIN'S SUMMER FICTION OPEN

Glimmer Train Press, Inc., 1211 NW Glisan St., Suite 207, Portland OR 97209. (503)221-0836. Fax: (503)221-0837. Web site: www.glimmertrain.org. Offered annually for unpublished stories as "a platform for all themes, all lengths (up to 2,000 words), all writers." Prize: 1st place: $2,000, publication in *Glimmer Train Stories*, and 20 copies of that issue; 2nd place: $1,000, and possible publication in *Glimmer Train Stories*; 3rd place: $600, and possible publication in *Glimmer Train Stories*. Entry fee: $20/story. Deadline: the month of June. Open to any writer. Make your submissions online at www.glimmertrain.org. Winners will be notified and results posted on October 1.

◻ GLIMMER TRAIN'S VERY SHORT FICTION SUMMER AWARD

Glimmer Train Press, Inc., 1211 NW Glisan St., Suite 207, Portland OR 97209. (503)221-0836. Fax: (503)221-0837. **Contact:** Linda Swanson-Davies, editor. Award to encourage the art of the very short story. "We want to read your original, unpublished, very short story (3,000 words or less)." Prize: $1,200 and publication in *Glimmer Train Stories* and 20 author's copies (1st place); $500; $300. Entry fee: $15 reading fee. Deadline: the month of August. Open to any writer. Make your submissions online at www.glimmertrain.org. Winners will be notified, and top 25 places will be posted by December 1.

◻ GLIMMER TRAIN'S VERY SHORT FICTION WINTER AWARD

Glimmer Train Press, Inc., 1211 NW Glisan St., Suite 207, Portland OR 97209. (503)221-0836. Fax: (503)221-0837. **Contact:** Linda Swanson-Davies. Award offered to encourage the art of the very short story. "We want to read your original, unpublished, very short story (3,000 words or less)." Prize: $1,200 and publication in *Glimmer Train Stories* and 20 author's copies (1st place); $500; $300. Entry fee: $15 reading fee. Deadline: the month of February. Open to any writer. Make your submissions online at www.glimmertrain. org. Winners will be notified, and top 25 places will be posted by June 1.

◖ GLIMMER TRAIN'S WINTER FICTION OPEN

Glimmer Train Press, Inc., 1211 NW Glisan St., Suite 207, Portland OR 97209. (503)221-0836. Fax: (503)221-0837. Web site: www.glimmertrain.org. Offered annually for unpublished stories "a platform for all themes, all lengths (up to 2,000 words), and all writers." Prize: 1st place: $2,000, publication in *Glimmer Train Stories*, and 20 copies of that issue; 2nd place: $1,000, possible publication in *Glimmer Train Stories*; 3rd place: $600, possible publication in *Glimmer Train Stories*. Entry fee: $20/story. Deadline: the month of December. Make your submissions online (www.glimmertrain.org). Winners will be notified and results posted on April 1.

⃞Ｎ GOLDENBERG PRIZE FOR FICTION

Bellevue Literary Review, NYU School of Medicine, 550 First Avenue, New York NY 10016. (212)263-3973. Fax: (212)263-3206. E-mail: info@blreview.org. Web site: www.blreview.org. **Contact:** Stacy Bodziak, Managing Editor. "Prize is created to honor outstanding writing related to themes of health, healing, illness, the mind and the body." Annual. Competition/award for short stories. Prize: $1,000 and publication in the Spring issue of *Bellevue Literary Review*. Fiction prizes have been judged by Ray Gonzalez (2006 prize) and Amy Hempel (2007 prize).Entry fee: $15. Send credit card information through Web site. Make checks payable to *Bellvue Litery Review*. Guidelines available in February. Accepts inquiries by e-mail, phone. Deadline is August. Entries should be unpublished. Length: Maximum 5,000 words. Writers may submit own work. Winners notified by e-mail. Winners announced November-December.

THE GOODHEART PRIZE FOR FICTION

Shenandoah: The Washington and Lee University Review, Mattingly House, 2 Lee Ave., Lexington VA 24450-2116. (540)458-8765. Fax: (540)458-8461. E-mail: shenandoah@wlu.edu. Web site: shenandoah.wlu.edu. **Contact:** Lynn Leech, managing editor. Awarded to best story published in *Shenandoah* during a volume year. Prize: $1,000. Judged by writer whose identity is revealed after the prize winner has been selected. No entry fee. All stories published in the review are automatically considered for the prize. Winners are notified by mail or e-mail each Spring. Results are available on Web site. "Read *Shenandoah* to familiarize yourself with the work we publish."

◖ THE GREAT BLUE BEACON SHORT-SHORT STORY CONTEST

The Great Blue Beacon: The Newsletter for Writers of All Genres and Skill Levels, 1425 Patriot Drive, Melbourne FL 32940-6881. (321)253-5869. E-mail: ajircc@juno.com. **Contact:** A.J. Byers, editor/publisher. Award to "recognize outstanding short-short stories." Prize: $50 (first prize), $25 (second prize), $10 (third prize) and publication of winning entry in *The Great Blue Beacon*. Judged by outside panel of judges. Entry fee: $5 ($4 for subscribers). Make checks out to A.J. Byers. Guidelines available periodically when announced. Length: 1,000 words or fewer. Cover letter and first page of ms should include name, address, phone, e-mail, word count and title. Deadline: TBA. Entries must be unpublished. Open to any writer. Two-three contests a year for short-short stories. Receives 50-75 entries per contest. For guidelines, send SASE or e-mail. Accepts inquiries by e-mail and phone. Results announced two months after contest deadline. Winners notified by SASE or e-mail. For contest results, send SASE or e-mail.

⃞ ◎ GREAT CANADIAN STORY CONTEST

Storyteller, Canada's Short Story Magazine, 3687 Twin Falls Place, Ottawa ON K1V 1W6 Canada. (613)822-9734. E-mail: info@storytellermagazine.com. Web site: www.storytellermagazine.com. **Contact:** Terry Tyo, publisher/managing editor. "Purpose of competition is to publish great Canadian stories. Stories must have a uniquely Canadian element (theme, setting, history, institution, politics, social phenomenon, etc.)." Prize: Varies from year to year. Short list determined by editors; readers choose from short list. Entry fee: $5 Canadian (make cheque or money order payable to TYO Communications). Deadline: sometime in mid-April every year. Entries must be unpublished. Canadian citizens or residents only. Guidelines available in February by SASE or on Web site. Length: 2,000-6,000 words. No simultaneous submissions or e-mail submissions. *Storyteller* cannot return mss unless accompanied by SASE. "Read the magazine. The short list comprises our summer issue, so all stories must be suitable for publication in *Storyteller* to qualify. Results announced on or around July 1st. Winners notified by phone or e-mail. For contest results, send SASE or visit Web site.

◖ GREAT LAKES COLLEGES ASSOCIATION NEW WRITERS AWARD

Great Lakes Colleges Association Inc., 535 W. William, Suite 301, Ann Arbor MI 48103. (734)661-2350. Fax: (734)661-2349. E-mail: shackelford@glca.org. **Contact:** Greg Wegner. Award for first publication in fiction or poetry. Writer must be nominated by publisher. Prize: Winners are invited to tour the GLCA colleges. An honorarium of $300 will be guaranteed the author by each GLCA member college they visit. Judged by professors from member colleges. No entry fee. Deadline: February 28. Open to any writer. Submit 4 copies of the book to Greg Wegner. Guidelines available after November 1. Accepts inquiries by fax and e-mail. Results announced in May. Letters go to publishers who have submitted.

GSU REVIEW WRITING CONTEST

GSU Review, Georgia State University, Campus Box 1894, MSC 8R0322, Unit 8, Atlanta GA 30303-3083. (404)651-4804. E-mail: gsu_review@langate.gsu.edu. Web site: www.review.gsu.edu. **Contact:** Christopher Bundy, editor. To promote quality work of emerging writers. Prize: Publication for finalists (up to 10 stories). $1,000 first prize; $250 second prize. Categories: fiction, poetry; receives more than 250 entries each. Judged by staff at *The Review* (finalists); 2006 winners were chosen by Dallas Hudgens (fiction) and Stephen Corey (poetry). Entry fee: $15, includes copy of Spring /Summer issue with contest results. Make checks payable to The GSU Review. Deadline: March 4. Entries must be unpublished. Length: should not exceed 7,500 words. Address fiction submissions to Jody Brooks, Fiction Editor; and poetry submissions to Jenny Sade-Orafai. Mss must be typed or letter-quality printed. On the first page of the ms include name, address, phone, e-mail, word count. Limit each submission to one short story. Guidelines available by SASE or on Web site. Contest open to all except faculty, staff, students of Georgia State University. US residents only. Winners notified by e-mail. "We look for engagement with language and characters we care about."

HAMMETT PRIZE

Internatonal Association of Crime Writers/North American Branch, P.O. Box 8674, New York NY 10116-8674. Fax: (815)361-1477. E-mail: mfrisque@igc.org. Web site: www.crimewritersna.org. **Contact:** Mary A. Frisque, executive director, North American Branch. Award established "to honor a work of literary excellence in the field of crime writing by a U.S. or Canadian author." Award for novels, story collections, nonfiction by one author. Prize: trophy. Judged by committee. "Our reading committee seeks suggestions from publishers and they also ask the membership for recommendations. Eligible books are read by a committee of members of the organization. The committee chooses five nominated books, which are then sent to three outside judges for a final selection. Judges are outside the crime writing field." No entry fee. For guidelines, send SASE or e-mail. Accepts inquiries by e-mail. Deadline: December 1. Entries must be previously published. To be eligible "the book must have been published in the U.S. or Canada during the calendar year." The author must be a U.S. or Canadian citizen or permanent resident. Nominations announced in January, winners announced in fall. Winners notified by mail, phone and recognized at awards ceremony. For contest results, send SASE or e-mail.

LORIAN HEMINGWAY SHORT STORY COMPETITION

P.O. Box 993, Key West FL 33041-0993. (305)294-0320. E-mail: calico2419@aol.com. Web site: www.shortstory competition.com. **Contact:** Carol Shaughnessy, co-director. Award to "encourage literary excellence and the efforts of writers who have not yet had major-market success." Competition for short stories. Prize: $1,000 (first prize), $500 (second prize), $500 (third prize), honorable mentions. Judged by a panel of writers, editors and literary scholars selected by author Lorian Hemingway. Guidelines available in January for SASE, by e-mail or on Web site. Accepts inquiries by SASE, e-mail or visit Web site. Deadline: May 15. Entries must be unpublished. Length: 3,000 words maximum. "Open to all writers whose work has not appeared in a nationally distributed publication with a circulation of 5,000 or more." Entry fee is $10 for each story postmarked by May 1, and $15 for stories postmarked between May 1 and May 15. "We look for excellence, pure and simple—no genre restrictions, no theme restrictions. We seek a writer's voice that cannot be ignored." Results announced at the end of July during Hemingway Days festival. Winners notified by phone prior to announcement. For contest results, send e-mail or visit Web site. "All entrants will receive a letter from Lorian Hemingway and a list of winners, via mail or e-mail, by October 1."

HIGHLIGHTS FOR CHILDREN FICTION CONTEST

Highlights for Children, 803 Church St., Honesdale PA 18431-1824. (570)253-1080. Fax: (570)251-7847. E-mail: eds@highlights-corp.com. Web site: www.highlights.com. **Contact:** Marileta Robinson, senior editor. Award "to honor quality stories (previously unpublished) for young readers and to encourage children's writers." Offered for stories for children ages 2-12; category varies each year. No crime or violence, please. Specify that ms is a contest entry. Prize: $1,000 to 3 winners, plus publication in *Highlights*. Categories: Short stories. Judged by *Highlights* editors, with input given by outside readers. No entry fee. "There is a different contest theme each year. We generally receive about 1,400 entries." Cover letter should include name, address, phone, e-mail, word count and title. "We prefer that these things appear on the first page of the manuscript as well." Deadline: January 1-February 28 (postmarked). Entries must be unpublished. Length: 500 words maximum for stories for beginning readers (to age 8) and 800 words for more advanced readers (ages 9-12). No minimum word count. Open to anyone 16 years of age or older. Results announced in June. Winners notified by mail or phone. For contest results, send SASE. See www.highlights.com for current theme and guidelines or send a SASE to *Highlights for Children*.

TONY HILLERMAN MYSTERY SHORT STORY CONTEST

Tony Hillerman Writers Conference and *Cowboys & Indians* magazine, 128 Grant Ave., Santa Fe NM 87501. E-mail: wordharvest@wordharvest.com. Web site: www.wordharvest.com. **Contact:** Anne Hillerman, contest administrator. "Purpose is to encourage mystery short stories set in the West or Southwest in the tradition of Tony Hillerman." Annual. Competition/award for short stories. Prize: $1,500 cash and publication in *Cowboys & Indians* magazine, a successful glossy national publication; signed Hillerman books; and tickets to the award banquet held in conjunction with the Tony Hillerman Writers Conference: Focus on Mystery in Albuqurque the first weekend of November. Category: mystery short story set in West or Southwest with at least one Native American or cowboy character. Receives about 260 entries per year. Entries are judged by a professional writer/editor with connections to both the conference and *Cowboys & Indians* magazine. Entry fee: $10; critiques available for $100. Make checks payable to Wordharvest. Guidelines available in June on Web site, in publication. Accepts inquiries by e-mail. Deadline: September 15, 2008. Entries should be unpublished. Open to all, as long as the entry is a previously unpublished mystery story that meets the guidelines. Length: 2,500 words. Cover letter should include name, address, phone, e-mail, word count, story title. Include only title on ms. Writers may submit own work. "Look at previous year's winner (published in March issue) for reference and info about the contest. Know that next year's winner must be different in terms of setting, plot and characters. Look at the magazine for info about the readers. Humor is a plus! Graphic sex, violence and four-letter words do not fit the magazine's tone." Winners notified by phone in October. Results made available to entrants on Web site.

TOM HOWARD/JOHN H. REID SHORT STORY CONTEST

Tom Howard Books, Mail to: Winning Writers, 351 Pleasant St., PMB 222, Northampton MA 01060-3961. (866)946-9748. Fax: (413)280-0539. E-mail: johnreid@mail.qango.com. Web site: www.winningwriters.com/tomstory. **Contact:** John H. Reid, award director. "Established in 1993, this award honors the best short stories, essays and other works of prose being written today." Annual. Prize: $1,200 (first prize), $800 (second prize), $400 (third prize). There will also be four High Distinction Awards of $200 each. The top ten entries will be published on the Winning Writers Web site and announced in Tom Howard Contest and News and the Winning Writers Newsletter. Categories: All entries are judged in one category. "We received 1,217 entries for the 2006 contest." Judged by a former journalist and magazine editor, John H. Reid. Mr. Reid has judged literary contests for over 15 years. He has published several novels, a collection of poetry, a guide to winning literary contests, and 15 books of film criticism and movie history. He is assisted by Dee C. Konrad, a leading educator and published author, who served as Associate Professor of English at Barat College of DePaul University and dean of Liberal Arts and Sciences for the year 2000-2001. Entry fee: $12 per entry. Make checks payable to Winning Writers. (U.S. funds only, please.) Guidelines available in Sept. on Web site. Prefers inquiries by e-mail. Deadline: March 31, 2008. "Both published and unpublished works are accepted. In the case of published work, the contestant must own the anthology and online publication rights." Open to all writers. Length: 5,000 words max per entry. Cover letter should include name, address, phone, e-mail, word count, story title, place(s) where story was previously published. Only the title should be on the actual ms. Writers may submit own work. "Read past winning entries at www.winningwriters.com/contests/tomstory/ts_pastwinners.php." Results announced May 15. Winners notified by e-mail. Results made available to entrants on Web site.

L. RON HUBBARD'S WRITERS OF THE FUTURE CONTEST

Author Services Inc., P.O. Box 1630, Los Angeles CA 90078. (323)466-3310. Fax: (323)466-6474. E-mail: contests@authorservicesinc.com. Web site: www.writersofthefuture.com. **Contact:** Judy, contest administrator. Established in 1983. Foremost competition for new and amateur writers of unpublished science fiction or fantasy short stories or novelettes. Offered "to find, reward and publicize new speculative fiction writers so they may more easily attain professional writing careers." Open to new and amateur writers who have not professionally published a novel or short novel, more than 1 novelette, or more than 3 short stories. Eligible entries are previously unpublished short stories or novelettes (under 17,000 words) of science fiction or fantasy. Guidelines for SASE or on Web site. Accepts inquiries by fax, e-mail, phone. Prize: awards quarterly: 1st place: $1,000; 2nd place: $750; and 3rd place: $500. Annual grand prize: $5,000. "Contest has four quarters. There shall be 3 cash prizes in each quarter. In addition, at the end of the year, the 4 first-place, quarterly winners will have their entries rejudged, and a grand prize winner shall be determined." Judged by K.D. Wentworth (initial judge), then by a panel of 4 professional authors. Deadline: December 31, March 31, June 30, September 30. Entries must be unpublished. Limit one entry per quarter. No entry fee; entrants retain all rights to their stories. Open to any writer. Manuscripts: white paper, black ink; double-spaced; typed; each page appropriately numbered with title, no author name. Include cover page with author's name, address, phone number, e-mail address (if available), as well as estimated word count and the title of the work. Results announced quarterly in e-newsletter. Winners notified by phone.

◎ INDIANA REVIEW ½ K (SHORT-SHORT/PROSE-POEM) CONTEST

Indiana Review, Ballantine Hall 465/Indiana University, 1020 E. Kirkwood Ave., Bloomington IN 47405-7103. (812)855-3439. Fax: (812)855-4253. E-mail: inreview@indiana.edu. Web site: www.indiana.edu/~inreview. **Contact:** Abdel Shakur, editor. Competition for fiction and prose poems no longer than 500 words. Prize: $1,000 plus publication, contributor's copies and a year's subscription. All entries considered for publication. Judged by *Indiana Review* staff and outside judges. Entry fee: $15 fee for no more than 3 pieces (includes a year's subscription, two issues). Make checks payable to *Indiana Review*. Deadline: June 8. Entries must be unpublished. Guidelines available in March for SASE, by phone, e-mail, on Web site, or in publication. Length: 500 words, 3 mss per entry. Open to any writer. Cover letter should include name, address, phone, e-mail, word count and title. No identifying information on ms. "We look for command of language and form." Results announced in August. Winners notified by mail. For contest results, send SASE or visit Web site.

☐ INDIANA REVIEW FICTION CONTEST

Indiana Review, BH 465/Indiana University, 1020 E. Kirkwood Ave., Bloomington IN 47405-7103. (812)855-3439. Fax: (812)855-4253. E-mail: inreview@indiana.edu. Web site: www.indiana.edu/~inreview. **Contact:** Tracy Truels, editor. Contest for fiction in any style and on any subject. Prize: $1,000, publication in the *Indiana Review* and contributor's copies. Judged by *Indiana Review* staff and outside judges. Entry fee: $15 fee (includes a year's subscription). Deadline: Mid-October. Entries must be unpublished. Mss will not be returned. No previously published work, or works forthcoming elsewhere, are eligible. Simultaneous submissions accepted, but in the event of entrant withdrawal, contest fee will not be refunded. Length: 15,000 words (about 40 pages) maximum, double spaced. Open to any writer. Cover letter must include name, address, phone number and title of story. Entrant's name should appear only in the cover letter, as all entries will be considered anonymously. Results announced January. Winners notified by mail. For contest results, send SASE. "We look for a command of language and structure, as well as a facility with compelling and unusual subject matter. It's a good idea to obtain copies of issues featuring past winners to get a more concrete idea of what we are looking for."

◎ INDIVIDUAL ARTIST FELLOWSHIP/MINI FELLOWSHIP

Kansas Arts Commission, 700 SW Jackson St., Suite 1004, Topeka KS 66603-3761. (785)296-3335. Fax: (785)296-4989. E-mail: kac@arts.state.ks.us. Web site: www.arts.state.ks.us. **Contact:** Tom Klocke, program consultant. "Awards are based on artistic merit and recognize sustained achievement and excellence." Fellowships awarded every other year in fiction, poetry and playwriting. Prize: $5,000 for fellowship; $500 for mini-fellowship. Judged by Kansas professionals in the field—generally, the panel meets in January. No entry fee. Deadline: October 13, 2008. Entries may be previously published or unpublished; do not submit work completed prior to 2001. Open to Kansas residents only. Undergraduate or graduate degree-seeking students are ineligible. Guidelines on Web site. Accepts inquiries by fax, e-mail, phone. Length: 30 pages mss for fiction and playwriting; 20 pages/mss for poetry. Competition receives 40-50 fellowship submissions; 10-15 mini-fellowship submissions. "Follow guidelines for application explicitly." Results announced in February each year. Winners notified by mail or phone.

◎ THE IOWA SHORT FICTION AWARD

Iowa Writers' Workshop, 102 Dey House, 507 N. Clinton St., Iowa City IA 52242-1000. (319)335-2000. Fax: (319)335-2055. Web site: www.uiowapress.org. **Contact:** Holly Carver, director. Award "to give exposure to promising writers who have not yet published a book of prose." Prize: publication by University of Iowa Press. Judged by Senior Iowa Writers' Workshop members who screen manuscripts; published fiction author of note makes final selections. No entry fee. Submission period: Aug. 1-Sept. 30. Entries must be unpublished, but stories previously published in periodicals are eligible for inclusion. "The manuscript must be a collection of short stories of at least 150 word-processed, double-spaced pages." Open to any writer. No application forms are necessary. Do not send original ms. Include SASE for return of ms. Announcement of winners made early in year following competition. Winners notified by phone.

☐ ◎ JOSEPH HENRY JACKSON AWARD

The San Francisco Foundation, Administered by Intersection for the Arts, 446 Valencia St., San Francisco CA 94103. (415)626-2787. Fax: (415)626-1636. Web site: www.theintersection.org. **Contact:** Kevin B. Chen, program director. Award "to encourage young, unpublished writers." Offered annually for unpublished, work-in-progress fiction (novel or short story), nonfiction or poetry by an author age 20-35, with 3-year consecutive residency in northern California or Nevada prior to submission. Prize: $2,000 and certificate. Categories: short stories, novels and short story collections, and poetry. No entry fee. Deadline: March 31. Entries must be unpublished. Work cannot exceed 40 double-spaced, typed pages. Entry form and rules available in mid-January for SASE. "Submit a serious, ambitious portion of a book-length manuscript." Results announced September. Winners will be announced in letter mailed to all applicants.

🔷 ◎ EZRA JACK KEATS/KERLAN COLLECTION MEMORIAL FELLOWSHIP

Ezra Jack Keats Foundation, University of Minnesota, 113 Andersen Library, 222 21st Ave. S., Minneapolis MN 55455. (612)624-4576. Fax: (612)625-5525. E-mail: clrc@tc.umn.edu. Web site: special.lib.umn.edu/clrc/. Competition for books of children's literature. Purpose is "to award a talented writer and/or illustrator of children's books who wishes to use Kerlan Collection for the furtherance of his or her artistic development. Special consideration will be given to someone who would find it difficult to finance the visit to the Kerlan Collection." Open to any writer and illustrator. Prize: $1,500 for travel to study at Kerlan Collection. Judged by panel of non-Kerlan Collection staff, area professionals, educators, etc. The Ezra Jack Keats Fellowship recipient will receive transportation costs and a per diem allotment. Applications for 2009 must be postmarked by December 30, 2008. For digital application materials, please visit http://special.lib.umn.edu/clrc/kerlan/awards.php. For paper copies of the application, send a large (6×9 or 9×12) self- addressed, $.87 postaged envelope.

🔵 E.M. KOEPPEL SHORT FICTION AWARD

Writecorner Press, P.O. Box 140310, Gainesville FL 32614-0310. Web site: www.writecorner.com. **Contact:** Mary Sue Koeppel, editor. Award for short stories. Prize: $1,100 first prize, and $100 for Editors' Choices. Judged by award-winning writers. Entry fee: $15 first story, $10 each additional story. Make checks payable to Writecorner Press. Send 2 title pages: One with title only and one with title, name, address, phone, e-mail, short bio. Place no other identification of the author on the ms that will be used in the judging. Guidelines available for SASE or on Web site. Accepts inquiries by e-mail and phone. Expects 300+ entries. Deadline: October 1-April 30. Entries must be unpublished. Open to any writer. Results announced in Summer. Winners notified by mail, phone in July (or earlier). For results, send SASE or check Web site.

🅽 LA BELLE LETTRE PROSE CONTEST

La Belle Lettre, 2122 S. Silver Lake Rd., Castle Rock WA 98611. E-mail: admin@labellelettre.com. Web site: www.labellelettre.com. **Contact:** Jennifer Hill, executive director. "La Belle Lettre's mission is to provide encouragement and support to writers. We aim to be a bridge to authors' literary accomplishments." Seasonal. Competition/award for short stories. Prize: 1st prize is $150 + critique; 2nd prize is $75 + critique; 3rd prize is $50 + critique; honorable mention recieves a critique. Seasonal contest categories vary from fiction/nonfiction, romance, mystery, children's, memoir/essay, to flash fiction. Entries are judged by La Belle Lettre staff who have been previously published, teach writing workshops, and have won multiple writing contests. Currently those judges are Jennifer Hill and Mary Stone. Entry fee: $8. Make checks payable to La Belle Lettere. Accepts inquiries by e-mail. Deadlines are as follows: Winter Romance Contest: February; Spring Children's Short Story: May; Summer Memoir/Personal Essay: August; Fall Holiday Fiction/Non-Fiction: November. Cover letter should include name, address, phone, e-mail, word count, novel/story title. "La Belle Lettre is looking for stories that reflect a strong point of view, vivid descriptions, and a story that from the begining draws readers into the adventure. Characters must be believable and linger in the judges' thoughts long after they put down the manuscript." Winners notified by mail. Results made available to entrants with SASE, by e-mail, on Web site.

🔷 ◎ THE LAWRENCE FOUNDATION AWARD

Prairie Schooner, 201 Andrews Hall, P.O. Box 880334, Lincoln NE 68588-0334. (402)472-0911. Fax: (402)472-9771. E-mail: kgrey2@unl.edu. Web site: http://prairieschooner.unl.edu. **Contact:** Hilda Raz, editor-in-chief. Offered annually for the best short story published in *Prairie Schooner* in the previous year. Prize: $1,000. Judged by editorial staff of *Praire Schooner*. No entry fee. Only work published in *Prairie Schooner* in the previous year is considered. Work is nominated by editorial staff. Results announced in the Spring issue. Winners notified by mail in February or March.

◎ LAWRENCE FOUNDATION PRIZE

Michigan Quarterly Review, 3574 Rackham Building, Ann Arbor MI 48109-1070. (734)764-9265. E-mail: mqr@u mich.edu. Web site: www.umich.edu/~mqr. **Contact:** Vicki Lawrence, managing editor. Competition for short stories. Prize: $1,000. Judged by editorial board. No entry fee. No deadline. "An annual cash prize awarded to the author of the best short story published in *Michigan Quarterly Review* each year. Stories must be already published in *Michigan Quarterly Review*. This is not a competition in which manuscripts are read outside of the normal submission process." Guidelines available for SASE or on Web site. Accepts inquires by e-mail and phone. Results announced in December. Winners notified by phone or mail.

🔷 ◎ STEPHEN LEACOCK MEMORIAL MEDAL FOR HUMOUR

Stephen Leacock Association, Box 854, Orrillia ON L3V 6K8 Canada. (705)835-3218 or (705)835-3408. Fax: (705)835-5171 or (705)835-3689. E-mail: drapson@encode.com or wayne@rural-roots.com. Web site: www.lea cock.com. **Contact:** Judith Rapson, award chair. Award for humorous writing by a Canadian, given in memory of Stephen B. Leacock, Canada's best-known writer of humorous fiction. Prize: silver medal and $10,000 given by TD Financial Group. Categories: novels, short story collections, drama, poetry, translations. Judged by five judges from across Canada, plus a local reading committee which has one vote. Entry fee: $100; make checks payable to Stephen Leacock Association. Entry must be a book published in the year prior to the presentation of the award and must be accompanied by a short biographical sketch and photograph of the author. Cover letter should include publisher's name, address, e-mail and name of contact person. Deadline: December 31. Authors must be Canadian citizens or landed immigrants; no more than two authors permitted for any given entry. Guidelines available in August for fax or on Web site. Book may be nominated by author or publisher. Books are judged primarily on humorous content but also on literary merit and general appeal. Results announced in April at luncheon in Orillia; winner required to attend Award Dinner in Orillia in June and deliver address. Results available for SASE, by fax, e-mail or on Web site.

LITERAL LATTÉ FICTION AWARD

Literal Latté, 200 East 10th Street Suite 240, New York NY 10003. (212)260-5532. E-mail: litlatte@aol.com. Web site: www.literal-latte.com. **Contact:** Edward Estlin, contributing editor. Award "to provide talented writers with three essential tools for continued success: money, publication and recognition." Offered annually for unpublished fiction. Guidelines for SASE or on Web site. Open to any writer. Prize: $1,000 and publication in *Literal Latté* (first prize), $300 (second prize), $200 (third prize), up to 7 honorable mentions. Judged by the editors. Entry fee: $10/story. Guidelines available for SASE, by e-mail or on Web site. Accepts inquiries by e-mail. Deadline: January 15. Entries must be unpublished. Length: 6,000 words maximum. Guidelines available for SASE, by e-mail or on Web site. Accepts inquiries by e-mail or on Web site. "The first-prize story in the first annual *Literal Latté* Fiction Awards has been honored with a Pushcart Prize." Winners notified by phone. List of winners available in late April for SASE or by e-mail.

⊕ ◻ LONG STORY CONTEST, INTERNATIONAL

White Eagle Coffee Store Press, P.O. Box 383, Fox River Grove IL 60021. (847)639-9200. E-mail: wecspress@aol.com. Web site: http://members.aol.com/wecspress. **Contact:** Frank E. Smith, publisher. Offered annually since 1993 for unpublished work to recognize and promote long short stories of 8,000-14,000 words (about 30-50 pages). Sample of previous winner: $5.95, including postage. Open to any writer, no restrictions on materials. Prize: (A.E. Coppard Prize) $500 and publication, plus 25 copies of chapbook; 40 additional copies sent to agents; and 10 press kits. Categories: No limits on style or subject matter. Entry fee: $15 fee, $10 for second story in same envelope. Guidelines available in April by SASE, e-mail or on Web site. Accepts inquiries by e-mail. Length: 8,000-14,000 words (30-50 pages double-spaced) single story; may have multiparts or be a self-contained novel segment. Deadline: December 15. Accepts previously unpublished submissions, but previous publication of small parts with acknowledgment is okay. Simultaneous submissions okay. Send cover with name, address, phone; second title page with title only. Submissions are not returned; they are recycled. "SASE for most current information." Results announced in late spring. Winners notified by phone. For contest results, send SASE or visit Web site in late spring. "Write with richness and depth."

◎ THE HUGH J. LUKE AWARD

Prairie Schooner, 201 Andrews Hall, P.O. Box 880334, Lincoln NE 68588-0334. (402)472-0911. Fax: (402)472-9771. E-mail: kgrey2@unl.edu. Web site: prairieschooner.unl.edu/ **Contact:** Hilda Raz, editor-in-chief. Offered annually for work published in *Prairie Schooner* in the previous year. Prize: $250. Judged by editorial staff of *Prairie Schooner*. No entry fee. Only work published in *Prairie Schooner* in the previous year is considered. Work is nominated by the editorial staff. Guidelines for SASE or on Web site. Results announced in the Spring issue. Winners notified by mail in February or March.

Ⓝ LUMINA

Sara Lawrence College, Sara Lawrence College Slonim House 1 Mead Way, Bronxville NY 10708. E-mail: lumina @slc.edu. Web site: http://pages.slc.edu/ ~ lumina/contest.html. **Contact:** Lani Scozzari, director. "We accept submissions from anyone who is not a Sarah Lawrence student. We are seeking short unpublished fiction, up to 5,000 words." Annual. Competition/award for short stories. Prize: First prize: $500; Second prize: $100; Third prize: $50. Plus publication and 2 copies of the journal. Initial reading done by Sarah Lawrence College MFA candidates and final decision to be made by Margot Livesey. Entry fee: $10. Cover letter should include e-mail.

⊕ ◎ MARSH AWARD FOR CHILDREN'S LITERATURE IN TRANSLATION

Marsh Christian Trust, Roehampton University, Froebel College, Roehampton Lane, London England SW15 5PJ United Kingdom. E-mail: G.Lathey@roehampton.ac.uk. **Contact:** Dr. Gillian Lathey. Award "to promote the publication of translated children's books in the UK." Biennial award for children's book translations. Judged by Patricia Crampton, Caroline Horn, Wendy Cooling, Elizabeth Hammill. No entry fee. Entries must be previously published. Entries should be translations into English first published in the UK. Entries must be nominated by publishers. Open to any writer. Guidelines available for SASE. Cover letter should include name, address, phone, e-mail and title. Accepts inquiries by e-mail. Results announced in January. Winners notified by mail and at presentation event.

◎ WALTER RUMSEY MARVIN GRANT

Ohioana Library Association, 274 E. First Ave., Suite 300, Columbus OH 43201. (614)466-3831. Fax: (614)728-6974. E-mail: ohioana@sloma.state.oh.us. Web site: www.ohioana.org. **Contact:** Linda Hengst. Award ''to encourage young, unpublished writers 30 years of age or younger.'' Competition for short stories. Prize: $1,000. No entry fee. Up to 6 pieces of prose may be submitted; maximum 60 pages, minimum 10 pages double-spaced, 12-point type. Deadline: January 31. Entries must be unpublished. Open to unpublished authors born in Ohio or who have lived in Ohio for a minimum of five years. Must be 30 years of age or younger. Guidelines for SASE. Winner notified in May or June. Award given in October.

◘ MASTERS LITERARY AWARDS

Titan Press, P.O. Box 17897, Encino CA 91416-7897. Web site: www.calwrierstv.com. Offered annually and quarterly for work published within 2 years (preferred) and unpublished work (accepted). Fiction, 15-page maximum; poetry, 5 pages or 150-lines maximum; and nonfiction, 10 pages maximum. ''A selection of winning entries may appear in our national literary publication.'' Winners may also appear on the Internet. Titan Press retains one-time publishing rights to selected winners. Prize: $1,000, and possible publication in the *Titan Press Internet* journal. Judged by 3 literary professionals. Entry fee: $15. Deadline: Ongoing (nominations made March 15, June 15, September 15, December 15). Any submission received prior to an award date is eligible for the subsequent award. Submissions accepted throughout the year. All entries must be in the English language. Guidelines for #10 SASE. ''Be persistent, be consistent, be professional.''

◎ THE JOHN H. MCGINNIS MEMORIAL AWARD

Southwest Review, P.O. Box 750374, Dallas TX 75275-0374. (214)768-1037. Fax: (214)768-1408. E-mail: swr@mail.smu.edu. Web site: www.southwestreview.org. **Contact:** Jennifer Cranfill, managing editor. Award for short fiction and nonfiction. Prize: $500. Judged by *Southwest Review*'s editor in chief and managing editor. No entry fee. Stories or essays must have been published in the *Southwest Review* prior to the announcement of the award. Pieces are not submitted directly for the award but for publication in the magazine. Open to any writer. Guidelines available for SASE and on Web site. Results announced in first issue of the year. Winners notified in January by mail, phone and e-mail.

◎ MEMPHIS MAGAZINE FICTION AWARDS

Memphis Magazine, P.O. Box 1738, Memphis TN 38101. (901)521-9000. E-mail: sadler@memphismagazine.com. Web site: www.memphismagazine.com. **Contact:** Marilyn Sadler, senior editor/contest coordinator. Annual. Competition/award for short stories. Prize: $1,000 grand prize and publication in *Memphis*; two $500 honorable mention awards. Judged by a panel of five, all with fiction writing experience and publications. Entry fee: $10/story. Guidelines available in April by phone, on Web site, in publication. Accepts inquiries by fax, e-mail, phone. Deadline: Aug. 1. Entries should be unpublished. ''Manuscripts may be previously published as long as previous publication was not in a national magazine with over 20,000 circulation or in a regional publication within Shelby County.'' Open to all authors who live within 150 miles of Memphis. Length: 3,000-4,500 words. Cover letter should include name, address, phone, story title. Do not put your name anywhere on the ms itself. Writers may submit own work. ''Each story should be typed, double-spaced, with unstapled, numbered pages. Stories are not required to have a Memphis or Southern theme, but we do want a compelling story and first-rate writing.'' Winners contacted in late September.

◎ MICHIGAN LITERARY FICTION AWARDS

University of Michigan Press, 839 Greene St., Ann Arbor MI 48104. Fax: (734)615-1540. E-mail: ump.fiction@umich.edu. Web site: www.press.umich.edu/fiction. Award to ''attract the work of writers of literary fiction looking for, and deserving, a second chance.'' Prize: $1,000 advance and publication. Categories: novels. No entry fee. Guidelines for SASE or on Web site. Accepts inquiries by e-mail. Deadline: July 1. Entries must be unpublished. Contest open to writers who have previously published at least one book-length work of literary fiction novel or story collection. Cover letter should include name, address, phone, e-mail and title; title only on every page of ms. Results announced in November. Winners notified by mail. For contest results, send SASE or visit Web site.

◎ A MIDSUMMER TALE

E-mail: editors@toasted-cheese.com. Web site: www.toasted-cheese.com. **Contact:** Theryn Fleming, editor. A Midsummer Tale is a summer-themed creative nonfiction contest. Topic changes each year. Check Web site for current focus and word limit. "We usually receive around 20 entries." Prize: First prize: $20 Amazon gift certificate, publication; Second prize: $15 Amazon gift certificate, publication; Third prize: $10 Amazon gift certificate, publication. Some feedback is often given to entrants. Categories: creative nonfiction. Judged by two Toasted Cheese editors who blind-judge each contest. Each judge has her own criteria for selecting winners. No entry fee. Guidelines, including the e-mail address to which you should send your entry and instructions for what to include and how to format, are available May 1 on Web site. Accepts inquiries by e-mail. Deadline: June 21. Entries must be unpublished. Open to any writer. Results announced July 31 on Web site. Winners notified by e-mail.

☻ MILKWEED EDITIONS NATIONAL FICTION PRIZE

Milkweed Editions, 1011 Washington Ave. S., Suite 300, Minneapolis MN 55415. (612)332-3192. Fax: (612)215-2550. E-mail: editor@milkweed.org. Web site: www.milkweed.org. **Contact:** The Editors. Annual award for unpublished works. "We are looking for a novel, novella, or a collection of short stories. Manuscripts should be of high literary quality and must be double-spaced and between 150-400 pages in length. Writers who need their work returned must include a SAS book mailer. Manuscripts not accompanied by a SAS book mailer will be recycled." Winner will be chosen from the mss Milkweed accepts for publication each year. All mss submitted to Milkweed will automatically be considered for the prize. Submission directly to the contest is no longer necessary. "Manuscript must be written in English. Writers should have previously published a book of fiction or 3 short stories (or novellas) in magazines/journals with national distribution." Catalog available on request for $1.50. Guidelines for SASE or online. Prize: Publication by Milkweed Editions, and a cash advance of $5,000 against royalties agreed upon in the contractual arrangement negotiated at the time of acceptance. Judged by Milkweed Editions. No entry fee. Deadline: rolling, but 2007 winner chosen by October 2006. Entries must be unpublished. "Please look at previous winners: *Visigoth*, by Gary Amdahl; *Crossing Bully Creek*, by Margaret Erhart; *Roofwalker*, by Susan Power; *Hell's Bottom, Colorado* by Laura Pritchett—this is the caliber of fiction we are searching for." Winners are notified by phone and announced in November.

◎ MILLION WRITERS AWARD

StorySouth, 898 Chelsea Ave., Columbus OH 43209. (614)545-0754. E-mail: storysouth@yahoo.com. Web site: www.storysouth.com. **Contact:** Jason Sanford, editor. Contest "to honor and promote the best fiction published annually in online journals and magazines. The reason for the Million Writers Award is that most of the major literary prizes for short fiction (such as the O. Henry Awards) ignore Web-published fiction. This award aims to show that world-class fiction is being published online and to promote this fiction to the larger reading and literary community." Prize: Cash prize and publicity for the author and story. Categories: short stories. Judged by *StorySouth* judges. No entry fee. Cover letter should include e-mail address, word count, title and publication where story was previously published. Guidelines available in December on Web site. Deadline: January. Entries must be previously published. All stories must be 1,000 words or longer. Open to any writer. Results announced in March on Web site. Winners notified by e-mail.

◎ THE MILTON CENTER POSTGRADUATE FELLOWSHIP

The Milton Center at *Image*, 3307 Third Ave. West, Seattle WA 98119. (206)281-2988. E-mail: miltoncenter@imagejournal.org. Web site: www.imagejournal.org/milton. **Contact:** Gregory Wolfe, director. Award "to bring emerging writers of Christian commitment to the Center, where their primary goal is to complete their first book-length manuscript in fiction, poetry or creative nonfiction." $25 application fee. Guidelines on Web site. Deadline: March 15. Open to any writer.

◖ THE MISSOURI REVIEW EDITORS' PRIZE CONTEST

Missouri Review, 1507 Hillcrest Hall, Columbia MO 65211. (573)882-4474. Fax: (573)884-4671. Web site: www.missourireview.org. **Contact:** Richard Sowienski, managing editor. Prize: $3,000 for fiction, poetry, essay and publication in *The Missouri Review*. Judged by *The Missouri Review* editors. Entry fee: $20; make checks payable to *Missouri Review*. Each fee entitles entrant to a one-year subscription to the journal, an extension of a current subscription, or a gift subscription. Guidelines and inquiries accepted on Web site. Expects to receive 1,800 entries. Deadline: October 1. Entries must be unpublished. Page length restrictions: 25 typed, double-spaced for fiction and essays; 10 for poetry. Open to any writer. Guidelines available in June for SASE. Outside of envelope should be marked "fiction" or "essay" or "poetry." On first page of submission include the author's name, address, e-mail address and telephone number. Results announced in January. Winners notified by phone and mail. For contest results, send SASE. "Send only fully realized work with a distinctive voice, style and subject."

⊞ ◎ BRIAN MOORE SHORT STORY AWARDS

Creative Writers Network, 109-113 Royal Ave., Belfast 6T1 1FF Ireland. E-mail: info@creativewritersnetwork.org. Web site: www.creativewritersnetwork.org. **Contact:** Administrator. Award to promote the short story form.

Prize: £500, £300, £200. Judged by established UK fiction writer. Entry fee: £5. Deadline: January 31, 2008. Entries must be unpublished. Open to writers born in Northern Ireland. Guidelines available in August/September 2007 by e-mail or on Web site. Accepts inquiries by e-mail. Results announced in April/May 2008. Winners notified by mail in March. List of winners available on Web site.

⚡ ◎ MUNICIPAL CHAPTER OF TORONTO IODE JEAN THROOP BOOK AWARD

Municipal Chapter of Toronto IODE (Imperial Order of the Daughters of the Empire), 40 St. Clair Ave., Suite 200, Toronto ON M4T 1M9 Canada. (416)925-5078. Fax: (416)925-5127. **Contact:** Jennifer Werry, education officer. To acknowledge authors and/or illustrators in the Greater Toronto Area. Prize: $1,000 to author and/or illustrator. Categories: short stories, novels, story collections. Judged by committee comprised of IODE education officer, president and other officers (approx. 5). No entry fee. Accepts inquiries by fax, phone. Cover letter should include name, address, phone, e-mail, title, place of original publication. Deadline: Nov. 1. Entries must be previously published. Open to books geared toward 6-12 year olds. Must be Canadian citizens. Authors/illustrators may submit their own work. "Submit books directly to the attention of Theo Heras at the Lillian Smith Library, Toronto. She compiles submissions and short lists them." Results announced in February and available by fax. Award given at annual dinner meeting in March.

◻ NATIONAL WRITERS ASSOCIATION NOVEL WRITING CONTEST

The National Writers Association, 10940 S. Parker Rd #508, Parker CO 80134. (303)841-0246. Fax: (303)841-2607. E-mail: contests@nationalwriters.com. Web site: www.nationalwriters.com. **Contact:** Sandy Whelchel, director. Annual contest "to help develop creative skills, to recognize and reward outstanding ability, and to increase the opportunity for the marketing and subsequent publication of novel manuscripts." Prize: 1st place: $500; 2nd place: $300; 3rd place: $200. Judges' evaluation sheets sent to each entry with SASE. Categories: Open to any genre or category. Judged by editors and agents. Entry fee: $35. Deadline: April 1. Entries must be unpublished. Length: 20,000-100,000 words. Open to any writer. Entry form and information available on Benefits section of Web site.

◻ NATIONAL WRITERS ASSOCIATION SHORT STORY CONTEST

The National Writers Association, 10940 S. Parker Rd. #508, Parker CO 80134. (303)841-0246. Fax: (303)841-2607. E-mail: contests@nationalwriters.com. Web site: www.nationalwriters.com. **Contact:** Sandy Whelchel, director. Annual contest "to encourage writers in this creative form and to recognize those who excel in fiction writing." Prize: 1st place: $200; 2nd place: $100; 3rd place: $50. Entry fee: $15. Deadline: postmarked by July 1. Entries must be unpublished. Length: 5,000 words maximum. Entry form and information available in January on Benefits section of Web site. Accepts inquiries by fax, phone and e-mail. Evaluation sheets sent to each entrant if SASE is provided. Results announced at the NWAF Summer Conference in June. Winners notified by phone or e-mail. List of winners available in *Authorship* or on Web site.

◻ ◎ NEVADA ARTS COUNCIL ARTIST FELLOWSHIPS

716 N. Carson St., Suite A, Carson City NV 89701. (702)687-6680. Fax: (775)687-6688. Web site: www.nevadaculture.org. **Contact:** Fran Morrow, artist service coordinator. Award "to honor Nevada individual artists and their artistic achievements and to support artists' efforts in advancing their careers." Prize: $5,000 ($4,500 immediately and $500 after public service event completed). Categories: fiction, nonfiction, poetry, playwriting and writing for children. Judged by peer panels of professional artists. No entry fee. Deadline: April. Open to Nevada residents only. Guidelines available by phone, e-mail or on Web site. Results announced in June. Winners notified by mail and phone. Entrants receive list of recipients. "Inquire about jackpot grants for Nevada residents' projects, up to $1,000."

◻ NEW ENGLAND WRITERS SHORT FICTION CONTEST

New England Writers, P.O. Box 5, Windsor VT 05089-0005. (802)674-2315. E-mail: newvtpoet@aol.com. Web site: www.newenglandwriters.org. **Contact:** Susan Anthony, director. Annual competition for short stories for publication in *The Anthology of New England Writers*. Prize: $300 Marjory Bartlett Sanger Award. Final judges are published writers and usually creative writing professors. Entry fee: $5/story (unlimited entries allowed). Send disposable mss. Length: 1,000 word limit. Deadline: postmarked by June 15. Entries must be unpublished. Open to any writer. Guidelines available for SASE or on Web site by January. Please send a 3×5 card with name, address and title(s) of fiction pieces with entry. Accepts inquiries by e-mail, phone. Results announced at annual New England Writers Conference in July. Winners notified right after conference. For contest results, visit Web site. "Strive for originality taken from your own life experience. We look for creative, concise work with an unexpected ending."

☐ NEW LETTERS LITERARY AWARDS

New Letters, 5101 Rockhill Rd., Kansas City MO 64110-2499. (816)235-1168. Fax: (816)235-2611. E-mail: newletters@umkc.edu. Web site: www.newletters.org. Award to "find and reward good writing from writers who need the recognition and support." Award has 3 categories (fiction, poetry and creative nonfiction) with 1 winner in each. Offered annually for previously unpublished work. Prize: 1st place: $1,500, plus publication; all entries are considered for publication. Judged by 2 rounds of regional writers (preliminary judging). Winners picked by an anonymous judge of national repute. Entry fee: $15/entry (includes year's subscription). Make checks payable to *New Letters* or send credit card information. Deadline: May 18. Entries must be unpublished. Open to any writer. Guidelines available in January for SASE, e-mail, on Web site and in publication. Cover letter should include name, address, phone, e-mail and title. Results announced in September. Winners notified by phone. For contest results, send SASE, e-mail or visit Web site.

☐ NEW MILLENNIUM WRITING AWARDS

New Millennium Writings, Room M2, P.O. Box 2463, Knoxville TN 37901. (423)428-0389. Fax: (865)428-2302. E-mail: DonWilliams7@charter.net. Web site: www.newmillenniumwritings.com/awards.html. **Contact:** Don Williams, editor. Award "to promote literary excellence in contemporary fiction." Offered twice annually for unpublished fiction, poetry, essays or nonfiction prose to encourage new fiction writers, poets and essayists and bring them to attention of publishing industry. Entrants receive an issue of *NMW* in which winners appear. Prize: $1,000 (fiction, poetry, nonfiction and short-short fiction, 1,000 words or less); winners published in *NMW* and on Web site. Judged by novelists and short story writers. Entry fee: $17 for each submission. Deadline: November 17 and June 17. Entries must be unpublished. Biannual competition. Length: 1,000-6,000 words. Guidelines available year round for SASE and on Web site at www.writingawards.com. "Provide a bold, yet organic opening line, sustain the voice and mood throughout, tell an entertaining and vital story with a strong ending. *New Millennium Writings* is a forward-looking periodical for writers and lovers of good reading. It is filled with outstanding poetry, fiction, essays and other speculations on subjects both topical and timeless about life in our astonishing times. Our pages brim with prize-winning essays, humor, full-page illustration, writing advice and poetry from writers at all stages of their careers. First-timers find their work displayed alongside such well-known writers as Shel Silverstein, Khaled Hosseini, Ted Kooser, Lucille Clifton, John Updike, Sharyn McCrumb, Lee Smith, Norman Mailer, Madison Smartt Bell and Cormac McCarthy." Results announced October and April. Winners notified by mail and phone. All entrants will receive a list of winners, plus a copy of the annual anthology. Send letter-sized SASE with entry for list.

☑ ◎ JOHN NEWBERY AWARD

American Library Association (ALA), Association for Library Service to Children, 50 E. Huron St., Chicago IL 60611. (312)280-2163. Fax: (312)944-7671. E-mail: alsc@ala.org. Web site: www.ala.org/alsc. **Contact:** ALSC, Attn: Newbery Medal. Prize: Medal. Judged by Newbery Award Selection Committee. No entry fee. Deadline: December 31. Entries must be previously published. Only books for children published in the U.S. during the preceeding year are eligible. Entry restricted to U.S. citizens, residents. Guidelines available on Web site, by fax, phone or e-mail. Accepts inquiries by fax and e-mail. Results announced at the ALA Midwinter Meeting. Winners notified by phone. For contest results, visit Web site in February or contact via phone, fax, e-mail or SASE.

⊕ ☑ ◎ THE NOMA AWARD FOR PUBLISHING IN AFRICA

P.O. Box 128, Witney, Oxon OX8 5XU. United Kingdom. E-mail: maryljay@aol.com. Web site: www.nomaaward.org. **Contact:** Mary Jay. Sponsored by Kodansha Ltd. Award "to encourage publication of works by African writers and scholars in Africa, instead of abroad as is still too often the case at present." Categories: scholarly or academic; books for children; literature and creative writing, including fiction, drama and poetry. Judged by a committee of African scholars and book experts and representatives of the international book community. Chairman: Walter Bgoya. No entry fee. Deadline: March 31. Entries must be previously published. Guidelines and entry forms available in December by fax, e-mail or on Web site. Submissions are through publishers only. "Publisher must complete entry form and supply six copies of the published work." Maximum number of entries per publisher is three. Results announced in October. Winners notified through publisher. List of winners available from Secretariat or on Web site. "The award is for an outstanding book. Content is the overriding criterion, but standards of publication are also taken into account."

◎ NORTH CAROLINA ARTS COUNCIL WRITERS' RESIDENCIES

109 E. Jones St., Raleigh NC 27601. (919)807-6512. Fax: (919)807-6532. E-mail: debbie.mcgill@ncmail.net. Web site: www.ncarts.org. **Contact:** Deborah McGill, literature director. Awards encourage and recognize North Carolina's finest creative writers. Every year we offer a 2-month residency for 1 writer at Headlands Center for the Arts (California) and a 1-month residency for 1 writer at Vermont Studio Center. Judged by panels of writers and editors convened by the residency centers. No entry fee. Deadline: early June; see Web site for details.

Writers must be over 18 years old, not currently enrolled in a degree-granting program on undergraduate or graduate level, must have been a resident of North Carolina for 1 full year as of application deadline and must plan to remain a resident for the following year. Please see Web site for other eligibility requirements. Guidelines available after March 1 by phone or online. Accepts inquiries by fax and e-mail. Results announced in the fall. Winners notified by phone. Other applicants notified by mail.

NORTHERN CALIFORNIA BOOK AWARDS

Northern California Book Reviewers Association, % Poetry Flash, 1450 Fourth St. #4, Berkeley CA 94710. (510)525-5476. Fax: (510)525-6752. E-mail: editor@poetryflash.org. Web site: www.poetryflash.org. **Contact:** Joyce Jenkins, executive director. "Award is to celebrate books published by Northern California authors in poetry, fiction, nonfiction, translation and children's literature." Annual. Competition/award for novels, story collections, translations. Prize: awards publicity from a professional publicist, $100 gift certificate, and reading at awards ceremony. Awards $1,000 for lifetime achievement award. Categories: novels and short story collections. Judged by members of the association, active book reviewers, and book editors. No entry fee. Deadline: Dec. 1 for books published in that calendar year. Entries should be previously published. Open to authors living in Northern California. Winners announced in April. Results made available to entrants with SASE, by fax, by e-mail, on Web site.

NOVEL MANUSCRIPT CONTEST

Writers' League of Texas, 1501 W. 5th St., #E-2, Austin TX 78703. (512)499-8914. Fax: (512)499-0441. E-mail: wlt@writersleague.org. Web site: www.writersleague.org. **Contact:** Kristy Bordine. Prize: First place winners meet individually with an agent at the Writers' League of Texas Agents Conference in June. Categories: mainstream fiction, mystery, thriller/action adventure, romance, science fiction/fantasy/horror, historical/western, narrative nonfiction, and children's long and short works. Judged by preliminary judges (first round), then agent or editor reads finalists' ms. Entry fee: $50 for score sheet with comments. Send credit card information or make check payable to Writer's League of Texas. Cover letter should include name, address, phone, e-mail, title. Entries must be unpublished. Submit first 10 pages of novel, double-spaced. Open to any writer. Guidelines available in January for by e-mail or on Web site. Accepts inquiries by e-mail. Results announced at the June conference. Results available on Web site.

NOVELLO LITERARY AWARD

Novello Festival Press, 310 N. Tryon St., Charlotte NC 28202. (704)432-0153. Web site: www.novellopress.org. **Contact:** A. Rogers, executive editor. "To recognize a writer of a book-length work of literary fiction or nonfiction who resides in North Carolina or South Carolina." Annual. Competition/award for novels, story collections. Prize: $1,000 advance against royalties, publication, national distribution of the winning book. Categories: Literary fiction/nonfiction (including novel, short story collection, memoir, biography, history). Receives about 100 entries per year. Judged by the editor(s), staff, advisory committee of the press, and others in the literary arts community whom they may designate. No entry fee. Guidelines available in Nov. on Web site and in regional writers resources. Submission period: Nov.-May 1. Entries should be unpublished. "Portions may be previously published (e.g. a short story within a collection)." Open to writers over the age of 18 who reside in NC or SC. Length: 200-400 pages, typed and double-spaced. Cover letter should include name, address, phone, e-mail, word count, novel/collection title. Identifying information may or may not be included on the actual ms; "this is not a blind competition." Writers may submit own work. No agent submissions. "Do not send genre fiction, poetry, or work for children. Literary fiction and/or literary nonfiction only." Results announced Oct. during The Novello Festival of Reading. Winners notified by mail, by phone. Winners announced Oct. Results made available to entrants on Web site.

THE FLANNERY O'CONNOR AWARD FOR SHORT FICTION

The University of Georgia Press, 330 Research Dr., Athens GA 30602-4901. Web site: www.ugapress.uga.edu. **Contact:** Andrew Berzanskis, coordinator. Does not return mss. Manuscripts must be 50,000-75,000 words (which is approximately 200-275 pages long). Authors do not have to be previously published. Prize: $1,000 and publication under standard book contract; selects two prize winners a year. Categories: Wants collections of short stories. Stories that have previously appeared in magazines or in anthologies may be included. Collections that include long stories or novellas (50-150 pages) are acceptable. However, novels or single novellas will not be considered. Stories previously published in a book-length collection of the author's own work may not be included. Entry fee: $20; checks payable to University of Georgia Press. Complete submission guidelines online. Submission Period: April 1-May 31. Open to all writers in English. "Manuscripts under consideration for this competition may be submitted elsewhere at the same time. Please notify us immediately, however, if your manuscript is accepted by another publisher while it is under review with our press. Authors may submit more than one manuscript to the competition as long as each submission is accompanied by a $20 entry fee, meets all eligibility requirements, and does not duplicate material sent to us in another manuscript." Winners are usually notified before the end of November. Entrants who have enclosed an SASE will receive a letter announcing the winners.

◎ FRANK O'CONNOR FICTION AWARD

descant, Texas Christian University, TCU Box 297270, Fort Worth TX 76129. (817)257-6537. Fax: (817)257-6239. E-mail: descant@tcu.edu. Web site: www.descant.tcu.edu. **Contact:** David Kuhne, editor. Annual award to honor the best published fiction in *descant* for its current volume. Prize: $500. No entry fee. Guidelines available for SASE or on Web site. Deadline: April 1. Entries must be previously published. Results announced in August. Winners notified by phone in July. For contest results, send SASE. Also offers the Gary Wilson Award for short fiction. Prize: $250. Send SASE for guidelines.

◎ (ALICE WOOD MEMORIAL) OHIOANA AWARD FOR CHILDREN'S LITERATURE

Ohioana Library Association, 274 E. First Ave., Suite 300, Columbus OH 43201. (614)466-3831. Fax: (614)728-6974. E-mail: ohioana@sloma.state.oh.us. Web site: www.ohioana.org. **Contact:** Linda Hengst, executive director. Offered to an author whose body of work has made, and continues to make, a significant contribution to literature for children or young adults and through their work as a writer, teacher, or administrator, or through their community service, interest in children's literature has been encouraged and children have become involved with reading. Nomination forms for SASE. Recipient must have been born in Ohio or lived in Ohio at least 5 years. Prize: $1,000. No entry fee. Deadline: December 31. Guidelines for SASE. Accepts inquiries by fax and e-mail. Results announced in August or September. Winners notified by letter in May. For contest results, call or e-mail.

⊠ ◎ OHIOANA BOOK AWARDS

Ohioana Library Association, 274 E. 1st Ave., Suite 300, Columbus OH 43201-3673. (614)466-3831. Fax: (614)728-6974. E-mail: ohioana@sloma.state.oh.us. Web site: www.ohioana.org. **Contact:** Linda Hengst, executive director. Offered annually to bring national attention to Ohio authors and their books, published in the last 2 years. (Books can only be considered once.) Categories: Fiction, nonfiction, juvenile, poetry, and books about Ohio or an Ohioan. Writers must have been born in Ohio or lived in Ohio for at least 5 years, but books about Ohio or an Ohioan need not be written by an Ohioan. Prize: certificate and glass sculpture. Judged by a jury selected by librarians, book reviewers, writers and other knowledgeable people. Each Spring the jury considers all books received since the previous jury. No entry fee. Deadline: December 31. Two copies of the book must be received by the Ohioana Library by December 31 prior to the year the award is given; literary quality of the book must be outstanding. No entry forms are needed, but they are available July 1 of each year. "We will be glad to answer letters or e-mails asking specific questions." Results announced in August or September. Winners notified by mail in May.

◯ OPEN WINDOWS

Ghost Road Press, 5303 E. Evans Ave. #309, Denver CO 80222. (303)758-7623. Fax: (303)671-5664. E-mail: info@ghostroadpress.com. Web site: ghostroadpress.com. **Contact:** Sonya Unrein, editor. This anthology series showcases new and established voices in poetry, fiction and creative nonfiction. The 2005 edition was a finalist for the Coloradio Book Award. Prizes: $500 + 4 copies for best story, creative nonfiction piece, and poem; 3 copies for 2nd prize; 2 copies for 3rd prize (9 winners total). Categories will be judged separatedly. The contest submission period is April 1 to June 30, 2007. (See Web site for 2008 dates.) Winners will be announced on September 15 on our Web site. Please do NOT send a SASE. There are two ways to enter. Send a labeled CD-ROM or an e-mail attachment (preferred) with the following items: The work(s) in a Word document with the title of the piece on every page in the right-hand corner—no author info on the work itself—double-spaced; a cover sheet with author name, address, phone number, and working e-mail address. The cover sheet should include a 30-40 word bio. If you are sending more than one poem, each poem should appear on its own page, as it should appear in its printed form. No 3.5 floppy disks; CDs only. For e-mail, please use an appropriate subject line, such as "Open Windows contest entry." You may pay submission fee (1 story or essay, up to 3 poems per $15) by check or online with Paypal on our Web site. No entries will be processed until payment is received.

◯ ORANGE BLOSSOM FICTION CONTEST

The Oak, 1530 Seventh St., Rock Island IL 61201. (309)788-3980. **Contact:** Betty Mowery, editor. Award "to build up circulation of publication and give new authors a chance for competition and publication along with seasoned writers." Prize: subscription to *The Oak*. Categories: short fiction. Judged by published authors. Entry fee: six 41¢ stamps. Deadline: April 1. "May be on any subject, but avoid gore and killing of humans or animals." Open to any writer. Guidelines available for SASE. Prefers name, address, contest deadline and title on ms; no cover letter. Guidelines for other contests available for SASE. "No reply will be made without SASE."

Results announced a week after deadline. Winners notified by mail. "Material is judged on content and tightness of writing as well as word lengths, since there is a 500-word limit. Always include a SASE with submissions. Entries without six 41¢ stamps will not be judged."

PATERSON FICTION PRIZE

The Poetry Center at Passaic County Community College, One College Blvd., Paterson NJ 07505-1179. (973)684-6555. Fax: (973)523-6085. E-mail: mgillan@pccc.edu. Web site: www.pccc.edu/poetry. **Contact:** Maria Mazziotti Gillan, executive director. Award "to encourage recognition of high-quality writing." Offered annually for a novel or collection of short fiction published the previous calendar year. Prize: $1,000. Judges rotate each year. No entry fee. Deadline: Submissions accepted after January 10. Open to any writer. Guidelines available for SASE, e-mail or on Web site. Accepts inquiries by e-mail or phone. Results announced in July. Winners notified by mail. For contest results, send SASE or visit Web site.

PEARL SHORT STORY PRIZE

*Pearl*Magazine, 3030 E. Second St., Long Beach CA 90803-5163. (562)434-4523. E-mail: Pearlmag@aol.com. Web site: www.pearlmag.com. **Contact:** Marilyn Johnson, fiction editor. Award to "provide a larger forum and help widen publishing opportunities for fiction writers in the small press and to help support the continuing publication of *Pearl*." Prize: $250, publication in *Pearl* and 10 copies of the journal. Judged by the editors of *Pearl*: Marilyn Johnson, Joan Jobe Smith, Barbara Hauk. Entry fee: $10/story. Include a brief bio and SASE for reply or return of mss. Accepts simultaneous submissions, but asks to be notified if story is accepted elsewhere. Submission period: April 1-May 31(postmark). Entries must be unpublished. "Although we are open to all types of fiction, we look most favorably on coherent, well-crafted narratives containing interesting, believable characters in meaningful situations." Length: 4,000 words maximum. Open to any writer. Guidelines for SASE or on Web site. Accepts queries by e-mail or fax. Results announced in September. Winners notified by mail. For contest results, send SASE, e-mail or visit Web site.

WILLIAM PEDEN PRIZE IN FICTION

The Missouri Review, 1507 Hillcrest Hall, Columbia MO 65211. (573)882-4474. Fax: (573)884-4671. Web site: www.missourireview.com. **Contact:** Speer Morgan. Offered annually "for the best story published in the past volume year of the magazine. All stories published in *The Missouri Review* are automatically considered." Prize: $1,000, and reading/reception. No entry fee. Submissions must have been previously published in the volume year for which the prize is awarded. No application process: All fiction published in *The Missouri Review* is automatically entered.

PEN CENTER USA ANNUAL LITERARY AWARDS

PEN Center USA, %Antioch University Los Angeles, 400 Corporate Pointe, Culver City CA 91030. (310)862-1555 ext. 361. Fax: (310)862-1556. E-mail: awards@penusa.org. Web site: www.penusa.org. Offered annually for fiction, creative nonfiction, poetry, children's/young adult literature, or translation published January 1-December 31 of 2007. Prize: $1,000 and honored at a ceremony in Los Angeles. Judged by panel of writers, editors and critics. Entry fee: $35. Guidelines available in July for SASE, fax, e-mail or on Web site. Accepts inquiries by fax, phone and e-mail. All entries must include 4 non-returnable copies of each submission and a completed entry form. Deadline: December 14. Entries must be professionally published or produced. Open to authors west of the Mississippi River, including all of Minnesota and Louisiana. Results announced in summer. Winners notified by phone and mail. For contest results, send SASE or visit Web site.

POCKETS FICTION-WRITING CONTEST

Upper Room Publications, 1908 Grand Ave. AV, P.O. Box 340004, Nashville TN 37203-0004. (615)340-7333. Fax: (615)340-7267. E-mail: pockets@upperroom.org. Web site: www.pockets.org. *Pockets* is a devotional magazine for children between the ages of 6 and 11. Contest offered annually for unpublished work to discover new children's writers. Prize: $1,000 and publication in *Pockets*. Categories: short stories. Judged by *Pockets* staff and staff of other Upper Room Publications. No entry fee. Guidelines available for #10 SASE or on Web site. Deadline: Must be postmarked between March 1-August 15. Entries must be unpublished. Because the purpose of the contest is to discover new writers, previous winners are not eligible. No violence, science fiction, romance, fantasy or talking animal stories. Word length 1,000-1,600 words. Open to any writer. Winner announced November 1 and notified by U.S. mail. Contest submissions accompanied by SASE will be returned Nov. 1. "Send SASE with 4 first-class stamps to request guidelines and a past issue, or go to www.pockets.org."

KATHERINE ANNE PORTER PRIZE IN SHORT FICTION

The University of North Texas Press, Dept. of English, P.O. Box 311307, Denton TX 76203. (940)565-2142. Fax: (940)565-4590. E-mail: kdevinney@unt.edu. Web site: www.unt.edu/untpress. **Contact:** Karen DeVinney, managing editor. "Purpose is to encourage and promote short fiction." Annual. Competition/award for story collections. Prize: $1,000 and publication by UNT Press. Categories: short fiction, which may be a combination of short-shorts, short stories and novellas. A single novella alone will not be accepted. Judged by anonymous judge (2006 was Dan Chaon). Entry fee: $20. Make checks payable to UNT Press. Guidelines available in Jan. with SASE, by fax, by phone, by e-mail, on Web site, in publication. Accepts inquiries by fax, e-mail, phone. Submission period: July & August. Entries should be unpublished. "Unpublished and previously published stories, or a combination of both, are accepted; however, the submitted collection itself must be unpublished. If a portion is previously published, permissions are needed." Open to all. Length: 27,500-50,000 words. Cover letter should include name, address, phone, e-mail, word count, novel/story title, place(s) where story or stories were previously published. None of this information should appear on the actual manuscript. Writers may submit own work. "Simply follow the rules and do your best." Results announced in January. Winners notified by mail, by phone, by e-mail. Results made available to entrants with SASE, by fax, by e-mail, on Web site.

⒩ POSTROMANTIC POETRY AND SHORT STORY

2537 Hawthorne Way, Saline MI 48176. (734)944-7742. E-mail: postromanticism@aol.com. Web site: http://postromanticism.com. **Contact:** Claudia Moscovici, director. "Postromanticism began as a movement in art—painting and sculpture—and we would like to expand it to poetry and fiction. The purpose of the contest is to find and publish on postromanticism.com, the official Web site of the postromantic movement, quality poetry and short fiction that fits with our vision and complements the postromantic art. For short story contest, our standards are broad. We're looking for good writing that focuses on important aspects of the human condition—love, family, suffering. We're not seeking genre fiction or experimental fiction. We invite entries for mainstream writing with a lyrical feel, fresh outlook, interesting, believable characters and engaging plot." Competition/award for short stories. Prize: The first prize winner wins $100 and online publication of his or her short story on the official Web site of the postromantic movement, postromanticism.com. We will also publish online the fifteen most appropriate poems and ten most appropriate short stories for each of our two annual contests (October 15 and March 15). Entries are judged based on the quality of the writing and the compatibility of the writing and style with the ideals of the postromantic movement. Entry fee: $10. Make checks payable to Claudia Moscovici, Postromanticism.org. Guidelines available in January. Accepts inquiries by e-mail. Entries should be unpublished. Length: 3,000 word maximum. Cover letter should include name, address, phone, e-mail, word count, novel/story title. "Look at postromanticism.com before you submit to get a sense of what this movement is about. Ultimately, however, you'll be judged by similar standards to those used by literary agents and mainstream publishers: a compelling plot, believable and engaging characters, elegant prose. Touches of humor can also add a lot to a short story. Please include SASE if you desire a reply by mail or your submission returned." Winners notified by mail, e-mail.

⒩ PRAIRIE SCHOONER BOOK PRIZE SERIES

Prairie Schooner, 201 Andrews Hall, PO Box 880334, Lincoln NE 68588-0334. Web site: http://prairieschooner.unl.edu. **Contact:** Attn: Fiction. Annual. Competition/award for story collections. Prize: $3,000 and publication through the University of Nebraska Press for one book of short fiction and one book of poetry; one runner-up in each category will receive a $1,000 prize. Entry fee: $25. Make checks payable to *Prairie Schooner*. Deadline: Submissions were accepted between January 15 and March 15 for 2007 contest; check Web site for 2008 dates. Entries should be unpublished. Send full manuscript (the author's name should not appear anywhere on the ms). Send two cover pages: one listing only the title of the ms, and the other listing the title, author's name, address, telephone number, and e-mail address. Send SASE for notification of results. All mss will be recycled. You may also send an optional SAS postcard for confirmation of receipt of ms. Winners notified by phone, by e-mail. Results made available to entrants on Web site, in publication.

◎ PRAIRIE SCHOONER GLENNA LUSCHEI AWARDS

Prairie Schooner, 201 Andrews Hall, P.O. Box 880334, Lincoln NE 68588-0334. (402)472-0911. Fax: (402)472-9771. E-mail: kgrey@unl.edu. Web site: www.unl.edu/schooner/psmain.htm. **Contact:** Hilda Raz, editor-in-chief. Awards to honor work published the previous year in *Prairie Schooner*, including poetry, essays and fiction. Prize: $250 in each category. Judged by editorial staff of *Prairie Schooner*. No entry fee. For guidelines, send SASE or visit Web site. "Only work published in *Prairie Schooner* in the previous year is considered." Work nominated by the editorial staff. Results announced in the Spring issue. Winners notified by mail in February or March.

◎ PUSHCART PRIZE

Pushcart Press, P.O. Box 380, Wainscott NY 11975. (516)324-9300. Web site: www.pushcartprize.com. **Contact:** Bill Henderson, president. Award to "publish and recognize the best of small press literary work." Prize: Publication in *Pushcart Prize: Best of the Small Presses* anthology. Categories: short stories, poetry, essays on any subject. No entry fee. Deadline: December 1. Entries must be previously published. Must have been published during the current calendar year. Open to any writer. Nomination by small press publishers/editors only.

QUEBEC WRITERS' FEDERATION BOOK AWARDS

Quebec Writers' Federation, 1200 Atwater, Montreal QC H3Z 1X4 Canada. (514)933-0878. E-mail: admin@qwf.org. Web site: www.qwf.org. **Contact:** Lori Schubert, executive director. Award "to honor excellence in writing in English in Quebec." Prize: $2,000 (Canadian) in each category. Categories: fiction, poetry, nonfiction, first book and translation. Each prize judged by panel of 3 jurors, different each year. $20 entry fee. Guidelines for submissions sent to Canadian publishers and posted on Web site in March. Accepts inquiries by e-mail. Deadline: May 31, August 15. Entries must be previously published. Length: must be more than 48 pages. "Writer must have resided in Quebec for 3 of the previous 5 years." Books may be published anywhere. Winners announced in November at Annual Awards Gala and posted on Web site.

DAVID RAFFELOCK AWARD FOR PUBLISHING EXCELLENCE

National Writers Association, 10940 S. Parker Rd. #508, Parker CO 80134. (303)841-0246. Fax: (303)841-2607. E-mail: contests@nationalwriters.com. Web site: www.nationalwriters.com. **Contact:** Sandy Whelchel, executive director. Award to "assist published authors in marketing their work and promoting them." Prize: publicity tour, including airfare, and services of a publicist (valued at $5,000). Categories: novels and short story collections. Judged by publishers and agents. Entry fee: $100. Deadline: May 1. Published works only. Open to any writer. Guidelines for SASE, by e-mail or on Web site. Winners announced in June at the NWAF conference and notified by mail or phone. List of winners available for SASE or visit Web site.

SIR WALTER RALEIGH AWARD

North Carolina Literary and Historical Association, 4610 Mail Service Center, Raleigh NC 27699-4610. (919)807-7290. Fax: (919)733-8807. **Contact:** Michael Hill, awards coordinator. "To promote among the people of North Carolina an interest in their own literature." Prize: statue of Sir Walter Raleigh. Categories: novels and short story collections. Judged by university English and history professors. No entry fee. Guidelines available in August for SASE. Accepts inquiries by fax. Deadline: July 15. Entries must be previously published. Book must be an original work published during the 12 months ending June 30 of the year for which the award is given. Writer must be a legal or physical resident of North Carolina for the 3 years preceding the close of the contest period. Authors or publishers may submit 3 copies of their book to the above address. Results announced in October. Winners notified by mail. For contest results, send SASE.

RANDOM HOUSE, INC. CREATIVE WRITING COMPETITION

Random House Inc., 1745 Broadway, New York NY 10019. (212)782-8319. Fax: (212)940-7590. E-mail: worldofexpression@randomhouse.com. Web site: www.worldofexpression.org. **Contact:** Melanie Fallon Hauska, director. Offered annually for unpublished work to NYC public high school seniors. Three categories: poetry, fiction/drama and personal essay. Prize: 72 awards given in literary (3) and nonliterary (2) categories. Awards range from $500-10,000. Categories: short stories and poems. Judged by various city officials, executives, authors, editors. No entry fee. Guidelines available in October on Web site and in publication. Deadline: February 1. Entries must be unpublished. Word length: 2,500 words or less. Applicants must be seniors (under age 21) at a New York high school. No college essays or class assignments will be accepted. Results announced mid-May. Winners notified by mail and phone. For contest results, send SASE, fax, e-mail or visit Web site.

THE REA AWARD FOR THE SHORT STORY

Dungannon Foundation, 53 W. Church Hill Rd., Washington CT 06794. Web site: www.reaaward.org. **Contact:** Elizabeth Rea, president. "Sponsored by the Dungannon Foundation, the Rea Award was established in 1986 by Michael M. Rea to honor a living U.S. or Canadian writer who has made a significant contribution to the short story form." Prize: $30,000. Categories: short stories. Judged by 3 jurors (2006 jurors were Ann Beattie, Richard Ford, and Joyce Carol Oates). No entry fee. Award cannot be applied for. The recipient is selected by an annually appointed jury. Award announced in fall annually. List of winners available on Web site. 2006 winner was John Updike.

THE RED HOUSE CHILDREN'S BOOK AWARD

(formerly The Children's Book Award), Federation of Children's Book Groups, The Old Malt House, Aldbourne, Marlborough, Wiltshire SN8 2DW United Kingdom. E-mail: marianneadey@aol.com. Web site: www.redhousechildrensbookaward.co.uk. **Contact:** Marianne Adey, national coordinator. Purpose of award is "to find out what children choose among books of fiction published in the United Kingdom." Prize: silver bowl, portfolio of children's letters and pictures. Categories: Books for Younger Children, Books for Younger Readers, Books for Older Children. No entry fee. Deadline: Closing date is Dec. 31. Entries must be previously published. UK authors only. Either author or publisher may nominate title. Guidelines available on Web site. Accepts inquiries by fax, e-mail and phone. Results announced in June for books published the previous year. Winners notified at event/banquet and via the publisher. For contest results, visit Web site.

HAROLD U. RIBALOW AWARD

Hadassah Magazine, 50 W. 58th St., New York NY 10019. (212)451-6289. Fax: (212)451-6257. E-mail: tblunt@h adassah.org. **Contact:** Tom Blunt, Ribalow Prize Coordinator. Offered annually for English-language books of fiction (novel or short stories) on a Jewish theme published the previous calendar year. Books should be submitted by the publisher. "Harold U. Ribalow was a noted writer and editor who devoted his time to the discovery and encouragement of young Jewish writers." Prize: $3,000 and excerpt of book in *Hadassah Magazine*. No entry fee. Deadline: March 1. Book should have been published the year preceding the award.

THE SCARS/CC&D EDITOR'S CHOICE AWARDS

Scars Publications and Design, 829 Brian Court, Gurnee IL 60031-3155. E-mail: editors@scars.tv. Web site: http://scars.tv. **Contact:** Janet Kuypers, editor/publisher. Award "to showcase good writing in an annual book." Prize: publication of story/essay and 1 copy of the book. Categories: short stories. Entry fee: $18/short story. Deadline: revolves for appearing in different upcoming books as winners. Entries may be unpublished or previously published. Open to any writer. For guidelines, visit Web site. Accepts inquiries by e-mail. Length: "We appreciate shorter works. Shorter stories, more vivid and more real storylines in writing have a good chance." Results announced at book publication, online. Winners notified by mail when book is printed. For contest results, send SASE or e-mail or look at the contest page at Web site."

SCIENCE FICTION WRITERS OF EARTH (SFWOE) SHORT STORY CONTEST

Science Fiction Writers of Earth, P.O. Box 121293, Fort Worth TX 76121-1293. E-mail: sfwoe@flash.net. Web site: www.flash.net/~sfwoe. **Contact:** Gilbert Gordon Reis, SFWoE administrator. Award to "promote the art of science fiction/fantasy short story writing." Prize: $200, $100, $50, $25. Also $75 paid to place the winning story on the SFWoE Web Site for 180 days. Categories: short story. Judged by author Edward Bryant. Entry fee: $5 for membership and first entry; $2 each for additional entries (make checks payable to SFWoE). Cover letter or entry form from Web site should include name, address, phone, e-mail address, word count and title. Same information should appear on ms title page. Deadline: October 30. Entries must be unpublished. The author must not have received payment for a published piece of fiction. Stories should be science fiction or fantasy, 2,000-7,500 words. Guidelines available for SASE, e-mail or on Web site. Accepts inquiries by e-mail and mail. "Visit our Web site and read the winning stories. Read our online newsletter to know what the judge looks for in a good story. Contestants enjoy international competition." Results announced after January 31. Winners notified by mail, phone or e-mail. "Each contestant is mailed the contest results, judge's report, and a listing of the top 10 contestants." Send separate SASE for complete list of the contest stories and contestants (or print from Web site).

SCRIPTAPALOOZA TELEVISION WRITING COMPETITION

7775 Sunset Blvd., PMB #200, Hollywood CA 90046. (323)654-5809. E-mail: info@scriptapalooza.com. Web site: www.scriptapaloozatv.com. "Seeking talented writers who have an interest in American television writing." Prize: $500 to top winner in each category (total $1,500), production company consideration. Categories: sitcoms, pilots, one-hour dramas and reality shows. Entry fee: $40; accepts Paypal credit card or make checks payable to Scriptapalooza. Deadline: April 15 and November 15 of each year. Entries must be unpublished. Length: standard television format whether one hour, one-half hour or pilot. Open to any writer 18 or older. Guidelines available now for SASE or on Web Site. Accepts inquiries by e-mail, phone. "Pilots should be fresh and new and easy to visualize. Spec scripts should stay current with the shows, up-to-date story lines, characters, etc." Winners announced February 15 and August 15. For contest results, visit Web Site.

MICHAEL SHAARA AWARD FOR EXCELLENCE IN CIVIL WAR FICTION

Civil War Institute at Gettysburg College, 300 North Washington Street, Campus Box 435, Gettysburg, PA 17325 (717)337-6590. Fax: (717)337-6596. E-mail: civilwar@gettysburg.edu. Web site: http://www.gettysburg.edu/civilwar. Contact: Tina Grim. Offered annually for fiction published January 1-December 31 "to encourage examination of the Civil War from unique perspectives or by taking an unusual approach." All Civil War novels are eligible. Nominations should be made by publishers, but authors and critics can nominate as well. Prize: $5,000, which includes travel stipend. No entry fee. Deadline: December 31. Entries must be previously published. "Judged for presentation of unique perspective, use of unusual approach; effective writing; contribution to existing body of Civil War literature. Competition open to authors of Civil War novels published for the first time in the year designated by the award (i.e. for 2007 award, only novels published in 2007 are eligible). Guidelines available on Web site. Accepts inquiries by fax, e-mail, and phone. Cover letter should include name, address, phone, e-mail, and title. Need 10 copies of novel. "Enter well before deadline." Results announced in Spring. Winners notified by phone. For contest results, visit Web site.

SHORT GRAIN WRITING CONTEST

Grain Magazine, Box 67, Saskatoon SK S7K 3K1 Canada. (306)244-2828. Fax: (306)244-0255. E-mail: grainmag @sasktel.net. Web site: www.grainmagazine.ca. **Contact:** Kent Bruyneel. Competition for postcard (flash) fiction, prose poems, dramatic monologues, nonfiction. Prize: 3 prizes of $500 in each category, plus publication. Entry fee: $ 30 fee for 2 entries in any additional categories, plus $8 for 3 additional entries; US and international entries $36, ($6 postage) in US funds (non-Canadian). Entrants receive a one-year subscription. Guidelines available by fax, e-mail, on Web Site or for SASE. Deadline: February 28. Contest entries must be either an original postcard story (narrative fiction in 500 words or less); prose poem (lyric poem written as a prose paragraph or paragraphs in 500 words or less); dramatic monologue (a self-contained speech given by a single character in 500 words or less); or essay or creative nonfiction piece (5,000 words or less). Cover document for each entry should include name, address, phone, e-mail, word count and title; title only on ms. Results announced in May. Winners notified by phone, e-mail, fax or mail. For contest results, send SASE, e-mail, fax or visit Web Site.

JOHN SIMMONS SHORT FICTION AWARD

University of Iowa Press, 102 Dey House, 507 N. Clinton St., Iowa City IA 52242-1000. (319)335-2000. Fax: (319)335-2055. Web site: www.uiowapress.org. **Contact:** Holly Carver, director. Award "to give exposure to promising writers who have not yet published a book of prose." Offered annually for a collection of short stories. Anyone who has not published a book of prose fiction is eligible to apply. Prize: Publication by the University of Iowa Press. Judged by Senior Iowa Writers' Workshops members who screen manuscripts; published fiction author of note makes final two selections. No entry fee. For guidelines, send SASE or visit Web site. Accepts inquiries by fax, phone. No application forms are necessary. A SASE must be included for return of ms. Submission period: August 1-September 30. "Individual stories can be previously published (as in journals), but never in *book* form." Stories must be in English. Length: "at least 150 word-processed, double-spaced pages; 8-10 stories on average for ms." Results announced early in year following competition. Winners notified by phone.

SKIPPING STONES HONOR AWARDS

P.O. Box 3939, Eugene OR 97403-0939. Phone/fax: (541)342-4956. E-mail: editor@skippingstones.org. Web site: www.skippingstones.org. **Contact:** Arun N. Toké, executive editor. Annual awards to "promote multicultural and/or nature awareness through creative writings for children and teens." Prize: honor certificates; seals; reviews; press release/publicity. Categories: short stories, novels, story collections, poetry and nonfiction. Judged by "a multicultural committee of teachers, librarians, parents, students and editors." Entry fee: $50 ($25 for small, low-income publishers/self-publishers). Deadline: February 1. Entries must be previously published. Open to previously published books and resources that appeared in print during a two year period prior to the deadline date. Guidelines for SASE or e-mail and on Web site. Accepts inquiries by e-mail, fax, phone. "We seek authentic, exceptional, child/youth friendly books that promote intercultural, international, intergenerational harmony and understanding through creative ways. Writings that come out of your own experiences and cultural understanding seem to have an edge." Results announced in May each year. Winners notified through personal notifications, press release and by publishing reviews of winning titles in the summer issue. For contest results, send SASE, e-mail or visit Web site.

SKIPPING STONES YOUTH AWARDS

Skipping Stones Magazine, P.O. Box 3939, Eugene OR 97403-09 39. Phone/fax: (541)342-4956. E-mail: editor@s kippingstones.org. Web site: www.skippingstones.org. **Contact:** Arun N. Toké, executive editor. Annual awards to "promote creativity and multicultural and nature awareness in youth." Prize: publication in Autumn issue, honor certificate, subscription to magazine, plus 5 multicultural or nature books. Categories: short stories. Entry fee: $3/entry, make checks payable to *Skipping Stones*. Cover letter should include name, address, phone and e-mail. Deadline: June 20. Entries must be unpublished. Length: 1,000 words maximum. Open to any writer between 7 and 17. Guidelines available by SASE, e-mail or on Web site. Accepts inquiries by e-mail or phone. "Be creative. Do not use stereotypes or excessive violent language or plots. Be sensitive to cultural diversity." Results announced in the September-October issue. Winners notified by mail. For contest results, visit Web site. Everyone who enters receives the issue which features the award winners.

THE BERNICE SLOTE AWARD

Prairie Schooner, 201 Andrews Hall, P.O. Box 880334, Lincoln NE 68588-0334. (402)472-0911. Fax: (402)472-9771. E-mail: kgrey2@unl.edu. Web site: http://prairieschooner.unl.edu. **Contact:** Hilda Raz, editor-in-chief.

Offered annually for the best work by a beginning writer published in *Prairie Schooner* in the previous year. Prize: $500. Categories: short stories, essays and poetry. Judged by editorial staff of *Prairie Schooner*. No entry fee. For guidelines, send SASE or visit Web site. "Only work published in the journal during the previous year will be considered." Work is nominated by the editorial staff. Results announced in the Spring issue. Winners notified by mail in February or March.

☐ ◎ KAY SNOW WRITING AWARDS

Willamette Writers, 9045 SW Barbur Blvd., Suite 5A, Portland OR 97219. (503)452-1592. Fax: (503)452-0372. E-mail: wilwrite@teleport.com. Web site: www.willamettewriters.com. **Contact:** Pat MacAodha. Contest offered annually to "offer encouragement and recognition to writers with unpublished submissions." Acquires right to publish excerpts from winning pieces 1 time in their newsletter. Prize: 1st place: $300; 2nd place: $150; 3rd place: $50; excerpts published in Willamette Writers newsletter, and winners acknowledged at banquet during writing conference. Student writers win $50 in categories for grades 1-5, 6-8, and 9-12. $500 Liam Callen Memorial Award goes to best overall entry. Entry fee: $15 fee; no fee for student writers. Deadline: May 15. Guidelines for #10 SASE, fax, by e-mail or on Web site. Accepts inquires by fax, phone and e-mail. Winners notified by mail and phone. For contest results, send SASE. Prize winners will be honored at the two-day August Willamette Writers' Conference. Press releases will be sent to local and national media announcing the winners, and excerpts from winning entries may appear in our newsletter.

◎ SOCIETY OF MIDLAND AUTHORS AWARD

Society of Midland Authors, P.O. Box 10419, Chicago IL 60610-0419. E-mail: tomfrisbie@aol.com. Web site: http://midlandauthors.com. **Contact:** Thomas Frisbie, president. "Established in 1915, the Society of Midland Authors Award (SMA) is presented to one title in each of six categories 'to stimulate creative effort,' one of SMA's goals, to be honored at the group's annual awards banquet in May." Annual. Competition/award for novels, story collections. Prize: cash prize of at least $300 and a plaque that is awarded at the SMA banquet. Categories: children's nonfiction and fiction, adult nonfiction and fiction, adult biography, and poetry. Received about 125 entries last year for adult fiction category. Judging is done by a panel of three judges for each category that includes a mix of experienced authors, reviewers, book sellers, university faculty and librarians. No entry fee. Guidelines available in September-November with SASE, on Web site, in publication. Accepts inquiries by e-mail, phone. Deadline: Feb. 1, 2008. Entries should be previously published. "The contest is open to any title with a recognized publisher that has been published within the year prior to the contest year." Open to any author with a recognized publisher who lives in a Midland state, which includes Illinois, Iowa, Kansas, Michigan, Minnesota, Missouri, Nebraska, North Dakota, South Dakota, Ohio and Wisconsin. SMA only accepts published work accompanied by a completed award form. Writers may submit own work. Entries can also be submitted by the publisher's rep. "Write a great story and be sure to follow contest rules by sending a copy of the book to each of the three judges for the given category who are listed on SMA's Web site." Results announced at the SMA Awards Banquet each May. Other announcements follow in the media. Winners notified by mail, by phone. Results made available to entrants on Web site, in our monthly membership newsletter. Results will also go to local media in the form of press releases.

◎ SOUTH DAKOTA ARTS COUNCIL

711 E. Wells Avenue, Pierre SD 57501-3369. (605)773-3301. E-mail: sdac@state.sd.us. Web site: www.artscouncil.sd.gov. **Contact:** Dennis Holub, executive director. "Individual Artist Grants (up to $3,000) and Artist Collaboration Grants (up to $6,000) are planned for fiscal 2007." No entry fee. Deadline: March 1. Open to South Dakota residents only. Students pursuing an undergraduate or graduate degree are ineligible. Guidelines and application available on Web site or by mail. Applicants must submit application form with an original signature; current résumé no longer than 5 pages; appropriate samples of artistic work (see guidelines); up to 5 pages additional documentation; SASE with adequate postage for return of ms (if desired).

☐ SOUTHWEST WRITERS (SWW) CONTESTS

SouthWest Writers (SWW), 3721 Morris St. NE, Suite A, Albuquerque NM 87111-3611. (505)265-9485. Fax: (505)265-9483. E-mail: SWriters@aol.com. Web site: www.southwestwriters.org. **Contact:** Jeanne Shannon, chair. The SouthWest Writers (SWW) Contest encourages and honors excellence in writing. There are 20 catagories, including a Spanish category, in which writers may enter their work. (Please see Category Specific Guidelines on Web site for more details.) Prize: Finalists in all categories are notified by mail and are listed on the SWW Web site with the title of their entry. First, second and third place winners in each category also receive cash prizes of $150, $100, and $50 (respectively), as well as a certificate of achievement. First place winners also compete for the $1,000 Storyteller Award. Winners will be honored at a contest awards banquet (date and time TBA). Categories: Eleven categories—broken down by genre—are for short story and novel writers. For novels: Mainstream and Literary; Mystery, Suspense, Thriller, or Adventure; Romance; Science

Fiction, Fantasy, or Horror; Historical or American Frontier/Western; Middle Grade (4th-6th grade) or Young Adult (7th grade and up); Spanish Language Nonfiction article/essay. For short stories: Science Fiction, Fantasy, or Horror; Mainstream and Literary; Mystery or Romance; Other Genres: Historical, Western, etc; Middle Grade (4th-6th grade) or Young Adult (7th grade and up). Judged by editors and agents (most from New York publishing houses) who are chosen by the contest chairs. Judges critique the top three entries in each category. All entries also receive a written critique by a qualified consultant (usually, but not always, a published author). Entry fee: $29 for members, $44 for nonmembers (make checks payable to SouthWest Writers). No cover letter is required; send signed copy of the SWW Contest Entry Form. Personal information should not appear anywhere else on ms. NOVELS: The first 20 pages or less, beginning with the prologue and/or first chapter, plus a 1-page synopsis. SHORT STORIES: 5,000 words or less. (For all children's writing, you must type *Middle Grade* or *Young Adult* in the top right corner of the first page.) Please follow detailed instructions for submission in Category Specific Guidelines on Web site. Deadline: May 1. Entries must be unpublished. Open to all writers from around the world. All entries should be submitted in English and follow standard ms format. "Entrants should read the SWW Contest Entry Form, General Contest Rules and the Category Specific Guidelines for complete information. A Tips & Resources page (as well as all contest info/entry form) is also available on the SWW Web site." Guidelines available in January by SASE, e-mail, on Web site or in SouthWest Sage SWW newsletter. Accepts inquiries by e-mail, phone.

◎ SPUR AWARDS

Western Writers of America, Inc., 1080 Mesa Vista Hall, MSC06 3770, 1 University of New Mexico Alberquerque NM 87131. (505)277-5234. E-mail: wwa@unm.edu. Web site: www.westernwriters.org. **Contact:** Awards Coordinator. Purpose of award is "to reward quality in the fields of western fiction and nonfiction." Prize: Trophy. Categories: short stories, novels, poetry and nonfiction. No entry fee. Deadline: December 31. Entries must be published during the contest year. Open to any writer. Guidelines available in Sept./Oct. for SASE or by phone. Inquiries accepted by e-mail or phone. Results announced annually in Summer. Winners notified by mail. For contest results, send SASE.

◎ STONY BROOK SHORT FICTION PRIZE

Department of English, State University of New York, Stony Brook NY 11794-5350. (631)632-7400. Web site: www.stonybrook.edu/fictionprize. **Contact:** John Westermann. Award "to recognize excellent undergraduate fiction." Prize: $1,000 and publication on Web site. Categories: Short stories. Judged by faculty of the Department of English & Creative Writing Program. No entry fee. Guidelines available on Web site. Inquiries accepted by e-mail. Expects 300 entries. Deadline: March 1. Word length: 7,500 words or less. "Only undergraduates enrolled full time in American or Canadian colleges and universities for the 2006-2007 academic year are eligible. Proof required. Students of all races and backgrounds are encouraged to enter. Guidelines for SASE or on Web site. Ms should include name, permanent address, phone, e-mail, word count and title. Winners notified by phone; results posted on Web site by June.

🖤 ◎ THEODORE STURGEON MEMORIAL AWARD FOR BEST SHORT SF OF THE YEAR

Center for the Study of Science Fiction, English Department, University of Kansas, Lawrence KS 66045. (785)864-3380. Fax: (785)864-1159. E-mail: jgunn@ku.edu. Web site: www.ku.edu/~sfcenter. **Contact:** James Gunn, professor and director. Award to "honor the best science fiction short story of the year." Prize: Trophy. Winners receive expense-paid trip to the University (in 2007 to Kansas City, MO) and have their names engraved on permanent trophy. Categories: short stories. Judged by jury. No entry fee. Entries must be previously published. Guidelines available in December by phone, e-mail or on Web site. Accepts inquiries by e-mail and fax. Entrants for the Sturgeon Award are by nomination only. Results announced in July. For contest results, send SASE.

🖤 ◻ SUBTERRAIN ANNUAL LITERARY AWARDS COMPETITION: THE LUSH TRIUMPHANT

subTERRAIN Magazine, P.O. Box 3008 MPO, Vancouver BC V6B 3X5 Canada. (604)876-8710. Fax: (604)879-2667. E-mail: subter@portal.ca. Web site: www.subterrain.ca. **Contact:** Jenn Farrell, managing editor. Offered annually to foster new and upcoming writers. Prize: $500 (Canadian) cash prizes in each category, publication in summer issue, and 1-year subscription to *subTERRAIN*. Runners up also receive publication. Categories: short stories, poetry, nonfiction. Judged by an editorial collective. Entry fee: $20. Entrants may submit as many entries in as many categories as they like. Guidelines on Web Site. "Contest kicks off in November." Deadline: May 15. Entries must be unpublished. Length: Fiction: 3,000 words maximum; Poetry: max 3 poems per entry, max 45 lines per poem; creative nonfiction: max 4,000 words. Results announced on Web Site. Winners notified by phone call and in press release. "All entries must be previously unpublished material. Submissions will not be returned, so do not send originals. If you would like to receive information regarding the outcome of the contest prior to their publication in the magazine, please include a regular letter-size SASE with your entry. If submitting from outside Canada, please include International Reply Coupons to cover return postage."

◎ SYDNEY TAYLOR MANUSCRIPT COMPETITION

Association of Jewish Libraries, 204 Park St., Montclair NJ 07042. (973)744-3836. Fax: (201)862-0362. E-mail: aidonna@aol.com. Web site: www.jewishlibraries.org. **Contact:** Aileen Grossbert, coordinator. Award "to identify and encourage writers of fiction for ages 8-11 with universal appeal of Jewish content; story should deepen the understanding of Judaism for all children, Jewish and non-Jewish, and reveal positive aspects of Jewish life. No short stories or plays. Length: 64-200 pages." Judged by 5 AJL member librarians. Prize: $1,000. No entry fee. Guidelines available by SASE, e-mail or on Web site. Deadline: December 30. Entries must be unpublished. Cover letter should include name, address, phone, e-mail and title. Results announced April 15. Winners notified by phone or e-mail. For contest information, send e-mail or visit Web site. Check Web site for more specific details and to download release forms which must accompany entry.

◖ THE PETER TAYLOR PRIZE FOR THE NOVEL

Knoxville Writers' Guild and University of Tennessee Press, P.O. Box 2565, Knoxville TN 37901. Web site: www.knoxvillewritersguild.org. Offered annually for unpublished work to discover and publish novels of high literary quality. Guidelines for SASE or on Web site. Only full-length, unpublished novels will be considered. Short story collections, translations, or nonfiction cannot be considered. Prize: $1,000, publication by University of Tennessee Press (a standard royalty contract). Judged by a widely published novelist who chooses the winner from a pool of finalists. 2007 judge: Kelly Cherry. Entry fee: $25, payable to KWG. Multiple and simultaneous submissions okay. Manuscripts should be a minimum of 40,000 words and should be of letter-quality print on standard white paper. Text should be double-spaced, paginated and printed on one side of the page only. Please do not use a binder; use two rubber bands instead. Please use a padded mailer for shipping. The mss should be accompanied by two title pages: one with the title only; the other with the title and author's name, address and phone number. The author's name or other identifying information should not appear anywhere else on the ms. Manuscripts will not be returned. Each ms must be accompanied by a self-addressed, stamped postcard for confirmation of receipt, along with an SASE for contest results. No FedEx or UPS, please. Deadline: February 1-April 30. Entries must be unpublished. The contest is open to any U.S. resident writing in English. Members of the Knoxville Writers' Guild, current or former students of the judge, and employees and students of the University of Tennessee system are not eligible. Contest results will be announced in November.

◎ TEDDY CHILDREN'S BOOK AWARD

Writers' League of Texas, 1501 W. 5th St., Suite E-2, Austin TX 78703-5155. (512)499-8914. Fax: (512)499-0441. E-mail: wlt@writersleague.org. Web site: www.writersleague.org. **Contact:** Kristy Bordine, membership administrator. Award established to "honor an outstanding book for children published by a member of the Writers' League of Texas." Prize: $1,000. Categories: long works and short works. Entry fee: $25. Deadline: May 31. Entries should be previously published children's books (during the period of January 1 to December 31, 2007) by Writers' League of Texas members. League members reside all over the U.S. and in some foreign countries. Persons may join the league when they send in their entries. Guidelines available in January for SASE, fax, e-mail, or visit Web site. Results announced in September. Winners notified at ceremony.

◖ THREE CHEERS AND A TIGER

E-mail: editors@toasted-cheese.com. Web site: www.toasted-cheese.com. **Contact:** Stephanie Lenz, editor. Purpose of contest is to write a short story (following a specific theme) within 48 hours. Prize: Amazon gift certificates and publication. Categories: short stories. Blind-judged by two *Toasted Cheese* editors. Each judge uses her own criteria to choose entries. No entry fee. Cover letter should include name, address, e-mail, word count and title. Information should be in the body of the e-mail. It will be removed before the judging begins. Entries must be unpublished. Contest offered biannually. Word limit announced at the start of the contest. Contest-specific information is announced 48 hours before the contest submission deadline. Open to any writer. Accepts inquiries by e-mail. "Follow the theme, word count and other contest rules. We have more suggestions at our Web site." Results announced in April and October. Winners notified by e-mail. List of winners on Web site.

◗ ◎ THE THURBER PRIZE FOR AMERICAN HUMOR

Thurber House, 77 Jefferson Ave., Columbus OH 43215. (614)464-1032. Fax: (614)280-3645. E-mail: mkendall@thurberhouse.org. Web site: www.thurberhouse.org. **Contact:** Missie Kendall, special events, media manager. Award "to give the nation's highest recognition of the art of humor writing." Prize: $5,000. Judged by well-known members of the national arts community. Entry fee: $65 per title. Deadline: April 2. Published submissions or accepted for publication in U.S. for the first time. Primarily pictorial works such as cartoon collections are not considered. Word length: no requirement. Work must be nominated by publisher. Guidelines available for SASE. Accepts inquiries by phone and e-mail. Results announced in November. Winners notified in person at the Algonquin Hotel in New York City. For contest results, visit Web site.

🔁 ⬜ TICKLED BY THUNDER ANNUAL FICTION CONTEST

Tickled By Thunder, 14076-86A Ave., Surrey BC V3W 0V9 Canada. E-mail: info@tickledbythunder.com. Web site: www.tickledbythunder.com. **Contact:** Larry Lindner, editor. Award to encourage new writers. Prize: $150 Canadian, 4-issue subscription (one year) plus publication. Categories: short stories. Judged by the editor and other writers. Entry fee: $10 Canadian (free for subscribers but more than one story requires $5 per entry). Deadline: February 15. Entries must be unpublished. Word length: 2,000 words or less. Open to any writer. Guidelines available for SASE, e-mail, on Web site. Accepts inquiries by e-mail. Results announced in May. Winners notified by mail. For contest results, send SASE.

🔁 ◎ TORONTO BOOK AWARDS

Toronto Protocol, City Clerk's Office, 100 Queen St. West, City Hall, 10th Floor, West Tower, Toronto ON M5H 2N2 Canada. (416)392-8191. Fax: (416)392-1247. E-mail: bkurmey@toronto.ca. Web site: www.toronto.ca/book_awards. **Contact:** Bev Kurmey, protocol officer. The Toronto Book Awards honor authors of books of literary or artistic merit that are evocative of Toronto. Annual award for short stories, novels, poetry or short story collections. Prize: $15,000. Each short-listed author (usually 4-6) receives $1,000 and the winner receives the remainder. Categories: No separate categories—novels, short story collections, books of poetry, biographies, history, books about sports, children's books—all are judged together. Judged by jury of five who have demonstrated interest and/or experience in literature, literacy, books and book publishing. No entry fee. Cover letter should include name, address, phone, e-mail and title of entry. Six copies of the entry book are also required. Deadline: February 28. Entries must be previously published. Guidelines available in September on Web site. Accepts inquires by fax, e-mail, phone. Finalists announced in June; winners notified in September at a gala reception. More information and results available on Web site.

🌐 ◎ THE TROLLOPE SOCIETY SHORT STORY PRIZE

The Trollope Society, Maritime House, Old Town, Clapham, London England SW4 OWJ United Kingdom. E-mail: pamela.singtone@tvdox.com. Web site: www.trollopestoryprize.org. **Contact:** Pamela Neville-Sington. Competition to "encourage interest in the novels of Anthony Trollope among young people; the emphasis is on reading and writing—for fun." Prize: $1,400 to the winner; story published in the Society's quarterly journal *Trollopiana* and on Web site; occasionally a runner up prize of $140. Categories: short stories. Judged by a panel of writers and academics. No entry fee. Guidelines available on Web site. Deadline: January 15. Length: 3,500 words maximum. Open to students worldwide, 21 and under. Guidelines available in May on Web site. Accepts inquiries by e-mail, phone. Cover letter should include name, address, phone, e-mail, word count and title. Results announced in March each year. Winners notified by e-mail.

🌐 ⬜ ◎ UPC SCIENCE FICTION AWARD

Technical University of Catalonia, Board of Trustees, Gran Capita 2-4, Edifici NEXUS 08034, Barcelona Spain. E-mail: consell.social@upc.edu. Web site: www.upc.edu/sciencefiction. **Contact:** Anna Serra Hombravella, secretary. "The award is based on the desire for integral education at UPC, since it unifies the concepts of science and literature." Prize: £6,000 (about $16,000 US). Judged by professors of the university and science fiction writers. No entry fee. Submissions may be made in Spanish, English, Catalan or French. The author must sign his work with a pseudonym and enclose a sealed envelope with full name, personal ID number, address and phone. The pseudonym and title of work must appear on the envelope. Deadline: September 14. Entries must be unpublished. Length: 70-115 pages, double-spaced, 30 lines/page, 70 characters/line. Open to any writer. Guidelines available in January for SASE, e-mail, phone, or on Web site. Results announced in December. Winners notified by phone in November. List of winners sent to all entrants; also available for SASE and on Web site, or by e-mail.

◎ VIOLET CROWN BOOK AWARD

Writers' League of Texas, 1501 W. Fifth St., Suite E-2, Austin TX 78703-5155. (512)499-8914. Fax: (512)499-0441. E-mail: wlt@writersleague.org. Web site: www.writersleague.org. **Contact:** Kristy Bordine, membership administrator. Award "to recognize the best books published by Writers' League of Texas members from January 1 through December 31, 2007 in fiction, nonfiction, literary poetry and literary prose categories." Prize: three $1,000 cash awards and 3 trophies. Entry fee: $25. Send credit card information or make checks payable to Writers' League of Texas. "Anthologies that include the work of several authors are not eligible." Deadline: May 31. Entries must be previously published. "Entrants must be Writers' League of Texas members. League members reside all over the U.S. and in some foreign countries. Persons may join the League when they send in their entries." Publisher may also submit entry in author's name. Guidelines available after January for SASE, fax, e-mail or on Web site. Accepts inquiries by fax, e-mail or on phone. Results announced in September. Winners notified at awards ceremony. For contest results, send SASE or visit Web site. "Special citations are presented to finalists."

KURT VONNEGUT FICTION PRIZE

North American Review, University of Northern Iowa, 1222 W. 27th St., Cedar Falls IA 50614-0516. (319)273-6455. Fax: (319)273-4326. E-mail: nar@uni.edu. Web site: webdelsol.com/NorthAmReview/NAR/HTMLpages/NARToday.htm Prize: 1st: $1,000; 2nd: $100; 3rd: $50. All winners and finalists will be published. Judged by acclaimed writer. Entry fee: $18 (includes a 1-yr subscription). Send two copies of one story (7,000 words max). No names on mss. Include cover letter with name, address, phone, e-mail, title. Stories will not be returned, so do not send SASE for return. For acknowledgment of receipt, please include a SASE. Make your check or money order out to *North American Review*. If you are outside the U.S., please make sure the entry fee is in U.S. currency and routed through a U.S. bank. Deadline: Dec. 31. Entries must be unpublished. Simultaneous submission is not allowed. Stories entered must not be under consideration for publication elsewhere. Open to any writer. For list of winners, send business-sized SASE. Winners will be announced on Web site and in writers' trade magazines.

EDWARD LEWIS WALLANT BOOK AWARD

Irving and Fran Waltman, 3 Brighton Rd., West Hartford CT 06117. (860)232-1421. **Contact:** Mrs. Fran Waltman, co-sponsor. To recognize an American writer whose creative work of fiction has significance for the American Jew. Prize: $500 and a scroll. Judged by panel of 3 judges. No entry fee. Accepts inquiries by phone. Writers may submit their own work. Deadline: Dec. 31. Entries must be previously published. Open to novels or story collections. Open to all American writers. Winner announced in Jan./Feb. and notified by phone.

THE ROBERT WATSON LITERARY PRIZE IN FICTION AND POETRY

(formerly The Greensboro Review Literary Award in Fiction and Poetry) *The Greensboro Review*, 3302 Hall for Humanities and Research Administration, UNCG, P.O. Box 26170, Greensboro NC 27402-6170. (336)334-5459. E-mail: anseay@uncg.edu. Web site: www.uncg.edu/eng/mfa. **Contact:** Allison Seay, assistant editor. Offered annually for fiction (7,500 word limit) and poetry; the best work is published in the Spring issue of *The Greensboro Review*. Sample issue for $5. Prize: $500 each for best short story and poem. Judged by editors of *The Greensboro Review*. No entry fee. Guidelines for SASE or on Web site. Deadline: September 15. Entries must be unpublished. No simultaneous submissions or submissions by e-mail. Open to any writer. Winners notified by mail, phone or e-mail. List of winners published in Spring issue. "All manuscripts meeting literary award guidelines will be considered for cash award as well as for publication in the Spring issue of *The Greensboro Review*."

WISCONSIN INSTITUTE FOR CREATIVE WRITING FELLOWSHIP

University of Wisconsin—Madison, Creative Writing/English Dept., 6195B H.C. White Hall, 600 N. Park St., Madison WI 53706. (608)263-3374. E-mail: rfkuka@wisc.edu. Web site: www.creativewriting.wisc.edu. **Contact:** Ron Kuka, program coordinator. Fellowship provides time, space and an intellectual community for writers working on first books. Receives approximately 300 applicants a year for each genre. Prize: $25,000 for a 9-month appointment. Judged by English Department faculty and current fellows. Entry fee: $20, payable to the Department of English. Applicants should submit up to 10 pages of poetry or one story of up to 30 pages and a résumé or vita directly to the program during the month of February. An applicant's name must not appear on the writing sample (which must be in ms form) but rather on a separate sheet along with address, social security number, phone number, e-mail address and title(s) of submission(s). Candidates should also supply the names and phone numbers of two references. Accepts inquiries by e-mail and phone. Deadline: February. "Candidates must not yet have published, or had accepted for publication, a book by application deadline." Open to any writer with either an M.F.A. or Ph.D. in creative writing. Please enclose a SASE for notification of results. Results announced by May 1. "Send your best work. Stories seem to have a small advantage over novel excerpts."

TOBIAS WOLFF AWARD IN FICTION

Bellingham Review, Mail Stop 9053, Western Washington University, Bellingham WA 98225. (360)650-4863. E-mail: bhreview@cc.wwu.edu. Web site: www.wwu.edu/~bhreview. **Contact:** Fiction Editor. Offered annually for unpublished work. Guidelines for SASE or online. Prize: $1,000, plus publication and subscription. Categories: novel excerpts and short stories. Entry fee: $15 for 1st entry; $10 each additional entry. Guidelines available in August for SASE or on Web site. Deadline: Contest runs: Dec. 1-March 15. Entries must be unpublished. Length: 8,000 words or less per story or chapter. Open to any writer. Winner announced in August and notified by mail. For contest results, send SASE.

JOHN WOOD COMMUNITY COLLEGE ADULT CREATIVE WRITING CONTEST

1301 S. 48th St., Quincy IL 62305. Fax: (214)228-9483. E-mail: jmcgovern@jwcc.edu. Web site: www.jwcc.edu. **Contact:** Janet McGovern, education specialist. Award to "promote new writing." Prize: Cash prizes dictated by the number of entries received. Categories: Categories include traditional rhyming poetry, limerick or haiku, light or humerous poetry, nonfiction, fiction. Entry fee: $5/poem; $7/fiction or nonfiction. "No identification should appear on manuscripts, but send a separate 3×5 card for each entry with name, social security number (in order to print checks for cash prizes), address, phone number, e-mail address, word count, title of work and category in which each work should be entered. You may use one check or money order and place all entries in the same envelope." Guidelines available after July for SASE, fax, e-mail, phone or on Web site. Entries must be unpublished. Open to any writer. Winners notified by mail in late June. For contest results, send SASE, fax, e-mail or visit Web site www.jwcc.edu.

WORLD FANTASY AWARDS

World Fantasy Awards Association, P.O. Box 43, Mukilteo WA 98275-0043. E-mail: sfexecsec@gmail.com. Web site: www.worldfantasy.org. **Contact:** Peter Dennis Pautz, president. Awards "to recognize excellence in fantasy literature worldwide." Offered annually for previously published work in several categories, including life achievement, novel, novella, short story, anthology, collection, artist, special award-pro and special award-nonpro. Works are recommended by attendees of current and previous 2 years' conventions and a panel of judges. Prize: Bust of HP Lovecraft. Judged by panel. No entry fee. Guidelines available in December for SASE or on Web site. Deadline: June 1. Entries must be previously published. Published submissions from previous calendar year. Word length: 10,000-40,000 for novella, 10,000 for short story. "All fantasy is eligible, from supernatural horror to Tolkien-esque to sword and sorcery to the occult, and beyond." Cover letter should include name, address, phone, e-mail, word count, title and publications where submission was previously published. Results announced November 1 at annual convention. For contest results, visit Web site.

WRITER'S DIGEST ANNUAL SHORT SHORT STORY COMPETITION

Writer's Digest, 4700 E. Galbraith Rd., Cincinnati OH 45236. E-mail: short-short-competition@fwpubs.com. Web site: www.writersdigest.com. **Contact:** Terri Boes, contest administrator. Annual. Competition/award for short-shorts. Prize: 1st place receives $3,000 and option for free "Best Seller Publishing Package" from Trafford Publishing; 2nd place receives $1,500; 3rd place receives $500; 4th-10th place receive $100; 11th-25th place receive $50 gift certificate for Writer's Digest Books. The names and story titles of the 1st-10th place winners will be printed in the June issue of *Writer's Digest*, and winners will receive the latest edition of *Novel & Short Story Writer's Market*. Judged by the editors of *Writer's Digest*. Entry fee: $12/story. Make checks payable to Writer's Digest. Deadline: Dec. 1. Entries should be unpublished. "*Writer's Digest* reserves the one-time publication rights to the 1st-25th place winning entries to be published in a *Writer's Digest* publication." Open to all except employees of F+W Publications, Inc., and their immediate families and *Writer's Digest* contributing editors and correspondents as listed on the masthead. Length: 1,500 words or fewer. Type the word count on the first page of your entry, along with your name, address, phone number and e-mail address. All entries must be typewritten and double-spaced on one side of 8½×11 A4 white paper. Mss will not be returned. Enclose a self-addressed, stamped postcard with your entry if you wish to be notified of its receipt. Write, see publication, or visit Web site for official entry form. Writers may submit own work. Results announced June. Winners notified in Feb. Results made available to entrants on Web site, in publication.

WRITER'S DIGEST ANNUAL WRITING COMPETITION

Writer's Digest, 4700 E. Galbraith Rd., Cincinnati OH 45236. (513)531-2690, ext. 1328. E-mail: writing-competition@fwpubs.com. Web site: www.writersdigest.com. **Contact:** Terri Boes, contest administrator. Annual. Competition/award for short stories, articles, poems, scripts. Prize: Grand prize is $3,000 cash and an all-expenses-paid trip to New York City to meet with editors and agents. *Writer's Digest* will fly you and a guest to The Big Apple, where you'll spend 3 days and 2 nights in the publishing capital of the world. While you're there, a *Writer's Digest* editor will escort you to meet and share your work with four editors or agents. You'll also receive a free Diamond Publishing Package from Outskirts Press. First place in each category receives $1,000 cash, a ms critique and marketing advice from a *Writer's Digest* editor or advisory board member, and $100 worth of Writer's Digest Books. Second place in each category receives $500 cash, plus $100 worth of Writer's Digest Books. Third place in each category receives $250 cash, plus $100 worth of Writer's Digest Books. Fourth place in each category receives $100 cash, the latest editon of *Writer's Market Deluxe*, and a 1-yr subscription to *Writer's Digest*. Fifth place in each category receives $50 cash, the latest edition of *Writer's Market Deluxe*, and a 1-yr subscription to *Writer's Digest*. Sixth-tenth place in each category receives $25 cash. First through tenth place winners also receive a copy of *Writer's Market Deluxe* and a one-year subscription to Writer's Digest mgazine. All other winners receive distinctive certificates honoring their accomplishment. Categories: Inspirational Writing (spiritual/religious); Article: Memoir/Personal Essay; Article: Magazine Feature; Short Story: Genre; Short Story: Mainstream/Literary; Poetry: Rhyming; Poetry: Non-rhyming; Script: Stage Play; Script: TV/Movie; Children's Fiction. Judged by the editors of *Writer's Digest*. Entry fee: $10 for first poem, $5 each additional poem; all other entries are $15 for first ms, $10 each additional ms. Make checks payable to

Writer's Digest. Accepts inquiries by e-mail. Deadline: May 15. Entries should be unpublished. "Entries in the Magazine Feature Article category may be previously published. *Writer's Digest* retains one-time publication rights to the grand prize and first place winning entries in each category to be published in a *Writer's Digest* publication." Open to all writers except employees of F + W Publications, Inc, and their immediate families, *Writer's Digest* contributing editors and correspondents as listed on the masthead, Writer's Online Workshops instructors, and Grand Prize winners from the previous three years. Length: 2,000 words max for Memoir/Personal Essay, Feature Article, and Children's Fiction; 2,500 words max for Insipirational Writing; 4,000 words max for Short Story categories; 32 lines max for Poetry categories; 15 pages in standard format plus 1-pg synopsis for Script categories. Write, visit Web site, or see publication for official entry form. Your name, address, phone number, and competition category must appear in the upper left-hand corner of the first page, otherwise your entry is disqualified. See additional guidelines in publication or on Web site. Winners notified by mail. Winners notified by Oct. Results made available to entrants on Web Site after the issue has been published.

⬭ WRITER'S DIGEST POPULAR FICTION AWARDS

Writer's Digest, 4700 East Galbraith Rd., Cincinnati OH 45236. (513)531-2690, ext. 1328. E-mail: popularfictiona wards@fwpubs.com. **Contact:** Terri Boes, contest administrator. Annual. Competition/award for short stories. Prizes: Grand Prize is $2,500 cash, $100 worth of Writer's Digest Books, plus a ms critique and marketing advice from a *Writer's Digest* editor or advisory board member; First Prize in each of the five categories receives $500 cash, $100 worth of Writer's Digest Books, plus a ms critique and marketing advice from a *Writer's Digest* editor or advisory board member; Honorable Mentions receive promotion in *Writer's Digest* and the next edition of *Novel & Short Story Writer's Market*. Categories: Romance, Mystery/Crime, Sci-Fi/Fantasy, Thriller/Suspense, Horror. Judged by *Writer's Digest* editors. Entry fee: $12.50. Make checks payable to *Writer's Digest*. Accepts inquiries by mail, e-mail, phone. Deadline: Nov. 1. Entries should be unpublished. Open to all "except employees of F + W Publications, Inc., and their immediate family members, *Writer's Digest* contributing editors and correspondents as listed on our masthead, Writer's Online Workshops instructors, and Grand Prize Winners from the previous three years in any *Writer's Digest* competitions." Length: 4,000 words or fewer. Entries must be accompanied by an Official Entry Form or facsimile. Your name, address, phone number and competition category must appear in the upper left-hand corner of the first page of your manuscript, otherwise it is disqualified. Writers may submit own work. Results announced in the July issue of *Writer's Digest*. Winners notified by mail before March 1.

◎ WRITERS' FELLOWSHIP

NC Arts Council, Department of Cultural Resources, Raleigh NC 27699-4632. (919)807-6512. Fax: (919)807-6532. E-mail: debbie.mcgill@ncmail.net. Web site: www.ncarts.org. **Contact:** Deborah McGill, literature director. Fellowships are awarded to support the creative development of NC writers and to stimulate the creation of new work. Prize: $8,000. Categories: short stories, novels, literary nonfiction, literary translation, spoken word. Work for children also invited. Judged by a panel of literary professionals appointed by the NC Arts Council, a state agency. No entry fee. Deadline: November 1, 2008. Mss must not be in published form. We receive approximately 300 applications. Word length: 20 double-spaced pages (max). The work must have been written within the past 5 years. Only writers who have been full-time residents of NC for at least 1 year as of the application deadline and who plan to remain in the state during the grant year may apply. Guidelines available in late August on Web site. Accepts inquiries by fax, e-mail, phone. Results announced in late summer. All applicants notified by mail.

⊕ ⬭ WRITERS' FORUM SHORT STORY COMPETITION

Writers International Ltd., P.O. Box 3229, Bournemouth BH1 1ZS United Kingdom. E-mail: editorial@writers-forum.com. Web site: www.writers-forum.com. **Contact:** Zena O'Toole, editorial assistant. "The competition aims to promote the art of short story writing." Prize: Prizes are £300 for 1st place, £150 for 2nd place and £100 for 3rd place. Categories: short stories. Judged by a panel who provides a short list to the editor. Entry fee: £10 or £7 for subscribers to *Writers' Forum*. Cover letter should include name, address, phone, e-mail, word count and title. Entries must be unpublished. "The competition is open to all nationalities, but entries must be in English." Length: 1,500-3,000 words. Open to any writer. Guidelines available for e-mail, on Web site and in publication. Accepts inquiries by fax, e-mail, phone. Make entry fee cheques payable to Writers International Ltd., or send credit card information. Winners notified by mail. List of winners available in magazine.

⬭ WRITERS' JOURNAL ANNUAL FICTION CONTEST

Val-Tech Media, P.O. Box 394, Perham MN 56573. (218)346-7921. Fax: (218)346-7924. E-mail: writersjournal@writersjournal.com. Web site: www.writersjournal.com. **Contact:** Leon Ogroske, editor (editor@writersjournal.com). Offered annually for previously unpublished fiction. Open to any writer. Prize: 1st Place: $500; 2nd

Place: $200; 3rd Place: $100, plus honorable mentions. Prize-winning stories and selected honorable mentions published in *Writers' Journal*. Entry fee: $15 reading fee. Guidelines and entry forms available for SASE and on Web site. Accepts inquiries by fax, e-mail and phone. Deadline: January 30. "Writer's name must not appear on submission. A separate cover sheet must include name of contest, title, word count and writer's name, address, phone and e-mail (if available)." Results announced in July/August. Winners notified by mail. A list of winners is published in July/August issue and posted on Web site or available for SASE.

WRITERS' JOURNAL ANNUAL HORROR/GHOST CONTEST

Val-Tech Media, P.O. Box 394, Perham MN 56573. (218)346-7921. Fax: (218)346-7924. E-mail: writersjournal@writersjournal.com. Web site: www.writersjournal.com. **Contact:** Leon Ogroske, editor. Offered annually for previously unpublished works. Open to any writer. Prize: 1st place: $250; 2nd place: $100; 3rd place: $75, plus honorable mentions. Prize-winning stories and selected honorable mentions published in *Writers' Journal*. Entry fee: $7. Guidelines available for SASE, by fax, phone, e-mail, on Web site and in publication. Accepts inquiries by e-mail, phone, fax. Deadline: March 30. Entries must be unpublished. Length: 2,000 words. Cover letter should include name, address, phone, e-mail, word count and title; just title on ms. Results announced in September annually. Winners notified by mail. For contest results, send SASE, fax, e-mail or visit Web site.

WRITERS' JOURNAL ANNUAL ROMANCE CONTEST

Val-Tech Media, P.O. Box 394, Perham MN 56573. (218)346-7921. Fax: (218)346-7924. E-mail: writersjournal@writersjournal.com. Web site: www.writersjournal.com. **Contact:** Leon Ogroske, editor. Offered annually for previously unpublished works. Open to any writer. Prize: 1st place: $250; 2nd place: $100; 3rd place: $50, plus honorable mentions. Prize-winning stories and selected honorable mentions published in *Writers' Journal*. Entry fee: $7 fee. No limit on entries per person. Guidelines for SASE, by fax, phone, e-mail, on Web site and in publication. Accepts inquiries by fax, e-mail, phone. Deadline: July 30. Entries must be unpublished. Length: 2,000 words maximum. Open to any writer. Cover letter should include name, address, phone, e-mail, word count and title; just title on ms. Results announced in January/February issue. Winners notified by mail. Winners list published in *Writer's Journal* and on Web site. Enclose SASE for winner's list or send fax or e-mail.

WRITERS' JOURNAL ANNUAL SHORT STORY CONTEST

Val-Tech Media, P.O. Box 394, Perham MN 56573. (218)346-7921. Fax: (218)346-7924. E-mail: writersjournal@writersjournal.com. Web site: www.writersjournal.com. **Contact:** Leon Ogroske. Offered annually for previously unpublished short stories less than 2,000 words. Open to any writer. Guidelines for SASE and online. Prize: 1st place: $350; 2nd place: $125; 3rd place: $75, plus honorable mentions. Prize-winning stories and selected honorable mentions published in *Writers' Journal* November/December issue. Winners notified by mail. Winners list published in *Writers' Journal* and on Web site. Entry fee: $10 reading fee. Deadline: May 30.

Conferences & Workshops

Why are conferences so popular? Writers and conference directors alike tell us it's because writing can be such a lonely business—at conferences writers have the opportunity to meet (and commiserate) with fellow writers, as well as meet and network with publishers, editors and agents. Conferences and workshops provide some of the best opportunities for writers to make publishing contacts and pick up valuable information on the business, as well as the craft, of writing.

The bulk of the listings in this section are for conferences. Most conferences last from one day to one week and offer a combination of workshop-type writing sessions, panel discussions and a variety of guest speakers. Topics may include all aspects of writing from fiction to poetry to scriptwriting, or they may focus on a specific type of writing, such as those conferences sponsored by the Romance Writers of America for writers of romance or by SCBWI for writers of children's books.

Workshops, however, tend to run longer—usually one to two weeks. Designed to operate like writing classes, most require writers to be prepared to work on and discuss their fiction while attending. An important benefit of workshops is the opportunity they provide writers for an intensive critique of their work, often by professional writing teachers and established writers.

Each of the listings here includes information on the specific focus of an event as well as planned panels, guest speakers and workshop topics. It is important to note, however, some conference directors were still in the planning stages for 2008 when we contacted them. If it was not possible to include 2008 dates, fees or topics, we have provided information from 2007 so you can get an idea of what to expect. For the most current information, it's best to send a self-addressed, stamped envelope to the director in question about three months before the date(s) listed or check the conference Web site.

FINDING A CONFERENCE

Many writers try to make it to at least one conference a year, but cost and location count as much as subject matter or other considerations when determining which conference to attend. There are conferences in almost every state and province and even some in Europe open to North Americans.

To make it easier for you to find a conference close to home—or to find one in an exotic locale to fit into your vacation plans—we've divided this section into geographic regions. The conferences appear in alphabetical order under the appropriate regional heading.

Note that conferences appear under the regional heading according to where they will be held, which is sometimes different from the address given as the place to register or send for information. The regions are as follows:

Northeast (page 488): Connecticut, Maine, Massachusetts, New Hampshire, New York, Rhode Island, Vermont

Midatlantic (page 495): Washington DC, Delaware, Maryland, New Jersey, Pennsylvania

Midsouth (page 496): North Carolina, South Carolina, Tennessee, Virginia, West Virginia

Southeast (page 499): Alabama, Arkansas, Florida, Georgia, Louisiana, Mississippi, Puerto Rico

Midwest (page 503): Illinois, Indiana, Kentucky, Michigan, Ohio

North Central (page 506): Iowa, Minnesota, Nebraska, North Dakota, South Dakota, Wisconsin

South Central (page 507): Colorado, Kansas, Missouri, New Mexico, Oklahoma, Texas

West (page 512): Arizona, California, Hawaii, Nevada, Utah

Northwest (page 517): Alaska, Idaho, Montana, Oregon, Washington, Wyoming

Canada (page 520)

International (page 522)

To find a conference based on the month in which it occurs, check out our Conference Index by Date at the back of this book.

LEARNING AND NETWORKING

Besides learning from workshop leaders and panelists in formal sessions, writers at conferences also benefit from conversations with other attendees. Writers on all levels enjoy sharing insights. Often, a conversation over lunch can reveal a new market for your work or let you know which editors are most receptive to the work of new writers. You can find out about recent editor changes and about specific agents. A casual chat could lead to a new contact or resource in your area.

Many editors and agents make visiting conferences a part of their regular search for new writers. A cover letter or query that starts with "I met you at the Green Mountain Writers Conference," or "I found your talk on your company's new romance line at the Moonlight and Magnolias Writer's Conference most interesting . . ." may give you a small leg up on the competition.

While a few writers have been successful in selling their manuscripts at a conference, the availability of editors and agents does not usually mean these folks will have the time there to read your novel or six best short stories (unless, of course, you've scheduled an individual meeting with them ahead of time). While editors and agents are glad to meet writers and discuss work in general terms, usually they don't have the time (or energy) to give an extensive critique during a conference. In other words, use the conference as a way to make a first, brief contact.

SELECTING A CONFERENCE

Besides the obvious considerations of time, place and cost, choose your conference based on your writing goals. If, for example, your goal is to improve the quality of your writing, it will be more helpful to you to choose a hands-on craft workshop rather than a conference offering a series of panels on marketing and promotion. If, on the other hand, you are a science fiction novelist who would like to meet your fans, try one of the many science fiction conferences or "cons" held throughout the country and the world.

Look for panelists and workshop instructors whose work you admire and who seem to be writing in your general area. Check for specific panels or discussions of topics relevant to what you are writing now. Think about the size—would you feel more comfortable with a small workshop of eight people or a large group of 100 or more attendees?

If your funds are limited, start by looking for conferences close to home, but you may want to explore those that offer contests with cash prizes—and a chance to recoup your expenses. A few conferences and workshops also offer scholarships, but the competition is stiff and writers interested in these should find out the requirements early. Finally, students may want to look for conferences and workshops that offer college credit. You will find these options included in the listings here. Again, send a self-addressed, stamped envelope for the most current details.

NORTHEAST (CT, MA, ME, NH, NY, RI, VT)

BOOKEXPO AMERICA/WRITER'S DIGEST BOOKS WRITERS CONFERENCE

4700 East Galbraith Rd., Cincinnati OH 45236. (513) 531-2690. Fax: (513) 891-7185. E-mail: publicity@fwpubs.com. Web site: www.writersdigest.com/bea or www.bookexpoamerica.com/writersconference. **Contact:** Greg Hatfield, publicity manager. Estab. 2003. Annual. Conference duration: one day, May 28, 2008. Average attendance: 600. "The purpose of the conference is to prepare writers hoping to get their work published. We offer instruction on the craft of writing, as well as advice for submitting their work to publications, publishing houses and agents. We provide breakout sessions on these topics, including expert advice from industry professionals, and offer workshops on fiction and nonfiction, in the various genres (literary, children's, mystery, romance, etc.). We also provide attendees the opportunity to actually pitch their work to agents." Site: The conference facility varies from year to year, as we are part of the BookExpo America trade show. The 2008 conference will take place in Los Angeles. Themes and panels have included Writing Genre Fiction, Children's Writing, Brutal Truths About the Book Publishing Industry, Crafting a Strong Nonfiction Book Proposal, Crafting Your Novel Pitch, and Secrets to Irresistible Magazine Queries. Past speakers included Jodi Picoult, Jerry B. Jenkins, Jonathan Karp, Steve Almond, John Warner, Susan Burmeister-Brown, Linda Swanson-Davies, Donald Maass and Michael Cader.
Costs The price in 2007 was $199, which included a 6-month subscription to WritersMarket.com.
Additional Information Information available in February. For brochure, visit Web site. Agents and editors participate in conference.

BREAD LOAF WRITERS' CONFERENCE

Middlebury VT 05753. (802)443-5286. Fax: (802)443-2087. E-mail: blwc@middlebury.edu. Web site: www.middlebury.edu/~blwc. **Contact:** Noreen Cargill, administrative manager. Estab. 1926. Annual. Last conference held August 15-26, 2007. Conference duration: 11 days. Average attendance: 230. For fiction, nonfiction, poetry. Site: Held at the summer campus in Ripton, Vermont (belongs to Middlebury College). 2007 faculty and staff included William Kittredge, Percival Everett, Sigrid Nunez, Joanna Scott, Susan Orlean.
Costs In 2007, $2,260 (included room and board). Fellowships available.
Accommodations Accommodations are at Ripton. Onsite accommodations included in fee.
Additional Information 2008 conference information available December 2007 on Web site. Accepts inquiries by fax, e-mail and phone.

ENVIRONMENTAL WRITERS' CONFERENCE AND WORKSHOP

in honor of Rachel Carson, St. Thomas Aquinas College, 125 Route 340, Sparkill NY 10976. (845)398-4247. Fax: (845)398-4224. E-mail: info@new-cue.org. Web site: www.new-cue.org. **Contact:** Barbara Ward Klein, President. Estab. 1999. Biennial (on the "even" year). Conference held June 10-13, 2008. Conference duration: Tuesday-Friday. Average attendance: 100. Participants can expect to hear award-winning authors, to enjoy guided outdoor activities and (if selected) to read from their own work at morning sessions. Site: The 2008 Environmental Writers' Conference and Workshops will be held once again at The Spruce Point Inn in Boothbay Harbor, Maine. The Inn is one of the finest in New England and Boothbay Harbor is the largest boating harbor north of Boston. A call for submissions will be posted with registration information in early September, 2007. In addition, there will be featured speakers each day of the Conference/Workshop. Previous speakers included Bill McKibben, Linda Lear, Carl Safina, Lawrence Buell, Robert Finch, Jean Craighead George, Joe Bruchac, Deborah Cramer, Andrea Cohen and Tom Horton. In addition, there were 15 concurrent sessions led by college/university faculty and published authors.
Costs Registration costs for 2008 have not been posted. In 2006, registration was $388-$430 and included all meals, program events and speakers but did *not* include accomodations and travel.
Accommodations Rooms at the Spruce Point Inn are $99-150/night (dbl. occupancy); rooms nearby are $70-125/night (dbl. occupancy).
Additional Information Readings of papers accepted for presentation at the event are limited to 15 minutes and will be elegible for inclusion in archives housed at the Thoreau Institute Library at Walden Woods. Deadline for paper submissions January 15, 2008. "The events are interdisciplinary, encouraging participants from colleges and universities, governmental agencies, public and private organizations as well as amateur and pub-

lished writers. This is an opportunity to participate and to enjoy the company of like-minded individuals in one of the most beautiful coastal locations on the eastern seaboard."

GOTHAM WRITERS' WORKSHOP

WritingClasses.com (online division), 555 8th Avenue, Suite 1402, New York NY 10018. (212)974-8377. Fax: (212)307-6325. E-mail: dana@write.org. Web site: www.writingclasses.com. **Contact:** Dana Miller, director of student affairs. Estab. 1993. "Classes held throughout the year. There are four terms, beginning in January, April, June/July, September/October." Conference duration: 10-week, 6-week, 1-day, and online courses offered. Average attendance: approximately 1,300 students per term, 6,000 students per year. Offers craft-oriented creative writing courses in fiction writing, screenwriting, nonfiction writing, memoir writing, novel writing, children's book writing, playwriting, poetry, songwriting, mystery writing, science fiction writing, romance writing, television writing, documentary film writing, feature article writing, travel writing, creative writing, and business writing. Also, Gotham Writers' Workshop offers a teen program, private instruction and classes on selling your work. Site: Classes are held at various schools in New York City as well as online at www.writingclasses.com. View a sample online class on the Web site.

Costs 10-week and online courses—$420 (includes $25 registration fee); 6-week courses-$320 (includes $25 registration fee); 1-day courses—$150 (includes $25 registration fee). Meals and lodging not included.

Additional Information "Participants do not need to submit workshop material prior to their first class." Sponsors a contest for a free 10-week online creative writing course (value = $420) offered each term. Students should fill out a form online at www.writingclasses.com to participate in the contest. The winner is randomly selected. For brochure send e-mail, visit Web site, call or fax. Accepts inquiries by e-mail, phone, fax. Agents and editors participate in some workshops.

GREAT RIVER ARTS

33 Bridge Street, P.O. Box 48, Bellows Falls VT 05101. (802)463-3330. Fax: (802)463-3322. E-mail: grai@sover.n et. Web site: www.greatriverarts.org. **Contact:** Carol Barber, administrator. Estab. 1999. Year-round workshops. Conference duration: 2-5 days. Average attendance: 6-8 per class. Master class and workshops in the visual and literary arts. Site: Classes are held in the Bellows Falls, Vermont/Walpole, New Hampshire region located on the shores of the Connecticut River. Classes are given in poetry, memoir, fiction and children's book arts.

Costs 2007 rates were $500-750. Does not include lodging or meals.

Accommodations Provides list of area hotels.

Additional Information Participants may need to submit material prior to arrival depending on course. Brochures for 2008 available in February/March 2007 by e-mail, phone, fax and on Web site. Accepts inquiries by e-mail, phone, fax.

GREEN MOUNTAIN WRITERS CONFERENCE

47 Hazel St., Rutland VT 05701. (802)236-6133. E-mail: ydaley@sbcglobal.net. Web site: www.vermontwriters. com. **Contact:** Yvonne Daley, director. Estab. 1999. Annual. Check Web site for 2008 conference dates; last conference was July 30-August 3, 2007. Conference duration: 5 days. Average attendance: 40. "The conference is an opportunity for writers at all stages of their development to hone their skills in a beautiful, lakeside environment where published writers across genres share tips and give feedback." Site: Conference held at an old dance pavillion on a 5-acre site on a remote pond in Tinmouth, VT. Past features include Place in story: The Importance of Environment; Creating Character through Description, Dialogue, Action, Reaction, and Thought; The Collision of Real Events and Imagination. Previous staff has included Yvonne Daley, Ruth Stone, Verandah Porche, Grace Paley, David Huddle, Sydney Lea, Joan Connor, Tom Smith and Howard Frank Mosher.

Costs $500 before June 15, $525 after. Fee includes lunch, snacks, beverages, readings.

Accommodations Offers list of area hotels and lodging.

Additional Information Participants' mss can be read and commented on at a cost. Sponsors contests. Conference publishes a literary magazine featuring work of participants. Brochures available in January on Web site or for SASE, e-mail. Accepts inquiries by SASE, e-mail, phone. "We aim to create a community of writers who support one another and serve as audience/mentors for one another. Participants often continue to correspond and share work after conferences." Further information available on Web site, by e-mail or by phone.

HIGHLIGHTS FOUNDATION WRITING FOR CHILDREN

814 Court St., Honesdale PA 18431. (570)253-1192. Fax: (570)253-0179. E-mail: contact@highlightsfoundation. org. Web site: www.highlightsfoundation.org. **Contact:** Kent Brown, executive director. Workshops geared toward those interested in writing for children; beginner, intermediate and advanced levels. Dozens of Classes include: Writing Poetry, Book Promotion, Characterization, Developing a Plot, Exploring Genres, The Publishing Business, What Makes a Good Book, and many more. Annual workshop. Held July 14-21, 2007, at the Chautauqua Institution, Chautauqua, NY. Registration limited to 100.

Costs $2,200, less discount for early registration; Includes tuition, meals, conference supplies. Cost does not include housing. Call for availability and pricing. Scholarships are available for first-time attendees. Phone, e-mail, or visit our Web site for more information.

IWWG MEET THE AGENTS AND EDITORS: THE BIG APPLE WORKSHOPS
% International Women's Writing Guild, P.O. Box 810, Gracie Station, New York NY 10028-0082. (212)737-7536. Fax: (212)737-9469. E-mail: iwwg@iwwg.com. Web site: www.iwwg.com. **Contact:** Hannelore Hahn, executive director. Estab. 1976. Biannual. Workshops held the second weekend in April and the second weekend in October. Average attendance: 200. Workshops to promote creative writing and professional success. Site: Private meeting space of Scandinavia House, mid-town New York City. Saturday: 1-day writing workshop. Sunday afternoon: open house/meet the agents, independent presses and editors.
Costs $130 for members; $155 for non-members for the weekend.
Accommodations Information on transportation arrangements and overnight accommodations available.
Additional Information Accepts inquiries by fax, e-mail, phone.

IWWG SUMMER CONFERENCE
% International Women's Writing Guild, P.O. Box 810, Gracie Station, New York NY 10028-0082. (212)737-7536. Fax: (212)737-9469. E-mail: iwwg@iwwg.org. Web site: www.iwwg.org. **Contact:** Hannelore Hahn, executive director. Estab. 1976. Annual. Conference held for one week in June. Average attendance: 450, including international attendees. Conference to promote writing in all genres, personal growth and professional success. Conference is held "on the tranquil campus of Skidmore College in Saratoga Springs, NY, where the serene Hudson Valley meets the North Country of the Adirondacks." 65 different workshops are offered every day.
Costs $945 single/$860 double (members); $1,025 single/$890 double (non-members) for weeklong program, includes room and board. Weekend and also 5-day overnight accommodations are also available. Commuters are welcome, too.
Accommodations Conference attendees stay on campus. Transportation by air to Albany, NY, or Amtrak train available from New York City.
Additional Information Conference information available with SASE. Accepts inquiries by fax, e-mail.

THE MACDOWELL COLONY
100 High St., Peterborough NH 03458. (603)924-3886. Fax: (603)924-9142. E-mail: admissions@macdowellcolony.org. Web site: www.macdowellcolony.org. **Contact:** Admissions Director. Estab. 1907. Open to writers and playwrights, composers, visual artists, film/video artists, interdisciplinary artists and architects. Site: includes main building, library, 3 residence halls and 32 individual studios on over 450 mostly wooded acres, 1 mile from center of small town in southern New Hampshire. Available up to 8 weeks year-round. Provisions for the writer include meals, private sleeping room, individual secluded studio. Accommodates variable number of writers, 10 to 20 at a time.
Costs "There are no residency fees. Grants for travel to and from the Colony are available based on need. The MacDowell Colony is pleased to offer grants up to $1,000 for writers in need of financial assistance during a residency at MacDowell. At the present time, only artists reviewed and accepted by the literature panel are eligible for this grant." Application forms available. Application deadline: January 15 for summer (June 1-Sept. 30), April 15 for fall (Oct. 1-Jan. 31), September 15 for winter/spring (Feb. 1-May 31). Submit 6 copies of a writing sample, no more than 25 pages. For novel, send a chapter or section. For short stories, send 2-3, work in progress strongly recommended. Brochure/guidelines available; SASE appreciated.

MARYMOUNT MANHATTAN COLLEGE WRITERS' CONFERENCE
Marymount Manhattan College, 221 E. 71st St., New York NY 10021. (212)774-4810. Fax: (212)774-4814. E-mail: lfrumkes@mmm.edu. **Contact:** Alexandra Smith and Dana Thompson. Estab. 1993. Annual. June. Conference duration: "Actual conference is one day, and there is a three-day intensive preceeding." Average attendance: 200. "We present workshops on several different writing genres and panels on publicity, editing and literary agents." Site: College/auditorium setting. 2006 conference featured 2 fiction panels, a children's book writing panel, a mystery/thriller panel and a literary agent panel. 2006 3-day intensive included fiction writer Erica Jong, magazine writer and editor Pamela Fiori, and memoir writer Malachy McCourt. Keynote speakers for 2006 were Joyce Carol Oates and Lewis Lapham. The conference itself included more than 50 authors.
Costs $165, includes lunch and reception.
Accommodations Provides list of area lodging.
Additional Information 2008 conference information will be available in March by fax or phone. Also accepts inquiries by e-mail. Editors and agents sometimes attend conference.

◎ MEDICAL FICTION WRITING FOR PHYSICIANS

SEAK, Inc., P.O. Box 729, Falmouth MA 02541. (508)548-7023. Fax: (508)540-8304. E-mail: mail@seak.com. Web site: www.seak.com. **Contact:** Karen Babitsky, Director of Marketing. Estab. 2000. Annual. Last conference: October 27-28, 2007. Conference Duration: 2 days. Average attendance: 150. Workshop focuses on writing medical fiction and is geared for physicians. Site: Sea Crest Ocean Front Resort, Falmouth MA on Cape Cod. 2007 speakers are Michael Palmer, MD; Tess Garritsen, MD; and 13 literary agents.

Accommodations Provides list of area hotels and lodging options.

Additional Information Accepts inquiries by e-mail, phone, fax. Agents and editors attend this conference.

NEW ENGLAND WRITERS CONFERENCE

P.O. Box 5, 151 Main St., Windsor VT 05089-0005. (802)674-2315. E-mail: newvtpoet@aol.com. Web site: www.newenglandwriters.org. **Contact:** Susan Anthony, directors. Estab. 1986. Annual. Conference held third Saturday in July. Conference duration: 1 afternoon. Average attendance: 150. The purpose is "to bring an affordable literary conference to any writers who can get there and to expose them to emerging excellence in the craft." Site: The Old South Church on Main St. in Windsor, VT. Offers panel and seminars by prominent authors, agents, editors or publishers; open readings, contest awards and book sales/signings. Featured guest speakers have included Reeve Lindbergh, Rosanna Warren and John Kenneth Galbraith.

Costs $20 (includes refreshments). No pre-registration required.

Accommodations Provides a list of area hotels or lodging options.

Additional Information Sponsors poetry and fiction contests as part of conference (award announced at conference). Conference information available in May. For brochure send SASE or visit Web site. Accepts inquiries by SASE, e-mail, phone. "Be prepared to listen to the speakers carefully and to network among participants."

NY STATE SUMMER WRITERS INSTITUTE

Skidmore College, 815 N. Broadway, Saratoga Springs NY 12866. (518)580-5593. Fax: (518)580-5548. E-mail: cmerrill@skidmore.edu. Web site: www.skidmore.edu/summer. **Contact:** Christine Merrill, program coordinator. Estab. 1987. Annual. Conference duration: Two-week or four-week session. Average attendance: 80 per two-week session. This event features fiction, nonfiction, poetry and short story workshops. College credit is available for four-week attendees. Site: held on Skidmore campus—dorm residency and dining hall meals. "Summer in Saratoga is beautiful." Past faculty has included Amy Hempel, Nick Delbanco, Margot Livesey, Jay McInerney, Rick Moody and Lee K. Abbott. Visiting faculty has included Joyce Carol Oates, Russell Banks, Ann Beattie, Michael Cunningham and Michael Ondaatje.

Costs Tuition is $1,000 for 2 weeks and $2,000 for 4 weeks. Room and board is additional—$630 for 2 weeks and $1,260 for 4 weeks. "These are 2006 rates. Visit Web site for updated fees for our 2007 institute."

Additional Information "Writing samples are required with applications: fiction, 5-20 pages; poetry, 2-3 poems; nonfiction prose, 5-20 pages."

◎ ODYSSEY FANTASY WRITING WORKSHOP

P.O. Box 75, Mont Vernon NH 03057-1420. Phone/fax: (603)673-6234. E-mail: jcavelos@sff.net. Web site: www.sff.net/odyssey. **Contact:** Jeanne Cavelos, director. Estab. 1996. Annual. Last workshop held June 11 to July 20, 2007. Conference duration: 6 weeks. Average attendance: limited to 16. "A workshop for fantasy, science fiction and horror writers that combines an intensive learning and writing experience with in-depth feedback on students' manuscripts. The only workshop to combine the overall guidance of a single instructor with the varied perspectives of guest lecturers. Also, the only such workshop run by a former New York City book editor." Site: conference held at Saint Anselm College in Manchester, New Hampshire. Previous guest lecturers included: George R.R. Martin, Harlan Ellison, Ben Bova, Dan Simmons, Jane Yolen, Elizabeth Hand, Terry Brooks, Craig Shaw Gardner, Patricia McKillip and John Crowley.

Costs In 2007: $1,700 tuition, $700 housing (double room), $1,400 (single room); $25 application fee, $500-600 food (approximate), $150 processing fee to receive college credit.

Accommodations "Workshop students stay at Saint Anselm College Apartments and eat at college."

Additional Information Students must apply and include a writing sample. Students' works are critiqued throughout the 6 weeks. Workshop information available in October. For brochure/guidelines send SASE, e-mail, visit Web site, call or fax. Accepts inquiries by SASE, e-mail, fax, phone.

THE PUBLISHING GAME

Peanut Butter and Jelly Press, P.O. Box 590239, Newton MA 02459. E-mail: alyza@publishinggame.com. Web site: www.publishinggame.com. **Contact:** Alyza Harris, manager. Estab. 1998. Monthly. Conference held monthly, in different locales across North America: Boston, New York City, Philadelphia, Washington DC, Boca Raton, San Francisco, Los Angeles, Toronto, Seattle, Chicago. Conference duration: 9 a.m. to 4 p.m. Maximum attendance: 18 writers. "A one-day workshop on finding a literary agent, self-publishing your book, creating a publishing house and promoting your book to bestsellerdom!" Site: "Elegant hotels across the country. Boston locations alternate between the Four Seasons Hotel in downtown Boston and The Inn at Harvard in historic Harvard Square, Cambridge." Fiction panels in 2005 included Propel Your Novel from Idea to Finished Manuscript; How to Self-Publish Your Novel; Craft the Perfect Book Package; How to Promote Your Novel; Selling Your Novel to Bookstores and Libraries. Workshop led by Fern Reiss, author and publisher of The Publishing Game series.

Costs $195.

Accommodations "All locations are easily accessible by public transportation." Offers discounted conference rates for participants who choose to arrive early. Offers list of area lodging.

Additional Information Brochures available for SASE. Accepts inquiries by SASE, e-mail, phone, fax, but e-mail preferred. Agents and editors attend conference. "If you're considering finding a literary agent, self-publishing your novel or just want to sell more copies of your book, this conference will teach you everything you need to know to successfully publish and promote your work."

ROBERT QUACKENBUSH'S CHILDREN'S BOOK WRITING & ILLUSTRATING WORKSHOPS

460 E. 79th St., New York NY 10021-1443. (212)744-3822. Fax: (212)861-2761. E-mail: rqstudios@aol.com. Web site: www.rquackenbush.com. **Contact:** Robert Quackenbush, director. Estab. 1982. Annual. Workshop to be held during second week of July. Conference duration: Four days. Average attendance: 10. Workshops to promote writing and illustrating books for children. "Focus is generally on picture books, easy-to-read and early chapter books. Come prepared with stories and/or illustrations to be developed or in a finished state ready to present to a publisher. And be ready to meet a lot of nice people to help you." Site: Held at the Manhattan studio of Robert Quackenbush, author and illustrator of more than 180 books for children. All classes led by Robert Quackenbush.

Costs $650 tuition covers all the costs of the workshop but does not include housing and meals. A $100 nonrefundable deposit is required with the $550 balance due two weeks prior to attendance.

Accommodations A list of recommended hotels and restaurants is sent upon receipt of deposit.

Additional Information Class is for beginners and professionals. Critiques during workshop. Private consultations also available at an hourly rate. "Programs suited to your needs; individualized schedules can be designed. Write or phone to discuss your goals and you will receive a prompt reply." Conference information available 1 year prior to conference. For brochure, send SASE, e-mail, visit Web site, call or fax. Accepts inquiries by fax, e-mail, phone, SASE.

REMEMBER THE MAGIC IWWG ANNUAL SUMMER CONFERENCE

International Women's Writing Guild, P.O. Box 810, Gracie Station, New York NY 10028-0082. (212)737-7536. Fax: (212)737-9469. Web site: www.iwwg.com. **Contact:** Hannelore Hahn. Estab. 1978. Annual. Conference held in the summer. Conference duration: 1 week. Average attendance: 500. The conference features 65 workshops held every day on every aspect of writing and the arts. Site: Saratoga Springs, 30 minutes from Albany, NY, and 4 hours from New York City. Conference is held "on the tranquil campus of Skidmore College in Saratoga Springs, where the serene Hudson Valley meets the North Country of the Adirondacks."

Costs $1,004 single, $869 double (members); $1,034 single, $899 double (non-members). Five day, weekend and commuter rates are also available. Includes meals and lodging.

Accommodations Modern, air-conditioned and non-air-conditioned dormitories—single and/or double occupancy. Equipped with spacious desks and window seats for gazing out onto nature. Meals served cafeteria-style with choice of dishes. Variety of fresh fruits, vegetables and salads have been found plentiful, even by vegetarians. Conference information is available now. For brochure send SASE, e-mail, visit Web site or fax. Accepts inquiries by SASE, e-mail, phone or fax. "The conference is for women only."

SCBWI WINTER CONFERENCE, NYC

(formerly SCBWI Midyear Conference), 8271 Beverly Blvd., Los Angeles CA 90048. (323)782-1010. Fax: (323)782-1892. E-mail: conference@scbwi.org. Web site: www.scbwi.org. **Contact:** Stephen Mooser. Estab. 2000. Annual. Conference held in February. Average attendance: 800. Conference is to promote writing and illustrating for children: picture books; fiction; nonfiction; middle grade and young adult; network with professionals; financial planning for writers; marketing your book; art exhibition; etc. Site: Manhattan.

Costs See Web site for current cost and conference information.

SCBWI/HOFSTRA CHILDREN'S LITERATURE CONFERENCE

University College for Continuing Education, Hofstra University, Hempstead NY 11549. (516)463-7600. Web site: www.hofstra.edu/ucce/childLitConf. **Contact:** Connie C. Epstein, Adrienne Betz and Judith Reed, co-organizers. Estab. 1985. Annual. Average attendance: 200. Conference to encourage good writing for children. "Purpose is to bring together various professional groups—writers, illustrators, librarians, teachers—who are interested in writing for children." Site: The conference takes place at the Student Center Building of Hofstra University, located in Hempstead, Long Island. "Each year we organize the program around a theme. This year's theme is "The Rhythm of the Book." We have two general sessions, an editorial panel and six break-out groups held in rooms in the Center." Previous agents/speakers have included: Paula Danziger and Anne M. Martin and a panel of children's book editors critique randomly selected first-manuscript pages submitted by registrants. Special interest groups are offered in picture books, nonfiction and submission procedures, with others in fiction.

Costs $82 (previous year) for SCBWI members; $87 for nonmembers. Lunch included.

SEACOAST WRITERS ASSOCIATION SPRING AND FALL CONFERENCES

59 River Road, Stratham NH 03885-2358. E-mail: patparnell@comcast.net. **Contact:** Pat Parnell, conference coordinator. Annual. Conferences held in May and October. Conference duration: 1 day. Average attendance: 60. "Our conferences offer workshops covering various aspects of fiction, nonfiction and poetry." Site: Chester College of New England in Chester, New Hampshire.

Costs Appr. $50.

Additional Information "We sometimes include critiques. It is up to the speaker." Spring meeting includes a contest. Categories are fiction, nonfiction (essays) and poetry. Judges vary from year to year. Conference and contest information available for SASE December 1, April 1, and September 1. Accepts inquiries by SASE, e-mail and phone. For further information, check the Web site www.seacoastwritersassociation.org.

THE SOUTHAMPTON COLLEGE WRITERS CONFERENCE

239 Montauk Highway, Southampton NY 11968. (631)632-5030. Fax: (631)632-2578. E-mail: southamptonwrite rs@stonybrook.edu. Web site: www.stonybrook.edu/writers. **Contact:** Adrienne Unger, administrative coordinator. Estab. 1975. Annual. Conference held in July. Conference duration: 12 days. Average attendance: 95. The primary work of the conference is conducted in writing workshops in the novel, short story, poem, play, literary essay and memoir. Site: The seaside campus of Southampton College is located in the heart of the Hamptons, a renowned resort area only 70 miles from New York City. During free time, participants can draw inspiration from Atlantic beaches or explore the charming seaside towns. Faculty has included Frank McCourt, Billy Collins, Bharati Mukherjee, Roger Rosenblatt, Ursula Hegi, Alan Alda, and Jules Feiffer, Melissa Bank and Matt Klam.

Costs Application fee: $25; tuition, room and board: $2,050; tuition only: $1,450 (includes breakfast and lunch).

Accommodations On-campus housing—doubles and small singles with shared baths—is modest but comfortable. Housing assignment is by lottery. Supplies list of lodging alternatives.

Additional Information Applicants must complete an application form and submit a writing sample of unpublished, original work up to 20 pages (15 pages for poetry). See Web site for details. Brochures available in December by fax, phone, e-mail and on Web site. Accepts inquiries by SASE, e-mail, phone and fax. Editors and agents attend this conference.

VERMONT COLLEGE POSTGRADUATE WRITERS' CONFERENCE

36 College St., Montpelier VT 05602. (802)223-2133. Fax: (802)828-8585. E-mail: roger.weingarten@tui.edu. Web site: www.tui.edu/conferences. **Contact:** Roger Weingarten, director. Estab. 1995. Annual. August 8-14. Conference duration: 6 days. Average attendance: 65. This workshop covers the following areas of writing: novels, short stories, creative nonfiction, poetry, poetry manuscript and translation. Site: Union Institute & University's historic Vermont College campus in Montpelier. Workshops are centered on craft and often include exercises. 2007 facutly include Short Story: Ellen Lesser, Pamela Painter, and Michael Martone; Novel: Rikki Ducornet, Victoria Redel; Creative Nonfiction: Sue William Silverman and Larry Sutin; Poetry Manuscript: Richard Jackson, Clare Rossini, and Charles Harper Webb; Poetry: Nancy Eimers, Mary Ruefle, Bruce Weigl and Roger Weingarter.

Costs Tuition is $800-875; private dorm room: $330; shared dorm room is $180; meals: $140.

Accommodations Shuttles from airport available.

Additional Information Workshop material must be submitted 6 weeks prior to conference. Submit 25 pages of prose, 6 pages of poetry, 50 pages of poetry ms. Brochures available at Web site. "This conference is for advanced writers with postgraduate degrees or equivalent experience. Workshops are limited to 5-7 participants. Scholarship support available. Contact director."

VERMONT STUDIO CENTER

P.O. Box 613, Johnson VT 05656. (802)635-2727. Fax: (802)635-2730. E-mail: writing@vermontstudiocenter.o rg. Web site: www.vermontstudiocenter.org. **Contact:** Michael Schiavo, writing program coordinator. Estab. 1984. Ongoing residencies. Conference duration: From 2-12 weeks. "Most residents stay for 1 month." Average attendance: 53 writers and visual artists/month. "The Vermont Studio Center is an international creative community located in Johnson, Vermont, and serving more than 500 American and international artists and writers each year (50 per month). A Studio Center Residency features secluded, uninterrupted writing time, the companionship of dedicated and talented peers, and access to a roster of two distinguished Visiting Writers each month. All VSC Residents receive three meals a day, private, comfortable housing and the company of an international community of painters, sculptors, poets, printmakers and writers. Writers attending residencies at the Studio Center may work on whatever they choose—no matter what month of the year they attend." Visiting writers have included Ron Carlson, Donald Revell, Jane Hirshfield, Rosanna Warren, Chris Abani, Bob Shacochis, Tony Hoagland, and Alice Notley.

Costs "The cost of a 4-week residency is $3,500. Many applicants receive financial aid."

Accommodations Provided.

Additional Information Conferences may be arranged with visiting writers of the resident's genre. If conference scheduled, resident may submit up to 15 pages of ms. "We have competitions for full fellowships three times a year. The deadlines are February 15, June 15 and October 1. Writers should submit manuscripts of 15 pages. Application fee is $25." Writers encouraged to visit Web site for more information. May also e-mail, call, fax.

WESLEYAN WRITERS CONFERENCE

Wesleyan University, 294 High St., room 207, Middletown CT 06459. (860)685-3604. Fax: (860)685-2441. E-mail: agreene@wesleyan.edu. Web site: www.wesleyan.edu/writers. **Contact:** Anne Greene, director. Estab. 1956. Annual. Conference held the third week of June. Average attendance: 100. For fiction techniques, novel, short story, poetry, screenwriting, nonfiction, literary journalism, memoir. Site: The conference is held on the campus of Wesleyan University, in the hills overlooking the Connecticut River. Meals and lodging are provided on campus. Features daily seminars, lectures and workshops; optional mss consultations and guest speakers on a range of topics including publishing. "Both new and experienced writers are welcome."

Costs In 2006, day students' rate $980 (included tuition, meals) boarding students' rate of $1,190 (included tuition, meals and room for 5 nights).

Accommodations "Participants can fly to Hartford or take Amtrak to Meriden, CT. We are happy to help participants make travel arrangements." Overnight participants stay on campus or in hotels.

Additional Information "Award-winning faculty. Participants are welcome to attend seminars in a range of genres if they are interested. Scholarships and teaching fellowships are available, including the Joan Jakobson Scholarships for new writers of fiction, poetry and nonfiction and the Jon Davidoff Scholarships for journalists." Accepts inquiries by e-mail, phone, fax.

WRITER'S VOICE OF THE WEST SIDE YMCA

5 West 63rd Street, New York NY 10023. (212)875-4124. Fax: (212)875-4184. E-mail: graucher@ymcanyc.org. **Contact:** Glenn Raucher. Estab. 1981. Workshop held 6 times/year. Conference duration: 8 weeks; 2 hours, one night/week. Average attendance: 12. Workshop on "fiction, poetry, writing for performance, nonfiction, multi-genre, playwriting and memoir." Special one-day intensives throughout the year. Frequent Visiting Author readings, which are free and open to the public. Site: Workshop held at the Westside YMCA.

Costs $400/workshop, $320 for summer session, free for West Side Y members.

Additional Information For workshop brochures/guidelines send e-mail or call. Accepts inquiries by SASE, e-mail, fax, phone. "The Writer's Voice of the Westside Y is the largest non-academic literary arts center in the U.S."

YADDO

Box 395, Saratoga Springs NY 12866-0395. (518)584-0746. Fax: (518)584-1312. E-mail: yaddo@yaddo.org. Web site: www.yaddo.org. **Contact:** Candace Wait, program director. Estab. 1900. Two seasons: large season is in mid-May-August; small season is late September-May (stays from 2 weeks to 2 months; average stay is 5 weeks). Average attendance: Accommodates approximately 32 artists in large season, 12-15 in the small season. "Those qualified for invitations to Yaddo are highly qualified writers, visual artists, composers, choreographers, performance artists and film and video artists who are working at the professional level in their fields. Artists who wish to work collaboratively are encouraged to apply. An abiding principle at Yaddo is that applications for residencies are judged on the quality of the artists' work and professional promise." Site: includes four small lakes, a rose garden, woodland.

Costs No fee is charged; residency includes room, board and studio space. Limited travel expenses are available to artists accepted for residencies at Yaddo.

Accommodations Provisions include room, board and studio space. No stipends are offered.

Additional Information To apply: Filing fee is $20 (checks payable to Corporation of Yaddo). Two letters of recommendation are requested. Applications are considered by the Admissions Committee and invitations are issued by March 15 (deadline: January 1) and October 1 (deadline: August 1). Information available for SASE (63¢ postage), by e-mail, fax or phone and on Web site. Accepts inquiries by e-mail, fax, SASE, phone.

MIDATLANTIC (DC, DE, MD, NJ, PA)

BAY TO OCEAN WRITERS' CONFERENCE

Chesapeake College, Wye Mills, MD 21679. (410)820-8822. E-mail: clj@goeaston.net. Web site: www.talb.lib.m d.us/baytoocean. **Contact:** Carolyn Jaffe. Estab. 1998. Annual. Conference held in February. Conference duration: 1 day. Average attendance: 100. Conference focuses on publishing, agenting, marketing, craft, fiction, journalism, memoir-writing, children's literature, screen writing, travel writing, nonfiction and freelance writing. Site: Chesapeake College, Near Easton on Maryland's historic Eastern Shore. Accessible to individuals with disabilities. 2007 featured 22 writers and instructors and a choice of 15 programs, including filmmaker Doug Sandler; authors Mary Jo Putney, Rebecca York, Candice Poarch, Mala and Roger Burt, Margaret Meacham, and Donna Andrews; Sheila Buckmaster, senior editor of *National Geographic Traveler*; publishers Gregg Wilhelm; literary agent Gail Ross; writers Austin Camacho, Dr. Ann Hennessy, Bonna Nelson, Judy Reveal and Diane Marquette; and actor David Foster.

Costs $80; includes sessions, continental breakfast and networking lunch.

Additional Information Brochures available in December at www.talb.lib.md.us/baytoocean. Accepts inquiries by e-mail and phone. Agents and editors attend this conference. Conference is for writers of all levels, especially new to intermediate writers.

HIGHLIGHTS FOUNDATION FOUNDERS WORKSHOPS

814 Court St., Honesdale PA 18431. (570)253-1192. Fax: (570)253-0179. E-mail: contact@highlightsfoundation. org. Web site: www.highlightsfoundation.org. **Contact:** Kent L. Brown Jr., executive director. Estab. 2000. Workshops held seasonally from March through November. Conference duration: 3-7 days. Average attendance: limited to 8-15. Conference focuses on children's writing: fiction, nonfiction, poetry, promotions, picture books, writing from nature, young adult novels, and much more. "Our goal is to improve, over time, the quality of literature for children by educating future generations of children's authors." Recent faculty/speakers have included Joy Cowley, Patricia Lee Gauch, Carolyn Yoder, Sandy Asher, Rebecca Dotlich, Carolyn Coman, Jane Resh Thomas, Rich Wallace and Peter Jacobi.

Costs Range from $545 and up, including meals, lodging, materials.

Accommodations "Participants stay in guest cabins on the wooded grounds surrounding Highlights Founders' home adjacent to the house/conference center, near Honesdale, PA."

Additional Information "Some workshops require pre-workshop assignment." Brochure available for SASE, by e-mail, on Web site, by phone, by fax. Accepts inquiries by phone, fax, e-mail, SASE. Editors attend conference. "Applications will be reviewed and accepted on a first-come, first-served basis. Applicants must demonstrate specific experience in writing area of workshop they are applying for—writing samples are required for many of the workshops."

MONTROSE CHRISTIAN WRITER'S CONFERENCE

5 Locust Street, Montrose Bible Conference, Montrose PA 18801-1112. (570)278-1001 or (800)598-5030. Fax: (570)278-3061. E-mail: mbc@montrosebible.org. Web site: www.montrosebible.org. **Contact:** Donna Kosik, MBC Secretary/Registrar. Estab. 1990. Annual. Conference held in July 2007. Average attendance: 85. "We try to meet a cross-section of writing needs, for beginners and advanced, covering fiction, poetry and writing for children. It is small enough to allow personal interaction between conferees and faculty. We meet in the beautiful village of Montrose, Pennsylvania, situated in the mountains. The Bible Conference provides hotel/ motel-like accommodation and good food. The main sessions are held in the chapel with rooms available for other classes. Fiction writing has been taught each year."

Costs In 2007 registration (tuition) was $150.

Accommodations Will meet planes in Binghamton, NY and Scranton, PA. On-site accomodations: room and board $255-300/conference; $55-65/day including food (2007 rates). RV court available.

Additional Information "Writers can send work ahead of time and have it critiqued for a small fee." The attendees are usually church related. The writing has a Christian emphasis. Conference information available April 2007. For brochure send SASE, visit Web site, e-mail, call or fax. Accepts inquiries by SASE, e-mail, fax, phone.

SANDY COVE CHRISTIAN WRITERS CONFERENCE

60 Sandy Cove Rd., North East MD 21901-5436. (800)234-2683. Fax: (410)287-3196. E-mail: info@sandycove. org or jim@jameswatkins.com. Web site: www.sandycovewriters.com. **Contact:** Jim Watkins, director of conference. Estab. 1982. Annual. Last conference held September 30-October 3, 2007. Average attendance: 160. Focus is on "all areas of writing from a Christian perspective such as: periodicals, devotionals, fiction, juvenile fiction, Sunday School curriculum, screenwriting, self-publishing, Internet writing, etc." Site: "Sandy Cove is conveniently located mid-way between Baltimore and Philadelphia, just off I-95." Located on 220 acres of

Maryland woodland, near headwaters of the Chesapeake Bay. Visit Web site for current date and faculty.
Costs In 2007, costs were full package: $499 per person (single room occupancy) or $440 per person (double room occupancy)—includes lodging, meals, materials, seminars, sessions, private appointments and 2 ms evaluations. Add $15/night for bay-view room.
Accommodations No arrangements for transportation. "Hotel-style rooms, bay view available. Suites available for additional fee."
Additional Information "Manuscript critiques from editors and professional writers offered. See Web site for details. Also offers 1-day student training for high school and college age students."

WASHINGTON INDEPENDENT WRITERS (WIW) WASHINGTON WRITERS CONFERENCE

1001 Connecticut Ave. NW, Ste. 70, Washington DC 20036. (202)775-5150. Fax: (202)775-5810. E-mail: info@washwriter.org. Web site: www.washwriter.org. **Contact:** Donald Graul Jr., executive director. Estab. 1975. Annual. Conference held in June. Conference duration: Saturday. Average attendance: 450. "Gives participants a chance to hear from and talk with dozens of experts on book and magazine publishing as well as meet one-on-one with literary agents." Site: George Washington University Cafritz Center. Past keynote speakers included Erica Jong, Diana Rehm, Kitty Kelley, Lawrence Block, John Barth, Stephen Hunter. 2007 Keynote Speaker, Francine Prose.
Additional Information Send inquiries to info@washwriter.org.

WINTER POETRY & PROSE GETAWAY IN CAPE MAY

18 North Richards Ave., Ventnor NJ 08406. (609)823-5076. E-mail: info@wintergetaway.com. Web site: www.wintergetaway.com. **Contact:** Peter E. Murphy, founder/director. Estab. 1994. Annual. 2008 dates: January 18-21. Conference duration: Four-day event. Average attendance: 200. Open to all writers, beginners and experienced over the age of 18. Workshops offered include Writing New Stories, Revising a Short Story Toward Publication, Focusing Your Fiction, Finishing Your Novel, as well as workshops in Creative Nonfiction and Turning Memory into Memoir. Workshops meet from 9-4 Saturday & Sunday and 9-12 on Monday. The Getaway also features workshops in poetry writing, song writing, writing for children, painting and photography. Other special features include extra-supportive sessions for beginners. There are usually 10 or fewer participants in each workshop and fewer than 7 in each of the prose workshops. Previous staff have included Renée Ashley, Christian Bauman, Anndee Hochman, Laura McCullough, Joyce McDonald, Carol Plum-Ucci and Robbie Clipper Sethi.
Costs Cost for 2007 was $350. Rooms at the hotel were $215 for a double and $360 for a single and included breakfast and lunch. A $25 "early bard" discount is available if full payment is made by November 15.
Accommodations "The Grand Hotel on the Oceanfront in Historic Cape May, NJ. Participants stay in comfortable rooms, most with an ocean view, perfect for thawing out the muse. Hotel facilities include a pool, sauna, and whirlpool, as well as a lounge and disco for late evening dancing for night people."
Additional Information "Individual critiques available." Brochure and registration form available by mail or on Web site. "The Winter Getaway is known for its challenging and supportive workshops that encourage imaginative risk-taking and promote freedom and transformation in the participants' writing."

MIDSOUTH (NC, SC, TN, VA, WV)

AMERICAN CHRISTIAN WRITERS CONFERENCES

P.O. Box 110390, Nashville TN 37222. (800)21-WRITE. Fax: (615)834-7736. E-mail: ACWriters@aol.com. Web site: www.ACWriters.com. **Contact:** Reg Forder, director. Estab. 1988. Annual. Conferences held throughout the year in over 2 dozen cities. Conference duration: 2 days. Average attendance: 30-80. Conference's purpose is to promote all forms of Christian writing. Site: Usually located at a major hotel chain like Holiday Inn.
Costs $109 for 1 day; $199 for 2 days. Plus meals and accommodations.
Accommodations Special rates available at host hotel.
Additional Information Conference information available for SASE, e-mail, phone or fax. Accepts inquiries by fax, e-mail, phone, SASE.

◎ BLUE RIDGE MOUNTAINS CHRISTIAN WRITERS CONFERENCE

(800)588-7222. E-mail: ylehman@bellsouth.net. Web site: www.lifeway.com/christianwriters. **Contact:** Yvonne Lehman, director. Estab. 1999. Annual. Last conference held May 20-24, 2007. Average attendance: 240. All areas of Christian writing, including fiction, nonfiction, scriptwriting, devotionals, greeting cards, etc. For beginning and advanced writers. Site: LifeWay Ridgecrest Conference Center, 18 miles east of Asheville, NC. "Companies represented this year include AMG Publications, Broadman and Holman, Focus on the Family, Howard Publishers, Upper Room, LifeWay Christian Resources, Lawson Falle Greeting Cards & Gift Books,

Christian Film & TV, Crosswalk, Evangel, Christian Writers Guild, Light and Life, Living Ink Books, NavPress, WestBow Press, MovieGuide, Hartline Literary Agency, Les Stobbe Agency, Bethany House, God Allows U-turns, Forevermore, Publisher's Weekly, Lifeline Journal Magazine, Hensley Publishing, Veggie Tales. '' Faculty includes professional authors, agents and editors.

Costs In 2007: $315, which includes all sessions, breaks, and a special Wednesday evening banquet. Additional on-campus meal package available for $98/person.

Accommodations LifeWay Ridgecrest Conference Center. See Web site for on-campus room rates.

Additional Information Sponsors contests for unpublished in categories for poetry and lyrics, articles and short stories, novels and novellas, nonfiction, greeting cards and scripts. Awards include trophy and $200 scholarship toward next year's conference. See Web site for critique service and daily schedule—offering keynote sessions, continuing classes and workshops.

HIGHLAND SUMMER CONFERENCE

Box 7014, Radford University, Radford VA 24142-7014. (540)831-5366. Fax: (540)831-5951. E-mail: jasbury@radford.edu. Web site: www.radford.edu/~arsc **Contact:** Jo Ann Asbury, assistant to director. Estab. 1978. Annual. Conference held first 2 weeks of June. Conference duration: 2 weeks. Average attendance: 25. Three hours graduate or undergraduate credits. Site: The Highland Summer Conference is held at Radford University, a school of about 9,000 students. Radford is in the Blue Ridge Mountains of southwest Virginia, about 45 miles south of Roanoke, VA. ''The HSC features one (two weeks) or two (one week each) guest leaders each year. As a rule, our leaders are well-known writers who have connections, either thematic or personal or both, to the Appalachian region. The genre emphasis depends upon the workshop leader(s). In the past we have had as guest lecturers Nikki Giovanni, Sharyn McCrumb, Gurney Norman, Denise Giardinia, George Ella Lyon, Jim Wayne Miller, Wilma Dykeman and Robert Morgan.''

Costs ''The cost is based on current Radford tuition for 3 credit hours plus an additional conference fee. On-campus meals and housing are available at additional cost. 2005 conference tuition was $594 for in-state undergraduates, $678 for graduate students.''

Accommodations ''We do not have special rate arrangements with local hotels. We do offer accommodations on the Radford University Campus in a recently refurbished residence hall. (In 2005 cost was $24.04-33.44 per night.)''

Additional Information ''Conference leaders typically critique work done during the two-week conference, but do not ask to have any writing submitted prior to the conference beginning.'' Conference information available after February for SASE. Accepts inquiries by e-mail, fax.

HILTON HEAD ISLAND WRITERS RETREAT

52 Brams Point Road, Hilton Head Island SC 29926. E-mail: bob@bobmayer.org. Web site: www.bobmayer.org. **Contact:** Bob Mayer. Estab. 2002. Every 3 months. Last conference: November 2007. Conference duration: 4 days. Site: Held at the Marriott Beach & Golf Resort, oceanside, Hilton Head Island.

Costs $550 in 2007.

Accommodations At Marriott.

Additional Information Participants will submit cover letter, one-page synopsis, and first 15 pages of ms.

N KILLER NASHVILLE

P.O. Box 680686, Franklin TN 37068-0686. (615)599-4032. E-mail: contact@killernashville.com. Web site: www.KillerNashville.com. **Contact:** Clay Stafford, regional president, Southeast Mystery Writers of America. Estab. 2006. Annual. Next event: September 2008. Conference duration: 2-3 days. Average attendance: 150. ''Conference designed for writers and fans of mysteries and thrillers, including authors (fiction and nonfiction), playwrights, and screenwriters. Killer Nashville sponsors include Mystery Writers of America, Southeast Mystery Writers of America, American Blackguard, Barnes & Noble Booksellers, First Tennessee Bank, Landmark Booksellers. Event includes book signings and panels. Many opportunities for authors to sign books.'' Past panelists included authors Carol Higgins Clark, P.J. Parrish, Reed Farrel Coleman, Gwen Hunter, Kathryn Wall; authors/screenwriters Alexandra Sokoloff, Steven Womack, Clay Stafford; attorney Helen Wu (Yu Leseberg/King Holmes Paterno & Berlinger), agent Carey Nelson Burch (William Morris Agency), publicist Eddie Lightsey (American Blackguard Public Relations).

Costs Many free events; Saturday conference $55 (includes buffet lunch).

Additional Information ''Additional information about registration is provided at www.KillerNashville.com.''

NORTH CAROLINA WRITERS' NETWORK FALL CONFERENCE

P.O. Box 954, Carrboro NC 27510-0954. (919)967-9540. Fax: (919)929-0535. E-mail: mail@ncwriters.org. Web site: www.ncwriters.org. **Contact:** Cynthia Barnett, executive director. Estab. 1985. Annual. Average attendance: 450. ''The conference is a weekend full of classes, panels, readings and informal gatherings. The Network serves writers at all stages of development from beginning, to emerging, to established. We also encourage readers who might be considering writing. We have several genres represented. In the past we have offered fiction, nonfiction, poetry, screenwriting, writing for children, journalism and more. We always invite New York editors and agents and offer craft classes in editing, pitching and marketing." Site: "We hold the conference at a conference center with hotel rooms available."

Costs "Conference registration fee for NCWN members is approximately $250 and includes at least two meals."
Accommodations "Special conference hotel rates are available, but the individual makes his/her own reservations."
Additional Information For brochure, e-mail us or visit our Web site. Online secure registration available at www.ncwriters.org.

OUTDOOR WRITERS ASSOCIATION OF AMERICA ANNUAL CONFERENCE

OWWA, 121 Hickory St., Suite 1, Missoula MT 59801. (406)728-7434. Fax: (406)728-7445. E-mail: owaa@montana.com. Web site: www.owaa.org. **Contact:** Eileen King, meeting planner. Estab. 1927. Annual. Conference held June 16-19, 2007, in Roanoke, Virginia. Average attendance: 700-750. Conference concentrates on outdoor communications (all forms of media). Featured speakers have included Don Ranley, University of Missouri, Columbia; Brig. General Chuck Yeager; Nina Leopold Bradley (daughter of Aldo Leopold); Secretary of the Interior, Gail Norton; Bill Irwin, the only blind man to hike the Appalachian Trail.
Costs $325 for nonmembers; "applicants must have prior approval from the Executive Director." Registration fee includes cost of most meals.
Accommodations List of accommodations available after February. Special room rates for attendees.
Additional Information Sponsors contests, "but all is done prior to the conference and you must be a member to enter them." Conference information available February 2007. For brochure visit Web site, send e-mail, call or fax. Accepts inquiries by e-mail, fax.

SEWANEE WRITERS' CONFERENCE

735 University Ave., Sewanee TN 37383-1000. (931)598-1141. E-mail: cpeters@sewanee.edu. Web site: www.sewaneewriters.org. **Contact:** Cheri B. Peters, creative writing programs manager. Estab. 1990. Annual. 2007 conference held in July. Average attendance: 120. "We offer genre-based workshops in fiction, poetry and playwriting and a full schedule of readings, craft lectures, panel discussions, talks, Q&A sessions and the like." Site: "The Sewanee Writers' Conference uses the facilities of Sewanee: The University of the South. Physically, the University is a collection of ivy-covered Gothic-style buildings, located on the Cumberland Plateau in mid-Tennessee." Invited editors, publishers and agents structure their own presentations, but there is always opportunity for questions from the audience." 2007 faculty included fiction writers Richard Bausch, John Casey, Tony Earley, Diane Johnson, Randall Kenan, Alison Lurie, Jill McCorkle, and Claire Messud; Poets Brad Leithauser, Charles Martin, Mary Jo Salter, Alan Shapiro, Mark Strand, and Greg Williamson; and playwrights Lee Blessing and Melanie Marnich.
Costs Full conference fee (tuition, board and basic room) is $1,600; a single room costs an additional $85.
Accommodations Participants are housed in university dormitory rooms. Motel or B&B housing is available but not abundantly so. The cost of shared dormitory housing is included in the full conference fee. Complimentary chartered bus service is available—on a limited basis—on the first and last days of the conference.
Additional Information "We offer each participant (excepting auditors) the opportunity for a private manuscript conference with a member of the faculty. These manuscripts are due one month before the conference begins." Conference information available begining in Mid-January. The application season runs from January 15 to May 1, or until all spaces have been filled. Early application is encouraged. For brochure send address and phone number, e-mail, visit Web site or call. "The conference has available a limited number of fellowships and scholarships; these are awarded on a competitive basis."

STELLARCON

Box I-1, Elliott University Center, UNCG, Greensboro NC 27412. E-mail: info@stellarcon.org. Web site: www.stellarcon.org. **Contact:** Mike Monaghan, convention manager. Estab. 1976. Annual. Last conference held March 9-11, 2007. Average attendance: 500. Conference focuses on "general science fiction and fantasy (horror also) with an emphasis on literature." Site: Downtown Radisson, High Point, NC. See Web site for 2008 speakers.
Costs See Web site for 2008 rates.
Accommodations "Lodging is available at the Radisson."
Additional Information Accepts inquiries by e-mail. Agents and editors participate in conference.

VIRGINIA FESTIVAL OF THE BOOK

145 Ednam Dr., Charlottesville VA 22903. (434)924-6890. Fax: (434)296-4714. E-mail: vabook@virginia.edu. Web site: www.vabook.org. **Contact:** Nancy Damon, programs director. Estab. 1995. Annual. Festival held in

March. Average attendance: 22,000. Festival held to celebrate books and promote reading and literacy. Site: Held throughout the Charlottesville/Albemarle area.

Costs See Web site for 2008 rates.

Accommodations Overnight accomodations available.

Additional Information ''Authors must 'apply' to the festival to be included on a panel.'' Conference information is available on the Web site, e-mail, fax or phone. For brochure visit Web site. Accepts inquiries by e-mail, fax, phone. Authors, agents and editors participate in conference. ''The festival is a five-day event featuring authors, illustrators and publishing professionals. The featured authors are invited to convene for discussions and readings or write and inquire to participate. All attendees welcome.''

WILDACRE WRITERS WORKSHOP

233 S. Elm St., Greensboro NC 27401-2602. (336)370-9188. Fax: (336)370-9188. E-mail: judihill@aol.com. Web site: www.Wildacres.com. **Contact:** Judith Hill, director. Estab. 1985. Annual. Residential workshop held second week in July. Conference duration: 1 week. Average attendance: 110. Workshop focuses on novel, short story, poetry, creative nonfiction. Site: Beautiful retreat center on top of a mountain in the Blue Ridge Mountains of North Carolina. Faculty 2006: Ann Hood, Ron Rash, Gail Adams, Luke Whisnant, Rand Cooper, Thorpe Moeckel, Janice Fuller, Rebecca McClanahan, Philip Gerard.

Costs $550 (everything is included: workshop, ms critique, double room, all meals).

Accommodations Vans available, $50 round trip.

Additional Information ''New people must submit a writing sample to be accepted. Those attending send their manuscript one month prior to arrival.'' Workshop information is available mid-January. For brochure send e-mail or visit Web site. Accepts inquiries by e-mail and phone. Agents and editors participate in conference.

SOUTHEAST (AL, AR, FL, GA, LA, MS, PR [PUERTO RICO])

ALABAMA WRITERS' CONCLAVE

137 Sterline Dr., Hueytown AL 35023. E-mail: harrisjc@bellsouth.net. Web site: www.alabamawritersconclave. org. **Contact:** Jimmy Carl Harris, program chair; Don Johnson, treasurer. Estab. 1923. Last event held July 20-22, 2007. Average attendance: 80-100. Conference to promote all phases of writing. Also offers ms critiques and eight writing contests. Site: Dixon Conference Center and Auburn Hotel at Auburn University, Auburn, Alabama.

Costs Fees for conference are $150 (member)/$175 (nonmember), includes 2 meals. Critique fee $25 (member)/ $30 (nonmember). Membership $25.

Accommodations Special conference rate, $89 (+tax)/night at Auburn Hotel.

Additional Information ''We have major speakers and faculty members who conduct intensive, energetic workshops. Our annual writing contest guidelines and all other information is available at www.alabamawritersconcl ave.org.''

ARKANSAS WRITERS' CONFERENCE

AR Penwomen Pioneer Branch of the National League of American Penwomen, 6817 Gingerbread Lane, Little Rock AR 72204. (501)565-8889. Fax: (501)565-7220. E-mail: pvining@aristotle.net. Web site: http://groups.yah oo.com/group/arpenwomen. **Contact:** Send SASE to: Peggy Vining, at the address listed above. Estab. 1944. Annual. Conference held first weekend in June. Average attendance: 175. ''We have a variety of subjects related to writing. We have some general sessions, some more specific, but we try to vary each year's subjects.''

Costs Registration: $15; luncheon: $19; banquet: $20; contest entry $10 (2006 rates).

Accommodations ''We meet at a Holiday Inn Presidential in Little Rock. Rooms available at reduced rate.'' Holiday Inn has a bus to bring our attendees from the airport. Rooms average $79.

Additional Information ''We have 36 contest categories. Some are open only to Arkansans, most are open to all writers. Our judges are not announced before the conference. All are qualified, many from out of state.'' Conference information available February 15. For brochures or inquiries send SASE with full mailing address, call or fax. ''We have had 226 people attending from 12 states—over 2,000 contest entries from 40 states and New Zealand, Mexico and Canada.''

AWP ANNUAL CONFERENCE AND BOOKFAIR

MS 1E3, George Mason University, Fairfax VA 22030. (703)993-4301 Fax: (703)993-4302. E-mail: awpconf@gmu .edu. Web site: www.awpwriter.org. **Contact:** Matt Scanlon, director of conferences. Estab. 1967. Annual. Conference held January 30-February 2, 2008, in New York City. Conference duration: 4 days. Average attendance: 4,000. The annual conference is a gathering of 4,000+ students, teachers, writers, readers and publishers. All genres are represented. Site: This year the conference will be held at Hilton New York. ''We will offer

175 panels on everything from writing to teaching to critical analysis.'' In 2007, Lee Smith, John Barth, Kaye Gibbons, C.D. Wright, Ann Beattie, and Robert Olen Butler were special speakers.
Costs Early registration fees: $40 student; $140 AWP member; $160 non-member.
Accommodations Provide airline discounts and rental-car discounts. Special rate at Hilton.
Additional Information Check Web site for more information.

FLORIDA FIRST COAST WRITERS' FESTIVAL
D315 4501 Capper Rd., Jacksonville FL 32218. (904)766-6731. Fax: (904)713-4858. E-mail: dathomas@fccf.edu. Web site: opencampus.fccj.org/WF/. **Contact:** Dana Thomas, conference coordinator. Estab. 1985. Annual. Festival held in April 18-19, 2008. Average attendance: 300-350. All areas; mainstream plus genre. Site: Held at Crowne Plaza Hotel in Jacksonville.
Costs $100-$380, depending on days attended and meal packages.
Accommodations Check Web site for updated hotel rates.
Additional Information Sponsors contests for short fiction, poetry, novels, memoirs, playwriting. Conference information available in January. For brochures/guidelines visit Web site, e-mail, fax, call. Accepts inquiries by e-mail, phone, fax. E-mail contest inquiries to dathomas@fccj.edu.

GEORGIA WRITERS ASSOCIATION'S SPRING FESTIVAL OF WORKSHOPS
1071 Steeple Run, Lawrenceville GA 30043. (678)407-0703. Fax: (678)407-9917. E-mail: festival2007@georgiaw riters.org. Web site: www.georgiawriters.org; link to festival page:www.georgiawriters.org/Festival-2007.htm. **Contact:** Geri Taran. Estab. 1995. Annual. Last conference held May 5, 2007. Conference duration: 1 day. Average attendance: 200. Conference is comprehensive—all genres and business aspects of a writing career, and agents, publishers, editors. Approximately 20 workshops, 4 each hour running concurrently. Site: Smyrna Community Center (Atlanta vicinity), large main area, separate rooms for sessions. Presenters/speakers have included Bobbie Christmas, Michael Lucker, Peter Bowerman, Eric Haney, Barbara LeBey, David Fulmer and many others.
Costs 2007: $85 at the door; $75 in advance; $95 includes annual membership expiring on June 30, 2008 ($45 annual dues).

HOW TO BE PUBLISHED WORKSHOPS
P.O. Box 100031, Birmingham AL 35210-3006. (205)907-0140. E-mail: mike@writing2sell.com. Web site: www. writing2sell.com. **Contact:** Michael Garrett. Estab. 1986. Workshops are offered continuously year-round at various locations. Conference duration: 1 session. Average attendance: 10-15. Workshops to ''move writers of category fiction closer to publication.'' Focus is not on how to write, but how to get published. Site: Workshops held at college campuses and universities. Themes include marketing, idea development and manuscript critique.
Costs $55-89.
Additional Information ''Special critique is offered, but advance submission is not required.'' Workshop information available on Web site. Accepts inquiries by e-mail.

N MONTEVALLO LITERARY FESTIVAL
Sta. 6420, University of Montevallo, Montevallo AL 35115. (205)665-6420. Fax: (205)665-6422. E-mail: murphyj @montevallo.edu. Web site: www.montevallo.edu/english. **Contact:** Dr. Jim Murphy, director. Estab. 2003. Annual. Last festival held: April 13-14, 2007. Festival duration: 2 days. Average attendance: 60-100. ''Readings, panels, and workshops on all literary genres and on literary editing/publishing. Workshops with manuscript critiques in fiction, poetry, and drama.'' Site: Several sites on a bucolic liberal arts university campus. 2007 fiction workshop leader was John Dufresne. Past fiction workshop faculty included Patricia Foster, Tom Franklin, Sheri Joseph, Sena Jeter Naslund, Brad Vice, Brad Watson. See Web site for 2008 dates and speakers.
Costs In 2007: $45 for festival, including meals; $95 for festival, including meals and workshop.
Accommodations Free on-campus parking. Offers overnight accommodations at Ramsay Conference Center on campus. Rooms $40/night. Call (205)665-6280 for reservations. Visit www.montevallo.edu/cont_ed/ramsay.s htm for information.
Additional Information Workshop participants submit up to 5 pages of poetry/up to 15 pages of prose; e-mail as Word doc to Jim Murphy (murphyj@montevallo.edu) at least 2 weeks prior to festival. Information for upcoming festival available in Feb. For brochure, visit Web site. Accepts inquiries by mail (with SASE), e-mail, phone, and fax. Editors participate in conference. ''This is a friendly, relaxed 2-day festival dedicated to bringing literary writers and readers together on a personal scale.''

NATCHEZ LITERARY AND CINEMA CELEBRATION
P.O. Box 1307, Natchez MS 39121-1307. (601)446-1208. Fax: (601)446-1214. E-mail: carolyn.smith@colin.edu. Web site: www.colin.edu/NLCC. **Contact:** Carolyn Vance Smith, co-chairman. Estab. 1990. Annual. Conference

held February 22-25, 2007. Average attendance: 3,000. Conference focuses on "all literature, including film scripts." Site: 500-seat auditorium, various sizes of break-out rooms. Theme: "Southern Accents, Language in the Deep South." Scholars will speak on food and drink in history, literature, film and real life.

Costs "About $100, includes a meal, receptions, book signings, workshops. Lectures/panel discussions are free."

Accommodations "Groups can ask for special assistance. Usually they can be accommodated." Call 866-296-6522.

Additional Information "Participants need to read selected materials prior to attending writing workshops. Thus, pre-enrollment is advised." Conference information is available in Fall. For brochure send SASE, e-mail, visit Web site, call or fax. Accepts inquiries by SASE, e-mail, phone and fax. Agents and editors participate in conference.

OXFORD CONFERENCE FOR THE BOOK

Center for the Study of Southern Culture, The University of Mississippi, University MS 38677-1848. (662)915-5993. Fax: (662)915-5814. E-mail: aabadie@olemiss.edu. Web site: www.olemiss.edu/depts/south. **Contact:** Ann J. Abadie, associate director. Estab. 1993. Annual. Conference held in March or April. Average attendance: 300. "The conference celebrates books, writing and reading and deals with practical concerns on which the literary arts depend, including literacy, freedom of expression and the book trade itself. Each year's program consists of readings, lectures and discussions. Areas of focus are fiction, poetry, nonfiction and—occasionally—drama. We have, on occasion, looked at science fiction and mysteries. We always pay attention to children's literature." Site: University of Mississippi campus. Annual topics include Submitting Manuscripts/Working One's Way into Print; Finding a Voice/Reaching an Audience; The Endangered Species: Readers Today and Tomorrow. In 2006, among the more than 50 program participants were T.A. Barron, Ellen Douglas, Barry Hannah, Larry L. King, James Meek, Lewis Nordan, Jack Pendarvis, George Saunders, Annalyn Swan and Natasha Trethewey. Also on the program were publisher Sara Gorham and agent Alex Glass. The 2007 program, set for March 22-24, will be dedicated to the late author Larry Brown.

Costs "The conference is open to participants without charge."

Accommodations Provides list of area hotels.

Additional Information Brochures available in February by e-mail, on Web Site, by phone, by fax. Accepts inquiries by e-mail, phone, fax. Agents and editors participate in conference.

MARJORIE KINNAN RAWLINGS: WRITING THE REGION

P.O. Box 12246, Gainesville FL 32604. (888)917-7001. Fax: (352)373-8854. E-mail: shakes@ufl.edu. Web site: www.writingtheregion.com. **Contact:** Norma M. Homan, executive director. Estab. 1997. Annual. Last conference held July 25-29, 2007. Conference duration: 5 days. Average attendance: 120. Conference concentrates on fiction, writing for children, poetry, nonfiction, drama, screenwriting, writing with humor, setting, character, etc. Site: Conference held at historic building, formerly the Thomas Hotel.

Costs $385 for 5 days including meals; $365 "early bird" registration (breakfast and lunch); $130 single day; $80 half day.

Accommodations Special conference rates at area hotels available.

Additional Information Optional trip and dinner at Rawlings Home at Crosscreek offered. Evening activities and banquets also planned. Manuscript consultation on an individual basis by application only and $100 additional fee. Sponsors essay contest for registrants on a topic dealing with Marjorie Kinnan Rawlings. Call for brochures/ guidelines. Accepts inquiries by fax, e-mail. Call toll free 888-917-7001.

SCBWI SOUTHERN BREEZE FALL CONFERENCE

Writing and Illustrating for Kids, P.O. Box 26282, Birmingham AL 35260. E-mail: jskittinger@bellsouth.net. Web site: www.southern-breeze.org. **Contact:** Jo Kittinger, co-regional advisor. Estab. 1992. Annual. Conference held in October (usually the third Saturday). Conference duration: One-day Saturday conference. Average attendance: 140. "All Southern Breeze SCBWI conferences are geared to the production and support of quality children's literature." Keynote speakers TBA.

Costs About $110 for SCBWI members, $135 for non-members.

Accommodations "We have a room block with a conference rate. The conference is held at a nearby school."

Additional Information "The fall conference offers approximately 28 workshops on craft and the business of writing, including a basic workshop for those new to the children's field." Ms critiques are offered; mss must be sent by deadline. Conference information is included in the Southern Breeze newsletter, mailed in September. Brochure is available for SASE, by e-mail or visit Web site for details. Accepts inquiries by SASE or e-mail. Agents and editors attend/participate in conference. "Familiarize yourself with the works of the speakers before the event."

◎ SCBWI SOUTHERN BREEZE SPRING CONFERENCE

Springmingle '08, P.O. Box 26282, Birmingham AL 35260. E-mail: jskittinger@bellsouth.net. Web site: www.southern-breeze.org. **Contact:** Jo Kittinger, co-regional advisor. Estab. 1992. Annual. Conference held in February or March each year. Average attendance: 90. "All Southern Breeze SCBWI conferences are geared to the production and support of quality children's literature." Site: Event is held "in a hotel in the Atlanta, GA area." Speakers generally include editors, agents, authors, art directors and/or illustrators of children's books.

Costs "About $200; SCBWI non-members pay $10-15 more. Some meals are included."

Accommodations "We have a room block with a conference rate in the hotel conference site. Individuals make their own reservations."

Additional Information There will be ms critiques available this year for an additional fee. Manuscripts must be sent ahead of time. Conference information is included in the Southern Breeze newsletter, mailed in January. Brochure is available for SASE, by e-mail or visit Web site in January for details. Accepts inquiries by SASE, e-mail.

SOUTHEASTERN WRITERS ASSOCIATION

SWA, 161 Woodstone Dr., Athens GA 30605. E-mail: purple@southeasternwriters.com. Web site: www.southeasternwriters.com. **Contact:** Sheila Hudson, registrar. Estab. 1975. Annual. Conference held third week of June every year. Average attendance: 75 (limited to 100). Conference offers classes in fiction, nonfiction, juvenile, inspirational writing, poetry, etc. Site: Epworth-by-the-Sea, St. Simons Island, GA.

Costs 2007 costs: $359 early bird tuition, $399 after April 15, $125 daily tuition. Three days' tuition required for free manuscript conferences. Conference tuition includes $35 annual membership fee.

Accommodations Offers overnight accommodations. 2006 rates were approximately $650/single to $425/double and including motel-style room and 3 meals/day per person. Off site lodging also available.

Additional Information Sponsors numerous contests in several genres and up to 3 free ms evaluation conferences with instructors. Agents and editors participate in conference panels and/or private appointments. Complete information is available on the Web site in March of each year, including registration forms. E-mail or send SASE for brochure.

TENNESSEE WILLIAMS/NEW ORLEANS LITERARY FESTIVAL

938 Lafayette St., Suite 514, New Orleans LA 70113. (504)581-1144. E-mail: info@tennesseewilliams.net. Web site: www.tennesseewilliams.net. **Contact:** Paul J. Willis, executive director. Estab. 1987. Annual. Conference held in late March. Average attendance: "10,000 audience seats filled." Conferences focus on "all aspects of the literary arts including editing, publishing and the artistic process. Other humanities areas are also featured, including theater and music." Site: "The festival is based at historic Le Petit Theatre du Vieux Carré and continues at other sites throughout the French Quarter."

Costs "Ticket prices range from $10 for a single event to $60 for a special event. Master classes are $35 per class. Theatre events are sold separately and range from $10-25."

Accommodations "Host hotel is the Monteleone Hotel."

Additional Information "In conjunction with the University of New Orleans, we sponsor a one-act play competition. Entries are accepted from September 1 through December 15. There is a $25 fee which must be submitted with the application form. There is a $1,000 cash prize and a staged reading at the festival, as well as a full production of the work at the following year's festival." Conference information is available in late January. For brochure send e-mail, visit Web site or call. Accepts inquiries by e-mail and phone. Agents and editors participate in conference.

WRITE IT OUT

P.O. Box 704, Sarasota FL 34230-0704. (941)359-3824. E-mail: rmillerwio@aol.com. Web site: www.writeitout.com. **Contact:** Ronni Miller, director. Estab. 1997. Workshops held 2-3 times/year in March, June, July and August. Conference duration: 5-10 days. Average attendance: 4-10. Workshops on "fiction, poetry, memoirs. We also offer intimate, motivational, in-depth free private conferences with instructors." Site: Workshops in Italy in a Tuscan villa, in Sarasota at a hotel, and in Cape Cod at an inn. Theme: "Feel It! Write It!" Past speakers included Arturo Vivante, novelist.

Costs 2006 fees: Italy, $1,795; Cape Cod, $800. Price includes tution, room and board in Italy. Cape Cod just tuition. Airfare not included.

Additional Information "Critiques on work are given at the workshops." Conference information available year round. For brochures/guidelines e-mail, call or visit Web site. Accepts inquiries by phone, e-mail. Workshops have "small groups, option to spend time writing and not attend classes, with personal appointments with instructors."

◎ WRITING STRATEGIES FOR THE CHRISTIAN MARKET

2712 S. Peninsula Dr., Daytona Beach FL 32118-5706. (386)322-1111. Fax: (386)322-1111. E-mail: rupton@cfl.rr .com. Web site: www.ruptonbooks.com. **Contact:** Rosemary Upton. Estab. 1991. Independent studies with manual. Includes Basics I, Marketing II, Business III, Building the Novel. Critique by mail with SASE. Question and answer session via e-mail or U.S. mail. Critique shop included once a month, except summer (July and August). Instructor: Rosemary Upton, novelist.

Costs $30 for manual and ongoing support.

Additional Information "Designed for correspondence students as well as the classroom experience, the courses are economical and include all materials, as well as the evaluation assignments." Those who have taken Writing Strategies instruction are able to attend an on-going monthly critiqueshop where their peers critique their work. Manual provided. For brochures/guidelines send SASE, e-mail, fax or call. Accepts inquiries by fax, e-mail. Independent study by mail only offered at this time.

MIDWEST (IL, IN, KY, MI, OH)

ANTIOCH WRITERS' WORKSHOP

P.O. Box 494, Yellow Springs OH 45387. (937)475-7357. E-mail: info@antiochwritersworkshop.com. Web site: www.antiochwritersworkshop.com. **Contact:** Laura Carlson, director. Estab. 1984. Annual. Conference held July 7-13, 2007; July 12-18, 2008. Conference duration: 1 week. Average attendance: 80. Workshop concentration: poetry, nonfiction, fiction, personal essay, memoir, mystery. Site: Workshop located in the idyllic Glen Helen Nature Preserve and in locations around the charming village of Yellow Springs. Past faculty have included Sue Grafton, Natalie Goldberg, Sena Jeter Naslund, Ann Hagedorn, Katrina Kittle, Silas House, and Ralph Keyes.

Costs Tuition is $735 (regular) or $675 (alumni and local participants), which includes a nonrefundable $125 registration fee.

Accommodations Accomodations are available in local homes through the village host program ($150 for the week) or at area hotels and B&Bs.

Additional Information Intensive sessions for beginning and experienced writers, small group lunches with faculty, optional ms critiques.

COLUMBUS WRITERS CONFERENCE

P.O. Box 20548, Columbus OH 43220. (614)451-3075. Fax: (614)451-0174. E-mail: AngelaPL28@aol.com. Web site: www.creativevista.com. **Contact:** Angela Palazzolo, director. Estab. 1993. Annual. Conference held in August. Average attendance: 250+. "In addition to agent and editor consultations, the conference covers a wide variety of fiction and nonfiction topics presented by writers, editors and literary agents. Writing topics have included novel, short story, children's, young adult, poetry, historical fiction, science fiction, fantasy, humor, mystery, playwriting, working with an agent, working with an editor, screenwriting, magazine writing, travel, humor, cookbook, technical, queries, book proposals, and freelance writing." The Conference has included many writers and editors, including Chuck Adams, Tracy Bernstein, Sheree Bykofsky, Oscar Collier, Lisa Cron, Jennifer DeChiara, Tracey E. Dils, Hallie Ephron, Karen Harper, Scott Hoffman, Jeff Kleinman, Simon Lipskar, Noah Lukeman, Donald Maass, Lee Martin, Erin McGraw, Kim Meisner, Doris S. Michaels, Rita Rosenkrantz, and Nancy Zafris.

Costs To be announced.

Additional Information To receive a brochure, contact the conference by e-mail, phone, or postal mail, or visit www.creativevista.com.

◎ FESTIVAL OF FAITH AND WRITING

Calvin College/Department of English, 1795 Knollcrest Circle SE, Grand Rapids MI 49546. (616)526-6770. E-mail: ffw@calvin.edu. Web site: www.calvin.edu/festival. **Contact:** English Dept. Estab. 1990. Biennial. Conference usually held in April of even years. Conference duration: 3 days. Average attendance: 1,800. The Festival of Faith and Writing encourages serious, imaginative writing by all writers interested in the intersections of literature and belief. Site: The festival is held at Calvin College in Grand Rapids, MI, 180 miles north of Chicago. Focus is on fiction, nonfiction, memoir, poetry, drama, children's, young adult, literary criticism, film and song lyrics. Past speakers have included Annie Dillard, John Updike, Katherine Paterson, Elie Wiesel, Joyce Carol Oates, Leif Enger, Salman Rushdie, and Marilynne Robinson.

Costs Registration: consult Web site. Registration includes all sessions during the 3-day event but does not include meals, lodging or evening concerts.

Accommodations Shuttles are available to and from select local hotels. Consult festival Web site for a list of hotels with special conference rates.

Additional Information Agents and editors attend the festival and consult with prospective writers.

Conferences

KENTUCKY WRITER'S WORKSHOP

Pine Mountain State Resort Park, 1050 State Park Rd., Pineville KY 40977. (606)337-3066. Fax: (606)337-7250. E-mail: dean.henson@ky.gov. Web site: http://parks.ky.gov/resortparks/pm/index.htm. **Contact:** Dean Henson, event coordinator. Estab. 1995. Annual. Workshop held each March. Average attendance: 50-65. "Focuses on writing in various genres, including fiction, mystery, poetry, novels, short stories, essays, etc." Site: Pine Mountain State Resort Park (a Kentucky State Park).

Costs Registration fee is $30 for non-package participants.

Accommodations Special all-inclusive event packages are available. Call for information.

Additional Information Brochures available 2 months in advance by e-mail or phone. Accepts inquiries by SASE, e-mail, phone, fax. "Our conference features successful and celebrated Kentucky authors speaking and instructing on various topics of the writing endeavor. This workshop is designed to help developing authors improve their writing craft."

KENYON REVIEW WRITERS WORKSHOP

The Kenyon Review, Kenyon College, Gambier OH 43022. (740)427-5207. Fax: (740)427-5417. E-mail: reacha@kenyon.edu. Web site: www.kenyonreview.org. **Contact:** Anna Duke Reach, director. Estab. 1990. Annual. Workshop held late June. Conference duration: 8 days. Average attendance: 40-50. Participants apply in poetry, fiction or creative nonfiction, and then participate in intensive daily workshops which focus on the generation and revision of significant new work. Site: The conference takes place on the campus of Kenyon College in the rural village of Gambier, Ohio. Students have access to college computing and recreational facilities and are housed in campus housing. Workshop leaders have included David Baker, Ron Carlson, Rebecca McClanahan, Rosanna Warren, and Nancy Zafris.

Costs $1,195 including room and board.

Accommodations The workshop operates a shuttle from Gambier to the airport in Columbus, Ohio. Offers overnight accommodations. Participants are housed in Kenyon College student housing. The cost is covered in the tuition.

Additional Information Application includes a writing sample. Admission decisions are made on a rolling basis. Workshop information is available November 1. For brochure send e-mail, visit Web site, call, fax. Accepts inquiries by SASE, e-mail, phone, fax.

MIDWEST WRITERS WORKSHOP

Dept. of Journalism, Ball State University, Muncie IN 47306. (765)282-1055. Fax: (765)285-5997. E-mail: info@midwestwriters.org. Web site: www.midwestwriters.org. **Contact:** Jama Bigger. Estab. 1974. Annual. Workshops to be in July. Average attendance: 150. Site: Conference held at New Alumni Center, Ball State University.

Costs $275 for 3-day workshop; $90 for 1-day Intensive Session including opening reception, hospitality room and closing banquet.

Accommodations Special hotel rates offered.

Additional Information Manuscript evaluation for extra fee. Conference brochures/guidelines are available for SASE.

OPEN WRITING WORKSHOPS

Creative Writing Program, Department of English, Bowling Green State University, Bowling Green OH 43403. (419)372-8370. Fax: (419)372-6805. E-mail: mmcgowa@bgsu.edu. Web site: www.bgsu.edu/departments/creative-writing/. "Check our Web site for next workshop dates." Conference duration: 1 day. Average attendance: 10-15. Workshop covers fiction and poetry. Site: Workshops are held in a conference room, roundtable setting, on the campus of Bowling Green State University. Provides close reading and ms critique. 2005 faculty included fiction writer Wendell Mayo and poet/editor Karen Craigo.

Costs $50 for workshop; does not include lodging or other services; $35 for alums and students.

Accommodations Parking provided on campus.

Additional Information Participants need to submit workshop material prior to conference. Fiction or non-fiction: 1 story, 15 pages double-spaced maximum; send 2 copies. Poetry: 3 poems, a total of 100 lines for all 3; send 2 copies. "Deadlines are set about 3 weeks before the workshop. This gives us time to copy all the manuscripts and mail to all participants with detailed instructions." For brochure or inquiries, e-mail, visit Web site, call or fax. "These are no-nonsense workshops whose purpose is to 'open' doors for writers who are writing in comparative isolation. We provide guidance on preparation of manuscripts for publication as well."

READERS AND WRITERS HOLIDAY CONFERENCE

Central Ohio Fiction Writers (COFW), P.O. Box 1981, Westerville OH 43086-1981. E-mail: slsham@yahoo.com. Web site: www.cofw.org. **Contact:** Stephanie Shamroski, president. Estab. 1990. Annual. Conference held in Columbus, OH. 2007 Conference dates September 28-29. Average attendance: 120. COFW is a chapter of Romance Writers of America. The conference focuses on all romance subgenres and welcomes published writers, pre-published writers and readers. Conference theme: celebrates and fosters writers at every stage of their careers. Best-selling authors provide motivation and instruction; workshops, speakers, and materials cover a broad spectrum of topics. Two national agents and one editor will speak and take short appointments. Appointments to early registrants who have completed at least one manuscript.

Costs Price will include Saturday lunch.

Accommodations See www.cofw.org for exact location. There will be a special conference rate for hotel rooms.

Additional Information Registration form and information available on Web site or by e-mail.

◎ 𝒢 SPACE (SMALL PRESS AND ALTERNATIVE COMICS EXPO)

Back Porch Comics, P.O.Box 20550, Columbus OH 43220. E-mail: bpc13@earthlink.net. Web site: www.backporchcomics.com/space.htm. **Contact:** Bob Corby. Next conference/trade show to be held in the spring (see Web site for exact date). Conference duration: 2 days. "The Midwest's largest exhibition of small press, alternative and creator-owned comics." Site: 2007 held at the Aladdin Shrine Complex multipurpose room in Columbus, Ohio. 2007 special guests were Dave Sim and Gerhard.

Additional Information For 2008 brochure, visit Web site. Editors participate in conference.

WALLOON WRITERS' RETREAT

P.O. Box 304, Royal Oak MI 48068-0304. (248)589-3913. Fax: (248)589-9981. E-mail: johndlamb@ameritech.net. Web site: www.springfed.org. **Contact:** John D. Lamb, director. Estab. 1999. Annual. Last conference held September 27-30, 2007. Average attendance: 75. Focus includes fiction, poetry and creative nonfiction. Site: Michigania is owned and operated by the University of Michigan Alumni Association. Located on Walloon Lake. Attendees stay in spruce-paneled cabins, and seminars are held in a large conference lodge with fieldstone fireplaces and dining area. Past faculty included Billy Collins, Jacquelyn Mitchard, Jane Hamilton, Thomas Lux, Joyce Maynard, Craig Holden, Laurel Blossom.

Costs Single occupancy is $600, $535 (3 days, 2 nights, all meals included). $360 non-lodging.

Accommodations Shuttle rides from Traverse City Airport or Pellston Airport. Offers overnight accommodations. Provides list of area lodging options.

Additional Information Optional: Attendees may submit 3 poems or 5 pages of prose for conference with a staff member. Brochures available mid-June by e-mail, on Web site or by phone. Accepts inquiries by SASE, e-mail, phone. Editors participate in conference. "Walloon Lake in Northern Michigan is the same lake at which Ernest Hemingway spent the first 19 years of his life at his family's Windemere Cottage. The area plays a role in some of his early short stories, notably in a couple Nick Adams stories."

WESTERN RESERVE WRITERS & FREELANCE CONFERENCE

Lakeland Community College, 7700 Clocktower Dr., Kirtland OH 44094. (440) 525-7000. E-mail: deencr@aol.com. **Contact:** Deanna Adams or Nancy Piazza, co-coordinators. Estab. 1983. Biannual. Last conference held September 17, 2005. Conference duration: One day. Average attendance: 120. "The Western Reserve Writers Conferences are designed for all writers, aspiring and professional, and offer presentations in all genres— nonfiction, fiction, poetry, essays, creative nonfiction and the business of writing, including Web sites and freelancing ." Site: Located in the main building of Lakeland Community College, the conference is easy to find and just off the I-90 freeway. The Fall 2006 conference featured Plain Dealer columnist Regina Brett as keynote speaker. Also featured presenters such as renowned mystery writer Les Roberts; newsman and author, Jack Marschall; and other prolific writers. Presentations included book proposals, contracts/copyrights, public speaking, tips on completing your novel, and when and how to get an agent.

Costs Fall conference, including lunch: $75. Spring conference, no lunch: $55.

Additional Information Brochures for the 2007 conferences will be available in February (for spring conference) and July 2007 (for fall). Also accepts inquiries by e-mail and phone, or see Web site. Editors and agents often attend the conferences.

◎ WRITE-TO-PUBLISH CONFERENCE

9118 W Elmwood Dr., Suite 1G, Niles IL 60714-5820. (847)296-3964. Fax: (847)296-0754. E-mail: lin@writetopublish.com. Web site: www.writetopublish.com. **Contact:** Lin Johnson, director. Estab. 1971. Annual. Conference held in early June. Average attendance: 275. Conference on "writing all types of manuscripts for the Christian market." Site: Wheaton College, Wheaton, IL.

Costs $425.

Accommodations In campus residence halls or discounted hotel rates. Cost $225-310.

Additional Information Optional ms evaluation available. College credit available. Conference information available in January. For brochures/guidelines, visit Web site, or e-mail brochure@writetopublish.com. Accepts inquiries by e-mail, fax, phone.

Conferences

WRITERS ONLINE WORKSHOPS

F + W Publications, Inc., 4700 E. Galbraith Rd., Cincinnati OH 45236. (800)759-0963. Fax: (513)531-0798. E-mail: wdwowadmin@fwpubs.com. Web site: www.writersonlineworkshops.com. **Contact:** Joe Stollenwerk, educational services manager. Estab. 2000. Online workshop; ongoing. Conference duration: From 4-28 weeks. Average attendance: 10-15 per class. "We have workshops in fiction, nonfiction, memoir, poetry, proposal writing and more." Site: Internet-based, operated entirely on the Web site. Current fiction-related courses include Fundamentals of Fiction, Focus on the Novel, Focus on the Short Story, Advanced Novel Writing, Advanced Story Writing, Creating Dynamic Characters, Writing Effective Dialogue, Writing the Novel Proposal, Essentials of Mystery Writing, Essentials of Science Fiction Writing, Essentials of Romance Writing, and Marketing Short Stories. New in 2007-2008: First Draft in 35 Days, Essentials of Writing to Inspire, What's My Genre?, Voice and Viewpoint, and others.

Costs $119-579.

Additional Information Additional information always available on Web site. Accepts inquiries by e-mail and phone.

NORTH CENTRAL (IA, MN, NE, ND, SD, WI)

GREAT LAKES WRITERS FESTIVAL

Lakeland College, P.O. Box 359, Sheboygan WI 53082-0359. (920)565-1276. Fax: (920)565-1260. E-mail: elderk @lakeland.edu. Web site: www.greatlakeswritersfestival.org. **Contact:** Karl Elder, coordinator. Estab. 1991. Annual. Last conference held Nov. 2-3, 2006. Conference duration: 2 days. "Festival celebrates the writing of poetry, fiction and creative nonfiction." Site: Lakeland College is a small, 4-yr. liberal arts college of 235 acres, a beautiful campus in a rural setting, founded in 1862. No themes or panels, just readings and workshops. 2006 faculty included Marilyn Taylor and Sebastian Matthews.

Costs Free and open to the public. Participants may purchase meals and must arrange for their own lodging.

Accommodations Does not offer overnight accommodations. Provides list of area hotels or lodging options.

Additional Information All participants who would like to have their writing considered as an object for discussion during the festival workshops must submit it to Karl Elder electronically by Oct. 15. Participants may submit material for workshops in one genre only (poetry, fiction or creative nonfiction). Sponsors contest. Contest entries must contain the writer's name and address on a separate title page, be in type, and be submitted as clear, hard copy on Friday at the festival registration table. Entries may be in each of three genres per participant, yet only one poem, one story, and/or one nonfiction piece may be entered. There are two categories—high school students on one hand, all other on the other—of cash awards for first place in each of the three genres. The judges reserve the right to decline to award a prize in one or more of the genres. Judges will be the editorial staff of *Seems*, excluding the festival coordinator, Karl Elder. Information available in September. For brochure, visit Web site. Editors participate in conference. "Much information is available on the festival Web site."

GREEN LAKE WRITERS CONFERENCE

W2511 State Hwy 23, Green Lake WI 54941. (800)558-8898. Fax: (920)294-3848. E-mail: program@glcc.org. Web site: www.glcc.org. **Contact:** Pat Zimmer, program cordinator. Estab. Annual. Conference held early August. Workshops include nonfiction (short), nonfiction (long), fiction, poetry, and inspirational/devotional. Evening critique groups and editors on hand.

Costs Daily commuter program fee $150. Meals and lodging extra.

Additional Information Brochures available in January on Web site, and by e-mail, phone and fax.

INTERNATIONAL MUSIC CAMP CREATIVE WRITING WORKSHOP

1930 23rd Ave. SE, Minot ND 58701. Phone/fax: (701)838-8472. E-mail: info@internationalmusiccamp.com. Web site: www.internationalmusiccamp.com. **Contact:** Dr. TImothy Wollenzien, camp director. Estab. 1956. Annual. Last conference held June 24-30, 2007. Average attendance: 35. "The workshop offers students the opportunity to refine their skills in thinking, composing and writing in an environment that is conducive to positive reinforcement. In addition to writing poems, essays and stories, individuals are encourgaged to work on their own area of interest with conferencing and feedback from the course instructor." Site: International Peace Garden on the border between the US and Canada. "Similar to a university campus, several dormitories, classrooms, lecture halls and cafeteria provide the perfect site for such a workshop. The beautiful and picturesque International Peace Garden provides additional inspiration to creative thinking." 2006 instructor was Colin Kapelovitz, Dickinson State University, ND.

Costs $320, includes tuition, room and board. Early bird registration (postmarked by May 15) $295.

Accommodations Airline and depot shuttles are available upon request. Housing is included in the $295 fee.

Additional Information Conference information is available in September. For brochure visit Web site, e-mail, call or fax. Accepts inquiries by e-mail, phone and fax. Agents and editors participate in conference.

IOWA SUMMER WRITING FESTIVAL

C215 Seashore Hall, University of Iowa, Iowa City IA 52242-1802. (319)335-4160. E-mail: iswfestival@uiowa.e du. Web site: www.uiowa.edu/~iswfest. **Contact:** Amy Margolis, director. Estab. 1987. Annual. Festival held in June and July. Workshops are one week or a weekend. Average attendance: limited to 12/class—over 1,500 participants throughout the summer. "We offer workshops across the genres, including novel, short story, poetry, essay, memoir, humor, travel, playwriting, screenwriting, writing for children and more. All writers 21 and over are welcome. You need only have the desire to write." Site: University of Iowa campus. Guest speakers are undetermined at this time. Readers and instructors have included Lee K. Abbott, Marvin Bell, Lan Samantha Chang, Janet Desaulniers, Hope Edelman, Bret Anthony Johnston, and many more.

Costs $500-525 for full week; $250 for weekend workshop. Discounts available for early registration. Housing and meals are separate.

Accommodations Iowa House, $70/night; Sheraton, $88/night, Heartland Inn, $62/night (rates subject to change).

Additional Information Conference information available in February. Accepts inquiries by fax, e-mail, phone. "Register early. Classes fill quickly."

WRITERS INSTITUTE

610 Langdon St., Room 621, Madison WI 53703. (608)262-3447. Fax: (608)265-2475. Web site: www.dcs.wisc. edu/lsa/writing. **Contact:** Christine DeSmet. Estab. 1989. Annual. Conference usually held in April. Site: Pyle Center. Average attendance: 200.

Costs $215 includes materials, breaks.

Accommodations Provides a list of area hotels or lodging options.

Additional Information Sponsors contest. Submit 1-page writing sample and $10 entry fee. Conference speakers are judges. For brochure send e-mail, visit Web site, call, fax. Accepts inquiries by SASE, e-mail, phone, fax. Agents and editors participate in conference.

SOUTH CENTRAL (CO, KS, MO, NM, OK, TX)

AGENTS & EDITORS CONFERENCE

Writers' League of Texas, 1501 W. Fifth St., Suite E-2, Austin TX 78703. (512)499-8914. Fax: (512)499-0441. E-mail: wlt@writersleague.org. Web site: www.writersleague.org. **Contact:** Kristy Bordine, membership director. Estab. 1982. Conference held in June. Conference duration: Friday-Sunday. Average attendance: 300. "Each Summer the League holds its annual Agents & Editors Conference, which provides writers with the opportunity to meet top literary agents and editors from New York and the West Coast." Open to writers of both fiction and nonfiction. Topics include: Finding and working with agents and publishers; writing and marketing fiction and nonfiction; dialogue; characterization; voice; research; basic and advanced fiction writing/focus on the novel; business of writing; also workshops for genres. Agents/speakers have included Malaika Adero, Stacey Barney, Sha-Shana Crichton, Jessica Faust, Dena Fischer, Mickey Freiberg, Jill Grosjean, Anne Hawkins, Jim Hornfischer, Jennifer Joel, David Hale Smith and Elisabeth Weed. Agents and editors will be speaking and available for meetings with attendees.

Costs $245-295. Contests and awards programs are offered separately.

Additional Information Brochures/guidelines are available on request.

ANNUAL RETREATS, WORKSHOPS AND CLASSES

1501 W. Fifth St., Suite E-2, Austin TX 78703-5155. (512)499-8914. Fax: (512)499-0441. E-mail: wlt@writersleag ue.org. Web site: www.writersleague.org. **Contact:** Kristy Bordine, membership director. "Classes and workshops provide practical advice and guidance on various aspects of fiction, creative nonfiction and screenwriting." Site: Writers' League of Texas resource center or as indicated on Web site. Some classes are by e-mail. "Topics for workshops and classes have included E-publishing; Creative Nonfiction; Screenwriting Basics; Novel in Progress; Basics of Short Fiction; Technique; Writing Scenes; Journaling; Manuscript Feedback; Essays; Newspaper Columns." Instructors include Suzy Spencer, Barbara Burnett Smith, Scott Wiggerman, Diane Fanning, Marion Winik, Emily Vander Veer, Annie Reid, Bonnie Orr, Jan Epton Seale, Susan Wade, Lila Guzman, Laurie Lynn Drummond, David Wilkinson, John Pipkin, Ann McCutchan and Dao Strom.

Costs $45-$250.

Additional Information Available at www.writersleague.org.

ASPEN SUMMER WORDS WRITING RETREAT & LITERARY FESTIVAL

110 E. Hallam St., #116, Aspen CO 81611. (970)925-3122. Fax: (970)925-5700. E-mail: info@aspenwriters.org. Web site: www.aspenwriters.org. **Contact:** Jamie Abbot, director of programs. Estab. 1976. Annual. 2007 conference held June 24-28. Conference duration: 5 days. Average attendance: writing retreat, 150; literary festival, 300+, 1,800 visitors. Retreat includes intensive workshops in fiction (begining through advanced), creative nonfiction, poetry, screenwriting, magazine writing and food writing, plus a "Reader's Retreat" which in 2007 will focus on African Literature. Literary festival features approximately 18 events (craft talks, author readings, and interviews; publishing panel discussions; agent/editor meeting; and social gatherings) for readers and writers. Festival theme for 2007 is Africa: The Origin of Stories. Retreat faculty for 2007: Amy Bloom (advanced fiction), Gary Ferguson (creative nonfiction), Robert Bausch (fiction), Percival Everett (fiction), Bharti Kirchner (food and magazine writing), Dorianne Laux (poetry), John Romano (screenwriting), Danzy Senna (fiction for beginners). Festival presenters for 2007: Ngugi Wa Thiong'o, Chimamanda Adiche, Wole Soyinka, Henry Louis Gates Jr., and Alaa Al Aswany.

Costs $475/retreat; $250/2 day symposia; $175/2-day reader's retreat. Tuition includes daily continental breakfast and lunch, plus one evening reception. $200 festival pass; retreat students receive a $50 discount when they sign up for the literary festival. Festival registration includes two wine and hors d'oeuvres receptions. $35/ private meetings with agents and editors.

Accommodations Discount lodging at the conference site will be available. 2007 rates to be announced. 2006 room rates were $125/single room in a shared 2-bedroom condo or $165/1-bedroom condo. Free shuttle around town.

Additional Information Application deadline: April 1. Mss must be submitted by May 25th for review by faculty, for most workshops. 10 page limit for workshop application mss. A limited number of partial-tuition scholarships are available. Deadline for agent/editor meeting registration is May 25th. Brochures available for SASE, by e-mail and phone request, and on Web site.

◎ EAST TEXAS CHRISTIAN WRITER'S CONFERENCE

East Texas Baptist University, School of Humanities, 1209 N. Grove, Marshall TX 75670. (903)923-2269. E-mail: jhopkins@etbu.edu or jcornish@etbu.edu. Web site: www.etbu.edu/News/CWC. **Contact:** Joy Cornish. Estab. 2002. Annual. Conference held first Friday and Saturday of June each year. Conference duration: 2 days (Friday & Saturday). Average attendance: 125. "Primarily we are interested in promoting quality Christian writing that would be accepted in mainstream publishing." Site: "We use the classrooms, cafeterias, etc. of East Texas Baptist University." Past conference themes were Back to Basics, Getting Started in Fiction, Writers & Agents, Writing Short Stories, Writing for Newspapers, The Significance of Style, Writing Fillers and Articles, Writing Devotionals, Blogging for Writers, Christian Non-Fiction, Inspirational Writing and Editor and Author Relations. Past conference speakers/workshop leaders were David Jenkins, Bill Keith, Pete Litterski, Joy Early, Jr., Mary Lou Redding, Denny Boultinghouse, Vickie Phelps, Michael Farris, Susan Farris, Pamela Dowd, Donna Walker-Nixon, Lexie Smith, Janet Crews, Kay Coulter, John Krueger and Leonard Goss.

Costs $60 for individual; $50 students. Price includes meal.

Additional Information "We have expanded to include publishers, small presses, publish-on-demand opportunities, e-publishing and agents. A bookstore is provided with a variety of materials for writers."

◎ EMINENCE AREA ARTS COUNCIL SHORT STORY WORKSHOP

P.O. Box 551, Eminence MO 65466-0551. (573)226-5655. E-mail: hilma@socket.net. **Contact:** Hilma Hughes, administrator. Estab. 1989. Annual. Last workshop held May 24-26, 2007. Conference duration: 3 days. Average attendance: 12. "The Short Story Workshop focuses on fiction of any genre." Workshop centers on the process of writing; participants leave with a finished short story. Site: Museum and Art Gallery conference room. We have large tables with chairs for participants. There is already a large-screen TV and VCR for the leaders to use. The museum is accessible to the physically challenged. Workshop led by Dr. C.D. Albin.

Costs $45.

Accommodations EAAC provides list of area lodging.

Additional Information Accepts inquiries by e-mail or phone. "We are a small rural community on the scenic Riverways. The workshops are an excellent opportunity to rest, relax and get away from the rush of daily life. Many participants have valued this part of the experience as much as the learning and writing process."

FORT BEND WRITERS GUILD WORKSHOP

12523 Folkcrest Way, Stafford TX 77477-3529. E-mail: roger@rogerpaulding.net. Web site: www.fortbendwriter sguild.com. **Contact:** Roger Paulding. Estab. 1997. Annual. Conference will be held in March. Conference duration: 1 day. Average attendance: 75. Focuses on fiction (novels) and screenwriting. Site: Held at Holiday Inn Southwest, Houston.

Costs $55 (including buffet lunch) before February 28; $65 thereafter; $75 at door on day of workshop. Check Web site for updated prices.

Additional Information Sponsors a contest. Submit for novel competition first 20 pages plus one-page synopsis, entry fee $15 plus $15 membership fee; for short story competition 10 pages complete, $10 each. ''Judges are published novelists.'' First prize: $350, second place: $250, third place: $150. Not necessary to attend workshop in order to win. For brochure send SASE, e-mail or check Web site.

◎ THE GLEN WORKSHOP

Image, 3307 Third Avenue W, Seattle WA 98119. (206)281-2988. Fax: (206)281-2335. E-mail: glenworkshop@imagejournal.org. Web site: www.imagejournal.org. Estab. 1991. Annual. Workshop held in August. Conference duration: 1 week. Average attendance: 140-150. Workshop focuses on ''fiction, poetry and spiritual writing, essay, memoir. Run by *Image*, a literary journal with a religious focus. The Glen welcomes writers who practice or grapple with religious faith.'' Site: 2006 conference held in Santa Fe, NM in the first week of August and features ''presentations and readings by the faculty.'' Faculty has included Erin McGraw (fiction), Lauren F. Winner (spiritual writing), Paul Mariani and Andrew Hudgins (poetry) and Jeanne Murray Walker (playwriting).

Costs $630-920, including room and board; $365-455 for commuters (lunch only).

Accommodations Arrange transportation by shuttle. Accommodations included in conference cost.

Additional Information Prior to arrival, participants may need to submit workshop material depending on the teacher. ''Usually 10-25 pages.'' Conference information is available in February. For brochure send SASE, e-mail, visit Web site, call or fax. ''Like *Image*, the Glen is grounded in a Christian perspective, but its tone is informal and hospitable to all spiritual wayfarers.''

◎ GLORIETA CHRISTIAN WRITERS CONFERENCE

Glorieta Conference Center, 3311 Candelaria NE, Ste. I, Albuquerque NM 87107-1952. (800)433-6633. Fax: (505)899-9282. E-mail: info@classervices.com. Web site: www.glorietacwc.com. **Contact:** Linda Jewell, seminar manager. Estab. 1997. Annual. Conference held October 17-21, 2007 and October 22-26, 2008. Conference duration: 5 days. Average attendance: 350. For ''beginners, professionals, fiction, poetry, writing for children, drama, magazine writing, nonfiction books.'' To train Christian writers in their craft, provide them with an understanding of the industry, and give opportunities to meet with publishers. Site: ''Located just north of historic Santa Fe, NM, conference center with hotels and dining hall with buffet-style meals.'' Plans ''continuing course for fiction writers and numerous one-hour workshops.''

Costs 2007 rates were $450 for early registration or $495 regular registration plus applicable tax; meals and lodging were additional and range from $200-500 depending on housing and meal plans. For lodging and meals contact Glorieta LifeWay Confrence Center at 800/797-4222.

Additional Information ''The craft of writing is universal, but attendees should be aware this conference has a Christian emphasis.''

◎ TONY HILLERMAN WRITERS CONFERENCE

304 Calle Oso, Santa FE NM 87501. (505)471-1565. E-mail: wordharvest@yahoo.com. Web site: http://sfworkshops.com. **Contact:** Jean Schaumberg, co-director. Estab. 2004. Annual. November. Conference duration: 4 days. Average attendance: 160. Site: Albuquerque Hyatt Regency. Previous faculty included Tony Hillerman, David Morrell, Michael McGarrity, and Jonathan and Faye Kellerman.

Costs Previous year's costs: $395 per-registration.

Accommodations Previous year $99 per night at the Hyatt Regency (plus parking).

Additional Information Sponsors on-site mini contest, $1,500 short story contest with *Cowboys & Indians Magazine* and a $10,000 first mystery novel contest with Thomas Dunne Books. Brochures available in July for SASE, by phone, e-mail, fax and on Web site. Accepts inquiries by SASE, phone, e-mail.

NATIONAL WRITERS ASSOCIATION FOUNDATION CONFERENCE

10940 S. Parker Rd. #508, Parker CO 80138. (303)841-0246. Fax: (303)841-2607. E-mail: conference@nationalwriters.com. Web site: www.nationalwriters.com. **Contact:** Sandy Whelchel, executive director. Estab. 1926. Annual. Conference held in June. Conference duration: 3 days. Average attendance: 200-300. For general writing and marketing.

Costs $200 (approximately).

Additional Information Awards for previous contests will be presented at the conference. Conference information available annually in December. For brochures/guidelines send SASE, visit Web site, e-mail, fax or call.

THE NEW LETTERS WEEKEND WRITERS CONFERENCE

University of Missouri-Kansas City, College of Arts and Sciences Continuing Ed. Division, 5300 Rockhill Rd., Kansas City MO 64110-2499. (816)235-2736. Fax: (816)235-5279. Web site: www.newletters.org. **Contact:** Robert Stewart. Estab. mid-'70s as The Longboat Key Writers Conference. Annual. Conference held in June. Conference duration: 3 days. Average attendance: 75. For "craft and the creative process in poetry, fiction, screenwriting, playwriting and journalism; but the program also deals with matters of psychology, publications and marketing. The conference is appropriate for both advanced and beginning writers." Site: "The conference meets at the beautiful Diastole conference center of The University of Missouri-Kansas City."

Costs Several options are available. Participants may choose to attend as a non-credit student or they may attend for 1-3 hours of college credit from the University of Missouri-Kansas City. Conference registration includes continental breakfasts, Saturday and Sunday lunch. For complete information, contact the university.

Accommodations Information on area accommodations is made available.

Additional Information Those registering for college credit are required to submit a ms in advance. Manuscript reading and critque are included in the credit fee. Those attending the conference for non-credit also have the option of having their ms critiqued for an additional fee. Accepts inquiries by phone, fax.

NIMROD ANNUAL WRITERS' WORKSHOP

University of Tulsa, 600 S. College Ave., Tulsa OK 74104. (918)631-3080. Fax: (918)631-3033. E-mail: nimrod@utulsa.edu. Web site: www.utulsa.edu/nimrod. **Contact:** Eilis O'Neal, managing editor. Estab. 1978. Annual. Conference held in October. Conference duration: 1 day. Average attendance: 100-150. Workshop in fiction and poetry. "Prize winners (*Nimrod*/Hardman Prizes) conduct workshops as do contest judges." Past judges: Rosellen Brown, Stanley Kunitz, Toby Olson, Lucille Clifton, W.S. Merwin, Ron Carlson, Mark Doty, Anita Shreve and Francine Prose.

Costs Approximately $50. Lunch provided. Scholarships available for students.

Additional Information *Nimrod International Journal* sponsors *Nimrod*/Hardman Literary Awards: The Katherine Anne Porter Prize for fiction and The Pablo Neruda Prize for poetry. Poetry and fiction prizes: $2,000 each and publication (1st prize); $1,000 each and publication (2nd prize). Deadline: must be postmarked no later than April 30.

SAN JUAN WRITERS WORKSHOP

P.O. Box 841, Ridgeway CO 81432. (806)438-2385. E-mail: inkwellliterary@mac.com. Web site: http://homepage.mac.com/inkwellliterary. **Contact:** Jill Patterson, director. Estab. 2002. Annual. Workshop held July or August each year. Last conference was July 21-29, 2007. Conference duration: up to 10 days. Average attendance: 40 per session. Focuses on fiction, poetry, creative nonfiction in each session. Sessions focus on generating new material, workshopping manuscripts, revising and submitting for publication. "The goal of the San Juan Workshops is to remove writers from the hectic pace of everyday life and give them the inspiration, space and quiet to attend to their writing." Site: "The Workshops are held for one week, each summer, in Ouray, CO, Switzerland of America. In this cozy mountain village, everything is within walking distance, including the Ouray Hot Springs Pool, Cascade Falls, the local movie theater in the historical Wright Opera House, several fine restaurants, lodging and the Community Center where workshop events take place." 2007 panels included Generating New Material, Craft and Critique, Revising and Submitting for Publication. Panelists in 2007 included Emily Fox Gordon, Bob Hicok, Pamela Painter, Pam Houston, Gary Short, Philip Gerard, Scott Russell Sanders, Andrew Hudgins, and Robert Olen Butler.

Costs $350-475, includes workshop instruction, faculty readings, breakfast each day and admission to all receptions. "All sessions will require an additional, non-refundable application fee of $25. There are substantial discounts for attending multiple sessions. There are also $100 scholarships available."

Accommodations Offers shuttle to/from airport in Montrose, CO. Provides a list of hotels.

Additional Information Accepts inquiries by SASE, e-mail, phone. "There are social activities, including mountain cookout, concerts in the local park, the annual pub crawl, champagne brunch and readings." See Web site for more information.

SOUTHWEST WRITERS CONFERENCE

3271 Morris NE Ste A, Albuquerque NM 87111. (505)265-9485. Fax: (505)265-9483. E-mail: swwriters@juno.com. Web site: www.southwestwriters.org. **Contact:** Conference Chair. Estab. 1983. Annual. Conferences held throughout the year. Average attendance: 50. "Conferences concentrate on all areas of writing and include appointments and networking." Workshops and speakers include writers, editors and agents of all genres for all levels from beginners to advanced.

Costs $99 and up (members); $159 and up (nonmembers); includes conference sessions and lunch.

Accommodations Usually have official airline and discount rates. Special conference rates are available at hotel. A list of other area hotels and motels is available.

Additional Information Sponsors an annual contest judged by authors, editors and agents from New York, Los Angeles, etc., and from other major publishing houses. Twenty categories. Deadline: See Web site. Entry fee is $29 (members) or $44 (nonmembers). For brochures/guidelines send SASE, visit Web site, e-mail, fax, call.

"An appointment (10 minutes, one-on-one) may be set up at the conference with the editor/agent of your choice on a first-registered/first-served basis."

STEAMBOAT SPRINGS WRITERS GROUP

Steamboat Arts Council, P.O. Box 774284, Steamboat Springs CO 80477. (970)879-8079. E-mail: sswriters@cs.com. Web site: www.steamboatwriters.com. **Contact:** Harriet Freiberger, director. Estab. 1982. Annual conference. Group meets year-round on Thursdays, 12:00 to 2:00 at Arts Depot; guests welcome. Conference held in July. Conference duration: 1 day. Average attendance: 30. "Our conference emphasizes instruction within the seminar format. Novices and polished professionals benefit from the individual attention and camaraderie which can be established within small groups. A pleasurable and memorable learning experience is guaranteed by the relaxed and friendly atmosphere of the old train depot. Registration is limited." Site: Restored train depot.

Costs $40 before June 1, $50 after. Fee covers all conference activities, including lunch.

Accommodations Lodging available at Steamboat Resorts.

Additional Information Optional dinner and activities during evening preceding conference. Accepts inquiries by e-mail, phone, mail.

TAOS SUMMER WRITERS' CONFERENCE

Department of English Language and Literature MSC03 2170, 1 University of New Mexico, Albuquerque NM 87131-0001. (505)277-5572. Fax: (505)277-2950. E-mail: taosconf@unm.edu. Web site: www.unm.edu/~taosconf. **Contact:** Sharon Oard Warner, director. Estab. 1999. Annual. Held each year in mid-July. Average attendance: 180. Workshops in novel writing, short story writing, screenwriting, poetry, creative nonfiction, publishing, and special topics such as yoga and writing and writing for social change. Master classes in novel, memoir and poetry. For beginning and experienced writers. "Taos itself makes our conference unique. We also offer daily visits to the D.H. Lawrence Ranch, the Harwood Museum and other local historical sites." Site: Workshops and readings are all held at the Sagebrush Inn Conference Center, part of the Sagebrush Inn, an historic hotel and Taos landmark since 1929.

Costs Weeklong workshop tuition is $600, includes a Sunday evening New Mexican buffet dinner, a Friday evening barbecue and other special events. Weekend workshop tuition is $300.

Accommodations We offer a discounted car rental rate through the Sagebrush Inn or the adjacent Comfort Suites. Conference participants receive special discounted rates $59-99/night. Room rates at both hotels include a full, hot breakfast.

Additional Information "We offer three Merit Scholarships, the Taos Resident Writer Award, the Hispanic Writer Award and one D.H. Lawrence Fellowship. Scholarship awards are based on submissions of poetry, fiction and creative nonfiction." They provide tuition remission; transportation and lodging not provided. To apply for a scholarship, submit 10 pages of poetry, nonfiction or fiction along with registration and deposit. Applicants should be registered for the conference. The Fellowship is for emerging writers with one book in print, provides tuition remission and cost of lodging. Brochures available late winter. "The conference offers a balance of special events and free time. If participants take a morning workshop, they'll have the afternoons free and vice versa. We've also included several outings, including a tour of the Harwood Arts Center and a visit to historic D.H. Lawrence Ranch outside Taos."

TEXAS CHRISTIAN WRITERS' CONFERENCE

First Baptist Church, 6038 Greenmont, Houston TX 77092. (713)686-7209. E-mail: marthalrogers@sbcglobal.net. **Contact:** Martha Rogers. Estab. 1990. Annual. Conference held in August. Conference duration: 1 day. Average attendance: 60-65. "Focus on all genres." Site: Held at the First Baptist Church fellowship center and classrooms. 2007 faculty: Sally Stuart, Kathy Ide, Lena Nelson Dooley, Terry Whalin, and Diann Mills as Keynote speaker. Additional faculty: Anita Highman, Janice Thompson, Kathleen Y'Barbo.

Costs $60 for members of IWA, $75 nonmembers, discounts for seniors (60+) and couples, meal at noon, continental breakfast and breaks.

Accommodations Offers list of area hotels or lodging options.

Additional Information Open conference for all interested writers. Sponsors a contest for short fiction; categories include articles, devotionals, poetry, short story, book proposals, drama. Fees: $8 member, $10 nonmember. Conference information available with SASE or e-mail to Martha Rogers. Agents participate in conference.

THUNDER WRITER'S RETREATS

Durango CO 81301-3408. (970)385-5884. Fax: (970)247-5327. E-mail: thunder@thunderforwriters.com. Web site: www.thunderforwriters.com. **Contact:** Michael Thunder. Estab. 2000. On demand, per client's need. Conference duration: 1-2 weeks. Average attendance: 1 individual/session. Focus is on fiction and scriptwriting. Site: Durango, Colorado, "beautiful mountain environment."

Costs $1,000/week coaching fee. Meals and lodging are dependent on the writer's taste and budget.

Accommodations Provides a list of area hotels or lodging options.

Additional Information "These writer's retreats are geared toward concepting a project or project development. Usually writers stay one week and receive 10 hours of one-on-one coaching. The rest of their time is spent writing. One and sometimes two interviews are required to design a course of action adapted to the writer's needs." Please call, e-mail, fax or send SASE for more information.

MARK TWAIN CREATIVE WRITING WORKSHOPS

University House, 5101 Rockhill Rd., Kansas City MO 64110-2499. (816)235-1168. Fax: (816)235-2611. E-mail: BeasleyM@umkc.edu. Web site: www.newletters.org. **Contact:** Betsy Beasley, adminstrative associate. Estab. 1990. Annual. Held first 3 weeks of June, from 9:30 to 12:30 each weekday morning. Conference duration: 3 weeks. Average attendance: 40. "Focus is on fiction, poetry and literary nonfiction." Site: University of Missouri-Kansas City Campus. Panels planned for next conference include the full range of craft essentials. Staff includes Robert Stewart, editor-in-chief of *New Letters* and BkMk Press, and Michael Pritchett, creative writing professor.

Costs Fees for regular and noncredit courses.

Accommodations Offers list of area hotels or lodging options.

Additional Information Submit for workshop 6 poems/one short story prior to arrival. Conference information is available in March by SASE, e-mail or on Web site. Editors participate in conference.

◎ WRITERS WORKSHOP IN SCIENCE FICTION

Lawrence KS 66045-2115. (785)864-3380. Fax: (785)864-1159. E-mail: jgunn@ku.edu. Web site: www.ku.edu/~sfcenter. **Contact:** James Gunn, professor. Estab. 1984. Annual. Workshop held in late June to early July. Conference duration: 2 weeks. Average attendance: 10-14. The workshop is "small, informal and aimed at writers on the edge of publication or regular publication." For writing and marketing science fiction and fantasy. Site: "Housing is provided and classes meet in university housing on the University of Kansas campus. Workshop sessions operate informally in a lounge." Past guests included Frederik Pohl, SF writer and former editor and agent; John Ordover, writer and editor; George Zebrowski, Pamela Sargent, Kij Johnson and Christopher McKittrick, writers; Lou Anders, editor. A novel workshop in science fiction and fantasy is also available.

Costs $400 tuition. Housing and meals are additional.

Accommodations Several airport shuttle services offer reasonable transportation from the Kansas City International Airport to Lawrence. During past conferences, students were housed in a student dormitory at $14/day double, $28/day single.

Additional Information "Admission to the workshop is by submission of an acceptable story. Two additional stories should be submitted by the end of May. These three stories are distributed to other participants for critiquing and are the basis for the first week of the workshop; one story is rewritten for the second week. The workshop offers a 3-hour session manuscript critiquing each afternoon. The rest of the day is free for writing, study, consultation and recreation." Information available in December. For brochures/guidelines send SASE, visit Web site, e-mail, fax, call. The workshop concludes with The Campbell Conference, a round-table discussion of a single topic, and the presentation of the Campbell and Sturgeon Awards for the Best SF Novel and Short Story of the Year. "The Writers Workshop in Science Fiction is intended for writers who have just started to sell their work or need that extra bit of understanding or skill to become a published writer."

WEST (AZ, CA, HI, NV, UT)

◎ ✐ ALTERNATIVE PRESS EXPO (APE)

Comic-Con International, P.O. Box 128458, San Diego CA 92112-8458 . (619)491-2475. Fax: (619)414-1022. E-mail: cci-info@comic-con.org. Web site: www.comic-con.org/ape/. **Contact:** Eddie Ibrahim, director of programming. Annual. Last conference held April 21-22, 2007, in San Francisco. Conference duration: 2 days. "Hundreds of artists and publishers converge for the largest gathering of alternative and self-published comics in the country." Includes panels on graphic novels, Web comics, how to pitch your comic to publishers, and the traditional APE 'queer cartoonists' panel. Site: Large conference or expo center in host city. Check Web site for 2008 location. 2007 special guests included Kevin Huizenga, Karl Christian Krumpholz, Hope Larson, Francoise Mouly, Art Spiegelman, Brian Lee O'Malley, Gene Yang.

Costs $7 single day; $10 both days.

Accommodations Does not offer overnight accommodations. Provides list of area hotels or lodging options on Web site.

Additional Information For brochure, visit Web site. Editors participate in conference.

BLOCKBUSTER PLOT INTENSIVE WRITING WORKSHOPS

708 Blossom Hill Rd. #146, Los Gatos CA 95032. Fax: (408)356-1798. E-mail: martha@blockbusterplots.com. Web site: www.blockbusterplots.com. **Contact:** Martha Alderson, instructor. Estab. 2000. Held four times per year. Conference duration: 2 days. Average attendance: 6-8. Workshop is intended to help writers create an action, character and thematic plotline for a screenplay, memoir, short story, novel or creative nonfiction. Site: a house.

Costs $135 per day.

Accommodations Provides list of area hotels and lodging options.

Additional Information Brochures available by fax, e-mail or on Web site. Accepts inquiries by SASE, e-mail and fax.

JAMES BONNET'S STORYMAKING: THE MASTER CLASS

P.O. Box 841, Burbank CA 91503-0841. (310)572-9410. Fax: (818)567-0038. E-mail: bonnet@storymaking.com. Web site: www.storymaking.com. **Contact:** James Bonnet. Estab. 1990. Conference held February, May, July, October. Conference duration: 2 days. Average attendance: 25. Conferences focus on fiction, mystery and screenwriting. Site: In 2007, Sportsmen's Lodge, Studio City, California and Hilton Resort, Palm Springs, California and Nans Sous Ste. Anne, France. Topics for next conference include The High Concept Great Idea, The Creative Unconscious, Metaphor, The Archetypes, The Fundamentals of Plot, Structure, Genre, Character, Complications, Crisis, Climax, Conflict, Suspense and more. James Bonnet (author) is scheduled to participate as speaker.

Costs $350 per weekend.

Accommodations Provides a list of area hotels or lodging options.

Additional Information For brochure send SASE, e-mail, visit Web site, call or fax. Accepts inquiries by SASE, e-mail, phone and fax. "James Bonnet, author of *Stealing Fire From the Gods*, teaches a story structure and storymaking seminar that guides writers from inspiration to final draft."

⊚ IWWG EARLY SPRING IN CALIFORNIA CONFERENCE

International Women's Writing Guild, P.O. Box 810, Gracie Station NY 10028-0082. (212)737-7536. Fax: (212)737-7536. E-mail: iwwg@iwwg.com. Web site: www.iwwg.com. **Contact:** Hannelore Hahn, executive editor. Estab. 1982. Annual. Conference held second week in March. Average attendance: 60. Conference to promote "creative writing, personal growth and networking." Site: Bosch Bahai School, a redwood forest mountain retreat in Santa Cruz, CA.

Costs $350 for weekend program with room and board ($330 for members); $100 per day for commuters ($80 for members).

Accommodations Accommodations are all at conference site.

Additional Information Conference information is available after August. For brochures/guidelines, send SASE. Accepts inquiries by e-mail, fax, phone.

MENDOCINO COAST WRITERS CONFERENCE

College of the Redwoods, 1211 Del Mar Drive, Fort Bragg CA 95437. (707)964-6810. E-mail: info@mcwc.org. Web site: http://mcwc.org. **Contact:** Barbara Lee, registrar. Estab. 1989. Annual. Last conference held August 10-12, 2006. Average attendance: 100. "We hope to encourage the developing writer by inviting presenters who are both fine writers and excellent teachers." Site: College of the Redwoods is a small community college located on the gorgeous northern California coast. Focuses are fiction, poetry, creative nonfiction—special areas have included children's (2003), mystery (2002), social awareness. In 2006 faculty included David Skibbins, Jody Gehrman, Paul Levine, Gerald Haslam.

Costs Before June 9, 2006: $300 (2 days); $375 (3 days). After June 9, 2006: $375 (2 days); $410 (3 days).

Additional Information Brochures for the conference will be available in March by SASE, phone, e-mail or on the Web site. Agents and editors participate in the conference. "The conference is small, friendly and fills up fast with many returnees."

⊚ MORMON WRITERS' CONFERENCE

Association for Mormon Letters, P.O. Box 1315, Salt Lake City UT 84110-1315. (801)582-2090. E-mail: aml@aml-online.org. Web site: www.aml-online.org. **Contact:** Conference Chair. Estab. 1999. Annual. Conference held on a Saturday in late fall. Conference duration: one day. Average attendance: 100. The conference usually covers anything to do with writing by, for or about Mormons, including fiction, nonfiction, theater, film, children's literature. Site: Last few years it has been in Orem, UT. "Plenary speeches, panels and instructional presentations by prominent authors and artists in the LDS artistic community."

Costs $15 for general public, $5 for AML members and for students who are not AML members, free to AML student members; catered lunch additional $15 with pre-registration.

Additional Information For brochures/guidelines send SASE, e-mail, visit Web site. Accepts inquiries by SASE, e-mail.

MOUNT HERMON CHRISTIAN WRITERS CONFERENCE

P.O. Box 413, Mount Hermon CA 95041-0413. (831)335-4466. Fax: (831)335-9413. E-mail: info@mhcamps.org. Web site: www.mounthermon.org/writers. **Contact:** David R. Talbott, director of adult ministries. Estab. 1970. Annual. Conference held March 14-18, 2008. Average attendance: 450. "We are a broad-ranging conference for all areas of Christian writing, including fiction, children's, poetry, nonfiction, magazines, books, educational curriculum and radio and TV scriptwriting. This is a working, how-to conference, with many workshops within the conference involving on-site writing assignments." Site: "The conference is sponsored by and held at the 440-acre Mount Hermon Christian Conference Center near San Jose, California, in the heart of the coastal redwoods. Registrants stay in hotel-style accommodations, and full board is provided as part of the conference fees. Meals are taken family style, with faculty joining registrants. The faculty/student ratio is about 1:6 or 7. The bulk of our faculty are editors and publisher representatives from major Christian publishing houses nationwide."

Costs Registration fees include tution, conference sessions, resource notebook, refreshment breaks, room and board and vary from $735 (economy) to $1,100 (deluxe), double occupancy (2007 rates).

Accommodations Airport shuttles are available from the San Jose International Airport. Housing is not required of registrants, but about 95% of our registrants use Mount Hermon's own housing faciltes (hotel-style double-occupancy rooms). Meals with the conference are required and are included in all fees.

Additional Information Registrants may submit 2 works for critique in advance of the conference. No advance work is required, however. Conference brochures/guidelines are available online only in December. Accepts inquiries by e-mail, fax. "The residential nature of our conference makes this a unique setting for one-on-one interaction with faculty/staff. There is also a decided inspirational flavor to the conference, and general sessions with well-known speakers are a highlight. Come rested, with plenty of business cards and samples of works in progress or just completed."

PIMA WRITERS' WORKSHOP

Pima Community College, 2202 W. Anklam Road, Tucson AZ 85709-0170. (520)206-6084. Fax: (520)206-6020. E-mail: mfiles@pima.edu. **Contact:** Meg Files, director. Estab. 1988. Annual. Conference held in May. Average attendance: 300. "For anyone interested in writing—beginning or experienced writer. The workshop offers sessions on writing short stories, novels, nonfiction articles and books, children's and juvenile stories, poetry, screenplays." Site: Sessions are held in the Center for the Arts on Pima Community College's West campus. Past speakers include Michael Blake, Ron Carlson, Gregg Levoy, Nancy Mairs, Linda McCarriston, Jerome Stern, Connie Willis, Larry McMurtry, Barbara Kingsolver and Robert Morgan.

Costs $75 (can include ms critique). Participants may attend for college credit, in which case fees are $104 for Arizona residents and $164 for out-of-state residents. Meals and accommodations not included.

Accommodations Information on local accommodations is made available and special workshop rates are available at a specified motel close to the workshop site (about $70/night).

Additional Information Participants may have up to 20 pages critiqued by the author of their choice. Manuscripts must be submitted 3 weeks before the workshop. Conference brochure/guidelines available for SASE. Accepts inquiries by e-mail. "The workshop atmosphere is casual, friendly and supportive, and guest authors are very accessible. Readings, films and panel discussions are offered as well as talks and manuscript sessions."

SAN DIEGO STATE UNIVERSITY WRITERS' CONFERENCE

SDSU College of Extended Studies, 5250 Campanile Drive, San Diego CA 92182-1920. (619)594-2517. Fax: (619)594-8566. E-mail: jgreene@mail.sdsu.edu. Web site: www.ces.sdsu.edu. **Contact:** Jim Greene, facilitator. Estab. 1984. Annual conference held in January. Conference duration: 2 days. Average attendance: 375. Covers fiction, nonfiction, scriptwriting, and e-books. Held at the Doubletree Hotel in Mission Valley. Each year the conference offers a variety of workshops for beginning, intermediate, and advanced writers. This conference allows the individual writer to choose which workshop best suits his/her needs. In addition to the workshops, editor reading appointments and agent/editor consultation appointments are available for additional fees, so attendees can meet with editors and agents one-on-one to discuss specific issues. A reception is offered Saturday immediately following the workshops, offering attendees the opportunity to socialize with the faculty (editors, agents, speakers) in a relaxed atmosphere. Last year, about 70 faculty attended.

Costs In 2007: $365-485. (2008 cost will be published with fall update of Web site.) Includes lunch and reception Saturday evening.

Accommodations Doubletree Hotel, (800)222-TREE. Attendees must make their own travel arrangements.
Additional Information Complete conference information is available at www.ces.sdsu.edu/writers.

SANTA BARBARA CHRISTIAN WRITERS CONFERENCE

P.O. Box 42429, Santa Barbara CA 93140. (805)682-0316. E-mail: cwgsb@sbcglobal.net. **Contact:** Opal Dailey, director. Estab. 1997. Conference held October 7, 2006. Conference duration: 1 day. Average attendance: 60-70. Site: Westmont College, "liberal arts Christian College. Beautiful campus in the Montecito Foothills at Santa Barbara.
Costs $89 for 2007. Includes continental breakfast, lunch and afternoon snack.
Additional Information Conference information available in May. For brochure, send SASE or call. Accepts inquiries by e-mail, SASE and phone. Agents and editors participate in conference.

◎ SCBWI/SUMMER CONFERENCE ON WRITING & ILLUSTRATING FOR CHILDREN

(formerly SCBWI/International Conference on Writing & Illustrating for Children), 8271 Beverly Blvd., Los Angeles CA 90048. (323)782-1010. Fax: (323)782-1892. E-mail: conference@scbwi.org. Web site: www.scbwi.org. **Contact:** Lin Oliver, executive director. Estab. 1972. Annual. Conference held in August. Conference duration: 4 days. Average attendance: 800. Writer and illustrator workshops geared toward all levels. Covers all aspects of children's magazine and book publishing.
Costs Approximately $400; includes all 4 days and one banquet meal. Does not include hotel room.
Accommodations Information on overnight accommodations made available.
Additional Information Ms and illustration consultations are available. Brochure/guidelines available on Web site.

SQUAW VALLEY COMMUNITY OF WRITERS

P.O. Box 1416, Nevada City CA 95959-1416. (530)470-8440. E-mail: info@squawvalleywriters.org. Web site: www.squawvalleywriters.org. **Contact:** Brett Hall Jones, executive director. Estab. 1969. Annual. Conference held in August. Conference duration: 7 days. Average attendance: 124. "The writers workshops in fiction, nonfiction and memoir assist talented writers by exploring the art and craft as well as the business of writing." Offerings include daily morning workshops led by writer-teachers, editors, or agents of the staff, limited to 12-13 participants; seminars; panel discussions of editing and publishing; craft colloquies; lectures; and staff readings. Past themes and panels included Personal History in Fiction, Narrative Structure, Roots, and Anatomy of a Short Story. Past faculty and speakers included Dorothy Allison, Bill Barich, Max Byrd, Louis Edwards, Anne Lamont, Marting J. Smith, Anthony Swofford, Mark Childress, Janet Fitch, Richard Ford, Karen Joy Fowler, Lynn Freed, Dagoberto Gilb, Molly Giles, Glen David Gold, Sands Hall, James D. Houston, Louis B. Jones, Alice Sebold, Amy Tan, Al Young.
Costs Tuition is $725, which includes 6 dinners.
Accommodations The Community of Writers rents houses and condominiums in the Valley for participants to live in during the week of the conference. Single room (one participant): $550/week. Double room (twin beds, room shared by conference participant of the same sex): $350/week. Multiple room (bunk beds, room shared with 2 or more participants of the same sex): $200/week. All rooms subject to availability; early requests are recommended. Can arrange airport shuttle pick-ups for a fee.
Additional Information Admissions are based on submitted ms (unpublished fiction, a couple of stories or novel chapters); requiries $25 reading fee. Submit ms to Brett Hall Jones, Squaw Valley Community of Writers, P.O. Box 1416, Nevada City, CA 95959. Deadline: May 10. Notification: June 10. Brochure/guidelines available February by phone, e-mail or visit Web site. Accepts inquiries by SASE, e-mail, phone. Agents and editors attend/participate in conferences.

◎ STEINBECK FESTIVAL

1 Main Street, Salinas CA 93901. (831)796-3833. Fax: (831)796-3828. Web site: www.steinbeck.org. Estab. 1980. Annual. Conference held August 2-5, 2007. Average attendance: 1,000 "over 4-day period." Conference focuses on the life and writings of John Steinbeck. Multi-day festival includes speakers, bus and walking tours, events and museum admission. Site: National Steinbeck Center, a museum with permanent, multimedia exhibition about John Steinbeck and changing art and cultural exhibits.
Costs Fees range from $17 to $75 per person, depending on the programs offered.
Accommodations Provides a list of area hotel and lodging options.

TMCC WRITERS' CONFERENCE

TMCC Workforce Development and Continuing Education Division, 5270 Neil Road Rm 216, Reno NV 89502. (775)829-9010. Fax: (775)829-9032. E-mail: asefchick@tmcc.edu or mikedcroft@sbcglobal.net. Web site: www.tmccwriters.com. Estab. 1990. Annual. 2007 conference held in March. Average attendance: 125. Conference focuses on fiction (literary and mainstream), poetry, memoirs, screenwriting, marketing to agents, publishers. Site: Truckee Meadows Community College in Reno, Nevada. "We strive to provide a well-rounded event for fiction writers and poets."

Costs 4-day Track A $389; 2-day Track B $139. "Scholarships based on merit and financial need are awarded every December."

Accommodations Hotel shuttle service from Reno airport available. Discounted room rate available through John Ascuaga's Nugget. Overnight accommodations available at site for conference rate of $85/night, plus tax and energy fee.

Additional Information If participating in Track A, attendees should submit first chapter (5,000 words maximum) by January 15. Brochures available November by e-mail, phone, mail, fax or on Web site. Accepts inquires by e-mail or phone. Agent will participate in conference. "This conference features an informal, friendly atmosphere where questions are encouraged. A Writers' Reception session allows for participants to mix with event speakers. No-host lunches with presenters (limited to first 9 sign-ups per lunch) will also be held. The 4-day Track A keeps each critique group small."

UCLA EXTENSION WRITERS' PROGRAM

10995 Le Conte Avenue, #440, Los Angeles CA 90024-2883. (310)825-9415 or (800)388-UCLA. Fax: (310)206-7382. E-mail: writers@UCLAextension.edu. Web site: www.uclaextension.edu/writers. **Contact:** Cindy Lieberman, program manager. Courses held year-round with one-day or intensive weekend workshops to 12-week courses. Writers Studio held in February. A 9-month master class is also offered every fall. "The diverse offerings span introductory seminars to professional novel and script completion workshops. The annual Writers Studio and a number of 1-, 2- and 4-day intensive workshops are popular with out-of-town students due to their specific focus and the chance to work with industry professionals. The most comprehensive and diverse continuing education writing program in the country, offering over 500 courses a year, including screenwriting, fiction, writing for the youth market, poetry, nonfiction, playwriting and publishing. Adult learners in the UCLA Extension Writers' Program study with professional screenwriters, fiction writers, playwrights, poets and nonfiction writers, who bring practical experience, theoretical knowledge and a wide variety of teaching styles and philosophies to their classes." Site: Courses are offered in Los Angeles on the UCLA campus and in the 1010 Westwood Center in Westwood Village, as well as online.

Costs Vary from $95 for one-day workshops to about $450 for quarterly courses to $3,250 for the 9-month master class.

Accommodations Students make own arrangements. The program can provide assistance in locating local accommodations.

Additional Information Writers Studio information available October. For brochures/guidelines/guide to course offerings, visit Web site, e-mail, fax or call. Accepts inquiries by e-mail, fax, phone. "Some advanced level classes have manuscript submittal requirements; instructions are always detailed in the quarterly UCLA Extension course catalog. The UCLA Extension Screenwriting Competition is now in its second year, featuring prizes and industry recognition to the top three winners. An annual fiction prize, The James Kirkwood Prize in Creative Writing, has been established and is given annually to one fiction writer who has produced outstanding work in a Writers' Program course."

WILD WRITING WOMEN WRITING WORKSHOP

110 Forrest Ave. Fairfax, CA 94930. (541)941-4759. E-mail: writing@lisaalpine.com. Web site: www.wildwritingwomen.com. **Contact:** Lisa Alpine. Estab. 2003. Annual. Fall 2007. Conference duration: 2 days. Average attendance: 50. Designed for serious and would-be serious writers both men and women, the conference includes classes on travel writing, chronicling your family legacy, the writer's voice, personal essay, real-time travelogues, food writing, understanding contracts, self-publishing and more. Site: Historic Fort Mason on San Francisco Bay, featuring breathtaking views of the Golden Gate Bridge. "We've arranged a panel discussion with magazine and book editors, a panel with the WWW on how to run a successful writing group, a travel photography discussion and slide show presentation, creativity exercises and more." Classes will be taught by members of Wild Writing Women, LCC, the acclaimed San Francisco writing group and authors of *Wild Writing Women: Stories of World Travel*, an award-winning anthology of travelogues, winners of The Lowell Thomas Gold Award and The Natja Award for Best Online Travel Magazine.

Costs $350. Includes all classes and panels, lunch and a wine mixer.

Accommodations Provides list of hotels and lodging options.

Additional Information Brochures for the conference will be available in 2007 by phone, e-mail and on Web site. Accepts inquiries by e-mail and phone.

WRITE FROM THE HEART

9827 Irvine Avenue, Upper Lake CA 95485. (707)275-9011. E-mail: Halbooks@HalZinaBennet.com. Web site: www.HalZinaBennet.com. **Contact:** Hal. Offered 4 to 6 times a year. Conference duration: 3-5 days. Also, year-long mentorships. Average attendance: 15-30. "Open to all genres, focusing on accessing the author's most individualized sources of imagery, characterization, tensions, content, style and voice." Site: Varies; California's Mt. Shasta, Mendocino California coast, Chicago, Colorado. Panels include Creativity and Life Experiences: Sourcing Story and Character from What You Have Lived, Getting Happily Published, and more. Instructor: Hal Zina Bennett.

Costs $250 and up.

Accommodations No arrangements for transportation. Provides list of area hotels.

Additional Information Brochures available. Request by SASE, e-mail, phone, fax or on Web site. Editors participate in conference. "Hal is a personal writing coach with over 200 successfully published clients, including several bestsellers. His own books include fiction, nonfiction, poetry, published by mainstream as well as smaller independent publishers."

WRITERS STUDIO AT UCLA EXTENTION

1010 Westwood Blvd., Los Angeles CA 90024. (310)825-9415. E-mail: writers@uclaextension.edu. Web site: www.uclaextension.edu/writers. **Contact:** Corey Campbell. Estab. 1997. Annual in February. Conference duration: 4 days; 10 a.m. to 6 p.m. Average attendance: 150-200. Intensive writing workshops in the areas of creative writing, screenwriting and television writing. Site: Conducted at UCLA Extension's 1010 Westwood Center.

Cost Fee is $725 after December 8.

Accommodations Information on overnight accommodations is available.

Additional Information For more information, call number (310)825-9415 or send an e-mail to writers@uclaextension.edu.

WRITING AND ILLUSTRATING FOR YOUNG READERS WORKSHOP

BYU, conferences and workshops, 348 HCEB, BYU, Provo UT 84602-1532. (801)422-2568. Fax: (801)422-0745. E-mail: cw348@byu.edu. Web site: http://wifyr.byu.edu. **Contact:** Conferences & Workshops. Estab. 2000. Annual. 5-day workshop held in June of each year. The workshop is designed for people who want to write or illustrate for children or teenagers. Participants focus on a single market during daily four-hour morning writing workshops led by published authors or illustrators. Afternoon workshop sessions include a mingle with the authors, editors and agents. Workshop focuses on fiction for young readers: picture books, book-length fiction, fantasy/science fiction, nonfiction, mystery, illustration and general writing. Site: Conference Center at Brigham Young University in the foothills of the Wasatch Mountain range.

Costs $450, full registration includes all workshops and breakout sessions plus a banquet on Thursday evening. $120, afternoon-only registration includes all afternoon workshop sessions plus the banquet on Thursday evening.

Accommodations Local lodging, airport shuttle. Lodging rates: $49-95/night.

NORTHWEST (AK, ID, MT, OR, WA, WY)

BOUCHERCON

507 S. 8th Street, Philadelphia PA 19147. (215)923-0211. Fax: (215)923-1789. E-mail: registration@bouchercon2007. Web site: www.bouchercon.com; www.bouchercon2007.com. Conference held September 27-30, 2007, in Anchorage, AK. The Bouchercon is "the world mystery and detective fiction event." Site: Anchorage Hilton Hotel. See Web site for details. Special guests include Ann Rule, Alexander McCall Smith.

Costs $200 (prior to July 1, 2007), $250 (after July 1) registration fee covers writing workshops, panels, reception, etc.

Additional Information Sponsors Anthony Award for published mystery novel; ballots due prior to conference. Information available on Web site.

CLARION WEST WRITERS' WORKSHOP

340 15th Avenue E, Suite 350, Seattle WA 98112-5156. (206)322-9083. E-mail: info@clarionwest.org. Web site: www.clarionwest.org. **Contact:** Leslie Howle, executive director. Estab. 1983. Annual. Workshop usually held in late June through July. Average attendance: 18. "Conference to prepare students for professional careers in science fiction and fantasy writing." Deadline for applications: April 1. Site: Conference held in Seattle's University district, an urban site close to restaurants and cafes, but not too far from downtown. Faculty: 6 teachers (professional writers and editors established in the field). "Every week a new instructor—each a well-known writer chosen for the quality of his or her work and for professional stature—teaches the class, bringing a unique perspective on speculative fiction. During the fifth week, the workshop is taught by a professional editor."

Costs Workshop tuition: $1,700 ($100 discount if application received by March 1). Dormitory housing: $1,200, some meals included.

Accommodations Students stay on site in workshop housing at one of the University of Washington's sorority houses.

Additional Information "Students write their own stories every week while preparing critiques of all the other students' work for classroom sessions. This gives participants a more focused, professional approach to their writing. The core of the workshop remains science fiction, and short stories (not novels) are the focus." Conference information available in Fall 2008. For brochure/guidelines send SASE, visit Web site, e-mail or call. Accepts inquiries by e-mail, phone, SASE. Limited scholarships are available, based on financial need. Students must submit 20-30 pages of ms with $30 for e-mail applications fee by mail to qualify for admission.

FLATHEAD RIVER WRITERS CONFERENCE

P.O. Box 7711, Kalispell MT 59904. E-mail: conference@authorsoftheflathead.org. **Contact:** Tom Kuffle. Estab. 1990. Annual. Next conference: intense workshops October 10-12, 2007, Conference October 13-14, 2007. Attendance limited to 100. Deals with all aspects of writing, including short and long fiction and nonfiction. Site: Grouse Mountain Lodge in Whitefish, MT. Recent speakers: Cricket Pechstein (agent), and Sandy Novack-Gottshall (fiction).

Costs Cost of general weekend conference; includes breakfast and lunch, not lodging. Approximately $100 per night.

Additional Information "We limit attendance to 100 in order to assure friendly, easy access to presentations."

◎ HEART TALK

Women's Center for Ministry, Western Seminary, 5511 SE Hawthorne Blvd., Portland OR 97215-3367. (503)517-1931 or (877)517-1800, ext. 1931. Fax: (503)517-1889. E-mail: wcm@westernseminary.edu. Web site: www.westernseminary.edu/women/. **Contact:** Kenine Stein, administrative associate. Estab. 1998. Every other year (alternates with speaker's conferences). March 12-15, 2008 will be a speakers conference with Carol Kent and team from Speak Up With Confidence. Original and mini-advanced seminars, with probable writing workshops included in mini-advanced. Last writing conference was March 2007. Conference duration: writing, 1 day; speaking, 3-4 days. Average attendance: 100+. "Heart Talk provides inspirational training for women desiring to write for publication and/or speak publicly." Site: "Western Seminary has a chapel plus classrooms to accommodate various size groups. The campus has a peaceful park-like atmosphere with beautiful lawns, trees and flowers." Topics in 2007 ranged from writing inspirational shorts, gift books, storyboarding, to book proposals, publishing alternatives, marketing, self-editing, being own publicist, and more. 2007 keynote speaker was Deborah Headstrom-Page. Workshops by Athena Dean, Sue Miholer, Elizabeth Jones, Carla Williams, Maxine Marsolini, and Karla Dornacher. Editors available for 1:1 consultation included Rebekah Clark, Athena Dean, Elizabeth Jones, Renee Sanford, and Carla Williams.

Costs $55 in 2007; box lunch can be ordered.

Additional Information Conference information available in January by e-mail, phone, fax and on Web site. For inquiries, contact by mail, e-mail, phone. Conference "is open to Christian women who desire to write for publication. Please view our Web site for Heart Talk 2007 Writer's Conference details. They will be posted as they become available. E-mail us to be added to our Heart Talk mailing list."

SAGEBRUSH WRITERS WORKSHOP

P.O. Box 1255, Big Timber MT 59011-1255. (406)932-4227. E-mail: sagebrsh@ttc-cmc.net. **Contact:** Gwen Petersen, director. Estab. 1997. Annual. Workshop usually held in April or May. Conference duration: 2½ days. Average attendance: 25-30. "Each year, the workshop has a different focus." Conference features "intensive personal instruction, good food, advance critiques, well-published authors/instructors, agents/editors, book sales and signings, readings." Site: American Legion, Carnegie Library or other venue, Big Timber, MT. Faculty consists of one writer/instructor and 2 guest speakers.

Costs $190 (2005), included Friday evening banquet dinner with guest speakers, all snacks at breaks.

Accommodations Offers shuttle from airport by arrangement with Sagebrush. Provides a list of area hotels and/or lodging options.

Additional Information "Submissions optional but encouraged—up to 10 pages." Workshop information is available February. For brochure send SASE, e-mail, call or fax. Accepts inquiries by SASE, e-mail, phone and fax. Agents and editors participate in conference.

SITKA CENTER FOR ART AND ECOLOGY

P.O. Box 65, Otis OR 97368. (541)994-5485. Fax: (541)994-8024. E-mail: info@sitkacenter.org. Web site: www.sitkacenter.org. **Contact:** Laura Young, program manager. Estab. 1970. "Our workshop program is open to all levels and is held annually from late May until late November. We also have a residency program from Septem-

ber through May." Average attendance: 10-16/workshop. A variety of workshops in creative process, including book arts and other media. Site: The Center borders a Nature Conservancy Preserve, the Siuslaw National Experimental Forest and the Salmon River Estuary, located just north of Lincoln City, OR.
Costs "Workshops are generally $50-300; they do not include meals or lodging."
Accommodations Does not offer overnight accommodations. Provides a list of area hotels or lodging options.
Additional Information Brochure available in February of each year by SASE, phone, e-mail, fax or visit Web site. Accepts inquiries by SASE, e-mail, phone, fax.

SITKA SYMPOSIUM
P.O. Box 2420, Sitka AK 99835-2420. (907)747-3794. Fax: (907)747-6554. E-mail: island@ak.net. Web site: www.islandinstitutealaska.org. **Contact:** Carolyn Servid, director. Estab. 1984. Annual. Conference held in June. Conference duration: 6 days. Enrollment limited to 60. Conference "to consider the relationship between writing and the ideas of selected theme focusing on social and cultural issues." Site: The Symposium is held in downtown Sitka, in the heart of southeast Alaska's striking coastal mountains and temperate rain forest. Many points of visitor interest are within walking distance. Guest speakers have included Alison Deming, Scott Russell Sanders, Rina Swentzell, Barry Lopez, William Kittredge, Gary Synder, Lorna Goodison, Terry Tempest Williams, Robert Hass, Wendell Berry and Linda Hogan.
Costs $365.
Accommodations Accommodation info is listed on Symposium brochure and Web site.
Additional Information Conference brochures/guidelines are available for SASE or online. Accepts inquiries by e-mail and fax.

SOUTH COAST WRITERS CONFERENCE
P.O. Box 590, 29392 Ellensburg Avenue, Gold Beach OR 97444. (541)247-2741. Fax: (541)247-6247. E-mail: scwc@socc.edu. Web site: www.socc.edu/scwriters. **Contact:** Janet Pretti, coordinator. Estab. 1996. Annual. Conference held President's Day weekend. Workshops held Friday and Saturday. Average attendance: 100. "We try to cover a broad spectrum: fiction, historical, poetry, children's, nature." Site: "Friday workshops are held at The Event Center on the Beach. Saturday workshops are held at the high school." 2007 keynote speaker will be Larry Brooks. Other presenters Shinan Barclay, Jim Coffee, Linda Crew, Roger Dorband, Jayel Gibson, Phil Hann, Rachel Ellen Koski, Bonnie Leon, John Noland, Joanna Rose, and J.D. Tynan.
Costs $55 before January 31; $65 after. Friday workshops are an additional $40. No meals or lodging included.
Accommodations Provides list of area hotels.
Additional Information Sponsors contest. "Southwestern scholarship open to anyone. This year's scholarship topic is 'Breaking Rules.' Contact SCWC for details."

THUNDER ARM WRITING RETREAT WITH NORTH CASCADES INSTITUTE
North Cascades Institute, 810 Highway 20, Sedro-Wooley WA 98284-9394. (360)856-5700 ext. 209. Fax: (360)856-1934. E-mail: nci@ncascades.org. Web site: www.ncascades.org. **Contact:** Deb Martin, registrar. Estab. 1999. Annual. 2006 conference was held October 10-14. Conference duration: 4 days. Average attendance: 32. Led by three outstanding authors and poets, the Institute's Thunder Arm Writing Retreat engages amateur and professional writers alike with lectures, discussions, readings and writing exercises centered on the natural world. "Nature writing, at its simplest, strives to explore basic principles at work in nature and to convey these in language that introduces readers to the facility and wonder of their own place in the world." Site: North Cascades Enviromental Learning Center on Diablo Lake in North Cascades National Park. Past faculty includes: Barbara Kingsolver, Robert Michael Pyle, William Kittredge, Ann Zwinger, Gary Ferguson, Kathleen Dean Moore, and William Dietrich.
Costs 2006 costs were $575 (double occupancy), $495 (commuter), $725 (single). All options include meals.
Additional Information For conference information, visit Web Site, e-mail or call.

TIN HOUSE SUMMER WRITERS WORKSHOP
P.O. Box 10500, Portland OR 97296. (503)219-0622. Fax: (503)222-1154. E-mail: emily@tinhouse.com. Web site: www.tinhouse.com. **Contact:** Lee Montgomery, conference coordinator. Estab. 2003. Annual in July. Conference duration: 1 week. Average attendance: 100. A weeklong intensive of panels, seminars, workshops and readings led by the editors of *Tin House* magazine and Tin House Books, and their guests—prominent contemporary writers of fiction, nonfiction, poetry and film. Site: The workshop will be held at Reed College in scenic Portland, OR, just minutes from downtown and the airport. Facilities include bookstore, library, mail service, an art gallery, print shop and athletic facilities. Each afternoon agents, editors, writers and filmmakers will discuss ideas and offer a range of discussions on topics and issues concerning the craft and business of riting. See Web site for specifics. 2007 faculty included Charles Baxter, T.C. Boyle, Annie Proulx, Colson Whitehead, Aimee Bender, Dorothy Allison.

Costs 2006 tuition was $950; food and lodging $550. Application fee $35. Scholarships available.

Additional Information Attendees must submit writing sample and attend by invitation. Deadline: April 1, then rolling while space allows. Admission is based on the strength and promise of the writing sample—up to 15 pages of fiction. Brochures available in February for SASE, by fax, phone, e-mail and on Web site. Accepts inquiries by SASE, e-mail, phone, fax. Agents and editors attend conference.

WILLAMETTE WRITERS CONFERENCE

9045 SW Barbur Blvd., Suite 5-A, Portland OR 97219-4027. (503)452-1592. Fax: (503)452-0372. E-mail: wilwrite @willamettewriters.com. Web site: www.willamettewriters.com. **Contact:** Bill Johnson, office manager. Estab. 1981. Annual. Conference held in August. Conference duration: 3 days. Average attendance: 600. "Williamette Writers is open to all writers, and we plan our conference accordingly. We offer workshops on all aspects of fiction, nonfiction, marketing, the creative process, screenwriting, etc. Also we invite top notch inspirational speakers for keynote addresses. Recent theme was 'The Writers Way.' We always include at least one agent or editor panel and offer a variety of topics of interest to both fiction and nonfiction writers and screenwriters." Recent editors, agents and film producers in attendance have included: Donald Maass, Donald Maass Literary Agency; Angela Rinaldi; Kim Cameron.

Costs Cost for 3-day conference including meals is $395 members; $425 nonmembers.

Accommodations If necessary, these can be made on an individual basis. Some years special rates are available.

Additional Information Conference brochure/guidelines are available in May for catalog-size SASE, e-mail, fax, phone or on Web site. Accepts inquiries by fax, e-mail, phone, SASE.

WRITE ON THE SOUND WRITERS' CONFERENCE

Edmonds Arts Commission, 700 Main Street, Edmonds WA 98020. (425)771-0228. Fax: (425)771-0253. E-mail: wots@ci.edmonds.wa.us. **Contact:** Kris Gillespie, conference organizer. Estab. 1986. Annual. Last conference held October 7-8 2007. Conference duration: 2 days. Average attendance: 180. "Conference is small—good for networking—and focuses on the craft of writing." Site: "Edmonds is a beautiful community on the shores of Puget Sound, just north of Seattle. View brochure at www.ci.edmonds.wa.us/artscommission."

Costs $104 by Sept. 21, $125 after Sept. 21 for 2 days, $68 for 1 day (2005); includes registration, morning refreshments and 1 ticket to keynote lecture.

Additional Information Brochures available August 1. Accepts inquiries by e-mail, fax.

WRITING IT REAL IN PORT TOWNSEND

(formerly the Colorado Mt. Writer's Workshop), 394 Colman Drive, Port Townsend, WA 98368. (360)385-7839. Web site: http://writingitreal.com/wirconference2007.htm. Established 1999. Annual. Last conference held June 21-25, 2007. Conference duration: 4 days. Average Attendance: 35. Named one of the top retreats by *Personal Journaling Magazine*, this conference focuses on fiction, poetry and personal essay. The conference is designed to lift writers, novice or experienced, to the next level. Site: Held at a hotel (housing there or around town) in Port Townsend, WA. Features personal writing. Faculty includes Sheila Bender, Susan Reich, Jack Heffron.

Costs $475 ($425 if paid in full by April 1). Accommodations and meals separate. Daily activities include craft talks, small group manuscript workshop, hands-on exercises for creating new work, instructor and group responses, readings.

CANADA

BLOODY WORDS MYSTERY CONFERENCE

Phone/fax: (416)497-5293. E-mail: soles@sff.net. Web site: www.bloodywords.com. **Contact:** Caro Soles, chair. Estab. 1999. Annual. Conference held June 6-8, 2008. Average attendance: 300. Focus: Mystery/true crime/ forensics, with Canadian slant. Purpose: To bring readers and writers of the mystery genre together in a Canadian setting. Site: Toronto, ON: Eaton Center Downtown Marriott. Conference includes two workshops and two tracks of panels, one on factual information such as forensics, agents, scene of the crime procedures, etc. and one on fiction, such as "Death in a Cold Climate," "Murder on the Menu," "Elementary, My Dear Watson," and a First Novelists Panel. Guests of honor in 2008: Rosemary Aubert and Carolyn Hart.

Costs 2007 fee: $175 (Canadian)/$165 (US), included the banquet and all panels, readings, dealers' room and workshop.

Accommodations Offers block of rooms in hotel; list of optional lodging available. Check Web site for details.

Additional Information Sponsors short mystery story contest—5,000 word limit; judges are experienced editors of anthologies; fee is $5 (entrants must be registered). Conference information is available now. For brochure visit Web site. Accepts inquiries by e-mail and phone. Agents and editors participate in conference. "This is a conference for both readers and writers of mysteries, the only one of its kind in Canada. We also run 'The Mystery Cafe,' a chance to get to know 15 authors, hear them read and ask questions (half hour each).''

BOOMING GROUND
Buch E-462, 1866 Main Mall, Creative Writing Program, UBC, Vancouver BC V6T 121 Canada. (604)822-2469. Fax: (604)822-3616. E-mail: bg@arts.ubc.ca. Web site: bg.arts.ubc.ca. **Contact:** Andrew Gray, director. Estab. 1998. Average attendance: 30 per session. Conference on ''fiction, poetry, nonfiction, children's writing. We offer three sessions of online-only mentorships each year in January, May and September. Online mentorships offer 16 weeks of work with an instructor, allowing up to 120 pages of material to be created. Site: Online and by e-mail.
Costs $775 (Canadian) for online-only mentorships; Some scholarships available.
Accommodations Not available.
Additional Information Workshops are based on works-in-progress. Writers must submit ms with application for jury selection. For brochures/guidelines visit Web site, e-mail, fax or call. Accepts inquiries by phone, fax, e-mail. ''Classes are offered for writers at all levels—from early career to mid-career. All student work is evaluated by a jury. Our mentorships are ideal for long-form work such as novels, collections of poetry and short fiction.''

HUMBER SCHOOL FOR WRITERS SUMMER WORKSHOP
Humber Institute of Technology and Advanced Learning, 3199 Lake Shore Blvd. West, Toronto ON M8V 1K8 Canada. (416)675-6622 ext. 3448. Fax: (416)251-7167. E-mail: antanas.sileika@humber.ca. Web site: www.humber.ca/creativeandperformingarts. **Contact:** Antanas Sileika, director. Annual. Workshop held July. Conference duration: 1 week. Average attendance: 100. Focuses on fiction, poetry, creative nonfiction. Site: Humber College's Lakeshore campus in Toronto. Panels cover success stories, small presses, large presses, agents. Faculty: Changes annually. 2006 included Francine Prose, Alistair Macleod, David Bezmozgis, Joseph Boyden, Wayson Choy, Bruce Jay Friedman, Isabel Huggan, Kim Moritsugu, Olive Senior and others.
Costs Workshop fee is $950 Canadian ($800 US).
Accommodations Provides lodging. Residence fee is $350 Canadian ($280 US).
Additional Information Participants ''must submit sample writing no longer than 15 pages approximately 4 weeks before workshop begins.'' Brochures available mid-February for e-mail, phone, fax. Accepts inquiries by e-mail, phone, fax. Agents and editors participate in conference.

MARITIME WRITERS' WORKSHOP
UNB Arts Centre, P.O. Box 4400, Fredericton NB E3B 5A3 Canada. Phone/fax: (506)453-4623. E-mail: atitus@unb.ca. Web site: http://extend.unb.ca/pers_cult/writers/index.php. **Contact:** Andrew Titus, coordinator. Estab. 1976. Workshop held annually in July. Average attendance: 50. ''We offer small groups of 10, practical manuscript focus. Novice writers welcome. Workshops in fiction, poetry, mystery/suspense, and francophone literature. The annual Maritime Writers' Workshop is a practical, wide-ranging program designed to help writers develop and refine their creative writing skills. This weeklong program will involve you in small group workshops, lectures and discussions, public readings and special events, all in a supportive community of writers who share a commitment to excellence. Workshop groups consist of a maximum of 10 writers each. Instructors are established Canadian authors and experienced teachers with a genuine interest in facilitating the writing process of others. For over a quarter century, Maritime Writers' Workshop has provided counsel, encouragement and direction for hundreds of developing writers.'' Site: University of New Brunswick, Fredericton campus.
Costs 2006: $495 tuition.
Accommodations On-campus accommodations and meals.
Additional Information ''Participants must submit 10-20 manuscript pages which form a focus for workshop discussions.'' Brochures available after March. No SASE necessary. Accepts inquiries by e-mail and fax.

SAGE HILL WRITING EXPERIENCE
Box 1731, Saskatoon SK S7K 3S1 Canada. Phone/fax: (306)652-7395. E-mail: sage.hill@sasktel.net. Web site: www.sagehillwriting.ca. **Contact:** Steven Ross Smith. Annual. Workshops held in July and May. Conference duration: 10-14 days. Average attendance: Summer, 30-40; Fall, 6-8. ''Sage Hill Writing Experience offers a special working and learning opportunity to writers at different stages of development. Top quality instruction, low instructor-student ratio and the beautiful Sage Hill setting offer conditions ideal for the pursuit of excellence in the arts of fiction, nonfiction, poetry and playwriting.'' Site: The Sage Hill location features ''individual accommodation, in-room writing area, lounges, meeting rooms, healthy meals, walking woods and vistas in several directions.'' Various classes are held: Introduction to Writing Fiction & Poetry; Fiction Workshop; Fiction Colloquium, Poetry Workshop; Poetry Colloquium; Playwriting Lab.

Costs Summer program, $1,095 (Canadian) includes instruction, accommodation, meals and all facilities. Fall Fiction Colloquium: $1,395 (Canadian).

Accommodations On-site individual accommodations for Summer and Fall programs located at Lumsden, 45 kilometers outside Regina.

Additional Information Application requirements for Introduction to Creative Writing: A 5-page sample of your writing or a statement of your interest in creative writing; list of courses taken required. For workshop and colloquium programs: A résumé of your writing career and a 12-page sample of your work-in-progress, plus 5 pages of published work required. Application deadline for the Summer Program is in April. Spring program deadline in March. Guidelines are available after January for SASE, e-mail, fax, phone or on Web site. Scholarships and bursaries are available.

◪ THE VICTORIA SCHOOL OF WRITING

Suite 306-620 View St., Victoria BC V8W 1J6 Canada. (250)595-3000. E-mail: info@victoriaschoolofwriting.org. Web site: www.victoriaschoolofwriting.org. **Contact:** Jill Margo, director. Conference held the third week in July annually. "Five-day intensive workshop on beautiful Vancouver Island with outstanding author-instructors in fiction, poetry, nonfiction, work-in-progress and other genres."

Costs $595 (Canadian).

Accommodations On site.

Additional Information Workshop brochures available. Accepts inquiries by e-mail, phone or Web site.

◪ THE WRITERS' RETREAT

15 Canusa St., Stanstead QC J0B 3E5 Canada. (819) 876-2065. E-mail: info@writersretreat.com. Web site: www.writersretreat.com. **Contact:** Micheline Cote, director. Estab. 2000. Year-round. The Writers' Retreat offers residency and literary services including private mentoring, workshops, editing and placement service to residents only; selected locations with on-site editor. Site: The headquarters are located in Quebec on the Vermont/Quebec border with additional retreats located in Ouray, Colorado; Santa Cruz, California; Santa Fe, New Mexico; Prince Edward Island and New Brunswick, Canada. The Writers' Retreat workshops feature instruction in fiction and nonfiction writing and screenwriting. "Our sole purpose is to provide an ambiance conducive to creativity for career and emerging writers." Residency includes a private studio, breakfast, reference books, wireless Internet, critique, on site editor.

Costs Residency varies between $575-$2,000 per week depending on location. Workshop tuition varies from $195-$1,500, depending on the format.

Additional Information Accepts inquiries by SASE, e-mail and phone.

◪ ◎ WRITING WITH STYLE

The Banff Centre, P.O. Box 1020, Banff AB T1L 1H5 Canada. (800)565-9989. E-mail: arts_info@banffcentre.ca. Web site: www.banffcentre.ca. **Contact:** Office of the Registrar. Semiannual. Writing workshop. "This writing program is offered to developing writers who may or may not be published." Conference held April 2008. Conference duration: 1 week. Average attendance: 30-40 participants. "Each faculty member is a writer of a different genre which may include short fiction, poetry, memoir, children's fiction, science fiction, crime writing, young adult, etc." Site: "The Banff Centre is a centre for creative excellence where professional and developing artists engage in formal and informal dialogues with peers and mentors for the purpose of advancing their creative practices. As inspirational as it is beautiful, the mountain setting (in Banff National Park) is a unique feature of the Centre." September genres include short fiction, memoir, travel writing, and nature writing. September 2007 faculty: Audrey Thomas, Steven Heighton, and Candace Savage.

Costs Workshop fee: please see Web site for up-to-date information, www.banffcentre.ca/writing/.

Accommodations Offers overnight accommodations. Accommodation fee: $357 (single occupancy room only option). "Onsite only, hotel style which also serve as private work spaces. Computers should be brought along for private use. Public computers available on campus."

Additional Information "At time of application, writers must submit writing samples and statement of expectations. Application fee: $56 Canadian. Brochure currently available for e-mail and on Web site. For inquiries, contact by SASE, e-mail, phone, fax. Other more advanced writing programs are also offered at The Banff Centre."

INTERNATIONAL

ART WORKSHOPS IN GUATEMALA

4758 Lyndale Ave. S, Minneapolis MN 55419-5304. (612)825-0747. E-mail: info@artguat.org. Web site: www.art guat.org. **Contact:** Liza Fourre, director. Estab. 1995. Annual. Workshops held year-round. Maximim class size: 10 students per class. Workshop titles include: Fiction Writing: Shaping and Structuring Your Story with Gladys

Swan; New Directions in Travel Writing with Richard Harris; Poetry: Snapshots in Words with Rosanne Lloyd; and Creative Writing: Journey of the Soul with Sharon Doubiago.
Costs $1,645 (includes tuition, lodging in a lovely colonial style B&B, and ground transportation, and some pretty interesting field trips).
Accommodations All transportation and accommodations included in price of conference.
Additional Information Conference information available now. For brochure/guidelines visit Web site, e-mail, fax or call. Accepts inquiries by e-mail, phone.

⊕ DINGLE WRITING COURSES

Ballintlea, Ventry, Co Kerry Ireland. 353 66 9159815. E-mail: info@dinglewritingcourses.ie. Web site: www.ding lewritingcourses.ie. **Contact:** Abigail Joffe and Nicholas McLachlan. Estab. 1996. Annual. Conference held 3 or 4 weekends per year. Average attendance: 14. Creative writing weekends for fiction, poetry, memoir, novel, writing for children, etc. Site: "Residential centre at Inch on the Dingle Peninsula." Recent faculty included Niall Williams, Paula Meehan and Andrew O'Hagan.
Costs 350€ for a weekend (Friday evening to Sunday evening) includes all meals, accommodation, tuition.
Accommodations "We arrange taxis on request; cost not included in fee." Provides overnight accommodations. "Large communal eating facility and workroom; spectacular views." Also provides list of area lodging.
Additional Information Some workshops require material submitted in advance. Brochures available in May by e-mail, phone, fax or on Web site. Accepts inquiries by e-mail, phone, fax.

⊕ PARIS WRITERS WORKSHOP/WICE

20, Bd. du Montparnasse, Paris 75015 France. (331)45.66.75.50. Fax: (331)40.65.96.53. E-mail: pww@wice-paris.org. Web site: www.wice-paris.org. **Contact:** Marcia Lebre, director. Estab. 1987. Annual. Conference held June-July. Average attendance: 50. "Conference concentrates on fiction, nonfiction and poetry. Visiting lecturers speak on a variety of issues important to beginning and advanced writers. 2007 writers in residence were Alice Mattison (novel), A. Manette Ansay (short fiction), Kurt Brown (poetry), Phillip Lopate (creative nonfiction), Jake Lamar (writing intensive tutorial). Located in the heart of Paris on the Bd. du Montparnasse, the stomping grounds of such famous American writers as Ernest Hemingway, Henry Miller and F. Scott Fitzgerald. The site consists of four classrooms, a resource center/library and private terrace."
Costs 650 Euros (525 Euros for early bird registration by May 17)—tuition only.
Additional Information "Students submit 1 copy of complete manuscript or work-in-progress which is sent in advance to writer-in-residence. Each student has a one-on-one consultation with writer-in-residence." Conference information available late fall. For brochures/guidelines visit Web site, e-mail, call or fax. Accepts inquiries by SASE, phone, e-mail, fax. "Workshop attracts many expatriate Americans and other English-language writers from all over Europe and North America. We are an intimate workshop with an exciting mix of more experienced, published writers and enthusiastic beginners."

◎ WRITING, CREATIVITY AND RITUAL: A WOMAN'S RETREAT

995 Chapman Road, Yorktown Heights NY 10598. (914)926-4432. E-mail: emily@emilyhanlon.com. Web site: www.awritersretreat.com. **Contact:** Emily Hanlon. Estab. 1998. Annual. Last retreat held in Costa Rica, Sept. 24-Oct. 6, 2006. Average attendance: 20 is the limit. Women only. Retreat for all kinds of creative writing and anyone interested in creativity and spirituality. Site: (In 2006) Samasati Retreat Center was an ideal setting for a gathering of women passionate about their writing and eager to connect with others of like mind and heart. Called by one writer who has been to Samasati "as close to heaven as you can get." Samasati is situated on 250 acres of virgin tropical forest overlooking the Caribbean Sea. "Here we will open doorways to new stories, characters, techniques and a deeper creativity." The Samasati Retreat Center is in a primary and secondary rain forest that is natural habitat to hundreds of species of birds, butterflies and wildlife; at an elevation of 650 feet, the climate is delightfully cool even on hot days. The retreat includes days to explore the rain forest, walk the magnificent beaches and swim in Carribean waters. There are Yoga classes, bird watching, river and sea kayaking, scuba diving, coral reefs, horseback riding on the beach, hiking at Samasati Biological Reserve, Dolphin Connections, as well as Indian Reserves and National Parks and a Wildlife Refuge.
Costs Range from $3,150 to $4,100 depending on choice of room and payment schedule. 12 days, includes room, workshop materials, all meals, and some sightseeing adventures. See Web Site.
Additional Information Conference information free and available online. Accepts inquiries by e-mail, phone. "More than just a writing workshop or conference, the retreat is an exploration of the creative process through writing, 3-hour writing workshops daily, plus creativity workshops and time to write and explore." Please e-mail or call if you would like to be put on the Ireland mailing list.

ZOETROPE: ALL-STORY SHORT STORY WRITERS' WORKSHOP

916 Kearny St., San Francisco CA 94133. (415)788-7500. E-mail: info@all-story.com. Web site: www.all-story.c om. **Contact:** Michael Ray, editor. Estab. 1997. Annual. Last workshop was August 18-25, 2007. Conference

duration: 1 week. Average attendance: 20. Workshop focuses on fiction, specifically short stories. Site: Francis Ford Coppola's gorgeous Blancaneaux Lodge in Belize, on the banks of the Privassion River. Guests stay in luxurious private cabanas and villas, all with spa baths and decks with hammocks and river views. Past instructors include Philip Gourevitch, National Book Award finalist Susan Straight, Pulitzer Prize-winner Robert Olen Butler, and George Saunders.

Costs Ranges from $2,500 to $3,550, depending on accommodations. That fee is all-inclusive, including accommodations, food, workshop, day excursions, all transfers to and from Belize city, and a camp T-shirt.

Additional Information Please submit a completed application and an original work of short fiction less than 5,000 words by August 15. Application forms are available on the Web site. Brochures available now for SASE, by fax, phone, e-mail, and on Web site. Accepts inquiries by phone, fax, e-mail and for SASE. Editors attend the conference.

Publishers and Their Imprints

The publishing world is constantly changing and evolving. With all of the buying, selling, reorganizing, consolidating and dissolving, it's hard to keep publishers and their imprints straight. To help you make sense of these changes, we offer this breakdown of major publishers (and their divisions)—who owns whom and which imprints are under each company umbrella. Keep in mind that this information is constantly changing. We have provided the Web site of each publisher so you can continue to keep an eye on this ever-evolving business.

HARLEQUIN ENTERPRISES

www.eharlequin.com

Harlequin
Harlequin American Romance
Harlequin Bianca
Harlequin Blaze
Harlequin Deseo
Harlequin Everlasting Love
Harlequin Ginger Blossom
Harlequin Historical
Harlequin Intrigue
Harlequin Jazmin
Harlequin Julia
Harlequin Medical Romance
Harlequin NEXT
Harlequin Presents
Harlequin Romance
Harlequin Superromance

HQN Books

LUNA

Mills & Boon
Mills & Boon Historical Romance
Mills & Boon Medical Romance
Mills & Boon Modern Xtra-Sensual

MIRA

Kimani Press
Kimani Press Arabesque Inspirational Romance
Kimani Press Arabesque Romance
Kimani Press Kimani Romance
Kimani TRU
Kimani Press New Spirit
Kimani Press Romance Sepia

Red Dress Ink

Silhouette
Silhouette Bombshell
Silhouette Desire
Silhouette Nocturne
Silhouette Romance
Silhouette Romantic Suspense
Silhouette Special Edition

SPICE

Steeple Hill
Steeple Hill Café
Steeple Hill Love Inspired

Steeple Hill Love Inspired Historical
Steeple Hill Love Inspired Suspense
Steeple Hill Women's Fiction

Worldwide Library
Rogue Angel
Worldwide Mystery

HARPERCOLLINS

www.harpercollins.com

HarperCollins Australia/New Zealand
Angus & Robertson
Collins
Fourth Estate
Harper Perennial
HarperCollins
HarperSports
Voyager

HarperCollins Canada
HarperCollinsPublishers
HarperPerennial Canada
HarperTrophyCanada
Phyllis Bruce Books

HarperCollins Children's Books Group
Amistad
Eos
Greenwillow Books
HarperCollins Children's Audio
HarperCollins Children's Books
HarperFestival
HarperEntertainment
HarperTeen
HarperTrophy
Joanna Cotler books
Julie Andrews Collection
Katherine Tegen Books
Laura Geringer Books
Rayo

HarperCollins General Books Group
Amistad
Avon
Avon A
Avon Red
Caedmon
Collins
Collins Design

Dark Alley
Ecco
Eos
Harper Paperbacks
Harper Perennial
Harper Perennial Modern Classics
HarperAudio
HarperCollins
HarperCollins e-Books
HarperEntertainment
HarperLuxe
HarperSanFrancisco
HarperTorch
Morrow Cookbooks
Rayo
William Morrow

HarperCollins UK
Collins
General Books
   HarperFiction
      Voyager
   HarperNonfiction
      HarperCollins Audio
      HarperEntertainment
      HarperSport
      HarperThorsons Harper Element
      Tolkien and Estates
   HarperCollins Children's Books
Press Books
   FourthEstate
   HarperPerennial
   HarperPress

Zondervan
Vida
Zonderkidz
Zondervan

Resources

HOLTZBRINCK PUBLISHERS

www.holtzbrinck.com

Farrar, Straus & Giroux
Faber & Faber, Inc.
Farrar, Straus & Giroux Books for Young
    Readers
Hill & Wang (division)
North Point Press

Henry Holt and Co. LLC
Books for Young Readers
Metropolitan Books
Owl Books
Times Books

Pan MacMillan
Boxtree
MacMillan
MacMillan Children's Books

Campbell Books
Priddy Books
Pan
Picador
Sidgwick & Jackson

St. Martin's Press
Griffin Books
Let's Go
Minotaur
St. Martin's Paperbacks
St. Martin's Press
Thomas Dunne Books
Truman Talley Books

Tom Doherty Associates
Forge
Tor Books

PENGUIN GROUP (USA), INC.

www.penguingroup.com

Penguin Adult Division
Ace Books
Alpha Books
Avery
Berkley Books
Dutton
Gotham Books
HPBooks
Hudson Street Press
Jeremy P. Tarcher
Jove
New American Library
Penguin
Penguin Press
Perigree
Plume
Portfolio

Putnam
Riverhead Books
Sentinel
Viking

Young Readers Division
Dial Books for Young Readers
Dutton Children's Books
Firebird
Frederick Warne
Grosset & Dunlap
Philomel
Price Stern Sloan
Puffin Books
Putnam
Razorbill
Speak
Viking Children's Books

RANDOM HOUSE, INC.

www.randomhouse.com

Bantam Dell Publishing Group
Bantam Hardcover
Bantam Mass Market

Bantam Trade Paperback
Crimeline
Delacorte Press

Dell
Delta
Domain
DTP
Fanfare
Island
Spectra
The Dial Press

Crown Publishing Group

Clarkson Potter
Crown Business
Crown Publishers, Inc.
Harmony Books
Potter Style
Potter Craft
Shaye Arehart Books
Three Rivers Press

Doubleday Broadway Publishing Group

Broadway Books
Currency
Doubleday
Doubleday Image
Doubleday Religious Publishing
Harlem Moon
Main Street Books
Morgan Road Books
Spiegel & Grau
Nan A. Talese

Knopf Publishing Group

Alfred A. Knopf
Anchor Books
Everyman's Library
Pantheon Books
Schocken Books
Vintage Books

Random House Publishing Group

Ballantine Books
Del Rey
Del Rey/Lucas Books
Fawcett
Ivy
The Modern Library
One World
Random House Trade Group
Random House Trade Paperbacks

Reader's Circle
Striver's Row Books
Villard Books
Wellspring

Random House Audio Publishing Group

Listening Library
Random House Audio
Random House Audio Assets
Random House Audio Dimensions
Random House Price-less
Random House Audio Roads
Random House Audio Voices

Random House Children's Books

Golden Books
Kids@Random

Random House Direct, Inc.

Bon Apetit
Gourmet Books
Pillsbury

Random House Information Group

Fodor's Travel Publications
Living Language
Prima Games
The Princeton Review
Random House Español
Random House Puzzles & Games
Random House Reference Publishing

Random House International

Areté
McClelland & Stewart Ltd.
Plaza & Janés
Random House Australia
Random House of Canada Ltd.
Random House of Mondadori
Random House South Africa
Random House South America
Random House United Kingdom
Transworld UK
Verlagsgruppe Random House

Random House Large Print

Random House Value Publishing

Waterbrook Press

Fisherman Bible Study Guides
Shaw Books
Waterbrook Press

SIMON & SCHUSTER

www.simonsays.com

Simon & Schuster Adult Publishing

Atria Books
Free Press
Howard Books
Pocket Books
Scribner
Simon & Schuster
Strebor
The Touchstone & Fireside Group

Simon & Schuster Audio

Pimsleur
Simon & Schuster Audioworks
Simon & Schuster Sound Ideas

Simon & Schuster Children's Publishing

Aladdin Paperbacks
Atheneum Books for Young Readers
Libros Para Niños
Little Simon®
Little Simon Inspirations
Margaret K. McElderry Books
Simon & Schuster Books for Young Readers
Simon Pulse
Simon Spotlight®
Simon Spotlight Entertainment

Simon & Schuster International

Simon & Schuster Australia
Simon & Schuster Canada
Simon & Schuster UK

HACHETTE BOOK GROUP USA

www.hachettebookgroupusa.com

Center Street

FaithWords

Hachette Book Group Digital Media

Hachette Audio

Little, Brown and Company

Back Bay Books
Bulfinch Press

Little, Brown Books for Young Readers

LB Kids
Megan Tingley Books

Grand Central Publishing

Business Plus
5-Spot
Forever
Orbit
Springboard Press
Twelve
Vision
Wellness Central
Yen Press

Canadian Writers Take Note

While much of the information contained in this section applies to all writers, here are some specifics of interest to Canadian writers:

Postage: When sending an SASE from Canada, you will need an International Reply Coupon ($3.50). Also be aware, a GST tax is required on postage in Canada and for mail with postage under $5 going to destinations outside the country. Since Canadian postage rates are voted on in January of each year (after we go to press), contact a Canada Post Corporation Customer Service Division (located in most cities in Canada) or visit www.canadapost.ca for the most current rates.

Copyright: For information on copyrighting your work and to obtain forms, write Canadian Intellectual Property Office, Industry Canada, Place du Portage I, 50 Victoria St., Room C-114, Gatineau, Quebec K1A 0C9 or call (866)997-1936. Web site: www.cipo.gc.ca.

The public lending right: The Public Lending Right Commission has established that eligible Canadian authors are entitled to payments when a book is available through a library. Payments are determined by a sampling of the holdings of a representative number of libraries. To find out more about the program and to learn if you are eligible, write to the Public Lending Right Commission at 350 Albert St., P.O. Box 1047, Ottawa, Ontario K1P 5V8 or call (613)566-4378 or (800)521-5721 for information. Web site: www.plr-dpp.ca/. The Commission, which is part of The Canada Council, produces a helpful pamphlet, *How the PLR System Works*, on the program.

Grants available to Canadian writers: Most province art councils or departments of culture provide grants to resident writers. Some of these, as well as contests for Canadian writers, are listed in our Contests and Awards section. For national programs, contact The Canada Council, Writing and Publishing Section, 350 Alberta St., P.O. Box 1047, Ottawa, Ontario K1P 5V8 or call (613)566-4414 or (800)263-5588 for information. Fax: (613)566-4410. Web site: www.canadacouncil.ca.

For more information: Contact The Writer's Union of Canada, 90 Richmond St. E, Suite 200, Toronto, Ontario M5C 1P1; call them at (416)703-8982 or fax them at (416)504-9090. E-mail: info@writersunion.ca. Web site: www.writersunion.ca. This organization provides a wealth of information (as well as strong support) for Canadian writers, including specialized publications on publishing contracts; contract negotiations; the author/editor relationship; author awards, competitions and grants; agents; taxes for writers, libel issues and access to archives in Canada.

Printing & Production

Terms Defined

I n most of the magazine listings in this book, you will find a brief physical description of each publication. This material usually includes the number of pages, type of paper, type of binding and whether or not the magazine uses photographs and/or illustrations.

Although it is important to look at a copy of the magazine to which you are submitting, these descriptions can give you a general idea of what the publication looks like. This material can provide you with a feel for the magazine's financial resources and prestige. Do not, however, rule out small, simply produced publications, as these may be the most receptive to new writers. Watch for publications that have increased their page count or improved their production from year to year. This is a sign the publication is doing well and may be accepting more fiction.

You will notice a wide variety of printing terms used within these descriptions. We explain here some of the more common terms used in our listing descriptions. We do not include explanations of terms such as Mohawk and Karma which are brand names and refer to the paper manufacturer.

PAPER

A5: An international paper standard; 148×210 mm or 5.8×8.3 in.

acid-free: Paper that has low or no acid content. This type of paper resists deterioration from exposure to the elements. More expensive than many other types of paper, publications done on acid-free paper can last a long time.

bond: Bond paper is often used for stationery and is more transparent than text paper. It can be made of either sulphite (wood) or cotton fiber. Some bonds have a mixture of both wood and cotton (such as "25 percent cotton" paper). This is the type of paper most often used in photocopying or as standard typing paper.

coated/uncoated stock: Coated and uncoated are terms usually used when referring to book or text paper. More opaque than bond, it is the paper most used for offset printing. As the name implies, uncoated paper has no coating. Coated paper is coated with a layer of clay, varnish or other chemicals. It comes in various sheens and surfaces depending on the type of coating, but the most common are dull, matte and gloss.

cover stock: Cover stock is heavier book or text paper used to cover a publication. It comes in a variety of colors and textures and can be coated on one or both sides.

CS1/CS2: Most often used when referring to cover stock, CS1 means paper that is coated only on one side; CS2 is paper coated on both sides.

newsprint: Inexpensive absorbent pulp wood paper often used in newspapers and tabloids.

text: Text paper is similar to book paper (a smooth paper used in offset printing), but it has been given some texture by using rollers or other methods to apply a pattern to the paper.

vellum: Vellum is a text paper that is fairly porous and soft.

Some notes about paper weight and thickness: Often you will see paper thickness described in terms of pounds such as 80 lb. or 60 lb. paper. The weight is determined by figuring how many pounds in a ream of a particular paper (a ream is 500 sheets). This can be confusing, however, because this figure is based on a standard sheet size and standard sheet sizes vary depending on the type of paper used. This information is most helpful when comparing papers of the same type. For example, 80 lb. book paper versus 60 lb. book paper. Since the size of the paper is the same it would follow that 80 lb. paper is the thicker, heavier paper.

Some paper, especially cover stock, is described by the actual thickness of the paper. This is expressed in a system of points. Typical paper thicknesses range from 8 points to 14 points thick.

PRINTING

There are many other printing methods but these are the ones most commonly referred to in our listings.

letterpress: Letterpress printing is printing that uses a raised surface such as type. The type is inked and then pressed against the paper. Unlike offset printing, only a limited number of impressions can be made, as the surface of the type can wear down.

offset: Offset is a printing method in which ink is transferred from an image-bearing plate to a "blanket" and from the blanket to the paper.

sheet-fed offset: Offset printing in which the paper is fed one piece at a time.

web offset: Offset printing in which a roll of paper is printed and then cut apart to make individual sheets.

BINDING

case binding: In case binding, signatures (groups of pages) are stitched together with thread rather than glued together. The stitched pages are then trimmed on three sides and glued into a hardcover or board "case" or cover. Most hardcover books and thicker magazines are done this way.

comb binding: A comb is a plastic spine used to hold pages together with bent tabs that are fed through punched holes in the edge of the paper.

perfect binding: Used for paperback books and heavier magazines, perfect binding involves gathering signatures (groups of pages) into a stack, trimming off the folds so the edge is flat and gluing a cover to that edge.

saddle stitched: Publications in which the pages are stitched together using metal staples. This fairly inexpensive type of binding is usually used with books or magazines that are under 80 pages.

Smythe-sewn: Binding in which the pages are sewn together with thread. Smythe is the name of the most common machine used for this purpose.

spiral binding: A wire spiral that is wound through holes punched in pages is a spiral bind. This is the binding used in spiral notebooks.

Glossary

Advance. Payment by a publisher to an author prior to the publication of a book, to be deducted from the author's future royalties.

Adventure story. A genre of fiction in which action is the key element, overshadowing characters, theme and setting. The conflict in an adventure story is often man against nature. A secondary plot that reinforces this kind of conflict is sometimes included. In Allistair MacLean's *Night Without End*, for example, the hero, while investigating a mysterious Arctic air crash, also finds himself dealing with espionage, sabotage and murder.

All rights. The rights contracted to a publisher permitting a manuscript's use anywhere and in any form, including movie and book club sales, without additional payment to the writer.

Amateur sleuth. The character in a mystery, usually the protagonist, who does the detection but is not a professional private investigator or police detective.

Anthology. A collection of selected writings by various authors.

Association of Authors' Representatives (AAR). An organization for literary agents committed to maintaining excellence in literary representation.

Auction. Publishers sometimes bid against each other for the acquisition of a manuscript that has excellent sales prospects.

Backlist. A publisher's books not published during the current season but still in print.

Biographical novel. A life story documented in history and transformed into fiction through the insight and imagination of the writer. This type of novel melds the elements of biographical research and historical truth into the framework of a novel, complete with dialogue, drama and mood. A biographical novel resembles historical fiction, save for one aspect: Characters in a historical novel may be fabricated and then placed into an authentic setting; characters in a biographical novel have actually lived.

Book producer/packager. An organization that may develop a book for a publisher based upon the publisher's idea or may plan all elements of a book, from its initial concept to writing and marketing strategies, and then sell the package to a book publisher and/or movie producer.

Cliffhanger. Fictional event in which the reader is left in suspense at the end of a chapter or episode, so that interest in the story's outcome will be sustained.

Clip. Sample, usually from a newspaper or magazine, of a writer's published work.

Cloak-and-dagger. A melodramatic, romantic type of fiction dealing with espionage and intrigue.

Commercial. Publishers whose concern is salability, profit and success with a large reader-ship.

Contemporary. Material dealing with popular current trends, themes or topics.

Contributor's copy. Copy of an issue of a magazine or published book sent to an author whose work is included.

Copublishing. An arrangement in which the author and publisher share costs and profits.

Copyediting. Editing a manuscript for writing style, grammar, punctuation and factual accuracy.

Copyright. The legal right to exclusive publication, sale or distribution of a literary work.

Cover letter. A brief letter sent with a complete manuscript submitted to an editor.

"Cozy" (or "teacup") mystery. Mystery usually set in a small British town, in a bygone era, featuring a somewhat genteel, intellectual protagonist.

Cyberpunk. Type of science fiction, usually concerned with computer networks and human-computer combinations, involving young, sophisticated protagonists.

Electronic rights. The right to publish material electronically, either in book or short story form.

E-zine. A magazine that is published electronically.

Electronic submission. A submission of material by e-mail or on computer disk.

Ethnic fiction. Stories and novels whose central characters are black, Native American, Italian-American, Jewish, Appalachian or members of some other specific cultural group. Ethnic fiction usually deals with a protagonist caught between two conflicting ways of life: mainstream American culture and his ethnic heritage.

Experimental fiction. Fiction that is innovative in subject matter and style; avant-garde, non-formulaic, usually literary material.

Exposition. The portion of the storyline, usually the beginning, where background information about character and setting is related.

Fair use. A provision in the copyright law that says short passages from copyrighted material may be used without infringing on the owner's rights.

Fanzine. A noncommercial, small-circulation magazine usually dealing with fantasy, horror or science-fiction literature and art.

Fictional biography. The biography of a real person that goes beyond the events of a person's life by being fleshed out with imagined scenes and dialogue. The writer of fictional biographies strives to make it clear that the story is, indeed, fiction and not history.

First North American serial rights. The right to publish material in a periodical before it appears in book form, for the first time, in the United States or Canada.

Flash fiction. See short short stories.

Galleys. The first typeset version of a manuscript that has not yet been divided into pages.

Genre. A formulaic type of fiction such as romance, western or horror.

Gothic. This type of category fiction dates back to the late 18th and early 19th centuries. Contemporary gothic novels are characterized by atmospheric, historical settings and feature young, beautiful women who win the favor of handsome, brooding heroes-simultaneously dealing successfully with some life-threatening menace, either natural or supernatural. Gothics rely on mystery, peril, romantic relationships and a sense of foreboding for their strong, emotional effect on the reader. A classic early gothic novel is Emily Bronte's Wuthering Heights. The gothic writer builds a series of credible, emotional crises for his ultimately triumphant heroine. Sex between the woman and her lover is implied rather than graphically detailed; the writer's descriptive talents are used instead to paint rich, desolate, gloomy settings in stark mansions and awesome castles. He composes slow-paced, intricate sketches that create a sense of impending evil on every page.

Graphic novel. A book (original or adapted) that takes the form of a long comic strip or heavily illustrated story of 40 pages or more, produced in paperback. Though called a novel, these can also be works of nonfiction.

Hard science fiction. Science fiction with an emphasis on science and technology.

Hard-boiled detective novel. Mystery novel featuring a private eye or police detective as the protagonist; usually involves a murder. The emphasis is on the details of the crime and the tough, unsentimental protagonist usually takes a matter-of-fact attitude towards violence.

High fantasy. Fantasy with a medieval setting and a heavy emphasis on chivalry and the quest.

Historical fiction. A fictional story set in a recognizable period of history. As well as telling the stories of ordinary people's lives, historical fiction may involve political or social events of the time.

Horror. Howard Phillips (H.P.) Lovecraft, generally acknowledged to be the master of the horror tale in the 20th century and the most important American writer of this genre since Edgar Allan Poe, maintained that "The oldest and strongest emotion of mankind is fear, and the oldest and strongest kind of fear is fear of the unknown. These facts few psychologists will dispute, and their admitted truth must establish for all time the genuineness and dignity of the weirdly horrible tale as a literary form." Lovecraft distinguishes horror literature from fiction based entirely on physical fear and the merely gruesome. "The true weird tale has something more than secret murder, bloody bones or a sheeted form clanking chains according to rule. A certain atmosphere of breathless and unexplainable dread of outer, unknown forces must be present; there must be a hint, expressed with a seriousness and portentousness becoming its subject, of that most terrible concept of the human brain-a malign and particular suspension or defeat of the fixed laws of Nature which are our only safeguards against the assaults of chaos and the daemons of unplumbed space." It is that atmosphere-the creation of a particular sensation or emotional level-that, according to Lovecraft, is the most important element in the creation of horror literature. Contemporary writers enjoying considerable success in horror fiction include Stephen King, Robert Bloch, Peter Straub and Dean Koontz.

Hypertext fiction. A fictional form, read electronically, which incorporates traditional elements of storytelling with a nonlinear plot line, in which the reader determines the direction of the story by opting for one of many author-supplied links.

Imprint. Name applied to a publisher's specific line (e.g. Owl, an imprint of Henry Holt).

Interactive fiction. Fiction in book or computer-software format where the reader determines the path the story will take by choosing from several alternatives at the end of each chapter or episode.

International Reply Coupon (IRC). A form purchased at a post office and enclosed with a letter or manuscript to a international publisher, to cover return postage costs.

Juveniles, Writing for. This includes works intended for an audience usually between the ages of two and 18. Categories of children's books are usually divided in this way: (1) picture and storybooks (ages two to nine); (2) easy-to-read books (ages seven to nine); (3) middle-age [also called "middle grade"] children's books (ages eight to 12); (4) young adult books (ages 12 to 18).

Libel. Written or printed words that defame, malign or damagingly misrepresent a living person.

Literary fiction. The general category of fiction which employs more sophisticated technique, driven as much or more by character evolution than action in the plot.

Literary fiction vs. commercial fiction. To the writer of literary, or serious, fiction, style and technique are often as important as subject matter. Commercial fiction, however, is written with the intent of reaching as wide an audience as possible. Commercial fiction is sometimes called genre fiction because books of this type often fall into categories, such as western, gothic, romance, historical, mystery and horror.

Literary agent. A person who acts for an author in finding a publisher or arranging contract terms on a literary project.

Mainstream fiction. Fiction which appeals to a more general reading audience, versus literary or genre fiction. Mainstream is more plot-driven than literary fiction and less formulaic than genre fiction.

Malice domestic novel. A mystery featuring a murder among family members, such as the murder of a spouse or a parent.

Manuscript. The author's unpublished copy of a work, usually typewritten, used as the basis for typesetting.

Mass market paperback. Softcover book on a popular subject, usually around 4×7, directed to a general audience and sold in drugstores and groceries as well as in bookstores.

Middle reader. Juvenile fiction for readers aged 8-13, featuring heavier text than picture books and some light illustration.

Ms(s). Abbreviation for manuscript(s).

Multiple submission. Submission of more than one short story at a time to the same editor. Do not make a multiple submission unless requested.

Mystery. A form of narration in which one or more elements remain unknown or unexplained until the end of the story. The modern mystery story contains elements of the serious novel: a convincing account of a character's struggle with various physical and psychological obstacles in an effort to achieve his goal, good characterization and sound motivation.

Narration. The account of events in a story's plot as related by the speaker or the voice of the author.

Narrator. The person who tells the story, either someone involved in the action or the voice of the writer.

New Age. A term including categories such as astrology, psychic phenomena, spiritual healing, UFOs, mysticism and other aspects of the occult.

Noir. A style of mystery involving hard-boiled detectives and bleak settings.

Nom de plume. French for "pen name"; a pseudonym.

Nonfiction novel. A work in which real events and people are written [about] in novel form, but are not camouflaged, as they are in the roman a' clef. In the nonfiction novel, reality is presented imaginatively; the writer imposes a novelistic structure on the actual events, keying sections of narrative around moments that are seen (in retrospect) as symbolic. In this way, he creates a coherence that the actual story might not have had. *The Executioner's Song*, by Norman Mailer, and *In Cold Blood*, by Truman Capote, are notable examples of the nonfiction novel.

Novella (also novelette). A short novel or long story, approximately 20,000-50,000 words.

#10 envelope. 4×9½ envelope, used for queries and other business letters.

Offprint. Copy of a story taken from a magazine before it is bound.

One-time rights. Permission to publish a story in periodical or book form one time only.

Outline. A summary of a book's contents, often in the form of chapter headings with a few sentences outlining the action of the story under each one; sometimes part of a book proposal.

Over the transom. A phrase referring to unsolicited manuscripts, or those that come in "over the transom."

Payment on acceptance. Payment from the magazine or publishing house as soon as the decision to print a manuscript is made.

Payment on publication. Payment from the publisher after a manuscript is printed.

Pen name. A pseudonym used to conceal a writer's real name.

Periodical. A magazine or journal published at regular intervals.

Plot. The carefully devised series of events through which the characters progress in a work of fiction.

Police procedural. A mystery featuring a police detective or officer who uses standard professional police practices to solve a crime.

Popular fiction. Generally, a synonym for category or genre fiction; i.e., fiction intended to appeal to audiences for certain kinds of novels. Popular, or category, fiction is defined as such primarily for the convenience of publishers, editors, reviewers and booksellers who must identify novels of different areas of interest for potential readers.

Print on demand (POD). Novels produced digitally one at a time, as ordered. Self-publishing through print on demand technology typically involves some fees for the author. Some authors use POD to create a manuscript in book form to send to prospective traditional publishers.

Proofreading. Close reading and correction of a manuscript's typographical errors.

Proofs. A typeset version of a manuscript used for correcting errors and making changes, often a photocopy of the galleys.

Proposal. An offer to write a specific work, usually consisting of an outline of the work and one or two completed chapters.

Protagonist. The principal or leading character in a literary work.

Psychological novel. A narrative that emphasizes the mental and emotional aspects of its characters, focusing on motivations and mental activities rather than on exterior events. The psychological novelist is less concerned about relating what happened than about exploring why it happened. The term is most often used to describe 20th-century works that employ techniques such as interior monologue and stream of consciousness. Two examples of contemporary psychological novels are Judith Guest's *Ordinary People* and Mary Gordon's *The Company of Women*.

Public domain. Material that either was never copyrighted or whose copyright term has expired.

Pulp magazine. A periodical printed on inexpensive paper, usually containing lurid, sensational stories or articles.

Query. A letter written to an editor to elicit interest in a story the writer wants to submit.

Reader. A person hired by a publisher to read unsolicited manuscripts.

Reading fee. An arbitrary amount of money charged by some agents and publishers to read a submitted manuscript.

Regency romance. A subgenre of romance, usually set in England between 1811-1820.

Remainders. Leftover copies of an out-of-print book, sold by the publisher at a reduced price.

Reporting time. The number of weeks or months it takes an editor to report back on an author's query or manuscript.

Reprint rights. Permission to print an already published work whose rights have been sold to another magazine or book publisher.

Roman à clef. French "novel with a key." A novel that represents actual living or historical characters and events in fictionalized form.

Romance novel. A type of category fiction in which the love relationship between a man and a woman pervades the plot. The story is often told from the viewpoint of the heroine, who meets a man (the hero), falls in love with him, encounters a conflict that hinders their relationship, then resolves the conflict. Romance is the overriding element in this kind of story: The couple's relationship determines the plot and tone of the book. The theme of the novel is the woman's sexual awakening. Although she may not be a virgin, she has never before been so emotionally aroused. Despite all this emotion, however, characters and plot both must be well developed and realistic. Throughout a romance novel, the reader senses the sexual and emotional attraction between the heroine and hero. Lovemaking scenes, though sometimes detailed, are not generally too graphic, because more emphasis is placed on the sensual element than on physical action.

Royalties. A percentage of the retail price paid to an author for each copy of the book that is sold.

SAE. Self-addressed envelope.

SASE. Self-addressed stamped envelope.

Science fiction [vs. fantasy]. It is generally accepted that, to be science fiction, a story must have elements of science in either the conflict or setting (usually both). Fantasy, on the other hand, rarely utilizes science, relying instead on magic, mythological and neomythological beings and devices and outright invention for conflict and setting.

Second serial (reprint) rights. Permission for the reprinting of a work in another periodical after its first publication in book or magazine form.

Self-publishing. In this arrangement, the author keeps all income derived from the book, but he pays for its manufacturing, production and marketing.

Sequel. A literary work that continues the narrative of a previous, related story or novel.

Serial rights. The rights given by an author to a publisher to print a piece in one or more periodicals.

Serialized novel. A book-length work of fiction published in sequential issues of a periodical.

Setting. The environment and time period during which the action of a story takes place.

Short short story. A condensed piece of fiction, usually under 1,000 words.

Simultaneous submission. The practice of sending copies of the same manuscript to several editors or publishers at the same time. Some editors refuse to consider such submissions.

Slant. A story's particular approach or style, designed to appeal to the readers of a specific magazine.

Slice of life. A presentation of characters in a seemingly mundane situation which offers the reader a flash of illumination about the characters or their situation.

Slush pile. A stack of unsolicited manuscripts in the editorial offices of a publisher.

Social fiction. Fiction written with the purpose of bringing about positive changes in society.

Soft/sociological science fiction. Science fiction with an emphasis on society and culture versus scientific accuracy.

Space opera. Epic science fiction with an emphasis on good guys versus bad guys.

Speculation (or Spec). An editor's agreement to look at an author's manuscript with no promise to purchase.

Speculative fiction (SpecFic). The all-inclusive term for science fiction, fantasy and horror.

Splatterpunk. Type of horror fiction known for its very violent and graphic content.

Subsidiary. An incorporated branch of a company or conglomerate (e.g. Alfred Knopf, Inc., a subsidiary of Random House, Inc.).

Subsidiary rights. All rights other than book publishing rights included in a book contract, such as paperback, book club and movie rights.

Subsidy publisher. A book publisher who charges the author for the cost of typesetting, printing and promoting a book. Also called a vanity publisher.

Subterficial fiction. Innovative, challenging, nonconventional fiction in which what seems to be happening is the result of things not so easily perceived.

Suspense. A genre of fiction where the plot's primary function is to build a feeling of anticipation and fear in the reader over its possible outcome.

Synopsis. A brief summary of a story, novel or play. As part of a book proposal, it is a comprehensive summary condensed in a page or page and a half.

Tabloid. Publication printed on paper about half the size of a regular newspaper page (e.g. *The National Enquirer*).

Tearsheet. Page from a magazine containing a published story.

Techno-Thriller. This genre utilizes many of the same elements as the thriller, with one major difference. In techno-thrillers, technology becomes a major character. In Tom Clancy's *The Hunt for Red October* for example, specific functions of the submarine become crucial to plot development.

Theme. The dominant or central idea in a literary work; its message, moral or main thread.

Thriller. A novel intended to arouse feelings of excitement or suspense. Works in this genre are highly sensational, usually focusing on illegal activities, international espionage, sex and violence. A thriller is often a detective story in which the forces of good are pitted against the forces of evil in a kill-or-be-killed situation.

Trade paperback. A softbound volume, usually around 5×8, published and designed for the general public, available mainly in bookstores.

Traditional fantasy. Fantasy with an emphasis on magic, using characters with the ability to practice magic, such as wizards, witches, dragons, elves and unicorns.

Unsolicited manuscript. A story or novel manuscript that an editor did not specifically ask to see.

Urban fantasy. Fantasy that takes magical characters such as elves, fairies, vampires or wizards and places them in modern-day settings, often in the inner city.

Vanity publisher. See subsidy publisher.

Viewpoint. The position or attitude of the first- or third-person narrator or multiple narrators, which determines how a story's action is seen and evaluated.

Western. Genre with a setting in the West, usually between 1860-1890, with a formula plot about cowboys or other aspects of frontier life.

Whodunit. Genre dealing with murder, suspense and the detection of criminals.

Work-for-hire. Work that another party commissions you to do, generally for a flat fee. The creator does not own the copyright and therefore cannot sell any rights.

Young adult. The general classification of books written for readers 12-18.

Zine. Often one- or two-person operations run from the home of the publisher/editor. Themes tend to be specialized, personal, experimental and often controversial.

Genre Glossary

Definitions of Fiction Subcategories

The following were provided courtesy of The Extended Novel Writing Workshop, created by the staff of Writers Online Workshops (www.writersonlineworkshops .com).

MYSTERY SUBCATEGORIES

The major mystery subcategories are listed below, each followed by a brief description and the names of representative authors, so you can sample each type of work. Note that we have loosely classified "suspense/thriller" as a mystery category. While these stories do not necessarily follow a traditional "whodunit" plot pattern, they share many elements with other mystery categories. In addition, many traditional mysteries are marketed as suspense/ thriller because of this category's current appeal in the marketplace. Since the lines between categories are frequently blurred, it seems practical to include them all here.

Classic Mystery (Whodunit). A crime (almost always a murder or series of murders) is solved. The detective is the viewpoint character; the reader never knows any more or less about the crime than the detective, and all the clues to solving the crime are available to the reader.

Amateur detective. As the name implies, the detective is not a professional detective (private or otherwise), but is almost always a professional something. This professional association routinely involves the protagonist in criminal cases (in a support capacity), gives him or her a special advantage in a specific case, or provides the contacts and skills necessary to solve a particular crime. (Jonathan Kellerman, Patricia Cornwell, Jan Burke)

Courtroom Drama. The action takes place primarily in the courtroom; the protagonist is generally a defense attorney out to prove the innocence of his or her client by finding the real culprit. (Scott Turow, Steve Martini, Richard North Patterson, John Grisham)

Cozy. A special class of the amateur detective category that frequently features a female protagonist. (Agatha Christie's Miss Marple stories are the classic example.) There is less on-stage violence than in other categories and the plot is often wrapped up in a final scene where the detective identifies the murderer and explains how the crime was solved. In contemporary stories, the protagonist can be anyone from a chronically curious housewife to a mystery-buff clergyman to a college professor, but he or she is usually quirky, even eccentric. (Susan Isaacs, Andrew Greeley, Lillian Jackson Braun)

Espionage. The international spy novel is less popular since the end of the cold war, but stories can still revolve around political intrigue in unstable regions. (John le Carré, Ken Follett)

Resources

Heists and Capers. The crime itself is the focus. Its planning and execution are seen in detail and the participants are fully-drawn characters that may even be portrayed sympathetically. One character is the obvious leader of the group (the "brains"); the other members are often brought together by the leader specifically for this job and may or may not have a previous association. In a heist, no matter how clever or daring the characters are, they are still portrayed as criminals and the expectation is that they will be caught and punished (but not always). A caper is more light hearted, even comedic. The participants may have a noble goal (something other than personal gain) and often get away with the crime. (Eric Ambler, Tony Kenrick, Leslie Hollander)

Historical. May be any category or subcategory of mystery, but with an emphasis on setting, the details of which must be diligently researched. But beyond the historical details (which must never overshadow the story), the plot develops along the lines of its contemporary counterpart. (Candace Robb, Caleb Carr, Anne Perry)

Juvenile/Young adult. Written for the 8-12 age group (Middle Grade) or the 12 and up age group (Young Adult), the crime in these stories may or may not be murder, but it is serious. The protagonist is a kid (or group of kids) in the same age range as the targeted reader. There is no graphic violence depicted, but the stories are scary and the villains are realistic. (Mary Downing Hahn, Wendy Corsi Staub, Cameron Dokey, Norma Fox Mazer)

Medical thriller. The plot can involve a legitimate medical threat (such as the outbreak of a virulent plague) or the illegal or immoral use of medical technology. In the former scenario, the protagonist is likely to be the doctor (or team) who identifies the virus and procures the antidote; in the latter he or she could be a patient (or the relative of a victim) who uncovers the plot and brings down the villain. (Robin Cook, Michael Palmer, Michael Crichton, Stanley Pottinger)

Police procedurals. The most realistic category, these stories require the most meticulous research. A police procedural may have more than one protagonist since cops rarely work alone. Conflict between partners, or between the detective and his or her superiors is a common theme. But cops are portrayed positively as a group, even though there may be a couple of bad or ineffective law enforcement characters for contrast and conflict. Jurisdictional disputes are still popular sources of conflict as well. (Lawrence Treat, Joseph Wambaugh, Ridley Pearson, Julie Smith)

Private detective. When described as "hard-boiled," this category takes a tough stance. Violence is more prominent, characters are darker, the detective—while almost always licensed by the state—operates on the fringes of the law, and there is often open resentment between the detective and law enforcement. More "enlightened" male detectives and a crop of contemporary females have brought about new trends in this category. (For female P.I.s—Sue Grafton, Sara Paretsky; for male P.I.s—John D. MacDonald, Lawrence Sanders, Robert Parker)

Suspense/Thriller. Where a classic mystery is always a whodunit, a suspense/thriller novel may deal more with the intricacies of the crime, what motivated it, and how the villain (whose identity may be revealed to the reader early on) is caught and brought to justice. Novels in this category frequently employ multiple points of view and have a broader scope than a more traditional murder mystery. The crime may not even involve murder—it may be a threat to global economy or regional ecology; it may be technology run amok or abused at the hands of an unscrupulous scientist; it may involve innocent citizens victimized for personal or corporate gain. Its perpetrators are kidnappers, stalkers, serial killers, rapists, pedophiles, computer hackers, or just about anyone with an evil intention and the means to carry it out. The protagonist may be a private detective or law enforcement official, but is just as likely to be a doctor, lawyer, military officer or other individual in a unique position to identify the villain and bring him or her to justice. (James Patterson, John J. Nance, Michael Connelly)

Technothriller. These are replacing the traditional espionage novel, and feature technology as an integral part of not just the setting, but the plot as well. (Tom Clancy, Stephen Coonts)

Woman in Jeopardy. A murder or other crime may be committed, but the focus is on the woman (and/or her children) currently at risk, her struggle to understand the nature of the danger, and her eventual victory over her tormentor. The protagonist makes up for her lack of physical prowess with intellect or special skills, and solves the problem on her own or with the help of her family (but she runs the show). Closely related to this category is the Romantic Suspense. But, while the heroine in a romantic suspense is certainly a "woman in jeopardy," the mystery or suspense element is subordinate to the romance. (Mary Higgins Clark, Mary Stewart, Jessica Mann)

ROMANCE SUBCATEGORIES

These categories and subcategories of romance fiction have been culled from the *Romance Writer's Sourcebook* (Writer's Digest Books) and Phyllis Taylor Pianka's *How to Write Romances* (Writer's Digest Books). We've arranged the "major" categories below with the subcategories beneath them, each followed by a brief description and the names of authors who write in each category, so you can sample representative works.

Category or Series. These are published in "lines" by individual publishing houses (such as Harlequin and Silhouette); each line has its own requirements as to word length, story content and amount of sex. (Debbie Macomber, Nora Roberts, Glenda Sanders)

Christian. With an inspirational, Christian message centering on the spiritual dynamic of the romantic relationship and faith in God as the foundation for that relationship; sensuality is played down. (Janelle Burnham, Ann Bell, Linda Chaikin, Catherine Palmer, Dee Henderson, Lisa Tawn Bergen)

Glitz. So called because they feature (generally wealthy) characters with high-powered positions in careers that are considered to be glamorous—high finance, modeling/acting, publishing, fashion—and are set in exciting or exotic (often metropolitan) locales such as Monte Carlo, Hollywood, London or New York. (Jackie Collins, Judith Krantz)

Historical. Can cover just about any historical (or even prehistorical) period. Setting in the historical is especially significant, and details must be thoroughly researched and accurately presented. For a sampling of a variety of historical styles try Laura Kinsell (*Flowers from the Storm*), Mary Jo Putney (*The Rake and the Reformer*) and Judy Cuevas (*Bliss*). Some currently popular periods/themes in historicals are:
Gothic: historical with a strong element of suspense and a feeling of supernatural events, although these events frequently have a natural explanation. Setting plays an important role in establishing a dark, moody, suspenseful atmosphere. (Phyllis Whitney, Victoria Holt)
Historical fantasy: with traditional fantasy elements of magic and magical beings, frequently set in a medieval society. (Amanda Glass, Jayne Ann Krentz, Kathleen Morgan, Jessica Bryan, Taylor Quinn Evans, Carla Simpson, Karyn Monk)
Early American: usually Revolution to Civil War, set in New England or the South, but "frontier" stories set in the American West are quite popular as well. (Robin Lee Hatcher, Elizabeth Lowell, Heather Graham)

Native American: where one or both of the characters are Native Americans; the conflict between cultures is a popular theme. (Carol Finch, Elizabeth Grayson, Karen Kay, Kathleen Harrington, Genell Dellim, Candace McCarthy)

Regency: set in England during the Regency period from 1811-1820. (Carol Finch, Elizabeth Elliott, Georgette Heyer, Joan Johnston, Lynn Collum)

Multicultural. Most currently feature African-American or Hispanic couples, but editors are looking for other ethnic stories as well. Multiculturals can be contemporary or historical, and fall into any sub-category. (Rochelle Alers, Monica Jackson, Bette Ford, Sandra Kitt, Brenda Jackson)

Paranormal. Containing elements of the supernatural or science fiction/fantasy. There are numerous subcategories (many stories combine elements of more than one) including:

Time travel: One or more of the characters travels to another time—usually the past—to find love. (Jude Devereaux, Linda Lael Miller, Diana Gabaldon, Constance O'Day Flannery)

Science fiction/Futuristic: S/F elements are used for the story's setting: imaginary worlds, parallel universes, Earth in the near or distant future. (Marilyn Campbell, Jayne Ann Krentz, J.D. Robb [Nora Roberts], Anne Avery)

Contemporary fantasy: From modern ghost and vampire stories to "New Age" themes such as extraterrestrials and reincarnation. (Linda Lael Miller, Anne Stuart, Antoinette Stockenberg, Christine Feehan)

Romantic Comedy. Has a fairly strong comic premise and/or a comic perspective in the author's voice or the voices of the characters (especially the heroine). (Jennifer Crusie, Susan Elizabeth Phillips)

Romantic Suspense. With a mystery or psychological thriller subplot in addition to the romance plot. (Mary Stewart, Barbara Michaels, Tami Hoag, Nora Roberts, Linda Howard, Catherine Coulter)

Single title. Longer contemporaries that do not necessarily conform to the requirements of a specific romance line and therefore feature more complex plots and nontraditional characters. (Mary Ruth Myers, Nora Roberts, Kathleen Gilles Seidel, Kathleen Korbel)

Young Adult. Focus is on first love with very little, if any, sex. These can have bittersweet endings, as opposed to the traditional romance happy ending, since first loves are often lost loves. (YA historical—Nancy Covert Smith, Louise Vernon; YA contemporary—Mary Downing Hahn, Kathryn Makris)

SCIENCE FICTION SUBCATEGORIES

Peter Heck, in his article "Doors to Other Worlds: Trends in Science Fiction and Fantasy," which appears in the 1996 edition of *Science Fiction and Fantasy Writer's Sourcebook* (Writer's Digest Books), identifies some science fiction trends that have distinct enough characteristics to be defined as categories. These distinctions are frequently the result of marketing decisions as much as literary ones, so understanding them is important in deciding where your novel idea belongs. We've supplied a brief description and the names of authors who write in each category. In those instances where the author writes in more than one category, we've included titles of appropriate representative works.

Hard science fiction. Based on the logical extrapolation of real science to the future. In these stories the scientific background (setting) may be as, or more, important than the characters. (Larry Niven)

Social science fiction. The focus is on how the characters react to their environments. This category includes social satire. (George Orwell's *1984* is a classic example.) (Margaret Atwood, *The Handmaid's Tale*; Ursula K. Le Guin, *The Left Hand of Darkness*; Marge Piercy, *Woman on the Edge of Time*)

Military science fiction. Stories about war that feature traditional military organization and tactics extrapolated into the future. (Jerry Pournelle, David Drake, Elizabeth Moon)

Cyberpunk. Characters in these stories are tough outsiders in a high-tech, generally near-future society where computers have produced major changes in the way that society functions. (William Gibson, Bruce Sterling, Pat Cadigan, Wilhelmina Baird)

Space opera. From the term "horse opera," describing a traditional good-guys-vs-bad-guys western, these stories put the emphasis on sweeping action and larger-than-life characters. The focus on action makes these stories especially appealing for film treatment. (The Star Wars series is one of the best examples, also Samuel R. Delany.)

Alternate history. Fantasy, sometimes with science fiction elements, that changes the accepted account of actual historical events or people to suggest an alternate view of history. (Ted Mooney, *Traffic and Laughter*; Ward Moore, *Bring the Jubilee*; Philip K. Dick, *The Man in the High Castle*)

Steampunk. A specific type of alternate history science fiction set in Victorian England in which characters have access to 20th-century technology. (William Gibson; Bruce Sterling, *The Difference Engine*)

New Age. A category of speculative fiction that deals with subjects such as astrology, psychic phenomena, spiritual healing, UFOs, mysticism and other aspects of the occult. (Walter Mosley, *Blue Light*; Neil Gaiman)

Science fantasy. Blend of traditional fantasy elements with scientific or pseudo-scientific support (genetic engineering, for example, to "explain" a traditional fantasy creature like the dragon). These stories are traditionally more character driven than hard science fiction. (Anne McCaffrey, Mercedes Lackey, Marion Zimmer Bradley)

Science fiction mystery. A cross-genre blending that can either be a more-or-less traditional science fiction story with a mystery as a key plot element, or a more-or-less traditional whodunit with science fiction elements. (Philip K. Dick, Lynn S. Hightower)

Science fiction romance. Another genre blend that may be a romance with science fiction elements (in which case it is more accurately placed as a subcategory within the romance genre) or a science fiction story with a strong romantic subplot. (Anne McCaffrey, Melanie Rawn, Kate Elliot)

Young Adult. Any subcategory of science fiction geared to a YA audience (12-18), but these are usually shorter novels with characters in the central roles who are the same age as (or slightly older than) the targeted reader. (Jane Yolen, Andre Norton)

FANTASY SUBCATEGORIES

Before we take a look at the individual fantasy categories, it should be noted that, for purposes of these supplements, we've treated fantasy as a genre distinct from science fiction. While these two are closely related, there are significant enough differences to warrant their separation for study purposes. We have included here those science fiction categories that have strong fantasy elements, or that have a significant amount of crossover (these categories appear in both the science fiction and the fantasy supplements), but "pure" science fiction categories are not included below. If you're not sure whether your novel is fantasy or science fiction, consider this definition by Orson Scott Card in *How to Write Science Fiction and Fantasy* (Writer's Digest Books):

> "Here's a good, simple, semi-accurate rule of thumb: If the story is set in a universe that follows the same rules as ours, it's science fiction. If it's set in a universe that doesn't follow our rules, it's fantasy.
> Or in other words, science fiction is about what could be but isn't; fantasy is about what couldn't be."

But even Card admits this rule is only "semi-accurate." He goes on to say that the real boundary between science fiction and fantasy is defined by how the impossible is achieved: "If you have people do some magic, impossible thing [like time travel] by stroking a talisman or praying to a tree, it's fantasy; if they do the same thing by pressing a button or climbing inside a machine, it's science fiction."

Peter Heck, in his article "Doors to Other Worlds: Trends in Science Fiction and Fantasy," which appears in the 1996 edition of the *Science Fiction and Fantasy Writer's Sourcebook* (Writer's Digest Books), does note some trends that have distinct enough characteristics to be defined as separate categories. These categories are frequently the result of marketing decisions as much as literary ones, so understanding them is important in deciding where your novel idea belongs. We've supplied a brief description and the names of authors who write in each category, so you can sample representative works.

Arthurian. Re-working of the legend of King Arthur and the Knights of the Round Table. (T.H. White, *The Once and Future King*; Marion Zimmer Bradley, *The Mists of Avalon*)

Contemporary (also called "urban") fantasy. Traditional fantasy elements (such as elves and magic) are incorporated into an otherwise recognizable modern setting. (Emma Bull, *War for the Oaks*; Mercedes Lackey, *The SERRAted Edge*; Terry Brooks, the Knight of the Word series)

Dark fantasy. Closely related to horror, but generally not as graphic. Characters in these stories are the "darker" fantasy types: vampires, witches, werewolves, demons, etc. (Anne Rice; Clive Barker, *Weaveworld, Imajica*; Fred Chappell)

Fantastic alternate history. Set in an alternate historical period (in which magic would not have been a common belief) where magic works, these stories frequently feature actual historical figures. (Orson Scott Card, *Alvin Maker*)

Game-related fantasy. Plots and characters are similar to high fantasy, but are based on a particular role-playing game. (Dungeons and Dragons; Magic: The Gathering; Dragonlance Chronicles; Forgotten Realms; Dark Sun)

Heroic fantasy. The fantasy equivalent to military science fiction, these are stories of war and its heroes and heroines. (Robert E. Howard, the Conan the Barbarian series; Elizabeth Moon, *Deed of Paksenarion*; Michael Moorcock, the Elric series)

High fantasy. Emphasis is on the fate of an entire race or nation, threatened by an ultimate evil. J. R. R. Tolkien's Lord of the Rings trilogy is a classic example. (Terry Brooks, David Eddings, Margaret Weis, Tracy Hickman)

Historical fantasy. The setting can be almost any era in which the belief in magic was strong; these are essentially historical novels where magic is a key element of the plot and/or setting. (Susan Schwartz, *Silk Road and Shadow*; Margaret Ball, *No Earthly Sunne*; Tim Powers, *The Anubis Gates*)

Juvenile/Young adult. Can be any type of fantasy, but geared to a juvenile (8-12) or YA audience (12-18); these are shorter novels with younger characters in central roles. (J.K. Rowling, C.S. Lewis)

Science fantasy. A blend of traditional fantasy elements with scientific or pseudo-scientific support (genetic engineering, for example, to "explain" a traditional fantasy creature like the dragon). These stories are traditionally more character driven than hard science fiction. (Anne McCaffrey, Mercedes Lackey, Marion Zimmer Bradley)

HORROR SUBCATEGORIES

Subcategories in horror are less well defined than in other genres and are frequently the result of marketing decisions as much as literary ones. But being familiar with the terms used to describe different horror styles can be important in understanding how your own novel might be best presented to an agent or editor. What follows is a brief description of the most commonly used terms, along with names of authors and, where necessary, representative works.

Dark Fantasy. Sometimes used as a euphemistic term for horror in general, but also refers to a specific type of fantasy, usually less graphic than other horror subcategories, that features more "traditional" supernatural or mythical beings (vampires, werewolves, zombies, etc.) in either contemporary or historical settings. (Contemporary: Stephen King, *Salem's Lot*; Thomas Tessier, *The Nightwalker*. Historical: Brian Stableford, *The Empire of Fear*; Chelsea Quinn Yarbro, *Werewolves of London*.)

Hauntings. "Classic" stories of ghosts, poltergeists and spiritual possessions. The level of violence portrayed varies, but many writers in this category exploit the reader's natural fear of the unknown by hinting at the horror and letting the reader's imagination supply the details. (Peter Straub, *Ghost Story*; Richard Matheson, *Hell House*)

Juvenile/Young Adult. Can be any horror style, but with a protagonist who is the same age as, or slightly older than, the targeted reader. Stories for middle grades (eight to 12 years old) are scary, with monsters and violent acts that might best be described as "gross," but stories for young adults (12-18) may be more graphic. (R.L. Stine, Christopher Pike, Carol Gorman)

Psychological horror. Features a human monster with horrific, but not necessarily supernatural, aspects. (Thomas Harris, *The Silence of the Lambs, Hannibal*; Dean Koontz, *Whispers*)

Splatterpunk. Very graphic depiction of violence—often gratuitous—popularized in the 1980s, especially in film. (*Friday the 13th, Halloween, Nightmare on Elm Street*, etc.)

Supernatural/Occult. Similar to the dark fantasy, but may be more graphic in its depiction of violence. Stories feature satanic worship, demonic possession, or ultimate evil incarnate in an entity or supernatural being that may or may not have its roots in traditional mythology or folklore. (Ramsey Campbell; Robert McCammon; Ira Levin, *Rosemary's Baby*; William Peter Blatty, *The Exorcist*; Stephen King, *Pet Sematary*)

Technological horror. "Monsters" in these stories are the result of science run amok or technology turned to purposes of evil. (Dean Koontz, *Watchers*; Michael Crichton, *Jurassic Park*)

Professional Organizations

AGENTS' ORGANIZATIONS

Association of Authors' Agents (AAA), 20 John St., London WC1N 2DR, United Kingdom. (44)(20)7405-6774. E-mail: aaa@apwatt. Web site: www.agentsassoc.co.uk.

Association of Authors' Representatives (AAR), 676A 9th Ave., #312, New York NY 10036. (212)840-5777. E-mail: aarinc@mindspring.com. Web site: www.aar-online.org.

Association of Talent Agents (ATA), 9255 Sunset Blvd., Suite 930, Los Angeles CA 90069. (310)274-0628. Fax: (310)274-5063. E-mail: shellie@agentassociation.com. Web site: www.agentassociation.com.

WRITERS' ORGANIZATIONS

Academy of American Poets, 584 Broadway, Suite 604, New York NY 10012-5243. (212)274-0343. Fax: (212)274-9427. E-mail: academy@poets.org. Web site: www.poets.org.

American Crime Writers League (ACWL), 17367 Hilltop Ridge Dr., Eureka MO 63205. Web site: www.acwl.org.

American Medical Writers Association (AMWA), 40 W. Gude Dr., Suite 101, Rockville MD 20850-1192. (301)294-5303. Fax: (301)294-9006. E-mail: amwa@amwa.org. Web site: www.amwa.org.

American Screenwriters Association (ASA), 269 S. Beverly Dr., Suite 2600, Beverly Hills CA 90212-3807. (866)265-9091. E-mail: asa@goasa.com. Website: www.asascreenwriters.com.

American Translators Association (ATA), 225 Reinekers Lane, Suite 590, Alexandria VA 22314. (703)683-6100. Fax: (703)683-6122. E-mail: ata@atanet.org. Web site: www.atanet.org.

Education Writers Association (EWA), 2122 P St. NW, Suite 201, Washington DC 20037. (202)452-9830. Fax: (202)452-9837. E-mail: ewa@ewa.org. Web site: www.ewa.org.

Garden Writers Association (GWA), 10210 Leatherleaf Ct., Manassas VA 20111. (703)257-1032. Fax: (703)257-0213. Web site: www.gardenwriters.org.

Horror Writers Association (HWA), 244 5th Ave., Suite 2767, New York NY 10001. E-mail: hwa@horror.org. Web site: www.horror.org.

The International Women's Writing Guild (IWWG),P.O. Box 810, Gracie Station, New York NY 10028-0082. (212)737-7536. Fax: (212)737-9469. E-mail: dirhahn@iwwg.org. Web site: www.iwwg.com.

Mystery Writers of America (MWA), 17 E. 47th St., 6th Floor, New York NY 10017. (212)888-8171. Fax: (212)888-8107. E-mail: mwa@mysterywriters.org. Web site: www.mysterywriters.org.

National Association of Science Writers (NASW), P.O. Box 890, Hedgesville WV 25427. (304)754-5077. Fax: (304)754-5076. E-mail: diane@nasw.org. Web site: www.nasw.org.

National Association of Women Writers (NAWW), 24165 IH-10 W., Suite 217-637, San Antonio TX 78257. Web site: www.naww.org.

Organization of Black Screenwriters (OBS). Web site: www.obswriter.com.

Outdoor Writers Association of America (OWAA), 121 Hickory St., Suite 1, Missoula MT 59801. (406)728-7434. Fax: (406)728-7445. E-mail: krhoades@owaa.org. Web site: www.owaa.org.

Poetry Society of America (PSA), 15 Gramercy Park, New York NY 10003. (212)254-9628. Web site: www.poetrysociety.org.

Poets & Writers, 72 Spring St., Suite 301, New York NY 10012. (212)226-3586. Fax: (212)226-3963. Web site: www.pw.org.

Romance Writers of America (RWA), 16000 Stuebner Airline Rd., Suite 140, Spring TX 77379. (832)717-5200. E-mail: info@rwanational.org. Web site: www.rwanational.org.

Science Fiction and Fantasy Writers of America (SFWA), P.O. Box 877, Chestertown MD 21620. E-mail: execdir@sfwa.org. Web site: www.sfwa.org.

Society of American Business Editors & Writers (SABEW), University of Missouri, School of Journalism, 385 McReynolds, Columbia MO 65211. (573)882-7862. Fax: (573)884-1372. E-mail: sabew@missouri.edu. Web site: www.sabew.org.

Society of American Travel Writers (SATW), 1500 Sunday Dr., Suite 102, Raleigh NC 27607. (919)861-5586. Fax: (919)787-4916. E-mail: satw@satw.org. Web site: www.satw.org.

Society of Children's Book Writers & Illustrators (SCBWI), 8271 Beverly Blvd., Los Angeles CA 90048. (323)782-1010. Fax: (323)782-1892. E-mail: scbwi@scbwi.org. Web site: www.scbwi.org.

Washington Independent Writers (WIW), 1001 Connecticut Ave. NW, Suite 701, Washington DC 20036. (202)775-5150. Fax: (202)775-5810. E-mail: info@washwriter.org. Web site: www.washwriter.org.

Western Writers of America (WWA). E-mail: wwa@unm.edu. Web site: www.westernwriters.org.

INDUSTRY ORGANIZATIONS

American Booksellers Association (ABA), 200 White Plains Rd., Tarrytown NY

Resources

10591. (914)591-2665. Fax: (914)591-2720. E-mail: info@bookweb.org. Web site: www.bookweb.org.

American Society of Journalists & Authors (ASJA), 1501 Broadway, Suite 302, New York NY 10036. (212)997-0947. Fax: (212)937-2315. E-mail: execdir@asja.org. Web site: www.asja.org.

Association for Women in Communications (AWC), 3337 Duke St., Alexandria VA 22314. (703)370-7436. Fax: (703)370-7437. E-mail: info@womcom.org. Web site: www.womcom.org.

Association of American Publishers (AAP), 71 5th Ave., 2nd Floor, New York NY 10003. (212)255-0200. Fax: (212)255-7007. Or, 50 F St. NW, Suite 400, Washington DC 20001. (202)347-3375. Fax: (202)347-3690. Web site: www.publishers.org.

The Association of Writers & Writing Programs (AWP), The Carty House, Mail stop 1E3, George Mason University, Fairfax VA 22030. (703)993-4301. Fax: (703)993-4302. E-mail: services@awpwriter.org. Web site: www.awpwriter.org.

The Authors Guild, Inc., 31 E. 32nd St., 7th Floor, New York NY 10016. (212)563-5904. Fax: (212)564-5363. E-mail: staff@authorsguild.org. Web site: www.authorsguild.org.

Canadian Authors Association (CAA), Box 419, Campbellford ON K0L 1L0 Canada. (705)653-0323. Fax: (705)653-0593. E-mail: admin@canauthors.org. Web site: www.canauthors.org.

Christian Booksellers Association (CBA), P.O. Box 62000, Colorado Springs CO 80962-2000. (800)252-1950. Fax: (719)272-3510. E-mail: info@cbaonline.org. Web site: www.cbaonline.org.

The Dramatists Guild of America, 1501 Broadway, Suite 701, New York NY 10036. (212)398-9366. Fax: (212)944-0420. Web site: www.dramaguild.com.

National League of American Pen Women (NLAPW), 1300 17th St. NW, Washington DC 20036-1973. (202)785-1997. Fax: (202)452-8868. Website: www.americanpenwomen.org.

National Writers Association (NWA), 10940 S. Parker Rd., #508, Parker CO 80134. (303)841-0246. Fax: (303)841-2607. E-mail: anitaedits@aol.com. Web site: www.nationalwriters.com.

National Writers Union (NWU), 113 University Place, 6th Floor, New York NY 10003. (212)254-0279. Fax: (212)254-0673. E-mail: nwu@nwu.org. Web site: www.nwu.org.

PEN American Center, 588 Broadway, Suite 303, New York NY 10012-3225. (212)334-1660. Fax: (212)334-2181. E-mail: pen@pen.org. Web site: www.pen.org.

The Playwrights Guild of Canada (PGC), 54 Wolseley St., 2nd Floor, Toronto ON M5T 1A5 Canada. (416)703-0201. Fax: (416)703-0059. E-mail: info@playwrightsguild.ca. Web site: www.playwrightsguild.com.

Volunteer Lawyers for the Arts (VLA), One E. 53rd St., 6th Floor, New York NY 10022. (212)319-2787. Fax: (212)752-6575. Web site: www.vlany.org.

Women in Film (WIF), 8857 W. Olympic Blvd., Suite 201, Beverly Hills CA 90211. (310)657-5144. E-mail: info@wif.org. Web site: www.wif.org.

Women in the Arts Foundation (WIA), 32-35 30th St., D24, Long Island City NY 11106. (212)941-0130. E-mail: reginas@anny.org. Web site: www.anny.org/2/orgs/womenin arts/.

Women's National Book Association (WNBA), 2166 Broadway, #9-E, New York NY 10024. (212)208-4629. Web site: www.wnba-books.org.

Writers Guild of Alberta (WGA), 11759 Groat Rd., Edmonton AB T5M 3K6 Canada. (780)422-8174. Fax: (780)422-2663. E-mail: mail@writersguild.ab.ca. Web site: writ ersguild.ab.ca.

Writers Guild of America-East (WGA), 555 W. 57th St., Suite 1230, New York NY 10019. (212)767-7800. Fax: (212)582-1909. Web site: www.wgaeast.org.

Writers Guild of America-West (WGA), 7000 W. Third St., Los Angeles CA 90048. (323)951-4000. Fax: (323)782-4800. Web site: www.wga.org.

Writers Union of Canada (TWUC), 90 Richmond St. E., Suite 200, Toronto ON M5C 1P1 Canada. (416)703-8982. Fax: (416)504-9090. E-mail: info@writersunion.ca. Web site: www.writersunion.ca.

Literary Agents Category Index

Agents listed in this edition of *Novel & Short Story Writer's Market* are indexed below according to the categories of fiction they represent. Use it to find agents who handle the specific kind of fiction you write. Then turn to those listings in the alphabetical Literary Agents section for complete contact and submission information.

Action/Adventure

Acacia House Publishing Services, Ltd. 156
Ahearn Agency, Inc., The 157
Alive Communications, Inc. 157
Ampersand Agency, The 158
August Agency, LLC, The 160
Authentic Creations Literary Agency 161
Barrett Books, Inc., Loretta 162
Brown, Ltd., Curtis 166
Browne, Ltd., Pema 166
Congdon Associates Inc., Don 170
D4EO Literary Agency 171
Dystel & Goderich Literary Management 174
Farber Literary Agency, Inc. 176
Farris Literary Agency, Inc. 176
Finch Literary Agency, Diana 177
Halsey North, Reece 179
Hartline Literary Agency 180
Harwood Limited, Antony 180
Hawkins & Associates, Inc., John 181
Henshaw Group, Richard 181
Jabberwocky Literary Agency 183
JCA Literary Agency 183

Klinger, Inc., Harvey 184
KT Public Relations & Literary Services 186
LA Literary Agency, The 186
Lampack Agency, Inc., Peter 187
Larsen/Elizabeth Pomada, Literary Agents, Michael 187
Lazear Agency, Inc. 189
Levine Literary Agency, Paul S. 190
Lippincott Massie McQuilkin 191
Literary Group, The 191
Lord Literary Management, Julia 192
Marshall Agency, The Evan 195
Mendel Media Group, LLC 196
Morrison, Inc., Henry 196
Muse Literary Management 197
Naggar Literary Agency, Inc., Jean V. 197
Picard, Literary Agent, Alison J. 199
Prospect Agency LLC 201
Quicksilver Books: Literary Agents 201
Raines & Raines 202
Rotrosen Agency LLC, Jane 205
Russell & Volkening 206
Sanders & Associates, Victoria 207

Scribe Agency, LLC 207
Serendipity Literary Agency, LLC 208
Simmons Literary Agency, Jeffrey 210
Talcott Notch Literary 214
Triada U.S. Literary Agency, Inc. 215
Weiner Literary Agency, Cherry 218
Winsun Literary Agency 219
Writers House 219

Comic Books/Cartoon
Ampersand Agency, The 158
Brown, Ltd., Curtis 166
Harwood Limited, Antony 180
Levine Literary Agency, Paul S. 190
Lippincott Massie McQuilkin 191
Pevner, Inc., Stephen 199
Regal Literary Agency 202
Scribe Agency, LLC 207

Confession
Ampersand Agency, The 158
Artists and Artisans Inc. 160
Brown, Ltd., Curtis 166
DeChiara Literary Agency, The Jennifer 172
Harwood Limited, Antony 180
Lazear Agency, Inc. 189
Levine Literary Agency, Paul S. 190
Lippincott Massie McQuilkin 191
March Tenth, Inc. 195
Serendipity Literary Agency, LLC 208
Simmons Literary Agency, Jeffrey 210

Contemporary Issues
Ahearn Agency, Inc., The 157
Alive Communications, Inc. 157
Barrett Books, Inc., Loretta 162
Books & Such Literary Agency 164
Brandt & Hochman Literary Agents, Inc. 164

Brown, Ltd., Curtis 166
Browne, Ltd., Pema 166
Clark Associates, Wm. 169
Halsey North, Reece 179
Hartline Literary Agency 180
Jabberwocky Literary Agency 183
JCA Literary Agency 183
Koster Literary Agency, LLC, Elaine 185
Larsen/Elizabeth Pomada, Literary Agents, Michael 187
Literary Group, The 191
Mendel Media Group, LLC 196
Picard, Literary Agent, Alison J. 199
Sanders & Associates, Victoria 207
Stauffer Associates, Nancy 212
Weiner Literary Agency, Cherry 218
Writers House 219

Detective/Police/Crime
Acacia House Publishing Services, Ltd. 156
Ahearn Agency, Inc., The 157
Alive Communications, Inc. 157
Ampersand Agency, The 158
Appleseeds Management 159
August Agency, LLC, The 160
Authentic Creations Literary Agency 161
Barrett Books, Inc., Loretta 162
Blumer Literary Agency, Inc., The 163
BookEnds, LLC 164
Brown, Ltd., Curtis 166
Browne & Miller Literary Associates 166
Congdon Associates Inc., Don 170
DeChiara Literary Agency, The Jennifer 172
D4EO Literary Agency 171
DHS Literary, Inc. 173
Dystel & Goderich Literary Management 174
Farris Literary Agency, Inc. 176
Finch Literary Agency, Diana 177
Halsey North, Reece 179

Harwood Limited, Antony 180
Hawkins & Associates, Inc., John 181
Henshaw Group, Richard 181
J de S Associates, Inc. 183
Jabberwocky Literary Agency 183
JCA Literary Agency 183
Klinger, Inc., Harvey 184
Koster Literary Agency, LLC, Elaine 185
KT Public Relations & Literary Services 186
LA Literary Agency, The 186
Lampack Agency, Inc., Peter 187
Langlie, Literary Agent, Laura 187
Larsen/Elizabeth Pomada, Literary Agents, Michael 187
Lazear Agency, Inc. 189
Levine Literary Agency, Paul S. 190
Literary Group, The 191
Lowenstein-Yost Associates 192
Maass Literary Agency, Donald 193
McGrath, Helen 196
Mendel Media Group, LLC 196
Morrison, Inc., Henry 196
Muse Literary Management 197
Naggar Literary Agency, Inc., Jean V. 197
Picard, Literary Agent, Alison J. 199
Pistek Literary Agency, LLC, Alicka 200
Prospect Agency LLC 201
Raines & Raines 202
Regal Literary Agency 202
Robbins Literary Agency, B.J. 204
Rotrosen Agency LLC, Jane 205
Russell & Volkening 206
Scribe Agency, LLC 207
Seligman, Literary Agent, Lynn 208
Simmons Literary Agency, Jeffrey 210
Spencerhill Associates 211
Spieler Agency, The 211
Spitzer Literary Agency, Inc., Philip G. 211
Talcott Notch Literary 214

Triada U.S. Literary Agency, Inc. 215
Vesel Literary Agency, Beth 216
Ware Literary Agency, John A. 217
Weiner Literary Agency, Cherry 218
Winsun Literary Agency 219
Writers House 219
Zachary Shuster Harmsworth 220
Zeckendorf Assoc., Inc., Susan 221

Erotica

Brown Literary Agency 165
Brown, Ltd., Curtis 166
D4EO Literary Agency 171
Harwood Limited, Antony 180
Levine Literary Agency, Paul S. 190
Lowenstein-Yost Associates 192
Marshall Agency, The Evan 195
Mendel Media Group, LLC 196
Perkins Associates, L. 198
Pevner, Inc., Stephen 199
Picard, Literary Agent, Alison J. 199
Prospect Agency LLC 201
Scribe Agency, LLC 207
Writers House 219

Ethnic

Ahearn Agency, Inc., The 157
Ampersand Agency, The 158
Amster Literary Enterprises, Betsy 158
August Agency, LLC, The 160
Barer Literary, LLC 161
Barrett Books, Inc., Loretta 162
Bleecker Street Associates, Inc. 163
Blumer Literary Agency, Inc., The 163
Brandt & Hochman Literary Agents, Inc. 164
Brown, Ltd., Curtis 166
Browne & Miller Literary Associates 166
Castiglia Literary Agency 168
Clark Associates, Wm. 169
DeChiara Literary Agency, The Jennifer 172

DHS Literary, Inc. 173
Dunham Literary, Inc. 174
Dystel & Goderich Literary Management 174
Elmo Agency, Inc., Ann 175
Finch Literary Agency, Diana 177
Freymann Literary Agency, Sarah Jane 178
Halsey North, Reece 179
Harris Literary Agency, Inc., The Joy 180
Harwood Limited, Antony 180
Hawkins & Associates, Inc., John 181
Henshaw Group, Richard 181
Jabberwocky Literary Agency 183
Koster Literary Agency, LLC, Elaine 185
Langlie, Literary Agent, Laura 187
Larsen/Elizabeth Pomada, Literary Agents, Michael 187
Lazear Agency, Inc. 189
Levine Literary Agency, Paul S. 190
Literary Group, The 191
Lowenstein-Yost Associates 192
March Tenth, Inc. 195
Marshall Agency, The Evan 195
Mendel Media Group, LLC 196
Naggar Literary Agency, Inc., Jean V. 197
Pevner, Inc., Stephen 199
Picard, Literary Agent, Alison J. 199
Pistek Literary Agency, LLC, Alicka 200
Prospect Agency LLC 201
Regal Literary Agency 202
Rhodes Literary Agency, Jodie 203
Robbins Literary Agency, B.J. 204
Russell & Volkening 206
Sanders & Associates, Victoria 207
Schiavone Literary Agency, Inc. 207
Scribe Agency, LLC 207
Seligman, Literary Agent, Lynn 208
Serendipity Literary Agency, LLC 208

Triada U.S. Literary Agency, Inc. 215
Writers House 219
Zachary Shuster Harmsworth 220
Zeckendorf Assoc., Inc., Susan 221

Experimental

Brown, Ltd., Curtis 166
Harris Literary Agency, Inc., The Joy 180
Harwood Limited, Antony 180
Hawkins & Associates, Inc., John 181
Larsen/Elizabeth Pomada, Literary Agents, Michael 187
Levine Literary Agency, Paul S. 190
Pevner, Inc., Stephen 199
Scribe Agency, LLC 207
Ahearn Agency, Inc., The 157

Family Saga

Alive Communications, Inc. 157
Ampersand Agency, The 158
Artists and Artisans Inc. 160
August Agency, LLC, The 160
Authentic Creations Literary Agency 161
Barer Literary, LLC 161
Barrett Books, Inc., Loretta 162
Blumer Literary Agency, Inc., The 163
Books & Such Literary Agency 164
Brown, Ltd., Curtis 166
Browne & Miller Literary Associates 166
DeChiara Literary Agency, The Jennifer 172
Dystel & Goderich Literary Management 174
Elmo Agency, Inc., Ann 175
Halsey North, Reece 179
Harris Literary Agency, Inc., The Joy 180
Hartline Literary Agency 180
Harwood Limited, Antony 180

Hawkins & Associates, Inc., John 181
Henshaw Group, Richard 181
Jabberwocky Literary Agency 183
JCA Literary Agency 183
Klinger, Inc., Harvey 184
Koster Literary Agency, LLC, Elaine 185
KT Public Relations & Literary Services 186
LA Literary Agency, The 186
Lampack Agency, Inc., Peter 187
Larsen/Elizabeth Pomada, Literary Agents, Michael 187
Lazear Agency, Inc. 189
Levine Literary Agency, Paul S. 190
Lippincott Massie McQuilkin 191
Literary Group, The 191
March Tenth, Inc. 195
Morrison, Inc., Henry 196
Naggar Literary Agency, Inc., Jean V. 197
Picard, Literary Agent, Alison J. 199
Pistek Literary Agency, LLC, Alicka 200
Prospect Agency LLC 201
Rhodes Literary Agency, Jodie 203
Rotrosen Agency LLC, Jane 205
Sanders & Associates, Victoria 207
Schiavone Literary Agency, Inc. 207
Simmons Literary Agency, Jeffrey 210
Weiner Literary Agency, Cherry 218
Winsun Literary Agency 219
Writers House 219

Fantasy

Ampersand Agency, The 158
Brown, Ltd., Curtis 166
Canton Smith Agency 167
Dawson Associates, Liza 172
DeChiara Literary Agency, The Jennifer 172
Harwood Limited, Antony 180
Henshaw Group, Richard 181
Jabberwocky Literary Agency 183

KT Public Relations & Literary Services 186
Larsen/Elizabeth Pomada, Literary Agents, Michael 187
Lazear Agency, Inc. 189
Literary Group, The 191
Maass Literary Agency, Donald 193
Perkins Associates, L. 198
Raines & Raines 202
Rubie Literary Agency, The Peter 206
Scribe Agency, LLC 207
Seligman, Literary Agent, Lynn 208
Spectrum Literary Agency 210
Sternig & Byrne Literary Agency 212
Triada U.S. Literary Agency, Inc. 215
Weiner Literary Agency, Cherry 218
Writers House 219

Feminist

Ahearn Agency, Inc., The 157
Blumer Literary Agency, Inc., The 163
Brown, Ltd., Curtis 166
Browne, Ltd., Pema 166
DeChiara Literary Agency, The Jennifer 172
Harris Literary Agency, Inc., The Joy 180
Harwood Limited, Antony 180
Hawkins & Associates, Inc., John 181
Koster Literary Agency, LLC, Elaine 185
LA Literary Agency, The 186
Langlie, Literary Agent, Laura 187
Larsen/Elizabeth Pomada, Literary Agents, Michael 187
Lazear Agency, Inc. 189
Levine Literary Agency, Paul S. 190
Lippincott Massie McQuilkin 191
Literary Group, The 191
Lowenstein-Yost Associates 192
Mendel Media Group, LLC 196

Naggar Literary Agency, Inc., Jean V. 197
Picard, Literary Agent, Alison J. 199
Sanders & Associates, Victoria 207
Scribe Agency, LLC 207
Seligman, Literary Agent, Lynn 208
Spieler Agency, The 211
Writers House 219
Zachary Shuster Harmsworth 220

Glitz

August Agency, LLC, The 160
Brown, Ltd., Curtis 166
Browne, Ltd., Pema 166
DeChiara Literary Agency, The Jennifer 172
Dystel & Goderich Literary Management 174
Harris Literary Agency, Inc., The Joy 180
Harwood Limited, Antony 180
Hawkins & Associates, Inc., John 181
Jabberwocky Literary Agency 183
Langlie, Literary Agent, Laura 187
Larsen/Elizabeth Pomada, Literary Agents, Michael 187
Lazear Agency, Inc. 189
Levine Literary Agency, Paul S. 190
Lippincott Massie McQuilkin 191
Mendel Media Group, LLC 196
Pevner, Inc., Stephen 199
Picard, Literary Agent, Alison J. 199
Sanders & Associates, Victoria 207
Scribe Agency, LLC 207
Seligman, Literary Agent, Lynn 208
Spieler Agency, The 211
Writers House 219
Zachary Shuster Harmsworth 220

Hi-Lo

Brown, Ltd., Curtis 166
Harris Literary Agency, Inc., The Joy 180
Harwood Limited, Antony 180

Hawkins & Associates, Inc., John 181
Lazear Agency, Inc. 189
Writers House 219

Historical

Ahearn Agency, Inc., The 157
Alive Communications, Inc. 157
Ampersand Agency, The 158
August Agency, LLC, The 160
Barer Literary, LLC 161
Barrett Books, Inc., Loretta 162
Bleecker Street Associates, Inc. 163
Blumer Literary Agency, Inc., The 163
Books & Such Literary Agency 164
Brandt & Hochman Literary Agents, Inc. 164
Brown, Ltd., Curtis 166
Browne & Miller Literary Associates 166
Browne, Ltd., Pema 166
Clark Associates, Wm. 169
Dawson Associates, Liza 172
DeChiara Literary Agency, The Jennifer 172
Delbourgo Associates, Inc., Joelle 173
D4EO Literary Agency 171
English Literary Agency, The Elaine P. 176
Farris Literary Agency, Inc. 176
Finch Literary Agency, Diana 177
Grosjean Literary Agency, Jill 179
Halsey North, Reece 179
Harris Literary Agency, Inc., The Joy 180
Hartline Literary Agency 180
Harwood Limited, Antony 180
Hawkins & Associates, Inc., John 181
Henshaw Group, Richard 181
J de S Associates, Inc. 183
Jabberwocky Literary Agency 183
JCA Literary Agency 183
Kneerim & Williams 185

Koster Literary Agency, LLC, Elaine 185

KT Public Relations & Literary Services 186

LA Literary Agency, The 186

Lampack Agency, Inc., Peter 187

Langlie, Literary Agent, Laura 187

Larsen/Elizabeth Pomada, Literary Agents, Michael 187

Lazear Agency, Inc. 189

Levine Literary Agency, Paul S. 190

Lippincott Massie McQuilkin 191

Lord Literary Management, Julia 192

Lowenstein-Yost Associates 192

Maass Literary Agency, Donald 193

March Tenth, Inc. 195

Marshall Agency, The Evan 195

Mendel Media Group, LLC 196

Morrison, Inc., Henry 196

Naggar Literary Agency, Inc., Jean V. 197

Picard, Literary Agent, Alison J. 199

Pistek Literary Agency, LLC, Alicka 200

Raines & Raines 202

Rees Literary Agency, Helen 202

Regal Literary Agency 202

Rhodes Literary Agency, Jodie 203

Rotrosen Agency LLC, Jane 205

Rubie Literary Agency, The Peter 206

Schiavone Literary Agency, Inc. 207

Seligman, Literary Agent, Lynn 208

Serendipity Literary Agency, LLC 208

Spectrum Literary Agency 210

Spencerhill Associates 211

Triada U.S. Literary Agency, Inc. 215

Weiner Literary Agency, Cherry 218

Writers House 219

Zachary Shuster Harmsworth 220

Zeckendorf Assoc., Inc., Susan 221

Horror

Anubis Literary Agency 159

Brown, Ltd., Curtis 166

DeChiara Literary Agency, The Jennifer 172

D4EO Literary Agency 171

Halsey North, Reece 179

Harwood Limited, Antony 180

Henshaw Group, Richard 181

Jabberwocky Literary Agency 183

Literary Group, The 191

Maass Literary Agency, Donald 193

Marshall Agency, The Evan 195

Perkins Associates, L. 198

Pevner, Inc., Stephen 199

Picard, Literary Agent, Alison J. 199

Rotrosen Agency LLC, Jane 205

Schiavone Literary Agency, Inc. 207

Scribe Agency, LLC 207

Seligman, Literary Agent, Lynn 208

Sternig & Byrne Literary Agency 212

Triada U.S. Literary Agency, Inc. 215

Writers House 219

Humor/Satire

Ahearn Agency, Inc., The 157

Alive Communications, Inc. 157

Artists and Artisans Inc. 160

August Agency, LLC, The 160

Blumer Literary Agency, Inc., The 163

Brown, Ltd., Curtis 166

Canton Smith Agency 167

DeChiara Literary Agency, The Jennifer 172

D4EO Literary Agency 171

Farber Literary Agency, Inc. 176

Farris Literary Agency, Inc. 176

Harris Literary Agency, Inc., The Joy 180

Harwood Limited, Antony 180

Henshaw Group, Richard 181

Jabberwocky Literary Agency 183

Langlie, Literary Agent, Laura 187

Larsen/Elizabeth Pomada, Literary Agents, Michael 187
Lazear Agency, Inc. 189
Levine Literary Agency, Paul S. 190
Lippincott Massie McQuilkin 191
Literary Group, The 191
March Tenth, Inc. 195
Marshall Agency, The Evan 195
Mendel Media Group, LLC 196
Pevner, Inc., Stephen 199
Picard, Literary Agent, Alison J. 199
Schiavone Literary Agency, Inc. 207
Scribe Agency, LLC 207
Seligman, Literary Agent, Lynn 208
Winsun Literary Agency 219
Writers House 219

Juvenile

Ampersand Agency, The 158
Brown, Ltd., Curtis 166
Browne, Ltd., Pema 166
Canton Smith Agency 167
DeChiara Literary Agency, The Jennifer 172
D4EO Literary Agency 171
Dunham Literary, Inc. 174
Farber Literary Agency, Inc. 176
J de S Associates, Inc. 183
Langlie, Literary Agent, Laura 187
Lazear Agency, Inc. 189
Maccoby Literary Agency, Gina 193
Mendel Media Group, LLC 196
Picard, Literary Agent, Alison J. 199
Prospect Agency LLC 201
Schiavone Literary Agency, Inc. 207
Serendipity Literary Agency, LLC 208
Talcott Notch Literary 214
Triada U.S. Literary Agency, Inc. 215
Winsun Literary Agency 219
Writers House 219

Literary

Acacia House Publishing Services, Ltd. 156

Ahearn Agency, Inc., The 157
Alive Communications, Inc. 157
Altshuler Literary Agency, Miriam 157
Ampersand Agency, The 158
Amster Literary Enterprises, Betsy 158
Artists and Artisans Inc. 160
August Agency, LLC, The 160
Authentic Creations Literary Agency 161
Barer Literary, LLC 161
Barrett Books, Inc., Loretta 162
Bender Literary Agency, Faye 162
Bernstein Literary Agency, Meredith 162
Bleecker Street Associates, Inc. 163
Blumer Literary Agency, Inc., The 163
Brandt & Hochman Literary Agents, Inc. 164
Brown, Ltd., Curtis 166
Browne & Miller Literary Associates 166
Browne, Ltd., Pema 166
Bykofsky Associates, Inc., Sheree 167
Castiglia Literary Agency 168
Chelius Literary Agency, Jane 168
Clark Associates, Wm. 169
Congdon Associates Inc., Don 170
Coover Agency, The Doe 170
Dawson Associates, Liza 172
DeChiara Literary Agency, The Jennifer 172
Delbourgo Associates, Inc., Joelle 173
D4EO Literary Agency 171
DHS Literary, Inc. 173
Dunham Literary, Inc. 174
Dystel & Goderich Literary Management 174
Ellison Agency, The Nicholas 175
Farber Literary Agency, Inc. 176
Finch Literary Agency, Diana 177
Fletcher & Parry 177

Freymann Literary Agency, Sarah Jane 178
Gelfman Schneider Literary Agents, Inc. 178
Grosjean Literary Agency, Jill 179
Halsey North, Reece 179
Harris Literary Agency, Inc., The Joy 180
Hartline Literary Agency 180
Harwood Limited, Antony 180
Hawkins & Associates, Inc., John 181
Henshaw Group, Richard 181
Hill Bonnie Nadell, Inc., Frederick 182
Imprint Agency, Inc. 182
J de S Associates, Inc. 183
Jabberwocky Literary Agency 183
JCA Literary Agency 183
Klinger, Inc., Harvey 184
Kneerim & Williams 185
Koster Literary Agency, LLC, Elaine 185
KT Public Relations & Literary Services 186
LA Literary Agency, The 186
Lampack Agency, Inc., Peter 187
Langlie, Literary Agent, Laura 187
Larsen/Elizabeth Pomada, Literary Agents, Michael 187
Lazear Agency, Inc. 189
Lescher & Lescher, Ltd. 189
Levine Greenberg Literary Agency, Inc. 190
Levine Literary Agency, Paul S. 190
Lippincott Massie McQuilkin 191
Lord Literary Management, Julia 192
Lowenstein-Yost Associates 192
Maass Literary Agency, Donald 193
Maccoby Literary Agency, Gina 193
Mann Agency, Carol 193
Manus & Associates Literary Agency, Inc. 194
March Tenth, Inc. 195
Marshall Agency, The Evan 195

McGrath, Helen 196
Mendel Media Group, LLC 196
Naggar Literary Agency, Inc., Jean V. 197
Nelson Literary Agency 198
Perkins Associates, L. 198
Pevner, Inc., Stephen 199
Picard, Literary Agent, Alison J. 199
Pistek Literary Agency, LLC, Alicka 200
Prospect Agency LLC 201
Rees Literary Agency, Helen 202
Regal Literary Agency 202
Rein Books, Inc., Jody 203
Rhodes Literary Agency, Jodie 203
Rittenberg Literary Agency, Inc., Ann 204
Robbins Literary Agency, B.J. 204
Rubie Literary Agency, The Peter 206
Russell & Volkening 206
Sanders & Associates, Victoria 207
Schiavone Literary Agency, Inc. 207
Scribe Agency, LLC 207
Seligman, Literary Agent, Lynn 208
Serendipity Literary Agency, LLC 208
Sherman Associates, Inc., Wendy 209
Simmons Literary Agency, Jeffrey 210
Slopen Literary Agency, Beverley 210
Spieler Agency, The 211
Spitzer Literary Agency, Inc., Philip G. 211
Stauffer Associates, Nancy 212
Strothman Agency, LLC, The 213
Triada U.S. Literary Agency, Inc. 215
Vesel Literary Agency, Beth 216
Watkins Loomis Agency, Inc. 218
Waxman Literary Agency, Inc. 218
Weingel-Fidel Agency, The 218
Winsun Literary Agency 219
Writers House 219

Zachary Shuster Harmsworth 220
Zeckendorf Assoc., Inc., Susan 221

Mainstream/Contemporary

Acacia House Publishing Services, Ltd. 156
Ahearn Agency, Inc., The 157
Alive Communications, Inc. 157
Altshuler Literary Agency, Miriam 157
Ampersand Agency, The 158
Artists and Artisans Inc. 160
August Agency, LLC, The 160
Authentic Creations Literary Agency 161
Barer Literary, LLC 161
Barrett Books, Inc., Loretta 162
Blumer Literary Agency, Inc., The 163
BookEnds, LLC 164
Books & Such Literary Agency 164
Brandt & Hochman Literary Agents, Inc. 164
Brown, Ltd., Curtis 166
Browne & Miller Literary Associates 166
Browne, Ltd., Pema 166
Bykofsky Associates, Inc., Sheree 167
Castiglia Literary Agency 168
Clark Associates, Wm. 169
Congdon Associates Inc., Don 170
DeChiara Literary Agency, The Jennifer 172
Delbourgo Associates, Inc., Joelle 173
D4EO Literary Agency 171
DHS Literary, Inc. 173
Dunham Literary, Inc. 174
Dystel & Goderich Literary Management 174
Ellison Agency, The Nicholas 175
Elmo Agency, Inc., Ann 175
Farber Literary Agency, Inc. 176
Farris Literary Agency, Inc. 176
Finch Literary Agency, Diana 177
Freymann Literary Agency, Sarah Jane 178
Gelfman Schneider Literary Agents, Inc. 178
Grosjean Literary Agency, Jill 179
Halsey North, Reece 179
Harris Literary Agency, Inc., The Joy 180
Harwood Limited, Antony 180
Hawkins & Associates, Inc., John 181
Henshaw Group, Richard 181
Hill Bonnie Nadell, Inc., Frederick 182
J de S Associates, Inc. 183
Jabberwocky Literary Agency 183
JCA Literary Agency 183
Klinger, Inc., Harvey 184
Kneerim & Williams 185
Koster Literary Agency, LLC, Elaine 185
KT Public Relations & Literary Services 186
LA Literary Agency, The 186
Lampack Agency, Inc., Peter 187
Larsen/Elizabeth Pomada, Literary Agents, Michael 187
Lazear Agency, Inc. 189
Levine Greenberg Literary Agency, Inc. 190
Levine Literary Agency, Paul S. 190
Lippincott Massie McQuilkin 191
Lord Literary Management, Julia 192
Lowenstein-Yost Associates 192
Maass Literary Agency, Donald 193
Maccoby Literary Agency, Gina 193
Manus & Associates Literary Agency, Inc. 194
March Tenth, Inc. 195
Marshall Agency, The Evan 195
McGrath, Helen 196
Mendel Media Group, LLC 196
Naggar Literary Agency, Inc., Jean V. 197
Pevner, Inc., Stephen 199

Picard, Literary Agent, Alison J. 199
Pistek Literary Agency, LLC, Alicka 200
Prospect Agency LLC 201
Psaltis Literary 201
Rees Literary Agency, Helen 202
Rein Books, Inc., Jody 203
Rhodes Literary Agency, Jodie 203
Robbins Literary Agency, B.J. 204
Rotrosen Agency LLC, Jane 205
Russell & Volkening 206
Schiavone Literary Agency, Inc. 207
Scribe Agency, LLC 207
Seligman, Literary Agent, Lynn 208
Simmons Literary Agency, Jeffrey 210
Spectrum Literary Agency 210
Spencerhill Associates 211
Spitzer Literary Agency, Inc., Philip G. 211
Teal Literary Agency, Patricia 214
Triada U.S. Literary Agency, Inc. 215
Weiner Literary Agency, Cherry 218
Weingel-Fidel Agency, The 218
Winsun Literary Agency 219
Writers House 219
Zachary Shuster Harmsworth 220
Zeckendorf Assoc., Inc., Susan 221

Military/War

Brown, Ltd., Curtis 166
Harwood Limited, Antony 180
Hawkins & Associates, Inc., John 181
Lazear Agency, Inc. 189
Writers House 219

Multimedia

Brown, Ltd., Curtis 166
Harris Literary Agency, Inc., The Joy 180
Harwood Limited, Antony 180
Hawkins & Associates, Inc., John 181
Lazear Agency, Inc. 189

Mystery/Suspense

Acacia House Publishing Services, Ltd. 156
Ahearn Agency, Inc., The 157
Alive Communications, Inc. 157
Ampersand Agency, The 158
Amster Literary Enterprises, Betsy 158
Appleseeds Management 159
August Agency, LLC, The 160
Authentic Creations Literary Agency 161
Axelrod Agency, The 161
Barrett Books, Inc., Loretta 162
Bernstein Literary Agency, Meredith 162
Bleecker Street Associates, Inc. 163
Blumer Literary Agency, Inc., The 163
BookEnds, LLC 164
Brandt & Hochman Literary Agents, Inc. 164
Brown, Ltd., Curtis 166
Browne & Miller Literary Associates 166
Browne, Ltd., Pema 166
Bykofsky Associates, Inc., Sheree 167
Castiglia Literary Agency 168
Chelius Literary Agency, Jane 168
Congdon Associates Inc., Don 170
Dawson Associates, Liza 172
DeChiara Literary Agency, The Jennifer 172
Delbourgo Associates, Inc., Joelle 173
D4EO Literary Agency 171
DHS Literary, Inc. 173
Dystel & Goderich Literary Management 174
English Literary Agency, The Elaine P. 176
Farber Literary Agency, Inc. 176
Farris Literary Agency, Inc. 176
Gelfman Schneider Literary Agents, Inc. 178

Grosjean Literary Agency, Jill 179
Halsey North, Reece 179
Harris Literary Agency, Inc., The Joy 180
Hartline Literary Agency 180
Harwood Limited, Antony 180
Hawkins & Associates, Inc., John 181
Henshaw Group, Richard 181
Imprint Agency, Inc. 182
J de S Associates, Inc. 183
JCA Literary Agency 183
Klinger, Inc., Harvey 184
Koster Literary Agency, LLC, Elaine 185
KT Public Relations & Literary Services 186
Lampack Agency, Inc., Peter 187
Langlie, Literary Agent, Laura 187
Larsen/Elizabeth Pomada, Literary Agents, Michael 187
Lazear Agency, Inc. 189
Lescher & Lescher, Ltd. 189
Levine Greenberg Literary Agency, Inc. 190
Levine Literary Agency, Paul S. 190
Literary Group, The 191
Lord Literary Management, Julia 192
Lowenstein-Yost Associates 192
Maass Literary Agency, Donald 193
Maccoby Literary Agency, Gina 193
Manus & Associates Literary Agency, Inc. 194
Marshall Agency, The Evan 195
McGrath, Helen 196
Mendel Media Group, LLC 196
Naggar Literary Agency, Inc., Jean V. 197
Picard, Literary Agent, Alison J. 199
Pistek Literary Agency, LLC, Alicka 200
Prospect Agency LLC 201
Quicksilver Books: Literary Agents 201
Raines & Raines 202

Rees Literary Agency, Helen 202
Regal Literary Agency 202
Rhodes Literary Agency, Jodie 203
Robbins Literary Agency, B.J. 204
Rotrosen Agency LLC, Jane 205
Russell & Volkening 206
Scribe Agency, LLC 207
Seligman, Literary Agent, Lynn 208
Simmons Literary Agency, Jeffrey 210
Slopen Literary Agency, Beverley 210
Spectrum Literary Agency 210
Spieler Agency, The 211
Spitzer Literary Agency, Inc., Philip G. 211
Sternig & Byrne Literary Agency 212
Talcott Notch Literary 214
Teal Literary Agency, Patricia 214
Triada U.S. Literary Agency, Inc. 215
Ware Literary Agency, John A. 217
Weiner Literary Agency, Cherry 218
Winsun Literary Agency 219
Writers House 219
Zachary Shuster Harmsworth 220
Zeckendorf Assoc., Inc., Susan 221

Occult

Brown, Ltd., Curtis 166
Harwood Limited, Antony 180
Lazear Agency, Inc. 189
Writers House 219

Picture Books

Brown, Ltd., Curtis 166
Browne, Ltd., Pema 166
DeChiara Literary Agency, The Jennifer 172
D4EO Literary Agency 171
Dunham Literary, Inc. 174
Harwood Limited, Antony 180
Lazear Agency, Inc. 189
Mendel Media Group, LLC 196
Muse Literary Management 197
Picard, Literary Agent, Alison J. 199

Prospect Agency LLC 201
Raines & Raines 202
Russell & Volkening 206
Serendipity Literary Agency, LLC
  208
Winsun Literary Agency 219
Writers House 219

Plays
Brown, Ltd., Curtis 166
Harwood Limited, Antony 180
Lazear Agency, Inc. 189

Poetry
Brown, Ltd., Curtis 166
Lazear Agency, Inc. 189

Poetry in Translation
Lazear Agency, Inc. 189

Psychic/Supernatural
Ahearn Agency, Inc., The 157
August Agency, LLC, The 160
Barrett Books, Inc., Loretta 162
Brown, Ltd., Curtis 166
Hawkins & Associates, Inc., John
  181
Henshaw Group, Richard 181
Jabberwocky Literary Agency 183
Lazear Agency, Inc. 189
Literary Group, The 191
Maass Literary Agency, Donald 193
McGrath, Helen 196
Naggar Literary Agency, Inc., Jean
  V. 197
Pevner, Inc., Stephen 199
Picard, Literary Agent, Alison J. 199
Scribe Agency, LLC 207
Weiner Literary Agency, Cherry 218
Winsun Literary Agency 219
Writers House 219

Regional
Ahearn Agency, Inc., The 157
Blumer Literary Agency, Inc., The
  163

Brown, Ltd., Curtis 166
Dawson Associates, Liza 172
DeChiara Literary Agency, The
  Jennifer 172
Delbourgo Associates, Inc., Joelle
  173
Grosjean Literary Agency, Jill 179
Harris Literary Agency, Inc., The Joy
  180
Hartline Literary Agency 180
Harwood Limited, Antony 180
Jabberwocky Literary Agency 183
Koster Literary Agency, LLC, Elaine
  185
Levine Literary Agency, Paul S. 190
Lippincott Massie McQuilkin 191
Stauffer Associates, Nancy 212
Writers House 219

Religious/Inspirational
Alive Communications, Inc. 157
Books & Such Literary Agency 164
Brown, Ltd., Curtis 166
Browne & Miller Literary Associates
  166
Browne, Ltd., Pema 166
Farris Literary Agency, Inc. 176
Hartline Literary Agency 180
Harwood Limited, Antony 180
Hawkins & Associates, Inc., John
  181
Larsen/Elizabeth Pomada, Literary
  Agents, Michael 187
Laube Agency, The Steve 188
Lazear Agency, Inc. 189
Levine Literary Agency, Paul S. 190
Marshall Agency, The Evan 195
Mendel Media Group, LLC 196
Seymour Agency, The 209
Spencerhill Associates 211
Winsun Literary Agency 219

Romance
Ahearn Agency, Inc., The 157
Ampersand Agency, The 158

Authentic Creations Literary Agency 161

Axelrod Agency, The 161

Bernstein Literary Agency, Meredith 162

Bleecker Street Associates, Inc. 163

BookEnds, LLC 164

Books & Such Literary Agency 164

Brandt & Hochman Literary Agents, Inc. 164

Brown Literary Agency 165

Brown, Ltd., Curtis 166

Browne & Miller Literary Associates 166

Browne, Ltd., Pema 166

Canton Smith Agency 167

D4EO Literary Agency 171

Elmo Agency, Inc., Ann 175

English Literary Agency, The Elaine P. 176

Farris Literary Agency, Inc. 176

Grosjean Literary Agency, Jill 179

Hartline Literary Agency 180

Harwood Limited, Antony 180

Henshaw Group, Richard 181

Hopkins Literary Associates 182

KT Public Relations & Literary Services 186

Langlie, Literary Agent, Laura 187

Larsen/Elizabeth Pomada, Literary Agents, Michael 187

Lazear Agency, Inc. 189

Levine Literary Agency, Paul S. 190

Literary Group, The 191

Lowenstein-Yost Associates 192

Maass Literary Agency, Donald 193

Marshall Agency, The Evan 195

McGrath, Helen 196

Mendel Media Group, LLC 196

Nelson Literary Agency 198

Picard, Literary Agent, Alison J. 199

Pistek Literary Agency, LLC, Alicka 200

Prospect Agency LLC 201

Rosenberg Group, The 205

Rotrosen Agency LLC, Jane 205

Seligman, Literary Agent, Lynn 208

Seymour Agency, The 209

Spectrum Literary Agency 210

Spencerhill Associates 211

Teal Literary Agency, Patricia 214

Triada U.S. Literary Agency, Inc. 215

Weiner Literary Agency, Cherry 218

Winsun Literary Agency 219

Writers House 219

Science Fiction

Anubis Literary Agency 159

Brown, Ltd., Curtis 166

Dawson Associates, Liza 172

D4EO Literary Agency 171

Halsey North, Reece 179

Harwood Limited, Antony 180

Henshaw Group, Richard 181

Jabberwocky Literary Agency 183

KT Public Relations & Literary Services 186

Lazear Agency, Inc. 189

Maass Literary Agency, Donald 193

Marshall Agency, The Evan 195

McGrath, Helen 196

Perkins Associates, L. 198

Prospect Agency LLC 201

Raines & Raines 202

Rubie Literary Agency, The Peter 206

Schiavone Literary Agency, Inc. 207

Scribe Agency, LLC 207

Seligman, Literary Agent, Lynn 208

Spectrum Literary Agency 210

Sternig & Byrne Literary Agency 212

Triada U.S. Literary Agency, Inc. 215

Weiner Literary Agency, Cherry 218

Writers House 219

Short Story Collections

Brown, Ltd., Curtis 166

Congdon Associates Inc., Don 170

Harris Literary Agency, Inc., The Joy 180

Hawkins & Associates, Inc., John 181

Lazear Agency, Inc. 189

Writers House 219

Spiritual

Brown, Ltd., Curtis 166

Harris Literary Agency, Inc., The Joy 180

Harwood Limited, Antony 180

Lazear Agency, Inc. 189

Writers House 219

Sports

Authentic Creations Literary Agency 161

Brown, Ltd., Curtis 166

Browne & Miller Literary Associates 166

DeChiara Literary Agency, The Jennifer 172

D4EO Literary Agency 171

Farris Literary Agency, Inc. 176

Harwood Limited, Antony 180

Hawkins & Associates, Inc., John 181

Henshaw Group, Richard 181

Jabberwocky Literary Agency 183

JCA Literary Agency 183

LA Literary Agency, The 186

Lazear Agency, Inc. 189

Levine Literary Agency, Paul S. 190

Literary Group, The 191

Mendel Media Group, LLC 196

Picard, Literary Agent, Alison J. 199

Robbins Literary Agency, B.J. 204

Russell & Volkening 206

Spitzer Literary Agency, Inc., Philip G. 211

Triada U.S. Literary Agency, Inc. 215

Writers House 219

Thriller

Acacia House Publishing Services, Ltd. 156

Ahearn Agency, Inc., The 157

Alive Communications, Inc. 157

Ampersand Agency, The 158

Amster Literary Enterprises, Betsy 158

August Agency, LLC, The 160

Authentic Creations Literary Agency 161

Barrett Books, Inc., Loretta 162

Bernstein Literary Agency, Meredith 162

Bleecker Street Associates, Inc. 163

Blumer Literary Agency, Inc., The 163

BookEnds, LLC 164

Brandt & Hochman Literary Agents, Inc. 164

Brown, Ltd., Curtis 166

Browne & Miller Literary Associates 166

Congdon Associates Inc., Don 170

Dawson Associates, Liza 172

DeChiara Literary Agency, The Jennifer 172

D4EO Literary Agency 171

DHS Literary, Inc. 173

Dystel & Goderich Literary Management 174

Elmo Agency, Inc., Ann 175

English Literary Agency, The Elaine P. 176

Farber Literary Agency, Inc. 176

Farris Literary Agency, Inc. 176

Finch Literary Agency, Diana 177

Halsey North, Reece 179

Hartline Literary Agency 180

Harwood Limited, Antony 180

Hawkins & Associates, Inc., John 181

Henshaw Group, Richard 181

Imprint Agency, Inc. 182

Jabberwocky Literary Agency 183

JCA Literary Agency 183

Klinger, Inc., Harvey 184

Koster Literary Agency, LLC, Elaine 185

KT Public Relations & Literary Services 186
LA Literary Agency, The 186
Lampack Agency, Inc., Peter 187
Langlie, Literary Agent, Laura 187
Lazear Agency, Inc. 189
Levine Greenberg Literary Agency, Inc. 190
Levine Literary Agency, Paul S. 190
Literary Group, The 191
Lowenstein-Yost Associates 192
Maass Literary Agency, Donald 193
Maccoby Literary Agency, Gina 193
Manus & Associates Literary Agency, Inc. 194
McGrath, Helen 196
Mendel Media Group, LLC 196
Naggar Literary Agency, Inc., Jean V. 197
Pevner, Inc., Stephen 199
Picard, Literary Agent, Alison J. 199
Pistek Literary Agency, LLC, Alicka 200
Prospect Agency LLC 201
Quicksilver Books: Literary Agents 201
Raines & Raines 202
Rees Literary Agency, Helen 202
Regal Literary Agency 202
Rhodes Literary Agency, Jodie 203
Robbins Literary Agency, B.J. 204
Rotrosen Agency LLC, Jane 205
Rubie Literary Agency, The Peter 206
Russell & Volkening 206
Sanders & Associates, Victoria 207
Scribe Agency, LLC 207
Serendipity Literary Agency, LLC 208
Simmons Literary Agency, Jeffrey 210
Spencerhill Associates 211
Spitzer Literary Agency, Inc., Philip G. 211
Talcott Notch Literary 214

Triada U.S. Literary Agency, Inc. 215
Ware Literary Agency, John A. 217
Weiner Literary Agency, Cherry 218
Winsun Literary Agency 219
Writers House 219
Zachary Shuster Harmsworth 220
Zeckendorf Assoc., Inc., Susan 221

Translation

Brown, Ltd., Curtis 166
Harris Literary Agency, Inc., The Joy 180
Harwood Limited, Antony 180
Hawkins & Associates, Inc., John 181
Lazear Agency, Inc. 189
Writers House 219

Westerns/Frontier

Brown, Ltd., Curtis 166
D4EO Literary Agency 171
DHS Literary, Inc. 173
Farris Literary Agency, Inc. 176
Harwood Limited, Antony 180
Hawkins & Associates, Inc., John 181
J de S Associates, Inc. 183
Lazear Agency, Inc. 189
Levine Literary Agency, Paul S. 190
Literary Group, The 191
Marshall Agency, The Evan 195
Prospect Agency LLC 201
Raines & Raines 202
Weiner Literary Agency, Cherry 218
Writers House 219

Women's

Amster Literary Enterprises, Betsy 158
Axelrod Agency, The 161
Bernstein Literary Agency, Meredith 162
Bleecker Street Associates, Inc. 163
BookEnds, LLC 164

Brown Literary Agency 165
Brown, Ltd., Curtis 166
Castiglia Literary Agency 168
Chelius Literary Agency, Jane 168
Congdon Associates Inc., Don 170
Elmo Agency, Inc., Ann 175
Gelfman Schneider Literary Agents, Inc. 178
Halsey North, Reece 179
Harris Literary Agency, Inc., The Joy 180
Hawkins & Associates, Inc., John 181
Hopkins Literary Associates 182
Imprint Agency, Inc. 182
Lazear Agency, Inc. 189
Levine Greenberg Literary Agency, Inc. 190
Lowenstein-Yost Associates 192
Maass Literary Agency, Donald 193
Manus & Associates Literary Agency, Inc. 194
Nelson Literary Agency 198
Rhodes Literary Agency, Jodie 203
Rosenberg Group, The 205
Rotrosen Agency LLC, Jane 205
Sherman Associates, Inc., Wendy 209
Writers House 219

Young Adult

Ampersand Agency, The 158
Barer Literary, LLC 161
Bender Literary Agency, Faye 162

Brandt & Hochman Literary Agents, Inc. 164
Brown, Ltd., Curtis 166
Browne, Ltd., Pema 166
Canton Smith Agency 167
DeChiara Literary Agency, The Jennifer 172
D4EO Literary Agency 171
Dunham Literary, Inc. 174
Farber Literary Agency, Inc. 176
Finch Literary Agency, Diana 177
Fletcher & Parry 177
Harris Literary Agency, Inc., The Joy 180
Harwood Limited, Antony 180
Hawkins & Associates, Inc., John 181
Imprint Agency, Inc. 182
J de S Associates, Inc. 183
Koster Literary Agency, LLC, Elaine 185
Langlie, Literary Agent, Laura 187
Lazear Agency, Inc. 189
Maccoby Literary Agency, Gina 193
Mendel Media Group, LLC 196
Muse Literary Management 197
Picard, Literary Agent, Alison J. 199
Prospect Agency LLC 201
Rhodes Literary Agency, Jodie 203
Schiavone Literary Agency, Inc. 207
Scribe Agency, LLC 207
Talcott Notch Literary 214
Triada U.S. Literary Agency, Inc. 215
Writers House 219

Conference Index by Date

Our conference index organizes all conferences listed in this edition by the month in which they are held. If a conference bridges two months, you will find its name and page number under both monthly headings. If a conference occurs multiple times during the year (seasonally, for example), it will appear under each appropriate monthly heading. Turn to the listing's page number for exact dates and more detailed information.

January

Annual Retreats, Workshops and Classes 507

Booming Ground 521

Gotham Writers' Workshop 489

How to Be Published Workshops 500

Publishing Game, The 491

San Diego State University Writers' Conference 514

Sitka Center for Art and Ecology 518

Southwest Writers Conference 510

Winter Poetry & Prose Getaway in Cape May 496

Writers Online Workshops 506

Yaddo 494

February

Annual Retreats, Workshops and Classes 507

Art Workshops in Guatemala 522

AWP Annual Conference and Bookfair 499

Bay to Ocean Writers' Conference 495

Bonnet's Storymaking: The Master Class, James 513

How to Be Published Workshops 500

Natchez Literary and Cinema Celebration 500

Publishing Game, The 491

SCBWI Southern Breeze Spring Conference 502

SCBWI Winter Conference, NYC 492

Sitka Center for Art and Ecology 518

South Coast Writers Conference 519

Southwest Writers Conference 510

UCLA Extension Writers' Program 516

Writers Online Workshops 506

Writers Studio at UCLA Extension 517

Yaddo 494

March

Annual Retreats, Workshops and Classes 507

Art Workshops in Guatemala 522

AWP Annual Conference and Bookfair 499

Florida First Coast Writers' Festival 500

Heart Talk 518
Highlights Foundation Founders
  Workshops 495
Hilton Head Island Writers Retreat
  497
How to Be Published Workshops
  500
IWWG Early Spring in California
  Conference 513
Kentucky Writer's Workshop 504
Mount Hermon Christian Writers
  Conference 514
Oxford Conference for the Book 501
Publishing Game, The 491
SCBWI Southern Breeze Spring
  Conference 502
Sitka Center for Art and Ecology 518
Southwest Writers Conference 510
Stellarcon 498
TMCC Writers' Conference 515
Virginia Festival of the Book 498
Western Reserve Writers &
  Freelance Conference 505
Williams/New Orleans Literary
  Festival, Tennessee 502
Write It Out 502
Writers Online Workshops 506
Yaddo 494

April
Alternative Press Expo (APE) 512
Annual Retreats, Workshops and
  Classes 507
Art Workshops in Guatemala 522
Eminence Area Arts Council Short
  Story Workshop 508
Festival of Faith and Writing 503
Florida First Coast Writers' Festival
  500
Fort Bend Writers Guild Workshop
  508
Gotham Writers' Workshop 489
Highlights Foundation Founders
  Workshops 495
How to Be Published Workshops
  500

IWWG Meet the Agents and Editors
  490
Montevallo Literary Festival 500
Oxford Conference for the Book 501
Publishing Game, The 491
Sagebrush Writers Workshop 518
SCBWI/Hofstra Children's
  Literature Conference 492
Sitka Center for Art and Ecology 518
Southwest Writers Conference 510
Writers Online Workshops 506
Writing With Style 522
Yaddo 494

May
Annual Retreats, Workshops and
  Classes 507
Blue Ridge Mountains Christian
  Writers Conference 496
Bonnet's Storymaking: The Master
  Class, James 513
BookExpo America/Writer's Digest
  Books Writers Conference 488
Booming Ground 521
Georgia Writers Association's
  Spring Festival of Workshops 500
Highlights Foundation Founders
  Workshops 495
How to Be Published Workshops
  500
Pima Writers' Workshop 514
Publishing Game, The 491
Sagebrush Writers Workshop 518
Seacoast Writers Association Spring
  and Fall Conferences 493
Sitka Center for Art and Ecology 518
Southwest Writers Conference 510
SPACE (Small Press and Alternative
  Comics Expo) 505
Writers Online Workshops 506
Yaddo 494

June
Agents & Editors Conference 507
Annual Retreats, Workshops and
  Classes 507

Arkansas Writers' Conference 499

Aspen Summer Words Writing Retreat & Literary Festival 508

Bloody Words Mystery Conference 520

Clarion West Writers' Workshop 517

East Texas Writer's Conference 508

Environmental Writers' Conference and Workshop 488

Gotham Writers' Workshop 489

Highland Summer Conference 497

Highlights Foundation Founders Workshops 495

Hilton Head Island Writers Retreat 497

How to Be Published Workshops 500

International Music Camp Creative Writing Workshop 506

Iowa Summer Writing Festival 507

IWWG Summer Conference 490

Kenyon Review Writers Workshop 504

Marymount Manhattan College Writers' Conference 490

National Writers Association Foundation Conference 509

New Letters Weekend Writers Conference, The 509

Odyssey Fantasy Writing Workshop 491

Outdoor Writers Association of America Annual Conference 498

Paris Writers Workshop/WICE 523

Publishing Game, The 491

Remember the MAGIC IWWG Annual Summer Conference 492

Sitka Center for Art and Ecology 518

Sitka Symposium 519

Southeastern Writers Association 502

Southwest Writers Conference 510

Twain Creative Writing Workshops, Mark 512

Washington Independent Writers (WIW) Washington Writers Conference 496

Wesleyan Writers Conference 494

Write It Out 502

Writers Online Workshops 506

Writers Workshop in Science Fiction 512

Write-To-Publish Conference 505

Writing and Illustrating for Young Readers Workshop 517

Writing It Real in Port Townsend 520

Yaddo 494

July

Alabama Writers' Conclave 499

Annual Retreats, Workshops and Classes 507

Antioch Writers' Workshop 503

Art Workshops in Guatemala 522

Bonnet's Storymaking: The Master Class, James 513

Clarion West Writers' Workshop 517

Gotham Writers' Workshop 489

Highlights Foundation Founders Workshops 495

Highlights Foundation Writing for Children 489

How to Be Published Workshops 500

Humber School for Writers Summer Workshop 521

International Music Camp Creative Writing Workshop 506

Iowa Summer Writing Festival 507

Maritime Writers' Workshop 521

Midwest Writers Workshop 504

Montrose Christian Writer's Conference 495

New England Writers Conference 491

NY State Summer Writers Institute 491

Odyssey Fantasy Writing Workshop 491

Paris Writers Workshop/WICE 523

Publishing Game, The 491

Quackenbush's Children's Book Writing & Illustrating Workshiops, Robert 492

Rawlings: Writing the Region, Marjorie Kinnan 501

Remember the MAGIC IWWG Annual Summer Conference 492

Sage Hill Writing Experience 521

San Juan Writers Workshop 510

Sewanee Writers' Conference 498

Sitka Center for Art and Ecology 518

Southampton College Writers Conference, The 493

Southwest Writers Conference 510

Steamboat Springs Writers Group 511

Taos Summer Writers' Conference 511

Tin House Summer Writers Workshop 519

Victoria School of Writing, The 522

Wildacre Writers Workshop 499

Write It Out 502

Writers Institute 507

Writers Online Workshops 506

Writers Workshop in Science Fiction 512

Yaddo 494

Mendocino Coast Writers Conference 513

Publishing Game, The 491

Remember the MAGIC IWWG Annual Summer Conference 492

San Juan Writers Workshop 510

SCBWI/Summer Conference on Writing & Illustrating for Children 515

Sitka Center for Art and Ecology 518

Southwest Writers Conference 510

Squaw Valley Community of Writers 515

Steinbeck Festival 515

Texas Christian Writers' Conference 511

Vermont College Postgraduate Writers' Conference 493

Willamette Writers Conference 520

Write It Out 502

Writers Online Workshops 506

Yaddo 494

August

Annual Retreats, Workshops and Classes 507

Bread Loaf Writers' Conference 488

Columbus Writers Conference 503

Glen Workshop, The 509

Green Lake Writers Conference 506

Green Mountain Writers Conference 489

Highlights Foundation Founders Workshops 495

How to Be Published Workshops 500

September

Annual Retreats, Workshops and Classes 507

Booming Ground 521

Bouchercon 517

Gotham Writers' Workshop 489

Highlights Foundation Founders Workshops 495

Hilton Head Island Writers Retreat 497

How to Be Published Workshops 500

Killer Nashville 497

Medical Fiction Writing for Physicians 491

Publishing Game, The 491

Sitka Center for Art and Ecology 518

Southwest Writers Conference 510

Walloon Writers' Retreat 505

Western Reserve Writers & Freelance Conference 505

Writers Online Workshops 506

Writing, Creativity and Ritual: A
   Woman's Retreat 523
Writing With Style 522
Yaddo 494
Zoetrope: All-Story Short Story
   Writers' Workshop 523

October
Annual Retreats, Workshops and
   Classes 507
Flathead River Writers Conference
   518
Glorieta Christian Writers
   Conference 509
Gotham Writers' Workshop 489
Highlights Foundation Founders
   Workshops 495
How to Be Published Workshops
   500
IWWG Meet the Agents and Editors
   490
Nimrod Annual Writers' Workshop
   510
Publishing Game, The 491
Readers and Writers Holiday
   Conference 504
Sandy Cove Christian Writers
   Conference 495
Santa Barbara Christian Writers
   Conference 515
SCBWI Southern Breeze Fall
   Conference 501
Seacoast Writers Association Spring
   and Fall Conferences 493
Sitka Center for Art and Ecology 518
Southwest Writers Conference 510
Thunder Arm Writing Retreat with
   North Cascades Institute 519

Write From the Heart 516
Write on the Sound Writers'
   Conference 520
Writers Online Workshops 506
Writing, Creativity and Ritual: A
   Woman's Retreat 523
Yaddo 494

November
Annual Retreats, Workshops and
   Classes 507
Bonnet's Storymaking: The Master
   Class, James 513
Great Lakes Writers Festival 506
Highlights Foundation Founders
   Workshops 495
Hillerman Writers Conference, Tony
   509
How to Be Published Workshops
   500
Mormon Writers' Conference 513
Publishing Game, The 491
Sage Hill Writing Experience 521
Sitka Center for Art and Ecology 518
Southwest Writers Conference 510
Writers Online Workshops 506
Yaddo 494

December
Hilton Head Island Writers Retreat
   497
How to Be Published Workshops
   500
Publishing Game, The 491
Sitka Center for Art and Ecology 518
Southwest Writers Conference 510
Writers Online Workshops 506
Yaddo 494

Category
Index

Our category index makes it easy for you to identify publishers who are looking for a specific type of fiction. Publishers who are not listed under a fiction category either accept all types of fiction or have not indicated specific subject preferences. Also not appearing here are listings that need very specific types of fiction, e.g., "fiction about fly fishing only."

To use this index to find markets for your work, go to category title that best describes the type of fiction you write and look under either Magazines or Book Publishers (depending on whom you're targeting). Finally, read individual listings *carefully* to determine the publishers best suited to your work.

For a listing of agenst and the types of fiction they represent, see the Literary Agents Category Index beginning on page 557.

ADVENTURE

Magazines

Adirondack Review, The 326
Advocate, PKA'S Publication 347
Aguilar Expression, The 224
Allegheny Review, The 225
American Feed Magazine 327
Anti Muse 328
Armchair Aesthete, The 228
Art Times 348
Backroads 349
Barbaric Yawp 229
Bear Deluxe Magazine, The 349
Beginnings Publishing Inc. 230
Big Country Peacock Chronicle 330
Big Muddy: A Journal of the
  Mississippi River Valley 231
Blueline 233
Broken Pencil 235
Brutarian 309
Bryant Literary Review 235
Buffalo Carp 235

Burst 330
Cadet Quest Magazine 350
cc&d, Children, Churches & Daddies
  magazine: The Unreligious,
  NONfamily-oriented literary and
  art magazine 237
Chrysalis Reader 239
Clubhouse Magazine 351
Country Connection, The 310
Cricket 352
Dan River Anthology 310
Down in the Dirt 311
Downstate Story 243
Eureka Literary Magazine 245
Fifty Something Magazine 353
First Line 311
Foliate Oak Literary Magazine 248
Green Mountains Review 252
Gud Magazine 253
Harpur Palate 254
Highlights for Children 354
Iconoclast 256

Irreantum 312

Karamu 260

Kentucky Monthly 355

London Magazine, The 314

MacGuffin, The 266

Magazine of Fantasy & Science Fiction, The 356

Maisonneuve 357

New Works Review 336

newWitch 358

Nimrod 272

North Central Review, YOUR Undergraduate Literary Journal 272

Northwoods Journal 273

Oak, The 315

Ohio Teachers Write 274

Open Wide Magazine 275

Oracle Story & Letters 316

Outlooks 359

Palo Alto Review 277

Pink Chameleon, The 339

Pockets 360

PSI 318

Riverwind 289

Rose & Thorn Literary E-Zine, The 340

Short Stuff 292

Silent Voices 319

Slate & Style 319

Sleepingfish 292

Spider 361

Stand Magazine 295

Stone Soup 296

Storyteller, The 320

Sword Review, The 343

Tabard Inn, Tales of Questionable Taste 320

Thema 300

Timber Creek Review 322

Toasted Cheese 343

Trail of Indiscretion 322

Virginia Quarterly Review 323

Washington Running Report 363

Weber Studies 323

Book Publishers

B & H Publishing 371

Bantam Dell Publishing Group 372

Bantam Doubleday Dell Books for Young ReadersBantam Doubeday Dell Bks for Yng Rdrs 372

Berkley Publishing Group, The 374

Bethany House Publishers 374

Black Heron Press 375

Borealis Press, Ltd. 376

Calamari Press 378

Cave Books 380

Clarion Books 381

Covenant Communications, Inc. 382

Dan River Press 383

Dial Books For Young Readers 385

Doubleday 385

Dutton 386

Fort Ross Inc. Russian-American Publishing Projects 391

Front Street 391

Geringer Books, Laura 392

Glencannon Press, The 393

HarperCollins Children's Books 397

Holiday House, Inc. 399

Holt & Co. Books for Young Readers, Henry 399

Houghton Mifflin Books for Children 399

Ivy Publications 403

JourneyForth 403

Komenar Publishing 405

Kregel Publications 405

Lifetime Books 407

Little, Brown and Co. Books for Young Readers 408

McElderry Books, Margaret K.McElderry, Margaret 411

Medallion Press, Inc. 411

Milkweed for Young Readers 413

New Victoria Publishers 416

Oak Tree Press 417

Palari Publishing 418

Paradise Cay Publications, Inc. 420

Piñata Books 423

Pipers' Ash, Ltd. 424

Port Town Publishing 426
Putnam's Sons, G.P. 427
Random House Trade Publishing Group 428
Red Dress Ink 430
Salvo Press 431
Science & Humanities Press 432
Soho Press, Inc. 436
SynergEbooks 439
Triumvirate Publications 442
WindRiver Publishing, Inc. 446
Worldwide Library 447

CHILDRENS/JUVENILE

Magazines
Advocate, PKA'S Publication 347
Big Country Peacock Chronicle 330
Cadet Quest Magazine 350
Clubhouse Jr. 351
Clubhouse Magazine 351
Cricket 352
DotLit 333
Fun For Kidz 311
Funny Paper, The 312
Highlights for Children 354
Oracle Story & Letters 316
Soleado 320
Spider 361
Toasted Cheese 343

Book Publishers
Absey & Co. 368
Barefoot Books 373
Barron's Educational Series, Inc. 373
Bethany House Publishers 374
Candlewick Press 379
Carnifex Press 379
Carolrhoda Books, Inc. 379
Covenant Communications, Inc. 382
Cricket Books 382
Dial Books For Young Readers 385
Dutton Children's Books 387
Eerdmans Books for Young Readers 387

Farrar, Straus & Giroux Books for Young Readers 389
Front Street 391
Geringer Books, Laura 392
Glencannon Press, The 393
Harcourt, Inc 395
HarperCollins Children's Books 397
Hendrick-Long Publishing Co., Inc. 398
Holiday House, Inc. 399
Holt & Co. Books for Young Readers, Henry 399
Houghton Mifflin Books for Children 399
Hyperion Books for Children 400
Ion Imagination Publishing 402
Ivy Publications 403
Kregel Publications 405
Lamb Books, Wendy 406
Lee & Low Books 407
Lerner Publishing Group 407
Lifetime Books 407
Little, Brown and Co. Books for Young Readers 408
McElderry Books, Margaret K.McElderry, Margaret 411
Moody Publishers 415
Mould Publishing, Paul 415
Oak Tree Press 417
Peachtree Children's Books 420
Peachtree Publishers, Ltd. 421
Pelican Publishing Co. 421
Pipers' Ash, Ltd. 424
Pippin Press 424
Port Town Publishing 426
Puffin Books 427
Pureplay Press 427
Random House Children's Books 428
Ransom Publishing Ltd. 429
Ravenhawk Books 429
Scholastic Canada, Ltd. 432
Scholastic Press 432
Tradewind Books 441
Tricycle Press 441

Turtle Books 442
White Mane Kids 445

COMICS/GRAPHIC NOVELS

Magazines

Albedo One 307
Anti Muse 328
Five-Trope 334
Fluent Ascension 335
Foliate Oak Literary Magazine 248
Lady Churchill's Rosebud Wristlet 314
Opium Magazine 337
Oracle Story & Letters 316
Pindeldyboz 281
Sleepingfish 292
Weber Studies 323
Wild Violet 344

Book Publishers

Calamari Press 378
Dark Horse Comics 384
Fantagraphics Books 389
Holloway House Publishing Co. 399
Insomniac Press 401
NBM Publishing 416
Papercutz 419

EROTICA

Magazines

Anti Muse 328
Ascent Aspirations 328
Broken Pencil 235
Brutarian 309
Burst 330
First Class 246
Fluent Ascension 335
Furnace Review, The 335
Gargoyle 249
Gud Magazine 253
Happy 254
Ledge Magazine, The 263
London Magazine, The 314
Metal Scratches 267

newWitch 358
Open Wide Magazine 275
Outlooks 359
Quarter After Eight 285
Silent Voices 319
Tabard Inn, Tales of Questionable Taste 320
Tales of the Talisman 321
Thirteenth Warrior Review, The 343
Writers' Forum 363

Book Publishers

Brown Skin Books 378
Ellora's Cave Publishing, Inc. 388
Holloway House Publishing Co. 399
Monsoon Books 414
Mould Publishing, Paul 415
New Victoria Publishers 416
Pedlar Press 421
Spice 437
Virgin Books 444

ETHNIC/MULTICULTURAL

Magazines

Advocate, PKA'S Publication 347
African American Review 224
Aguilar Expression, The 224
Aim Magazine 347
Allegheny Review, The 225
American Feed Magazine 327
Anti Muse 328
Any Dream Will Do Review 308
Apalachee Review 227
Apple Valley Review, A Journal of Contemporary Literature 328
Art Times 348
Baltimore Review, The 229
Big Country Peacock Chronicle 330
Big Muddy: A Journal of the Mississippi River Valley 231
Binnacle, The 308
Black Lace 308
Boston Review 350
Briar Cliff Review, The 234

Brillant Corners 234
Broken Pencil 235
Bryant Literary Review 235
cc&d, Children, Churches & Daddies magazine: The Unreligious, NONfamily-oriented literary and art magazine 237
Center 237
Cezanne's Carrot 331
Chaffin Journal 237
Chariton Review, The 238
Clubhouse Jr. 351
Colorado Review 240
Convergence 331
Cream City Review, The 242
Creative With Words Publications 310
Cricket 352
Crucible 242
Dan River Anthology 310
DisciplesWorld 352
Down in the Dirt 311
Downstate Story 243
Eclipse 243
Ecotone, Reimagining Place 244
Epoch 244
Eureka Literary Magazine 245
Feminist Studies 246
Fifty Something Magazine 353
First Line 311
Flint Hills Review 247
Fluent Ascension 335
Foliate Oak Literary Magazine 248
Gargoyle 249
Georgetown Review 250
Gertrude 250
Global City Review 251
Green Hills Literary Lantern, The 335
Gud Magazine 253
Gulf Coast 253
Happy 254
Harpur Palate 254
Hawai'i Pacific Review 255
Hayden's Ferry Review 255
Heartlands Today, The 255

Highlights for Children 354
Home Planet News 256
Iconoclast 256
Illya's Honey 258
Indiana Review 258
Irreantum 312
Jabberwock Review, The 259
Karamu 260
Kenyon Review, The 260
Kit-Cat Review, The 261
Ledge Magazine, The 263
London Magazine, The 314
Long Story, The 264
Louisiana Review, The 265
MacGuffin, The 266
Maisonneuve 357
Missouri Review, The 269
Mobius 269
Na'Amat Woman 358
New Letters 270
New Orphic Review, The 271
newWitch 358
Nimrod 272
North Central Review, YOUR Undergraduate Literary Journal 272
North Dakota Quarterly 273
Obsidian III 274
Ohio Teachers Write 274
Open Wide Magazine 275
Oracle Story & Letters 316
Pacific Coast Journal 276
Painted Bride Quarterly 277
Palo Alto Review 277
Paperplates 338
Passages North 278
Paterson Literary Review 279
Pikeville Review 280
Pisgah Review 281
Pleiades 281
Pockets 360
Pointed Circle 282
Porcupine Literary Arts Magazine 282
Puerto Del Sol 285
Quarter After Eight 285

Quarterly West 285
Rainbow Curve 286
Raven Chronicles, The 287
River Styx 289
Riverwind 289
R-KV-R-Y 339
Rockford Review, The 290
Rose & Thorn Literary E-Zine, The 340
Saranac Review, The 291
Silent Voices 319
Sleepingfish 292
So to Speak 293
Soleado 320
Sonora Review 293
Southwestern American Literature 295
Spider 361
Stand Magazine 295
Steel City Review: A Pittsburgh-based magazine of Short Fiction 341
Stone Soup 296
Straylight 296
Struggle 297
Sulphur River Literary Review 298
Sword Review, The 343
Tabard Inn, Tales of Questionable Taste 320
Talking River Review 298
Tampa Review 299
Thema 300
Timber Creek Review 322
Toasted Cheese 343
Transition 301
Virginia Quarterly Review 323
Weber Studies 323
Wild Violet 344
Windhover 304
Workers Write! 304
Xavier Review 304
Yemassee 304
ZYZZYVA 305

Book Publishers

Arcade Publishing 369
Arte Publico Press 370
Aunt Lute Books 370
Ballantine Books 371
Bancroft Press 372
Barking Dog Books 373
Borealis Press, Ltd. 376
Branden Publishing Co., Inc. 377
Calyx Books 378
Carolrhoda Books, Inc. 379
Charlesbridge Publishing 380
Chronicle Books for Children 380
Circlet Press, Inc. 380
Coffee House Press 381
Coteau Books 382
Doubleday 385
Feminist Press at the City University of New York, The 390
Front Street 391
Gertrude Press 392
Gival Press 392
Glencannon Press, The 393
Holloway House Publishing Co. 399
Houghton Mifflin Books for Children 399
Ingalls Publishing Group, Inc. 401
Insomniac Press 401
Interlink Publishing Group, Inc. 402
Kensington Publishing Corp. 404
Komenar Publishing 405
Lee & Low Books 407
Lifetime Books 407
Little, Brown and Co. Books for Young Readers 408
Medallion Press, Inc. 411
Monsoon Books 414
Oak Tree Press 417
Palari Publishing 418
Panther Creek Press 419
Red Hen Press 430
River City Publishing 430
Seal Press 433
Soho Press, Inc. 436
Spice 437
Spout Press 437
Third World Press 439
Tindal Street Press, Ltd. 440

EXPERIMENTAL

Magazines

Abiko Annual With James Joyce, The 307

Adirondack Review, The 326

Advocate, PKA'S Publication 347

African American Review 224

Aguilar Expression, The 224

Alaska Quarterly Review 224

Albedo One 307

Allegheny Review, The 225

Alsop Review, The 327

American Feed Magazine 327

Anti Muse 328

Apalachee Review 227

Apple Valley Review, A Journal of Contemporary Literature 328

Ascent Aspirations 328

Barbaric Yawp 229

Bathtub Gin 229

Bellingham Review 230

Big Muddy: A Journal of the Mississippi River Valley 231

Binnacle, The 308

Bitter Oleander, The 232

Bomb Magazine 350

Boston Review 350

Boulevard 233

Brillant Corners 234

Broken Bridge Review 234

Broken Pencil 235

Brutarian 309

Bryant Literary Review 235

Buffalo Carp 235

Burst 330

Cafe Irreal, The 330

cc&d, Children, Churches & Daddies magazine: The Unreligious, NONfamily-oriented literary and art magazine 237

Center 237

Cezanne's Carrot 331

Chapman 238

Chariton Review, The 238

Chicago Review 239

Chrysalis Reader 239

Coal City Review 240

Colorado Review 240

Confrontation 241

Convergence 331

Cream City Review, The 242

Crucible 242

Dan River Anthology 310

Diagram 333

DotLit 333

Down in the Dirt 311

Downstate Story 243

Dreams & Visions 311

Eclipse 243

Ecotone, Reimagining Place 244

Epoch 244

Eureka Literary Magazine 245

Fiction 246

Fifty Something Magazine 353

Five-Trope 334

Flaunt Magazine 353

Florida Review 247

Fluent Ascension 335

Foliate Oak Literary Magazine 248

Frank 248

Furnace Review, The 335

Gargoyle 249

Georgetown Review 250

Ginosko 251

Global City Review 251

Grain Literary Magazine 251

Green Hills Literary Lantern, The 335

Green Mountains Review 252

Gud Magazine 253

Gulf Coast 253

Happy 254

Harpur Palate 254

Hawai'i Pacific Review 255

Hayden's Ferry Review 255

Heaven Bone 256

Home Planet News 256

Iconoclast 256

Idaho Review, The 257

Illya's Honey 258

Indiana Review 258

Inkwell Magazine 259
Iris 259
Irreantum 312
Isotope 259
Jabberwock Review, The 259
Karamu 260
Kenyon Review, The 260
Kit-Cat Review, The 261
Lady Churchill's Rosebud Wristlet 314
Lake Effect 262
Literal Latté 263
London Magazine, The 314
MacGuffin, The 266
Madison Review, The 266
Maisonneuve 357
Metal Scratches 267
Mid-American Review 267
Minnesota Review, The 268
Mobius 269
New Letters 270
New Orphic Review, The 271
Nimrod 272
North Central Review, YOUR Undergraduate Literary Journal 272
North Dakota Quarterly 273
Northwest Review 273
Northwoods Journal 273
Oak, The 315
Ohio Teachers Write 274
Open Wide Magazine 275
Opium Magazine 337
Outer Art 338
Pacific Coast Journal 276
Painted Bride Quarterly 277
Palo Alto Review 277
Paradoxism 317
Paumanok Review, The 339
Phantasmagoria 280
Pikeville Review 280
Pindeldyboz 281
Pisgah Review 281
Pleiades 281
Portland Review 283
Prism International 284

Puerto Del Sol 285
Quarter After Eight 285
Quarterly West 285
Rainbow Curve 286
Red Rock Review 287
Rejected Quarterly, The 288
River Styx 289
Rock & Sling: A Journal of Literature, Art and Faith 290
Rockford Review, The 290
Rose & Thorn Literary E-Zine, The 340
Santa Monica Review 291
Silent Voices 319
Sleepingfish 292
So to Speak 293
Soleado 320
Sonora Review 293
Stand Magazine 295
Stone Soup 296
storySouth 342
Straylight 296
Struggle 297
Sulphur River Literary Review 298
Sycamore Review 298
Tabard Inn, Tales of Questionable Taste 320
Tampa Review 299
Thema 300
Thirteenth Warrior Review, The 343
Transcendent Visions 322
Versal 302
Weber Studies 323
Wild Violet 344
William and Mary Review, The 302
Windhover 304
Xavier Review 304
Yemassee 304
ZYZZYVA 305

Book Publishers

Ageless Press 368
Anvil Press 369
Barking Dog Books 373
Black Heron Press 375
Calamari Press 378

Calyx Books 378
Coffee House Press 381
Doubleday 385
Empyreal Press 388
Eros Books 389
FC2 390
Gertrude Press 392
Insomniac Press 401
Komenar Publishing 405
Livingston Press 408
Low Fidelity Press 409
Omnidawn Publishing 417
Panther Creek Press 419
Pathwise Press 420
Paycock Press 420
Pedlar Press 421
Post-Apollo Press, The 426
Random House Trade Publishing
    Group 428
Red Hen Press 430
Small Beer Press 435
Spout Press 437
Starcherone Books 438
Stone Bridge Press 438
Woodley Memorial Press 446

FAMILY SAGA

Magazines

Adirondack Review, The 326
Allegheny Review, The 225
American Feed Magazine 327
Beginnings Publishing Inc. 230
Big Country Peacock Chronicle 330
Big Muddy: A Journal of the
    Mississippi River Valley 231
Bryant Literary Review 235
Buffalo Carp 235
cc&d, Children, Churches & Daddies
    magazine: The Unreligious,
    NONfamily-oriented literary and
    art magazine 237
Foliate Oak Literary Magazine 248
Irreantum 312
New Works Review 336

North Central Review, YOUR
    Undergraduate Literary Journal
    272
Oracle Story & Letters 316
Pink Chameleon, The 339
William and Mary Review, The 302

Book Publishers

Bancroft Press 372
Dan River Press 383
Mira Books 414
Monsoon Books 414
Mountain State Press 415
Piatkus Books 423
Pureplay Press 427
SynergEbooks 439

FANTASY

Magazines

Advocate, PKA'S Publication 347
Albedo One 307
AlienSkin Magazine 326
Allegheny Review, The 225
Allegory 327
American Feed Magazine 327
Anti Muse 328
Apalachee Review 227
Armchair Aesthete, The 228
Art Times 348
Ascent Aspirations 328
Asimov's Science Fiction 348
Barbaric Yawp 229
Big Country Peacock Chronicle 330
Broken Pencil 235
Brutarian 309
Bryant Literary Review 235
Burst 330
Cafe Irreal, The 330
cc&d, Children, Churches & Daddies
    magazine: The Unreligious,
    NONfamily-oriented literary and
    art magazine 237
Cezanne's Carrot 331
Challenging Destiny 331
Country Connection, The 310

Cricket 352

Dan River Anthology 310

Dargonzine 332

Down in the Dirt 311

Dragons, Knights & Angels, The Magazine of Christian Fantasy and Science Fiction 333

Dreams & Visions 311

Eureka Literary Magazine 245

Fifty Something Magazine 353

First Line 311

Gud Magazine 253

Happy 254

Harpur Palate 254

Hawai'i Pacific Review 255

Heaven Bone 256

Highlights for Children 354

Irreantum 312

Lady Churchill's Rosebud Wristlet 314

Lamp-Post, The 262

Literal Latté 263

London Magazine, The 314

Lone Star Stories, Speculative Fiction and Poetry 336

Magazine of Fantasy & Science Fiction, The 356

Midnight Times 336

Mobius 269

New Orphic Review, The 271

newWitch 358

North Central Review, YOUR Undergraduate Literary Journal 272

Northwoods Journal 273

Oak, The 315

Ohio Teachers Write 274

On Spec 316

Oracle Story & Letters 316

Oracular Tree, The 338

Outer Darkness 317

Palo Alto Review 277

Paradox 277

Pink Chameleon, The 339

Postscripts: The A to Z of Fantastic Fiction 283

Rejected Quarterly, The 288

Rockford Review, The 290

Rose & Thorn Literary E-Zine, The 340

Silent Voices 319

Slate & Style 319

Soleado 320

Spider 361

Stone Soup 296

Summerset Review, The 342

Sword Review, The 343

Talebones 321

Tales of the Talisman 321

Tampa Review 299

Thema 300

Tickled by Thunder 301

Toasted Cheese 343

Trail of Indiscretion 322

Washington Running Report 363

Weird Tales 323

Wild Violet 344

Windhover 304

Zahir 324

Book Publishers

Ageless Press 368

Baen Publishing Enterprises 371

Ballantine Books 371

Bantam Dell Publishing Group 372

Bantam Doubleday Dell Books for Young ReadersBantam Doubeday Dell Bks for Yng Rdrs 372

Ben Bella Books 374

BL Publishing 375

Carnifex Press 379

Circlet Press, Inc. 380

Clarion Books 381

Coteau Books 382

Dan River Press 383

DAW Books, Inc. 384

Del Rey Books 385

Dial Books For Young Readers 385

Dragon Moon Press 386

Edge Science Fiction and Fantasy Publishing 387

Ellora's Cave Publishing, Inc. 388

Fort Ross Inc. Russian-American
  Publishing Projects 391
Geringer Books, Laura 392
Greenwillow Books 394
HarperCollins Children's Books 397
Holt & Co. Books for Young Readers,
  Henry 399
Images SI, Inc. 401
ImaJinn Books 401
Komenar Publishing 405
Last Knight Publishing Company
  406
Little, Brown and Co. Books for
  Young Readers 408
McElderry Books, Margaret
  K.McElderry, Margaret 411
Medallion Press, Inc. 411
Moody Publishers 415
New Victoria Publishers 416
Oak Tree Press 417
Port Town Publishing 426
Random House Trade Publishing
  Group 428
Ravenhawk Books 429
Silhouette Nocturne 434
Silver Leaf Books, LLC 435
Small Beer Press 435
Spectra Books 436
St. Martin's Press 437
SynergEbooks 439
Timberwolf Press, Inc. 440
Triumvirate Publications 442
Twilight Times Books 442
Tyrannosaurus Press 442
Warner Books 445
Willowgate Press 445
WindRiver Publishing, Inc. 446
Wizards of the Coast 446

FEMINIST

Magazines

Advocate, PKA'S Publication 347
African American Review 224
Allegheny Review, The 225
American Feed Magazine 327
Anti Muse 328
Apalachee Review 227
Art Times 348
Ascent Aspirations 328
Big Muddy: A Journal of the
  Mississippi River Valley 231
Briar Cliff Review, The 234
Bryant Literary Review 235
cc&d, Children, Churches & Daddies
  magazine: The Unreligious,
  NONfamily-oriented literary and
  art magazine 237
Convergence 331
Crucible 242
Down in the Dirt 311
Eureka Literary Magazine 245
Feminist Studies 246
Foliate Oak Literary Magazine 248
Furnace Review, The 335
Gertrude 250
Global City Review 251
Green Hills Literary Lantern, The
  335
Happy 254
Hawai'i Pacific Review 255
Home Planet News 256
Illya's Honey 258
Iris 259
Irreantum 312
Jabberwock Review, The 259
Karamu 260
Kenyon Review, The 260
Lady Churchill's Rosebud Wristlet
  314
Long Story, The 264
Minnesota Review, The 268
Mobius 269
North Central Review, YOUR
  Undergraduate Literary Journal
  272
North Dakota Quarterly 273
Northwest Review 273
Obsidian III 274
Ohio Teachers Write 274
Open Wide Magazine 275
Pacific Coast Journal 276

Painted Bride Quarterly 277
Palo Alto Review 277
Paperplates 338
Pikeville Review 280
Pleiades 281
Rainbow Curve 286
River Styx 289
R-KV-R-Y 339
Roanoke Review 289
So to Speak 293
Southern Humanities Review 294
Struggle 297
Sulphur River Literary Review 298
Tabard Inn, Tales of Questionable
    Taste 320
Talking River Review 298
Timber Creek Review 322
Toasted Cheese 343
Transcendent Visions 322
Virginia Quarterly Review 323
Weber Studies 323
Wild Violet 344
Yemassee 304

Book Publishers
Aunt Lute Books 370
Ballantine Books 371
Bancroft Press 372
Calyx Books 378
Coteau Books 382
Doubleday 385
Empyreal Press 388
FC2 390
Feminist Press at the City University
    of New York, The 390
Gertrude Press 392
Ingalls Publishing Group, Inc. 401
Little, Brown and Co. Books for
    Young Readers 408
New Victoria Publishers 416
Oak Tree Press 417
Pedlar Press 421
Pipers' Ash, Ltd. 424
Red Hen Press 430
Seal Press 433
Soho Press, Inc. 436

Third World Press 439
Tindal Street Press, Ltd. 440

GAY
Magazines
Adirondack Review, The 326
Allegheny Review, The 225
Anti Muse 328
Art Times 348
Big Country Peacock Chronicle 330
cc&d, Children, Churches & Daddies
    magazine: The Unreligious,
    NONfamily-oriented literary and
    art magazine 237
Cezanne's Carrot 331
Convergence 331
Down in the Dirt 311
Feminist Studies 246
First Line 311
Flint Hills Review 247
Fluent Ascension 335
Foliate Oak Literary Magazine 248
Furnace Review, The 335
Gargoyle 249
Gertrude 250
Global City Review 251
Happy 254
Home Planet News 256
Illya's Honey 258
Jabberwock Review, The 259
Karamu 260
Kenyon Review, The 260
Minnesota Review, The 268
Mobius 269
North Central Review, YOUR
    Undergraduate Literary Journal
    272
Ohio Teachers Write 274
Open Wide Magazine 275
Painted Bride Quarterly 277
Paperplates 338
Pleiades 281
Quarter After Eight 285
Rainbow Curve 286
River Styx 289

R-KV-R-Y 339
Roanoke Review 289
Straylight 296
Tabard Inn, Tales of Questionable
   Taste 320
Toasted Cheese 343
Transcendent Visions 322
Wild Violet 344
Yemassee 304

Book Publishers
Arsenal Pulp Press 369
Ballantine Books 371
Bancroft Press 372
Calyx Books 378
Coteau Books 382
Doubleday 385
Ellora's Cave Publishing, Inc. 388
Empyreal Press 388
FC2 390
Gertrude Press 392
Gival Press 392
Insomniac Press 401
Kensington Publishing Corp. 404
Little, Brown and Co. Books for
   Young Readers 408
Monsoon Books 414
Palari Publishing 418
Pedlar Press 421
Plume 425
Red Hen Press 430
Seal Press 433
Starcherone Books 438
Stone Bridge Press 438
Torquere Press 441

GLITZ
Magazines
American Feed Magazine 327
North Central Review, YOUR
   Undergraduate Literary Journal
   272

Book Publishers
Bancroft Press 372
Medallion Press, Inc. 411

HISTORICAL
Magazines
Adirondack Review, The 326
Advocate, PKA'S Publication 347
Aim Magazine 347
Allegheny Review, The 225
American Feed Magazine 327
Ancient Paths 226
Anti Muse 328
Apalachee Review 227
Armchair Aesthete, The 228
Art Times 348
Barbaric Yawp 229
Bear Deluxe Magazine, The 349
Big Country Peacock Chronicle 330
Big Muddy: A Journal of the
   Mississippi River Valley 231
Briar Cliff Review, The 234
Broken Pencil 235
Bryant Literary Review 235
Buffalo Carp 235
Caribbean Writer, The 237
cc&d, Children, Churches & Daddies
   magazine: The Unreligious,
   NONfamily-oriented literary and
   art magazine 237
Chaffin Journal 237
Chapman 238
Chrysalis Reader 239
Copperfield Review, The 332
Country Connection, The 310
Cricket 352
Dan River Anthology 310
Down in the Dirt 311
Downstate Story 243
Ecotone, Reimagining Place 244
Eureka Literary Magazine 245
Fifty Something Magazine 353
Flint Hills Review 247
Foliate Oak Literary Magazine 248
Furnace Review, The 335
Harpur Palate 254
Hawai'i Pacific Review 255
Highlights for Children 354
Home Planet News 256

Illya's Honey 258
Irreantum 312
Karamu 260
Kentucky Monthly 355
Kenyon Review, The 260
London Magazine, The 314
Louisiana Review, The 265
MacGuffin, The 266
Minnesota Review, The 268
Mobius 269
Na'Amat Woman 358
Nassau Review 269
New Orphic Review, The 271
newWitch 358
North Central Review, YOUR
    Undergraduate Literary Journal
    272
North Dakota Quarterly 273
Ohio Teachers Write 274
108, Celebrating Baseball 359
Oracle Story & Letters 316
Pacific Coast Journal 276
Pakn Treger 359
Palo Alto Review 277
Paradox 277
Paumanok Review, The 339
Pockets 360
Portland Monthly 360
Portland Review 283
Purpose 318
Queen's Quarterly 319
Rejected Quarterly, The 288
Rose & Thorn Literary E-Zine, The
    340
RPPS/Fullosia Press 341
Saranac Review, The 291
Short Stuff 292
Silent Voices 319
Soleado 320
Spider 361
Stand Magazine 295
Stone Soup 296
Storyteller, The 320
Struggle 297
Sword Review, The 343

Tabard Inn, Tales of Questionable
    Taste 320
Talking River Review 298
Tampa Review 299
Thema 300
Timber Creek Review 322
Toasted Cheese 343
Transition 301
Virginia Quarterly Review 323
Washington Running Report 363
Weber Studies 323
William and Mary Review, The 302
Windhover 304
Writers' Forum 363
Xavier Review 304
Yemassee 304

Book Publishers

Academy Chicago Publishers 368
Avalon Books 370
Ballantine Books 371
Bancroft Press 372
Bantam Doubleday Dell Books for
    Young ReadersBantam Doubeday
    Dell Bks for Yng Rdrs 372
Barbour Publishing, Inc. 373
Barking Dog Books 373
Beil, Publisher, Inc., Frederic C. 374
Berkley Publishing Group, The 374
Bethany House Publishers 374
Borealis Press, Ltd. 376
Branden Publishing Co., Inc. 377
Carolrhoda Books, Inc. 379
Cave Books 380
Clarion Books 381
Coteau Books 382
Covenant Communications, Inc. 382
Crossway Books 383
Dan River Press 383
Doubleday 385
Dutton 386
Ellora's Cave Publishing, Inc. 388
Empire Publishing Service 388
Forge and Tor Books 391
Front Street 391
Geringer Books, Laura 392

Gival Press 392
Glencannon Press, The 393
Harbor House 395
Harlequin Historicals 396
HarperCollins Children's Books 397
Holiday House, Inc. 399
Holt & Co. Books for Young Readers, Henry 399
Houghton Mifflin Books for Children 399
Howells House 400
Ingalls Publishing Group, Inc. 401
Ivy Publications 403
JourneyForth 403
Kensington Publishing Corp. 404
Komenar Publishing 405
Kregel Publications 405
Lifetime Books 407
Little, Brown and Co. Books for Young Readers 408
MacAdam/Cage Publishing, Inc. 410
McBooks Press 411
McElderry Books, Margaret K.McElderry, Margaret 411
Medallion Press, Inc. 411
Milkweed for Young Readers 413
Mira Books 414
Monsoon Books 414
Moody Publishers 415
Mould Publishing, Paul 415
Mountain State Press 415
New Victoria Publishers 416
Palari Publishing 418
Pelican Publishing Co. 421
Piatkus Books 423
Pineapple Press, Inc. 423
Pipers' Ash, Ltd. 424
Pippin Press 424
Plume 425
Port Town Publishing 426
Pureplay Press 427
Random House Trade Publishing Group 428
Red Hen Press 430
River City Publishing 430

Science & Humanities Press 432
Soho Press, Inc. 436
St. Martin's Press 437
SynergEbooks 439
TCU Press 439
Third World Press 439
Triumvirate Publications 442
Twilight Times Books 442
Willowgate Press 445
Wind River Press 446
WindRiver Publishing, Inc. 446

HORROR

Magazines

Aguilar Expression, The 224
Albedo One 307
AlienSkin Magazine 326
Allegheny Review, The 225
Allegory 327
American Feed Magazine 327
Anti Muse 328
Apex Science Fiction and Horror Digest 308
Armchair Aesthete, The 228
Ascent Aspirations 328
Barbaric Yawp 229
Bear Deluxe Magazine, The 349
Big Country Peacock Chronicle 330
Broken Pencil 235
Brutarian 309
Buffalo Carp 235
cc&d, Children, Churches & Daddies magazine: The Unreligious, NONfamily-oriented literary and art magazine 237
Dan River Anthology 310
deathlings.com 333
Down in the Dirt 311
Downstate Story 243
Gud Magazine 253
Happy 254
Harpur Palate 254
Irreantum 312
Lone Star Stories, Speculative Fiction and Poetry 336

Magazine of Fantasy & Science Fiction, The 356
Metal Scratches 267
Midnight Times 336
Mobius 269
newWitch 358
Nocturnal Lyric, The 314
Nocturnal Ooze 337
North Central Review, YOUR Undergraduate Literary Journal 272
On Spec 316
108, Celebrating Baseball 359
Open Wide Magazine 275
Outer Darkness 317
Paradox 277
Paumanok Review, The 339
Postscripts: The A to Z of Fantastic Fiction 283
Rose & Thorn Literary E-Zine, The 340
Silent Voices 319
Strand Magazine, The 363
Sword Review, The 343
Tabard Inn, Tales of Questionable Taste 320
Tales of the Talisman 321
Toasted Cheese 343
Trail of Indiscretion 322
Weird Tales 323
Wild Violet 344
William and Mary Review, The 302
Writers' Forum 363

Book Publishers
Bantam Dell Publishing Group 372
BL Publishing 375
Carnifex Press 379
Dan River Press 383
Ellora's Cave Publishing, Inc. 388
Forge and Tor Books 391
Fort Ross Inc. Russian-American Publishing Projects 391
Gothic Chapbook Series 393
Harbor House 395
ignotus Press 400
ImaJinn Books 401
Kensington Publishing Corp. 404
Leisure Books 407
Medallion Press, Inc. 411
Monsoon Books 414
Pocol Press 425
Port Town Publishing 426
Random House Trade Publishing Group 428
Ravenhawk Books 429
Silver Leaf Books, LLC 435
St. Martin's Press 437
SynergEbooks 439
Triumvirate Publications 442
Warner Books 445
Willowgate Press 445

HUMOR/SATIRE
Magazines

Advocate, PKA'S Publication 347
Allegheny Review, The 225
American Feed Magazine 327
Ancient Paths 226
Anti Muse 328
Apalachee Review 227
Apple Valley Review, A Journal of Contemporary Literature 328
Armchair Aesthete, The 228
Art Times 348
Backroads 349
Bathtub Gin 229
Bear Deluxe Magazine, The 349
Bellingham Review 230
Big Country Peacock Chronicle 330
Big Muddy: A Journal of the Mississippi River Valley 231
Binnacle, The 308
Blueline 233
Briar Cliff Review, The 234
Broken Pencil 235
Brutarian 309
Bryant Literary Review 235
Buffalo Carp 235
Burst 330
Caribbean Writer, The 237

Center 237
Cezanne's Carrot 331
Chaffin Journal 237
Chapman 238
Clubhouse Magazine 351
Country Connection, The 310
Creative With Words Publications 310
Cricket 352
Dan River Anthology 310
Dana Literary Society Online Journal 332
Downstate Story 243
Dreams & Visions 311
Eureka Literary Magazine 245
Fiction 246
Fifty Something Magazine 353
First Line 311
Fluent Ascension 335
Foliate Oak Literary Magazine 248
Funny Paper, The 312
Furnace Review, The 335
Gertrude 250
Green Hills Literary Lantern, The 335
Green Mountains Review 252
Gud Magazine 253
Happy 254
Harpur Palate 254
Hawai'i Pacific Review 255
Hayden's Ferry Review 255
Heartlands Today, The 255
Highlights for Children 354
Iconoclast 256
Idiot, The 257
Illya's Honey 258
Inkwell Magazine 259
Irreantum 312
Isotope 259
Karamu 260
Kenyon Review, The 260
Krax Magazine 313
London Magazine, The 314
MacGuffin, The 266
Maisonneuve 357
Mature Years 357

Missouri Review, The 269
Mobius 269
Na'Amat Woman 358
Nassau Review 269
New Delta Review 270
New Letters 270
New Works Review 336
newWitch 358
North Central Review, YOUR Undergraduate Literary Journal 272
North Dakota Quarterly 273
Nuthouse 315
Oak, The 315
Ohio Teachers Write 274
108, Celebrating Baseball 359
Open Wide Magazine 275
Opium Magazine 337
Outlooks 359
Pacific Coast Journal 276
Pakn Treger 359
Palo Alto Review 277
Pearl 279
Pegasus Review, The 318
Pikeville Review 280
Pink Chameleon, The 339
Playboy Magazine 359
Pleiades 281
Portland Review 283
Purpose 318
Quarter After Eight 285
Quarterly West 285
Rejected Quarterly, The 288
Riverwind 289
Roanoke Review 289
Rockford Review, The 290
Rose & Thorn Literary E-Zine, The 340
Short Stuff 292
Silent Voices 319
Slate & Style 319
Socket Shocker Magazine 319
Soleado 320
Southern Humanities Review 294
Spider 361
Stone Soup 296

Storyteller, The 320
Strand Magazine, The 363
Struggle 297
Sulphur River Literary Review 298
Summerset Review, The 342
Sycamore Review 298
Tabard Inn, Tales of Questionable
    Taste 320
Talebones 321
Talking River Review 298
Texas Review, The 299
Thema 300
Thirteenth Warrior Review, The 343
Tickled by Thunder 301
Timber Creek Review 322
Toasted Cheese 343
Trail of Indiscretion 322
Transcendent Visions 322
Transition 301
Virginia Quarterly Review 323
Washington Running Report 363
Weber Studies 323
Wild Violet 344
William and Mary Review, The 302
Windhover 304
Workers Write! 304
Yemassee 304
ZYZZYVA 305

Book Publishers

Acme Press 368
Ageless Press 368
Ballantine Books 371
Bancroft Press 372
Bantam Doubleday Dell Books for
    Young ReadersBantam Doubeday
    Dell Bks for Yng Rdrs 372
Barking Dog Books 373
Black Heron Press 375
Bridge Works Publishing Co. 377
Clarion Books 381
Coteau Books 382
Covenant Communications, Inc. 382
Dan River Press 383
Davenport, Publishers, May 384
Doubleday 385
Front Street 391
Geringer Books, Laura 392
Gertrude Press 392
Glencannon Press, The 393
Greenwillow Books 394
HarperCollins Children's Books 397
Holiday House, Inc. 399
Houghton Mifflin Books for Children
    399
ignotus Press 400
Insomniac Press 401
Ivy Publications 403
Komenar Publishing 405
Little, Brown and Co. Books for
    Young Readers 408
Luath Press Ltd. 410
Medallion Press, Inc. 411
Meriwether Publishing, Ltd. 412
Milkweed for Young Readers 413
Monsoon Books 414
New Victoria Publishers 416
Oak Tree Press 417
Panther Creek Press 419
Pedlar Press 421
Pippin Press 424
Quixote Press 427
Random House Trade Publishing
    Group 428
Ravenhawk Books 429
Red Dress Ink 430
Science & Humanities Press 432
SynergEbooks 439
Willowgate Press 445
WindRiver Publishing, Inc. 446

LESBIAN

Magazines

Allegheny Review, The 225
Anti Muse 328
Art Times 348
Black Lace 308
cc&d, Children, Churches & Daddies
    magazine: The Unreligious,
    NONfamily-oriented literary and
    art magazine 237

Cezanne's Carrot 331
Convergence 331
Down in the Dirt 311
Feminist Studies 246
First Line 311
Fluent Ascension 335
Foliate Oak Literary Magazine 248
Furnace Review, The 335
Gargoyle 249
Gertrude 250
Global City Review 251
Happy 254
Home Planet News 256
Illya's Honey 258
Iris 259
Karamu 260
Kenyon Review, The 260
Minnesota Review, The 268
Mobius 269
North Central Review, YOUR
    Undergraduate Literary Journal
    272
Ohio Teachers Write 274
Open Wide Magazine 275
Painted Bride Quarterly 277
Paperplates 338
Quarter After Eight 285
Rainbow Curve 286
River Styx 289
R-KV-R-Y 339
Roanoke Review 289
So to Speak 293
Straylight 296
Tabard Inn, Tales of Questionable
    Taste 320
Toasted Cheese 343
Transcendent Visions 322
Wild Violet 344
Yemassee 304

Book Publishers
Aunt Lute Books 370
Bancroft Press 372
Calyx Books 378
Ellora's Cave Publishing, Inc. 388
FC2 390

Gertrude Press 392
Gival Press 392
New Victoria Publishers 416
Torquere Press 441

LITERARY
Magazines

Abiko Annual With James Joyce,
    The 307
Advocate, PKA'S Publication 347
African American Review 224
Agni 224
Alaska Quarterly Review 224
Albedo One 307
Alimentum, The Literature of food
    225
Allegheny Review, The 225
Alsop Review, The 327
American Feed Magazine 327
American Literary Review 226
Ancient Paths 226
Anti Muse 328
Antigonish Review, The 227
Apalachee Review 227
Apple Valley Review, A Journal of
    Contemporary Literature 328
Arkansas Review 227
Art Times 348
Ascent Aspirations 328
Ballyhoo Stories 228
Baltimore Review, The 229
Barbaric Yawp 229
Bathtub Gin 229
Beginnings Publishing Inc. 230
Bellevue Literary Review 230
Bellingham Review 230
Bellowing Ark 231
Beloit Fiction Journal 231
Big Country Peacock Chronicle 330
Big Muddy: A Journal of the
    Mississippi River Valley 231
Black Warrior Review 232
Blueline 233
Boston Review 350
Boulevard 233

Briar Cliff Review, The 234
Brillant Corners 234
Broken Bridge Review 234
Bryant Literary Review 235
Buffalo Carp 235
Button 236
Byline 236
Caribbean Writer, The 237
cc&d, Children, Churches & Daddies
    magazine: The Unreligious,
    NONfamily-oriented literary and
    art magazine 237
Center 237
Cezanne's Carrot 331
Chaffin Journal 237
Chapman 238
Chariton Review, The 238
Chicago Quarterly Review 239
Chicago Review 239
Chrysalis Reader 239
Cincinnati Review, The 240
Coal City Review 240
Colorado Review 240
Confrontation 241
Connecticut Review 241
Convergence 331
Cream City Review, The 242
Crucible 242
Dan River Anthology 310
descant 243
Diagram 333
Dislocate 243
DotLit 333
Down in the Dirt 311
Downstate Story 243
Dreams & Visions 311
Eclipse 243
Ecotone, Reimagining Place 244
Emrys Journal 244
Epoch 244
Eureka Literary Magazine 245
Failbetter.com 334
Fairfield Review, The 334
Faultline 245
Fiction 246
First Class 246

First Line 311
Five-Trope 334
Florida Review 247
Fluent Ascension 335
Flyway 247
Foliate Oak Literary Magazine 248
Front & Centre 249
Funny Paper, The 312
Furnace Review, The 335
Gargoyle 249
Georgetown Review 250
Gertrude 250
Ginosko 251
Glimmer Train Stories 251
Global City Review 251
Grain Literary Magazine 251
Granta 252
Green Hills Literary Lantern, The
    335
Green Mountains Review 252
GSU Review 253
Gud Magazine 253
Gulf Coast 253
Gulf Stream Magazine 253
Happy 254
Harvard Review 254
Hawai'i Pacific Review 255
Hayden's Ferry Review 255
Heartlands Today, The 255
Home Planet News 256
Iconoclast 256
Idaho Review, The 257
Illuminations 257
Illya's Honey 258
Image 258
Indiana Review 258
Inkwell Magazine 259
Iris 259
Irreantum 312
Isotope 259
Italian Americana 313
Jabberwock Review, The 259
Journal, The 260
Karamu 260
Kenyon Review, The 260
Kit-Cat Review, The 261

Lady Churchill's Rosebud Wristlet 314
Lake Effect 262
Laurel Review, The 262
Ledge Magazine, The 263
Listening Eye, The 263
Literal Latté 263
Literary Review, The 264
Long Story, The 264
Louisiana Literature 264
Louisville Review, The 265
Lunch Hour Stories 265
Lutheran Journal, The 356
MacGuffin, The 266
Madison Review, The 266
Manoa 267
Metal Scratches 267
Michigan Quarterly Review 267
Mid-American Review 267
Midnight Times 336
Mindprints 268
Minnesota Review, The 268
Missouri Review, The 269
Mobius 269
Na'Amat Woman 358
Nassau Review 269
Nerve Cowboy 270
New Delta Review 270
New Letters 270
New Madrid 271
New Orphic Review, The 271
New Works Review 336
North Central Review, YOUR Undergraduate Literary Journal 272
North Dakota Quarterly 273
Northwest Review 273
Northwoods Journal 273
Obsidian III 274
Ohio Teachers Write 274
One-Story 275
Open Wide Magazine 275
Opium Magazine 337
Oracle Story & Letters 316
Oracular Tree, The 338
Other Voices 275

Outer Art 338
Oyez Review 276
Pacific Coast Journal 276
Painted Bride Quarterly 277
Palo Alto Review 277
Paperplates 338
Paradoxism 317
Paris Review, The 278
Passages North 278
Paterson Literary Review 279
Paumanok Review, The 339
Pearl 279
Pegasus Review, The 318
Pennsylvania English 279
Phantasmagoria 280
Pikeville Review 280
Pindeldyboz 281
Pink Chameleon, The 339
Pinyon 281
Pisgah Review 281
Pleiades 281
Pointed Circle 282
Polyphony H.S. 282
Porcupine Literary Arts Magazine 282
Portland Monthly 360
Post Road 283
Prairie Journal, The 284
Prism International 284
Puerto Del Sol 285
Quarter After Eight 285
Quarterly West 285
Queen's Quarterly 319
Rainbow Curve 286
Rambler, The 286
Rattapallax 287
Raven Chronicles, The 287
Red Rock Review 287
Redivider 288
Reflections Literary Journal 288
Rejected Quarterly, The 288
River Styx 289
Riverwind 289
R-KV-R-Y 339
Roanoke Review 289

Rock & Sling: A Journal of Literature, Art and Faith 290
Rockford Review, The 290
Rose & Thorn Literary E-Zine, The 340
Santa Monica Review 291
Saranac Review, The 291
Seattle Review, The 291
Sewanee Review, The 291
Sleepingfish 292
Slow Trains Literary Journal 341
Snreview 341
So to Speak 293
Sonora Review 293
South Carolina Review 293
Southern Review, The 294
Southwest Review 294
Southwestern American Literature 295
Steel City Review: A Pittsburgh-based magazine of Short Fiction 341
Storie 296
storySouth 342
Storyteller, The 320
Straylight 296
Struggle 297
subTERRAIN 297
Sulphur River Literary Review 298
Summerset Review, The 342
Sun, The 298
Sword Review, The 343
Sycamore Review 298
Tabard Inn, Tales of Questionable Taste 320
Talking River Review 298
Tampa Review 299
Taproot Literary Review 299
Texas Review, The 299
The Reader 300
Thema 300
Third Coast 301
Thirteenth Warrior Review, The 343
Tickled by Thunder 301
Timber Creek Review 322
Toasted Cheese 343

Transition 301
Verbsap.com, Concise Prose. Enough Said. 344
Versal 302
Virginia Quarterly Review 323
Weber Studies 323
Wild Violet 344
William and Mary Review, The 302
Willow Springs 303
Windhover 304
Workers Write! 304
Writers' Forum 363
Xavier Review 304
Yemassee 304
Zahir 324

Book Publishers

Ageless Press 368
Algonquin Books of Chapel Hill 369
Anvil Press 369
Arcade Publishing 369
Arsenal Pulp Press 369
Arte Publico Press 370
Baker Books 371
Ballantine Books 371
Bancroft Press 372
Barking Dog Books 373
Beil, Publisher, Inc., Frederic C. 374
Berkley Publishing Group, The 374
Birch Brook Press 374
BkMk Press 375
Black Heron Press 375
Bleak House Books 376
Books for All Times, Inc. 376
Borealis Press, Ltd. 376
Branden Publishing Co., Inc. 377
Bridge Works Publishing Co. 377
Broadway Books 378
Calamari Press 378
Calyx Books 378
Cave Books 380
Christchurch Publishers Ltd. 380
Chronicle Books 380
City Lights Books 381
Coffee House Press 381
Coteau Books 382

Covenant Communications, Inc. 382
Crossway Books 383
Dan River Press 383
Daniel and Co., John 384
Davenport, Publishers, May 384
Dial Press 385
Doubleday 385
Dutton 386
ECW Press 387
Empyreal Press 388
Eros Books 389
Farrar, Straus & Giroux 389
Farrar, Straus & Giroux Paperbacks 390
Feminist Press at the City University of New York, The 390
Front Street 391
Geringer Books, Laura 392
Gertrude Press 392
Gival Press 392
Goose Lane Editions 393
Graywolf Press 394
Greenwillow Books 394
Grove/Atlantic, Inc. 394
HarperCollins Children's Books 397
Holiday House, Inc. 399
Houghton Mifflin Books for Children 399
Houghton Mifflin Co. 400
Howells House 400
Insomniac Press 401
Knopf, Alfred A. 405
Komenar Publishing 405
Little, Brown and Co. Adult Trade Books 408
Livingston Press 408
Lost Horse Press 409
Low Fidelity Press 409
Luath Press Ltd. 410
MacAdam/Cage Publishing, Inc. 410
MaCrae Books, John 410
Mariner Books 411
Medallion Press, Inc. 411
Milkweed Editions 412
Monsoon Books 414

NeWest Publishers Ltd. 417
Norton Co., Inc., W.W. 417
Orca Book Publishers 418
Other Press 418
Palari Publishing 418
Panther Creek Press 419
Pathwise Press 420
Paycock Press 420
Pedlar Press 421
Permanent Press/Second Chance Press, The 422
Piatkus Books 423
Picador USA 423
Pineapple Press, Inc. 423
Pipers' Ash, Ltd. 424
Plume 425
Pocol Press 425
Post-Apollo Press, The 426
Prairie Journal Press 426
Pureplay Press 427
Putnam's Sons, G.P. 427
Rager Media 427
Ravenhawk Books 429
Red Dress Ink 430
Red Hen Press 430
River City Publishing 430
Riverhead Books 431
Ronsdale Press 431
Salvo Press 431
Sarabande Books, Inc. 431
Science & Humanities Press 432
Seal Press 433
Seven Stories Press 433
Small Beer Press 435
Soho Press, Inc. 436
Southern Methodist University Press 436
Spectra Books 436
Spice 437
Spire Press 437
Spout Press 437
St. Martin's Press 437
Starcherone Books 438
Stone Bridge Press 438
Talese, Nan A. 439
Third World Press 439

Tin House Books 440
Tindal Street Press, Ltd. 440
Titan Press 441
Twilight Times Books 442
Unbridled Books 443
University of Michigan Press 443
University Press of New England 443
Véhicule Press 443
Vintage Anchor Publishing 444
Willowgate Press 445
Wind River Press 446
WindRiver Publishing, Inc. 446
Woodley Memorial Press 446
Yellow Shoe Fiction Series 447

MAINSTREAM/ CONTEMPORARY

Magazines

Advocate, PKA'S Publication 347
African American Review 224
Aguilar Expression, The 224
Aim Magazine 347
Allegheny Review, The 225
American Feed Magazine 327
American Literary Review 226
Ancient Paths 226
Anti Muse 328
Any Dream Will Do Review 308
Apalachee Review 227
Apple Valley Review, A Journal of Contemporary Literature 328
Armchair Aesthete, The 228
Art Times 348
Ascent Aspirations 328
Baltimore Review, The 229
Barbaric Yawp 229
Beginnings Publishing Inc. 230
Bellowing Ark 231
Beloit Fiction Journal 231
Big Muddy: A Journal of the Mississippi River Valley 231
Binnacle, The 308
Briar Cliff Review, The 234
Brillant Corners 234
Broken Bridge Review 234
Bryant Literary Review 235
Buffalo Carp 235
Burst 330
Caribbean Writer, The 237
Cezanne's Carrot 331
Chaffin Journal 237
Chariton Review, The 238
Chrysalis Reader 239
Colorado Review 240
Confrontation 241
Dan River Anthology 310
DisciplesWorld 352
Downstate Story 243
Dreams & Visions 311
Ecotone, Reimagining Place 244
Epoch 244
Eureka Literary Magazine 245
Fifty Something Magazine 353
First Line 311
Foliate Oak Literary Magazine 248
Furnace Review, The 335
Gargoyle 249
Gertrude 250
Ginosko 251
Grain Literary Magazine 251
Green Hills Literary Lantern, The 335
Green Mountains Review 252
Gulf Stream Magazine 253
Harpur Palate 254
Hawai'i Pacific Review 255
Heartlands Today, The 255
Home Planet News 256
Iconoclast 256
Illya's Honey 258
Indiana Review 258
Iris 259
Irreantum 312
Jabberwock Review, The 259
Karamu 260
Kentucky Monthly 355
Kenyon Review, The 260
Lake Effect 262
London Magazine, The 314
Louisiana Literature 264

Lunch Hour Stories 265
MacGuffin, The 266
Manoa 267
Midnight Times 336
Mindprints 268
Missouri Review, The 269
Mobius 269
Nassau Review 269
New Delta Review 270
New Letters 270
New Orphic Review, The 271
New Works Review 336
newWitch 358
North Central Review, YOUR
    Undergraduate Literary Journal
    272
Northwoods Journal 273
Oak, The 315
Ohio Teachers Write 274
108, Celebrating Baseball 359
Open Wide Magazine 275
Opium Magazine 337
Oracle Story & Letters 316
Palo Alto Review 277
Paperplates 338
Passages North 278
Paumanok Review, The 339
Pearl 279
Pennsylvania English 279
Phantasmagoria 280
Pikeville Review 280
Pink Chameleon, The 339
Pisgah Review 281
Playboy Magazine 359
Pleiades 281
Porcupine Literary Arts Magazine
    282
Puerto Del Sol 285
Quarter After Eight 285
Quarterly West 285
Queen's Quarterly 319
Red Rock Review 287
Rejected Quarterly, The 288
River Styx 289
Riverwind 289
Roanoke Review 289

Rose & Thorn Literary E-Zine, The
    340
Shenandoah 292
Short Stuff 292
Silent Voices 319
Snreview 341
So to Speak 293
Socket Shocker Magazine 319
Soleado 320
Sonora Review 293
South Carolina Review 293
Southwestern American Literature
    295
St. Anthony Messenger 362
St. Joseph's Messenger & Advocate
    of the Blind 362
Stand Magazine 295
Steel City Review: A Pittsburgh-
    based magazine of Short Fiction
    341
Storyteller, The 320
Straylight 296
Sulphur River Literary Review 298
Sword Review, The 343
Sycamore Review 298
Tabard Inn, Tales of Questionable
    Taste 320
Talking River Review 298
Tampa Review 299
Tea, A Magazine 321
Texas Review, The 299
Thema 300
Thirteenth Warrior Review, The 343
Tickled by Thunder 301
Timber Creek Review 322
Toasted Cheese 343
Verbsap.com, Concise Prose.
    Enough Said. 344
Virginia Quarterly Review 323
Washington Running Report 363
Weber Studies 323
William and Mary Review, The 302
Workers Write! 304
Writers' Forum 363
Xavier Review 304
ZYZZYVA 305

Book Publishers

Absey & Co. 368
Academy Chicago Publishers 368
Ageless Press 368
Arcade Publishing 369
Arte Publico Press 370
Baker Books 371
Ballantine Books 371
Bancroft Press 372
Bantam Doubleday Dell Books for Young ReadersBantam Doubeday Dell Bks for Yng Rdrs 372
Barbour Publishing, Inc. 373
Black Heron Press 375
Books for All Times, Inc. 376
Borealis Press, Ltd. 376
Calyx Books 378
Chronicle Books for Children 380
Coffee House Press 381
Coteau Books 382
Covenant Communications, Inc. 382
Dan River Press 383
Doubleday 385
Dutton 386
Ellora's Cave Publishing, Inc. 388
Eros Books 389
Forge and Tor Books 391
Fort Ross Inc. Russian-American Publishing Projects 391
Gertrude Press 392
Glencannon Press, The 393
Goose Lane Editions 393
Harbor House 395
HarperTorch 397
Holiday House, Inc. 399
Holt & Co. Books for Young Readers, Henry 399
Howells House 400
Insomniac Press 401
Kensington Publishing Corp. 404
Komenar Publishing 405
Little, Brown and Co. Adult Trade Books 408
MacAdam/Cage Publishing, Inc. 410
MaCrae Books, John 410

Mariner Books 411
McElderry Books, Margaret K.McElderry, Margaret 411
Medallion Press, Inc. 411
Meriwether Publishing, Ltd. 412
Mid-List Press 412
Milkweed for Young Readers 413
Mira Books 414
Monsoon Books 414
Oak Tree Press 417
Orca Book Publishers 418
Palari Publishing 418
Panther Creek Press 419
Permanent Press/Second Chance Press, The 422
Piatkus Books 423
Pineapple Press, Inc. 423
Pipers' Ash, Ltd. 424
Plume 425
Pocol Press 425
Port Town Publishing 426
Putnam's Sons, G.P. 427
Random House Trade Publishing Group 428
Ravenhawk Books 429
Red Dress Ink 430
Red Hen Press 430
Riverhead Books 431
Science & Humanities Press 432
Soho Press, Inc. 436
St. Martin's Press 437
SynergEbooks 439
Third World Press 439
Tindal Street Press, Ltd. 440
Titan Press 441
Twilight Times Books 442
Villard Books 444
Vintage Anchor Publishing 444
Warner Books 445
Willowgate Press 445
Wind River Press 446
Woodley Memorial Press 446

MILITARY/WAR
Magazines

Allegheny Review, The 225
Anti Muse 328

Big Country Peacock Chronicle 330
Big Muddy: A Journal of the
    Mississippi River Valley 231
Bryant Literary Review 235
Furnace Review, The 335
New Works Review 336
North Central Review, YOUR
    Undergraduate Literary Journal
    272
Oracle Story & Letters 316
Paradox 277
RPPS/Fullosia Press 341
Tabard Inn, Tales of Questionable
    Taste 320
Weber Studies 323

Book Publishers

Academy Chicago Publishers 368
Ballantine Books 371
Bancroft Press 372
Branden Publishing Co., Inc. 377
Dan River Press 383
Glencannon Press, The 393
Harbor House 395
Ivy Publications 403
McBooks Press 411
Medallion Press, Inc. 411
Monsoon Books 414
Mountain State Press 415
Pipers' Ash, Ltd. 424
Pureplay Press 427
Science & Humanities Press 432
SynergEbooks 439
Timberwolf Press, Inc. 440
Triumvirate Publications 442
Twilight Times Books 442
Willowgate Press 445
WindRiver Publishing, Inc. 446

MYSTERY/SUSPENSE

Magazines

Advocate, PKA'S Publication 347
Aguilar Expression, The 224
Allegheny Review, The 225
American Feed Magazine 327
Apalachee Review 227
Armchair Aesthete, The 228
Ascent Aspirations 328
Bear Deluxe Magazine, The 349
Beginnings Publishing Inc. 230
Big Country Peacock Chronicle 330
Big Muddy: A Journal of the
    Mississippi River Valley 231
Broken Pencil 235
Brutarian 309
Bryant Literary Review 235
Buffalo Carp 235
Burst 330
cc&d, Children, Churches & Daddies
    magazine: The Unreligious,
    NONfamily-oriented literary and
    art magazine 237
Chrysalis Reader 239
Clubhouse Magazine 351
Creative With Words Publications
    310
Cricket 352
Down in the Dirt 311
Downstate Story 243
Dreams & Visions 311
Eureka Literary Magazine 245
Fifty Something Magazine 353
First Line 311
Hardboiled 312
Harpur Palate 254
Hitchcock's Mystery Magazine,
    Alfred 354
Irreantum 312
London Magazine, The 314
Nassau Review 269
New Works Review 336
newWitch 358
North Central Review, YOUR
    Undergraduate Literary Journal
    272
Northwoods Journal 273
108, Celebrating Baseball 359
Open Wide Magazine 275
Outer Darkness 317
Pakn Treger 359
Palo Alto Review 277

Paradox 277

Paumanok Review, The 339

Pink Chameleon, The 339

Playboy Magazine 359

Postscripts: The A to Z of Fantastic Fiction 283

PSI 318

Queens Mystery Magazine, Ellery 360

Rejected Quarterly, The 288

Rose & Thorn Literary E-Zine, The 340

RPPS/Fullosia Press 341

Short Stuff 292

Silent Voices 319

Soleado 320

Spider 361

St. Joseph's Messenger & Advocate of the Blind 362

Stone Soup 296

Storyteller, The 320

Strand Magazine, The 363

Sword Review, The 343

Tabard Inn, Tales of Questionable Taste 320

Thema 300

Tickled by Thunder 301

Timber Creek Review 322

Toasted Cheese 343

Virginia Quarterly Review 323

Washington Running Report 363

Weber Studies 323

Writers' Forum 363

Book Publishers

Academy Chicago Publishers 368

Ageless Press 368

Avalon Books 370

B & H Publishing 371

Baker Books 371

Ballantine Books 371

Bancroft Press 372

Bantam Doubleday Dell Books for Young ReadersBantam Doubeday Dell Bks for Yng Rdrs 372

Berkley Publishing Group, The 374

Bleak House Books 376

Bridge Works Publishing Co. 377

Clarion Books 381

Coteau Books 382

Covenant Communications, Inc. 382

CrossTIME 383

Dan River Press 383

Dutton 386

ECW Press 387

Ellora's Cave Publishing, Inc. 388

Empire Publishing Service 388

Forge and Tor Books 391

Fort Ross Inc. Russian-American Publishing Projects 391

Gaslight Publications 392

Glencannon Press, The 393

Greenwillow Books 394

Gryphon Books 394

Harlequin Intrigue 396

HarperTorch 397

Houghton Mifflin Books for Children 399

Ingalls Publishing Group, Inc. 401

Insomniac Press 401

Jireh Publishing Company 403

JourneyForth 403

Kensington Publishing Corp. 404

Komenar Publishing 405

Kregel Publications 405

Little, Brown and Co. Books for Young Readers 408

Llewellyn Publications 409

Luath Press Ltd. 410

McElderry Books, Margaret K.McElderry, Margaret 411

Medallion Press, Inc. 411

Monsoon Books 414

Moody Publishers 415

Mortalis 415

Mould Publishing, Paul 415

New Victoria Publishers 416

Oak Tree Press 417

Palari Publishing 418

Panther Creek Press 419

Permanent Press/Second Chance Press, The 422

Piatkus Books 423
Pippin Press 424
Poisoned Pen Press 425
Port Town Publishing 426
Pureplay Press 427
Putnam's Sons, G.P. 427
Random House Trade Publishing
    Group 428
Ravenhawk Books 429
Salvo Press 431
Science & Humanities Press 432
Silver Dagger Mysteries 434
Silver Leaf Books, LLC 435
Soho Press, Inc. 436
Spice 437
St. Martin's Press 437
Steeple Hill 438
SynergEbooks 439
Timberwolf Press, Inc. 440
Tindal Street Press, Ltd. 440
Triumvirate Publications 442
Twilight Times Books 442
Warner Books 445
Willowgate Press 445
WindRiver Publishing, Inc. 446

NEW AGE/MYSTIC/ SPIRITUAL

Magazines
Allegheny Review, The 225
American Feed Magazine 327
Anti Muse 328
Apalachee Review 227
Ascent Aspirations 328
Bryant Literary Review 235
cc&d, Children, Churches & Daddies
    magazine: The Unreligious,
    NONfamily-oriented literary and
    art magazine 237
Cezanne's Carrot 331
Down in the Dirt 311
Irreantum 312
North Central Review, YOUR
    Undergraduate Literary Journal
    272

Oracular Tree, The 338
Rose & Thorn Literary E-Zine, The
    340
Toasted Cheese 343
Weber Studies 323
Wild Violet 344

Book Publishers
Ageless Press 368
Bancroft Press 372
CrossTIME 383
Harbor House 395
ignotus Press 400
Mountain State Press 415
SynergEbooks 439
Twilight Times Books 442

PSYCHIC/ SUPERNATURAL/ OCCULT

Magazines
Allegheny Review, The 225
American Feed Magazine 327
Anti Muse 328
Any Dream Will Do Review 308
Ascent Aspirations 328
Barbaric Yawp 229
Big Country Peacock Chronicle 330
Bryant Literary Review 235
cc&d, Children, Churches & Daddies
    magazine: The Unreligious,
    NONfamily-oriented literary and
    art magazine 237
Cezanne's Carrot 331
Dan River Anthology 310
Down in the Dirt 311
Downstate Story 243
Eureka Literary Magazine 245
Happy 254
Irreantum 312
Magazine of Fantasy & Science
    Fiction, The 356
Midnight Times 336
Nocturnal Ooze 337

North Central Review, YOUR
    Undergraduate Literary Journal
    272
Northwoods Journal 273
Outer Darkness 317
Thema 300
Toasted Cheese 343
Trail of Indiscretion 322
Weber Studies 323
Weird Tales 323
Wild Violet 344
Zahir 324

Book Publishers
CrossTIME 383
Dan River Press 383
Harbor House 395
ignotus Press 400
ImaJinn Books 401
Llewellyn Publications 409
Ravenhawk Books 429
Silhouette Nocturne 434
Spice 437
Triumvirate Publications 442
Twilight Times Books 442

REGIONAL

Magazines
Advocate, PKA'S Publication 347
Anti Muse 328
Apple Valley Review, A Journal of
    Contemporary Literature 328
Arkansas Review 227
Barbaric Yawp 229
Bellingham Review 230
Big Country Peacock Chronicle 330
Big Muddy: A Journal of the
    Mississippi River Valley 231
Blueline 233
Boston Review 350
Briar Cliff Review, The 234
Broken Bridge Review 234
Bryant Literary Review 235
Chaffin Journal 237
Confrontation 241

Convergence 331
Cream City Review, The 242
Creative With Words Publications
    310
Crucible 242
Dan River Anthology 310
Downstate Story 243
Eureka Literary Magazine 245
First Line 311
Flint Hills Review 247
Green Hills Literary Lantern, The
    335
Gulf Coast 253
Hawai'i Pacific Review 255
Hayden's Ferry Review 255
Heartlands Today, The 255
Heaven Bone 256
Illya's Honey 258
Indiana Review 258
Irreantum 312
Jabberwock Review, The 259
Karamu 260
Kelsey Review 313
Louisiana Literature 264
Louisiana Review, The 265
North Carolina Literary Review 272
North Central Review, YOUR
    Undergraduate Literary Journal
    272
Northwoods Journal 273
Ohio Teachers Write 274
Palo Alto Review 277
Passages North 278
Pikeville Review 280
Pleiades 281
Pointed Circle 282
Portland Review 283
Prairie Journal, The 284
Raven Chronicles, The 287
Riverwind 289
Roanoke Review 289
Rockford Review, The 290
Rose & Thorn Literary E-Zine, The
    340
So to Speak 293
Southern Humanities Review 294

Southwestern American Literature 295

Steel City Review: A Pittsburgh-based magazine of Short Fiction 341

storySouth 342

Straylight 296

Struggle 297

Sycamore Review 298

Talking River Review 298

Thema 300

Timber Creek Review 322

Transition 301

Weber Studies 323

Workers Write! 304

Xavier Review 304

Yemassee 304

Book Publishers

Arsenal Pulp Press 369

Bancroft Press 372

Barking Dog Books 373

Beil, Publisher, Inc., Frederic C. 374

Birch Brook Press 374

Coteau Books 382

Covenant Communications, Inc. 382

Ingalls Publishing Group, Inc. 401

Lost Horse Press 409

Monsoon Books 414

Panther Creek Press 419

Piatkus Books 423

Pineapple Press, Inc. 423

Pipers' Ash, Ltd. 424

Plexus Publishing, Inc. 424

Port Town Publishing 426

Red Dress Ink 430

River City Publishing 430

Science & Humanities Press 432

Tindal Street Press, Ltd. 440

Twilight Times Books 442

University Press of New England 443

Véhicule Press 443

Willowgate Press 445

RELIGIOUS/ INSPIRATIONAL

Magazines

Allegheny Review, The 225

Ancient Paths 226

Annals of St. Anne de Beaupré, The 348

Barbaric Yawp 229

Big Country Peacock Chronicle 330

Buffalo Carp 235

Cadet Quest Magazine 350

Cezanne's Carrot 331

Church Educator 309

Clubhouse Jr. 351

Clubhouse Magazine 351

DisciplesWorld 352

Dragons, Knights & Angels, The Magazine of Christian Fantasy and Science Fiction 333

Dreams & Visions 311

Evangel 353

Irreantum 312

Liguorian 355

LIVE 356

London Magazine, The 314

Lutheran Journal, The 356

Mature Years 357

Messenger of the Sacred Heart, The 357

newWitch 358

North Central Review, YOUR Undergraduate Literary Journal 272

Nova Science Fiction Magazine 315

Ohio Teachers Write 274

Pegasus Review, The 318

Pink Chameleon, The 339

Pockets 360

Prayerworks 318

Purpose 318

Rock & Sling: A Journal of Literature, Art and Faith 290

Rose & Thorn Literary E-Zine, The 340

Seek 361

Silent Voices 319
St. Anthony Messenger 362
St. Joseph's Messenger & Advocate
   of the Blind 362
Storyteller, The 320
Sword Review, The 343
Tabard Inn, Tales of Questionable
   Taste 320
Thema 300
Xavier Review 304

Book Publishers

B & H Publishing 371
Baker Books 371
Barbour Publishing, Inc. 373
Branden Publishing Co., Inc. 377
Covenant Communications, Inc. 382
Dan River Press 383
Doubleday 385
Doubleday Religious Publishing 386
Eerdmans Publishing Co., William
   388
Harvest House Publishers 398
ignotus Press 400
Jireh Publishing Company 403
Kregel Publications 405
Meriwether Publishing, Ltd. 412
Moody Publishers 415
Mountain State Press 415
Norton Co., Inc., W.W. 417
Pipers' Ash, Ltd. 424
Ravenhawk Books 429
Steeple Hill 438
SynergEbooks 439
WindRiver Publishing, Inc. 446

ROMANCE

Magazines

Advocate, PKA'S Publication 347
Aguilar Expression, The 224
Allegheny Review, The 225
Any Dream Will Do Review 308
Beginnings Publishing Inc. 230
Big Country Peacock Chronicle 330
Brillant Corners 234
Broken Pencil 235
Buffalo Carp 235
Burst 330
Copperfield Review, The 332
Dan River Anthology 310
Downstate Story 243
Eureka Literary Magazine 245
Fifty Something Magazine 353
First Line 311
Irreantum 312
London Magazine, The 314
Louisiana Review, The 265
Lutheran Journal, The 356
newWitch 358
North Central Review, YOUR
   Undergraduate Literary Journal
   272
Northwoods Journal 273
Ohio Teachers Write 274
Open Wide Magazine 275
Oracle Story & Letters 316
Outer Darkness 317
Palo Alto Review 277
Pink Chameleon, The 339
PSI 318
Rejected Quarterly, The 288
Rose & Thorn Literary E-Zine, The
   340
Short Stuff 292
Silent Voices 319
St. Joseph's Messenger & Advocate
   of the Blind 362
Storyteller, The 320
Summerset Review, The 342
Toasted Cheese 343
Virginia Quarterly Review 323
Writers' Forum 363

Book Publishers

Avalon Books 370
Ballantine Books 371
Barbour Publishing, Inc. 373
Berkley Publishing Group, The 374
Borealis Press, Ltd. 376
Carnifex Press 379
Covenant Communications, Inc. 382

CrossTIME 383
Dan River Press 383
Ellora's Cave Publishing, Inc. 388
Eros Books 389
Fort Ross Inc. Russian-American
    Publishing Projects 391
Harbor House 395
Harlequin American Romance 395
Harlequin Blaze 395
Harlequin Everlasting 396
Harlequin Historicals 396
Harlequin Intrigue 396
Harlequin Mills & Boon, Ltd. 397
Harlequin Superromance 397
HarperTorch 397
ImaJinn Books 401
Ingalls Publishing Group, Inc. 401
Kensington Publishing Corp. 404
Leisure Books 407
Lionhearted Publishing, Inc. 408
Love Spell 409
Medallion Press, Inc. 411
Mills & Boon Medical Romance 413
Mills & Boon Modern Romance 413
Mills & Boon Modern Xtra-Sensual
    414
Mills & Boon Romance 414
New Victoria Publishers 416
Oak Tree Press 417
Piatkus Books 423
Pipers' Ash, Ltd. 424
Port Town Publishing 426
Pureplay Press 427
Ravenhawk Books 429
Red Dress Ink 430
Science & Humanities Press 432
Silhouette Books 433
Silhouette Desire 433
Silhouette Intimate Moments 434
Silhouette Nocturne 434
Silhouette Special Edition 434
Steeple Hill 438
SynergEbooks 439
Warner Books 445
Worldwide Library 447

SCIENCE FICTION
Magazines

Advocate, PKA'S Publication 347
Albedo One 307
AlienSkin Magazine 326
Allegheny Review, The 225
Allegory 327
American Feed Magazine 327
Analog Science Fiction & Fact 347
Ancient Paths 226
Anti Muse 328
Any Dream Will Do Review 308
Apex Science Fiction and Horror
    Digest 308
Armchair Aesthete, The 228
Art Times 348
Ascent Aspirations 328
Asimov's Science Fiction 348
Barbaric Yawp 229
Beginnings Publishing Inc. 230
Big Country Peacock Chronicle 330
Broken Pencil 235
Bryant Literary Review 235
Buffalo Carp 235
Burst 330
Cafe Irreal, The 330
cc&d, Children, Churches & Daddies
    magazine: The Unreligious,
    NONfamily-oriented literary and
    art magazine 237
Cezanne's Carrot 331
Challenging Destiny 331
Chrysalis Reader 239
Cosmos, A Magazine of Ideas,
    Science, Society and the Future
    352
Cricket 352
Dan River Anthology 310
Down in the Dirt 311
Downstate Story 243
Dragons, Knights & Angels, The
    Magazine of Christian Fantasy
    and Science Fiction 333
Dreams & Visions 311
Eureka Literary Magazine 245

First Class 246
First Line 311
Foliate Oak Literary Magazine 248
Gud Magazine 253
Happy 254
Harpur Palate 254
Home Planet News 256
Iconoclast 256
Irreantum 312
La Kancerkliniko 261
Lady Churchill's Rosebud Wristlet 314
Lamp-Post, The 262
Literal Latté 263
Lone Star Stories, Speculative Fiction and Poetry 336
Magazine of Fantasy & Science Fiction, The 356
Maisonneuve 357
Midnight Times 336
Mobius 269
North Central Review, YOUR Undergraduate Literary Journal 272
Northwoods Journal 273
Nova Science Fiction Magazine 315
Ohio Teachers Write 274
On Spec 316
Outer Darkness 317
Pacific Coast Journal 276
Palo Alto Review 277
Paradox 277
Paumanok Review, The 339
Pink Chameleon, The 339
Playboy Magazine 359
Postscripts: The A to Z of Fantastic Fiction 283
Rejected Quarterly, The 288
Rockford Review, The 290
Rose & Thorn Literary E-Zine, The 340
Short Stuff 292
Silent Voices 319
Soleado 320
Spider 361

Steel City Review: A Pittsburgh-based magazine of Short Fiction 341
Stone Soup 296
Struggle 297
Sword Review, The 343
Tabard Inn, Tales of Questionable Taste 320
Talebones 321
Tales of the Talisman 321
Thema 300
Tickled by Thunder 301
Toasted Cheese 343
Trail of Indiscretion 322
Wild Violet 344
William and Mary Review, The 302
Writers' Forum 363
Zahir 324

Book Publishers

Ageless Press 368
Baen Publishing Enterprises 371
Bancroft Press 372
Ben Bella Books 374
BL Publishing 375
Black Heron Press 375
Carnifex Press 379
Circlet Press, Inc. 380
Clarion Books 381
Crossquarter Publishing Group 383
CrossTIME 383
Dan River Press 383
DAW Books, Inc. 384
Del Rey Books 385
Dragon Moon Press 386
Edge Science Fiction and Fantasy Publishing 387
Ellora's Cave Publishing, Inc. 388
Forge and Tor Books 391
Fort Ross Inc. Russian-American Publishing Projects 391
Gryphon Books 394
Images SI, Inc. 401
ImaJinn Books 401
Komenar Publishing 405

Last Knight Publishing Company 406

Little, Brown and Co. Books for Young Readers 408

Luath Press Ltd. 410

Medallion Press, Inc. 411

Moody Publishers 415

New Victoria Publishers 416

Pipers' Ash, Ltd. 424

Port Town Publishing 426

Ravenhawk Books 429

Salvo Press 431

Science & Humanities Press 432

Silver Leaf Books, LLC 435

Small Beer Press 435

Spectra Books 436

St. Martin's Press 437

SynergEbooks 439

Timberwolf Press, Inc. 440

Triumvirate Publications 442

Twilight Times Books 442

Tyrannosaurus Press 442

Warner Books 445

Willowgate Press 445

WindRiver Publishing, Inc. 446

SHORT STORY COLLECTIONS

Book Publishers

Absey & Co. 368

Ageless Press 368

Anvil Press 369

Arcade Publishing 369

Ballantine Books 371

Barking Dog Books 373

Beil, Publisher, Inc., Frederic C. 374

Ben Bella Books 374

BkMk Press 375

BL Publishing 375

Books for All Times, Inc. 376

Borealis Press, Ltd. 376

Branden Publishing Co., Inc. 377

Breakaway Books 377

Bridge Works Publishing Co. 377

Calamari Press 378

Calyx Books 378

Chronicle Books 380

Coffee House Press 381

Coteau Books 382

Dan River Press 383

Daniel and Co., John 384

Doubleday 385

Dutton 386

ECW Press 387

Empyreal Press 388

Eros Books 389

Feminist Press at the City University of New York, The 390

Gertrude Press 392

Gival Press 392

Goose Lane Editions 393

Graywolf Press 394

Helicon Nine Editions 398

Lifetime Books 407

Livingston Press 408

Lost Horse Press 409

Low Fidelity Press 409

Luath Press Ltd. 410

Panther Creek Press 419

Pathwise Press 420

Paycock Press 420

Pedlar Press 421

Pipers' Ash, Ltd. 424

Plume 425

Pocol Press 425

Prairie Journal Press 426

Quixote Press 427

Ravenhawk Books 429

Red Dress Ink 430

Red Hen Press 430

River City Publishing 430

Ronsdale Press 431

Science & Humanities Press 432

Small Beer Press 435

Southern Methodist University Press 436

Spire Press 437

Spout Press 437

Starcherone Books 438

SynergEbooks 439

Third World Press 439

Tin House Books 440
Tindal Street Press, Ltd. 440
Titan Press 441
University of Michigan Press 443
Véhicule Press 443
Vintage Anchor Publishing 444
Willowgate Press 445
Wind River Press 446
Wizards of the Coast 446
Woodley Memorial Press 446

THRILLER/ESPIONAGE

Magazines

American Feed Magazine 327
Anti Muse 328
Big Country Peacock Chronicle 330
Bryant Literary Review 235
Buffalo Carp 235
Cricket 352
Irreantum 312
New Works Review 336
North Central Review, YOUR
   Undergraduate Literary Journal
   272
Oracle Story & Letters 316
Pink Chameleon, The 339
Rose & Thorn Literary E-Zine, The
   340
RPPS/Fullosia Press 341
Sword Review, The 343
Toasted Cheese 343
William and Mary Review, The 302
Writers' Forum 363

Book Publishers

Ballantine Books 371
Bantam Doubleday Dell Books for
   Young ReadersBantam Doubeday
   Dell Bks for Yng Rdrs 372
Berkley Publishing Group, The 374
Christchurch Publishers Ltd. 380
Dutton 386
ECW Press 387
Ellora's Cave Publishing, Inc. 388
Forge and Tor Books 391

Fort Ross Inc. Russian-American
   Publishing Projects 391
HarperTorch 397
Houghton Mifflin Books for Children
   399
Insomniac Press 401
JourneyForth 403
Kensington Publishing Corp. 404
Leisure Books 407
Little, Brown and Co. Books for
   Young Readers 408
Meriwether Publishing, Ltd. 412
Mira Books 414
Monsoon Books 414
Oak Tree Press 417
Palari Publishing 418
Piatkus Books 423
Pipers' Ash, Ltd. 424
Plume 425
Putnam's Sons, G.P. 427
Random House Trade Publishing
   Group 428
Salvo Press 431
Science & Humanities Press 432
Soho Press, Inc. 436
St. Martin's Press 437
Timberwolf Press, Inc. 440
Warner Books 445
WindRiver Publishing, Inc. 446

TRANSLATIONS

Magazines

Adirondack Review, The 326
Agni 224
Alaska Quarterly Review 224
Antigonish Review, The 227
Apalachee Review 227
Apple Valley Review, A Journal of
   Contemporary Literature 328
Big Country Peacock Chronicle 330
Big Muddy: A Journal of the
   Mississippi River Valley 231
Bitter Oleander, The 232
Boston Review 350
Bryant Literary Review 235

Cafe Irreal, The 330
Caribbean Writer, The 237
Chariton Review, The 238
Convergence 331
Cream City Review, The 242
Eureka Literary Magazine 245
Faultline 245
Fiction 246
Flint Hills Review 247
Fluent Ascension 335
Gargoyle 249
Global City Review 251
Green Mountains Review 252
Gulf Coast 253
Hawai'i Pacific Review 255
Image 258
Indiana Review 258
Irreantum 312
Isotope 259
Jabberwock Review, The 259
Kenyon Review, The 260
Lady Churchill's Rosebud Wristlet 314
MacGuffin, The 266
Madison Review, The 266
Manoa 267
Mid-American Review 267
New Delta Review 270
New Letters 270
New Works Review 336
Nimrod 272
North Central Review, YOUR Undergraduate Literary Journal 272
Northwest Review 273
Painted Bride Quarterly 277
Palo Alto Review 277
Paperplates 338
Pikeville Review 280
Pindeldyboz 281
Pleiades 281
Prism International 284
Puerto Del Sol 285
Quarter After Eight 285
Quarterly West 285
River Styx 289

So to Speak 293
storySouth 342
Struggle 297
Sulphur River Literary Review 298
Sycamore Review 298
Tampa Review 299
Understanding 301
Virginia Quarterly Review 323
Weber Studies 323
Weird Tales 323
William and Mary Review, The 302
Willow Springs 303
Xavier Review 304

Book Publishers
City Lights Books 381
Clarion Books 381
Eros Books 389
Feminist Press at the City University of New York, The 390
Interlink Publishing Group, Inc. 402
Italica Press 402
Luath Press Ltd. 410
Milkweed Editions 412
Monsoon Books 414
Stone Bridge Press 438
Tin House Books 440

WESTERN
Magazines
Advocate, PKA'S Publication 347
Allegheny Review, The 225
Anti Muse 328
Armchair Aesthete, The 228
Bear Deluxe Magazine, The 349
Beginnings Publishing Inc. 230
Big Country Peacock Chronicle 330
Bryant Literary Review 235
Buffalo Carp 235
Copperfield Review, The 332
Cricket 352
Dan River Anthology 310
Downstate Story 243
Fifty Something Magazine 353
First Line 311

New Works Review 336
North Central Review, YOUR
    Undergraduate Literary Journal
    272
Northwoods Journal 273
Ohio Teachers Write 274
Oracle Story & Letters 316
Palo Alto Review 277
Paradox 277
Paumanok Review, The 339
Pink Chameleon, The 339
PSI 318
Rose & Thorn Literary E-Zine, The
    340
Short Stuff 292
Silent Voices 319
Storyteller, The 320
Tabard Inn, Tales of Questionable
    Taste 320
Thema 300
Tickled by Thunder 301
Timber Creek Review 322
Toasted Cheese 343
Weber Studies 323
Writers' Forum 363

Book Publishers
Avalon Books 370
B & H Publishing 371
Barbour Publishing, Inc. 373
Berkley Publishing Group, The 374
Crossway Books 383
Dan River Press 383
Ellora's Cave Publishing, Inc. 388
Forge and Tor Books 391
Glencannon Press, The 393
Jameson Books. Inc. 403
JourneyForth 403
Kensington Publishing Corp. 404
Leisure Books 407
Lifetime Books 407
Medallion Press, Inc. 411
Mould Publishing, Paul 415
New Victoria Publishers 416
Plume 425
Science & Humanities Press 432

St. Martin's Press 437
SynergEbooks 439

YOUNG ADULT/TEEN
Magazines

Advocate, PKA'S Publication 347
Creative With Words Publications
    310
DotLit 333
Dragons, Knights & Angels, The
    Magazine of Christian Fantasy
    and Science Fiction 333
Irreantum 312
Liguorian 355
Listen Magazine 356
Lutheran Journal, The 356
Magazine of Fantasy & Science
    Fiction, The 356
Oracle Story & Letters 316
Pink Chameleon, The 339
Storyteller, The 320
Struggle 297
Sword Review, The 343
Writers' Forum 363

Book Publishers

Bancroft Press 372
Barron's Educational Series, Inc.
    373
Berkley Publishing Group, The 374
Bethany House Publishers 374
BL Publishing 375
Borealis Press, Ltd. 376
Candlewick Press 379
Carnifex Press 379
Carolrhoda Books, Inc. 379
Chronicle Books for Children 380
Coteau Books 382
Covenant Communications, Inc. 382
Cricket Books 382
CrossTIME 383
Dan River Press 383
Dial Books For Young Readers 385
Dutton Children's Books 387

Writer's Digest

DISCOVER A WORLD OF WRITING SUCCESS!

Are you ready to be praised, published, and paid for your writing? It's time to invest in your future with *Writer's Digest!* Beginners and experienced writers alike have been relying on *Writer's Digest*, the world's leading magazine for writers, for more than 80 years — and it keeps getting better!

Each issue is brimming with:

- technique articles geared toward specific genres, including fiction, nonfiction, business writing and more
- business information specifically for writers, such as organizational advice, tax tips, and setting fees
- tips and tricks for rekindling your creative fire
- the latest and greatest markets for print, online and e-publishing
- and much more!

NO RISK!
Send No Money Now!

☐ **Yes!** Please rush me my FREE issue of *Writer's Digest* — the world's leading magazine for writers. If I like what I read, I'll get a full year's subscription (6 issues, including the free issue) for only $19.96. That's 44% off the newsstand rate! If I'm not completely satisfied, I'll write "cancel" on your invoice, return it and owe nothing. The FREE issue is mine to keep, no matter what!

Name (please print)
_____

Address
_____

City _____ State _____ ZIP _____

E-mail (to contact me regarding my subscription)
_____

☐ YES! Also e-mail me *Writer's Digest*'s FREE e-newsletter and other information of interest. *(We will not sell your e-mail address to outside companies.)*

Subscribers in Canada will be charged an additional US$10 (includes GST/HST) and invoiced. Outside the U.S. and Canada, add US$10 and remit payment in U.S. funds with this order. Annual newsstand rate: $35.94. Please allow 4-6 weeks for first-issue delivery.

Writer's Digest www.writersdigest.com

J7FNMK

Get a FREE TRIAL ISSUE of Writer's Digest

Packed with creative inspiration, advice, and tips to guide you on the road to success, *Writer's Digest* offers everything you need to take your writing to the next level! You'll discover how to:

- create dynamic characters and page-turning plots
- submit query letters that publishers won't be able to refuse
- find the right agent or editor
- make it out of the slush-pile and into the hands of publishers
- write award-winning contest entries
- and more!

See for yourself — order your FREE trial issue today!

RUSH! Free Issue!

Writer's Digest
PO BOX 421365
PALM COAST FL 32142-7104

Eerdmans Books for Young Readers 387

Farrar, Straus & Giroux Books for Young Readers 389

Front Street 391

Geringer Books, Laura 392

Glencannon Press, The 393

Harbor House 395

Harcourt, Inc 395

HarperCollins Children's Books 397

Hendrick-Long Publishing Co., Inc. 398

Holt & Co. Books for Young Readers, Henry 399

Houghton Mifflin Books for Children 399

Hyperion Books for Children 400

Ingalls Publishing Group, Inc. 401

Ivy Publications 403

JourneyForth 403

Kregel Publications 405

Lamb Books, Wendy 406

Lerner Publishing Group 407

Lifetime Books 407

Little, Brown and Co. Books for Young Readers 408

Llewellyn Publications 409

McElderry Books, Margaret K.McElderry, Margaret 411

Medallion Press, Inc. 411

Monsoon Books 414

Moody Publishers 415

Mould Publishing, Paul 415

Oak Tree Press 417

Orca Book Publishers 418

Peachtree Children's Books 420

Peachtree Publishers, Ltd. 421

Piñata Books 423

Pipers' Ash, Ltd. 424

Port Town Publishing 426

Puffin Books 427

Pureplay Press 427

Ransom Publishing Ltd. 429

Ravenhawk Books 429

Red Deer Press 429

Scholastic Canada, Ltd. 432

Science & Humanities Press 432

Silver Dagger Mysteries 434

Silver Leaf Books, LLC 435

SynergEbooks 439

TCU Press 439

Third World Press 439

Twilight Times Books 442

White Mane Kids 445

WindRiver Publishing, Inc. 446

General Index

A

Abel Literary Agency, Inc., Dominick 156
Abiko Annual With James Joyce, The 307
Absey & Co. 368
Absinthe Literary Review, The 326
Acacia House Publishing Services, Ltd. 156
Academy Chicago Publishers 368
Acme Press 368
Adirondack Review, The 326
Adventures 347
Advocate, PKA'S Publication 347
African American Review 224
Ageless Press 368
Agents & Editors Conference 507
Agents Ink! 156
Agni 224
Aguilar Expression, The 224
Ahearn Agency, Inc., The 157
AIM Magazine Short Story Contest 449
Aim Magazine 347
Alabama State Council on the Arts Individual Artist Fellowship 449
Alabama Writers' Conclave 499
Alaska Quarterly Review 224
Albedo One 307
Algonquin Books of Chapel Hill 369
Algren Short Fiction Contest, Nelson 449

AlienSkin Magazine 326
Alimentum, The Literature of Food 225
Alive Communications, Inc. 157
Allegheny Review, The 225
Allegory 327
Alsop Review, The 327
Alternative Press Expo (APE) 512
Altshuler Literary Agency, Miriam 157
American Association of University Women Award in Juvenile Literature 449
American Christian Writers Conferences 496
American Drivel Review, The 226
American Feed Magazine 327
American Literary Review 226
American Literary Review Short Fiction Award 449
American Markets Newsletter Short Story Competition 449
American Scandinavian Foundation Translation Prize 450
Ampersand Agency, The 158
Amster Literary Enterprises, Betsy 158
Analog Science Fiction & Fact 347
Ancient Paths 226
Anderson Foundation Fiction Award, The Sherwood 450

Annals of St. Anne de Beaupré, The 348

Annual Atlantic Writing Competition 450

Annual Book Competition 450

Annual Fiction Contest 450

Annual Juvenile Fiction Contest 451

Annual Retreats, Workshops and Classes 507

Anti Muse 328

Antigonish Review, The 227

Antioch Writers' Workshop 503

Anubis Literary Agency 159

Anvil Press 369

Any Dream Will Do Review 308

Apalachee Review 227

Apex Science Fiction and Horror Digest 308

Apple Valley Review, A Journal of Contemporary Literature 328

Appleseeds Management 159

Arcade Publishing 369

Arcadia 159

Ariel Starr Productions, Ltd. 369

Arkansas Review 227

Arkansas Writers' Conference 499

Armchair Aesthete, The 228

Arrowhead Regional Arts Council Individual Artist Career Development Grant 451

Arsenal Pulp Press 369

Art of Music Annual Writing Contest, The 451

Art Times 348

Art Workshops in Guatemala 522

Arte Publico Press 370

Artists and Artisans Inc. 160

Ascent Aspirations 328

Asimov's Science Fiction 348

Aspen Summer Words Writing Retreat & Literary Festival 508

Asted/Grand Prix de Litterature Jeunesse du Quebec-Alvine-Belisle 451

Athenaeum Literary Award, The 451

Atlantic Monthly, The 349

August Agency, LLC, The 160

Aunt Lute Books 370

Authentic Creations Literary Agency 161

Avalon Books 370

AWP Annual Conference and Bookfair 499

AWP Award Series in the Novel, Creative Nonfiction and Short Fiction 452

AWP Intro Journals Project 452

Axelrod Agency, The 161

B

B & H Publishing 371

Babel 329

Babybug 349

Backroads 349

Backwards City Review 228

Baen Publishing Enterprises 371

Baker Books 371

Ballantine Books 371

Ballyhoo Stories 228

Baltimore Review, The 229

Bancroft Press 372

Bantam Dell Publishing Group 372

Bantam Doubleday Dell Books for Young Readers 372

Barbaric Yawp 229

Barbour Publishing, Inc. 373

Barcelona Review, The 329

Bard Fiction Prize 452

Barefoot Books 373

Barer Literary, LLC 161

Barking Dog Books 373

Barrett Books, Inc., Loretta 162

Barron's Educational Series, Inc. 373

Bathtub Gin 229

Bay to Ocean Writers' Conference 495

Bear Deluxe Magazine, The 349

Beginnings Publishing Inc. 230

Beil, Publisher, Inc., Frederic C. 374

Bellevue Literary Review 230

Bellingham Review 230

Bellowing Ark 231
Beloit Fiction Journal 231
Ben Bella Books 374
Bender Literary Agency, Faye 162
Bennett Fellowship, George 452
Berkley Publishing Group, The 374
Bernstein Literary Agency, Meredith 162
Best Lesbian Erotica 453
"Best of Ohio Writer" Contest 453
Bethany House Publishers 374
Big Country Peacock Chronicle 330
Big Muddy: A Journal of the Mississippi River Valley 231
Bigscore Productions, Inc. 162
Bilingual Review 232
Binghamton University John Gardner Fiction Book Award 453
Binnacle, The 308
Birch Brook Press 374
Bitter Oleander, The 232
BkMk Press 375
BL Publishing 375
Black Award, Irma S. and James H. 453
Black Heron Press 375
Black Lace 308
Black Memorial Prizes, James Tait 453
Black Warrior Review 232
Blair, Publisher, John F. 375
Bleak House Books 376
Bleecker Street Associates, Inc. 163
Blockbuster Plot Intensive Writing Workshops 513
Bloody Words Mystery Conference 520
Blue Ridge Mountains Christian Writers Conference 496
Blueline 233
Blumer Literary Agency, Inc., The 163
Boardman Tasker Award for Mountain Literature, The 453
Bogg 233
Bomb Magazine 350

Bonnet's Storymaking: The Master Class, James 513
Book World Magazine 233
BookEnds, LLC 164
BookExpo America/Writer's Digest Books Writers Conference 488
Books & Such Literary Agency 164
Books for All Times, Inc. 376
Booming Ground 521
Borealis Press, Ltd. 376
Boson Books 377
Boston Review 350
Bouchercon 517
Boulevard 233
Boulevard Short Fiction Contest for Emerging Writers 454
Branden Publishing Co., Inc. 377
Brandt & Hochman Literary Agents, Inc. 164
Braun Associates, Inc., Barbara 165
Bread Loaf Writers' Conference 488
Breakaway Books 377
Briar Cliff Review Poetry, Fiction & Creative Nonfiction Competition, The 454
Briar Cliff Review, The 234
Bridge Works Publishing Co. 377
Bridport Prize, The 454
Brillant Corners 234
Broadway Books 378
Broken Bridge Review 234
Broken Pencil 235
Brown (Aust) Pty Ltd, Curtis 165
Brown Literary Agency 165
Brown, Ltd., Curtis 166
Brown Skin Books 378
Browne & Miller Literary Associates 166
Browne, Ltd., Pema 166
Brutarian 309
Bryant Literary Review 235
Buffalo Carp 235
Burnaby Writers' Society Contest 454
Burst 330
Bush Artist Fellows Program 454

General Index

Button 236
Bykofsky Associates, Inc., Sheree 167
Byline 236
ByLine Magazine Awards 455

C

Cadet Quest Magazine 350
Cafe Irreal, The 330
Caine Prize for African Writing, The 455
Calamari Press 378
Calliope 351
Calyx 236
Calyx Books 378
Campbell Memorial Award for Best Science Fiction Novel of the Year, John W. 455
Canadian Writer's Journal 351
Candlewick Press 379
Canton Smith Agency 167
Cappon Fiction Award, The Alexander Patterson 455
Caribbean Writer, The 237
Carnifex Press 379
Carolrhoda Books, Inc. 379
Castiglia Literary Agency 168
Cave Books 380
cc&d, Children, Churches & Daddies magazine: The Unreligious, NONfamily-oriented literary and art magazine 237
Center 237
Cezanne's Carrot 331
Chaffin Journal 237
Challenging Destiny 331
Chapman 238
Characters 309
Chariton Review, The 238
Charlesbridge Publishing 380
Chattahoochee Review, The 238
Chelius Literary Agency, Jane 168
Chicago Quarterly Review 239
Chicago Review 239
Christchurch Publishers Ltd. 380
Christoper Awards, The 455

Chronicle Books 380
Chronicle Books for Children 380
Chrysalis Reader 239
Church Educator 309
Cimarron Review 239
Cincinnati Review, The 240
Circlet Press, Inc. 380
City Lights Books 381
City of Toronto Book Awards 456
City Slab 309
Claremont Review, The 240
Clarion Books 381
Clarion West Writers' Workshop 517
Clark Associates, Wm. 169
Clubhouse Jr. 351
Clubhouse Magazine 351
CNW/FFWA Annual Florida State Writing Competition 456
Coal City Review 240
Coffee House Press 381
Collin, Literary Agent, Frances 169
Collins Literary Agency 169
Colorado Review 240
Columbus Writers Conference 503
Confrontation 241
Congdon Associates Inc., Don 170
Connecticut Review 241
Connor Literary Agency 170
Conseil de la Vie Francaise en Amerique/Prix Champlain 456
Convergence 331
Coover Agency, The Doe 170
Copper Canyon Press 382
Copperfield Review, The 332
Cosmos, A Magazine of Ideas, Science, Society and the Future 352
Coteau Books 382
Cottonwood 241
Country Connection, The 310
Covenant Communications, Inc. 382
Crazyhorse 242
Crazyhorse Fiction Prize 456
Cream City Review, The 242

Creative With Words Publications 310
Cricket 352
Cricket Books 382
Crossquarter Publishing Group 383
CrossTIME 383
Crossway Books 383
Crucible 242
Crucible Poetry and Fiction Competition, The 457
Curtis Associates, Inc., Richard 171

D

Dail Literary Agency, Inc., Laura 172
Dan River Anthology 310
Dan River Press 383
Dana Literary Society Online Journal 332
Daniel and Co., John 384
Dargonzine 332
Darhansoff, Verrill, Feldman Literary Agents 172
Dark Horse Comics 384
Davenport, Publishers, May 384
DAW Books, Inc. 384
Dawson Associates, Liza 172
Dead of Winter 457
deathlings.com 333
DeChiara Literary Agency, The Jennifer 172
Del Rey Books 385
Delbourgo Associates, Inc., Joelle 173
descant 243
D4EO Literary Agency 171
DHS Literary, Inc. 173
Diagram 333
Dial Books For Young Readers 385
Dial Press 385
Dingle Writing Courses 523
DisciplesWorld 352
Dislocate 243
DotLit 333
Doubleday 385
Doubleday Books for Young Readers 386

Doubleday Canada 386
Doubleday Religious Publishing 386
Down in the Dirt 311
Downstate Story 243
Dragon Moon Press 386
Dragons, Knights & Angels, The Magazine of Christian Fantasy and Science Fiction 333
Dreams & Visions 311
Dunham Literary, Inc. 174
Dutton 386
Dutton Children's Books 387
Dystel & Goderich Literary Management 174
Dobie/Paisano Fellowships 457

E

East Texas Writer's Conference 508
Eaton Literary Agency's Annual Awards Program 457
Eclipse 243
Ecotone, Reimagining Place 244
ECW Press 387
Edge Science Fiction and Fantasy Publishing 387
Eerdmans Books for Young Readers 387
Eerdmans Publishing Co., William 388
Ellenberg Literary Agency, Ethan 175
Ellison Agency, The Nicholas 175
Ellora's Cave Publishing, Inc. 388
Elmo Agency, Inc., Ann 175
Emerging Voices Rosenthal Fellowship 457
Emerging Writers Network Short Fiction Contest 457
Emily Contest, The 458
Eminence Area Arts Council Short Story Workshop 508
Empire Publishing Service 388
Empyreal Press 388
Emrys Journal 244
English Literary Agency, The Elaine P. 176

Environmental Writers' Conference and Workshop 488
Epoch 244
Eros Books 389
Esquire 353
Eureka Literary Magazine 245
Evangel 353
Evansville Review 245

F

Failbetter.com 334
Fairfield Review, The 334
Fantagraphics Books 389
Farber Literary Agency, Inc. 176
Farrar, Straus & Giroux 389
Farrar, Straus & Giroux Books for Young Readers 389
Farrar, Straus & Giroux Paperbacks 390
Farris Literary Agency, Inc. 176
Faulkner Award for Excellence in Writing, The Virginia 458
Faultline 245
FC2 390
Feminist Press at the City University of New York, The 390
Feminist Studies 246
Festival of Faith and Writing 503
Fiction 246
Fifty Something Magazine 353
Finch Literary Agency, Diana 177
First Class 246
First Line 311
Fish One Page Prize 458
Fish Short Story Prize 458
Five Points 246
Five-Trope 334
Flathead River Writers Conference 518
Flaunt Magazine 353
Fletcher & Parry 177
Flint Hills Review 247
Florida Academic Press 390
Florida First Coast Writers' Festival 500

Florida First Coast Writers' Festival Novel, Short Fiction, Playwriting & Poetry Awards 458
Florida Review 247
Florida State Writing Competition 459
Fluent Ascension 335
Flyway 247
Foley Literary Agency, The 177
Foliate Oak Literary Magazine 248
Forge and Tor Books 391
Fort Bend Writers Guild Workshop 508
Fort Ross Inc. Russian-American Publishing Projects 391
Francis Short Story Award, H.E. 459
Frank 248
FreeFall Magazine 248
Fresh Boiled Peanuts 249
Freymann Literary Agency, Sarah Jane 178
Front & Centre 249
Front Street 391
Fun For Kidz 311
Funny Paper, The 312
Furnace Review, The 335

G

Gargoyle 249
Gaslight Publications 392
Gelfman Schneider Literary Agents, Inc. 178
Georgetown Review 250
Georgia Review, The 250
Georgia Writers Association's Spring Festival of Workshops 500
Geringer Books, Laura 392
Gertrude 250
Gertrude Press 392
Ginosko 251
Gislason Agency, The 178
Gival Press 392
Gival Press Novel Award 459
Gival Press Short Story Award 459
Glasgow Prize for Emerging Writers, The 459

Glen Workshop, The 509
Glencannon Press, The 393
Glimmer Train Stories 251
Glimmer Train's Fall Short-Story
    Award for New Writers 460
Glimmer Train's Family Matters
    (April) 460
Glimmer Train's Family Matters
    (October) 460
Glimmer Train's Spring Short-Story
    Award for New Writers 460
Glimmer Train's Summer Fiction
    Open 460
Glimmer Train's Very Short Fiction
    Summer Award 460
Glimmer Train's Very Short Fiction
    Winter Award 460
Glimmer Train's Winter Fiction
    Open 461
Global City Review 251
Glorieta Christian Writers
    Conference 509
Goldenberg Prize for Fiction 461
Golvan Arts Management 179
Goodheart Prize for Fiction, The 461
Goodman Associates 179
Goose Lane Editions 393
Gotham Writers' Workshop 489
Gothic Chapbook Series 393
Grain Literary Magazine 251
Granta 252
Graywolf Press 394
Great Blue Beacon Short-Short Story
    Contest, The 461
Great Canadian Story Contest 461
Great Lakes Colleges Association
    New Writers Award 461
Great Lakes Writers Festival 506
Great River Arts 489
Green Hills Literary Lantern, The
    335
Green Lake Writers Conference 506
Green Mountain Writers Conference
    489
Green Mountains Review 252
Greene Bark Press 394

Greensboro Review, The 252
Greenwillow Books 394
Griffin, The 252
Grosjean Literary Agency, Jill 179
Grove/Atlantic, Inc. 394
Gryphon Books 394
GSU Review 253
GSU Review Writing Contest 462
Gud Magazine 253
Gulf Coast 253
Gulf Stream Magazine 253

H
Halsey North, Reece 179
Hammett Prize 462
Happy 254
Harbor House 395
Harcourt, Inc 395
Hardboiled 312
Harlequin American Romance 395
Harlequin Blaze 395
Harlequin Everlasting 396
Harlequin Historicals 396
Harlequin Intrigue 396
Harlequin Mills & Boon, Ltd. 397
Harlequin Superromance 397
HarperCollins Canada Ltd. 397
HarperCollins Children's Books 397
HarperCollins General Books Group
    397
HarperTorch 397
Harpur Palate 254
Harris Literary Agency, Inc., The Joy
    180
Hartline Literary Agency 180
Harvard Review 254
Harvest House Publishers 398
Harwood Limited, Antony 180
Hawai'i Pacific Review 255
HAWK Publishing Group 398
Hawkins & Associates, Inc., John
    181
Hayden's Ferry Review 255
Heart Talk 518
Heartlands Today, The 255
Heaven Bone 256

General Index

Helicon Nine Editions 398

Hemingway Short Story Competition, Lorian 462

Hendrick-Long Publishing Co., Inc. 398

Henshaw Group, Richard 181

Highland Summer Conference 497

Highlights for Children 354

Highlights for Children Fiction Contest 462

Highlights Foundation Founders Workshops 495

Highlights Foundation Writing for Children 489

Hill Bonnie Nadell, Inc., Frederick 182

Hillerman Mystery Short Story Contest, Tony 463

Hillerman Writers Conference, Tony 509

Hilton Head Island Writers Retreat 497

Hitchcock's Mystery Magazine, Alfred 354

Holiday House, Inc. 399

Holloway House Publishing Co. 399

Holt & Co. Books for Young Readers, Henry 399

Holt, Henry 399

Home Planet News 256

Hopkins Literary Associates 182

Houghton Mifflin Books for Children 399

Houghton Mifflin Co. 400

How to Be Published Workshops 500

Howard/John H. Reid Short Story Contest, Tom 463

Howells House 400

Hubbard's Writers of the Future Contest, L. Ron 463

Humber School for Writers Summer Workshop 521

Hyperion Books for Children 400

I

Iconoclast 256

Idaho Review, The 257

Idiot, The 257

ignotus Press 400

Illuminations 257

Illya's Honey 258

Image 258

Images SI, Inc. 401

ImaJinn Books 401

Imprint Agency, Inc. 182

Indiana Review 258

Indiana Review ½ K (Short-Short/ Prose-Poem) Contest 464

Indiana Review Fiction Contest 464

Individual Artist Fellowship/Mini Fellowship 464

Ingalls Publishing Group, Inc. 401

Inkwell Magazine 259

Insomniac Press 401

Interlink Publishing Group, Inc. 402

International Music Camp Creative Writing Workshop 506

Inverted-A 402

Ion Imagination Publishing 402

Iowa Short Fiction Award, The 464

Iowa Summer Writing Festival 507

Iris 259

Irreantum 312

Isotope 259

Italian Americana 313

Italica Press 402

Ivy Publications 403

IWWG Early Spring in California Conference 513

IWWG Meet the Agents and Editors 490

IWWG Summer Conference 490

J

J de S Associates, Inc. 183

Jabberwock Review, The 259

Jabberwocky Literary Agency 183

Jackson Award, Joseph Henry 464

Jameson Books. Inc. 403

JCA Literary Agency 183

Jireh Publishing Company 403
Journal, The 260
JourneyForth 403

K

Kaeden Books 404
Kaleidoscope 354
Karamu 260
Kearney Street Books 404
Keats/Kerlan Collection Memorial
  Fellowship, Ezra Jack 465
Kelsey Review 313
Kennesaw Review 335
Kensington Publishing Corp. 404
Kentucky Monthly 355
Kentucky Writer's Workshop 504
Kenyon Review, The 260
Kenyon Review Writers Workshop
  504
Kerem 261
Kern Literary Agency, The Natasha
  184
Killer Nashville 497
Kirchoff/Wohlberg, Inc., Authors'
  Representation Division 184
Kit-Cat Review, The 261
Klinger, Inc., Harvey 184
Kneerim & Williams 185
Knoll, Publishers, Allen A. 405
Knopf, Alfred A. 405
Koeppel Short Fiction Award, E.M.
  465
Komenar Publishing 405
Koster Literary Agency, LLC, Elaine
  185
Kraas Literary Agency 186
Krax Magazine 313
Kregel Publications 405
KT Public Relations & Literary
  Services 186

L

LA Literary Agency, The 186
La Belle Lettre Prose Contest 465
La Kancerkliniko 261

Lady Churchill's Rosebud Wristlet
  314
Ladybug 355
Lake Effect 262
Lamb Books, Wendy 406
Lampack Agency, Inc., Peter 187
Lamp-Post, The 262
Landfall/University of Otago Press
  262
Langlie, Literary Agent, Laura 187
Larsen/Elizabeth Pomada, Literary
  Agents, Michael 187
Last Knight Publishing Company
  406
Laube Agency, The Steve 188
Laurel Review, The 262
Lawrence Foundation Award, The
  465
Lawrence Foundation Prize 465
Lazear Agency, Inc. 189
Le Forum 263
Leacock Memorial Medal for
  Humour, Stephen 465
Leapfrog Press 406
Leaping Dog Press 407
Leavitt Agency, The Ned 189
Ledge Magazine, The 263
Lee & Low Books 407
Leisure Books 407
Lerner Publishing Group 407
Lescher & Lescher, Ltd. 189
Levine Greenberg Literary Agency,
  Inc. 190
Levine Literary Agency, Paul S. 190
Lifetime Books 407
Liguorian 355
Lionhearted Publishing, Inc. 408
Lippincott Massie McQuilkin 191
Listen Magazine 356
Listening Eye, The 263
Literal Latté 263
Literal Latté Fiction Award 466
Literary Group, The 191
Literary Review, The 264
Little, Brown and Co. Adult Trade
  Books 408

Little, Brown and Co. Books for Young Readers 408

LIVE 356

Livingston Press 408

Llewellyn Publications 409

London Magazine, The 314

Lone Star Stories, Speculative Fiction and Poetry 336

Long Story Contest International 466

Long Story, The 264

Lord Literary Management, Julia 192

Lord Literistic, Inc., Sterling 192

Lost Horse Press 409

Louisiana Literature 264

Louisiana Review, The 265

Louisville Review, The 265

Love Spell 409

Low Fidelity Press 409

Lowenstein-Yost Associates 192

Luath Press Ltd. 410

Luke Award, The Hugh J. 466

Lumina 466

Lunch Hour Stories 265

Lutheran Journal, The 356

M

Maass Literary Agency, Donald 193

MacAdam/Cage Publishing, Inc. 410

Maccoby Literary Agency, Gina 193

MacDowell Colony, The 490

MacGuffin, The 266

MaCrae Books, John 410

Madison Review, The 266

Magazine of Fantasy & Science Fiction, The 356

Maisonneuve 357

Malahat Review, The 266

Mann Agency, Carol 193

Manoa 267

Manus & Associates Literary Agency, Inc. 194

March Tenth, Inc. 195

Marcil Literary Agency, Inc., The Denise 195

Marine Techniques Publishing, Inc. 410

Mariner Books 411

Maritime Writers' Workshop 521

Marsh Award for Children's Literature in Translation 466

Marshall Agency, The Evan 195

Marvin Grant, Walter Rumsey 467

Marymount Manhattan College Writers' Conference 490

Masters Literary Awards 467

Mature Years 357

McBooks Press 411

McElderry Books, Margaret K.McElderry, Margaret 411

McGrath, Helen 196

McGinnis Memorial Award, The John H. 467

McSweeney's Internet Tendency, Timothy 336

Medallion Press, Inc. 411

Medical Fiction Writing for Physicians 491

Memphis Magazine Fiction Awards 467

Mendel Media Group, LLC 196

Mendocino Coast Writers Conference 513

Meriwether Publishing, Ltd. 412

Messenger of the Sacred Heart, The 357

Metal Scratches 267

Michigan Literary Fiction Awards 467

Michigan Quarterly Review 267

Mid-American Review 267

Mid-List Press 412

Midnight Times 336

Midsummer Tale, A 467

Midwest Writers Workshop 504

Milkweed Editions 412

Milkweed Editions National Fiction Prize 468

Milkweed for Young Readers 413

Million Writers Award 468
Mills & Boon Medical Romance 413
Mills & Boon Modern Romance 413
Mills & Boon Modern Xtra-Sensual 414
Mills & Boon Romance 414
Milton Center Postgraduate Fellowship, The 468
Mindprints 268
Minnesota Review, The 268
Mira Books 414
Mississippi Review 268
Missouri Review Editors' Prize Contest, The 468
Missouri Review, The 269
Mobius 269
Monsoon Books 414
Montevallo Literary Festival 500
Montrose Christian Writer's Conference 495
Moody Publishers 415
Moore Short Story Awards, Brian 468
Mormon Writers' Conference 513
Morrison, Inc., Henry 196
Mortalis 415
Mould Publishing, Paul 415
Mount Hermon Christian Writers Conference 514
Mountain State Press 415
Mslexia 358
Municipal Chapter of Toronto Jean Throop IODE Book Award 469
Muse Literary Management 197

N

Na'Amat Woman 358
Naggar Literary Agency, Inc., Jean V. 197
Nassau Review 269
Natchez Literary and Cinema Celebration 500
National Writers Association Foundation Conference 509
National Writers Association Novel Writing Contest 469

National Writers Association Short Story Contest 469
NBM Publishing 416
Nelson Literary Agency 198
Nelson Publishers, Thomas 416
Nerve Cowboy 270
Nevada Arts Council Artist Fellowships 469
New Delta Review 270
New England Writers Conference 491
New England Writers Short Fiction Contest 469
New Letters 270
New Letters Literary Awards 470
New Letters Weekend Writers Conference, The 509
New Madrid 271
New Methods 314
New Millennium Writing Awards 470
New Orphic Review, The 271
New Victoria Publishers 416
New Works Review 336
New Writer, The 271
New Yorker, The 358
Newbery Award, John 470
NeWest Publishers Ltd. 417
newWitch 358
Nimrod 272
Nimrod Annual Writers' Workshop 510
Nocturnal Lyric, The 314
Nocturnal Ooze 337
Noma Award for Publishing in Africa, The 470
Noon 272
North Carolina Arts Council Writers' Residencies 470
North Carolina Literary Review 272
North Carolina Writers' Network Fall Conference 497
North Central Review, YOUR Undergraduate Literary Journal 272
North Dakota Quarterly 273

Northern California Book Awards 471
Northwest Review 273
Northwoods Journal 273
Norton Co., Inc., W.W. 417
Notre Dame Review 274
Nova Science Fiction Magazine 315
Novel Manuscript Contest 471
Novello Literary Award 471
Nuthouse 315
Nuvein Online 337
NY State Summer Writers Institute 491

O

Oak, The 315
Oak Tree Press 417
Ober Associates, Harold 198
Obsidian III 274
O'Connor Award for Short Fiction, The Flannery 471
O'Connor Fiction Award, Frank 472
Odyssey Fantasy Writing Workshop 491
Ohio Teachers Write 274
Ohioana Award for Children's Literature (Alice Wood Memorial) 472
Ohioana Book Awards 472
Omnidawn Publishing 417
On Spec 316
108, Celebrating Baseball 359
One-Story 275
Open Minds Quarterly 316
Open Spaces 275
Open Wide Magazine 275
Open Windows 472
Open Writing Workshops 504
Opium Magazine 337
Oracle Story & Letters 316
Oracular Tree, The 338
Orange Blossom Fiction Contest 472
Orca Book Publishers 418
Orient Paperbacks 418
Orphan Leaf Review, The 316
Other Press 418

Other Voices 275
Our Child Press 418
Outdoor Writers Association of America Annual Conference 498
Outer Art 338
Outer Darkness 317
Outlooks 359
Oxford Conference for the Book 501
Oxford Magazine 338
Oyez Review 276
Oyster Boy Review 276

P

Pacific Coast Journal 276
pacific REVIEW 276
Painted Bride Quarterly 277
Pakn Treger 359
Palari Publishing 418
Palo Alto Review 277
Panther Creek Press 419
Papercutz 419
Paperplates 338
Papyrus Publishers & Letterbox Service 420
Paradise Cay Publications, Inc. 420
Paradox 277
Paradoxism 317
Paris Review, The 278
Paris Writers Workshop/WICE 523
Parks Agency, The Richard 198
Parting Gifts 278
Passages North 278
Paterson Fiction Prize 473
Paterson Literary Review 279
Pathwise Press 420
Paumanok Review, The 339
Paycock Press 420
PBW 339
Peachtree Children's Books 420
Peachtree Publishers, Ltd. 421
Pearl 279
Pearl Short Story Prize 473
Peden Prize in Fiction, William 473
Pedlar Press 421
Pegasus Review, The 318
Pelican Publishing Co. 421

Pemmican Publications 421
PEN Center USA Annual Literary
    Awards 473
Penguin Group USA 422
Pennsylvania English 279
Peregrine 280
Perkins Associates, L. 198
Permanent Press/Second Chance
    Press, The 422
Pevner, Inc., Stephen 199
Phantasmagoria 280
Philip Publishers, David 422
Piatkus Books 423
Picador USA 423
Picard, Literary Agent, Alison J. 199
Pikeville Review 280
Pima Writers' Workshop 514
Piñata Books 423
Pinch, The 280
Pindeldyboz 281
Pineapple Press, Inc. 423
Pink Chameleon, The 339
Pinyon 281
Pipers' Ash, Ltd. 424
Pippin Press 424
Pisgah Review 281
Pistek Literary Agency, LLC, Alicka
    200
Playboy Magazine 359
Pleiades 281
Plexus Publishing, Inc. 424
Plume 425
Pockets 360
Pockets Fiction-Writing Contest 473
Pocol Press 425
Pointed Circle 282
Poisoned Pen Press 425
Polyphony H.S. 282
Porcupine Literary Arts Magazine
    282
Port Town Publishing 426
Porter Prize in Short Fiction,
    Katherine Anne 473
Portland Monthly 360
Portland Review 283
Post Road 283

Post-Apollo Press, The 426
Postromantic Poetry and Short Story
    474
Postscripts: The A to Z of Fantastic
    Fiction 283
Potomac Review 284
Prairie Journal Press 426
Prairie Journal, The 284
Prairie Schooner Book Prize Series
    474
Prairie Schooner Glenna Luschei
    Awards 474
Prayerworks 318
Priest Literary Agency, Aaron M.
    200
Prism International 284
Prospect Agency LLC 201
Psaltis Literary 201
PSI 318
Publishing Game, The 491
Puerto Del Sol 285
Puffin Books 427
Pureplay Press 427
Purpose 318
Pushcart Prize 474
Putnam's Sons, G.P. 427

Q
Quackenbush's Children's Book
    Writing & Illustrating
    Workshiops, Robert 492
Quarter After Eight 285
Quarterly West 285
Quebec Writers' Federation Book
    Awards 475
Queens Mystery Magazine, Ellery
    360
Queen's Quarterly 319
Quicksilver Books: Literary Agents
    201
Quixote Press 427

R
Raffelock Award for Publishing
    Excellence, David 475
Rager Media 427

Rainbow Curve 286

Raines & Raines 202

Raleigh Award, Sir Walter 475

Rambler, The 286

Random House Children's Books 428

Random House, Inc. 428

Random House, Inc. Creative Writing Competition 475

Random House Trade Publishing Group 428

Ransom Publishing Ltd. 429

Rattapallax 287

Raven Chronicles, The 287

Ravenhawk Books 429

Rawlings: Writing the Region, Marjorie Kinnan 501

Rea Award for the Short Story, The 475

Readers and Writers Holiday Conference 504

Realpoetik 340

Red Deer Press 429

Red Dress Ink 430

Red Hen Press 430

Red House Children's Book Award, The 475

Red Rock Review 287

Red Wheelbarrow 287

Redbook Magazine 361

Redivider 288

Rees Literary Agency, Helen 202

Reflections Literary Journal 288

Regal Literary Agency 202

Rein Books, Inc., Jody 203

Rejected Quarterly, The 288

Remember the MAGIC IWWG Annual Summer Conference 492

Rhodes Literary Agency, Jodie 203

Ribalow Award, Harold U. 476

Rising Tide Press, New Mexico 430

Rittenberg Literary Agency, Inc., Ann 204

River City Publishing 430

River Styx 289

Riverhead Books 431

Riverside Literary Agency 204

Riverwind 289

R-KV-R-Y 339

Roanoke Review 289

Robbins Literary Agency, B.J. 204

Rock & Sling: A Journal of Literature, Art and Faith 290

Rockford Review, The 290

Ronsdale Press 431

Rose & Thorn Literary E-Zine, The 340

Rosenberg Group, The 205

Rosenstone/Wender 205

Rotrosen Agency LLC, Jane 205

RPPS/Fullosia Press 341

Rubie Literary Agency, The Peter 206

Russell & Volkening 206

S

Sage Hill Writing Experience 521

Sagebrush Writers Workshop 518

Salvo Press 431

San Diego State University Writers' Conference 514

San Juan Writers Workshop 510

Sanders & Associates, Victoria 207

Sandy Cove Christian Writers Conference 495

Sanskrit 290

Santa Barbara Christian Writers Conference 515

Santa Monica Review 291

Sarabande Books, Inc. 431

Saranac Review, The 291

Scars/CC&D Editor's Choice Awards, The 476

SCBWI Southern Breeze Fall Conference 501

SCBWI Southern Breeze Spring Conference 502

SCBWI Winter Conference, NYC 492

SCBWI/Hofstra Children's Literature Conference 492

SCBWI/Summer Conference on Writing & Illustrating for Children 515

Schiavone Literary Agency, Inc. 207

Scholastic Canada, Ltd. 432

Scholastic Press 432

Science & Humanities Press 432

Science Fiction Writers of Earth (SFWoE) Short Story Contest 476

Scribe Agency, LLC 207

Scriptapalooza Television Writing Competition 476

Seacoast Writers Association Spring and Fall Conferences 493

Seal Press 433

Seattle Review, The 291

Seek 361

Seligman, Literary Agent, Lynn 208

Serendipity Literary Agency, LLC 208

Seven Stories Press 433

Sewanee Review, The 291

Sewanee Writers' Conference 498

Seymour Agency, The 209

Shaara Award for Excellence in Civil War Fiction, Michael 476

Shenandoah 292

Sherman Associates, Inc., Wendy 209

Short Grain Writing Contest 477

Short Stuff 292

Siegel, International Literary Agency, Inc., Rosalie 209

Silent Voices 319

Silhouette Books 433

Silhouette Desire 433

Silhouette Intimate Moments 434

Silhouette Nocturne 434

Silhouette Special Edition 434

Silver Dagger Mysteries 434

Silver Leaf Books, LLC 435

Simmons Literary Agency, Jeffrey 210

Simmons Short Fiction Award, John 477

Simon & Schuster 435

Simon & Schuster Adult Publishing Group 435

Sitka Center for Art and Ecology 518

Sitka Symposium 519

Skipping Stones Honor Awards 477

Skipping Stones Youth Awards 477

Slate & Style 319

Sleepingfish 292

Slopen Literary Agency, Beverley 210

Slote Award, The Bernice 477

Slow Trains Literary Journal 341

Small Beer Press 435

Snow Writing Awards, Kay 478

Snowy Egret 293

SNReview 341

So to Speak 293

Society of Midland Authors Award 478

Socket Shocker Magazine 319

Soho Press, Inc. 436

Soleado 320

Sonora Review 293

South Carolina Review 293

South Coast Writers Conference 519

South Dakota Arts Council 478

Southampton College Writers Conference, The 493

Southeastern Writers Association 502

Southern Humanities Review 294

Southern Methodist University Press 436

Southern Review, The 294

Southwest Review 294

SouthWest Writers Conference 510

SouthWest Writers (SWW) Contests 478

Southwestern American Literature 295

SPACE (Small Press and Alternative Comics Expo) 505

Speak Up 295

Spectra Books 436

Spectrum Literary Agency 210

Spencerhill Associates 211

Spice 437

Spider 361

Spieler Agency, The 211

Spire Press 437

Spitzer Literary Agency, Inc., Philip G. 211

Spout Press 437

Spur Awards 479

Squaw Valley Community of Writers 515

St. Anthony Messenger 362

St. Joseph's Messenger & Advocate of the Blind 362

St. Martin's Press 437

Stand Magazine 295

Standard 362

Staple Magazine 295

Starcherone Books 438

Stauffer Associates, Nancy 212

Steamboat Springs Writers Group 511

Steel City Review: A Pittsburgh-based magazine of Short Fiction 341

Steele-Perkins Literary Agency 212

Steeple Hill 438

Steinbeck Festival 515

Stellarcon 498

Sternig & Byrne Literary Agency 212

Stone Bridge Press 438

Stone Soup 296

Stony Brook Short Fiction Prize 479

Storie 296

Story Bytes 342

storySouth 342

Storyteller, The 320

Strand Magazine, The 363

Straylight 296

Strickler Author Management, Pam 212

Strong International Literary Agency, Rebecca 213

Strothman Agency, LLC, The 213

Struggle 297

Studio 320

Sturgeon Memorial Award for Best Short SF of the Year 479

subTERRAIN 297

subTERRAIN Annual Literary Awards Competition: The Lush Triumphant 479

Sulphur River Literary Review 298

Summerset Review, The 342

Sun, The 298

Swetky Agency, The 213

Sword Review, The 343

Sycamore Review 298

SynergEbooks 439

T

Tabard Inn, Tales of Questionable Taste 320

Talcott Notch Literary 214

Talebones 321

Tales of the Talisman 321

Talese, Nan A. 439

Talking River Review 298

Tampa Review 299

Taos Summer Writers' Conference 511

Taproot Literary Review 299

Taylor Manuscript Competition, Sydney 480

Taylor Prize for the Novel, The Peter 480

TCU Press 439

Tea, A Magazine 321

Teal Literary Agency, Patricia 214

Teddy Children's Book Award 480

Tessler Literary Agency, LLC 215

Texas Christian Writers' Conference 511

Texas Review, The 299

The Reader 300

Thema 300

Third Coast 301

Third World Press 439

Thirteenth Warrior Review, The 343

Three Cheers and a Tiger 480

3 Seas Literary Agency 215

Thunder Arm Writing Retreat with North Cascades Institute 519

Thunder Writer's Retreats 511

Thurber Prize for American Humor, The 480

Tickled by Thunder 301

Tickled by Thunder Annual Fiction Contest 481

Timber Creek Review 322

Timberwolf Press, Inc. 440

Tin House Books 440

Tin House Summer Writers Workshop 519

Tindal Street Press, Ltd. 440

Titan Press 441

TMCC Writers' Conference 515

Toasted Cheese 343

Toronto Book Awards 481

Torquere Press 441

Tradewind Books 441

Trail of Indiscretion 322

Transcendent Visions 322

Transition 301

Triada U.S. Literary Agency, Inc. 215

Tricycle Press 441

Trident Media Group 216

Triumvirate Publications 442

Trollope Society Short Story Prize, The 481

Turtle Books 442

Twain Creative Writing Workshops, Mark 512

Twilight Times Books 442

Tyrannosaurus Press 442

U

UCLA Extension Writers' Program 516

Unbridled Books 443

Understanding 301

Unity House 443

University of Michigan Press 443

University Press of New England 443

UPC Science Fiction Award 481

V

Véhicule Press 443

Verbsap.com, Concise Prose. Enough Said. 344

Vermont College Postgraduate Writers' Conference 493

Vermont Studio Center 493

Versal 302

Vesel Literary Agency, Beth 216

Victoria School of Writing, The 522

Villard Books 444

Vintage Anchor Publishing 444

Violet Crown Book Award 481

Virgin Books 444

Virginia Festival of the Book 498

Virginia Quarterly Review 323

Vision Books Pvt Ltd. 444

Vonnegut Fiction Prize, Kurt 482

W

Wade & Doherty Literary Agency 216

Wales Literary Agency, Inc. 217

Walker and Co. 444

Wallant Book Award, Edward Lewis 482

Walloon Writers' Retreat 505

Ware Literary Agency, John A. 217

Warner Books 445

Washington Independent Writers (WIW) Washington Writers Conference 496

Washington Running Report 363

Watkins Loomis Agency, Inc. 218

Watson Literary Prizes in Fiction and Poetry, The Robert 482

Waxman Literary Agency, Inc. 218

Weber Studies 323

Weiner Literary Agency, Cherry 218

Weingel-Fidel Agency, The 218

Weird Tales 323

Wesleyan Writers Conference 494

Western Reserve Writers & Freelance Conference 505

Whiskey Island Magazine 302

White Mane Kids 445

Wild Violet 344
Wild Writing Women Writing
    Workshop 516
Wildacre Writers Workshop 499
Willamette Writers Conference 520
William and Mary Review, The 302
Williams/New Orleans Literary
    Festival, Tennessee 502
Williard & Maple 303
Willow Review 303
Willow Springs 303
Willowgate Press 445
Wilshire Book Co. 445
Wind River Press 446
Windhover 304
WindRiver Publishing, Inc. 446
Winsun Literary Agency 219
Winter Poetry & Prose Getaway in
    Cape May 496
Wisconsin Institute for Creative
    Writing Fellowship 482
Wizards of the Coast 446
Wolff Award in Fiction, Tobias 482
Woman's Weekly 363
Wood Community College Adult
    Creative Writing Contest, John
    482
Woodley Memorial Press 446
Wordserve Literary Group 219
Workers Write! 304
World Fantasy Awards 483
Worldwide Library 447
Write From the Heart 516
Write It Out 502
Write on the Sound Writers'
    Conference 520
Writer's Digest Annual Short Short
    Story Competition 483
Writer's Digest Annual Writing
    Competition 483
Writer's Digest Popular Fiction
    Awards 484
Writers' Fellowship 484
Writers' Forum 363

Writers' Forum Short Story
    Competition 484
Writers House 219
Writers Institute 507
Writers' Journal 364
Writers' Journal Annual Fiction
    Contest 484
Writers' Journal Annual Horror/
    Ghost Contest 485
Writers' Journal Annual Romance
    Contest 485
Writers' Journal Annual Short Story
    Contest 485
Writers Online Workshops 506
Writers' Retreat, The 522
Writers Studio at UCLA Extension 517
Writer's Voice of the West Side
    YMCA 494
Writers Workshop in Science Fiction
    512
Write-to-Publish Conference 505
Writing and Illustrating for Young
    Readers Workshop 517
Writing, Creativity and Ritual: A
    Woman's Retreat 523
Writing It Real in Port Townsend
    520
Writing Strategies for the Christian
    Market 503
Writing With Style 522

X
Xavier Review 304

Y
Yaddo 494
Yellow Shoe Fiction Series 447
Yemassee 304

Z
Zachary Shuster Harmsworth 220
Zahir 324
Zebra Books 447
Zeckendorf Assoc., Inc., Susan 221
Zoetrope: All-Story Short Story
    Writers' Workshop 523
ZYZZYVA 305

NOTES

NOTES

NOTES

NOTES

NOTES

NOTES

NOTES

NOTES

NOTES

NOTES